ROUTLEDGE HANDBOOK OF MENTAL HEALTH LAW

Mental health law is a rapidly evolving area of practice and research, with growing global dimensions. This work reflects the increasing importance of this field, critically discussing key issues of controversy and debate, and providing up-to-date analysis of cutting-edge developments in Africa, Asia, Europe, the Americas, and Australia.

This is a timely moment for this book to appear. The United Nations Convention on the Rights of Persons with Disabilities (2006) sought to transform the landscape in which mental health law is developed and implemented. This Convention, along with other developments, has, to varying degrees, informed sweeping legislative reforms in many countries around the world. These and other developments are discussed here. Contributors come from a wide range of countries and a variety of academic backgrounds including ethics, law, philosophy, psychiatry, and psychology. Some contributions are also informed by lived experience, whether in person or as family members. The result is a rich, polyphonic, and sometimes discordant account of what mental health law is and what it might be.

The Handbook is aimed at mental health scholars and practitioners as well as students of law, human rights, disability studies, and psychiatry, and campaigners and law- and policy-makers.

Brendan D. Kelly is Professor of Psychiatry at Trinity College Dublin, Ireland.

Mary Donnelly is Professor of Law at University College Cork, Ireland.

ROUTLEDGE HANDBOOKS IN LAW

About the Series
Routledge Handbooks in Law present state-of-the-art surveys of important and emerging topics in Law and Legal Studies, providing accessible yet thorough assessments of key fields, themes and recent developments in research.

All chapters for each volume are specially commissioned, and written by leading and emerging scholars in the field. Carefully edited and organized, Routledge Handbooks in Law provide indispensable reference tools for students and researchers seeking a comprehensive overview of new and exciting topics in the relevant subject areas. They are also valuable teaching resources as accompaniments to textbooks, anthologies, and research-orientated publications.

ROUTLEDGE HANDBOOK OF COMMERCIAL SPACE LAW
Edited by Lesley-Jane Smith, Ingo Baumann and Dr. Susan Wintermuth

ROUTLEDGE HANDBOOK OF MENTAL HEALTH LAW
Edited by Brendan D. Kelly and Mary Donnelly

For more details, visit: https://www.routledge.com/Routledge-Handbooks-in-Law/book-series/RHL

ROUTLEDGE HANDBOOK OF MENTAL HEALTH LAW

Edited by Brendan D. Kelly and Mary Donnelly

LONDON AND NEW YORK

Designed cover image: DrAfter123

First published 2024
by Routledge
4 Park Square, Milton Park, Abingdon, Oxon OX14 4RN

and by Routledge
605 Third Avenue, New York, NY 10158

Routledge is an imprint of the Taylor & Francis Group, an informa business

© 2024 selection and editorial matter, Brendan D. Kelly and Mary Donnelly; individual chapters, the contributors

The right of Brendan D. Kelly and Mary Donnelly to be identified as the authors of the editorial material, and of the authors for their individual chapters, has been asserted in accordance with sections 77 and 78 of the Copyright, Designs and Patents Act 1988.

With the exception of Chapters 1, 21, 35 and 36, no part of this book may be reprinted or reproduced or utilised in any form or by any electronic, mechanical, or other means, now known or hereafter invented, including photocopying and recording, or in any information storage or retrieval system, without permission in writing from the publishers.

Chapters 1, 21 and 36 of this book are available for free in PDF format as Open Access at www.taylorfrancis.com. It has been made available under a Creative Commons Attribution-Non Commercial-No Derivatives (CC-BY-NC-ND) 4.0 license.

Chapter 35 of this book is available for free in PDF format as Open Access at www.taylorfrancis.com. It has been made available under a Creative Commons Attribution (CC-BY) 4.0 license.

Trademark notice: Product or corporate names may be trademarks or registered trademarks, and are used only for identification and explanation without intent to infringe.

British Library Cataloguing-in-Publication Data
A catalogue record for this book is available from the British Library

Library of Congress Cataloging-in-Publication Data
Names: Kelly, Brendan (Lawyer), editor. | Donnelly, Mary (Law teacher), editor.
Title: Routledge handbook of mental health law / edited by Brendan D. Kelly and Mary Donnelly.
Description: Abingdon, Oxon [UK]; New York, NY: Routledge, 2023. | Series: Routledge handbooks in law | Includes bibliographical references and index. |
Identifiers: LCCN 2023022224 | ISBN 9781032128375 (hardback) | ISBN 9781032128405 (paperback) | ISBN 9781003226413 (ebook)
Subjects: LCSH: Mental health laws. | Insanity (Law) | Convention on the Rights of Persons with Disabilities and Optional Protocol (2007 March 30)
Classification: LCC K640 .R68 2023 | DDC 344.04/4–dc23/eng/20230724
LC record available at https://lccn.loc.gov/2023022224

ISBN: 978-1-032-12837-5 (hbk)
ISBN: 978-1-032-12840-5 (pbk)
ISBN: 978-1-003-22641-3 (ebk)

DOI: 10.4324/9781003226413

Typeset in Galliard
by Deanta Global Publishing Services, Chennai, India

The Open Access version of chapter 1 was funded by Trinity College Dublin.

The Open Access version of chapter 21 was funded by The University of Dublin.

The Open Access version of chapter 35 was funded by Wellcome Trust.

The Open Access version of chapter 36 was funded by Australian Research Council and University of Melbourne.

CONTENTS

List of contributors   *x*
List of figures   *xiii*
List of tables   *xiv*

    Introduction to Routledge Handbook of Mental Health Law   1
    Mary Donnelly and Brendan D. Kelly

PART 1
Background and context   **15**

1   History and development of mental health law   17
     Brendan D. Kelly

2   Independent mental health monitoring: Evaluating the Care Quality Commission in England's approach to regulation, rights, and risks   34
     Judy Laing

3   The relationship between ethics and law in mental healthcare   55
     Louise Campbell

PART 2
European and international standards   **81**

4   The European Court's incremental approach to the protection of liberty, dignity and autonomy   83
     Anna Nilsson

Contents

5   The United Nations Convention on the Rights of Persons with
    Disabilities and mental health laws: Requirements and responses   101
    Suzanne Doyle Guilloud

6   Responses to the World Health Organization's QualityRights initiative   124
    Richard M. Duffy

PART 3
Specific groups   147

7   Children's mental health care: Decision-making and human rights   149
    Camilla Parker

8   People with learning disability: Scotland and beyond   166
    Jill Stavert

9   Mental health laws and older adults   179
    Penelope Weller

10 Abuse, neglect, and adult safeguarding in the context of mental health
    and disability   193
    Laura Pritchard-Jones

11 The use of trans-related diagnoses in health care and legal gender
    recognition: From disease- to identity-based models   212
    Pieter Cannoot and Sarah Schoentjes

12 Personality disorder in mental health law and criminal law   233
    Ailbhe O'Loughlin

PART 4
Forensic psychiatry and criminal law   253

13 Mental illness and criminal law: Irreconcilable bedfellows?   255
    Jill Peay

14 The principles of forensic psychology and criminal law—an American
    perspective   272
    Eric Y. Drogin

15 Mental capacity in forensic psychiatry in a comparative context   285
    Stefano Ferracuti and Giovanna Parmigiani

16 Capturing mental health issues in international criminal law and justice: The input of the International Criminal Court   306
Caroline Fournet

PART 5
Issues, controversies, challenges   **325**

17 Decision-making capacity in mental health law   327
Alex Ruck Keene and Katherine Reidy

18 Risk of harm and involuntary psychiatric treatment   342
Matthew Large, Sascha Callaghan and Christopher James Ryan

19 Compulsory community treatment: Is it the least restrictive alternative?   356
John Dawson

20 Socio-economic inclusion and mental health law   371
Terry Carney

21 The right to mental health care in mental health legislation   384
Brendan D. Kelly

22 Mental health, discrimination and employment law   403
Mark Bell

23 Family in mental health law: Responding to relationality   421
Mary Donnelly

24 Consenting for prevention: The ethics of ambivalent choice in psychiatric genomics   438
Camillia Kong

PART 6
Developments in specific regions and jurisdictions   **457**

25 Change or improvement? Mental health law reform in Africa   459
Heléne Combrinck

26 Mental health law and practice in Ghana: An examination of the implementation of Act 846   477
Lily Kpobi, Charlotte Kwakye-Nuako, and Leveana Gyimah

27 Regulating mental health care in South Africa: Assessing the right to legal capacity and the right to the highest attainable standard of health in South African law and policy 493
Elizabeth Kamundia and Ilze Grobbelaar-du Plessis

28 Untapped potential of China's mental health law reform 511
Bo Chen

29 Colonization, history and the evolution of mental health legislation in India, Pakistan, Sri Lanka and Bangladesh 527
Sangeeta Dey and Graham Mellsop

30 India's Mental Healthcare Act, 2017: A promise for transformation and radical change 540
Arjun Kapoor and Manisha Shastri

31 An alternative to mental health law: The Mental Capacity Act (Northern Ireland) 2016 556
Gavin Davidson

32 Argentina, Chile, Colombia, and Peru: The relationship of mental health law and legal capacity 571
Pablo Marshall

33 Mental health policies in Spanish and Portuguese-speaking South American countries 587
Carla Aparecida Arena Ventura

PART 7
Future directions 615

34 Interdisciplinary collaboration in the mental health sector: The role of the law 617
Bernadette McSherry

35 The Mental Health and Justice project: Reflections on strong interdisciplinarity 629
Gareth Owen

36 'Digitising the Mental Health Act': Are we facing the app-ification and platformisation of coercion in mental health services? 645
Piers Gooding

37 Mental health law: A global future? 665
    Jean V. McHale

38 The future of mental health law: Abolition or reform? 685
    Kay Wilson

39 The future of mental health law: The need for deeper examination and
    broader scope 704
    Tania L. Gergel

Index 727

CONTRIBUTORS

Mark Bell, Regius Professor of Laws, School of Law, Trinity College Dublin, Ireland.

Sascha Callaghan, Senior Lecturer, Sydney Law School, University of Sydney, Australia.

Louise Campbell, Lecturer in Medical Ethics and Law, School of Medicine, University of Galway, Ireland.

Pieter Cannoot, Assistant Professor of Law and Diversity, Ghent University, Belgium.

Terry Carney, Emeritus Professor, Sydney Law School, University of Sydney, Australia.

Bo Chen, Lecturer, School of Law, Minjiang University, Fuzhou, China.

Heléne Combrinck, Associate Professor, Faculty of Law, North-West University, South Africa.

Gavin Davidson, Professor of Social Care, School of Social Sciences, Education and Social Work, Queen's University Belfast, Northern Ireland.

John Dawson, Emeritus Professor, Faculty of Law, University of Otago, New Zealand.

Sangeeta Dey, Consultant Psychiatrist, Mental Health Services for Older People, Waikato, Te Whatu Ora – Health New Zealand.

Mary Donnelly, Professor of Law, School of Law, Arás na Laoi, University College Cork, Ireland.

Eric Y. Drogin, Affiliated Lead of Psycholegal Studies, Psychiatry, Law, and Society Program, Brigham and Women's Hospital, Harvard Medical School, Department of Psychiatry, USA.

Richard M. Duffy, Consultant Perinatal Psychiatrist, Specialist Perinatal Mental Health Service, Rotunda Hospital, Dublin; Consultant Liaison Psychiatrist, Mater Misericordiae University Hospital, Dublin, Ireland.

Contributors

Stefano Ferracuti, Full Professor of Forensic Psychopathology, Department of Human Neuroscience, Faculty of Medicine and Dentistry, Sapienza University of Rome, Italy.

Caroline Fournet, Professor of Law, Law School, University of Exeter, UK.

Tania L. Gergel, Senior Research Fellow, Department of Psychological Studies, The Institute of Psychiatry, Psychology and Neuroscience, King's College London, UK.

Piers Gooding, Associate Professor, La Trobe Law School, Melbourne, Australia.

Ilze Grobbelaar-du Plessis, Associate Professor, Department of Public Law, University of Pretoria, South Africa.

Suzanne Doyle Guilloud, Independent Researcher.

Leveana Gyimah, Lecturer/Psychiatrist, Pantang Hospital, Mental Health Authority, Ministry of Health, Ghana.

Elizabeth Kamundia, Assistant Director, Research, Advocacy and Outreach Directorate, Kenya National Commission on Human Rights, Kenya.

Arjun Kapoor, Programme Manager and Research Fellow, Centre for Mental Health Law and Policy, Indian Law Society, India.

Alex Ruck Keene, Barrister, 39 Essex Chambers, London and Visiting Professor, King's College London, UK.

Brendan D. Kelly, Professor of Psychiatry, Department of Psychiatry, Trinity College Dublin, Trinity Centre for Health Sciences, Tallaght University Hospital, Ireland.

Camillia Kong, Senior Lecturer and Institute of Humanities and Social Sciences Fellow, School of Law, Queen Mary University of London, UK.

Lily Kpobi, Research Fellow/Psychologist, Regional Institute for Population Studies, University of Ghana, Ghana.

Charlotte Kwakye-Nuako, Lecturer/Lawyer, Department of Forensic Science, University of Cape Coast, Ghana.

Judy Laing, Professor of Mental Health Law, Rights, and Policy, University of Bristol Law School, UK.

Matthew Large, Conjoint Professor, Discipline of Psychiatry and Mental Health, University of New South Wales, Australia.

Pablo Marshall, Associate Professor of Law, School of Law, Universidad Austral de Chile, Chile.

Jean V. McHale, Professor of Healthcare Law, Centre for Health Law Science and Policy, University of Birmingham, UK.

Bernadette McSherry, Emeritus Professor of Law, Melbourne Law School, University of Melbourne, Australia.

Graham Mellsop, Emeritus Professor, University of Auckland, New Zealand.

Contributors

Anna Nilsson, Associate Lecturer in Health Law, Faculty of Law, Lund University, Sweden.

Ailbhe O'Loughlin, Senior Lecturer in Law, York Law School, University of York, UK.

Gareth Owen, Reader/Honorary Consultant Psychiatrist, Institute of Psychiatry, Psychology and Neuroscience, Department of Psychological Medicine, King's College London, UK.

Camilla Parker, Legal & Policy Consultant, Just Equality, UK.

Giovanna Parmigiani, Reseach Fellow/Psychiatrist, Department of Human Neuroscience, Faculty of Medicine and Dentistry, Sapienza University of Rome, Italy.

Jill Peay, Emeritus Professor of Law, London School of Economics and Political Science, UK.

Laura Pritchard-Jones, Senior Lecturer, School of Law, Keele University, UK.

Katherine Reidy, Registrar in Psychiatry, Department of Psychiatry, Trinity College Dublin, Trinity Centre for Health Sciences; Linn Dara Child and Adolescent Mental Health Services, Cherry Orchard Hospital, Dublin, Ireland.

Christopher James Ryan, Conjoint Associate Professor, University of Sydney and University of New South Wales, Australia.

Sarah Schoentjes, FWO (Flanders Research Foundation) PhD Research Fellow, Ghent University, Belgium

Manisha Shastri, Research Associate, Centre for Mental Health Law and Policy, Indian Law Society, India

Jill Stavert, Professor of Mental Health and Capacity Law; Director, Centre for Mental Health and Capacity Law; Lead, Centre for Mental Health Practice, Policy and Law Research, School of Health and Social Care, Edinburgh Napier University, Scotland.

Carla Aparecida Arena Ventura, Full Professor, University of São Paulo at Ribeirão Preto College of Nursing, Brazil.

Penelope Weller, Professor of Law, Graduate School of Business and Law, College of Business and Law, RMIT University, Australia.

Kay Wilson, Post-Doctoral Research Fellow, Melbourne Law School, University of Melbourne, Australia.

FIGURES

10.1	Key adult safeguarding legislation in England	197
15.1	Capacity to consent to treatment	286
15.2	Variables that influence decisional capacity	287
15.3	Criteria for involuntary hospitalization in European countries	289
15.4	Decisional capacity: clinical and forensic dimensions	295
18.1	Number of people (false positives) needed to detain one person (true positive) with a future harmful act determined by an excellent risk assessment tool with a sensitivity and specificity of 75%	351
35.1	Scheme for Mental Health and Justice project policy lab on reform of the Mental Health Act	636

TABLES

6.1	Tools created by the World Health Organization's QualityRights initiative	125
6.2	The World Health Organization's QualityRights assessment themes, standards and criteria	128
6.3	Research carried out using the World Health Organization's QualityRights material	136
15.1	Selected instruments to assess decisional capacity to consent to treatment	288
15.2	Selected instruments to assess decisional capacity to consent to research	288
15.3	Selected instruments to assess decisional capacity to stand trial	292
15.4	Selected instruments to assess criminal responsibility	293
15.5	Selected instruments to assess financial capacity	297
18.1	Contingency table generated by risk assessment and outcome	346
32.1	Relevant legal reforms in selected Latin American jurisdictions	572
32.2	List of acronyms (for Chapter 32)	575
32.3	Safeguards for involuntary hospitalisation in Argentina and Chile	582
33.1	Documents selected by country on the theme "Mental health legislation, regulations and implementation guides" (World Health Organization MiNDbank [More Inclusiveness Needed in Disability and Development] platform)	590
33.2	Documents by categories (World Health Organization MiNDbank [More Inclusiveness Needed in Disability and Development] platform)	600

INTRODUCTION TO ROUTLEDGE HANDBOOK OF MENTAL HEALTH LAW

Mary Donnelly and Brendan D. Kelly

Introduction

The relationship between mental illness, psychiatry, and law is complex, contested, and filled with possibility. This Handbook reflects our view that we can and should demand more from mental health law in providing a framework to protect the rights and advance the recovery of people experiencing mental illness. We also recognise the limits of law and that legal measures may have unforeseen and undesirable consequences. This is why we must interrogate not just legal frameworks but also the range of factors that influence how these operate in practice. This is a timely moment for the expansive exploration of mental health law undertaken in this Handbook. The advent of the United Nations (UN) Convention on the Rights of Persons with Disabilities (CRPD), which came into force in 2008, sought to transform the landscape in which mental health law is developed and implemented. This has meant that mental health law reform has been on political agendas in a very wide range of countries, quite literally from Australia to Zambia.

At the same time, discussion and debate continue regarding how we should respond to mental illness and the role of psychiatry in such responses (Burns, 2013; Rose, 2019). Regrettably, this debate often takes place against a backdrop of media misinformation (especially regarding risk and dangerousness) as well as ongoing systemic neglect of people with severe mental illnesses (Kelly, 2022). We believe strongly in the power of debate. While there may be plausible political reasons to advance a position as absolute or incontestable, much of the time, reality will be more nuanced. Answers are unlikely to be clear, permanent, or impervious to dissent, but we can still bring integrity, openness, and ethical involvement to the debates, the formulation of solutions, and the re-evaluation of our positions as legislation, practices, and technology evolve. Thus, the foundational values underlying this volume are tolerance, interdisciplinarity, and listening.

Having said this, we also recognise that every editor, like every author, approaches their task in a way which reflects their own experiences, professional and personal. We edit this Handbook as a combination of a practising psychiatrist and an academic lawyer/family member. In this Introduction, we take the chance to set out some thoughts about how we approach mental health law before turning to introduce the rich and varied views of our contributors. First, a brief note on terminology. We have not sought uniformity and so there

DOI: 10.4324/9781003226413-1

will be differences across different chapters. In this Introduction, we adopt the term 'mental illness' which we understand to mean a complex and changeable condition where a person's state of mind affects their thinking, perceiving, emotion, or judgement and seriously impairs their mental function.

The Scope of Mental Health Law

The first task of editors in compiling a Handbook on mental health law is to consider the perimeters of the discipline. As is pointed out in several chapters, 'traditional' mental health law is concerned primarily with regulating the involuntary admission of people experiencing mental illness to a hospital or other facility and the medical or psychiatric treatment of these people. Many jurisdictions (57% of World Health Organization Member States) have laws of this kind (WHO, 2020). As summarised by Lady Hale, writing extra-judicially, such laws can be seen as an attempt 'to reconcile three overlapping but often competing goals: protecting the public, obtaining access to the services people need, and safeguarding users' civil rights' (2007: 19). The balance struck between these objectives varies significantly across different jurisdictions and mental health law reform projects often involve realignment of objectives in light of changing social and political contexts (Donnelly, 2023). Alongside this civil law formulation, many jurisdictions address aspects of mental illness as part of their criminal code (whether through legislation or common law rules such as the M'Naghten Rules). Here, too, a balance is being sought, this time between attribution of criminal responsibility and the legal 'forgiveness' which arises from a finding of insanity and/or diminished responsibility.

While recognising the ongoing importance of these formulations of mental health law, we favour a broader view, operating on the basis that mental health law encompasses all aspects of law which have an impact on the rights, interests, and wellbeing of someone living with mental illness. Thus, we regard mental health law as including human rights, employment and equality law, health law, housing and social care/welfare law, as well as safeguarding and capacity law. This blurs the boundaries of the discipline but ultimately it provides a clearer picture of the expanse of law that needs to be interrogated to determine if it meets the needs of people with mental illness.

Mental health law operates on multiple levels and involves a wide range of actors and stakeholders. We begin with the person experiencing mental illness who should be, although is not always, at the heart of all relevant legal frameworks. We also have their family, friends, and supporters whose lives will be impacted, especially in situations of severe mental illness. Then there are the courts, tribunals, and other quasi-judicial bodies and the regulators who oversee the operation of the law. The day-to-day practice of the law typically involves a range of professionals including psychiatrists, psychologists, nurses and other health professionals, legal professionals, and social workers. Advocates and peer supporters also play an increasingly important role in providing information and facilitating access to law. Each stakeholder brings a different perspective to bear so that there is no single conception of mental health law but rather a kaleidoscope of competing and overlapping versions. This means that mental health law (and in particular critical evaluation of how it is working and how it should be changed) must be a multi-disciplinary endeavour, underpinned always by the central involvement of stakeholders who have lived experience of mental illness.

Introduction

The Role of Human Rights

The past two decades have seen a decisive and very welcome shift towards a greater human rights focus in mental health law. The recognition of human rights as a normatively relevant element in responses to mental illness emerged initially, and rather tentatively, through regional human rights instruments such as the European Convention on Human Rights (ECHR). While to modern eyes, the decision of the European Court of Human Rights (ECtHR) in *Winterwerp v the Netherlands* (1979) may seem unduly focused on a medical model of disability, in its day the decision constituted an important message to states that arbitrary deprivations of liberty would not be tolerated simply because a person had a mental illness. We have come a long way since *Winterwerp* and the CRPD has clearly played a very significant role in this respect. Many chapters in this Handbook refer to the CRPD and for some contributors, the CRPD provides the foundational normative framework for critical engagement.

There can be little doubt that the CRPD injected new energy into debates on the role and scope of mental health law (Gooding, 2017; Wilson, 2021). However, some elements of the CRPD have proved contentious and none more so than the approach of the Committee on the Rights of Persons with Disabilities (the Committee) to mental illness (Freeman et al., 2015; Wilson, 2021; 2022). In General Comment No. 1 (GC No 1, 2014), Guidelines on Art. 14 (Guidelines, 2015), and concluding observations on country reports, the Committee has been clear that all laws that allow for substitute decision-making (GC No. 1, 2014: para. 28) and/or compulsory admission (Guidelines, 2015: para. 10) or treatment (GC No. 1, 2014: para. 42) are contrary to the CRPD and must immediately be repealed. There is no accompanying requirement that States Parties have in place alternative safeguarding or protective mechanisms for people with severe mental illness. There are structural reasons for this; the rights of autonomy and liberty (both of which are undeniably impacted by mental health laws) are civil and political rights and so subject to immediate realisation while the positive rights in the CRPD which can ground alternative approaches are generally socio-economic in nature and so are subject to progressive realisation. Nonetheless, the Committee's focus on just one aspect of the dyadic relationship between negative and positive rights carries with it a whiff of libertarianism. Thus far, States Parties have largely resisted the Committee's injunctions, sometimes by issuing reservations or declarations on ratification, and sometimes by simply ignoring the Committee's interpretation.

We believe that respect for human rights must be at the heart of mental health law. In this regard, while we recognise that the traditional liberal rights of autonomy and liberty must continue to play a role in holding mental health law to account, it is important not to restrict understandings of human rights to these rights. One of the strengths of the CRPD is its identification of positive rights, with rights such as the rights to health and to live in the community offering very significant potential to improve the lives of people with mental illness and to reduce and possibly ultimately eliminate the need for coercive practices. While there is a long way to go in delivering on positive rights, some jurisdictions are taking steps in this direction. The Indian Mental Healthcare Act 2017 includes a statutory right to access mental healthcare and to treatment by mental health services run or funded by the state (s. 18(1)). The Act elaborates on what the right means, stating that mental health services must be affordable and of good quality, available in sufficient quantity, and accessible geographically and without discrimination and provided in a manner that is acceptable to persons with mental illness and their families and carers (s. 18(2)). The Victorian Mental Health and

Wellbeing Act 2022 goes further. This Act shifts the legislative focus away from coercion (although it does not outlaw coercive practices) and onto delivering the highest attainable standard of mental health and wellbeing and sets out detailed legislative objectives in pursuit of this goal. These include promoting conditions in which people can experience good mental health and wellbeing and can recover from mental illness or psychological distress, reducing inequities in access to and delivery of mental health services, and providing for 'comprehensive, compassionate, safe and high-quality mental health and wellbeing services' (s. 12). Clearly, these kinds of legislative initiatives can only work if the necessary infrastructure is put in place to deliver on them. Nonetheless, we hope that these examples become part of a wider trend towards a re-conceptualisation of mental health law to make it more attentive to positive rights.

The Role of Risk

It is over 30 years since Ulrich Beck first outlined the concept of a risk society (Beck, 1992) and, if anything, our consciousness of risk has increased in the interim (Gardner, 2009). Risk has long played a central role in mental health law and practice. Most traditional mental health laws use risk of harm to oneself or others as a basis for involuntary admission (usually alongside a therapeutic ground) and there is continual pressure on clinicians (from families, health workers, police, courts, and others) to detain people who are considered to be 'at risk'. Failing to detain or releasing someone who then turns out to do harm to themselves or someone else can lead not only to harm or death, but also imprisonment, family anger, criticism by courts and coroners, and media condemnation.

The problem with this, as is clear from a wide range of meta-analyses of risk predictions of both self-harm and harm to others (Large et al, this vol.), is that clinicians have proven not to be very good at assessing risk, and risk-assessment 'tools' have not been able to enhance the quality of risk-assessment to any substantial extent. The unreliability of risk prediction has normative implications. Even if one does not share the Committee on the Rights of Persons with Disabilities' view that all involuntary admission should immediately stop, it seems incontrovertible that there should be a plausible and defensible reason to take such a step (which undeniably restricts the individual's right to liberty). It is difficult to see that risk prediction meets this basic standard. While risk continues to play a role in mental health law, it reinforces public perceptions of linkage between mental illness and dangerousness notwithstanding countless studies which rebut this. This stigmatises people with mental illness and limits what the mental health system can deliver. Breaking the link between risk and mental illness will not be easy but ultimately it may be the case that only legislation that eschews risk entirely will resolve this matter and eliminate pressure for societal misuse of psychiatry to absorb risk.

The Limits of Law

It would be remiss to introduce this Handbook without recognising the limits of law. Mental health law is just one part of a complex system which also incorporates policies, planning and programmes, financing and resourcing, staffing, education and training, research and review (Minas and Cohen, 2007). The Royal Commission into Victoria's Mental Health Law describes complex systems as 'a group of visible and invisible interconnected parts that function together to achieve a goal' (Report Vol. 1: 55). This interconnectedness means that system change cannot be achieved simply by directing the system to produce an outcome (for example by introducing new legislation); instead, as the Royal Commission recognised,

Introduction

change is achieved by 'shifting the underlying conditions that hold the most influence over how the system, and those people within the system, operate' (Report Vol. 1: 58).

This placing of mental health law means that we can only evaluate law – and develop ways to improve it – by looking at how it operates within the broader system. Any analysis of mental health legislation that fails to recognise the complicated lived realities of mental health, mental illness, consensual treatment, and coercive interventions will always be incomplete. Any policy reform that fails to acknowledge the effects of socio-political factors on the development of illness, provision of treatment, and outcomes of care will always be inadequate. And any legislative initiative, no matter how theoretically elegant, that does not study outcomes in the real world will likely prove irrelevant and might well corrode the very rights it seeks to protect. This has implications for how we approach the necessary task of measuring and evaluating mental health law. We need conceptual debate and innovative thinking but we also need empirical and grounded engagement with messy realities.

The Handbook in Outline

Our main goal in bringing together contributors for this Handbook was to represent as wide a range of perspectives as possible. The result is a rich, polyphonic, and sometimes discordant account of what mental health law is and what it might be. Contributors come from at least 18 different countries and we are especially pleased that the Handbook includes contributors from low-income countries which have often been under-represented in mental health law scholarship. Contributors come from a variety of academic backgrounds, including ethics, law, philosophy, psychiatry, and psychology and some contributions are also informed by lived experience, whether through personal experience or as family members. These different perspectives are reflected throughout the seven parts of this Handbook, which begins by establishing the background and context for the discussion to follow.

Part 1: Background and Context

The Handbook starts by looking back. Brendan D. Kelly shows how the historical use and misuse of mental health legislation demonstrates a clear need to pro-actively ensure that laws are just and fair, not least because, while legislation has always been part of a broader social system of care, it has commonly failed people with mental illness. Having recounted the role of mental health law in the past, Kelly moves to the present, pointing out that, at the start of the twentieth century, current legislation continues to over-emphasise the risk purportedly presented by people with mental illness and that this injustice needs to be addressed. The second contextual chapter concerns the role of monitoring. Judy Laing uses the work of the Care Quality Commission in England as the basis for an exploration of the role of monitoring bodies in maintaining standards and ensuring human rights compliance in mental health settings. Laing's analysis reinforces the importance of monitoring but also shows the myriad challenges which monitoring bodies face in carrying out this necessary work.

The final context-setting chapter is Louise Campbell's careful discussion of the relationship between ethics and law in mental healthcare. Campbell recognises that mental healthcare is fraught with ethical challenges. She shows how an emphasis on benefit, for example through a focus on best interests, can sometimes obscure the 'equally salient' ethical obligation to avoid harm and that this can lead to ethically problematic outcomes. In order to avoid these, Campbell advocates greater reliance on clinical ethics mechanisms and better ethics education which she hopes will help decision-making by 'broadening the scope of the discussion, incorporating multiple perspectives and promoting accountability, fairness and inclusiveness'.

Part 2: European and International Standards

Part 2 of the book focuses on European and international standards and engages with a triumvirate of transnational bodies: the European Court of Human Rights (ECtHR), the United Nations (especially the Committee on the Rights of Persons with Disabilities), and the World Health Organization (WHO). Anna Nilsson begins this Part with an analysis of the ECtHR's incremental approach to rights protection in mental health, with particular focus on the protection of liberty, dignity, and autonomy. She identifies a trend towards stricter scrutiny of practices and notes the role of the CRPD in the ongoing development of ECtHR jurisprudence. Nilsson concludes by identifying an urgent need for ECtHR to engage in discrimination analysis and to introduce positive obligations on states to develop voluntary crisis support services aimed at preventing the human rights violations associated with compulsory mental health interventions.

Suzanne Doyle Guilloud's chapter shifts the focus to the CRPD. Having recounted the drafting dynamics of the CRPD, the chapter goes on to explore those elements of the Convention most relevant to people with psychosocial disabilities. In a wide-ranging analysis, Doyle Guilloud identifies the varied responses to CRPD requirements by regional and state actors. These have included avoidance, through the use of reservations and declarations, by several states; rejection/refusal to engage in England and Wales; and 'acceptance (almost)' in Peru. Doyle Guilloud recognises that tensions around the CRPD will continue to play out in multiple fora but concludes by calling on States Parties to honour the promise they made when signing up to the Convention. Richard M. Duffy retains the global focus in a chapter which analyses responses to the World Health Organization's QualityRights Initiative. This Initiative, which commenced in the wake of the CRPD, produced a wide range of documents including a QualityRights tool kit to assist in developing mental health policy. Duffy describes the materials available, discusses their strengths and weaknesses, and identifies the importance of ongoing research to investigate the real-world impact of the training materials and ongoing engagement to ensure that any failings identified can be remedied.

These three chapters highlight not only specific positions and initiatives linked with the bodies discussed but also their varied and differing roles at transnational level. Each contributes in its own way to the complex, multi-layered, overlapping concatenation of standards, commitments, and initiatives that shapes the cluttered, rich, and sometimes contradictory landscape of mental health legislation. The next Part moves from this broad perspective to a series of different foci, exploring the positions of specific groups within this wider and sometimes bewildering framework.

Part 3: Specific Groups

Some of the complexity of mental health law arises from the fact that the needs and interests of different groups require different legal approaches. This Part looks at some of these groups, identifying relevant questions for mental health law specific to each group. The discussion begins with Camilla Parker's consideration of children's (people aged under 18 years) mental healthcare, with a focus on decision-making and the role of human rights. Parker identifies the triangular relationship (between State, parent, and child) which operates in mental health decision-making and which is also reflected in the key relevant human rights standards, which in this context includes the United Nations Convention on the Rights of the Child as well as the CRPD and ECHR. Parker argues that insufficient attention has been paid to the dynamics of this triangular relationship and that a better understanding is needed if we are to promote and protect the rights of children who need mental healthcare. Jill Stavert takes up the theme of difference from the perspective of people with learning disabilities. This group has traditionally been included within the ambit of mental health legislation (even where the person does not actually have a mental illness). Focusing on two recent reviews of mental health law in Scotland, Stavert recognises the strength of the arguments in favour of expressly excluding people with learning disabilities from mental health legislation if they do not have a mental illness. However, she also sounds a note of caution, noting the risk that people with learning disabilities could fall through the broader disability system and end up becoming subject to the criminal justice system.

Different issues again arise in Penelope Weller's exploration of how mental health laws impact on older adults. Weller begins by identifying the gendered nature of mental illness in this group, with older women being disproportionately impacted. Weller shows how traditional legal approaches to decision-making are ill-suited to older adults. However, she holds out hope for the potential of supported decision-making provided that such frameworks are adequately resourced and adapted to be sensitive to the needs and preferences of older adults. Continuing this theme, Laura Pritchard-Jones examines abuse, neglect, and adult safeguarding in the context of mental health and disability. This chapter explores the nature of abuse and neglect and explains why this is a very real concern for people with mental health problems or cognitive disabilities. Focusing on the position in England, Pritchard-Jones interrogates legal safeguarding duties and powers and asks how well these are understood and applied in practice. She articulates the clear ethical tensions which arise in seeking to balance protection of rights to autonomy and choice with protection from abuse or neglect – tensions which are addressed in different ways between jurisdictions, between different groups, and over time.

The chapter by Pieter Cannoot and Sarah Schoentjes addresses an important issue which has triggered a good deal of recent controversy. This is the role of trans-related mental health diagnoses in providing access to healthcare (such as gender affirming hormonal treatment and surgery) and legal gender recognition. This chapter shows how social and legal recognition of trans persons has evolved from a model based on disease and psycho-pathologisation to one based on de-pathologisation and identity. Cannoot and Schoentjes argue that while there has been significant pushback in certain States, this movement has been largely successful in bringing tangible improvements for trans people. This articulation of positive change, albeit uneven and incomplete, is a welcome reminder of the possibility of progress and responsivity in this field.

The final chapter in Part 3 explores the long-running and difficult question of how (and where) to address personality disorder. Ailbhe O'Loughlin tracks the issue across mental health law and criminal law, noting that 'significant advances have been made in understanding the aetiology and life-course of personality disorder'. This means that the view of personality disorder as untreatable no longer convinces. Nonetheless, as O'Loughlin recounts, 'thorny normative issues' remain which can mean that people diagnosed with personality disorders can find themselves excluded from both the protections of mental health law and those of the criminal law. This deeply worrying situation looks set to continue because as O'Loughlin notes, legal reforms 'continue to be hampered by risk aversion towards offenders diagnosed with mental disorders'. O'Loughlin's dual focus chapter provides a bridge to the closer analysis of forensic psychiatry and criminal law in Part 4.

Part 4: Forensic Psychiatry and Criminal Law

As Jill Peay recognises in the first chapter of Part 4, criminal law and psychiatry are 'problematic bedfellows'. Peay's comprehensive analysis identifies the inevitability of difficulties in trying to fit people with mental illness into a system constituted to deal with the mentally 'ordered' and in which the criminal law's need for certainty conflicts with the ambiguities and nuances of psychiatry. In spite of these problems, Peay sees signs of progress. She identifies the increased significance afforded to subjectivity in the criminal law which, she argues, aligns more closely with psychiatry's attempts to understand the subjective experience of patients.

Peay's chapter is followed by Eric Y. Drogin's distillation of the principles of forensic psychology and criminal law. Based on his experience of the United States criminal system, Drogin identifies five basic principles which he argues should apply to forensic psychologists interacting with the criminal justice system: forensic psychologists should address the issues identified by counsel, maintain assigned professional roles, investigate malingering whenever feasible, strive to keep errors to a bare minimum, and convey that ethical obligations are not negotiable. Moreover, Drogin cautions that psychologists need to accomplish this within an adversarial system that creates pressures to compromise professional integrity. Discussions in this adversarial system commonly centre on the contested issue of 'mental capacity', which is the subject of the next chapter. Stefano Ferracuti and Giovanna Parmigiani explore mental capacity in forensic psychiatry, drawing comparisons with capacity in other areas of law. Ferracuti and Parmigiani investigate various tools that assist in the task of capacity assessment but emphasise the importance of recognising all aspects of the broader context in which such evaluations occur, noting the need for care in applying instruments that have the possibility to limit individual freedom.

To conclude Part 4, Caroline Fournet takes up a transnational theme in a contribution that centres on the role of mental health in international criminal law with a particular focus on the operations of the International Criminal Court (ICC). Fournet shows how mental health issues have been incorporated into international criminal law through the inclusion of the infliction of mental harm as an element in the legal definition of a war crime and analyses the (generally cautious) way in which this has been interpreted by the ICC. Fournet also explores the response of the ICC to the use of mental illness/lack of capacity as a defence to charges of war crimes, including a fascinating account of the issues arising from the trial of former child soldier Dominic Ongwen.

Part 5: Issues, Controversies, Challenges

Part 5 of the book highlights specific issues, controversies, and challenges in a field that often seems to comprise *only* issues, controversies, and challenges. The discussion begins with Alex Ruck Keene and Katherine Reidy's exploration of the contested issue of decision-making capacity in mental health law. Drawing on the examples provided by two jurisdictions, England and Wales and Ireland, Ruck Keene and Reidy note the limited formal role played by decision-making capacity in mental health law but also recognise that 'soft law' and professional practice may operate quite differently. Ruck Keene and Reidy argue that further 'confidence tests' are needed before switching to an entirely capacity-based mental health law.

The discussion of capacity is followed by the equally contentious issue of risk. Having identified the central role of risk in much mental health legislation, Matthew Large, Sascha

Introduction

Callaghan, and Christopher James Ryan provide a powerful critique of risk assessment as a defensible scientific practice. Drawing on a range of empirical studies, Large and colleagues show that risk-based laws lead to the unnecessary and inappropriate detention of many people who would not cause or experience harm. For this reason, they argue that clinicians need to be cautious in interpreting risk of harm criteria in mental health legislation and that mental health legislation needs to be updated to take account of the weakness of risk assessment in mental health. A key lesson for legislators and policymakers can be drawn directly from this contribution: 'risk' is risky. Still further controversy is associated with the role of compulsory community treatment which is interrogated by John Dawson's chapter. Dawson discusses relevant legal frameworks, systems, research, and case-law, and asks whether the restrictions imposed through compulsory community treatment orders (CTOs) can be justified under human rights law. He concludes that the answer to this depends on whether compulsory community care can be considered to be the least restrictive alternative, i.e. whether the CTO constitutes an alternative to the greater restrictions that apply where there is a hospital admission. Based on evidence that CTOs generally do not fulfil this role, Dawson concludes that such orders should be approached with great caution.

Terry Carney broadens our focus by exploring what law can do to deliver socio-economic inclusion for people with mental health conditions or psychosocial disabilities. The controversy here lies not with the idea of socio-economic inclusion which, as Carney states, is generally recognised as a virtuous goal. Rather, it lies in the difficulties with defining and realising this goal and the resulting doubts regarding its conceptual utility. Following a careful analysis of the elements of inclusion, Carney argues that law has an important but limited contribution to make in advancing socio-economic inclusion. He identifies the need for a 'joined-up' framework which integrates the 'often separate conceptual domains of regulatory (law), distributive (economic), discretionary spending (services), and "soft policies" ("new regulation")'. This, he argues, would help advance broader dialogue on the politics of socio-economic inclusion and equality.

This need for broader dialogue is strongly endorsed in the next chapter. Brendan D. Kelly identifies the emergence of two 'cultures' with respect to the right to mental healthcare. Kelly argues that organisations such as the UN and the WHO issue high-level declarations without addressing the social, medical, and scientific basis for mental healthcare while healthcare professionals working on the ground regard these declarations as too detached from reality to be useful and so largely ignore them. He cites the example of the WHO and UN High Commissioner for Human Rights' draft *Guidance on Mental Health, Human Rights and Legislation* (2022) which avoids addressing 'hard cases' and which, he argues, prioritises ideology over providing practical, workable standards which will help deliver on the right to mental healthcare. Continuing the theme of broader rights, Mark Bell takes up the neglected issue of mental health-based discrimination in employment law. Bell begins by identifying the scale of challenges which people with mental illness face in the labour market. He identifies the potential of anti-discrimination law to address some of these challenges, noting the contribution which the CRPD has made to advancing understandings of anti-discrimination law in this context. However, Bell also recognises the limits of anti-discrimination measures and, like Carney, he recognises the need to consider questions of inclusion which, he argues, requires better enforcement of employers' obligations to prevent psychosocial risks to workers.

A different kind of inclusion provides the basis for Mary Donnelly's exploration of the role of family and relationality in mental health law. Donnelly argues that mental illness is almost always experienced relationally and that mental health law (and policy) has implications not just for people with mental illness but also for their families (which she uses to include family of choice). Donnelly identifies various reforms, including a greater role for nominated supporters and for advance planning, which will improve the way law responds to the role played by family. However, she also advocates the creation of mechanisms for broader engagement with families (alongside users of mental health services) in researching, planning, and structuring mental health systems. The final chapter in this section stays with the theme of family, addressing the controversial and largely neglected topic of psychiatric genomics. Drawing on her own family experience, Camillia Kong engages in a nuanced exploration of the ethical questions that arise in choosing to participate in genomic research which might be regarded as implicitly indicating the undesirability of constitutive parts of one's own or one's child's identity and way of functioning in the world. Kong notes that the relevant questions are typically framed as binary, with respect and acceptance of disability being contrasted to disrespect and attempts at medical amelioration. She seeks to bridge the binary and to create an 'ethical space' which allows for recognition of the 'complex dialectic between equally compelling (and perhaps incommensurable) imperatives'. Kong's contribution serves as a compelling argument for reflection, tolerance, and ethical engagement with complicated issues in this field.

Part 6: Developments in Specific Regions and Jurisdictions

Part 6 explores developments in specific regions and jurisdictions, demonstrating themes from other chapters applied in specific jurisdictions and regions and also raising other issues, including the role of colonialism, the challenges faced by low-income countries, and the impact of cultural norms in formulating responses to mental illness. We begin with three chapters from Africa. Heléne Combrinck provides an instructive overview of the treatment of disability rights in the African Charter on Human and Peoples' Rights. This is followed by her comparative analysis of disability and mental health law reforms in three African jurisdictions: Uganda, Zambia, and Kenya. Combrinck concludes that all three jurisdictions have made some progress on the road to meaningful reform. However, she also notes that, at the time of writing, only the Kenyan Act is operational and so she identifies the importance of ongoing scrutiny of all three Acts.

Combrinck's chapter is followed by Lily Kpobi, Charlotte Kwakye-Nuako, and Leveana Gyimah's comprehensive analysis of mental health law and practice in Ghana. This analysis is centred on Act 846, which was passed in 2012 after several years of advocacy. Kpobi and colleagues believe that Act 846 has the potential to facilitate an improved approach to mental healthcare in Ghana although they recognise that this can only be achieved if the legislation is scaffolded by enhanced infrastructure and supported by resources. In fact, the need for funding is expressly recognised in Act 846 which legislates for the establishment of a Mental Health Fund and dictates the sources of finance for this fund as well as its management. However, Kpobi and colleagues note that, notwithstanding ongoing advocacy in this regard, the necessary levy to finance this fund has not yet been introduced. Elizabeth Kamundia and Ilze Grobbelaar-du Plessis' analysis of mental healthcare in South Africa provides an interesting case study of mental health legislation (the Mental Health Care Act 2002) which includes an express right to care, treatment, and rehabilitation services and which is also underpinned by a constitutional right to access healthcare services. While recognising that this is a positive aspect of South African law, Kamundia and Grobbelar-du Plessis' evaluation of South African

Introduction

law and policy with reference to CRPD norms leads them to conclude that the South African mental health system deviates in significant ways from a human rights-based approach to mental healthcare.

From Africa, we move to several instructive chapters on mental health law in Asia. Bo Chen outlines the untapped potential of China's mental health law reform, focusing on China's Mental Health Law, which entered into force in 2013. While recognising the progress which this law makes in narrowing the scope of involuntary admission and treatment, Chen argues that the law reform has not fully achieved its potential because the popular practice of 'medical protective admission' (admissions by family members based on clinical evaluations of capacity or insight), which had provided the main basis for admission before the new Act, is still widely accepted in both medical practice and judicial proceedings. Sangeeta Dey and Graham Mellsop take both historical and contemporary perspectives in their exploration of colonisation, history, and the evolution of mental health legislation in India, Pakistan, Sri Lanka, and Bangladesh. In a wide-ranging review, Dey and Mellsop explore the colonial legacy and subsequent evolution of legislation in these jurisdictions and identify common challenges which need to be factored into processes of reform. These include stigma, lack of infrastructure, and lack of funding, all of which mean that clinicians in these countries face additional dilemmas to those faced by clinicians in higher-income countries.

The third Asian chapter is Arjun Kapoor and Manisha Shastri's analysis of the Indian Mental Healthcare Act 2017. As Kapoor and Shastri note, this legislation, which was enacted to comply with India's obligations under the CRPD, holds out a 'promise for transformation and radical change'. However, as they also identify, implementation is central and, to date, this has been poor, mainly because of a lack of political will to put in place the legal and regulatory infrastructure needed for the operationalisation of the law. In such circumstances, it becomes necessary to find ways to hold states to account. Kapoor and Shastri identify the need for 'collective action and a multi-pronged approach by civil society', including recourse to the courts where necessary.

Continuing the theme of law reform, Gavin Davidson's chapter addresses the Mental Capacity Act (Northern Ireland) 2016. This ambitious measure seeks to 'fuse' mental health and mental capacity law, replacing separate mental health law with a capacity-based framework which applies equally to all. Despite its innovative and progressive aspects, Davidson points to ongoing uncertainties, including the exclusion of children from the Act and how the Act will interact with the criminal justice system. More significantly, the Act is only partially implemented, and Davidson notes the uncertainty as to when (and whether) it will be implemented in full.

Finally, we turn to Latin America. Pablo Marshall provides an overview of legal changes in both mental health law and legal capacity that have been happening in four jurisdictions: Argentina, Chile, Colombia, and Peru. In a comprehensive contribution, Marshall identifies the efforts in all four jurisdictions to incorporate the standards of the CRPD, including supported decision-making, advance decision-making, and respect for will and preferences. However, he points out that outstanding issues remain, including ongoing provision for involuntary hospitalisation, although he also notes interesting developments in this respect in Peru. More data on outcomes will hopefully follow in the years ahead which will allow for empirical analysis of how the new laws are working in practice. Marshall's exploration of these reforms is complemented by Carla Aparecida Arena Ventura's account of mental health policies in Spanish- and Portuguese-speaking South American countries. Ventura's analysis is based on documents collected through the platform WHO MiNDbank (More Inclusiveness

Needed in Disability and Development), pertaining to Argentina, Bolivia, Brazil, Chile, Colombia, Ecuador, Paraguay, Peru, Uruguay, and Venezuela. Based on this analysis, specific thematic categories are presented and discussed, including recognition of rights, community-oriented service, regulations for psychiatric hospitalisation, financing of mental health, and benefit programs for wellbeing and the promotion of rights. Ventura identifies signs of movement on all fronts but she also notes that policy challenges continue to be experienced across all the jurisdictions analysed.

Overall, this Part of the book demonstrates a number of important features of the contemporary relationship between psychiatry and law, including the impact of human rights developments on mental health and capacity legislation, points of commonality between jurisdictions, specific differences in regional reforms, and the ubiquity of certain contentious issues such as tensions between liberty and the need for treatment, problems with stigma, and fundamental issues with resources for basic mental health services as well as more ambitious reforms.

Part 7: Future Directions

The final Part of this Handbook looks to the future. All the chapters focus on key issues for the development of this field and point to future directions for research, reform, and legislative change. Some contributors use concrete examples of specific initiatives in order to explore particular issues, while others widen our focus to question the very existence of this field in the first place.

Bernadette McSherry begins the Part by identifying the need for interdisciplinary collaboration within the mental health sector and the importance of ensuring that the lived experience of people who use mental health services is at the heart of this endeavour. Using specific examples from the state of Victoria in Australia, McSherry argues that the law can play a useful role in supporting collaborations of this kind, including by playing a co-ordinating role and requiring inclusion of all voices. The theme of collaborative engagement is taken up in Gareth Owen's chapter. Owen reflects on the strong interdisciplinarity which underpinned the Mental Health and Justice Project (MHJ), a five-year, Wellcome Trust-funded project for which Owen was the project lead. Owen recognises the value of strongly interdisciplinary projects which he argues 'offer multi-faceted opportunities for outputs, influences and impacts' and also play an important educational role for the participants. However, he also recognises that there are inherent tension points in such projects and therefore there is a need for what he calls 'dynamic balance' which allows for adaptive learning. Owen's recounting of the MHJ experience makes a valuable contribution to advancing understanding of the normative contribution of, and methodological approaches to, strongly interdisciplinary projects.

Piers Gooding's chapter presents a necessary evaluation of an area of rapid change that does not often feature in mental health law discussions. Gooding examines the role of digital technology, focusing on the position in England and Wales where there is an explicit policy goal to 'digitise the Mental Health Act'. He identifies three elements to this: (1) remote medical assessments of persons facing involuntary intervention, (2) the remote operation of tribunals that authorise involuntary interventions, and (3) the rise of digital platforms for Mental Health Act assessment setup. Gooding argues that while the courts have been responsive to the first two developments, insufficient attention has been paid to the third. He identifies the need for safeguards in procurement and commission of private sector actors

Introduction

to do mental health work and in respect of the proliferation of such platforms. This chapter reminds us to be attentive to the range of future challenges for mental health law, many of which will be of a different nature to those faced in the past.

The final three chapters in this part address fundamental questions which speak to the essence of mental health law. Jean V. McHale's chapter provides a carefully modulated meditation on the global future of mental health law. She begins by considering the future of mental health law as a separate area of scholarship and identifies the possibility that we may see mental health law assimilated into another related area of law, such as health, human rights, or disability law. In terms of global reach, McHale identifies a space for mental health law to operate through a global prism, although she also recognises the need for some caution in seeking to expand mental health law into this space. Nonetheless, there are benefits to exploring the nature and potential of global mental health not least because this helps us to think about how to deal with the challenges of 'conflicting rights and collective responsibilities'. Kay Wilson poses perhaps the ultimate contemporary question in the next chapter, asking whether the future of mental health law should involve its abolition or its reform. Having outlined how the debate in this respect was ignited by the Committee on the Rights of Persons with Disabilities, Wilson argues in favour of reform which she understands to include moves to decrease coercion and increase social supports. This chapter also presents an 'interpretive compass' of the CRPD, which draws on the CRPD principles of dignity (including autonomy), equality and non-discrimination, and participation, and sets out an argument as to how these can assist in working with the CRPD.

The final chapter in the Handbook is written by Tania L. Gergel, a philosopher who combines research and analysis with insights from lived experience. Gergel identifies the need for deeper examination and broader scope in mental health law, drawing attention to two areas which fall outside of the traditional remit of mental health law but which, she argues, are centrally important to the human rights of people with mental illness. These are the criminalisation of suicide, and the legalisation of euthanasia for mental disorder or 'psychological suffering'. Both issues merit substantially more attention than they currently receive, and this contribution will undoubtedly stimulate deeper engagement with them. More generally, Gergel argues that a broad view of mental health law is needed, recognising the clinical, social, and environmental landscapes in which it operates, a position which as editors we strongly endorse. Gergel also uses her chapter to respond to some of the other chapters in the Handbook, bringing her insights to bear on arguments made. For this reason, this chapter constitutes a fitting conclusion to the Handbook.

Conclusion

It has been a great pleasure to bring together this group of scholars to debate and interrogate mental health law and we thank all contributors for their engagement and enthusiasm. We hope that this volume will advance scholarship and practice in this field, enhance interdisciplinary dialogue, and – ultimately – help protect and promote the rights of people with mental illness, including positive rights to health, housing, and inclusion.

References

Beck, U. (1992) *Risk Society: Towards a New Modernity*. London: Sage Publications.
Burns, T. (2013) *Our Necessary Shadow: The Nature and Meaning of Psychiatry*. London: Allen Lane.

Donnelly, M. (2023) Making the Future Happen: Law Reform Lessons from the Victorian Royal Commission. In Y. Maker and K. Wilson, eds. *The Future of Mental Health, Disability and Criminal Law*. Abingdon: Routledge.

Freeman, M. et al. (2015) Reversing Hard Won Victories in the Name of Human Rights: A Critique of the General Comment on Article 12 of the UN Convention on the Rights of Persons with Disabilities. *Lancet Psychiatry* 2(9): 844–850.

Gardner, D. (2009) *Risk: The Science and Politics of Fear*. London: Virgin Books.

Gooding, P. (2017) *A New Era for Mental Health Law and Policy: Supported Decision-Making and the UN Convention on the Rights of Persons with Disabilities*. Cambridge: Cambridge University Press.

Hale, B. (2007) Justice and Equality in Mental Health Law: The European Experience. *International Journal of Law and Psychiatry* 30: 18–28.

Kelly, B. (2022) *In Search of Madness: A Psychiatrist's Travels through the History of Mental Illness*. Dublin: Gill Books.

Minus, H. and Cohen, A. (2007) Why Focus on Mental Health Systems? *International Journal of Mental Health Systems* 1(1). https://doi.org/10.1186/1752-4458-1-1.

Mental Health Care Act 2017 (India).

Mental Health and Wellbeing Act (Victoria).

Rose, N. (2019) *Our Psychiatric Future*. Cambridge: Policy Press.

Royal Commission into Victoria's Mental Health System Final Report, PP 202, Session 2018-2021 (February 2021). https://finalreport.rcvmhs.vic.gov.au/.

United Nations Convention on the Rights of Persons with Disabilities (2006) A/RES/61/106/Annex 1.

United Nations Committee on the Rights of Persons with Disabilities, *General Comment No. 1 on Article 12: Equal Recognition before the Law*, (2014) CRPD/C/GC/1.

United Nations Committee on the Rights of Persons with Disabilities, Guidelines on Article 14 (September 2015).

Wilson, K. (2021) *Mental Health Law: Abolish or Reform?* Oxford: Oxford University Press.

Wilson, K. (2022) The CRPD and Mental Health Law: The Conflict about Abolition, the Practical Dilemmas of Implementation and the Untapped Potential. In F. Felder, L. Davy and R. Kayess, eds. *Disability Law and Human Rights*. Switzerland: Palgrave Macmillan: 171–197.

World Health Organisation. *Mental Health*. Atlas 2020. https://www.who.int/publications/i/item/9789240036703.

World Health Organization/Office of the United Nations High Commissioner for Human Rights. (2022) *Guidance on Mental Health, Human Rights, and Legislation (Draft)*. Geneva: World Health Organization/Office of the United Nations High Commissioner for Human Rights.

PART 1

Background and context

1
HISTORY AND DEVELOPMENT OF MENTAL HEALTH LAW

Brendan D. Kelly

Introduction

This chapter examines the history and development of mental health law, with particular emphasis on legislation designed to govern the treatment of mental illness. Such legislation has traditionally focused on admission without consent to psychiatric inpatient facilities, treatment without consent in such settings, and mechanisms to ensure standards of care (e.g., inspection regimes). Certain jurisdictions have, on occasion, expanded the remit of mental health legislation to include such matters as authorising compulsory treatment in the community, articulating a right to mental health care, and various other matters.

This chapter starts with an overview of mental illness in history, presents an exploration of early efforts to control people deemed to be 'mentally ill', outlines the emergence of asylums and more focused legislation in the nineteenth century, documents increased emphasis on human rights during the twentieth century, uses Ireland's and India's current mental health legislation as examples of contemporary mental health law, and indicates likely future developments in this area.

Throughout this chapter, original language and terminology from the past and from various archives, reports, and publications have been maintained, except where explicitly indicated otherwise. This reflects an attempt to optimise fidelity to historical sources and does not reflect an endorsement of the broader use of such terminology in contemporary settings. Language evolves constantly in this field, as social attitudes change.

The history of mental illness: the emergence of psychiatry

Mental illness has been a constant feature of human history since records began. Every society has described conditions akin to 'madness', 'lunacy', or mental illness and has developed varied responses at the levels of individuals, families, communities, and countries. Early explanations often prioritised religious interpretations of hearing voices, having visions, or behaving strangely (Scull, 2015). Responses varied across societies and over time: while some people who 'heard voices' were hailed as saints or mystics, most were dismissed as 'mad',

This chapter has been made available under a CC-BY-NC-ND license.

persecuted, confined, ostracised, or constrained to lives of wandering, loneliness, destitution, and early death (Kelly, 2022).

There was a significant shift in this position in medical texts written in the tradition of Hippocrates (c.460–c.370 BCE), a Greek physician, developing the idea of four 'humours': black bile, yellow bile, phlegm, and blood. Health resulted when the humours were in balance; disease resulted when they were not. This approach linked health, including mental health, with the physical body. Hippocrates highlighted the particular importance of the brain in determining our responses to the world and, in turn, shaping 'madness':

> by the same organ we become mad and delirious, and fears and terrors assail us, some by night, and some by day, and dreams and untimely wanderings, and cares that are not suitable, and ignorance of present circumstances, desuetude, and unskilfulness. All these things we endure from the brain, when it is not healthy, but is more hot, more cold, more moist, or more dry than natural, or when it suffers any other preternatural and unusual affection.
>
> *(quoted in Kelly, 2022; p. 10)*

This paradigm located mental illness in the body and brain, rather than the heavens, and represented a key shift in thinking about those who were 'mad and delirious'.

Even as Hippocratic theory grew in popularity, traditional and folkloric explanations often persisted alongside evolving medical thought. In China, demonic possession and disturbances to cosmic forces were commonly invoked to explain madness, while supernatural therapies also continued in the Islamic tradition, although the Islamic hospitals of the eighth century made additional medical provision for people with mental illness.

In England, Bethlem Royal Hospital ('Bedlam') was founded in the thirteenth century as the Priory of St Mary of Bethlehem and, by 1403, housed six insane men, among others (Shorter, 1997). Over subsequent centuries, private 'madhouses' emerged in many countries and were followed, in the nineteenth century, by an extraordinary wave of public asylum-building across much of the world. This trend stemmed from genuine concern about the mentally ill, philanthropic impulses to assist the afflicted, a burgeoning belief in the power of medicine to heal the mentally ill, and a desire for legitimacy among asylum doctors who were keen for professional recognition of their new branch of medicine: psychiatry.

This enthusiasm for large mental hospitals was misguided in retrospect, but was generally well intentioned at the time, seeking to correct a clear injustice against the mentally ill, many of whom were homeless, destitute, and profoundly neglected. Understandings of mental illness changed in parallel with evolving systems of care – systems that were driven by a perceived social need for containment as much as by medical discoveries, by a desire for control over the 'insane' rather than scientific understanding of their condition.

The desire to control the mentally ill stemmed in part from fear. In 1904, German psychiatrist Emil Kraepelin (1856–1926) wrote that 'all the insane are dangerous, in some degree, to their neighbours, and even more so to themselves':

> Mental derangement is the cause of at least a third of the total number of suicides, while sexual crimes and arson, and, to a less extent, dangerous assaults, thefts, and impostures are often committed by those whose minds are diseased. Numberless families are ruined by their afflicted members, either by the senseless squandering of their means, or because long illness and inability to work have gradually sapped the power of

caring for a household. Only a certain number of those who do not recover succumb at once. The greater part live on for dozens of years, imbecile and helpless, imposing a heavy and yearly increasing burden on their families and communities, of which the effects strike deeply into our national life.

(Kraepelin, 1904; pp. 2–3)

Kraepelin was gravely mistaken about these risks, but his views were widely shared, resulting in mass institutionalisation of people with mental illness in certain countries and, later, their persecution and murder in Nazi Germany (Kelly, 2022).

More broadly, at the start of the twentieth century, multiple countries had built large psychiatric hospitals that were now filled with patients whom doctors could not treat effectively. Other regions offered virtually no care to many people with severe illness who continued to be excluded, ignored, and neglected by their communities and societies. At this point, the problem of mental illness seemed intractable, diffuse, and widespread, with no ready solution to hand.

As a result of this situation, a series of novel biological therapies were introduced in the asylums during the first half of the twentieth century, fuelled primarily by a desire to discharge patients from the grossly outsized institutions – a desire informed more by therapeutic desperation than reliable science. New treatments included insulin coma therapy and lobotomy, both of which were eventually abandoned due to lack of efficacy and the extraordinary harm they caused. Other treatments from that era, such as electro-convulsive therapy (ECT), remained in use, but on a more limited scale. The introduction of anti-psychotic medication in the 1950s helped improve symptoms and discharge patients, but large institutions remained in place in many countries because anti-psychotics managed, rather than cured, severe mental illnesses.

One of the recurring problems was – and still is – the shifting definition of 'insanity' or 'mental illness'. This dilemma stems from the fact that most diagnoses in psychiatry are based on symptoms rather than biological tests, and are therefore subject to change and redefinition over time.

In an effort to bring some reliability to this field, the World Health Organization (WHO) added mental disorders to the sixth edition of its *International Statistical Classification of Diseases, Injuries, and Causes of Death* in 1949 (World Health Organization, 1949). The American Psychiatric Association (APA) followed suit three years later with its *Diagnostic and Statistical Manual of Mental Disorders* (American Psychiatric Association, 1952). Both of these symptom-based diagnostic systems have gone through several revisions over the past decades, but while they have facilitated research and treatment to a substantial degree, they remain imperfect, contested, and continually under revision (Katshnig, 2010). Diagnostic systems are necessary and better than nothing, but they manage rather than solve psychiatry's core problem of symptom-based diagnosis, rather than definitive biological tests for mental illness.

In the meantime, and somewhat improbably, psychiatric treatments advanced substantially, with medications such as antidepressants proving effective for depression (among other disorders), psychological therapies such as cognitive-behaviour therapy (CBT) expanding their remits substantially, and various other approaches emerging over time, often by chance rather than design. The result is that treatments today are extremely useful but imperfect for most psychiatric conditions, mental health services exist but are often inadequate in many parts of the world, and the biological basis of most mental illnesses remains stubbornly unclear, despite substantial research (Kelly, 2020).

Control and mental illness: the role of legislation

Throughout the historical evolution of these ideas about mental illness, the building of asylums, the emergence of psychiatry as a medical discipline, and the development of recent therapies, the idea of controlling the mentally ill has been the only constant feature of societal responses to mental illness. In the fourth century BCE, Plato, in his *Laws* (Book XI), emphasised the need for control of the 'mad' in 'a well-ordered state':

> If a man is mad he shall not be at large in the city, but his relations shall keep him at home in any way which they can; or if not, let them pay a penalty – he who is of the highest class shall pay a penalty of one hundred drachmae, whether he be a slave or a freeman whom he neglects; and he of the second class shall pay four-fifths of a mina; and he of the third class three-fifths; and he of the fourth class two-fifths.
>
> Now there are many sorts of madness, some arising out of disease, which we have already mentioned; and there are other kinds, which originate in an evil and passionate temperament, and are increased by bad education; out of a slight quarrel this class of madmen will often raise a storm of abuse against one another, and nothing of that sort ought to be allowed to occur in a well-ordered state.

This desire to manage and control all aspects of the lives of people with mental illness was widespread and sustained over many centuries, and persists today.

In Ireland, early laws specified the obligation of families to look after the insane, the elderly, and people with physical disabilities (Kelly, 2003). Legal texts from between the seventh and ninth centuries forbade exploitation of the insane, ruled that a contract with a person of unsound mind was invalid, and made provision for land owned by the insane. Early Irish law also dealt with offences committed by persons of unsound mind and made provisions governing childbirth and responsibility for offspring of the mentally ill (Kelly, 2016a).

The first piece of modern mental health law was, arguably, the *Statute De Prerogativa Regis*, introduced under Edward II of England in 1324 (Fennell, 2010). This statute gave the King wardship over the lands of 'idiots' and, later, 'lunatics'. Subsequent legislation generally focused on criminals and the homeless, so the first law to deal specifically with the needs of 'pauper lunatics' in that jurisdiction was the Vagrancy Act, 1744, which provided for the incarceration of the 'furiously mad'.

Following these developments, mental health law evolved at different rates and on slightly different trajectories in various jurisdictions around the world (Hayes et al., 1993). Despite these often subtle variations, the impulse to manage, control, and (to varying degrees) treat people with mental illness is evident in virtually every jurisdiction over the past two hundred years (Porter, 1991). During the nineteenth and twentieth centuries, the two key, linked mechanisms for achieving these goals in many countries were the building of asylums and the introduction of dedicated laws aimed at containing or treating people with mental illness in them.

Plato's suggestion that 'if a man is mad', his 'relations shall keep him at home in any way which they can' is also reflected consistently throughout this history. In 1817, before a system of public asylums was widely established in Ireland, a parliamentary committee heard evidence about the plight of the mentally ill in rural family homes:

> There is nothing so shocking as madness in the cabin of the peasant, where the man is out labouring in the fields for his bread, and the care of the woman of the house is scarcely sufficient for the attendance on the children. When a strong young man or woman gets the complaint [mental illness], the only way they have to manage is by making a hole in the floor of the cabin not high enough for the person to stand up in, with a crib over it to prevent his getting up, the hole is about five feet deep, and they give this wretched being his food there, and there he generally dies. Of all human calamity, I know of none equal to this, in the country parts of Ireland which I am acquainted with.
> *(Select Committee on the Lunatic Poor in Ireland, 1817; p. 23)*

As in many other countries, the governmental response to this dreadful situation was to pass a series of laws governing the management of people with mental illness and directing the erection of public institutions designed to house, contain, and treat them. This belief in institutional solutions was unshakeable. In 1858, the Lunatic Asylums, Ireland, Commission emphasised that 'it is of the utmost importance that cases of insanity should as speedily as possible be removed to an asylum' (Lunatic Asylums, Ireland, Commission, 1858; p. 12). Attitudes were similar in other jurisdictions.

As a consequence of this position, multiple laws were introduced across Europe, Asia, the Americas, Africa, Oceania, and elsewhere, generally providing for public asylums to contain people with mental illness and govern their management and treatment (see, for example, Grob, 1973; Somasundaram, 1987; Swartz, 1995; Kirkby, 1999; Scull, 2015; Kelly, 2016a). To take just one example, relevant legislation in Great Britain (and its various constituent jurisdictions as they evolved) included the Madhouses Act (1774), County Asylums Act (1808), Lunatics Act (1845), Lunacy Act (1890), Mental Deficiency Act (1913), and, later, Mental Treatment Act (1930) and the Mental Health Acts of 1959, 1983, and 2007 (Fennell, 2010).

The end result of this frenzied legislative zeal, which reached fever pitch in the mid-nineteenth century, was that, at the start of the twentieth century, the legal situation of the mentally ill in many countries was enormously complicated owing to multiple pieces of overlapping legislation that were poorly understood and often contradictory. People with mental illness were in an impossible situation. In many parts of the world, majorities still received no care whatsoever, while in countries with large mental hospitals, their position was more complex but no less distressing. Patients in these hospitals were abandoned by communities that would not accept them back, stranded in institutions that now focused on custody rather than care (let alone cure), and lacked any clear avenue for redress. Even if patients could access the courts, virtually nobody understood the relevant laws and fewer cared. Asylum patients were both captive and lost at the same time.

To compound matters, and despite the surfeit of obscure legal instruments, families often remained central to managing the mentally ill outside the formal institutions. George Fielding Blandford (1829–1911), a relatively enlightened English asylum doctor, argued, in 1871, that 'common law' permitted restraint of the mentally ill by their families or friends.

He wrote that 'a man [sic] does not necessarily come under the cognizance of the lunacy laws because he happens to be a lunatic':

> He may be a lunatic for years, and may be tended and restrained in his own house, or in that of a relative or friend, provided that his own friends or relations take care of him, and take care of him properly. It is the common law of the land that a man's friends may restrain him from harm, or protect him, if he is unable to protect himself. But if the lunatic is not taken care of by his own friends, or if they neglect him, and he is found to be wandering at large or improperly confined or maintained, then the Lunacy Acts reach him.
>
> *(Blandford, 1871; p. 381)*

This situation was replicated in many countries around the world: families remained central to day-to-day management and control of the mentally ill who were not placed in mental hospitals, prisons, poor houses, or other institutions. Blandford emphasised the importance of early treatment to avoid admission to an asylum:

> Now, in the earliest stages, insanity is a very curable disorder; but through the obstinacy of friends it happens over and over again that the curable stage is past and gone long before any remedial measures have been taken, and the patient is brought to us a confirmed and hopeless lunatic, requiring care not cure, to be shut up in restraint for the term of his natural life.
>
> *(Blandford, 1871, pp. 360–361)*

The emergence of complicated mental health legislation throughout the nineteenth century served the mentally ill poorly. This was not the intent of such initiatives, but it was their effect. One Irish report stated, in 1891, that 'good lunacy laws should make it possible to obtain care and treatment in asylums with ease, but they should make unnecessary detention difficult' (Committee on Lunacy Administration (Ireland), 1891; p. 36). That is not how mental health legislation operated in practice for much of the nineteenth and twentieth centuries, as the social hunger for institutions pushed up admission rates across the world, resulting in the large asylums of the early and mid-twentieth century and asylum doctors' increasingly desperate efforts to find a cure.

Continual changes in legislation constituted a form of social control that affected not only patients but also staff in mental hospitals over this period (Leiba, 1998). After treatments such as insulin coma and lobotomy were eventually abandoned in the mid-twentieth century, and new forms of medication started to arrive, the issue of institutional reform became more urgent. Discharge was increasingly possible, and many societies became less tolerant of institutions of all kinds including mental hospitals.

Change was uneven over the following decades, with certain jurisdictions remaining essentially static, others opting for incremental reform, and some implementing dramatic measures to dismantle their psychiatric institutions in one fell swoop. In Italy, psychiatrist Franco Basaglia (1924–1980) was dismayed by what he saw in Italian mental hospitals: grossly untherapeutic environments, indiscriminate physical restraint, and routine disempowerment of patients (Kelly, 2022). In 1964, Basaglia presented a report to the First International Congress of Social Psychiatry in London, titled 'The Destruction of the Mental Hospital as a Place of Institutionalisation'. Basaglia continued to work and campaign in this vein for a sustained period, seeking profound changes to the treatment of mental illness and psychiatric institutions in Italy.

The clearest consequence of Basaglia's work was the 'closure' of the Italian asylums as a result of the Italian Mental Health Act of 1978, also known as the 'Basaglia Law'. This legislation directed the closure of psychiatric hospitals throughout Italy and their replacement with community-based services, although some acute inpatient care was retained, chiefly in general hospitals. The changes in Italy were dramatic and remain controversial today, not least owing to the emergence of private psychiatric facilities in areas where public beds are scarce (Amaddeo and Barbui, 2018). It is also notable that, despite his appeal in Italy, Basaglia's work was relatively neglected in Anglophone countries (Burns, 2019). Basaglia's international impact might have been greater if more of his writings had been translated from Italian and if biological ideas had not emerged as a dominant theme in psychiatry over the relevant decades.

Even so, Basaglia's work showed that mental health law could be changed substantially over a relatively short period of time, and that this could have significant impact, even if some of the consequences in Italy remain unclear or even paradoxical. This realisation was followed by a new era of activism on the topic of mental health law and rights by the United Nations (UN) and WHO (as an agency of the UN). These developments underscored both broader social changes in the 1980s and 1990s, and the power of mental health law to produce changes to mental health systems, as Basaglia had shown in Italy.

The United Nations and World Health Organization

In 1991, the UN published its *Principles for the Protection of Persons with Mental Illness and the Improvement of Mental Health Care* (United Nations, 1991). These principles endorse a human rights approach to mental health legislation, stating that 'there shall be no discrimination on the grounds of mental illness' (Principle 1(4)) and 'every person with a mental illness shall have the right to exercise all civil, political, economic, social and cultural rights as recognized in the Universal Declaration of Human Rights, the International Covenant on Economic, Social and Cultural Rights, the International Covenant on Civil and Political Rights, and in other relevant instruments' (Principle 1(5)).

This was a welcome, overdue endorsement of the rights of people with mental illness and an implicit admission that the observance of these rights requires additional protection, owing to historical mistreatment and neglect. With this in mind, the UN *Principles* go on to address a number of areas of particular concern to the mentally ill.

In relation to admission without consent, the *Principles* state that:

> a person may (a) be admitted involuntarily to a mental health facility as a patient; or (b) having already been admitted voluntarily as a patient, be retained as an involuntary patient in the mental health facility if, and only if, a qualified mental health practitioner authorized by law for that purpose determines, in accordance with Principle 4 ['Determination of mental illness'], that that person has a mental illness and considers:
>
> (a) That, because of that mental illness, there is a serious likelihood of immediate or imminent harm to that person or to other persons; or

(b) That, in the case of a person whose mental illness is severe and whose judgement is impaired, failure to admit or retain that person is likely to lead to a serious deterioration in his or her condition or will prevent the giving of appropriate treatment that can only be given by admission to a mental health facility in accordance with the principle of the least restrictive alternative.

(United Nations, 1991; Principle 16(1))

In the case of (b), 'a second such mental health practitioner, independent of the first, should be consulted where possible. If such consultation takes place, the involuntary admission or retention may not take place unless the second mental health practitioner concurs'. This position and even some of this wording are now reflected in specific pieces of mental health legislation around the world (World Health Organization, 2005; see below).

In relation to treatment without consent, the *Principles* state that, subject to specified exceptions:

a proposed plan of treatment may be given to a patient without a patient's informed consent if the following conditions are satisfied:

(a) The patient is, at the relevant time, held as an involuntary patient;
(b) An independent authority, having in its possession all relevant information, including the information specified in paragraph 2 above [regarding diagnosis, treatment, alternatives, and adverse effects], is satisfied that, at the relevant time, the patient lacks the capacity to give or withhold informed consent to the proposed plan of treatment or, if domestic legislation so provides, that, having regard to the patient's own safety or the safety of others, the patient unreasonably withholds such consent; and
(c) The independent authority is satisfied that the proposed plan of treatment is in the best interest of the patient's health needs.

(United Nations, 1991; Principle 11(6))

The UN *Principles* contain various other provisions, including a requirement for reviews of involuntary admissions 'as soon as possible' after admission occurs (paragraph 17(2)).

Overall, the UN *Principles* sought to influence and inform national mental health legislation in order to better safeguard rights while also permitting admission and treatment without consent under specific circumstances and subject to independent review. While the idea of 'best interest' is no longer as prevalent as it was, many of these UN *Principles* are still clearly reflected in national mental health law today (see below).

Five years after the 1991 UN *Principles*, the WHO Division of Mental Health and Prevention of Substance Abuse provided more detail on this theme in *Mental Health Care Law: Ten Basic Principles* (Division of Mental Health and Prevention of Substance Abuse, 1996a). This document is based largely on the UN *Principles* as well as 'a comparative analysis of national mental health laws in a selection of 45 countries worldwide conducted by WHO in recent years' (p. 1).

The WHO's *Ten Basic Principles* include 'promotion of mental health and prevention of mental disorders'; 'access to basic mental health care'; 'mental health assessments in accordance with internationally accepted principles'; 'provision of the least restrictive type of mental health care'; 'self-determination'; 'right to be assisted in the exercise of self-determination'; 'availability of review procedure'; 'automatic periodical review mechanism'; 'qualified decision-maker' (i.e., official or surrogate decision-makers should be qualified for the role); and 'respect of the rule of law' (p. 1).

In relation to mental health legislation more specifically, the *Ten Basic Principles* take a broad approach and recommend 'maintaining legal instruments and infrastructures (human resources, sites, etc.) to support community-based mental health care involving settings for patients with various degrees of autonomy' (paragraph 4). For decisions 'affecting integrity (treatment) and/or liberty (hospitalization) with a long-lasting impact', however, 'there should be an automatic periodical review mechanism' (paragraph 8).

In respect of the 'rule of law',

decisions should be made in keeping with the body of law in force in the jurisdiction involved and not on another basis nor on an arbitrary basis [...]

1. Depending on the legal system of the country, the body of law may be found in different types of legal instruments (e.g. constitutions, international agreements, laws, decrees, regulations, orders) and/or in past court rulings (precedents);
2. The law applicable is the law in force at the time in question, as opposed to retroactive or draft legal instruments;
3. Laws should be public, accessible and made understandable.

(Division of Mental Health and Prevention of Substance Abuse, 1996a; paragraph 10)

One of the most interesting aspects of the UN *Principles* (1991) and the WHO's *Ten Basic Principles* (1996) is their implicit acceptance of admission and treatment without consent in certain circumstances and their acceptance that such practices are governed by national mental health legislation. Similar assumptions underlie later WHO publications, including their *Guidelines for the Promotion of Human Rights of Persons with Mental Disorders*, which note that 'international instruments supporting even the most basic rights of persons with mental disorders have been very long in coming' (p. v) and which provide guidance about implementing the relevant principles at national level (Division of Mental Health and Prevention of Substance Abuse, 1996b). Many of these rights-based considerations were underscored in the 2001 WHO World Health Report which was devoted to *Mental Health: New Understanding, New Hope* (World Health Organization, 2001) and the 2005 *WHO Resource Book on Mental Health, Human Rights and Legislation* (World Health Organization, 2005).

A more critical stance became apparent in the WHO's 2004 document on *The Role of International Human Rights in National Mental Health Legislation* (Department of Mental Health and Substance Dependence, 2004). In relation to 'informed consent and the right to refuse treatment', this document states that:

the common practice in many countries of permitting family members to consent on behalf of the patient, without any formal process for determining the legal incapacity of the patient consistent with these requirements, violates the human rights of dignity and autonomy as recognized in the Universal Declaration of Human Rights as elaborated upon in [the 1991 UN] Principles.

(Department of Mental Health and Substance Dependence, 2004; p. 35)

This document also noted that the UN *Principles* outlined 'a number of major exceptions' to UN Principle 11, that 'no treatment shall be given' without informed consent:

A meeting of disability rights experts convened by UN Special Rapporteur Bengt Lindqvist at Almåsa, Sweden in November 2000, pursuant to UN Human Rights Commission Resolution 2000/51 to recommend improvements in international human rights protections, has called into question whether Principle 11 may violate the anti-discrimination provision of international human rights conventions. The conference members adopted a resolution finding that any law is 'inherently suspect' as a form of discrimination if it permits coercive treatment for individuals with disabilities and not all other people. This is an issue that has yet to receive additional attention by international human rights oversight bodies.

(Department of Mental Health and Substance Dependence, 2004; pp. 36–37)

Two years later, the UN *Convention on the Rights of Persons with Disabilities* (CRPD) stated, among other provisions, 'that the existence of a disability shall in no case justify a deprivation of liberty' (United Nations, 2006; article 14(1)(b)). Differing interpretations of this and other sections of the CRPD are explored in various contributions to this volume. For the present chapter, focused on the evolution of mental health legislation, it is sufficient to note the incremental shift in tone from the UN and WHO over past decades, moving from acceptance of admission and treatment without consent (provided certain conditions are met under national mental health legislation) to the current, somewhat ambiguous position reflected in the CRPD.

This lack of clarity in the CRPD has led to highly diverse interpretations of its provisions (Doyle Guilloud, 2019). This is unfortunate and divisive in itself, but also has the regrettable consequence of diverting attention away from other parts of the Convention which are more widely agreed upon, and which affect far greater numbers of people. These include the CRPD's broader protections of other rights and its extensive requirements in relation to equality and non-discrimination. It is a matter of regret that these areas are often overshadowed by diametrically opposed views about specific parts of the CRPD which are, in any case, likely to defy definitive interpretation on the basis of their wording.

Human rights in mental health legislation

To summarise so far, mental health legislation has, for most of its history, generally focused on managing and controlling people with mental illness, rather than treating their conditions. The idea of institutional care based on national legislation emerged most strongly in the nineteenth century and declined in the twentieth but left a mark on legislation and services in many countries. At the international level, the language of the UN and WHO shifted in recent decades, but national legislation is slower to change and will likely continue to reflect national positions, rather than international ones, for the foreseeable future (i.e., continue to provide for admission and treatment without consent in certain circumstances and subject to review, among other provisions).

Even so, there is evidence that certain aspects of UN and WHO publications are reflected in national legislation but are drawn upon in a selective fashion rather than implemented to the letter. Ireland is a good example of this growing influence of international bodies, including not only the UN and WHO, but also the European Court of Human Rights and the European Convention on Human Rights (ECHR) of the Council of Europe. With this in mind, it is useful to look at Ireland as an example of the historical development of transnational influences on national mental health law.

In 1995, the Irish Government sought to reform mental health legislation explicitly to 'ensure full compliance with our obligations under the European Convention' (Department of Health, 1995; p. 15). The need for reform in Ireland came more urgently into focus in 2000 when the lack of automatic review of detention under Ireland's Mental Treatment Act, 1945, was the focus of a landmark case in the European Court of Human Rights.[1] Under a 'friendly settlement', the Irish Government undertook to compensate the applicant and noted its obligations under the ECHR. Ireland's subsequent Mental Health Bill, 1999, was the culmination of a lengthier process of reform, which had commenced prior to this case, but which was pursued with considerably greater urgency afterwards, confirming the ECHR as a key driver of reform (Kelly, 2016b).

Ireland's Mental Health Bill, 1999, led to the current Mental Health Act, 2001, which, in common with most national mental health legislation, permits admission and treatment without consent under certain circumstances. Even the detailed criteria for involuntary admission in Ireland, however, clearly reflect international recommendations, especially the 1991 UN *Principles*. Ireland's legislation permits admission without consent when a person has:

mental illness, severe dementia or significant intellectual disability where:

(a) because of the illness, disability or dementia, there is a serious likelihood of the person concerned causing immediate and serious harm to himself or herself or to other persons, or

(b) (i) because of the severity of the illness, disability or dementia, the judgment of the person concerned is so impaired that failure to admit the person to an approved centre would be likely to lead to a serious deterioration in his or her condition or would prevent the administration of appropriate treatment that could be given only by such admission, and (ii) the reception, detention and treatment of the person concerned in an approved centre would be likely to benefit or alleviate the condition of that person to a material extent.

(Mental Health Act, 2001; Section 3(1))

These wordings closely echo those of the UN *Principles*, which permit admission without consent if the 'person has a mental illness' and (a) 'because of that mental illness, there is a serious likelihood of immediate or imminent harm to that person or to other persons', or (b)

---

1 *Croke v Ireland* 33267/96 [2000] ECHR 680 (http://www.bailii.org/eu/cases/ECHR/2000/680.html).

in the case of a person whose mental illness is severe and whose judgement is impaired, failure to admit or retain that person is likely to lead to a serious deterioration in his or her condition or will prevent the giving of appropriate treatment that can only be given by admission to a mental health facility in accordance with the principle of the least restrictive alternative.

(United Nations, 1991; Principle 16(1))

While the Irish wording is similar to that of the UN, it is not identical, owing to other influences on Irish mental health law including domestic legislation, case-law, the ECHR, and various other considerations, Nonetheless, the imprint of the UN is clear not only in the criteria for involuntary admission, but also in the broader principles of the Irish Act, which include 'the need to respect the right of the person to dignity, bodily integrity, privacy and autonomy' (Section 4(3)) and 'best interests':

In making a decision under this Act concerning the care or treatment of a person (including a decision to make an admission order in relation to a person), the best interests of the person shall be the principal consideration with due regard being given to the interests of other persons who may be at risk of serious harm if the decision is not made.

(Mental Health Act, 2001; Section 4(1))

This is consistent with both broader Irish law and the 1991 UN *Principles* which require 'that the proposed plan of treatment is in the best interest of the patient's health needs' (Principle 11(6)).

Overall, Irish legislation is a good example of the substantial impact of international bodies and standards on national mental health legislation in certain countries, even if such impact is necessarily incomplete, tempered by other aspects of national law, and subject to interpretation and change over time. Similar influences are evident in other jurisdictions (World Health Organization, 2005); Ireland is simply presented here as one example to illustrate the history of this trend over recent decades.

The systematic impact of the CRPD on national mental health legislation is not yet fully clear, although it is likely to be similar to the impact of previous UN and WHO documents, at least in certain jurisdictions. Hopefully, the CRPD itself, rather than some of its interpretations, will have widespread impact, chiefly because the Convention offers a once-in-a-generation opportunity to improve the lives of people with mental illness and re-shape mental health legislation in an historically positive way.

Giving effect to the CRPD in national mental health legislation is, however, a complex task. India's Mental Healthcare Act, 2017, is a good example of some of the opportunities and ambiguities that can be involved in this process (see Kapoor and Shastri, this vol.).

India's new mental health legislation was commenced on 29 May 2018 and introduces many changes, including a new definition of 'mental illness'; revised measures governing 'capacity', 'advance directives', and 'nominated representatives'; revised procedures for 'independent admission' (voluntary admission) and 'supported admission' (admission and treatment without patient consent); and *de facto* decriminalization of suicide. Overall, India's 2017 Act is a comprehensive, encouraging piece of law, albeit with inevitable complications, caveats, and possible paradoxical effects.

Most interestingly, India's new legislation seeks explicitly to comply with the CRPD, which gives it particular relevance to the present chapter and to the history of mental health legislation in general. The preamble to the 2017 Act notes that 'India has signed and ratified the said Convention on the 1st day of October, 2007', and 'it is necessary to align and harmonise the existing laws with the said Convention'. This is an historic, ambitious undertaking, not only because of the content of the CRPD itself, but also because of the diversity of interpretations that exist. As a result, any commitment to implement the CRPD is a considerable, if admirable, task.

The full content of India's legislation is explored in detail elsewhere, including its headline articulation of a right to mental health care, which is consistent with both the CRPD and previous documents from the UN and WHO (Duffy and Kelly, 2020; Kapoor and Shastri, this vol.). The legislation also accords with the CRPD in many other ways that are frequently innovative, constructive, subtle, and useful for other jurisdictions to study. As a result, India's 2017 Act is, arguably, the best effort to date to give effect to the Convention in national mental health legislation and, as such, merits close attention.

Despite these achievements, the Indian legislation demonstrates certain limitations to its adherence with the CRPD, which point to potentially similar issues elsewhere. For example, the 2017 Act includes a model of supported decision-making that is consistent with the CRPD in principle, but which, if taken to its logical conclusion, can result in substitute decision-making. In relation to 'Admission and treatment of persons with mental illness, with high support needs, in mental health establishment, up to thirty days (supported admission)', the Act states:

> If a person with the mental illness admitted under this section requires nearly hundred per cent support from his nominated representative in making a decision in respect of his treatment, the nominated representative may temporarily consent to the treatment plan of such person on his behalf.
>
> *(Section 89(7))*

This constitutes a form of substitute decision-making and therefore might not comply with the CRPD, at least according to the interpretation of the UN Committee on the Rights of Persons with Disabilities (Committee on the Rights of Persons with Disabilities, 2014). This position is by no means agreed, but the Committee has expressed a clear view along these lines.

This issue illustrates the dilemma presented by the CRPD to national mental health legislation, even when such legislation tries to accord with the Convention as best as possible. Other contributions to the present volume explore this issue further and in different ways, but the fundamental question is: To what extent should the diversity of interpretations of the CRPD impede progressive realisation of its core provisions? India chose to move ahead with implementation, despite uncertainties of this nature and despite resource challenges across mental health services on the ground. Notwithstanding the linguistic ambiguities of parts of India's 2017 Act (and, indeed, the CRPD), it is difficult to argue against India's model of pragmatic realisation. Even if progress is imperfect, some progress is better than none – and India has made considerable advances with its legislation.

From an historical perspective, and in addition to the influence of international bodies on national legislation, it is notable that mental health law in Ireland, India, and many other jurisdictions continues to reflect one of the most controversial features of the history of such laws: the role of perceived dangerousness as a justification for involuntary admission and treatment. The inclusion of risk in these criteria is hugely questionable, not least because future behaviour is essentially impossible to predict (Large et al., 2008; Large et al., this vol.). This issue, too, is explored elsewhere in the present volume, so, for this chapter which focuses on history, it is sufficient to note that the persistence of dangerousness criteria continues to present cause for concern.

The root issue here is that psychiatry's evidence base rests on treating mental illness, not identifying or managing risk (Kelly, 2022). This is – strangely – reflected to a degree in some aspects of national legislation, including Ireland's criteria for involuntary admission. Under the Mental Health Act, 2001, the requirement that treatment 'would be likely to benefit or alleviate' mental disorder applies *only* to involuntary admissions of persons with mental disorder that occur on the basis that 'failure to admit [...] would be likely to lead to a serious deterioration [or] prevent the administration of appropriate treatment' (Section 3(1)). It does *not* apply to involuntary admissions of persons with mental disorder that occur on the basis of 'a serious likelihood of the person concerned causing immediate and serious harm' (Section 3(1)). For the latter, there is no treatment requirement.

As a result, it is legally possible to involuntarily admit someone with mental disorder in Ireland on the basis of risk even if treatment will not benefit them. This needs to change because it would be unethical and because it reflects one of the many unwelcome legacies of the history of mental health legislation: an excessive focus on 'risk' which we cannot measure.

Just as Plato insisted that the 'mad' should 'not be at large in the city' in the fourth century BCE, just as Blandford urged families and friends to 'restrain' the mentally ill in the nineteenth century, and just as Kraepelin argued that everyone with mental illness was 'dangerous, in some degree' at the start of the twentieth century, current legislation still over-emphasises the risk purportedly presented by people with mental illness. This injustice remains apparent in mental health legislation across most jurisdictions today and is no more defensible in the twenty-first century than it was in the times of Plato, Blandford, and Kraepelin. This, and much else, needs to change.

Future directions for mental health legislation

In 2017, the WHO published a report titled *Advancing the Right to Health: The Vital Role of Law* (World Health Organization, 2017). In the document, the WHO 'aims to raise awareness about the role that the reform of public health laws can play in advancing the right to health and in creating the conditions for people to live healthy lives' (p. 1). The WHO emphasises the importance of the 'rule of law':

> The rule of law refers to the principle that law-making processes should be transparent, laws should be enforced fairly, courts and tribunals should be independent, and the administration of law and its substantive content should be consistent with international human rights standards.
>
> *(World Health Organization, 2017; p. 7)*

While the WHO sees a 'vital role' for law across all areas of health, law already has an established role in the field of mental health, albeit a controversial, contested, but nonetheless persistent role. In order to better understand current mental health legislation, and to plan for the future, it is useful to reflect on the history of such legislation, especially its unintended consequences (e.g., disproportionate growth of asylums in the nineteenth century) and its positive potential (e.g., re-shaping legislation to protect rights, rather than just limiting them).

Most of the history of mental health legislation presented in this chapter reflects the geographical and language biases across much of the literature on this topic. Legislative developments in Ireland and India are presented as examples, reflecting one high-income country in the Global North and one lower middle-income country in the Global South. Other examples might equally have been chosen to illustrate these and other points, especially in low-income countries.

It is a matter of regret that many jurisdictions are still under-represented in the historiography of mental health legislation and in the current literature about mental health law in general. The present volume seeks to address this imbalance, at least in part, by including contributions from regions that are commonly under-represented. This does not address biases and omissions in the historiography, but will hopefully help minimise such biases and omissions in the future.

This chapter has focused chiefly on traditional roles of mental health legislation, concerning admission and treatment without consent, and the contexts in which these occur. Mental health legislation in various jurisdictions also deals with other topics including, but not limited to, mechanisms to ensure standards of care (e.g., inspection regimes), authorising compulsory treatment in the community, articulating a right to mental health care, and various other matters. Many of these issues are explored in other contributions to this volume.

Future work on the history of mental health legislation could usefully focus on dimensions of this history that have been relatively neglected to date (e.g., gender, sexuality, race, language, religion, colonialism, etc.), jurisdictions and regions that remain under-represented in the literature (e.g., Africa), the use of institutions other than mental hospitals for containment of people with mental illness (e.g., prisons), and the relationship (if any) between the recent emphasis on human rights (e.g., by the UN and WHO) and personal experience of mental illness: Even when human rights statements clearly inform mental health legislation, does this make a positive difference in the lives of people with mental illness and their families?

Finally, the issue of human dignity, which is central to rights, has not received the attention it merits in the history of mental health legislation or considerations of its current effects (Kelly, 2016c; Plunkett and Kelly, 2021). An enhanced focus on dignity could help ensure that decisions made under mental health legislation actively facilitate people with mental disorder to exercise their capabilities, promote human rights, and deliver much-needed mental health care (Kelly, 2014). Dignity matters.

The history of mental health legislation supports the over-arching importance of laws that are just and fair, but also suggests that some rights might be better protected, and some needs better met, through mental health policy, social policy, and broader societal awareness and reform. Mental health legislation matters deeply, but it is just one part of a social system of care that has, too often, failed the mentally ill. We can and must do better.

References

Amaddeo, F. and Barbui, C. (2018) 'Celebrating the 40th anniversary of the Italian mental health reform', *Epidemiology and Psychiatric Sciences*, 27(4), pp. 311–313. https://doi.org/10.1017/S2045796018000112

American Psychiatric Association. (1952) *Diagnostic and statistical manual of mental disorders.* Washington, DC: American Psychiatric Association.

Blandford, G.F. (1871) *Insanity and its treatment: Lectures on the treatment, medical and legal, of insane patients.* Edinburgh: Oliver and Boyd.

Burns, T. (2019) 'Franco Basaglia: A revolutionary reformer ignored in Anglophone psychiatry', *Lancet Psychiatry*, 6(1), pp. 19–21. https://doi.org/10.1016/S2215-0366(18)30426-7

Committee on Lunacy Administration (Ireland). (1891) *First and second reports of the committee appointed by the lord lieutenant of Ireland on lunacy administration (Ireland).* Edinburgh: Neill & Co. for Her Majesty's Stationery Office.

Committee on the Rights of Persons with Disabilities. (2014) *General comment no. 1. Article 12: Equal recognition before the law.* New York: United Nations.

Department of Health. (1995) *White paper: A new mental health act.* Dublin: The Stationery Office.

Department of Mental Health and Substance Dependence. (2004) *The role of international human rights in national mental health legislation.* Geneva: World Health Organization.

Division of Mental Health and Prevention of Substance Abuse. (1996a) *Mental health care law: Ten basic principles.* Geneva: World Health Organization.

Division of Mental Health and Prevention of Substance Abuse. (1996b) *Guidelines for the promotion of human rights of persons with mental disorders.* Geneva: World Health Organization.

Doyle Guilloud, S. (2019) 'The right to liberty of persons with psychosocial disabilities at the United Nations: A tale of two interpretations', *International Journal of Law and Psychiatry*, 66, p. 101497. https://doi.org/10.1016/j.ijlp.2019.101497

Duffy, R.M. and Kelly, B.D. (2020) *India's mental healthcare act, 2017: Building laws, protecting rights.* Singapore: Springer.

Fennell, P. (2010) 'Mental health law: History, policy, and regulation', in Gostin, L., Bartlett, P., Fennell, P., McHale, J. and Mackay, R. (eds), *Principles of mental health law and policy.* Oxford: Oxford University Press, pp. 3–70.

Grob, G.N. (1973) *Mental institutions in America: Social policy to 1875.* New York: Free Press.

Hayes, R., Boerma, B. and Ovadia, F.T. (1993) 'Mental health and the law: An introduction', *International Journal of Mental Health*, 22(4), pp. 3–21.

Katshnig, H. (2010) 'Are psychiatrists an endangered species? Observations on internal and external challenges to the profession', *World Psychiatry*, 9(1), pp. 21–28. https://doi.org/10.1002/j.2051-5545.2010.tb00257.x

Kelly, B.D. (2014) 'Dignity, human rights and the limits of mental health legislation', *Irish Journal of Psychological Medicine*, 31(2), pp. 75–81. https://doi.org/10.1017/ipm.2014.22

Kelly, B.D. (2016a) *Hearing voices: The history of psychiatry in Ireland.* Dublin: Irish Academic Press.

Kelly, B.D. (2016b) *Mental illness, human rights and the law.* London: RCPsych Publications.

Kelly, B.D. (2016c) *Dignity, mental health and human rights: Coercion and the law.* Abingdon, Oxon: Routledge.

Kelly, B.D. (2020) 'Psychiatry's future: Biology, psychology, legislation, and "the fierce urgency of now"', *Indian Journal of Psychological Medicine*, 42(2), pp. 189–192. https://doi.org/10.4103/IJPSYM.IJPSYM_492_19

Kelly, B.D. (2022) *In search of madness: A psychiatrist's travels through the history of mental illness.* Dublin: Gill Books.

Kelly, F. (2003) *A guide to early Irish law.* Dublin: School of Celtic Studies, Dublin Institute for Advanced Studies.

Kirkby, K.C. (1999) 'History of psychiatry in Australia, pre-1960', *History of Psychiatry*, 10(38), pp. 191–204. https://doi.org/10.1177/0957154X9901003802

Kraepelin, E. (1904) *Lectures on clinical psychiatry.* New York: William Wood and Company.

Large, M.M., Ryan, C.J., Nielssen, O.B. and Hayes, R.A. (2008) 'The danger of dangerousness: Why we must remove the dangerousness criterion from our mental health acts', *Journal of Medical Ethics*, 34(12), pp. 877–881. http://doi.org/10.1136/jme.2008.025098

Leiba, T. (1998) 'The effects of mental health legislation 1890–1990', *International History of Nursing Journal*, 3(4), pp. 12–18.

Lunatic Asylums, Ireland, Commission. (1858) *Report of the commissioners of inquiry into the state of the lunatic asylums and other institutions for the custody and treatment of the insane in Ireland: With minutes of evidence and appendices (part 1 – report, tables, and returns).* Dublin: Thom and Sons, for Her Majesty's Stationery Office.

Plunkett, R. and Kelly, B.D. (2021) 'Dignity: The elephant in the room in psychiatric inpatient care? A systematic review and thematic synthesis', *International Journal of Law and Psychiatry*, 75, p. 101672. https://doi.org/10.1016/j.ijlp.2021.101672

Porter, R. (ed.) (1991) *The Faber book of madness*. London: Faber and Faber.

Scull, A. (2015) *Madness in civilization: A cultural history of insanity from the Bible to Freud, from the madhouse to modern medicine*. London: Thames & Hudson, Ltd.

Select Committee on the Lunatic Poor in Ireland. (1817) *Report from the select committee on the lunatic poor in Ireland with minutes of evidence taken before the committee and an appendix*. London: House of Commons.

Shorter, E. (1997) *A history of psychiatry: From the era of the asylum to the age of Prozac*. New York: John Wiley and Sons, Inc.

Somasundaram, O. (1987) 'The Indian Lunacy Act, 1912: The historic background', *Indian Journal of Psychiatry*, 29(1), pp. 3–14.

Swartz, S. (1995) 'The Black insane in the Cape, 1891–1920', *Journal of Southern African Studies*, 21(3), pp. 399–415.

United Nations. (1991) *Principles for the protection of persons with mental illness and the improvement of mental health care*. Geneva: Office of the United Nations High Commissioner for Human Rights.

United Nations. (2006) *Convention on the rights of persons with disabilities*. New York: United Nations.

World Health Organization. (1949) *International statistical classification of diseases, injuries, and causes of death. Sixth revision of the international list of diseases and causes of death*. Geneva: World Health Organization.

World Health Organization. (2001) *Mental health: New understanding, new hope*. Geneva: World Health Organization.

World Health Organization. (2005) *WHO resource book on mental health, human rights and legislation*. Geneva: World Health Organization.

World Health Organization. (2017) *Advancing the right to health: The vital role of law*. Geneva: World Health Organization.

2
INDEPENDENT MENTAL HEALTH MONITORING

Evaluating the Care Quality Commission in England's approach to regulation, rights, and risks

Judy Laing

Introduction

The following quote from Phil Fennell encapsulates the development of mental health law in England and Wales, and the tensions and struggles within it to balance the rights of patients with the interests of the mental health professionals who treat them and the wider public interest:

> The history of mental health law charts the development of an increasingly complex codification of clinical authority whereby mental health professionals are given the authority to detain and treat mentally disordered people without consent where necessary to prevent harm to the patient or others. It is the story of the creation of and subsequent dismantling of the asylum system of care as the basis of social responses to mental disorder. ... It is also the history of a struggle for rights on the part of psychiatry's often reluctant clientele. ... In the period since the 1770s a specialized system of courts, tribunals and commissions has been developed to rule authoritatively on the scope of the rights of mentally disordered and mentally incapacitated people, and of the powers of those who have charge over them.
>
> *(Fennell, 2010, p. 4)*

This chapter focuses on one component of this complex mental health system, namely the role of independent oversight bodies – so-called 'commissions' – to inspect mental health facilities, monitor the operation of mental health law, and protect the rights of mentally ill persons detained under the legislation. Independent watchdogs form part of the mental health landscape in many jurisdictions, albeit they may be constituted differently, have distinct powers and duties, and adopt a range of diverse approaches to their monitoring work. For example, recent legislation in the Australian state of Victoria – the Mental Health and Wellbeing Act 2022 – created a new independent body, the Mental Health and Wellbeing Commission, with powers to publish data, launch investigations, and hear complaints from carers and families, as well as people in the mental health system (Maylea, 2022). A Mental Health Commission was established under the Mental Health Act 2001 in Ireland to regulate standards of mental health care, and it also operates the Mental Health Tribunal system to vindicate the rights of patients who are involuntarily detained.[1] In New Zealand, a different system of District Inspectors (lawyers appointed by the Minister of Health) monitor compliance with various provisions of the Mental Health (Compulsory Assessment and Treatment) Act 1992 and act as an important safeguard to protect the rights of detained patients (Thom & Prebble, 2013, p. 131).

This chapter explores the system of mental health monitoring and regulation in England through the work of the Care Quality Commission (CQC). The CQC is a large independent oversight body with three primary functions. First, it has a very wide remit to regulate all health and social care services in England, ensuring the quality and safety of care in hospitals, ambulances, dentists, and care homes, including psychiatric hospitals and social care institutions.

Second, it has a statutory responsibility to monitor the operation of the Mental Health Act 1983 (MHA) (as amended in 2007) which applies in regulated mental health settings. The MHA regulates the process of compulsory admission and treatment in hospital for a mental disorder in England and Wales. Section 120(1) of the MHA imposes a duty on the 'regulatory authority' to 'keep under review and, where appropriate, investigate the exercise of the powers and the discharge of the duties conferred or imposed by this Act'. Moreover, Section 120(3) requires the regulatory authority 'to make arrangements for persons authorised by it to visit and interview patients in private' and under Section 120(4) to 'investigate any complaint as to the exercise of the powers' under the MHA. This gives the CQC, as the relevant 'regulatory authority', considerable power to (1) proactively monitor places where persons are deprived of their liberty under the Act in England by visiting and speaking to detained patients in private; and (2) a reactive duty to investigate complaints about the MHA from patients and carers. The CQC publishes its findings on this work in annual monitoring reports on the MHA (CQC, 2022a).

The CQC's regulatory care standards work in England also includes oversight of the Mental Capacity Act 2005 (MCA) and operation of the Deprivation of Liberty safeguards (so-called DoLS).[2] The MCA sets out a legal framework in England and Wales to authorise care and treatment when a person lacks mental capacity to consent. The MCA also governs the process for authorising deprivations of liberty in care homes and hospitals on a similar legal basis. The CQC will check on the use of DoLS as part of its regulatory function by visiting places where they are used, which includes psychiatric hospitals and care homes, and it has published guidance to raise awareness of the legal responsibilities placed on providers by the MCA (CQC, 2011). Its findings on this work are published in its annual assessment of health and social care in England, the State of Care report (CQC, 2022b), though these are less prominent than the MHA monitoring work findings, which are communicated in a separate report.

Additionally, the CQC is one of 21 bodies designated as a member of the UK National Preventive Mechanism (NPM). The UK NPM was established in March 2009 after the

---

1 See www.mhcirl.ie/what-we-do (accessed 8 March 2023).
2 See further www.cqc.org.uk/help-advice/mental-health-capacity/about-mental-capacity-act (accessed 8 March 2023).

UK ratified the Optional Protocol to the Convention Against Torture (OPCAT) in 2003. OPCAT recognises that people in detention are vulnerable and requires States to set up a national-level body that can support efforts to prevent ill-treatment.[3] This national mechanism has a remit to visit all places where people are deprived of their liberty, which includes prisons, police custody, immigration detention and psychiatric and social care facilities. Most other countries which are signatories to the OPCAT designated one body to carry out the NPM role. The advantage of the UK NPM is that it has wide-ranging, multi-disciplinary and specialist expertise for a range of detention contexts; for example, HM Inspectorate of Prisons visits prisons in England and Wales as a member of the NPM, HM Inspectorate of Constabulary and Fire and Rescue Services inspects police custody facilities, and the CQC visits health and social care settings in England. The NPM function adds a further layer of protection and oversight against ill-treatment in psychiatric and social care settings as the CQC must examine the treatment of people in detention in accordance with international human rights standards and make recommendations to government authorities to strengthen protection against torture (see further Murray et al., 2011). This NPM function applies to the CQC's work related to the MHA and the MCA (including the DoLS), as persons may be deprived of their liberty and detained under these legal frameworks. It is worth noting here that the Mental Welfare Commission for Scotland,[4] Healthcare Inspectorate Wales,[5] and Northern Ireland Regulation and Quality Improvement Authority[6] have similar responsibilities for monitoring mental health and care standards in their respective jurisdictions in the UK and they are also members of the UK NPM, alongside the CQC and other independent inspection bodies in the UK.

This chapter explores the role of the CQC as a national mental health monitoring mechanism in England within this wider international human rights framework, focusing on the requirements of the OPCAT to protect persons who are deprived of their liberty from torture, inhuman and degrading treatment. As the former UN Special Rapporteur for Torture has emphasised in a 2013 report on *Torture in Healthcare Settings*:

> examining abuses in health-care settings from a torture protection framework provides the opportunity to solidify an understanding of these violations and to highlight the positive obligations that States have to prevent, prosecute and redress such violations.
>
> *(2013, para. 82)*

Human rights frameworks to prevent ill-treatment

The prohibition on torture is one of the few absolute and non-derogable human rights and there are overlapping national, regional and international frameworks that protect this right and should inform the work of national mental health monitoring bodies, including the CQC.

---

3 Article 1 states that the objective of the protocol is 'to establish a system of regular visits undertaken by independent international and national bodies to places where people are deprived of their liberty, in order to prevent torture, and other cruel, inhuman, or degrading treatment or punishment'.
4 See www.mwcscot.org.uk (accessed 12 February 2023).
5 See www.hiw.org.uk (accessed 12 February 2023).
6 See www.rqia.org.uk (accessed 12 February 2023).

The Human Rights Act 1998 (HRA) and European Convention on Human Rights (ECHR)

Human rights are legally defined and protected in the UK by the Human Rights Act 1998 (HRA). The HRA gives effect to the fundamental rights and freedoms guaranteed under the European Convention on Human Rights (ECHR), drafted in the wake of the Second World War in post-war Europe. Article 3 of the ECHR guarantees freedom from torture, inhuman or degrading treatment. Article 3 has been described by the European Court of Human Rights in *Labita v Italy* (2000, para. 119) as 'enshrining one of the most fundamental values of democratic societies' and is an absolute right, which means it cannot be restricted or limited in any way. Torture is defined in *Selmouni v France* (1999) as the intentional infliction of severe mental or physical pain or suffering; inhuman treatment is treatment which causes intense physical or mental suffering (*Kudla v Poland* (2000)); and degrading treatment means treatment that is extremely humiliating and undignified (*Price v United Kingdom* (2011)). In *Mursic v Croatia* (2016) the European Court of Human Rights said it must reach a minimum level of severity to contravene Article 3, considering the duration, effects, nature, and characteristics of the victim.

The ECHR was drafted and adopted by the Council of Europe, an international organisation founded to uphold human rights, democracy and the rule of law. The European Committee for the Prevention of Torture, Inhuman and Degrading Treatment or Punishment (CPT) was established in 1987 under the European Convention for the Prevention of Torture, Inhuman or Degrading Treatment or Punishment as a specialised independent monitoring body of the Council of Europe, to 'examine the treatment of persons deprived of their liberty' and protect them from torture, inhuman or degrading treatment or punishment.[7] Both European conventions are closely connected, though academics assert that the rights of people with mental disabilities were 'not foremost in the minds of [the ECHR] framers', so these rights have been developed within a much broader international human rights framework (Bartlett et al., 2007, p. 23). Notably, United Nations treaties provide further human rights protection in this context and together these instruments are important indicators of the evolution of human rights norms more generally. This is particularly so in relation to the growing significance of disability rights since the adoption of the UN Convention on the Rights of Persons with Disabilities in 2006, which is explored further below.

The United Nations Convention Against Torture (UN CAT) and its Optional Protocol (OPCAT)

Torture, cruel, inhuman or degrading treatment are absolutely prohibited in similar terms under international human rights treaties, including the United Nations Convention Against Torture and other Cruel, Inhuman or Degrading Treatment (UN CAT) and the OPCAT, which provide additional protection against torture for those who are deprived of their liberty. The UN CAT sets out substantive human rights commitments to prevent torture and ill-treatment and the Treaty is monitored by the UN Committee against Torture. The OPCAT 'is primarily focussed on establishing mechanisms to further the realization of the

---

[7] See www.coe.int/en/web/cpt (accessed 12 February 2023).

pre-existing commitment of States parties to the UN Convention Against Torture' (Murray et al., 2011, p. 11). States that have ratified the OPCAT must also allow the UN Sub-Committee on Prevention of Torture (SPT) to visit their places of detention and examine the treatment of people held there (Article 4(1)). The SPT has stated that 'an essential element for preventing torture and ill-treatment is the existence of a fully developed system of independent inspection visits to all places where people may be deprived of their liberty' (SPT, 2010a, para. 12).

OPCAT affirms a broad understanding of 'deprivation of liberty' in Article 4(2) which includes psychiatric and social care settings:

> any form of detention or imprisonment or the placement of a person in a public or private custodial setting which that person is not permitted to leave at will by order of any judicial, administrative or other authority.

The SPT has produced guidelines to advise States that are signatories to the OPCAT on the establishment of a NPM and to help steer the NPM's work (2010b). Monitoring under the OPCAT entails both procedural and substantive elements which are crucial to the work of NPMs, including the CQC. As the guidelines for NPMs recommend, the former strand encompasses all aspects relating to how the visits are conducted, such as the independence and composition of the team, the regularity of the visit, the ability to conduct unannounced visits and to talk with detainees in private. The substantive aspects refer to the benchmarks against which the institution in question is being evaluated and include issues such as the conditions of detention, which are explored in more depth below.

In 2016, the SPT published a statement on its approach to the rights of persons institutionalised and treated medically without informed consent (SPT, 2016). The document sets out the SPT's views on the rights of persons who are in detention owing to their health status, recognising that compulsory detention may be necessary for persons with a serious mental disorder in some circumstances:

> placement in a psychiatric facility may be necessary to protect the detainee from discrimination, abuse and health risks stemming from the illness.... Restraints, physical or pharmacological, are forms of deprivation of liberty and, subject to all the safeguards and procedures applicable to a deprivation of liberty, should be considered as measures only of last resort for safety reasons.
>
> *(SPT, 2016, paras. 8 & 9)*

Additionally, the document outlines the exceptional circumstances when a person deprived of their liberty may be treated without their consent (SPT, 2016, para. 14). This document provides an indication of the SPT's position on institutionalisation and deprivation of liberty in these settings, though it stands at odds with the approach of another UN Treaty monitoring body, the Committee on the Rights of Persons with Disabilities, which is explored below.

The United Nations Convention on the Rights of Persons with Disabilities (CRPD)

Torture and inhuman treatment are also prohibited under Article 15 of the United Nations Convention on the Rights of Persons with Disabilities (CRPD). The CRPD protects the rights of persons with mental and physical disabilities and promotes a 'paradigm shift' by viewing persons with disabilities as 'subjects' with rights who can claim those rights and make decisions for themselves as active members of society (see further Bartlett, 2014). The CRPD promotes respect for the inherent dignity, autonomy and independence of persons with disabilities and Article 12 guarantees equal recognition before the law for persons with disabilities and the enjoyment of legal capacity on an equal basis with others in all aspects of life (see further Gooding, 2015). The Committee on the Rights of Persons with Disabilities (established under Article 34) is tasked with monitoring implementation of the CRPD and providing guidance to States parties on the treaty's interpretation and implementation. Its work has been helpful in some respects as it has clarified the content of some of the rights contained in the CRPD, including Article 12.[8] It has, however, yet to make any specific recommendations on Article 15, though it has issued guidelines on deinstitutionalisation to support States to realise Article 19 on living independently and being included in the community. The guidance states explicitly that:

> States parties should recognize institutionalization as a form of violence against persons with disabilities. It exposes persons with disabilities to forced medical intervention with psychotropic medications, such as sedatives, mood stabilizers, electro-convulsive treatment, and conversion therapy, infringing articles 15, 16 and 17. It exposes persons with disabilities to the administration of drugs and other interventions without their free, prior and informed consent, in violation of articles 15 and 25.
>
> *Institutionalization contradicts the right of persons with disabilities to live independently and be included in the community.*
> *States parties should abolish all forms of institutionalization, end new placements in institutions and refrain from investing in institutions.*
>
> (2022, paras. 6–8, emphasis added)

The Committee regards Article 14, which protects the right to liberty and security of persons with disabilities, as central to the implementation of Article 19. The Committee's guidance on Article 14 reaffirms its opposition to deprivation of liberty on the grounds of mental impairment and repeats its call for States parties to repeal laws which allow for the involuntary commitment of persons with mental disabilities in mental health institutions on the grounds of actual or perceived impairments (2015, para. 10). The views of the CRPD Committee are abundantly clear: all forms of institutionalisation of persons with mental disabilities should be abolished.

Scholars suggest that the CRPD and UN CAT should be read 'hand in glove' (Perlin & Schriver, 2014, p. 195) and the CRPD has created an opportunity for international and domestic monitoring bodies to review their standards and practices, to re-evaluate the definition of torture and pay additional attention to the circumstances and experiences of people with disabilities (Karsay & Lewis, 2012). For example, Lea et al. (2018) advocate for an expanded disability-aware definition of 'sites of detention' for OPCAT monitoring in Australia, to encapsulate both disability-specific and mainstream settings in which people

---

8 The Committee has issued several General Comments thus far, including on Articles 5, 6, 9, 12, 24 and 27. See further www.ohchr.org/en/treaty-bodies/crpd/general-comments (accessed 12 February 2023).

may be deprived of their liberty. Lawson (2012) maintains that human rights law demands that disabled people should not be discriminated against while in detention, and how failures to provide reasonable accommodations to disabled detainees may amount to torture and inhuman treatment. She asserts that this should be reflected more clearly in the guidance provided by international monitoring bodies for monitoring places of detention. McSherry and Maker state there is growing impetus for more effective regulation of restraint for persons with mental disabilities since the CRPD was introduced, particularly considering the repeated concerns expressed by the UN Committee which monitors implementation of the CRPD in its concluding observations and reports (2021, p. 3). Weller (2019) takes this a step further, arguing for a more expansive definition of torture and ill-treatment to reflect that 'routine' care practices, such as the use of restraint and seclusion may, in contemporary understanding, be characterised as such. Finally, O'Mahoney (2012) argues that Article 12 requires a move away from institutional care to a supported decision-making model that facilitates the exercise of legal capacity. Accordingly, international monitoring bodies should further embed the right to independent living and inclusion in the community in their standards, in line with Article 19 of the CRPD. These views are supported by the former UN Special Rapporteur for Torture, Juan E. Méndez, in his 2013 report on *Torture in Healthcare Settings*, where he called on States parties to the UN CAT to review the anti-torture framework in line with the CRPD for persons with psychosocial disabilities; to impose a ban on all forced and non-consensual treatment of persons with disabilities; and replace forced treatment and commitment by services in the community (2013, para. 89).

Mental disability and ill-treatment

It is essential to closely scrutinise and reappraise the work of independent monitors in this context, as there are concerns that health and care settings have traditionally been neglected by torture prevention mechanisms, which has led to people with mental disabilities being exposed to torture and ill-treatment 'with impunity' (Karsay & Lewis, 2012, p. 816). Persons with a mental disability in social care and psychiatric institutions are in a position of powerlessness and vulnerability, segregated from society and detained for varying lengths of time under domestic mental health or capacity legislation. Despite an overlapping web of international and domestic legal safeguards, persons with mental disabilities are subjected to practices including involuntary commitment, forced and non-consensual administration of psychiatric drugs or electroshock therapy, and prolonged use of restrictive practices such as segregation, restraint and seclusion, which may amount to inhuman and degrading treatment. For example, in *Gorobet v Moldova* (2011) the European Court of Human Rights found a breach of Article 3 when the applicant had been subjected to a prolonged period of confinement and forced psychiatric treatment where there was no medical necessity. The Court has stated that compulsory medical interventions, such as forced feeding and forced psychiatric treatment, cannot in principle be regarded as inhuman or degrading treatment under Article 3 ECHR, as long as there is a convincing therapeutic necessity in accordance with accepted medical practice (*Jalloh v Germany* (2006); *Herczegfalvy v Austria* (1992)). In *V.C. v Slovakia* (2011) the European Court of Human Rights concluded that the imposition of forced sterilisation without the consent of a mentally competent patient is incompatible with the requirement of respect for freedom and human dignity, one of the fundamental principles on which the Convention is based. Accordingly, the Court found a breach of Article 3 where the applicant was sterilised without her informed consent immediately after giving birth via C-section, as the medical staff had 'shown a gross disregard for her right to autonomy and choice as a patient'.

The CRPD Committee is clearly of the view that these practices violate the rights of persons with mental disabilities and there is now growing concern, particularly since the advent of the CRPD, about the risks faced by persons with mental disabilities in these institutions from such routine care practices. As McSherry and Maker (2021, p. 3) have pointed out, 'some forms are inherently dangerous and may involve serious deprivations of liberty, interference with physical and mental integrity and loss of dignity'. The former UN Special Rapporteur for Torture's Report on *Torture in Healthcare Settings* (2013) recognised the evolving nature of the right to be protected against torture and ill-treatment, illustrating some of these abusive practices that take place in healthcare settings and describing how the torture and ill-treatment framework applies in these circumstances. Indeed, the Special Rapporteur was sympathetic to the CRPD Committee's position and challenged the use of the medical necessity doctrine, stating that it:

> continues to be an obstacle to protection from arbitrary abuses in health-care settings. It is therefore important to clarify that treatment provided in violation of the terms of the Convention on the Rights of Persons with Disabilities – either through coercion or discrimination – cannot be legitimate or justified under the medical necessity doctrine.
> *(2013, para. 35)*

This view is shared by the former UN Special Rapporteur for Health who said in his 2019 Thematic Report:

> Coercion is widely used in mental health-care services and there is evidence that the prevalence of coercive measures in mental health-care services is growing. These tendencies risk eroding trust in mental health services, damaging the image and reputation of mental health service providers and, most importantly, continue to raise serious concerns about systemic human rights violations in the field of mental health care.
> *(Human Rights Council, 2019, para. 48)*

In addition to concerns about violations arising from coercive and restrictive practices, persons with mental disabilities have also been subjected to inhuman and degrading treatment due to the poor conditions and standards of care (*Keenan v UK* (2002); *McGlinchey and others v UK* (2003)). For example, in *Stanev v Bulgaria* (2012) Mr Stanev had a diagnosis of schizophrenia and had been living in the community. The authorities decided he should be moved to a care home as none of his relatives were willing to act as his guardian. His state benefits were paid to the care home which was in a remote area, and it was a long way from his hometown. He argued the physical conditions in the home were poor and there was no access to the community or daily activities. After visiting the care home in 2003, the European CPT found that the deplorable living conditions and lack of therapeutic activities could be said to amount to inhuman and degrading treatment. In 2012, the European Court of Human Rights found that his indefinite and involuntary detention in the home by the State amounted to an unlawful deprivation of liberty contrary to Article 5 of the ECHR (which guarantees the right to liberty and security of the person), and the deplorable conditions in the home amounted to degrading treatment, in breach of the absolute prohibition on torture in Article 3. As a result of decisions such as these, national authorities are obliged to improve conditions in psychiatric and social care institutions and respect the human rights of people who are living there.

Regrettably, however, there is widespread evidence of continued ill-treatment and abuse of persons with mental disabilities, particularly those who are deprived of their liberty in psychiatric hospitals and care homes. As noted above, the use of restrictive practices, such as physical and chemical restraint, segregation and seclusion in mental health settings is common, but it is controversial and can lead to human rights abuses (McSherry & Maker, 2021). A Disability Rights Monitor Report in 2020 on the Covid-19 pandemic highlighted how the rights of persons with mental disabilities in institutions were breached during lockdown with excessive use of sedation, seclusion, social isolation and overmedication (2020). Human Rights Watch found evidence that men, women and children with mental health conditions are locked and chained in 60 countries across the globe (2020). An investigation by the CQC in 2020 on the use of restrictive practices in hospital and care settings for persons with learning disabilities and autistic people in England found too many examples of inhuman and undignified care (CQC, 2020). The CQC found excessive and inappropriate use of restraint falling outside permitted guidelines, including chemical restraint with rapid tranquilisation, and mechanical restraint, such as the use of handcuffs and belts. International human rights monitors have also criticised the use of restrictive practices in psychiatric settings in the UK. For example, the European CPT commented in a periodic visit report to the UK in 2017 on the high levels of rapid tranquilisation and manual restraint, and inappropriate use of long-term seclusion in secure hospital settings (CPT, 2017).

In the last decade, there has been criminal abuse by staff of residents with a learning disability in Winterbourne View hospital in 2011 (Department of Health, 2012) and Whorlton Hall specialist hospital in 2019 (Murphy, 2020), to name but a few. Verbal, physical and mental ill-treatment of patients uncovered in September 2022 at the Edenfield Centre, a psychiatric hospital in Manchester (Quince, 2022), has, once again, brought these issues into sharp focus, and remind us of the need to remain vigilant and ensure robust safeguards are in place to detect and prevent such abuse. These ongoing concerns led the government in England to set up a rapid review of in-patient mental health services in January 2023 to consider how safety risks and failures in patient care can be better identified (Caulfield, 2023).

A brief look back at mental health monitoring in England

This 'struggle' for rights that Phil Fennell refers to throughout the history of mental health law has been fuelled by concerns about ill-treatment and the conditions of detention in psychiatric and social care institutions, with repeated calls for external oversight. Abuse and ill-treatment in these settings is not a new phenomenon. A brief look back through time reveals that the system of central mental health care regulation through inspection and visits was originally introduced in England in the Madhouses Act in 1774, whereby external Commissioners were given powers to inspect private madhouses acting on behalf of the public. Despite criticisms of the Commissioners' lax and 'ineffectual approach' (Fennell, 2010, p. 10) this model endured and led to the birth of the Commissioners in Lunacy in the mid-nineteenth century. Their functions included the licensing and frequent inspection of asylums, which had expanded rapidly in number during that time. Although the Mental Health Act 1959 replaced this specialist inspection body with a system of visits by the Health Advisory Service, a series of inquiries into abuse and ill-treatment at psychiatric hospitals in the late 1960s and early 1970s led to the Boynton Committee review in 1980 to investigate abuse and ill-treatment at Rampton special hospital.[9] The report called for the reintroduction of a specialist commission to inspect and visit detained patients, which was accepted by Patrick Jenkin MP, the then Secretary of State for Social Services in a statement in parliament:

> Sound and effective monitoring systems are essential to the proper running of all health services in this country, including those institutions that hold Mental Health Act patients.
>
> *(Jenkin, 1980)*

Accordingly, the reformed MHA in 1983 reinstated a specialist commission – the Mental Health Act Commission (MHAC) – as a new independent body to monitor the operation of the Act in England and Wales. This MHA also introduced other measures to strengthen patient rights and safeguards against neglect and ill-treatment in psychiatric hospitals, including the requirement for a second medical opinion to authorise invasive treatments and access to an independent tribunal to review the grounds for continued detention, in line with Article 5(4) of the ECHR, as confirmed in the case of *X v UK* (1982).

The MHAC had statutory jurisdiction to visit hospitals and interview patients in private, and deal with complaints concerning their treatment. Commissioners came from a variety of professional backgrounds, spanning psychiatry, psychology, social work, and law, and included people with lived experience of compulsory detention. Having carried out the inspection, Commissioners completed a report, provided feedback and made recommendations to the relevant unit/facility. The MHAC focused on protecting individual patients whose rights are restricted under mental health legislation; however, it attempted to drive improvements in standards by commenting more generally in its biennial reports on the conditions of care for patients detained in psychiatric settings (Laing, 2014; Shaw et al., 2007). The MHAC's biennial reports also demonstrated a deep concern for human rights, which became an important feature of its safeguarding work (MHAC, 2008). However, the MHAC's remedial powers were limited as it could only investigate complaints when hospital managers had not been able to satisfactorily resolve the issue and it was unable to award any remedies to complainants. Furthermore, its role was hampered by its lack of enforcement powers. It could not compel providers to make specific changes and relied heavily on persuasion and the co-operation of mental healthcare providers to implement its recommendations (McHale, 2003; Clayton, 2002).

The Care Quality Commission (CQC): regulating standards of health and social care

From 31 March 2009, by virtue of the Health and Social Care Act 2008, the MHAC ceased to exist, and its functions were transferred to the CQC. This followed an arms-length bodies review by the government at the time to reduce the number of quangos in the health service and release resources to the front line (National Audit Office, 2008). The government's main rationale for the change was to enhance professional regulation, improve patient safe-

---

9 See further this news item on the publication of the Boynton report www.theguardian.com/news/2017/nov/12/from-the-observer-archive-this-week-in-1980 (accessed 1 September 2023).

guards, create an integrated regulator and harmonise standards across health and adult social care (National Audit Office, 2008).

All health and social care providers in England (including mental health care providers) must be registered by the CQC and before the CQC will grant a license to operate, the providers must show that their services meet the fundamental standards for quality and safety as set out in regulations. These were revised in 2015 and include, *inter alia*, ensuring service users are treated with dignity and respect, and protected from abuse and improper treatment; care and treatment must be appropriate, reflect service users' needs and preferences, and only be provided with consent and in a safe way; complaints must be properly investigated and appropriate action taken in response.[10] The CQC discharges this regulatory function by employing inspectors with relevant expertise to visit providers, talk to the people who use it and the staff, observe how the care is provided and check the provider's records. Unlike the MHAC, it can take enforcement action when providers are failing to meet the fundamental standards, which includes issuing warning notices and/or financial penalties, as well as shutting providers down where there are serious concerns. Some of the CQC's regulations have offences attached which means that, as part of the enforcement action, CQC will be able to bring prosecutions if they are breached. These include Regulation 11 which requires all care and treatment to be provided with the consent of the service user. The CQC has taken enforcement action if care standards are not being met and has shut down care homes and hospitals for failures to meet the care standards. For example, it took enforcement action to close Winterbourne View and Whorlton Hall hospitals as a result of the providers failing to ensure that residents were adequately protected from risk, including the risks of unsafe practices by its own staff.[11] In 2022, the CQC issued a financial sanction to a Mental Health Trust in Birmingham for failing to adhere to the fundamental standards in Regulation 11 on assessing mental capacity and seeking patient consent prior to treatment.[12] This punitive function should serve as a stronger deterrent and help to drive up standards of care.

The Care Quality Commission (CQC): mental health monitoring and human rights

Protecting the human rights of people who are detained under the MHA is an additional and distinct part of the CQC's work. An examination of the CQC's work in this regard offers helpful insights into evaluating similar systems and functions in other jurisdictions. The statutory functions of the CQC are akin to those of the MHAC following the transfer of responsibilities; however, the CQC's remit is much broader than that of the MHAC. As noted above, it also has responsibility for oversight of the DoLS and use of the MCA in all health and care services in England. This is significant when we consider the meaning of deprivation of liberty, the range of situations where persons with a mental disability may be deprived of their liberty and the potential impact of the CRPD.

---

10 The fundamental care standards are set out in the Health and Social Care Act 2008 (Regulated Activities) Regulations 2014 and the Care Quality Commission (Registration) Regulations 2009.
11 See CQC Press Release 18 July 2011 located at www.cqc.org.uk and www.cqc.org.uk/location/1-894121431/inspection-summary (accessed 8 March 2023).
12 See www.cqc.org.uk/press-release/university-hospitals-birmingham-nhs-foundation-trust-pays-fixed-penalties-ps8000 (accessed 8 March 2023).

Independent mental health monitoring

The CQC's duty to monitor the MHA and the DoLS relates directly to its role as a member of the UK NPM under the OPCAT. This additional NPM function is explicitly acknowledged by the CQC in its work on monitoring the MHA. The NPM role is set out in an appendix to recent annual MHA monitoring reports (CQC, 2022a). There is a distinct focus within the CQC on its MHA inspection visits and it has designated MHA reviewers with relevant expertise tasked with MHA monitoring alongside other staff who carry out the regulatory inspections (Laing, 2015).

SPT guidelines for National Preventive Mechanisms

As noted above, the SPT guidelines to all NPMs expand on what the concept of prevention means, stipulating that it requires a system of regular proactive visits, not just reactive by responding only to complaints or concerns (SPT, 2010b). Article 1 of OPCAT requires that visits carried out by NPMs and SPT are 'regular', but there is no guidance provided as to what that means. The SPT guidelines explain that NPMs should be able to conduct private interviews and carry out unannounced visits at all times, carried out by monitors with relevant skills and expertise (SPT, 2010b). The question remains as to how frequent the visits need to be to reach the requisite standards of regularity envisaged in the OPCAT. The SPT has not stipulated how often NPMs should be making on-site visits, with its guidelines providing only that the visits must make an 'effective contribution' towards preventing ill-treatment (SPT, 2010b, para. 34). Consequently, there is huge variability across NPMs as to what regularity requires, as a recent review of NPM visiting practices in Europe demonstrates (Hardwick & Murray, 2019). The CQC carries out a combination of focused and comprehensive inspections, but it is not always clear how many site visits take place to each provider and within what timescale. It launched a consultation in May 2022 on introducing a more flexible and responsive approach to regulation based on risk, which places less reliance on on-site physical visits.[13] It says it wants to use a wider source of evidence, tools and techniques to assess quality, although on-site inspections will still form an integral part of their work when they have information about significant risks to people's safety. It is not known yet how this will translate on the ground or how it will impact on the CQC's MHA monitoring work; nevertheless, it is concerning that less time will be spent by inspectors visiting and talking directly with people with lived experience who are in hospitals and care homes, including mental health care. If it leads to a significant diminution in on-site visits and in-person interviews with patients who are deprived of their liberty in hospitals and care homes, it will undermine the CQC's ability to carry out regular and effective preventive monitoring, as required by the OPCAT.

SPT guidelines for NPMs also provide guidance on the expertise and composition of the inspection team to ensure visits are effective. The SPT recommends 'members of the NPM should collectively have the expertise and experience necessary for its effective functioning' (SPT, 2010b, para. 17), and that 'healthcare experts' be part of visiting delegations at the national level (SPT, 2010b, para. 21). The CQC's designated mental health reviewers continue to bring mental health and social care experience and expertise to the role, in line with the NPM criteria for capability and professional knowledge. The CQC's broad remit ensures

---

13 See www.cqc.org.uk/get-involved/consultations/consultation-changes-more-flexible-responsive-regulation-consultation (accessed 8 March 2023).

that its inspectors can also look at mental health patients who are detained informally in hospitals and care homes. It is therefore well placed to assess whether health and social care organisations ensure that people are supported by an appropriate package of care that spans the different services they use.

Under the CRPD, States parties are required to 'closely consult with' and 'actively involve' persons with disabilities in decision-making processes related to them (Article 4 (3)). This can greatly add to the effectiveness of torture prevention work as such individuals are 'experts by experience' and have a particular role to play during visits, as they may be able to pick up on ill-treatment which may not be as visible to other monitors who lack lived experience of being detained (Steinerte et al., 2012). Equally, their presence on the monitoring team may help to establish trust between the monitor and the patient/resident and could result in reports on visits which are more reflective of the needs of those deprived of their liberty in such institutions (Mental Disability Advocacy Center, 2010, p. 15). The CQC recognises the value of involving people with lived experience as Experts by Experience are directly engaged in the inspection work.[14] Their involvement is a vital step towards a more holistic understanding of the impact of deprivation of liberty and quality of care in individual settings, in line with the ethos of the CRPD.

The CQC further engages with those with lived experience by drawing on the feedback and suggestions of a service user reference panel (SURP), a Deprivation of Liberty Advisory Group and a Mental Health Act monitoring group.[15] The SURP is made up of people who are, or have been, detained patients, and it brings an important 'lived experience' perspective to help guide the CQC's monitoring work. This is supplemented by the other groups whose members include representative bodies, voluntary and community groups, to advise the CQC on its work in relation to the MHA and MCA.

As the SPT guidelines for NPMs makes clear, a preventive human rights-based approach is not just about visits and checking for human rights breaches, but also to offer proposals as to how to reduce the likelihood and future risk of torture/ill-treatment and formulate good practice/guidance (SPT, 2010b, paras. 35, 36, 38). The CQC aims to do so in England through publication of ad hoc themed reports and guidance to providers; for example, it has published information for care providers in 2020 on responding to 'Closed Cultures', identifying that some services are higher risk, especially during the pandemic, as there were no visitors and acute staff and financial pressures.[16] It has also produced some themed reports relevant to DoLS/MCA on the experiences of residents in care homes. For example, a review of dementia care in the *Cracks in the Pathway* report (CQC, 2014) highlighted concerns about privacy and dignity (through behaviour and disrespectful language used as well as care environments, e.g., lack of personalisation of rooms and clothing, inability to summon help/assistance, and lost hearing aids/dentures not replaced) in addition to poor staff training and concerns about staffing levels and staff changes. The report highlighted what action the CQC would take in response to the findings, including training for inspectors to 'promote a culture that is based on strong values' (CQC, 2014, p. 13).

---

14 See further www.cqc.org.uk/about-us/jobs/experts-experience (accessed 8 March 2023).
15 See further www.cqc.org.uk/get-involved/how-we-involve-you/panels-advisory-groups. (accessed 8 March 2023).
16 For further information on the CQC's closed cultures work see www.cqc.org.uk/publications/themes-care/our-work-closed-cultures/closed-cultures-summer-2022-update (accessed 8 March 2023).

Protecting and promoting human rights standards

The explicit procedural requirements for NPMs explored above may be difficult for some monitoring bodies to translate on the ground, particularly for national monitors with more generic remits and reactive functions (Steinerte et al., 2012). The applicable standards against which the provider is being measured also raise challenges for national monitors such as the CQC. The standards are often found in a variety of different sources, including international and regional treaties and national legislation and policies (Steinerte & Murray, 2009). For example, in the case of OPCAT, Article 19(b) requires that NPMs, when making recommendations, take into consideration the relevant norms of the United Nations and the SPT has further clarified that this especially includes norms in the field of torture and ill-treatment prevention as well as recommendations and comments made by the SPT itself (SPT, 2010b).

The need for clearly articulated and agreed standards which recognise and capture the experiences and circumstances of persons with mental disabilities is vital. They are also important to provide clarity for inspectors, care providers and people who are detained, and to promote transparency and consistency (Steinerte et al., 2012). The CRPD may provide an important and up-to-date framework, but the challenge for national monitoring bodies is how to 'translate' these various legal obligations into practically applicable standards to be utilised during a visit to a psychiatric hospital or care home, particularly when there is conflicting guidance from the UN on institutionalisation and the nature and scope of the rights to be protected in these settings. The CRPD Committee's view on abolishing institutionalisation is clear, but it compounds the challenges for national monitors, as it is at odds with the comments of other UN Treaty bodies and experts on deprivation of liberty in health and social care settings, notably the approach of the SPT to the rights of persons in institutions and medical treatment without informed consent (SPT, 2016).

Moreover, the CRPD Committee's interpretation of Article 12 has been contentious; their views have been challenged and are not universally supported (Dawson, 2015). This creates further confusion and uncertainty about their interpretation and implementation (Weller, 2019; O'Mahoney, 2012). Recent proposals to reform mental health law in England have been circumspect and effectively side-stepped the provisions of the CRPD, with the prominent Chair of an Independent Review in 2018 on modernising the MHA going so far as to say:

> We agree with the positive vision for disabled people that is set out within the Convention. ... However, we also need to make it clear that *we do not share all the goals of the Committee on the Rights of Persons with Disabilities* (the Committee) which is the UN body that oversees the CRPD.... The Committee's interpretation of the CRPD is not shared by all UN bodies. The European Court of Human Rights does not agree that the CRPD prevents involuntary treatment and detention. ... *We also want to make it clear that we believe that the Committee's interpretation of the CRPD goes too far.*
> (Department of Health and Social Care, 2018, p. 61, emphasis added)

There is scant (if any) mention of the CRPD in any of the CQC's annual reports or guidance and very little evidence of direct engagement with the OPCAT: it focuses instead on national human rights and equality frameworks which are directly enforceable in a domestic context. It states that it is committed to equality and human rights as articulated in the HRA and Equality Act 2010, which underpin its work as a regulator to register and inspect services.[17] It has sought to incorporate a human rights approach into its regulatory approach and standards since 2014, based on the 'FREDA' Principles, i.e., fairness, respect, equality, dignity and autonomy, plus recognition of the right to life.[18] It also publishes additional good practice resources for care providers to reinforce the centrality of human rights in the provision of care and services (CQC, 2018). This experience in England suggests that national bodies tend to focus on implementation of domestic legislation, mental health services and local issues, whereas the international visiting body – SPT – brings a broader perspective to monitor compliance with international standards and obligations (Steinerte et al., 2012). As noted above, academics have argued that the CRPD should require a reappraisal of monitoring standards to take account of the particular circumstances of the treaty for persons with mental disabilities in hospitals, care homes and the wider community, but there is very little evidence in England to date that this sort of reappraisal is taking place.

The SPT carried out its first country visit to the UK in September 2019 and recommended greater public visibility for UK NPM bodies and their work (SPT, 2021). With that in mind it is noteworthy that the CQC's MHA monitoring power is firmly grounded in statute, but there is nothing comparable grounded in the MCA currently for monitoring the DoLS.[19] The precise nature and extent of the CQC's work as a NPM in the MCA and DoLS context is unclear. Unlike the MHA-related activity, the MCA work no longer appears in a distinct annual report,[20] but is subsumed within the CQC's larger Annual State of Care Report, which reports voluminously on the findings of the CQC's extensive regulatory and care standards functions (CQC, 2022b). Regular reporting on the MCA/DoLS in the State of Care Report is generally brief, and there is a lack of published qualitative data on resident/service user experiences of DoLS in hospitals and care homes. There is only a small section on the CQC's website with information on MCA/DoLS responsibilities and very little reported data available on their oversight work in this area.[21] Overall, the CQC's role to monitor mental health and capacity legislation and its membership of the UK NPM is not as prominent or widely known as its role as a health and social care regulator (SPT, 2021) and there is no mention of the CQC's NPM role in the statute that created it.

The SPT report to the UK NPM was also critical of the lack of formal legislative basis for the UK NPM which impacts on its credibility and effectiveness (SPT, 2021). The UN Committee against Torture has been equally critical of this, stating in its 2019 Concluding Observations on the UK's Sixth Periodic Report that:

> The Committee is concerned that while each of the 21 bodies that are members of the United Kingdom National Preventive Mechanism operate under their own statu-

---

17 See www.cqc.org.uk/about-us/our-strategy-plans/equality-human-rights (accessed 12 February 2023).
18 www.cqc.org.uk/guidance-providers/all-services/our-human-rights-approach (accessed 12 February 2023).
19 Note that a similar provision is proposed for the new Liberty Protection Safeguards, which will eventually replace the DoLS under the Mental Capacity (Amendment) Act 2018, although the implementation date is not known. See further www.gov.uk/government/publications/liberty-protection-safeguards-factsheets/liberty-protection-safeguards-what-they-are (accessed 12 February 2023).
20 The CQC previously published separate DoLS reports until 2015, available here: www.cqc.org.uk/guidance-providers/all-services/mental-capacity-act-deprivation-liberty-safeguards (accessed 8 March 2023).
21 See www.cqc.org.uk/guidance-providers/all-services/mental-capacity-act-deprivation-liberty-safeguards (accessed 8 March 2023).

tory provisions, the Mechanism itself is not provided for in legislation and the legislation creating many of the member bodies does not refer to their mandate under the Mechanism. The Committee also remains concerned that the absence of legislation impedes the Mechanism's independence.

(Committee Against Torture, 2019, para. 16)

The SPT recommends that NPM functions should be viewed as separate from the 'business as usual' function and noted that the preventive function is not always prioritised by NPM members. The CQC and Ofsted, the independent inspector for schools, are both cited as examples in the SPT report of NPM members who do not prioritise this aspect of their work (SPT, 2021, para. 80). These concerns call into question the CQC's ability to adequately protect the rights of psychiatric patients and discharge its obligations as a member of the UK NPM to prevent torture and ill-treatment in places of detention.

The CQC has a vast remit as the super health and social care regulator in England, and the MHA, MCA and related NPM monitoring work create additional burdens on an already stretched body. Research in the early period after the transition of mental health monitoring to the CQC suggested that the human rights focus of the MHA inspection work had been diluted (Laing, 2015) and the work of the CQC has been subject to further scrutiny and critique since then from a range of sources (National Audit Office, 2017; Laing, 2015). The CQC has been repeatedly censured for its failure to identify and target mistreatment of patients with learning disabilities post Winterbourne View in 2011. More recently an independent review into CQC's inspection of Whorlton Hall hospital again highlighted significant failures in its approach to inspection and regulation, which failed to detect ill-treatment and abuse in the hospital (Murphy, 2020). As noted earlier, these mounting concerns led to the establishment in January 2023 of an independent review on reducing risk and improving care and safety in mental health in-patient settings (Caulfield, 2023).

The CQC's MHA complaint function has also been called into question in a recent review of the government's proposals to reform the MHA (Parliament, House of Commons, House of Lords, 2023). An Independent Review of the MHA in 2018 recommended that the CQC and government should 'take steps to improve the systems that handle complaints from patients and their carers … to improve transparency and effectiveness across the system' (DHSC, 2018, p. 98). Similar criticisms and calls for reform have been made in other jurisdictions, for example in Australia, where mental health service users have faced an equally complex system which is difficult to navigate (McSherry, 2011). A parliamentary joint committee on the Draft Mental Health Bill's report in January 2023 also highlighted the challenges faced by patients detained under the MHA to access effective complaints (Parliament, House of Commons, House of Lords, 2023). To help counteract this, the joint committee recommended the creation of a new role of Mental Health Commissioner (akin to the role of the Children's Commissioner for England[22]) at a national level to promote the interests of those who are detained, and their families and carers. The Commissioner would work in conjunction with the CQC to make recommendations on reforming mental health law and to provide advice and support on navigating complaints processes (Parliament, House of Commons, House of Lords, 2023, Chapter 2). This national-level advocacy role could provide some clar-

---

22 For further information on the work of the Children's Commissioner to promote and protect the rights of children see www.childrenscommissioner.gov.uk (accessed 8 March 2023).

ity and help to strengthen the support systems for detained patients. It could also help to raise the profile of mental health, care and treatment, though its success will depend on its remit, powers and resources, and the credibility it has with key stakeholders, notably the CQC, other government departments, mental health care providers, patients, carers and the wider public.

Conclusion

Independent monitoring of psychiatric hospitals and care homes is an essential part of the struggle to prevent ill-treatment of persons with mental disabilities who are deprived of their liberty. This chapter has used the work of the CQC in England as a way of exploring the way in which human rights standards are enforced on the ground in mental health and care home settings. Despite the progress and positive initiatives in recent years and an increasing focus in the work of the CQC on OPCAT and human rights, there are still too many reports and instances of inequality across services, human rights abuses, and undignified and inhuman care for persons with mental disabilities in care homes and hospitals in England. For example, the Parliamentary Joint Committee on Human Rights (Parliament, House of Commons, House of Lords, 2022) and Health and Social Care Committee (Parliament, House of Commons, House of Lords, 2021) have both recently reported on ongoing human rights concerns in psychiatric institutions and care homes in England, which were heightened during the pandemic due to the social isolation, segregation, and restrictions on visiting. At an international level, the European CPT country report on the UK in 2022 was critical of conditions and practices of the UK NPM (CPT, 2022) and the UN SPT has urged greater visibility and prominence for the vital NPM work (SPT, 2021). The government's response to the SPT report has been disappointing however, stating that it is for the NPM to 'take the lead in promoting its role as a key component in preventing torture and ill-treatment' and it was silent on the implications for psychiatric and social care institutions (UK Government, 2021, para. 47).

Looking back through time we see that instances of ill-treatment and abuse of persons with mental disabilities in institutions is endemic, leading to a string of reports, reviews, and calls for stricter monitoring and tighter regulation to safeguard the rights of detained patients. Independent commissions have been a key feature of the history of mental health law in England, and their work has focused on visiting persons in detention to inspect conditions and detect ill-treatment. But they are not a panacea, and their work has, at times, been heavily criticised. At a national level, one of the most challenging issues is ensuring that monitoring of psychiatric hospitals and care homes is effectively prioritised and resourced (Steinerte et al., 2012). Even the CQC, whose work is focused exclusively on health and social care services and settings in England, has been criticised by the SPT for failing to prioritise its NPM-related human rights monitoring work. The organisation has also been dogged by criticisms about inconsistent inspections and persistent failures with the timeliness of some of its activities (NAO, 2017). Arguably, the MHA monitoring work is eclipsed by the CQC's wider regulatory activity, though conversely, these activities should complement each other and enable the regulator to take a more holistic view of the range of care pathways and settings for persons with mental disabilities. For example, this wider view no doubt helped to inform its findings on the poor experiences and fragmented nature of dementia care in the *Cracks in the Pathway* thematic review (CQC, 2014).

Ultimately, this examination of the CQC shows that monitoring, detection and preventive work of specialist commissions can only achieve so much – systemic and cultural changes are also needed across the sector to bring about meaningful and enduring change and reduce the risk of ill-treatment and abuse in the longer term. As the Shadow Minister for Mental Health in England stated in parliament in response to the recent abuse uncovered at the Edenfield Centre in Manchester, more must be done by the government to tackle the 'toxic culture' in these settings and services (Allin-Khan, 2022). The SPT recognises in its guidelines that NPMs can contribute to systemic change by making recommendations and publishing guidance to providers and the State to promote good, positive and safe practices. But their work in this area is compounded by a lack of agreed and clearly articulated international standards on psychiatric institutions and social care homes, and variability in focus on the distinct needs of persons with mental disabilities in national-level NPM monitoring work.

With the 'paradigm shift' introduced by the CRPD and increasing recognition of the experiences and circumstances of persons with mental disabilities, there is a need for regular review and monitoring of standards and approaches. This should recognise the range of settings where persons with mental disabilities may be deprived of their liberty as well as reevaluating the ways in which they may be subjected to torture and ill-treatment (Steinerte et al., 2012; Lea et al., 2018). The CRPD Committee could provide further advice through authoritative interpretation of the relevant provisions of the CRPD. However, evidence suggests that the Committee's views are controversial, and not universally shared or supported (Torture in Healthcare Settings, 2014). Moreover, there are inconsistent approaches from UN bodies and experts in this area, which create further challenges for national bodies to effectively monitor how the applicable international human rights standards are implemented on the ground. Thus, the 'struggle' to protect the rights of persons with mental disabilities who are deprived of their liberty in hospitals and care homes will continue for some considerable time to come.

References

Allin-Khan, R. (2022) *Edenfield centre: Treatment of patients*, Hansard House of Commons Debates, 13 October, 720, c. 253. Available at: https://hansard.parliament.uk/commons/2022-10-13/debates/D624F0ED-AD0D-48A4-A416-20F5354600D2/EdenfieldCentreTreatmentOfPatients (Accessed 8th March 2023).

Bartlett, P. (2014) Implementing a Paradigm Shift: Implementing the CRPD in the Context of Mental Disability Law. In *Torture in Healthcare Settings: Reflections on the Special Rapporteur on Torture's 2013 Thematic Report*, Washington, DC: Centre for Human Rights and Humanitarian Law, American University Washington College of Law, pp. 169–180.

Bartlett, P. et al. (2007) *Mental disability and the European Convention on Human Rights*, c

Care Quality Commission (2011) *A new system of registration: The Mental Capacity Act 2005 guidance for providers*, London: Care Quality Commission.

Care Quality Commission (2014) *Cracks in the pathway: People's experiences of dementia care as they move between care homes and hospitals*. Available at: https://www.cqc.org.uk/sites/default/files/20141009_cracks_in_the_pathway_final_0.pdf (Accessed 8th March 2023).

Care Quality Commission (2018) *Equally outstanding: Equality & human rights good practice resource*, London: Care Quality Commission.

Care Quality Commission (2020) *Out of sight – Who cares?* Available at: https://www.cqc.org.uk/sites/default/files/20201218_rssreview_report.pdf (Accessed 8th March 2023).

Care Quality Commission (2022a) *Monitoring the Mental Health Act in 2021/22*, London: Care Quality Commission.

Care Quality Commission (2022b) *State of care 2021/22*, London: Care Quality Commission. https://www.cqc.org.uk/publication/state-care-202122 (Accessed 19th July 2023).

Caulfield, M. (2023) *Mental health update*, Hansard House of Commons Debates, 23 January, Statement UIN HCWS512. Available at: https://questions-statements.parliament.uk/written-statements/detail/2023-01-23/hcws512 (Accessed 8th March 2023).

Clayton, M. (2002) The Separation of the Mental Health Act Commission's Functions: Inspectors, Visitors and Advocacy, *Journal of Mental Health Law*, July, pp. 97–104.

Committee Against Torture (2019) *Concluding observations on the sixth periodic report on the United Kingdom of Great Britain and Ireland CAT/C/GBR/CO/6*. Available at: https://documents-dds-ny.un.org/doc/UNDOC/GEN/G19/154/71/PDF/G1915471.pdf?OpenElement (Accessed 8th March 2023).

Committee for the Prevention of Torture (2022) *Report to the government of United Kingdom on the periodic visit to the United Kingdom carried out by the European Committee for the Prevention of Torture and Inhuman or Degrading Treatment or Punishment*. Available at: https://rm.coe.int/1680a72b71 (Accessed 8th March 2023).

Committee on the Rights of Persons with Disabilities (2015) *Guidelines on article 14 of the Convention on the Rights of Persons with Disabilities A/72/55*.

Committee on the Rights of Persons with Disabilities (2022) *Guidelines on deinstitutionalisation, including in emergencies, CRPD/C/5*.

Dawson, J. (2015) A realistic approach to assessing mental health laws' compliance with the UN CRPD, *International Journal of Law and Psychiatry*, 40, pp. 70–79.

Department of Health (2012) *Transforming care: A national response to Winterbourne View hospital Department of Health review: Final report*, Department of Health.

Department of Health and Social Care (2018) *Modernising the mental health act: Increasing choice, reducing compulsion final report of the independent review of the Mental Health Act 1983*. Available at: https://assets.publishing.service.gov.uk/government/uploads/system/uploads/attachment_data/file/778897/Modernising_the_Mental_Health_Act_-_increasing_choice__reducing_compulsion.pdf (Accessed 8th March 2023).

Disability Rights Monitor (2020) *Disability rights during the pandemic: A global report on findings of the Covid-19 disability rights monitor*, Disability Rights Monitor. Available at: https://covid-drm.org/assets/documents/Disability-Rights-During-the-Pandemic-report-web.pdf (Accessed 8th March 2023).

European Committee for the Prevention of Torture, Inhuman or Degrading Treatment or Punishment. (2017) *Report to the government of the United Kingdom on the visit to the United Kingdom carried out by the European Committee for the Prevention of Torture and Inhuman or Degrading Treatment or Punishment CPT/Inf (2017)9*. Available at: https://rm.coe.int/168070a774 (Accessed 8th March 2023).

Fennell, P. (2010) Mental health law: History, policy and regulation. In Bartlett, P. et al. (Eds.), *Principles of mental health law and policy*, Oxford: Oxford University Press, pp. 3–70.

Gooding, P. (2015) Navigating the 'flashing amber lights' of the right to legal capacity in the United Nations convention on the rights of persons with disabilities: Responding to major concerns, *Human Rights Law Review*, 15(1), pp. 45–71.

Hardwick, N. and Murray, R. (2019) Regularity of OPCAT visits by NPMs in Europe *Australian Journal of Human Rights*, 25(1), pp. 66–90.

Human Rights Council (2019) *Report of the Special Rapporteur on the right of everyone to the enjoyment of the highest attainable standard of physical and mental health, A/HRC/41/34*. Available at: https://documents-dds-ny.un.org/doc/UNDOC/GEN/G19/105/97/PDF/G1910597.pdf?OpenElement (Accessed 8th March 2023).

Human Rights Watch (2020) *Living in chains: Shackling of people with psychosocial disabilities worldwide*. Available at: https://www.hrw.org/report/2020/10/06/living-chains/shackling-people-psychosocial-disabilities-worldwide (Accessed 8th March 2023).

Jenkin, M. (1980) *Rampton Hospital*. Hansard House of Commons Debates, 11 November, 992, c. 193. Available at: https://api.parliament.uk/historic-hansard/commons/1980/nov/11/rampton-hospital (Accessed 8th March 2023).

Karsay, D. and Lewis, O. (2012) Disability, torture and ill-treatment: Taking stock and ending abuses, *The International Journal of Human Rights*, 16(6), pp. 816–830.

Laing, J. (2014) Protecting the rights of patients in psychiatric settings: A comparison of the work of the mental health act commission with the CQC, *Journal of Social Welfare and Family Law*, 36(2), pp. 149–167.

Laing, J. (2015) Perspectives on monitoring mental health legislation in England: A view from the front-line, *Medical Law Review*, 23(3), pp. 400–426.

Lawson, A. (2012) Disability equality, reasonable accommodation and the avoidance of ill-treatment in places of detention: the role of supranational monitoring and inspection bodies, *The International Journal of Human Rights Law*, 16(6), pp. 845–864.

Lea, M. et al. (2018) A disability aware approach to torture prevention? Australian OPCAT ratification and improved protections for people with disability, *Australian Journal of Human Rights*, 24(1) pp. 70–96.

Maylea, C. (2022) Victoria, Australia is getting a new Mental Health and Wellbeing bill, *Journal of Bioethical Inquiry*, 19, pp. 527–532.

McHale, J. (2003) Standards, quality and accountability the NHS and mental health: A case for joined-up thinking? *The Journal of Social Welfare and Family Law*, 25(4), pp. 369–382.

McSherry, M. (2011) Who do I turn to? Resolving complaints by mental health consumers and carers, *JLM*, 18, pp. 669–676.

McSherry, M. and Maker, Y. (Eds.). (2021) *Restrictive practices in health care and disability settings: Legal, policy and practical responses*, Abingdon: Routledge.

Mental Disability Advocacy Centre (2010) Recommendations by the mental disability advocacy center to the European Committee for the Prevention of Torture, on aligning its standards to the UN Convention on the Rights of Persons with Disabilities.

Mental Health Act Commission (2008) Risk, Rights and Recovery Twelfth Biennial Report 2005–2007, London: The Stationery Office.

Murphy, G. (2020) *CQC inspections and regulation of Whorlton Hall 2015–2019: An independent review*, England: CQC.

Murray, R. et al. (2011) *The optional protocol to the UN Convention against Torture*, Oxford: Oxford University Press.

National Audit Office (2008) *Releasing resources to the frontline: The Department of Health's review of its arm's length bodies*. Available at: https://www.nao.org.uk/reports/releasing-resources-to-the-frontline-the-department-of-healths-review-of-its-arms-length-bodies/ (Accessed 8th March 2023).

National Audit Office (2017) *Care quality commission regulating health and social care*. Available at: https://www.nao.org.uk/reports/care-quality-commission-regulating-health-and-social-care/ (Accessed 8th March 2023).

O'Mahoney, C. (2012) Legal capacity and detention: Implications of the UN disability convention for the inspection standards of human rights monitoring bodies, *The International Journal of Human Rights*, 16(6), pp. 883–901.

Parliament, House of Commons (2021) *Health and social care committee, the treatment of autistic people and individuals with learning disabilities, fifth report of session 2021–22 (HC 2021-22 21)*. Available at: https://committees.parliament.uk/publications/6669/documents/71689/default/ (Accessed 8th March 2023).

Parliament, House of Commons, House of Lords (2022) *Joint committee on human rights, protecting human rights in care settings, fourth report of session 2022–23 (HC 2022-23 216)*. Available at: https://committees.parliament.uk/publications/23214/documents/169544/default/ (Accessed 8th March 2023).

Parliament, House of Commons, House of Lords (2023) *Joint committee on the draft Mental Health Bill 2022, session 2022–23 (HC 2022-23 696)*. Available at: https://committees.parliament.uk/publications/33599/documents/182904/default/ (Accessed 8th March 2023).

Perlin, M. L. and Schriver, M. R. (2014) 'You that hide behind walls: The relationship between the convention on the rights of persons with disabilities and the convention against torture and the treatment of institutionalised forensic patients' in *Torture in Healthcare Settings: Reflections on the Special Rapporteur on Torture's 2013 Thematic Report*, Washington, DC, Centre for Human Rights and Humanitarian Law, American University Washington College of Law, pp. 195–217.

Quince, W. (2022) *Edenfield Centre: Treatment of patients*, Hansard House of Commons Debates, 13 October, 720, c. 251. Available at: https://hansard.parliament.uk/commons/2022-10-13/debates/D624F0ED-AD0D-48A4-A416-20F5354600D2/EdenfieldCentreTreatmentOfPatients (Accessed 8th March 2023).

Report of the Special Rapporteur on torture and other cruel, inhuman or degrading treatment or punishment (2013) A/HRC/22/53.

Shaw, I. et al. (2007) *Understanding treatment without consent: An analysis of the work of the Mental Health Act commission*, Farnham: Ashgate.

Steinerte, E. and Murray, R. (2009) Same but different? National human rights commissions and ombudsman offices and national preventive mechanisms under the optional protocol to the UN convention against torture, *Essex Human Rights Review*, 6(1), p. 95.

Steinerte, E. et al. (2012) Monitoring those deprived of their liberty in psychiatric and social care institutions and national practice in the UK, *The International Journal of Human Rights*, 16(6), pp. 865–882.

Subcommittee on Prevention of Torture (2010a) *Report on the visit of the Subcommittee on Prevention of Torture and Other Cruel, Inhuman or Degrading Treatment or Punishment to Mexico*, CAT/OP/MEX/1.

Subcommittee on Prevention of Torture (2010b) *Guidelines on national preventive mechanisms*, CAT/OP/12/5.

Subcommittee on Prevention of Torture (2016) *Approach of the Subcommittee on Prevention of Torture and Other Cruel, Inhuman or Degrading Treatment or Punishment regarding the rights of persons institutionalised and treated medically without informed consent*, CAT/OP/27/2.

Subcommittee on the Prevention of Torture (2021) *Visit to the United Kingdom of Great Britain and Northern Ireland undertaken from 9 to 18 September 2019: recommendations and observations addressed to the state party*, CAT/OP/GBR/ROSP/1. Available at: https://s3-eu-west-2.amazonaws.com/npm-prod-storage-19n0nag2nk8xk/uploads/2021/06/CAT.OP_.GBP_.ROSP_.R1.FINAL-VERSION_SPT-report-to-UK-govt-3.pdf (Accessed 8th March 2023).

UK Government (2021) *The UK's response to the Subcommittee on the Prevention of Torture and Other Cruel Inhuman or Degrading Treatment or Punishment's visit report from October 2020*. Available at: https://assets.publishing.service.gov.uk/government/uploads/system/uploads/attachment_data/file/993044/annex-B-uk-response-to-spt-visit-report.pdf (Accessed 8th March 2023).

Thom, K. and Prebble, K. (2013) District inspectors: Watchdogs of patients' rights. In Dawson, J. and Gledhill, K. (Eds.), *New Zealand's mental health act in practice*, Wellington: Victoria University Press, pp. 131–146.

Torture in healthcare settings: Reflections on the Special Rapporteur on Torture's 2013 thematic report (2014) Washington: Centre for Human Rights and Humanitarian Law, American University Washington College of Law.

Weller, P. (2019) Monitoring and the convention on the rights of persons with disabilities, *Australian Journal of Human Rights*, 25(1), pp. 130–149.

3
THE RELATIONSHIP BETWEEN ETHICS AND LAW IN MENTAL HEALTHCARE

Louise Campbell

Introduction

Mental healthcare is fraught with ethical challenges. In no other domain of clinical practice is the tension between what the law permits and the question of what "ought to be done" so explicit. We expect the law to be ethical (Daw, 2015: 103), yet law can at best aspire to an ethical minimum; it cannot compel "ethical excellence" (Van der Burg, 1997: 102–3; 112). At worst, law permits practices which cause harm. Treatment and care which are genuinely person-centred, evidence-based and founded on respect for the person who is being cared for can effect profound change in the lives of people with mental and psychosocial disabilities. Conversely, mental healthcare which is not built around these principles can cause enormous harm and exacerbate the difficulties experienced by the person being treated. The balance between providing appropriate treatment which is effective in reducing the burden of mental illness and avoiding further harm to the person receiving treatment is exceptionally fine.

Healthcare law and healthcare ethics serve different purposes (Miola, 2007: 194) and may usefully be conceptualised as distinct "sources of authority" in situations in which someone is trying to determine what he or she "ought to do or ought to have done" (Brassington, 2018: 225).[1] Yet they are so profoundly entangled that it is increasingly difficult "to determine where one ends and the other begins" (Fovargue and Brazier, 2006: 21; van der Berg, 1997: 92; Harrington, 2017: 176). In the domain of clinical practice, health law establishes the parameters of what is permissible for the health and social care professions, while ethics determines which among a number of *legally permissible* options is preferable or "best", furnishing principles and tools for analysing and working through problems which arise when values collide or legitimate viewpoints come into conflict.

Ethical and legal issues in mental healthcare are rarely discussed in conjunction, despite the fact that most of the legal cases which come before the courts in this area of clinical practice have a significant ethical component. Lack of clarity about the nature of ethics as

---

1 Brassington identifies three such sources of authority: law, what he terms "morality" and "professional codes" (2018: 225), claiming that both law and professional codes of conduct are "written with a moral aim in mind".

it applies to clinical practice has often led to the ethical dimension of particular cases being subsumed within discussions of legal concepts or points of law. The aim of this chapter is therefore to provide a sketch of the relationship between ethics and law as they mutually shape mental health practice and to draw attention to the distinctive role of ethics in clarifying and resolving challenging clinical cases. Clinical ethics as a discipline involves analysing available options from a multiplicity of perspectives in the interests of determining the most justifiable or "least worst" course of action in a given decision-making context. Ethical scrutiny of the reasons given to support a given decision may eliminate bias, ensure robustness and minimise the harm to patients associated with unidimensional decision-making. This is particularly important in light of the discretion afforded to mental health professionals by the law, the tendency of members of the judiciary to defer to clinical authority and the obligation on clinicians to comply with the ethical principles of the Convention on the Rights of Persons with Disabilities.

The evolution of mental health law

Mental health law emerged as a discrete field only in the late nineteenth century (Wilson, 2021: 36; Kelly, this vol.), giving "structure and substance" to two "nebulous" doctrines, the "police powers" of the state and the doctrine of *parens patriae*,[2] which in conjunction furnish its conceptual foundations and allow it to justify creating exceptions to the liberal ideology of non-interference (Wilson, 2021: 34). Underpinned by the doctrine of necessity, the concept of *parens patriae*, with its moral overtones, legitimates the role of the state in ensuring access to treatment for people who need it, notwithstanding the fact that they may not be able to provide consent (Wilson, 2021: 35), while the police powers of the state allow it to intervene to protect the public from harm in specific circumstances (Fennell, 2008: 255; Wilson, 2021: 34).[3] Historically, however, the law has served to exclude, oppress and "disable" people with psychosocial disabilities by depriving them of rights which others are free to exercise, such as the right to refuse medical treatment (Lawson and Priestly, 2017: 14). Those who have been subjected to unwanted, unproven, harmful or barbaric treatments or institutionalised for protracted periods without justification were failed spectacularly by the law,[4] even as psychiatry as a nascent profession boasted of "advances" in the treatment of mental illness. Revelations of the abuse and dehumanising treatment experienced by patients

---

2 The doctrine of *parens patriae* is the idea that it is the responsibility of the state to protect the rights of those who are unable to advocate on their own behalf.
3 Brenda Hale describes mental health law in terms of a "perpetual struggle" to reconcile three related but often competing goals: protecting the public, ensuring access to appropriate services and safeguarding the civil rights of people with mental impairments (Hale, 2007: 19).
4 For reasons of space I will restrict my discussion to the legal landscape in England and Wales, acknowledging the immensity of the challenge to provide equitable access to appropriate services for people with mental disorder at a global level. Mezzina and colleagues observe that "[t]he abandonment of many of those in need is still the reality" worldwide. They point to the lack of a welfare state "safety net" and of affordable services in many low- and medium-income countries, exacerbated by social exclusion and discrimination, and to inequities of access to adequate care in high-income countries, noting that even in these countries "when accessing care, there is often poor care quality with persistent risk of stigmatization, social exclusion and loss of rights" (Mezzina et al., 2019: 484). Drew et al. argue that, particularly in low- and middle-income countries, people with mental and psychosocial disabilities continue to experience violations of their civil, cultural, economic, political and social rights (Drew et al., 2011: 1664).

in psychiatric hospitals galvanised the anti-psychiatry movement, bolstered calls for de-institutionalisation and provided a powerful impetus to the reform of mental health law during the second half of the twentieth century.

Conceptualising the history of mental health law in terms of a dialectic between the polarised approaches of *medicalism* (or medical discretion) and *legalism* may be a "cliché" (Wilson, 2021: 41), but it offers an explanation for society's understanding of how the purpose of mental health law has changed over time (Brown, 2016: 1). Medicalism refers to the view that the substantive aim of mental health law is to provide care and treatment for people with mental disorder, with the law remaining as open-ended as possible in order to allow clinicians maximum discretion to act in the "best interests" of their patients (Brown, 2016: 2). Legalism, conversely, is the view that the imposition of legal duties and responsibilities on healthcare professionals is needed to protect patients from excessive medical authority and ensure that their rights are respected (Brown, 2016: 2). Rooted in the biomedical model of illness, medicalism seeks to remove barriers to accessing care, including "cumbersome" procedural requirements, while legalism is more concerned with preventing wrongful deprivation of liberty (Dhanda, 2016: 441). Thus, on a legalist interpretation, the purpose of mental health law is to establish procedural safeguards to guarantee the rights of those who are subject to it, including the restriction of the statutory definition of mental disorder, recognition of the right to refuse treatment, strict statutory criteria for detention and judicial review of decisions to detain (Brown, 2016: 2). The "new legalism" spearheaded by Larry Gostin in the late 1970s sought to protect people with mental disorder from discrimination and looked to the European Convention on Human Rights to guarantee the rights of those detained under mental health legislation to due process regarding their detention (Fennell, 2010: 16–17). It was underpinned by two principles: the principle that people with mental impairment should have "enforceable rights" to the care they needed – the "ideology of entitlement" – and the principle of the "least restrictive alternative", namely, the right to be treated in a setting which restricted their rights and freedoms as minimally as possible (Fennell, 2010: 17; Brown 2016: 7).[5]

The most basic principle of medicine and of all healthcare – to do no harm – entails a fundamental commitment to respecting human rights (Pūras, 2018: 521). Human rights draw their force from a contractarian foundation based on a "codification of those aspects of the prevailing morality which are seen as essential to its common life and therefore properly protected against challenge" (Montgomery, 2006: 9). Human rights law can be a powerful tool for advancing the rights and freedoms of persons with mental disorder, not only because it recognises that people have human rights simply in virtue of their humanity – and irrespective of their "disability" – but also because it permits international scrutiny of non-compliant domestic mental health policy and practices (Gostin, 2001: 264; Richardson, 2010: 181). However, the international human rights instruments which predated the Convention on the Rights of Persons with Disabilities (CRPD) failed people with disabilities (Lewis 2010: 113), with the European Convention on Human Rights exhibiting a "'friendliness' towards medical paternalism" (Montgomery, 2006: 10), while the European Court of Human Rights

---

5 Brown argues that this move to legalism was observable in the case law of the European Court of Human Rights during the 1980s, noting that "[o]ne of the most important articulations of legalism was the manner in which the ECtHR built on the right under Article 5(4) to have the lawfulness of one's detention reviewed speedily by a court" (Brown, 2016: 3).

showed a similar reluctance to question medical authority (Brown, 2016: 5).[6] While both medicalist and legalist approaches – what Amita Dhanda calls "therapy-dominant" and "autonomy-dominant" models of legislation (Dhanda, 2016: 439–41) – were well-intentioned, both have the same fundamental flaw: they both silence the voice of the person with disability, allowing others to determine her priorities and needs and relegating her to a "bystander" in her own life (Dhanda, 2016: 442; see Brown, 2016: 7).

Voice, inclusion and the Convention on the Rights of Persons with Disabilities

The CRPD is the first comprehensive and legally binding international framework for the protection of the human rights of people with disabilities, including mental and psychosocial disabilities (Drew et al., 2011: 1665; Doyle-Guilloud, this vol.). Underpinned by a social model of disability which reconceptualises disability as a result of the interaction between an individual and her environment (Barton-Hanson, 2018: 279–80), the treaty "challenges centuries of legally-sanctioned prejudice" (Pūras and Gooding, 2019:42) by placing the human rights of people with disabilities at the forefront of the legal reform agenda (Fennell, 2010: 14). Under the CRPD, people with disabilities are no longer perceived as recipients of medical and social welfare, but as legal agents and bearers of rights; it is social organisation and discriminatory attitudes which "disable" people, not any impairments they may happen to have (Brown 2016: 6). In demanding, not formal equality between people with and without disabilities, but "equality of outcome", the CRPD calls for the recasting of the "physical and the normative world[s]" to eliminate discrimination and ensure for people with disabilities full and meaningful participation in all aspects of social life (Dhanda, 2016: 442–3). As such, the CRPD has an explicitly ethical aim, insofar as it seeks to ground disability policy upon a foundation of "moral principles or values", namely the principles of equality, dignity, autonomy and participation (Degener, 2017: 34–5).

Because States Parties are required to "modify or abolish"[7] domestic legislation which is not in compliance with these principles, the entry into force of the CRPD has prompted an upsurge of initiatives to review and reform mental health laws in a number of jurisdictions (Wilson, 2022: 188). Articles 13–16 of the CRPD explicitly mandate the creation of legal frameworks and oversight mechanisms to protect the rights of people with mental and psychosocial disabilities (Drew et al., 2011: 1672) and the emphasis on the necessity of moving from regimes of substituted decision-making to models of supported decision-making[8] will require significant changes to existing legislation (Callaghan and Ryan, 2014:

---

6 This is exemplified by the ruling in *Herczegfalvy v Austria* (1992) which stated that "a method which is a therapeutic necessity cannot be regarded as inhuman or degrading", tempered by the caveat that the court "must nevertheless satisfy itself that the medical necessity has been convincingly shown to exist" (*Herczegfalvy v Austria* (1992) EHRR 437, 484 (82) at 82).
7 Convention on the Rights of Persons with Disabilities, Art. 4.
8 The Mental Capacity Act (2005) contains provisions which rely in part on the practice of substituted decision-making, which allows a third party to substitute her decision for the decision of the person who lacks capacity, subject to certain restrictions, including the need to be guided by the wishes and preferences of the person on behalf of whom a decision is being made. Conversely, supported decision-making is based on the concept of providing support to enable a person to make her own decisions wherever possible (Barton-Hanson, 2018: 281).

760). Whether and how existing laws which permit involuntary treatment and detention can be reformed to make them compliant with the CRPD is a matter of ongoing debate. Tina Minkowitz argues that the "new paradigm" represented by the CRPD requires respecting the autonomy of people with disabilities rather than "vesting decision-making authority in another person" and insists that both treatment without consent and deprivation of liberty for purposes of treatment violate this requirement and may in some situations amount to torture (Minkowitz, 2010: 171–172). She maintains that it is not possible to reform mental health laws which permit these practices and that they should be abolished (Minkowitz, 2010: 177; Minkowitz, 2017: 78). Others argue for reform rather than abolition of existing mental health legislation and call for a "pragmatic rather than an ideological approach to maximising the rights of people with mental impairments" (Wilson 2021: 167; Dawson, 2015: 79). Callaghan and Ryan argue that, in certain circumstances and subject to stringent safeguards, substituted judgement which respects the rights, will and preferences of service users may do more justice to the requirements of Article 12 than the notion of providing a person with 100% support – a notion which "strains ordinary understandings of what support involves" and begins to resemble a "legal fiction" (Callaghan and Ryan, 2014: 757).[9] They suggest that failure to acknowledge the "full spectrum of decision-making processes" in mental healthcare may in fact undermine the rights of people with mental disorder because it limits the ability of lawmakers to ensure that appropriate safeguards are in place (Callaghan and Ryan, 2014: 760).[10] Wilson describes models of decision-making support based on the principles of the CRPD which are aimed at enhancing significantly the participation of people with mental impairment and which strive to balance the negative rights to liberty and freedom from non-interference with the positive rights to life, health, education, employment and social inclusion, but acknowledges that such initiatives will require increased resources and a central role for advocacy and education (Wilson 2021: 174ff, Dawson, 2015: 71ff).[11]

The paradox of coercive care

Ensuring that people who seek or require treatment have access to it in an appropriate environment (Department of Health, 2014: 6) is a laudable goal of mental health legislation. People who are diagnosed with mental disorder are often acutely unwell and in need of support to manage their symptoms. But by "codifying" clinical authority, mental health law

---

9 Similar concerns have been raised in relation to the "best interpretation" of best interests, the "fallback" approach adopted in General Comment 1, which sidesteps the acknowledgement that "there are things that we do not, and cannot, know" about the interests of a person whose capacity is profoundly impaired. See Donnelly (2016), 326–7.
10 "Safeguards such as tribunal oversight of substituted decisions would be overly intrusive in the case of ordinary supported decision-making, but would be an indispensable protection for the rights of persons who are the subject of substituted decision-making, and a separate category of oversight for substituted decisions will be necessary to ensure that such interventions are "appropriate and tailored" to an individual's circumstances as required by the CRPD" (Callaghan and Ryan, 2014: 760).
11 Dawson draws attention to an internal inconsistency in the text of the CRPD, which describes human rights as indivisible but does not provide clarity in relation to the question of whether a person's negative or positive rights should prevail in circumstances in which these rights come into conflict. For example, involuntary psychiatric treatment "could both limit a person's autonomy and promote their social inclusion, health, and standard of living" and may thus promote his or her rights "under the Convention as a whole" (Dawson, 2015: 71).

gives healthcare professionals the power to detain people with mental disorder, to administer treatment against their wishes and to subject them to restrictive practices such as seclusion and restraint (Fennell, 2010: 23).[12] Coercion is thus a central component of psychiatric treatment and interventions, regulated by law and seen as a legitimate form of patient management (Arboleda-Florez, 2011: 83–4; Mann et al., 2021: 2). Effectively, what mental health law does is specify "the point at which coercion becomes lawful" (Richardson, 2010: 182).

Treating people with mental disorder who do not want to be treated for mental disorder is the most ethically fraught issue in mental health law (Monaghan, in (eds.) Kallert et al., 2011: 33). Coercion of any kind is antithetical to some of the most cherished values in many contemporary societies, particularly the values of liberty and autonomy enshrined in the Western liberal tradition (Hem et al., 2018: 93), yet coercive measures are still widely used in mental healthcare settings (Allikmets et al., 2020: 723) and are perceived in certain contexts as ethically obligatory, and thus ethically justifiable (Kjellin et al., 1997: 1567). What makes the problem of involuntary treatment so intractable is the contradiction at its heart: a given intervention in a specific context may be *both* "right" and "wrong", both ethically permissible and impermissible. While involuntary detention and treatment can be damaging and traumatising for people with mental disorder, withholding treatment for serious mental impairment because a person does not have the capacity to consent to it can also result in profound suffering and may be tantamount to discrimination (Wilson, 2022: 192, 177). Administering treatment without a person's consent may advance her positive right to receive care, while undermining her negative right to freedom from interference in the decisions she makes about what happens to her own body. It is this collision of positive and negative rights which generates the paradox of "coercive care"[13] and makes the process of justification so ethically precarious. Whether it is ever ethically justifiable to hospitalise and treat a person with mental disorder despite her objection, and if so, under what circumstances, is a complex and controversial question which gives rise to significant human rights concerns (Bartlett, 2011: 517) and must be addressed by all stakeholders in the field of mental healthcare (Ryan and Bartels, 2021: 279).

Treatment is involuntary when someone other than the person being treated provides consent to an intervention to which the person him- or herself objects (Callaghan and Ryan, 2014: 753) and it is compulsory if it is administered in spite of the person's refusal. In mental healthcare, the term "coercion" denotes a broad set of practices ranging from different types of treatment pressures to "interpersonal leverage", whereas the term "compulsion" refers more narrowly to the legally regulated use of force to make a person accept treatment which he or she has refused (Szmukler 2015: 259). Coercion exists on a spectrum, encompassing both formal measures regulated by mental health legislation and informal measures intended to secure compliance from patients (Grey, 2019: 14; McSherry and Freckelton, 2015: 3). Practices involving compulsion and coercion vary widely across and even within jurisdictions (Szmukler, 2015: 259),[14] but in most countries, mental health legislation permits depriva-

---

12 Physical restraint may be defined as "any direct contact where the intervener's intention is to prevent, restrict, or subdue movement of the body of another person" (Department of Health (DH), 2014; p. 26, cited in Cusack et al., 2018: 1162). Chemical restraint achieves the same ends through the administration of medication.
13 I have borrowed this term from McSherry and Freckelton (2015).
14 Szmukler notes that in England the rate of coercive practices doubled between 1995 and 2015 (Szmukler, 2015: 259).

tion of liberty, detention, interference with a person's privacy, restrictions on freedom of movement and non-consensual use of medication which may alter the person's thinking or personality (Hem et al., 2018: 94). Alongside more formal measures, "soft" forms of coercion such as negotiation, education and persuasion are all routinely deployed in the treatment of people with mental disorder (Arboleda-Florez, in Kallert et al., 2011: 94). In mental healthcare, power is exercised along a continuum ranging from covert coercion to explicit or overt coercion, with covert forms of coercion concealing the exercise of power through the use of "diversion strategies" such as ignoring, distracting or bargaining with patients (Vatne and Fagermoen, 2007: 44).[15] Even where coercive measures are not explicitly used, many people receiving treatment for mental disorder exist constantly under the shadow of coercion, consenting to treatment out of fear that non-compliance will result in treatment being administered involuntarily (Szmukler, 2015: 259). Not only is coercion itself detrimental to trust and communication between clinicians and patients (Hem et al., 2018: 105), it invariably makes the therapeutic relationship "even more unbalanced than when [treatment] is consensual and informed" (McSherry and Freckelton, 2010: 7).[16] Whether visible or invisible, exercising power in these ways – even if it is seen as justifiable in the context of the benefits of treatment – can leave people who are being treated for mental disorder feeling disempowered, devalued, humiliated and "othered" (Vatne and Fagermoen, 2007: 45; see Freeth, 2007: 43).

Justification of involuntary treatment

Mental health legislation differs across jurisdictions in the justifications provided for the use of involuntary detention and treatment. Justifications most commonly provided in law include promoting the welfare of the person with mental disorder herself and the protection of those to whom she might pose a risk, including herself. In England and Wales, mental health legislation provides for involuntary detention in a hospital if a person is "suffering from a mental disorder of a nature or degree which warrants the detention of the patient in a hospital for assessment (or for assessment followed by medical treatment)",[17] if treatment is deemed necessary for the person's own health or safety or for the protection of others (Mental Health Act 1983 as amended by Mental Health Act 2007, s. 2.2 (a–b)).[18] The law provides for involuntary treatment if the person is "suffering from a mental disorder of a nature or degree which makes it appropriate to receive medical treatment in a hospital", if

---

15 Vatne and Fagermoen describe a slippage in mental health nursing practice from a starting point of caring for the patient to the perception of the patient as "deviant" and requiring correction in order to enable her to return to more "normal" behaviour (Vatne and Fagermoen, 2007: 44).
16 While there is limited evidence that some people who have been subjected to involuntary treatment regard it in retrospect as a positive measure, high-quality evidence of its effectiveness is lacking and the question of whether or not it improves outcomes for people with mental disorder in the longer term is unresolved (Brissos et al., 2017: 36).
17 For Bartlett and Sandland, the "extraordinary flexibility" of the language used in s. 2.2 (a) is problematic from a civil rights perspective insofar as it gives clinicians very little guidance, and very broad discretion, in interpreting the law (Bartlett and Sandland, 2014: 253).
18 Detention must be the least restrictive option available, with all other less restrictive alternatives having been explored and rejected before the person is detained, and it must be a proportionate response to the situation based on a balancing of the interests of the person herself against the interests of society (Bartlett and Sandland, 2014: 252).

such treatment is necessary for the health or safety of the patient or for the protection of others and it cannot be provided unless she is detained under the law, and if appropriate medical treatment is available (Mental Health Act 1983 as amended by Mental Health Act 2007, s. 3.2 (a,c,d)).[19] As Peter Bartlett points out, the "starting point" of the legislation in England and Wales is that the consent of service users is not required for treatment administered for mental disorder (Bartlett, 2011: 521), with the exception of neurosurgery and electroconvulsive therapy (ECT) (Mental Health Act 1983, s.63).

Whereas at common law, an adult with decision-making capacity can refuse medical treatment for any reason, mental health legislation in many jurisdictions denies people with mental illness this right, if they are deemed to be a risk to themselves or others (Callaghan and Ryan, 2014: 750). In England and Wales, a capable refusal of treatment by a person who has been detained under the Mental Health Act 2007 can be overridden in the interests of the person's health or safety or for the protection of others, with no legal requirement that "the risk to the patient or to others be significant nor the harm serious" (Richardson, 2011: 156). As Bartlett points out, it is one thing to allow patients who have capacity to decide to accept treatment with significant risks and uncertain outcomes, but "quite another to compel them to do so" (Bartlett 2011: 534) and many people with mental disorders have had treatments imposed on them in good faith and "for their own good" which in retrospect have been found to have harmed them (Szmukler and Dawson in Kallert et al., 2011: 115).

Because capacity plays little or no role in these decisions (Szmukler and Dawson, 2011: 99), it can be argued that the law treats people with mental illness less favourably than people with physical illnesses, ultimately amounting to discrimination against people with mental impairment (Szmuckler and Dawson, 2011: 117). The lawful imposition of an intervention on a person who has met the threshold for decision-making capacity but refuses treatment, when the decisions of people who have capacity and refuse treatment for physical conditions are respected, creates an "ethical asymmetry" which further stigmatises people with mental illness (Borecky et al., 2019: 78; Bartlett, 2011: 540; Richardson, 2011: 146–7). Whereas the autonomy and personal values of people with medical conditions are recognised, the same privilege is not afforded to people with mental illness (Richardson 2011). The legislation thereby encourages a culture of exclusion and non-participation (Weller, 2010: 59).[20] While the failure to legislate for decision-making on behalf of people who lack capacity would be tantamount to "condemning incapable people to remain untreated" (Richardson 2011: 155), commentators such as Richardson call for a reconsideration of laws which undermine the human rights of people with mental disorder and further entrench the discrimination and stigma they experience. Others urge a revision of healthcare policy to limit involuntary hospitalisation and treatment to those who cannot, even with support, make their own decisions about their health (Borecky et al., 2019; Szmukler and Dawson, 2011; Wilson 2021: 196)[21].

---

19 Ambiguity in the language of s. 3.2 raises a number of questions, including the question of what is meant by "available", how effective treatment needs to be if it is to be deemed "appropriate" (as opposed to "minimal" or "optimal") and how predictable the efficacy of treatment should be (Bartlett and Sandland, 2014: 254; see also Fennell, 2010: 33).
20 Richardson argues that if mental disorder is to be treated differently from physical disorder then "the justification for that apparent discrimination must be specifically and expressly spelt out" (Richardson, 2011: 156).
21 According to Richardson, involuntary treatment should only be administered in exceptional circumstances when the person has capacity. She suggests that the jurisprudence of the ECtHR, particularly in relation to article 8 of the European Convention on Human Rights "contains quite enough respect for patient auton-

Involuntary pharmacological treatment

Refusal of treatment for symptoms of mental disorder is a multifaceted phenomenon.[22] Like medications for many physical illnesses, psychiatric drugs are complex and the process of determining what will be effective or optimal for a given individual is often a matter of trial and error (Bartlett and Sandland, 2014: 401). There are legitimate reasons why patients might want to decline psychiatric medication (ibid: 403). The harms associated with psychopharmacological treatment for mental illness have been well documented, while their benefits are not "clear-cut" (Bartlett, 2011: 517; Tjannso, 2004: 432; Gøtzsche, 2015: 1–2). Second-generation antipsychotic medications have been shown to have a response rate of 41% and to reduce significantly the risk of relapse (Leucht et al., 2012: 101),[23] yet antipsychotics, particularly neuroleptics, have a panoply of side effects which interfere with the way a person lives her life and can lead to a perceived reduction in quality of life (Wykes et al., 2017: 2369).[24] While side effects vary from drug to drug, the most common side effects of neuroleptics include severe weight gain, drooling, impotence, insomnia, chronic drowsiness, memory problems and an inability to concentrate (Wykes et al., 2017: 2369). Extra-pyramidal side effects include movement disorders such as tardive dyskinesia, akathesia and dystonia, which occur in 35–55% of patients (Bartlett, 2011: 517), QT prolongation and sudden cardiac death (Taipale et al., 2020: 61). Neuroleptics are associated with physical morbidity and mortality, increased stigma and, predictably, non-adherence (Wykes et al., 2017: 2370, 2375), with the side-effect profile a central determinant of medication cessation and nonadherence (Bartlett, 2011: 518; Di Bonaventura et al., 2012: 5–6).

People who are prescribed neuroleptic drugs vary in their perception of the tolerability of these side effects, with side effects which are not associated with medical consequences often having the most significant life impact (Wykes et al., 2017: 2375). Resource constraints, a lack of reasonable alternatives and over-reliance on medication for the management of symptoms mean that many people in crisis will end up living with the side effects of psychotropic drugs for years, often with deleterious consequences for their physical health. Medication prescribed for moderate or severe depression is also associated with a range of side effects including gastro-intestinal problems, weight loss, nervousness and anxiety, sexual dysfunction, mania, hypomania and hallucinations (SSRIs) and an increased risk of cardiovascular problems (tryclic medications) (Bartlett and Sandland, 2014: 400–1). The adverse effects

---

omy to suggest that domestic policy makers should seriously reassess the traditional approach to involuntary treatment in the case of capable individuals with mental disorder" (Richardson, 2011: 153).

22 For reasons of space, more controversial therapies such as ECT or psychosurgery cannot be discussed here. Psychotherapy falls "largely outside the scope of common law regulation" (Bartlett and Sandland, 2014: 405).

23 In their review, Leucht and colleagues found that antipsychotic maintenance treatment reduced relapse rates from 57% to 22% within a ten-month period, while lithium reduced relapse rates from 81% to 36%, or from 61% to 40% after excluding studies in which lithium was suddenly discontinued (Leucht et al., 2012: 101). Taipale et al. found that, over the course of a twenty-year period, antipsychotic use was not only not associated with an increased risk of hospitalisation for somatic and cardiovascular problems in patients with schizophrenia, but was associated with a decreased risk of all-cause, cardiovascular and suicide mortality (Taipale et al., 2020: 65).

24 While this is the case with many forms of medication, a focus on the side effects of psychiatric medication is warranted here given the fact that these treatments are more likely to be administered without consent in psychiatry than in general medicine.

which are of greatest relevance to the people for whom the medication is prescribed are often inadequately identified in the process of explaining what the treatment involves (Bartlett, 2011: 519; Wykes et al., 2017). Communication, trust and the quality of the therapeutic relationship are therefore additional determinants of medication refusal (Bartlett, 2011: 519). In light of all of these factors, Peter Bartlett argues that "reasonable certainty", not only in relation to the diagnosis of mental disorder itself, but also to the likely outcome of the intervention and the "therapeutic necessity"[25] of treatment, should be required when considering the administration of involuntary treatment. Absent this certainty, the infringement of human rights is unjustifiable because adequate grounds cannot be provided for the intervention itself and the harm caused by overriding autonomy cannot be balanced against a benefit which is merely speculative, while the harms may be significant (Bartlett, 2011: 535). Worryingly, the courts in England and Wales have tended to opt for a reading of both law and evidence which favours compulsory treatment (Bartlett and Sandland, 2014: 403).

Ethical losses in mental healthcare

Ethical justification is necessary in situations in which treatment is administered without a person's consent or against his or her wishes (Olsen, 2003: 707), and whether or not the legal rationale for involuntary treatment provides adequate justification for the use of coercive practices has been the subject of intense debate. Justification for the use of involuntary treatment has focused primarily on improving the wellbeing of people with mental disorder – the principle of beneficence – yet "the net result [of coercion] may not be beneficent at all" (Hem et al., 2018: 100). The good intentions which well-established practices are founded upon often mask unintended harms which "undermine the intended benefits" (Borecky et al., 2019: 71). Testimonies of survivors of psychiatric institutionalisation and involuntary treatment provide harrowing accounts of the experience of coercion from a first-person perspective. Cath Roper describes the structural violence experienced by people who have received treatment for mental illness against their wishes, violence which operates on many levels. It undermines autonomy, interferes with a person's bodily integrity, causes physical and psychological harm and leads to a pathologising of identity and a distortion of one's sense of being in the world (Roper, 2019: 4–7). It has an effect on one's experience of agency and one's understanding of oneself as "actor, not only acted-upon" (Minkowitz, 2015: 1). Detention in hospital gives rise to "major disruption" in a person's life and increases the stigma experienced by people who are "already acknowledged to be the most stigmatised and disadvantaged group in society", potentially contributing to a "vicious cycle" of homelessless, poverty and isolation experienced by many people with mental disorder (Royal College of Psychiatrists, 2006: 2.7–2.8).

---

25 Bartlett points out that the standard of medical necessity came under scrutiny in the Court of Appeal for England and Wales in *R(N) v (M)* [2002]:

The answer to that question will depend on a number of factors, including (a) how certain is it that the patient does suffer from a treatable mental disorder; (b) how serious a disorder is it; (c) how serious a risk is presented to others; (d) how likely is it that, if the patient does suffer from such a disorder, the proposed treatment will alleviate the condition; (e) how much alleviation is there likely to be; (f) how likely is it that the treatment will have adverse consequences for the patient; and (g) how severe may they be.

([2002] EWHC 1911 (Admin) at 19)

Despite widespread acknowledgement of the importance of using the least restrictive measures in the mental healthcare setting and the dearth of empirical data relating to the benefits and risks associated with coercive interventions such as restraint and seclusion (Mann et al., 2021: 2), these measures are still routinely used in many jurisdictions, resulting in physical and psychological harm to both patients and staff (Alikmets et al., 2020: 723).[26] While staff may resort to using restraint or seclusion out of fear for their own safety or the safety of others (Cusack et al., 2018: 1173),[27] these "forms of management" are perceived as harmful, not only by patients, but often also by healthcare staff themselves. The administration of coercive treatment can profoundly traumatise people who are subjected to it, or retraumatise service users who are survivors of abuse (Cusack et al., 2018: 1173; Knowles et al., 2015: 463; Brophy et al., 2016: 8), and this trauma can linger for years (Oaks in Kallert et al., 2011: 187). Studies show that people with mental impairment are distressed, humiliated and dehumanised by restraint use, experience a loss of dignity and feel that their wishes are ignored (Cusack et al., 2018: 1167–71). The upshot of all of this is that, ultimately, mental health treatment is itself a risk factor for iatrogenic harm (Freuh et al., 2005: 1123). Whether this harm is the result of "inappropriate use" of the legislation (Royal College of Psychiatrists, 2006: 2.6) or simply a consequence of outdated, unreflective, reactive clinical practice, it must be acknowledged and corrected.

High stakes concepts

Best interests

Two distinct legal regimes govern the treatment and care of people with mental impairment in England and Wales. Both the Mental Capacity Act (2005) and the Mental Health Act 1983 (amended by the Mental Health Act 2007) provide for the non-consensual treatment of people who lack capacity, but each act contains different safeguards. Under Part IV of the Mental Health Act, not just involuntary, but also compulsory treatment can be administered without consent (Richardson 2010: 198), irrespective of capacity but subject to a second opinion provided by a Second Opinion Appointed Doctor (SOAD) (MHA 2007, s. 58), whereas under the Mental Capacity Act, a proposed treatment is lawful in the absence of consent if it is judged to be in the "best interests" of the person whose capacity is lacking or impaired, provided that he or she is not resisting treatment (Fennell, 2010: 26). As a common law principle, best interests plays no explicit role in mental health legislation in England and Wales,[28] although it has become relevant to decision-making in relation to involuntary treatment because of the second opinion safeguard in Part IV of the Mental Health Act and additionally in case law relating to the Human Rights Act 1998 (Fennell, 2008: 256; 262–3; Fennell, 2010: 33).

---

26 Empirical data in relation to the benefits and risks associated with both coercive measures and alternatives to coercion is sparse (Mann et al., 2021: 2; Hem et al., 2018: 104), while studies of practical, accessible and effective alternatives to seclusion are limited (Alikmets et al., 2020: 723).
27 Cusack and colleagues note that staff often overestimate risk based on the behaviour of the person receiving treatment and argue that fear may prevent them from looking for alternative ways to enhance the therapeutic potential of the encounter (Cusack et al., 2018: 173).
28 The concept of best interests appears in case law under the Human Rights Act (1998), which requires that the courts give effect to the rights enumerated in the European Convention on Human Rights (Fennell, 2008: 257–8).

Originating in the context of children's rights (Dhanda, 2016: 455; Birchley, 2021: 2), best interests is both a bioethical concept and a legal construct, ultimately grounded in a duty-based ethics concerned with establishing principles and rules for action (Birchley, 2021: 10).[29] Initially the legality of a doctor's adjudication of whether a treatment was in a patient's best interests rested only on the Bolam test, namely the requirement that the decision was supported by a responsible body of medical opinion within a given area of specialisation (Quigley, 2008: 234; Fennell, 2008: 264; Coggon, 2016: 397). Criticism of this reduction of legality to the requirement to act non-negligently was reflected in subsequent case law (Fennell 2008: 264), and the "de-Bolamised" concept of best interests which plays a central role in the Mental Capacity Act (2005) requires that the "objective" interests of the person who lacks capacity must be considered, with safeguards in place to ensure the fairness and proportionality of decisions made on behalf of the person (Foster and Miola, 2015: 510; Johnston 2013: 563). Best interests in the Mental Capacity Act may be understood, not as a stand-alone concept but rather as a set of principles which instructs decision-makers to take into account a variety of factors when making decisions on behalf of someone who lacks capacity (Coggon, 2008: 220; 225),[30] including the wishes, feelings, values and beliefs of the person who lacks capacity.[31] *Aintree* marked a sea-change in the courts' approach to interpreting best interests and led to the emergence over time of a "judicially created, patient-centred best interests standard [...which focuses] on the values of the patient and her global rather than just her medical interests" (Coggon, 2016: 409). The judgment explicitly rejected a medicalised interpretation of best interests in favour of a more holistic approach to decision-making, stated most clearly in paragraph 45:

> the purpose of the best interests test is to consider matters from the patient's point of view [..., meaning that], insofar as it is possible to ascertain the patient's wishes and feelings, his beliefs and values or the things which [are] important to him, it is those which should be taken into account because they are a component in making the choice which is right for him as an individual human being.[32]

Nonetheless, critics continue to argue that at law the weight given to these considerations "still remains largely within the discretion of the best interests decision maker" (Series, 2016: 1103; Weller 2010, 63).[33] Given that the legislative intention behind the Mental Capacity Act is to instruct decision-makers to apply the best interests checklist taking into account *all* of the circumstances of the case, without giving any one factor greater emphasis than the others (Bartlett and Sandland, 2014: 189; Barton-Hanson, 2018: 295), the Act provides

---

29 The principle that decisions made on behalf of a person who lacks capacity must be made in his or her best interests is codified in England and Wales by the Mental Capacity Act 2005 and has a foundation in common law dating back to *Re F (Mental Patient: Sterilisation)* in 1990 (Series, 2016: 1106).
30 Coggon argues that mental capacity law is underpinned by a commitment to achieving patient-centred care, which he defines as "care that honours where possible the patient's own, reflectively-endorsed values" (Coggon, 2016: 397), irrespective of whether or not she has decision-making capacity.
31 Mental Capacity Act, s4.
32 *Aintree University Hospitals NHS Foundation Trust v James* [2013] UKSC 67, para. 45.
33 For Series, the idea that someone other than the person receiving care can ascertain better than the person herself what constitutes her best interests is indicative of the paternalism at the heart of the Mental Capacity Act 2005 (Series, 2016: 1102).

no guidance in relation to how much weight should be given to the views of the person whose best interests are being considered, potentially leading to a demotion of her wishes and feelings, uncertainty in the application of the test and a lack of consistency in the case law handed down by the Court of Protection (Barton-Hanson, 2018: 277–8).[34] While the Mental Capacity Act and the accompanying Code of Practice contain measures to optimise the objectivity of the test, the phrase "to know what is best for someone" can be said to contain a "colonising presumption" (Mezzina et al., 2019: 493) which risks steering best interests tests towards an approach which is overprotective and paternalistic (Fennell, 2008: 265), reinforcing the medical model of decision-making (Barton-Hanson, 2018: 294). In practice the concept of best interests is still open to being interpreted in two ways: either as emphasising the decision-maker's ability to determine what is in the best interests of the patient, or as seeking to reflect to the greatest extent possible the individual's own preferences and values (Richardson, 2011: 142; see Fennell, 2008: 265). Like substituted judgement, best interests decision-making runs the risk of attempting to "divine" what the person who is the subject of the judgement would "really" have wanted.[35]

While the courts recognise that best interests "goes wider than medical necessity",[36] encompassing "medical, emotional and all other welfare issues",[37] this recognition has the potential to increase clinical discretion which is already wide as a result of the broad definition of treatment for mental disorder, by "extending beyond the medical the range of interests which may be served by treatment without consent" (Fennell, 2008: 259, 262; see also Bartlett and Sandland, 2014: 406–7). Fennell argues that the concept of best interests in the Mental Capacity Act provides a range of justifications for treatment without consent which is potentially as wide as the provisions of the Mental Health Act (Fennell, 2008: 266–7). Reference to "best interests" invokes what Fennell refers to as a "feelgood" response "almost on a par with the related concept of 'human dignity'", yet both of these concepts are inescapably coloured by the social and cultural values of the decision-maker (Fennell, 2008: 266).[38] In the courts, judges grappling with the questions of best interests must draw, not merely on their own personal values (Callaghan and Ryan, 2014: 758), but also on "relevant values that are current within society, in order to estimate the moral significance and acceptability of the judgement" (Holm and Edgar, 2008: 205). Margaret Quigley suggests that the best interests test in the Mental Capacity Act allowed members of the judiciary in England and Wales to broaden the category of decisions which come under the jurisdiction of the courts, in effect substituting a professional judicial standard for the professional medical standard to which the courts had deferred since *Bolam* (Quigley, 2008: 235–6). Quigley's concern is that, while "bad" – paternalistic – decision-making by a clinician will only affect his or her patients, "bad judgements by the courts legally bind all doctors to make bad decisions" and

---

34 Barton-Hanson refers to reports published by the House of Lords Select Committee on the Mental Capacity Act 2005 and the Law Commission which "clearly point to how the person's wishes and feelings are overlooked in favour of medical judgment or other factors, including resources" (House of Lords Select Committee on the Mental Capacity Act 2005, 2014; Law Commission, 2015; para. 12.42) (Barton-Hanson, 2018: 277–8).
35 Victorian Law Reform Commission [17.112], no. 49, cited in Callaghan and Ryan, 2014: 758.
36 *R (N) v Dr M and Others* [2002] EWCA Civ 1789.
37 Butler-Sloss P in *Re A (male patient: sterilisation)* [2000] 1 FLR 549, [2000] 1 FCR 193, at 100.
38 Given the fact that values influence interpretation, each concept can be used to justify incompatible conclusions about which outcome best promotes an individual's dignity or best interests (Fennell, 2008: 266).

she argues that optimal implementation of the best interests standard is not simply a matter of shifting the locus of authority from the medical profession to the judiciary (Quigley, 2008: 238). Ultimately, it is open to question whether the concept of best interests could ever shed its paternalistic overtones and become more than "a legal fiction, necessary in order to resolve reasonable disagreement and … get something done" (Holm and Edgar, 2008: 206), or whether it should be dispensed with entirely (McSherry and Freckelton, 2015: 9). All of these concerns notwithstanding, however, the current best interests standard may yet prove fit for service insofar as it draws attention to the rights of service users as individuals and to the need for what Mary Donnelly terms "principled, open and accountable decision-making" in a world in which there are "no perfect solutions" (Donnelly, 2016: 332).

Insight

While Fennell describes best interests as a "portmanteau concept" capable of justifying "a broad range of compulsory interventions in the name of treatment for mental disorder" (Fennell, 2008: 267), IanFreckelton argues along similar lines that the concept of insight has the potential to become a "portmanteau" for many different components of mental disorder (Freckelton, 2010: 213). The concepts of insight and "insightlessness" are "extra-legislative descriptors" (Freckelton, 2010: 203) which are regularly relied upon by experts, both in determinations of whether a person does or does not have decision-making capacity and in decisions about whether or not to detain and treat someone under the Mental Health Act 1983 (Gurbai et al., 2020:11; Case, 2016: 360). "Insight" is a clinical term with no legal basis[39] which has three central components – recognition that one has a mental disorder, acknowledgement that certain mental events are associated with mental disorder and compliance with treatment (David, cited in Freckelton, 2010: 208) – but it can also refer to acceptance of the fact that one has a mental disorder, acceptance of the need for, and the efficacy of, treatment and an ability to identify potential signs of relapse (Freckelton, 2010: 208). Despite the appearance of a shared understanding of the term between psychiatrists, the concept lacks transparency (Case, 2016: 364) and is often used "without adequate specification as to its meaning" and without reliance on any standardised scales or instruments to quantify it (Gurbai et al., 2020: 7; 10; Guidry-Grimes, 2019: 180). Insight "lies on a spectrum" and may be affected by a range of factors, including stigma, family pressures, stress, intelligence levels, disability and religious affiliation (Freckelton, 2010: 210–11). Paula Case suggests that the language of insight, used in abstraction from its clinical context, can mask value judgements and paternalistic assumptions, ultimately undermining the presupposition of capacity at the heart of the Mental Capacity Act (2005) (Case, 2016: 360; 362).[40] Given the conceptual ambiguity of the concept and how high the stakes are for those whose insight is being assessed, there is an urgent need for clarity in the definition and application of the term among clinicians and legal professionals (Guidry-Grimes, 2019: 180; Freckelton, 2010: 313).

---

39 "Lack of insight" was originally associated with a diagnosis of schizophrenia, but through a process of "diagnostic creep" it has come to apply to a range of conditions.
40 Case examines the implications of the "extensive reliance" of the law on the expert testimony of psychiatrists in relation to determining capacity, arguing that "experts' liberal deployment of the concept of 'insight' … has the potential to corrupt the assessment of capacity in the Court of Protection (and in practice)" (Case, 2016: 364).

Considered from a therapeutic perspective, insight is associated with a concern for the future well-being of a person with mental disorder but, if it is improperly assessed, it fails to provide an acceptable justification for involuntary detention or treatment and may undermine therapeutic goals (Diesfeld, 2003: 67). Analysing the role played by the concept of insight in the published judgements of the Court of Protection between 2007 and 2018, Gurbai and colleagues distinguish five patterns in the use of the term "insight" among expert witnesses (most of whom were psychiatrists), noting that evidence to support a finding of lack of insight was often absent, while the concepts of insight and capacity were often used interchangeably or alongside one another without any supporting information about the relationship between them (ibid, 2021: 8; David, 2020: 521).[41] Despite the availability of guidance which states clearly that insight and capacity are distinct concepts and that a person may have decision-making capacity even if she is described as lacking insight into her condition (NICE, 2018: 1.4.24), none of the judgements analysed by Gurbai and colleagues satisfied the four requirements set out in the guideline (Gurbai et al., 2020: 11).[42]

This lack of consistency and specificity is concerning precisely because reliance on the concept of insight increases the discretion afforded by the law to psychiatrists to determine "who meets the required threshold of involuntary detention and treatment" (Diesfeld, 2003; 69). McGorry and McConville point out that conflicts arising from the therapeutic process (or relationship) itself are commonly interpreted as a lack of insight on the part of the patient, "rather than [as] a relative divergence of views between clinician and patient" (McGorry and McConville, 1999: 132).[43] In assessing insight, stigma and misconceptions about people with mental illness may colour clinicians' perception of patients' credibility as reporters of their own experience and deprive patients of "epistemic trust", with profound ethical implications for how the patient is treated as an epistemic agent (Guidry-Grimes, 2019: 178; 181),[44] while at the same time privileging a process of assessment which may be vulnerable to bias and inaccuracies. Assessments of insight may minimise the patient's own perspective, discount her experience and dismiss what may be genuine concerns about treatment, all of which "exacerbate her vulnerability as a knower" (Guidry-Grimes, 2019: 180; Wilson, 2021: 46), further entrenching the power asymmetry between clinicians and patients in mental healthcare.[45] Guidry-Grimes argues that, while insight assessments should not carry

---

41 In the jurisprudence of the Court of Protection, the term "insight" can mean unwillingness or inability to believe or accept that one has a mental disorder, inability to understand that one has a mental disorder, inability to recognise or understand relevant risks, inability to recognise or understand one's need for care or support or, finally, inability to understand the value or importance of treatment (Gurbai et al., 2020: 6–8).
42 The guidance states clearly that "if a practitioner believes a person's insight/lack of insight is relevant to their assessment of the person's capacity, they must clearly record what they mean by insight/lack of insight in this context and how they believe it affects/does not affect the person's capacity" (NICE, 2018, 1.4.24).
43 McGorry and McConville equate the assessment of insight with a "judgement of a discrepancy between the perspective of the clinician and the perspective of the patient, [...which uses] a framework derived from the assessor's perspective" (McGorry and McConville, 1999: 132).
44 "A patient's assessed level of insight can directly impact how comfortable clinicians feel trusting the patient's testimony, which in turn affects how much they trust the patient as a decision-maker" (Guidry-Grimes, 2019: 180). This "presumptive distrust" on the part of clinicians in turn fosters patients' apprehension about the healthcare system and perpetuates the view of the patient as untrustworthy, leading to a "vicious cycle of mistrust" which undermines the therapeutic relationship (Guidry-Grimes, 2019: 178).
45 Richardson suggests that, although they cannot make a finding of incapacity on the basis of "irrational" reasoning, in individual cases the courts seem to be willing to interpret the criteria for capacity in ways which

such high stakes, insight is not an "unsalvageable" concept, but should be seen as a complex phenomenon which accommodates many different forms and degrees of self-knowledge, "allowing for reasonable interpretations that go beyond standard biomedical views of the patient's condition" (Guidry Grimes, 2019: 181).[46]

Risk

Risk to self or to others is the primary rationale given for treating people who have decision-making capacity without their consent.[47] The law in many jurisdictions provides for the preventive detention of people with mental disorder without their consent, even if they have committed no offence, on the grounds that they pose a potential risk to others. Assessment of a person's risk of violence is an increasingly important part of psychiatric practice (Singh et al., 2014: 180).[48] George Szmukler has described risk assessment in mental healthcare as "essentially a moral enterprise" in which the benefits of containing risk to society at large are weighed against costs incurred by a small proportion of the population, namely, those with mental disorders who are considered potentially dangerous (Szmukler, 2003: 205–6). Szmukler and others have argued that the legal provision for preventive detention is discriminatory because no such provision exists for people without a mental disorder who may be perceived as dangerous (Szmukler, 2003: 207; Daw, 2015: 101). The threat of preventive detention runs the risk of further disenfranchising members of an already marginalised group within society and may deter people who could benefit from accessing mental health services (including those who may pose a risk) from seeking treatment (Szmukler, 2003: 206). More general ethical concerns arising from the practice of risk assessment include the prioritising of control and containment – the "public protection interest" – above the therapeutic interests of the patient, the reinforcement of stereotypes which represent people with mental disorder as dangerous and the unwarranted diversion of mental health resources towards a minority who are perceived as dangerous (Szmukler, 2003: 206). For Szmukler, treatment without consent or against a person's wishes may be justified if she lacks decision-making capacity and treatment is deemed to be in her "best (health) interests", but no similar justification can be provided on the basis of a putative risk to others (Szmukler, 2003: 207).

Reducing uncertainty comes at a cost (Szmukler and Rose, 2013: 125). Essentially the dangerousness criterion justifies detaining many people with mental illness who will never become dangerous in order to contain the few who will (Large et al., 2008: 879). Risk factors for dangerousness or violence are "derived from population-level analyses and lead to

---

enable them to "avoid the need to respect decisions which they regard as not truly autonomous [namely, those based on delusional beliefs]". In this respect, she suggests, lack of capacity may be as open to manipulation as the concept of mental disorder itself (Richardson, 2010: 193). Elsewhere she argues that lack of insight may be a "real hurdle" to the promotion of autonomy in the field of mental healthcare (Richardson, 2011: 154).

46 Minkowitz (2015) asks what a shift from "a system overseen by medical professionals to one where different professions complement each other and the role of medicine is much less significant" would look like: a set of practices in which people's lived experience of "madness, trauma or psychosocial disability" would be accommodated within the knowledge base.
47 For reasons of space, I will restrict this discussion to a brief examination of the concept of risk to others.
48 Penelope Weller argues that, in a "stressed" system, refusal of treatment is more likely to function as an indicator of risk of violence or dangerousness and to be interpreted as a proxy indicator of both lack of capacity and the need for treatment (Weller, 2010: 57–8).

conclusions framed in terms of probabilities" (Szmukler, 2003: 207; Szmukler and Rose, 2013: 133). Singh and colleagues argue that that rates of violence in high-risk groups depend on local factors and that no general assumptions can be made about the probability of violent behaviour (Singh et al., 2014: 184; compare Large et al., 2008: 879). While a range of structured risk assessment instruments (SRAIs) is available to enable psychiatrists, psychologists and other healthcare professionals to determine the risk of individual patients acting violently by scoring them on a list of variables associated with violence (Singh et al., 2014: 180), the predictive accuracy of different instruments varies significantly across settings. As a result, there is no existing mechanism to enable practitioners "to systematically identify local base rates for different forms of violence in different psychiatric populations" (Singh et al., 2014: 184; compare Szmukler and Rose, 2013: 130), and without a reasonable estimate of the base rate for the population in question, healthcare professionals will be unable to predict the probability of a member of one of the three risk categories committing a future violent act (Singh et al., 2014: 184). Labels such as "high", "moderate" and "low" risk tend to be interpreted inconsistently by clinicians and others, prompting the question of whether high-risk categorisations should be used at all (ibid.). Singh et al. urge caution in the use of probabilistic risk estimates as a basis for "decisions related to individual liberty and public safety" and call for explicit acknowledgement of the possible sources of error associated with the use of individual risk assessments (Singh et al., 2014: 185).[49]

Given the malleability of concepts such as "insight", "best interests" and "risk", the extent of the discretion enjoyed by clinicians and the way in which stigma influences the perception of people with mental illness, clinicians should be especially vigilant in conducting assessments in all three domains. This vigilance is ethical, not clinical, because the use of these "high stakes" concepts[50] potentially has such profound implications for patients' liberty and autonomy (Diesfeld 2003: 67).

Law, ethics and clinical practice

Legal theorists have charted a "decline in formal legal values" spanning the last three-quarters of a century: a "de-formalisation" of law involving a move away from the system of "general, abstract norms applicable to all legal subjects" characteristic of nineteenth-century law in liberal jurisdictions to an emphasis on broader, more open-ended standards which "allowed high levels of executive discretion and professional autonomy" in decision-making, particularly in medicine (Harrington, 2017: 164–5).[51] The Bolam test formalised a pattern of judicial deference to clinical authority by allowing professional opinion to function "as a black box … [which allowed the law] to conceal the indeterminacy of its own decision-making in areas of moral and political controversy" (Harrington, 2017: 165).[52] Applying the Bolam test allowed the courts to abstain from further scrutinising the actions of a doctor who had followed even a "minority" of professional opinion, creating an exception for

---

49 In relation to risk to the person him- or herself, Boreky and colleagues draw attention to the issue of "overconfidence" in the process of psychiatric risk assessment and caution against a tendency to minimise the "personal costs" of psychiatric treatment (see Borecky et al., 2019: 77).
50 I am borrowing this term from Laura Guidry-Grimes' discussion of insight (2019: 180ff).
51 Such values included rationality, consistency and legal equality (see Harington 2017: 163ff).
52 Following McLean, Harrington argues that *Bolam* incorporated "clinical irrationality … into law" (Harrington, 2017: 171).

medicine compared with other professions (Harrington, 2017: 169). Open-ended tests carried out "in good faith", such as tests of best interests or welfare, depended on context and factual knowledge and were "strongly shaped by professional expertise", creating "legal asymmetries" between doctors and patients (Harrington, 2017: 166; 169). Confronted with "difficult" cases, the courts demonstrated a reluctance to codify principles or articulate precise rules, defaulting instead to the concept of best interests as a way of resolving disputes (Montgomery, 2006: 202–3).

Van der Burg argues that the relationship between healthcare ethics and health law which emerged in the latter part of the twentieth century rested on mutual opposition to the paternalism of the Bolam era and an insistence that the moral standards implicit in the practice of individual doctors be subject to public scrutiny and external oversight (Van der Burg, 1997: 94–5, 97).[53] Within this "strategic alliance", ethics provided law with reasoned arguments, while law furnished ethics with "institutional authority and the prospect of enforcement" (Harrington 2017: 176).[54] Challenges to Bolam mounted by legal reformers during the 1980s drew attention to a ceding of legal sovereignty and a loss of control over clinical decision-making, with judgments sacrificing legal coherence "in the face of medical 'fact'" (McLean, 1999: 110; Harrington, 2017: 169). Scholars of English law such as McLean and Kennedy saw in the Bolam era a tradition of principled reasoning being replaced with "clinical irrationality" (Harrington, 2017: 169). As John Harrington points out, it was not that decisions were not being made according to principles during the Bolam era; the problem was that these principles were not *articulated*. *Bolam* absolved doctors of the obligation to give reasons (Harrington, 2017: 172). In ethics, conversely, legal scholars such as Kennedy and McLean saw an "ideal of law restored to its true form" (Harrington, 2017: 164) and called upon law to "follow ethics in taking a principled approach to the promotion of fundamental values", particularly autonomy (Harrington, 2017: 177), resulting in the emergence of a new "ethically-informed healthcare law which challenged the profession-centered model" (Harrington, 2017: 162; Foster and Miola, 2015: 515).

While historically the "abstentionism" and deference of the courts may have been rooted in the assumption that judges and healthcare professionals had "complementary roles" in an integrated system intended to ensure that healthcare was "governed by sound moral principles" (Montgomery, 2006: 205–6), established patterns of judicial non-intervention and deference to medical opinion in the Bolam era and afterwards may also be interpreted as refusal by the courts to engage in debates in which law should have assumed its proper place (Foster and Miola, 2015: 529). Building on an earlier analysis of thirty years of case law by José Miola, Foster and Miola claim that many of the salient issues which arise in medical law cases are *ethical* – not medical – in nature and argue that the courts have responded to these cases either by downgrading their ethical content and reframing it as a matter of legal inter-

---

53 Both disciplines aimed to produce rules or principles rather than endorse practices which were more open-ended (Harrington, 2017: 176; Van der Burg, 1997: 100–101). The emphasis on patient rights – particularly autonomy – and on the importance of levelling the power differential between doctors and patients reflected the larger ideology of political liberalism, prompting the suggestion that the "mission" of both healthcare ethics and health law during this period was to implement the programme of liberalism in the healthcare arena (Van der Burg, 1997: 99).
54 Harrington argues that medical ethics played an important role in supporting the challenges to medical paternalism put forward by legal scholars in the early days of medical law reform, serving as a "model for law to emulate" (Harrington, 2017: 177; 164).

pretation or by "abrogating" responsibility for the decision to the regulatory authority itself, essentially leaving it to the individual clinician to interpret his or her regulatory guidance appropriately, even though in fact this guidance often refers back to the law (Miola, 2007: 187; Foster and Miola, 2015: 507, 509, 529).[55] Distinguishing between legal decisions, ethical decisions and moral decisions, Foster and Miola define "legal" decisions as those with which health professionals must comply because the law "mandates or proscribes a certain course of action", while "moral" decisions are those which rest entirely on the conscience of the individual practitioner (Foster and Miola, 2015: 506–7; 512).[56] Somewhere in between are "ethical" decisions, which the law allows the medical profession to regulate *via* the development of professional standards and mechanisms to enforce adherence, "reflect[ing] the corporate morality of the profession" (ibid.). In cases relating to this category of decisions, which are the domain of "professional" – as opposed to philosophical – medical ethics (Foster and Miola, 2015: 506–7), Foster and Miola argue that the law is better placed "in terms of structure and legitimacy" than the medical profession to be the "final arbiter". They suggest that the courts need to "start engaging in ethical debate" (Foster and Miola, 2015: 529–30), although what exactly this might look like is left an open question.[57]

A role for ethics

Ultimately, in spite of the idealisation of ethics by academic legal scholars, the role played by ethics in healthcare delivery is poorly understood by many clinicians and legal professionals. This is significant because how ethics is "done" in clinical practice, or whether it is done at all, can have profound implications for the treatment of individual patients. Among the "context-free" ethical principles which liberal academic legal reformers wanted to see "balanced" in judicial decisions (McLean, 1999: 3; Brassington, 2018: 244, 241) are the canonical principles of biomedical ethics identified in 1979 by Beauchamp and Childress. Properly speaking, respect for autonomy, beneficence (promoting welfare or well-being), non-maleficence (avoiding harm) and justice are less action-guiding principles than well-established values which have underpinned healthcare policy and clinical decision-making for at least forty years. While they might have conceptual utility in the theoretical analysis of ethical issues arising in healthcare practice, however, they are less helpful in addressing and resolving ethical disagreement at the clinical coal-face because concepts such as "doing what is best", "fairness" and "avoiding harm" cannot be univocally defined and their interpretation depends on a number of contextual factors, including – crucially – the value-system of the decision-maker (Adshead and Cave, 2021: 24). Underpinned by a scaffolding of ethical

---

55 The law's deference to guidance published by professional medical associations such as the British Medical Association is problematic in situations in which such guidance differs from the regulatory guidance published by the General Medical Council (see Miola, 2007).
56 Of note, there are some regulatory constraints on the exercise of conscientious objection.
57 Ultimately the question of "ownership" over decision-making in relation to ethical matters in healthcare (Foster and Miola, 2015: 530) not only misses the point but further obscures the needs, wishes and preferences, and the fragility and vulnerability of many of the people at the centre of these decisions. The point is not to claim authority for decision-making; it is to ensure that the "least worst" decision is made in every case. There is no reason why such decisions cannot be made by ethically competent clinicians without the need to have recourse to the courts, particularly since Foster and Miola themselves acknowledge that autonomy has often been interpreted in an "embarrassingly simplistic" way by the courts (Foster and Miola, 2015: 516; see also Quigley, 2008 and Dunn and Foster, 2010).

terms such as "autonomy", "best interests" and "fairness", regulatory guidance leaves room for reasonable disagreement between professionals, and clinicians may draw different conclusions from the same guidance (Brassington, 2018: 238).[58] The same action – take, for example, the administration of involuntary treatment – "may in some instances be considered to be a harm, in some instances not to be a harm, and in some instances to be a justified harm", depending on one's perspective (Coggon, 2008: 222).[59]

José Miola laments the proliferation of ethical discourse available to practitioners, suggesting that the profusion of guidance, academic discussion and media analysis makes it possible "to 'ethically' justify any opinion that one cares to hold" (Miola, 2007: 212). In the context of clinical practice, however, the task of ethics as a discipline is not to provide unambiguous direction or definitive answers to the question of what should be done, but to *evaluate reasons* for choosing a particular course of action and to ensure that these reasons are robust and adequately justified. A position is only as justifiable as the quality of the ethical reasoning which supports it – itself dependent on the quality of information available to decision-makers – and legitimate disagreement between stakeholders is to be expected given the range of values at play in the clinical setting. It is a strength, not a shortcoming, of ethics that there is no "objectivity" in ethical discourse because this indeterminacy necessitates an appeal to multiple perspectives, a vital component in balanced decision-making given the danger that reasoning may be distorted by personal, interpersonal or organisational biases (Adshead and Cave, 2021: 24). Many ethically challenging clinical decisions involve choosing between alternatives which are each associated with harm and identifying the "better" option in such situations is a complex and time-consuming process. While adequate reasons may be adduced to justify diametrically opposed courses of action in some situations (Skorupski, 1999: 71), close scrutiny of the context in which a given decision has to be made and an exploration of the reasons provided by decision-makers may ultimately lead to a negotiated consensus about the "least worst" option (Adshead and Cave, 2021: 23). This is exactly how the practice of clinical ethics works.

Clinical ethics is a multidisciplinary, collaborative approach to the resolution of ethically challenging issues arising in clinical practice.[60] Commentators are increasingly acknowledging the potentially useful role formal clinical ethics support services can play in supporting clinicians to make ethically competent decisions in situations in which the best course of action is unclear or contested.[61] In a recent case discussion which illustrates the way clinical

---

58 Adshead and Cave observe that mental health practice is "remarkable" insofar as it operates "within a legal framework that directly empowers doctors to make significant compromises between these principles" (Adshead and Cave, 2021: 21).
59 In a pluralist society, a variety of harms are viewed as "legitimate" and individuals are free to decide which of these harms or risks to accept (Coggon, 2008: 222).
60 Clinical ethics consultation may be facilitated by a specifically appointed committee, a small group or an individual ethics consultant. Margaret Urban Walker describes clinical ethics consultation as an "interaction which (…) renders authority more self-conscious and responsibility clearer (…) [and maintains] a certain kind of reflective space within an institution" (Urban Walker, cited in Andre 2002: 67).
61 Guidry-Grimes argues that the provision of education to clinical staff in relation to the "meaning and potential pitfalls of insight assessments" may allow clinical ethics support services to more effectively support healthcare teams who "encounter so-called 'difficult' patients who seem to lack insight" (2019: 181). Foster and Miola argue for a role for "rightly directed" clinical ethics committees in addressing and exploring "conundra" in clinical practice which do not need to involve the courts, while acknowledging that "the final recourse would always be to the courts" (Foster and Miola, 2015: 525).

ethics works in mental health practice, Silva and colleagues describe a decision taken by a clinical team in a high-security hospital to compel nasogastric administration of clozapine on four occasions against the wishes of a severely ill patient (Silva et al., 2017: 231ff).[62] The painstaking nature of the process by which the decision was made to restrain the patient while administering the medication as a treatment of last resort illustrates the granularity of the analysis required to arrive at the "least worst" option in complex cases of this nature and the ethical precariousness of the conclusion reached.[63] Ultimately, whether an intervention is in fact the "least worst" option can only be determined after the event, and the radical contingency of the conditions under which these kinds of decision are made obligate clinicians to ensure that due diligence is done to minimise the harm which will inevitably result. Interventions which "interfere" with a person's autonomy or bodily integrity are described by Roper as "dirty hands" acts and she argues compellingly that the "dirty feature" of any such act "does not simply disappear on grounds that it is part of a morally justifiable act", but must be noted – and "regretted" – with a view ultimately to restoring the person's autonomy (Roper, 2019: 12; see Sjostrand and Helgesson, 2008: 117).[64]

Several studies examining the use of coercive practices in mental healthcare have found that ethical questions are routinely reduced to medical, psychological or legal problems, with some evidence that the use of coercive measures is not universally perceived by clinicians as ethically problematic (Hem et al., 2018: 105; Sjostrand et al., 2015: 7). Hem et al. suggest that ethics education and capacity-building among mental health professionals would enable clinicians to develop an "ethical vocabulary" which may assist them in confronting ethical challenges in their everyday work, helping to make implicit values and assumptions explicit and potentially identifying alternatives to coercion (Hem et al., 2018: 105).[65] Devitt and Kelly emphasise the importance of incorporating ethical values, human rights principles and sensitivity to the need to balance competing rights into professional practice training, to counter the attitudes and culture which lead to the use of coercion. Although the vast majority of health and social care professionals working in the mental health setting "have a real and honest concern about the people in their care" (Bartlett and Sandland, 2014: 19), they are often "under-trained, over-worked and placed in environments which ... do not prevent abuse and possibly even facilitate it" (Devitt and Kelly, 2019: 53).[66] Empowering health professionals to act reflectively and flexibly in their interactions with the people they are caring for may result in a less confrontational, more "dialogical" version of paternalism which

---

62 While it is not clear from this discussion whether or not a formal clinical ethics consultation was initiated, the approach taken by the team mirrors the approach a clinical ethics committee or consultant would have taken in this situation.
63 Extensive consultation between a range of healthcare and legal professionals, the patient's family and an independent advocate was required to determine the justifiability of the intervention, which caused distress for some members of the team even though it ultimately had a significant benefit for the patient.
64 For Roper, the agent of the "dirty hands" act is morally compromised, even if the act can be ethically justified.
65 Adshead and Cave suggest that the most difficult aspect of ethically challenging situations in mental healthcare may perhaps be "not that the moral principles falter, but that professionals do not always take enough time to reflect on them" (Adshead and Cave, 2021: 24).
66 Wilson argues that many mental health professionals "understand the delicate balance" between the harms and benefits of involuntary detention and treatment and agree that these interventions are overused, but claims that the real problem is the lack of available alternatives within the mental health system, overreliance on medication and restricted opportunities to "intervene earlier using less coercive approaches in the community" (Wilson, 2021: 201).

responds to the patient's needs and at the same time empowers her to exercise "supported autonomy" instead of reacting on impulse (Hem, 2018: 106; see Vatne and Fagermoen, 2007: 47). To achieve this requires both a readiness to drive culture change within healthcare organisations and responsiveness to "external" drivers of change such as legislation, codes of practice, standard-setting, routine inspections and sanctions (Devitt and Kelly, 2019: 53).

Conclusion

Many important issues, for reasons of space, have not been addressed in this chapter. My aim has been to draw attention to the role of ethics in mental health practice as it is shaped by the law, particularly in light of the entry into force of the CRPD. Given the discretion afforded to mental health professionals by the law, there is an ethical obligation to ensure that decision-making in mental healthcare is inclusive, collaborative and fair, that the legitimacy of the perspective of the person receiving treatment is recognised, that "high-stakes" concepts are used consistently and with an understanding of their implications, and that due diligence is done to minimise harm to people with mental disorder. Minimising harm is perhaps the single most important ethical imperative in mental healthcare. If it is true, as Rosanna Daw suggests, that the concept of "doing no harm" has received less attention in mental health law – and, by extension, in practice – than its companion principles (Daw, 2015: 103), it is time for this to change.

References

Adshead, Gwen and Cave, Jeremy (2021). "An introduction to clinical ethics in psychiatry". *British Journal of Psychiatric Advances* 27(1), 20–25.
Allikmets, Silvia, Marshall, Caryl, Murad, Omar and Gupta, Kamal (2020). "Seclusion: A patient perspective". *Issues in Mental Health Nursing* 41(8), 723–745.
Andre, Judith (2002). *Bioethics as Practice*. Chapel Hill and London: University of North Carolina Press.
Arboleda-Florez, Julio (2011). "Psychiatry and the law – Do the fields agree in their views on coercive treatment?" In: Kallert et al (eds.), 83–96.
Bartlett, Peter (2011). "The necessity must be convincingly shown to exist; standards for compulsory treatment for mental disorder under the Mental Health Act 1983". *Medical Law Review* 19(4), 514–547.
Bartlett, Peter and Sandland, Ralph (2014). *Mental Health Law: Policy and Practice* (4th edition). Oxford: Oxford University Press.
Barton-Hanson, Renu (2018). "Reforming best interests: The road towards supported decision-making". *Journal of Social Welfare and Family Law* 40(3), 277–298.
Beauchamp, Tom (2021). "The philosophical dimension". In: Bloch and Green (eds.), 41–75.
Birchley, Giles (2021). "The theorisation of 'best interests' in bioethical accounts of decision-making". *BMC Medical Ethics* 22(68), 1–18.
Blanck, Peter and Flynn, Eilionoir (2017). *Routledge Handbook of Disability Law and Human Rights*. London and New York: Routledge.
Bloch, Sydney and Green, Stephen A (2021). *Psychiatric Ethics*. Oxford: Oxford University Press.
Borecky, Adam, Thomsen, Calvin and Dubov, Linda (2019). "Reweighing the ethical tradeoffs in the involuntary hospitalization of suicidal patients". *The American Journal of Bioethics* 19(10), 71–83.
Brassington, Iain (2018). "On the relationship between medical ethics and the law". *Medical Law Review* 26(2), 225–245.
Brissos, Sofia, Vicente, Felipe, Oliveira, João Miguel, Sobreira, Gonçalo Santos, Gameiro, Zita, Moreira, Cátia Alves, Pinto da Costa, Mariana, Queirós, Marta, Mendes, Eva, Renca, Susana, Prata-Ribeiro, Henrique, Scopel Hoffmann, Maurício and Vieira, Fernando (2017). "Compulsory psychiatric

treatment checklist: Instrument development and clinical application". *International Journal of Law and Psychiatry* 54, 36–45.

Brown, Jennifer (2016). "The changing purpose of mental health law: From medicalism to legalism and the new legalism". *International Journal of Law and Psychiatry* 47, 1–9.

Brophy, Lisa M, Roper, Catherine E, Hamilton, Bridget E, Tellez, Juan José and McSherry, Bernadette M (2016). "Consumers and carer perspectives on poor practice and the use of seclusion and restraint in mental health settings: Results from Australian focus groups". *International Journal of Mental Health Systems* 10(6), 1–10.

Callaghan, Sasha M and Ryan, Christopher (2014). "Is there a future for involuntary treatment in rights-based mental health law?" *Psychiatry, Psychology and Law* 21(5), 747–766.

Carolyn, Johnston (2013). "The weight attributed to patient values in determining best interests". *Journal of Medical Ethics* 39(9), 562–564.

Case, Paula (2016). "Dangerous liaisons: Psychiatry and law in the court of protection expert discourses of insight (and compliance)". *Medical Law Review* 24(3), 360–378.

Charland, Louis C (2021). "A historical perspective". In: Bloch and Green (eds.), 11–39.

Coggon, John (2016). "Mental capacity law, autonomy, and best interests: An argument for conceptual and practical clarity in the court of protection". *Medical Law Review* 24(3), 396–414.

Coggon, John (2008). "Best interests, public interest, and the power of the medical profession". *Health Care Analysis* 16(3), 219–232.

Cusack, Pauline, Cusack, Frank Patrick, McAndrew, Sue, McKeown, Mick and Duxbury, Joy (2018). "An integrative review exploring the physical and psychological harm inherent in using restraint in mental health inpatient settings". *International Journal of Mental Health Nursing* 27(3), 1162–1176.

Dale, O, Haigh, R, Blazdell, J and Sethi, F (2020). "Social psychiatry, relational practice and learning from COVID-19". *Mental Health Review Journal* 25(4), 297–300.

David, Anthony S (2020). "Insight and psychosis: The next 30 years". *The British Journal of Psychiatry* 217(3), 521–523.

Daw, Rowena (2015). "The case for a fusion law: Challenges and issues". In: McSherry and Freckelton (eds.), 93–113.

Dawson, John (2015). "A realistic approach to assessing mental health laws' compliance with the UNCRPD". *International Journal of Law and Psychiatry* 40, 70–79.

Degener, Theresia (2017). "A human rights model of disability". In: Blanck and Flynn (eds.), 31–49.

Department of Health (2015). *Report of the Expert Group on the Review of the Mental Health Act 2001.* Dublin: Government of Ireland.

Devitt, P and Kelly, B (2019). "A human rights foundation for ethical mental health practice". *Irish Journal of Psychological Medicine* 36(1), 47–54.

Dhanda, Anita (2016). "From duality to indivisibility: Mental health care and human rights". *South African Journal on Human Rights* 32(3), 438–456.

Di Bonaventura, Marco, Gabriel, Susan, Dupclay, Leon, Gupta, Shaloo and Kim, Edward (2012). "A patient perspective of the impact of medication side effects on adherence: Results of a cross-sectional nationwide survey of patients with schizophrenia". *BMC Psychiatry* 12(20), 1–7.

Diesfeld, Kate (2003). "Insight: Unpacking the concept in mental health law". *Psychiatry, Psychology and Law* 10(1), 63–70.

Donnelly, Mary (2016). "Best interests in the mental capacity act: Time to say goodbye?" *Medical Law Review* 24(3), 318–332.

Dunn, Michael and Foster, Charles (2010). "Autonomy and welfare as amici curiae". *Medical Law Review* 18(1), 86–95.

Drew, N, Funk, M, Tang, S, Lamichhane, J, Chávez, E, Katontoka, S, Pathare, S, Lewis, O, Gostin, L and Saraceno, B (2011). "Human rights violations of people with mental and psychosocial disabilities: An unresolved global crisis". *Lancet* 378(9803), 1664–1675.

Fennell, Philip (2008). "Best interests and treatment for mental disorder". *Health Care Analysis* 16(3), 255–267.

Fennell, Philip (2010). "Institutionalising the community: The codification of clinical authority and the limits of rights-based approaches". In: McSherry and Weller (eds.), 13–50.

Foster, Charles and Miola, Jose (2015). "Who's in charge? The relationship between medical law and medical ethics and medical morality". *Medical Law Review* 23(4), 505–530.

Fovargue, S and Brazier, M (2006). "Editorial". *Clinical Ethics* 1(1), 21.
Freckelton, Ian (2010). "Extra-legislative factors in involuntary status decision-making". In: McSherry and Weller (eds.), 203–230.
Freeth, Rachel (2007). *Humanising Psychiatry and Mental Health Care*. Oxford and New York: Radcliffe Publishing.
Freeman, Melvyn Colin, Kolappa, Kavitha, Caldas de Almeida, Jose Miguel, Kleinman, Arthur, Makhashvili, Nino, Phakathi, Sifiso, Saraceno, Benedetto and Thornicroft, Graham (2015). "Reversing hard won victories in the name of human rights: A critique of the general comment on article 12 of the UN convention on the rights of persons with disabilities". *The Lancet Psychiatry* 2(9), 844–50.
Frueh, Christopher, Knapp Rebecca, G, Cusack, Karen J, Grubaugh, Anouk L, Sauvageot Julie, A, Cousins Victoria, C, Yim, Eunsil, Robins Cynthia, S, Monnier, Jeannine and Hiers, Thomas G (2005). "Patients' reports of traumatic or harmful experiences within the psychiatric setting." *Psychiatric Services* 56(9), 1123–1133.
Gøtzsche, Peter C, Young, Allen H and Crace, John (2015). "Does long term use of psychiatric drugs cause more harm than good?" *BMJ* 350, 1–3.
Gostin, Laurence O (2001). "Beyond moral claims: A human rights approach in mental health". *Cambridge Quarterly of Healthcare Ethics* 10(3), 264–274.
Guidry-Grimes, Laura (2019). "Ethical complexities in assessing patients' insight". *Journal of Medical Ethics* 45(3), 178–182.
Gurbai, Sandor, Fitton, Emily and Martin, Wayne (2020). "Insight under scrutiny in the court of protection: A case law survey". *Frontiers in Psychiatry* 11, 1–12.
Gray, R (2019). *Service Users' Experiences of Coercion and Autonomy in Inpatient Mental Health Services*. Unpublished Ph.D dissertation.
Hale, Brenda (2007). "Justice and equality in mental health law: The European experience". *International Journal of Law and Psychiatry* 30(1), 18–28.
Harrington, John (2017). *Towards a Rhetoric of Medical Law*. London and New York: Routledge.
Hem, Marit Helene, Gjerberg, Elizabeth, Husum, Tonje Lossius and Pedersen, Reidar (2018). "Ethical challenges when using coercion in mental healthcare: A systematic literature review". *Nursing Ethics* 25(1), 92–110.
Herring, Jonathan (2016). *Medical Law and Ethics*. Oxford: OUP.
Herczegfalvy v Austria (1992). EHRR, 437, 484(82).
Holm, S and Edgar, A (2008). "Best interest: A philosophical critique". *Health Care Analysis* 16, 197–207.
House of Lords. Select Committee. (2014). "Post-legislative scrutiny of the mental capacity act 2005".
Javed, A and Fountoulakis, KN (2019). *Advances in Psychiatry*. New York: Springer International Publishing.
Kallert, Thomas W, Mezzich, Juan E and Monahan, John (2011). *Coercive Treatment in Psychiatry: Clinical, Legal and Ethical Perspectives*. Chichester: Wiley-Blackwell.
Kallert, Thomas W (2011). "Mental health care and patients' rights – Are these two fields currently compatible?" In: Kallert et al (eds.), 121–145.
Kjellin, Lars, Andersson, Kristina, Candefjord, Inga-Lill, Palmstierna, Tom and Walisten, Thula (1997). "Ethical benefits and costs of coercion in short-term inpatient psychiatric care". *Psychiatric Services* 48(12), 1567–1570.
Knowles, SF, Hearne, J and Smith, I (2015). "Physical restraint and the therapeutic relationship". *The Journal of Forensic Psychiatry & Psychology*, 26(4), 461–475.
Large, MM, Ryan, CJ, Nielssen, OB and Hayes, RA (2008). "The danger of dangerousness: why we must remove the dangerousness criterion from our mental health acts". *Journal of Medical Ethics* 34(12), 877–881.
Lawson, Anna and Priestly, Mark (2017). "The social model of disability: Questions for law and legal scholarship?" In: Blank and Flynn (eds.), 3–15.
Leucht, Setefan, Hierl, Sandra, Kissling, Werner, Dold, Markus and Davis, John M (2012). "Putting the efficacy of psychiatric and general medicine medication into perspective: Review of meta-analyses". *The British Journal of Psychiatry* 200(2), 97–106.
Lewis, O (2010). "The expressive, educational and proactive roles of human rights: An analysis of the United Nations convention on the rights of persons with disabilities". In: McSherry and Weller (eds.).

Mann, K, Gröschel, S, Singer, S, Breitmaier, J, Claus, S, Fani, M, Rambach, S, Salize, HJ and Lieb, K (2021). "Evaluation of coercive measures in different psychiatric hospitals: The impact of institutional characteristics". *BMC Psychiatry* 21, 419, 1–11.

McGorry, Patrick D and McConville, Scott B (1999). "Insight in psychosis: An elusive target". *Comprehensive Psychiatry* 40(2), 131–142.

McLean, Sheila (1999). *Old Law, New Medicine; Medical Ethics and Human Rights*. London: Pandora Publishing.

McSherry, Bernadette and Weller, Penelope (eds.) (2010) *Rethinking Rights-Based Mental Health Law*. Oxford: Hart Publishing.

Mezzina, R, Rosen, A, Amering, M and Javed, A (2019). "The practice of freedom: Human rights and the global mental health agenda". In Javad and Foutoulakis (eds.), 483–515.

Minkowitz, Tina (2010). "Abolishing mental health laws to comply with the convention on the rights of persons with disabilities". In McSherry and Weller (eds.).

Minkowitz, Tina (2015). "What would CRPD-compliant mental health legislation look like?" *Mad in America*, May 11, 2015. https://www.madinamerica.com/2015/05/what-would-crpd-compliant-mental-health-legislation-look-like/. Accessed September 9, 2022.

Minkowitz, Tina (2015). "Decision-making and moral injury". *Mad in America*, June 22, 2015. https://www.madinamerica.com/2015/06/decision-making-moral-injury/.

Minkowitz, Tina (2017). "CRPD and transformative equality". *International Journal of Law in Context* 13(1), 77–85.

Miola, Jose (2007). *Medical Ethics and Medical Law: A Symbiotic Relationship*. Oxford and Portland: Hart Publishing.

McSherry, Bernadette and Weller, Penelope (2010). *Rethinking Rights-Based Mental Health Laws*. Oxford and Portland, Oregon: Hart Publishing.

McSherry, Bernadette and Freckelton, Ian (2015). *Coercive Care: Rights, Law and Policy*. London and New York: Routledge.

McSherry, Bernadette and Freckelton, Ian (2015). "Coercive care: Rights, law and policy". In: McSherry and Freckelton (eds.), 3–13.

Montgomery, Jonathan (2006). "The legitimacy of medical law". In: McLean, Sheila (ed.), *First, Do No Harm: Law, Ethics and Healthcare*. London and New York: Routledge, 1–15.

National Institute for Health and Care Excellence. (2018). "Guideline on decision-making and mental capacity".

Oaks, David W (2011). "The moral imperative for dialogue with organisations of survivors of coerced psychiatric human rights violations". In: Kallert et al (eds.), 187–211.

Olsen, DP (2003). "Influence and coercion: Relational and rights-based ethical approaches to forced psychiatric treatment". *Journal of Psychiatric and Mental Health Nursing* 10(6), 705–712.

Pūras, Dainius (2018). "A human rights approach to mental health and people with disabilities". *Bulletin of the World Health Organization* 96(8), 520–521.

Pūras, Dainius and Gooding, Piers (2019). "Mental health and human rights in the 21st century". *World Psychiatry* 18(1), 42–43.

Quigley, Muireann (2008). "Best interests, the power of the medical profession, and the power of the judiciary". *Health Care Analysis* 16(3), 233–239.

Richardson, Genevra (2011). "Involuntary treatment, human dignity and human rights". In: Rioux, Marcia, Basser, Lee Ann and Jones, Melinda (eds.), *Critical Perspectives on Human Rights and Disability Law*. Nijhoff: Brill Publishing, 138–156.

Richardson, Genevra (2010). "Rights-based legalism: Some thoughts from the research". In: McSherry and Weller (eds.), 181–201.

Roper, Cath (2019). "Ethical peril, violence, and 'dirty hands': Ethical consequences of mental health laws." *Journal of Ethics in Mental Health* 10, 1–17.

Royal College of Psychiatrists (2006). "Memorandum submitted by the royal college of psychiatrists (MH 10)". https://publications.parliament.uk/pa/cm200607/cmpublic/mental/memos/uc1002.htm. Accessed September 9, 2022.

Ryan, Christopher James and Bartels, Jane (2021). "Involuntary hospitalisation". In: Bloch et al (eds.), 279–299.

Scorupski, John (1999). *Ethical Explorations*. Oxford: OUP.

Series, Lucy (2016). "The place of wishes and feelings in best interests decisions: Wye Valley NHS Trust v Mr B". *Modern Law Review* 79(6), 1101–1115.

Silva, E, Till, A and Adshead, G (2017). "Ethical dilemmas in psychiatry: When teams disagree". *BJPsych Advances* 23(4), 231–239.

Singh Jay, P, Fazel, Seena, Gueorguieva, Ralitza and Buchanan, Alec (2014). "Rates of violence in patients classified as high risk by structured risk assessment instruments". *The British Journal of Psychiatry* 204(3), 180–187.

Sjöstrand, Manne and Helgesson, Gert (2008). "Coercive treatment and autonomy in psychiatry". *Bioethics* 22(2), 113–120.

Sjöstrand, Manne, Sandman, Lars, Karlsson, Petter, Helgesson, Gert, Eriksson, Stefan and Juth, Niklas (2015). "Ethical deliberations about involuntary treatment: Interviews with Swedish psychiatrists". *BMC Medical Ethics* 16(37), 1–12.

Szmukler, George (2003). "Risk assessment: 'numbers' and 'values'". *Psychiatric Bulletin* 27(6), 205–207.

Szmukler, George and Dawson, John (2011). "Reducing discrimination in mental health law – The 'fusion' of incapacity and mental health legislation". In: Kallert et al (eds.), 97–119.

Szmuckler, George and Rose, Nicholas (2013). "Risk assessment in mental health care: Values and costs". *Behavioral Sciences and the Law* 31(1), 125–140.

Szmukler, George and Appelbaum, Paul (2008). "Treatment pressures, leverage, coercion, and compulsion in mental health care". *Journal of Medical Health* 17(3), 233–244.

Szmukler, George (2015). "Compulsion and coercion". *World Psychiatry* 14(3), 259–261.

Taipale, Heidi, Tanskanen, Antti, Mehtälä, Juha, Vattulainen, Pia, Correll, Christoph U and Tiihonen, Jari (2020). "20-year follow-up study of physical morbidity and mortality in relationship to antipsychotic treatment in a nationwide cohort of 62,250 patients with schizophrenia (FIN20)". *World Psychiatry* 19(1), 61–68.

Tjannso, T (2004). "The convention on human rights and biomedicine and the use of coercion in psychiatry". *Journal of Medical Ethics* 30(5), 430–434.

UK Mental Health Act (2007).

United Nations Committee on the Rights of Persons with Disabilities (2014). "General Comment No. 1 – Article 12: Equal recognition before the law (Adopted 11 April 2014)".

United Nations convention on the rights of persons with disabilities (2006).

Van der Burg, Wibren (1997). "Bioethics and law: A developmental perspective". *Bioethics* 11(2), 91–114.

Vatne, S and Fagermoen, MS (2007). "To correct and to acknowledge: Two simultaneous and conflicting perspectives of limit-setting in mental health nursing". *Journal of Psychiatric and Mental Health Nursing* 14(1), 41–48.

Weller, Penelope (2010). "Lost in translation: Human rights and mental health law". In: McSherry and Weller (eds.), 51–72.

Weller, Penelope (2015). "Towards a genealogy of coercive care". In: McSherry and Freckelton (eds.), 15–30.

Wilson, Kay (2021). *Mental Health Law: Abolish or Reform?* Oxford: Oxford University Press.

Wilson, Kay (2022). "The CRPD and mental health law: The conflict about abolition, the practical dilemmas of implementation and the untapped potential". In: Felder, Franziska, Davy, Laura and Keyess, Rosemary (eds.), *Disability Law and Human Rights*. Switzerland: Springer, 171–197.

Wykes, T, Evans, J, Paton, C, Barnes, TRE, Taylor, D, Bentall, R, Dalton, T, Ruffell, D, Rose, D and Vitoratou, S (2017). "What side effects are problematic for patients prescribed antipsychotic medication? The Maudsley Side Effects (MSE) measure for antipsychotic medication". *Psychological Medicine* 47(13), 2369–2378.

PART 2

European and international standards

4
THE EUROPEAN COURT'S INCREMENTAL APPROACH TO THE PROTECTION OF LIBERTY, DIGNITY AND AUTONOMY

Anna Nilsson

Introduction

In 1979, the European Court of Human Rights (ECtHR) delivered its first significant case on this topic, *Winterwerp v the Netherlands*, establishing the criteria to be met to justify the detention of persons with mental health problems in a psychiatric facility. These criteria still form the backbone of the Court's mental health jurisprudence and a recent study implies that they have had a significant impact on domestic mental health laws in Europe (Niveau, Jantzi and Godet, 2021). Since then, the Court's case law has grown and progressed particularly in relation to Article 5 (right to liberty), Article 3 (protection against inhuman and degrading treatment), and Article 8 (respect for private life) in the manner and pace with which applicants have submitted cases. The chapter discusses this development, each article in turn, and then engages with the critique levelled at the Court for its lenient approach to malpractices taking place within psychiatric institutions and for its reluctance to align its jurisprudence with the standards on mental health care set forth in the Convention on the Rights of Persons with Disabilities (CRPD).

Protection against arbitrary deprivation of liberty

The right to liberty is guaranteed in Article 5 of the European Convention on Human Rights (ECHR). The treaty text informs us that states parties to the Convention must ensure that no one is deprived of her liberty save in a number of situations listed in paragraphs 1(a)–(f). Paragraph 1(e) provides for the detention of persons of "unsound mind". The terminology reminds us that the ECHR was developed in the late 1940s, and the Court has held that the content of this phrase (i.e. what it denotes) is continually evolving in parallel with medical advances and as our attitudes to mental health problems change (*Winterwerp*, 1979, para. 37). To comply with Article 5, the detention must conform to the substantive and procedural rules prescribed by domestic law (*Stanev v Bulgaria*, 2012, para. 143). Mere compliance with domestic law is, however, not sufficient. The system for deprivation of liberty must also be "fair and proper" and include safeguards against arbitrariness and professional misjudgments (*Winterwerp*, 1979, para. 45; *H.L. v the United Kingdom*, 2004, para. 120–124). To facilitate such protection, the Court has insisted on a range of procedural safeguards. This includes the right to have the decision to detain reviewed by a court (*X v Finland*, para. 168), to have the opportunity to be heard in person or, where necessary, through representation (*Zagidulina v Russia*, 2013, para. 61–66) and to receive legal assistance in proceedings relating to the confinement, unless special circumstances speak against such an order (*M.S. v Croatia (no. 2)*, 2015, para. 152–153). The mere appointment of a lawyer is not sufficient. The Convention is designed to guarantee rights that are not theoretical or illusory, but practical and effective. Thus, a lawyer who, without good reason, refuses to follow the client's instructions and/or remains passive during court proceedings will not count as effective legal representation (*M.S.*, 2015, para. 156; *V.K. v Russia*, 2017, para. 35–36).

Paragraphs 2 and 4 of Article 5 set forth additional procedural guarantees against arbitrariness. Paragraph 2 obliges states to promptly inform anyone who is arrested of the reasons for the arrest in a language that he or she understands. The term "arrest" applies beyond the criminal context to persons apprehended and detained to facilitate medical treatment (*Van der Leer v the Netherlands*, 1990, para. 27–28). Information should be provided in simple, non-technical language that the person can understand, enabling him or her to make effective use of the right to judicial review (*Z.H. v Hungary*, 2012, para. 41–44). Paragraph 4 entitles all detainees to have the lawfulness of their detention decided speedily by a court and to have their release ordered if the detention is not lawful. Delays exceeding three to four weeks raise issues under Article 5.4. Consideration is, however, given to the complexity of the legal and factual issues under review. Moreover, persons who are confined for long periods are entitled to have their detention reviewed at reasonable intervals (*Stanev*, 2012, para. 171). The rationale behind these rules is that the individual should not run the risk of remaining in a psychiatric institution for a significant time after such detention has become unjustified.

The *Winterwerp* criteria

In addition to the procedural safeguards discussed above, the ECtHR has developed three minimum conditions that must be met if civil detention is to be lawful under Article 5.1(e). According to the first of these criteria, it must be "reliably shown" that the person concerned has a "true mental disorder" (*Winterwerp*, 1979, para. 39). Psychiatric detention requires medical evidence, a requirement that is intended to safeguard against the arbitrary detention of political opponents or people who behave in an antisocial manner. It is for domestic authorities to determine the procedure to be followed to obtain such medical evidence, and in urgent cases or where a person is acting violently, the medical assessment may take place after the person has been detained, though without delay. A medical consultation with the person or, in case the person refuses to talk to a doctor, his or her medical file, is, however, indispensable and seen as a safeguard against arbitrariness (*Varbanov v Bulgaria*, 2000, para. 47–48). The medical opinion must furthermore be based on the current state of mental health of the person concerned and not solely on past events. The question of whether medical expertise is sufficiently recent has not been answered by the Court in a static way but depends on the specific circumstances of the case before it (*M.B. v Poland*, 2021, para. 64–66). Consideration is, for example, given to whether the person cooperates with those making the assessment.

The second criterion for lawful detention under Article 5.1(e) requires that the person's condition is of a "kind or degree warranting compulsory confinement" (*Winterwerp*, 1979, para. 39). The condition should attain a certain level of seriousness and confinement within the psychiatric care facility should be appropriate. The Court has clarified that the fact that an individual reads the Bible all night, drops out of university, fails to support himself financially and voices unrealistic ideas about a future political career are not sufficient reasons to conclude that they are of unsound mind warranting compulsory hospitalisation (*Rakevich v Russia*, 2003, para. 29; *Plesó v Hungary*, 2012, para. 7–12 and 65). The individual must be in need of therapy, medication or other forms of clinical treatment to cure or alleviate his condition, or in need of supervision to prevent serious self-harming behaviour or violence against others (*Bergmann v Germany*, 2016, para. 97). People who are believed to pose a risk to others may be detained irrespective of whether their condition is likely to improve with clinical treatment, at least as long as the detention takes place in an environment that offers support and protection against violent or self-harming behaviour (*Hutchinson Reid v the United Kingdom*, 2003, para. 52–56).

Given that deprivation of liberty is such a serious measure, the Court has emphasised that it can only be justified where other, less severe measures have been considered and found to be insufficient to safeguard the individual or public interests at stake (*Varbanov*, 2000, para. 46). Moreover, the principle of proportionality applies, meaning that domestic authorities must strike a fair balance between the competing interests of protecting the health and lives of its citizens on the one hand, and securing the right to liberty and self-determination of the person in need of treatment on the other. Involuntary hospitalisation must carry true health benefits that compensate for the harms connected to such hospitalisation (*Plesó*, 2012, para. 66). The third *Winterwerp* criterion concerns the length of the detention and asserts that the validity of continued confinement depends upon the persistence of mental disorder (para. 39). Still, domestic authorities are permitted to take some time to prepare the release, as long as the release is not unreasonably delayed (*Johnson v the United Kingdom*, 1997, para. 61–67).

An essential principle that permeates the Court's entire body of case law, and one that also applies in mental health cases, is that of subsidiarity. In *Winterwerp*, the Court stated that national authorities enjoy a certain amount of discretion (a margin of appreciation) when evaluating the evidence adduced before them in order to determine whether an individual has a true mental disorder of the kind or degree warranting compulsory care (1979, para. 40). In many cases, the Court has refrained from scrutinising the national authorities' assessments on these matters. When applicants have challenged the content of psychiatric expert opinions, the Court has often held that it is primarily for the domestic courts to assess the scientific quality of such opinions and accepted the courts' evaluations (e.g. *Herczegfalvy v Austria*, 1992, para. 63–64; *Glien v Germany*, 2013, para. 88–91; *K.C. v Poland*, 2014, para. 69). As will be discussed further below, this lenient approach is highly problematic. In a fair number of more recent cases, the Court has begun to limit the discretion afforded to states and has engaged in stricter scrutiny regarding whether the *Winterwerp* criteria have been met and whether voluntary and less restrictive forms of care have proven insufficient to protect the person concerned or others. This shift is justified by what have now become stock phrases in the Court's jurisprudence on persons with mental health problems. Namely that "individuals suffering from a mental illness constitute a particularly vulnerable group", such that "any interference with their rights must be subject to strict scrutiny", and only "very weighty reasons" can justify a restriction of their rights (e.g. *Pleshó*, 2012; para. 65; *M.S.*, 2015, para. 147; *D.R. v Lithuania*, 2018, para. 88).

An appropriate facility for detention

Article 5 says nothing about the manner or the conditions of the detention. In its early case law, the Court held that this provision is not in principle concerned with the conditions of detention and cannot, for example, be interpreted to include a right to treatment (*Winterwerp*, 1979, para. 51; *Ashingdane v the United Kingdom*, 1985, para. 44 and 47–48). Since then, the Court has gradually modified its position in this respect and attached increasing weight to the need to provide a therapeutic environment. In 1998, the Court found, for the first time, a violation of Article 5.1(e) on account of the conditions of detention (*Aerts v Belgium*, 1998). The case concerned a man who spent seven months in a psychiatric wing of an ordinary prison because the social-protection centre in which he was supposed to stay had no available places. During this time, he had very little contact with medically qualified staff, and spent most of his time in a common room that made him extremely anxious. The European Committee for the Prevention of Torture and Inhuman or Degrading Treatment or Punishment (CPT), who visited the place at that time, described the standard of care as falling "in every respect, below the minimum acceptable from an ethical and humanitarian point of view" (CPT, 1994, para. 191). In its subsequent case law, the Court has on several occasions confirmed that psychiatric wings of ordinary prisons are not appropriate places for the detention of persons with mental health problems as they do not provide proper treatment and thus deprive the persons concerned of their prospect of rehabilitation and release (e.g. *O.H. v Germany*, 2011, para. 88–95; *B. v Germany*, 2012, para. 82–84; *L.B. v Belgium*, 2012, para. 95–102; *Claes v Belgium*, 2013, para. 120–121). The mere fact that a service is part of the prison structure does not, however, automatically disqualify the site as an appropriate facility for persons with mental health problems. What matters, for the purposes of Article 5, is not the title of the institution but the conditions at the facility in question, including the individual's access to adequate treatment (*Bergmann*, 2016, para. 124–128). Put differently, there must be some relationship between the basis for detention and the place and the conditions of its execution. As a general rule, detention of a person with mental health problems must be effected in a hospital, clinic or similar appropriate institution to comply with the Convention (*Stanev*, 2012, para. 147). This arguably also applies in situations in which the individual's condition is not amenable to treatment (*Hutchinson Reid*, 2003, para. 52 and 55).

What kind of treatment must the individual be provided with, then? The Court discussed this question at length in *Rooman v Belgium* (2019), a case concerning a man who, following the end of his prison sentence, was detained in a high-security unit at a social-protection facility because of the risk that he may reoffend. The facility was located in the French-speaking region of the country. Mr Rooman was German-speaking and had only a poor command of the French language. According to a psychiatric assessment in 2005, he was in need of psychotherapeutic treatment over several years. However, due to difficulties in finding German-speaking specialists, he received very little therapeutic treatment. He saw a psychologist 18 times and received no other treatment for his mental condition. The Court found this to be insufficient. The level of treatment provided must go beyond basic care. Mere access to a general practitioner and medication will not suffice. Rather, the range and quality of the treatment provided should be at a level comparable to that which is provided to the population as a whole. In particular, it is important that an individualised programme is put in place, one that is tailored to meet the detainee's specific mental health condition and with a view to preparing him or her for life in society (para. 147 and 209). Still, domestic authorities enjoy a certain latitude to determine the details of the therapeutic programme. Applying these principles to the circumstances in the case, the Court held that in the context of mental health care, the dialogue between the psychiatrist and the patient is key to facilitating appropriate treatment. As Mr Rooman was willing to undergo therapy, the authorities had a duty to provide such treatment in German. The few instances of therapy were not enough. The failure to provide the applicant with treatment was all the more unjustifiable in view of the fact that German is one of Belgium's official languages, and as such overcoming the language problem did not seem to place an unreasonable burden on the state. Consequently, the detention of Mr Rooman for 13 years without providing access to therapy amounted to a violation of Article 5 (para. 237–243). The Court did not speculate about what results might have been achieved through therapy had it taken place during the first decade of Mr Rooman's detention. Having noted that the obligation to provide treatment is just as important in situations where a condition is considered to be "incurable", the Court concluded that absence of treatment was sufficient to find a violation of the Convention (para. 235–237). In this case, the therapeutic neglect not only rendered deprivation of liberty unlawful under the Convention, but it also amounted to inhuman and degrading treatment in violation of Article 3. The next section discusses in greater depth what protection this provision affords to persons with mental health problems.

Protection against inhuman and degrading treatment

Article 3 of the Convention prohibits in absolute terms torture and inhuman or degrading treatment or punishment. In order to fall within the scope of Article 3, the act or omission under scrutiny must attain a minimum level of severity. The assessment of this minimum is relative; it depends on all the circumstances of the case, such as the duration of the treatment, its physical and mental effects and, in some cases, the sex, age and state of health of the victim (*Stanev*, 2012, para. 201–202). For persons committed to psychiatric hospitals or forensic care, the level of suffering must go beyond that inevitable element of suffering or humiliation connected with detention per se. Far from all such deprivations of liberty can be said to interfere with human dignity or subject the individual to the kind of distress or hardship that raise issues under Article 3 (*Stanev*, 2012, para. 204). On the other hand, the Court has also held that detainees with mental health problems are more vulnerable than others, which must be taken into account (*Rooman*, 2019, para. 145). A key question has been whether any of the coercive measures to which persons with mental health problems are subjected in psychiatric hospitals may constitute inhuman or degrading treatment. For many years, this hardly seemed to be the case. In *Herczegfalvy* (1992), the Court held that:

> it is for the medical authorities to decide, on the basis of the recognised rules of medical science, on the therapeutic methods to be used, if necessary by force, to preserve the physical and mental health of patients who are entirely incapable of deciding for themselves

and that "as a general rule, a measure which is a therapeutic necessity cannot be regarded as inhuman or degrading" (para. 82). The case concerned a man who had been forcibly administered food and neuroleptics, isolated and attached with handcuffs to a security bed for weeks during his stay in a Viennese psychiatric hospital in the 1980s. One episode stands out as particularly austere. The parties' descriptions of the course of events diverge and conclusive evidence is lacking. Yet, it is undisputed that Mr Herczegfalvy was to be injected with sedatives, that he fell into a rage over the proposed treatment, that an emergency team was called in to overpower him, that the injection was carried out and that Mr Herczegfalvy collapsed after the incident and developed pneumonia and nephritis (Report of the Commission, *Herczegfalvy v Austria*, 1991 para. 88–89, 245–246). Still, the Court concluded that the evidence before it was insufficient to disprove that the treatment was justified according to the psychiatric principles accepted at the time (para. 83). The outcome is perhaps even more remarkable in view of the Court's assertion that involuntary patients' experience of inferiority and powerlessness called for increased vigilance in the review (para. 82). For many years, the lenient approach in *Herczegfalvy* set the tone for the Court's jurisprudence on coercive care, and its principles still influence the Court's argumentation (e.g. *Wilkinson v the United Kingdom*, 2006, para. 19–20; *D.D. v Lithuania*, 2012, para. 173–176; *M.S.*, 2015, para. 103). As will be discussed below, the Court has, however, begun to subject malpractices in psychiatric settings to stricter review.

Living conditions

The poor standards of many civil and forensic psychiatric establishments constitute a serious problem in several parts of Europe. This includes problems with overcrowding, inadequate heating, dilapidated and damaged sanitary facilities and lack of proper ventilation and access to daily outdoor activities (e.g. CPT, 2021, para. 70–73; 2020, para. 20–23; 2019a, para. 22–26). The Court has condemned such living conditions as degrading treatment in the prison and pre-trial detention context since the beginning of the millennium *(Kalashnikov v Russia*, 2002, para. 97–103; *Nevmerzhitsky v Ukraine*, 2005, para. 86–88). In 2012, the Court condemned for the first time the living conditions of a social care institution, accommodating persons with mental health problems, as amounting to degrading treatment in violation of Article 3 (*Stanev*, 2012, para. 213). In this case, the Court was particularly concerned about the fact that the building in which the applicant spent seven years was inadequately heated so that residents had to sleep with their coats on in the winter, that the food was insufficient and of poor quality and that the toilets were in a deplorable state (para. 209). Moreover, staff did not return clothes to the same people after they were washed, which was likely to arouse a feeling of inferiority among the residents. Taken together, these living conditions amounted to degrading treatment (para. 212). The Court reached the same conclusion in a more recent case about a man who spent nine years within dilapidated forensic institutions with widespread damp and lack of central heating (*Strazimiri v Albania*, 2020, para. 106). This in combination with the fact that the applicant did not benefit from regular out-of-room activities, and had only received medication but no therapeutic treatment, led the ECtHR to conclude that there was a violation of Article 3 (para. 107–112).

Restraints

Misuse of restraints is another area of concern in several countries in Europe. This includes the use of physical force, mechanical restraints (e.g. straps and "net-beds") and sedation for illegitimate purposes, for excessive periods and/or in view of other patients (e.g. CPT, 2020, para. 33 and 39–40; 2019a, para. 63; 2019b, para. 122–128). The Court has accepted that physical restraints may sometimes be necessary and legitimate, i.e. in situations in which no other measures are available to calm down an agitated individual and to prevent him or her from harming himself or herself or others. Such measures must, however, be proportionate to their purposes and never prolonged beyond what is strictly necessary. In addition, their administration must be accompanied with procedural safeguards to prevent abuse (*M.S.*, 2015, para. 104–105). As noted above, the Court found no violation of the Convention in *Herczegfalvy* (1992), characterising the use of handcuffs and the violent treatment of the applicant by the hospital staff as merely "worrying" (para. 83). Since then, the Court has condemned the use of handcuffs within psychiatric care, pointing to the fact that handcuffing is not a standard method of restraining persons with mental health problems and an ineffective means to prevent self-harm (*Kucheruk v Ukraine*, 2007, para. 142–144).

In *Bureš v the Czech Republic* (2012), the Court found the use of a multiple-point restraint belt for two hours immediately on arrival at a psychiatric hospital to be in breach of Article 3. The government sought to justify the measure with reference to the applicant's restlessness. Mere restlessness, the Court argued, is not a good enough reason to strap someone to a bed for hours. The Court went on to critique the authorities for using belts as a matter of routine, without trying alternative methods to calm people down (para. 96–97). Similarly, the Court has held that the fact that someone refuses hospitalisation, yells and appears suspicious, tense and distanced is not sufficient reason to resort to restraints (*M.S.*, 2015, para. 107–108). As regards duration of restraints, the Court has refrained from specifying a time at which the use of such means becomes excessive, as this will depend on the circumstances of each specific case. According to the Court, even strapping someone to a restraint bed for 22 hours and 50 minutes can be justified if it is shown to be necessary to prevent violent or self-harming behaviour (*Aggerholm v Denmark*, 2020, para. 105). If, on the other hand, the person calms down after some hours, then the continued application of restraints due to "potential dangerousness" is unjustified and in violation of Article 3 (ibid., para. 111–115).

Medical treatment

Administration of medical treatment may interfere with the protection granted under Article 3 in, at least, three ways: failure to provide appropriate of treatment; unethical administration of treatment; and treatment against the person's will. In 2001, the Court pointed for the first time to the lack of appropriate medical care as a key reason to find a violation of Article 3 (*Keenan v the United Kingdom*, 2001, para. 114–116). The case concerned a prison inmate with a history of mental health problems who committed suicide whilst in prison in connection with a period of disciplinary confinement in a cell. In *Dybeku v Albania* (2007), the Court affirmed that Article 3 imposes an obligation on states to protect the well-being of persons deprived of their liberty (para. 41). This includes an obligation to accommodate the needs and vulnerability associated with mental health problems. Keeping an offender with significant mental health problems in a shared cell in an ordinary prison, which had a detrimental impact on his health, without access to proficient psychiatric care, amounted to inhuman and degrading treatment (para. 45–52). To support this conclusion, due consideration was given to the applicant's condition, his vulnerability, the inadequacy of the care provided and the length of the detention. Mr Dybeku was sentenced to life imprisonment. By contrast, *Blokhin v Russia* (2016) concerned a 12-year-old child with attention-deficit hyperactivity disorder who was sent to a juvenile detention centre for 30 days. During detention, he shared a bedroom with seven other boys and was denied medical treatment for his mental health condition. The absence of treatment in combination with his young age and mental health condition sufficed in this case to find a violation of Article 3 (para. 148–149).

Thus far, the Court has not rejected any particular treatment method as inhuman or degrading per se or when imposed without consent. Several applicants have argued that forced administration of, for example, neuroleptics violated Article 3, but without success. In *Buckley v the United Kingdom* (1997), the patient died due to cardiac failure associated with the administration of the drug. The ensuing domestic inquiry, however, found no medical negligence on the part of the doctors, which led the Commission to dismiss the complaint as manifestly ill-founded (para. 4). The Court has also rejected such claims with reference to the applicant's failure to prove that he had actually been treated with outdated drugs (*Shtukaturov v Russia*, 2008, para. 128). Whilst these cases illustrate the Court's reluctance to address the issue of forced medication head on, they should not be taken to imply that maladministration of psychiatric treatment can never constitute inhuman and degrading treatment. All forms of medical practice are open to abuse, and some psychiatric psychopharmacological treatment involves a considerable amount of pain and suffering, indeed arguably an amount that meets the minimum threshold for ill-treatment under Article 3.

The third way in which medical treatment may interfere with Convention rights is if such treatment is administered against the person's will. Such issues have mainly been adjudicated in relation to Article 8 and are discussed in the next section. As Wicks (2001) has explained, violations of Article 3 have been more connected to the concept of human dignity than with individual self-determination and autonomy (pp. 22–23).

Respect for personal autonomy

Respect for personal autonomy is a fundamental imperative in contemporary bioethics and an important principle undergirding the Court's jurisprudence (*Pretty v the United Kingdom*, 2002, para. 61). Conscious decisions deserve respect even if they entail a risk to the person's health or life. Treatment decisions are value sensitive, meaning that the "right" choice depends on the values and costs the person concerned attaches to the consequences of the decision. How does the person concerned value the potential benefits of a certain treatment? Does he or she think that they outweigh the adverse effects associated with the treatment in question? The results of such balancing naturally differ between individuals, and between doctors and their clients. Hence, to facilitate protection of personal choices, there must be room for disagreement. The Court expressed this point eloquently in its case law regarding the right of Jehovah's Witnesses to refuse blood transfusions:

> The freedom to accept or refuse specific medical treatment, or to select an alternative form of treatment, is vital [...] For this freedom to be meaningful, patients must have the right to make choices that accord with their own views and values, regardless of how irrational, unwise or imprudent such choices may appear to others.
> *(Jehovah's Witnesses of Moscow v Russia, 2010, para. 136)*

This does not mean that every "yes" or "no" expressed by a patient constitutes a consent or refusal that deserves respect. To be valid, treatment choices must be free and informed. "Free" decisions are those that are obtained without threats or improper inducements. To facilitate informed decisions, states should ensure that doctors provide their patients with "full, accurate and comprehensible information about the patient's condition and the treatment proposed" (*X.*, 2012, para. 132). Describing electroconvulsive therapy as "sleep therapy" would be an example in which this standard is not met. Moreover, only persons who are considered to have decision-making capacity enjoy the right to refuse medical care under the Convention. Whilst the Court has recognised that the administration of treatment against someone's will always constitutes an interference with that person's physical integrity (*Storck v Germany*, 2005, para. 143–144), such interferences may be justified in situations in which the person lacks decision-making capacity according to the rule established in *Herczegfalvy*. At least if the person is held to be "entirely incapable" of deciding for himself or herself, the rule leaves physicians with significant clinical discretion to determine, on the basis of medical standards, what methods to be used (para. 82). Given the importance attached to mental capacity, it would have been useful if the Court had elaborated on what constitutes such capacity in the mental health context. But alas, such specificity is absent. Instead, domestic authorities enjoy a wide margin of appreciation to determine these matters. National authorities have the benefit of direct contact with the persons concerned and are therefore, the Court argues, better placed than an international court to determine such issues (*Shtukaturov*, 2008, para. 87).

A growing respect for the personal wishes of persons with mental health problems

Many European states still allow a guardian or other legal representative to consent to medical treatment on behalf of persons who are considered to lack mental capacity for such decisions. The Court has accepted that there are situations in which "the wishes of a person with impaired mental faculties may validly be replaced by those of another person" (*Stanev*, 2012, para. 130). Even so, the Court has declared that depriving someone of their legal capacity, completely or partially, constitutes a serious interference with Article 8 that can only be justified under exceptional circumstances (*Shtukaturov*, 2008, para. 90; *Ivinović v Croatia*, 2014, para. 38). In *Shtukaturov*, the Court struck down for the first time a decision depriving a person with mental health problems of his legal capacity, i.e. his capacity to exercise his rights and obligations within a legal system. In this case, Mr Shtukaturov was deprived of his legal capacity altogether, which made him fully dependent on his official guardian in almost all areas of life. The guardian did, for example, "consent" to Mr Shtukaturov's hospitalisation against his will. The Court clarified that guardians cannot consent to hospitalisation against the individual's will. Such committals are to be viewed as deprivation of liberty. To safeguard against arbitrariness, the *Winterwerp* criteria and the procedural protection package developed in relation to Article 5.1(e) apply (1979, para. 112–116).

In *Shtukaturov*, the Court also laid the foundation for its future jurisprudence on legal capacity. To begin with, the Court clarified that a diagnosis, even a serious one, is not a sufficient reason to deny someone the right to self-determination. Making an analogy with the *Winterwerp* criteria, the Court held that the condition must be of a "kind and degree" warranting deprivation of legal capacity to be justified (2008, para. 94). Besides, capacity assessments must be based on reliable and conclusive evidence, such as a recent medical report explaining what kind of actions the person is unable to understand or control and how this affects his or her social life, health, pecuniary interests and so on (ibid., para. 93–94; *Sýkora v the Czech Republic*, 2012, para. 103 and 111). The very fact that an individual resists treatment cannot be taken as proof of a lack of insight into his or her condition. As noted above, there must be room for disagreement between the doctor and the client. Domestic authorities must instead enquire into the reasons behind an individual's refusal of hospitalisation and/or treatment (*Plesó*, 2012, para. 67–68; *D.R.*, 2018, para. 95). This is important given that studies suggest that the majority of those who are committed to inpatient psychiatric care possess the relevant skills to consent to medical treatment (Grisso and Applebaum, 1995; Calcedo-Barba et al., 2020).

In addition, the *Shtukaturov* judgment set forth procedural guarantees for domestic processes divesting someone of his or her legal capacity. Whilst acknowledging that states are free to make some procedural adjustments in cases involving persons with mental health problems, such measures must not affect "the very essence of the right to a fair trial" as guaranteed by the Convention (2008, para. 68). Just like in cases concerning deprivation of liberty according to Article 5.1(e), the Court emphasised that the participation of the individual concerned is crucial, not only to enable him to argue his own case, but also to allow the judge to form an opinion about the person's mental capacity (para. 72; *A.N. v Lithuania*, 2016, para. 90–91 and 95–98). Hence, only very weighty reasons could justify an exclusion of the person concerned from such hearings.

Even if the Court accepts that the wishes of those who are held to lack mental capacity may be overruled under certain circumstances, it has acknowledged that personal preferences of those deprived of their legal capacity should nevertheless be given due consideration. Just because a person fails to meet domestic standards for mental capacity does not mean that he or she does not have personal preferences that deserve respect. In *Stanev* – a case about a man who was placed in a social care institution by his guardian – the Court criticised the state for not taking due account of the wishes of the person concerned when deciding on protective measures. The primary response to a need of social assistance must not be measures involving deprivation of liberty. On the contrary, "any protective measure should reflect as far as possible the wishes of persons capable of expressing their will", and failure to consult with the person concerned "could give rise to situations of abuse and hamper the exercise of the rights of vulnerable persons" (2012, para. 153).

In the clinical setting, the Court has stressed that doctors' discretionary powers to force medication on their patients must be constrained and subject to scrutiny. Administration of medication in defiance of the person's will interferes with his or her right to respect for physical integrity and must accordingly be based on domestic law that guarantees proper safeguards against arbitrariness. Domestic regimes, which authorise forced treatment of all patients who are subject to involuntary hospitalisation without providing patients with any remedies to challenge the lawfulness of the medication or to have it discontinued, fail to comply with Article 8 (*X.*, 2012, para. 218–222). Thus, even if the Court accepts that treatment without consent can be legitimate under certain circumstances, patients must be protected from overmedication and similar forms of unprofessionalism. Similarly, in *Shopov v Bulgaria*, the Court found that treatment without consent for over five years without regular judicial supervision violated the Convention (2010, para. 45–48).

Balancing respect for autonomy and protection of life

Whether and to what extent states may use compulsory powers to protect people from harming themselves or putting their life at risk has long been a topic of jurisprudential and moral discussion. As noted above, the Convention protects "mentally competent" persons' right to refuse treatment also in situations in which such refusals might be fatal. Whether this extends to people who are deprived of their liberty is somewhat unclear. In *Nevmerzhitsky* (2005) the Court restated the *Herczegfalvy* rule (i.e. that therapeutically necessary measures cannot in principle be regarded as inhuman or degrading) and asserted that the same applies to force-feeding to save the life of a detainee who consciously refuses to take food (para. 94). This seems to suggest that the interest in protecting life outweighs the right to refuse treatment in this context. However, it should be noted that the applicant had not claimed that he should have been left without any food or medicine regardless of the possibly fatal consequences. His complaint concerned the fact that he had been force-fed even though such an intervention had not been necessary to protect his health and life, and that the feeding had been administered in an unprofessional and humiliating manner. The Court agreed on both these points (para. 95–98). Thus, whilst there can be little doubt that, as a general rule, competent patients retain their right to refuse treatment, even if they are detained in a psychiatric facility, it remains unclear under what circumstances this extends to life-saving interventions.

To some extent, the Court has upheld the distinction between competent and incompetent decision-makers also in relation to suicide. In its jurisprudence on assisted suicide, the Court has, for example, acknowledged a right to decide when and by what means to end one's life for everyone who is in a position to make such a decision and take appropriate action (*Haas v Switzerland*, 2011, para. 51). Yet, the *Winterwerp* criteria certainly seem to permit states to hospitalise a person with a mental health problem at risk of such acts. In its jurisprudence under Article 5.1(e), the Court has paid little, if any, attention to whether a risk of suicide reflects a conscious choice or not. Rather, the presence of such a risk constitutes a strong argument in favour of permitting compulsory hospitalisation in contrast to situations in which there is no immediate risk to the person's life (*Plesó*, 2012, para. 66). Congruent with that line of argumentation, the Court has held that, under certain circumstances, states are even obliged to take operational measures to prevent individuals from ending their lives. This includes situations in which persons with mental health problems have been detained in prisons (*Keenan*, 2001, para. 91–96) or placed in psychiatric facilities, voluntarily or involuntarily (*Hiller v Austria*, 2016, para. 48; *Fernandes de Oliveira v Portugal*, 2019, para. 124). In such situations, domestic authorities must do what can reasonably be expected of them to prevent a real and immediate risk of suicide materialising. To determine whether the risk is real and immediate, consideration is given to the gravity of the mental condition, previous attempts to commit suicide or self-harm, suicidal thoughts or threats and signs of physical or mental distress (*Oliveira*, para. 115).

More important, I believe, is that the *Oliveira* judgment recognises that prediction of suicide is extremely difficult and complete prevention is "an impossible task" (para. 131). Research on suicide shows that we do not know what distinguishes people who actually commit suicide from those who do not (other than undertaking the act itself, of course). Certain factors are associated with suicide, such as those enumerated by the Court. This information makes it possible for doctors and others to identify persons at increased risk, but it does not enable them to effectively identify *who* (within a group of people at increased risk) will actually engage in serious self-harm within the coming days, weeks or months. Suicides are rare events, even among those at elevated risk. A systematic review of the clinical factors associated with suicide has calculated the predictive value of risk assessments of inpatient suicide to be below two per cent (Large et al., 2011, p. 26). This means that if 100 individuals are classified as being at risk of suicide, 98 of them will not take their own lives, which seriously undermines the utility of risk-assessment tools in the clinical context (Large, Ryan and Nielssen, 2011). The Court seems to be aware of this problem. In *Oliveira* (para. 112) as well as in *Hiller* (2016, para. 55), the Court also took note of the trend in international law and practice to encourage open treatment regimes, and acknowledged the danger that fervent use of coercive protective measures could result in violations of Articles 3, 5 and 8.

A move to stricter scrutiny

For decades, the Court has been heavily (and rightfully) criticised for its lenient approach to malpractices taking place within psychiatric institutions (e.g. Fennell, 1998, pp. 323–324; Niveau and Materi, 2007, p. 66; Bartlett, 2011 and 2012; Waddington and McSherry, 2016). Whilst the Court has been relatively good at insisting on the establishment of procedural safeguards against arbitrariness at the domestic level, at the same time, it has been remarkably deferential to domestic authorities and medical practitioners as regards the question of whether the substantive criteria set forth in *Winterwerp* (1979), *Herczegfalvy* (1992) and other case law have been met. This is particularly problematic in view of the fact that statutory tests for compulsory psychiatric care in many European countries are malleable and that domestic judges are not always well equipped or inclined to challenge medical reports. As explained by Bartlett (2012), if procedural protections should have any meaning, the criteria for compulsory care must be clear and review bodies must be competent and willing to scrutinise whether the criteria are met in individual cases (p. 832).

As discussed in this chapter, a shift towards stricter scrutiny seems to have occurred in the Court's jurisprudence over the last decade. In *Plesó* (2012), for example, the Court condemned the compulsory hospitalisation of the applicant even though two doctors had asserted the need for such an intervention. In addition, the Court criticised the domestic statutory criteria for compulsory hospitalisation for being too vague and the authorities for being indifferent to the reasons behind Mr Plesó's treatment refusal as well as for their failure to consider whether less restrictive forms of care would be an option (para. 65–69). Similarly, in *N. v Romania* (2017, para. 153–156) and *D.R.* (2018, para. 94–97), the Court slated the responsible domestic authorities for their failure to conduct independent assessments of whether the applicants' condition warranted detention, taking less restrictive alternatives into account. As discussed above, the Court has also engaged in stricter scrutiny of patients' living conditions in psychiatric facilities, the use of restraints and access to adequate medical care under Article 3.

This trend towards stricter review in mental health cases has primarily been defended by the argument that persons with mental health problems belong to a vulnerable group. The Court has not been particularly elaborate about what constitutes a vulnerable group or in what sense the members of such groups are vulnerable. Social factors (e.g. past discrimination, stigmatisation and social marginalisation) may give rise to the relevant kind of vulnerability, as may personal characteristics like age and mental condition (Mjöll Arnardóttir, 2017, pp. 164–166). Strict scrutiny of mental health cases also fits with the general idea of subsidiarity and the view that the intensity of the Court's review depends, among other things, on the quality of the domestic system (e.g. Mowbray, 2015). If the domestic system fails to offer clear criteria for compulsory care, fair procedures and other safeguards against arbitrariness, then it is reasonable for the Court to engage in stricter review to ensure that the rights set forth in the Convention are effective in practice.

The call to align the ECHR with the CRPD

For quite some time now, scholars, representatives from the disability movement and other human rights actors have urged the Court to align its interpretation of the ECHR with the CRPD (e.g. Abello Jiménez, 2015, pp. 310–313; Flynn, 2016, pp. 99–101; Council of Europe Commissioner for Human Rights, 2018 and 2021). The CRPD sets out a new vision for mental health care with equal treatment and respect for personal choice as core standards. In contrast to the ECHR, the CRPD contains no provisions explicitly legitimising civil detention. On the contrary, its Article 14.1(b) asserts that the fact that a person has a mental or psychosocial disability cannot justify deprivation of liberty. In addition, Article 12(2) of the CRPD states that people with disabilities enjoy legal capacity "on an equal basis with others" in all spheres of life. In other words, people with disabilities have the same right to make decisions about their health care treatment as people without disabilities. To what extent these provisions prohibit compulsory mental health interventions is still a matter of contention between different stakeholders and within legal scholarship (Nilsson, 2021, pp. 14–18 and 22–24). The Committee on the Rights of Persons with Disabilities (CRPD Committee) has interpreted the CRPD to outlaw all forms of compulsory mental health care. In its first General Comment (2014), the Committee declared that compulsory mental health interventions constitute "an ongoing violation [of the CRPD] found in mental health laws across the globe, despite empirical evidence indicating its lack of effectiveness" and notwithstanding the fact that persons subjected to such practices "have experienced deep pain and trauma as a result" (para. 42). Targeting persons with mental health problems for coercive care is arbitrary and constitutes disability-based discrimination. Other actors, including the vast majority of the states parties to the CRPD, interpret the treaty differently, arguing that compulsion is sometimes necessary to protect the health and lives of patients or to prevent violence against others, and, if coupled with appropriate legal safeguards, it is lawful under such circumstances. This latter position is more in line with the jurisprudence of the ECtHR and thus far, the Court has not been inclined to revise its case law to bring it into line with the CRPD Committee's interpretation of the CRPD (Lewis, 2017). Whilst the Court has acknowledged that it may consider the CRPD when interpreting the ECHR, it is for the Court to decide how much weight to attach to its standards (*N.*, 2017, para. 147). In *Rooman* (2019), the Court clarified that Article 5 of the ECHR, as currently interpreted, "does not contain a prohibition of detention on the basis of impairment, in contrast to what is proposed by the UN Committee on the Rights of Persons with Disabilities" (para. 205).

Even so, the Court has used CRPD-like expressions and ideas in its reasoning. The duty put on states to accommodate detention facilities to meet the needs of persons with mental health problems (*Dybeku*, 2007, and *Blokhin*, 2016), for example, resemble the CRPD's notion of reasonable accommodation (Article 2, CRPD). Reasonable accommodation recognises that people have different abilities and needs, which is why public services, including prison services, need to ensure that persons with disabilities are not worse off but enjoy the same level of protection as non-disabled detainees. The increased weight attached to the wishes of persons with mental health problems would be another example of the implicit effect of the CRPD on the Court's reasoning. Whether the CRPD will have a more profound impact on the Court's jurisprudence on compulsory hospitalisation and treatment remains to be seen. Thus far, such arguments have been reserved for separate opinions (e.g. Judge Sajó in *Ruiz Rivera v Switzerland*, 2014; and Judge Pinto de Albuquerque in *Kuttner v Austria*, 2015).

The urgent need to engage in discrimination analysis

Until now, the Court has not addressed the question of whether compulsory psychiatric care, or certain forms of such care, may constitute discrimination on the basis of disability or mental health status. In *Shtukaturov* (2008), the applicant tried to convince the Court that his incapacitation and involuntary hospitalisation violated the prohibition of discrimination in

Article 14 of the ECHR, but without success. The Court noted that the discrimination claim was based on the same circumstances as the complaint under the substantive provisions. Having already found violations of Articles 5, 6 and 8, the Court saw no need for a separate examination under Article 14 (para. 134). The same conclusion was recently reached in *N. v Romania (no. 2)* (2021, para. 77–79). This unwillingness to engage in discrimination analysis is not limited to mental health cases; rather it is symptomatic of the Court's non-discrimination jurisprudence. Unless the Court considers that inequality is a key aspect of a case, it typically refrains from human rights claims under Article 14 and focuses its analysis on whether there has been a violation of any of the substantive provisions (e.g. *Evans v the United Kingdom*, 2007, para. 93–96; *V.C. v Slovakia*, 2011, para. 176–180). The general application of this approach does not, however, make it less problematic. The violations Mr Shtukaturov was exposed to were clearly linked to his status as a person with a mental health problem, and it is difficult to imagine such abuses occurring in a tolerant and inclusive society, free from stereotypical views of persons with mental health problems as unable to make decisions and suitable for institutional care. In view of this, I find it difficult to see how inequality was not at the heart of this case.

A similar argument can be made in favour of analysing other mental health cases from a non-discrimination perspective. Compulsory mental health care is an exception to the rule that all medical interventions must be based on consent from the person concerned, affecting persons with mental health problems only or disproportionately. Hence, we have a case of prima facie discrimination of persons with mental health problems that warrants justification to be compatible with Article 14 (*Molla Sali v Greece*, 2018, para. 133–135; *Cînţa v Romania*, 2020, para. 66). The harmful effects of coercive psychiatry are well known. Unfathomable abuses have taken place behind closed doors in psychiatric hospitals, and ill-treatment is still a problem (e.g. CPT, 2020, para. 16–18). In addition, targeting persons with mental health problems for coercive care risks fuelling stigma and prejudice against this group as particularly dangerous and/or unable to take care of themselves (Nilsson, 2021, pp. 121–122). The magnitude of these harms will of course vary from state to state, depending on, among other things, the quality of the care provided in the country in question, the prevalence of public prejudice against persons with mental health problems and the level of social exclusion experienced by this group. The arguments against compulsory mental health care are certainly stronger in a domestic context in which the quality of care is low and public prejudice towards and social exclusion of persons with mental health problems are widespread. Whether or not the reasons against compulsory care outweigh those in favour of such care in an individual case is currently determined by the *Winterwerp* criteria as discussed above. Discrimination analysis could contribute to these standards by insisting that attention is paid to issues of redistributive justice. Articles 3, 5 and 8 oblige states to ensure that everyone, including persons with mental health problems, enjoy a certain (minimum) level of protection of their dignity, liberty and autonomy. Discrimination analysis, on the other hand, would focus on ensuring that persons with mental health problems enjoy an *equal* level of respect for dignity, liberty, and autonomy as persons without such problems in the health care context.

Such a comparative focus could help the Court to ensure that it does not accept rights infringements in the mental health context that it would not accept had the victim not been diagnosed with a mental health problem. In addition, discrimination analysis could serve as a reminder of the need to consider the inequality-related harms associated with compulsory mental health care, like stigma, social exclusion and marginalisation. Thus, whilst Article 5.1(e) may prevent the Court from outlawing compulsory hospitalisation under all circumstances, nothing prevents the Court from engaging in discrimination analysis in mental health cases taking into account the full range of harms associated with abuses taking place within coercive psychiatry. Again, the first steps towards a fully-fledged discrimination analysis in the mental health context have been taken in separate opinions such as the partly dissenting opinion of Judge Motoc in *N. (no. 2)* concerning depravation of legal capacity.

Concluding remarks

This chapter has illustrated how the protection of the right to liberty, to respect for dignity and for personal autonomy has developed incrementally in the Court's jurisprudence over the years, from a lenient approach to abuses taking place within psychiatric institutions towards stricter review of such malpractices. Within the Council of Europe, the Committee on Bioethics has been working for several years to develop an additional protocol to the Convention on Human Rights and Biomedicine (1997, the Oviedo Convention) codifying the rules and principles established in the Court's jurisprudence discussed in this chapter. The protocol, which is still only a draft, aims to protect the dignity and rights of persons with mental health problems in relation to involuntary hospitalisation and treatment (Committee on Bioethics, 2018a, Article 1). In addition to codifying the Court's jurisprudence, the draft protocol adds something new. Article 3 obliges states to develop less restrictive alternative forms of care.

The Bioethics Committee's work has met with strong opposition from the Parliamentary Assembly of the Council of Europe (2019), the Council's Commissioner for Human Rights (2018) and civil society (Committee on Bioethics, 2015, pp. 93–99) (see Doyle-Guilloud, this vol.). Drawing on the CRPD, they argue that Council of Europe member states should not permit compulsory care at all, as it conflicts with the CRPD Committee's interpretation of the CRPD. If anything, these critics believe, the protocol should provide guidance on how member states can avoid the use of coercive care and develop voluntary care and support services instead. The critics are certainly correct that more time and resources ought to be invested in support services. A growing body of evidence shows the successful operation of voluntary crisis support services (Barbui et al., 2020; Gooding, McSherry and Roper, 2020; Gooding, 2021). It includes initiatives to reduce or eliminate the use of locked doors and restraints in psychiatric hospitals, as well as to utilise peer support groups and advance planning tools to help people prevent and manage crises. The evidence suggests that a fair share of today's coercive measures would not be necessary if alternative services were developed, which, in turn, makes a compelling case for the Court to consider introducing a positive obligation along the lines of Article 3 of the draft protocol in its jurisprudence. Instead of merely focusing on whether compulsion was necessary in view of alternative forms of care already in place in the state in question, the Court could consider whether the state has done enough to provide voluntary support services to prevent the need for compulsory interventions altogether. To be sure, this would involve a significant shift in the Court's jurisprudence. Regardless of whether the Court would be prepared to go in that direction, it could support the development of voluntary mental health services by continuing to insist that coercive measures must be necessary and proportionate to their aims, and by being explicit about the many harms, including stigma and social exclusion, associated with coercive care.

Literature

Abello Jiménez, A.E. (2015) 'Criminalizing disability: The urgent need of a new reading of the European Convention on Human Rights', *American University International Law Review*, 30(2), pp. 285–313.
Barbui, C., Purgato, M., Abdulmalik, J., Caldas-de-Almeida, J.M., Eaton, J., Gureje, O., Hanlon, C., Nosè, M., Ostuzzi, G., Saraceno, B., Saxena, S., Tedeschi, F. and Thornicroft, G. (2020) 'Efficacy of interventions to reduce coercive treatment in mental health services: Umbrella review of randomised evidence', *The British Journal of Psychiatry*, 218(4), pp. 185–195.
Bartlett, P. (2011) 'The necessity must be convincingly shown to exist: Standards for compulsory treatment for mental disorder under the mental health act 1983', *Medical Law Review*, 19(4), pp. 514–547.
—— (2012) 'A mental disorder of a kind or degree warranting confinement: Examining justifications for psychiatric detention', *International Journal of Human Rights*, 16(6), pp. 831–844.
Calcedo-Barba, A., Fructuoso, A., Martinez-Raga, J., Paz, S., Sánchez de Carmona, M. and Vicens, E. (2020) 'A meta-review of literature reviews assessing the capacity of patients with severe mental disorders to make decisions about their healthcare', *BMC Psychiatry*, 20(1), p. 339.
Fennell, P. (1998) 'Doctor knows best? Therapeutic detention under common law, the Mental Health Act, and the European convention', *Medical Law Review*, 6(3), pp. 322–353.
Flynn, E. (2016) 'Disability, deprivation of liberty and human rights norms: Reconciling European and international approaches', *International Journal of Mental Health and Capacity Law*, 22, pp. 75–101.
Gooding, P., McSherry, B. and Roper, C. (2020) 'Preventing and reducing "coercion" in mental health services: An international scoping review of English-language studies', *Acta Psychiatrica Scandinavica*, 142(1), pp. 27–39.
Grisso, T. and Appelbaum, P.S. (1995) 'The MacArthur Treatment Competence Study. III: Abilities of patients to consent to psychiatric and medical treatments', *Law and Human Behavior*, 19(2), pp. 149–174.
Large, M., Ryan, C. and Nielssen, O. (2011) 'The validity and utility of risk assessment for inpatient suicide', *Australasian Psychiatry*, 19(6), pp. 507–512.
Large, M., Smith, G., Sharma, S., Nielssen, O. and Singh, S.P. (2011) 'Systematic review and meta-analysis of the clinical factors associated with the suicide of psychiatric in-patients', *Acta Psychiatrica Scandinavica*, 124(1), pp. 18–29.
Lewis, O. (2017) 'Council of Europe', in: Lawson, A. and Waddington, L. (eds.), *The UN convention on the rights of persons with disabilities: A comparative analysis of the role of courts*. Oxford. Oxford University Press, pp. 89–130.
Mjöll Arnardóttir, O. (2017) 'Vulnerability under article 14 of the European convention on human rights', *Oslo Law Review*, 4(3), pp. 150–171.
Mowbray, A. (2015) 'Subsidiarity and the European convention on human rights', *Human Rights Law Review*, 15(2), pp. 313–341.
Nilsson, A. (2021) *Compulsory mental health care and the CRPD: Minding equality*. Oxford: Hart Publishing.
Niveau, G. and Materi, J. (2007) 'Psychiatric commitment: Over 50 years of case law from the European Court of Human Rights', *European Psychiatry*, 22(1), pp. 59–67.
Niveau, G., Jantzi, C. and Godet, T. (2021) 'Psychiatric commitment: Sixty years under the scrutiny of the European Court of Human Rights', *Frontiers in Psychiatry*, 12, article 656791.
Waddington, L. and McSherry, B. (2016) 'Exceptions and exclusions: The right to informed consent for medical treatment of people with psychosocial disabilities in Europe', *European Journal of Health Law*, 23(3), pp. 279–304.
Wicks, E. (2001) 'The right to refuse medical treatment under the European Convention on Human Rights', *Medical Law Review*, 9(1), pp. 17–40.

Case law

Aerts v Belgium, 30 July 1998, Reports of Judgments and Decisions 1998-V.
Aggerholm v Denmark, no. 45439/18, 15 September 2020.

A.N. v Lithuania, no. 17280/08, 31 May 2016.
Ashingdane v the United Kingdom, 28 May 1985, Series A no. 93.
B. v Germany, no. 61272/09, 19 April 2012.
Bergmann v Germany, no. 23279/14, 7 January 2016.
Blokhin v Russia [GC], no. 47152/06, 23 March 2016.
Buckley v the United Kingdom, Commission (dec.), no. 28323/95, 26 February 1997.
Bureš v the Czech Republic, no. 37679/08, 18 October 2012.
Cînța v Romania, no. 3891/19, 18 February 2020.
Claes v Belgium, no. 43418/09, 10 January 2013.
D.D. v Lithuania, no. 13469/06, 14 February 2012.
D.R. v Lithuania, no. 691/15, 26 June 2018.
Dybeku v Albania, no. 41153/06, 18 December 2007.
Evans v the United Kingdom [GC], no. 6339/05, ECHR 2007-I.
Fernandes de Oliveira v Portugal [GC], no. 78103/14, 31 January 2019.
Glien v Germany, no. 7345/12, 28 November 2013.
Haas v Switzerland, no. 31322/07, ECHR 2011.
Herczegfalvy v Austria, 24 September 1992, Series A no. 244.
Hiller v Austria, no. 1967/14, 22 November 2016.
H.L. v the United Kingdom, no. 45508/99, ECHR 2004-IX.
Hutchinson Reid v the United Kingdom, no. 50272/99, ECHR 2003-IV.
Ivinović v Croatia, no. 13006/13, 18 September 2014.
Jehovah's Witnesses of Moscow v Russia, no. 302/02, 10 June 2010.
Johnson v the United Kingdom, 24 October 1997, Reports of Judgments and Decisions 1997-VII.
Kalashnikov v Russia, no. 47095/99, ECHR 2002-VI.
K.C. v Poland, no. 31199/12, 25 November 2014.
Keenan v the United Kingdom, no. 27229/95, ECHR 2001-III.
Kucheruk v Ukraine, no. 2570/04, 6 September 2007.
Kuttner v Austria, no. 7997/08, 16 July 2015.
L.B. v Belgium, no. 22831/08, 2 October 2012.
M.B. v Poland, no. 60157/15, 14 October 2021.
Molla Sali v Greece [GC], no. 20452/14, 19 December 2018.
M.S. v Croatia (no. 2), no. 75450/12, 19 February 2015.
N. v Romania, no. 59152/08, 28 November 2017.
N. v Romania (no. 2), no. 38048/18, 16 November 2021.
Nevmerzhitsky v Ukraine, no. 54825/00, ECHR 2005-II (extracts).
O.H. v Germany, no. 4646/08, 24 November 2011.
Plesó v. Hungary, no. 41242/08, 2 October 2012.
Pretty v the United Kingdom, no. 2346/02, ECHR 2002-III.
Rakevich v Russia, no. 58973/00, 28 October 2003.
Rooman v Belgium [GC], no. 18052/11, 31 January 2019.
Ruiz Rivera v Switzerland, no. 8300/06, 18 February 2014.
Shopov v Bulgaria, no. 11373/04, 2 September 2010.
Shtukaturov v Russia, no. 44009/05, ECHR 2008.
Stanev v Bulgaria [GC], no. 36760/06, ECHR 2012.
Storck v Germany, no. 61603/00, ECHR 2005-V.
Strazimiri v Albania, no. 34602/16, 21 January 2020.
Sýkora v the Czech Republic, no. 23419/07, 22 November 2012.
Van der Leer v the Netherlands, 21 February 1990, Series A no. 170-A.
Varbanov v Bulgaria, no. 31365/96, ECHR 2000-X.
V.C. v Slovakia, no. 18968/07, ECHR 2011 (extracts).
V.K. v Russia, no. 9139/08, 4 April 2017.
Wilkinson v the United Kingdom (dec.), no. 14659/02, 28 February 2006.
Winterwerp v. the Netherlands, 24 October 1979, Series A no. 33.
X. v Finland, no. 34806/04, ECHR 2012 (extracts).
Zagidulina v Russia, no. 11737/06, 2 May 2013.
Z.H. v Hungary, no. 28973/11, 8 November 2012.

Treaties

Convention for the Protection of Human Rights and Fundamental Freedoms, 4 November 1950, ETS. 5, entered into force 3 September 1953.

Convention for the Protection of the Human Rights and Dignity of the Human Being with regard to the Application of Biology and Medicine (1997) ETS 164, entered into force 1 December 1999.

Convention on the Rights of Persons with Disabilities, 13 December 2006, 2515 UNTS. 3, entered into force 3 May 2008.

Reports and other documents

Committee on the Rights of Persons with Disabilities (2014) 'General comment no. 1 on article 12: Equal recognition before the law', UN doc. CRPD/C/GC/1.

Commissioner for Human Rights (2018) 'Comments on the draft additional protocol to the convention on human rights and biomedicine concerning the protection of human rights and dignity of persons with mental disorder with regard to involuntary placement and involuntary treatment'.

——— (2021) 'Third party intervention under Article 36, paragraph 3, of the European convention on human rights in the case Eugeniu Clipea and Virginia Iapara v the Republic of Moldova, Application No. 39468/17', CommDH(2021)19.

Council of Europe's Committee on Bioethics (2015) 'Additional protocol on the protection of the human rights and dignity of persons with mental disorders with regard to involuntary placement and involuntary treatment: compilation of comments received during the public consultation', DH-BIO/INF(2015)20 6.

——— (2018a) 'Draft Additional Protocol concerning the protection of human rights and dignity of persons with mental disorder with regard to involuntary placement and involuntary treatment', DH-BIO/INF (2018) 7.

European Committee for the Prevention of Torture and Inhuman or Degrading Treatment or Punishment (CPT) (1994) 'Report to the Belgian Government on the visit to Belgium carried out from 14 to 23 November 1993', CPT/Inf (94) 15.

——— (2019a) 'Report to the Russian Government on the visit to the Russian Federation carried out from 19 to 29 October 2018', CPT/Inf (2019) 26.

——— (2019b) 'Report to the Slovak Government on the visit to the Slovak Republic carried from 19 to 28 March 2018', CPT/Inf (2019) 2.

——— (2020) 'Report to the Bulgarian Government on the visit to Bulgaria carried from 10 to 21 August 2020', CPT/Inf (2020) 39.

——— (2021) 'Report to the Armenian Government on the visit to Armenia carried from 2 to 12 December 2019', CPT/Inf(2021) 10.

Gooding, P. (2021) 'Compendium report: Good practices in the Council of Europe to promote voluntary measures in mental health', commissioned by the Committee of Bioethics of the Council of Europe.

Parliamentary Assembly of the Council of Europe (2019) 'Recommendation 2158, ending coercion in mental health: The need for a human rights-based approach'.

5
THE UNITED NATIONS CONVENTION ON THE RIGHTS OF PERSONS WITH DISABILITIES AND MENTAL HEALTH LAWS

Requirements and responses

Suzanne Doyle Guilloud

Introduction

The United Nations (UN) Convention on the Rights of Persons with Disabilities (hereinafter 'the CRPD') opened for signature on 30 March 2007 and entered into force on 3 May 2008. It has been ratified by 184 States. Ninety-nine of those have also ratified its Optional Protocol, which recognises the competence of the Committee on the Rights of Persons with Disabilities (hereinafter 'the CRPD Committee') to receive and consider communications from or on behalf of individuals or groups of individuals claiming violations of provisions of the CRPD, as well as for the Committee to carry out an inquiry where it receives reliable information 'indicating grave or systematic violations' by a State Party (Article 6(1)).

Prior to the adoption of the CRPD, international instruments addressing the topic of psychosocial disability reflected a paternalistic and ableist approach, which medicalised and 'othered' those with that identity (see, for example, United Nations, 1971, 1975, 1991). This was generally uncontentious for UN member states, as reflected by the high rate of the adoption of those instruments. Conversely, the norms and standards that these instruments espoused – removal of legal capacity, deprivation of liberty, violations of bodily integrity – were rejected and contested by advocates within the disability community (Jones, 2005; Kampf, 2008; Kanter, 2003; Perlin, 2007). The pre-CRPD situation is summarised by Bartlett as amounting to an assumption that control of people with psychosocial disabilities was, at least in some circumstances, justified and that the issue was simply 'determining the bounds of permitted compulsion' (Bartlett, 2012, p. 752).

The CRPD, in particular its recognition of the equal legal personhood of persons with disabilities and their right to liberty on an equal basis with others, changes all of that and requires a 'paradigm shift'. It requires radical, paradigmatic shifts in legislative and policy responses to psychosocial disability which eliminate the option of coercion in mental healthcare provision and instead requires States Parties to fully recognise the decision-making rights of persons with psychosocial disabilities and to affirm the validity and visibility of their lives lived in the community.

This chapter will set out a brief history of the drafting of the CRPD. It will then engage in depth with the specific provisions of the CRPD which have the greatest amount of consequence for mental health laws. The responses of both the Council of Europe (CoE) and individual States will then be examined, and conclusions drawn regarding the current dynamic of opposition and reform in this area of the law.

The drafting of the CRPD – innovation and participation

The drafting and adoption of the CRPD was the product of a developed consensus that while previous international human rights instruments had *de jure* applied to persons with disabilities, in reality, those mechanisms simply did not meet the needs of the disability community (Stein and Lord, 2009). This gave rise to what one commentator has called a 'regulatory vacuum' (Manca, 2017, p. 592). Similar language is used by Arnardóttir (2009, pp. 51–53) to describe the human rights landscape for people with disabilities before the CRPD, where she outlines previous unsuccessful efforts to secure these rights by way of the classical non-discrimination clauses, e.g. Articles 2 and 26 of the International Covenant on Civil and Political Rights (ICCPR) and Article 2(2) of the International Covenant on Economic, Social and Cultural Rights (ICESCR).

The CRPD was the first human rights treaty of the 21st century and reimagined the creation of human rights norms as an active, iterative and – above all – participatory endeavour. I (Doyle, 2012) and others (Dhanda, 2006; Grandia, 2014; Kayess and French, 2008; Minkowitz, 2012, 2006) have written about the process which led to the finalisation and adoption of various provisions of the CRPD which are relevant to mental health laws, particularly the rights to equal legal personhood, to liberty and security of the person, to live independently and be included in the community, and to health. Those analyses recount a number of aspects of the negotiations that contributed to the development of the obligations which the CRPD now imposes on States Parties regarding persons with psychosocial disabilities. These include the fact that the CRPD drafting sessions placed those who would be impacted by the treaty at the centre of the negotiations, giving effect to the disability community's decades-long refrain of 'nothing about us without us'. This is reflected in the text of the CRPD by way of Article 4(3), which states:

> In the development and implementation of legislation and policies to implement the present Convention, and in other decision-making processes concerning issues relating to persons with disabilities, States Parties shall closely consult with and actively involve persons with disabilities, including children with disabilities, through their representative organizations.

There was also innovation on the part of disabled person's organisations (DPOs), with the International Disability Caucus (IDC) being formed. This was a collective of non-governmental organisations (NGOs) led by DPOs which developed out of the pre-CRPD International Disability Alliance. Where a particular issue was determined to be exclusive to a specific group of people with disabilities, the organisation that represented that group played the central role in establishing the IDC's position. Decisions were made by consensus and once a position was agreed on, all IDC members had to support this position. No indication of any internal disagreement was to be publicly conveyed to other actors such as national governments (Reina, 2008).

In contrast to the united voice offered by the disability movement, Bartlett has noted that there was an absence of any medical representative body during the CRPD negotiations. He suggests that this 'affected the tenor of the negotiations'. He also raises the concern that this has consequences for implementation of CRPD if those stakeholders feel they are being presented with a *fait accompli* which has the potential to 'fundamentally alter their conditions of practice' (Bartlett, 2012, p. 757). Freeman takes up this point and notes 'the near-total absence of clinical experts on the Committee' suggests that 'service user input was not broad enough to represent a range of different service user views' (Freeman et al., 2015, p. 848).

While it would clearly have been desirable to have greater participation from the medical community during the negotiation process in order to obtain some level of 'buy-in', it is also important to place the CRPD in its historical context. This treaty was intended to give voice to those who had felt marginalised and disempowered within their societies and within the general human rights discourse. It was grounded in a sense that previous human rights instruments had not sufficiently accounted for the discrimination experienced by people with disabilities as illustrated by the previous thematic instruments which had come before it on the topic of disability. Particularly in the context of persons with psychosocial disabilities, the replication of power dynamics which they may have experienced in domestic legal structures and/or clinical settings could have been very problematic. Indeed, a dominating presence of medical groups could conceivably have given rise to inverse criticisms regarding the validity of the CRPD's normative content. It is also important to remember that participation in the CRPD negotiations was always open to medical bodies. Indeed, new civil society organisations were admitted up until the final drafting session.

CRPD fundamentals

The definition of disability

Article 1 of the CRPD reads:

> Persons with disabilities include those who have long-term physical, mental, intellectual or sensory impairments which in interaction with various barriers may hinder their full and effective participation in society on an equal basis with others.

Its Preamble makes clear that this is not an exhaustive list of persons with disabilities and recognises that:

> disability is an evolving concept and that disability results from the interaction between persons with impairments and attitudinal and environmental barriers that hinders their full and effective participation in society on an equal basis with others.

The Preamble also recognises further 'the diversity of persons with disabilities'. This approach to disability and impairment can find its normative roots in the social model of disability. This is a theory of disability which is to be contrasted with the medical model. The latter co-locates the source of 'disablement' in impairment and informed most of the pre-CRPD international legal instruments cited above. A full exposition of the history and development of the social model is not possible here, and Kayess and French (2008, p. 5) provide a concise summary of its core elements:

> the social model of disability locates the experience of disability in the social environment, rather than impairment, and carries with it the implication of action to dismantle the social and physical barriers to the participation and inclusion of persons with disability. The social model of disability is a generic term for a broad theory of disability that began to emerge from the mid 1960s principally from within the disability rights movement in the United Kingdom. It involved disability activist academics reinterpreting 'disability' as social oppression, and radically refocusing the agenda away from cure, treatment, care and protection to acceptance of impairment as a positive dimension of human diversity, and to the problematisation and rejection of a social norm that results in exclusion.

Further, it is notable that the CRPD does not directly define disability. It instead defines 'persons with disabilities', a term which has been both embraced and rejected by various sections of the disability community. In its General Comment on Article 5 (Equality and Non-discrimination) (Committee on the Rights of Persons with Disabilities, 2018, para. 73(b)), the CRPD Committee has stated that States Parties' anti-discrimination laws must be:

> based on a definition of disability that includes those who have long-term physical, including psychosocial, intellectual or sensory impairments, and should include past, present, future and presumed disabilities, as well as persons associated with persons with disabilities. Persons victimized by disability-based discrimination seeking legal redress should not be burdened by proving that they are 'disabled enough' in order to benefit from the protection of the law. … In that regard, a broad impairment-related definition of disability is in line with the Convention.

Salie suggests that the omission or non-definition of disability within the CRPD was intentional and serves to demonstrate the fact that 'disability is not an internal flaw in the individual, but is socially constructed when society is not inclusive enough to facilitate the accessibility needs of all people' (Salie, 2014, p. 67). De Búrca characterises the concept of disability the CRPD contains as 'a soft threshold definition in the form of guidance which is open-ended and inclusive' (de Búrca, 2010, p. 191).

This formulation of the central concept of the CRPD could be seen as an attempt to reflect the fact that the 'person' at the centre of the disability has, historically, been forgotten by both society and the law. Such an approach to the concept of disability is also consistent with the concept of 'personhood' which, as will be demonstrated below, has taken a central role within the normative model upon which the CRPD is based – that of the equality of the individual and their consequent equality before the law.

Human rights model of disability

It is notable that the CRPD Committee, in this construction of persons with disabilities, has placed to the fore the existence of an impairment without encircling that with reference to the barriers that result in the 'disablement' of the individual. This 'embracing' of impairment goes to the human rights model of disability as Degener (2016, p. 54) explains:

The CRPD was initially drafted as a human rights convention that replaces the medical model of disability with the social model of disability. However, the drafters went beyond the social model of disability and codified a treaty that is based on the human rights model of disability. While the medical model of disability reduces the disabled individual to her impairment, the social model dissects disability as a social construct and debunks exclusion and denial of rights on the basis of impairment as ideological constructions of disability. The human rights model builds on the social model in that it is built on the premise that disability is a social construct but it develops it further.

The CRPD Committee further expanded on the implications of the CRPD's human rights model of disability in its General Comment on Equality and Non-discrimination where it explained that this model gives rise to a new conceptualisation of equality – inclusive equality (Committee on the Rights of Persons with Disabilities, 2018, para. 11). This 'extends and elaborates on the content of equality' and requires:

> (a) a fair redistributive dimension to address socioeconomic disadvantages; (b) a recognition dimension to combat stigma, stereotyping, prejudice and violence and to recognize the dignity of human beings and their intersectionality; (c) a participative dimension to reaffirm the social nature of people as members of social groups and the full recognition of humanity through inclusion in society; and (d) an accommodating dimension to make space for difference as a matter of human dignity.

Both this conceptualisation of equality – with its focus on stereotyping and an acceptance of difference – as well as the influence on the social model of constructions of disability in the CRPD, has particular resonance for systems of coercive mental healthcare provision, as will now be explained.

The CRPD's prohibition on disability-based detention and treatment

Determining the CRPD's position on mental health laws which provide for deprivation of liberty and psychiatric treatment in the absence of informed consent requires an examination of both the relevant provisions of the CRPD as well as the jurisprudence of the CRPD Committee – the body charged with monitoring the implementation of the treaty by States Parties.

Of central importance to the CRPD's implications for mental health laws is its 'paradigm shift' towards a recognition of universal legal capacity in Article 12. This provides:

1. States Parties reaffirm that persons with disabilities have the right to recognition everywhere as persons before the law.
2. States Parties shall recognize that persons with disabilities enjoy legal capacity on an equal basis with others in all aspects of life.
3. States Parties shall take appropriate measures to provide access by persons with disabilities to the support they may require in exercising their legal capacity.

Article 12(4) then goes on to require States Parties to put in place 'appropriate and effective safeguards' for 'all measures that relate to the exercise of legal capacity' in order to ensure that such measures 'respect the rights, will and preferences of the person'. The drafting history of

Article 12 is set out in detail by Dhanda (2006), Minkowtiz (2006) and de Bhailís and Flynn (2017) and is beyond the scope of this chapter, but it is sufficient to note that it was one of the most contentious provisions during the CRPD negotiations. This debate, both in terms of its requirements as well as its implications for mental health laws – which are emblematic of laws which refuse to recognise the legal capacity of the individual – has continued (Dawson, 2015; Flynn and Arstein-Kerslake, 2014, 2014; Freeman et al., 2015; Gooding, 2013).

For its part, the CRPD Committee has been clear on its interpretation of the requirements of Article 12. Equal recognition before the law was the subject of the CRPD Committee's first General Comment (Committee on the Rights of Persons with Disabilities, 2014). A General Comment is an authoritative, if not legally binding, interpretation of a particular provision of a treaty by its monitoring body. Within that document, the CRPD Committee makes clear that Article 12 affirms the distinction between legal capacity – the right to be recognised as a decision-maker before the law – and mental capacity – what can be thought of as the decision-making capacity of an individual (Committee on the Rights of Persons with Disabilities, 2014, para. 14). The General Comment takes the position that while mental capacity may change and fluctuate due to factors such as a person's age, impairment or emotional state, the legal capacity of every individual is unassailable. In light of this legal principle, supported decision-making should be made available to everyone, regardless of the level of support they may require. Such support should be based on the will and preference of the person, not on what is perceived as being in his or her objective best interests (Committee on the Rights of Persons with Disabilities, 2014, para. 29(a) & (b)).

Of particular relevance to mental health laws, the General Comment (Committee on the Rights of Persons with Disabilities, 2014, para. 9) states that:

> persons with cognitive or psychosocial disabilities have been, and still are, disproportionately affected by substitute decision-making regimes and denial of legal capacity. The Committee reaffirms that a person's status as a person with a disability or the existence of an impairment (including a physical or sensory impairment) must never be grounds for denying legal capacity or any of the rights provided for in article 12. All practices that in purpose or effect violate article 12 must be abolished in order to ensure that full legal capacity is restored to persons with disabilities on an equal basis with others.

Later on it specifically refers to the implications of Article 12 for mental healthcare (Committee on the Rights of Persons with Disabilities, 2014, para. 42):

> States parties must abolish policies and legislative provisions that allow or perpetuate forced treatment, as it is an ongoing violation found in mental health laws across the globe, despite empirical evidence indicating its lack of effectiveness and the views of people using mental health systems who have experienced deep pain and trauma as a result of forced treatment. The Committee recommends that States parties ensure that decisions relating to a person's physical or mental integrity can only be taken with the free and informed consent of the person concerned.

In analysing the application of universal legal capacity and supported decision-making in the context of persons with psychosocial disabilities, Gooding (2013, p. 440) suggests that Article 12 requires that:

instead of focusing on the point at which a person is incapable of consenting to medical treatment, or the point at which a substitute decision-maker is legally empowered, the emphasis shifts to identifying when a person who has some decision-making impairment, or is at risk of losing the capacity to make decisions, should be provided with support. For individuals, this might mean identifying social isolation and providing a personal advocate, or perhaps working to facilitate an existing informal support network, or even establishing a new informal support network around them.

The recognition of every individual's equal legal personhood is affirmed and supported in the specific context of its challenge to mental health laws which authorise coercion by Article 14 – the right to liberty and security of the person. This requires States Parties to ensure that persons with disabilities, on an equal basis with others, are not deprived of their liberty 'unlawfully or arbitrarily' and 'that the existence of a disability shall in no case justify a deprivation of liberty' (Article 14(1)(b)). In its Concluding Observations – the assessment of a States Party's compliance with the CRPD when they come before the CRPD Committee for periodic reviews – the CRPD Committee has been unambiguous in its interpretation of Article 14, taking the position that it imposes an absolute prohibition on disability-based detention, whether as a sole ground or in combination with other factors such as 'need for treatment' or 'dangerousness' to self or others. As I have set out in detail elsewhere (Doyle Guilloud, 2019), this interpretation of the right to liberty of persons with psychosocial disabilities has not been shared by all other bodies within the UN human rights structure, with the Human Rights Committee being the most notable dissenter. That Committee has interpreted the liberty provision contained in Article 9 of the International Covenant on Civil and Political Rights as permitting deprivations of liberty 'for the purpose of protecting the individual … from serious harm or preventing injury to others' provided that it was 'only as a measure of last resort and for the shortest appropriate period of time' (UN Human Rights Committee, 2014, para. 19).

Partly as a response to this authoritative opposition voice on liberty in the context of psychosocial disability within the UN human rights infrastructure, in 2015 the CRPD Committee adopted Guidelines on Article 14 (Committee on the Rights of Persons with Disabilities, 2017a) which sought to concretise the requirements of the right to liberty under the CRPD. Within this document, the CRPD Committee links the prohibition on detention on the basis of disability with the principle of equality and non-discrimination contained in Article 5 of the CRPD. The Guidelines (2017a, para. 6) are strident in their rejection of any lawful basis for mental health laws and state that:

> The Committee has established that article 14 does not permit any exceptions whereby persons may be detained on the grounds of their actual or perceived impairment. However, the legislation of several States parties, including mental health laws, still provide for instances in which persons may be detained on the grounds of their actual or perceived impairment, provided there are other reasons for their detention, including that they are deemed dangerous to themselves or others. That practice is incompatible with article 14; it is discriminatory in nature and amounts to arbitrary deprivation of liberty.

To date, the CRPD Committee has found a violation of Article 14(1)(b) in only one individual communication brought under its Optional Protocol (*Noble v. Australia*, 2016). In that case it found that the detention of the author of the communication for 10 years due a finding of unfitness to plead to a criminal charge was contrary to Article 14(1)(b) as this had been 'decided on the basis of the assessment by the State party's authorities of potential consequences of his intellectual disability, in the absence of any criminal conviction, thereby converting his disability into the core cause of his detention' (*Noble v. Australia*, 2016, para. 8.7). Further, as his later conditional release was 'a direct consequence' of his detention, this also amounted to a violation of Article 14(1)(b) of the CRPD (*Noble v. Australia*, 2016, para. 8.8).

The then Special Rapporteur on the Rights of Persons with Disabilities, Catalina Devandas Aguilar's thematic reports on equal recognition before the law (Special Rapporteur on the rights of persons with disabilities, 2017) and deprivation of liberty on the basis of disability (Special Rapporteur on the rights of persons with disabilities, 2019) bolster the CRPD Committee's position on the incompatibility of mental health laws as they currently exist in many jurisdictions. In an unequivocal call for systemic reform, she stated that:

> Mental health legislation as it exists today must be repealed, as it creates a separate legal regime for persons with psychosocial disabilities, contrary to the obligations of States under the Convention. Regulation of the practice of mental health services should focus on acceptability and quality, while the rights and freedoms of persons with psychosocial disabilities must be the same as those of others in all areas of law, including legal capacity and liberty and security of the person.
> *(Special Rapporteur on the rights of persons with disabilities, 2017, para. 52)*

The Special Rapporteur also emphasised the negative role of prejudice against persons with psychosocial disabilities, pointing in particular to 'the baseless belief that they are prone to violence' when 'evidence shows that they are actually more likely to be victims of violence'. She linked this misconception to how both service providers and the general public react in situations involving persons with psychosocial disabilities, 'leading to social distance, discriminatory behaviour and recourse to coercive practices' (Special Rapporteur on the rights of persons with disabilities, 2019, para. 27). This call for the elimination of current mechanisms of deprivation of liberty and forced treatment have also been made by the Special Rapporteur on the right of everyone to the enjoyment of the highest attainable standard of physical and mental health as then was, Dainius Pūras, where he echoed the language of the CRPD in calling for a 'paradigm shift' in the field of mental health 'which abandons outdated measures resulting in the forced confinement of persons with intellectual and psychosocial disabilities in psychiatric institutions'. The Special Rapporteur also called on 'States, international organizations and other stakeholders to undertake concerted efforts to radically reduce the use of institutionalization in mental health-care settings, with a view to eliminating such measures and institutions' (Special Rapporteur on the right of everyone to the enjoyment of the highest attainable standard of physical and mental health, 2018, para. 51).

Within its 2015 Guidelines on Article 14, the CRPD Committee emphasised the link between the right to liberty and the right to equal recognition before the law. It also pointed to the connection between the prohibition on disability-based detention and Articles 19 and 25 of the CRPD. These provisions can be seen as completing the normative template of the CRPD's alternative to coercive systems of mental healthcare provision.

Article 19 of the CRPD provides for the right of persons with disabilities to live independently and be included in the community, with choices equal to others. This includes the right to choose 'where and with whom to live on an equal basis with others' (Article 19(a)), as well as the right to support services to achieve this right and 'to prevent isolation or segregation from the community'. It therefore stands in opposition to any suggestion that States Parties can validly retain a power to compel a person to live in an institutional setting such as a psychiatric hospital. In its General Comment No. 5 on Article 19 (Committee on the Rights of Persons with Disabilities, 2017b, para. 97(g)), the CRPD Committee stated that in order to ensure full implementation of the right, States Parties are required to:

> Adopt clear and targeted strategies for deinstitutionalization, with specific time frames and adequate budgets, in order to eliminate all forms of isolation, segregation and institutionalization of persons with disabilities; special attention should be paid to persons with psychosocial and/or intellectual disabilities and children with disabilities currently in institutions.

At the time of writing, the CRPD Committee is engaged in a process of drafting 'Guidelines on Deinstitutionalization, including in emergencies' which are intended to provide States Parties with more detailed instructions on Article 19 and supplements General Comment No. 5 (Committee on the Rights of Persons with Disabilities, 2022).

Article 25 provides that persons with disabilities 'have the right to the enjoyment of the highest attainable standard of health without discrimination on the basis of disability'. Of central importance to the validity of mental health laws which provide for compulsory treatment is the requirement in Article 25(d) that healthcare should be of the same quality for persons with disabilities as to others, 'including on the basis of free and informed consent'. In its General Comment on Article 12, the CRPD Committee emphasised the link between recognition of equal legal personhood and the right to health and confirmed that States Parties 'have an obligation to require all health and medical professionals (including psychiatric professionals) to obtain the free and informed consent of persons with disabilities prior to any treatment' (Committee on the Rights of Persons with Disabilities, 2014, para. 41). It used similar language in its General Comment on equality and non-discrimination (Committee on the Rights of Persons with Disabilities, 2018, para. 66).

In his report on the right of everyone to mental health, the then Special Rapporteur on the right of everyone to the enjoyment of the highest attainable standard of physical and mental health highlighted the central importance of certain key principles to CRPD-compatible reform:

> The evolving normative context around mental health involves the intimate connection between the right to health, with the entitlement to underlying determinants, and the freedom to control one's own health and body. That is also linked to the right to liberty, freedom from non-consensual interference and respect for legal capacity.
> *(Special Rapporteur on the right of everyone to the enjoyment of the highest attainable standard of physical and mental health, 2017, para. 31)*

Referencing the CRPD, the Special Rapporteur linked State failures to offer 'treatment and integration in the community' as a 'primary driver of coercion and confinement' (Special

Rapporteur on the right of everyone to the enjoyment of the highest attainable standard of physical and mental health, 2017, para. 32).

The CRPD Committee's instructions to States Parties on mental health laws can be most concisely found in the following statement (Committee on the Rights of Persons with Disabilities, 2017a, para. 10):

> Involuntary commitment of persons with disabilities on health-care grounds contradicts the absolute ban on deprivation of liberty on the basis of impairment (art. 14 (1) (b)) and the principle of free and informed consent of the person concerned for health care (art. 25). The Committee has repeatedly stated that States parties should repeal provisions that allow for the involuntary commitment of persons with disabilities in mental health institutions based on actual or perceived impairment. Involuntary commitment in mental health facilities carries with it the denial of the person's legal capacity to decide about care, treatment and admission to a hospital or institution, and therefore violates article 12 in conjunction with article 14.

The requirements of the CRPD in relation to questions of torture or cruel, inhuman or degrading treatment or punishment (Article 15), exploitation, violence and abuse (Article 16), as well as the protection of the physical and mental integrity of the person (Article 17) are clearly of importance when considering the validity of policies and practices (such as physical/chemical restraint and seclusion in the operation of mental laws) but are beyond the constraints of this chapter, which is limited to dealing with the fundamental validity of such laws. Those questions are also dealt with by other commentators (Bartlett and Schulze, 2017; Lewis and Campbell, 2017; McSherry, 2017).

Responses to the CRPD

The Council of Europe

The European Convention on Human Rights (ECHR) and its application to mental health laws is examined in detail by Nilsson in this collection, and I have assessed the challenge that Article 14 in particular poses to Council of Europe member states that have also ratified the CRPD elsewhere (Doyle, 2017). My analysis here will therefore be confined to the manner in which the European Court of Human Rights and other Council of Europe structures have responded to the requirements of the CRPD. It is important to note at this point that the Council of Europe is not a State Party to the CRPD. Unlike the European Union which has 'confirmed' (ratified) the CRPD, it does not qualify as a 'regional integration organization' in accordance with the requirements of Article 44 of the CRPD. Nevertheless, in the case of *Glor v. Switzerland* (2009) the European Court of Human Rights, referencing the CRPD, stated that 'there is a European and worldwide consensus on the need to protect people with disabilities from discriminatory treatment' (*Glor v. Switzerland*, 2009, para. 53).

The European Court of Human Rights and the CRPD

In light of the internal conflict between UN treaty bodies mentioned above, it is notable that the Strasbourg Court has increasingly referenced the CRPD rather than the ICCPR on the question of liberty and disability in more recent decisions (e.g. *N. v. Romania – 59152/08*, 2017). Favalli notes that in many cases in which the European Court of Human Rights

(ECtHR) refers to provisions of the CRPD, this is done in a manner which solely strengthens its assessment, 'assuming an ancillary role in the ECtHR case law' (Favalli, 2018, p. 527). Nevertheless, she concludes that the CRPD has become the main interpretative tool, setting the standard for the protection of the rights of persons with disabilities in the CoE (Favalli, 2018, p. 530). As such, she considers that the ECtHR has begun 'a process of recognising the core principles of the UN Convention as ... regional customary law' (Favalli, 2018, p. 521). Lewis (2018, p. 126) is less sure of what he describes as 'jurisprudential osmosis' between the CRPD and the ECtHR. He notes: that:

> Where the Court has cited the CRPD, it has generally done so without integrating CRPD insights into its legal reasoning. Where the Court has disagreed with the CRPD or its interpretation by the CRPD Committee it has been less inclined to rely upon it, or even cite it.
>
> *(Lewis, 2018, p. 126)*

He goes on to posit that the ECtHR may wish to avoid becoming deeply entangled in interpreting the norms of the CRPD while they are still contested by some States Parties to the CRPD, particularly in the area of mental health detention and forced treatment, 'preferring instead to wait until the international policy dust has settled' (Lewis, 2018, p. 127).

Whatever the speed at which real engagement with the CRPD by the ECtHR takes place, in accordance with the doctrine of *lex specialis*, and given the acknowledgement by the ECtHR of the implications of the CRPD for its jurisprudence, for any level of reconciliation between the ECHR and the CRPD (and specific rapprochement on the question of the rights of persons with psychosocial disabilities) to occur, the direction of travel will be from Strasbourg to Geneva.

Medical model entrenchment – the proposed Additional Protocol to the Oviedo Convention

Of relevance for Council of Europe member states, and weighing against any major normative shifts on the part of the ECtHR, are the proposals to adopt an 'Additional Protocol concerning the protection of human rights and dignity of persons with mental disorders' to the Council of Europe Convention on Human Rights and Biomedicine ('the Oviedo Convention') – its treaty on bioethics which entered into force in 1999. The Working Document of the Protocol (Council of Europe Committee on Bioethics, 2015), which was published for consultation by the Committee on Bioethics in June 2015, provided for the involuntary detention and treatment of persons with a 'mental disorder' based on need for treatment or dangerousness to others. The proposed Protocol also endorsed the concept of legal incapacity. The proposals were criticised by the Parliamentary Assembly of the Council of Europe (Council of Europe Parliamentary Assembly, 2016) which stated in its Recommendation on the matter that it had 'serious doubts about the added value of a new legal instrument in this field' (para. 3) and questioned the compatibility of the proposed Protocol with the CRPD. The Assembly called on the Committee on Bioethics to withdraw the proposal and instead focus on promoting alternatives to involuntary measures in psychiatry (para. 11). Of note also are the Assembly's comments regarding the obligation of the Council of Europe – *qua* Council of Europe – and the CRPD where it stated (para. 9):

[The Parliamentary Assembly] also notes that there is resistance from some member States with regard to accepting the above interpretation [of Article 14] of the CRPD Committee. However, it considers that the Council of Europe's position ought to be independent from the position of some of its member States. Ignoring the interpretation of the CRPD by its monitoring body established under international law would not only undermine the Council of Europe's credibility as a regional human rights organisation, but would also risk creating an explicit conflict between international norms at the global and European levels.

This concern to ensure that Council of Europe law is consistent with the requirements of the CRPD is important and could be interpreted as a soft 'nudge' by the Parliamentary Assembly to the ECtHR in terms of the future interpretation of the ECHR on this point. This positive move is somewhat tempered by the fact that the Council of Europe's Committee of Ministers, in its Reply to the Parliamentary Assembly's Recommendation (Committee of Ministers, 2016), endorsed the continued development of the Additional Protocol, albeit with consultation with disability rights organisations.

For their part, the CRPD Committee, the Special Rapporteur on the rights of persons with disabilities, the Special Rapporteur on torture and other cruel, inhuman or degrading treatment or punishment and the Office of the High Commissioner for Human Rights – Regional Office for Europe all raised objections to the drafting of such a Protocol (Council of Europe Committe on Bioethics, 2015). The European Network of (Ex-)Users and Survivors of Psychiatry (ENUSP) and Mental Health Europe (MHE) also expressed deep concern about the continued drafting of the Protocol ('Statement of ENUSP and Mental Health Europe on Additional Protocol', 2017).

As requested by both the Parliamentary Assembly and the Committee of Ministers, the Committee on Bioethics agreed at a plenary session in December 2016 to the inclusion of disability rights organisations as observers to the relevant meetings relating to the drafting of the proposed Additional Protocol. This development is potentially relevant to the fact that at its May 2018 session, the Committee published an updated version of the proposed Protocol for the opinion of a number of Council of Europe bodies and committees (Council of Europe Committee on Bioethics, 2018). It is notable for the addition of multiple references to the 'primary use' of 'less restrictive and intrusive measures' than involuntary detention and the addition of this principle to a provision on alternative measures (Article 3). This principle of 'least restrictive environment' had previously been included in a provision on necessity and proportionality. It is possible that this redrafting was based on the increased emphasis placed on least restrictive alternatives by the ECtHR in decisions such as *Stanev v. Bulgaria* (*Stanev v. Bulgaria – 36760/06 [2012] ECHR 46*, 2012) and *Pleso v. Hungary* (*Pleso v. Hungary – 41242/08 – HEJUD [2012] ECHR 1767*, 2012).

Despite these redrafting efforts, the decision on the part of the Committee of Ministers to pursue the proposed Additional Protocol denotes a level of internal inconsistency within the CoE, particularly given the guarded receptivity of the ECtHR to CRPD norms and further evidenced the divide which still existed between the Council of Europe and the Committee on the Rights of Persons with Disabilities on the question of the rights of persons with psychosocial disabilities. It goes to Lewis and Campbell's (2017, p. 47) point that:

> It is perilous to attempt to layer the CRPD neatly onto the ECHR. This is because the two treaties not only say different things, but they speak to different audiences and have different purposes.

They raise the concern that the passage of the Additional Protocol, although having no direct effect on the ECtHR, could influence the Court's jurisprudence 'as it would indicate a Europe-wide consensual about turn from the CRPD position' (Lewis and Campbell, 2017, p. 57).

It is notable, however, that Portugal and Bulgaria, who are both States Parties to the CRPD and member states of the Council of Europe, have voiced their objection to the proposed Additional Protocol. While Portugal voiced its objection during closed meetings, Bulgaria did so publicly during its periodic review before the CRPD Committee ('Bulgaria Stands Up for the Rights of People with Disabilities', 2018) in September 2018.

In what could be interpreted as a response to concerns raised, as well as an attempt to justify its approach, in October 2018 the Committee on Bioethics published a document seeking to answer frequently arising questions in relation to the proposed Additional Protocol (Council of Europe Committee on Bioethics, 2019). Within this document the Committee attributed the decision to draft the Additional Protocol to the large number of cases which have come before the ECtHR in the previous five years where findings of violations of Article 5(1)(e) have been made 'because of the lack of effective procedural safeguards for persons subject to involuntary placement and/or involuntary treatment' (p. 1). Having referenced the CRPD, the Committee characterised the Protocol not as promoting the use of involuntary measures, but as instead aiming at 'preventing abuses and at minimizing the use of such measures ...' (p. 2) in circumstances where:

> [a]ll Council of Europe members States having explicitly referred to this issue in their report on the implementation of the UN Convention on the Rights of Persons with Disabilities (CRPD) in recent years ... have indicated that they provide some form ... of involuntary placement and/or involuntary treatment.
> *(Council of Europe Committee on Bioethics, 2019, p. 1)*

In the context of whether the draft protocol discriminates against persons with 'mental disorders', the Committee stated (p. 2):

> The existence of a mental disorder is not a criterion which would justify any involuntary measure. Under the draft text, involuntary measures may only be used if the person's mental health condition represents a significant risk of serious harm to his or her health or to others, if the measure has a therapeutic purpose and if any voluntary measure is insufficient to address the risk(s).
>
> This is in line with the wording of the UN Human Rights Committee's General comment No. 35 on Article 9 of the International Covenant of Civil and Political Rights.

As such, as between the differing constructions of the right to liberty of persons with psychosocial disabilities which the CRPD Committee and the Human Rights Committee have arrived at, the Committee on Bioethics sided with the latter body.

However, more recent events resulting from the sustained advocacy of disability rights organisations have led to a substantive shift in approach regarding the Additional Protocol. In June 2019 the Parliamentary Assembly adopted a Resolution (Council of Europe Parliamentary Assembly, 2019) calling for an end to coercion in mental health and CRPD-compatible reform in Council of Europe Member States. Subsequently, in June 2021 the

CRPD Committee and the UN Special Rapporteur on the rights of persons with disabilities issued an Open Letter to the Council of Europe (Committee on the Rights of Persons with Disabilities and Special Rapporteur on the Rights of Persons with Disabilities, 2021), calling on it to discontinue the drafting process and instead develop a Committee of Ministers Recommendation to its Member States on the need to move away from coercive approaches and to build up a non-coercive framework.

In September 2021, the Grand Chamber refused a request for an advisory opinion on the proposed Additional Protocol, citing lack of competence. However, in delivering its decision, it pointed to its case law as being 'characterised by the Court's dynamic approach to interpreting the Convention, which in this field is guided *inter alia* by evolving legal and medical standards, national and international' ('Request for an advisory opinion under Article 29 of the Convention for the Protection of Human Rights and Dignity of the Human Being with regard to the Application of Biology and Medicine: Convention on Human Rights and Biomedicine', 2021, para. 69), which has been interpreted by many as an implied reference to the requirements of the CRPD in this area.

The Committee on Bioethics sent the draft protocol to the Committee of Ministers for a vote in the latter part of 2021. In a major victory for those advocating a CRPD-based approach to mental healthcare provision, in May 2022 the Committee of Ministers made a formal decision to suspend the process for the adoption of the draft Protocol. It instead gave a deadline of 31 December 2024 for the Steering Committee for Human Rights in the fields of Biomedicine and Health (which replaced the Committee on Bioethics in January 2022) to produce both a draft recommendation promoting the use of voluntary measures in mental healthcare services as well as a report on the case law of the European Court of Human Rights relevant to mental health. No decision on the continuation of the procedure for the adoption of an Additional Protocol will be made until these documents are examined by the Committee of Ministers. The Committee of Ministers also instructed the Steering Committee to include the United Nations Office of the High Commissioner for Human Rights, as well as a number of NGOs working in the field of disability rights, in the drafting process. The Committee of Ministers also committed themselves to preparing a declaration 'affirming the commitment of the Council of Europe to improving the protection and the autonomy of persons in mental health care services' (Committee of Ministers, 2022). While the draft Additional Protocol has not been withdrawn, this represents a major shift in approach which has the potential to recalibrate the governing Council of Europe bioethical Convention towards closer alignment with the CRPD.

Council of Europe Commissioner for Human Rights

The approach of the Committee on Bioethics is to be contrasted with that of the Council of Europe Commissioner for Human Rights. The Commissioner is charged with promoting awareness of and respect for human rights within the Council of Europe and engages in country monitoring visits as well as thematic reporting on specific issues. Previous Commissioners have published thematic reports relating to recognition of legal capacity and the right to live independently and be included in the community of persons with disabilities. The current Commissioner published a Human Rights Comment in 2021 within which she reiterated her opposition to the proposed Additional Protocol to the Oviedo Convention and instead called for the elimination of coercion in mental healthcare provision, as well as emphasising the barriers that persons with psychosocial disabilities face in accessing justice (Council of Europe Commissioner for Human Rights, 2021).

In June of 2021 the Commissioner lodged a third-party intervention in the ECtHR case of *Clipea & Iapara v. the Republic of Moldova* (Application No. 39468/17). In that submission, she noted the growing consensus by the CRPD Committee, the Special Rapporteur on the rights of persons with disabilities, the Special Rapporteur on the rights to physical and mental health – and even the World Health Organization – on the need to put an end to coercive practices such as involuntary detention and treatment. She stated that:

> While the [ECHR] provides for a mental health exception under Article 5, in the opinion of the Commissioner the evolution of the international consensus has reached such a level as to warrant a less tolerant approach to institution-based mental health systems and coercion when viewed from the angles of Articles 3 and 8.

The Commissioner called for a reinterpretation of Article 3 (prohibition on torture or inhuman or degrading treatment or punishment) which, as Nilsson highlights elsewhere in this collection, provides a wide margin of discretion for compulsory medical treatment based on therapeutic necessity, as well as Article 8 (right to respect for private and family life) of the ECHR – which 'reflects the fundamental shift in attitudes towards mental health globally' and avoids 'a widening gap between the protections afforded to persons with psychosocial disabilities under the European Convention on Human Rights and the United Nations Convention on the Rights of Persons with Disabilities'.

It is not yet possible to determine the final outcome of the internal dialogue which is currently taking place between the various Council of Europe structures regarding the mental health laws. The recent Decision of the Committee of Ministers on the proposed Additional Protocol to the Oviedo Convention indicates some level of political receptivity to the requirements of the CRPD, and this is supported by other bodies such as the Commissioner for Human Rights. Yet any meaningful change in this area would have to involve a reinterpretation of the ECHR by the Council of Europe – given the constraints which exist on such innovation in the context of Article 5, this is more likely to come about in the manner recently proposed by the Commissioner in her third-party intervention.

Domestic responses

The response of States Parties to the interpretation of the requirements of the CRPD in the area of mental health laws by the CRPD Committee are varied and cannot be completely captured here. However, it is useful to examine three examples of how this issue has been dealt with at the domestic level.

Avoidance: reservations and declarations

A number of States have chosen to lodge reservations and/or interpretative declarations which are in effect reservations intended to either limit or completely absolve them of any obligation to reform their mental health laws. For example, Norway lodged a declaration in relation to Article 12 which states its interpretation that the CRPD allows for situations of guardianship/substitute decision-making. In relation to Article 14, its declaration states:

Norway recognises that all persons with disabilities enjoy the right to liberty and security of person, and a right to respect for physical and mental integrity on an equal basis with others. Furthermore, Norway declares its understanding that the Convention allows for compulsory care or treatment of persons, including measures to treat mental illnesses, when circumstances render treatment of this kind necessary as a last resort, and the treatment is subject to legal safeguards.

It is interesting to note the approach of Norway with regard to this issue. The above provision is titled 'Articles 14 and 25'. It therefore seems that Norway is seeking to link restrictions on the right to liberty with a purported vindication of the right to health, echoing the arguments of Freeman et al. (2015, p. 846). Norway has not yet been the subject of its first Concluding Observations but submitted its initial report to the CRPD Committee in December 2015. Therein it addresses its declaration in the context of Article 14 and states that its interpretation of Article 14 is that the CRPD 'does not lay down a prohibition against necessary compulsory admission or treatment of persons with mental illness as long as any deprivation of liberty and treatment is justified by objective criteria that go beyond the existence of a mental illness' (Committee on the Rights of Persons with Disabilities, 2015, para. 111). This represents a clear divergence from the *travaux préparatoires* of the CRPD as well as the CRPD Committee's jurisprudence on this point. Norway goes on to affirm its position that the declaration is:

in line with the wording in Article 14 and in accordance with the prevalent understanding of the Convention among the States Parties. The fact that the declaration accords with the prevalent understanding of the Convention among the States Parties is reflected in the States Parties' reports to the Committee on the Rights of Persons with Disabilities and with the Committee's concluding remarks to these reports.

This statement therefore suggests that Norway has based its interpretation of the requirements of Article 14 not on the CRPD Committee's interpretation but on the understandings which other States Parties have proffered. Such an approach to interpreting treaty obligations is inconsistent with the CRPD, Article 46(1) of which provides that:

Reservations incompatible with the object and purpose of the present Convention shall not be permitted.

This provision finds its roots in Article 31(1) of the Vienna Convention on the Law of Treaties which states:

A treaty shall be interpreted in good faith in accordance with the ordinary meaning to be given to the terms of the treaty in their context and in the light of its object and purpose.

As such, Norway's position seems unlikely to stand up to scrutiny when the CRPD Committee issues its Concluding Observations in respect of its initial report.

The Netherlands has also lodged a specific declaration with respect to Article 14 which stated its understanding that the CRPD 'allows for compulsory care or treatment of persons, including measures to treat mental illnesses, when circumstances render treatment of this kind necessary as a last resort, and the treatment is subject to legal safeguards'. The Netherlands only ratified the CRPD in June 2016 and submitted an initial report to the CRPD Committee in July 2018. It has therefore not been the subject of a Concluding Observation. But compatibility issues like those arising for Norway would seem to arise. Similar limiting reservations and declarations have been lodged by Australia, Canada, Ireland and Poland, with other States such as Georgia, Kuwait, Libya, Uzbekistan and Venezuela lodging such broad declarations regarding their understanding of the implications of the CRPD, particularly in relation to legal capacity, as to also potentially be included in this list.

Kanter remarks that the small number of express declarations or reservations in respect of Article 14 in particular could be due to the fact that most States Parties do not fully understand its meaning and therefore do not see the need for the lodging of such limiting measures or, more probably, that States Parties 'simply assume that they may continue their current practices of involuntary treatment and detention' (Kanter, 2014, p. 143). This latter theory goes to the wider question of State Parties' views on the CRPD Committee's authority in the area of mental health laws, and therefore the consequent potential for domestic reform.

It is also important to note the potential role that objections by other State Parties to reservations can have. An example of this is that of the reservation lodged by El Salvador which sought to retain domestic constitutional supremacy on the interpretation of its laws after ratification. On foot of this, a number of States Parties (Germany, Austria, Czech Republic, the Netherlands, Portugal, Slovakia, Sweden and Switzerland) objected over the course of a number of years to the reservation on grounds of its incompatibility with the norms, object and purpose of the CRPD, as well as on the grounds of its vagueness. On 18 March 2015, the Government of El Salvador informed the Secretary-General that it had decided to withdraw the reservation.

While it is not possible to engage in a comprehensive review of all the reform processes that have been undergone in specific jurisdictions in this chapter, it is useful to point to two contrasting examples of how States that have ratified the CRPD have responded to its requirements.

Refusal: England and Wales

In its initial review of the UK, the CRPD Committee stated its concern that the Mental Health Act 1983 which applies in England and Wales 'provides for involuntary, compulsory treatment and detention both inside and outside hospitals on the basis of actual or perceived impairment' and recommended that the UK '[r]epeal legislation and practices that authorize non-consensual involuntary, compulsory treatment and detention of persons with disabilities on the basis of actual or perceived impairment' (Committee on the Rights of Persons with Disabilities, 2017c, paras. 34 & 35(a)). An Independent Review was chaired by Regius Professor of Psychiatry at King's College London and, at that time, president of the Royal Society of Medicine, Professor Sir Simon Wessely. It consulted with service users, carers, special-interest groups and professionals and recommended the setting out of central principles in reformed legislation – including 'choice and autonomy', ensuring the powers contained in the Act are 'used in the least restrictive way', a requirement for therapeutic benefit to ensure that 'patients are supported to get better, so they can be discharged from the Act' and 'ensuring patients are viewed and treated as rounded individuals'. Yet despite the CRPD Committee's recent recommendations, any suggestion at more fundamental reform was rejected, with the Chair stating his position as follows:

Implementing our proposals will go a substantial part of the way to addressing the concerns motivating the CRPD Committee. But in rejecting the last steps that they propose – the abolition of all mental health legislation ... I wish to be clear. It is true that we do not currently have the legislative space that would be required for such a radical step. But to use this as a reason would be disingenuous. The reason is simpler – I don't agree with it, and I am far from sure that is what most service users want either, as well as many others.

Neither the subsequent government White Paper (Department of Health and Social Care, 2021a) nor the government response to the consultation on that document (Department of Health and Social Care, 2021b) make any reference to the CRPD, beyond a listing of it in the glossary of the former. Unsurprisingly, the Draft Mental Health Bill which was published in late June 2022 shows no evidence of incorporating any of the requirements of the CRPD.

Acceptance (almost): Peru

In recent years, Peru has engaged in a process of fundamental reform of both its mental health and mental capacity laws, due in large part to the advocacy of Peruvian DPOs and their civil society partners. Legislative Decree No. 1384 was published in 2018 and was the result of a drafting process which saw government, academia and civil society work collaboratively (Encalada, 2021, p. 126). It reforms the Civil Code, the Civil Procedural Code and the Notary Act to recognise the full legal capacity, and abolishes guardianship and other restrictions on the legal capacity of persons with disabilities. The reform also creates various regimes of supported decision-making. Crucially, the new law removed the power of a guardian to authorise the admission to an institution of a person who was deemed to lack decision-making capacity (SODIS – Sociedad y Discapacidad (Disability and Society), 2021, p. 5).

Subsequently in 2019, Peru adopted a new Mental Health Act – Law No. 30947. This provides for a rights-based model of mental healthcare provision which is based in the community on a voluntary basis. Encalada (2021, p. 133) explains that this new law 'neither refers to involuntary hospitalization and treatment, nor seclusion and restraints'. The law also provides for the recognition of systems of supported decision-making, including chosen 'informal supporters', as well as the provision for advance mental healthcare planning.

The possibility of hospitalization is retained 'when it provides greater therapeutic benefits for the individual compared to other possible interventions'. The new legislation also provides for the removal of a requirement for informed consent in cases of 'psychiatric emergencies' – in such circumstances a person can be 'interned' in a health setting. Encalada (2021, pp. 136–137) notes that the definition of an 'emergency' in this case would not include the perceived risk of the individual to others. Further, where that provision is relied upon, there is an obligation on professionals to ensure 'real, considerable and relevant efforts to obtain the manifestation of the will of the person, including the provision of decision-making support'.

The Peruvian reforms cannot be said to comply completely with the requirements of the CRPD in relation to the rights of persons with psychosocial disabilities, retaining as they do some scope for involuntary detention and treatment. But the participatory nature of the legal capacity reform process, as well as the shift in the primary purpose of mental health legislation to enunciating the rights of the individual rather than the regulation of coercive practices, demonstrates the influence of the CRPD and its potential to reshape States Parties' approaches to mental healthcare, albeit imperfectly. Yet the real test of Peru's reforms will be in their implementation, particularly the way in which 'psychiatric emergencies' are interpreted and therefore the extent to which involuntary measures are relied upon. Due to the recency of these reforms, that cannot yet be assessed.

Conclusion

The requirements of the CRPD in the area of mental health law are a profound challenge to most existing systems of regulation of mental health provision. It requires a fundamental recalibration of the way in which persons with psychosocial disabilities are positioned within the legal system – recognising their right to make decisions on an equal basis with others, invalidating practices which deprive them of their liberty or right to informed consent and obliging States Parties to reimagine non-coercive approaches to the provision of mental healthcare.

This reform imperative is now in the process of engaging with rival and opposing conceptualisations of the role of the State, professionals and service providers. In the case of a regional organisation like the Council of Europe, this has produced internal division and incoherence. Yet there are more recent signs that the norms of the CRPD are beginning to infiltrate policy. However, more substantive changes in the interpretative jurisprudence of the European Court of Human Rights will be required before fundamental incompatibilities on mental health laws could be said to be addressed. At the domestic level, the response has varied from complete rejection, to outright refusal, to major (if not complete) shifts in law and policy on mental healthcare.

What is clear is that the tension that exists between the human rights model of disability and mental health laws which provide for coercion will continue to play out in multiple fora over the coming years. States Parties made a commitment to persons with psychosocial disabilities when they signed up to the CRPD. After centuries of discrimination and segregation, that promise now needs to be honoured.

Literature

Arnardóttir, O.M., 2009. A future of multidimensional disadvantage equality? In: *The UN Convention on the Rights of Persons with Disabilities: European and Scandanavian Perspectives, International Studies in Human Rights.* Brill | Nijhoff, pp. 41–66. https://doi.org/10.1163/ej.9789004169715.i-320.19

Bartlett, P., 2012. The United Nations Convention on the Rights of Persons with Disabilities and mental health law. *Mod. Law Rev.* 75(5), 752–778. https://doi.org/10.1111/j.1468-2230.2012.00923.x

Bartlett, P., Schulze, M., 2017. Urgently awaiting implementation: The right to be free from exploitation, violence and abuse in article 16 of the Convention on the Rights of Persons with Disabilities (CRPD). *Int. J. Law Psychiatry* 53, 2–14. https://doi.org/10.1016/j.ijlp.2017.05.007

Dawson, J., 2015. A realistic approach to assessing mental health laws' compliance with the UNCRPD. *Int. J. Law Psychiatry Ment. Capacities Leg. Respons.* 40, 70–79. https://doi.org/10.1016/j.ijlp.2015.04.003

de Bhailís, C., Flynn, E., 2017. Recognising legal capacity: Commentary and analysis of Article 12 CRPD. *Int. J. Law Context* 13(1), 6–21. https://doi.org/10.1017/S174455231600046X

de Búrca, G., 2010. The European Union in the negotiation of the UN disability convention. *Eur. Law Rev.* 35, 174.

Degener, T., 2016. Disability in a human rights context. *Laws* 5(3), 35. https://doi.org/10.3390/laws5030035

Dhanda, A., 2006. Legal capacity in the disability rights convention: Stranglehold of the past or lodestar for the future symposium: The United Nations Convention on the Rights of Persons with Disabilities. *Syracuse J. Int. Law Commer.* 34, 429–462.

Doyle Guilloud, S., 2019. The right to liberty of persons with psychosocial disabilities at the United Nations: A tale of two interpretations. *Int. J. Law Psychiatry* 66, 101497. https://doi.org/10.1016/j.ijlp.2019.101497

Doyle, S., 2017. Article 14 of the CRPD in light of article 5 of the ECHR: The challenge for Council of Europe member states regarding the involuntary detention of persons with mental disabilities. In: O'Mahony, C., Quinn, G. (Eds.), *Disability Law and Policy: An Analysis of the UN Convention*. Clarus Press, Dublin, pp. 151–163.

Doyle, S., 2012. The new paradigm for involuntary detention: Article 14 of the UN Convention on the Rights of Persons with Disabilities. In: De Londras, F., Mullally, S. (Eds.), *The Irish Yearbook of International Law*. Hart Pub., Oxford; Portland, OR, pp. 71–118.

Encalada, A.V., 2021. The potential of the legal capacity law reform in Peru to transform mental health provision. In: Stein, M.A., Mahomed, F., Patel, V., Sunkel, C. (Eds.), *Mental Health, Legal Capacity, and Human Rights*. Cambridge University Press, pp. 124–139. https://doi.org/10.1017/9781108979016.011

Favalli, S., 2018. The United Nations Convention on the Rights of Persons with Disabilities in the case law of the European Court of Human Rights and in the Council of Europe disability strategy 2017–2023: 'From zero to hero'. *Hum. Rights Law Rev.* 18(3), 517–538. https://doi.org/10.1093/hrlr/ngy026

Flynn, E., Arstein-Kerslake, A., 2014. Legislating personhood: Realising the right to support in exercising legal capacity. *Int. J. Law Context* 10(1), 81–104. https://doi.org/10.1017/S1744552313000384

Freeman, M.C., Kolappa, K., de Almeida, J.M.C., Kleinman, A., Makhashvili, N., Phakathi, S., Saraceno, B., Thornicroft, G., 2015. Reversing hard won victories in the name of human rights: A critique of the general comment on article 12 of the UN Convention on the Rights of Persons with Disabilities. *Lancet Psychiatry* 2(9), 844–850. https://doi.org/10.1016/S2215-0366(15)00218-7

Gooding, P., 2013. Supported decision-making: A rights-based disability concept and its implications for mental health law. *Psychiatry Psychol. Law* 20(3), 431–451. https://doi.org/10.1080/13218719.2012.711683

Grandia, L., 2014. Imagine: To be a part of this. In: Sabatello, M., Schulze, M. (Eds.), *Human Rights and Disability Advocacy*. University of Pennsylvania Press, pp. 146–156. https://doi.org/10.9783/9780812208740.146

Jones, M., 2005. Can international law improve mental health? Some thoughts on the proposed Convention on the Rights of People with Disabilities. *Int. J. Law Psychiatry* 28(2), 183–205. https://doi.org/10.1016/j.ijlp.2005.03.003

Kampf, A., 2008. The disabilities convention and its consequences for mental health laws in Australia. *Law Context Bundoora Vic.* 26, 10–36.

Kanter, A.S., 2014. *The Development of Disability Rights under International Law: From Charity to Human Rights*. Taylor & Francis Group, London.

Kanter, A.S., 2003. The globalization of disability rights law. *Syracuse J. Int. Law Commer.* 30, 241.

Kayess, R., French, P., 2008. Out of darkness into light? Introducing the Convention on the Rights of Persons with Disabilities. *Hum. Rights Law Rev.* 8(1), 1–34. https://doi.org/10.1093/hrlr/ngm044

Lewis, O., 2018. Council of Europe. In: *The UN Convention on the Rights of Persons with Disabilities in Practice*. Oxford University Press, Oxford. https://doi.org/10.1093/oso/9780198786627.003.0004

Lewis, O., Campbell, A., 2017. Violence and abuse against people with disabilities: A comparison of the approaches of the European Court of Human Rights and the United Nations Committee on the Rights of Persons with Disabilities. *Int. J. Law Psychiatry* 53, 45–58. https://doi.org/10.1016/j.ijlp.2017.05.008

Manca, L., 2017. Article 33 [National implementation and monitoring]. In: *The United Nations Convention on the Rights of Persons with Disabilities: A Commentary*. Springer International Publishing, Cham, pp. 591–606. https://doi.org/10.1007/978-3-319-43790-3_37

McSherry, B., 2017. Regulating seclusion and restraint in health care settings: The promise of the Convention on the Rights of Persons with Disabilities. *Int. J. Law Psychiatry* 53, 39–44. https://doi.org/10.1016/j.ijlp.2017.05.006

Minkowitz, T., 2012. CRPD advocacy by the world network of users and survivors of psychiatry: The emergence of an user/survivor perspective in human rights (SSRN scholarly Paper No. ID 2326668). Social Science Research Network, Rochester, NY. https://doi.org/10.2139/ssrn.2326668

Minkowitz, T., 2006. The United Nations Convention on the Rights of Persons with Disabilities and the right to be free from nonconsensual psychiatric interventions. *Syracuse J. Int. Law Commer.* 34, 405–428.

Perlin, M.L., 2007. International human rights law and comparative mental disability law: The universal factors. *Syracuse J. Int. Law Commer.* 34, 333.

Reina, M.V., 2008. How the international disability caucus worked during negotiations for a UN human rights convention on disability [WWW Document]. *Glob. Action Aging.* http://globalag.igc.org/agingwatch/events/CSD/2008/maria.htm (accessed 3.10.22).

Salie, M., 2014. The voice of the user/survivor. In: Okpaku, S.O. (Ed.), *Essentials of Global Mental Health*. Cambridge University Press, Cambridge, pp. 63–71. https://doi.org/10.1017/CBO9781139136341.009

Stein, M.A., Lord, J.E., 2009. Future prospects for the United Nations Convention on the Rights of Persons with Disabilities. In: Arnardóttir, O.M., Quinn, G. (Eds.), *The UN Convention on the Rights of Persons with Disabilities: European and Scandanavian Perspectives*. Brill | Nijhoff, pp. 17–40. https://doi.org/10.1163/ej.9789004169715.i-320.14

Case Law

Glor v. Switzerland, 13444/04, [2009] ECHR 2181
N. v. Romania - 59152/08, 28 November 2017
Noble v. Australia, CRPD/C/16/D/7/2012, 10 October 2016
Pleso v. Hungary - 41242/08 - HEJUD [2012] ECHR 1767, 2012
Stanev v. Bulgaria - 36760/06 [2012] ECHR 46, 2012

Treaties

Convention for the Protection of Human Rights and Fundamental Freedoms, 4 November 1950, ETS. 5, entered into force 3 September 1953.

Convention for the Protection of the Human Rights and Dignity of the Human Being with regard to the Application of Biology and Medicine (1997) ETS 164, entered into force 1 December 1999.

Convention on the Rights of Persons with Disabilities, 13 December 2006. 2515 UNTS. 3, entered into force 3 May 2008.

United Nations, 1991. Principles for the Protection of Persons with Mental Illness.

United Nations, 1975. Declaration on the Rights of Disabled Persons.

United Nations, 1971. Declaration on the Rights of Mentally Retarded Persons.

Bulgaria Stands Up for the Rights of People With Disabilities, 2018. Human Rights Watch. https://www.hrw.org/news/2018/09/06/bulgaria-stands-rights-people-disabilities (accessed 3.13.22).

Committee of Ministers, 2016. The case against a council of Europe legal instrument on involuntary measures in psychiatry: Reply to recommendation.

Committee of Ministers, 2022. Committee for bioethics (DH-BIO) draft additional protocol to the convention on human rights and biomedicine concerning the protection of human rights and dignity of persons with regard to involuntary placement and involuntary treatment within mental healthcare services and its draft explanatory report, CM/Del/Dec(2022)1434/4.2.

Committee on the Rights of Persons with Disabilities, 2022. *Call for submissions: Draft guidelines on deinstitutionalization, including in emergencies committee on the rights of persons with disabilities.* https://www.ohchr.org/en/calls-for-input/2022/call-submissions-draft-guidelines-deinstitutionalization-including-emergencies (accessed 26.7.22).

Committee on the Rights of Persons with Disabilities, 2018. General comment no. 6 (2018) on equality and non-discrimination.

Committee on the Rights of Persons with Disabilities, 2017a. Annex to the biannual report of the committee on the rights of persons with disabilities - Guidelines on the right to liberty and security of persons with disabilities (No. A/72/55).
Committee on the Rights of Persons with Disabilities, 2017b. General comment no. 5 (2017) on living independently and being included in the community.
Committee on the Rights of Persons with Disabilities, 2017c. Concluding observations on the initial report of the United Kingdom of Great Britain and Northern Ireland (No. CRPD/C/GBR/CO/1).
Committee on the Rights of Persons with Disabilities, 2015. Consideration of reports submitted by states parties under article 35 of the convention Initial reports of states parties due in 2015: Norway (No. CRPD/C/NOR/1). Committee on the rights of persons with disabilities.
Committee on the Rights of Persons with Disabilities, 2014. General comment no. 1 (2014) - Article 12: Equal recognition before the law.
Committee on the Rights of Persons with Disabilities, Special Rapporteur on the Rights of Persons with Disabilities, 2021. Open letter to the Secretary-General of the Council of Europe, the Committee of Ministries of the Council of Europe, the Committee on Bioethics of the Council of Europe, the Steering Committee for Human Rights, the Commissioner of Human Rights, the Parliamentary Assembly of the Council of Europe and other organizations and entities of the Council of Europe.
Council of Europe Commissioner for Human Rights, 2021. Reform of mental health services: An urgent need and a human rights imperative [WWW Document]. Comm. Hum. Rights. https://www.coe.int/en/web/commissioner/blog/-/asset_publisher/xZ32OPEoxOkq/content/reform-of-mental-health-services-an-urgent-need-and-a-human-rights-imperative (accessed 3.11.22).
Council of Europe Committee on Bioethics, 2015. Additional Protocol on the protection of the human rights and dignity of persons with mental disorders with regard to involuntary placement and involuntary treatment: Compilation of comments received during the public consultation (No. DH-BIO/INF (2015) 20). Council of Europe, Strasbourg.
Council of Europe Committee on Bioethics, 2019. Draft Additional Protocol concerning the protection of human rights and dignity of persons with mental disorder with regard to involuntary placement and involuntary treatment: Frequently asked questions (No. DH-BIO/INF (2018) 10). Council of Europe, Strasbourg.
Council of Europe Committee on Bioethics, 2018. Draft Additional Protocol concerning the protection of human rights and dignity of persons with mental disorder with regard to involuntary placement and involuntary treatment: As revised by the 13th DH-BIO (Strasbourg, 23 – 25 May 2018) (No. DH-BIO/INF (2018) 7). Council of Europe, Strasbourg.
Council of Europe Committee on Bioethics, 2015. Working document concerning the protection of human rights and dignity of persons with mental disorder with regard to involuntary placement and involuntary treatment. Council of Europe Committee on Bioethics, Strasbourg.
Council of Europe Parliamentary Assembly, 2019. Resolution 2291 (2019) - Ending coercion in mental health: The need for a human rights-based approach.
Council of Europe Parliamentary Assembly, 2016. The case against a Council of Europe legal instrument on involuntary measures in psychiatry (No. Doc. 14007). Council of Europe Parliamentary Assembly.
Department of Health and Social Care, 2021a. Reforming the Mental Health Act (No. CP 355).
Department of Health and Social Care, 2021b. Reforming the Mental Health Act: Government response [WWW Document]. GOV.UK. https://www.gov.uk/government/consultations/reforming-the-mental-health-act/outcome/reforming-the-mental-health-act-government-response (accessed 3.16.22).
Request for an advisory opinion under Article 29 of the Convention for the Protection of Human Rights and Dignity of the Human Being with regard to the Application of Biology and Medicine: Convention on Human Rights and Biomedicine, 2021.
SODIS - Sociedad y Discapacidad (Disability and Society), 2021. Legislative Decree No. 1384 legislative decree that recognizes and regulates the legal capacity of persons with disabilities on equal basis.
Special Rapporteur on the right of everyone to the enjoyment of the highest attainable standard of physical and mental health, 2018. Report on deprivation of liberty and the right to health (No. A/HRC/38/36).

Special Rapporteur on the right of everyone to the enjoyment of the highest attainable standard of physical and mental health, 2017. Report on the right of everyone to mental health (No. A/HRC/35/21).

Special Rapporteur on the Rights of Persons with Disabilities, 2019. Deprivation of liberty of persons with disabilities (No. A/HRC/40/54).

Special Rapporteur on the Rights of Persons with Disabilities, 2017. The right of persons with disabilities to equal recognition before the law (No. A/HRC/37/56).

Statement of ENUSP and Mental Health Europe on Additional Protocol, 2017. Mental Health Europe. https://www.mhe-sme.org/statement-of-enusp-and-mental-health-europe-on-additional-protocol/ (accessed 3.13.22).

UN Human Rights Committee, 2014. General comment no. 35 Article 9 (Liberty and security of person).

6
RESPONSES TO THE WORLD HEALTH ORGANIZATION'S QUALITYRIGHTS INITIATIVE

Richard M. Duffy

Introduction

The United Nations (UN) Convention on the Rights of Persons with Disabilities (CRPD) (2006) is potentially driving the biggest change in the treatment of individuals with mental illness since the advent of psychopharmacology. The vast majority of consequences of this change are positive. The inclusion of mental illness under the broader umbrella of disability has wide-ranging benefits and promotes the protection of individuals' rights that has been sadly deficient within mental healthcare. Many countries have revised their mental health legislation in line with the CRPD. For example, India replaced their Mental Health Act 1987, which had been drafted in 1950, with legislation that explicitly attempts to concord with the CRPD (Duffy and Kelly, 2019). This one change impacted the mental healthcare of over 17% of the world's population.

As the agency of the UN responsible for international public health, the World Health Organization (WHO) has taken a central role in facilitating the realisation of the CRPD. While legislative reform is a major priority for the WHO (World Health Organization, 2021), it is the lives of individuals with mental illness that they wish to improve. The WHO recognises that there are many factors that may limit the realisation of legislative change including, *inter alia*, the availability of trained personnel, a government's ability to perform regulatory functions, the rule-of-law situation and funding of regulatory institutions (Clarke, 2016). Consequently, the WHO has not solely focused on CRPD concordant legislation. To embed the CRPD into systems, services and practices in the treatment of individuals with mental illness the WHO has developed the QualityRights Initiative (Funk and Bold, 2020). The first section of this chapter describes the current QualityRights material and discusses some of the concerns that have been raised in relation to it. The second section discusses the research that has been done to date using the material.

The WHO's QualityRights Initiative's goal is to use 'a multicomponent framework and strategies to promote mental health systems, services, and practices that prioritize respect for human rights, in line with the United Nations Convention on the Rights of Persons with Disabilities (CRPD)' (Funk and Bold, 2020, p. 69). The QualityRights Initiative has been developed within the Policy, Law and Human Rights Unit in the WHO's Department of Mental Health and Substance Use. The QualityRights Initiative describes five objectives:

1. Build capacity to understand and promote human rights, recovery and independent living in the community.
2. Create community-based and recovery-oriented services in line with the Convention on the Rights of Persons with Disabilities.
3. Improve the quality and human rights conditions in in-patient and out-patient mental health and related services.
4. Develop a civil society movement to conduct advocacy and influence policy-making.
5. Reform national policies and legislation in line with best practice, the CRPD and other international human rights standards.

To realise these objectives the programme has developed training and assessment tools. These resources are targeted at the full range of individuals involved in the field of mental health; this includes, *intra alia*, people with lived experience, their families and carers, academics, policy makers, nongovernmental organisations and organisations representing persons with psychosocial disabilities. The wide range of tools available is summarised in Table 6.1. In the first half of this chapter, the resources available will be examined and in the second half the research that has been conducted to date using the QualityRights materials will be discussed.

Table 6.1 Tools created by the World Health Organization's QualityRights initiative

General area	*Specific documents*
Service transformation tools	The WHO QualityRights assessment tool kit
	Transforming services and promoting human rights
Training tools	Human rights
	Mental health, disability and human rights
	Recovery and the right to health
	Legal capacity and the right to decide
	Freedom from coercion, violence and abuse
	Supported decision-making and advance planning
	Strategies to end seclusion and restraint
	Recovery practices for mental health and well-being
Evaluation tools	Evaluation of the WHO QualityRights training on mental health, human rights and recovery: pre-training questionnaire
	Evaluation of the WHO QualityRights training on mental health, human rights and recovery: post-training questionnaire
Guidance tools	One-to-one peer support by and for people with lived experience
	Peer support groups by and for people with lived experience
	Civil society organizations to promote human rights in mental health and related areas
	Advocacy for mental health, disability and human rights
Self-help tools	Person-centred recovery planning for mental health and well-being – self-help tool

Source: Based on WHO QualityRights – Training and guidance tools (WHO, 2019a)

It is worth taking some time at this stage to discuss the interpretation of the CRPD used in the QualityRights material. The authors interpret the CRPD as totally prohibiting all involuntary treatment on the basis of mental illness. This interpretation is not required based on the text of the CRPD alone. However, the UN Committee on the Rights of Persons with Disabilities (2014), who are responsible for interpreting the CRPD, in General Comment No. 1, stated that 'forced treatment by psychiatric and other health and medical professionals is a violation of the right to equal recognition before the law' (p. 11). This is also in line with the UN Special Rapporteur on torture, Nils Melzer, who has repeatedly raised concerns about involuntary treatment (UN General Assembly, 2018). Many groups representing individuals with psychosocial disabilities, including Disability Rights International and the International Disability Caucus, have also strongly lobbied for this interpretation and sought such provisions through the drafting of the CRPD (Melish, 2014). However, this perspective was controversial during the drafting of the CRPD (MacQuarrie and Laurin-Bowie, 2014) and is not universally accepted throughout the UN (Szmukler, 2019). Many ratifying states also do not fully support this interpretation of the CRPD; some of the countries included declarations and reservations with their ratification which permit involuntary treatments. For example,

Norway seeks to permit involuntary treatment in certain circumstances with a declaration that states:

> Norway declares its understanding that the Convention allows for compulsory care or treatment of persons, including measures to treat mental illnesses, when circumstances render treatment of this kind necessary as a last resort, and the treatment is subject to legal safeguards.
>
> *(United Nations Treaty Collection, 2020)*

Ireland also makes a similar declaration in relation to Articles 12 and 14.

Appelbaum (2019) and Freeman et al. (2015) articulate many of the concerns raised about the Committee on the Rights of Persons with Disabilities' interpretation of the CRPD which has been used by the QualityRights Initiative. They argue an interpretation precluding any involuntary interventions stands to deprive individuals with severe mental illness of treatment. They describe the personal, financial, reputational and occupational damage that may occur when an individual's freedom and autonomy is protected at the expense of their well-being. Freeman et al. (2015), in particular, argue that an individual's right to health, justice, liberty and even life could be violated by this interpretation of Article 12. The resultant increase in stigma and discrimination, and the potential impact on the rights of others are also highlighted. Funk and Bold (2020) attempt to address many of these issues; however, they do not directly examine many of the acute situations described by Applebaum and Freeman. Instead they opt to describe preventive measures that can be taken to avoid coercion, highlight the lack of evidence base for involuntary treatments and articulate the views of advocacy groups opposing forced treatments.

Funk and Drew (2019) also highlight how measures that are intended to be applied in exceptional circumstances often become common practice. The European Network of (Ex-) Users and Survivors of Psychiatry et al. (2019) also draws attention to the fact that the threat of involuntary treatment colours all psychiatric care. Many individuals may adhere to treatment for fear that they will be treated against their will if they do not. This creates a cohort of individuals receiving *de facto* involuntary treatment, generally without the protections or review mechanisms that are present for individuals receiving formal involuntary treatment.

The QualityRights assessment tool kit

The WHO's 'QualityRights tool kit to assess and improve quality and human rights in mental health and social care facilities' was published in 2012. To date the majority of research conducted using the QualityRights material has utilised this tool. This document received input from a wide range of professionals, service users and organisations supporting individuals with psychosocial disabilities. The tool kit was designed to be appropriate for low-, middle-, and high-income countries. It is designed to be used in out-patient as well as in-patient settings; this is a very important factor as often the focus of mental health reform is on in-patient care while the majority of individuals receive care as out-patients. Legislation also often focuses on in-patient care facilities only and the WHO assessment tool that predated the QualityRights Initiative was sparse in terms of out-patient care (WHO, 2005). In terms of diagnosis the scope of the tool is broad: it seeks to be used in services addressing the needs of individuals with mental, neurological or intellectual impairments and those with substance use disorders. In addition to this, the tool kit seeks to influence policy, service planning and legislation.

The toolkit assesses five themes based on articles of the CRPD. Each theme is made up of multiple standards and within each standard are specific criteria. Overall there are 25 standards and 111 criteria. These are described in Table 6.2.

In addition to laying out the themes, standards and criteria, the tool kit identifies national and international groups that could use it to conduct evaluations. Suggested organisations include:

- the United Nations Subcommittee on the Prevention of Torture and other Cruel, Inhuman or Degrading Treatment or Punishment,
- the Committee for the Prevention of Torture and Inhuman or Degrading Treatment or Punishment, set up under the Council of Europe's European Convention for the Prevention of Torture and Inhuman or Degrading Treatment or Punishment,
- Disability Rights International,
- the Mental Disability Advocacy Centre and
- the Global Initiative on Psychiatry.

The tool kit describes how to conduct an assessment, from initiating and planning a project, to selecting and training individuals, collecting data and managing ethical considerations. It describes in detail how to collect data from a wide variety of sources including: direct observation of the facility, review of the facility's policies, guidelines, standards, records of specific events and individuals' charts, and interviews with service users, carers and staff. Finally, it describes how to report and make use of the results.

QualityRights training material

In late 2019, the QualityRights training material was launched.

> These resources aim to support countries in transforming their health systems and services toward a person-centred, recovery-oriented, and human rights-based approach

Table 6.2 The World Health Organization's QualityRights assessment themes, standards and criteria

Theme	Standard	Number of criteria
The right to an adequate standard of living	The building is in good physical condition.	4
	The sleeping conditions of service users are comfortable and allow sufficient privacy.	6
	The facility meets hygiene and sanitary requirements.	4
	Service users are given food, safe drinking-water and clothing that meet their needs and preferences.	4
	Service users can communicate freely, and their right to privacy is respected.	5
	The facility provides a welcoming, comfortable, stimulating environment conducive to active participation and interaction.	4
	Service users can enjoy fulfilling social and personal lives and remain engaged in community life and activities.	5
The right to enjoyment of the highest attainable standard of physical and mental health (Article 25 of the CRPD)	Facilities are available to everyone who requires treatment and support.	3
	The facility has skilled staff and provides good-quality mental health services.	6
	Treatment, psychosocial rehabilitation and links to support networks and other services are elements of a service user driven recovery plan and contribute to a service user's ability to live independently in the community.	6
	Psychotropic medication is available, affordable and used appropriately.	5
	Adequate services are available for general and reproductive health.	6
The right to exercise legal capacity and the right to personal liberty and the security of person (Articles 12 and 14 of the CRPD)	Service users' preferences regarding the place and form of treatment are always a priority.	3
	Procedures and safeguards are in place to prevent detention and treatment without free and informed consent.	6
	Service users can exercise their legal capacity and are given the support they may require to exercise their legal capacity.	7
	Service users have the right to confidentiality and access to their personal health information.	4

(*Continued*)

Table 6.2 (Continued)

Theme	Standard	Number of criteria
Freedom from torture or cruel, inhuman or degrading treatment or punishment and from exploitation, violence and abuse (Articles 15 and 16 of the CRPD)	Service users have the right to be free from verbal, mental, physical and sexual abuse and physical and emotional neglect.	5
	Alternative methods are used in place of seclusion and restraint as means of de-escalating potential crises.	5
	Electroconvulsive therapy, psychosurgery and other medical procedures that may have permanent or irreversible effects, whether performed at the facility or referred to another facility, must not be abused and can be administered only with the free and informed consent of the service user.	6
	No service user is subjected to medical or scientific experimentation without his or her informed consent.	4
	Safeguards are in place to prevent torture or cruel, inhuman or degrading treatment and other forms of ill-treatment and abuse.	6
The right to live independently and be included in the community (Article 19 of the CRPD)	Service users are supported in gaining access to a place to live and have the financial resources necessary to live in the community.	3
	Service users can access education and employment opportunities.	3
	The right of service users to participate in political and public life and to exercise freedom of association is supported.	3
	Service users are supported in taking part in social, cultural, religious and leisure activities.	3

in line with the CRPD and the vision outlined by WHO Director General Tedros Ghebreyesus in the foreword to the QualityRights materials.

(Funk and Bold, 2020, p71)

The training material is aimed at service users, professionals working in the field of mental health, carers, advocates and any other relevant individuals. This training and guidance material includes five core modules and three specialised training modules (Table 6.1). Each module is divided into topics; the core modules take between six and ten hours to deliver while the specialised modules take 14–16 hours. It is designed to be delivered by a multidisciplinary team including individuals with lived experience. For each module there is a course guide, course slides, notes for facilitators, learning objectives and resources. These modules are not simply based on didactic teaching but rather utilise debate and case-based discussions that examine these practices and principles on personal and emotive levels.

The training material was conceptualised by WHO, input was also sought from over 20 key international experts including: the UN Special Rapporteur on the rights of persons with disabilities, the UN Special Rapporteur on the right of everyone to the enjoyment of the highest attainable standard of health, multiple groups representing users and survivors of psychiatry services, and legal and mental health experts. Modules were reviewed by an extensive list of professionals and individuals with lived experience from across the globe. The training material describes how the inclusion of individuals from such diverse geographical locations attempts to ensure that the modules are applicable in a wide range of contexts. The documents explicitly attempt to shift mental healthcare away from the medical model through the involvement of a wide range of specialities.

As part of the training material, the QualityRights Initiative also includes videos, many made by external agencies; their use clearly communicates the human impact of substandard mental healthcare that is sadly common practice. This collaborative approach, with so many participating groups, and in combination with the long list of supporting statements from different organisations, included at the start of each module, demonstrates the prevalence of the deficiencies in mental healthcare and the commonality of the reforms being sought.

The human rights module (WHO, 2019a) addresses: what human rights are, the relationship between different rights and violations of these rights. Topics five and six in this module are particularly helpful in regard to mental health; they highlight populations that are at risk of human rights violations and the consequences of such practices. The material includes clear and emotive examples. The final topic attempts to inspire personal action from participants; it gives individuals space for reflection and examples of steps that they can take.

The 'Mental health, disability and human rights' module (WHO, 2019b) discusses discrimination and denial of human rights in the context of disability. It describes the different models that have been used in relation to disabilities, which provides a helpful context for discussions on the topic. It also introduces the CRPD, including a description of each article with practical examples. It draws on detailed scenarios to examine the CRPD in practice and then explores Articles 12, 16 and 19 in detail.

The 'Legal capacity and the right to decide' module (WHO, 2019c) really begins to challenge the standard practices of in-patient mental healthcare in many countries. It addresses legal capacity, supported decision making, advance directives and mechanisms to prevent involuntary treatment. It also briefly discusses the highly important topic of gender and capacity. This module includes a really helpful description of different supported decision-making models used internationally; these provide workable ideas and examples to support services as they move from substitute to supported decision making. The module sets forth in unambiguous terms the arguments against any form of involuntary treatment, and at times there is limited or idealised discussions of the alternatives; however, these may become more practical as the topics are discussed in a group setting.

The fourth core module, 'Recovery and the right to health' (WHO, 2019d), seeks to equip participants to understand mental health and well-being, examines barriers to care and defines and promotes recovery. One of the most helpful aspects of this module is the clear understanding of the interconnectedness between physical and mental health. It also provides very broad definitions of both mental and physical health, far removed from a more medical model; this may prompt an overdue re-evaluation of the care provided by some mental health services.

The 'Freedom from coercion, violence and abuse' module (WHO, 2019e) attempts to help participants understand the impact of these practices, to identify power dynamics and to develop different approaches for diffusing conflictual and tense situations. During the module there are options to have individuals share their lived experience or to use videos describing people's experience of coercion. There are very helpful sections examining the reasons why violence, coercion and abuse occur and analysing power dynamics within mental healthcare. The second half of the module explores mechanisms to avoid coercion or violence; these contain some excellent, and sadly underutilised, suggestions including emergency response teams, individualised plans, supportive environments, comfort rooms and communication advice to de-escalate individuals.

The first of the specialised training modules addresses 'Recovery practices for mental health and well-being'; this expands on many of the ideas covered in the fourth core module (WHO, 2019f). This is a 16-hour module which gives a detailed description of the recovery model. One of the most challenging and potentially helpful sections covers positive risks in recovery. In addition to this, there are sections on making a recovery plan and developing a recovery wheel, both of which are excellent resources.

The second specialised module addresses 'Strategies to end seclusion and restraint'; this builds on much of the material discussed in the 'Freedom from coercion, violence and abuse' module (WHO, 2019g), but as this module is 15 hours long it allows greater space to develop and explore these ideas. This should be essential reading for any service that uses seclusion and restraint as the practices and approaches described are practical, effective and require minimal resources. The document also importantly describes the personal experience of seclusion and restraint. Some of the literature in this area primarily focuses on physical and mechanical restraint but this material considers the use of medication throughout.

The 'Supported decision-making and advance planning' module (WHO, 2019h) builds on the 'Legal capacity and the right to decide' module; again, it is able to explore this topic in enhanced detail. Supported decision making, advance directives and nominated representatives are examined in depth. There is a brief discussion of a 'Ulysses Clause', a mechanism whereby individuals can opt into involuntary treatment. However, despite discussing this the authors of the module state that:

> According to article 12 of the CRPD, people have the right to legal capacity *at all times*. Therefore, people should retain their right to make decisions directly and to change their mind, even if an advance plan has been drafted. The fact that people develop advance plans does not mean they are 'legally incapable'.
> *(WHO, 2021h, p. 51)*

This complicates the use and questions the validity of a Ulysses Clause. The module appears to only see such a mechanism as useful in a context where an individual cannot communicate their will or preference. This tool also provides a number of useful templates and resources.

Evaluation tools

Pre- and post-training questionnaires have been developed to evaluate the impact of the course; these comprise 17 questions, each scored on a five point scale (Funk *et al.*, 2017). The post-training evaluation also includes an assessment of the trainers and material and space for qualitative feedback.

Guidance tools

The QualityRights Initiative has published four guidance tools. The document entitled 'Peer support groups by and for people with lived experience' (WHO, 2019i) describes what such groups are and their benefits, and discusses how to set up and run them. It provides many helpful practical tips and shares experiences of facilitating groups. The guidance module 'One-to-one peer support by and for people with lived experience' (WHO, 2019j) provides extensive information on what the role of a peer supporter is, and what the benefits of such support can be. It addresses many of the misconceptions that exist about peer support, examines ethical considerations and describes some of the potential roles. It also considers some very practical steps including: developing a job description for a peer supporter, interviewing and hiring, conditions of work and interactions with mental health services.

The guidance module addressing advocacy (WHO, 2019k) describes how to run an advocacy campaign. It is a powerful tool for anyone advocating for disability rights; it may be of particular relevance to clinicians, as many of the topics covered in it are highly relevant, yet often far removed from their original training. The document is full of practical examples and manageable steps, and it provides templates and tools. It considers topics like lobbying governments and politicians, working with the media, generating debate within communities and identify resources and funding. The fourth guidance document published by the QualityRights Initiative is entitled 'Civil society organizations to promote human rights in mental health and related areas' (WHO, 2019l). This document describes what a civil society (or non-state) organisation is, discusses how one can be set up and then considers operations, monitoring, evaluation, reporting and sustainability.

Self-help tool

The QualityRights Initiative has developed an excellent resource for individuals with psychosocial disabilities. Their 'Person-centred recovery planning for mental health and well-being' document (WHO, 2019m) draws on documents from the Nottinghamshire Healthcare NHS Trust. This includes wellness and recovery planning, advance mental health directives and many of the elements from WRAP (wellness recovery action plan).

This document focuses on recovery and attempts to provide an individual with mental health difficulties, or individuals who support them, with tools to promote recovery. The definition of recovery described departs from more medical conceptualisations of mental illness and focuses on holistic goals, meaning, purpose and agency rather than on symptoms. Consequently, this definition is inherently personal. The document supports individuals in making a Personal Recovery Plan, which they suggest may cover five domains:

1. Plan for pursuing dreams and goals.
2. How to keep yourself well.
3. Plan for difficult times.
4. Plan for responding to a crisis.
5. Plan for after a crisis.

Under each of these headings are tables that can be filled out by an individual to assist them in planning. For example, in relation to 'pursuing dreams and goals' the document uses tables to break down large key goals into smaller steps; it also has a table that assists people in identifying goals by focusing on personal strengths. The 'keeping well or wellness plan' section helps individuals to identify triggers and helpful practices and to develop a schedule in order to remain well. The 'planning for difficult times' section has excellent tables that support people in identifying their individuals' signs of emotional distress, and planning actions that can help address them. It also encourages keeping a regular record of these sensitivities and signs of distress to help individuals understand how events impact them and build their recovery skills.

The section that plans a crisis response is the largest section in the document; it helps an individual make an advance directive for mental healthcare. This includes identifying signs that an individual is in crisis, persons to be contacted in an emergency and people they do not want involved in their care. There are boxes that can be filled out to identify things they want supporters to take care of, things that people can do that are helpful, and unhelpful measures. There are sections which provide important medical information like current medication, medication preferences, allergies and important personal and social factors.

This section does not shy away from issues relating to risk; it demonstrates a nuanced understanding of the complexity that often comes with a mental health crisis and includes sections for individuals to identify their relevant background, signs of relapse, family and carers, treatment and support preferences, and plans should the level of risk increase. It concludes with a section for individuals to sign and have this document witnessed. In some jurisdictions this would have a significant legal weight. For example, this aligns well with the provisions for advance directives and nominated representatives described in Section 5-17 of India's Mental Healthcare Act, 2017 (Duffy and Kelly, 2019). Even in jurisdictions without a legal obligation to follow an advance mental healthcare directive, the WHO tool has space for the individual making the directive to give the rationale for the decisions. Consequently, it creates a valuable record for individuals receiving and providing care. The final section provides multiple useful tools for attempting to maintain recovery and to assist individuals in reflecting on things that may have been learned from any recent crisis.

Areas of concern about elements of the QualityRights Initiative

Funk and Bold (2020) acknowledge how polarised the current debate on the total prohibition of coercive treatment is. The QualityRights material repeatedly states that it seeks to bring about an end to what it sees as abusive practices and describes involuntary treatment in the community or in hospital as a form of violence and coercion; this is most notable in the module on freedom from coercion, violence and abuse (WHO, 2019e). The difficulties with this perspective are deepened by the hesitancy of the QualityRights Initiative to address exceptional or high-risk circumstances. Multiple levels of excellent de-escalation tools are discussed, including communication skills and special response teams, but they give no serious consideration to what to do when these are exhausted aside from involving 'law enforcement bodies (e.g. the police force) to guarantee the security of all' (WHO, 2019g, p. 21). To a degree, this is understandable as exceptional involuntary treatments could all too easily become common place. Many of the case examples in the QualityRights training material include idealised outcomes where adequate supports by compassionate trained professionals result in the resolution of crises without any restrictive practices. There is not adequate exploration of cases that are not resolved through such techniques and it is unclear what is proposed in instances where there is a serious and immediate risk. The fifth core training module (WHO, 2019e) states that

> it is considered legitimate to use physical force in self-defence or to defend another person when the use of force is proportionate to the attempted act of violence. However, in many services, responses to behaviour that is perceived as violent are not in self-defence and are out of proportion with the threat of harm.
>
> *(p. 15)*

There is no discussion of how the magnitude of risk would be classified, what form this defence might take, if an individual would have a right to review the steps taken in 'self-defence' or what would be considered proportional (especially in the context of ongoing risk). Could this defence involve physical restraint or seclusion or is the criminal justice system the only acceptable avenue for dealing with such challenges? Many of the critics of the Committee on the Rights of Persons with Disabilities interpretation of the CRPD have highlighted how this has the potential to criminalise individuals with mental illness (Freeman et al. 2015, Scholten and Gather, 2018). In elements of the QualityRights training material there appears to be a worrying acceptance of this fact (Duffy and Kelly 2020; Hoare and Duffy, 2021). This is particularly true when one of the common faults found with services evaluated using the QualityRights tool kit is that police were involved in restraining individuals receiving treatment (Nomidou, 2013).

The tool kit states that while it

> does not endorse long-stay facilities as an appropriate setting for treatment and care, as long as this type of facility continues to exist in countries all over the world, there is a need to prevent violations and promote the rights of those residing in them.
>
> *(WHO, 2012, p. 3)*

This is an excellent pragmatic approach. However, while the majority of countries still permit involuntary care, the tool kit opts to not approach this topic in the same manner; it does not describe the 'proportional' self-defence measures or any mechanism to review or limit these practices. Many of these were addressed in the, now withdrawn, WHO resource book on mental health, human rights and legislation (WHO, 2005). With coercive measures legally permitted in so many countries it appears somewhat idealistic not to describe the protections and limitations that may inform them, even if this is accompanied with an acknowledgement that the QualityRights Initiative fully opposes such practices.

A further problematic element throughout the QualityRights material is that legal practices that are currently part of mental health services like seclusion, restraint or electroconvulsive therapy are listed alongside illegal acts like assault, verbal abuse and 'forced sterilisation' (Hoare and Duffy, 2021). There are merits in debating if seclusion and restraint have any place in mental healthcare, but to equate them with other gross violations of human rights appears overly simplistic. Unlike illegal acts like assault or verbal abuse, seclusion and restraint are practices that have been long established, used with therapeutic intent, described by legislation and subject to review procedures; and unlike practices that were once legal but still grossly clear violations of individuals' rights, like forced sterilisation, these practices are time limited and when appropriately used seek to reduce acute risk. Seclusion and restraint have undoubtedly led to many severe violations of individuals' rights, but to state that in all contexts they are gross violations of human rights is unhelpful, especially when the only suggested alternative is the involvement of law enforcement.

The dismissal of a Ulysses Clause as non-concordant with the CRPD is unhelpful and, if widely adopted, places individuals with severe mental illness in a very insecure situation (Philip et al., 2019). The authors of the training module on 'Supported decision-making and advance planning' (WHO, 2019h) give an authority to current preference for treatment that totally invalidates consistent, carefully considered choices made previously by an individual about their own health. It also leaves an individual at high risk of relapse with no way of addressing this should it occur.

Within the QualityRights material, occasionally a straw man argument is used. Often when describing the medical model, the use of medication or the use of restraint, extreme examples are portrayed as the norm. For example, the 'traditional or clinical' understanding of recovery is described using extremely pejorative terms or the description of medication is nearly universally negative (Hoare and Duffy, 2021). While the QualityRights Initiative does not oppose medication (Moro et al., 2022), such a description undermines the role of an evidence-based treatment.

The limited reference to the QualityRights material in WHO's Mental Health Action Plan 2013–2030 (WHO, 2021) and the fact that the views concerning capacity and involuntary treatment lack consensus within the UN (Szmukler, 2019), both call into question the status of the QualityRights Initiative within the WHO.

Research using the QualityRights material

To date there have been several projects that have conducted research using the QualityRights material. The majority of these have evaluated healthcare systems or hospitals using the QualityRights tool kit but increasingly it has included other elements of the WHO's material. Table 6.3 describes the research done to date and some of the key projects are discussed in more detail below.

India

Pathare et al. (2021) have conducted the most extensive interventional trial to date, in Gujarat, India. This study demonstrated the positive impact the QualityRights Initiative can have, even in the context of limited resources. This project implemented the QualityRights programme at six public mental health establishments, three in general hospitals and three in stand-alone mental health facilities. These were compared to three other centres that did not receive the QualityRights training. Intervention occurred over a period of one year with assessments occurring approximately six months before and after training. Delivery of the QualityRights programme comprised five elements:

1. The WHO QualityRights tool kit was used to assess the services; this occurred at baseline and one year following intervention.
2. Measures were put in place to improve infrastructure including sanitation, hygiene and food quality, and service users monitored the progress.
3. Training was delivered to professionals, family members and service users on recovery, rights, communication and avoiding coercive practices.
4. Peer groups were established for service users and family members.
5. Policies were introduced to attempt to limit restrictive practices and enhance the rights of individuals receiving treatment.

The first element occurred in the intervention and control group, but elements two to five only undertaken in the intervention group. Following the initial assessment using a WHO QualityRights tool kit the intervention and control groups were given feedback on their

Table 6.3 Research carried out using the World Health Organization's QualityRights material

Reference	Methodology	Setting	Key findings
Nomidou, 2013	Cross-sectional study with control group (urology ward)	In-patient care in a single hospital, Greece	Lower level of adherence compared to the medical setting. Significant omission and violations across all themes
Elnemais Fawzy, 2015	Cross-sectional study	In-patient care, single hospital, Egypt	Significant omission and violations across all themes
Minoletti et al., 2015a*	Cross-sectional study	Public out-patients in 15 departments, Chile	Areas of high concordance with standards but also some areas with significant deficiencies
Minoletti et al., 2015b*	Cross-sectional study including comparison of two cohorts	Public out-patients in 15 departments, Chile	Demonstrated that service users and family members have a lower perception of the standard of services compared to staff.
Rekhis et al., 2017	Cross-sectional study	In-patient care, only psychiatric hospital in Tunisia	Significant omission and violations across all themes, most severely in regard to the right to live independently and be included in the community. Area of greatest concordance was in relation to the right to the enjoyment of the highest attainable standards of physical and mental health.
WHO, 2018	Cross-sectional study	In 75 facilities in 25 European countries	Only 28% of the standards assessed were achieved in full, some of the failings underpinned by outdated legislation. Many common deficiencies identified across all themes.
Pathare et al., 2021	Interventional study with control group	Stand-alone mental health facilities and psychiatric units in general hospitals in India	Service quality improved in the intervention group, enhanced staff attitudes and greater empowerment of service users was also seen.
Carta et al., 2020 (note two phases to this study)	Interventional study without control group	Mental health, legal and administrative professionals in Tunisia	Training in QualityRights material improved knowledge and attitudes. A minority of the findings were statistically significant
	Cross sectional study	Mental health professionals, service users and their families in Tusnia	Significant omission and violations across all themes most severely in regard to the right to live independently. No improvement from prior study (Rekhis et al., 2017)

(*Continued*)

Table 6.3 (Continued)

Reference	Methodology	Setting	Key findings
Winkler et al., 2020	Cross-sectional study	Nationwide study of in-patient units in the Czech Republic, including child and adolescent services	No hospital fully met the QualityRights criteria. There were major shortcomings in terms of accessibility and many had insufficient standards of living. Privacy was often compromised and there was a lack of availability to communications technology.
Muhia et al., 2021	Cross-sectional study	In-patient and out-patient services in Kenya's largest psychiatry hospital	Progress towards CRPD concordant care had been initiated across all themes. But deficiencies were found in relation to infrastructure, staffing, protection of service users' capacity, the presence of physical and verbal abuse and community reintegration.
Lantta et al., 2021	Cross-sectional study	In-patient care, national sample, Finland	All wards fully or partially fulfilled every item on the checklist.
Moro et al., 2022	Cross-sectional study	The Gambia, Ghana, Liberia and Sierra Leone	Significant omission and violations across all themes; right to exercise legal capacity and the right to personal liberty and security were almost absent and the right to live independently was severely limited.

Note: *Only abstract available in English; full paper written in Spanish

results. However, in the intervention group there was an implementation group comprised of experts from a range of disciplines, including experts by experience. This team assisted services in developing a strategic plan to address deficiencies in each of the domains identified. In addition to the use of the tool kit, surveys of staff, service users and their carers were conducted at baseline and follow-up.

At follow-up the control group demonstrated a significantly better level of adherence to the standards in themes one, two and four. This may highlight that theme three, regarding legal capacity, and theme five, regarding community living, may be the most difficult to address and may require more concerted systematic interventions. Analysing the surveys conducted revealed that in the control group there were improved attitudes towards service users by staff, enhanced empowerment of service users, greater satisfaction with services and reduced burden on carers. It should be noted that this project targeted a geographical area with an identified need to improve quality of mental healthcare and human rights. There was also pre-existing motivation at a political level. Both of these factors may have benefited the results.

Finland

Lantta et al. (2021) used the QualityRights tool kit to evaluate the quality of mental healthcare and realisation of human rights for individuals receiving in-patient care in Finland. This is one of the main studies that has occurred in a high-income context; in addition to Finland being a wealthy country, it has one of the highest levels of mental health professionals per capita in Europe (World Health Organization, 2021). This cross-sectional observational study occurred in 13 wards in eight hospitals. Only publicly funded wards where coercive measures were used were included. As recommended by the tool kit, document analysis, observations and group interviews were employed to generate the data. Service users, family members and staff were interviewed. The findings of the study are based on data collected from 45 in-patients, 130 staff and 5 family members. Unfortunately, this strongly under-represented the perspectives of patients and families. Every ward was either fully or partial concordant with every item on the checklist. The four lowest scoring items were:

- Alternative methods are used in place of seclusion and restraint as means of de-escalating potential crises.
- Service users' preferences regarding the place and form of treatment are always the priority.
- Procedures and safeguards are in place to prevent detention and treatment without free and informed consent.
- The facility provides a welcoming, comfortable, stimulating environment conducive to active participation and interaction.

The first item on this list, regarding de-escalation, was the least concordant with the vast majority of units only partially fulfilling the item.

Egypt

Elnemais Fawzy (2015) conducted a cross-sectional study at a 1,474-bed publicly funded hospital in Cairo. Egypt had revised its mental health legislation in 2009 and the authors felt that this was an important window in which to evaluate concordance with the themes and standards of the QualityRights tool kit. The researchers interviewed 36 patients, 58 staff and 15 family members as well as reviewing documents and carrying out an independent assessment. Many steps were taken to get a comprehensive picture of the hospital: visits were made at different times of the day, some were unannounced, night staff were intentionally included and patients were recruited from all the wards in the hospital and included individuals who required acute, long stay, voluntary and involuntary admissions.

This study identified many items that needed to be addressed under each theme. Under theme one, 'The Right to an Adequate Standard of Living', issues that arose included: the lack of air conditioning, insufficient activities, reduced accessibility for individuals with physical disabilities, limited privacy, water for hygiene and drinking, no food choice and reduced personal freedoms including phone use. Under theme two, 'The Right to the Enjoyment of the Highest Attainable Standard of Physical and Mental Health', the researchers identified insufficient staffing levels, with poor staff morale and limited team cohesion. No staff were aware of the CRPD. Under theme three, 'The Right to Exercise Legal Capacity and to Personal Liberty and the Security of Person', patients reported having limited awareness of their rights, feeling that doctors did not take their preference seriously. Frequent use of chemical restraint and labelling of patients as dangerous was common, and incomplete records were kept regarding restraints. Theme four, 'Freedom from Torture or Cruel, Inhuman or Degrading Treatment or Punishment and from Exploitation, Violence and Abuse' had a large number of identified deficiencies. These included excessively rigid and overly controlled daily routines, patients' fear of punishment by staff, limited access to appeals and complaints procedure, and patients experiencing verbal and physical abuse. The analysis of theme five, 'The Right to Live Independently and Be Included in the Community' brought to light the lack of information on occupational and rehabilitative opportunities, and staff were unconvinced of the patients' right to vote. Positives were also noted across all themes.

This study demonstrated how basic many of the unmet needs can be; it helped describe the magnitude of the problem and illustrated many of the issues in significant detail. The wide range of perspectives is highly informative.

Greece

Nonidou (2013) was one of the first authors to use the QualityRights tool kit to evaluate a mental health facility and also evaluated a urology ward as a comparison. This study was carried out in a 20-bed ward in Greece. While the number of individuals included was smaller than subsequent studies, an in-depth analysis of the collected data was conducted. A wide range of patients, staff and relatives were chosen. The particular unit lacked policies to review, an area of concern in itself. Factors that were identified as non-concordant in relation to standards of living included: lack of accessibility for individuals with blindness, lack of recreational activities, lack of privacy, insufficient safety procedures and equipment, absent emergency policies or health and safety measures, poor temperature regulation, failures to meet dietary requirements or provide options, a lack of financial autonomy and restrictions of phone use. Many of these echoed the themes that emerged in the later Egyptian study (Elnemais Fawzy, 2015).

Significant deficiencies were identified regarding the standards relating to the right to health. Staff described dissatisfaction, burnout and stigma for working in mental health. For patients, health promotion, screening and vaccination were absent; individualised care plans and treatment preferences were not well documented, were not available to the patients and prescribing was idiosyncratic. There were highly limited recovery-orientated services and no access to rehabilitation services. Patients were actively disempowered, there was no co-creation of treatment plans, there was a lack of patient education and the complaints procedure was obscure.

There were also significant omissions and violations in relation to capacity and liberty. Police were often involved in physical restraint, chemical and mechanical restraint were widely used and consent for admission was often not obtained from voluntary patients. Individuals were unaware of their right to appeal, they had a lack of information about legal options and some were refused legal representation.

There were less omissions in relation to freedom from torture. However, as this is a non-derogable right, violations in this area are of particular seriousness. De-escalation techniques were not used, police assisted with restraint and patients were often labelled as dangerous. Regarding the right to live independently, patients were often neglected and deprived of their liberty, there was no access to occupational or recreational services and limited supports in sourcing accommodation.

This study also used a urology clinic as a control group, demonstrating how the mental health services were less concordant with the QualityRights standards. Some of these contrasts are stark, in particular the variation in the ward conditions. However, the paper describes clear human rights violations and does not need to enhance its findings with a somewhat artificial comparison. While it is informative, they are not directly comparable settings.

Tunisia

Carta et al. (2020) have conducted one of the more ambitious projects. While the QualityRights tool kit has been widely used in observational studies, this study completed an audit cycle in the only psychiatric hospital in Tunisia, providing follow-up data. In addition to the evaluation, an intensive one-week course based on the QualityRights principles was delivered to 19 individuals, including staff of the participating centre. The 'knowledge and attitudes regarding human rights in mental health and the CRPD' of the training participants was measured before and after the course. The authors carried out the second service evaluation using the tool kit, five months after delivering the training. This was compared to the prior evaluation carried out four years earlier (Rekhis et al., 2017). This process has two advantages: there are two separate evaluations of the same centre and the effectiveness of training based on the QualityRights principles is assessed.

The educational component of the study included professionals working in the field of mental health. A 26-item multiple choice questionnaire was used, and each item was scored on a 5-point Likert scale. This questionnaire has also been used in the evaluation of QualityRights E-training (Funk *et al.*, 2017). Participants who received the training demonstrated a general increased level of sensitivity towards the patients' view and reduced support for coercive practices; however, a statistically significant difference in scores was only seen in 5 of the 26 items.

The observational assessment of the facility drew on interviews from staff, patients and carers; 20 of each were interviewed. Each criterion, standard and theme was given one of four scores: 'Completely achieved', 'Partially achieved', 'Achievement initiated' and 'Not started'. Four of the five themes were graded as: 'Achievement initiated' while theme five, the right to live independently and be included in the community, was graded as 'not started'; this was a decline since the evaluation in 2014. However, the authors noted that the later assessment was conducted by trained staff, some of whom were external to the hospital. Of the 25 standards, 2 were 'Completely achieved', 3 'Partially achieved', 11 classified as 'Achievement initiated' and 9 'Not started'. The presentation of the data in this structured style, in contrast to other studies, allows for increased ease of comparison across sites but reduces the richness and usefulness of the data for that specific site.

Chile

Both of the Minolette papers (2015a; 2015b) were only available in Spanish but the abstracts have been translated into English. These projects included some of the largest groups of participants with 146 patients, 64 carers and 148 staff interviewed. Both papers also contribute to the QualityRights research, as they analyse care received in out-patients. Research and legislation are often heavily weighted towards in-patient services and out-patient practice can be neglected.

The paper in *Revista Médica* (2015a) identified the presence of 'discrimination-free health care, availability of psychotropic medications, [and] lack of abuse or neglect' as the key positive findings, while 'support to cope with community living, access to education or work and participation in community activities, respect for user treatment preferences and [a lack of] preventative measures to avoid maltreatment and cruelty' were the main areas where improvement was needed.

The second paper (2015b) found that staff in the study were significantly more likely to rate services as good or concordant to standards compared to patients or family members.

Limitations of the research to date

The studies identified various limitations. Multiple studies overestimated the degree of adherence to international standards and minimised problems; Elnemais Fawzy (2015) and Nomidou (2013) identified that patients and family may minimise concerns and potential issues for fear of punishment. In those studies many of the patients refused to participate for that very reason, and staff were also reluctant to talk freely. A discrepancy was noted between the scores and the observed reality; this demonstrates that the utility of the tool kit is in the process rather than the scores alone. This will be of particular relevance in environments where there are established human rights deficiencies or where there is a significant power imbalance between staff and patients. Carta et al. (2020) highlight the importance of external staff carrying out the assessment and in particular conducting the interviews with patients and families; this may help reduce the fears that individuals have when reporting concerns. It is vital that service users and their carers feel empowered to contribute to evaluations as they are often most aware of limitations within the service (Minelotti et al., 2015)

A common critique of research concerning human rights in mental health in low- and middle-income countries was well articulated in Elnemais Fawzy's (2015) study who said, 'You are looking for mental health patients forgotten rights in a country where its citizens are struggling to prove their fundamental rights'. As the QualityRights tool kit is more broadly used, it will be important to decide what realises a better standard of care for individuals. Aspirational goals, aiming for a possibly unattainable standard, run the risk of being ignored as impractical, while more realistic goals employing a pragmatic margin of appreciation may lead to an acceptance of substandard practices. The most effective approach may vary from location to location.

Few of the papers that use the tool kit discuss the potential for recall bias. Nomidou (2013) is an exception by highlighting that disenfranchised staff will be more likely to give negative reports. Moro et al. (2022) also highlight the potential for cultural bias to have a significant role due to the subjective elements present in the tool kit.

One of the major limitations in the research to date is the lack of a convenient or natural control group to compare to mental health services. Nimidou (2013) attempted to address this by comparing a urology clinic to a mental health service. Some criteria were not directly comparable, but others were relevant to both services. For example, Nimidou describes therapeutic restraint as occurring in the urology clinic; what this means and if this form of restraint ever happens in a mental health setting is unclear.

Strengths of research to date

The current research demonstrates how the QualityRights tool kit is more effective in assessing the actual experience of individuals, rather than simply the theoretical context of the health service, as was the case with the checklist in the WHO resource book on mental health, human rights and legislation (WHO, 2005). For example, Elnemais Fawzy (2015) highlights the discrepancy between legislative provisions, policy and practice. Carta et al. (2020) also used the tool kit to evaluate the impact of legislative change in Tunisia, and captured the discordance between legislative change and the ground reality. The QualityRights tool kit is also useful in describing the power dynamics in the services (Muhia et al., 2021); many of the situations described resonate with Goffman's findings (1961) from over 60 years ago.

The presence of these standards allows for repeated evaluations over time, as occurred in Tunisia (Carta et al., 2020; Rekhis et al., 2017) and the Czech Republic (Winkler et al, 2020; WHO, 2018). Carta et al. (2020) demonstrated that assessment in itself may not produce change. Following on from an evaluation it is vital that changes are proposed and that individuals take responsibility for the implementation of changes. For example, Winkler et al. (2020) proposed facility and system-level interventions following their evaluation.

Conclusion

If the CRPD is to be fully realised for individuals with mental health difficulties, the QualityRights Initiative will be a large part of driving that change. The tool kit and training modules currently contain many excellent measures to begin the transition towards CRPD concordant mental healthcare. Internationally services would benefit from delivering this training and aligning their reviews of mental health services with the tool kit's themes, standards and criteria. The potential benefits of this are huge considering the magnitude of the deficiencies described by the research to date.

The current studies published have been highly informative but more interventional studies are needed to demonstrate how the failings that have been identified can be remedied. Studies evaluating the impact of the training materials are also needed and will hopefully demonstrate their effectiveness in improving the quality of mental healthcare received by individuals.

There are unanswered questions around coercive practices that will need to be addressed. The QualityRights Initiative's CRPD-informed position may present challenges. The potential for the criminalisation of individuals with mental illness is worrying and some of the QualityRights material appears to be accepting of this risk. The inability for someone to receive treatment against their will, even if this is their strongly articulated longstanding preference, will be disempowering for some individuals and brings a high level of uncertainty. It is also unclear how services should proceed when supportive non-coercive measures prove ineffective.

There are no simple answers to these questions and the QualityRights material is helping service users and providers reflect on them in a more informed way and hopefully come to more humane and compassionate answers. The material should have an important place in mental healthcare internationally and have the potential to greatly improve the quality of life for people with psychosocial disabilities.

References

Appelbaum, P. S. (2019) 'Saving the UN Convention on the Rights of Persons with Disabilities - from Itself', *World Psychiatry*, 18(1), pp. 1–2. doi: 10.1002/wps.20583.

Carta, M. G. et al. (2020) 'Implementing WHO-Quality Rights Project in Tunisia: Results of an Intervention at Razi Hospital', *Clinical Practice and Epidemiology in Mental Health*, 16(1), pp. S125–S133. doi: 10.2174/1745017902016010125.

Clarke, D. (2016) 'Law, Regulation and Strategizing for Health', in G. Schmets, D. Rajan and S. Kadandale (eds.) *Strategizing National Health in the 21st Century: A Handbook*. Geneva: World Health Organization, pp. 1–44.

Duffy, R. M. and Kelly, B. D. (2019) 'India's Mental Healthcare Act, 2017: Content, Context, Controversy', *International Journal of Law and Psychiatry*, 62, pp. 169–178. doi: 10.1016/j.ijlp.2018.08.002.

Duffy, R. M. and Kelly, B. D. (2020) 'World Health Organization and Mental Health Law', in *India's Mental Healthcare Act, 2017: Building Laws, Protecting Rights*. Singapore: Springer, pp. 25–48. doi: 10.1007/978-981-15-5009-6_3.

Elnemais Fawzy, M. (2015) 'Quality of Life and Human Rights Conditions in a Public Psychiatric Hospital in Cairo', *International Journal of Human Rights in Healthcare*, 8(4), pp. 199–217. doi: 10.1108/IJHRH-02-2015-0006.

European Network of (Ex-) Users and Survivors of Psychiatry, Absolute Prohibition Campaign, Center for Human Rights of Users and Survivors of Psychiatry et al. (2019) *Open Letter to WPA*. Available at: http://psychrights.org/countries/UN/190301WNUSPOpen-Letter-to-WPA-1.pdf (Accessed 2 June 2022).

Freeman, M. C. et al. (2015) 'Reversing Hard Won Victories in the Name of Human Rights: A Critique of the General Comment on Article 12 of the UN Convention on the Rights of Persons with Disabilities', *The Lancet Psychiatry*, 2(9), pp. 844–850. doi: 10.1016/S2215-0366(15)00218-7.

Funk, M. et al. (2017) *QualityRights e-Training on Mental Health, Human Rights and Recovery: Pre and Post Training Evaluation*. Geneva: QualityRights Initiative.

Funk, M., & Drew, N. (2019). Practical strategies to end coercive practices in mental health services. *World Psychiatry: Official Journal of the World Psychiatric Association (WPA)*, 18(1), 43–44. https://doi.org/10.1002/wps.20600

Funk, M. and Bold, N. D. (2020) 'WHO's QualityRights Initiative: Transforming Services and Promoting Rights in Mental Health', *Health and Human Rights*, 22(1), pp. 69–75.

Funk, M. and Drew, N. (2017) 'WHO QualityRights: Transforming Mental Health Services', *The Lancet Psychiatry*, 4(11), pp. 826–827. doi: 10.1016/S2215-0366(17)30271-7.

Goffman, E. (1961) *Asylums: Essays on the Condition of the Social Situation of Mental Patients and Other Inmates*. New York: Anchor Books.

Hoare, F. and Duffy, R. (2021) 'The World Health Organization's QualityRights Materials for Training, Guidance and Transformation: Preventing Coercion But Marginalising Psychiatry', *The British Journal of Psychiatry*, 218(5), pp. 240–242.doi: 10.1192/bjp.2021.20.

Lantta, T., Anttila, M. and Välimäki, M. (2021) 'Quality of Mental Health Services and Rights of People Receiving Treatment in Inpatient Services in Finland: A Cross-Sectional Observational Survey with the WHO QualityRights Tool Kit', *International Journal of Mental Health Systems*, 15(1), p. 70. doi: 10.1186/s13033-021-00495-7.

MacQuarrie, A. and Laurin-Bowie, C. (2014) 'Our Lives, Our Voices: People with Intellectual Disabilities and Their Families', in M. Sabatello and M. Schulze (eds.) *Human Rights and Disability Advocacy*. Philadelphia: University of Pennsylvania Press, pp. 25–44.

Melish, T. J. (2014) 'An Eye Towards Effective Enforcement: Technical-Comparative Approach to the Negotiations', in M. Sabatello and M. Schulze (eds.) *Human Rights and Disability Advocacy*. Philadelphia: University of Pennsylvania Press, pp. 70–96.

Minoletti, A. et al. (2015a) '[A Survey About Quality of Care and User's Rights in Chilean Psychiatric Services] [Spanish]', *Revista Médica de Chile*, 143(12), pp. 1585–1592. [Spanish]. doi: 10.4067/S0034-98872015001200012.

Minelotti, A. et al. (2015b) '[Differences on Perceptions of Quality of Care and Respect for Rights in Mental Health Between User, Family and Staff] [Spanish]', *Revista de la Facultad de Ciencias Medicas (Cordoba, Argentina)*, 72(4), pp. 261–269.

Moro, M. F. et al. (2022) 'Quality of care and respect of human rights in mental health services in four West African countries: Collaboration between the mental health leadership and advocacy programme and the World Health Organization QualityRights initiative', *BJPsych Open*, 8(1), p. e31. doi: 10.1192/bjo.2021.1080.

Muhia, J. et al. (2021) 'A Human Rights Assessment of a Large Mental Hospital in Kenya', *The Pan African Medical Journal*, 40, p. 199. doi: 10.11604/pamj.2021.40.199.30470.

Nomidou, A. (2013) 'Standards in Mental Health Facilities—An in Depth Case Study in Greece Using the WHO QualityRights Tool', *Journal of Public Mental Health*, 12(4), pp. 201–211. doi: 10.1108/JPMH-06-2013-0046.

Pathare, S. et al. (2021) 'Systematic Evaluation of the QualityRights Programme in Public Mental Health Facilities in Gujarat, India', *The British Journal of Psychiatry*, 218(4), pp. 196–203. doi: 10.1192/bjp.2019.138.

Philip, S. et al. (2019) 'Advance Directives and Nominated Representatives: A Critique', *Indian Journal of Psychiatry*, 61(Suppl 4), pp. S680–S685. doi: 10.4103/psychiatry.IndianJPsychiatry_95_19.

Rekhis, M. et al. (2017) 'Rights of People with Mental Disorders: Realities in Healthcare Facilities in Tunisia', *The International Journal of Social Psychiatry*, 63(5), pp. 439–447. doi: 10.1177/0020764017712301.

Scholten, M. and Gather, J. (2018) 'Adverse Consequences of Article 12 of the UN Convention on the Rights of Persons with Disabilities for Persons with Mental Disabilities and an Alternative Way Forward', *Journal of Medical Ethics*, 44(4), pp. 226–233. doi: 10.1136/medethics-2017-104414.

Szmukler, G. (2019) '"Capacity" "Best Interests", "Will and Preferences" and the UN Convention on the Rights of Persons with Disabilities', *World Psychiatry*, 18(1), pp. 34–41. doi: 10.1002/wps.20584.

United Nations Committee on the Rights of Persons with Disabilities (2014) *General Comment, No. 1: Article 12: Equal Recognition Before the Law*. New York: United Nations.

United Nations General Assembly (2006) *Convention on the Rights of Persons with Disabilities*. New York. United Nations General Assembly.

United Nations General Assembly (2018) *Interim Report of the Special Rapporteur on Torture and Other Cruel, Inhuman or Degrading Treatment or Punishment, 20 July*. New York: United Nations General Assembly.

United Nations Treaty Collection (2020) *Status of Treaties, Chapter IV Human Rights, Section 15 Convention on the Rights of Persons with Disabilities*. Available at: https://treaties.un.org/doc/Publication/MTDSG/Volume%20I/Chapter%20IV/IV-15.en.pdf. (Accessed 10 July 2020).

Winkler, P. et al. (2020) 'Adherence to the Convention on the Rights of People with Disabilities in Czech Psychiatric Hospitals: A Nationwide Evaluation Study', *Health and Human Rights*, 22(1), pp. 21–33.

World Health Organization (2005) *WHO Resource Book on Mental Health, Human Rights and Legislation*. Geneva: World Health Organization.

World Health Organization (2012) *WHO QualityRights Tool Kit to Assess and Improve Quality and Human Rights in Mental Health and Social Care Facilities*. Geneva: World Health Organization.

World Health Organization (2018) *Mental Health, Human Rights and Standards of Care: Assessment of the Quality of Institutional Care for Adults with Psychosocial and Intellectual Disabilities in the WHO European Region*. Copenhagen: World Health Organization.

World Health Organization (2019a) *Human Rights, WHO QualityRights Core Training - For All Services and All People, Course Guide*. Geneva: World Health Organization.

World Health Organization (2019b) *Mental Health, Disability and Human Rights, WHO QualityRights Core Training - For All Services and All People, Course Guide*. Geneva: World Health Organization.

World Health Organization (2019c) *Legal Capacity and the Right to Decide, WHO QualityRights Core Training - For All Services and All People, Course Guide*. Geneva: World Health Organization.

World Health Organization (2019d) *Recovery and the Right to Health, WHO QualityRights Core Training - For All Services and All People, Course Guide*. Geneva: World Health Organization.

World Health Organization (2019e) *Freedom from Coercion, Violence and Abuse, WHO QualityRights Core Training - For All Services and All People, Course Guide*. Geneva: World Health Organization.

World Health Organization (2019f) *Recovery Practices for Mental Health and Well-Being, WHO QualityRights Specialized Training, Course Guide*. Geneva: World Health Organization.

World Health Organization (2019g) *Strategies to End Seclusion and Restraint, WHO QualityRights Specialized Training, Course Guide*. Geneva: World Health Organization.

World Health Organization (2019h) *Supported Decision-Making and Advance Planning, WHO QualityRights Specialized Training, Course Guide*. Geneva: World Health Organization.

World Health Organization (2019i) *Peer Support Groups by and for People with Lived Experience, WHO QualityRights Guidance Module*. Geneva: World Health Organization.

World Health Organization (2019j) *One-to-One Peer Support by and for People with Lived Experience, WHO QualityRights Guidance Module*. Geneva: World Health Organization.

World Health Organization (2019k) *Advocacy for Mental Health, Disability and Human Rights, WHO QualityRights Guidance Module*. Geneva: World Health Organization.

World Health Organization (2019l) *Civil Society Organizations to Promote Human Rights in Mental Health and Related Areas, WHO QualityRights Guidance Module*. Geneva: World Health Organization.

World Health Organization (2019m) *Person-Centred Recovery Planning for Mental Health and Well-Being Self-Help Tool*. Geneva: World Health Organization.

World Health Organization (2021) *Mental Health Atlas 2020*. Geneva: World Health Organization.

PART 3
Specific groups

7
CHILDREN'S MENTAL HEALTH CARE
Decision-making and human rights

Camilla Parker

Introduction

Although human rights apply to everyone, whatever their age, there are significant differences in how they are interpreted and applied in relation to those who have not yet reached the age of 18 ('children'), as compared to those who have. Albeit entitled to enjoy the same rights as adults, children's rights can be restricted in circumstances and manner that would not be permitted once they have attained their 18th birthday, thereby reaching the age of majority. Whereas by affirming that they are 'fully-fledged rights holders' (Sutherland, 2016, 1), the adoption of the United Nations (UN) Convention on the Rights of the Child (CRC) might have settled the long-standing debates on whether children have rights (MacDonald, 2011 para. 1.36), it does not extend to recognising them as fully fledged decision-makers. Due to their minority status, key decisions may be made about them, not by them.

Being a minor is equated with dependency, thereby justifying differential treatment. This is made clear by the Preamble to the CRC which states that 'the child, by reason of his physical and mental immaturity, needs special safeguards and care'. The need for such special treatment is that 'because of their youth, inexperience and lack of political power, children are not well placed to protect their own interests, or to take care of themselves' (Sutherland, 2016, 21). However, the incentive to protect is not the only distinguishing feature of children's rights (States have obligations to protect adults as well). It is also the recognition that adults (usually parents) have responsibilities both for children's welfare and development and to protect them 'against the worst dangers which threaten as a result of their relative inexperience and incompletely developed understanding' (Feldman, 2002, 266).

Accordingly, two interrelated features of children's rights are that while affirming children as rights-holders (like adults), children are regarded as requiring special protection due to their minority status and that their parents (or others who have undertaken parental responsibilities) are recognised as having the primary role in providing such protection. What therefore distinguishes children's rights from those of adults is the tensions arising from the need to accommodate three key factors: (a) the State's protective role in relation to children (which exists because they are minors); (b) the responsibilities of parents for the upbringing of their child; and (c) the developing agency of the child (which should calibrate the extent of the protective powers of parents and the State).

This chapter explores how this interplay between State, parent and child is reflected in human rights standards and the extent to which this impacts upon decision-making in the context of children's mental health care, in particular their admission to hospital and treatment for mental disorder ('inpatient psychiatric care'). The first part considers provisions of the CRC and the Convention on the Rights of Persons with Disabilities (CRPD) relevant to the decision-making powers of the State, parent and child, highlighting the need for greater attention to be given to the developing agency of the child and the extent to which this determines the decision-maker (State, parent or child). The second part examines the differing interpretations on what constitutes a deprivation of liberty, in particular the relevance of consent to the child's care arrangements – comparing the UN human rights framework approach to that of the European Convention on Human Rights (ECHR). By way of illustration, both parts include examples of the development of the law relating to children's mental health care in the United Kingdom (UK) (specifically England and Wales, the jurisdictions in which the Mental Health Act (MHA) 1983 applies). Unless stated otherwise, the term 'national law' will refer to these two countries. It should also be noted that the term 'children' is used throughout the text (unless stated otherwise) to mean individuals aged under 18. This is to reflect the approach adopted by the CRC and other human rights standards. However, increasingly older children, especially those aged 16 and 17, are referred to in national law as 'young people'.

Although the discussion on human rights standards is not limited to these three treaties, particular attention is given to the CRC, the CRPD and the ECHR given their significant influence and relevance to children's mental health care. Both the CRC and CRPD cover a wide range of civil, political, economic, social and cultural rights. Both have reached near global recognition with the CRC having been ratified by all members of the UN except the USA (see: https://indicators.ohchr.org/). The CRC is focused on children, including children with disabilities (they are referred to specifically in Article 23). The CRPD applies to individuals of all ages who have long-term mental or intellectual impairments which 'in the interaction with various barriers may hinder their full and effective participation in society on an equal basis with others' (CRPD, Article 1). The ECHR, which applies to people of all ages, has been ratified by the 46 members of the Council of Europe and there are plans for the European Union to do so too (www.coe.int/en/web/human-rights-convention). As discussed in the second part, the European Court of Human Rights (ECtHR) has developed extensive jurisprudence on the interpretation of 'deprivation of liberty' under Article 5 of the ECHR.

Dynamics of decision-making in children's mental health care

Within the human rights framework, the State's protective function in relation to children is engaged via the principle of the best interests of the child. Article 3(1) of the CRC requires that in 'all actions concerning children…the best interests of the child shall be a primary consideration' and is regarded by the Committee on the Rights of the Child (CCRC) as one of the four general principles of the CRC 'for interpreting and implementing all the rights of the child' (CRC/GC/14 para. 1). This principle forms an integral feature of international human rights. It has been endorsed by the ECtHR (*Neulinger and Shuruk v Switzerland* (2010) para. 135). Moreover, whereas the CRPD Committee (CCRPD) regards the best interests principle as an aberration so far as adults are concerned (CRPD/C/GC/1 para. 21), it is enshrined in the CRPD for those yet to reach adulthood, with Article 7(2) stating that 'the best interests of the child shall be a primary consideration' in all actions concerning disabled children.

The discussion below further examines the CRC's interpretation of the principle of the best interests of the child and its relationship with Article 5 of the CRC which seeks to 'balance the rights of the child, the parents and the state' (Sutherland, 2020, 18). This is followed by consideration of how the approach adopted by the CCRPD in relation to two significant aspects of mental health care (non-consensual interventions and the importance of distinguishing between legal capacity and mental capacity) might relate to children. Finally, the relevance of a child's decision-making ability in national law is noted.

Best interests and the evolving capacities of the child under the CRC

While, as acknowledged by the CCRC, the concept of the best interests of the child is not new and is enshrined in 'many national and international laws' (CRC/GC/14 para. 2), its application as envisaged by the CCRC differs from the traditional notion of best interests that was dictated by an adult centric view of what was 'best' for the child.

The concept of best interests as crafted by the CRC is complex. It seeks to incorporate the decision-making role of parents without undermining children's rights. Article 5 provides the linchpin for this objective. It is through this right that the CRC gives explicit recognition to the inter-relationship between the protective role of the State, parental responsibilities and the developing agency of the child.

Described as 'a unique provision of international human rights law' (Lansdown, 2020, 36), Article 5 requires States to respect the role of parents (and others who have acquired parental responsibilities) in assisting children to exercise their CRC rights by providing 'appropriate direction and guidance'. However, such direction and guidance is to be 'in a manner consistent with the evolving capacities of the child' (a term which refers to 'processes of maturation and learning whereby children progressively acquire knowledge, competencies and understanding' which includes 'acquiring understanding about their rights and about how they can best be realized' (CRC/C/GC/7, para. 17)). Accordingly, the CRC creates a framework within which the dynamics between State, child and parent can operate, as the following points illustrate.

First, while States are required to ensure that children receive the care and protection that they need, they are also expected to do so in a manner which respects the 'primary responsibility' of parents for caring for children (Articles 3(2) and 18(1)). Parents' decisions also fall within the CRC in that they, like States, are expected to act in the best interests of their child (Article 18(1)).

Second, the views of the child are integral to determining a child's best interests. Such views are to be given 'due weight according to their age and maturity' in accordance with Article 12 of the CRC, which in turn engages consideration of the 'evolving capacities of the child' given that 'as the child matures, his or her views shall have increasing weight in the assessment of his or her best interests' (CRC/C/GC/14 paras 43–44). If the decision does not accord with the child's wishes 'the reason for that should be clearly stated' (CRC/C/GC/14 para. 19). In relation to parents, Article 5 expects their decision-making powers to be calibrated by the developing agency of the child (their actions to be 'in a manner consistent with the evolving capacities of the child', making adjustments which 'take account of a child's interests and wishes as well as the child's capacities for autonomous decision–making and comprehension of his or her best interests' (CRC/C/GC/7/Rev1 para. 17)). The CCRC observes:

> the more the child knows, has experienced and understands, the more the parent, legal guardian or other persons legally responsible for him or her have to transform direction and guidance into reminders and advice, and later to an exchange on an equal footing.
> *(CRC/C/GC/14, para. 44)*

Third, Article 5 of the CRC not only enshrines the notion that parental decision-making will diminish in line with the evolving capacities of their child, it also places an important limitation on parents' actions in that the respect owed to parents by States is in relation to parental direction and guidance that is 'appropriate'. This reaffirms that parents are to act in the best interests of the child. It also necessitates that parents act 'in a manner consistent with and in conformity with the rights embodied in the CRC' (Lansdown, 2020, 41). Moreover, there may be cases in which 'parental direction is so far outwith normal parameters that the State Party may treat it as inappropriate' (Sunderland, 2020, 30).

Accordingly, the decision-making framework envisaged by the CRC is that while States must respect the decision-making powers of parents, this is balanced against the requirement on States to protect children, which includes ensuring that parents' decisions do not undermine the rights of their child. It therefore makes clear that there are limits to both State and parental powers. However, no precise boundaries are drawn. This gives rise to two questions, the first of which is how a child's capacity for decision-making is to be assessed, an area long recognised as requiring further attention (Lansdown, 2005).

The second question is in what circumstances (if any) the child's wishes prevail, irrespective of the outcome of that decision (for example, where the child refuses life-saving treatment). While the CCRC considers that recognition should be given to the right of the child to give or refuse consent 'if able to demonstrate sufficient understanding' (CRC/C/GC/20 para. 39), it is not clear whether a refusal would be upheld, irrespective of the consequences. For example, in its General Comment on the best interests of the child, the CCRC states that there may be cases 'where "protection" factors affecting a child (e.g. which may imply limitation or restriction of rights) need to be assessed in relation to measures of "empowerment" (which implies full exercise of rights without restriction)'. In such cases the CCRC considers that 'the age and maturity of the child should guide the balancing of the elements', noting the assessment of maturity includes the child's 'physical, emotional, cognitive and social development' (CRC/GC/14 para. 83). Such comments return us to the first question of how to assess a child's decision-making abilities.

Non-consensual care, mental health and children's rights

Within the human rights framework, the State's protective role is not confined to those of minority status. As illustrated by the UN's *Principles for the Protection of Persons with Mental Illness and the Improvement of Mental Health Care* (1991) and decisions of ECtHR, such as *Herczegfalvy v Austria* (1993), the traditional human rights framework deemed non-consensual interventions to be justified if necessary to protect people on grounds of their mental disorder and/or mental incapacity. Today, however, the CRPD provides a strong platform for those dissenting from the notion that detention in hospital and treatment without consent on grounds of the person's mental disorder, or mental incapacity, sit comfortably (or at all) with respect for human rights. The CCRPD holds that compliance with the CRPD requires the abolition of laws that permit non-consensual interventions on the basis of a person's 'mental disorder' or 'mental incapacity' (CRPD/C/GC/1). However, it should be noted that not all UN bodies adopt this approach (see for example the Subcommittee on the prevention of torture (CAT/OP/27/2)), while (as discussed below) the ECHR specifically permits detention on grounds of 'unsound mind' ('mental disorder' in contemporary language).

It is noteworthy, however, that notwithstanding its prohibition of non-consensual interventions on grounds of the person's mental disorder or mental incapacity, the CCRPD raises no such objections to decisions being made on behalf of individuals on grounds of their minority status. The reason for this appears to lie with the CCRPD's interpretation of legal capacity (which it defines as 'ability to hold rights and duties (legal standing) and to exercise those rights and duties (legal agency)') as discussed in its General Comment 1 on States' obligations under Article 12 (Equal recognition before the law) (CRPD/C/GC/1). Although not stated explicitly, the CCRPD's view seems to be that all adults have legal capacity, but those aged under 18 do not. General Comment 1 states in paragraph 8 that Article 12 'affirms that all persons with disabilities have full legal capacity'. However, this affirmation is watered down in relation to children with disabilities. Paragraph 36, which focuses on children with disabilities, notes:

> While article 12 of the Convention protects equality before the law for all persons regardless of age, article 7 of the Convention recognizes the developing capacities of children and requires that 'in all actions concerning children with disabilities, the best interests of the child…be a primary consideration (para. 2) and that their views [be] given due weight in accordance with their age and maturity' (para. 3).
> *(CRPD/C/GC/1, para. 36)*

The paragraph then adds that to comply with Article 12, States 'must examine their laws to ensure that the will and preferences of children with disabilities are respected on an equal basis with other children'. For those aged under 18, what the CCRPD expects, therefore, is not full legal capacity but equal treatment, as compared to non-disabled children.

On one level, this approach is understandable given that the CRPD is focused on challenging the long-standing disability discrimination that is ingrained in many laws, policies and practice across the globe (CRPD/C/GC/1 para. 15). The CCRPD is therefore seeking to 'ensure that the right of persons with disabilities to legal capacity is not restricted on an unequal basis with others' (CRPD/C/GC/1 para. 7) and for children with disabilities this means that they are to be treated on an equal basis with non-disabled children. However, as Sandland observes, the CCRPD appears to do 'what it censures in others' by recognising 'disabled children *have* the right to equality before the law, but does not allow disabled children to *exercise* that right' (Sandland, 2017, 99).

The likely explanation for the CCRPD's approach is the principle of the best interests of the child, which as noted above (in contrast to adults) is enshrined in the CRPD (Article 7(2)) as well as the CRC (Article 3(1)). Indeed, the common interests of these two treaties are underlined by the CCRC and the CCRPD's joint statement:

> The Committees urge the States parties to apply the concept of the 'best interests of the child' contained in article 3 of the CRC and 7 of the CRPD to children with dis-

abilities with a careful consideration of their evolving capacities, their circumstances and in a manner that ensures children with disabilities are informed, consulted and have a say in every decision-making process related to their situation.

(Joint Statement, March 2022, para. 4)

The Committees' statement makes clear that while the views of those aged under 18 are to be taken into account (as required by Article 7(3) of the CRPD and Article 12 of the CRC), others can make decisions for them. The emphasis therefore is on the child's active participation. Important as this is, there is a marked silence as to the potential for a child's 'evolving capacities' to have attained a level at which the child becomes the arbiter of his or her best interests and therefore the decision-maker, not merely a participant in the decision-making process.

Identifying the decision-makers: legal capacity versus decisional capacity

In the CCRPD's General Comment 1, the CCRPD criticises States for their conflation of the concepts of 'legal capacity' (which as noted above, is concerned with having rights and being able to exercise them) and 'mental capacity' (referred to as 'the decision-making skills of a person'). The CCRPD view is that individuals are being discriminated against on grounds of their disability because through a finding of mental incapacity (where individuals are 'considered to have impaired decision-making skills, often because of a cognitive or psychosocial disability'), their legal capacity to make a particular decision is removed. This distinction between the differing elements of capacity provides an important insight into how (and why) children are treated differently from adults. This can be illustrated by considering an example of national law.

In England and Wales, by dint of having reached the age of majority, adults are deemed to have the legal capacity to make decisions about all aspects of care and treatment. Under the Mental Capacity Act (MCA) 2005 they are presumed to have the mental capacity to make such decisions (MCA 2005, s1). However, if they are found to lack such capacity (applying the statutory criteria (MCA 2005 s2 and s3)), decisions are made on their behalf, in their best interests as determined under the MCA 2005 (sections 4 and 5). Accordingly, under the MCA 2005, legal capacity and mental capacity go hand in hand – individuals who lack the mental capacity to make decisions for themselves will no longer have the legal capacity to make those decisions. In relation to adults, the MCA 2005 therefore falls foul of the CCRPD's criticism of conflating legal capacity with mental capacity. However, the relationship between legal capacity and mental capacity differs in respect of children.

The first difference concerns the presumption of legal capacity. As Lansdown notes, societies treat children differently from adults in that whereas adults are presumed to have autonomy (meaning the right to self-determination, such as the right to consent to, or refuse medical treatment), children are not (Lansdown, 2009, 21). In other words, they are presumed to lack legal capacity.

The second difference is the basis on which a child is determined to have the ability to make a particular decision (referred to as 'decisional capacity', to distinguish this question from the MCA 2005's concept of 'mental capacity'). Whereas adults are presumed to be able to decide for themselves, the starting point for children is usually that they are presumed to be *unable* to decide for themselves. Where the presumption lies (whether the law's starting point is that they do, or do not, have the ability to decide for themselves) and the test to be applied depends on the child's age. For children aged 16 and 17, the MCA 2005 applies so that, like adults, they are presumed to have the mental capacity to make the relevant decision unless they are shown to lack such capacity. In contrast, children aged under 16 are assumed to be unable to make decisions for themselves unless they are found to be '*Gillick* competent'. This term derives from the House of Lords' decision in *Gillick v West Norfolk & Wisbech Area Health Authority* ('*Gillick*') which established that a child 'of sufficient intelligence and understanding' could give valid consent to medical treatment. The concept of *Gillick* competence is used widely and understood to mean that the '*Gillick* child' can consent (albeit as noted below, not necessarily refuse) medical treatment and other interventions relevant to their care and treatment. However, as Daly observes, while this concept 'ostensibly' guides these decision-making processes, what it entails 'is little understood – it has proven notoriously hard to define' (Daly, 2020, 53).

The third difference concerns a child's right to make decisions for themselves (in CRPD-speak 'legal agency', being the aspect of legal capacity referring to the right to exercise rights). The fact that a child has the requisite decisional capacity (mental capacity for 16- and 17-year-olds, or *Gillick* competence for under 16s) does not always mean that they have the legal agency to decide for themselves. In other words, their views (the CRPD refers to 'will and preferences') may not determine the outcome. For example, the long-standing position in national law that those yet to reach the age of majority do not have the final say on their treatment decisions, was reaffirmed by the Court of Appeal in 2021. It held that the protective power under the inherent jurisdiction of the court means that the welfare of the child is the overriding principle so that whereas on reaching adulthood individuals have the right to refuse medical treatment 'before that age the court must act upon its objective assessment of the young person's best interests, even if this conflicts with sincere and considered views' (*E & F (Minors: Blood Transfusion)* (2021) para. 73).

Decisional capacity: a child's inpatient psychiatric care under national law

The matters discussed above are relevant when determining the legal authority for a child's inpatient psychiatric care under national law. Whereas the Mental Health Act (MHA) 1983 sets out the circumstances in which individuals can be detained in hospital and treated for mental disorder (broadly defined under section 1: 'disorder or disability of the mind or brain') without their consent, it should only be engaged as a last resort. For children, a key question will be whether they, or their parents, are able and willing to consent to the proposed inpatient psychiatric care. If they are, the child can be admitted and treated 'informally': in other words, without adherence to the statutory criteria and procedural safeguards of the MHA 1983.

Children with the requisite decisional capacity (mental capacity if 16 and over, *Gillick* competence if under 16) can consent or refuse their admission to hospital and treatment for mental disorder, irrespective of their parents' views (MHA 1983 s131, Code of Practice to the MHA 1983 para. 19.39). Accordingly, if the child refused admission, the MHA 1983 would be required to authorise the child's inpatient psychiatric care. In contrast, for children who lack the requisite decisional capacity, it may be possible for parents to give consent on their child's behalf (so obviating the need to apply the MHA 1983). However, whether a parent may do so depends on whether the child's hospitalisation gives rise to a deprivation of liberty. This is discussed below.

Determining a deprivation of liberty and the relevance of consent

The process for determining a deprivation of liberty is inextricably linked to the interpretation of the decision-making powers of the State, the child and the child's parent(s) and how they relate to one another. As discussed below, this is an area in which there are significant differences in approach as between UN human rights standards, the ECHR and national law.

The importance of the right to liberty

Our right to liberty and not to be arbitrarily deprived of our liberty, is a fundamental right enshrined in major human rights treaties such as the International Convention on Civil and Political Rights (ICCPR, Article 9), the CRC (Article 37), the CRPD (Article 14) and the ECHR (Article 5). It applies to everyone, of whatever age. Unlike the ICCPR, the CRC and the CRPD, Article 5 of the ECHR specifies the circumstances in which individuals may be deprived of their liberty. This includes 'the lawful detention of persons…of unsound mind' – or in more modern-day parlance: 'mental disorder'. It is therefore at loggerheads with the CCRPD's view that Article 14 of the CRPD establishes an 'absolute ban of deprivation of liberty on the basis of impairment' (which includes mental disorder) (CCRPD, 2015), albeit, as noted above, there is no consensus on this point.

A common feature of these human rights treaties is their requirement for strict procedural safeguards to be in place to ensure against arbitrary detention. In addition to requiring any deprivation of liberty to be lawful, the ICCPR, CRC and ECHR specify that anyone deprived of their liberty is entitled to challenge the lawfulness of their detention. These provisions are incorporated into the CRPD which also provides that people with disabilities who are deprived of their liberty 'are, on an equal basis with others, entitled to guarantees in accordance with human rights law' (Article 14(2)). The CRC includes the additional provision that a child's deprivation of liberty is 'only used as a measure of last resort and for the shortest period of time' (Article 37(b)).

Given that the procedural guarantees set out under international human rights standards are only triggered if the arrangements give rise to a deprivation of liberty, clarity on what constitutes a deprivation of liberty is essential if individuals' rights are to be protected. Although varying in approaches on how these are expressed, three core requirements for a deprivation of liberty to arise can be identified in human rights standards on the right to liberty. These are: the restrictions placed on the person having reached a certain level, the lack of consent to such restrictions and the direct, or indirect, responsibility of the State for the situation (see for example CCPR/C/GC/35 paras 5-8). However, as discussed below, there is a lack of consistency in how to determine whether these three requirements are met.

Deprivation of liberty and children's institutional care

The UN Global Study on Children Deprived of Liberty (the Global Study) notes that 'A person is deprived of personal liberty if he or she is confined to such a narrowly bounded location, which he or she cannot leave at will' (Nowak, 2019, 61). Drawing on ECtHR jurisprudence the study adds:

> Criteria which play a role in distinguishing whether a certain restriction of freedom of movement reaches the level of interfering also with the right to personal liberty include

the type and place where a person is held, the degree of supervision, the extent of isolation and the availability of contacts.

(Nowak, 61)

Across the UN bodies the consensus appears to be that a child's placement into institutional care will amount to a deprivation of liberty. This is the position adopted by the Human Rights Committee in its General Comment on deprivation of liberty under Article 9 of the ICCPR (CCPR/C/GC/35, para. 62), citing the UN Rules for the Protection of Juveniles Deprived of their Liberty (1990) and the CCRC's General Comment 10 (CRC/C/GC/10). The UN Rules define a deprivation of liberty as 'any form of detention or imprisonment or the placement of a person in a public or private custodial setting, from which this person is not permitted to leave at will, by order of any judicial, administrative or other public authority', thereby making clear the wide range of settings in which a deprivation of liberty might occur (para. 11(b)). The CCRC refers specifically to institutions when clarifying that children considered to be deprived of their liberty under the CRC include those 'placed in institutions for the purposes of care, protection or treatment, including mental health, educational, drug treatment, child protection or immigration institutions' (CCR/C/GC/10, para. 11). Hospitals providing mental health care for children ('psychiatric hospitals') are regarded as falling within the definition of an institution, as made clear by the Global Study's inclusion of such settings in its survey of institutions where children are deprived of their liberty. It observes that:

Most countries permit the commitment of children to psychiatric hospitals/wards or other mental health or social care facilities or regimes, without free and informed consent (understood and applied from a child-rights perspective).

(Nowak, 196)

Moreover, the Global Study holds that a child's placement 'in any form of institution' is regarded as constituting a deprivation of liberty, even if the placement has been made by the child's parents (Nowak, 68). Although not stated explicitly, this view would seem to be shared by the Human Rights Committee given that a footnote to its statement that a child's placement in an institution amounts to a deprivation of liberty contrasts this position with parents' 'normal supervision of children'. Noting that such supervision 'may involve a degree of control over movement, especially of younger children, that would be inappropriate for adults', the Human Rights Committee observes 'but that does not constitute a deprivation of liberty' and adds 'neither do the ordinary requirements of daily school attendance constitute a deprivation of liberty' (CCPR/C/GC/35, para. 62, footnote 176).

Whereas UN human rights standards equate a child's admission to a psychiatric hospital with a deprivation of liberty, to date, no such assumptions are made by either the ECtHR or national law. Both require a more detailed analysis of the specific circumstances of each case. This is explored further below.

Determining a deprivation of liberty under the ECHR

For over 40 years, the ECtHR's starting point when considering if a deprivation of liberty has arisen, is to consider the individual's 'concrete situation', namely to assess the specific restrictions placed on the person, taking into account 'a whole range of criteria such as the type, duration, effects and manner of implementation of the measure in question' (*Guzzardi v Italy* (1980) (*Guzzardi*) para. 92). Like the Human Rights Committee (CCPR/C/GC/35 paras 35 and 60), the ECtHR distinguishes between restriction of liberty (movement) and deprivation of liberty, but notes that the difference between the two 'is merely one of degree or intensity, and not one of nature or substance' (*Guzzardi*, para. 93). In doing so, the ECtHR acknowledges not only that determining whether curtailing an individual's freedoms amounts to a deprivation of liberty may not be easy, but also underlines that restrictions on a person's liberty can easily move into the territory of a deprivation of liberty.

Consideration of the person's specific circumstances continues to be the ECtHR's first step when seeking to determine whether a deprivation of liberty has arisen. However, since *Storck v Germany* (2005) (*Storck*), in which the German Government argued that there was no deprivation of liberty because the young adult had consented to her placement in a private psychiatric unit, the ECtHR now applies a three-pronged test, summarised as follows:

> (a) the objective component of confinement in a particular restricted place for a not negligible length of time: (b) the subjective component of lack of valid consent; and (c) the attribution of responsibility to the State.
>
> (P v Cheshire West and Chester Council; P and Q v Surrey County Council *(2014)* (*Cheshire West*)
> *para. 37)*

These '*Storck* components' articulate the three features of a deprivation of liberty, which as noted above, are common to human rights standards (the restrictions imposed, lack of consent and State responsibility). In *Storck*, having found that the restrictions placed on the applicant meant that she was 'objectively' deprived of her liberty, the ECtHR observed that this 'objective element' was not the only relevant criteria as there will be no deprivation of liberty unless 'as an additional subjective element' the person 'has not validly consented to the confinement in question' (*Storck*, para. 73).

Accordingly, if the person is considered to have been confined 'in a particular restricted place for a not negligible length of time' ('the confinement condition'), the 'subjective element' must then be addressed, which is whether valid consent has been given to the confinement ('the lack of valid consent condition'). The third condition is that the deprivation of liberty 'is imputable to the State' ('the State responsibility condition'), the threshold for which is low. It can be met either 'owing to the direct involvement of public authorities in the applicant's detention' or where the State has failed in some way to meet its positive obligation to protect the person's right to liberty against interferences with their liberty by other people (*Storck*, paras 74 and 79).

Whether, and if so how, the *Storck* tri-partite test applies to children has not yet been addressed by the ECtHR. Despite extensive jurisprudence concerning the circumstances in which an individual's care arrangements amount to a deprivation of liberty (see for example *Stanev v Bulgaria* (2012), *Shtukaturov v Russia* (2008)), no such case has come before the ECtHR in relation to under 18s since *Nielsen v Denmark* (1988) (*Nielsen*). In a highly controversial decision, as illustrated by the minority dissenting judgment and subsequent criticism from a long list of legal scholars (see for example Feldman, 2002, 459; Fortin, 2009, 68; and Kilkelly, 1999, 36–37), the ECtHR held that a 12-year-old boy's placement in a children's psychiatric hospital, by his mother and against his wishes, did not amount to a deprivation of liberty because it 'was a responsible exercise by his mother of her custodial rights in the interests of the child' (*Nielsen*, para. 73). An additional frustration is that the ECtHR's rationale for this decision is difficult to discern.

Today, the ECtHR would have plenty of justification for distancing itself from *Nielsen*, given that it was decided over 30 years ago (so very much at the formative stage of the ECtHR's approach to deprivation of liberty in health and social care settings and pre-dating the CRC). The relevance of this decision is questioned by the Global Study which asserts that contrary to *Nielsen*, 'it is today beyond doubt' that parental consent has no bearing 'in defining whether a child is deprived of liberty or not' as well as holding that the child's consent is also irrelevant (Nowak, 68). Nonetheless, for the reasons elaborated below, it is suggested that the ECtHR's future adjudication on the relevance of consent (whether by parent or child) to what constitutes a child's deprivation of liberty is not so easy to predict.

Determining a child's deprivation of liberty: a national approach

Within the UK, the Supreme Court confirmed that, like adults, in determining whether the care arrangements for children give rise to a deprivation of liberty, the tri-partite test set out by the ECtHR in *Storck* should be applied (*Re D (A Child) (2019) (Re D)*). Although all three *Storck* components must be present for a deprivation of liberty to arise for the purpose of Article 5 of the ECHR, the main areas of judicial debate have concerned the first two conditions in *Storck* (the confinement condition and the lack of valid consent condition), both of which engage questions about the decision-making role of parents. Both conditions were considered by the Supreme Court in *Re D* which concerned a young man ('D') who had various conditions, including autism and a mild learning disability and when aged 16 was placed in a residential unit by his local authority, with the agreement of his parents (Children Act 1989, s20). In the light of the majority decision in *Re D* (Lady Hale giving the leading judgment, with which Lady Black and Lady Arden agreed), the following observations can be made.

First, determining whether the confinement condition is met turns upon a comparison between the restrictions imposed on that child as part of the care arrangements and the restrictions that parents would reasonably be expected to apply to a child of the same age. Therefore the 'crux of the matter' is:

> Do the restrictions fall within normal parental control for a child of this age or do they not? If they do, they will not fall within the scope of article 5 [of the ECHR]; but if they go beyond normal parental control, article 5 will apply (subject to the question of whether parental consent negates limb (b) of the *Storck* criteria…).
>
> *(para. 39)*

Repeating the view expressed by the Supreme Court in an earlier case that the living arrangements of 'mentally disabled people' had to be compared with those placed on non-disabled people (*Cheshire West*, para. 41), Lady Hale stated:

> It follows that a mentally disabled child who is subject to a level of control beyond that which is normal for a child of his age has been confined within the meaning of article 5. Limb (a) of the three Storck criteria for a deprivation of liberty…has been met.
>
> *(para. 42)*

Accordingly, whereas for adults receiving care and support, the test (known as the 'acid test') for the confinement condition is whether they are 'under continuous supervision and control' and 'not free to leave' (*Cheshire West* para. 49), for children this is gauged by comparing the restrictions imposed on the child with those that would be expected for a child of the same age (without disabilities).

Second, in relation to whether parental consent has any bearing on whether the lack of valid consent condition is met, the Supreme Court moves national law closer to the UN position, albeit via a different and more circumscribed route. As noted above, the consensus amongst the UN human rights standards is that parents cannot consent to their child's placement in an institution (a term which includes a psychiatric hospital). Having found that D was confined (the *Storck* confinement condition being met), the question was whether D's parents could consent to the confinement on his behalf (D lacked the capacity to do so). The conclusion was that they could not because the ECtHR has not adopted 'a general principle of substituted consent' (in other words, the ECtHR does not recognise the power of one person to consent to another's confinement).

The difference between the UN and the UK Supreme Court is that whereas for the UN a child's admission to a psychiatric hospital is automatically a deprivation of liberty, for the Supreme Court, the question of a potential deprivation of liberty only arises if the restrictions placed on the child are considered to meet the *Storck* confinement condition. A second important difference is that the Supreme Court's ruling only relates to 16- and 17-year-olds. Under national law it is still possible for parents to consent to the confinement of a child aged under 16 where that child is not competent to decide for him or herself (*Re D (A Child) (Deprivation of Liberty)* (2015)).

Third, observations made by the justices of the Supreme Court highlight the continuing debate on the rationale for *Nielsen*. Lady Hale considered that *Nielsen* 'clearly turned on the comparative normality of the restrictions imposed upon the freedom of a 12-year-old boy' (*Re D*, para. 38). In holding that parents cannot consent to their 16- or 17-year-old child's confinement, Lady Hale rejected the interpretation of *Nielsen* as being one of substituted consent (whereby parental consent is given to the confinement on behalf of the child). In contrast, Lord Carnwath (giving the minority judgment in *Re D*) supports the view expressed by other senior members of the judiciary that *Nielsen* concerns the proper exercise of parental consent, noting that this 'seems to me the more natural interpretation' (para. 149).

As Lord Carnwath commented, it is 'a little artificial' to attempt to analyse the reasoning of *Nielsen* through the prism of *Storck*'s tri-partite test given that it pre-dates *Storck* (*Re D* para. 147). Nonetheless, the ECtHR's subsequent observations on its decision in *Nielsen* suggest that factors relevant to both the *Storck* confinement condition and *Storck* lack of consent condition were at play (albeit this leaves the question as to which (if either) was the deciding factor unresolved). For example, with a nod to the comparator approach to the confinement condition, the ECtHR has recently noted that there was no violation of Article 5 in *Nielsen* because conditions in the hospital were similar to those 'in many hospital wards where children with physical disorders are treated' (*Gard v UK* para. 99). In relation to the relevance of parental consent, in *Stanev v Bulgaria* (2012), the ECtHR referred to *Nielsen*, explaining that as the child applicant had been admitted to hospital by his mother 'in good faith' it had concluded that this 'entailed the exercise of exclusive custodial rights over a child who was not capable of expressing a valid opinion' (*Stanev*, para. 122). Such comments indicate that the ECtHR has not ruled out the possibility of parents consenting to their child's confinement.

Fourth, under national law there is a stark difference between children aged under 16 and those aged 16 and over, with that difference pertaining to the interpretation of the decision-making powers of parents. In practice, like adults, the placement of a child aged 16 and over will give rise to a deprivation of liberty unless that child is willing and able to consent to this. This is because the proposed inpatient psychiatric care is likely to meet the confinement condition (the restrictions on the child exceeding 'normal parental control'), for which there will be no consent if that 16- or 17-year-old either declines, or lacks the capacity, to give consent (the lack of consent condition will therefore be met) and the State responsibility condition will also be met (the admission will be to a hospital provided and/or funded by the National Health Service). In such cases, the procedural safeguards outlined by human rights standards, such as Article 5 of the ECHR must be engaged (usually this will be via detention under the MHA 1983, otherwise an application for a court order would be required).

In contrast, for children aged under 16, where parents have consented to their child's confinement, that child will not be considered to be deprived of their liberty (the lack of consent condition not being met) and therefore the guarantees set out under Article 5 of the ECHR are not engaged. Parental consent therefore negates what would otherwise be a deprivation of liberty. Although the courts have emphasised that parental consent is limited to where parents are acting in the proper exercise of their parental responsibilities (*Re D (A Child) (Deprivation of Liberty)* (2015)) how to determine whether parental consent to a child's confinement is within, or outwith, the scope of parental powers is not clear.

Determining a deprivation of liberty: relevance of consent under the ECHR

How the ECtHR might approach the question of consent (whether by the child or the parent) is debatable. As noted above, comments by the ECtHR on *Nielsen* suggest that the ECtHR has not ruled out the possibility of parents consenting to their child's confinement. However, if the ECtHR does adopt this approach, it is suggested that in the light of ECHR jurisprudence and the development of international human rights (the introduction of the CRC and the CRPD) since *Nielsen*, the ECtHR will give careful scrutiny to the circumstances of the case, in particular, the views of the child. Reasons for this suggestion are as follows.

First, as Lady Hale noted in *Re D* (para. 42), the cases in which the ECtHR has found that the consent of a third party (the adult's legal guardian) means that the person confined is not deprived of their liberty are where 'evidence showed that the person concerned was willing to stay where he or she was and was capable of expressing a view'. As argued elsewhere, an analysis of these cases (see for example *Shtukaturov v Russia* (2008)) shows that where the person confined has indicated an objection to the placement, for example expressing a desire to leave, or trying to escape, the ECtHR has concluded that there was no valid consent and a deprivation of liberty had arisen (Parker 2021). The importance of focusing on the views of the child is underscored by both Article 12 of the CRC and Article 12 of the CRPD. Moreover, Article 12 of the CRC and Article 7 of the CRPD establish that children have the right to express their views freely on all matters affecting them, with their views being 'given due weight' in accordance with their age and maturity.

Second, as the ECtHR affirmed in *Nielsen* (para. 72), there are limits to the decision-making powers of parents. In this regard particular attention should be given to Article 5 of the CRC. As noted above, while it requires States to respect the rights and responsibilities of parents to direct and guide the child in exercising rights, the decision-making powers of parents are calibrated by the evolving capacities of the child. The CCRC expects parents 'to take into account the child's views, in accordance with their age and maturity' and 'to continually adjust the levels of support and guidance they offer to a child', such adjustments taking into account the 'child's interests and wishes as well as the child's capacities for autonomous decision-making and comprehension of his or her best interests' (CRC/C/GC/7/Rev1, paras 3 and 17). Moreover, as Sutherland observes, Article 5 is an acknowledgement of the important role of parents in their child's life, not an acceptance of 'unfettered parental authority': it is for the State to decide whether the guidance and direction is appropriate and 'in a manner consistent with the evolving capacities of the child' (Sutherland, 2020, 28).

Another unresolved issue in relation to deprivation of liberty under the ECHR is whether children can consent to their confinement. It has been stated that the ECtHR assumes that children lack the capacity to consent, or object to, their placement (Liefaard, 2019, 327). This view seems to be based on the ECtHR's observation in *Storck* that the applicant is 'considered to have the capacity to consent or object to her admission and treatment in hospital' given that at the time of her admission she had 'attained the age of majority' (*Storck*, para. 75). Given that the case concerned a young adult, it is suggested that the ECtHR was simply reaffirming the presumption of capacity for adults. As her complaint related to her time in hospital when she was an adult, the applicant was assumed to have capacity to decide whether she wished to receive inpatient care. Certainly, in England and Wales the courts are of the view that it is possible for children to consent to their confinement where they have the decisional capacity to do so (*A Local Authority v D* (2016)). In such cases, however, it will important to be alive to factors that adversely affect the validity of the child's consent, for example, if the child feels under pressure to agree to the arrangements giving rise to the confinement (*Re T (A Child)* (2021), para. 161).

Whatever stance the ECtHR takes with regard to the relevance of the child's consent to determining a deprivation of liberty, what is clear is that the child's compliance would not be enough (*HL v United Kingdom* (2004)).

Conclusion

This chapter started with the observation that the source of the difference between children's rights and those of adults is the interplay between the protective role of the State, the responsibilities of parents for the upbringing of their child and the growing agency of the child. The above analysis has shown the importance of this triangular relationship within human rights standards, particularly within the CRC which includes an express recognition of the dynamics between the decision-making powers of the parents and State and the evolving capacities of the child (Article 5). However, how this relationship between State, parent and child is expected to operate in practice is less clear.

The first part of this chapter highlighted two unresolved issues. First, a long-standing question is how to determine whether a child's evolving capacities have developed to the point where that child is able to make the particular decision for him or herself ('decisional capacity'). Current human rights standards provide little guidance for States on how to determine when this point has been reached (referring to broad concepts such the maturity of the child). Second, there is a lack of clarity on whether (and if so, in what circumstances) the child's attainment of decisional capacity means that they are regarded as the decision-maker so that the child's decision is upheld, notwithstanding the views of the parents or the State. Although both the CRC and the CRPD emphasise the importance of the child's wishes (in CRPD terminology 'will and preferences'), the circumstances in which the child's wishes will determine the outcome of the particular decision are not spelt out. Such matters are pertinent to deliberations on what circumstances the provision of non-consensual psychiatric care to a child might be justified (as noted, the CCRPD holds that the grounds of mental disorder or mental incapacity are insufficient justification).

The second part examined what constitutes a child's deprivation of liberty within human rights standards, a question of crucial importance given that a finding of a deprivation of liberty engages significant safeguards. In this regard, there is a striking difference between the human rights standards of the UN and the approach adopted in England and Wales (as noted above, the ECHR position is uncertain given that the ECtHR has not adjudicated on such matters since the 1988 decision of *Nielsen*). Whereas under the UN human rights framework, a child's admission to a psychiatric hospital equates to a deprivation of liberty (thereby engaging right to liberty safeguards) irrespective of consent (whether given by the child or a parent), under national law the presence of consent can negate a finding of a deprivation of liberty.

The most controversial and uncertain area is the national courts' current position that (whereas not possible for those aged 16 and over) parents can consent to the confinement of children aged under 16. Controversial, because this means that this age group is excluded from the protections afforded to older children and adults. Uncertain, given the absence of criteria for how to balance the decision-making powers of parents against the protective function of the State and the agency of the child. Children aged under 16 are deemed to lack decisional capacity unless they demonstrate that they are *Gillick* competent (but there is no consistent guidance on what is required of the child). How to determine whether giving consent to their child's confinement falls within parents' decision-making powers (or exceeds this, so the State must intervene), is similarly lacking in adequate guidance.

To date there has been little attention given to the dynamics of decision-making powers as between the State, parents and the child. A better understanding of the tensions they create and how they might be resolved is essential if we are to ensure the protection and promotion of the rights of children in need of mental health care.

References

Daly, A. (2020) 'Assessing Children's Capacity – Reconceptualising Our Understanding through the UN Convention on the Rights of the Child'. In: Sutherland, E. and Barnes Macfarlene, L.-A., (eds), *Implementing Article 3 of the United Nations Convention on the Rights of the Child, Best Interests, Welfare and Well-Being*, Cambridge, Cambridge University Press, pp. 52–79.

Feldman, D. (2002) *Civil Liberties and Human Rights in England and Wales* (2nd edn), Oxford, Oxford University Press.

Fortin, J. (2009) *Children's Rights and the Developing Law* (3rd edn), Cambridge, Cambridge University Press, 2009).

Kilkelly, U. (1999) *The Child and the European Convention on Human Rights*, London and New York, Routledge.

Lansdown, G. (2005) *The Evolving Capacities of the Child*, Florence, UNICEF Innocenti Research Centre.

Lansdown, G. (2009) *See Me, Hear Me: A Guide to Using the UN Convention in the Rights of Persons with Disabilities to Promote the Rights of Children*, London, Save the Children.

Lansdown, G. (2020) 'The Scope and Limitations of the Concept of Evolving Capacities within the CRC'. In: Sutherland, E. and Barnes Macfarlene, L.-A., (eds), *Implementing Article 3 of the United Nations Convention on the Rights of the Child, Best Interests, Welfare and Well-Being*, Cambridge, Cambridge University Press, pp. 36–51.

Liefaard, T. (2019) 'Deprivation of Liberty of Children'. In: Kilkelly, U. and Liefaard, T., (eds), *International Human Rights of Children*, Singapore, Springer. doi: 10.1007/978-981-10-3182-3.
MacDonald, A. (2011) *The Rights of the Child Law and Practice*, Bristol, Family Law (Jordon Publishing Ltd).
Nowak, M. (2019) *United Nations Global Study on Children Deprived of Liberty*, Geneva, United Nations. https://childrendeprivedofliberty.info/wp-content/uploads/2020/09/Full-Global-Study_Revised-Version.pdf
Parker, C. (2021) 'Deprivation of Liberty, Parental Consent and the Rights of the Child'. In: Clough, B. and Herring, J., (eds), *Disability, Care and Family Law*, London and New York, Routledge, pp. 99–119.
Sandland, R. (2017) 'A Clash of Conventions? Participation, Power an the Rights of Disabled Children'. *Social Inclusion*, 5(3), pp. 93–103. doi: 10.17645/si.v5i3.955.
Sutherland, E. (2016) 'Introduction'. In: Sutherland, E. and Barnes Macfarlene, L.-A., (eds), *Implementing Article 3 of the United Nations Convention on the Rights of the Child, Best Interests, Welfare and Well-Being*, Cambridge, Cambridge University Press, pp. 1–17.
Sutherland, E. (2020) 'The Enigma of Article 5 of the United Nations Convention on the Rights of the Child Central or Peripheral?' In: Sloan, B. and Fenton-Glynn, C., (eds), *Parental Guidance, State Responsibility and Evolving Capacities Article 5 of the United Nations Convention on the Rights of the Child*, Leiden, The Netherlands, Brill Nijhoff, pp. 13–35.

Cases

A Local Authority v D [2016] EWHC 3473 (Fam)
E & F (Minors: Blood Transfusion) [2021] EWCA Civ 1888
Gard and Others v UK, App No 39793/17 (2017)
Gillick v West Norfolk & Wisbech Area Health Authority [1986] AC 112
Guzzardi v. Italy, App No 7367/76 (1980)
Herczegfalvy v Austria, App No 10533/83 (1993)
HL v United Kingdom, App No 45508/99 (2004)
Neulinger and Shuruk v Switzerland, App No 41615/07 (2010)
Nielsen v Denmark, App No 10929/84 (1988)
P v Cheshire West and Chester Council; P and Q v Surrey County Council [2014] UKSC 19
Re D (A Child) [2019] UKSC 42
Re D (A Child) (Deprivation of Liberty) [2015] EWHC 922 (Fam)
Re T (A Child) [2021] UKSC 35
Shtukaturov v Russia, App No 44009/05 (2008)
Stanev v Bulgaria, App No 36760/06 (2012)
Storck v Germany, No 61603/00 (2005)

Legislation

Children Act 1989
Mental Health Act 1983 (MHA 1983)
Mental Capacity Act 2005 (MCA 2005)

International human rights publications

CRC/C/GC/7/Rev 1, Committee on the Rights of the Child, General Comment No. 7 (2005) *Implementing child rights in early childhood*
CRC/C/GC/10, Committee on the Rights of the Child, General Comment No. 10 (2007) *Children's rights in juvenile justice*
CRC/GC/14, Committee on the Rights of the Child, General Comment No. 14 (2013) *on the right of the child to have his or her best interests taken as a primary consideration*
CRC/C/GC/20, Committee on the Rights of the Child, General Comment No. 20 (2016) *on the implementation of the rights of the child during adolescence*

CCPR/C/GC/35, Human Rights Committee of the UN International Covenant on Civil and Political Rights, General Comment No 35 (2014): *Article 9 (Liberty and security of person)*
CCRPD 2015, Committee on the Rights of Persons with Disabilities *Guidelines on article 14 of the Convention on the Rights of Persons with Disabilities – the right to liberty and security of persons with disabilities* (2015)
CRPD/C/GC/1, Committee on the Rights of Persons with Disabilities, General Comment No. 1 (2014) *Article 12; Equal recognition before the law*
Joint Statement, The rights of children with disabilities, Committee on the Rights of the Child and Committee on the Rights of Children with Disabilities, March 2022
Subcommittee on the prevention of torture (CAT/OP/27/2) *Subcommittee on Prevention of Torture and Other Cruel, Inhuman or Degrading Treatment or Punishment, Approach of the Subcommittee on Prevention of Torture and Other Cruel, Inhuman or Degrading Treatment or Punishment regarding the rights of persons institutionalized and treated medically without informed consent* (2016)
United Nations, *Principles for the Protection of Persons with Mental Illness and the Improvement of Mental Health Care* (General Assembly resolution 46/119 of 17 December 1991)
United Nations, Rules for the Protection of Juveniles Deprived of their Liberty, 1990 (adopted by the UN General Assembly on 14 December 1990 (Resolution 45/113)

8
PEOPLE WITH LEARNING DISABILITY
Scotland and beyond

Jill Stavert

Introduction

In Scotland 'learning disability' currently falls within the statutory definition of 'mental disorder' used by both the Adults with Incapacity (Scotland) Act 2000 (AWIA) (AWIA.1(6)) and Mental Health (Care and Treatment) (Scotland) Act 2003 (MHA) (MHA.359) along with mental illness and personality disorder. This raises two issues. Firstly, it raises the wider Convention on the Rights of Persons with Disabilities (CRPD)-related issue, associated also more generally with persons with psychosocial and cognitive disabilities, of the legitimacy of non-consensual interventions based on diagnosis (Committee on the Rights of Persons with Disabilities 2014, 2015). Secondly, in relation to mental health legislation which authorises and regulates non-consensual psychiatric treatment, it also begs the question, one which has been discussed for the best part of the last three decades in Scotland, of whether learning disability, which is not of itself a condition capable of cure or management through medical treatment, ought to fall within the remit of mental health legislation. Since 2018 these questions have been central to two Scottish legislative reviews.

Invoking a social and human rights model of disability Article 5 CRPD makes it clear that persons with disabilities are entitled to enjoy life, with the underpinning rights, on an equal basis with others. Article 1 CRPD states that 'Persons with disabilities include those who have long-term physical, mental, intellectual or sensory impairments which in interaction with various barriers may hinder their full and effective participation in society on an equal basis with others', therefore encompassing persons with a diagnosis of 'learning disability'[1] and highlighting that such diagnosis and related impairments must not stand in the way of equal life and rights enjoyment (Committee on the Rights of Persons with Disabilities 2014, 2018).

The CRPD approach requires a reconceptualising of approaches in law, policy and practice, and supporting human rights and notions of equality and non-discrimination (Committee on the Rights of Persons with Disabilities 2014, 2018; Clough 2018; Stavert 2018). The pre-CRPD, or alternative to CRPD, approach accepts that the rights of persons with learning disabilities may be restricted on the basis of impairments related to the diagnosis. Whilst the safeguard exists that such restriction must be objectively and reasonably justified it is otherwise acceptable if the same restrictions apply to other persons with disabilities (Nilsson 2014; Human Rights Committee 2002, 2004; Committee on Economic Social and Cultural Rights 2009). The CRPD, on the other hand, requires that such impairments are not used to justify rights restrictions but are instead overcome with support, such as support for the exercise of legal capacity (supported decision-making), universal design and reasonable accommodation. This allows for enjoyment of the whole range of rights – civil, political, economic, social and cultural – on an equal basis with others.

This chapter will consider the existing mental health and capacity law and human rights frameworks impacting on the rights of persons with learning disabilities in Scotland and their ability to achieve rights equality and provide for the needs of persons with learning disabilities. It will also look at CRPD requirements and how these are being, or may be, implemented in order to achieve this for persons with learning disabilities. Such law has been recently reviewed again given human rights developments. In doing so, whilst some of its observations will apply to Scotland only, many will also have implications for other jurisdictions which are attempting to locate support for persons with learning disabilities within legal frameworks which fully respects their equal enjoyment of rights.

Scotland and persons with learning disabilities: the human rights framework

The international human rights treaties which are most likely to impact on Scotland's mental health and capacity law and how it operates in relation to persons with learning disabilities are the European Convention on Human Rights (ECHR) and the CRPD. At present the ECHR has greater leverage in terms of enforceable rights. The UK-wide Human Rights Act 1998 (Human Rights Act 1998. 2, 3, 6) and the Scotland Act 1998 (Scotland Act 1998. 29(2)(d), 57(2)) allows individuals to enforce their rights through the national courts or tribunals, public bodies (including the courts and tribunals) must act in accordance with individuals' ECHR rights, courts and tribunals must interpret the law in accordance with European Court of Human Rights jurisprudence and provisions in devolved Scottish legislation (which includes mental health and capacity legislation) that are incompatible with ECHR rights are invalid and unenforceable.

ECHR rights are, however, predominantly civil and political rights. Whilst they may protect persons with learning disabilities from unwarranted and excessive intrusions on their autonomy they are of limited value when it comes to actively seeking services and support. The CRPD, on the other hand, identifies the full range of civil, political, social, economic and cultural rights and directs how they must apply in relation to persons with disabilities. This not only provides safeguards against unwarranted intrusions of individual autonomy, it also identifies those rights that underpin accessing support and services to enable persons with disabilities to have the opportunity to better engage in society and enjoy rights on an equal basis with others. As already mentioned, diagnosis and related impairments must not be permitted to prevent equal life and rights enjoyment and the CRPD makes it clear that challenges that persons with disabilities may experience when it comes to enjoying rights on an equality basis with others should be overcome with support.

At present, CRPD rights are not incorporated into the UK or Scottish legal framework as ECHR rights are but the Scottish Government, following recommendations from its National Taskforce on Human Rights Leadership March 2021 report (Scottish Government, 2021), has stated that it will incorporate the CRPD, along with other international human rights treaties, into national law. The details of how, and the extent to which, this will actually be achieved are not clear at present but it does reflect what appears to be an increasing commitment to realise CRPD rights in Scotland. This followed earlier indications in its CRPD Delivery Plan 2016 (Scottish Government 2016) and urging from the Scottish Parliament that the Scottish Government does commit to CRPD implementation (Scottish Parliament 2016), a recent Scottish Government review of the AWIA and requirement to reflect the CRPD in the AWIA in Scotland's previous Mental Health Strategy 2017–2027(Scottish Government 2017) and the Independent Review of Learning Disability and Autism in the Mental Health Act (Rome Review) (Rome Review 2019).

CRPD compliance was also central to the terms of reference of the 2019–2022independent Scottish Mental Health Law Review (Scott Review) which was established by the Scottish Government (Scottish Government 2019) and absorbed the work of the Rome Review.

Meanwhile, therefore, the CRPD remains persuasive even if its rights are not yet legally enforceable. There is evidence of the public, private and voluntary sectors endeavouring to adhere to aspects of the CRPD within the existing legal framework, particularly in relation to the Article 12 CRPD (equal recognition before the law) requirements relating to support for the exercise of legal capacity, examples being Mental Welfare Commission for Scotland guidance on supported decision-making (Mental Welfare Commission for Scotland 2016) and sheriff court AWIA directions (Sheriffdom of Lothian and Borders 2016). Significantly, the importance of the CRPD has also been embraced by various learning disability representative organisations in Scotland (People First (Scotland) 2017; Scottish Commission for People with Learning Disabilities 2020).

Scotland and persons with learning disabilities: the legal framework

Scotland, as a devolved region of the UK, has legislative competence in relation to mental health and capacity law and at the time of its enactment such legislation was internationally regarded as representing good practice in terms of its human rights-based and person-centred approach.

As stated above, persons with learning disabilities currently fall within the definition of 'mental disorder' in the MHA and AWIA. At this juncture it is worth noting that the term 'mental disorder' does now carry certain stigmatising connotations and this was revisited by the Scott Review (Scott Review 2022).

The MHA's primary function is to authorise and regulate under civil law the non-consensual care and treatment for persons with mental disorder who are assessed as having significantly impaired decision-making ability as a result of their mental disorder. The MHA applies to children and adults and, in particular, it permits:

1. A medical practitioner to authorise emergency detention in hospital for up to 72 hours to determine what medical treatment is required (MHA, 36). The criteria for this are that if the person is not detained in hospital there would be a significant risk to their health, safety or welfare or another person's safety and that short-term detention would invoke an undesirable delay (MHA, 36(5)).
2. An approved medical practitioner (being a medical practitioner with special experience in the diagnosis and treatment of mental disorder) to authorise short-term detention for up to 28 days (MHA, 44). The criteria for this are that the person has a mental disorder, that their ability to make decisions about the provision of medical treatment

is significantly impaired because of the mental disorder, that it is necessary to detain the person in hospital to determine what medical treatment should be given to them or to give them medical treatment, and that absent of such detention there would be a significant risk to the person or the safety of any other person (MHA, 44(4)).
3. A mental health officer (a social worker with specific qualifications in mental health) to apply to the Mental Health Tribunal for Scotland for a Compulsory Treatment Order (MHA, 63). The criteria here are that the person has a mental disorder and that medical treatment is available which would be likely to prevent the mental disorder worsening or alleviate its symptoms or effects, that if the medical treatment is not provided there would be a significant risk to the person's health, safety or welfare of the patient or to another person's safety, that the person's ability to make decisions about the provision of such medical treatment is significantly impaired because of the mental disorder, and that compulsory treatment is necessary (MHA, 64(5)).

The AWIA authorises interventions relating to the physical and mental health, welfare, financial and property matters of a person aged 16 years and older where they are deemed to lack capacity or, as the Act states, an 'incapable adult' (AWIA, 1(6)). It notably allows for 'medical treatment' to be authorised by doctors, dentists, opticians and registered nurses (AWIA, 47) and for the sheriff court to grant one-off intervention orders and guardianship orders for incapable adults (AWIA, 53, 57). It also regulates the making and operation of welfare and financial powers of attorney (AWIA, 15, 16). Both types of powers of attorney may be granted by the adult when they have capacity and welfare powers of attorney come into effect when the adult loses capacity whilst financial (or continuing) powers of attorney may, at the adult's discretion, come into effect either upon or prior to their losing capacity to manage their financial and property affairs.

Both Acts are underpinned by similar human rights-based principles which must be followed when deciding and carrying out interventions under the Acts (AWIA, 1; MHA, 1, 2). These principles were mainly informed by the ECHR and seek to preserve individual autonomy requiring account to be taken of the individual's wishes and feelings and views of named persons, carers, guardians and welfare attorneys and adopting the least restrictive alternative. A further principle is that any intervention must only be authorised under the legislation where it will provide a benefit which is not otherwise available (AWIA, 1(2); MHA, 1(3)(f)).

The MHA, apart from having additional requirements related to psychiatric compulsion such as necessity and significant risk to the person or others (MHA, 36, 44, 64), also stresses the importance of patient participation including provision of appropriate information and support to enable this to be effective (MHA, 1(3)(c) and (d)) as well as non-discrimination (MHA, 1(3)(g)) and taking the patient's background and characteristics into consideration (MHA, 1(3)(h)). It also identifies specific forms of support for the exercise of legal capacity to ensure that the person's wishes and feelings can be made known, such as psychiatric advance statements, named persons and independent advocacy.

The AWIA similarly requires those exercising functions under the Act to encourage the adult to exercise whatever skills they may have concerning their property, financial affairs and personal welfare (Adults with Incapacity (Scotland) Act. 1(5)). However, apart from a reference to independent advocacy in applications to the sheriff court (Adults with Incapacity (Scotland) Act, 3(5A)), it does not actively identify forms of support for exercising legal capacity.

All of this falls short of the requirements of the CRPD oversight body, the Committee on the Rights of Persons with Disabilities (UN Committee on the Rights of Persons with Disabilities 2014). In interpreting Article 12 CRPD, the committee directs that support for the exercise of legal capacity must transcend capacity and diagnosis so that the person's own will and preferences are heard on an equal basis with others. Its concern is that mental capacity (decision-making) assessments and diagnoses may be accompanied by biases and misconceptions about a disabled person's capabilities and ability to make valid decisions. Access to support for the exercise of legal capacity must not therefore be dependent upon the presence of mental disorder or diagnosis. However, the MHA links the making and coming into effect of psychiatric advance statements with capacity assessments and the duty on health boards and local authorities to provide independent advocacy with the existence of 'mental disorder' (MHA, 275–276C, 259–259A). Named persons are also at liberty to put forward their own views as opposed to those of the patient. Moreover, and importantly, the MHA and AWIA principles are non-hierarchical and the principle requiring the person's wishes and feelings to be taken into account must compete with the other principles, thus not necessarily allowing for prominence to be given to the person's views (Stavert 2015, 2021).

Developing mental health and capacity law in Scotland: the actual and the aspired

The Mental Health (Care and Treatment) (Scotland) Act 2003

The Millan Committee, whose 2001 Report and recommendations (Scottish Executive 2001) are largely reflected in the MHA, considered the issue of whether there should continue to be provision for learning disability within mental health law. It ultimately concluded that there should be an expert review on this and, in the meantime, learning disability would continue to be provided for under mental health legislation. This was reiterated in the 2009 McManus Review report (in relation to limited aspects of the MHA) (Scottish Government 2009) and, at the time of enactment of the Mental Health (Scotland) Act 2015 (which made some amendments to the MHA) the Scottish Government repeated its earlier promise to take this forward which was fulfilled by its establishing the Rome Review in 2018.

The Rome Review's remit was broadly to consider the operation of the MHA and whether people with autism and learning disability are well served by it. After wide consultation and seeking of evidence and expert advice in which persons with lived experience were actively involved, the Rome Review concluded that a number of human rights issues were present in relation to people with learning disability and their care and treatment under the MHA. These included questions about proportionality and necessity in relation to respect for the right to liberty in that persons with learning disability are more likely to be detained under the MHA for twice as long as others (Rome Review 2019; Welsh and Morrison 2017). This has a corresponding impact on other aspects of the autonomy of persons with learning disability relating to their compulsory care and treatment in hospital, and also on community Compulsory Treatment Orders (Rome Review 2019; Welsh and Morrison 2017) with similar findings relating to offenders with learning disability. It noted that this loss of liberty and autonomy inevitably leads to a loss of independence. Questions relating to autonomy, dignity and personal and mental integrity also arose in that persons with learning disabilities were often compelled to be in inadequate environments (Rome Review 2019; Mental Welfare Commission for Scotland 2016; Scottish Government 2018) and that there was evidence that antipsychotic medications were being used to manage 'problem' behaviours and prescribed for adults with learning disabilities at much higher rates than for people with psychosis (Rome Review 2019; Scottish Learning Disability Observatory Newsletter 2017). The Scott Review also received evidence relating to a lack of available advocacy for persons with learning disability, domination of the medical model of disability, inpatient wards not being adapted to the needs of persons with learning disability and, more generally, a failure of the current legislation to cater for long-term conditions such as learning disability (Scott Review 2022).

More widely, and beyond the remit of the MHA as it currently stands, the Rome Review noted health inequalities relevant to respect for the right to the highest attainable standard of physical and mental health in terms of the physical and mental health profile of persons with learning disability differing from that of the general population and access to health services being more limited than for others (Rome Review 2019; Cooper et al. 2015; Truesdale and Brown 2017). Issues around the right to respect for private and family life (Article 8 ECHR) and independent living (Article 19 CRPD) also arose as a result of the long-term removal from family and community and long-term denial of independent living (Rome Review 2019; MacDonald 2018) as well as inequality in terms of the right to life with lower life expectancy for persons with learning disabilities (Rome Review 2019; O'Leary et al. 2017) and challenges regarding access to civil and criminal justice, housing and education.

Acknowledging the limited applicability of ECHR rights in meeting the wider needs of persons with learning disability, the Rome Review took the stance that the CRPD should be used to enhance and broaden the rights identified in the ECHR (Rome Review 2019). Whilst this has been suggested previously as a possibility within the existing legal framework (Stavert 2018) the Scottish Government's commitment to giving legal effect to the CRPD adds real weight to this.

The review therefore made a number of recommendations adopting the CRPD description of disability and interpretation of discrimination. These included (a) that learning disability and autism are removed from the definition of mental disorder in the MHA; (b) working towards removing discrimination on the basis of disability in the law in relation to detention and compulsory treatment; (c) supporting access to positive rights (which includes the right to independent living); (d) ensuring equity, non-discrimination and fairness in decisions about support, care, treatment and detention for people with learning disability and autism who need support, including in the criminal justice system; (d) a human rights assessment framework to inform all decision-making; (e) duties on public authorities to provide a range of services, environments and professionals to meet the needs of persons with learning disability and autistic persons; (f) a rebuttable presumption in favour of the individual's will and preferences; and (g) an opt-out right to independent advocacy.

The Adults with Incapacity (Scotland) Act 2000

In terms of guardianship orders authorised under the AWIA, the most common primary diagnosis for new orders and renewals is learning disability, 47% of all applications according to the Mental Welfare Commission for Scotland's most recent monitoring report (Mental Welfare Commission 2021). Indefinite guardianship orders are decreasing. However, notwithstanding this, the restrictions on liberty and other aspects of autonomy associated with guardianship arrangements, the extent to which these are necessary and lack of identified support in the Act for ensuring that the person's voice is actually heard are of concern and raise issues relating to Articles 5 and 8 ECHR and Articles 12, 14 and 19 CRPD (McKay and Stavert 2017).

The coronavirus pandemic and persons with learning disabilities

Whilst the MHA and AWIA are currently somewhat lacking in terms of achieving rights equality and meeting the needs of persons with learning disability, this rights inequality was brought into sharp relief by the Covid-19 pandemic.

Scottish Covid-19 measures designed to relieve pressure on health and social care services simply exacerbated existing inequities relating to persons with disabilities including those with learning disability. With the exception of a reduction of some legal formalities in relation to the appointment of Named Persons, emergency measures relating to the MHA (Coronavirus Act 2020) did not come into force as they were deemed unnecessary. However, patients who were subject to applications to the telephone hearings adopted by the Mental Health Tribunal and adults subject to the 'stop the clock' measures relating to renewal of guardianship orders or 'section 47' certificates authorising medical treatment under the AWIA included those with learning disability, and questions of proportionality of restrictions arose in connection with this.

In terms of the wider rights enjoyment of persons with learning disabilities, notably the right to life and to health, it has already been noted that persons with learning disability experience significantly worse health outcomes and excess mortality in comparison with the general population. Certainly during the first wave of the pandemic in Scotland such inequalities were also reflected in the higher Covid infection rates, more severe outcomes and increased mortality (Scottish Learning Disabilities Observatory).

What was also worrying was the early guidance issued by the Scottish Government to support clinicians and other professionals in their response to the pandemic. Whilst it was not directed specifically at persons with mental disabilities, including learning disability, it did place persons with learning disabilities at particular risk of discrimination in terms of access to healthcare (Stavert and McKay 2020; McKay et al. 2022). In particular, on 3 April 2020 documents relating to clinical and ethical advice and support were issued (Scottish Government 2020a, 2020b) and it is unclear whether these were subsequently updated to take into account concerns about them. Their focus was on addressing demand potentially exceeding healthcare resources and prioritisation of access to critical care and treatments such as ventilators. Despite clear messages from the Committee on the Rights of Persons with Disabilities and the Special Envoy of the UN Secretary General on Disability and Accessibility (Committee on the Rights of Persons with Disabilities/Special Envoy of the UN Secretary General on Disability and Accessibility 2020a; Committee on the Rights of Persons with Disabilities 2020b) there was little or no reference to human rights in such guidance. The clinical advice did make recommendations that anticipatory care planning conversations should take place with those who are at higher risk from Covid-19 and that speciality teams should be encouraged to discuss treatment escalation and limitation plans with patients and/or their families at the earliest opportunity. However, it appeared to focus more on identifying who was less entitled to critical care and who should be encouraged to agree to 'Do not attempt cardiopulmonary resuscitation' (DNACPR), based on value judgements about the quality of their life and who would therefore benefit more from the treatment, rather than respecting individual autonomy and supporting the exercise of this. Several organisations, including the Mental Welfare Commission, Scottish Human Rights Commission, the Health and Social Care Alliance and

Centre for Mental Health and Capacity Law (Edinburgh Napier University), raised significant concerns about such guidance (Scottish Human Rights Commission 2020; Alliance 2020; Centre for Mental Health and Capacity Law 2020a, 2020b; McKay et al. 2022).

Another concern arose in connection with the adequacy of support in the community and emergency measures relating to social care assessments of the rights to the highest attainable standard of physical and mental health, to autonomy, dignity and independent living. The UK Coronavirus Act removed the statutory duty on local authorities in Scotland to assess social care needs where it would be impractical to do this or where to do so would cause unnecessary delay in providing community care services to an individual. Several subsequent reports highlighted the adverse effect of such measures on persons with learning disabilities in terms of loss of social and other supports, isolation, loss of independence and corresponding disproportionate effect on mental health (Scottish Government 2021; Scottish Commission for People with Learning Disabilities; McKay at al. 2022).

Article 2 ECHR and Article 11 CRPD are clear that the state has an obligation to protect life and to take all necessary measures to ensure the protection and safety of persons, including those with disabilities, in emergency situations. They acknowledge that states may introduce measures in legislation, policy and practice to address emergencies which reduce human rights safeguards. The rights to life or to be free from torture and inhuman or degrading treatment are always absolute and untouchable even in emergencies (Article 15(2) ECHR; Articles 10 and 11 CRPD) and whilst other rights such as the right to liberty, respect for private and family life/autonomy/to exercise legal capacity, to a fair hearing/access to justice, to the highest attainable standard of physical and mental health and community living may be limited, this must be lawful, necessary and proportionate, such proportionality including non-discrimination on the basis of a disability. The effect of restrictions, even if applied to everyone, must not disproportionately adversely impact on persons with disabilities (Committee on the Rights of Persons with Disabilities/Special Envoy of the UN Secretary General on Disability and Accessibility 2020a).

Paradigm shifts: implications for Scotland and beyond

This chapter started by raising the issues of diagnosis being the catalyst for non-consensual interventions under mental health and capacity legislation for persons with mental disabilities in general and also, more specifically, whether it is appropriate to use mental health legislation, which focuses on the authorisation and regulation of psychiatric care and treatment, to ensure the needs and rights of persons with learning disability. The CRPD approach to the rights of persons with disabilities requires that the existence of a diagnosis of mental disability or related impairment should not trigger involuntary psychiatric care and treatment. Mental health law which permits involuntary treatment on the basis of diagnosis and related impairment clearly therefore treats all persons with mental disability unequally in terms of limiting autonomy relative to others. This inequality is compounded for persons with learning disabilities given that learning disability is a lifelong condition which is not susceptible to medical treatment or management as was identified by, amongst others, the Rome and Scott Reviews and has already been mentioned in this chapter. Unfortunately, it is impossible at this stage to predict how these challenges will be specifically addressed in Scotland. That being said, some observations can be made at this stage.

On the subject of diagnosis and non-consensual interventions in relation to all persons with mental disabilities, including those with learning disabilities, the principles that underpin decisions about and the implementation of interventions authorised under existing Scottish mental health and capacity legislation reflect ECHR safeguards for persons with mental disabilities. They provide limited assurance that the views of persons subject to such interventions will be taken into account in light of the requirement for this holding no precedence over other principles and limited support for the exercise of legal capacity being identified. Moreover, meeting the wider needs and accompanying rights, notably economic, social and cultural rights, of persons with mental disabilities is not effectively reflected in the legislation.

The Rome Review recommended adopting a CRPD definition of disability that emphasises obstacles to equal rights enjoyment as the cause of disability as opposed to diagnosis of a disability and related impairment (Rome Review 2019). It also recommended removing discrimination more broadly in relation to psychiatric detention and compulsory treatment, supporting access to positive rights and ensuring equity, non-discrimination and fairness in decisions about all types of support, care, treatment and detention and a rebuttable presumption in favour of an individual's will and preferences (Rome Review2019). The Scott Review wasinvolved in similar considerations (Scott Review 2022), recognising that this needs to be addressed so as to ensure equality of rights enjoyment for all persons with mental disabilities. Moreover, recent experience during the Covid-19 pandemic makes it clear that this must be done in a manner which is robust enough to endure even during times of national emergency (Stavert and McKay 2020; McKay et al. 2022).

In terms of whether, more specifically, the use of mental health legislation to support persons with learning disability without mental illness is desirable, there appears to be support across the UK and Ireland to remove learning disability and autism from the remit of such law. The Rome Review was not convinced by arguments that use of the MHA is the way to support persons with learning disability and autism. Noting that persons with learning disability and autism were disproportionately adversely impacted by the Act, as was mentioned above, it recommended removing learning disability from the definition of 'mental disorder' in the MHA and separate legislation to support persons with learning disability and autism. This separate legislation would not authorise detention or compulsory care and treatment but should promote and protect the broad range of rights in order to ensure that needs of persons with disability in terms of support and inclusion are met (Rome Review 2019). The 2018 review of the English and Welsh Mental Health Act (Wessely Review) whilst also recognising that persons with learning disabilities were unequally affected by the Act in terms of inappropriate detention and treatment, and that such legislation currently does not ensure that necessary support is necessarily forthcoming, concluded that separate legislation for persons with learning disability was unnecessary. It considered that removal of discrimination, safeguards to prevent unnecessary detention and restriction and better and tailored support and treatment, including adequate community options, that addresses the needs of persons with learning disabilities was required (Department of Health and Social Care 2018). Interestingly, however, it appears that the resultant bill intended to reform the English and Welsh Mental Health Act in fact removes learning disability and autism from the definition of mental disorder, thus effectively removing this group of persons from the scope of the legislation (Prime Minister's Office, 2022). Similarly, the 2014 Expert Group Review of the Irish Mental Health Act 2001 concluded that the specific inclusion of 'significant intellectual disability' in the definition of mental disorder should not continue if ECHR and CRPD compliance is to be achieved. It noted that the detention of persons with intellectual disability who do not have mental illness in psychiatric institutions is inappropriate and, indeed, criticised by the European Committee for the Prevention of Torture (Department of Health 2014).

The Scott Review did not ultimately follow the Rome recommendations that learning disability be removed from the definition of 'mental disorder' in the MHA (Scott Review 2022). Nor did it recommend that separate legislation to meet the needs of persons with learning disability and autistic people (Scott Review 2022). . It acknowledged that if the opportunities for persons with learning disabilities to lead fulfilling and enabled lives on an equal basis with others are to be made available in the same way as for others, then it cannot be achieved through inappropriately and disproportionately restricting their autonomy through the use of coercive measures under mental health and capacity law and access to support to live independently where this would not happen for others. It considered that this can be achieved through broadening the purpose and scope of mental health and capacity law to focus on enablement and prioritisation of the voice and choices of persons with 'mental disorder' (which may or may not include learning disability within its definition) with accompanying enforceable civil, political, economic social and cultural rights to ensure the wider needs beyond psychiatric care and treatment (Scott Review, 2022). The Scottish Government has, however, stated that it is introducing a Learning Disability Autism and Neurodiversity (Scotland) Bill to cater for the rights and needs of this community. To this end, it has established specialist, including lived experience, advisory groups to inform the bill's content although at present the precise objective of, and rights to be protected under, the bill remain to be clarified. The Scottish Government has also highlighted the need to significantly reduce out-of-area placements and delayed hospital discharges given the challenges and inequities these create (Scottish Government 2018, 2022). At the same time, as was identified by the Rome Review, it is important to ensure that such approaches do not result in increased numbers of persons with learning disability inappropriately falling within the criminal justice system or, where this is appropriate, falling within the criminal justice system without meaningful support and adjustments to secure their rights, including access to justice. In this respect lessons can possibly be learned from New Zealand where its Mental Health (Compulsory Assessment and Treatment) Act 1992, although its repeal and replacement is currently being considered, introduced a new definition of 'mental disorder' which excluded individuals with an intellectual disability only from the Act's compulsory measures. However, it was subsequently necessary to later enact the Intellectual Disability (Compulsory Care and Rehabilitation) Act 2003 to fill the legislative gap left by the 1992 Act resulting in some persons with intellectual disabilities who had been charged with, or convicted of, an offence and thought to present a risk not being cared for under mental health legislation and being discharged into the community. The 2003 Act places responsibility on the disability sector rather than the mental health or criminal justice system and provides various rights and safeguards for individuals who are receiving care and rehabilitation under it. All these challenges will have to be addressed if CRPD compliance is to be achieved, or at least concrete steps in the direction of compliance are to be taken.

Note

1 This term is used as opposed to 'intellectual disabilities' because this chapter focuses primarily on Scotland where the term 'learning disability' is currently referred to in Scottish legislation.

References

ALLIANCE, 2020, 'Comments on Draft COVID-19 Clinical and Ethical Guidance', 14 April. Available at https://www.alliance-scotland.org.uk/blog/news/the-alliance-comments-on-draft-covid-19-clinical-and-ethical-guidance/ (Accessed 1 April 2022)

Centre for Mental Health and Capacity Law, 2020a, *Comment on Scottish Government CMO COVID-19 Guidance: Clinical Advice (Version 2:3)*, 3 April. Available at: http://blogs.napier.ac.uk/cmhcl-mhts/2020/04/08/comment-on-cmo-covid-19-guidance-clinical-advice-version-23-3rd-april-2020/ (Accessed 1 April 2022)

Centre for Mental Health and Capacity Law, 2020b, *Comment on Scottish Government CMO COVID-19 Guidance: Ethical Advice and Support Framework (Version 2:2)*, 6 April. Available at: http://blogs.napier.ac.uk/cmhcl-mhts/2020/04/06/comment-on-scottish-government-cmo-covid-19-guidance-ethical-advice-and-support-framework-version-22/ (Accessed 1 April 2022)

Clough, BA, 2018, 'New Legal Landscapes: (Re)Constructing the Boundaries of Mental Capacity Law', *Medical Law Review* 26(2), pp. 246–75.

Committee on Economic Social and Cultural Rights, 2009, *General Comment 20: Non-Discrimination in Economic, Social and Cultural Rights (Art. 2(2))*, E/C.12/GC/20, 2 July 2009; 16 IHRR 925.

Committee on the Rights of Persons with Disabilities (CRPD), 2014, *General Comment No. 1 (2014), Article 12: Equal Recognition Before the Law*, 19 May 2014, CRPD/C/GC/1. Available at: https://documents-dds-ny.un.org/doc/UNDOC/GEN/G14/031/20/PDF/G1403120.pdf?OpenElement (Accessed 25 March 2022)

Committee on the Rights of Persons with Disabilities, 2015, *Guidelines on Article 14 of the Convention on the Rights of Persons with Disabilities: the Right to Liberty and Security of Persons with Disabilities, Adopted during the Committee's 14th Session, Held in September 2015*, Geneva, September 2015.

Committee on the Rights of Persons with Disabilities (CRPD), 2018, *General Comment No. 6 (2018), Equality and Non-Discrimination*, 24 April 2018, CRPD/C/GC/6. Available at: https://tbinternet.ohchr.org/_layouts/15/treatybodyexternal/Download.aspx?symbolno=CRPD/C/GC/6&Lang=en (Accessed 25 March 2022)

Committee on the Rights of Persons with Disabilities and the Special Envoy of the United Nations Secretary-General on Disability and Accessibility, 2020a, *Joint Statement: Persons with Disabilities and COVID-19*. Available at: https://www.ohchr.org/EN/NewsEvents/Pages/DisplayNews.aspx?NewsID=25765&LangID=E (Accessed 1 April 2022)

Committee on the Rights of Persons with Disabilities, 2020b, *Statement on Covid-19 and the Human Rights of Persons with Disabilities*, 9 June 2020. Available at: https://www.ohchr.org/en/news/2020/06/statement-covid-19-and-human-rights-persons-disabilities?LangID=E&NewsID=25942 (Accessed 1 April 2022)

Cooper, SA, McLean, G, Guthrie, B et al., 2015, 'Multiple Physical and Mental Health Comorbidity in Adults with Intellectual Disabilities: Population-Based Cross-Sectional Analysis', *BMC Family Practice* 16, p. 110. https://doi.org/10.1186/s12875-015-0329-3

Department of Health, 2014, *Report of the Expert Group on the Review of the Mental Health Act 2001*, December 2014. Available: af32aee7c6ce4747aef4962b11d716d8.pdf (assets.gov.ie) (Accessed 30 May 2022)

Department of Health and Social Care, 2018, 'Modernising the Mental Health Act: Increasing Choice, Reducing Compulsion', https://assets.publishing.service.gov.uk/government/uploads/system/uploads/attachment_data/file/778897/Modernising_the_Mental_Health_Act_-_increasing_choice__reducing_compulsion.pdf

Human Rights Committee, *Gillot and others v France* (932/2000), A/57/40 at 270 (2002), 15 July 2002; 10 IHRR 22 (2003).

Human Rights Committee, *Guido Jacobs v Belgium* (943/2000), CCPR/C/81/D/943/2000 (2004), 17 August 2004.

'Independent Review of Learning Disability and Autism in the Mental Health Act' (Rome Review), Final Report, December 2019. Available at: https://webarchive.nrscotland.gov.uk/20200313205853/https://www.irmha.scot/ (Accessed 29 March 2022)

MacDonald, A, 2018, *Coming Home A Report on Out-of-Area Placements and Delayed Discharge for People with Learning Disabilities and Complex Needs*, Scottish Government.

McKay, C and Stavert, J, 2017, 'Scotland's Mental Health and Capacity Law: The Case for Report', Mental Welfare Commission for Scotland/Edinburgh Napier University. Available at: https://www.mwcscot.org.uk/sites/default/files/2019-06/scotland_s_mental_health_and_capacity_law_0.pdf (Accessed 1 April 2022)

McKay, C, et al., 2022, *Research Report for COVID-19 Public Inquiry: Corrected draft*, May 2022. Available at: https://www.covid19inquiry.scot/sites/default/files/2023-03/Portfolio_3_McKay _et_al_Edinburgh_Napier_University_Health_Social_Care.pdf (Accessed 11 July 2023)

Mental Welfare Commission for Scotland, 2016, *Good Practice Guide: Supported Decision-Making*, Edinburgh. Available at: https://www.mwcscot.org.uk/sites/default/files/2019-06/mwc_sdm _draft_gp_guide_10__post_board__jw_final.pdf (Accessed 28 March 2022)

Mental Welfare Commission for Scotland, 2016, *No through Road: People with Learning Disabilities in Scotland*. Available at: https://www.mwcscot.org.uk/sites/default/files/2019-06/no_through _road.pdf (Accessed 29 March 2022)

Mental Welfare Commission for Scotland, Adults with Incapacity Act Monitoring Report 2020/1, November 2021. Available at: https://www.mwcscot.org.uk/sites/default/files/2021-11/AWI _MonitoringReport_2020-21.pdf (Accessed 1 April 2022)

Nilsson, A (2014), 'Objective and Reasonable? Scrutinising Compulsory Mental Health Interventions from Non-discrimination Perspective', *Human Rights Law Review* 14(3), p. 459.

O'Leary, L, Cooper, S and Hughes-McCormack, L, 2017, 'Early Death and Causes of Death of People with Intellectual Disabilities: A Systematic Review', *Journal of Applied Research in Intellectual Disabilities*, https://doi.org/10.1111/jar.12417.

People First (Scotland), 2017, *The Case for a New Legal Framework to Cover the Lives of People with Learning Disabilities in Scotland*. Available at: https://peoplefirstscotland.org/people-first-scotland/information/ (Accessed 29 March 2022)

Prime Minister's Office, 2022, *The Queen's Speech 2022*, London, 10 May 2022. Available at: https:// assets.publishing.service.gov.uk/government/uploads/system/uploads/attachment_data/file /1074113/Lobby_Pack_10_May_2022.pdf (Accessed 30 May 2022)

Scottish Commission for People with Learning Disabilities, 2020, *Position Statement: Incorporation of the United Nations Convention on the Rights of Persons with Disabilities*, December 2020. Available at: https://www.scld.org.uk/wp-content/uploads/2020/12/SCLD-UNCRPD-Incorporation -Statement-updated-LATEST_090721.pdf (Accessed 29 March 2022)

Scottish Commission for People with Learning Disabilities (SCLD), 'The Equality and Human Rights Implications of the COVID-19 Emergency for People with Learning/ Intellectual Disabilities', Available at: https://www.scld.org.uk/wp-content/uploads/2020/06/The-Equality-and-Human -Rights-Implications-of-the-COVID-19-emergency-SCLD-Submission_designed.pdf

Scottish Executive New Directions: Report of the Review of the Mental Health (Scotland) Act 1984, January 2011, SE/2001/56. Available at: https://www.mhtscotland.gov.uk/mhts/files/Millan _Report_New_Directions.pdf (Accessed 25 March 2022)

Scottish Government, Limited Review of the Mental Health (Care and Treatment) (Scotland) Act 2003: Report, 2009.

Scottish Government, 2016, *A Fairer Scotland for Disabled People: Our Delivery Plan to 2021 for the United Nations Convention on the Rights of Persons with Disabilities*, December 2016. Available at: Our Delivery Plan to 2021 for the United Nations Convention on the Rights of Persons with Disabilities (Accessed 30 March 2022).

Scottish Government, 2017, *Mental Health Strategy 2017–2027*, March 2017. Available at: https:// www.gov.scot/publications/mental-health-strategy-2017-2027/documents/ (Accessed 25 March 2022)

Scottish Government, 2018, *Coming home: A Report on Out-of-Area Placements and Delayed Discharge for People with Learning Disabilities and Complex Needs*, November 2018. Available at: https://www. gov.scot/binaries/content/documents/govscot/publications/research-and-analysis/2018/11/ coming-home-complex-care-needs-out-area-placements-report-2018/documents/00543272-pdf /00543272-pdf/govscot%3Adocument/00543272.pdf (Accessed 11 July 2023)

Scottish Government, 2019, *Review of Mental Health and Incapacity Legislation in Scotland*, September 2019. Available at: https://www.gov.scot/binaries/content/documents/govscot/publications /agreement/2019/09/mental-health-legislation-review-terms-of-reference/documents/mental -health-legislation-review-terms-of-reference/mental-health-legislation-review-terms-of-reference /govscot%3Adocument/Review%2Bof%2Bmental%2Bhealth%2Blegislation%2B-%2Bterms%2Bof %2Breference.pdf (Accessed 29 March 2022)

Scottish Government, 2020a, *COVID-19 Guidance: Clinical Advice*, 3rd April 2020, Version 2:3. Available at: Coronavirus (COVID-19): clinical guidance for managing patients-gov.scot (nrscotland.gov.uk) (Accessed 1 April 2022)

Scottish Government, 2020b, *COVID-19 Guidance: Ethical Advice and Support Framework*, 3rd April 2020, Version 2:2. Available at: https://www.gov.scot/publications/coronavirus-covid-19-ethical-advice-and-support-fram9ework/ (Accessed 1 April 2022)

Scottish Government, 2021, *National Taskforce on Human Rights: Leadership* Report, March 2021. Available at: https://www.gov.scot/publications/national-taskforce-human-rights-leadership-report/ (Accessed 1 April 2022)

Scottish Government, 2021, *Learning/Intellectual Disability and Autism: Transformation Plan*, March 2021. Available at: https://www.gov.scot/publications/learning-intellectual-disability-autism-towards-transformation/documents/ (Accessed 31 March 2022)

Scottish Government, 2022, *Coming Home Implementation: Report from the Working Group on Complex Care and Delayed Discharge*, February 2022. Available at: https://www.gov.scot/publications/coming-home-implementation-report-working-group-complex-care-delayed-discharge/ (Accessed 11 July 2023)

Scottish Human Rights Commission, 2020, *Letter to Equalities and Human Rights Committee on COVID-19 Emergency Legislation*, 28 April. Available at: https://www.scottishhumanrights.com/media/2012/letter-in-response-to-ehric-committee-270420.pdf (Accessed 1 April 2022)

Scottish Learning Disabilities Observatory Newsletter Volume 4, May 2017. Available at: https://www.sldo.ac.uk/media/1693/may-2017-newsletter.pdf (Accessed 29 March 2022)

Scottish Learning Disabilities Observatory the Impact of COVID -19 on People with Learning/Intellectual Disabilities in Scotland. Available at: https://www.sldo.ac.uk/our-research/life-expectancy-and-mortality/covid-19/ (Accessed 1 April 2022)

Scottish Mental Health Law Review (Scott Review), 2022, *Final Report, September 2022*.

Scottish Parliament, 8 December 2016, *Minutes of Proceedings, Parliamentary Year 1, No. 53, Session 5*. Available at: https://archive2021.parliament.scot/S5_BusinessTeam/Chamber_Minutes_2016 1208.pdf (Accessed 30 March 2022)

Sheriffdom of Lothian and Borders, *Practice Note No 1 of 2016, Applications under the Adults with Incapacity (Scotland) Act 2000*, Edinburgh, 11 March 2016

Stavert, J, 2015, 'The Exercise of Legal Capacity, Supported Decision-Making and Scotland's Mental Health and Incapacity Legislation: Working with CRPD Challenges' *Laws* 4(2), pp. 296–313. https://doi.org/10.3390/laws4020296

Stavert, J, 2018, 'Paradigm Shift or Paradigm Paralysis? National Mental Health and Capacity Law and Implementing the CRPD in Scotland', *Laws* 7(3), 26. https://doi.org/10.3390/laws7030026

Stavert, J, 2021, 'Supported Decision-Making and Paradigm Shifts: Word Play or Real Change?' *Frontiers in Psychiatry*, 11 January 2021. https://doi.org/10.3389/fpsyt.2020.571005

Stavert, J and McKay, C, 2020, 'Scottish Mental Health and Capacity Law: The Normal, Pandemic and "New Normal"', *International Journal of Law and Psychiatry* 71. https://doi.org/10.1016/j.ijlp.2020.101593

Truesdale, M and Brown, M, 2017, 'People with Learning Disabilities in Scotland: 2017 Health Needs Assessment Update', July. Available at: http://www.healthscotland.scot/media/1690/people-with-learning-disabilities-in-scotland.pdf (Accessed 29 March 2022)

Welsh, H and Morrison, G, 2017, 'Learning Disability and the Scottish Mental Health Act', Advances in Mental Health and Intellectual Disabilities 11(2), pp. 74–82.

9
MENTAL HEALTH LAWS AND OLDER ADULTS

Penelope Weller

Introduction

The health and social care needs of older adults with psychosocial disabilities and mental health problems raise important questions about the rationale, structure and application of the law. Generally, the term 'mental health law' refers to the specific laws that apply to the treatment and detention of people with acute mental health problems. In reality, most mental health treatment for older adults, including the provision of treatment and care for mental health problems or psycho-social distress, is governed by the general laws relating to the provision of medical treatment. Examining these laws from the perspective of older adults and the care they receive, offers pertinent insights into the regulation of mental health care. The salient areas of law are all those that apply if a person is deemed unable to make decisions for themselves, including mental health legislation. Mental health legislation is typically used if an older adult is admitted to hospital for involuntary psychiatric treatment. The objective of the following analysis, however, is to consider the full suite of laws relevant to the provision of health and mental health care of older persons, that is, the laws that are most often engaged in the day-to-day provision of care. Despite the detail of the law differing significantly across the jurisdictions, if the law is viewed as this meta level, the broadly similar principles that structure the law in developed jurisdictions can be assessed.

Decisions about mental health care and treatment for older adults occur in a uniquely complex social, clinical, pharmacological and legal matrix. Older adults as a group experience high levels of both cognitive decline and mental health problems. The prevalence of cognitive decline in particular influences the way the law responds to older adults and therefore the way they experience health and mental health care. The aim of this chapter is to examine some of the tensions associated with current laws, including the way negative assumptions about ageing influence the way the law is used. The chapter begins with a discussion of the health and mental health profile of older adults and the unique clinical and legal challenges that are associated with their care and treatment. The second part considers the law of informed consent and its application in the context of aged care. The third part outlines the principles of mental capacity law and its limitations, while the fourth part considers guardianship and mental health laws. The final part turns to an examination of supported decision-making and its recent incorporation into legislation in some jurisdictions. The chapter recognises that supported decision-making is a promising but undeveloped area of law and practice. Threaded through each section is the observation that a major barrier to change in this area is the persistence of ageism and its intersection with sexism and mentalism. The United Nations have stressed that a fully developed human rights approach is necessary to address the human rights abuses experienced by older adults (Chinsung Chung Report, 2009). Negative attitudes about the inevitability of frailty and assumptions about cognitive decline impact the experience of older adults. In this regard, the World Health Organization reports that one in two people in Europe hold ageist attitudes and one in three older people have experienced ageism (WHO, 2021). The literature shows that ageism, sexism and mentalism combine to create negative attitudes towards ageing and dependency. Negative attitudes influence the way the law is perceived and implemented by those who use it. There is therefore a need for targeted research into the way law is understood and implemented so that those who are providing care and treatment for older adults are better equipped to provide optimal care.

Older people and mental health

It is not possible to consider the topic of mental health law and older people without examining the context in which mental health care and treatment occurs. Providing appropriate health and mental health care for older adults is a pressing health care issue of global significance. According to the United Nations, there are 703 million persons over the age of 65, with older people accounting for more than one-fifth of the population in 17 countries. By 2050, 1 in 6 people in the world will be over the age of 65 (UN, 2019). Increasing years are not an indicator of decline and dysfunction. Particularly in developed nations, those who have enjoyed a good standard of living throughout life are likely to continue to enjoy good health, maintain functional ability, and continue to work and participate in society. How one ages is a function of social and physiological processes that are shaped by the many intersecting factors, contexts and identities that make up individual lives (Hall, 2019). Moreover, if one accepts, following Friedman (2000), that a measure of a good or valuable life is that people continue to undertake activities that are of value to them (Friedman, 2000:37), many people continue to live valuable lives well into their older years (WHO, 2015).

Ageing has distinctive features that give rise to distinctive clinical and legal problems (WHO, 2021). In Europe, the number of people who need some form of assistance with daily living varies significantly from country to country. In all cases the rate increases considerably in the over-75 age group (WHO, 2015:69). With respect to mental health, 20% of those over 60 experience some form of mental or neurological disorder (Hamilton et al., 2021). Advanced age, frailty, cognitive impairment, mental and physical comorbidities and social isolation are all associated with poor mental health. Ageing is also a gendered phenomenon. Because women live longer than men, groups of older adults are disproportionately made up of women. Women experience greater levels of dysfunction and spend more years with functional limitations. Women report poorer health and mental health outcomes than men. Women are disproportionately represented amongst those who experience mental or neurological disorder such as depression, dementia and anxiety, making up two-thirds of those with a diagnosis of Alzheimer's disease (Hamilton et al., 2021:2). Women are also disproportionately affected by poverty as they age, often influenced by lifetime experiences of gender discrimination and/or violence. Poverty later in life may reflect the reality of economic dependency, lower lifetime wages, interrupted work and unpaid care. These factors make older women more vulnerable to homelessness, more vulnerable to poor mental health, and more likely to have decisions made on their behalf. As women age, gender and ageism combine to amplify discrimination and marginalisation.

As a consequence, women are 40% more likely than men to be placed in care homes and facilities (McCann et al., 2012). Serious questions are raised about the adequacy of care in such places, particularly with respect to deprivation of liberties and physical and chemical restraint. Multiple global failures of the Covid-19 response have unscored the dire state of residential aged care arrangements (Peisah, 2020). Prior to Covid-19 the inappropriate use of antipsychotic medications was identified as a key problem. In aged care facilities, antipsychotic medications are commonly used to 'manage' a range of behavioural problems such as aggression, agitation, wandering, anxiety and depression (Peisah and Skladzien, 2014), despite evidence that such medications are no more effective than non-pharmaceutical approaches to behavioural problems. In Australia, prescriptions for antipsychotic medication are high and increase markedly if a person enters care (Harrison et al., 2020). Antipsychotic medication is often associated with harmful extrapyramidal side effects, somnolence, sedation, hip fracture and pneumonia (Kalisch Ellet and Lim, 2020). Their long-term use is associated with faster cognitive decline and increased risk of adverse events including death (Harrison et al., 2020:336). The behavioural 'problems' that are treated with antipsychotics are too often associated with poorly designed environments that facilitate confusion and cognitive decline (Byrne, 2020) and poorly resourced facilities that employ unskilled or under-skilled staff. In these circumstances, problematic behaviours can be understood as expressions of distress, anger, hunger, loneliness or pain (Ballard and Corbett, 2020). These perspectives point to the need for properly resourced and regulated aged care systems and facilities which actively support and facilitate appropriate and lawful decision-making practices.

The scope and limitations of informed consent

The first legal principle is the principle of informed consent. Informed consent refers to a person's voluntary decision to accept health care treatment or some other intervention. It is therefore axiomatic that informed consent must be obtained before treatment can be provided (Beauchamp and Childress, 2001). Modern informed consent law is understood as having a close relationship with the protection of human dignity, autonomy and self-determination. These connections have been repeatedly recognised by domestic courts (Pritchard Jones, 2019).

Informed consent law requires the communication of appropriate information about the nature and purpose of the treatment being proposed. The information must be provided in a way that the person is able to understand (Farrell and Brazier, 2016). Information should include details on expected and possible side effects and unwanted outcomes. Since the decision in *Montgomery v Lanarkshire Health Board* (2015), information about any reasonable alternatives to or variations in the proposed treatment should be discussed (Heywood and Miola, 2017). The rationale for the provision of the information is sometimes expressed as a measure that protects the clinician from a negligence claim. The latter analysis overlooks the significance of autonomy in western jurisprudence, where the ability to make rational autonomous decisions is taken to be a marker of autonomy and freedom (Farrell et al., 2017). In the era of human rights, informed consent law reflects an understanding of the right to autonomy, bodily integrity and dignity of a person which is given substance by the requirement to provide information in a way that considers the person and their particular circumstances, including their need for decision-making support and assistance.

The first hurdle related to the practice of gaining informed consent is a prevailing assumption that older persons do not wish to be involved in treatment decisions. Several studies have observed that diagnoses of dementia, for example, are not discussed with older persons (Downs, 1997). This is so even when the individual does want to know more about their condition or diagnosis (Holroyd, Turnbull, & Wolf, 2002). In a study by Marzanski (2000), for example, two-thirds of a cohort of 30 participants with dementia claimed they never had the opportunity to discuss their dementia with a medical professional. Only five had done so and only one participant had been told of their diagnosis. Several participants reported being given untrue information or being treated in a disrespectful way by their clinicians (Marzanski, 2000, 109). The research suggests that the very fact that the person has dementia leads to the assumption that they lack decision-making ability in all areas (Pritchard-Jones, 2019:3). Carney and Grey (2015) provide sociological explanation of the dynamic of silence. They argue that society assigns an inferior social status to those who show signs of biological ageing. Inferior status has a cumulative social and economic effect which in turn results in a reduction in the ability of older people to speak for themselves. The burdens of ageism and sexism combine to make it almost impossible for many older persons to elicit information about their clinical condition, participate in an informed discussion and arrive at a decision about how to resolve the problem (Carney and Grey, 2015:127).

Where informed consent is sought, the law is supposed to be alert to the dilemmas of vulnerability. If the person has not received the information, is unduly influenced by another person in making of decision or, as is discussed below, lacks mental capacity to understand the information, the decision is not legally valid. These aspects of informed consent law protect autonomy by ensuring that vulnerable people are not experiencing exploitation and abuse. They do so by imposing on clinicians a duty to identify if a person is not making a true decision for themselves. In theory, the discovery of vulnerability should trigger another set of legal actions, such as the appointment of an alternative decision-maker. In practice, clinicians (and other gatekeepers) are often reluctant to find older persons incapable of making treatment decisions, even where concerns about exploitation are recognised (Benbow & Jolley, 2012; Werner & Doron, 2017). Clinicians who are in this situation are faced with a practical dilemma. On one hand, they have an obligation to provide salient information in a way that the person can understand. If information is communicated well, people with cognitive deficits or other difficulties may well be able to provide informed consent to particular procedures. On the other, deciding that a person's decision is not valid requires a different path of action, one that is likely to elicit the heavy stigma associated with loss of autonomy. While the weight of procedure should be balanced towards autonomy, if closer inquiry into the situation of a potentially vulnerable person is avoided because of the ramification of that inquiry, it is possible that critical needs are overlooked.

The obligation to be alert to questions of influence may be particularly problematic for individuals who need assistance and support to present at clinical interview, or to work through the relevant information and come to a decision. In legal terms, it may be argued that decisions reached with support are (a) not made independently and are therefore not true decisions, or (b) have required a level of support that points to a lack of mental capacity. Typically, older adults receive support for decision-making on an informal basis, with progressive ageing being accompanied by increasing reliance on family members. In a study of couples in which one person is experiencing dementia, Samsi and Manthorpe found that many regarded joint decision-making as an inherent part of their relationship (2013:955). Moreover, the researchers observed that decision-making approaches shifted from joint decision-making to 'substituted' decision-making as the dementia worsened. Where there was a trusted relationship, the fact that another person made the decisions was often welcomed by the person with dementia (2013:959). The law's insistence on the absence of external influence, however, may mean that clinicians or other gatekeepers question the validity of decisions that are made with the active support of other people. The legal question is whether there is undue influence such that a person's decision may not be regarded as their own true decision (Quinn, 2000). Assessing whether this is the case may be very difficult when people engage in embedded, relational, decision-making. Nevertheless, to deny the validity of these arrangements by assuming the person is not making a true decision, may amount to discrimination on the basis of age and disability. As is discussed more fully below, the law's assumption that true decisions are those made in isolation from others is itself being questioned by feminist scholars.

Decision-making with older adults is complicated by other contextual factors that may impact on cognition, permanently or intermittently (Jones and Davis, 2021). Older people may need time to understand and appreciate the information. Their decision-making ability may be compromised by stress, lack of sleep, transient clinical conditions or new medication. Older people may speak a first language other than English, typically losing facility with their second language as cognitive function declines. Communication is further inhibited by common communication problems such as hearing loss or loss of clear speech if, for example, a person is affected by stroke. On a different level, older people may lack basic information about common medical treatment, common medical conditions and contemporary standards of care. They may have misconceptions about the objective of treatment. Such attitudes may reflect the person's lifetime opportunity for education or the realities of social isolation. Communication difficulties may manifest or be compounded by social and economic precarity or situations of abuse. Clinicians who are unaware of the multiple difficulties faced by already marginalised older people may mistake passive or coerced agreement to treatment as a valid consent or overlook clinical signs of stress or compromised cognition.

Decision-making is also heavily influenced by context. For older people, a key point of disruption and possible loss of autonomy and dignity may occur if they are placed in care. For many older people the shift to residential care may represent a loss of consistent support for everyday decisions and activities as well as more complex treatment and care decisions. Older people who move into institutional care may experience the collapse of those informal systems of support. Family members may think of themselves as a supporter or decision-maker but are not recognised by the care facilities. They may be listed as decision-makers but do not have formal status and are therefore overlooked. They may be listed as formal decision-makers but not actually called in to provide support when critical decisions are made. In theory, older people who have been making their own decisions about treatment should continue to do so. If the person had been relying on family members to keep attuned to everyday decision-making and to assist with treatment decisions, the shift to care may be extremely disorienting.

Recent examinations of informed consent practice in aged care facilities suggests that informed consent, either from the person or their designated decision-maker, may not be routinely obtained (Rendina et al., 2009; Molenda and Lusis, 2015). For example, in a recent study into antipsychotic use in an age care facility in Australia, Harrison et al. (2020) found that written consent was obtained for only one resident out of a cohort of 146 with verbal consent being documented for 23 residents (16%). Six patients (4%) were given antipsychotic medication against the express direction of the person's lawful representative. In addition, it had been recommended by qualified practitioners that 91 residents (62%) should have their medication reviewed, but this had not occurred (Harrison et al., 2020). There are no special laws or legal exceptions for the provision of medication in aged care facilities. In theory, informed consent law applies unless there are other decision-making arrangements in place. The provision of routine medication, including psychotropic medication, aimed at behavioural control without the proper consent of the residents or those who are legally entitled to give consent on their behalf is unlawful.

Mental capacity principles

Informed consent law anticipates that the person giving consent has mental capacity such that mental capacity is a threshold requirement for informed consent (Appelbaum and Gutheil, 2019). The concept was developed in the common law and then codified in statute. The statutory recognition of mental capacity has reinforced the salience of the principle, meaning that questions about whether an older person is able to make decisions for themselves is typically resolved by a consideration of cognitive capabilities.

Mental capacity principles in law have a complicated relationship with the idea of autonomy (Skowron, 2019). The first principle of mental health law is that all adult people, including older people, are presumed to have the capacity to consent to or to refuse medical treatment unless and until that presumption is rebutted (Donnelly, 2010:93). While there are some variations in the definition, mental capacity is a functional test that refers to the ability of a person to understand, retain, use and weigh information relevant to a particular question to arrive at and communicate a decision (Donnelly, 2010:139). Assumptions about mental capacity should not be made on the basis of age or appearance or other status characteristics such as race or disability. Moreover, the law recognises that a person's decision-making ability may fluctuate, can be enhanced by support and is influenced by the quality and accessibility of information that is provided (Curtice, 2020). The high incidence of neurological disorder in older people means that questions about mental capacity will be raised. It cannot be assumed, however, that those who are aged, or have a diagnosis such as dementia, lack mental capacity. Recent international research shows, for example, that approximately 22% of those who are affected by dementia retain the cognitive ability to give informed consent (Beattie et al., 2019).

The courts have made clear that in order to avoid discrimination the standard for capacity should not be too high. As was observed in the Sheffield City Council case (2005, para. 89), it may otherwise operate as an 'unfair, unnecessary and indeed discriminatory bar against the mentally disabled'. Similarly, Lady Hale observed in Wilkinson's case (2002) that:

> Our threshold of capacity is rightly a low one. It is better to keep it that way and allow some non-consensual treatment of those who have capacity than to set such a high threshold for capacity that many would never qualify.
>
> *(446, para. 80)*

In particular, Lady Hale noted that the ability to understand, retain, use and weigh the information should be interpreted broadly. Similarly, Justice McDonald in King's College Hospital NHS Foundation Trust (2015) clarified that:

> It is not necessary for a person to use and weigh every detail of the respective options available to them in order to demonstrate capacity, merely the salient features ... Even though a person may be unable to use and weigh some information relevant to the decision in question, they may nonetheless be able to use and weigh other elements sufficiently to be able to make a capacitous decision.
>
> *(para. 37)*

In the latter case Justice McDonald took the opportunity to step through the 'cardinal' legal principles. In summary these are that mental capacity is decision specific, it cannot be determined before all efforts for support have been provided, the outcome of the decision is not relevant even if the decision is unwise and that, at least with respect to the Mental Capacity Act 2005 (England and Wales), incapacity must have a causal connection to the disturbance of the mind (paras 23–39).

It is clear that people can be regarded as retaining decision-making capacity even if they reject medical or psychiatric interpretations of their behaviour or condition (Re MB, 1997).

The law does not require a person's decisions to be sensible, rational or well considered. The test is not whether a person can make a balanced or rational decision but whether they can apply the information to their own situation. As recognised by the Supreme Court in Canada in *Starson v Swayze* (2003) the right to refuse unwanted medical treatment was regarded by the court as fundamental to a person's dignity or autonomy. The impact of this analysis is the conclusion that people with mental capacity are entitled to make unwise decisions, cannot be compelled to undergo medical treatment 'for their own good' and are entitled to reject treatment without providing a rational reason or indeed any reason at all (Rioux et al., 2013). Conversely, it cannot be determined that a person lacks capacity because the decision they make is not in their best interests, appears to be irrational or is not a decision that another person would make.

Determining the validity of a decision that others would think is unwise when there are doubts about the person's cognitive abilities is a profound task (Ryan, 2012). Either way, the erroneous application of these difficult legal standards holds a dual danger for older persons. People may be assessed as having mental capacity when in fact they are unable to make a true decision. On the other hand, people may be assessed as lacking in mental capacity when they are able to understand and wish to make their own decisions. An erroneous determination of mental incapacity denies a person the dignity of making decisions for themselves, compelling them instead to undergo or forgo medical treatment that clinicians or another person have decided is best.

Mental capacity law purports to offer a deliberate, evidence-based assessment of cognitive function as the basis of the law's determination. Discussing the operation of the mental capacity jurisdiction as it applies to older adults in England and Wales, Herring (2016) argues that mental capacity law operates as a legal fiction that deems certain individuals incapable, whether or not that is the case (Herring, 2016:28). Rather than identifying mental incapacity, he claims that mental capacity assessments operate as a legal mechanism that enables, justifies and provides a process for over-ruling choices and preferences that are not convenient to others. Hall (2019) takes the argument a step further to argue that determinations of mental capacity work to allocate scarce resources. She observes that questions about mental capacity typically arise when there is an intense need for care, coupled with a decreased ability of the care system to recognise and respond to that need, resulting in a determination that the person is capable (Hall, 2019:2). The failure of the system to identify incapacity leaves supposedly 'capable' but vulnerable older people exposed to both self-neglect and exploitation by others because they are technically able to make decisions but in practice cannot exercise mental capacity (Lock, 2015:42). Even the Court of Appeal in England and Wales recognises there is 'a jurisdictional hinterland' in which 'vulnerable adults' who are in fact incapable of making decisions for themselves are deemed to fall outside that ambit of the MCA Act (Vulnerable Adults with Capacity case, 2012, para. 1). With respect to clinical decisions, it is often observed that the capacity of those who agree with medical advice is unquestioned, while the rational abilities of those who question or disagree with medical advice triggers a mental capacity assessment.

Substitute decision-making and mental health law

Mental capacity considerations have implications for other legal mechanisms relevant to health care decision-making. Modern law permits those with mental capacity to create enduring medical powers of attorney or advance directives that enable individuals to set out their wishes regarding future treatment and/or appoint another person to make decisions on their behalf in the event that they lose mental capacity. Such measures usually require legal advice and assistance and may have limited utility if the need for them has not been anticipated (Purser et al., 2019). Advance directives are commonly used in health settings to assist older people to express and assert their wishes about future treatment, especially with respect to end of life care (WHO, 2021). While they have gained wider acceptance in recent years, they remain poorly understood and underutilised, especially with respect to mental health care.

The conclusion that a person lacks mental capacity usually results in the appointment of another person to make decisions on their behalf. Such laws have moved towards limited guardianship corresponding with specific areas of decision-making. Some require substitute decision-makers to adopt an objective best interest approach, others use subjective best interest and others privilege assessments of what the person would have wanted were they able to make the decision. Typically, a family member is appointed to fulfil this role. At their best, guardianship arrangements formalise positive relationships of support that have long sustained the decision-making of the older person. In other instances, it is possible that such appointments serve to entrench relationships of exploitation and abuse. If a guardian has authority to make decisions in health care, they are able to provide consent to any needed mental health treatment.

In some instances, compulsory treatment powers under mental health legislation will be utilised, enabling clinicians to place those who meet the civil commitment criteria in general or specialist psycho-geriatric wards and institutions. Mental health legislation is typically formulated using risk criteria, raising questions about the relationship between risk and capacity (Curley et al., 2019). Some scholars argue that the human rights infringements association with compulsory mental health treatment can be minimised by the inclusion of capacity in the civil commitment criteria so that compulsory treatment only applies to those who lack mental capacity (Szmukler and Kelly, 2016). The salient point is that the law generally permits those who demonstrate mental capacity to accept or reject proposed medical treatment, while alternative arrangements are made for those who are unable to demonstrate such abilities. If this standard is applied to mental health legislation, it is argued, the discriminatory aspects of mental health law would be reduced and there would be better alignment with the general principles that govern health law (Szmukler and Dawson, 2011). According to commentary associated with the Convention on the Rights of Persons with Disabilities

(CRPD), however, mental capacity criteria is itself inherently discriminatory because it is the basis upon which legal capacity is denied (Arstein-Kerslake and Flynn, 2016). There remains considerable controversy about the meaning and application of the CRPD (Pritchard-Jones, 2019). One point of almost universal acceptance, however, is recognition that supported decision-making will ameliorate the most egregious feature of the current legal framework.

Supported decision-making and the law

As feminist scholars have long pointed out, the elements of mental capacity law rely on a model of rational decision-making that valorises the liberal ideals of self-sufficiency, independence and control (Harding, 2018). In this model, self-sufficiency stands as the foundation of legal and social autonomy (Fineman, 2004). Rosie Harding argues that as a consequence, 'there is little room in the legal imaginary for the complexities of relationships, or in the influence of social connection on decisions that people make' (Harding, 2018:17). This is because the definition of independent autonomy necessarily excludes any consideration of how relationships, structures and resources impinge and contribute to the ability to present oneself as a fully functioning and independent adult (Fineman, 2019:59). Moreover, they screen out the way in which individual preference, cultural influences and social bonds shape our decisions (Quinn and Mahler, 2021).

Promoting a rich version of autonomy, feminist scholars argue that decision-making in health care is essentially relational because every human relies on others to help them make decisions (Mackenzie and Stoljar, 2020). The reality for those who are dependent in some way is that the assistance and support is visible and treated with suspicion. In contrast to the notion of rational autonomy, respect for autonomy which is defined through the lens of relational autonomy elicits an obligation to imagine the other person's situation. It requires an effort to understand what it is like for her, in the context of her cares, values and concerns. It asks carers, clinicians and other medical staff to understand the experience of illness and mental illness from the patient's perspective (Mackenzie and Stoljar, 2020).

Relational autonomy provides an important normative rationale for supported decision-making. Supported decision-making is the provision of support in a way that enables people to make legally recognised decisions, albeit with the support of another person. When supported decision-making is recognised as a legitimate response, evidence of a person's cognitive decline does not trigger a process of exclusion, it provides the basis for the initiating support calibrated to the needs of the person. Support provided in this way is premised on the idea that everyone has the right to make their own decisions and to receive whatever support they require to do so. Rather than penalising older adults for their failure to be independent, support for decision-making opens the way for new forms of decision-making relationships and practices that are attuned to the way older adults make decisions. As is explained above, because of requirements in the law with respect to undue influence, legislative change is required to give legal form to supported decision-making measures.

The point of supported decision-making laws is to validate or sanction the provision of support for older people and others who may need assistance with decision-making, without compromising the legal status of those decisions. In Victoria, Australia, there are now four pieces of state legislation that set out legally recognised relationships of support. The Powers of Attorney Act 2014 (Vic) makes provision for supportive attorneys; the Guardianship and Administration Act 2019 (Vic) makes provision for supportive guardianship orders and supportive administration orders; the Medical Treatment Planning and Decisions Act 2016

(Vic) permits the appointment of a medical support person; while the Mental Health Act 2014 (Vic) similarly allows the appointment of a nominated person. Various guides are being produced to support those who will take up these roles. The Mental Health Act 2014 (Vic) has a number of additional features that have been referred to as elements of a supported decision-making approach. These are a right to be informed of rights, access to independent mental health advocates, a right to make an advance statement and a right to a second psychiatric opinion. All of these rights continue under the Mental Health and Wellbeing Act 2022 which came into force on 1 September 2023. While the overall impact of these strategies has been modest, the Mental Health Act 2014 (Vic) provides an expansive legislative model that could be translated into other contexts, such as aged care facilities. Other jurisdictions are also experimenting with legal recognition of supported decision-making. Using a tiered model, the Assisted Decision-Making (Capacity) Act 2015 in Ireland provides three levels of supported decision-making. There may be a 'decision-making assistant' who assists a person to make decisions. In this instance the person retains ultimate decision-making responsibility. There is a 'co-decision-maker' who has joint decision-making responsibility with the person and a 'decision-making representative' who is appointed by the Court to make decisions on behalf of a person (Donelly, 2019). It is relevant to note that both these frameworks anticipate a determination of mental incapacity in order to move to a substituted decision-making arrangement.

There are several points of uncertainty associated with the formalisation of supported decisions arrangements. First, the instances cited above are formal legal mechanisms. They do not engage with nor validate the informal everyday relationships that generally provide support to older people. In the absence of dedicated advocacy and legal support, it is likely that families will be legally unprepared to exercise the new powers. If this is the case, transitions from home care to institutional care will remain instances of disruption. The success of such law will depend on the quality of the dissemination and implementation effort that accompanies law reform. Second, the legal frameworks say little about the quality of the interactions that are necessary to build a decision-making relationship. If decision-making support is understood narrowly there is a danger that the interaction will be blunt and transactional, rather than imbued with the delicacy that is derived from a rich understanding of relational autonomy. As Herring and Wall explain:

> Autonomous decision-making is … built upon the interaction between cognition (giving practical reason content) and emotion (giving practical reason vision). If a person has no desires, goals, values or standards, they have no tools with which to engage the information that is relevant to a particular decision. In order to make a decision that reflects an exercise of autonomy by them, they need to have some understanding of what they want, some conception of what is good.
>
> *(Herring and Wall, 2015:711)*

The challenge is to create a decision-making practice within the legal framework that recognises the human dimension of decision-making while acknowledging that decision-making is closely associated with the concepts of personal identity, integrity and dignity (Hall, 2019:6). In this sense, Herring and Wall (2015) argue the exercise of autonomy in decision-making is not simply a matter of comprehension but is also a matter of evaluative judgement, self-respect and self-care (Herring and Wall, 2015:711). The latter formula veers dangerously towards a stance that could undermine the right to make one's own decisions. There is, however, a viable model at hand. Relational decision-making in the health care context has a close correlation with the principles of informed consent if it is accepted that informed consent law, in its true substance, reflects an understanding of the right to autonomy, bodily integrity and dignity of a person which is given substance by considering the person and their particular circumstances, including their need for appropriate support and assistance.

With respect to the question of advice about support for medical treatment decision-making under Victoria's new supported decision-making laws, the Office of the Public Advocate (OPA) advises those who feel uncertain about making decisions on their own first, that health practitioners are obliged to explain what the medical treatment is, why it is needed, what might be bad about the treatment and if there are other choices. The OPA also explains that clinicians have an obligation to explain the information in different ways, explain it slowly and give the person time to think about the information. They also explain that medical supporters can assist the person to talk with doctors, nurses and other health practitioners. The OPA (2020) guidance on supported decision-making includes a case study about the provision of support to an individual with dementia. The strategies suggested include the need for a supporter to develop a close relationship with the person so that the supporter knows and understands the person's priorities, using tools like a visual wall calendar to reduce confusion, participating in clinical meetings so that information can be communicated to the person in ways they are able to understand and retain after the meeting, and taking an active role in meetings by asking questions and clarifying information so that any new information becomes accessible to the person (OPA, 2020:12).

As supported decision-making practice becomes better known these common-sense strategies should become the norm in any decision-making encounter that concerns a person who wishes to have support with decision-making. There are several caveats to the promise of these schemes. The first is the question of dignity. Some older adults may be reluctant to receive formal decision-making support because it requires an acknowledgement of their declining abilities. From this perspective a deep culture of support is required to ensure that support is a normal part of everyday living. The next two caveats relate to adequate resourcing. Sufficient resources must be provided to educate clinicians, services and family members about the rights and entitlements supported decision-making law creates. Law can fail completely if it is not implemented in an appropriate way. If this is the case the default setting will be substituted decision-making. Sufficient support must also be provided to family members and professional supporters to ensure that older adults who need support are able to receive it. A dedicated support workforce is likely to be required. Once the resourcing question is addressed, however, the most difficult barrier to appropriate decision-making for older adults may be negative attitudes about the abilities of older people. It is hoped that supported decision-making laws themselves will play a role in shifting these negative perceptions.

Conclusion

Protecting the human rights of older adults is a continuing challenge (Megret, 2011). This chapter has outlined some of the dilemmas that surround decision-making for older adults with respect to mental health care. The analysis shows that traditional decision-making law is poorly adapted to the needs of older adults, but that an emerging sensibility about the importance of supported decision-making has the potential to shift decision-making practice. Healthy ageing is facilitated by good decision-making. The effort towards support for decision-making is an important step in ensuring that older adults receive appropriate decision-making support. It should be a shared expectation that systems of care actively seem to support the autonomy, intrinsic capacity and resilience of older adults.

Reference List

Appelbaum, P.S., and Gutheil, T.G. (2019) *Clinical Handbook of Psychiatry and the Law*. 5th ed. Baltimore: Walters Kluwer.

Arstein-Kerslake, A., and Flynn, E. (2016) 'The general comment on article 12 of the convention on the rights of persons with disabilities; a roadmap for equality before the law', *The International Journal of Human Rights*, 20(4), pp. 417–490. https://doi.org/10.1080/13642987.2015.1107052.

Ballard, C., and Corbett, A. (2020) 'Reducing psychotropic drug use in people with dementia living in nursing homes', *International Psychogeriatrics*, 32(3), pp. 291–294.

Beauchaum, T., and Childress, J. (2001) *Principles of Biomedical Ethics*. 5th ed. Oxford: OUP.

Beattie, E. et al (2019) 'Supporting autonomy of nursing home residents with dementia in the informed consent process', *Dementia: The International Journal of Social Research and Practice*, 18(7–8), pp. 821–835.

Benbow, S., and Jolley, D. (2012) 'Dementia: Stigma and its effects', *Neurodegenerative Diseases*, 2(2), pp. 165–172.

Byrne, G. (2020) 'Prescribing psychotropic medications in residential aged care facilities', *Medical Journal of Australia*, 212(7), pp. 304–305.

Carney, G., and Grey, M. (2015) 'Unmasking the "elderly mystique": Why it is time to make the personal political in ageing research,' Journal of Aging Studies, 35, pp. 123–134. https://doi.org/10.1016/j.jaging.2015.08.007.

Curtice, M. (2020) 'Fluctuating capacity: The concept of micro- and macro-decisions', *BJPsych Advances*, 26(4), pp. 238–244. https://doi.org/10.1192/bja.2020.

Chinsung Chung Report (2009) 'Implementation of sections III and IV of the annex to human rights council resolution 5/1 of 18 June 2007: Agenda and annual programme of work, including new priorities: The necessity of a human rights approach and effective united nations mechanism for the human rights of the older person, working paper prepared by Chinsung Chung, member of the human rights council advisory committee (Chinsung Chung Report)', 4 December 2009, A/HRC/AC/4/CRP.1.

CRPD,y (*Convention on the Rights of Persons with Disabilities: Resolution/adopted by the General Assembly*, 24 January 2007, A/RES/61/106. https://www.refworld.org/docid/45f973632.html.

Curleya, A. et al (2019) 'Age, psychiatry admission status and linear mental capacity for treatment decisions', *International Journal of Law and Psychiatry*, 66, p. 101469. https://doi.org/10.1016/j.ijlp.2019.101469.

Donnelly, M. (2010) *Healthcare Decision-Making and the Law: Autonomy Capacity and Limits of Liberalism*. Cambridge: Cambridge University Press.

Donnelly, M. (2019) 'Deciding in dementia: The possibilities and limits of supported decision-making International', *International Journal of Law and Psychiatry*, 66, p. 101466. https://doi.org/10.1016/j.ijlp.2019.101466.

Downs, M. (1997) 'The emergence of the person in dementia research', *Ageing and Society*, 17(5), pp. 597–607.

Farrell, A., and Brazier, M. (2016) 'Not so new directions in the law of consent? Examining Montgomery v Lanarkshire Health Board', *Journal of Medical Ethics*, 42(2), pp. 85–88.

Farrell, A., et al (2017) *Health Law Frameworks and Context*. Cambridge: Cambridge University Press.

Fineman, M. (2004) *The Autonomy Myth: A Theory of Dependency*. New York: The New Press.

Fineman, M. (2019) 'Vulnerability in law and bioethics', *Journal of Health Care for the Poor and Underserved*, 30(5), pp. 52–61.

Friedman, M. (2000) 'Autonomy, social disruption and women', in: MacKenzie, C. and Stoljar, N. (eds) *Relational Autonomy: Feminist Perspectives on Autonomy, Agency and the Social Self*, pp. 25–51. Oxford: OUP.

Gaffney-Rhys, R. 'Sheffield City Council v E and another - Capacity to marry and the rights and responsibilities of married couples', *Child and Family Law Quarterly*, 18(1), pp. 139–150.

Hall, M. (2009) 'Capacity, vulnerability, risk, and consent', in: O'Connor, D. and Purves, B. (eds) *Decision-Making, Personhood and Dementia, Exploring the Interface*. London: Jessica Kingsley Publishers.

Hall, M. (2019) 'Relational autonomy, vulnerability theory, older adults and the law: Making it real', *Elder Law Review*, 12, pp. 1–22.

Hamilton, M. et al (2021) 'Understanding barriers to the realization of human rights among older women with mental health conditions', *The American Journal of Geriatric Psychiatry*, 29(2), pp. 1–5.

Harding, R. (2018) *Duties to Care, Dementia, Relationality and Law*. Cambridge: CUB.

Harrison, F. et al (2020) 'Prolonged use of antipsychotic medications in long-term aged care in Australia: A snapshot from the HALT project', *International Psychogeriatrics*, 32(3), pp. 335–345.

Harrison, S. et al (2020) 'The dispensing of psychotropic medicines to older people before and after they enter residential aged care', *Medical Journal of Australia*, 212(7), pp. 309–313. https://doi-org.ezproxy.lib.rmit.edu.au/10.5694/mja2.50501.

Herring, J. (2016) *Vulnerable Adults and the Law*. Oxford: Oxford University Press.

Herring, J., and Wall, J. (2015) 'Autonomy, capacity and vulnerable adults: Filling the gaps in the Mental Capacity Act', *Legal Studies*, 35(4), pp. 698–719.

Heywood, R., and Miola, J. (2017) 'The changing face of pre-operative medical disclosure: Placing the patient at the heart of the matter', *Law Quarterly Review*, 133(April), pp. 296–321.

Holroyd, S., Turnbull, Q., and Wolf, A. (2002) 'What are patients and their families told about the diagnosis of dementia? Results of a family survey, *International Journal of Geriatric Psychiatry*, 17(2), pp. 218–221.

Jones, H., and Davis, D. (2021) 'What you need to know about: Delirium in older adults in hospital', *British Journal of Hospital Medicine*, Dec, 2021. https://doi.org/10.12968/hmed.2020.0603.

Kalisch Ellet, L., and Lim, R. (2020) 'We need to do better: Most people with dementia living in aged care facilities use antipsychotics for too long, for off-label indications and without documented consent', *International Psychogeriatrics*, 32(3), pp. 299–302.

King's college hospital NHS Foundation Trust that, under s 3(1)(c) of the Mental Capacity Act: [2015] EWCOP 80.

Lock, D. (2015) 'Decision-making, mental capacity and undue influence: Action by public bodies to explore the grey areas between capacity and incapacity', *Judicial Review*, 20(1), pp. 42–49.

Mackenzie, C., and Stoljar, N. 'Relational autonomy in feminist bioethics', in: Rogers, W. et al (eds) *Routledge Companion to Feminist*. Routledge, Taylor and Francis Group. DOI https://10.4324/9781003016885-7

Marzanski, M. (2000) 'Would you like to know what is wrong with you? On telling the truth to patients with dementia', *Journal of Medical Ethics*, 26(2), pp. 108–113.

McCann, M., Donnelly, M., and O'Reilly, D. (2012) 'Gender differences in care home admission risk: Partner's age explains the higher risk for women', *Age and Ageing*, 41(3), pp. 416–419.

Megret, F. (2011) 'The human rights of older persons: A growing challenge', *Human Rights Law Review*, 11(1), pp. 37–66.

Molenda, D., and Lusis, S. (2015) 'Informed consent for psychotropic medication use: A novel approach to changing physician behavior', *Journal of the American Medical Directors Association*, 16(12), pp. 1097–1099.

Montgomery v Lanarkshire Health Board [2015], UKSC 11 2015 2, WLR 768.

OPA, Office of the Public Advocate. (2020) *Supported Decision Making in Victoria*. https://www.publicadvocate.vic.gov.au/joomlatools-files/docman-files/general/Supported_Decision_Making_in_Victoria.pdf.

Purser, K., Cockburn, T., and Ulrick, E. (2019) 'Examining access to formal justice mechanisms for vulnerable older people in the context of enduring powers of attorney', *Elder Law Review*, 12(1), pp. 1–32.

Peisah, C., and Skladzien, E. (2014) *The Use of Restraints and Psychotropic Medications in People with Dementia, A Report for Alzheimer's Australia* (Dementia Australia Paper 38, March 2014). https://dementia.org.au.

Peisah, C. et al (2020) 'Advocacy for the human rights of older people in the COVID pandemic and beyond: A call to mental health professionals', *International Journal of Psychogeriatrics*, 32(10), pp. 1199–1204.

Pritchard-Jones, L. (2019) 'Exploring the potential and the pitfalls of the United Nations convention on the rights of persons with disabilities and general comment no. 1 for people with dementia', *International Journal of Law and Psychiatry*, 66, 101467. https://doi.org/10.1016/j.ijlp.2019.101467.
Quinn, M.J. (2000) 'Undoing undue influence', *Journal of Elder Abuse and Neglect*, 12(2), pp. 9–17.
Quinn, G., and Mahler, C. (2021) 'Reducing the burden of ageism, mentalism, and ableism: Transforming the narrative for older persons with mental health conditions and psychosocial disability', *The American Journal of Geriatric Psychiatry*, 29(10), pp. 993–994.
Re MB (An Adult: Medical Treatment) [1997] 2 FLR 426.
Rendina, N. et al (2009) 'Substitute consent for nursing home residents prescribed psychotropic medication', *International Journal of Geriatric Psychiatry*, 24(3), pp. 226–231.
Rioux, M. et al (2013) 'Negotiating capacity: Legally constructed entitlements and protection', in: McSherry,B. and Freckelton, I. (eds) *Coercive Care: Rights, Law and Policy*, pp. 51–75. London and New York: Routledge.
Ryan, C. (2012) 'Playing the ferryman: Psychiatry's role in end-of-life decision-making', *Australian and New Zealand Journal of Psychiatry*, 46(10), pp. 932–935.
Samsi, K., and Manthorpe, J. (2013) 'Everyday decision-making in dementia: Findings from a longitudinal interview study of people with dementia and family carers', International Psychogeriatrics, 25(6), pp. 949–996. https://doi.org/10.1017/S1041610213000306.
Sheffield City Council v E and another [2004] EWHC, 2808 (Fam), [2005] 2 WLR 953,
Skowron, P. (2019) 'The relationship between autonomy and adult mental capacity in the law of England and Wales', *Medical Law Review*, 27(1), pp. 32–58. https://doi.org/10.1093/medlaw/fwy016.
Starson v Swayze [2003] 1 Scientific Review 722.
Szmukler, G., and Dawson, J. (2011) 'Reducing discrimination in mental health law: The fusion of incapacity and mental health legislation', in: Kallert, T., Mezzich, J., and Monahan, J. (eds) *Coercive Treatment in Psychiatry*, pp 97–120. London: Wiley and Sons.
Szmukler, G., and Kelly, B. (2016) 'We should replace conventional mental health law with capacity-based law', *British Journal of Psychiatry*, 209(6), pp. 449–453.
UN, United Nations (2019) World population ageing 2019, department of economic and social affairs. Geneva: United Nations. ST/ESA/SER.A/430. un.org/en/development/desa/population/publications/pdf/ageing/WorldPopulationAgeing2019-Highlights.pdf.
Vulnerable adults with capacity case (2012), Re L(vulnerable adults with capacity: Courts jurisdiction (No 2) [2012] EWCA Civ 253.
Werner, P., and Doron, I. (2017) 'Alzheimer's disease and the law: Positive and negative consequences of structural stigma and labelling in the legal system', *Aging and Mental Health*, 21(11), pp. 1206–1213.
Wilkinson's case: R (Wilkinson) v Broadmoor Hospital authority [2002] 1 WLR 419.
WHO (2021) *Global Report on Ageism, Global Report on Ageism*. Geneva: World Health Organization. https://www.who.int/teams/social-determinants-of-health/demographic-change-and-healthy-ageing/combatting-ageism/global-report-on-ageism.
WHO, World Health Organisation (2015) *World Report on Health and Aging*. Geneva: World Health Organisation. https://apps.who.int/iris/bitstream/handle/10665/186463/9789240694811_eng.pdf;jsessionid=336E1853D741666A8B245B334A64238A?sequence=1.

10
ABUSE, NEGLECT, AND ADULT SAFEGUARDING IN THE CONTEXT OF MENTAL HEALTH AND DISABILITY

Laura Pritchard-Jones

Introduction

History is littered with instances of the abuse and neglect of people with mental or cognitive disabilities across community and institutional settings both in the United Kingdom and beyond. From emerging concerns about 'granny battering' in the 1970s (Burston, 1975), the rise of debates about elder abuse and self-neglect in America in the 1990s and 2000s, to the horrific abuse and murder of Steven Hoskin in Cornwall in 2006 (Flynn, 2007), and the abuse and neglect of mental health patients at Ely Hospital, Cardiff, in the 1960s (Howe, 1969), to the deaths of Joanna, 'Jon', and Ben, three adults with learning disabilities at Cawston Park Hospital, Norfolk, in 2019–20 (Flynn, 2021), it appears that abuse and neglect of people with learning disabilities, mental health conditions, or other cognitive or mental disabilities is widespread and commonplace. While the focus of this chapter is predominantly on the situation in England and Wales, it should be noted at the outset that such abuse is present in many communities and many countries. In 2022, for example, the Council of Europe's Committee for the Prevention of Torture and Inhuman or Degrading Treatment or Punishment (CPT) held talks with Bulgarian officials regarding the repeated findings in CPT reports of abuse and ill-treatment at Bulgarian mental health hospitals and social welfare institutions (Council of Europe, 4 November 2021). Likewise, the importance of Article 19 of the United Nations Convention on the Rights of Persons with Disabilities (the right to independent living) lies partly in the fact that adults with disabilities – often cognitive or mental disabilities – have historically been subjected to mass institutionalisation (UNCRPD, 2017), much of which has been abusive and corrosive of their rights.

Identifying and responding to such abuse and neglect also presents challenges; people with mental or cognitive disabilities may face difficulties reporting abuse, or experience 'psychiatric disqualification' whereby they are not believed, or their evidence may be perceived as unreliable because of their disabilities (Carr et al., 2019). Moreover, abuse which has been uncovered in many care homes and hospitals such as that revealed by the BBC documentary *Panorama* at Winterbourne View in the United Kingdom is also the very antithesis of what patients should expect from an institution where they have been taken, sometimes against their will, to be cared for. Cassie's story exemplifies such sentiments. Cassie was a woman in her mid-50s who had a learning disability and had lived in an 'unstimulating' care home since she was a child. During her time at this care home, she had been raped, most likely by a care worker, which had led to her contracting HIV. Moreover, as Cassie had difficulties communicating, this fact was only discovered following routine medical appointments. As Cassie's mother commented in the safeguarding inquiry into her daughter's care (or lack of), 'They're supposed to be specialists. I trusted them' (Flynn, 2018a, p. 6).

Despite many cases of such abuse and neglect among adults with mental or cognitive disabilities coming to light over the years, adult safeguarding – the prevention of and protection from abuse and neglect among adults, particularly those with needs for care and support – in England and Wales has only recently developed into an area of law and practice in its own right. This is in comparison to child safeguarding, a firmer focus on which emerged in the 1980s. It is thus unsurprising that early schemes and processes for adult safeguarding in the late 1990s and early 2000s in England and Wales were therefore modelled, to a large extent, on child safeguarding processes and the centralisation of the protection imperative that is so clearly at the forefront of child safeguarding. This is notwithstanding the clear differences between the needs of adults compared to those of children. Moreover, adult safeguarding has – traditionally – been seen as the poor relation to child safeguarding (HMICFRS, 2019); a sentiment that perhaps partially explains *why* history is so littered with such examples of the abuse and neglect of adults with disabilities. This chapter is therefore a timely opportunity to take stock of three aspects connected with mental health law and treatment. The first is to explore abuse and neglect and how it affects adults with mental health, cognitive, or intellectual disabilities. The second is the legal framework around adult safeguarding. Lastly – because adult safeguarding depends as much on professional implementation of legal powers as on the existence of a robust legal framework in itself – is the extent to which the laws and policies that *do* exist work in practice to safeguard adults with mental health conditions from abuse and neglect. In much the same way that the abuse of people with mental health or cognitive impairments is not solely an English and Welsh phenomenon, many of the issues that arise under these legal frameworks and their translation into practice are similarly mirrored in other jurisdictions.

Abuse, neglect, and mental health

In order to understand abuse and neglect in the context of mental health, it is first necessary to understand what we mean by abuse and neglect more generally and how it impacts adults with mental health, cognitive, or intellectual disabilities. Definitions of what constitutes abuse typical fall into two kinds. The first are those concerned with evaluating what abuse is on a conceptual level and are often – understandably – linked to some sort of harm (Department of Health, 1993). These ideas often explain abuse and neglect as a violation of or having an adverse effect on a person's human rights (Department of Health, 2000; Law Commission, 2011), or – in some narrower definitions – conduct that harms a person where there is or should be an expectation of trust (Action on Elder Abuse, 2004; Dixon et al., 2010). The second kind of definitions are those that seek to identify taxonomies or types of abuse. In England, for example, the Care and Support Statutory Guidance (Department of Health and Social Care, 2022, Ch 14) states that abuse can be physical, sexual, financial, psychological, discriminatory, organisational, and can include domestic violence, modern slavery, and neglect, including self-neglect. Furthermore, even within these taxonomies, adult safeguarding has seen a proliferation of language used to identify different types of abuse, such as 'cuckooing'[1], 'county lines',[2] and 'mate crime',[3] and which are often forms of exploitation that disproportionately affect people with mental or cognitive disabilities (Landman, 2014).

Statistical evidence suggests that such abuse, neglect, and exploitation is a common concern among people with mental health disabilities. In England, the annual Safeguarding Adults Collection (SAC) statistics, for example, collate information about safeguarding concerns received and enquiries undertaken each year in every local authority. In 2020–21 there were an estimated 152,270 adult safeguarding enquiries across all local authorities; 39,070 of these enquiries related to individuals who required support with memory and cognition, a learning disability, or for adults who had mental health support needs (NHS Digital, 2021a). These high rates of suspected abuse and neglect are mirrored by the wider literature. In their international review exploring prevalence rates of abuse against people with disabilities, Hughes et al. (2012) found that those with mental illnesses were particularly at risk of violence; the pooled prevalence rate of any violence against a person with mental illness was 24.3%, while Cambridge (1999) highlights that organisational or institutional abuse against people with learning disabilities – that which occurs in care homes or residential facilities, for example – often involves multiple different types of abuse such as physical, emotional, or sexual. This picture is mirrored internationally, with higher rates of neglect and physical, emotional, or psychological abuse documented in the institutional care of older adults with dementia in other countries (Bužgová and Ivanová, 2009; Kangasniemi et al., 2022). COVID-19, and the response to the pandemic through lockdowns, suspension of social care duties in many countries, enforced shielding and isolation, and mandatory suspension of visits by friends, relatives, professionals, and regulators to care homes and hospitals, has also exacerbated this situation; this picture has also been mirrored globally (Beaulieu, Genessa, and St-Martin, 2020). There have been increased concerns about deteriorating mental health among adults, as well as increased concerns about being able to gain access to organisations and environments such as care homes or a person's own home where there is suspected abuse (Local Government Association, 2021; Pritchard-Jones et al., 2022; Spivakovsky and Steele, 2022).

At this point it is also briefly worth considering the specific position of adults with mental health or cognitive disabilities who live in or are patients in institutional settings such as care homes, nursing homes, or mental health hospitals. In the UK alone, it is estimated that nearly half a million people – predominantly with dementia – live in care homes (Statista, May 2021), and over 50,000 adults with learning disabilities live in some form of supported living accommodation or care home (Public Health England, 2020). Elsewhere, for example, the USA has 1.7 million beds in nursing homes (CDC, undated), while China has over 8 million beds in care homes or welfare institutions (Statista, September 2021). In many ways adults in these settings might also be seen as doubly disadvantaged or at risk of abuse and neglect. First, not only are they at risk of direct abuse and neglect from the staff that care for

---

1 Where a person takes over another's property in order to exploit them.
2 Recruiting adults or children – often those considered 'at risk' – to traffic and deal drugs into more rural communities.
3 Where someone, often with mental health conditions or learning disabilities, is befriended by another person, and this is used to then exploit them financially, physically, or sexually.

them, but often this is because the very environment around them is abusive or toxic itself; one where 'closed cultures' and restrictive practices as the norm prevail, making it even more difficult to identify and respond to such abuse. As the current statutory guidance to the Care Act 2014 notes in England, organisational abuse includes:

> neglect and poor care practice within an institution or specific care setting such as a hospital or care home, for example…This may range from one off incidents to on-going ill-treatment. It can be through neglect or poor professional practice as a result of the structure, policies, processes and practices within an organisation.
> *(Department of Health and Social Care, 2022, para. 14.17)*

The abuse and neglect of people with mental health, cognitive, or intellectual disabilities who are patients of, or live in, these types of organisational or institutional settings has a longstanding history. This is undoubtedly linked to historical perceptions among many communities of adults with such disabilities as 'monsters' or 'deviants' in need of control (Sandland, 2013; Jarrett, 2020), and who find themselves in settings where 'normal moral concerns' are neutralised through a process of depersonalisation of adults with such disabilities (Wardhaugh and Wilding, 1993, p. 6). In 1969, for example, an investigation was commissioned into the mistreatment of adults with mental health conditions at Ely Hospital, a large psychiatric hospital in Cardiff. The inquiry identified far-reaching and individualised instances of abusive behaviour such as ill-treatment, inhumane and threatening behaviour towards patients, theft of food, clothes, and other items belonging to the patients, indifference to complaints, and general lack of care by the medical team based at the hospital. Beyond this, however, the investigation found that a toxic culture prevailed, which culminated in hospital staff and management having 'an unduly casual attitude towards death' of patients, all of whom had mental illnesses or disabilities (Department of Health and Social Security, 1969, para. 78(b)). A look at the history of psychiatric hospitals and treatment globally shows that such concerns and reports of abuse, ill-treatment, and high mortality rates can also be found in many countries, particularly in psychiatric institutions and asylums (Geller, 2006; Prior, 2012).

Since the Ely Hospital inquiry in the 1960s, reports of similar serious abuse and neglect by both publicly and privately run care providers of people with mental illnesses, dementia, or learning disabilities, continue to emerge in England and Wales. To name a few, these include the Oxfordshire Learning Disability NHS Trust (Verita, 2015), Southern Health NHS Foundation Trust (Pascoe, 2021), Nye Bevan Lodge (Gibbs, Evans, and Rodway, 1987), Cawston Park Hospital in Norfolk (Flynn, 2021), Atlas Homes Ltd (Flynn, 2019), Whorlton Hall in Durham (Murphy, 2022), Mendip House in Somerset (Flynn, 2018b), Winterbourne View in South Gloucestershire (Flynn and Citarella, 2012), Purbeck Care Home in Dorset (DBPSAB, 2015), the 24 south-east Wales care homes owned by Dr N Das and Dr P Das that were investigated as part of Operation Jasmine (Flynn, 2015), and Orchid View in West Sussex (WSSAB, 2014). It is therefore unsurprising that some commentators have suggested that this risk of abuse, combined with the controlled and controlling environments in which individuals live when they reside in institutions and the 'huge asymmetry of power between service user and service provider' (Williams and Keating, 2000, p. 35), as well as the general reluctance of mental health services to tackle abuse, arguably means that institutions – in which people with mental or cognitive disabilities are much more likely to be living or treated – could be considered a form of abuse in themselves (Whitelock, 2009;

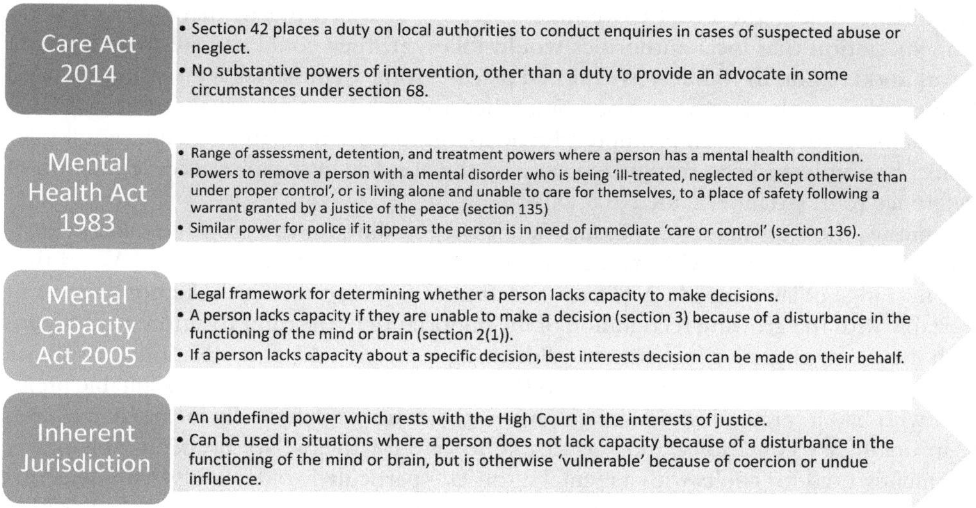

Abuse, neglect, and adult safeguarding

Care Act 2014
- Section 42 places a duty on local authorities to conduct enquiries in cases of suspected abuse or neglect.
- No substantive powers of intervention, other than a duty to provide an advocate in some circumstances under section 68.

Mental Health Act 1983
- Range of assessment, detention, and treatment powers where a person has a mental health condition.
- Powers to remove a person with a mental disorder who is being 'ill-treated, neglected or kept otherwise than under proper control', or is living alone and unable to care for themselves, to a place of safety following a warrant granted by a justice of the peace (section 135).
- Similar power for police if it appears the person is in need of immediate 'care or control' (section 136).

Mental Capacity Act 2005
- Legal framework for determining whether a person lacks capacity to make decisions.
- A person lacks capacity if they are unable to make a decision (section 3) because of a disturbance in the functioning of the mind or brain (section 2(1)).
- If a person lacks capacity about a specific decision, best interests decision can be made on their behalf.

Inherent Jurisdiction
- An undefined power which rests with the High Court in the interests of justice.
- Can be used in situations where a person does not lack capacity because of a disturbance in the functioning of the mind or brain, but is otherwise 'vulnerable' because of coercion or undue influence.

Figure 10.1 Key adult safeguarding legislation in England

Series, 2022). Moreover, additional research worldwide highlights that a particular risk factor for institutional abuse is a higher level of need for support with memory, cognition, and activities of daily living, suggesting that those with the most complex mental health, intellectual, or cognitive disabilities, may also be the most vulnerable to abuse or neglect (Kamavarapu et al., 2017; Yon et al., 2019). Yet such instances of abuse and neglect may also be the most difficult to identify given the difficulties adults with such complex needs might face in reporting abuse of this kind, together with the fact that such abuse often roots itself where there are closed and inward-looking cultures within institutions.

The legal framework for adult safeguarding in England

Historical developments

As explained above, the focus on adult safeguarding in law and policy is a recent development, even if acknowledgement of the abuse and neglect of adults with mental health conditions or cognitive disabilities is not (Sherwood-Johnson, 2016). In England, the earliest specific guidance on safeguarding adults at risk of abuse or neglect, *No Secrets* (Department of Health, 2000), was published in 2000, with its Welsh counterpart, *In Safe Hands* (Welsh Assembly Government, 2000), also published in the same year. This was the framework for ensuring multi-agency procedures were in place across local authorities to respond to the abuse of 'vulnerable'[4] adults. The *No Secrets* guidance, however, had only the status of formal

---

4 A vulnerable adult in *No Secrets* was an adult 'who is or may be in need of community care services by reason of mental or other disability, age or illness; and who is or may be unable to take care of him or herself, or unable to protect him or herself against significant harm or exploitation' (para. 2.3). The term has now been replaced in some legal frameworks by 'adult at risk' – see, for example, section 42 of the Care Act 2014, and section 126 of the Social Services and Well-being (Wales) Act 2014.

policy guidance under the Local Government Act 1972, which meant that although there was an expectation that local authorities would follow it, they could deviate from it where there was good reason to. While – as explored below – some minimal legal provisions beyond *No Secrets* did exist, there remained no comprehensive and systematic legal powers available for safeguarding adults, which prompted Mandelstam to note that 'In England, [adult safeguarding] has hitherto been recognized only by the absence in social services legislation of any reference to it' (Mandelstam, 2013, p. 41).

Historically, the legal framework around adult safeguarding for the protection and prevention of abuse among adults with mental or cognitive disabilities in England and Wales thus rested on a range of laws outside *No Secrets* and *In Safe Hands*, ones which did not seem to sit comfortably with the growing recognition of the importance of the right to autonomy for people with mental or cognitive impairments. For example, section 47 of the National Assistance Act 1948 gave powers to remove a person with needs for care and support to a suitable premises and who had a 'grave chronic disease', was 'aged, infirm or physically incapacitated', was living in unsanitary conditions, and was unable to care for themselves properly. This power was frequently used for adults with a mental disorder – particularly older adults with dementia – and often resulted in higher mortality rates (Wolfson et al., 1990). Unsurprisingly, section 47 was severely criticised as unethical and a violation of peoples' rights (Hobson, 1998). The use of section 47 in relation to adults with mental disabilities was further confused when the Mental Health Act 1983 (MHA) came into force. Not only does the latter Act provide a range of assessment, detention, and treatment provisions – explored elsewhere in this collection – and which can clearly be of relevance in situations where someone with a 'mental disorder' is being abused, but section 135 of the 1983 Act also gives powers to remove a person with a mental disorder who is being 'ill-treated, neglected or kept otherwise than under proper control', or is living alone and unable to care for themselves, to a place of safety following a warrant granted by a justice of the peace. Police have a similar power under section 136 if it appears the person is in need of immediate 'care or control'. The use of this latter power is more common than the section 135 power; in 2020–21, for example, there were 20,153 recorded place of safety detentions under section 136, but only 909 recorded under section 135 (NHS Digital, 2021b).

In essence, the pre-2000 legal landscape designed to protect adults with mental or cognitive disabilities – or, indeed, *any* adults – from abuse or neglect, was piecemeal. As will be shown below, it arguably still is. Moreover, it largely did not fit with the increased concern for ensuring human rights-compliant approaches in healthcare law and practice that was beginning to emerge in the early 2000s, following the passing of the Human Rights Act 1998. Similar criticisms around coercive adult safeguarding procedures have also been made – and continue to be made – in other jurisdictions; for example, the criminalisation of and mandatory duties to report suspected elder abuse in America. This has led to concerns expressed by Kohn (2009; 2012) that such measures automatically reduce the amount of control older adults have over their lives and are unethical.

The Care Act 2014

Concerns about the piecemeal approach to adult safeguarding in England and Wales led the Law Commission in its 2011 review of adult social care law to comment that:

[t]he existing legal framework for adult protection is 'neither systematic nor coordinated, reflecting the sporadic development of safeguarding policy over the last 25

years'…there is no single or coherent statutory framework for adult protection in England and Wales. Instead, it must be discerned through reference to a wide range of law.

(Law Commission, 2011, para. 9.1, references omitted)

It is these concerns that, in turn, prompted the inclusion of specific legal obligations in relation to adult safeguarding in the Care Act 2014. The primary adult safeguarding duty is now to be found under section 42 of that Act. This places a duty on local authorities to undertake an inquiry if it suspects that an adult in its area has needs for care and support, is at risk of or experiencing abuse or neglect, and as a result of their needs is unable to protect themselves against the abuse, neglect, or risk of it. This obligation arises regardless of whether they have any services in place to meet their needs. Having needs for care and support includes adults with mental health, cognitive, or intellectual disabilities. However, unlike other legislation in the UK,[5] section 42 provides no substantive powers of intervention in situations of actual or suspected abuse, but is effectively a gatekeeper clause, which has the purpose of effecting an inquiry, usually by the local authority. This inquiry might be delegated to another party or organisation, but the local authority retains overall responsibility for ensuring it is conducted, and the timescales within which this should be done.

Moreover, the Care Act 2014 also now places a legal obligation on local Safeguarding Adults Boards (SABs)[6] to undertake Safeguarding Adults Reviews (SARs) where a person in their area has died from abuse or neglect or is still alive and suffered serious abuse or neglect, and there is reasonable cause for concern about how the SAB, members of it, or other persons with relevant functions worked together to safeguard the adult (section 44, Care Act 2014). In addition to these, section 68 of the Care Act also places a duty on local authorities to provide independent advocacy for people at the centre of safeguarding reviews or inquiries where they may have substantial difficulties understanding or retaining information, using and weighing information, or communicating their views and wishes, and where it appears there is nobody else appropriate to support and represent the adult. Given its alignment with the test for mental capacity under the Mental Capacity Act 2005 (MCA) as explored below in the context of safeguarding, section 68 is therefore particularly relevant for people with mental health, cognitive, or intellectual impairments, although there is very limited evidence or data as to its use.

In many ways, then, the Care Act 2014 is the *most* important legal tool in respect of adult safeguarding by identifying when a duty arises, what that duty is (an inquiry, review, or advocacy) and by whom (the local authority or SAB). On the other hand, it is, in many ways, also the *least* important legal framework; it offers no powers to a local authority or any of its partner organisations to do anything where they find evidence of abuse, neglect, or the risk of it, beyond undertaking an inquiry or providing advocacy. This remains within

---

5 The Social Services and Well-being (Wales) Act 2014, for example, provides for an Adult Support and Protection Order (section 127), which allows a justice of the peace to grant an order authorising someone to speak to a suspected adult at risk privately, to ascertain whether that person is making decisions freely, and what action should be taken. On some organisations there is also a mandatory duty to report to the local authority if they suspect an adult is at risk of abuse or neglect (section 128).
6 These are regional bodies which have strategic oversight for leading adult safeguarding activity in their area. They should have representatives from a wide range of organisations.

the domain of the rest of the civil and criminal law. In particular, much rests on the duties and powers available under the MCA: in the latest SAC statistics, for example, 44,550 adults at the centre of the safeguarding inquiry under section 42 lacked mental capacity to make decisions related to the inquiry (NHS Digital, 2021a). As will be explored further below, analyses of Safeguarding Adults Reviews also often highlight failings in professional and legal literacy, especially around the use of the MCA and, indeed, the MHA in safeguarding adults with mental health, cognitive, or intellectual disabilities.

The Mental Capacity Act 2005

As outlined previously in this edited collection, the MCA provides the main legal framework in England and Wales which supports, but also ultimately controls and regulates, decision-making among adults with a mental health, cognitive, or intellectual disability. This Act establishes a set of principles that govern anything done under the legislation (section 1). The first group of these principles relate to capacity itself, and include first and foremost a presumption of capacity (section 1(2)), that a person must not be assumed to lack capacity to make decisions simply because they make an unwise decision (section 1(3)), and that a person is not to be taken to lack capacity unless they have been provided with all practicable support to make a decision (section 1(4)). The second group of these principles relate to the processes which are invoked once a person lacks capacity, and require anything done to be in their best interests (section 1(5)), and in deciding what is in their best interests consideration must be given as to any less restrictive alternatives (section 1(6)). Beyond these principles, the Act also provides the legal framework by which a person's mental capacity to make decisions must be assessed. To establish that a person lacks capacity to make a particular decision at a particular time, they must be unable to understand information relevant to that decision, or retain that information, or use and weigh that information in a balance to reach a decision, or communicate their decision (section 3(1)). This inability to make a decision must be because of an impairment or disturbance in the functioning of the mind or brain (section 2(1)), such as alcohol or drug abuse, dementia, learning disabilities, mental health conditions, or acquired brain injuries (Department for Constitutional Affairs, 2007, para. 4.12).[7] If a person does lack capacity to make a decision then a decision can be made on their behalf in their best interests, but section 4 requires that, *inter alia*, the person's wishes, feelings, values, and beliefs are taken into consideration in making this decision, as are the views of anyone engaged in caring for them (section 4(6) and (7)).

Despite the extensive territory now occupied by the MCA and its clear relevance for adult safeguarding in situations where someone with mental health conditions or cognitive impairments may be unable to make a decision, the way it operates – particularly in situations where there is abuse or neglect *together with* a 'disturbance in the functioning of the mind or brain' – is not always entirely clear. In precisely these types of situations it may not always be clear what the relationship is between the 'disturbance in the functioning of the mind or brain' – to use the language of the Act itself – and the abuse or neglect, and therefore what the joint impact of this is on the person's decision-making or their ability to make a decision. Legally this is significant, as it is only in the former situation that the MCA has any jurisdiction. In *Leicester*

---

7 At the time of writing, the Government are consulting on a new draft code of practice to the Mental Capacity Act; however, this element is replicated in the new draft Code (HM Government, 2022, para. 4.46).

City Council v MPZ [2019] EWCOP 64, for example, 'Mary' (a pseudonym) had diagnoses of Emotionally Unstable Personality Disorder and Dependent Personality Disorder resulting from severe childhood trauma, including sexual abuse. In adulthood, she had entered into a relationship with a man over whom there were concerns about sexual abuse and exploitation. In deciding whether Mary lacked capacity to make decisions about – among other things – sexual relationships, the evidence suggested that Mary did not understand that she had the right to say no to a sexual relationship. In effect, she did not understand that she could refuse or withhold consent to sex. The evidence suggested that she understood in theory that people generally could say no, but not that *she herself* could say no. However, Mary would only lack capacity under the MCA if she was unable to understand this information because of her personality disorders. If it was not possible – on the balance of probabilities – to establish this, or if her difficulties understanding this seemed to be because of the effect of the exploitative relationships or coercion from the sexual partners, this would not be covered by the MCA.

A similar situation arose in *London Borough of Redbridge v G* [2014] EWHC 485 (COP). G was an older lady with dementia who had been an active member of her community and church for many years. She had been befriended by two adults (C and F) whom she had met through her church and who had eventually moved into her home with her to care for her. There were increasing concerns about G potentially being financially and psychologically abused, including concerns that the carers were coercing her to leave her property and finances to them. As with *Leicester City Council v MPZ*, the local authority sought orders under the MCA to the effect that G lacked capacity because of her dementia; however, it was not immediately clear, or easy to decide, whether G lacked capacity as a result of her dementia or whether her decision-making was coerced by C and F and because of their influence, only the former being covered by the MCA. The Court of Protection in both cases decided that Mary and G lacked capacity under the MCA, in effect because of their mental or cognitive disabilities.

The inherent jurisdiction

In situations such as Mary's or G's, where there is a confluence of abuse with a mental or cognitive disability, it is therefore unsurprising that this aspect of the MCA and its operation could be seen as a source of criticism. It requires artificial mental gymnastics by capacity assessors, and sometimes judges in the Court of Protection, as to what exactly is causing a person's inability to decide: a mental disorder, or the abuse and coercion. It is only in relation to the former that the MCA can be used. In 2012, in the important case of *DL v A Local Authority* [2012] EWCA Civ 253 the Court of Appeal thus identified a lacuna in the law: there was no legal scope for intervention where a person is unable to make a decision, but because of coercion, rather than a mental disorder. This lacuna was filled by the Court of Appeal which indicated that in such cases, the inherent jurisdiction – a theoretically limitless power vested in the High Court to make decisions in the interests of justice – could be used. According to Lord Justice McFarlane:

> There is, in my view, a sound and strong public policy justification for [the availability of the inherent jurisdiction]. The existence of 'elder abuse'…is sadly all too easy to contemplate…Where the facts justify it, such individuals require and deserve the protection of the authorities and the law so that they may regain the very autonomy that the appellant rightly prizes.
>
> *(DL v A Local Authority, para. 63)*

In such cases, the inherent jurisdiction is available where a person does not lack capacity under the MCA, i.e. because of a disturbance in the functioning of the mind or brain, but is otherwise 'vulnerable' (*Re SA* [2005] EWHC 2942) or incapacitated from making a decision because of undue influence, coercion, or abuse. It is therefore not uncommon to see cases where there is a confluence of a mental or cognitive disability, together with abuse and neglect, arrive at court for a final decision as to incapacity. When they do – of which *Leciester City Council v MPZ* and *London Borough of Redbridge v G* were two examples – they often require a final determination as to whether a person lacks capacity under the MCA, or if not, whether orders are available under the inherent jurisdiction on the basis of the person being a 'vulnerable adult' because of the abuse or coercion. It is this unsatisfactory gap in the statutory framework that the inherent jurisdiction has had to fill, which has led to some commentators seeking greater adult safeguarding powers than those that exist currently either in the Care Act, the MCA, or the MHA (Ruck Keene, 2017).

The law in practice

As mentioned in an earlier section of this chapter, adult safeguarding rests as much on professionals implementing and navigating the law correctly, as it does on having that robust legal framework for them to navigate in the first place. As Braye, Orr, and Preston-Shoot (2017, p. 326) note when writing in the context of the ethical complexity behind working with adults who self-neglect, '[h]ow practitioners understand the legal framework within which they work has a powerful influence on professional judgement'. This raises an interesting question that is not confined solely to England and Wales: what is, or should be, the role of laws in adult safeguarding, or protecting adults from abuse or neglect? Research suggests that following adult safeguarding procedures in, for example, mental health services, is often seen as an 'add on', or not central to professional roles (Fanneran, Kingston, and Bradley, 2013). However, in other settings – particularly institutional care – raising safeguarding concerns by whistleblowers, or family and friends of relatives, is fundamental to tackling abuse and neglect. This is especially pertinent given that many people with disabilities who live in these settings might have such complex needs that they are not in a position to report the abuse themselves, or identify it as abusive in the first place.

Yet notwithstanding this, in order to do anything to protect adults who may be experiencing abuse or neglect – whether this is undertaking a mental capacity assessment, putting measures in place to control who they might see, or admitting them for a mental health assessment – requires laws. It requires laws which grant professionals powers to do these things, and a detailed framework by which practitioners can act in accordance with such laws. It is precisely for this reason that the MCA was enacted in England and Wales. Until 2005 there had been longstanding concerns over the fact that no legal framework existed in order to determine whether a person lacked capacity; a legal situation which was described as 'a string bag, which can stretch further and hold more than a basket but which is essentially a group of holes' (Law Commission, 1995, para. 2.47). However, the law does not simply give powers to undertake actions that could be seen as protecting the adult; it also provides mechanisms by which professionals can be held accountable for the decisions they make. As this section of the chapter will show, professional accountability has been an increasing theme of adult safeguarding activity in recent years, including in situations where professionals fail to act in situations of abuse or neglect, notwithstanding the fact that there is a clear legal framework in place which would enable them – or indeed, require them – to do so.

Having therefore identified the most relevant areas of law in adult safeguarding where there is abuse or neglect among adults with mental health or cognitive disabilities in the previous section, this chapter now turn to a consideration of how these legal frameworks apply in practice. In doing so, this section of the chapter focuses on the primary legal frameworks outlined above: the Care Act 2014 and its associated guidance, the MCA and its interface with the inherent jurisdiction, and the MHA. It does not address each of these legal regimes separately, however, precisely because there are many common themes, misunderstandings, and challenges, that arise across professional implementation of all of them (Pritchard-Jones, 2020). Although the focus of this chapter is the domestic legal framework in England and Wales, it is also contended that many of the issues and themes identified – and particularly the ethical dilemmas that arise in implementing the law – are also highly relevant to other jurisdictions.

Many of the challenges that emerge in the research into the legal framework in England and Wales can be commonly identified as relating to professional literacy, both legal and ethical; that is, professional knowledge and understanding of the legal and ethical frameworks on which adult safeguarding activity rests. In 2020, for example, the Local Government Association (2020) published a national analysis of 231 Safeguarding Adults Reviews. A large number of the reviews in this analysis involved individuals with autism (n=23), a learning disability (n=57), and memory or cognition difficulties (n=69). However, it is notable that 161 of these SARs – some 70% of all SARs included – involved someone with a mental health condition. Across all 231 SARs, mental capacity was the top identified practice theme, and poor attention to mental capacity arose 138 times across all 231 reviews (Local Government Association, 2020, p. 73). One of the most common issues involving both the MCA and the MHA is a misunderstanding of the key principles among practitioners, when to undertake assessments, or how to navigate the legislation in conjunction with risk assessment or risk management among people with mental health, cognitive, or intellectual disabilities. For example, the presumption of capacity in section 1(2) of the MCA is often reported as not requiring any investigation as to whether a person's capacity might be compromised (Local Government Association, 2020). Likewise, section 1(4) – a person is not to be deemed to lack capacity simply because they make an unwise decision – is often interpreted erroneously as conferring a right to make unwise decisions, which also often results in practitioners not exploring whether a capacity assessment was needed in the first place. In one review, for example:

> A striking feature of this case was that in face of the evidently unwise decisions, increasing risk and self-neglect by X, and the dedication of a small group of professionals, how readily professionals both assumed he had mental capacity to make those decisions and avoided actively engaging with him in more probing discussions about the decisions and their consequences.
>
> *(Local Government Association, 2020, p. 118)*

This issue gets to the heart of a key ethical dilemma for professionals navigating the abuse and neglect of adults with mental health or cognitive disabilities: the balance between the ostensibly competing principles of autonomy versus protection, discussed below. However, it is also worth considering exactly what the relationship is between an unwise decision – for example, to remain in an abusive relationship – and capacity. Many pieces of capacity legislation include a principle to the effect that a person is not to be treated as lacking capacity simply because they make an unwise decision; see, for example, section 8(4) of the Assisted Decision-Making (Capacity) Act 2015 in Ireland, section 1(5) of the Mental Capacity Act (Northern Ireland) 2016, and section 3(4) of the Singaporean Mental Capacity Act 2008. It is clear that the ethos underpinning this sort of a provision is to avoid situations where individuals are identified as having made an unwise decision, leading to an automatic conclusion that they lack capacity to make that decision (similar to the 'concertina effect', discussed below). As Davis LJ noted in *DL v A Local Authority* (para. 76):

> It is…the essence of humanity that adults are entitled to be eccentric, entitled to be unorthodox, entitled to be obstinate, entitled to be irrational. Many are…there can be no power of public intervention simply because an adult proposes to make a decision, or to tolerate a state of affairs, which most would consider neither wise nor sensible.

However, the fact that someone is making an unwise decision or a series of unwise decisions, such as to remain in or embark on an abusive or exploitative relationship, may be a legitimate trigger for a capacity assessment. In effect, it may be evidence that a person's capacity to make that decision should be scrutinised more closely. This is also often what happens in practice in some domains, such as refusal of medical treatment for example; as Kong and Ruck Keene (2018, p. 99) note, 'many assessments come about when a person's choice diverges from the advice of professionals'. Yet as will be seen below, in situations where there is abuse or neglect of adults with mental health or cognitive disabilities, making an unwise decision is often conflated with having capacity to do so, with no fuller assessment as to a person's capacity to make that decision.

This issue has recently been identified in particular in relation to mental health treatment services where patients who are seeking to or who have attempted suicide are determined by practitioners to have the capacity to make the decision to take their own lives (Aves, 2022). Beyond the questionable legal position of this sort of a claim and the extent to which it relies on the MCA for something it is not legally intended to do (see Ruck Keene, 2020), the evidence suggests that this position – that the patient has the capacity to take their own life – is then used in turn to justify two things. First, it is used to justify failures to undertake a further capacity assessment to explore the impact of the person's mental health condition on their thinking and decision-making. Second, it is also used to justify not intervening to remove or minimise the risk of the patient actually committing suicide. This is notwithstanding that – as Ruck Keene (2020) points out – there is a clear operational duty under Article 2 of the European Convention on Human Rights to do so where practitioners are aware of a real and immediate risk to the person's life such as a suicide threat (*Savage v South Essex Partnership NHS Foundation Trust* [2008] UKHL 74). Such issues, and particularly the misuse and misinterpretation of the presumption of capacity, have been present since the entry into force of the MCA in 2007. Concerns regarding the interpretation of the MCA led the House of Lords Select Committee in 2014 to suggest that the presumption of capacity in section 1(2) of the Act in particular:

> is widely misunderstood by those involved in care. It is sometimes used to support non-intervention or poor care, leaving vulnerable adults exposed to risk of harm. In some cases this is because professionals struggle to understand how to apply the principle in practice. In other cases, the evidence suggests the principle has been deliberately misappropriated to avoid taking responsibility for a vulnerable adult.
>
> *(House of Lords Select Committee, 2014, para. 105)*

These findings around professional literacy and use of the legal frameworks are also replicated in analyses of SARs which explore the use – or misuse – of the MHA in cases where an adult has been abused or neglected. In Foss's (2021) review of SARs, for example, it was found that a common theme was failings in assessments under the MHA, inappropriately conducted risk assessments such as reliance on self-reported information, lack of professional curiosity around missed mental health or psychiatric appointments, as well as failing to make arrangements for access to statutory advocacy services. These findings regarding the use of the MHA, risk management, and professional curiosity by practitioners under the legislation are also evident in other similar reviews, including where there is a coexistence of mental health conditions with multiple exclusion homelessness, for example (Manthorpe and Martineau, 2019; Martineau et al., 2019). Lastly, such evidence has also been forthcoming in relation to the use (or lack thereof) of the court's inherent jurisdiction in cases where there is a confluence of a mental disability and abuse. Miss T (Isle of Wight Safeguarding Adults Board, 2016) died in 2015 following a long history of substance misuse, mental ill-health, and abusive relationships. She had been assessed both under the MCA and MHA on several occasions but there were repeated and grave concerns about the nature of her boyfriend, who would use drugs to control her. In particular, a consultant psychiatrist who assessed her in December 2014, 8 months before her death, felt that an application under the inherent jurisdiction would be appropriate because 'T's freedom of action was constrained by her past history of trauma and a lack of ability to make truly autonomous decisions' (Isle of Wight Safeguarding Adults Board, 2016, p. 12), and the local authority were advised as such by the head of a barristers' chambers, yet no application was made.

In many ways the findings of these reviews and the wider literature around the extent to which adult safeguarding is properly understood and embedded in mental health treatment is unsurprising. Research shows particular concerns about the extent to which adult safeguarding practice, legal literacy, and policies for appropriate adult safeguarding investigation and interventions have been embedded into mental health services. This naturally then impacts on the type of adult safeguarding activity that happens in this sector, and the extent to which concerns raised by patients or people with cognitive or mental health disabilities are taken seriously. In their survey looking at the extent to which adult safeguarding activity was embedded into mental health NHS services in England and Wales, for example, Fanneran, Kingston, and Bradley (2013) found that while most trusts did have leadership posts for adult safeguarding, there was limited frontline support for adult safeguarding activity, poor take-up of adult safeguarding training, defensive attitudes among staff, as well as limited knowledge and understanding of the MCA, particularly among mental health services (as opposed to learning disability services, which had better levels of legal literacy around the MCA). Evidence also suggests that fractured and fragmented approaches to adult safeguarding for adults with mental health, cognitive, or intellectual disabilities – who more often than not have input from multiple different services into their care – can exacerbate feelings of being disempowered in the safeguarding process (Carr et al., 2019; Hafford-Letchfield et al., 2021).

Beyond the issues around professional literacy outlined above, a further area of difficulty for practitioners involved in safeguarding adults with mental health, cognitive, or intellectual disabilities in navigating the law is the extent to which the wishes of the person being abused should be at the centre of any decision-making. In effect, to what extent, and when, should practitioners respect a person's wish to remain in an abusive situation? A key feature of developments in law and policy in adult safeguarding following the coming into force of the

Human Rights Act 1998 has been to place much greater emphasis on listening to the voice of the adult involved, and a respect for their rights. In effect, giving respect to the person's right to make their own autonomous decisions. Section 4(6)(a)–(b) of the MCA requires a consideration of the individual's past and present wishes and feelings, and the beliefs and values that would be likely to influence their decision if they had capacity. Likewise, section 4(7)(a)–(b) places an obligation on those making best interests decisions to take into account the views of anyone engaged in caring for the person who lacks capacity, or who has an interest in their welfare, or anyone named by them as to be consulted, and failing to do so will be a violation of the person's human rights.[8] The Care Act 2014 also requires local authorities to have regard to certain matters, such as the individual's views, wishes, feelings and beliefs, and the importance of beginning with the assumption that the individual is best placed to judge their own wellbeing (section 1(3)(a)–(b)), but also have regard to the need to protect people from abuse and neglect (section 1(3)(g)). It is this development in particular – the primacy given to the person's wishes – that has, in recent years, distinguished *adult* safeguarding from *child* safeguarding.

Yet evidence suggests widespread deviations in practice in the extent to which the person's wishes are considered, respected, and upheld. One of the central concerns outlined by the House of Lords Select Committee in their Post-Legislative Scrutiny of the MCA (House of Lords Select Committee, 2014), for example, was a regular lack of involvement in capacity assessments and best interests decision-making by both the individual concerned and their family or carers. This trend is replicated in broader empirical literature, for example, evidence of a lack of involvement by people living with dementia or their families in best interests decision-making regarding discharge from hospital or care planning, and inequalities in power dynamics where they had been involved, leading them to feel unvalued in the process (Emmett et al., 2013; Emmett et al., 2014). In addition to this, a 'concertina effect' sometimes emerges, 'whereby…the best interests decision had effectively already been made, and it appeared the assessment of (in)capacity was then carried out to provide the basis for that decision' (Williamson et al., 2012, p. 189). The 'concertina effect' may be particularly pronounced in situations where there are concerns that a person with mental health, cognitive, or intellectual disabilities apparently wants to stay in situations that expose them to abuse or neglect.

Underpinning these considerations is an ethical dilemma; that between respecting the right of people with mental health, cognitive, or intellectual disabilities to make autonomous decisions, and simultaneously recognising that there is also a duty to protect the person being abused or neglected. As His Honour Judge Mackie QC noted in *Davis v West Sussex County Council* (2012) EWHC 2152 (QB), '[t]hose working in this area face criticism for allegedly interfering when they intervene and for alleged neglect or worse when they do not' (para. 101). It is this view of autonomy and protection as being in opposition to each other that allows for misinterpretations of the MCA, particularly around capacity and unwise decisions, that have already been explored above in this chapter. Yet to reduce this point down

---

8 See, for example, *Winspear v City Hospitals Sunderland NHS Foundation Trust* [2015] EWHC 3250 (QB). Sections 5–6 of the MCA also provide a defence to anything done to a person if it is done in compliance with the legal framework in the statute. In *Winspear*, Baker J also held that failing to consult with Carl Winspear's mother, his main caregiver, was not in compliance with section 4 and therefore the defence was not available to those who acted.

to two competing principles that – at best – sit uncomfortably alongside each other, and – at worst – pull in opposite directions, obscures some more complex issues. First, autonomy and protection are not always competing principles. Adult safeguarding activity in relation to adults with mental health or cognitive disabilities relies on balancing them in a way that is both necessary and proportionate, for example, developing risk management plans in such a way as to mitigate some element of risk, while at the same time ensuring a person has the opportunity to develop their own skills in managing risk in relationships. Second, understanding that risk can be minimised but not eliminated entirely; as Munby J noted in a well-known judgment:

> The emphasis must be on sensible risk appraisal, not striving to avoid all risk, whatever the price, but instead seeking a proper balance and being willing to tolerate manageable or acceptable risks as the price appropriately to be paid in order to achieve some other good – in particular to achieve the vital good of the elderly or vulnerable person's happiness. What good is it making someone safer if it merely makes them miserable?
> (Local Authority X v MM and KM *[2007] EWHC 2003 (Fam) para. 120)*

Lastly, focussing exclusively on autonomy and protection and their role in adult safeguarding also obscures the fact that in navigating situations of abuse and neglect there are also further ethical considerations at play. For example, the most effective adult safeguarding relies on relationships of trust between professionals and the adults they support (Anka et al., 2017; Pritchard-Jones et al., 2022).

Conclusion

This chapter has sought to explore three interconnected aspects: what abuse and neglect is and how it affects people with mental health, cognitive, or intellectual disabilities; what the legal framework is in England and Wales to protect and prevent against such abuse; and how well that legal framework operates in practice. It is fair to say that the protection of adults has been somewhat late to the 'safeguarding party' that developed in the 1980s in relation to children. It was not until the early 2000s that specific adult safeguarding policies were devised and implemented; policies which had no legal force at that. Notwithstanding the progress made through the enactment of the MCA, and the reforms contained in the Care Act 2014, this *status quo* remains; adult safeguarding continues to rest on a complex patchwork of laws such as the MCA and MHA, and the Care Act, that are often misunderstood, misinterpreted, and misapplied. The lack of a systematic or robust adult safeguarding framework has also required the knotty involvement of the inherent jurisdiction of the High Court in situations where there is a confluence of mental disability and abuse or exploitation. Moreover, practitioners face professional, structural, and ethical challenges interpreting and implementing the law in situations where there is abuse and neglect in respect of adults with mental health, cognitive, or intellectual disabilities, and leave such adults at the risk of continued abuse.

It is clear that the abuse and neglect of adults with mental health or cognitive disabilities is a global problem, and as such the same challenges in identifying and responding to such abuse arise in many countries and communities. The abuse of people with such disabilities may be hidden, for example. Adults who experience it may not recognise it as abuse, or may face challenges in reporting it including psychiatric disqualification, or repercussions from those people abusing them. This may be particularly pronounced in historically closed settings such as care homes, nursing homes, and psychiatric hospitals. Beyond its identification, where abuse and neglect *is* present, practitioners face a plethora of issues in responding to it. For example, it is often difficult to navigate the relationship between a person ostensibly making an unwise decision with a lack of capacity; to what extent can, and should, an unwise decision indicate a cause for concern over a person's capacity in the first place? Moreover, given the often complex range of laws that exist to protect adults from abuse and neglect, practitioners can face challenges traversing professional and legal literacy in their respective jurisdictions. Finally, this area rests on clear ethical tensions; how can the right of adults with mental health or cognitive disabilities to make their own decisions be reconciled with the need to also protect those vulnerable to abuse?

References

Action on Elder Abuse. (2004). *Hidden Voices: Older People's Experience of Abuse*. London: Help the Aged.

Anka, A., Sorensen, P., Brandon, M. and Bailey, S. (2017). 'Social Work Intervention with Adults Who Self-Neglect in England: Responding to the Care Act 2014'. *Journal of Adult Protection*, 19(2), pp. 67–77.

Aves, W. (2022). '"If You Are Not a Patient They Like, Then You Have Capacity": Exploring Mental Health Patient and Survivor Experiences of being told "You Have the Capacity to End Your Life" [Internet]'. Psychiatry is Driving Me Mad. Available at: https://www.psychiatryisdrivingmemad.co.uk/post/if-you-are-not-a-patient-they-like-then-you-have-capacity (accessed 22 June 2022).

Beaulieu, M., Genesse., J. C. and St-Martin, K. (2020). 'COVID-19 and Residential Care Facilities: Issues and Concerns Identified by the International Network Prevention of Elder Abuse (INPEA)'. *Journal of Adult Protection*, 22(6), pp. 385–389.

Braye, S., Orr, D. and Preston-Shoot, M. (2017). Autonomy and Protection in Self-Neglect Work: The Ethical Complexity of Decision-Making. *Ethics and Social Welfare*, 11(4), pp. 320–335.

Burston, G. R. (1975). 'Letter: Granny Battering'. *British Medical Journal*, 3(5983), p. 592.

Bužgová, R. and Ivanová, K. (2009). 'Elder Abuse and Mistreatment in Residential Settings'. *Nursing Ethics*, 16(1), pp. 110–126.

Cambridge, P. (1999). 'The First Hit: A Case Study of the Physical Abuse of People with Learning Disabilities and Challenging Behaviours in a Residential Service'. *Disability and Society*, 14(3), pp. 285–308.

Carr, S., Hafford-Letchfield, T., Faulkner, A., Megele, C., Gould, D., Khisa, C., Cohen, R. and Holley, J. (2019). "Keeping Control': A User-Led Exploratory Study of Mental Health Service User Experiences of Targeted Violence and Abuse in the Context of Adult Safeguarding in England'. *Health and Social Care in the Community*, 27(5), pp. e781–e792.

CDC. (Undated). 'Nursing Home Care'. Available at: https://www.cdc.gov/nchs/fastats/nursing-home-care.htm (accessed 16 August 2022).

Council of Europe. (2021). 'European Committee for the Prevention of Torture and Inhuman or Degrading Treatment or Punishment (CPT): Public Statement Concerning Bulgaria'. (4 November 2021, CPT/Inf [2021] 26).

Davis v West Sussex County Council (2012) EWHC 2152 (QB).

DBPSAB. (2015). *Purbeck Care Home: Serious Case Review*. Dorset, Bournemouth & Poole Safeguarding Adults Board.

Department for Constitutional Affairs. (2007). *Mental Capacity Act 2005: Code Of Practice*. The Stationery Office.

Department of Health. (1993). *No Longer Afraid: The Safeguarding of Older People in Domestic Settings*. The Stationery Office.

Department of Health. (2000). *No Secrets: Guidance on Developing and Implementing Multi-agency Policies and Procedures to Protect Vulnerable Adults from Abuse*. The Stationery Office.

Department of Health and Social Care. (2022). *Care and Support Statutory Guidance*. The Stationery Office.
Department of Health and Social Security. (1969). *Report of the Committee of Inquiry into Allegations of Ill – Treatment of Patients and Other Irregularities at the Ely Hospital, Cardiff*. The Stationery Office.
Dixon, J., Manthorpe, J., Biggs, S., Mowlam, A., Tennant, R., Tinker, A. and McCreadie, C. (2010). 'Defining Elder Mistreatment: Reflections on the United Kingdom Study of Abuse and Neglect of Older People'. *Ageing and Society*, 30(3), pp. 403–420.
DL v A Local Authority [2012] EWCA Civ 253
Emmett, C., Poole, M., Bond, J. and Hughes, J. C. (2013). 'Homeward Bound or Bound for a Home? Assessing the Capacity of Dementia Patients to Make Decisions about Hospital Discharge: Comparing Practice with Legal Standards'. *International Journal of Law and Psychiatry*, 36(1), pp. 73–82.
Emmett, C., Poole, M., Bond, J. and Hughes, J. C. (2014). 'A Relative Safeguard? The Informal Roles That Families and Carers Play When Patients with Dementia Are Discharged from Hospital into Care in England and Wales'. *International Journal of Law, Policy and the Family*, 28(3), pp. 302–320.
Fanneran, T., Kingston, P. and Bradley, E. (2013). 'A National Survey of Adult Safeguarding in NHS Mental Health Services in England and Wales'. *Journal of Mental Health*, 22(5), pp. 402–411.
Flynn, M. (2007). *The Murder of Steven Hoskin: A Serious Case Review, Executive Summary*. Cornwall Adult Protection Committee. Available at: https://www.hampshiresab.org.uk/wp-content/uploads/2007-December-Serious-Case-Review-regarding-Steven-Hoskin-Cornwall.pdf (accessed 29 March 2022).
Flynn, M. (2015). *In Search of Accountability*. Welsh Government.
Flynn, M. (2018a). *Safeguarding Adult Review: Adult B (Cassie)*. Brent Safeguarding Adult Board. Available at: https://brentsafeguardingpartnerships.uk/adults/article.php?id=929&menu=1&sub_menu=7 (accessed 8 March 2022).
Flynn, M. (2018b). *Safeguarding Adult Review: Mendip House*. Somerset Safeguarding Adults Board.
Flynn, M. (2019). *Safeguarding Adults Review: Atlas Care Homes*. Torbay and Devon Safeguarding Adults Partnership.
Flynn, M. (2021). *Safeguarding Adults Review: Joanna, Jon & Ben*. Norfolk Safeguarding Adults Board. Available at: https://www.norfolksafeguardingadultsboard.info/assets/SARs/SAR-Joanna-Jon-and-Ben/SAR-Rpt-Joanna-JonBen_FINAL-PUBLICATION02-June2021.pdf (accessed 31 March 2022).
Flynn, M. and Citarella, V. (2012). *Winterbourne View: A Serious Case Review*. South Gloucestershire Safeguarding Adults Board.
Foss, D. (2021). 'An Analysis of Safeguarding Adults Reviews: What Is the Role of the Mental Health Act 1983 in Safeguarding Adults at Risk of Abuse and Neglect?' MA Thesis, Keele University, Keele.
Geller, J. (2006). 'A History of Private Psychiatric Hospitals in The USA: From Start to Almost Finished'. *Psychiatric Quarterly*, 77(1), pp. 1–41.
Gibbs, J., Evans, M. and Rodway, S. (1987). *Report of the Inquiry into Nye Bevan Lodge*. Southwark Borough Council.
Hafford-Letchfield, T., Carr, S., Faulkner, A., Gould, D., Khisa, C., Cohen, R. and Megele, C. (2021). 'Practitioner Perspectives on Service Users Experiences of Targeted Violence and Hostility in Mental Health and Adult Safeguarding'. *Disability and Society*, 36(7), pp. 1099–1124.
Her Majesty's Inspectorate of Constabulary and Fire and Rescue Services (HMICFRS). (2019). *The Poor Relation: The Police and CPS Response to Crimes Against Older People*. HMICFRS.
HM Government. (2022). *Mental Capacity Act 2005 Code of Practice Draft*. The Stationery Office. Available at: https://assets.publishing.service.gov.uk/government/uploads/system/uploads/attachment_data/file/1080137/draft-mental-capacity-act-code-of-practice.pdf (accessed 16 June 2022).
Hobson, S. J. (1998). 'The Ethics of Compulsory Removal under Section 47 of the 1948 National Assistance Act'. *Journal of Medical Ethics*, 24(1), pp. 38–43.
House of Lords Select Committee on the Mental Capacity Act 2005 Report of Session 2013-14. (2014). *Mental Capacity Act 2005 Post-Legislative Scrutiny*. The Stationery Office.

Howe, G. (1969). *Report of the Committee of Inquiry into Allegations of Ill-Treatment of Patients and Other Irregularities at the Ely Hospital, Cardiff*. HMSO.

Hughes, K., Bellis, M. A., Jones, L., Wood., S., Bates, G., Eckley, L., McCoy, E., Mikton, C., Shakespeare, T. and Officer, A. (2012). 'Prevalence and Risk of Violence Against Adults with Disabilities: A Systematic Review and Meta-analysis of Observational Studies'. *The Lancet*, 379(9826), pp. 1621–1629.

Isle of Wight Safeguarding Adults Board. (2016). *Learning Review – Miss T Isle of Wight Safeguarding Adults Board*. https://www.iowsab.org.uk/wp-content/uploads/2019/01/2880-Miss-T-final-report-for-publication-22.09-v9.pdf (accessed 21 August 2022).

Jarrett, S. (2020). *Those They Called Idiots*. Reaktion Books.

Kamavarapu, Y., Ferriter, M., Morton, S. and Völlm, B. (2017). 'Institutional Abuse – Characteristics of Victims, Perpetrators and Organisations: A Systematic Review'. *European Psychiatry*, 40, pp. 45–54.

Kangasniemi, M., Papinaho, O., Moilanen, T., Leino-Kilpi, H., Siipi, H., Suominen, S. and Suhonen, R. (2022). 'Neglecting the Care of Older People in Residential Care Settings: A National Document Analysis of Complaints Reported to the Finnish Supervisory Authority. *Health and Social Care in the Community*, 30(4), pp. e1313–e1324. https://doi.org/10.1111/hsc.13538.

Kohn, N. (2009). 'Outliving Civil Rights'. *Washington University Law Review*, 86, pp. 1053–1116.

Kohn, N. (2012). 'Elder (In)Justice: A Critique of the Criminalization of Elder Abuse'. *American Criminal Law Review*, 49, pp. 1–29.

Kong, C. and Ruck Keene, A. (2018). *Overcoming Challenges in the Mental Capacity Act 2005: Practical Guidance for Working with Complex Issues*. Jessica Kingsley Publisher.

Landman, R. (2014). "A counterfeit friendship': Mate Crime and People with Learning Disabilities'. *Journal of Adult Protection*, 16(6), pp. 355–366.

Law Commission. (1995). *Mental Incapacity: Law Com CP 231*. The Stationery Office.

Law Commission. (2011). *Adult Social Care: Law Com CP 326*. The Stationery Office.

Leicester City Council v MPZ [2019] EWCOP 64.

Local Authority X v MM and KM [2007] EWHC 2003 (Fam)

Local Government Association. (2020). *Analysis of Safeguarding Adult Reviews April 2017 –March 2019: Findings for Sector-Led Improvement*. Available at: https://www.local.gov.uk/sites/default/files/documents/National%20SAR%20Analysis%20Final%20Report%20WEB.pdf (accessed 3 June 2022).

Local Government Association. (2021). *COVID-19 Adult Safeguarding Insight Project - Third Report*. LGA. Available at: https://www.local.gov.uk/publications/covid-19-adult-safeguarding-insight-project-third-report-december-2021 (accessed 31 March 2022).

London Borough of Redbridge v G [2014] EWHC, 485 (COP).

Mandelstam, M. (2013). *Safeguarding Adults and the Law*. 2nd edn. Jessica Kingsley Publishers.

Manthorpe, J. and Martineau, S. (2019). 'Mental Health Law under Review: Messages from English Safeguarding Adults Reviews'. *Journal of Adult Protection*, 21(1), pp. 46–64.

Martineau, S., Cornes, M., Manthorpe, J., Ornelas, B. and Fuller, J. (2019). 'Safeguarding, Homelessness and Rough Sleeping: An Analysis of Safeguarding Adults Reviews'. The Policy Institute: King's College London. Available at: https://kclpure.kcl.ac.uk/portal/files/116649790/SARs_and_Homelessness_HSCWRU_Report_2019.pdf (accessed 16 June 2022).

Murphy, G. (2022). *CQC Inspections and Regulation of Whorlton Hall: Second Independent Report*. Available at: https://www.cqc.org.uk/sites/default/files/20201215_glynis-murphy-review-second-report.pdf (accessed 16 August 2022).

NHS Digital. (2021a). *Safeguarding Adults Collection Statistics: 2020–21*. Available at: https://digital.nhs.uk/data-and-information/publications/statistical/safeguarding-adults/2020-21 (accessed 31 March 2022).

NHS Digital. (2021b). *Mental Health Act Statistics, Annual Figures – 2020/1*. Available at: https://digital.nhs.uk/data-and-information/publications/statistical/mental-health-act-statistics-annual-figures/2020-21-annual-figures (accessed 3 June 2022).

Pascoe, N. (2021). *Right First Time. Independent Investigation into Southern Health NHS Foundation Trust*. Available at: https://www.england.nhs.uk/south-east/wp-content/uploads/sites/45/2021/09/Southern-Health-NHSFT-Stage-2-Final-Report-Right-First-Time-1-1.pdf (accessed 16 August 2022).

Prior, P. M. (2012). 'Introduction to Asylums, Mental Health Care and the Irish: Historical Studies 1800–2010'. In: Prior, P. M. (ed.) *Asylums, Mental Health Care and the Irish: Historical Studies 1800–2010*. Irish Academic Press, pp. 1–22.

Pritchard-Jones, L. (2020). 'The Care Act 2014 and the Mental Capacity Act 2005: Learning Lessons for the Future?' In: Braye, S. and Preston-Shoot, M. (eds). *The Care Act 2014: Wellbeing in Practice*. Learning Matters, pp. 98–112.

Pritchard-Jones, L., Mehmi, M., Eccleston-Turner, M. and Brammer, A. (2022). 'Exploring the Changes and Challenges of COVID-19 in Adult Safeguarding Practice: Qualitative Findings from a Mixed-Methods Project'. *Journal of Adult Protection*, Online First. https://doi.org/10.1108/JAP-01-2022-0002.

Public Health England. (2020). *People with Learning Disabilities in England*. Ch.5. Available at: https://www.gov.uk/government/publications/people-with-learning-disabilities-in-england/chapter-5-adult-social-care (accessed 16 June 2022).

Re SA [2005] EWHC 2942 (Fam)

Ruck Keene, A. (2017). 'Proposals for a Vulnerable Adults Bill'. Available at: https://www.mentalcapacitylawandpolicy.org.uk/wp-content/uploads/2018/04/Briefing-on-gaps-in-the-protection-of-vulnerable-adults.pdf (accessed 16 June 2022).

Ruck Keene, A. (2020, 26 May). 'Capacity and Suicide'. Available at: https://www.mentalcapacitylawandpolicy.org.uk/capacity-and-suicide/ (accessed 22 June 2022).

Sandland, R. (2013). 'Sex and Capacity: The Management of Monsters?' *Modern Law Review*, 76(6), pp. 981–1009.

Series, L. (2022). *Deprivation of Liberty in the Shadows of the Institution*. Bristol University Press.

Sherwood-Johnson, F. (2016). 'Discovery or Construction? Theorising the Roots of Adult Protection Policy and Practice'. *Social Work Education*, 35(2), pp. 119–130.

Spivakovsky, C. and Steele, L. (2022). 'Disability Law in a Pandemic: The Temporal Folds of Medico-Legal Violence'. *Social and Legal Studies*, 31(2), pp.175–196.

Statista. (2021a). 'Number of Beds in Nursing Homes and Social Welfare Institutions for the Elderly in China from 2010 to 2020'. (September 2021). Available at: https://www.statista.com/statistics/251917/number-of-beds-in-nursing-homes-for-elderly-in-china/#:~:text=The%20graph%20shows%20the%20number,been%20available%20for%20the%20elderly (accessed 16 August 2022).

Statista. (2021b). 'Number of People Living in Care Homes in the United Kingdom in 2020, by Country'. (May 2021). Available at: https://www.statista.com/statistics/1082379/number-of-people-living-in-care-homes-in-the-united-kingdom/ (accessed 16 June 2022).

UNCRPD. (2017). 'General Comment No.5 on Article 19 - The Right to Live Independently and Be Included in the Community'.Available at: https://www.ohchr.org/en/documents/general-comments-and-recommendations/general-comment-no5-article-19-right-live

Verita. (2015). *Independent Review into Issues That May Have Contributed to the Preventable Death of Connor Sparrowhawk*. NHS England, South Region & Oxfordshire Safeguarding Adults Board.

Wardhaugh, J. and Wilding, P. (1993). 'Towards and Explanation of the Corruption of Care'. *Critical Social Policy*, 13(37), pp. 4–31.

Welsh Assembly Government. (2000). *In Safe Hands: Implementing Adult Protection Procedures in Wales*. WAG.

Whitelock, A. (2009). 'Safeguarding in Mental Health: Towards a Rights-Based Approach'. *Journal of Adult Protection*, 11(4), pp. 30–42.

Williams, J. and Keating, F. (2000). 'Abuse in Mental Health Services: Some Theoretical Considerations'. *Journal of Adult Protection*, 2(3), pp. 32–39.

Williamson, T., Boyle, G., Heslop, P., Jepson, M. J., Swift, P.. and Williams, V. J. (2012). 'Listening to the Lady in the Bed: The Mental Capacity Act 2005 in Practice for Older People'. *Elder Law Journal*, 2(2), pp. 185–192.

Winspear v City Hospitals Sunderland NHS Foundation Trust [2015] EWHC 3250 (QB).

Wolfson, P., Cohen, M., Lindesay, J. and Murphy, E. (1990). 'Section 47 and Its Use with Mentally Disordered People'. *Journal of Public Health*, 12(1), pp. 9–14.

WSSAB. (2014). *Orchid View: Serious Case Review*. West Sussex Safeguarding Adults Board.

Yon, Y., Ramiro-Gonzalez, M., Mikton, C., Huber, M. and Sethi, D. (2019). 'The Prevalence of Elder Abuse in Institutional Settings: A Systematic Review and Meta-analysis'. *European Journal of Public Health*, 29(1), pp. 58–67.

11
THE USE OF TRANS-RELATED DIAGNOSES IN HEALTH CARE AND LEGAL GENDER RECOGNITION

From disease- to identity-based models

Pieter Cannoot and Sarah Schoentjes

Introduction

One of the most pressing issues facing trans persons[1] is their psycho-pathologisation in society and law (Cannoot, 2019a).[2] However, over the last decades, the social and legal recognition of trans persons has gradually evolved from a disease-based model to an identity-based model (Motmans, Nieder and Bouman, 2019). Indeed, an emerging fundamental right to gender self-determination has been increasingly recognised by human rights actors and in State practice around the world (Cannoot, 2019a). While a disease-based model assumes that, in the case of a trans person, normative gender identity development has been compromised which leads to distress, the identity-based model assumes that gender variance is an example of human diversity and that distress is induced by transphobic stereotypes in society (Motmans, Nieder and Bouman, 2019). As Ashley (2021, p. 1159) states, "people naturally develop gender identities, and some people turn out to be trans as a result". In both the disease-based model and the identity-based model, it is considered vital that trans persons have access to specific forms of health care, predominantly gender-affirming hormonal treatment and surgery, in order to establish (greater) congruence between their bodies, gender identity, and gender roles. Whereas in the disease-based model access to trans-specific health care is reserved for persons who have been diagnosed with the clinical distress mentioned

---

1 For the purpose of this chapter the term 'trans persons' refers to all persons whose gender identity does not (always) correspond to the expectations that society connects to the sex assigned to them at birth. This includes persons who identify outside the gender binary and persons who are agender. For further elaboration, see Cannoot, 2019a.
2 Suess Schwend (2020, p. 3) has defined pathologisation as follows: "Pathologization can be understood as the conceptualization of bodily characteristics, habits, practices, living forms, gestures, people, and groups of people as mentally disordered, ill, abnormal, or malformed".

above, identity-based models generally advance medical practice and treatment models that are centred around autonomy, informed consent, shared decision-making, and support. Indeed, although many trans persons are confronted with mental health problems, these tend to occur as a consequence of social stigma and internalised minority stress, rather than because of the fact that they identify as trans (Ashley, 2021; Schulz, 2018). While some (and certainly not all) trans persons wish to physically transition through hormonal and/or surgical treatment, a transition process often also entails exploring the psychological, social, and legal implications of being recognised in a different gender than the one assigned at birth (Schulz, 2018). Gender transitions are complex, nonlinear, lengthy, often costly, and highly individualised processes (Coleman et al., 2011).

The gradual evolution from a disease-based model to an identity-based model cannot only be observed in health care practice, but is also reflected in the procedures for obtaining legal gender recognition, and more specifically in the requirements that trans persons have to comply with before being able to change their registered sex. One of the common conditions has been a mandatory diagnosis of transsexuality, gender identity disorder, or gender dysphoria, or a mandatory psychological assessment (Theilen, 2014). This requirement for gender recognition clearly rests upon a disease-based model of trans identities, since it means the State only legally recognises those trans persons who have been diagnosed with a mental health condition, or who have the mental capacity to know that they are 'truly trans'. However, in recent years, a significant number of countries worldwide have abolished this requirement, moving instead towards a model of gender recognition based on self-determination (Castro-Peraza et al., 2019; Cannoot, 2019a; Cannoot and Decoster, 2020).

In this chapter, we address three forms of pathologisation and depathologisation of gender diversity and trans persons in society and law: (1) the inclusion of trans-related diagnoses in international medical classifications of diseases and mental disorders, (2) the role of these diagnoses in the access to trans-specific health care, and (3) the requirement to comply with pathologising conditions in order to obtain legal gender recognition. More specifically, we will elaborate on how trans persons have historically been othered through pathologising stereotypes and rhetoric and how, over the last few decades, a depathologisation movement has thoroughly challenged their social and legal exclusion, leading to a stronger protection of fundamental rights. While the depathologisation movement has been remarkably successful in deconstructing the conceptualisation of trans identities as mental disorders, we notice greater hesitancy towards full depathologisation in trans-specific health care and legal gender recognition.

The general psycho-pathologisation of trans persons and gender diversity

Pathologisation of gender diversity in international medical classifications

Sexologist Magnus Hirschfeld is generally credited as being the first scholar to introduce the term 'transsexuality' in his article *"Die Intersexuelle Konstitution"* in 1923. Although he addressed social phenomena such as cross-dressing and cross-gender identification, he mainly wanted to normalise homosexuality by clearly distinguishing it from cross-gender behaviour (Motmans, 2009). Widespread scientific and public interest in gender identity in general, and transsexuality in particular, significantly increased when trans persons started appearing in (American) popular media in the 1940s and 1950s (Pfäfflin, 2016; Drescher, Cohen-Kettenis, and Winter, 2012). Although the first forms of gender-affirming treatment and surgery date back to the 1910s (Pfäfflin, 2016), the work of endocrinologist and sexologist Harry Benjamin (1960s) is commonly regarded as the foundation of the modern medical approach to gender incongruence. In the 1960s, clinicians began to refuse surgery on demand, because of the professional risks of performing experimental medicine (Davy, Sørlie, and Suess Schwend, 2018). Medical professionals, such as Benjamin, therefore started to develop criteria for approval onto gender-affirming treatment programmes (Davy, Sørlie, and Suess Schwend, 2018). Benjamin strongly believed that the body of trans persons should be adapted to their gender identity through medical treatment, consisting of hormonal replacement and gender-affirming surgery (Motmans, 2009). Importantly, in his vision, this medical treatment should be reserved for 'true' trans persons, who were accordingly diagnosed by a psychiatrist. Since the 1960s, this medical approach has been the leading way through which Western societies have dealt with issues relating to incongruence between a person's assigned sex and gender identity, making a physical and social transition possible for persons who have been diagnosed with the condition of transsexuality or gender dysphoria. However, by linking a physical gender transition to a psycho-medical condition, trans persons became inherently pathologised. Being trans thus has been considered a medical condition to be treated rather than a fundamental aspect of identity (Silver, 2014; Davy, Sørlie, and Suess Schwend, 2018).

'Transsexuality' was first included in the third edition of the *Diagnostic Statistical Manual of Mental Disorders* (DSM-3) of the American Psychiatric Association in 1980, before being changed to 'gender identity disorder' in DSM-4. The fifth and current *Diagnostic Statistical Manual of Mental Disorders* (DSM-5) still includes a diagnosis for the situation where a person's gender identity does not match their sex assigned at birth. However, the DSM-4 diagnosis of 'gender identity disorder' was revised to 'gender dysphoria', in order to emphasise that gender incongruence in itself does not constitute a mental disorder. The diagnosis of 'gender dysphoria' rather refers to the clinically significant distress *associated* with the condition of gender incongruence. In other words, DSM-5 centralises the distress, not the gender (Motmans, Nieder and Bouman, 2019). For an adult or adolescent to be diagnosed with gender dysphoria in accordance with DSM-5, there must be a marked difference between the individual's expressed/experienced gender and the gender others would assign to that person, and it must continue for at least six months. This condition must cause clinically significant distress or impairment in social, occupational or other important areas of functioning. DSM-5 also includes separate diagnostic criteria for gender dysphoria with children. These have been strongly criticised, since trans children (i.e. before they reach adolescence) are not in need of trans-specific health care such as puberty blockers or cross-sex hormones (Suess Schwend, 2017; Coleman et al., 2022).

Although prior versions already included the diagnoses of transvestitism (eighth version) and transvestism (ninth version), the tenth edition of the World Health Organization's *International Classification of Mental and Behavioural Disorders* (ICD) placed 'transsexualism', 'dual-role transvestism', 'gender identity disorder of childhood', 'other gender identity disorders', and 'gender identity disorder, unspecified' under the new separate chapter of 'gender identity disorders'. However, the WHO's latest revision of the ICD (ICD-11) removed the diagnostic category of 'gender identity disorders' and replaced it with a diagnosis of 'gender incongruence' as a medical condition related to sexual health, which does not include the assumption of a mental disorder (Richards et al., 2016). According to ICD-11, gender incongruence of adolescence or adulthood is characterised by a marked and persistent incongruence between an individual´s experienced gender and the assigned sex, which often leads to a desire to 'transition', in order to live and be accepted as a person of the experienced gender, through hormonal treatment, surgery, or other health care services to make the individual's body align, as much as desired and to the extent possible, with the experienced gender. The diagnosis cannot be assigned prior to the onset of puberty. Gender variant behaviour and preferences alone are not a basis for assigning the diagnosis. Similarly to DSM-5, ICD-11 still maintains separate diagnostic criteria for gender incongruence in childhood.

Criticism of the inclusion of trans-related diagnoses in medical classifications

The inclusion of trans persons in international classifications of diseases and mental disorders, be it in the form of a diagnosis of transsexuality, gender identity disorder, gender dysphoria, or even gender incongruence as a condition related to sexual health, has been widely criticised by trans activists and in academic scholarship. The criticism often deploys standards of international human rights law, such as the prohibition of inhuman and degrading treatment, the right to respect for private life, the right to health and high-quality health care, the right to personal autonomy, and the prohibition of discrimination (Theilen, 2014; Davy, Sørlie, and Suess Schwend, 2018). As Suess Schwend (2020, p. 2) describes, many trans (and allied) activists and scholars consider the contemporary pathologising model of gender diversity in Western societies as a root cause for the social and labour discrimination, criminalisation and exposure to transphobic violence and homicides that many trans persons, and especially trans persons of colour, are confronted with (see also Schulz, 2018). Given the persistent social stigma that is associated with mental illness, pathologisation is also seen as the primary cause for the poor access to health care that is common among trans persons around the world (Castro-Peraza et al., 2019; Drescher, Cohen-Kettenis and Winter, 2012). Indeed, as Theilen (2014, p. 331) points out,

> trans persons face a myriad of problems in everyday life which stem precisely from the fact that gender diversity is not accepted as normal but rather regarded as something unusual, a deviation, a cause for concern – in short, an illness.

From a historical perspective, the classification of gender identity diagnoses as mental disorders appears to have been based on prevailing social attitudes, rather than on available scientific evidence (Drescher, Cohen-Kettenis, and Winter, 2012; Davy, 2015). In addition, trans-related diagnostic criteria in international medical classifications have only recently acknowledged the existence of non-binary gender identities. While the diagnosis in ICD-11 no longer implies a binary conceptualisation of gender, DSM-5 still only recognises the gender identity spectrum in a subsidiary way, preferring the concept of 'the opposite sex/gender'. Medical classifications of gender diversity have therefore been criticised for upholding a binary and heteronormative construction of gender and trans identities (Suess Schwend, 2020). One of the main objectives of trans depathologisation activism is thus a complete removal of all trans-related diagnostic codes from international medical classifications. Such removal would contribute to the elimination of the social stigmatisation of trans persons, much as the removal of homosexuality from DSM and ICD was a major factor in the (albeit still ongoing) social destigmatisation of LGB+ persons (Drescher, Cohen-Kettenis, and Winter, 2012).

While many calls for full trans depathologisation have been driven by regional and international activist groups and networks in the context of 'STP – International Campaign Stop Trans Pathologisation' (Castro-Peraza et al., 2019; Davy, Sørlie, and Suess Schwend, 2018), over the last decade support has also come from institutional human rights bodies, such as the Council of Europe and the United Nations (UN). For instance, in Resolution 2048 (2015) the Parliamentary Assembly of the Council of Europe found "the fact that the situation of transgender people is considered as a disease by international diagnosis manuals [to be] disrespectful of their human dignity and an additional obstacle to social inclusion" (Council of Europe Parliamentary Assembly, 2015). In 2018, the UN Independent Expert on Sexual Orientation and Gender Identity presented a thematic report on legal gender recognition and trans depathologisation which, *inter alia*, called for the end of classifying trans identities as disorders (UN Independent Expert, 2018). The UN Special Rapporteur on the right of everyone to the enjoyment of the highest attainable standard of physical and mental health has also pointed out that "mental health diagnoses have been misused to pathologize identities and other diversities" and that "the pathologization of lesbian, gay, bisexual, transgender and intersex persons reduces their identities to diseases, which compounds stigma and discrimination" (UN Special Rapporteur on the right to health, 2017, p. 11). The Yogyakarta Principles, which are considered to be a universal guide to human rights that applies generally recognised and binding international legal standards to the situation of LGBTIQ+ persons, also state that "notwithstanding any classifications to the contrary, a person's sexual orientation and gender identity are not, in and of themselves, medical conditions and are not to be treated, cured or suppressed" (Principle 18). States are called on to

> take all necessary legislative, administrative and other measures to ensure full protection against harmful medical practices based on sexual orientation or gender identity, including on the basis of stereotypes, whether derived from culture or otherwise, regarding conduct, physical appearance or perceived gender norms.
>
> *(Principle 18 A)*

Although the Yogyakarta Principles are not legally binding, they are considered to be very influential towards policymakers, courts and other human rights actors (Cannoot, 2019a).

Depathologising trans persons has also been one of the goals of the World Professional Association for Transgender Health (WPATH) (Müller, De Cuypere, and T'Sjoen, 2017). WPATH is especially known for the articulation of the Standards of Care (SOC) for trans health care, which are international clinical guidelines that aim to articulate professional consensus about psychiatric, psychological, medical, and surgical management of trans individuals (Schulz, 2018). The currently used version eight of the WPATH's SOC for the Health of Transgender and Gender Diverse People explicitly distinguishes between gender incongruence and gender dysphoria (Coleman et al., 2022), the latter referring to a state of discomfort or distress that may be experienced because a person's gender identity differs from that which is physically and/or socially attributed to their sex assigned at birth (Coleman et al., 2022, p. 252). While gender-affirming care can address the distress or dysphoria that trans individuals experience, the SOC 8 acknowledges that access to gender-affirming care should not be reserved to those individuals who have been diagnosed with gender dysphoria. The SOC 8 adopts a holistic, multidisciplinary approach to gender-affirming care, which suggests changes in gender expression and role, hormone therapy, surgery, voice and communication therapy, hair removal, reproductive and sexual health care, and mental health care as the main (medical) options for assisting trans and gender diverse individuals, next to social support and non-medical changes in gender expression. Since the adoption of version seven, the SOC have acknowledged that gender diverse individuals may not necessarily experience distress because of the incongruence between the sex assigned to them at birth and their gender identity (Müller, De Cuypere, & T'Sjoen, 2017). Indeed, experiencing anxiety or distress is not a condition that is necessarily inherently connected to being trans or experiencing incongruence between one's assigned sex and gender identity, but is often induced by pervasive and cisnormative gender stereotypes and transphobic responses by the individual's social environment (Suess Schwend, 2020; Castro-Peraza et al., 2019; Schulz, 2018). While an entire absence of distress or anxiety may be expected with those trans persons who do not seek gender-affirming medical treatment, there are certainly also trans persons who present themselves in gender clinics without reporting distress or impairment (Drescher, Cohen-Kettenis, and Winter, 2012). This is especially true for young persons who are aware of the possibility of gender transition, live in an accepting social environment and who have access to puberty-suppressing treatment (Drescher, Cohen-Kettenis, and Winter, 2012).

The role of trans-related diagnoses in the access to trans-specific health care
Mental health diagnoses or assessments in the context of trans health care

While the existence of trans-related diagnoses in international medical classifications is in and of itself an important issue from a depathologisation perspective, activist, and scholarly critiques also target the use of these diagnoses – predominantly DSM-5 – as a means of regulating the access to trans-specific medical treatment. Indeed, in many cases around the world (adult and adolescent) trans persons must meet the diagnostic criteria of gender dysphoria, as established in DSM-5 (Schulz, 2018), before being considered eligible for hormonal treatment and/or surgery.

As mentioned above, the WPATH SOC 8 aims to

> provide clinical guidance to health professionals to assist transgender and gender diverse (TGD) people in accessing safe and effective pathways to achieving lasting personal comfort with their gendered selves with the aim of optimizing their overall physical health, psychological well-being, and self-fulfillment.
> *(Coleman et al., 2022, p. 5)*

Contrary to version seven, the SOC 8 provides guidelines for gender-affirming treatment of *all* trans and gender diverse people, and not only those individuals presenting gender dysphoria (Coleman et al., 2022, p. 8). Assistance may include different types of care, including mental health services, and hormonal and surgical treatment. The aim of such treatment should be to partner with the individual to holistically address their social, mental and medical health needs in order to affirm their gender identity. As such, there is no 'one-size-fits-all' approach, and trans and gender diverse individuals may need to undergo all, some or none of the possible treatment options (Coleman et al., 2022, p. 7). The SOC 8 recommends that all (adult) trans and gender diverse individuals who seek access to gender-affirming care are assessed by a health care professional. According to the SOC, the role of the assessor is to assess whether the person concerned shows gender incongruence and to identify any co-existing mental health concerns, to offer information about the treatment options, to support the individual in considering the effects and the risks of treatment and to assess whether the person has the capacity to provide informed consent to the treatment. In any case, the SOC recognise that the decision should be shared between the health care professional and the individual concerned (Coleman et al., 2022, p. 31). Although SOC 8 generally acknowledges that gender incongruence is a highly individualised and unique experience (Coleman et al., 2022, pp. 5–6), it still recommends an assessment of the existence thereof and whether it is 'marked and sustained', before gender-affirming (hormonal and surgical) treatment is performed.

The SOC 8 thus does not require trans and gender diverse individuals to be diagnosed with gender dysphoria or to undergo an assessment by a *mental health* professional in order to have access to gender-affirming care. However, while, according to the SOC, mental health professionals may serve trans persons in different ways (e.g. in providing individual or family counselling, psychotherapeutic support throughout a gender transition or in exploring gender identity and gender roles, psychotherapy for underlying mental health issues, etc.), they may also still have the important task of assessing whether people seeking trans-specific health care present gender dysphoria and for that reason are eligible for hormonal treatment and/or gender-affirming surgery. Indeed, while the SOC 8 does not require a diagnosis or mental health assessment for accessing gender-affirming treatment, it does not oppose such a diagnosis- or assessment-based model either.

The use of a formal diagnosis or mental health assessment to grant access to trans-specific health care has been generally described as a gatekeeping model, leading to strong criticism (Schulz, 2018). Not only does such model psycho-pathologise trans persons seeking gender-affirming treatment, it may also pressure them to conform to an expected narrative of distress or bodily discomfort that does not match their individual experience (Schulz, 2018; Drescher, Cohen-Kettenis and Winter, 2012; Davy, 2015). Indeed, as a result of the model, those who do not report (sufficient) distress may be deemed unsuitable to receive medical services (Schulz, 2018). Trans health care users may feel similarly pressured to display a desire for a very stereotypical masculine or feminine appearance or gender role, even when this does not match their actual gender identity or expectations (Schulz, 2018; Davy, 2015). The diagnostic and assessment criteria therefore have essentialising effects and fail to take into account the complex reality of trans experiences (Davy, 2015). In sum, the gatekeeping model is viewed as a significant barrier when trans health care users have to educate the medical professional about being trans while 'proving' their identity and eligibility for treatment (Schulz, 2018).

However, despite the aforementioned calls by trans activists and human rights bodies to fully depathologise gender diversity and gender incongruence, diagnostic classifications concerning trans persons have often been retained and used in health care settings predominantly *because of* the fact that some trans people wish for medical interventions (Richards et al., 2016), and therefore should have access to health care and social security (Kraus, 2015). Indeed, while trans-related diagnostic terms have stigmatising effects, they also facilitate access to clinical care and insurance coverage (Motmans, Nieder and Bouman, 2019; Coleman et al., 2022) and therefore arguably contribute to realising the right to health. For this reason, (the uses of) trans-related diagnoses have also been supported by trans persons around the globe (Suess Schwend, 2020). Nevertheless, as former Council of Europe Commissioner for Human Rights Hammarberg already stated in 2009, neither a human rights nor a health care perspective requires a diagnosis in order to give access – on the basis of informed consent – to high-quality medical treatment for a situation in need of medical care (Hammarberg, 2009). Full trans depathologisation therefore does not necessarily contradict the desire of some trans persons to have access to trans-specific forms of health care. As Theilen (2014, p. 336) noted, the public coverage of several health care-related expenses regarding pregnancy illustrates that having a disease or diagnosis is not a necessary condition for being afforded access to State-funded health care. Many trans activists and scholars thus call for the universal provision of State-funded trans-specific health care on the basis of a human rights framework, rather than a diagnostic classification system (Davy, Sørlie, Suess Schwend, 2018). For instance, the 2012 Argentinian Gender Identity Law not only provided for the right to legal gender recognition on the basis of self-determination (i.e. without medical requirements) but also established a right to State-funded trans health care within an informed consent model (Davy, Sørlie, and Suess Schwend, 2018).

Besides, as the social taboo on trans health care is gradually disappearing, more and more trans persons are seeking access to health services. While existing health services may be growing, they often cannot cope with rising demand resulting in excessive waiting lists for health care users (Motmans, Nieder, and Bouman, 2019; Spanos et al., 2020). This also necessitates a move towards a more flexible, person-centred approach (Motmans, Nieder and Bouman, 2019), given the high rates of depression and suicidal thoughts or behaviour among trans persons awaiting health care (Spanos et al., 2020). Diagnostic or assessment requirements may also result in an additional financial burden, rendering trans-specific health care less accessible especially for the most vulnerable trans persons with limited financial resources (Schulz, 2018; Spanos et al., 2020). Moreover, since gender-affirming treatment is still required by a considerable number of jurisdictions in order to obtain legal gender recognition (Cannoot, 2019a), unnecessary obstacles in accessing such treatment may have strong legal implications. We will come back to this in the third part of this chapter.

Towards informed consent models in trans health care

Given the pathologising and other undesirable effects of a diagnosis- and assessment-based model and the gradual societal evolution towards the recognition of gender variance as a matter of human diversity, many trans (and allied) activists and scholars call for the adoption of so-called informed consent models (ICMs) in trans health care. ICMs are based on the paradigm that trans persons have access to those forms of medical treatment that they desire in order to seek congruence between their body and gender identity, without mandatorily undergoing a mental health intervention or referral by a mental health specialist (Schulz, 2018). The role for the medical professional is to assess the capacity of the health care user to make an informed decision about the desired bodily modifications, to provide them with all necessary information about the nature, risks, side-effects, benefits, and possible consequences of a certain form of gender-affirming treatment, and to obtain prior, free and informed consent (Schulz, 2018). To be clear, the term 'ICM' should not lead to the wrongful conclusion that in diagnosis- and assessment-based models, the medical professional should not obtain informed consent or may simply forgo any individualised assessment of the person's desires in terms of treatment outcomes. Nor should it lead to the conclusion that mental health professionals should never be involved in a gender transition process (Schulz, 2018; Spanos et al., 2020). Indeed, mental health professionals may still play a crucial role in supporting the trans person concerned in exploring their gender identity and gender expression, in dealing with reactions by the social environment, in assessing their desired treatment outcomes or potential risks and side-effects. Moreover, the person concerned may also have some secondary mental health problems that require assessment and assistance (Spanos et al., 2020).

As Ashley, St. Amand, and Rider (2021, p. 543) explain, ICMs should actually be conceptualised as a continuum. They propose three different models that differ in their level of commitment to the autonomy of the health care user concerned: strong ICMs, weak ICMs, and no-letter models. Between those models lies a spectrum that muddles any attempt at categorisation. A strong ICM only requires informed consent in order to have access to trans-specific (hormonal) treatment. The objective of the clinician concerned is to elucidate and meet the health care user's needs and desires in terms of embodiment. Naturally, the clinician should always check whether the health care user has the capacity to provide informed consent (Spanos et al., 2020). In a weak ICM, the individual autonomy and desires of the health care user concerned are placed at the centre of the treatment, yet an assessment of gender identity and/or gender dysphoria is still a requirement for eligibility. In a no-letter model, the comprehensive assessment of gender identity and/or gender dysphoria should not be performed by an external mental health professional, but may be done by the prescribing clinician. Contrary to strong and weak ICMs, a no-letter model does not emphasise personal autonomy. What are commonly regarded as ICMs, i.e. treatment models that do not include any assessment of gender identity, a mental health assessment, or a diagnosis of gender dysphoria, thus predominantly only correspond to what Ashley, St. Amand, and Rider qualify as *strong* ICMs. Nevertheless, given the fact that paternalism and pathologisation have historically plagued trans-specific health care (Ashley, St. Amand, and Rider, 2021), there is undeniable importance in explicitly designating (and advancing) any treatment model that operationalises a clear commitment to personal autonomy and collaborative decision-making as informed consent-based, even when it does not fully qualify as a *strong* ICM.

Since the (strong) ICM clearly departs from currently established medical practice in the West, it remains controversial. While the current WPATH SOC 8 does not oppose the use of (strong) informed consent models in trans-specific health care (Coleman et al., 2022, p. 31), the advised treatment model still includes the assessment of the person concerned by a health professional, which is *inter alia* aimed at identifying the presence of gender incongruence. However, it is clear that SOC 8 has moved significantly closer towards (at the very least weak) informed consent models, as it recommends respecting personal autonomy and informed consent, individualised care, and shared decision-making. In this light, the European Society for Sexual Medicine also stated in its recent position statement on trans health care that medical professionals should avoid being seen as gatekeepers, and should focus on informing and supporting the health care user concerned and assessing their capacity to provide informed consent (T'Sjoen et al., 2020).

From a human rights law perspective, (strong) ICMs for trans-specific health care do not seem to raise any important issues. Indeed, it is a well-known rule of biomedical ethics and international human rights law that medical treatment may only be carried out after a health care user has been informed of the purpose, nature, risks and consequences of the intervention, and has freely consented to it (Dunne, 2018b). Informed consent changes what would otherwise be a violation of fundamental rights into a legitimate medical intervention (Silver, 2014). In fact, human rights bodies are currently rather focused on pathologising and other restrictive practices in terms of trans health care than on more liberal treatment models. For instance, in Resolution 2048 (2015) the Parliamentary Assembly of the Council of Europe called for health care procedures such as hormonal treatment, surgery and psychological support that are effectively accessible for trans persons and reimbursed by public health insurance schemes. In the resolution, the Assembly encouraged States to explore alternative trans health care models, based on informed consent. Principle 17 of the aforementioned Yogyakarta Principles also calls on States to ensure access to the highest attainable standard of gender-affirming health care, on the basis of an individual's free, prior, and informed consent. However, while from a human rights law perspective ICMs do not raise any immediate concern, the issue of informed consent has recently come to play an important role in legal settings, especially in cases concerning adolescents (legal minors).

In current clinical practice, and as foreseen by the WPATH SOC 8, adolescents can also already have access to certain forms of trans-specific medical treatment. Indeed, the use of puberty-suppressing hormones has, for instance, become professionally accepted as a crucial part of health care for trans adolescents and treatment access has increased significantly (de Vries et al., 2021). However, despite a slowly growing body of evidence supporting the effectiveness and benefits of gender-affirming care for trans adolescents, the total number of scientific studies remains limited and there is a general shortage of longitudinal research (Coleman et al., 2022, p. 46). In this light, the renowned gender clinic of the Karolinska Hospital in Sweden, for instance, ended all use of puberty blockers and cross-sex hormones for minors outside of medical studies in 2021. At the same time, gender-affirming treatment for trans adolescents has been met with severe criticism among (conservative) policymakers, even to the extent of a legal ban (for instance in the US states of Arkansas and Alabama). Besides the issue of the availability of sufficient research on the benefits and risks of gender-affirming care for adolescents, the question whether, legally speaking, trans legal minors have the capacity to assess their best interests and therefore to provide informed consent to the treatment is also often raised. This question was recently brought before court in the United Kingdom, in the case of *Bell v Tavistock* (High Court, 'Bell v Tavistock', 2020; Court of Appeal, 'Bell v Tavistock', 2021). In the case, a person who had reversed their gender transition and a parent who objected to puberty-suppressing treatment for adolescents sued the country's only gender clinic that provides trans-specific treatment to adolescents. The petitioners claimed that minors should not be able to consent to trans-specific health care without court supervision. In December 2020, the High Court agreed that children under the age of 16 are highly unlikely to be able to consent to taking puberty blockers, since it considered it unlikely that they can understand the immediate and long-term consequences of the treatment, which it even qualified as 'experimental' (High Court, 'Bell v Tavistock', 2020; de Vries et al., 2021; Moreton, 2021). The Court also considered that, since many trans adolescents move onto irreversible hormonal treatment, minors also have to (be able to) foresee the consequences of such treatment when they consider taking puberty blockers. The concrete result of the judgment was that a minor under the age of 16 could no longer consent to treatment without court supervision (de Vries et al., 2021). In the case of 16- and 17-year-olds, clinicians could also still seek prior court authorisation, despite the legal presumption of competence for these minors concerned (Moreton, 2021). However, in September 2021 the Court of Appeal overturned the High Court's decision, criticising the latter's engagement with scientific evidence and considering that nothing about the nature or implications of treatment with puberty blockers indicated that it was not for medical professionals but for judges to decide on a minor's capacity to provide informed consent (Court of Appeal, 'Bell v Tavistock', 2021).

In a reaction to the High Court's decision, professionals associated with, *inter alia*, WPATH not only pointed out the flaws in the High Court's reasoning, especially regarding the presumed 'experimental' nature of puberty-suppressing hormonal treatment, but also "the extensive diagnostic and counselling work that precedes decisions around gender affirming treatment to minors" (de Vries et al., 2021). Indeed, the SOC 8 also recommends the performance of a comprehensive biopsychosocial assessment of adolescents who seek access to gender-affirming care, preferably by a mental health professional, before such treatment takes place (Coleman et al., 2022, p. 50). Similarly, the Court of Appeal's judgment referenced Tavistock's rigorous assessment processes before granting minors access to (reversible or irreversible) hormonal treatment (Court of Appeal, 'Bell v Tavistock', 2021, §75). This focus on the role of diagnostic work and assessment (of mental health) clearly is at odds with the objectives of trans depathologisation. While it is not expected that strong ICMs will soon be the norm in the clinical practice concerning trans adolescents, it remains to be seen how this attention in legal settings for a minor's capacity to provide informed consent to trans-specific hormonal and/or surgical treatment will respond to, on the one hand, the progressive move towards personal autonomy and (strong) ICMs in trans health care and, on the other hand, concerns over the availability of sufficient evidence of the benefits of gender-affirming treatment for adolescents, even among gender clinics.

The pathologisation of trans persons in procedures of legal gender recognition

Abusive requirements in gender recognition procedures

Access to gender recognition has far-reaching consequences for the human rights of trans persons. Beyond the validation inherent in the State legally recognising one's identity, a trans person's identity documents not matching their gender presentation makes them extremely vulnerable to discrimination in such varied domains as health care, employment, housing, education, etc. (Cannoot and Decoster, 2020). Since these domains are closely related to the exercise of various human rights, gender recognition is essential to ensure the human rights of trans persons (Lau, 2020). This is the reasoning that led the European Court of Human Rights (ECtHR) to declare that gender recognition is protected under Article 8 (the right to respect for private and family life) of the European Convention on Human Rights (ECHR) in 2002, in the case of *Christine Goodwin v United Kingdom* (Cannoot, 2019b).

In most countries where gender recognition is possible, however, these procedures are not based on self-determination, i.e. the simple declaration of one's gender identity, but instead depend on a variety of preconditions, some of which touch on human rights (UN Independent Expert, 2018). Consequently, a subset of those requirements are considered to be 'abusive', because they force trans persons to choose between the human rights protected and ensured by gender recognition, and those violated by the conditions for gender recognition (such as the rights to personal autonomy, respect for private life, physical integrity, etc.). The following requirements are generally defined as abusive: mandatory sterilisation, mandatory medical treatments such as hormone replacement therapy, gender-affirming surgery, a mandatory diagnosis or psychological assessment, mandatory divorce, loss of parental rights, mandatory waiting times, and 'real life experience', and in some cases, age restrictions (see UN Independent Expert, 2018; Council of Europe Committee of Ministers, 2010).

The requirement of a mandatory diagnosis shows how the pathologisation of trans identities also has consequences that extend to legal gender recognition procedures. This condition rests upon and reinforces the stereotype of trans persons as mentally ill, confused and delusional (Gazzola and Morrison, 2014). Trans persons can, allegedly, not be trusted to know their own gender; therefore, (cisgender) 'specialists' must confirm that they truly are trans, strongly limiting their right to private life and autonomy (Theilen, 2014). This requirement ignores the developments expanded upon above: the fact that much of the scientific field no longer considers being trans a mental illness, and that a diagnosis is therefore unnecessarily pathologising, as well as the fact that not all trans persons experience gender dysphoria.

This is not a fringe problem – in the vast majority of States that allow gender recognition, it is dependent on such a mental health diagnosis or mental health assessment (TGEU, 2021). Some States have amended this requirement, moving from a mandatory diagnosis of 'transsexuality' or 'gender identity disorder' to one of 'gender dysphoria', in accordance with the changes in DSM-5 and the general trend towards depathologisation of trans identities *in se* (Dunne, 2018a). However, the requirement of any mandatory mental health diagnosis means that the very act of the State recognising a trans person's identity is subordinate to them being diagnosed with a mental health condition, which remains deeply pathologising.

Pathologising procedures for legal gender recognition and international human rights law

This legal pathologisation has led a variety of international entities to recommend depathologisation in gender recognition procedures, often in the same documents in which they push for general depathologisation of trans identities and for depathologisation in trans health care. For instance, Principle 31 of the Yogyakarta Principles states that gender recognition should be based on self-determination and recommends that "no eligibility criteria, such as medical or psychological interventions, a psycho-medical diagnosis ... or any other third party opinion, shall be a prerequisite to change one's name, legal sex or gender". Mandatory diagnoses have also been called into question at the United Nations level. Both the UN High Commissioner for Human Rights and the UN Special Rapporteur on torture and other cruel, inhuman and degrading treatment, made reports expressing their concern about medical abusive requirements, which did not explicitly mention mandatory diagnoses but did respectively insist on "forced sterilization, forced gender reassignment and other medical procedures" (OHCHR, 2015) and "forced or otherwise involuntary gender reassignment surgery, sterilization or other coercive medical procedures" (UN Special Rapporteur on torture, 2016). In a 2018 report to the UN General Assembly, the Independent Expert on Sexual Orientation and Gender Identity recommended the abolition of all abusive requirements for gender recognition, including mandatory diagnosis. In his specific recommendations to Member States, he condemned any obligation to undergo "medical diagnosis, psychological appraisals or other medical or psychosocial procedures or treatment" (UN Independent Expert, 2018).

Similar recommendations have been made at the regional level. In Europe, the Parliamentary Assembly of the Council of Europe considered, in its Resolution 2048 (2015), that the following conditions for gender recognition violate trans persons' right to respect for private life and to physical integrity: "sterilisation, divorce, a diagnosis of mental illness, surgical interventions and other medical treatments" as well as "a period of 'life experience' in the gender of choice". Consequently, it recommended that States "abolish sterilisation and other compulsory medical treatment, as well as a mental health diagnosis, as a necessary legal requirement to recognise a person's gender identity in laws regulating the procedure for changing a name and registered gender". This view was confirmed at the EU level, by the European Parliament's Resolution on promoting gender equality in mental health and clinical research (2017), in which the Parliament stressed that transgender identities are not pathological, but are deplorably still considered mental health disorders and most Member States request such diagnoses for access to legal gender recognition and transgender-related healthcare, even though research has shown that the "gender identity disorder" diagnosis is a source of significant distress for transgender people.

In the Americas, the Inter-American Court of Human Rights (IACtHR) adopted an advisory opinion on Gender Identity, Equality, and Non-Discrimination of Same-Sex Couples (2017). In this advisory opinion, the IACtHR stated that gender recognition procedures should be "based solely on the free and informed consent of the applicant without requirements such as medical and/or psychological or other certifications that could be unreasonable or pathologizing". More specifically, the IACtHR recommended that applicants should not be

> subjected to medical or psychological appraisals related to their self-perceived gender identity, or other requirements that undermine the principle according to which gender identity is not to be proven. Consequently, the procedure should be based on the mere expression of the applicant's intention.

Pathologisation in gender recognition procedures: progress versus stagnation

It is therefore undeniable that recent years have seen significant progress regarding abusive requirements for gender recognition, including pathologisation in gender recognition procedures. An increasing number of countries worldwide have abolished, or seriously diminished, abusive requirements for gender recognition. Since Argentina's 2012 Gender Recognition Law (Ley establecese el derecho a la identidad de genero de las personas, 2012), for example, a significant number of Latin-American States – such as Bolivia, Brazil, Chile, Colombia, Costa Rica, Ecuador and Uruguay – have eliminated abusive requirements for gender recognition ('Advisory Opinion OC-24/17', 2017). In Europe, 11 countries – Belgium, Denmark, Finland, Ireland, Iceland, Luxembourg, Malta, Norway, Portugal, Spain and Switzerland – have abolished all pathologising requirements for gender recognition (for adults). Two more – France and Greece – have abolished the requirements of a mandatory diagnosis, but they still respectively impose a judicial procedure and mandatory divorce. With these exceptions, however, all Member States of the Council of Europe still require a mandatory diagnosis or psychological assessment as a condition for gender recognition. In a number of countries, a diagnosis or assessment is even the last requirement standing in the way of true self-determination. In the United Kingdom, public consultations about reforming the 2004 Gender Recognition Act in order to introduce a depathologised procedure based on gender self-determination, resulted in a highly polarised and often transphobic public debate, predominantly concerning the inclusion of trans women and other persons assigned male at birth in women-only spaces (Pearce, Erikainen, and Vincent, 2020). While the Scottish government still seems determined to move forward with the intended legal reform, the UK government decided that the requirement to provide evidence of having gender dysphoria will remain in place in England and Wales (Stonewall, 2020). At the same time, States like Hungary, Russia, and Poland have increasingly become more hostile towards trans persons, with the former even abolishing any possibility of legal gender recognition (Ben Chikha, 2022).

The widespread acceptance of mental health diagnoses or assessments in gender recognition procedures was also a key aspect of the ECtHR's justification for permitting such requirements in the case of *A.P., Garçon and Nicot v France* (2017). This judgment is best known as the one that declared mandatory sterilisation as a requirement for gender recognition to be in violation of the ECHR. This was unquestionably a positive development for the bodily autonomy of trans persons, and it led to easier access to gender recognition. However, this was not the only abusive requirement at stake in this case. Indeed, the second applicant submitted that requiring a diagnosis of a 'gender disorder' as a condition for gender recognition amounted to labelling trans persons as mentally ill, and that this infringed on trans persons' dignity. While the Court was aware of the international trend towards depathologisation of trans identities, it ruled that, since the vast majority of Council of Europe States required a mental health diagnosis or assessment for gender recognition, States enjoyed a wide margin of appreciation. In view thereof, the gatekeeping of gender recognition by mental health practitioners was justified by the aims of ensuring that persons did not unadvisedly change their legal identity and of "safeguarding the principle of the inalienability of civil status, the reliability and consistency of civil-status records, and legal certainty, given that this requirement also promotes stability in changes of gender in civil-status documents". Consequently, the Court found that a requirement of a diagnosis of gender identity disorder for gender recognition did not violate the right to private life protected under Article 8 ECHR.

The Court's conclusion that "ensuring that persons do not unadvisedly change their legal identity" is a legitimate aim is highly pathologising, since it does, in fact, come down to requiring an assessment of whether someone is 'really trans'. The Court's explicit support of this aim, especially since this assessment must be performed by a medical expert, consequently lends legitimacy to the idea that trans persons cannot be trusted to independently develop and understand their own identities, and that trans identities belong to the realm of pathology rather than identity. It is thus regrettable that the ECtHR has legitimised pathologisation in gender recognition procedures in *A.P., Garçon and Nicot*. The Court's authority and the binding nature of its judgments could have significantly precipitated progress towards depathologisation in Europe. However, this does not exclude the possibility that the developments expanded upon in this chapter may cause the Court to amend its reasoning in future cases on the same topic. Indeed, the Court has since ruled that a requirement of gender-affirming surgery for gender recognition – another abusive requirement that affects a trans person's bodily autonomy – violates Article 8 ECHR ('X. and Y. v Romania', 2021; Schoentjes and Cannoot, 2021). Other international human rights monitoring bodies – whether at the regional level or at the UN – could also be presented with similar cases, and rule in favour of depathologisation. As becomes apparent in many preparatory documents of gender recognition laws, every country that changes its legislation to abolish pathologisation in gender recognition procedures is an example to other States (Schoentjes, 2019). International soft law has a similar impact. We must not lose sight of the fact that progress towards depathologisation in gender recognition procedures has been significant in the past decade, and, while we may regret its slow and arduous nature, it is nonetheless likely that this trend will continue.

Pathologisation, discrimination, and intersectional exclusion

Pathologising requirements for gender recognition not only strongly interfere with a trans person's right to autonomy, they are also discriminatory, as pointed out by the IACtHR in its aforementioned advisory opinion. Indeed, mandatory diagnoses are synonymous with requiring a third party (who is often cisgender) to assess whether a person is 'truly trans'.

This practice not only pathologises trans identities and restricts trans persons' autonomy – it is also discriminatory and exclusionary. Firstly, as the IACtHR argued, psychological assessments discriminate between cisgender persons and trans persons, because cisgender persons do not need to undergo such an assessment to see their gender identity validated and recognised by the State. Secondly, it discriminates among trans persons. Indeed, not all trans persons experience gender dysphoria (Theilen, 2014), and granting gender recognition only to those who do is equivalent to declaring that only persons who experience gender dysphoria are 'truly trans'.

Furthermore, mandatory diagnoses can lead to particularly fraught situations regarding intersectionality. Indeed, the (often cisgender) practitioner's perception of whether the person in question can be trusted to know their own identity, or of whether they adequately perform gender roles, can play a big role in the diagnosis they pose. This leads to problems for intersectionally positioned trans persons, including (but not limited to) neurodivergent and mentally ill trans persons, gender-non-conforming and LGB+ trans persons, and trans minors.

Trans men on the autism spectrum, for example, may be suspected of being women and girls who feel like they do not fit in, and, when they are exposed to trans identities, start thinking that they would fit in better if they were men. This argument has become a prominent talking point in so-called 'gender-critical'[3] circles (e.g. Rowling, 2020), but even mental health practitioners who have bought into these ideas in a much more restrained manner may approach autistic trans persons with heightened suspicion (Strang et al., 2018). This attitude is often bolstered by studies that suggest that persons on the autism spectrum are proportionally more often LGBTQI+ than neurotypical persons – nonetheless, the leap to the assumption that they are in fact not truly trans is certainly premature (Nobili et al., 2018). Similarly, trans persons who suffer from clinical depression may be told that they are simply trying to find an inappropriate solution to their unhappiness. This specific intersection is rendered particularly complex by the fact that trans persons do have a higher-than-average rate of depression – likely caused by the transphobia they face on a regular basis (Theilen, 2014). Trans persons with particularly stigmatised personality disorders may be accused of faking or lying about their identity, and those with mental illnesses such as schizophrenia or psychosis, which influence one's perception of reality, may be considered to incorrectly perceive the reality of their gender identity (Mizock and Fleming, 2011).

As mentioned above, the intersectional impact of psychological assessments is also keenly felt by gender-non-conforming trans persons. Indeed, trans persons are considerably more likely to be taken seriously by their mental health practitioner if they present in a gender-conforming manner – that is, if their behaviour and gender presentation match the expectations of masculinity or femininity linked to their gender identity rather than their sex assigned at birth (Vincent, 2019). Since expectations of gender conformity still include attraction to 'the opposite gender', such reasoning can also lead to LGB+ trans persons being regarded with increased suspicion. This prevalent societal heteronormativity could lead practitioners and States to wish to stop people from 'transitioning into' homosexuality (Gonzalez-Salzberg, 2018).

---

3 As Pearce, Erikainen, and Vincent (2020, p. 681) note, the term 'gender-critical' denotes "less a critical approach to gender, and more an emphasis on claiming 'biologically defined' notions of femaleness and womanhood over gender identity and social concepts of gender".

Heterosexual trans persons, and especially heterosexual trans men who are perceived to 'merely' be butch lesbian women, on the contrary, may be suspected of struggling with their sexual orientation to such an extent that they attempt to force themselves into another gender. This argument – which is particularly common among transphobic feminists – posits that trans-affirming care is in fact a type of conversion therapy that turns lesbian women straight, despite all available evidence to the contrary (Motmans, 2009). Non-binary trans persons are also at risk of such exclusion. Since assumptions about what makes a person 'truly trans' are so deeply rooted in the gender binary pervading (Western) society, non-binary identities are still considered by many not to be real. And even if non-binary identities are recognised as such, they are still at risk of being simply considered a 'third gender' rather than as the broad spectrum they truly represent. Replacing the binary with a 'trinary' could lead to practitioners expecting non-binary persons to conform to certain expectations for this 'third gender' rather than accepting the diversity within this group (Theilen, 2018).

Another problem lies not with the practitioners, but with the State legislation itself. Indeed, some countries that have abolished the requirement of a psychological assessment for trans adults, do still require such an assessment for trans minors. Ireland, for example, only grants gender recognition to minors by way of a judicial procedure, which can only be completed if the minor provides a medical certificate signed by the child's primary medical practitioner and an endocrinologist or psychiatrist. This certificate must confirm the child's maturity, their understanding of the consequences of gender recognition, their free will, and the fact that they have transitioned or started transitioning into their preferred gender (Gender Recognition Act 2015). This last requirement again creates the risk of renewed pathologisation: while it does not define precisely what such a transition entails, it is entirely possible that individual doctors will require medical treatments before they provide the minor with such a certificate, as was the case with adults in Portugal (ILGA Portugal et al., 2017). Belgium and Portugal have similar provisions regarding gender recognition for trans minors. Both also demand a certificate by a child psychiatrist that asserts that the minor is mature enough to truly be convinced of their gender identity (*Wet tot hervorming van regelingen inzake transgenders 2017*; *Lei Direito à autodeterminação da identidade de género 2018*). Portugal furthermore requires this certificate to confirm that the minor gave their free and informed consent and that this decision is in their best interests. Such a certificate is quite questionable: while both laws exclude the need for a diagnosis of gender dysphoria, requiring the involvement of a psychiatrist keeps contributing to the psycho-pathologisation of trans minors (Bribosia and Rorive, 2018).

These non-exhaustive examples provide us with an idea of the different ways mental health practitioners – or the State itself – may invalidate trans persons' identities simply because of their intersectional positioning and may consequently withhold a diagnosis, and in turn, gender recognition, from a significant subset of trans persons. Consequently, mandatory diagnoses or psychological assessments risk barring intersectionally marginalised trans persons from gender recognition.

Conclusion

Social attitudes towards trans persons have traditionally led to trans identities being classified as mental disorders, rather than as an expression of human diversity. This association with mental illnesses, which are heavily stigmatised, in turn has increased the stigma against trans persons. Beyond the transphobia they face in their daily life, this stigma also has had implications for the realisation of their human rights. Indeed, access to trans-specific health care as well as to gender recognition has been widely made dependent upon a diagnosis of a gender identity disorder or gender dysphoria, or upon a psychological mental health assessment.

This disease-based model is increasingly being challenged by trans and allied activists, medical professionals, and scholars, as well as by international human rights institutions. This has created a growing trend towards the depathologisation of trans identities. In health care, the two biggest international classifications of diseases (DSM and ICD) have recently updated their definitions of trans identities to reflect the fact that they are not mental illnesses *in se*, and WPATH's SOC 8 strongly relies on personal autonomy, individualised care and shared decision-making. Nevertheless, the simple inclusion of trans identities in medical classifications has been heavily criticised as being pathologising in and of itself. Not all trans persons are equally opposed to such medical classifications and diagnoses, however. Indeed, in many countries, access to trans-specific health care and, crucially, to insurance coverage of this care, is dependent on being able to provide an official proof of diagnosis. Those trans persons consequently fear that removing medical classifications would negatively impact their access to necessary gender-affirming care. However, this issue could be resolved by moving from a medical model based on diagnoses towards one based on informed consent. In such models, the main goal is not to assess whether the person requesting care is 'truly' trans, but instead whether they have all the information to make an informed decision, as well as the capacity to consent to care. Consequently, (strong) ICMs provide a way to reconcile depathologisation and effective access to trans-specific health care.

In many States, a diagnosis or psychological assessment is still a precondition for gender recognition. This means that the State makes recognition of trans persons subordinate to their pathologisation. Furthermore, it can have a significant negative impact on access to gender recognition for intersectionally marginalised trans persons. The same human rights institutions that have called for depathologisation of trans identities in general and in health care, have therefore also extended that call to gender recognition procedures. This has led to an increasing number of countries amending their legislation in order to remove such pathologising requirements for gender recognition, showing how the trend towards depathologisation has also impacted gender recognition procedures. Despite this positive impact, pathologisation in gender recognition remains very common, and the ECtHR has even legitimised this form of gatekeeping.

This chapter has shown that the push towards depathologisation has had undeniably positive consequences. In a relatively short time span, it has succeeded in bringing about significant growth in support for trans persons in their everyday life, in accessing health care and in the law. Indeed, it is increasingly followed by international medical authorities, international human rights institutions and individual States. This, in turn, leads to the trend towards depathologisation gaining in strength and legitimacy. Nevertheless, the push for trans depathologisation does not come without criticism. As we illustrated in this chapter, in recent years opponents of a strong recognition of trans identity-based models have sought access to legal routes, such as (opposing) legislative reforms or court procedures in order to block greater acceptance of gender autonomy. It thus remains to be seen whether the impact of the trans depathologisation movement will keep growing, resulting in a heightened respect for and fulfilment of the human rights of trans persons worldwide.

References list

'Advisory Opinion OC-24/17 on Gender Identity, And Equality And Non-Discrimination of Same-Sex Couples' [2017] IACtHR. CorteIDH [Online]. Available at: https://corteidh.or.cr/docs/opiniones/seriea_24_eng.pdf (Accessed: 31 January 2022).

'A.P., Garçon and Nicot v France' [2017] ECtHR, Applications nos. 79885/12, 52471/13 and 52596/13. HUDOC [Online]. Available at: https://hudoc.echr.coe.int/eng?i=001-172913 (Accessed: 31 January 2022).

'Bell v Tavistock', [2020] EWHC 3274 (Admin)

'Bell v Tavistock', [2021] EWCA Civ 1363.

'Christine Goodwin v the United Kingdom', [2002] ECtHR, Application no. 28957/95. HUDOC [Online]. Available at: https://hudoc.echr.coe.int/eng?i=001-60596 (Accessed: 31 January 2022).

Ashley, F. (2021) 'The Misuse of Gender Dysphoria: Toward Greater Conceptual Clarity in Transgender Health', *Perspectives on Psychological Science*, 16(6), pp. 1159–1164, https://doi.org/10.1177/1745691619872987.

Ashley, F., St. Amand, C. M. and Rider, G. N. (2021) 'The Continuum of Informed Consent Models in Transgender Health', *Family Practice*, 38(4), pp. 543–544.

Ben Chikha, F. (2022) *Combating Rising Hate against LGBTI People in Europe*. Available at: https://pace.coe.int/pdf/1b6c0d268db2aeb5ea21ee59ccf0d29ce22f34d60784bef00d85be8b2f4190e1/doc.%2015425.pdf (Accessed: 1 February 2022).

Bribosia, E. and Rorive, I. (2018) 'Human Rights Integration in Action: Making Equality Law Work for Trans People in Belgium', in: Brems, E. and Ouald-Chaib, S. (eds.) *Fragmentation and Integration in Human Rights Law*. Cheltenham: Edward Elgar Publishing, pp. 111–138, https://doi.org/10.4337/9781788113922.00011.

Cannoot, P. (2019a) '#WontBeErased: The Effects of (de)pathologisation and (de)medicalisation on the Legal Capacity of Trans* Persons', *International Journal of Law and Psychiatry*, 66, https://doi.org/10.1016/j.ijlp.2019.101478.

Cannoot, P. (2019b) 'The Pathologisation of Trans* Persons in the ECtHR's Case Law on Legal Gender Recognition', *Netherlands Quarterly of Human Rights*, 37(1), pp. 14–35, https://doi.org/10.1177/0924051918820984.

Cannoot, P. and Decoster, A. (2020) 'The Abolition of Sex/Gender Registration in the Age of Gender Self-Determination: An Interdisciplinary, Queer, Feminist and Human Rights Analysis', *The International Journal of Gender, Sexuality and Law*, 1(1), https://doi.org/10.19164/ijgsl.v1i1.998.

Castro-Peraza, M. E., García-Acosta, J. M., Delgado, N., Perdomo-Hernández, A. M., Sosa-Alvarez, M. I., Llabrés-Solé, R. and Lorenzo-Rocha, N. D. (2019) 'Gender Identity: The Human Right of Depathologisation', *International Journal of Environmental Research and Public Health*, 16(6), https://doi.org/10.3390/ijerph16060978.

Coleman, E., et al. (2011) 'Standards of Care for the Health of Transsexual, Transgender, and Gender Nonconforming People, Version 7', *International Journal of Transgenderism*, 13(4), pp. 165–232.

Coleman, E., et al. (2022) 'Standards of Care for the Health of Transgender and Gender Diverse People, Version 8', *International Journal of Transgender Health*, https://doi.org/10.1080/26895269.2022.2100644.

Committee of Ministers of the Council of Europe (2010) *Recommendation CM/Rec(2010)5 of the Committee of Ministers to Member States on Measures to Combat Discrimination on Grounds of Sexual Orientation or Gender Identity*. Available at: https://www.coe.int/en/web/sogi/rec-2010-5 (Accessed: 20 January 2022).

Council of Europe Parliamentary Assembly (2015) *Resolution 2048 (2015) 'Discrimination against Transgender People in Europe'*. Available at: http://assembly.coe.int/nw/xml/XRef/Xref-XML2HTML-EN.asp?fileid=21736 (Accessed: 7 January 2022).

De Vries, A., Richards, C., Tishelman, A. C., Motmans, J., Hannema, S. E., Green, J. and Rosenthal, S. M. (2021) 'Bell v Tavistock and Portman NHS Foundation Trust [2020] EWHC 3274: Weighing Current Knowledge and Uncertainties in Decisions about Gender-Related Treatment for Transgender Adolescents', *International Journal of Transgender Health*, https://doi.org/10.1080/26895269.2021.1904330.

Davy, Z. (2015) 'The DSM-5 and the Politics of Diagnosing Transpeople', *Archives of Sexual Behavior*, 44(5), pp. 1165–1176.

Davy, Z., Sørlie, A. and Suess Schwend, A. (2018) 'Democratising Diagnoses? The Role of the Depathologisation Perspective in Constructing Corporeal Trans Citizenship', *Critical Social Policy*, 38(1), pp. 13–34.

Drescher, J., Cohen-Kettenis, P. and Winter, S. (2012) 'Minding the Body: Situating Gender Identity Diagnoses in the ICD-11', *International Review of Psychiatry*, 24(6), pp. 568–577.

Dunne, P. (2018a) *The Conditions for Obtaining Legal Gender Recognition: A Human Rights Evaluation*. Thesis. Trinity College Dublin. School of Law. Discipline of Law. Available at: http://www.tara.tcd.ie/handle/2262/84084 (Accessed: 20 January 2022).

Dunne, P. (2018b) 'Towards Trans and Intersex Equality: Conflict or Complimentarity', in Scherpe, J. M., Dutta, A. and Helms, T. (eds.) *The Legal Status of Intersex Persons*. Cambridge: Intersentia, pp. 217–240.

European Parliament (2017) *Resolution on Promoting Gender Equality in Mental Health and Clinical Research*. Available at: https://www.europarl.europa.eu/doceo/document/TA-8-2017-0028_EN.html (Accessed: 20 January 2022).

Gazzola, S. B. and Morrison, M. A. (2014) 'Cultural and Personally Endorsed Stereotypes of Transgender Men and Transgender Women: Notable Correspondence or Disjunction?', *International Journal of Transgenderism*, 15(2), pp. 76–99, https://doi.org/10.1080/15532739.2014.937041.

Gender Recognition Act 2015. Parliament of Ireland. Available at: http://www.irishstatutebook.ie/eli/2015/act/25/enacted/en/html.

Gonzalez-Salzberg, D. A. (2018) 'An Improved Protection for the (Mentally Ill) Trans Parent: A Queer Reading of AP, Garçon and Nicot v France', *The Modern Law Review*, 81(3), pp. 526–538, https://doi.org/10.1111/1468-2230.12344.

Hammarberg, T. (2009) *Human Rights and Gender Identity*. Strasbourg: Council of Europe.

ILGA Portugal et al. (2017) *A Lei de Identidade de Género: Impacto e Desafios da Inovação Legal na Área do (Trans)Género*. Available at: https://eeagrants.cig.gov.pt/resultados/a-lei-de-identidade-de-genero-impacto-e-desafios-da-inovacao-legal-na-area-do-transgenero/ (Accessed: 20 January 2022).

Kraus, C. (2015) 'Classifying Intersex in DSM-5: Critical Reflections on Gender Dysphoria', *Archives of Sexual Behavior*, 44(5), pp. 1147–1163.

Lau, H. (2020) 'Gender Recognition as a Human Right', in von Arnauld, A., von der Decken, K. and Susi, M. (eds.) *The Cambridge Handbook on New Human Rights: Recognition, Novelty, Rhetoric*. Cambridge: Cambridge University Press, pp. 193–206.

Lei No. 38/2018 de 7 de Agosto 2018 Direito A Autodeterminacao da Identidade de Genero e Expressao de Genero E A Protecao Das Caracteristicas Sexuais de Cada Pessoa. Parliament of Portugal. Available at: https://www.pgdlisboa.pt/leis/lei_mostra_articulado.php?nid=2926&tabela=leis&ficha=1.

Ley 26.743 Establecese el Derecho a la Identidad de Genero de las Personas 2012. Parliament of Argentina. Available at: https://www.argentina.gob.ar/normativa/nacional/ley-26743-197860.

Mizock, L. and Fleming, M. Z. (2011) 'Transgender and Gender Variant Populations with Mental Illness: Implications for Clinical Care', *Professional Psychology: Research and Practice*, 42(2), pp. 208–213, https://doi.org/10.1037/a0022522.

Moreton, K. (2021) 'A Backwards-Step for Gillick: Trans Children's Inability to Consent to Treatment for Gender Dysphoria—Quincy Bell & Mrs A v The Tavistock and Portman NHS Foundation Trust and Ors [2020] EWHC 3274 (Admin)', *Medical Law Review*, 29(4), pp. 699–715.

Motmans, J. (2009) *Leven als Transgender in België. De Sociale en Juridische Situatie van Transgender Personen in Kaart Gebracht*. Brussels: Institute for the Equality of Women and Men.

Motmans, J., Nieder, T. O. and Bouman, W. P. (2019) 'Transforming the Paradigm of Nonbinary Transgender Health: A Field in Transition', *International Journal of Transgenderism*, 20(2–3), pp. 119–125, https://doi.org/10.1080/15532739.2019.1640514.

Müller, S., De Cuypere, G. and T'Sjoen, G. (2017) 'Transgender Research in the 21st Century: A Selective Critical Review from a Neurocognitive Perspective', *American Journal of Psychiatry*, 174(12), pp. 1155–1162.

Nobili, A. et al. (2018) 'Autistic Traits in Treatment-Seeking Transgender Adults', *Journal of Autism and Developmental Disorders*, 48(12), pp. 3984–3994, https://doi.org/10.1007/s10803-018-3557-2.

Pearce, R., Erikainen, S. and Vincent, B. (2020) 'TERF Wars: An Introduction', *The Sociological Review Monographs*, 68(4), pp. 677–698, https://doi.org/10.1177/0038026120934713.

Pfäfflin, F. (2016) 'Transgenderism and Transsexuality: Medical and Psychological Viewpoints', in Scherpe, J. M. (ed.) *The Legal Status of Transsexual and Transgender Persons*. Cambridge: Intersentia, pp. 11–23.

Richard, C., Bouman, W. P., Seal, L., Barker, M. J., Nieder, T. O. and T'Sjoen, G. (2016) 'Non-binary or Genderqueer Genders', *International Review of Psychiatry*, 28(1), pp. 95–102.

Rowling, J. K. (2020) 'J.K Rowling Writes about Her Reasons for Speaking Out on Sex and Gender Issues', *JK Rowling*. Available at: https://www.jkrowling.com/opinions/j-k-rowling-writes-about-her-reasons-for-speaking-out-on-sex-and-gender-issues/ (Accessed: 9 January 2022).

Schoentjes, S. (2019) *The Evolution of Abusive Requirements for Gender Recognition in the Council of Europe's Most Progressive Member States*. Master Thesis. Ghent University. Available at: https://libstore.ugent.be/fulltxt/RUG01/002/782/645/RUG01-002782645_2019_0001_AC.pdf (Accessed: 21 January 2022).

Schoentjes, S. and Cannoot, P. (2021) 'X and Y v. Romania: The "Impossible Dilemma" Reasoning Applied to Gender Affirming Surgery as a Requirement for Gender Recognition', *Strasbourg Observers*. Available at: https://strasbourgobservers.com/2021/02/25/x-and-y-v-romania-the-impossible-dilemma-reasoning-applied-to-gender-affirming-surgery-as-a-requirement-for-gender-recognition/ (Accessed: 21 January 2022).

Schulz, S. L. (2018) 'The Informed Consent Model of Transgender Care: An Alternative to the Diagnosis of Gender Dysphoria', *Journal of Humanistic Psychology*, 58(1), pp. 72–92.

Silver, A. E. (2014) 'An Offer You Can't Refuse. Coercing Consent to Surgery through the Medicalisation of Gender Identity', *Columbia Journal of Gender and Law*, 26, pp. 488–526.

Strang, J. F. et al. (2018) '"They Thought It Was an Obsession": Trajectories and Perspectives of Autistic Transgender and Gender-Diverse Adolescents', *Journal of Autism and Developmental Disorders*, 48(12), pp. 4039–4055, https://doi.org/10.1007/s10803-018-3723-6.

Suess Schwend, A. (2017) 'Gender Diversity in Childhood: A Human Right', *Archives of Sexual Behavior*, 46(8), pp. 2519–2520.

Suess Schwend, A. (2020) 'Trans Health Care from a Depathologisation and Human Rights Perspective', *Public Health Reviews*, 41(3), https://doi.org/10.1186/s40985-020-0118-y.

Spanos, C. et al. (2020) 'The Informed Consent Model of Care for Accessing Gender-Affirming Hormone Therapy Is Associated with High Patient Satisfaction', *The Journal of Sexual Medicine*, 18(1), pp. 201–208.

Stonewall (2020) 'What Does the UK Government Announcement on the Gender Recognition Act Mean?', *Stonewall*. Available at: https://www.stonewall.org.uk/what-does-uk-government-announcement-gender-recognition-act-mean (Accessed: 31 January 2022).

Transgender Europe (2021) *Trans Rights Map 2021 Documents Alarming Loss in Trans Rights*. Available at: https://tgeu.org/trans-rights-map-2021/ (Accessed: 20 January 2022).

Theilen, J. T. (2014) 'Depathologisation of Transgenderism and International Human Rights Law', *Human Rights Law Review*, 14(2), pp. 327–342.

Theilen, J. T. (2018) 'Beyond the Gender Binary: Rethinking the Right to Legal Gender Recognition', *European Human Rights Law Review*, 3, pp. 249–257.

T'Sjoen, G., Arcelus, J., de Vries, A., Fisher, A., Nieder, T. O., Özer, M. and Motmans, J. (2020) 'European Society for Sexual Medicine Position Statement "Assessment and Hormonal Management in Adolescent and Adult Trans People, With Attention for Sexual Function and Satisfaction"', *The Journal of Sexual Medicine*, 17(4), pp. 570–584.

United Nations Independent Expert on Protection against Violence and Discrimination Based on Sexual Orientation and Gender Identity (2018) *Protection against Violence and Discrimination Based on Sexual Orientation and Gender Identity*. Available at: https://undocs.org/A/73/152 (Accessed: 7 January 2021).

United Nations Office of the High Commissioner for Human Rights (2015) *Report to the UNHRC on Discrimination and Violence against Individuals Based on Their Sexual Orientation and Gender Identity*. Available at: https://digitallibrary.un.org/record/797193 (Accessed: 20 January 2022).

United Nations Special Rapporteur on the Right of Everyone to the Enjoyment of the Highest Attainable Standard of Physical and Mental Health (2017) *Report of the Special Rapporteur on the*

Right of Everyone to the Enjoyment of the Highest Attainable Standard of Physical and Mental Health. Available at: https://undocs.org/A/HRC/35/21 (Accessed: 7 January 2021).

United Nations Special Rapporteur on Torture and Other Cruel, Inhuman or Degrading Treatment or Punishment (2016) *Report of the Special Rapporteur on Torture and Other Cruel, Inhuman or Degrading Treatment or Punishment to the General Assembly*. Available at: https://www.undocs.org/A/HRC/31/57 (Accessed: 20 January 2022).

Vincent, B. (2019) 'Breaking down Barriers and Binaries in Trans Healthcare: The Validation of Non-binary People', *International Journal of Transgenderism*, 20(2–3), pp. 132–137, https://doi.org/10.1080/15532739.2018.1534075.

Wet van 25/06/2017 tot Hervorming van Regelingen Inzake Transgenders Wat de Vermelding van een Aanpassing van de Registratie van Het Geslacht in de Akten van de Burgerlijke Stand en de Gevolgen Hiervan Betreft. Parliament of Belgium. Available at: https://www.ejustice.just.fgov.be/wet/wet.htm.

'X. and Y. v Romania', [2021] ECtHR, Applications nos. 2145/16 et 20607/16. HUDOC [Online]. Available at: https://hudoc.echr.coe.int/eng?i=001-207364 (Accessed: 31 January 2022).

12
PERSONALITY DISORDER IN MENTAL HEALTH LAW AND CRIMINAL LAW

Ailbhe O'Loughlin

Introduction

Over the last two decades, significant advances have been made in understanding the aetiology and life-course of personality disorder, and people given the diagnosis are no longer widely considered untreatable (Pickersgill, 2013). Nevertheless, thorny normative issues remain. Personality disorder has long been criticised as a 'moral judgement masquerading as a clinical diagnosis' (Blackburn, 1988, p. 511) and is associated with negative professional attitudes (Bowers et al., 2006). For people with lived experience of the diagnosis, it evokes stigma, shame, hopelessness, and rejection (Lamph et al., 2022). For offenders, a diagnosis can open the door to long-term detention under the Mental Health Act (MHA) 1983. Moreover, the evidence base for treating personality disorders common amongst offending populations continues to be limited. Consequently, offenders with personality disorder detained in hospital to protect the public often have limited prospects of reintegration into the community.

This chapter first explores the evolving psychiatric understandings of personality disorder and the persistent stigma that surrounds the diagnosis despite recent efforts to reduce it. It then evaluates the concept of 'treatability' in the former MHA 1983 and its replacement, 'appropriate medical treatment', and considers recent reform proposals from the Wessely Review (Department of Health and Social Care, 2018), the White Paper *Reforming the Mental Health Act* (Department of Health and Social Care and Ministry of Justice, 2021), and the Draft Mental Health Bill 2022. Finally, it explores how the intersections between mental health law, criminal law, and human rights law affect people with personality disorders.

By drawing these threads together, this chapter highlights key tensions in the law. For many people with personality disorder, their disorders are not sufficient to protect them from conviction and punishment in the criminal law, yet they can be detained and treated against their will under mental health law. In addition, their disorders can be deemed insufficiently treatable to warrant a therapeutic disposal at sentencing, yet they can be detained post-sentence in a psychiatric hospital on the basis that appropriate medical treatment is available for them. Consequently, people diagnosed with personality disorders seem to get a 'raw deal' (Pickard, 2015, p. 16). They can find themselves excluded both from legal protections accorded to people with mental disorders under criminal law and from legal protections accorded to people with no mental disorder under mental health law. This looks set to continue, as legal reforms in pursuit of person-centred and rights-respecting mental health care continue to be hampered by risk aversion within government towards offenders diagnosed with mental disorders.

Defining personality disorder: evolving clinical models

Personality disorder is a much-debated diagnosis in psychiatry and has undergone significant conceptual shifts over time. Debates in the psychiatric literature focus primarily on whether diagnostic systems should describe personality disorders as a set of categories, separate from each other and distinct from normal personality, or as extremes along a spectrum with normal personality and behaviour (Coolidge and Segal, 1998, p. 592). The revised fifth edition of the American Psychiatric Association's (2022) *Diagnostic and Statistical Manual of Mental Disorders* (DSM-V-TR) and the eleventh edition of the World Health Organization's (2022) *International Classification of Diseases* (ICD-11) have taken rather different directions on this question.[1]

DSM-V-TR contains two models of personality disorder. Section II, intended for clinical use, largely retains the approach of the previous edition (DSM-IV) and describes distinct categories of personality disorder. An alternative model in Section III, intended to inspire research, combines categories with dimensions. Finally, ICD-11 contains an almost entirely dimensional model – a significant departure from previous editions that followed a similar approach to the DSM. Consequently, the two leading manuals for diagnosing mental disorders now take very different approaches to the diagnosis of personality disorder.

Legal practitioners will have to grapple with these changes in psychiatric nosology, as both manuals are often relied upon as authoritative, if imperfect, catalogues of recognised psychiatric disorders for legal purposes (Slovenko, 2011; Bartlett, 2011; Ahuja, 2015). Changing the methods for diagnosing and describing personality disorders has proved controversial, and attempts to address longstanding concerns regarding the validity of the disorder and its moral undertones have only partially succeeded.

To demonstrate how personality disorder is currently defined, it is necessary to briefly explore the differences between these models and the rationales behind them.

Starting with DSM-V-TR, personality disorder is defined in Section II as:

> an enduring pattern of inner experience and behavior that deviates markedly from the norms and expectations of the individual's culture…This enduring pattern is inflexible and pervasive across a broad range of personal and social situations…leads to clinically significant distress or impairment in social, occupational, or other important areas of functioning…is stable and of long duration, and its onset can be traced back at least to adolescence or early adulthood.
>
> *(American Psychiatric Association, 2022, p. 736)*

---

1 The DSM is the standard diagnostic manual in the USA, while the ICD is the standard in the UK. WHO member states agreed to adopt ICD-11 on 25 May 2019. ICD-11 came into effect in February 2022, replacing ICD-10 (World Health Organization, 2022).

Section II divides personality disorders into categories. In Cluster A are the 'odd or eccentric' types: paranoid, schizoid, and schizotypal. In Cluster B are the 'dramatic, emotional or erratic' types: antisocial, borderline, histrionic, and narcissistic. In Cluster C are the 'anxious and fearful' types: avoidant, dependent, and obsessive-compulsive (American Psychiatric Association, 2022, p. 734). Two further, catch-all categories are described: 'other specified personality disorder' and 'unspecified personality disorder'. Each specified personality disorder comes with its own set of diagnostic criteria. For example, antisocial personality disorder (ASPD) is described as 'a pattern of disregard for, and violation of, the rights of others' (American Psychiatric Association, 2022, p. 733). Borderline personality disorder (BPD) is characterised by 'a pattern of instability in interpersonal relationships, self-image, and affects, and marked impulsivity' (American Psychiatric Association, 2022, p. 733).

The DSM-V-TR alternative model defines the essential features of a personality disorder as 'moderate or greater impairment in personality (self/interpersonal) functioning' and the presence of one or more 'pathological personality traits' (American Psychiatric Association, 2022, p. 881). While Section II uses the terms 'enduring', 'inflexible', and 'pervasive', the Section III alternative model describes impairments and traits as '*relatively* inflexible and pervasive across a broad range of personal and social situations'[2] and '*relatively* stable across time'[3] (American Psychiatric Association, 2022, p. 881). While Section II contains ten categories, Section III describes just six specific personality disorders using trait domains: antisocial, avoidant, borderline, narcissistic, obsessive-compulsive, and schizotypal (American Psychiatric Association, 2022, pp. 883–884). A trait domain is conceptualised as a spectrum with two opposing poles within which the trait applies in different degrees (rather than being present or absent) (American Psychiatric Association, 2022, pp. 899–901).

While the alternative DSM-V-TR model retains specific personality disorders, ICD-11 has radically abolished all categories of personality disorder except for 'borderline pattern'. Under ICD-11, a person is first assessed for the presence of a personality disorder. This is then assigned a severity rating (mild, moderate, or severe) and described using a set of six prominent personality traits: negative affectivity, detachment, dissociality, disinhibition, anankastia,[4] and 'borderline pattern' (Tyrer et al., 2019).

The variations in the diagnostic models reflect the difficulties in reaching a consensus on a new personality disorder model that both reflects advances in research on personality disorder and meets the needs of practitioners. Initially, the DSM-V Personality and Personality Disorders Work Group pursued a fully dimensional approach that would abandon the DSM-IV categories. It failed, however, to reach a consensus on which dimensional model to adopt (Zachar, Krueger, and Kendler, 2016). The Section III model was a compromise, but it failed to garner support from the American Psychiatric Association due to a lack of expert consensus and concerns that the model was too complex for clinical practice (Zachar, Krueger, and Kendler, 2016). The alternative model was included in DSM-V to allow for further research on its validity and clinical utility (Whooley, 2016; Zachar, Krueger, and Kendler, 2016).

While the initial proposals of the ICD-11 working group on personality disorder were met with some criticism, the process was comparatively smooth (Tyrer et al., 2019). While

---

2 Emphasis added.
3 Emphasis added.
4 This is similar to obsessive-compulsive personality disorder in DSM-V-TR.

the architects of the ICD-11 model initially intended to abolish all personality disorder categories, 'borderline pattern' was retained in response to criticisms that the new model disregarded significant advances in treatments for and research on BPD (Herpertz et al., 2017; Tyrer et al., 2019).

Implications of the new models

The DSM and ICD have long emphasised the enduring, inflexible, deeply engrained and pervasive qualities of personality disorders (Tyrer and Seivewright, 2008). David Pilgrim argues that this sense of immutability, coupled with the socially undesirable traits associated with a diagnosis, makes personality disorder particularly stigmatising. He argues that the diagnosis of an enduring 'abnormal' personality is 'a clear moralistic position involving a long-term lack of confidence in those individuals who recurrently act in ways that others find offensive, disappointing and troublesome' (Pilgrim, 2007, p.84). The validity of the personality disorder diagnosis has also come under fire following epidemiological studies showing high levels of co-morbidity between supposedly distinct personality disorders (First et al., 2002; Grant et al., 2005, 2008; Stinson et al., 2008) and between personality disorders and other disorders (First et al., 2002, p. 150).

The architects of the DSM-V alternative model and those of ICD-11 sought to respond to these critiques. Members of the DSM-V work group argued that a dimensional model would reduce stigma by 'recogniz[ing] and appreciat[ing] that the person is more than just the personality disorder and that there are aspects to personality that can be adaptive, even commendable, despite the presence of a personality disorder' (Widiger, Livesley, and Clark, 2009, p. 246). The architects of the ICD-11 model suggested that introducing a spectrum of severity would reduce stigma by counteracting the notion that personality disorder is immutable and untreatable and by producing a more nuanced, and accurate, description of the nature of the condition (Tyrer et al., 2011b, pp. 248–249).

Significantly, the DSM-V-TR alternative model and the ICD-11 have both shifted away from the view that personality disorders are lifelong, deep-seated disturbances that are separate from normal personality and from each other. These changes reflect recent clinical research indicating that some personality disorder traits decline with age (Lilienfeld, 2005) and variation and remission in symptoms during the life-course of the disorder (Zanarini et al., 2003; Gutiérrez et al., 2012).

Nevertheless, both models continue to use moral judgments and descriptions of socially undesirable behaviours as diagnostic criteria. The traits of ASPD in the DSM-V-TR alternative model include manipulativeness, callousness, deceitfulness and irresponsibility. Similar terms are used to describe the personality trait of 'dissociality' in ICD-11. In ICD-11, 'negative affectivity' includes a tendency to reject others' suggestions or advice, and 'anankastia' is characterised by stubbornness and a lack of spontaneity (World Health Organisation, 2022, sec. 6D11.0 and 6D11.4). Examples of behaviours associated with 'borderline pattern' include 'risky sexual behaviour, reckless driving, excessive alcohol or substance use' and 'binge eating' (World Health Organization, 2022, sec. 6D11.5). Thus, the argument that a personality disorder diagnosis is essentially tantamount to a declaration of disapproval or dislike still seems to hold true (Lewis and Appleby, 1988; Bowers et al., 2006).

Both systems continue to use the term 'personality disorder', which is stigmatising in itself (Sheehan, Nieweglowski and Corrigan, 2016). People with lived experience describe personality disorder as 'a dustbin label given to people who seem difficult' that means 'abnormal', 'untreatable' or 'bad and evil' (Castillo, 2003, pp. 69–70). While there is some evidence that clinical attitudes towards personality disorder have improved over time (Day et al., 2018), other studies show that the label continues to provoke negative attitudes amongst practitioners (Lam et al., 2016; Sheehan, Nieweglowski, and Corrigan, 2016). Professionals and people with lived experience associate the label with a sense of blame, shame, defectiveness, exclusion and permanence (Lamph et al., 2022). While a BPD diagnosis has afforded some people a sense of control and hope, these positive attitudes are expressed only where the diagnosis led to support (Horn, Johnstone, and Brooke, 2007; see also Lamph et al., 2022). Without such support, a diagnosis is experienced as 'the killing of hope' (Horn, Johnstone, and Brooke, 2007, p. 262).

While clinical advances have contributed to a sense that personality disorder is treatable, some scepticism remains (Pickersgill, 2013). Research evidence for the effectiveness of treatment is of moderate quality at best. The most comprehensively studied, and most commonly diagnosed, personality disorders are ASPD and BPD (Tyrer et al., 2011a, 2019). A recent systematic review of psychological treatments for ASPD concluded that 'there is insufficient evidence to support or refute the effectiveness of any psychological intervention' (Gibbon et al., 2020, p. 41). A review of pharmacological therapies drew the same conclusion (Khalifa et al., 2020, p. 32).

The evidence base for treating BPD is better, but it continues to be limited by deficiencies in study quality (Bateman, Gunderson, and Mulder, 2015). A recent metanalysis found beneficial effects of psychotherapy compared to treatment as usual, but the evidence was only of moderate quality and all trials had a high risk of bias (Storebø et al., 2020, p. 70). While dialectical behavioural therapy and mentalisation-based treatment were found to be more effective than treatment as usual in improving some symptoms, this finding was based on low-quality evidence. Thus, the true magnitude of treatment effects was uncertain (Storebø et al., 2020, pp. 70–71). A review of pharmacological interventions concluded that 'there is no evidence from [randomised controlled trials] that any drug reduces overall BPD severity' but that some did improve symptoms (Stoffers et al., 2010, p. 40). Again, the evidence was not robust. A more recent systematic review drew similar conclusions (Gartlehner et al., 2021).

This is not to say that existing therapies have been shown conclusively *not* to work. Rather, more robust research is needed. In the meantime, the National Institute for Health and Care Excellence (NICE) guideline on the treatment and management of ASPD recommends that clinicians consider group-based cognitive behavioural interventions, which are supported by some evidence (NCCMH et al. 2010, paras 8.4.2.1–2). It also recommends challenging therapeutic pessimism and negative attitudes towards patients and encouraging staff to develop 'a stronger belief in the effectiveness of their own personal skills' (NCCMH et al. 2010, para. 4.3.1). The NICE guideline on the treatment and management of BPD is also cautiously optimistic. It recommends that clinicians explore treatment options with patients 'in an atmosphere of hope and optimism, explaining that recovery is possible and attainable' (NCCMH et al. 2009, para. 10.1.4.1). The guideline recommends that psychotherapy should be delivered in a structured setting, and that clinicians consider dialectical behavioural therapy for self-harm (NCCMH et al. 2009, para. 5.12.1.1–3).

The diverging paths taken by DSM-V-TR and ICD-11 could have significant legal and social implications. Research on treatments for the DSM-V-TR personality disorders is likely to continue as these categories have been retained in the manual. However, research on the ICD-11 models may take a different direction, focused on specific traits or behaviours rather than categories. In addition, while the revised diagnostic systems are an improvement, they have not fully addressed the longstanding stigma attaching to personality disorders and the moral judgments that underlie the diagnosis.

Experts rely on the DSM and ICD as the basis for psychiatric diagnoses, and these have significant consequences across a range of legal contexts, including criminal law, medical law, and family law (Bartlett, 2011). The existence of three diagnostic systems increases the likelihood of experts disagreeing over diagnosis, or using different terminology to describe a similar condition. Disagreements can have a decisive impact in legal contexts that require expert consensus. In mental health law, the MHA 1983 generally requires two doctors to certify that they are satisfied that the criteria for detention are met. A key criterion is that the person must be suffering from a mental disorder. Experts basing their assessments on the DSM-V-TR criteria or the ICD-11 may come to different conclusions on this issue, as the criteria are not identical. An apparent lack of consensus could result, for example, in a prison sentence rather than a hospital disposal at sentencing. In the context of criminal law, a recognised psychiatric condition is required to demonstrate injury (*R. v. D*, 2006). Consequently, 'competing diagnoses or conflict between a diagnosis and non-diagnosis…can scupper a case that would have a realistic prospect of conviction in the absence of such conflict' (Finch, 2022, p. 371).

Moreover, legal actors who are not experts in psychiatric diagnosis will have to familiarise themselves with three different models. This raises the prospect of misinterpretations of psychiatric evidence that can undermine the authority of legal decisions. Commentary on the trial of Anders Breivik in Norway highlights how diagnostic disagreements between psychiatrists in high-profile cases can fuel anti-expert or anti-psychiatric commentary in the media, and lead to questionable legal decisions (Melle, 2013). Faced with contradictory psychiatric evidence, a trial court concluded in 2012 that Breivik was not psychotic, and found him legally accountable for killing 77 people. The decision has been criticised for relying on common-sense interpretations of Breivik's behaviour and for relying on the ICD-10 criteria for schizophrenia, seemingly overlooking DSM-IV criteria that could have led to the conclusion that Breivik was psychotic and therefore not legally accountable (Melle, 2013).

The problem of 'dangerous' people diagnosed with personality disorders

Concerns for the human rights or civil liberties of individuals who could be subject to long-term hospital detention with little prospect of release have long sat alongside demands for public protection from dangerous individuals. In 1999, the Fallon Inquiry into the personality disorder unit at Ashworth Special Hospital concluded that:

> there continues to be a wide diversity of opinion among experts from all the professions about the treatment and management of personality disorder and particularly severe personality disorder. There have always been dedicated enthusiasts convinced that they have the answer within their grasp, but there are also the sceptics, probably the majority, who point to the lack of credible evidence that treatment works.
> *(Fallon et al., 1999, para. 6.10.1)*

Little in this picture had changed since the 1957 report of the Royal Commission on the Law Relating to Mental Illness and Mental Deficiency (the Percy Commission) and the 1975 report of the Committee on Mentally Abnormal Offenders (the Butler Committee). While some progress has been made in respect of BPD, the picture is unlikely to be much different when it comes to ASPD.

Some jurisdictions have taken the step of entirely, or almost entirely, excluding people diagnosed with personality disorder from the scope of compulsory powers. In Ireland, a person cannot be involuntarily admitted to psychiatric hospital unless he or she suffers from mental disorder, defined as 'mental illness, severe dementia or significant intellectual disability' (Mental Health Act (Ireland) 2001, s.3). Involuntary admission based on a personality disorder alone is explicitly excluded (Mental Health Act (Ireland) 2001, s.8(2)(b)). Thus, a person diagnosed with a personality disorder can only be involuntarily admitted in Ireland if they have a comorbid condition that meets the mental disorder definition.

In New Zealand and in most Australian jurisdictions (except South Australia), a person must be suffering from 'mental illness' and require psychiatric treatment before he or she can be detained under mental health law (Gray et al., 2010; Dawson, 2018). Personality disorder does not fit easily within statutory definitions of mental illness that are tailored to psychosis, thought disorder or mood disorders. Consequently, people with personality disorders in these jurisdictions can only be detained short-term during acute mental health crises (Dawson, 2018).

Under the Australasian approach, the prison service bears responsibility for managing 'dangerous' offenders with personality disorders (Dawson, 2018, p. 624). Similarly, the Irish Mental Health Act 2001 implies that 'it is criminal law, rather than mental health law, that should provide for situations where a person's decisions possibly place others in jeopardy' (Reidy and Kelly, 2021, p. 3).

Dawson argues that the justification for the Australasian approach is that mental health law should not be used to facilitate the 'pure preventive detention of people considered "dangerous" but untreatable' but instead for 'those most likely to benefit from treatment' (Dawson, 2018, p. 84). Dawson traces this view back to the influential psychiatrist, Aubrey Lewis (1963, p. 1553), who was wary of the abuse of psychiatry and suggested that:

> psychiatrists have no wish to…act…as the agents of organized society in getting 'deviants' to conform. If society asks psychiatrists to do this, with 'psychopathic disorder' as the thin end of the wedge, it may be predicted that they will refuse.

By contrast, the trend in England and Wales has been towards expanding the scope of mental health law to facilitate the detention of people with personality disorder where they are considered to pose a risk to the public. In the 1990s, the New Labour Government sought to introduce new legislation to detain 'dangerous people with severe personality disorder', or DSPD, in psychiatric hospitals (Home Office and Department of Health, 1999). Under the MHA 1983 as originally enacted, a person could only be detained on the grounds of 'psychopathic disorder' if treatment in hospital was 'likely to alleviate or prevent a deterioration of [his or her] condition' (MHA 1983, former s.3(2)(b)). Psychopathic disorder was a legal rather than a psychiatric concept defined as 'a persistent disorder or disability of mind (whether or not including significant impairment of intelligence) which results in abnormally aggressive or seriously irresponsible conduct on the part of the person concerned.' The Government presented this 'treatability' requirement as a stumbling block to the detention of dangerous individuals in hospital on the grounds that personality disorders were considered untreatable by many psychiatrists (Peay, 2011b, p. 176. See further O'Loughlin, 2014).

New Labour's determination to remove perceived legal impediments to public protection drove the introduction of the MHA 2007 (Daw, 2007). The MHA 2007 amended the MHA 1983, replacing the old categories of mental illness, mental impairment and psychopathic disorder with the single diagnosis of 'mental disorder', broadly defined as 'any disorder or disability of the mind' (MHA 1983, s.1(2)). It replaced the 'treatability' requirement with the new, weaker test of whether 'appropriate medical treatment' is 'available' to the patient in hospital. The 'purpose' of this treatment must be to 'alleviate, or prevent a worsening of, the disorder or one or more of its symptoms or manifestations' (MHA 1983, s.145(4)). This test applies, *inter alia*, to civil detention for treatment under section 3 and to the transfer of prisoners to psychiatric hospital by the Justice Secretary under section 47 of the MHA 1983.

While awaiting amendments to the MHA 1983, a pilot DSPD Programme was established in both hospital and prison settings to develop treatment and management techniques for the DSPD group. The programme has since been expanded in prisons and in the community under the new title of the Offender Personality Disorder (OPD) Pathway (O'Loughlin, 2019; Skett and Lewis, 2019; Trebilcock et al., 2019). While some commentators point to high-profile cases of serious offending by former psychiatric patients such as Michael Stone as the impetus for the plans for the DSPD group (Seddon, 2008; Pickersgill, 2013), others highlight 'a longstanding frustration within government at the refusal of psychiatrists to address the problem of high risk offenders with personality disorder' (Maden, 2007, p. 8).

The DSPD group were not only conceived of as presenting a risk to the public, but also as disrupting the work of prisons and secure hospitals and threatening the authority of state institutions to maintain a safe custodial environment (O'Loughlin, 2019, p. 633). While the impact of the DSPD initiative on reoffending rates has yet to be fully evaluated, the reasons for its survival seem to hinge on its effectiveness in managing difficult prisoners at a reduced cost, and on its potential to provide a means for integrating difficult, high-risk offenders into existing systems of offender management and control (O'Loughlin, 2014, 2019; see further Trebilcock et al., 2019).

From 'treatability' to 'appropriate treatment' in the MHA 1983

The DSPD programme and legislative amendments were further designed to address the problem of individuals in special hospitals resisting treatment by refusing to engage with treatment in order to be found 'untreatable' and not detainable under the MHA 1983. As the Law Society has highlighted, however, 'treatability' was already given a very wide interpretation under the original MHA 1983, and the problems targeted by the DSPD proposals may therefore have been problems of culture rather than of law (The Law Society, 2002).

The case law under the old MHA 1983 raises the question of whether the removal of the treatability test was necessary in the first place. In *Hutchison Reid v. Secretary of State for Scotland* (1999), the House of Lords interpreted the test very broadly. It held that while the patient was not receiving treatment for his personality disorder, 'his detention in the hospital was preventing a deterioration of his condition because his abnormally aggressive or seriously irresponsible behaviour was being controlled or at least being modified' (*Hutchison Reid v. Secretary of State for Scotland* (1999), p. 531). As the patient's anger management showed improvement in the structured and medically supervised hospital environment, this was enough to satisfy the 'treatability' test. This approach was confirmed by the European Court of Human Rights (ECtHR) in *Hutchison Reid v. UK* (2003, para. 52), in which the Court held that compulsory confinement may be necessary not only where a person needs therapy, medication or other clinical treatment to cure or alleviate his condition, but also where the person needs control and supervision to prevent him, for example, causing harm to himself or other persons.

The new appropriate medical treatment test has been interpreted even more broadly than the old treatability test. 'Appropriate medical treatment' is defined tautologically as 'medical treatment which is appropriate in (the patient's) case, taking into account the nature and degree of the mental disorder and all other circumstances of his case' (s.3(4) MHA 1983). 'Medical treatment' is defined broadly and includes 'nursing, psychological intervention and specialist mental health habilitation, rehabilitation and care' (s.145(1) MHA 1983). The 'purpose' of treatment must be 'to alleviate, or prevent a worsening of, the disorder or one or more of its symptoms or manifestations' (s.145(4) MHA 1983). This sets a lower standard than the treatability test, as 'purpose is not the same as likelihood' (Department of Health, 2015, para. 23.4). Medical treatment may fulfil this criterion 'even though it cannot be shown in advance that any particular effect is likely to be achieved' (Department of Health, 2015, para. 23.4).

There is a very fine line between mere detention, which is impermissible under the MHA 1983, and appropriately 'therapeutic' detention, which is permissible. The MHA 1983 Code of Practice states that 'simply detaining someone, even in a hospital, does not constitute medical treatment' (Department of Health, 2015, para. 23.18). Nevertheless, 'appropriate treatment' for some patients may consist 'only of nursing and specialist day-to-day care…in a safe and secure therapeutic environment with a structured regime' (Department of Health, 2015, para. 23.17). For some, 'management of the undesirable effects of their disorder may be the most that can realistically be hoped for' (Department of Health, 2015, para. 23.16).

The courts in some cases have come 'perilously close to finding that detention is, itself, appropriate treatment' (Bartlett and Sandland, 2014, p. 255). In *MD v. Nottinghamshire Healthcare NHS Trust* (2010), the First-Tier Tribunal (Mental Health) held that a patient, who was not psychologically able to engage with therapy, had 'the potential to benefit from the milieu of the ward both for its short term effects and for the possibility that it would break through the defence mechanisms and allow him later to engage in therapy' (*MD*, para. 39). Thus, appropriate treatment was held to be available.

Judge Jacobs seemed to take a more cautious approach in *DL-H v. Devon Partnership NHS Trust and Secretary of State for Justice* (2010). He was concerned that 'medical treatment' was defined so broadly in the legislation that there was a 'danger that a patient for whom no appropriate treatment is available may be contained for public safety rather than detained for treatment' (*DL-H v. Devon Partnership NHS Trust and Secretary of State for Justice*, 2010, para. 33). To avoid this, he advised that tribunals 'must investigate behind assertions, generalisations and standard phrases' and consider specific questions:

What precisely is the treatment that can be provided? What discernible benefit may it have on this patient? Is that benefit related to the patient's mental disorder or to some unrelated problem? Is the patient truly resistant to engagement?
(*Devon Partnership NHS Trust and Secretary of State for Justice, 2010, para. 33*)

The reference to 'therapeutic benefit' seemed to set a higher standard than the legislation itself. However, in a subsequent case, Judge Jacobs said that his statements in *DL-H v. Devon* were merely intended to guide tribunals in their fact-finding mission. He further held that

> if the tribunal finds that the patient is not prepared to engage and will never be brought to engage, that will not necessarily be decisive. This is because the definition of treatment is so broad that it includes much that does not require the patient's engagement in formal therapy.
> (DL-H v. Partnerships in Care, 2013, para. 42)

In *WH v. Llanarth Court Hospital* (2015, para. 56), the Upper Tribunal confirmed the approach in the Code of Practice, holding that:

> it may in some circumstances be difficult to distinguish appropriate treatment from mere detention…If the purpose of the treatment the patient receives is to prevent a worsening of the symptoms or manifestations of his mental disorder, it is likely to constitute appropriate treatment even though the outcome of such treatment may have little or no beneficial effect on the patient.

Thus, whilst 'mere detention' cannot constitute appropriate treatment, it is sufficient for treatment to have a therapeutic 'purpose', even if it is unlikely to have any beneficial effect. This sets a very low standard. Surely treatment cannot have a 'therapeutic purpose' if it is known in advance that it is unlikely to any beneficial effect on the patient? In any event, tribunals are often able to find a therapeutic purpose on the facts of the case. As the judge remarked in *WH* (2015, para. 39), 'there has been no reported case where a tribunal has found that a patient's treatment in hospital constituted mere containment'.

This liberal approach may not now comply with the European Convention on Human Rights (ECHR). In *Rooman v. Belgium* (2019, para. 208), the Court, summarising its case law, held that:

> the administration of suitable therapy has become a requirement in the context of the wider concept of the 'lawfulness' of the deprivation of liberty. Any detention of mentally ill persons must have a therapeutic purpose, aimed specifically, and in so far as possible, at curing or alleviating their mental-health condition, including, where appropriate, bringing about a reduction in or control over their dangerousness. The Court has stressed that, irrespective of the facility in which those persons are placed, they are entitled to be provided with a suitable medical environment accompanied by real therapeutic measures, with a view to preparing them for their eventual release.

The ECtHR held that detaining the applicant in a hospital for 14 years without providing him with therapy in a language he could understand violated Articles 3 and 5 of the Convention. This was, at least in part, because he needed to engage with therapy to have any prospect of being discharged. Accordingly, *Rooman* falls in line with the ECtHR's case law on the prisoner's 'right to rehabilitation' and right to a 'hope' of release (van Zyl Smit, Weatherby, and Creighton, 2014; Vannier, 2016; Meijer, 2017; O'Loughlin, 2021a).

After *Rooman*, placing a person in a structured environment with the purpose of merely preventing a deterioration in his condition, or providing treatment that has little or no chance of having any beneficial effect may not be compliant with the ECHR. Such regimes could not be said to be oriented towards preparing the individual for release.

From appropriate treatment to therapeutic benefit?

The debate surrounding appropriate treatment has returned following the publication of *Modernising the Mental Health Act* (Department of Health and Social Care, 2018), the final report of the Independent Review of the Mental Health Act 1983 chaired by Professor Sir Simon Wessely. A Draft Mental Health Bill 2022 based on the proposals contained in a White Paper entitled *Reforming the Mental Health Act* (Department of Health and Social Care and Ministry of Justice, 2021) is currently undergoing scrutiny by a Joint Committee of members of the House of Commons and House of Lords.

The Wessely Review was conducted in a much calmer political climate than that facing its predecessor, the Expert Committee chaired by Professor Genevra Richardson commissioned in 1998 to review the MHA 1983 (Department of Health, 1999). In the Foreword to the Review, Professor Sir Wessely wryly comments that his Review's terms of reference included 'the problems of the rising rate of coercion, seen as something undesirable, as opposed to the aim of public policy' (Department of Health and Social Care, 2018, p. 8).

The Wessely Review proposed that the following purposes be enshrined on the face of the Mental Health Act: 'to confer and authorise the powers (including coercive powers) necessary for the treatment of mental disorder and to safeguard the dignity and rights of those who are made subject to the exercise of such powers and for related purposes' (Department of Health and Social Care, 2018, p. 67).

It further recommended four key principles to govern the use of compulsory powers:

1. Choice and autonomy
2. Least restriction
3. Therapeutic benefit
4. The person as an individual

(Department of Health and Social Care, 2018, p. 67)

Most relevant to personality disorder, the Review recommended strengthening the detention criteria under the Act by adding two new requirements: first, that 'treatment is available which would benefit the patient, and not just serve public protection, which cannot be delivered without detention'; and second, that 'there is a substantial likelihood of significant harm to the health, safety or welfare of the person, or the safety of any other person without treatment' (Department of Health and Social Care, 2018, p. 113).

Whilst proposing that 'treatment' be broadly defined, the Review sought to guard against the idea that detention in itself could be sufficient. It proposed that 'in situations of crisis, it may be reasonable for the main, but not the only, element of treatment to be to provide a safe therapeutic environment for a brief period of time' (Department of Health and Social Care, 2018, p. 113). Keeping a person 'off the streets' would not be enough, nor would long periods of detention be justified on the basis of 'general nursing input and self-care planning' or the 'assertion that the "ward routine" provides a therapeutic benefit' (Department of Health and Social Care, 2018, p. 113).

Thus, the Wessely Review recommended a move away from the minimalist requirements in the case law and Code of Practice and towards a requirement for more active therapeutic input. The proposed 'substantial risk of serious harm' test would also set a higher bar for detention than the current legislation, and would presumably set a lower bar for discharge.

The Review's recommendations were not restricted to a particular part of the Act, and it appears that the Review envisaged they would apply to people detained under civil (Part II) and criminal (Part III) powers. There was, however, little detailed consideration of the implications of proposed reforms for Part III patients.

While the current criteria for discharging unrestricted Part III patients are the same as for section 3 patients (MHA 1983, s.72(1)(b)), the criteria for making hospital orders (s.37, MHA 1983) and transfer directions (s.47, MHA 1983) without restrictions make no reference to risk.[5] Currently, an unrestricted patient detained under Part III of the MHA 1983 must be discharged by a Tribunal if the criteria under s.72(1)(b) of the Act are no longer met. If these criteria were strengthened along the lines recommended by the Wessely Review, it is likely that more hospital order patients would be discharged at their first review. But a patient serving a prison sentence[6] could continue to be detained in hospital, so long as their detention continued to be justified under Article 5(1)(a) (detention after conviction). This is also the case under the current MHA 1983.

In *Reforming the Mental Health Act* (Department of Health and Social Care and Ministry of Justice, 2021), the Government published plans to insert the Wessely Review's 'substantial likelihood of significant harm' requirement into sections 2 and 3 of the MHA 1983 Act and the community treatment order (CTO). The consultation paper also proposed to introduce a therapeutic benefit test for section 3 patients and CTO patients. It, however, took the questionable step of proposing to restrict these reforms to Part II patients. This was on the grounds that 'patients in the criminal justice system have a unique risk profile' and that changing the detention criteria would 'compromise [the Government's] ability to adequately protect the public from risk of harm from sometimes serious or violent offenders' (Department of Health and Social Care and Ministry of Justice, 2021, p. 27). The paper also suggested that the four Wessely Review principles may not be applicable to Part III patients due to public safety concerns (Department of Health and Social Care and Ministry of Justice, 2021, p. 21).

---

5 See, for example, the criteria for making a hospital order under s.37 of the Act: '(1) Where a person is convicted before the Crown Court of an offence punishable with imprisonment other than an offence the sentence for which is fixed by law,…or is convicted by a magistrates' court of an offence punishable on summary conviction with imprisonment, and the conditions mentioned in subsection (2) below are satisfied, the court may by order authorise his admission to and detention in such hospital as may be specified in the order… (2) The conditions referred to in subsection (1) above are that — (a) the court is satisfied, on the written or oral evidence of two registered medical practitioners, that the offender is suffering from mental disorder and that… (i) the mental disorder from which the offender is suffering is of a nature or degree which makes it appropriate for him to be detained in a hospital for medical treatment and appropriate medical treatment is available for him;…and (b) the court is of the opinion, having regard to all the circumstances including the nature of the offence and the character and antecedents of the offender, and to the other available methods of dealing with him, that the most suitable method of disposing of the case is by means of an order under this section.' A court can make a hospital order subject to restrictions on discharge under section 41 of the MHA 1983, and the Justice Secretary can make a transfer direction subject to restrictions under section 49.
6 Under the MHA 1983, there are two main routes into hospital for people serving a prison sentence: the section 45A hospital and limitation direction under section (attached by a sentencing court to a prison sentence) or the section 47 transfer direction (an order to transfer a sentenced prisoner to hospital made by the Secretary of State).

Personality disorder

The assumption that Part III patients are inherently dangerous is not based in evidence. Indeed, a study of 84 patients discharged from medium- or low-secure hospital wards identified that civil patients in secure settings were more frequently involved in incidents of aggression, sex offending and fire-setting than forensic patients (Galappathie, Khan and Hussain, 2017).

The Draft Mental Health Bill 2022 has since departed from this assumption of dangerous by extending its proposed reforms to the detention criteria under the MHA 1983 to people detained under Part II and Part III. It does not, however, propose to enshrine the Wessely Review principles on the face of the Act.

The Bill proposes to replace s.72(1)(b) with a new s.20(4) that would require the Tribunal to discharge a patient who is liable to be detained under the Act[7] where it is *not* satisfied that:

(a) the patient is suffering from psychiatric disorder of a nature or degree which makes it appropriate for the patient to receive medical treatment in a hospital; and
(b) serious harm may be caused to the health or safety of the patient or of another person unless the patient receives medical treatment,
(c) it is necessary, given the nature, degree and likelihood of the harm, and how soon it would occur, for the patient to receive medical treatment,
(d) the necessary treatment cannot be provided unless the patient continues to be liable to be detained, and
(e) appropriate medical treatment is available for the patient.

(proposed new section 20(4), Clause 3 and 4 of the Draft Bill)

These criteria are more stringent than the current s.72(1)(b) as they would require Tribunals to be satisfied that treatment is necessary to avoid 'serious harm' to the patient or to others, whereas the current criteria merely require treatment to be 'necessary for the health or safety of the patient or for the protection of other persons'. The wording of the Draft Bill is opaque, however, as it does not specify how likely the harm should be before detention for treatment is necessary. Should it be almost certain to occur, or more likely than not? Furthermore, as is the case under the current Act, the proposals give no further guidance on how the broad terms of 'nature', 'degree', 'health' and 'safety' are to be interpreted.

The proposed changes to the 'appropriate medical treatment' test in the Draft Bill are light-touch. The definition of 'appropriate medical treatment' in the Bill is almost identical to the current definition in the Act. The only difference is that 'reasonable prospect' has replaced 'purpose'. This means that a person detained under Part III of the MHA 1983 would have to be discharged (conditionally or absolutely) if the Tribunal was *not* satisfied that appropriate medical treatment was available and that this would have 'a reasonable prospect of alleviating, or preventing the worsening of, the disorder or one or more of its symptoms or manifestations'.

While 'purpose' in the current Act does not seem to require much more than hope that the treatment will have the desired effect, 'reasonable prospect' would seem to require an evaluation of the likelihood of treatment having such an effect. This, however, falls short of the requirement for a 'therapeutic benefit' proposed by the Wessely Review, where 'benefit' 'would include contributing to the patient's discharge, and not solely to public safety'

---

7 Apart from patients detained for assessment under section 2 of the Act.

(Department of Health and Social Care, 2018, p. 113). The Wessely Review's interpretation of 'treatment benefit' would fit better with the ECtHR's insistence on measures to prepare detainees for discharge in *Rooman*. The Government may, however, be reluctant to re-ignite the concerns that resulted in the watering down of the old 'treatability' test. Given the limited evidence for the effectiveness of treatments for ASPD, a more robust therapeutic benefit test could run the risk of limiting public protection powers.

Personality disorder and criminal law

The mental state of a person with personality disorder whose behaviour poses a risk to him or herself or to others can 'at one and the same time [be] deemed to meet the conditions required for criminal responsibility, and to warrant involuntary hospital admission' (Pickard, 2015, p. 16). As Hannah Pickard (2015, p. 16) argues, it is difficult to avoid the feeling that a person in this position

> gets a raw deal. For, whichever way he turns, he is subjected to the strong arm of the law – deemed sufficiently mentally well to be punished for his crimes, but not deemed sufficiently mentally well to retain the right to make his own decisions about matters of serious importance to his own life, including whether or not to continue it.

In addition, while individuals with personality disorder often do not benefit from the protections offered by the law to those who are deemed insane, they can nevertheless be detained in hospital under the MHA 1983 on the grounds that they have a mental disorder and pose a risk to others (Peay, 2011a, p. 232). The reasons behind and the implications of these seeming paradoxes are examined below.

As Pickard (2015) acknowledges, the purposes and rationales of civil and criminal law are distinct. The MHA 1983 is highly paternalistic, and aims to prevent people with mental disorder from harming themselves or others. Treatment choices are at the discretion of the treating clinician, and treatment for mental disorder can be imposed on a detained person without their consent under section 63 of the MHA 1983, even if they have capacity to refuse treatment under the Mental Capacity Act (MCA) 2005.[8]

Treatment for personality disorder is construed in a broad sense. It includes force-feeding where this is concurrent with or a necessary pre-requisite to treatment for mental disorder (*B v. Croydon Health Authority*, 1995), or where a hunger strike is a symptom or manifestation of personality disorder (*R v. Collins, ex p Brady*, 2001). More recently, kidney dialysis was held to be treatment 'for' a personality disorder as the person's physical condition and his non-compliance with treatment were both held to be 'manifestations' of his personality disorder (*A Healthcare v. CC*, 2020).

The MCA 2005, by contrast, seeks to *maximise* a person's ability to make their own decisions about medical treatment (Department for Constitutional Affairs, 2007, pp. 19–20). The threshold for someone to lack capacity under the MCA 2005 is therefore relatively high. People diagnosed with personality disorder tend to be found to have capacity under the

---

8 This power is subject to safeguards for certain treatments under sections 57–58A. Treatment must not breach Article 3 of the ECHR. See further Bartlett (2011b).

MCA 2005. Indeed, 94% of patients and prisoners on the DSPD programme were found to have capacity to consent to treatment (Burns et al. 2011, p. 93).

Conversely, the criminal law has been shaped by a judicial desire to *minimise* findings of non-responsibility and to resist challenges to the criminal law's authority to punish (Eigen, 1995; Wiener, 2003; Loughnan and Ward, 2014). While a personality disorder may constitute a 'disease of the mind' under the rules in *R. v. M'Naghten* (1843), only those who did not know the nature and quality of their act and/or that it was legally wrong can be found not guilty by reason of insanity (NGRI) (*R. v. Codère*, 1917; *R. v. Windle*, 1952). A defendant with a personality disorder who does not respond to moral reasons or who has problems exercising self-control is unlikely to be found insane (see Morse, 2008; Peay, 2011a). Indeed, between 1975 and 1988 there were just three findings of NGRI where the primary diagnosis was personality disorder, and in later research there were no successful pleas with this diagnosis (Law Commission, 2012, para. 3.38).

Diminished responsibility is more responsive to personality disorder, as it considers, *inter alia*, a person's capacity to form a rational judgment or to exercise self-control (Homicide Act 1957, s.2). When accepted, the plea avoids the mandatory life sentence for murder and leaves the choice of sentence to the judge's discretion. The proportion of successful pleas on the grounds of personality disorder are, however, relatively low. In 2005, 10% of successful pleas were based on personality disorder while 28% of successful pleas were based on paranoid schizophrenia (Ministry of Justice 2009, p. 15). In a later study, 73% of defendants with personality disorder who raised diminished responsibility were convicted of murder compared to just 12% of those diagnosed with schizophrenia (Mackay and Mitchell, 2017, Table 8).[9] Defendants with personality disorder who successfully raised diminished responsibility were also more likely to be regarded as deserving punishment, as all such defendants in the study received a prison sentence (Mackay and Mitchell, 2017, Table 8).

An individual with personality disorder may therefore expect to only have the effects of his or her mental disorder taken into account at sentencing, if at all. The Court of Appeal in the leading case of *R. v. Vowles* (2015, para. 54(iii)) advised judges that a hospital order with restrictions (MHA 1983, ss.37 and 41) would be warranted at sentencing where:

> (1) the mental disorder is treatable; (2) once treated there is no evidence [the offender] would be in any way dangerous; and (3) the offending is entirely due to that mental disorder.

Thus, the Court in *Vowles* created an additional risk-based treatability requirement in sentencing law that is narrower than the appropriate treatment requirement in the MHA 1983. The Court advised that offenders with personality disorder should be given prison sentences rather than hospital disposals. This was on the grounds that it is 'more difficult to attribute a reduction in culpability to a personality disorder'; that 'individuals with severe personality disorders are less likely to benefit from hospitalisation'; and that treatment was available in specialist prisons (*Vowles*, 2015, para. 50(iii)–(v)).

After *Vowles*, offenders with personality disorder seemed more likely to receive a prison sentence than a hospital order. However, subsequent cases adopted a more flexible approach (O'Loughlin, 2021b). In *R. v. Turner* (2015) and *R. v. Hoppe* (2016), two appellants diag-

---

9 Figures calculated by the author from data in Mackay and Mitchell (2017).

nosed with emotionally unstable personality disorder successfully appealed against indeterminate prison sentences. In both cases, the Court of Appeal chose to substitute hospital orders with restrictions based on psychiatric evidence that the appellants' disorders were treatable and that their offending was related to their mental disorders (O'Loughlin, 2021b). The psychiatric evidence in these cases may have reflected the stronger evidence base for the treatment of BPD, and it is unclear whether the same approach will be adopted for ASPD.

After *Vowles*, a person with a personality disorder may therefore be excluded from a hospital disposal at sentencing on the grounds that treatment is not expected to reduce risk to the public. Yet, the same person may later be detained under the MHA 1983 on the grounds, *inter alia*, that 'appropriate medical treatment' is 'available' in hospital. This is because the MHA 1983 can be used for the purposes of preventive detention after a prison sentence expires: a possibility that sits uncomfortably with the principle of proportionate punishment.

No routinely published data is available on how frequently sentenced prisoners are transferred to hospital by the Justice Secretary for the purposes of preventive detention under section 47 of the MHA 1983. But, according to data from one study, the majority (65%) of patients admitted to hospital units on the DSPD programme were serving determinate sentences (Trebilcock and Weaver, 2012). Most were admitted close to their expected release date, and 20% had been transferred to hospital less than two weeks before they expected to be released from prison (Trebilcock and Weaver 2012).[10] These patients were often angry and some refused to engage with treatment, and this had a negative impact on the work of hospital DSPD units (Burns et al., 2011, p. 219 and p. 225). While the OPD Pathway aims to identify eligible prisoners early in their sentences (NOMS and NHS England, 2015, p. 17) and late transfers have been criticised by the Court of Appeal, transfers late in sentence are still possible where the requirements of the MHA 1983 are 'scrupulously satisfied' (*R (TF) v. SS for Justice*, 2008).

Conclusions

Personality disorder is a controversial and contested diagnosis associated with negative moral judgments towards people whose behaviour is deemed disturbing, demanding, difficult, dangerous or merely eccentric. While advances in understanding and treating personality disorders are beginning to counteract the notion that they are permanent, the diagnosis continues to be associated with shame and exclusion. For BPD, the picture is more hopeful as the evidence to support treatment techniques continues slowly to improve. For ASPD or dissocial personality disorder, however, there is still little evidence of treatment effectiveness.

Attempts to confine the use of the MHA 1983 to people who need treatment have repeatedly encountered the problem of serious offenders whom the authorities are reluctant to discharge. The Wessley Review's attempt to counteract a culture of containment has met resistance from government, yet again on public protection grounds. Thus, the risk aversion that saw the introduction of the MHA 2007 and the DSPD Programme continues to impede progressive reforms to mental health law.

Meanwhile, people with personality disorder are largely found to have capacity to refuse treatment under the MCA 2005, yet they can have treatment imposed upon them under the

---

10 This figure has been calculated by the author from the data reported in Trebilcock and Weaver (2012). The data is based on 69 admissions to DSPD units in high-secure hospitals.

MHA 1983. They are frequently found criminally responsible and deserving of a prison sentence by criminal courts, yet can be detained under the MHA 1983 post-sentence. Offenders with personality disorder in England and Wales are therefore at the intersection between two overlapping coercive systems: the criminal justice system and the mental health system. In a context of risk aversion and flexible legal criteria for detention, compulsion may seem inevitable for offenders who are perceived to be dangerous by criminal justice and mental health authorities. The Draft Mental Health Bill 2022 is a step in the right direction, but more work is needed to move towards a system that is oriented towards discharge, rather than containment, and a greater tolerance for positive risk-taking.

References

A Healthcare v. CC [2020] EWHC 574 (Fam)
Ahuja, J. (2015) 'Liability for psychological and psychiatric harm: The road to recovery', *Medical Law Review*, 23(1), pp. 27–52.
American Psychiatric Association (2022) *Diagnostic and Statistical Manual of Mental Disorders : DSM-5-TR*. 5th ed. (text revision). Washington, DC: American Psychiatric Association.
B. v. Croydon Health Authority [1995] 1 All ER 683.
Bartlett, P. (2011) 'DSM-5 and ICD-11 on personality disorder: A lawyer's perspective', *Personality and Mental Health*, 5(2), pp. 144–151.
Bartlett, P. and Sandland, R. (2014) *Mental Health Law: Policy and Practice*. Oxford: Oxford University Press.
Bateman, A. W., Gunderson, J. and Mulder, R. (2015) 'Treatment of personality disorder', *The Lancet*, 385(9969), pp. 735–743.
Blackburn, R. (1988) 'On moral judgements and personality disorders: The myth of psychopathic personality revisited', *British Journal of Psychiatry*, 153(4), pp. 505–512.
Bowers, L. et al. (2006) 'Attitude to personality disorder among prison officers working in a dangerous and severe personality disorder unit', *International Journal of Law and Psychiatry*, 29(5), pp. 333–342.
Burns, T. et al. (2011) *Inclusion for DSPD: Evaluating Assessment and Treatment (IDEA). Final Report to NHS National R&D Programme on Forensic Mental Health*. London: Ministry of Justice.
Butler, R. A. (1975) *Report of the Committee on Mentally Abnormal Offenders*. London: H.M.S.O.
Castillo, H. (2003) *Personality Disorder: Temperament or Trauma?* London: Jessica Kingsley.
Coolidge, F. L. and Segal, D. L. (1998) 'Evolution of personality disorder diagnosis in the diagnostic and statistical manual of mental disorders', *Clinical Psychology Review*, 18(5), pp. 585–599.
Daw, R. (2007) 'The Mental Health Act 2007: The defeat of an ideal', *Journal of Mental Health Law*, 1(16), pp. 131–148.
Dawson, J. B. (2018) 'The Australasian approach to the definition of mental disorder in a Mental Health Act', *Medical Law Review*, 26(4), pp. 610–632.
Day, N. J. S. et al. (2018) 'Clinician attitudes towards borderline personality disorder: A 15-year comparison', *Personality and Mental Health*, 12(4), pp. 309–320.
Department for Constitutional Affairs (2007) *Mental Capacity Act 2005: Code of Practice*. London: TSO.
Department of Health (2015) *Mental Health Act 1983: Code of Practice*. London: TSO.
Department of Health (1999) *Report of the Expert Committee: Review of the Mental Health Act 1983*. London: Department of Health.
Department of Health and Social Care (2018) *Modernising the Mental Health Act: Increasing choice, reducing compulsion. Final report of the Independent Review of the Mental Health Act 1983 (The Wessely Review)*. London: Department of Health and Social Care.
Department of Health and Social Care and Ministry of Justice (2021) *Reforming the Mental Health Act*. London: HMSO.
DL-H v. Devon Partnership NHS Trust and Secretary of State for Justice [2010] UKUT 102 (AAC).
DL-H v. Partnerships in Care [2013] UKUT 500 (AAC), [2014] AACR 16.

Eigen, J. P. (1995) *Witnessing Insanity: Madness and Mad-Doctors in the English Court*. New Haven and London: Yale University Press.

Fallon, P. et al. (1999) *Report of the Commitee of Inquiry into the Personality Disorder Unit, Ashworth Special Hospital: Volume I. Cm 4194-ii*. London: The Stationery Office.

Finch, E. (2022) 'Psychological injury: Where's the harm in it?', *Criminal Law Review*, 5, pp. 358–376.

First, M. B. et al. (2002) 'Personality disorders and relational disorders: A research agenda for addressing crucial gaps in DSM', in: D.J. Kupfer, M.B. First and D.A. Regier (eds) *A Research Agenda for DSM-V*. Washington, DC: American Psychiatric Association, pp. 123–200.

Galappathie, N., Khan, S. T. and Hussain, A. (2017) 'Civil and forensic patients in secure psychiatric settings: A comparison', *BJPsych Bulletin*, pp. 156–159.

Gartlehner, G. et al. (2021) 'Pharmacological treatments for borderline personality disorder: A systematic review and meta-analysis', *CNS Drugs*, 35(10), pp. 1053–1067.

Gibbon, S. et al. (2020) 'Psychological interventions for antisocial personality disorder', *Cochrane Database of Systematic Reviews*, 9, Art. No.: CD007668.

Grant, B. F. et al. (2005) 'Co-occurrence of DSM-IV personality disorders in the United States: Results from the national epidemiologic survey on alcohol and related conditions', *Comprehensive Psychiatry*, 46(1), pp. 1–5.

Grant, B. F. et al. (2008) 'Prevalence, correlates, disability, and comorbidity of DSM-IV borderline personality disorder: Results from the Wave 2 National Epidemiologic Survey on alcohol and Related Conditions', *Journal of Clinical Psychiatry*, 69(4), pp. 533–545.

Gray, J. E. et al. (2010) 'Australian and Canadian Mental Health Acts compared', *Australian and New Zealand Journal of Psychiatry*, 44(12), pp. 1126–1131.

Gutiérrez, F. et al. (2012) 'Personality disorder features through the life course', *Journal of Personality Disorders*, 26(5), pp. 763–774.

Herpertz, S. C. et al. (2017) 'The challenge of transforming the diagnostic system of personality disorders', *Journal of Personality Disorders*, 31(5), pp. 577–589.

Home Office and Department of Health (1999) *Managing Dangerous People with Severe Personality Disorder: Proposals for Policy Development*. London: Home Office and Department of Health.

Horn, N., Johnstone, L. and Brooke, S. (2007) 'Some service user perspectives on the diagnosis of borderline personality disorder', *Journal of Mental Health*, 16(2), pp. 255–269.

Hutchison Reid v. Secretary of State for Scotland [1999] 2 A.C. 512.

Hutchison Reid v. UK, E. C. H. R., App. no. 50272/99 20 February 2003.

Khalifa, N. et al. (2020) 'Pharmacological interventions for antisocial personality disorder', *Cochrane Database of Systematic Reviews*, 9, Art. No.: CD007667.

Lam, D. C. K. et al. (2016) 'An experimental investigation of the impact of personality disorder diagnosis on clinicians: Can we see past the borderline?', *Behavioural and Cognitive Psychotherapy*, 44(3), pp. 361–373.

Lamph, G. et al. (2022) 'A qualitative study of the label of personality disorder from the perspectives of people with lived experience and occupational experience', *The Mental Health Review Journal Review*, 27(1), pp. 31–47.

Law Commission (2012) *Insanity and automatism: Supplementary material to the scoping paper*. Available at: <http://www.lawcom.gov.uk/wp-content/uploads/2015/06/insanity_scoping_supplementary.pdf>. Accessed 27 April 2022.

Lewis, A. (1963) 'Medicine and the affections of the mind', *British Medical Journal*, 2(5372), pp. 1549–1557.

Lewis, G. and Appleby, L. (1988) 'Personality disorder: The patients psychiatrists dislike', *The British Journal of Psychiatry*, 153, pp. 44–49.

Lilienfeld, S. O. (2005) 'Longitudinal studies of personality disorders: Four lessons from personality psychology', *Journal of Personality Disorders*, 19(5), pp. 547–556.

Loughnan, A. and Ward, T. (2014) 'Emergent authority and expert knowledge: Psychiatry and criminal responsibility in the UK', *International Journal of Law and Psychiatry*, 37(1), pp. 25–36.

Mackay, R. and Mitchell, B. (2017) 'The new diminished responsibility plea in operation: Some initial findings', *Criminal Law Review*, (1), pp. 18–35.

Maden, A. (2007) 'Dangerous and severe personality disorder: Antecedents and origins', *British Journal of Psychiatry*, 190(Suppl 49), pp. s8–s11.

MD v. Nottinghamshire Healthcare NHS Trust [2010] UKUT 59 (AAC).

Meijer, S. (2017) 'Rehabilitation as a positive obligation', *European Journal of Crime, Criminal Law and Criminal Justice*, 25(2), pp. 145–162.
Melle, I. (2013) 'The Breivik case and what psychiatrists can learn from it', *World Psychiatry*, 12(1), pp. 16–21.
Mental Health Act 1983, c.20. Available at: https://www.legislation.gov.uk/ukpga/1983/20/contents (Accessed 18 July 2023).
Mental Health Act (Ireland) 2001. Available at: https://www.irishstatutebook.ie/eli/2001/act/25/enacted/en/html (Accessed 18 July 2023).
Ministry of Justice (2009) *Summary: Intervention and Options, Coroners and Justice Bill: Homicide Clauses*. London: Ministry of Justice.
Morse, S. (2008) 'Psychopathy and criminal responsibility', *Neuroethics*, 1(3), pp. 205–212.
National Collaborating Centre for Mental Health, National Institute for Health and Clinical Excellence, British Psychological Society and Royal College of Psychiatrists (2009) *Borderline Personality Disorder: The NICE Guideline on Treatment and Management*. National clinical practice guideline number 78. London: British Psychological Society and Royal College of Psychiatrists.
National Collaborating Centre for Mental Health, National Institute for Health and Clinical Excellence, British Psychological Society, Royal College of Psychiatrists and National Institute for Health and Care Excellence (NICE) (2010) *Antisocial Personality Disorder: Treatment, Management and Prevention*. National clinical practice guideline number 77. London: British Psychological Society and Royal College of Psychiatrists.
NOMS and NHS England (2015), The offender personality disorder pathway strategy 2015. Available at: www.england.nhs.uk/commissioning/wp-content/uploads/sites/12/2016/02/opd-strategy-nov-15.pdf. Accessed 27 April 2022.
O'Loughlin, A. (2014) 'The offender personality disorder pathway: Expansion in the face of failure?', *Howard Journal of Criminal Justice*, 53(2), pp. 173–192.
O'Loughlin, A. (2019) 'De-constructing risk, therapeutic needs and the dangerous personality disordered subject', *Punishment and Society*, 21(5), pp. 616–638.
O'Loughlin, A. (2021a) 'Risk reduction and redemption: An interpretive account of the right to rehabilitation in the jurisprudence of the European Court of Human Rights', *Oxford Journal of Legal Studies*, 41(2), pp. 510–538.
O'Loughlin, A. (2021b) 'Sentencing mentally disordered offenders: Towards a rights-based approach', *Criminal Law Review*, 2, pp. 98–112.
Peay, J. (2011a) 'Personality disorder and the law: Some awkward questions', *Philosophy, Psychiatry, and Psychology*, 18(3), pp. 231–244.
Peay, J. (2011b) *Mental Health and Crime*. Abingdon: Routledge.
Percy Commission (1957) *Report of the Royal Commission on the Law Relating to Mental Illness and Mental Deficiency*. London: H.M.S.O.
Pickard, H. (2015) 'Choice, deliberation, violence: Mental capacity and criminal responsibility in personality disorder', *International Journal of Law and Psychiatry*, 40, pp. 15–24.
Pickersgill, M. (2013) 'How personality became treatable: The mutual constitution of clinical knowledge and mental health law', *Social Studies of Science*, 43(1), pp. 30–53.
Pilgrim, D. (2007) 'New "Mental Health" legislation for England and Wales: Some aspects of consensus and conflict', *Journal of Social Policy*, 36(1), pp.79–95.
R. v. Codère (1917) 12 Cr App R 21.
R. v. Collins, ex p Brady (2001) 58 B.M.L.R. 173; [2000] M.H.L.R. 17.
R. v. D [2006] EWCA Crim 1139.
R. v. Hoppe [2016] EWCA Crim 2258.
R. v. M'Naghten [1843] 8 Eng. Rep. 718.
R. (TF) v. SS for Justice [2008] EWCA Civ 1457.
R. v. Turner [2015] EWCA Crim 1249; [2015] Crim. L.R. 920.
R. v. Vowles and others [2015] EWCA Crim 45; [2015] 2 Cr. App. R. (S.).
R. v. Windle [1952] 2 QB 826.
Reidy, K. and Kelly, B. (2021) 'Involuntary status and mental capacity for treatment decisions under sections 4, 3, and 57 of Ireland's Mental Health Act, 2001: Analysis and recommendations for reform', *Irish Journal of Psychological Medicine*, pp. 1–6.
Rooman v. Belgium [2019] ECHR 109.

Seddon, T. (2008) 'Dangerous liaisons: Personality disorder and the politics of risk', *Punishment and Society*, 10(3), pp. 301–317.

Sheehan, L., Nieweglowski, K. and Corrigan, P. (2016) 'The stigma of personality disorders', *Current Psychiatry Reports*, 18(1), p. 11.

Skett, S. and Lewis, C. (2019) 'Development of the Offender Personality Disorder Pathway: A summary of the underpinning evidence', *Probation Journal*, 66(2), pp. 167–180.

Stinson, F. S. et al. (2008) 'Prevalence, correlates, disability, and comorbidity of DSM-IV Narcissistic personality disorder: Results from the Wave 2 national epidemiologic survey on alcohol and related conditions', *The Journal of Clinical Psychiatry*, 69(7), pp. 1033–1045.

Slovenko, R. (2011) 'The DSM in litigation and legislation', *Journal of the American Academy of Psychiatry and the Law*, 39(1), pp. 6–11.

Stoffers, J. et al. (2010) 'Pharmacological interventions for borderline personality disorder', *Cochrane Database of Systematic Reviews*, 6, Art. No.: CD005653.

Storebø, O. J. et al. (2020) 'Psychological therapies for people with borderline personality disorder', *Cochrane Database of Systematic Reviews*, 5, Art. No.: CD012955.

The Law Society (2002) 'Response to the draft mental health bill', *Journal of Mental Health Law*, 2, pp. 380–385.

Trebilcock, J. and Weaver, T. (2012) 'Changing legal characteristics of dangerous and severe personality disorder (DSPD) patients and prisoners', *Journal of Forensic Psychiatry and Psychology*, 23(2), pp. 237–243.

Trebilcock, J. et al. (2019) 'A more promising architecture? Commissioners' perspectives on the reconfiguration of personality disorder services under the offender personality disorder (OPD) pathway', *Mental Health Review Journal*, 24(4), pp. 306–316.

Tyrer, P. et al. (2011a) 'A classification based on evidence is the first step to clinical utility', *Personality and Mental Health*, 5(4), pp. 304–307.

Tyrer, P. et al. (2011b) 'The rationale for the reclassification of personality disorder in the 11th revision of the international classification of diseases (ICD-11)', *Personality and Mental Health*, 5(4), pp. 246–259.

Tyrer, P. et al. (2019) 'The development of the ICD-11 classification of personality disorders: An amalgam of science, pragmatism, and politics', *Annual Review of Clinical Psychology*, 15(1), pp. 481–502.

Tyrer, P. and Seivewright, H. (2008) 'Stable instability: The natural history of personality disorders', *Psychiatry*, 7(3), pp. 129–132.

Vannier, M. (2016) 'A right to hope? Life imprisonment in France', in: van Zyl Smit, D. and Appleton, C. (eds) *Life Imprisonment and Human Rights*. Oxford: Hart Publishing, pp. 189–214.

WH v. Llanarth Court Hospital [2015] UKUT 695 (AAC).

van Zyl Smit, D., Weatherby, P. and Creighton, S. (2014) 'Whole life sentences and the tide of European human rights jurisprudence: What is to be done?', *Human Rights Law Review*, 14(1), pp. 59–84.

Whooley, O. (2016) 'Measuring mental disorders: The failed commensuration project of DSM-5', *Social Science and Medicine*, 166, pp. 33–40.

Widiger, T. A., Livesley, W. J. and Clark, L. A. (2009) 'An integrative dimensional classification of personality disorder', *Psychological Assessment*, 21(3), pp. 243–255.

Wiener, M. J. (2003) *Reconstructing the Criminal: Culture, Law and Policy in England, 1830–1914*. Cambridge: Cambridge University Press.

World Health Organisation (2022) *ICD-11 2022 Release*. Available at: https://www.who.int/news/item/11-02-2022-icd-11-2022-release.

Zachar, P., Krueger, R. F. and Kendler, K. S. (2016) 'Personality disorder in DSM-5: An oral history', *Psychological Medicine*, 46(1), pp. 1–10.

Zanarini, M. C. et al. (2003) 'The longitudinal course of borderline psychopathology: 6-year prospective follow-up of the phenomenology of borderline personality disorder', *American Journal of Psychiatry*, 160(2), pp. 274–283.

PART 4
Forensic psychiatry and criminal law

PART 4

Bioethics, Health, and criminal law

13
MENTAL ILLNESS AND CRIMINAL LAW
Irreconcilable bedfellows?

Jill Peay

In 2011 Andrew Ashworth argued that the common law doctrine 'ignorance of the law is no defence to a criminal charge' was preposterous (2011:1). He based this in part on a fundamental lack of fairness and the doctrine's conflicts with other rule of law values. His article examined the impossibility of citizens being fully informed of the vast array of regulatory offences and offences of omission but extended the argument persuasively to other serious offences. He thus addressed the position of those who did not know the law but were nonetheless held culpable for their actions. What he did not address explicitly was the position of those who could not know the law by reason of mental incapacity, and what their fate should be.

The debate concerning the division between those who do not and those who cannot comply with the criminal law is longstanding. It crystallises most obviously with respect to those with assorted personality disorders who show a lack of restraint. Can it be known for certain whether such individuals committed their criminal offences by choice or without such conscious decision-taking; were they in essence 'bad' or 'mad'? This stark characterisation wholly misses the more recent subtleties of psychiatric understanding of those living with, for example, borderline personality disorder, where the inability to regulate intense emotions combined with poor impulse control are defining features of the disorder. Yet the criminal law would regard such offenders as law-breakers who, despite attributions of autonomy, have simply failed to adhere to the law's requirements. Immediately, the disciplinary conflict is clear between the psychiatric context with its understanding of an individual's needs, and that of the law seeking to judge and censure behaviour, with a societal framework in mind. This chapter will touch on these issues with respect to anti-social personality disorder, but its primary focus will be on the law relating to, and the actions of, those deemed 'ill', albeit the distinction between illnesses and disorders is easier to draw in theory than to untangle in practice.

Holding those with mental illness legally accountable for their criminal offending is problematic; it is arguably both discriminatory to exclude such individuals from the normal functioning of the law (Minkowitz, 2014) and anomalous to design laws specially to include them (see Loughnan, 2016 on the problematic separation of responsibility and non-responsibility). The standard approach to convicting an offender requires the state to prove

DOI: 10.4324/9781003226413-18

actus reus, mens rea and to rebut any relevant defences. And to do so to the requisite high standard, which in England and Wales used to be termed 'proof beyond a reasonable doubt' and is now proof so that the decision-maker is sure of the offender's guilt. Before a decision to prosecute is made, the Crown Prosecution Service must be satisfied not only that the evidence is sufficient so that there is a realistic prospect of conviction, but also that a prosecution is in the public interest. Liaison and Diversion Services can also be effective in diverting alleged offenders away from prosecution or imprisonment (Disley et al., 2021). Moreover, where a trial would be unjust because of the alleged perpetrator's unfitness to plead, defendants can be diverted away from the criminal justice system. At any of these hurdles, the prosecution of those with mental illness may come to a halt, leaving those whose mental illness is relevant to their offending and who are prosecuted, a relatively small group. Or are they? Figures from those detained in prisons in many jurisdictions suggest that the majority of offenders have mental health difficulties (Singleton et al., 1998; Fazel and Danesh, 2002; House of Commons Justice Committee, 2021). So why have such obvious vulnerabilities not diverted these offenders from conventional punishment? What is it about the law that causes us to pursue those with impaired abilities either to control themselves, or to think through their actions, or to be aware of the law's legal restraints? Why is accountability, and hence the state's ability to punish, pre-eminent? Indeed, why the desire to punish rather than to treat? These are age-old questions which will not be resolved here. My intention in this chapter is rather to explore some of the difficulties the criminal law encounters when it comes face-to-face with those who may have offended and who may have co-occurring mental health difficulties. In so doing it will explore law's problematic relationship with two mental condition defences, insanity and diminished responsibility, but it will also consider why issues relating to the role of psychiatrists, and of offenders' appreciation (or lack of it) of their own conditions, sit awkwardly within a criminal law context. These difficulties have been most memorably crystallised by Melle (2013:20) when she observed, 'The evaluation of what went on in a person's mind while committing a crime will, despite technical innovations, in the end continue to rely on personal evaluations and interpretations'.

It is worth diverting to two issues. First, whilst the criminal law presupposes that it only holds accountable those who are blameworthy, Ashworth's (2011) magisterial analysis makes plain that this is not true. To hold accountable those who do not, or even more persuasively, cannot understand the law's restraints is anathema. Thus the law, even on the face of it, does not deal fairly with all and particularly does not deal fairly with those who have vulnerabilities or inadequacies in the areas of cognition and understanding. Second, and in stark contrast, the 'man must be mad' test remains prevalent, and specifically as it relates to bizarre crimes. Yet, the superficial attraction of this belies both the criminal law's ability to grapple with those who are seriously disordered and the public's arguable intolerance of those who commit heinous crimes when disordered. In contrast, psychiatry, by definition, strives to heal minds with the understanding of disordered behaviour and an individual's subjective experience at its core (Nathan, 2021).

Most of those who appear before the criminal courts plead guilty (Peay and Player, 2018); like their 'ordered' compatriots, it is likely that most of those with mental disorder will also plead guilty, being subject to the same pressures and incentives to do so. In consequence, they do not gain the benefit of any mental condition defences, such as they are, and rely on the processes of mitigation and therapeutic disposal to accommodate their disabilities. The Sentencing Council's (2020) definitive guideline on mental disorders, developmental disorders or neurological impairments may improve the position regarding consistency, but it cannot address the prior problem of those with vulnerabilities pleading guilty to offences to which they may have a good defence (Peay and Player, 2018). And even where there is a trial, those with undiagnosed disorders or those who do not co-operate with assessment or trial, possibly because of those disorders, fare badly in a system which presupposes offenders will act in their own best interests and take advantage of the protections the criminal law offers. As examples of those who would satisfy 'the man must be mad' test, the cases of *Bravery* [2020] and *Hussein* [2021] illustrate well how a combination of autism and personality disorder can disrupt any alleviation of punitive outcomes.[1] Those whose crimes are perceived as manifestly dangerous, in the context of extreme forms of personality disorder, psychosis or autism, challenge the criminal law's adherence to fair labelling and just outcomes. Both the law, and the public, hold out an exemplar of what constitutes a disordered offender that is most likely grounded in myth rather than gritty, complex and uncomfortable reality.

Insanity

Testament to the difficulties of achieving a satisfactory balance between the demands of the criminal law and the needs and vulnerabilities of those with mental illness has been the longstanding nature of the M'Naghten Rules. These are the basis of the insanity defence in England and Wales. In the same way that the law presupposes knowledge of it, the law also presupposes sanity. Familiar to many, and dating back to 1843, the insanity defence requires the accused to establish, on a balance of probabilities, that at the time of committing the act, the accused 'was labouring under such a defect of reason, from disease of mind, as not to know the nature and quality of the act he was doing; or if he did know it, that he did not know he was doing what was wrong' (M'Naghten's Case (1843) 10 Cl. & F. 200, (1843) 8 ER 718). An accused using an insanity defence acknowledges the actus reus of the offence, and that it may or may not have been done with the requisite mens rea, either because if mens rea were present it was attributable to the mental disorder, or because the individual was incapable of forming the requisite mens rea. Thus, the perpetrator either did not have an 'understanding' of what they did, or if they did, they lacked the necessary knowledge of the legal wrongness of those acts. Hence, there should be no responsibility for the offence; a finding of 'not guilty by reason of insanity' results. As this is an acquittal the individual is unpunishable, although there are special disposal options, including compulsory confinement under the Mental Health Act 1983 (MHA 1983).

---

1 Bravery pleaded guilty to attempted murder, having thrown a 6-year-old French boy off the 10th-floor viewing platform of Tate Modern, https://www.judiciary.uk/wp-content/uploads/2020/06/Bravery-sentence-002.pdf. His actions were described as 'considered' rather than 'reactive' violence making him less suitable for a hospital disposal. He was sentenced to detention for life, with a tariff of 15 years, to be spent initially in a Young Offender Institution. Hussein, who brutally murdered two women in a park, had made a pact with King Lucifage Rofocal to sacrifice six women every six months in return for winning the Mega Millions Super Jackpot and being protected from any police knowledge of his actions, https://www.judiciary.uk/wp-content/uploads/2021/10/R-v-Hussein-Sentencing-Remarks.pdf. He did not give evidence at his trial, maintaining that he did not commit the murders despite overwhelming evidence, so any potential defence of diminished responsibility was unavailable to him. He was given two mandatory life sentences of imprisonment and a tariff of 35 years. The judge made no reduction in culpability for mental impairment or disorder, but said she had taken some account of the likelihood that he would struggle in prison, as a person with autism and other possible diagnoses.

The undeniably narrow legal scope of this test – it does not include failures of self-control, or emotional deficits – together with the stigma associated with a finding of 'insanity' and the fear of the outcomes that can follow, has resulted in its limited use. In the infamous case of Clarke [1972], the absent-minded shoplifter's actions were held not to be insane by using the concept of restraint in a somewhat novel context: a difference was argued between a failure to use the powers of reasoning that a rational mind retains and the inability to do so that insanity implies.

In England and Wales insanity defences are successful some 30 or so times a year. The Law Commission (2013), in its review of the insanity defence and automatism, concluded that updating the law was justified to bring it into better alignment with current psychiatric, medical and psychological developments, to address its incoherence on sane and insane automatism and to remedy insanity's stigmatic effect. Indeed, its obvious lack of relevance to those with learning disability or epilepsy made the use of the term 'insane' simply wrong.

The many and varied technical criticisms of the insanity defence were explored at length by the Law Commission (2013). Suffice it to illustrate here, one of the insanity defence's more bizarre aspects is that it currently includes as insane automatism 'sane' individuals who offend whilst sleepwalking (the peculiar medical and legal perspectives are discussed respectively in Ebrahim et al., 2005, and Wilson et al., 2005). The Law Commission (2013: para. 5.57) did however note that the lower courts have on occasions taken a generous interpretation, treating sleepwalking as 'sane automatism'. In contrast, the insanity defence excludes an offender like Coley [2013], discussed further below, who killed during a brief psychotic state brought about, in part, by the use of cannabis. For the purposes of the criminal law, intoxication trumps insanity if the offender is 'awake', but if the offender is asleep, and alcohol as an external trigger has in part brought about the sleepwalking, it may facilitate a finding of sane automatism (a complete acquittal). Since the insanity defence embraces both mental and physical disorders as bases for holding people not accountable, interactions between the two states can lead to significant inconsistency, if not utter indefensibility. Or as Lord Justice Davis commented, the internal/external distinction is 'illogical, little short of a disgrace, and should be abolished' (Law Commission, 2013: para. 1.46).

The Law Commission's proposals recognised that whilst the insanity defence is theoretically flawed, in practice it seemed to be working as practitioners managed the legal difficulties in the small number of cases in which it arose. Of course, a revised test with greater scope might be employed more frequently.[2] In the event the Law Commission provisionally proposed a test of 'not criminally responsible by reason of recognised medical condition' (2013); but it will require a total lack of capacity in the relevant abilities. Three criteria applicable at the time of the offence – the ability to make a rational judgment, to understand what you are doing is wrong or to control your body – would underpin such a finding; expert evidence would be required. And the defence would exclude acute voluntary intoxication and anti-social personality disorders. The Commission recommended shifting the burden of disproof of a medically recognised condition onto the prosecution once the defence had established on the balance of probabilities that an incapacity was present. As will be evident from the discussion below, the proposals shift the grounds for the defence onto similar territory as apply in diminished responsibility, albeit the defence would apply to all offences. Of

---

2 Contrasting the position with Norway below is interesting, as although Norway has had a similar number of insanity cases, it has a population some 10 times smaller.

course, its application will be very narrow, and arguably rightly so as it will result in a finding that the perpetrator is not criminally responsible, but subject to special disposal powers.

To date, there has been no movement on these proposals. One possible explanation is that potential reforms to fitness to plead (Law Commission, 2016a, 2016b), which have also been subject to delay, may 'soak up' some of the cases away from the limitations of the insanity defence.

Norway

An interesting counterpoint to the application of the M'Naghten Rules in England and Wales (albeit many common law jurisdictions use some variant of these rules) arises in Norway with respect to its Criminal Procedure Code. Until 2020, when Norway introduced a new insanity defence, an arguably extreme version of this defence operated based on a medical model. Insanity for criminal law purposes was identified exclusively with a medical or biological condition, which required that, at the time of the offence, the perpetrator was experiencing an active state of mental disorder, most likely psychosis, intellectual disability of a high degree or serious autism spectrum disorders (Gröning, 2021:195). What constitutes psychosis was determined according to the diagnostic manuals – either the *Diagnostic and Statistical Manual of Mental Disorders*, produced by the American Psychiatric Association, or the *International Classification of Diseases* produced by the World Health Organization (both now in new versions DSM-5 and ICD-11).[3] There was no requirement for a causative link between the mentally disordered state and the offence. Inevitably, the findings of medical experts were highly influential in court-based determinations of 'insanity'.

However, the insanity defence was subject to intense scrutiny following the Breivik case. In 2011 Breivik killed 77 people, largely by shooting, on the island of Utøya, but he had also exploded a fatal bomb in Oslo before driving to Utøya. A lengthy account of Breivik's life, these atrocities and their aftermath has been documented by Åsne Seierstad (2015) from chilling first-hand accounts. Breivik's mental state at the time of the murders was the subject of significant psychiatric evaluation; evaluations that were not consistent over time, with a diagnosis shifting from a psychotic condition, namely, paranoid schizophrenia (which would have seen him acquitted on grounds of being 'not criminally accountable' but subject to compulsory psychiatric confinement) to a severe narcissistic personality disorder (which could have found him culpable and punishable) (Melle, 2013). A finding of legal non-accountability in Norway is thus based on broader grounds than the M'Naghten Rules permit. Breivik's defence sought his acquittal on grounds of self-defence. As a right-wing extremist he had intended the mass murders to act as a catalyst for a media-focussed trial; and he resisted the idea that he might be found insane. Ultimately, the Court resolved the conflicting psychiatric evaluations by finding that Breivik did not meet the criteria for an ICD-10 classification of schizophrenia, rather than examining whether he satisfied any legal threshold for being sufficiently psychotic to be insane. He was found responsible for the murders and sentenced to 21 years in prison – the maximum penalty available in Norway. How long Breivik will serve will depend upon whether this period is subject to additional protective detention, an option available in the case of particularly serious acts.

---

3 https://www.psychiatry.org/psychiatrists/practice/dsm; https://icd.who.int/en.

Following his conviction, the Rieber-Mohn Commission was established to consider reforms to the insanity law (Gröning and Rieber-Mohn, 2015). The Commission was seemingly conscious of the adage that 'hard cases make bad law' and emphasised that the Breivik case ought not to have a decisive effect on the future shape of the law, which would routinely be applied in less serious cases. In the event the Commission was less radical in its recommendations than might have been anticipated. They wanted to retain the medical model but limit the application of the 'psychotic' condition to those where a certain level of seriousness was present, having a significant and confusing effect on the mind. However, they did recognise that other conditions could also affect thinking, functioning and understanding and could be as serious as a psychotic state, so other mentally disordered offenders could equally be held not legally accountable if their conditions met the requisite threshold of seriousness. This latter judgment was to be for the courts and not the medical experts.

However, and as documented by Gröning (2021), the Commission's careful recommendations did not find favour with the legislature. The Ministry of Justice and Public Security proposed that the psychosis criterion should be replaced – seemingly on the grounds of its potential stigma – and in the enacted version of its Bill adopted the elusive criterion of a 'severe divergent state of mind'. Any person under 15 years of age is not legally accountable for criminal acts in Norway, but the criterion of 'not accountable' was also to be applied to those who, at the time of the act, had a 'severe divergent state of mind' or a 'severe impairment of consciousness' or a 'high degree of intellectual disability'. Critically, the lack of accountability is linked to one of these three states by the words 'due to'. Moreover, s.20 of the Penal Code, which specifies these three conditions, further notes that when deciding whether a person is not accountable, emphasis should be placed 'on the degree of failure of understanding reality and functional ability'. Whilst psychotic conditions will clearly remain central to these determinations, other disorders which affect functional abilities and reality testing will be similarly embraced. Severe autism disorders and dementia will be counted in, but personality disorders will be excluded. Notably, conditions which have proved controversial under the M'Naghten Rules, such as epilepsy and sleepwalking, can be included under a 'severe impairment of consciousness' regardless of whether the condition was caused externally or internally.

It is necessary, under the new Norwegian law, for the courts to be satisfied not only that the defendant fell within one of the three categories, but also that they were not accountable due to that condition or conditions. Frustratingly, this further hurdle is left undefined, providing, as Gröning (2021:200) points out, the courts 'large room for discretion to define the threshold for insanity', with only the proviso that emphasis should be placed on the *degree* of failure of understanding reality and functional ability. Of course, good general functioning may trump any specific psychotic delusion. Moreover, a causative link per se is not required; rather the link is between the seriousness of the disorder and the defendant's functional abilities or their failure to understand reality. Separating the nature of the crime and a defendant's functional abilities has never been easy; there is often resistance, including within the courts, to accepting that those who can plan crimes, appear motivated and manage complicated tasks, can still be insane within the legal definition. But the new Norwegian law should confine experts to their area of expertise; namely, the defendant's mental condition and their functional and reality testing abilities. It will remain for the courts to decide whether this state passes the legal threshold for insanity. Tellingly, Gröning concludes that the shift from a medical to a legal model may not be as marked as first appears. Since it is the degree of severity of the medical condition which will trigger an opportunity for the insanity defence, medical experts will inevitably find themselves advising the courts as to whether any emerging threshold is passed – even if they only do so orally when judges struggle with cases that are not clear-cut. The shift from diagnostic characteristics to relevant symptoms is to be welcomed, but even this may not prove without its problems, particularly since the concept of accountability can include both 'did he understand factually that what he was doing was wrong?' and 'did he understand morally that what he was doing was wrong?'. The two are not always in perfect alignment.

Diminished responsibility

Diminished responsibility in England and Wales is a partial defence to murder (and only to murder) which, if successful, results in a conviction for manslaughter. This avoids the otherwise mandatory sentence of a life-term. How much of a life sentence is spent in prison depends on a number of factors. For now, what is important is that a conviction for manslaughter by reason of diminished responsibility enables, but does not require, a judge to make a therapeutic order as an alternative to a punitive sentence.

In its previous incarnation diminished responsibility verdicts often came about via a plea accepted by the Crown where prosecution and defence experts were of the opinion that the accused fell within the parameters of the then applicable law. A broadly defined 'abnormality of mind' had to 'substantially impair' an accused's mental responsibility for his acts or omissions (s.2 Homicide Act 1957). Although experts were supposedly not to be asked about whether the defendant was 'diminished', that is, they were not to be asked for an opinion on the ultimate issue to be decided by the jury, in practice, this did occur and counsel would not always be criticised for it. In many ways old diminished responsibility mirrored the difficulties Gröning (2021) anticipates with the new Norwegian insanity law. Under the new diminished responsibility law (s.2 as amended by the Coroners and Justice Act 2009) the territory has shifted. Now a series of criteria break down substantial impairment broadly into issues of 'understanding one's own conduct', 'forming a rational judgment' and 'exercising self-control' (Mackay, 2018). But critically, the required abnormality of mental functioning has to provide an explanation for the conduct by causing or being a significant contributory factor to the conduct alleged (s.2(1B) Homicide Act 1957). Notably, although this new causative link between abnormality and reprehensible conduct is present on the face of the statute, Mackay and Hughes (2021) have argued persuasively that its interpretation is ambiguous, and it is both unprincipled and unnecessary following the Supreme Court decision in *R v Golds* [2016]. This decision clarified that 'substantially', if any definition was required, means 'of consequence or weight', thereby stressing the need for a meaningful connection between the abnormality and the impairment. Indeed, Mackay and Hughes cite an empirical study of cases heard subsequent to the new provisions where commonly psychiatric reports make no mention of the newly required 'causation' element (2021:469). From the expert's perspective why would an opinion be required on causation (a notoriously difficult issue to argue; Buchanan and Zonana, 2009) when they have already provided an 'explanation' in terms of clinical criteria (on which they arguably are experts) with respect to the substantial impairment elements? As no causative element had been required under old diminished responsibility and many of the practitioners would have been used to working with that version of the law, their neglect of this provision is perhaps understandable. And to presuppose that a distinct causative connection was necessary for the purposes of mitigation, rather than conviction, would run counter to the ethos of a therapeutic disposal under the MHA 1983 which had never required a causal connection. Once again, the mismatch between criminal law and psychiatric expertise is evident; and defendants for whom no 'causal' connection is advanced may risk unjust conviction.

It is notable that new diminished responsibility has shifted verdicts from their former plea basis to more contested trials and more rejected defences (Mackay and Mitchell, 2017:35). Was this the intention of the reforms? It is clear that juries and judges had initial difficulties accepting that someone who had the capacity overtly to plan and execute a killing can still be eligible for a diminished responsibility verdict.[4] Psychiatric evidence that someone could both be acutely psychotic and still engage in superficially rational behaviour sat awkwardly with the court's approach to planning and motivation as precursors of culpable behaviour. This awkwardness may now have been remedied by the Supreme Court in *R v Golds* [2016: para. 49] in declaring that if psychiatric evidence is to be rejected, some rational basis for so doing must have been advanced in the trial.

Thus, the question hangs in the air, where psychiatric evidence asserts substantial impairment due to a mental abnormality, why do juries reject this and convict of murder? Is it because they have accepted other evidence which indicates that although the defendant could have been 'in the grip of a psychotic delusion' he was not in fact so, when he killed? And does this rejection of psychiatric evidence and the favouring of other explanations derive from an underlying anxiety about psychiatric evidence or from the persuasive impact of other explanations appealing to the jury's common sense? This is an issue discussed further below.

Psychiatry and uncertainty

In the same way that it is easy to be critical of the criminal law's shortcomings in dealing with the complexities of those with mental disorder, it is easy to suggest that psychiatrists do not enjoy the same levels of certainty in their profession as other medical specialists. The vulnerability of psychiatry to misdiagnosis was demonstrated in Rosenhan's study (1973) where pseudo-patients in the United States gained access to psychiatric hospitals and were not discharged for significant periods thereafter despite allegedly acting normally post-admission. Although published in the eminent journal *Science*, the first limb of the study has had its veracity roundly questioned by Cahalan (2019), albeit the central thesis, about the then reliability of psychiatric diagnosis, arguably holds true. However, what is as interesting about this study is its second, somewhat fortuitous, element. One research and teaching hospital invited Rosenhan to repeat the experiment over a three-month period, claiming that they would be able to spot any pseudo-presentations. In the event, and seemingly by mistake (Cahalan, 2019), Rosenhan sent no pseudo-patients, but of 193 patients where judgments were made, 19 presenting patients were identified as 'fakes' by at least one psychiatrist supported by another staff member.[5] These individuals could, of course, have been genuine malingerers. But equally, the hospital may have altered its threshold for diagnosis and assessed patients who were ill as sane, making false negative errors to supplement the

---

4 See Peay (2016) and the example of *Brennan* [2014] under the new provisions where the Court of Appeal pointed out errors of rationality in the judge's summing-up, and also the discussion of *Cooper* [2010] and *Fox* [2011].
5 This number reached 41 where only one staff member made the identification of a pseudo-patient with a high degree of confidence (Rosenhan, 1973: 252).

earlier false positives. Getting to the truth behind the Rosenhan study has proved elusive. Partial real-life replication attempts (see, for example, Slater, 2004) have been criticised on other grounds of unreliability. Yet, an essential truth remains: psychiatrists can and do disagree about diagnosis, either contemporaneously or over time, and can be misled. Studies of psychiatric decision-making generally that cross the *in-vivo/in-vitro* border are rare (for one such example, see Peay, 2003) but their lessons are telling. Such decision-making may be improving, but it is still susceptible to scrutiny. Indeed, one reputable *in vitro* study from Sweden illustrates the vulnerability and variability of psychiatric assessments of the need for compulsory care (Kullgren et al., 1996). The findings included significant rates of diagnosis in an arguably 'healthy' case, testifying to the tricky and uncertain territory in which psychiatry must function.

The idea that patients can mask symptoms (as opposed to manufacturing them) which can confound diagnosis was illustrated in the Mental Health Tribunal for Brady (2014). Brady was convicted of multiple murder and had various diagnoses including 'personality disorder of the psychopathic type' and 'mental illness of a psychotic nature', both in prison and before his death in Ashworth Hospital. Psychiatrists' interactions with this one notorious offender-patient and with the complexities of the relevant law over a prolonged period demonstrate the 'vortex of uncertainty' with which professionals grapple (Peay, 2019). Indeed, both the Tribunal and the medical witnesses agreed in the hearing that 'without the cooperation of the patient diagnosis is difficult' (MHT Brady, 2014 para. 119); and even with it, as Melle (2013) observes, personal interpretations provide scope for considerable uncertainty.

Such difficulties with diagnosis also reflect those in the Breivik case above. Diagnosing psychosis relies in part on the presence of delusions or hallucinations. But even if identified, these symptoms leave open the underlying causes of those phenomena; and the causes can, of course, be central to criminal law. In Breivik's case, his bizarre beliefs were initially attributed to psychosis; but a further assessment identified a narcissistic personality disorder accompanied by pathological lying, with his right-wing ideology underpinning his extreme beliefs. Given the significant interval of time between the first and second assessments of Breivik it is equally plausible that his presentation had changed in part due to his own desire not to be found insane (see Melle, 2013). Since reliance on DSM-IV merely required the presence of one delusion, it is understandable why the initial assessors may have favoured psychosis as the primary explanation. On the other hand, public condemnation of the suggestion that Breivik was 'insane' might have tipped the balance in his second assessment towards a finding that would hold him culpable. Should the mere presence of a single delusion – if that were the case – determine legal responsibility?

Context is critical. It has been argued (Bortolotti et al., 2014) that when assessing whether racist and anti-Islamic beliefs are merely ideological, or idiosyncratic to the point of being delusional (clearly racists can also be ill), one would need to know to what extent those beliefs were shared by others in the same reference group. Dangerous and, indeed, life-taking behaviour could arise from either or both belief systems; but a finding of non-responsibility should arguably only result where the deluded beliefs fundamentally affected the defendant's various decision-making skills. Having weird beliefs should not be excusatory unless they lead to a profound inability to control one's actions or justify the deluded taking of action in the mind of the perpetrator. Explaining why something has happened because of the subjective workings of someone's mind may be a necessary but insufficient justification for absolving that person of criminal responsibility.

Psychiatry and complexity

The problematic nature of a descent into the finer points of madness in a legal setting was highlighted in the Court's somewhat bizarre reasoning in *Fox* [2011]. There, a failure by Fox to follow his 'good voices', whilst not resisting command hallucinations to offend, seemed to imply in the Court's reasoning a capacity by Fox to choose and thus responsibility for his actions. At one level this looks like instrumental reasoning; but one can also see how a court might equally interpret a psychiatrist's conclusions as equally instrumental where, for example, it was argued that planned and seemingly motivated behaviour did not mean that the offender was not in the grip of psychosis and could exercise control. The former is simply verging on the side of a legal interpretation; the latter, a medical interpretation. Thus, descending to the level of delusions may simply enhance the fogginess, rather than clarify conflicting diagnoses.

Yet, the complexity of these issues for the courts is rarely confined to a 'simple' dispute among psychiatrists as to the diagnosis. People's lives, and their decision-making, have an obvious time dimension and are affected by competing and interacting factors that can disrupt and disturb 'reality testing', confounding any straightforward application of law. The case of *R v Coley* [2013] is illustrative. Coley was a young man – aged 17 – of good character and with no documented mental health problems. He was charged with the attempted murder of his next-door neighbour, an attack which occurred in the night after Coley had been watching violent videos and using cannabis. Coley's parents had the next-door neighbours' keys and their son, having dressed in dark clothing and put on a balaclava, gained entry to the neighbours' house using the keys and went upstairs to their bedroom where the (vicious) attack took place, with a 'Rambo style' knife Coley had taken with him. His assertion of a brief psychotic incident brought on in part by cannabis use, resulting in him lacking the intent to kill, was rejected by the jury. His prior indication that he wished to use automatism/insanity was denied by the judge as his intoxication was voluntary and an 'external' cause of his behaviour; and his behaviour – the taking of the keys and the dressing in dark clothing – indicated moreover a degree of planned behaviour incompatible with automatism. The psychiatric evidence suggested Coley could have suffered from a psychotic episode, however transient, wherein his mind had become detached from reality. The psychiatrists stressed that even in this state he would have been capable of complex organised behaviour. But it was discounted by the court as not complying with M'Naghten because of its external cause – it was not a 'disease of the mind' but rather a case of voluntary intoxication, leading to a temporary malfunctioning of the mind. What constitutes a disease of the mind is a question of law and not one of medical usage; and not all defects of reason constitute a disease of the mind, since a disease of the mind requires an 'internal' cause. Automatism was also discounted in Coley's case since his voluntary intoxication had induced a mental state that the defendant ought to have foreseen (Quick, 1973; Bailey, 1983; and Hennessy, 1989); and although irrational, his behaviour could not be described as involuntary.

Of course, many criminal offences are committed when defendants have been drinking or using drugs; intoxication undoubtedly has an impact on one's cognition, but the legal doctrine of 'prior fault' largely negates any amelioration the influence of intoxication might have on subsequent criminal behaviour. Voluntary intoxication, for policy reasons, does not constitute a defence beyond reducing some crimes of specific intent to a conviction for a crime of basic intent (DPP v Majewski, 1977). Those with co-occurring mental disorders are not immune from the ingestion of intoxicants, sometimes in combination with prescribed, non-prescribed or over-the-counter medication. Disentangling all these factors makes the application of criminal law to ordered offenders sufficiently challenging; doing so with those already subject to a mental illness or mental illnesses (again, co-morbidity is common) makes matters considerably more problematic. Coley's offence was recognised as 'isolated, motiveless and inexplicable' (Coley, 2013:28), yet not amenable to a psychiatric defence. He was convicted of attempted murder and sentenced to 18 years' youth custody, reduced to 15 on appeal on account of his age and impeccable character.

The law's reliance on clarity and certainty, even where these run contrary to professional opinions, can produce uncomfortable results. In other cases, the specific requirements of the law defer to a form of humane pragmatism or a sotto voce acceptance of psychiatric opinion. But in some cases, perhaps influenced by the abhorrent nature of the crime, psychiatric opinion is rejected, no matter how persuasive it is. Notably, such rejections do not always survive the considerations of the Court of Appeal (see *Brennan* [2014]).

Psychiatry and inter-disciplinary differences

Not surprisingly, deference to psychiatric opinion cannot be guaranteed. Indeed, the courts have been particularly critical of psychiatrists where they have not been ad idem with the courts' expectations. Such disciplinary misunderstandings can, in some circumstances, be creative (see Teubner et al., 2002). In others, not.

One such example arises in the area of fitness to plead. Unfitness is an area where the Law Commission has made substantial recommendations for change and has produced a draft Bill (Law Commission, 2016a, 2016b). One of the many justifications for reform in this area stemmed from the outdated nature of the test for unfitness (*R v Pritchard* [1836]) and its incompatibility with modern psychiatric thinking. In this context it is perhaps understandable that psychiatrists giving evidence about unfitness would find themselves at odds with the courts. However, psychiatrists have also, on occasions, been criticised for simply being unfamiliar with or unprepared for the courts' requirements with respect to unfitness (see, for example, *R v Walls* [2011]). Walls had no history of psychiatric illness per se but did suffer from extremely low to borderline intelligence and learning disability, either or both of which may have affected his ability to participate (meaningfully) in a criminal trial. He was charged with various offences including sexual assault on a child under 13. The judge, who had expressed concern at the start of the trial about the defence advocate's failure to obtain a psychological profile of the defendant, returned to the issue after the jury had convicted Walls, criticising the defence advocate on several grounds, including the failure mentioned at the start of the trial. The advocate responded that as the defendant held down a job and managed his life on a day-to-day basis, no need had been seen to obtain reports with respect to a possible issue of fitness to plead. As concerningly, in his summing-up the judge asked the jury to consider whether the defendant was 'effectively pretending that he is suffering from a degree of difficulty?' [2011:9]. After conviction, psychiatric reports were obtained for both the defence and the Crown, and the case went to the Court of Appeal to consider whether his conviction should be quashed on the basis that he should have been found unfit to plead. Neither the defence advocate, nor the judge, emerge from this saga with any great credit, and there is a sense of all the parties muddling through. The judge could have intervened to raise the issue of unfitness, or indeed, consider the appointment of an intermediary.

In the event, the conviction was upheld, arguably motivated as much by the court's pragmatic preference for the three-year community order Walls was successfully undergoing, in contrast to what would have been either a hospital order or a two-year supervision order had he been found unfit. The latter was deemed problematic in relation to 'the protection of the public' [2011:40]. But notably, the Court of Appeal was trenchant in its criticism of the psychiatric evidence; one psychiatrist was criticised for not being au fait with the law's requirements; and the other's conclusion that Walls was unfit was rejected by the Court, concluding that he was 'not unfit'. Resort to using the double negative is paradoxical in the light of the consistent psychiatric evidence (opinions, given his intellectual disabilities, that were more likely to have been robust over time than a retrospective diagnosis of, for example, psychosis). Thus, a lack of familiarity with the law underpins attributions of psychiatric uncertainty where experts give evidence outwith their own domain. Psychiatric professionals are simply vulnerable in court settings.

Thus, the criminal law seeks a degree of rigour and certainty in its application – even if in some areas it is prepared to continue to apply laws or doctrines that are manifestly risible, to achieve such predictability. And even after such doctrines have been roundly condemned – for example the internal/external causes of a disease of the mind – by one of its most authoritative legal bodies, the Law Commission. The courts 'test' evidence in an open setting; and no matter how unsatisfactory that process might be, it gives the law confidence in its own methods. In contrast, the psychiatric profession works with a constant appreciation that its diagnoses remain vulnerable; diagnoses are forged in largely private settings, albeit they will frequently involve multi-disciplinary teams. Clinicians are invariably reliant on how patients report their conditions – their symptoms and experiences – to them, together with observable symptoms and the clinician's experience of all the relevant factors. Whilst other branches of medicine can rely on diagnostic tests – the joy of a full blood analysis – psychiatry's tools are more subtle and influenced by both what the patient says and the experience of the clinician in hearing that. Psychiatry is not wholly devoid of tests, but it is significantly handicapped in this regard (see, for example, the TOMM, a test of memory malingering, cited in Peay, 2019:4); and, as Nathan (2021) observes, there are no routine physical tests for the diagnoses made in forensic psychiatry. Indeed, psychiatric experts do not work in terms of certainties, but much more in possibilities (Buchanan and Zonana, 2009). This is not an original point, but it does underpin why courts can appear questioning or even frankly critical of psychiatric experts. Lingering in the background is also the suspicion that psychiatrists can not only get things wrong but can also be actively fooled by patients, who either feign symptoms or exaggerate them.

Psychiatry, trust and malingering

Legal malingering in the context of mental disorder (Peay, 2019) has been described in several guises: actual, feared, claimed, attributed, mediated and resisted. Although probably infrequent, and underdiagnosis rather than false positives being the real problem, the criminal justice system's suspicions about being exploited have implications for issues of trust. The erosion of trust in experts has been the subject of a fascinating study by Davies (2018). In this context, where psychiatrists must assess the degree of disorder in an individual, with the vagaries of the clinician-patient interaction, and the courts then assess the confidence that the professional has in their diagnosis, trust is critical. Yet its intangibility is, as Davies argues, too easily trumped by powerful emotions: juries equally cannot be immune. And convictions being quashed on appeal, for example *Brennan* [2014], are testament to the possible consequences.

Clinician-patient interactions: resisting and embracing diagnoses

Another difficulty concerns the extent to which fundamentally honest individuals can convince themselves of their own ill-judged narratives. Or fail to recognise their own disabilities whether attributable, for example, to socio-cultural factors or the stigma associated with mental disability. The parallel vulnerability of individuals in convincing themselves that they are physically disordered, when the root cause lies within a psychological domain, is evidence of the powerful role minds play, as illustrated by the eminent neurologist Suzanne O'Sullivan (2018). But whatever the cause, the confidence of an individual in their own narrative and the practised coherence of it can make assessments by others even more difficult; and can be profoundly damaging to that individual. Drawing the line between disorder, deception and self-deception can be acutely problematic. Indeed, it is well known that those with Munchausen by Proxy Syndrome can seek out caring susceptible professionals who in turn unknowingly draw others into a web of deception motivated by a desire to help (Wood et al., 2001:141–142). One final illustration, the case of *Blackman* [2017], may help with an understanding of the complexities arising where psychiatry interfaces with criminal law.

Blackman, a Royal Marine, shot and killed an already badly wounded insurgent in Afghanistan in 2011. He was tried for murder before a court martial, convicted and given a life sentence with a tariff of 10 years. His defence was that the insurgent was already dead when he shot him. Video evidence of the incident contemporaneously recorded his damning admissions (*R v Blackman*, 2017, para. 22 (xvi)).[6] A psychiatric report prepared for sentencing noted that Blackman may have been suffering from an undetected combat stress disorder, which would be an extenuating factor. The sentence was appealed, and the Court Martial Appeal Court reduced the tariff to 8 years. Subsequently, the Criminal Cases Review Commission referred the case back to the court on the grounds of both conviction and sentence. Further psychiatric evidence was produced from two more psychiatrists concluding that Blackman was suffering from an adjustment disorder at the time of both the killing and the court martial. Such evidence made available the partial defence of diminished responsibility.

The prosecution accepted the evidence of the adjustment disorder but contested whether the disorder might have or had substantially impaired Blackman's responsibility for the killing. Thus, having the disorder was regarded as a necessary but not necessarily sufficient basis for reducing the conviction to manslaughter. Notably, the video evidence had limited capacity accurately to capture Blackman's mental state and its impact on his rationality and self-control.

Adjustment disorders were recognised under ICD-10. The three psychiatrists agreed his was of moderate severity. The symptoms can be masked and not apparent to others, or to the person suffering from it. Those with such disorders can plan and act with apparent rationality; but the disorder is capable of substantially impairing the capacity to form a rational judgment or exercise self-control. Failure to seek a psychiatric report prior to trial was attributed to Blackman's non-recognition of his psychiatric state, and because he would not want to rely on a psychiatric defence given the stigma perceived to attach to it, perceived weakness, and the likely end of his career.

---

6 Blackman said to his colleagues, after he shot the insurgent: 'Obviously this doesn't go anywhere, fellas. I've just broke the Geneva Convention'.

Two of the psychiatrists concluded, based on their diagnosis of the adjustment disorder (derived from their interviews with Blackman), together with factors relating, for example, to the particular conditions in which Blackman was functioning, that his responsibility was substantially impaired (*R v Blackman*, para. 40). The third reached that conclusion 'on balance'.

The Court of Appeal accepted the psychiatric evidence, observing how unfortunate it was that contemporaneous assessments of those charged with murder were not routinely obtained, despite exhortations from the courts that this should be the practice. They particularly noted the responsibility placed on the armed forces in respect of the mental health and welfare of troops (*R v Blackman*, para. 79). Having accepted that the evidence could have raised a doubt as to guilt in the minds of the Court Martial, they quashed the conviction for murder as unsafe. Reviewing the evidence for themselves, and in the light of Blackman's fresh preparedness to admit that he had intended to kill the insurgent (para. 10), they concluded that the impairment was sufficient to substitute a verdict of diminished responsibility manslaughter.

This brief synopsis cannot do justice to the Court's reasoning. However, they concluded that it was possible to have an adjustment disorder which did not affect one's capacity to plan but did affect the ability to form a rational judgment about adhering to moral standards or thinking through the consequences of one's actions. This was consistent with, for example, the psychiatric evidence in the earlier case of *Brennan* [2014], cited in *R v Golds* (2016 para. 47). They also concluded that Blackman's decision to kill was probably impulsive and that the adjustment disorder had substantially affected his ability to exercise self-control.

Four aspects are notable with respect to issues of uncertainty. First, the court only had to be satisfied on a balance of probabilities: this is entirely appropriate since psychiatric evidence would struggle to achieve the standards necessary to establish that the decision-makers were 'sure' of the perpetrator's guilt. Second, disorders can be masked from both sufferers and contemporaneous observers (albeit in Blackman's case there was non-psychiatric evidence that he had been observably affected: para. 105). Third, resistance to psychiatric explanations and their attributed stigma can result in legal proceedings being unnecessarily drawn out (Blackman, 2019). Finally, trying to assess the partial role of mental disorder in culpability is difficult enough; tackling this many years after the incident in question can only result in uncertainty. Rightly, uncertainty favours the defence, not the prosecution.

Conclusions

Criminal law and psychiatry are problematic bedfellows. It is not surprising that law reform in this area is a prolonged process, meaning that law's tools, in the interim, leave justice and fairness wanting. Interim informal resolution brings its own problems of inconsistency. In the process of reform those who offend in the context of mental disorder are not infrequently an afterthought for legislators; and even international instruments, for example the United Nations Convention on the Rights of Persons with Disabilities, do not give the area sufficient attention. Indeed, where law reform is achieved, it does not necessarily do justice to the issues a reform process has endeavoured to address.

Criminal law's approach of a progressive descent into functional detail, whilst admirable in its intentions, does not necessarily intersect well with what psychiatry is able to offer. Although ICD-11 and DSM-5 have granular detail, much of what psychiatrists do still relies on listening, interpretation and understanding. Trying to fit criminal law's focus on causation and culpability with psychiatrists' caution around causation, and ethical resistance around culpability, is problematic. And it is psychiatrists in the legal arena of a court who can find their expertise undermined.

One area of overlap beckons encouragingly; namely, subjectivity. The criminal law has increasingly focussed on subjectivity, bringing it potentially more into line with psychiatry's attempts to understand the subjective experience of patients. Improving the latter may help to reduce the likelihood of repetitive criminal behaviour, even where causality cannot or is unlikely to be established. Shifting from what an offender ought to have known, as a basis for criminal liability, to what they did know, places a more intense focus on this alleged perpetrator and his or her decision-making skills, and their capacity for control. It also helps to address the paradox wherein pre-conviction an offender's actions are deemed subject to autonomous choices, but post-conviction rehabilitative endeavours seek to change the pathologised individual. Moreover, given that the causes of any behaviour, whether criminal or not, are likely to be multi-factorial and not focussed solely within an individual, bringing the complexities and uncertainties that psychiatrists can contribute to understanding human behaviour may help to moderate criminal law's more robust approach. And in so doing, assist in changing destructive behaviour even where the exact causes of that behaviour cannot be ascertained. Perhaps compassion's effectiveness should rightly trump crude culpability. That said, maintaining a high threshold for the attribution of culpability, a rightly positive feature of an adversarial system, does not lie easily with creating space for psychological or psychiatric insights into an individual's behaviour.

Finally, there is the influence of unavoidable human factors. Those who offend with mental illness are undeniably awkward for both criminal law and the criminal justice process, with the former 'cognizant' of the latter's difficulties in reconciling punishment and treatment. Limited human benevolence, an understandable protective fear that permeates the system and inadequate resources to deal with the problems posed, all contribute to a field that creaks along, dependent often on pragmatic avoidance of the law's consequences. But sometimes a harsh infliction of criminal law on those who can't comply is the result of not being able adequately to separate this group from those who have the capacity to comply, but do not. This remains a critical challenge.

References

Ashworth, A. (2011) 'Ignorance of the law and duties to avoid it', *Modern Law Review*, 74(1), pp. 1–26.
Blackman, A. (2019) *Marine A: My Toughest Battle: The Truth about the Murder Conviction*. London: Mirror Books.
Bortolotti, L., Broome, M. and Mameli, M. (2014) 'Delusions and responsibility for action: Insights from the Breivik case', *Neuroethics*, 7(3), pp. 377–382.
Buchanan, A. and Zonana, H. (2009) 'Mental disorder as the cause of a crime', *International Journal of Law and Psychiatry*, 32(3), pp. 142–146.
Cahalan, S. (2019) *The Great Pretender*. Edinburgh: Canongate.
Davies, W. (2018) *Nervous States: How Feeling Took over the World*. London: Jonathan Cape.
Disley, E., Gkousis, E., Hulme, S., Morley, K., Pollard, J., Saunders, C., Sussex, J. and Sutherland, A. (2021) *Outcome evaluation of the national model for liaison and diversion*. Cambridge: RAND Europe.
DPP v Majewski [1977] AC 443
Ebrahim, I., Fenwick, P., Marks, R. and Peacock, K. (2005) 'Violence, sleepwalking and the criminal law: Part 1: The medical aspects', *Criminal Law Review*, 8, pp. 601–613.
Fazel, S. and Danesh, J. (2002) 'Serious mental disorder in 23,000 prisoners: A systematic review of 62 surveys', *Lancet*, 359(9306), pp. 545–550.
Gröning, L. (2021) 'Has Norway abandoned its medical model? Thoughts about the criminal insanity law reform post 22 July', *Criminal Law Review*, 3, pp. 191–202.

Gröning, L. and Rieber-Mohn, G. F. (2015) 'NOU 2014:10 - Proposal for new rules regarding criminal insanity and related issues, Norway post-22 July', *Bergen Journal of Criminal Law and Criminal Justice*, 3(1), pp. 109–131. https://doi.org/10.15845/bjclcj.v3i1.830.

House of Commons Justice Committee (2021) *Mental Health in Prison*. Fifth Report of Session 2021-2022, HC 72.

Kullgren, G., Jacobsson, L., Lynöe, N., Kohn, R. and Levav, I. (1996) 'Practices and attitudes among Swedish psychiatrists regarding the ethics of compulsory treatment', *Acta Psychiatrica Scandinavica*, 93, pp. 389–396.

Law Commission (2013) *Criminal Liability: Insanity and Automatism: A Discussion Paper*. https://s3-eu-west-2.amazonaws.com/lawcom-prod-storage-11jsxou24uy7q/uploads/2015/06/insanity_discussion.pdf.

Law Commission (2016a) *Unfitness to Plead - Volume 1: Report*. https://s3-eu-west-2.amazonaws.com/lawcom-prod-storage-11jsxou24uy7q/uploads/2016/01/lc364_unfitness_vol-1.pdf.

Law Commission (2016b) *Unfitness to Plead - Volume 2: Draft Legislation*. https://s3-eu-west-2.amazonaws.com/lawcom-prod-storage-11jsxou24uy7q/uploads/2016/01/lc364_unfitness_vol-2.pdf.

Loughnan, A. (2016) 'Asking (different) responsibility questions: Responsibility and non-responsibility in criminal law', *Bergen Journal of Criminal Law and Criminal Justice*, 4(1), pp. 25–47.

Mackay, R. (2018) 'The impairment factors in the new diminished responsibility plea', *Criminal Law Review*, 6, pp. 457–466.

Mackay, R. and Hughes, D. (2021) 'Explaining the 'explanation' requirement in the new diminished responsibility plea', *Criminal Law Review*, 6, pp. 461–477.

Mackay, R. and Mitchell, B. (2017) 'The new diminished responsibility plea in operation: Some initial findings', *Criminal Law Review*, 1, pp. 18–35.

In The Matter of an Application by Ian Stuart Brady, In The First-Tier Tribunal (Health, Education And Social Care) (Mental Health) 24th January 2014. https://www.judiciary.uk/judgments/ian-brady-mh-tribunal-240114/

Melle, I. (2013) 'The Breivik case and what psychiatrists can learn from it', *World Psychiatry*, 12(1), pp. 16–21.

Mental Health Act 1983, https://www.legislation.gov.uk/ukpga/1983/20/contents

Minkowitz, T. (2014) 'Rethinking criminal responsibility from a critical disability perspective: The abolition of insanity/incapacity acquittals and unfitness to plead, and beyond', *Griffith Law Review*, 23(3), pp. 434–466.

Nathan, T. (2021) *Dangerous Minds: A Forensic Psychiatrist's Quest to Understand Violence*. London: John Murray Press.

O'Sullivan, S. (2018) *Is It All in Your Head? True Stories of Imaginary Illness*. New York: Other Press.

Peay, J. (2003) *Decisions and Dilemmas: Working with Mental Health Law*. Oxford: Hart Publishing.

Peay, J. (2016) 'Responsibility, culpability and the sentencing of mentally disordered offenders: Objectives in conflict', *Criminal Law Review*, 3, pp. 152–165.

Peay, J. (2019) *Legal Malingering: A Vortex of Uncertainty*. LSE Law, Society and Economy Working Papers 10/2019 London School of Economics and Political Science, Law Department.

Peay, J. and Player, E. (2018) 'Pleading guilty: Why vulnerability matters', *Modern Law Review*, 81(6), pp. 929–957.

Rosenhan, D. (1973) 'On being sane in insane places', *Science*, 179(4070), pp. 250–258.

R v Bailey (1983) 77 Cr App R 76

R v Blackman [2017] EWCA Crim 190

R v Coley and others [2013] EWCA Crim 223

R v Golds [2016] UKSC 61

R v Hennessy [1989] 1 WLR 287

R v Pritchard (1836) 7 C&P 303

R v Quick [1973] QB 910

Seierstad, A. (2015) *One of US. The Story of a Massacre and Its Aftermath*. London: Virago, Little, Brown Book Group.

Sentencing Council (2020) *Definitive Guideline: Sentencing Offenders with Mental Disorders, Developmental Disorders or Neurological Impairments*. London: Sentencing Council.

Singleton, N., Meltzer, H. and Gatward, R. (1998) *Psychiatric Morbidity Among Prisoners in England and Wales*. London: Office for National Statistics. The Stationery Office.

Slater, L. (2004) *Opening Skinner's Box: Great Psychological Experiments of the 20th Century*. London: Bloomsbury Publishing.

Teubner, G., Nobles, R. and Schiff, D. (2002) 'The autonomy of law: An introduction to legal autopoiesis', in: Penner, J., Schiff, D. and Nobles, R. (eds) *Jurisprudence and Legal Theory: Commentary and Materials*. London: Butterworths, 897–954.

Wilson, W., Ebrahim, I., Fenwick, P. and Marks, R. (2005) 'Violence, sleepwalking and the criminal law: Part 2: The legal aspects', *Criminal Law Review*, 8, pp. 614–623.

Wood, H., Brown, J. and Wood, P. (2001) 'Differing approaches to the identification of Munchausen by proxy syndrome (MBPS): A case of professional training or role of experiential exposure', *Journal of Clinical Forensic Medicine*, 8(3), pp. 140–150.

14
THE PRINCIPLES OF FORENSIC PSYCHOLOGY AND CRIMINAL LAW—AN AMERICAN PERSPECTIVE

Eric Y. Drogin

Introduction

Having won considerable professional autonomy for themselves during the course of the preceding century, forensic psychologists have fashioned an impressive array of clinical procedures, research-based scholarship, and ethical standards as bases for their typically well-received participation in the criminal justice system. With this recognition and acceptance comes a formidable weight of responsibility, befitting those whose acknowledged goal is to support rather than co-opt a vital enterprise with its own distinct and deeply entrenched procedural, scholarly, and ethical traditions.

Five basic principles enable forensic psychologists to contribute to criminal law matters with a maximum degree of effectiveness. Forensic psychologists *address the issues identified by counsel*, avoiding confusion, embarrassment, or worse by performing the tasks requested of them instead of crafting and embarking upon potentially dissonant missions of their own. In turn, this calls upon forensic psychologists to *maintain assigned professional roles*, since testimony, consultation, and treatment are typically incompatible functions for forensic psychologists, who must accept the specific identities that were initially determined and see these through. Forensic psychologists *investigate malingering whenever feasible*, consciously aware that the integrity of the assessment process calls for objective investigation of the defendant's effort and veracity. Every time that forensic psychologists *strive to keep errors to a bare minimum*, they reflect necessary professionalism and enhance their own credibility. Opportunities to *convey that ethical obligations are not negotiable* should be taken when feasible, to the ultimate benefit of all parties concerned.

When forensic psychologists do their jobs, play the same part throughout the case, check to see if others are remaining on task, reduce their own mistakes, and stick to the rules, they contribute directly to the cause of justice and substantially increase the likelihood that they'll be invited back.

An American Perspective

Address the issues identified by counsel

The consequences of failing to address the issues identified by counsel may best be defined from the perspectives of the various parties who participate in any standard criminal trial. The judge wonders why certain issues either are or are not being addressed. The jury—should such evidence be deemed admissible and placed before them at all—wonders what these hitherto unheralded matters have to do with the role so painstakingly explained to them by the judge. The attorney who commissioned an expert opinion struggles to recognize in it those issues that were once deemed critical to success or failure. Opposing counsel must decide whether to sit back quietly and observe with glee the pending collapse of an adversary's mental health case, or instead to object to the introduction of any issues that were not properly stated and approved at an earlier stage of these proceedings. The defendant, perhaps only dimly aware of the technical implications of this new development, senses counsel's discomfort and can only imagine what new peril may be looming. The expert, having arrived to demonstrate the value of mental health science and to bask in the system's approval, now scrambles to salvage some prospect of legitimate influence as well as any hope of being invited back at some point in the future.

Absent some dramatic and unheralded abandonment of an earlier, agreed-upon strategy, this is not primarily the expert's fault. It is counsel who bears the ultimate responsibility for whatever does or does not occur when the case is finally presented. Woe betide the attorney who cuts an expert loose—how impressively seasoned and industrious that expert may be—with vague, impressionistic instructions along the lines of 'conduct a forensic evaluation', 'see what you can find out', or even 'address the usual issues in such cases'. Issues can emerge. Issues can disappear. Counsel never likes surprises, and counsel has not just the opportunity but the duty to prevent them whenever possible. From retention to examination to report writing to the development of expert testimony, each plateau of preparation calls for a periodic check-in with the expert, despite whatever issues of convenience or discoverability may intrude (Bullis, 2014).

Fortunately, identifying the appropriate issues for a given case is not particularly difficult, especially since these are often imposed by the court or otherwise dictated by familiar circumstance. The most prominent and frequently arising of these is 'competency to stand trial', or as it is known in England and Wales, 'fitness to plead' (Brown, 2019). It is a fundamental requirement that all criminal defendants be capable of grasping not only the nature and consequences of the proceedings against them, but also capable of rational participation in the conceptualization and execution of the defense itself (Collins, 2019).

The 'nature and consequences' element is often described as the 'cognitive' prong of trial competency (Felthous, 2011, p. 23), given its primary reliance upon the defendant's capacity to obtain, store, and retrieve knowledge. What charges am I facing? Where and when are criminal offenses alleged to have occurred? Who is the alleged victim? What are the meanings of such legally relevant notions as plea bargaining, probation, guilt, innocence, and conviction? What are the potential consequences of conviction? What are the interactive roles of the judge, jury, prosecutor, defense counsel, and witnesses?

The balance of conducting assessments for this issue concerns the 'rational participation' prong that is often described as the 'behavioral' prong of trial competency (Schwalbe and Medalia, 2007, p. 519), focusing as it does upon what the defendant is actually in a position to *do* with whatever knowledge has been acquired. How often have I met with counsel? Is counsel 'on my side' and expending sufficient effort in this matter? Do I plan to take counsel's legal advice? How would I determine whether to do so? Do I have any real choice in the matter? Am I in a position to testify? How am I likely to fare upon cross-examination? If a plea bargain—perhaps involving probation—is in the offing, do I have the capacity to gauge the desirability of that offer? Do I possess the ability to make good upon its requirements? Am I capable of meeting and maintaining the usual standards for proper comportment in the courtroom?

A defendant who displays significant deficits in either or both of the prongs of this construct will only be deemed incompetent if there exists a mental health substrate for this situation. In other words, incompetency must be predicated, at least in part, upon some identifiable psychiatric condition, and not merely a lack of general exposure to criminal matters (Reisner and Piel, 2018). Either during the initial proffer of trial competency evidence, or subsequent to a judicial finding of incompetency, the expert may also be asked to opine on the prospects for 'competency restoration'—often a somewhat misleading term when it comes to those defendants who could never have been considered competent at any point in their lives—and recommend a psychoeducational path toward achieving that goal within a designated timeframe (Heilbrun et al., 2019).

Distinct from the present-day and future focus of competency to stand trial, the issue of the 'criminal responsibility' or 'insanity' defense targets addresses behavior that may have occurred some days, weeks, months, or even years prior to the forensic psychological evaluation. In this instance, the goal is typically to determine whether, at the time of the alleged offense, the defendant was capable of recognizing the criminal nature of the activity in question (again, a 'cognitive' prong) and also whether the defendant possessed the ability to conform alleged behaviors to the requirements of the law (again, a 'behavioral' prong) (Baselice, Stevenson and Cohen, 2022).

Unlike competency to stand trial, criminal responsibility is typically a waivable issue (Frizzell and Mobbs, 2020), in that defendants are not compelled to raise it if, for example, they deem that it is not a winning strategy, or that the spectre of involuntary civil commitment is more forbidding than that of incarceration or a fine. Criminal responsibility can also take on different forms or aspects in different jurisdictions, including a limited focus upon whether defendants were acting on the basis of an 'irresistible impulse', or upon whether their behavior was somehow the 'product' of a 'mental disease or defect' (Fahey, Groschadl and Weaver, 2020). There are some jurisdictions that have chosen to eschew the notion of a free-standing 'insanity defense' altogether, leaving defendants instead to establish more traditionally that at the time in question they lacked the necessary element of intent (*mens rea*) for a specific criminal offense (Appelbaum, 2020).

Even if a defendant presents as competent to stand trial and does not assert a viable insanity defense, the issue of 'mitigation' may come into play. Mitigation is often available—sometimes established by statute or case law, and sometimes as a matter of common sense and custom—to reduce the sentence of someone who has either been found guilty at trial or who has entered into a plea agreement, perhaps to a lesser offense or otherwise to a stipulated lessening of penalties. In addition to flowing naturally from the results of an 'insanity' evaluation that failed to meet its mark, the mitigation evaluation may incorporate elements that perhaps had little if anything to do with the defendant's behavior at the time of the offense. Examples can include low intellectual functioning, chronic mental illness, economic deprivation, and prior subjection to abuse (Meixner, 2022). One form of mitigation actually focuses upon what may be the actions of victims themselves, concerning 'heat of passion' or 'extreme emotional disturbance' (Drogin and Marin, 2008; Johnston et al., 2022). In such situations, were defendants faced with a provocation so shocking and infuriating that they temporarily took leave of their senses, acting in a fashion that need not reflect any underlying mental illness and that would never have occurred under normal circumstances?

Another potentially vital issue may involve neither present competency nor prior culpability, but rather the ultimate admissibility of statements made by the defendant to law enforcement at or around the time of arrest. When the defendant was offered the requisite 'Miranda warning', or, in England and Wales, a 'police caution' (Sim and Lamb, 2018), was any waiver of such rights as the option to remain silent or the option to obtain the presence of counsel made in a knowing, intelligent, and voluntary fashion (Sharf et al., 2017)? In other words, was the defendant capable of understanding such rights, weighing the implications of such rights, and exercising—or declining to exercise—such rights free of physical or psychological coercion? Unlike the typical insanity defense, voluntary intoxication may be relevant here, in addition to standard concerns involving acute mental illness and cognitively related vocabulary deficits (Drogin, 2022). In some cases, the expert's contribution does not focus on the delivery or incorporation of a given 'Miranda warning' at all, but rather on whether the circumstances were sufficiently 'custodial', due to real or imagined inability to leave the scene of questioning, that such warnings *should* have been provided when in fact they were not (Taylor, 2015). There has also been some scholarly debate concerning whether it is problematically misleading to administer a 'Miranda warning' to someone who is *not* in custody (Maoz, 2012).

Clearly there may be some commonality among the assessment strategies employed by the expert in these and other specialized evaluations, including the all-important need for confidentiality with its rarefied forensic exceptions (van Kan and Kumar, 2020), but the end product as expressed in a forensic opinion potentially addresses distinct legal issues that may be premature, incompatible, irrelevant, and even outright counterproductive from counsel's point of view. Determining what is and is not germane to a specific criminal matter depends upon periodic, candid, and explicit communication between counsel and the expert as the case progresses toward trial (Bullis, 2014).

Maintain assigned professional roles

Forensic psychologists have an ample selection of roles to inhabit within the course of criminal proceedings. The most common and traditional of these roles is that of the 'testifying expert', who typically reviews available documentation, administers psychological tests, conducts interviews, composes a report, and testifies about relevant issues based upon the contents of that report. The testifying witness may not actually wind up testifying but stands ready to do so. Depending upon the circumstances of the case at hand, there may be a privity with counsel that excludes contact with any additional parties until cross-examination occurs in the courtroom—or in some instances, concerning cases in which the potential consequences are particularly dire, during a deposition taken prior to the date of trial (Drogin and Williams, 2018).

Counsel may need some help in identifying, selecting, retaining, and directing testifying witnesses. In this, a 'consulting expert' can play a crucial role (Drogin and Hagan, 2023). For this form of assistance to be most effective, a candid exposition of the current status of counsel's case, warts and all, is essential—particularly when counsel is a defense attorney, observed here in the course of instructing the consulting expert:

Here's what my client did that the prosecutor knows about. Here's what my client may get charged with in the next several weeks. Here's a copy of the report we received from the other side's expert, curriculum vitae included. Please let us know what's wrong with that report and which credentials are exaggerated or downright fraudulent. Here's a copy of the report we received from our own expert last week. We fired that expert and you're the only other person who will ever see this report. Please help us find an expert more sympathetic to my client's current diagnosis and the hospital where it was ascribed. If possible, this should be an expert our judge likes. Let's try to wrap this up before the end of next month, because the current judge retires then. The new judge we're about to get can't stand me and gave my client a maximum sentence in another matter ten years ago.

Although all of the preceding remarks reside well within the bounds of acceptable attorney ethics, none of them are utterances that counsel wants to see disclosed on the witness stand, or for that matter anywhere else. If the consulting expert were asked to perform double duty as a testifying expert, all communications with counsel could be subject to discovery, including cross-examination. The decision about which of these two roles the forensic psychologist will perform is one to be made by counsel with clarity and firmness—all the more so because of the established befuddlement of so many experts concerning these issues (Gutheil et al., 2012). If counsel wants a testifying expert to become a consulting expert, then this is easily arranged, as long as that change is deemed permanent, and as long as there is no risk of the expert being called to court in connection with prior duties in the case at hand. A transformation from a consulting expert into a testifying expert is never advisable, at least if counsel has been sufficiently disclosing to the consulting expert for that role to have been justified in the first place. Overall, 'taking both roles (consultant and testifying expert) can easily undermine the apparent, if not actual, objectivity of the clinician as a testifying witness' (Melton et al., 2018, p. 87).

In criminal matters, the use of the term 'treating expert' in criminal matters is as misleading as its practice is inadvisable. It has been recognized for over a quarter of a century, in forensic psychology and forensic psychiatry alike (Greenberg and Shuman, 1997; Strasburger, Gutheil and Brodsky, 1997), that there is an inherent conflict of interest when one attempts to provide therapeutic services to a defendant while at the same time—or previously, or subsequently—rendering an opinion with respect to that defendant's competency to stand trial, criminal responsibility, or other legally relevant status. Psychotherapy is a supportive, affiliative activity that fits poorly with the requisite willingness to render a negative, perhaps even literally fatal, forensic opinion regarding the same individual. Similarly, the therapeutic relationship can be strained to the point of utter ineffectiveness when the forensic evaluator, whose court-related duties may complicate or even threaten the life of the patient, now seeks to develop and oversee a clinical treatment plan (Gutheil and Drogin, 2013, pp. 5–6).

Arguments have been made in favor of enabling such dual roles in, for example, rural areas with a low professional census, or forensic hospitals that are charged by court order or statute with providing restoration services (American Academy of Psychiatry and the Law, 2005; American Psychological Association, 2013). These convenience-oriented allowances do not make such practices any less problematic. The forensically evaluated criminal defendant is often a cognitively challenged and anxious person with sharply curtailed autonomy and minimal financial resources, and thus especially vulnerable to the negative effects of such conflicts of interest. 'Tele-assessment', with a 'modest, though compelling, body of evidence' for its 'reliability, validity, and utility' (Wright and Raiford, 2021, p. 2), complemented by the proper apportionment of institutional duties, will go a long way toward making the notion of the 'treating expert' a relic of the past.

Investigate malingering whenever feasible

Malingering, despite its forensically relevant clinical implications, is not a mental disorder. In fact, it is essentially the opposite. Malingering reflects an attempt to exaggerate or to engage in wholesale fabrication of a psychiatric condition, for the specific purpose of obtaining some form of 'secondary gain'. Its relevance to forensic psychology and criminal law is underscored by no less an authoritative source than the current edition of the American Psychiatric Association's *Diagnostic and Statistical Manual of Mental Disorders* (2022), which advises that malingering be 'strongly considered' when, for example, 'the individual is referred by an attorney to the clinician for examination, or the individual self-refers while litigation or criminal charges are pending' (p. 835).

The potentially damning effects of a verified finding of malingering in criminal matters would be difficult to overstate. When a defendant's competency to stand trial or criminal responsibility is called into question, cognitive disability or major mental illness is typically cited as the reason. Apart from records that may convincingly describe the presence of some qualifying psychiatric condition in the past, the defendant's forensically informed legal fate largely rests upon just how convincing a present display of symptoms may be, as reflected in a combination of behavioral observations, interview performance, and psychological test results.

The last of these three sources of verification—or of disputation—is the particular purview of the forensic psychologist. What tends to distinguish psychology from other mental health professions is its mastery and widely applied utilization of psychological testing. Well-standardized, clinically proven, and research-supported assessment measures are commonly and convincingly touted as lending just the sort of objectivity that forensic evaluations require. Scales designed to identify malingering—some experts prefer such terms as 'measures of effort' or 'measures of feigning'—are built into a number of different psychological tests, and there is also a broad range of free-standing instruments primarily dedicated to ferreting out malingering and other forms of 'dissimulation', a term that refers to any of a host of aberrant response styles (Rogers, 2018, pp. 583–585). The way these tests work is often to troll for inconsistent answers, to determine if defendants are willing to endorse symptoms that rarely exist for even the most impaired of examinees, and to offer cognitive puzzles for which the most profound of intellectual shortcomings would be necessary as a basis for legitimate failure.

Unhelpful malingering assessment outcomes can be so devastating that forensic examiners may need to summon every ounce of professional resolve in order to withstand the desperate and sometimes starkly aggrieved pushback that may be mounted by counsel. Although '[t]he majority of attorneys are ethical individuals who value the objectivity of expert opinion' (Gutheil and Brodsky, 2016, p. 148), one particularly egregious and unfortunately unembellished example may serve to demonstrate how the attorney-expert relationship can unravel. In a murder case, counsel was informed that the client had failed a malingering screening test, but counsel did not register any particular surprise or concern at that juncture. When reminded of this finding, however, as trial approached, counsel proposed progressively unreasonable solutions. Counsel's first suggestion was that the expert undertake to report all of the other psychological test results, but not the malingering results. Told that such selective accounting was not permissible, counsel then suggested that this could be cured by refraining from mentioning any psychological test results at all. This solution, too, was rejected. When counsel revived this discussion sometime later, claiming to have consulted with an expert who insisted that one should never perform malingering testing in criminal matters, counsel was challenged to produce that expert. Counsel's highly experienced supervisor eventually interceded.

For the forensic psychological evaluation of those criminal defendants who are capable of grasping the instructions for malingering measures and who can understand the wording of the items those measures may contain, some form of standardized malingering assessment is indispensable. It is often helpful if counsel is made aware of the likelihood of such procedures before these occur. If malingering testing was feasible but not performed, vigorous cross-examination concerning this notion should be expected, and in a situation reminiscent of the above-noted distinction between the treating clinician and the testifying expert, the latter should not be surprised to be asked on the witness stand about being on the defendant's 'side', and about unquestioningly accepting the defendant's assertions without any objective assessment to place self-serving symptoms in context.

Strive to keep errors to a bare minimum

Forensic psychologists who contribute their expertise in the context of criminal proceedings are providing services that in some jurisdictions may literally amount to a matter of life and death. Occasional mistakes are virtually unavoidable. That does not mean, however, that complacency is acceptable. Given the heightened stakes inherent to criminal matters and the extended range of parties who may to varying degrees be affected—including defendants, alleged victims, the criminal justice system, and more generally society at large—forensic psychologists will want to take especial care that errors in both reports and testimony are reduced to the extent feasible.

'The quality of our reports is often the most tangible and visible measure of our professionalism. At a basic level, misspellings, typographical errors, and poor grammar suggest carelessness, if not a lack of respect for the reader' (Appelbaum, 2010, p. 43). Such errors can to some extent be flagged—although likely not repaired without further scrutiny—on the basis of spell-checking features that are built into every contemporary word-processing application. There exist other applications, specific to clinical use, that are sensitive to matters commonly arising in forensic practice and that are downloadable as an adjunct to basic, commonly bundled options (Lai et al., 2015).

Reliance on mechanical aspects of report generation may be what caused some typographical and other content errors in the first place. In addition to automatic warning devices, a simple checklist (Zwartz, 2018) for the author's own implementation may be the most effective tool for reducing mistakes. Have such elements as litigant names, listed offenses, examination dates, examination locations, test titles, and representations of test data been transferred faithfully from the forensic psychologist's contemporaneous notes? Another simple if potentially time-consuming remedy is to move beyond mere visual scanning—mechanical or otherwise—to reading the report draft aloud, thus adding an auditory component to the overall quality control process (University of North Carolina at Chapel Hill, 2022).

Some mistakes may have occurred long before the time comes for writing a report or preparing to testify. Concerning the substantial reliance on testing that is a hallmark of forensic psychological practice in criminal law matters, there has been an ongoing focus in the professional literature on test-scoring errors (Frederick and Tyner, 2013; Drogin and Biswas, 2016; Harrison, Geogan and Macoun, 2019), particularly in the context of examinations that are being conducted, in whole or in part, by supervised trainees (Oak et al., 2019; Lockwood et al., 2020). Given that 'errors in scoring psychological tests occur at every level, including transferring the items [*sic*] scores to another medium for scoring' (Frederick and Tyner, 2013, p. 1360), forensic psychologists are best advised not just to review what appears in a report or in notes, but also to review the underlying protocol-level data as well.

It may be the case that errors in report writing are only discovered after the document in question has already been proffered to counsel and then forwarded to the court. Under these circumstances, forensic psychologists may wish to consult counsel directly in order to determine collaboratively if the error is sufficiently significant to be highlighted at all, if it should only be addressed at a pending hearing or trial, or if an erratum notice, report supplement, or revised full report should be issued. Errors in witness testimony, which research has demonstrated can negatively affect juror perceptions of credibility (Tenney et al., 2007) can be subjected to the same *post hoc* interactive process with counsel, and then cured as needed in writing, via follow-up testimony, or perhaps both.

Convey that ethical obligations are not negotiable

As noted by Heilbrun, Grisso and Goldstein (2009, p. 120):

> Keep your ethical priorities in order. Attending to scientific and professional truths always comes before responsibility to the court, and those court obligations always precede responsibilities to retaining counsel and protecting one's self-esteem.

Easier said than done? Counsel's role, after all, occurs within the context of an adversarial system, and 'at their best, attorneys are in firm control' (Brodsky, 2013, p. 142). Nonetheless, the experienced trial attorney 'understands—and can grudgingly afford to respect, within limits—the testifying expert's codified obligations to assess, report, and testify within certain guild-determined boundaries' (Drogin and Hagan, 2023, p. 373). Forensic psychologists are not in a position, in criminal or any other matters, to plead ignorance of their ethical obligations, or to assert when being called to account for ethical transgressions that they were 'just following orders'.

This is particularly true given the constant promulgation of forensically oriented ethical guidance that can now be accessed by all criminal case evaluators, tailored in each instance to that individual's specific profession. What follows is a sampling of advice from the most prominent of these sources, the American Psychological Association's *Specialty Guidelines for Forensic Psychology* (2013). Each excerpt is accompanied here by a brief commentary on its relevance to examinations conducted in criminal matters.

Forensic psychologists 'strive to be unbiased and impartial, and avoid partisan presentation of unrepresentative, incomplete, or inaccurate evidence that might mislead finders of fact' (p. 9). This advice actually touches upon two separate strains of free-standing yet ultimately interrelated concern. The first of these is the need for forensic psychologists to conduct periodic, searching, unflinching self-examinations concerning the extent to which overt or implicit biases regarding certain defendant populations may be interfering with sound professional judgement. There has never been a point in the history of the helping professions at which more ample resources for this purpose have been made available. Diversity-, equity-, and inclusion-oriented continuing education programming is presently ubiquitous, and a great deal of it is geared specifically to the duties of forensic psychologists in criminal matters. Concerns regarding the presentation of evidence, on the other hand, may have much less to do with bias and partiality than with the occasional tendency of forensic psychologists to become caught up in counsel's adversarial quest at the expense of detached, objective, and purely scientifically based performance. Counsel can always seek out the services of a consulting expert if the testifying expert's reserve attitude and behavior appear to be impeding the pursuit of a specific legal outcome.

Forensic psychologists 'recognize the importance of obtaining a fundamental and reasonable level of knowledge and understanding of the legal and professional standards, laws, rules, and precedents that govern their participation in legal proceedings' (p. 9). The role of the testifying expert is to bring science to the criminal justice system, but on the criminal justice system's terms. To function effectively in any environment, psychologists need to develop a grasp of the needs of service recipients. Of course, while there is considerable professional risk in doing damage to a criminal case due to ignorance and overall lack of investment, there are, conversely, similar dangers to assuming that one knows enough about counsel's world that one can start to function *as* counsel. This extends to such counterproductive behaviors as jumping ahead of questions on direct and cross examination, attempting to sway counsel's litigation strategy, and conveying legal advice to defendants and other criminal justice system participants. 'Knowledge and understanding' about the work environment in which one is functioning do not translate into expertise outside the boundaries of one's own professional expertise.

Forensic psychologists 'strive to contribute a portion of their professional time for little or no compensation or personal advantage' (p. 12). It has never been anticipated that this goal would be reached on the basis of psychologists submitting an invoice but failing to obtain payment. The same can be said for those situations in which psychologists settle for a meager hourly rate because, despite their best efforts, they were unable to negotiate successfully for an initially sought-after level of compensation. Such billing failures are not the pathway to sincere *pro bono* service. It is difficult to determine what is meant by no 'personal advantage'. Presumably this does not refer to some form of barter. When we consider how word travels within what remains a fairly small community of forensic psychological practitioners, and when we contemplate the appreciation—and typically future engagements—that professional generosity typically engenders, avoiding 'personal advantage' might be every bit as complicated as achieving it.

Forensic psychologists 'carefully consider the appropriateness of conducting a forensic evaluation of an individual who is not represented by counsel' (p. 13). This status may not readily be apparent when forensic psychologists are first contacted by forensic examinees. As often as not, a letter, email message, text message, or telephone call from a non-lawyer was actually instigated by counsel in the first place. This could occur for any number of potentially overlapping reasons. Counsel may be too poorly connected to the local expert witness community, or to the local legal community from which advice about experts would normally emanate. Neither of these is a good sign. Perhaps counsel is simply too busy—an even worse sign. In some instances, this is a calculated approach on the part of counsel, who seeks, despite the sorts of concerns raised earlier in this chapter, to instigate a 'treating expert' situation. Sometimes it is potential examinees themselves who contact forensic psychologists, seeking to obtain some sort of 'general' examination and then disclose after the fact that this was for the purpose of obtaining a witness for an upcoming criminal hearing or trial.

Forensic psychologists 'only provide written or oral evidence about the psychological characteristics of particular individuals when they have sufficient information or data to form an adequate foundation for those opinions or to substantiate their findings' (p. 15). Purely secondhand forensic conclusions are a gratefully received windfall for the opposing criminal law practitioner. Cross-examinations under such circumstances tend almost to write themselves. 'So, when you met with the defendant, you ... oh, wait'. 'What behavioral observations were you able to make when you administered tests to gauge ... ah, yes, that's right'. How can forensic psychologists seek, for example, to provide an up-to-date and convincing diagnosis of a defendant based upon dated information that was derived, if at all, by other mental health professionals or even by laypersons? This is not, of course, to demean the value of collateral information, which is often critical to certain types of opinions in criminal matters; rather, the issue here is that when forensic psychologists seek to offer normal services based solely upon limited means of inquiry, they have chosen a very difficult path.

Forensic psychologists 'strive to conduct evaluations in settings that provide adequate comfort, safety, and privacy' (p. 16). This can be an exceptionally challenging goal to realize when, as is so often the case, the evaluation in question is going to consist of examinations that are conducted in the local jail. Forensic psychologists may have the time and the interpersonal skills to develop a working relationship with correctional personnel, which can lead to some forbearance and understanding when the time comes to schedule an appropriately quiet and removed meeting space. Of course, care must be taken—in some cases more importantly than others—that the space in question is not *too* removed. To this list of concerns can be added another: adequate time. When planning to develop a multi-hour encounter featuring rapport building, in-depth interviews, and extensive testing, forensic psychologists would do well to consider that it can often seem easier to break out of jails and prisons than to break into them. The merest incidence of backstage disturbance, day-to-day fluctuations in staffing, or misplaced memoranda can delay the proceedings and thus narrow the examination window to the point that a carefully plotted visit may need to be postponed outright until another, luckier day. In any event, well-managed surroundings tend to lead to increasingly valid results and thus increasingly compelling and defensible opinions.

Such guild-driven cautions and recommendations are not unique to forensic practice in the United States. For example, the British Psychological Society recently published *Psychologists as Expert Witnesses: Best Practice Guidelines for Psychologists* (2021). Similar to their American counterpart, these guidelines assert that forensic psychologists 'are expected to understand the legal processes in which they are involved, and how expert and professional witness evidence sits within such proceedings' (p. 10), should remain cognizant of potential concerns when evaluating those who are 'representing themselves with little or no input from a legal professional' (p. 15), are encouraged to determine how 'managing safety considerations should be considered for each setting, depending on specific risks and/or constraints' (p. 15), and 'need to ensure that they can provide an independent and impartial opinion' (p. 17), in addition to which detailed advice is proffered on how to negotiate and characterize the 'range of fees that expert witnesses can charge' (p. 24).

Although guidelines and codes have a necessary role to play in informing appropriate responses to ethical dilemmas, 'there are occasions when these sources of authority do not provide direction, are too general, may not apply to a specific forensic case, or are in conflict' (Otto, Goldstein and Heilbrun, 2017, p. 8). A good deal of the modern scholarship in this arena 'is dedicated to reminding researchers and clinicians that there is much more to professional ethics than mere compliance with codes and guidelines' (Drogin, 2019, p. 242).

In order to navigate the inevitable challenges raised by this form of work, 'psychologists involved in forensic practice must have both a personal commitment to maintaining high standards of ethical practice and the information and tools needed to achieve and maintain ethical practice' (Bush, Connell and Denney, 2020, p. 3).

Forensic psychology has become so entrenched in American criminal law proceedings that it is now difficult to imagine how such notions as competency to stand trial, criminal responsibility, mitigation, and Miranda waivers could be addressed without its input. Difficult, but not impossible. The twin histories of psychology and law are littered with examples of theories, protocols, and specialties once deemed indispensable but now scarcely recalled by anyone save academicians and rare book collectors. When forensic psychologists construe the issues presented to them by lawyers as mere suggestions, drift back and forth between roles without notice or consultation, fail to assess the propensity of individual defendants to malinger, proffer reports and testimony without an established system for reducing errors, and treat ethics as an option instead of an obligation, they may try the patience of the criminal justice system to such an extent that lawyers and judges will find new ways to solve old problems on their own. The principles espoused by this chapter are neither novel nor incompatible with established best practices, and can thus be incorporated into existing service routines with relative ease.

References

American Academy of Psychiatry and the Law (2005) *Ethics Guidelines for the Practice of Forensic Psychiatry*. Available at: https://www.aapl.org/ethics.htm (Accessed: 29 December 2022).

American Psychiatric Association (2022) *Diagnostic and Statistical Manual of Mental Disorders*. 5th edn. Washington, DC: American Psychiatric Association.

American Psychological Association (2013) 'Specialty guidelines for forensic psychology', *American Psychologist*, 68(1), pp. 7–19. doi: 10.1037/a0029889.

Appelbaum, K.L. (2010) 'Commentary: The art of forensic report writing', *Journal of the American Academy of Psychiatry and the Law*, 38(1), pp. 43–45.

Appelbaum, P.S. (2020) 'Kahler v. Kansas: The constitutionality of abolishing the insanity defense', *Psychiatric Services*, 72(1), pp. 104–106. doi: 10.1176/appi.ps.202000707.

Baselice, L., Stevenson, K.A. and Cohen, B. (2022) 'Connecting criminal conduct to mental illness in the insanity defense', *Journal of the American Academy of Psychiatry and the Law*, 50(3), pp. 480–482. doi: 10.29158/JAAPL.220059-22.

British Psychological Society (2021) *Psychologists as expert witnesses: Best practice guidelines for psychologists*. Available at: https://www.bps.org.uk/guideline/psychologists-expert-witnesses (Accessed: 30 December 2022).

Brodsky, S.L. (2013) *Testifying in Court: Guidelines and Maxims for the Expert Witness*. 2nd edn. Washington, DC: American Psychological Association.

Brodsky, S.L. and Gutheil, T.G. (2016) *The Expert Expert Witness: More Maxims and Guidelines for Testifying in Court*. 2nd edn. Washington, DC: American Psychological Association.

Brown, P. (2019) 'Unfitness to plead in England and Wales: Historical development and contemporary dilemmas', *Medicine, Science and the Law*, 59(3), pp. 187–196. doi: 10.1177/0025802419856761.

Bullis, R.K. (2014) 'Promoting communications between social scientists and lawyers', *The Jury Expert*, 26(4), pp. 40–142.

Bush, S.S., Connell, M. and Denney, R.L. (2020) *Ethical Practice in Forensic Psychology: A Guide for Mental Health Professionals*. 2nd edn. Washington, DC: American Psychological Association.

Collins, J.D. (2019) 'Re-evaluating competence to stand trial', *Law and Contemporary Problems*, 82(2), pp. 157–189.

Drogin, E.Y. (2019) *Ethical Conflicts in Psychology*. 5th edn. Washington, DC: American Psychological Association.

Drogin, E.Y. (2022) '"Hold my beer": When does it matter if intoxication is voluntary?', *Criminal Justice*, 37(3), pp. 56–57.

Drogin, E.Y. and Biswas, J. (2016) 'Forensic assessment', in Norcross, J.C., VandenBos, G.R. and Freedheim, D.K. (eds), *APA Handbook of Clinical Psychology, Vol. 3: Applications and Methods*. Washington, DC: American Psychological Association, pp. 167–188.

Drogin, E.Y. and Hagan, L.D. (2023) 'Trial consultation', in DeMatteo, D. and Scherr, K.C. (eds), *The Oxford Handbook of Psychology and Law*. New York: Oxford University Press, pp. 366–379.

Drogin, E.Y. and Marin, R. (2008) 'Extreme emotional disturbance (EED), heat of passion, and provocation: A jurisprudent science perspective', *Journal of Psychiatry and Law*, 36(1), pp. 133–147. doi: 10.1177/009318530803600212.

Drogin, E.Y. and Williams, C.S. (2018) 'Introduction to the legal system', in Gold, L. and Frierson, R. (eds), *The American Psychiatric Publishing Textbook of Forensic Psychiatry*. 3rd edn. Washington, DC: American Psychiatric Publishing, pp. 15–26.

Fahey, E.M., Groschadl, L. and Weaver, B. (2020) '"The angels that surrounded my cradle": The history, evaluation, and application of the insanity defense', *Buffalo Law Review*, 68(3), pp. 805–856.

Felthous, A.R. (2011) 'Competence to stand trial should require rational understanding', *Journal of the American Academy of Psychiatry and the Law*, 39(1), pp. 19–30.

Frederick, R.I. and Tyner, E.A. (2013) 'Rates of computational errors for scoring the SIRS primary scales', *Psychological Assessment*, 25(4), pp. 1367–1369. doi: 10.1037/a0033696.

Frizzell, W. and Mobbs, K. (2020) 'Competence to refuse an insanity defense', *Journal of the American Academy of Psychiatry and the Law*, 48(3), pp. 404–406. doi: 10.29158/JAAPL.200045L1-20.

Greenberg, S.A. and Shuman, D.W. (1997) 'Irreconcilable conflict between therapeutic and forensic roles', *Professional Psychology: Research and Practice*, 28(1), pp. 50–57. doi: 10.1037/0735-7028.28.1.50.

Gutheil, T.G., Commons, M.L., Drogin, E.Y., Hauser, M.J., Miller, P.M. and Richardson, A.M. (2012) 'Do forensic practitioners distinguish between testifying and consulting experts? A pilot study', *International Journal of Law and Psychiatry*, 35(5–6), pp. 452–455. doi: 10.1016/j.ijlp.2012.09.020.

Gutheil, T.G. and Drogin, E.Y. (2013) *The Mental Health Professional in Court: A Survival Guide*. Washington, DC: American Psychiatric Publishing.

Harrison, G.L., Geogan, L.D. and Macoun, S.J. (2019) 'Common examiner scoring errors on academic achievement measures', *Canadian Journal of School Psychology*, 34(2), pp. 98–112. doi: 10.1177/0829573518763484.

Heilbrun, K., Giallella, C., Wright, H.J., DeMatteo, D., Griffin, P.A., Locklair, B. and Desai, A. (2019) 'Treatment for restoration of competence to stand trial: Critical analysis and policy recommendations', *Psychology, Public Policy, and Law*, 25(4), pp. 266–283. doi: 10.1037/law0000210.

Heilbrun, K., Grisso, T. and Goldstein, A.M. (2009) *Foundations of Forensic Mental Health Assessment*. New York: Oxford University Press.

Johnston, E.L., Gliser, C.P., Haney, J.P., Formon, D.L., Hashimoto, N. and Rossbach, N. (2022) 'Extreme emotional disturbance: Legal frameworks and considerations for forensic evaluation', *Behavioral Sciences and the Law*, 40(6), pp. 733–755. doi: 10.1002/bsl.2580.

Lai, K.H., Topaz, M., Goss, F.R. and Zhou, L. (2015) 'Automated misspelling detection and correction in clinical free-text records', *Journal of Biomedical Informatics*, 55, pp. 188–195. doi: 10.1016/j.jbi.2015.04.008.

Lockwood, A.B., Sealander, K., Gross, T.J. and Lanterman, C. (2020) 'Teacher trainees' administration and scoring errors on the Kaufman Test of Educational Achievement', *Journal of Psychoeducational Assessment*, 38(5), pp. 551–563. doi: 10.1177/0734282919871144.

Maoz, A. (2012) 'Empty promises: Miranda warnings in noncustodial interrogations', *Michigan Law Review*, 119(7), pp. 1309–1340.

Meixner, J.B. (2022) 'Modern sentencing mitigation', *Northwestern University Law Review*, 116(6), pp. 1395–1479.

Melton, G.B., Petrila, J., Poythress, N.G., Slobogin, C.S., Otto, R.K., Mossman, D.M. and Condie, L.O. (2018) *Psychological Evaluations for the Courts: A Handbook for Mental Health Professionals and Lawyers*. 4th edn. New York: Guilford Press.

Oak, E., Viezel, K.D., Dumont, R. and Willis, J. (2019) 'Wechsler administration and scoring errors made by graduate students and school psychologists', *Journal of Psychoeducational Assessment*, 37(6), pp. 679–691. doi: 10.1177/0734282918786355.

Otto, R.K., Goldstein, A.M. and Heilbrun, K. (2017) *Ethics in Forensic Psychology Practice*. Hoboken, NJ: John Wiley and Sons, Inc.

Reisner, A.D. and Piel, J.L. (2018) 'Mental condition requirement in competency to stand trial assessments', *Journal of the American Academy of Psychiatry and the Law*, 46(1), pp. 86–92.

Rogers, R. (2018) 'Clinical assessment of response styles', in Rogers, R. and Bender, S.D. (eds), *Clinical Assessment of Malingering and Deception*. 4th edn. New York: Guilford Press, pp. 571–591.

Schwalbe, E. and Medalia, A. (2007) 'Cognitive dysfunction and competency restoration: Using cognitive remediation to help restore the unrestorable', *Journal of the American Academy of Psychiatry and the Law*, 35(4), pp. 518–525.

Sharf, A.J., Rogers, R., Williams, M.M. and Drogin, E.Y. (2017) 'Evaluating juvenile detainees' Miranda misconceptions: The discriminant validity of the Juvenile Miranda Quiz', *Psychological Assessment*, 29(5), pp. 556–567. doi: 10.1037/pas0000373.

Sim, M.P.Y. and Lamb, M.E. (2018) 'An analysis of how the police "caution" is presented to juvenile suspects in England', *Psychology, Crime and Law*, 24(8), pp. 851–972. doi: 10.1080/1068316X.2018.1442449.

Strasburger, L.H., Gutheil, T.G. and Brodsky, B.A. (1997) 'On wearing two hats: Role conflict in serving as both psychotherapist and expert witness', *American Journal of Psychiatry*, 154(4), pp. 448–456. doi: 10.1176/ajp.154.4.448.

Taylor, B. (2015) 'You have the right to be confused! Understanding *Miranda* after 50 years', *Pace Law Review*, 36(1), pp. 158–214.

Tenney, E.R., MacCoun, R.J., Spellman, B.A. and Hastie, R. (2007) 'Calibration trumps confidence as a basis for witness credibility', *Psychological Science*, 18(1), pp. 46–50. doi: 10.1111/j.1467-9280.2007.01847.x.

University of North Carolina at Chapel Hill (2022) *Reading Aloud*. Available at: https://writingcenter.unc.edu/tips-and-tools/reading-aloud (Accessed: 30 December 2022).

van Kan, C. and Kumar, S. (2020) 'Court-ordered assessments and routine access to confidential health information: Findings from a regional forensic mental health service', *Psychiatry, Psychology and Law*, 28(4), pp. 576–584. doi: 10.1080/13218719.2020.1805814.

Wright, A.J. and Raiford, S.E. (2021) *Essentials of Psychological Tele-Assessment*. Hoboken, NJ: John Wiley and Sons, Inc.

Zwartz, M. (2018) 'Report writing in the forensic context: Recurring problems and the use of a checklist to address them', *Psychiatry, Psychology and Law*, 25(4), pp. 578–588. doi: 10.1080/13218719.2018.1473172.

15
MENTAL CAPACITY IN FORENSIC PSYCHIATRY IN A COMPARATIVE CONTEXT

Stefano Ferracuti and Giovanna Parmigiani

Introduction

Mental capacity, often referred to with the term of "competence" or "capacity", consists of the ability of the person to decide independently and consciously. It is a multidimensional construct that underlies the presence of different neuropsychological functions (attention, memory, ability to reason in a logical deductive way, etc.), and which must always be carefully contextualized, since a person can be competent for some dimensions of his acts and not for others. Decision-making capacity takes on particular importance, for example, in making decisions regarding medical treatment, with respect to participation in an experimental research protocol, or, in forensic settings, in the ability to plead and stand trial or when the person is evaluated for reasons of insanity.

This chapter focuses on mental capacity evaluation in six areas:

1. Informed consent to medical treatment;
2. Informed consent to clinical research;
3. Capacity to stand trial;
4. Criminal responsibility;
5. Financial capacity;
6. Other decisional tasks (testamentary capacity, competence to marry, etc.).

Informed consent to treatment/research in vulnerable populations

Three criteria are required to ensure an adequate informed consent acquisition: full information disclosure, voluntariness, and patient's capacity to make a decision (Appelbaum, 2007). Decisional capacity refers to the ability to understand and retain the information disclosed, in order to reason about it and appreciate the possible consequences of one's own choices (Moynihan et al., 2018).

Following the widely accepted model of Grisso and Appelbaum (Appelbaum, 2007), decisional capacity consists of four elements: understanding, appreciating, reasoning, and expressing a choice (see Figure 15.1). The evaluation of capacity to consent to clinical

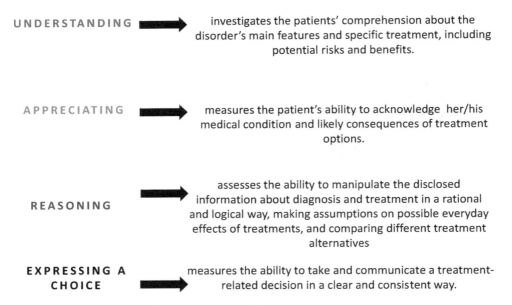

Figure 15.1 Capacity to consent to treatment

research, however, is different from that of treatment, because, for example, it investigates the understanding and retaining of information related to the possibility to receive a placebo or not benefitting directly from the experimental intervention, as well as the possibility to withdraw from the study at any time without negative consequences, or the risk of serious or unknown adverse events (Dunn and Jeste, 2001; Parmigiani et al., 2016). In addition, patients participating in clinical research might fail to comprehend the distinction between research and usual treatment, assuming that decisions about their treatment will be made only for their individual benefit, a process defined as therapeutic misconception (Dunn et al., 2006). Finally, requisites for decisional capacity tend to vary across jurisdictions and according to different research protocols or medical treatments (the higher the risk, the higher is the required decisional capacity level).

Patients affected by serious neuropsychiatric illnesses (Carpenter et al., 2000; Curley et al., 2019a; Curley et al., 2019; Kovnick et al., 2003; Okai et al., 2007) and neurodegenerative disorders (Appelbaum, 2010; Parmigiani et al., 2021) have been considered at higher risk of incapacity, although there is a considerable heterogeneity among diagnostic groups (Appelbaum, 2006; Jeste, Depp and Palmer, 2006). Regardless of diagnosis, mental incapacity has been associated with executive and global cognitive dysfunctions (Mandarelli et al., 2019; Mandarelli et al., 2012; Raymont et al., 2004), severity of psychiatric symptoms (Howe et al., 2005), impaired metacognition (Koren et al., 2005), and multiple environmental factors (Jeste et al., 2007; Palmer, 2006), including the complexity of disclosed information, type of clinical setting, and quality of consent forms and disclosing procedures (see Figure 15.2).

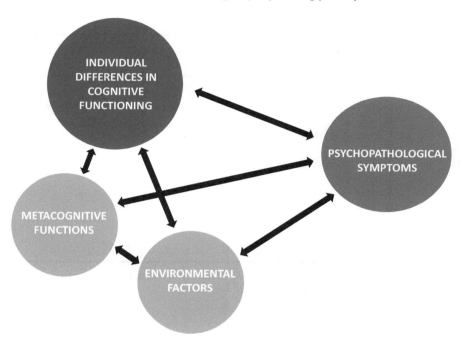

Figure 15.2 Variables that influence decisional capacity

Physicians tend to rely on their clinical judgment to assess patients' capacity to consent to treatment/research. However, unstructured evaluations tend to be unreliable, especially for those patients whose cognitive functioning is neither intact nor highly impaired but somewhere in the middle (Appelbaum, 2010). For example, Marson and colleagues (1997) found that the agreement among five physicians who reviewed videotapes of capacity assessments and evaluated the competence of patients affected by mild Alzheimer's Disease (AD) was no better than chance (kappa statistic, 0.14). To address this ethical issue, some clinical tools have been developed aimed at evaluating patients' decisional capacity (see Table 15.1 and Table 15.2), among which the most widely used are the MacArthur Competence Assessment Tool for Treatment (MacCAT-T) (Grisso and Appelbaum, 1998) and the MacArthur Competence Assessment Tool for Clinical Research (MacCAT-CR) (Appelbaum and Grisso, 2001).

Mental capacity to consent to treatment in involuntary psychiatric hospitalization

Involuntary psychiatric hospitalization (IPH) is often regarded as a necessary measure and as a last resort option in some cases, even though there have been attempts towards reducing or abolishing coercive treatments. Several concerns have been raised about the implications of non-consensual psychiatric care in terms of possible violations of personal rights, as well as limitations of personal autonomy (Mandarelli et al., 2019; Svindseth, Dahl and Hatling, 2007).

Table 15.1 Selected instruments to assess decisional capacity to consent to treatment

Instrument	Decisional ability construct	Scenario	Administration time	Format
MacCAT-T	Understanding Appreciation Reasoning Expressing a choice	Real	15–20 minutes	Semi-structured interview
CCTI (Gerstenecker et al., 2016a)	Choice Reasonableness Appreciation Rational reasons Understanding	Hypothetical		Clinical vignettes
ACE (Etchells et al., 1999)	Understanding Appreciating Choice	Real	15 minutes	Semi-structured interview

Note: MacCAT-T: MacArthur Competence Assessment Tool for Treatment; CCTI: Capacity to Consent to Treatment Instrument; ACE: Aid to Capacity Evaluation.

Table 15.2 Selected instruments to assess decisional capacity to consent to research

Instrument	Decisional ability construct	Scenario	Administration time	Format
MacCAT-CR	Understanding Appreciation Reasoning Expressing a choice	Real	15–20 minutes	Semi-structured interview
UBACC (Jeste et al., 2007)	Understanding	Real	5 minutes	10-item screening instrument
BACO (Parmigiani et al., 2016)	Understanding	Real	5 minutes	5-item screening instrument

Note: MacCAT-CR: MacArthur Competence Assessment Tool for Clinical Research; UBACC: University of California Brief Assessment of Capacity to Consent; BACO: Brief Assessment for Consent to Clinical Research.

Sheridan Rains et al. (2019) compared annual incidence of IPH between 2008 and 2017 in 22 countries across Europe, Australia, and New Zealand and found that the median rate of IPH was 106.4 (IQR 58.5 to 150.9) per 100,000 individuals, with Austria having the highest (282 per 100,000), while Italy showed the lowest rates (14.5 per 100,000). The authors found that a lower rate of absolute poverty, higher gross domestic product per capita, higher health care spending per capita, a higher proportion of foreign-born individuals in a population, and a large number of inpatient beds were associated with a higher incidence of IPH (Sheridan Rains et al., 2019). No evidence linking rates of IPH to differences in legislation was found (Salize and Dressing, 2004; Sheridan Rains et al., 2019), although studies evaluating the effect of legislation on IPH are needed (Bersani et al., 2020).

Despite the wide variation in IPH rates across countries (Salize and Dressing, 2004; Zinkler and Priebe, 2002), the clinical and socio-demographic characteristics of IPH patients are similar. Specifically, IPH is commonly associated with a diagnosis of psychosis (Cunningham, 2012; Ferracuti et al., 2021; Ng and Kelly, 2012; van der Post et al., 2012), the severity of psychiatric symptoms (Hustoft et al., 2013), male gender (Wheeler, Robinson and Robinson, 2005), low socioeconomic status (Webber and Huxley, 2004), and reduced insight (Kelly et al., 2004). The PROGRES-Acute project (Preti et al., 2009), in Italy, showed that patients with schizophrenia spectrum disorders accounted for more than half of IPH, whereas approximately one-fifth of the IPH patients was affected by bipolar disorder, and one-tenth by personality disorder. Depressive or anxiety disorders represented a very small percentage among IPH patients (Preti et al., 2009).

Three main criteria for IPH are applied in European countries: (a) mental illness and danger to others (Austria, Belgium, France, Germany, Luxemburg, and the Netherlands); (b) mental illness and danger to others or need for treatment (Denmark, Finland, Greece, Ireland, Portugal, and the United Kingdom); (c) mental illness and need for treatment (Italy, Spain, and Sweden) (Dressing and Salize, 2004) (see Figure 15.3).

Considerable inconsistencies among different legislative and procedural details for involuntary hospitalization have emerged across European Union Member States (Dressing and Salize, 2004; Kelly, 2019) indicating the need for cross-national harmonization of regulations. Despite the differences in the legal framework for involuntary hospitalization, the criteria for a valid informed consent/dissent to treatment are well acknowledged, and specific reliable clinical tools to measure such abilities exist (Appelbaum, 2007). However, studies investigating competence to consent to treatment in involuntarily hospitalized patients are scarce and lead to contrasting results (Appelbaum, Appelbaum and Grisso, 1998; Bellhouse et al., 2013; Bellhouse et al., 2013; Owen et al., 2009; Poythress, Cascardi and Ritterband, 1996). While Poythress et al. (1996) found no significant differences in capacity to consent to treatment between patients admitted voluntarily and involuntarily, Appelbaum et al. (1998) showed that involuntarily admitted subgroups scored worse on a scale measuring understanding of information. Cairns et al. (2005) found that 43.8% of all in-patients lacked capacity, and 9.5% of IPH patients had competence to consent to treatment. The presence of mania, psychosis, delusions, and poor insight have been associated with a higher risk of incapacity (Cairns et al., 2005; Mandarelli et al., 2018; Mandarelli et al., 2014; Owen et al., 2008). Owen and colleagues (2008) found that 60% (95% CI 55–65) among 338 patients hospitalized in three general adult acute psychiatric in-patient units lacked mental capacity

Mental illness and danger-criterion	Austria, Belgium, France, Germany, Luxembourg, The Netherlands
Mental illness and danger-criterion or Mental illness and need for treatment-criterion	Denmark, Finland, Greece, Ireland, United Kingdom, Portugal
Mental illness and need for treatment-criterion	Italy, Spain, Sweden

Figure 15.3 Criteria for involuntary hospitalization in European countries

to make treatment decisions. A systematic review by Curley and colleagues (2021) found that the prevalence of decision-making capacity among involuntary patients ranged from 7.7% to 42%, and among voluntary patients from 29% to 97.9%. Finally, Mandarelli et al. (2018) in a study assessing capacity to consent to treatment in 131 involuntarily hospitalized patients found that 22% showed high treatment decision-making capacity (DMC). Such patients presented an almost complete understanding and appreciation of their clinical condition, as well as of the risks and benefits of their treatment (or no treatment), an adequate capacity to reason about their therapy, and to express a choice (i.e., no hospitalization/treatment) in a clear and consistent way. This result led the authors to suggest that also in those countries where involuntarily commitment is based on the mental illness and need for treatment criterion there is always present a social dimension that refers not only to the principle of best interest for the patient but to a security problem for society.

Improving decisional capacity to consent to research

In order to maximize patients' mental capacities, and to avoid needlessly depriving them of their right to make decisions about their health care, some strategies have been suggested, such as:

a) Performing the evaluation in the patient's native language;
b) Identifying and correcting potentially treatable conditions, such as fever, sedation, dehydration, depression, and anxiety, that may impair capacity;
c) Optimizing the environment – for example, assessing patients affected by mild dementia early in the day to avoid sundowning or conducting consent discussions in quiet areas free from distractions; and
d) Enhancing the informed consent process to make the decisional task easier (Appelbaum, 2010).

In addition, several efforts have been made in developing educational interventions to enhance psychiatric and non-psychiatric patients' decisional capacity (Dunn and Jeste, 2001). A recent meta-analysis by Hostiuc and colleagues (2018) found that differences in decisional capacity between patients affected by schizophrenia and non-mentally-ill controls tend to decrease with the use of enhanced informed consent forms. Stable community patients affected by schizophrenia showed an improvement in their decisional capacity after one week of informed consent information training, although such improvement was not sustained one year later (Wang et al., 2016). Another study involving the administration of a brief educational intervention to a sample of patients affected by schizophrenia found that their performance was no longer significantly different from the healthy comparison group in any of the four dimensions of decisional capacity (Moser et al., 2006). A study employing multimedia disclosure and cognitive feedback to enhance decisional capacity among patients affected by AD and non-psychiatric comparison participants, found no significant effect of the enhanced consent procedure relative to routine consent (Palmer et al., 2018). Mittal and colleagues (2007) provided two enhanced consent procedures – a PowerPoint presentation and an enhanced printed consent form – to patients with AD or Mild Cognitive Impairment (MCI) and found an improvement in understanding in both conditions. However, this study led to dubious results because of the small sample size and the absence of a routine consent comparison condition. Finally, Rubright and colleagues (2010) observed that a memory and organizational aid added to a standard consent procedure improved capacity to consent to research in patients affected by AD. However, they used the performance of cognitively normal participants to calculate thresholds to examine whether the memory and organizational aid would improve AD participants' decisional capacity, without the decisional capacity judgment being confirmed by a psychiatrist with experience in competency assessment.

Mental capacity and competence to stand trial

Competence to stand trial represents one of the most common pretrial evaluations within the criminal domain of forensic psychiatry (Rogers and Johansson-Love, 2009) and comprises two underlying components: competence to assist counsel and decisional competence (Bonnie, 1992, 1993). One of the most acknowledged standards has been established by the United States Supreme Court's decision in *Dusky v United States* (1960). Specifically, the *Dusky*'s three prongs require the defendant to possess:

- A rational ability to consult one's own attorney;
- A factual understanding of the proceedings;
- A rational understanding of the proceedings.

A judgment of incompetence is generally associated with a diagnosis of psychotic disorder and active psychiatric symptoms such as delusions, hallucinations, conceptual disorganization, and unusual thoughts (Hoge, et al., 1997a; Hoge et al., 1997b; Viljoen, Zapf and Roesch, 2003).

A first generation of instruments to help forensic experts in the evaluation of competence to stand trial was introduced in the 1970s. However, they have limited data on their psychometric properties, a lack of normative data, and poor correspondence to the relevant legal standard (Rogers and Johansson-Love, 2009). In Table 15.3, a list of some of the most commonly and currently used tools to guide competence to stand trial assessment is presented.

Mental capacity and the notion of criminal responsibility

The insanity defense represents one of the most controversial and debated evaluations that forensic psychiatrists and psychologists perform. Despite differences between jurisdictions, in Western countries, the legal criteria for insanity often rely on the presence of cognitive and/or volitional impairment of the defendant at the time of the crime (Simon and Ahn-Redding, 2006).

In the Anglo-American systems the most acknowledged standards are the M'Naghten Rule (1843) and the Model Penal Code's test, also known as the American Law Institute (ALI) standard (American Law Institute, 1962). According to the M'Naghten Rule, which focuses on the cognitive component, a defendant is not found responsible if, due to a mental disorder, he did "not know the nature and quality of the act he was doing; or if he did know it, that he did not know what he was doing was wrong". The Model Penal Code, meanwhile, evaluates both the cognitive as well as the behavioral component, and states that:

Table 15.3 Selected instruments to assess decisional capacity to stand trial

Instrument	Decisional ability construct	Type	Dusky prong	Format
MacCAT- CA	Understanding	Hypothetical	Factual understanding	Clinical vignettes
	Reasoning	Hypothetical	Consult counsel	
	Appreciation	Case	Rational understanding	
ECST – R* (Rogers, Tillbrook, and Sewell, 2004)	Factual Understanding of the Courtroom Proceedings (FAC)	Case	Rational understanding	Clinical vignettes
	Rational Understanding of the Courtroom Proceedings (RAC)	Case	Consult counsel	
	Consult with Counsel (CWC)	Case		
CAST–MR (Everington and Luckasson, 1992)	Legal concepts	Case	Factual understanding	Semi-structured interview
	Understand case	Case	Factual understanding	
	Assist defense	Both	Consult counsel	

Note: MacCAT-CA: MacArthur Competence Assessment Tool for Criminal Adjudication; ECST – R: Evaluation of Competency to Stand Trial – Revised; CAST–MR: Competence Assessment for Standing Trial for Defendants with Mental Retardation.
* The ECST – R is the only measure to contain an assessment of symptom validity, or feigned incompetence, across four Atypical Presentation (ATP) scales.

a person is not responsible for criminal conduct if at the time of such conduct as a result of mental disease or defect he lacks substantial capacity either to appreciate the criminality (wrongfulness) of his conduct or to conform his conduct to the requirements of the law.

Offenders' criminal responsibility is based on their legal capacities, referring to their ability to act within the framework of the legal system. Depending on the jurisdiction, defendants' will be exculpated if, at the time of the crime, they were lacking only the capacity to fully acknowledge an act's illicit nature (cognitive prong – M'Naghten Rule) or also the capacity to self-determination according to this understanding (cognitive and volitional prong – ALI standard).

Several tools have been developed to structure and guide criminal responsibility evaluations (see Table 15.4), in order to improve their reliability and consistency. Disagreement among experts is in fact common, with a recent meta-analysis showing that forensic evaluators disagreed 25–35% of the time (Guarnera and Murrie, 2017). This is an issue that deserves to be addressed, considering the significant forensic and procedural implications of psychiatric evaluations, and a need for improved training and practice has been suggested (Gowensmith, Murrie and Boccaccini, 2013). Discrepancies between expert testimonies may stem from several factors, among which are:

Table 15.4 Selected instruments to assess criminal responsibility

Instrument	Domains of criminal responsibility	Cognitive/ volitional prong	Standard	Format
R-CRAS (Rogers, Dolmetsch and Cavanaugh, 1981)	Patient's reliability Organicity Psychopathology Cognitive control Behavioral control	C, V	ALI standard	30-item scale
MSE (Slobogin, Melton and Showalter, 1984)	Historical information Offense information Present Mental State Examination			Semi-structured interview (screening)
DIASS (Parmigiani et al., 2019)	Knowledge/ understanding Appreciating Reasoning Inhibitory control	C, V	ALI standard	Semi-structured interview
RSCRs (Cai et al., 2014)	Capacity of cognition Capacity of control	C, V	ALI standard	18-itemscale
CRS (Meyer et al., 2020)	Understanding Self-determination	C, V	ALI standard	Clinical vignettes

Note: R-CRAS: Rogers Criminal Responsibility Assessment Scales; MSE: Mental State at the Time of the Offense Screening Evaluation; DIASS: Defendant's Insanity Assessment Support Scale; RSCRs: Rating scale of criminal responsibility for mentally disordered offenders; CRS: Criminal Responsibility Scale.

1. The intrinsic limit of psychiatric diagnosis;
2. The different and non-standardized evaluation methodologies (Gowensmith et al., 2013; Kacperska et al., 2016);
3. The longitudinal variability of psychiatric symptoms, implicating that evaluations performed at different times can lead to different conclusions on the same case;
4. The absence of reliable biological markers available;
5. The relative scarcity of reliable and diagnostic tools to guide insanity assessments;
6. The paucity of research on insanity assessments which implies poor empirical support underlying such evaluations (Gowensmith et al., 2013);
7. The dialectic of the criminal trial, where different parties plead their case, which entails the possibility of different opinions, which the court or jury weighs.

However, caution is warranted in interpreting these findings (Guarnera and Murrie, 2017), since this analysis refers to those cases that went to trial. In some jurisdictions, when there is an agreement among experts, the cases may not go to trial.

Among the factors that have emerged in influencing forensic experts' decision-making are money, prestige, and the amount of public attention attracted by the case (Commons, Miller, and Gutheil, 2004). Regarding defendants' characteristics, a clinical judgment of not criminally responsible is commonly associated with a psychiatric history and with the presence of a psychotic disorder (Kois and Chauhan, 2018; Mandarelli, et al., 2019).

Several authors have proposed an incapacity-based approach to criminal responsibility (Matthews, 2004; Meynen, 2011, 2016; Parmigiani et al., 2017, 2019). Both concepts and assessment, in fact, have much in common, and the way in which incompetency is conceptualized and operationalized could serve as an example of how to conceive, and operationalize, insanity (Meynen, 2016). However, an adaptation and a contextualization regarding the specific situation of forensic assessments of criminal responsibility are needed, because of the following differences between these two types of evaluation:

1. The evaluation of criminal responsibility involves a retrospective assessment (the "state of mind at the time of the criminal act"), while the evaluation of competence to consent refers to a decision which has to be made at the moment or in the immediate future (Meynen, 2009).
2. Forensic assessments regard a criminal act and are carried out in a juridical environment, while informed consent acquisition is related to choosing about a treatment in a medical setting.
3. The purpose of the forensic evaluation is to ascertain that the subject can be held accountable, or responsible, for the act, while the medical evaluation focuses on the patient's autonomy regarding their decisions about treatment – autonomy and accountability being related, though not identical.
4. The insanity assessment refers to an act which is unlawful and could be punishable, while informed consent concerns a choice about a medical treatment, which is legal and admissible (Meynen, 2009, 2016).

Despite these limitations, these two models present the following similarities that must be acknowledged (see Figure 15.4):

1. Both evaluations involve a normative assessment by a health professional of a particular act/choice by an individual.
2. In both evaluations the decision-making process is performed in relation to the possible presence and influence of a mental disorder, or, more broadly, mental incapacity (Meynen, 2009).
3. In many jurisdictions, competency as well as responsibility are presumed: patients are considered competent and defendants are considered criminally accountable until proven otherwise (Meynen, 2016).
4. As the patient (to be considered competent to consent to treatment) must understand their diagnosis, treatment and risks and benefits, so the defendant (to be held responsible for the crime) must demonstrate their ability at the moment of the crime to have comprehended the situation, and any relevant information.
5. While the patient must possess the capacity to acknowledge their medical condition and likely consequences of treatment options, at the same time, the defendant must show to have acknowledged their options or alternative possibilities.
6. The patient must be capable of manipulating the disclosed information and make assumptions on possible everyday effects of treatments, and compare different treatment alternatives; similarly, the defendant should demonstrate to have processed information about their options and their possible consequences.

Mental capacity in forensic psychiatry

	Clinical	Forensic	Neuropsychological dimensions
Understanding	Diagnosis Therapy	Wrongfulness of the act: legal anc moral aspects of the act	Attention – Concentration Perception Language Memory – Learning
Appreciating	Diagnosis Therapy	The nature and possible options in the situations (e.g. in terms of threat, danger, risk)	Comparison Emotions Information processing (reality testing)
Reasoning	Consequential thinking Comparative thinking Generating consequences Logical coherence	Consequential thinking Comparative thinking Generating consequences Logical coherence	Motivations Executive functions: Abstract thinking Working memory Problem solving Cognitive flexibility
Expressing a choice/behavioral control	In a clear and consistent way	Ability to perform an action or to inhibit one's behavior	Motility Associative areas

Figure 15.4 Decisional capacity: clinical and forensic dimensions

7. As the patient must be able to make a choice about their treatment and express it in a clear and consistent way, the defendant must have possessed the capacity to perform or inhibit one's behavior (at least in those jurisdictions in which the insanity standard includes a control prong).

On the basis of this model, we developed an instrument, the Defendant's Insanity Assessment Support Scale (DIASS), which can be useful to support, structure, and guide the insanity assessment across different jurisdictions, in order to improve reliability and consistency of such evaluations (Parmigiani et al., 2019). It assesses four dimensions of offenders' mental capacity at the time of the crime: "Knowledge/understanding of the crime" (two items), "Appreciating the crime" (one item), "Reasoning" (three items), and "Control of voluntary motor activity" (two items). The first three dimensions refer to the "Epistemic component", while the fourth and one item of the first dimension refer to the "Control component".

At the end of the scale, there is a box referring to the final judgments on the Epistemic and Control components, which are scored on a three-point scale (intact, partially compromised, and compromised). The tool represents a step towards some standardization that will hopefully foster the exchange of ideas and research findings across jurisdictions and disciplines. This would represent a valuable development for an area that is of considerable medical, legal, and societal importance, but that regrettably continues to be understudied.

Financial capacity

Financial capacity has been defined as the "ability to independently manage one's financial affairs in a manner that is consistent with personal values and that promotes self-interest" (Marson et al., 2000). It refers to a broad range of conceptual, pragmatic, and judgmental abilities important to independent functioning of older adults (Marson et al., 2000).

Although financial capacity evaluations can be performed in all clinical and age groups, patients affected by dementia, depression, anxiety, psychotic disorders, and hypomania are considered at higher risk of incapacity (Pinsker et al., 2010; Spar, Hankin and Stodden, 1995), together with the elderly population due to the associated cognitive decline (Sousa et al., 2014). Total or partial cognitive decline can have serious consequences both in patients and in their families. In addition to the risk of making decisions that may endanger assets needed in the future for their long-term care or intended for their family members in their will, there is also the risk of being scammed (Marson et al., 2000).

The theoretical model developed by Marson and colleagues (Griffith et al., 2003; Marson et al., 2000) involves several domains of financial capacity – basic monetary skills, financial conceptual knowledge, cash transactions, checkbook management, bank statement management, financial judgment, bill payment, knowledge of personal assets/estate, and investment decision-making.

Apart from the impact of any medical condition or mental disorders, forensic evaluators need to consider past values and preferences (Sousa et al., 2014), cognition and emotional functioning (Pinsker et al., 2010), personality, and financial, social, and cultural aspects (Pinsker et al., 2010). Finally, the patient's premorbid functioning regarding financial issues must also be taken into consideration in order to detect whether the actual level of functioning represents a change regarding previous functioning.

Among the existing tools aimed at assessing financial capacity (Giannouli, Stamovlasis and Tsolaki, 2018; Marroni et al., 2017) the most widely used are the Financial Capacity Instrument (FCI) (Griffith et al., 2003; Marson et al., 2000) and the Financial Capacity Instrument Short-Form (FCI-SF) (Gerstenecker et al., 2016b) (for a review of assessing instruments see Ghesquiere, McAfee and Burnett, 2019). In Table 15.5, a list of some of the most commonly and currently used tools to guide financial capacity evaluation is presented.

The presence of impaired financial capacity is associated with a higher risk of financial exploitation and is often the basis for legal determinations of guardianship (which to a lesser extent may be requested also for impaired capacity to consent to treatment). A guardian can represent the person for some acts or for a whole range of possibilities. In psychiatric assessments it should be specified which type of act the person can carry out independently and which, on the other hand, needs supervision or replacement (McSwiggan, Meares and Porter, 2016). Great attention must be paid to understanding people's residual abilities and their potential strengths, in an attempt to provide advice on measures that are as less restrictive as possible of the person's personal freedom. In particular, the study of the cognitive functioning of the person can provide relevant information for the purpose of determining the possible degree of impairment. In this case, it may be necessary to carry out a neuropsychological evaluation, in addition to the usual screening tests, such as the Mini-Mental State Examination (MMSE). In fact, correlations between decisional capacity and global cognitive functioning are mixed, as it has been shown that a score of 19 or less on MMSE robustly predicts incapacity, but a higher score does not guarantee capacity (Karlawish, et al., 2005). Standardized tools for measuring financial and economic capacity can help correlate cognitive measures with the person's actual economic management capacity. Most guardianship measures are subject to temporal limitations and periodic reassessments, which allows the measures to be calibrated also on the trend of disorders, as in the case of psychiatric pathologies subject to change over time.

Table 15.5 Selected instruments to assess financial capacity

Instrument	Domains of financial activity	Intended recipients	Administration time	Format
FACT (Black et al., 2007)	Memory Reading/writing comprehension Calculating/attention Daily financial tasks General financial knowledge Understanding assets Financial insight Financial confidence Rational beliefs about money	Geriatric psychiatry patients	30 minutes	46 items in 9 domains
FCI	Basic monetary skills Financial conceptual knowledge Cash transactions Checkbook management Bank statement management Financial judgment	Patients with dementia	30–40 minutes in older controls with no cognitive impairment; 40–50 minutes in patients with dementia	14 tasks in 6 domains
FCI-SF	Mental calculation Financial conceptual knowledge Single checkbook/register Complex checkbook/register Bank statement management	Any older adults	15 minutes	37 items in 4 domains
SCIFC (Marson et al., 2009)	Basic monetary skills Financial conceptual knowledge Cash transactions Checkbook management Bank statement management Financial judgment Bill payment Knowledge of personal assets and estate	Older adults with cognitive impairment	Not stated	8 core items in 8 domains

(Continued)

Table 15.5 (Continued)

Instrument	Domains of financial activity	Intended recipients	Administration time	Format
FCAI (Kershaw and Webber, 2008)	Everyday financial abilities Financial judgment Estate management Cognitive functioning related to financial tasks Debt management Support resources	Adults with cognitive impairment	Not stated	41 items (questions and tasks) in 6 subscales
LFDRS (Lichtenberg et al., 2015)	Financial situational awareness Psychological vulnerability Current financial transaction Undue influence and financial exploitation	Adults aged 60 and over	15–40 minutes	61 items in 4 domains

Note: FACT: Financial Assessment and Capacity Test; FCI: Financial Capacity Instrument; FCI-SF: Financial Capacity Instrument Short-Form; SCIFC: Semi-Structured Clinical Interview for Financial Capacity; FCAI: Financial Competence Assessment Inventory; LFDRS: Lichtenberg Financial Decision Rating Scale

Other decisional tasks

In civil law, competence takes on particular aspects in relation to the type of issue the person has to deal with. It is widely accepted in forensic psychiatry that a person can be competent for one legal aspect and incompetent for another. Obviously, there is a wide variability in relation to the type of legislation in force and therefore the legal standards to which reference is made must first be known.

Generally speaking, it can be said that competence in civil law tends to refer to the actual ability of the person to appropriately evaluate their interest in relation to a specific type of legal act (Ciccone and Jones, 2017). The person must be able to adequately understand the situation in which they finds themselves, the consequences of their decision and consequent actions, and the rational management of available information and the communication of a choice (Fornari, 2018). In this perspective, the model of informed consent to treatment has widely transposable characteristics for acts of economic value, although not entirely transferrable.

The assessment of competence in the civil field is therefore substantially different from that carried out in the criminal field where a severe misunderstanding of the nature of the criminal act or an inability to behave in a manner compliant with the law is required to evaluate incompetence in the person.

A condition for assessing competence in the civil field is represented by the capacity to contract. In these cases, the person should demonstrate that they understand the terms of the contract, whether or not they can make a profit, and the duration of the contract. As in the case of testamentary problems, the contents of the document can provide relevant information. It is clear that a person suffering from a severely depressive condition or with a delusion of grandeur can underestimate or overestimate their belongings or the consequences of the contract. Persons with intellectual disabilities and major neurocognitive disorders may find it difficult to be accurate and critical in their decision making. The way in which the document is drafted must also be considered because it can provide data on the development of thought processes, on their logical coherence, or on the presence of pathological contents. If the grammatical and syntactic level of the document differs from the previous level of linguistic expression, the data can acquire relevance.

Particular problems often arise, e.g., for the ability to dispose of property by will, and are relatively frequent (Schulman et al., 2021). The deed is strictly personal and cannot be drawn up by a representative. The testamentary form changes according to the jurisdictions and as a general rule the person who draws it is not required to communicate its dispositions to anyone. It can be written in any language and must indicate the date and place. Testamentary capacity or the capacity to make a valid will is composed of several abilities: the ability to understand the nature of the act, the nature and extent of assets, an ability to comprehend and appreciate the claims of potential beneficiaries, understanding the impact of the distribution, and being free of a disorder of mind that influences the distribution (Sousa et al., 2014). The will can be rendered void for formal defects, for example if the date is missing, or if it is possible to prove that the person did not understand the nature of the act he was carrying out or the consequences thereof. People making wills should also have sufficient knowledge of their properties, relatives, and relations with relatives. In a testamentary evaluation, for example, a determining cognitive variable is the integrity of the person's autobiographical memory. Also in this case, it is not possible to follow a linear correlative criterion between illness and inability to dispose of property by will (Voskou et al., 2018). More than on the graveness and severity of the illness considered in and of itself, the emphasis must be placed on the influence that the illness had in preventing the person from adequately and congruously evaluating his own acts and consequently not being free to self-determinate (Kennedy, 2012).

Competence problems sometimes arise regarding the ability to consent to marriage (Glezer and Devido, 2017), especially if the person has a moderate or severe intellectual disability, a major neurocognitive disorder or severe mental illness. This issue has become more relevant for a large number of cases of arranged marriages between people with mental capacity problems and people trying to obtain a residence permit. It is clear that the competence to marry presents a high threshold of incapacity given the immediately accessible nature of the act.

The dementia epidemic of recent decades is raising the issue of competence to divorce more frequently (Filaković et al, 2011). People with cognitive impairment may not fully appreciate the consequences deriving from a divorce and the reasons should be adequately explicated also in light of the evolutionary condition of the pathological picture and what the person believes will happen once the divorce has been completed.

Conclusions

There are many different types of competence, with varying criteria depending on the relevant area of functioning. Regarding competence associated with criminal responsibility, legal systems generally require the presence of a psychotic condition and the crime to be an expression of the psychotic dimension (impairment of the cognitive and/or the volitional component).

Conversely, the evaluation of the capacity to stand trial depends on the interpretation of the accused's possibility of contextualizing themselves with respect to the legal procedure. It is one thing to have a general knowledge of the criminal proceedings (knowing that you have a lawyer, of being accused) and another thing to be able to choose the defense strategy to adopt, what type of defense to choose and which information to value and which to minimize. Depending on the definition, we will get different results. Central to the concept of capacity to consent to treatment (and with slight variation to research) the core feature is represented by the ability to choose what is best for one's self, after having been adequately informed. For the civil law dimension, competence is generally linked to the concept of financial capacity, and regards the evaluation of to what extent the subject is able to act in his best interests, which implies the involvement of the emotional dimension. Generally, the affective-social dimension has a great impact on competence, with the only exception of capacity to consent to treatment or research, where it plays a minor role compared to the cognitive functioning dimension.

In the application of legal instruments that can limit personal freedom, a balanced approach would require the finding of an equilibrium between personal care and collective interest.

References

American Law Institute, Model Penal code, Proposed Official Draft, (1962), American Psychological Association. *Standards for educational and psychological tests.* Washington, DC: American Psychological Association, 1974.

Appelbaum, B. C., Appelbaum, P. S. and Grisso, T. (1998), 'Competence to consent to voluntary psychiatric hospitalization: A test of a standard proposed by APA', *Psychiatric Services*, 49(9), pp. 1193–1196. doi: 10.1176/ps.49.9.1193

Appelbaum, P. S. (2006), 'Decisional capacity of patients with schizophrenia to consent to research: Taking stock', *Schizophrenia Bulletin*, 32(1), pp. 22–25. doi: 10.1093/schbul/sbi063

Appelbaum, P. S. (2007), 'Clinical practice: Assessment of patients' competence to consent to treatment', *New England Journal of Medicine*, 357(18), pp. 1834–1840. doi: 10.1056/NEJMcp074045

Appelbaum, P. S. (2010), 'Consent in impaired populations', *Current Neurology and Neuroscience Reports*, 10(5), pp. 367–373. doi: 10.1007/s11910-010-0123-5

Appelbaum, P. S. and Grisso, T. (2001) *MacArthur Competence Assessment Tool for Clinical Research (MacCAT-CR)*. Sarasota: Professional Resource Press.

Bellhouse, J. et al. (2013), 'Capacity-based mental health legislation and its impact on clinical practice: 1) admission to hospital', *Journal of Mental Health Law*, 1, pp. 9–23.

Bellhouse, J. et al. (2013), 'Capacity-based mental health legislation and its impact on clinical practice: 1) treatment in hospital', *Journal of Mental Health Law*, 1, pp. 24–37.

Bersani, F. S. et al. (2020), 'Legislative differences may influence the characteristics of involuntary hospitalised psychiatric patients', *Medicine, Science and the Law*, 60(3), pp. 235–236. doi: 10.1177/0025802420918487

Black, E. L. et al. (2007) 'A financial assessment & capacity test (FACT) for a psychogeriatric population: Development and concurrent validity', *Research Insights of the Regional Mental Health Care*, 4(5), pp. 1–23.

Bonnie, R. J. (1992), 'The competence of criminal defendants: A theoretical reformulation', *Behavioral Sciences and the Law*, 10(3), pp. 291–316. doi: 10.1002/bsl.2370100303

Bonnie, R. J. (1993), 'The competence of criminal defendants: Beyond Dusky and Drope', *University of Miami Law Review*, 47, pp. 539–601.

Cai, W. et al. (2014), 'The reliability and validity of the rating scale of criminal responsibility for mentally disordered offenders', *Forensic Science International*, 236, pp. 146–150. doi: 10.1016/j.forsciint.2013.12.018

Cairns, R. et al. (2005), 'Prevalence and predictors of mental incapacity in psychiatric in-patients', *British Journal of Psychiatry*, 187, pp. 379–385. doi: 10.1192/bjp.187.4.379

Carpenter, W. T. et al. (2000), 'Decisional capacity for informed consent in schizophrenia research', *Archives of General Psychiatry*, 57(6), pp. 533–538. doi: 10.1001/archpsyc.57.6.533

Ciccone, R. and Jones, J. C. W. (2017), 'Civil competencies', in Rosner, R. and Scott, C. L. (Eds.), *Principles and Practice of Forensic Psychiatry*. 3th edn. Boca Raton: Taylor & Francis, pp. 337–345.

Commons, M. L., Miller, P. M. and Gutheil, T. G. (2004), 'Expert witness perceptions of bias in experts', *Journal of the American Academy of Psychiatry and the Law*, 32(1), pp. 70–75.

Cunningham, G. (2012), 'Analysis of episodes of involuntary re-admission in Ireland (2007–2010)', *Irish Journal of Psychological Medicine*, 29(3), pp. 180–184. doi: 10.1017/S0790966700017225

Curley, A. et al. (2019a), 'Age, psychiatry admission status and linear mental capacity for treatment decisions', *International Journal of Law and Psychiatry*, 66, p. 101469. doi: 10.1016/j.ijlp.2019.101469

Curley, A. et al. (2019b), 'Categorical mental capacity for treatment decisions among psychiatry inpatients in Ireland', *International Journal of Law and Psychiatry*, 64, pp. 53–59. doi: 10.1016/j.ijlp.2019.02.001

Curley, A., Watson, C. and Kelly, B. D. (2021), 'Capacity to consent to treatment in psychiatry inpatients - A systematic review', *International Journal of Psychiatry in Clinical Practice*, 23, pp. 1–13. doi: 10.1080/13651501.2021.2017461

Dressing, H. and Salize, H. J. (2004), 'Compulsory admission of mentally ill patients in European Union member states', *Social Psychiatry and Psychiatric Epidemiology*, 39(10), pp. 797–803. doi: 10.1007/s00127-004-0814-9

Dunn, L. B. and Jeste, D. V. (2001), 'Enhancing informed consent for research and treatment', *Neuropsychopharmacology*, 24(6), pp. 595–607. doi: 10.1016/S0893-133X(00)00218-9

Dunn, L. B. et al. (2006), 'Assessment of therapeutic misconception in older schizophrenia patients with a brief instrument', *American Journal of Psychiatry*, 163(3), pp. 500–506. doi: 10.1176/appi.ajp.163.3.500

'Dusky v United States', [1960] 362 402, (US).

Etchells, E. et al. (1999), 'Assessment of patient capacity to consent to treatment', *Journal of General Internal Medicine*, 14(1), pp. 27–34. doi: 10.1046/j.1525-1497.1999.00277.x

Everington, C. and Luckasson, R. (1992) *Manual for Competence Assessment for Standing Trial for Defendants with Mental Retardation: CAST-MR*. Worthington: IDS Publishing.

Ferracuti, S. et al. (2021), 'Involuntary psychiatric hospitalization in Italy: Critical issues in the application of the provisions of law', *International Review of Psychiatry*, 33(1–2), pp. 119–125. doi: 10.1080/09540261.2020.1772581

Filaković, P. et al. (2011), 'Dementia and legal competency', *Collegium Antropologicum*, 35(2), pp. 463–469.

Fornari, U. (2018) *Trattato di Psichiatria Forense*. Torino: Wolters Kluwer.

Gerstenecker, A. et al. (2016a), 'Enhancing medical decision-making evaluations: Introduction of normative data for the capacity to consent to treatment instrument', *Assessment*, 23(2), pp. 232–239. doi: 10.1177/1073191115599053

Gerstenecker, A. et al. (2016b), 'Age and education corrected older adult normative data for a short form version of the financial capacity instrument', *Psychological Assessment*, 28(6), pp. 737–749. doi: 10.1037/pas0000159

Ghesquiere, A. R., McAfee, C. and Burnett, J. (2019), 'Measures of financial capacity: A review', *Gerontologist*, 59(2), pp. e109–e129. doi: 10.1093/geront/gnx045

Giannouli, V., Stamovlasis, D. and Tsolaki, M. (2018), 'Exploring the role of cognitive factors in a new instrument for elders' financial capacity assessment', *Journal of Alzheimer's Disease*, 62(4), pp. 1579–1594. doi: 10.3233/JAD-170812

Glezer, A. and Devido, J. J. (2017), 'Evaluation of the capacity to marry', *Journal of the American Academy of Psychiatry and the Law*, 45(3), pp. 292–297.

Gowensmith, W. N., Murrie, D. C. and Boccaccini, M. T. (2013), 'How reliable are forensic evaluations of legal sanity?', *Law and Human Behavior*, 37(2), pp. 98–106. doi: 10.1037/lhb0000001

Griffith, H. R. et al. (2003), 'Impaired financial abilities in mild cognitive impairment a direct assessment approach', *Neurology*, 60(3), pp. 449–457. doi: 10.1212/wnl.60.3.449

Grisso, T. and Appelbaum, P. S. (1998) *Assessing Competence to Consent to Treatment: A Guide for Physicians and Other Health Professionals*. New York: Oxford University Press.

Guarnera, L. A. and Murrie, D. C. (2017), 'Field reliability of competency and sanity opinions: A systematic review and metaanalysis', *Psychological Assessment*, 29(6), pp. 795–818. doi: 10.1037/pas0000388

Hoge, S. K. et al. (1997a), 'The MacArthur adjudicative competence study: Development and validation of a research instrument', *Law and Human Behavior*, 21(2), pp. 141–179. doi: 10.1023/a:1024826312495

Hoge, S. K. et al. (1997b), 'The MacArthur adjudicative competence study: Diagnosis, psychopathology, and competence-related abilities', *Behavioral Sciences and the Law*, 15(3), pp. 329–345. doi: 10.1002/(sici)1099-0798(199722/06)15:3<329::aid-bsl276>3.0.co;2-z

Hostiuc, S. et al. (2018), 'Testing decision-making competency of schizophrenia participants in clinical trials: A meta-analysis and meta-regression', *BMC Psychiatry*, 18(1), p. 2. doi: 10.1186/s12888-017-1580-z

Hustoft, K. et al. (2013), 'Predictors of involuntary hospitalizations to acute psychiatry', *International Journal of Law and Psychiatry*, 36(2), pp. 136–143. doi: 10.1016/j.ijlp.2013.01.006

Howe, V. et al. (2005), 'Competence to give informed consent in acute psychosis is associated with symptoms rather than diagnosis', *Schizophrenia Research*, 77(2–3), pp. 211–214. doi: 10.1016/j.schres.2005.03.005

Jeste, D. V., Depp, C. A. and Palmer, B. W. (2006), 'Magnitude of impairment in decisional capacity in people with schizophrenia compared to normal subjects: An overview', *Schizophrenia Bulletin*, 32(1), pp. 121–128. doi: 10.1093/schbul/sbj001

Jeste, D. V. et al. (2007), 'A new brief instrument for assessing decisional capacity for clinical research', *Archives of General Psychiatry*, 64(8), pp. 966–974. doi: 10.1001/archpsyc.64.8.966

Kacperska, I. et al. (2016), 'Reliability of repeated forensic evaluations of legal sanity', *International Journal of Law and Psychiatry*, 44, pp. 24–29. doi: 10.1016/j.ijlp.2015.08.028

Karlawish, J. H. T. et al. (2005), 'The ability of persons with Alzheimer disease (AD) to make a decision about taking an AD treatment', *Neurology*, 64(9), pp. 1514–1519. doi: 10.1212/01.WNL.0000160000.01742.9D

Kelly, B. D. (2019), 'Variations in involuntary hospitalisation across countries', *Lancet Psychiatry*, 6(5), pp. 361–362. doi: 10.1016/S2215-0366(19)30095-1

Kelly, B. D. et al. (2004), 'Clinical predictors of admission status in first episode schizophrenia', *European Psychiatry*, 19(2), pp. 67–71. doi: 10.1016/j.eurpsy.2003.07.009

Kennedy, K. M. (2012), 'Testamentary capacity: A practical guide to assessment of ability to make a valid will', *Journal of Forensic and Legal Medicine*, 19(4), pp. 191–195. doi: 10.1016/j.jflm.2011.12.029

Kershaw, M. M. and Webber, L. S. (2008), 'Assessment of financial competence', *Psychiatry, Psychology and Law*, 15(1), pp. 40–55. doi: 10.1080/13218710701873965

Kois, L. E. and Chauhan, P. (2018), 'Criminal responsibility: Meta-analysis and study space', *Behavioral Sciences and the Law*, 36(3), pp. 276–302. doi: 10.1002/bsl.2343

Koren, D. et al. (2005), 'The neuropsychological basis of competence to consent in first-episode schizophrenia: A pilot metacognitive study', *Biological Psychiatry*, 57(6), pp. 609–616. doi: 10.1016/j.biopsych.2004.11.029

Kovnick, J. A. et al. (2003), 'Competence to consent to research among long-stay inpatients with chronic schizophrenia', *Psychiatric Services*, 54(9), pp. 1247–1252. doi: 10.1176/appi.ps.54.9.1247

Lichtenberg, P. A. et al. (2015), 'A person-centered approach to financial capacity assessment: Preliminary development of a new rating scale', *Clinical Gerontologist*, 38(1), pp. 49–67. doi: 10.1080/07317115.2014.970318

M'Naghten's Case, 10 Cl. & Fin. 200, 8 Eng. Rep. 718 (H.L. 1843)

Mandarelli, G. et al. (2012), 'The relationship between executive functions and capacity to consent to treatment in acute psychiatric hospitalisation', *Journal of Empirical Research on Human Research Ethics*, 7(5), pp. 63–70. doi: 10.1525/jer.2012.7.5.63

Mandarelli, G. et al. (2014), 'Mental capacity in patients involuntarily or voluntarily receiving psychiatric treatment for an acute mental disorder', *Journal of Forensic Sciences*, 59(4), pp. 1002–1007. doi: 10.1111/1556-4029.12420

Mandarelli, G. et al. (2018), 'Treatment decision-making capacity in non-consensual psychiatric treatment: A multicentre study', *Epidemiology and Psychiatric Sciences*, 27(5), pp. 492–499. doi: 10.1017/S2045796017000063

Mandarelli, G. et al. (2019), 'Decisional capacity to consent to treatment and anaesthesia in patients over the age of 60 undergoing major orthopaedic surgery', *Medicine, Science and the Law*, 59(4), pp. 247–254. doi: 10.1177/0025802419865854

Mandarelli, G. et al. (2019), 'The admission experience survey Italian version (I-AES): A factor analytic study on a sample of 156 acute psychiatric in-patients', *International Journal of Law and Psychiatry*, 62, pp. 111–116. doi: 10.1016/j.ijlp.2018.12.006

Mandarelli, G. et al. (2019), 'The factors associated with forensic psychiatrists' decisions in criminal responsibility and social dangerousness evaluations', *International Journal of Law and Psychiatry*, 66, p. 101503. doi: 10.1016/j.ijlp.2019.101503

Marroni, S. P. et al. (2017), 'Instruments for evaluating financial management capacity among the elderly: An integrative literature review', *Revista Brasileira de Geriatria e Gerontologia*, 20(4), pp. 582–593. doi: 10.1590/1981-22562017020.160207

Marson, D. C. et al. (2009), 'Clinical interview assessment of financial capacity in older adults with mild cognitive impairment and Alzheimer's disease', *Journal of the American Geriatrics Society*, 57(5), pp. 806–814. doi: 10.1111/j.1532-5415.2009.02202.x

Marson, D. C. et al. (1997), 'Consistency of physician judgments of capacity to consent in mild Alzheimer's disease', *Journal of the American Geriatrics Society*, 45(4), pp. 453–457. doi: 10.1111/j.1532-5415.1997.tb05170.x

Marson, D. C. et al. (2000), 'Assessing financial capacity in patients with Alzheimer disease: A conceptual model and prototype instrument', *Archives of Neurology*, 57(6), pp. 877–884. doi: 10.1001/archneur.57.6.877

Matthews, S. (2004), 'Failed agency and the insanity defence', *International Journal of Law and Psychiatry*, 27(5), pp. 413–424. doi: 10.1016/j.ijlp.2004.06.006

McSwiggan, S., Meares, S. and Porter, M. (2016), 'Decision-making capacity evaluation in adult guardianship: A systematic review', *International Psychogeriatrics*, 28(3), pp. 373–384. doi: 10.1017/S1041610215001490

Meyer, L. F. et al. (2020), 'Criminal responsibility scale: Development and validation of a psychometric tool structured in clinical vignettes for criminal responsibility assessments in Brazil', *Frontiers in Psychiatry*, 11, p. 579243. doi: 10.3389/fpsyt.2020.579243

Meynen, G. (2009), 'Exploring the similarities and differences between medical assessments of competence and criminal responsibility', *Medicine, Health Care, and Philosophy*, 12(4), pp. 443–451. doi: 10.1007/s11019-009-9211-1

Meynen, G. (2011), 'Autonomy, criminal responsibility, and competence', *Journal of the American Academy of Psychiatry and the Law*, 39(2), pp. 231–236.

Meynen, G. (2016) *Legal Insanity: Explorations in Psychiatry, Law, and Ethics*. New York: Springer.

Mittal, D. et al. (2007), 'Comparison of two enhanced consent procedures for patients with mild Alzheimer disease or mild cognitive impairment', *American Journal of Geriatric Psychiatry*, 15(2), pp. 163–167. doi: 10.1097/JGP.0b013e31802dd379

Moser, D. J. et al. (2006), 'Using a brief intervention to improve decisional capacity in schizophrenia research', *Schizophrenia Bullettin*, 32(1), pp. 116–120. doi: 10.1093/schbul/sbi066

Moynihan, G. et al. (2018), 'An evaluation of functional mental capacity in forensic mental health practice: The Dundrum capacity ladders validation study', *BMC Psychiatry*, 18(1), p. 78. doi: 10.1186/s12888-018-1658-2

Ng, X. T. and Kelly, B. D. (2012), 'Voluntary and involuntary care: Three-year study of demographic and diagnostic admission statistics at an inner-city adult psychiatry unit', *International Journal of Law and Psychiatry*, 35(4), pp. 317–326. doi: 10.1016/j.ijlp.2012.04.008

Okai, D. et al. (2007), 'Mental capacity in psychiatric patients: Systematic review', *British Journal of Psychiatry*, 191, pp. 291–297. doi: 10.1192/bjp.bp.106.035162

Owen, G. S. et al. (2008), 'Mental capacity, diagnosis and insight in psychiatric in-patients: A cross-sectional study', *Psychological Medicine*, 39(8), pp. 1389–1398. doi: 10.1017/S0033291708004637

Owen, G. S. et al. (2009), 'Mental capacity and psychiatric in-patients: Implications for the new mental health law in England and Wales', *British Journal of Psychiatry*, 195(3), pp. 257–263. doi: 10.1192/bjp.bp.108.059782

Palmer, B. W. (2006), 'Informed consent for schizophrenia research: What is an investigator (or IRB) to do?', *Behavioral Sciences and the Law*, 24(4), pp. 447–452. doi: 10.1002/bsl.695

Palmer, B. W. et al. (2018), 'Multimedia aided consent for Alzheimer's disease research', *Clinical Gerontologist*, 41(1), pp. 20–32. doi: 10.1080/07317115.2017.1373177

Parmigiani, G. et al. (2016), 'Decisional capacity to consent to clinical research involving placebo in psychiatric patients', *Journal of Forensic Sciences*, 61(2), pp. 388–393. doi: 10.1111/1556-4029.13000

Parmigiani, G. et al. (2017), 'Free will, neuroscience, and choice: Towards a decisional capacity model for insanity defense evaluations', *Rivista di Psichiatria*, 52(1), pp. 9–15. doi: 10.1708/2631.27049

Parmigiani, G. et al. (2019), 'Translating clinical findings to the legal norm: The defendant's insanity assessment support scale (DIASS)', *Translational Psychiatry*, 9(1), p. 278. doi: 10.1038/s41398-019-0628-x

Parmigiani, G. et al. (2021), 'Decisional capacity to consent to treatment and research in patients affected by mild cognitive impairment: A systematic review and meta-analysis', *International Psychogeriatrics*, 15, pp. 1–14. doi: 10.1017/S1041610220004056

Parmigiani, G. et al. (2022), 'Validation of a new instrument to guide and support insanity evaluations: The defendant's insanity assessment support scale (DIASS)', *Translational Psychiatry*, 12(1), p. 115. doi: 10.1038/s41398-022-01871-8

Pinsker, D. M. et al. (2010), 'Financial capacity in older adults: A review of clinical assessment approaches and considerations', *Clinical Gerontologist*, 33(4), pp. 332–346. doi: 10.1080/07317115.2010.502107

Poythress, N. G., Cascardi, M. and Ritterband, L. (1996), 'Capacity to consent to voluntary hospitalization: Searching for a satisfactory Zinermon screen', *Bullettin of the American Academy of Psychiatry and the Law*, 24(4), pp. 439–452. doi: 10.1016/B978-0-08-006821-3.50006-4

Preti, A. et al. (2009), 'Patterns of admission to acute psychiatric in-patient facilities: A national survey in Italy', *Psychological Medicine*, 39(3), pp. 485–496. doi: 10.1017/S0033291708003607

Raymont, V. et al. (2004), 'Prevalence of mental incapacity in medical inpatients and associated risk factors: Cross-sectional study', *The Lancet*, 364(9443), pp. 1421–1427. doi: 10.1016/s0140-6736(04)17224-3

Rogers, R., Dolmetsch, R. and Cavanaugh, J. L. (1981), 'An empirical approach to insanity evaluations', *Journal of Clinical Psychology*, 37(3), pp. 683–687. doi: 10.1002/1097-4679(198107)37:3<683::aid-jclp2270370343>3.0.co;2-f

Rogers, R. and Johansson-Love, J. (2009), 'Evaluating competency to stand trial with evidence-based practice', *Journal of the American Academy of Psychiatry and the Law*, 37(4), pp. 450–460.

Rogers, R., Tillbrook, C. E. and Sewell, K. W. (2004) *Evaluation of Competency to Stand Trial-Revised (ECST-R) and Professional Manual*. Odessa, FL: Psychological Assessment Resources.

Rubright, J. et al. (2010), 'A memory and organizational aid improves Alzheimer disease research consent capacity: Results of a randomized, controlled trial', *American Journal of Geriatric Psychiatry*, 18(12), pp. 1124–1132. doi: 10.1097/JGP.0b013e3181dd1c3b

Salize, H. J. and Dressing, H. (2004), 'Epidemiology of involuntary placement of mentally ill people across the European Union', *British Journal of Psychiatry*, 184, pp. 163–168. doi: 10.1192/bjp.184.2.163

Sheridan Rains, L. et al. (2019), 'Variations in patterns of involuntary hospitalisation and in legal frameworks: An international comparative study', *The Lancet Psychiatry*, 6(5), pp. 403–417. doi: 10.1016/s2215-0366(19)30090-2

Shulman, K. et al. (2021), 'The role of the medical expert in the retrospective assessment of testamentary capacity', *Canadian Journal of Psychiatry. Revue Canadienne de Psychiatrie*, 66(3), pp. 255–261. doi: 10.1177/0706743720915007

Simon, R. J. and Ahn-Redding, H. (2006), *The Insanity Defense, the World Over*. Plymouth: Rowman & Littlefield.

Slobogin, C., Melton, G. B. and Showalter, C. R. (1984), 'The feasibility of a brief evaluation of mental state at the time of the offense', *Law and Human Behavior*, 8(3/4), pp. 305–320. doi: 10.1007/BF01044698

Sousa, L. B. et al. (2014), 'Financial and testamentary capacity evaluations: Procedures and assessment instruments underneath a functional approach', *International Psychogeriatrics*, 26(2), pp. 217–228. doi: 10.1017/S1041610213001828

Spar, J. E., Hankin, M. and Stodden, A. B. (1995), 'Assessing mental capacity and susceptibility to undue influence', *Behavioral Sciences and the Law*, 13(3), pp. 391–403. doi: 10.1002/bsl.2370130307

Svindseth, M. F., Dahl, A. A. and Hatling, T. (2007), 'Patients' experience of humiliation in the admission process to acute psychiatric wards', *Nordic Journal of Psychiatry*, 61(1), pp. 47–53. doi: 10.1080/08039480601129382

van der Post, L. et al. (2012), 'Factors associated with higher risks of emergency compulsory admission for immigrants: A report from the ASAP study', *International Journal of Social Psychiatry*, 58(4), pp. 374–380. doi: 10.1177/0020764011399970

Viljoen, J. L., Zapf, P. A. and Roesch, R. (2003), 'Diagnosis, current symptomatology, and the ability to stand trial', *Journal of Forensic Psychology Practice*, 3(4), pp. 23–37. doi: 10.1300/J158v03n04_02

Voskou, P. et al. (2018), 'Testamentary capacity assessment: Legal, medical, and neuropsychological issues', *Journal of Geriatric Psychiatry and Neurology*, 31(1), pp. 3–12. doi: 10.1177/0891988717746508

Wang, X. et al. (2016), 'Longitudinal informed consent competency in stable community patients with schizophrenia: A one-week training and one-year follow-up study', *Schizophrenia Research*, 170(1), pp. 162–167. doi: 10.1016/j.schres.2015.11.019

Webber, M. and Huxley, P. (2004), 'Social exclusion and risk of emergency compulsory admission: A case-control study', *Social Psychiatry and Psychiatric Epidemiology*, 39(12), pp. 1000–1009. doi: 10.1007/s00127-004-0836-3

Wheeler, A., Robinson, E. and Robinson, G. (2005), 'Admissions to acute psychiatric inpatient services in Auckland, New Zealand: A demographic and diagnostic review', *New Zeland Medical Journal*, 118(1226), p. U1752.

Zinkler, M. and Priebe, S. (2002), 'Detention of the mentally ill in Europe–A review', *Acta Psychiatrica Scandinavica*, 106(1), pp. 3–8. doi: 10.1034/j.1600-0447.2002.02268.x

16
CAPTURING MENTAL HEALTH ISSUES IN INTERNATIONAL CRIMINAL LAW AND JUSTICE

The input of the International Criminal Court

Caroline Fournet[1]

Introduction

The birth of contemporary international criminal law may be traced back to the aftermath of the Second World War and the establishment of the International Military Tribunal in Nuremberg (1945) and of the International Military Tribunal for the Far East in Tokyo (1946), set up to prosecute the individuals who bore the greatest responsibilities in the waging of the war and in the perpetration of atrocities during it. This initial legal and judicial reaction was regrettably followed by decades of apathy and it was only in the 1990s that international criminal law took a new and decisive turn with the creation of the International Criminal Tribunal for the former Yugoslavia (ICTY, 1993) and of the International Criminal Tribunal for Rwanda (ICTR, 1994), both entrusted with the mandate of prosecuting the individuals responsible for international crimes committed in the course of these designated conflicts. The adoption of the Statute of the International Criminal Court (ICC) in 1998 and its entry into force four years later (2002) confirmed this shift. The ICC is the first permanent international criminal court established specifically to prosecute individuals for international crimes, namely, genocide, crimes against humanity, war crimes and aggression. While it is subjected to strict jurisdictional rules, it still has a global aim and its Prosecutor can investigate on the territory of any of its States Parties.

Being a fairly young legal corpus, international criminal law is admittedly under constant evolution, one that perhaps mirrors the evolution of human rights concerns. An apt illustration of this evolution may be found in the increasing attention granted to mental health issues in international criminal law and justice, be it in the text of the law itself, in case law or in scholarly works (for earlier works, see Radosavljevic, 2013). The importance gradually

---

1 I would like to thank Brendan Kelly and Mary Donnelly for their support and extremely constructive feedback on earlier drafts. I would also like to extend my gratitude to Adina-Loredana Nistor (Faculty of Law, Rijksuniversiteit Groningen, Netherlands) for very useful suggestions and thought-provoking comments. Any remaining errors are my own.

gained by mental health issues in this context is such that broader academic scholarship on mental health law now needs to include international criminal law and case law: this is a crucial step in prompting a cross-fertilisation between the two legal fields and in generating a transfer of knowledge that would benefit them both. The growing interest for mental health issues in international criminal law and justice has already contributed to further capture the essence of international crimes as planned and organised crimes rather than as uncontrollable outbursts of violence, to understand the specific impact of atrocities on the mental health of the victims and witnesses, and to reflect on the mental capacity of the accused while rebutting the idea that such crimes can only be perpetrated by individuals who lack such capacity. A more systematic dialogue between international criminal law and mental health law would undoubtedly strengthen this path.

It is against this background that this chapter focuses specifically on the law applicable at the ICC – namely, on the Rome Statute of the International Criminal Court (ICC Statute), on the Elements of Crimes, on the Rules of Procedure and Evidence (RPE) and on the Regulations of the Court – to critically assess whether, and if so how, mental health issues are integrated within the text of contemporary international criminal law. This chapter also explores the case law of the Court to expose how mental health issues can emerge in the course of a trial, potentially affecting victims, witnesses and defendants, and to review how the judges have addressed them.

To conduct this research, all the ICC judgments – trial judgments and appeal judgments – were read in their entirety. As a safety net, the following keywords were also searched for: mental, health, expert(s), doctor(s), scientific, medicine, medical, clinical, psychology/ist(s)/ical, psychiatry/ist(s)/ic, trauma. The aim of the keyword search was to mitigate risks of bias and ensure that the findings presented in this chapter are entirely driven by how the Court has interpreted and/or dealt with mental health issues when they emerged before it. The analysis of this case law, in the light of the ICC Statute, the Elements of Crimes, the RPE and the Regulations of the Court, shows that there can be some discrepancies between the theory and the practice.

The following two sections will respectively show that the definitions of certain international crimes indirectly encompass mental health issues via the integration of mental harm as a legal ingredient of these crimes and that the psychological impact of atrocities – and notably of sexual violence – on the victims is recognised in the text of the law and increasingly acknowledged by the Court. When approaching mental health issues, judges do not deviate from the text of the law but appear to be exercising a degree of caution. The last two sections will focus on this judicial prudence, particularly discernible in the assessment of the testimonies of traumatised witnesses and of the mental capacity of the defendant, which will thus be explored in turn.

The textual incorporation of mental health issues in the definition of international crimes: mental harm as an explicit legal element

Mental harm, pain or suffering is explicitly mentioned in the definitions of some international crimes, whether war crimes, crimes against humanity or genocide.

Under the Rome Statute of the ICC, mental pain or suffering can be an element of torture, both as a crime against humanity (article 7(1)(f)) and as a war crime (article 8(2)(c)(i)). Torture as a crime against humanity is defined under article 7(2)(e) as 'the intentional infliction of severe pain or suffering, whether physical or *mental*, upon a person in the custody or under the control of the accused' (emphasis added). Likewise, torture as a war crime requires that '[t]he perpetrator inflicted severe physical or *mental pain or suffering* upon one or more persons' (Elements of Crimes; emphasis added). The mental aspect of the pain or suffering in the context of torture was acknowledged by the Court and, in its *Ongwen* judgment (2021), the Trial Chamber recalled that: '[t]he pain and suffering may be either physical or mental. The consequences of torture do not have to be visible, nor must the injury be permanent' (para. 2700).

Also prohibited as both a crime against humanity (article 7(1)(g)) and as a war crime (article 8(2)(e)(vi)) under the ICC Statute, the crime of rape includes within its legal elements an invasion that:

> was committed by force, or by threat of force or coercion, such as that caused by fear of violence, duress, detention, *psychological oppression* or abuse of power, against such person or another person, or by taking advantage of a coercive environment, or the invasion was committed against a person *incapable of giving genuine consent.*
> *(Elements of Crimes; emphases added)*

As noted by the *Ntaganda* Trial Chamber:

> The Elements of Crimes clearly seek to punish any act of penetration where committed under threat of force or coercion, such as that caused by the threat of violence, duress, detention, *psychological pressure* or abuse of power or, more generally, any act of penetration taking advantage of a coercive environment. The establishment of at least one of the coercive circumstances or conditions set out in the second element is therefore sufficient alone for penetration to amount to rape within the meaning of Articles 7(1)(g) and 8(2)(e)(vi) of the Statute.
> (Prosecutor v Ntaganda, *para. 934; emphasis added.*
> See also Prosecutor v Katanga, *2014, para. 965*)

Psychological pressure – and thus the mental state of the victim – at the time of the commission of the crime therefore explicitly constitutes a legal ingredient of the crime. This pressure element has been noted on several occasions by the different Trial Chambers of the ICC with respect to crimes of sexual violence, and notably the crime of sexual slavery, both as a crime against humanity and as a war crime, for which 'psychological control' and 'other forms of mental coercion' are among the factors to be taken into account for the determination of the exercise of a power of ownership, central to this particular crime (*Prosecutor v Ntaganda*, 2019, para. 952; *Prosecutor v Katanga*, 2014, para. 976).

In the case law, mental harm as a component of international crimes seems to be inextricably linked to crimes of sexual violence, as illustrated below with the analysis of two distinct crimes whose definitions expressly refer to mental harm: the genocidal act of causing serious bodily or mental harm to members of the group and other inhumane acts as crimes against humanity.

The genocidal act of 'causing serious bodily or mental harm to members of the group'

The definition of genocide exhaustively enumerates a number of acts constitutive of the crime, among which the act of 'causing serious bodily or mental harm to members of the group' (article II, Genocide Convention). While the ICC has yet to rule on the crime of genocide, the

ICTY and the ICTR both had opportunities to define this genocidal act. They found that '[t]he gravity of the suffering must be assessed on a case by case basis and with due regard for the particular circumstances' (*Prosecutor v Krstić*, 2001, para. 486) while 'using a common sense approach' (*Prosecutor v Kayishema and Ruzindana*, 1999, para. 108). Within this context, they have construed this phrase 'to mean harm that seriously injures the health, causes disfigurement or causes any serious injury to the external, internal organs or senses' (*Prosecutor v Kayishema and Ruzindana*, 1999, para. 109; *Prosecutor v Krstić*, 2001, para. 483; *Prosecutor v Semanza*, 2003, paras 320–22; *Prosecutor v Stakić*, 2003, para. 516; *Prosecutor v Ntagerura, Bagambiki, Imanishimwe*, 2004, para. 664; *Prosecutor v Seromba*, 2006, para. 317). They have also specified that 'serious harm need not cause permanent and irremediable harm' (*Prosecutor v Akayesu*, 1998, para. 502; *Prosecutor v Kayishema and Ruzindana*, 1999, para. 108; *Prosecutor v Rutaganda*, 1999, para. 51; *Prosecutor v Musema*, 2000, para. 156; *Prosecutor v Semanza*, 2003, paras 320–21), 'but it must involve harm that goes beyond temporary unhappiness, embarrassment or humiliation. It must be harm that results in a grave and long-term disadvantage to a person's ability to lead a normal and constructive life' (*Prosecutor v Krstić*, 2001, para. 486; *Prosecutor v Kajelijeli*, 2003, para. 738). In its *Kajelijeli* judgment (2003), the ICTR further held that mental harm involves 'more than minor or temporary impairment of mental faculties such as the infliction of strong fear or terror, intimidation or threat' (para. 815).

According to Meiches:

> In making these statements, the tribunals intended to both distinguish mental harm from everyday psychological stress and to include the possibility that acts of mental harm could extend beyond those explicitly specified by the court. However, these distinctions only raise further questions about the standards of evidence and interpretation used by international courts to understand and assess serious mental harm. For instance, the tribunal's articulation of mental harm as 'grave and long term disadvantage to a person's ability to lead a normal and constructive life' begs the question of what standards of health, development and mortality the court applies, what mechanisms it uses to judge the potential consequences that follow from a specific act of violence, and what it envisions as a 'normal life'.
>
> (Meiches, 2022, 29–30)

The Tribunals have not addressed the questions posed by Meiches and have generally delineated the scope of the genocidal act of causing serious bodily or mental harm by means of illustration. They have thus found that such harm would be constituted by acts of sexual violence and rape, by mutilations and interrogations combined with beatings and/or threats of death (*Prosecutor v Akayesu*, 1998, paras 706–7; *Prosecutor v Kayishema and Ruzindana*, 1999, paras 108–10; *Prosecutor v. Rutaganda*, 1999, para. 51; *Prosecutor v Musema*, 2000, para. 156; *Prosecutor v Semanza*, 2003, paras 320–21) as well as by acts of bodily or mental torture, inhumane or degrading treatment and persecution (*Prosecutor v Akayesu*, 1998, para. 504; *Prosecutor v Rutaganda*, 1999, para. 51).

Within the case law of the ICTR, emphasis has been put on the mental harm inflicted by acts of sexual violence. In its very first judgment in the *Akayesu* case the ICTR found that:

> rape and sexual violence certainly constitute infliction of serious bodily and mental harm on the victims and are even, according to the Chamber, one of the worst ways of inflicting harm on the victim as he or she suffers *both bodily and mental harm*. ... These

rapes resulted in physical and *psychological destruction* of Tutsi women, their families and their communities. Sexual violence was an integral part of the process of destruction, specifically targeting Tutsi women and specifically contributing to their destruction and to the destruction of the Tutsi group as a whole.

(Prosecutor v Akayesu, *1998, para. 731, emphases added*)

Reiterating the impact of the mental harm generated by these crimes, the Tribunal concluded that '[s]exual violence was a step in the process of destruction of the Tutsi group – destruction of the spirit, of the will to live, and of life itself' (*Prosecutor v Akayesu*, 1998, para. 732). This impact is however not confined to genocidal contexts and, as detailed below, the judicial interpretation of the crime against humanity of 'other inhumane acts' – which now encompasses injury to mental health – also expressly includes crimes of sexual violence.

The express reference to mental health in the definition of 'other inhumane acts' as crimes against humanity

Article 5(i) of the ICTY Statute, Article 3(i) of the ICTR Statute, Article 2(i) of the Statute of the Special Court for Sierra Leone (SCSL) and Article 5 of the Law on the Extraordinary Chambers in the Courts of Cambodia (ECCC) all feature 'other inhumane acts' in their list of crimes against humanity. Adding to these existing prohibitions, article 7(1)(k) of the ICC Statute went a step further to specifically proscribe 'other inhumane acts of a similar character intentionally causing great suffering, or serious injury to body or to *mental* or physical health' (emphasis added). The mental dimension of this crime is further reiterated in the Elements of Crimes, which – with respect to article 7(1)(k) – specify:

The crime of other inhumane acts is committed, either by act or omission, when the following two material elements are fulfilled:

1. The perpetrator inflicted great suffering, or serious injury to body or to mental or physical health, by means of an inhumane act.
2. Such act was of a character similar to any other act referred to in article 7, paragraph 1, of the Statute.

In practice, this means that mental harm – if it results from a behaviour that otherwise fulfils the definitional elements of crimes against humanity, namely, that is 'committed as part of a widespread or systematic attack directed against any civilian population, with knowledge of the attack' (article 7(1)) – could be prosecuted as an 'other inhumane act' as a crime against humanity. As noted in the *Ongwen* judgment (2021), 'Article 7(1)(k) of the Statute was included in recognition of the impossibility of exhaustively enumerating every inhumane act which could constitute a crime' (para. 2745) and it allows the Chamber to 'enter a conviction … if the perpetrator inflicts great suffering, or serious injury to body or to *mental* or physical health, by means of a course of conduct which, despite comprising also acts falling under one or more of the enumerated crimes, is, in its entirety, not identical, but is nonetheless "similar" in character in terms of nature and gravity, to those enumerated crimes' (para. 2747; emphasis added). Here also proceeding by means of examples, the Trial Chamber recalled:

International case-law suggests that serious beatings, subjection to deplorable conditions of detention and requiring persons to witness the beatings or killings of others can constitute other inhumane acts. Other international jurisdictions have also recognised forced marriage as an 'other inhumane act' falling under crimes against humanity.
(para. 2744)

The Trial Chamber took this opportunity to further elaborate on the crime of forced marriage – which is otherwise textually absent from the definition of crimes against humanity – and in particular on its impact on the mental health of the victims:

> Marriage creates a status based on a consensual and contractual relationship ... The central element, and underlying act of forced marriage is the imposition of this status on the victim, i.e. the imposition, regardless of the will of the victim, of duties that are associated with marriage – including in terms of exclusivity of the (forced) conjugal union imposed on the victim – as well as the consequent social stigma. Such a state, beyond its illegality, has also social, ethical and even religious effects which have a *serious impact on the victim's physical and psychological well-being*. The victim may see themselves as being bonded or united to another person despite the lack of consent. Additionally, a given social group may see the victim as being a 'legitimate' spouse. To the extent forced marriage results in the birth of children, this creates *even more complex emotional and psychological effects on the victim and their children* beyond the obvious physical effects of pregnancy and child-bearing.
> *(para. 2747; emphasis added)*

This finding is worth noting as it admittedly provides for an apt illustration of how other inhumane acts can cover acts that exert psychological pressure on the victims, inflict severe mental suffering and result in 'mental trauma' (para. 2749). It is thus a welcome step towards further recognition of the impact of atrocities on the mental health of the victims.

A gradual consideration of the psychological impact of crimes of sexual violence on the victims

The recognition of the long-lasting – if not permanent – mental harm caused to the victims by the perpetration of international crimes is a gradual process which – as for now – seems to focus extensively on the psychological impact of crimes of sexual violence, as reflected in the Rules of Procedure and Evidence, in Prosecutors' policy papers as well as in the case law.

Already at the International Criminal Tribunals, the Rules of Procedure and Evidence granted special attention to victims and witnesses of crimes of sexual violence. At the ICTY, Rule 34 (A) (ii) specified that the Victims and Witnesses Section was set up 'to provide counselling and support for them, in particular in cases of rape and sexual assault' while, at the ICTR, Rule 34(b) required the Victims and Witnesses Unit to adopt '[a] gender sensitive approach to victims and witnesses protective and support measures'. At the ICC, the guidance is admittedly more specific and under article 68 of the ICC Statute:

> 1. The Court shall take appropriate measures to protect the safety, physical *and psychological well-being*, dignity and privacy of victims and witnesses. In so doing, the Court shall have regard to all relevant factors, including age, gender as defined in article 7,

paragraph 3, and health, and the nature of the crime, in particular, but not limited to, where the crime involves *sexual or gender violence* or violence against children. The Prosecutor shall take such measures particularly during the investigation and prosecution of such crimes. ...

2. As an exception to the principle of public hearings provided for in article 67, the Chambers of the Court may, to protect victims and witnesses or an accused, conduct any part of the proceedings in camera or allow the presentation of evidence by electronic or other special means. In particular, such measures shall be implemented in the case of a *victim of sexual violence* or a child who is a victim or a witness, unless otherwise ordered by the Court, having regard to all the circumstances, particularly the views of the victim or witness. (emphases added)

Further instructions are given by the Rules of Procedure and Evidence and Rule 86 lays out the general principle that '[a] Chamber in making any direction or order, and other organs of the Court in performing their functions under the Statute or the Rules, shall take into account the needs of all victims and witnesses in accordance with Article 68, in particular, children, elderly persons, persons with disabilities and *victims of sexual or gender violence*' (emphasis added). Rule 88 (5) further requires a Chamber to be 'vigilant in controlling the manner of questioning a witness or victim so as to avoid any harassment or intimidation, paying *particular attention to attacks on victims of crimes of sexual violence*' (emphasis added).

Beyond the text of the law, the impact of crimes of sexual violence on the mental health of the victims has also been recognised by the different Offices of the Prosecutor, so much so that it can constitute key evidence in proving the crimes. In its *Best Practices Manual for the Investigation and Prosecution of Sexual Violence Crimes in Situations of Armed Conflict – Lessons from the International Criminal Tribunal for Rwanda* (2014), the ICTR Office of the Prosecutor specified that '[t]he presentation of evidence from expert witnesses and medical professionals with expertise ... in the dynamics of sexual assault and the impact of sexual assault victimization can be another important source of evidence' (60, para. 189). At the ICTY, the Prosecutors have also 'found that expert evidence can be useful for sentencing by demonstrating the impact of sexual violence crimes on victims' (Brammertz and Jarvis, 152).

In its *Policy Paper on Sexual and Gender-Based Crimes* (2014), the ICC's Office of the Prosecutor expressly stated that it 'will consult with experts, and, where appropriate, propose their testimony on different aspects, such as the socio-political, *psychological*, and medical aspects, of sexual and gender-based crimes' (36–37, para. 97; emphasis added).

These prosecutorial policies have had repercussions in practice: expert testimonies relating to the impact of crimes of sexual violence on the mental health of the victims of crimes of sexual violence have been heard in court and are cited in judgments. For instance, during the trial of Bemba Gombo, the ICC Trial Chamber heard the testimony of a forensic psychiatric who presented his expert report on sexual violence based on the medical examinations of 371 victims (*Prosecutor v Bemba Gombo*, 2011, 16, lines 1–10). As he explained in court, his report assessed 'four types of impact' of the physical violence (23, lines 16–25), including the 'psychological impact, i.e., what the person felt at the time and in the wake of the rape' and 'the psychiatric impact, in other words, disorders – psychiatric disorders – that were generated by the rape in the victim' (ibid.). He also stressed the particular long-lasting psychological consequences on girls:

> The younger victims, that is to say between six and 15 years of age ... did suffer psychological consequences that were much more serious than the adults because, you

see, these are children, people who are in the process of becoming who they are. The person has not yet found his or her identity, so when a person is subject to such an event this affects the person's growth. So these particular victims suffered much more serious psychological repercussions than the adults did.

(48, lines 1–22)

In its judgment (2016), the Trial Chamber explicitly relied on this report and testimony and referred on several occasions to the psychological and psychiatric consequences of the crimes on the victims. Among the psychological consequences, the Trial Chamber listed fear (note 1761), including fear of armed soldiers (para. 464) and fear of rejection by their families and communities (note 1761), anxiety (note 1761; para. 567), anger (note 1761), aggression (note 1761), guilt (note 1761; para. 567), isolation (note 1761), embarrassment and shame (note 1761), feelings of humiliation (para. 567), feeling of 'no longer [being] treated as a human being and [being] called the "Banyamulengué wife"' (para. 551), loss of confidence (note 1761) and washing rituals (note 1761). Among the psychiatric consequences, the Trial Chamber listed post-traumatic stress disorder (note 1761; para. 567), reactive depression (note 1761; paras 464 and 472), nightmares (para. 510), melancholia, neuroses, addictive behaviour and psychosomatic disorders (note 1761).

This was not an isolated instance and in its *Ongwen* judgment (2021), the ICC Trial Chamber also expressly acknowledged the 'severe physical *and mental* pain' suffered by the victims of sexual and physical violence (para. 221; emphasis added; see also paras 2309 and 3073). In so doing, it explicitly relied on the expert report of Professor Daryn Reicherter,

clinical professor for psychiatry and behavioural sciences at Stanford University School of Medicine, United States of America. He testified about a report he elaborated together with Ryan Matlow and the Human Rights in Trauma Mental Health Laboratory at Stanford University on mental health outcomes of rape and other forms of sexual violence, forced marriage and forced pregnancy. His testimony offered a detailed account of the methodology and terminology adopted by the report and its outcomes. Professor Reicherter's testimony was comprehensive, structured, clear and specific. He offered in particular information on the *psychological impact of rape and other forms of sexual violence on men and women* in the cultural context of the charged crimes.

(para. 600, emphasis added)

This increasing judicial recognition of – and emphasis on – the mental health repercussions of crimes of sexual violence on victims is obviously to be welcomed, encouraged and strengthened as a first step towards a more general acknowledgement of the psychological impact on victims of all international crimes and atrocities; a path that is starting to emerge with the attention given to victims and witnesses who come to testify at the Court and the consideration of their potential trauma.

The theoretical facilitation of the testimony of traumatised victims and witnesses v. the judicial caution due to 'the vagaries of human perception and recollection'

Rule 88 of the ICC's Rules of Procedure and Evidence contains the general principle that

a Chamber may, taking into account the views of the victim or witness, order special measures such as, but not limited to, *measures to facilitate the testimony of a trauma-*

tized victim or witness, a child, an elderly person or a victim of sexual violence (emphasis added).

A Chamber may thus

> hold a hearing on a motion or a request [for special measures], if necessary *in camera* or *ex parte*, to determine whether to order any such special measure, including but not limited to an order that a counsel, a legal representative, a psychologist or a family member be permitted to attend during the testimony of the victim or the witness.
> *(Rule 88(2); see e.g.* Prosecutor v Ntaganda, *2021, note 141)*

More generally, these facilitating measures may also include the admissibility of the testimony of a witness who suffers mental impairment due to trauma and psychological distress. Rule 66(2) indeed explicitly allows

> a person whose judgement has been impaired and who, in the opinion of the Chamber, does not understand the nature of a solemn undertaking (...) to testify without this solemn undertaking if the Chamber considers that the person is able to describe matters of which he or she has knowledge and that the person understands the meaning of the duty to speak the truth.

While the impact of trauma on testimonies falls outside the scope of this contribution (see Marschner, 2016; Smith, 2021; Schot, 2022), what is worth noting here is that several Rules clearly establish the duty for the Court to 'control the mode of questioning of such witnesses and to be cognizant of the vulnerabilities of the witnesses who appear before it' (Rohan, 2010, 542), while respecting 'the concurrent obligation to protect the accused's right to a fair trial' (ibid.). When assessing the impact of trauma on testimony, the Trial Chambers of the International Criminal Court have expressly followed the ICTY's approach according to which 'there is "no recognised rule of evidence that traumatic circumstances necessarily render a witness's evidence unreliable"' (*Prosecutor v Bemba Gombo*, 2016, para. 241) and 'witnesses who suffered trauma may have had particular difficulty in providing a coherent, complete, and logical account' (*Prosecutor v Lubanga Dyilo*, 2012, para. 103; *Prosecutor v Katanga*, 2014, para. 83; *Prosecutor v Bemba Gombo*, 2016, para. 230; *Prosecutor v Ntaganda*, 2019, paras 79 and 230). This approach does not, however, mean that a Chamber will not exercise a degree of caution in assessing the reliability of testimonies of traumatised witnesses providing identification evidence 'due to "the vagaries of human perception and recollection"', in particular, where identification is made in 'turbulent and traumatising circumstances' (*Prosecutor v Lubanga Dyilo*, 2014, para. 239; *Prosecutor v Bemba Gombo*, 2016, para. 241; *Prosecutor v Ntaganda*, 2019, para. 71).

While victims of sexual violence have been qualified as 'particularly vulnerable witnesses' (*Prosecutor v Katanga*, 2014, para. 204), trauma is evidently not confined to one category of crimes. Perhaps prompted by the wording of Rule 88 which specifically refers to children, the particular trauma of child soldiers has been expressly acknowledged in several instances. Articles 8(2)(b)(xxvi) and 8(2)(e)(vii) of the ICC Statute mirror article 4(3)(c) of Additional Protocol II and article 38 (2) and (3) of the Convention on the Rights of the Child in their prohibition of the recruitment and use of children under the age of 15 in armed conflicts, whether international or non-international in character. In its *Lubanga Dyilo* judgment (2012), the Trial Chamber referred to these instruments to recall that:

> The principal objective underlying these prohibitions historically is to protect children under the age of 15 from the risks that are associated with armed conflict, and first and foremost they are directed at securing their physical and *psychological well-being*. This includes not only protection from violence and fatal or non-fatal injuries during fighting, but also the *potentially serious trauma* that can accompany recruitment (including separating children from their families, interrupting or disrupting their schooling and exposing them to an environment of violence and fear).
>
> *(para. 605; emphases added)*

When reviewing the 'conditions of use of child soldiers', the Trial Chamber considered testimonial evidence according to which girls who had been abducted had been sexually abused, making note of the fact that the 'psychological and physical state of some of these young girls was catastrophic' (para. 890).

To reach its verdict in the *Lubanga Dyilo* case, the Trial Chamber 'called a psychologist who gave expert testimony on the psychological impact of a child having been a soldier and the effect of trauma on memory' (para. 105). In its judgment, it took into account 'the psychological impact of the events that have been described in evidence, and the trauma the children called by the prosecution are likely to have suffered' (para. 479) and accepted 'that some or all of them may have been exposed to violence in the context of war, and this may have had an effect on their testimony' (para. 479). The Chamber also explained that it:

> made appropriate allowance for any instances of imprecision, implausibility or inconsistency, bearing in mind the overall context of the case and the circumstances of the individual witnesses. ... Memories fade, and witnesses who were children at the time of the events, or who suffered trauma, may have had particular difficulty in providing a coherent, complete and logical account.
>
> *(para. 103; see also* Prosecutor v Ngudjolo Chui, *2012, para. 49;* Prosecutor v Ntaganda, *2019, paras 79 and 197, notes 1196 and 1360)*

Despite this 'appropriate allowance', the Chamber in this case ultimately found that 'the inconsistencies or other problems with their evidence has led to a finding that they are unreliable as regards the matters that are relevant to the charges in this case' (para. 479). While the initial approach not to exclude imprecise, implausible or inconsistent evidence given by traumatised witnesses seems sensible, practice shows that the Trial Chambers tend to err on the side of caution and to adopt a rather strict approach to issues of mental impairment due to trauma. As further developed in the next section, this judicial strictness also seems to apply to concerns as to the mental capacity of the defendant at the time of the commission of the criminal acts.

A strict approach to grounds for excluding criminal responsibility related to the mental health of the defendant

In international criminal law, concerns as to mental health do not solely relate to victims or witnesses. As a matter of principle, and to guarantee fairness of proceedings, the defendant must be fit to stand trial, both physically and mentally, so as to understand the proceedings that are initiated against him or her. Thus, in cases of voluntary admissions of guilt, article

65(1)(a) of the ICC Statute specifies that the Trial Chamber 'shall determine whether the accused understands the nature and consequences of the admission of guilt'. Put differently, the defendant must be mentally competent at the time of trial. The mental capacity of the defendant at the time of the commission of the crimes may also be assessed where a defence of mental disease or defect or a defence of intoxication – which, if constituted, could exclude criminal responsibility – is raised before the Court.

The defence of mental disease or defect

The Rome Statute marks 'the first codification of this defence in international law' (Cryer et al., 2019, 383) and under article 31(1)(a):

> a person shall not be criminally responsible if, at the time of that person's conduct:
>
> (a) The person suffers from a mental disease or defect that destroys that person's capacity to appreciate the unlawfulness or nature of his or her conduct, or capacity to control his or her conduct to conform to the requirements of law.

This defence thus encompasses three scenarios: 'when a person is unable to understand the nature of his or her conduct'; 'is incapable of understanding the unlawfulness of his or her conduct'; or 'understands the nature and wrongfulness of the conduct, but is unable, due to mental illness, to stop from acting as he or she did' (Cryer et al., 2019, 383). Yet, the formulation adopted in article 31(1)(a) 'is problematic' (Stahn, 2019, 149; see also Xavier, 2016, 802) as it explicitly refers to the person's (in)capacity 'to control his or her conduct to conform to the requirements of law' and thus overlooks the fact that 'atrocity crimes are often conformist rather than deviant' (ibid.). This misunderstanding aside, it would be erroneous to interpret this multiplicity of situations as indicating a wide approach to this defence: to the contrary, by requiring destruction – rather than mere impairment – of the person's capacity, article 31(1)(a) sets a high standard, 'albeit one which is consistent with the way most domestic jurisdictions deal with the matter' (Cryer et al., 2019, 384). Short of complete destruction of the person's capacity, this defence plea will be rejected. Further, while the Rules of Procedure and Evidence do envisage diminished mental capacity, this plea will only be considered in mitigation of punishment if it is substantial (Rule 145(2)(a)(i); see Eser, 2016, 1140).

If validly invoked, however, a plea of mental disease or defect will lead to an acquittal (Schabas, 2010, 485). While 'article 31(1)(a) fails to provide for a special verdict in the eventuality of a person being acquitted on the basis of mental incapacity' (Cryer et al., 2019, 384), Regulation of the Court 103(6) provides that:

> Arrangements shall be made by the Registrar for the detention of mentally ill persons and for those who suffer from serious psychiatric conditions. By order of the Chamber, a detained person who is determined to be mentally ill or who suffers from a serious psychiatric condition may be transferred to a specialised institution for appropriate treatment.

As mentioned above, this defence 'concerns the mental state of the accused at the time of commission of trial, and not at the time of the trial itself' (Schabas, 2010, 484; see *Prosecutor v Ongwen*, 2021, para. 2452) and there is 'no requirement that insanity is permanent. It is sufficient that the person's insanity was destroyed at the time of the impugned conduct' (Cryer et al., 2019, 383; see *Prosecutor v Ongwen*, 2021, para. 2453). Yet, for this defence to be successfully raised, it must be demonstrated 'that a person must be "one hundred per cent insane when he committed the acts, otherwise he will be regarded as mentally sane"' (Janssen, 2004, 85 in Stahn, 2019, 149); an '"all or nothing requirement" [which] poses particular difficulties in relation to child soldiers who may suffer from brainwashing or indoctrination at an early age' (Stahn, 2019, 149), as admittedly aptly illustrated during the trial of Dominic Ongwen. Stahn explains:

> The indoctrination may alter the perception of what is normal in relation to a reasonable adolescent or impede the ability to question choices. For instance, indoctrination may prevent the ability of a child soldier to develop an adequate moral standard.
>
> *(Stahn, 2019, 149)*

Dominic Ongwen, himself a former child soldier, was found guilty by Trial Chamber IX of 61 counts of war crimes and crimes against humanity (2021). This conviction was upheld by the Appeals Chamber in December 2022. From the outset, his Defence team contended that Ongwen suffered from an impairment of his mental capacity both at the time of the trial and at the time of the commissions of the alleged acts.

With respect to the defendant's mental capacity at the time of the trial, the Defence argued that 'Dominic Ongwen did not understand the charges against him at the time of his plea' (para. 75) and that the Trial Chamber had 'discriminated against Mr Ongwen' by considering him 'as if he were not a defendant with mental disabilities' (para. 107). The Trial Chamber strongly rebutted these allegations, considering them 'to be entirely untenable' (para. 109), and stressed that:

> in all its decisions, the Chamber assessed the specific situation of Dominic Ongwen, including his health, and in particular his mental health. Throughout the proceedings the Chamber has ensured that the accused received all the medical attention and care necessary. In December 2016, while rejecting a request by the Defence to order a medical examination in order to assess whether the accused is fit to stand trial, the Chamber ordered an examination 'making a diagnosis as to any mental condition or disorder that [the accused] may suffer'.
>
> *(para. 109)*

The Trial Chamber recalled the conclusions of this examination, which found that:

> while the accused suffered from various mental illnesses, 'he is oriented in time, oriented vis-à-vis his environment and himself. He has a good attention span and maintains his concentration after hours of interviewing.' Concerning his treatment by the responsible sections of the Court, the examiner stated that '[t]he current intervention strategy by the Detention Centre is more than adequate'.
>
> *(para. 110)*

With respect to the mental capacity of the defendant at the time of the commission of the crimes, the Defence invoked article 31(1)(a) of the Statute to raise mental disease or defect as a ground for excluding criminal responsibility (para. 2448), thus prompting the Trial Chamber to assess the validity of this plea in this case; an assessment which was guided by the testimonies of five mental health experts. While the Chamber recalled that it was '*exclusively competent*' to make [a judicial finding under article 31(1)(a)], including on the question of the presence of a mental disease or defect' (para. 2456; emphasis added), Dr Catherine Abbo (P-0445), Professor Gillian Mezey (P-0446), Professor Roland Weierstall-Pust (P-0447), Dr Dickens Akena (D-0041) and Professor Emilio Ovuga (D-0042) submitted reports and testified before it, thus assisting it in its determination of Ongwen's mental capacity (para. 593). In its judgment, the Trial Chamber dedicated a specific section to 'its analysis of the evidence provided by the experts, including as concerns the reliability of their reports and conclusions' (para. 593; see also paras 2456 and 2458–580). This assessment calls for a series of remarks.

In its judgment the Trial Chamber ultimately decided to rule out the Defence experts' reports. The Defence had relied on the conclusions of Dr Akena and Professor Ovuga to contend that Ongwen suffered from 'severe depressive illness, post-traumatic stress disorder ("PTSD") and dissociative disorder (including depersonalization and multiple identity disorder) as well as severe suicidal ideation and high risk of committing suicide', and from 'dissociative amnesia and symptoms of obsessive compulsive disorder' (para. 2450). The Trial Chamber however found that these expert reports were unreliable: as it explained, '[a] number of issues, in particular as concerns the methodology employed, affect the reliability of the evidence provided by Professor Ovuga and Dr Akena, to the extent that the Chamber cannot rely on it' (para. 2527).

First, the Trial Chamber ruled that the blurring of the roles of the two experts, both as treating physicians and forensic experts, 'negatively affect[ed] the reliability of the[ir] reports' (para. 2531). Second, the Trial Chamber considered 'that major doubts exist as to the validity of the methods employed by Professor Ovuga and Dr Akena' (para. 2535). Third, the Chamber found that 'there are unexplained contradictions in the evidence of Professor Ovuga and Dr Akena between the various statements and observations made, or between such statements and observations and the conclusions finally drawn' (para. 2536). Fourth, the Trial Chamber criticised the fact that 'Professor Ovuga and Dr Akena, in their work for the purposes of this trial, failed to take into account other sources of information about Dominic Ongwen which were readily available to them', deeming it 'an unjustifiable and fundamental failure that in itself invalidates the[ir] conclusions' (para. 2545). Fifth, the Chamber was 'not satisfied by the explanations provided by Professor Ovuga and Dr Akena for how they excluded malingering [also referred to as dissimilation, or 'faking bad'; para. 2559] in Dominic Ongwen, and [found] that the choice not to use further standardised methods to detect malingering remains questionable and undermined their analysis.' (para. 2566). The Chamber thus found 'the way in which they dismissed malingering as a possible explanation for the presence of symptoms of mental disorders apparent from the self-report of Dominic Ongwen unconvincing, and consider[ed] this to be a major factor militating against reliance on their reports' (para. 2568). Sixth, and finally, the Chamber opined that the reports of these two experts 'present very general analyses and findings, and are not clearly anchored on the relevant period and the more specific factual contexts in which Dominic Ongwen acted' (para. 2569).

Reaching entirely different findings with respect to the Prosecution mental health experts, the Trial Chamber referred on numerous occasions to their reports and testimonies to rebut those of the Defence experts, and to conclude that it could 'not rely on that evidence, and in particular not on the diagnoses of mental disorders in Dominic Ongwen which are advanced therein' (para. 2574). Relying explicitly on the evidence submitted by the Prosecution experts, the Trial Chamber ultimately found that 'Dominic Ongwen did not suffer from a mental disease or defect at the time of the conduct relevant under the charges' (para. 2580) and that article 31(1)(a) was thus not applicable in this case:

> based on the expert evidence of Professor Mezey, Dr Abbo and Professor Weierstall-Pust, who did not identify any mental disease or disorder in Dominic Ongwen during the period of the charges, further based on the corroborating evidence heard during the trial, which is incompatible with any such mental disease or disorder, and noting that the evidence of Professor Ovuga and Dr Akena cannot be relied upon, the Chamber finds that Dominic Ongwen did not suffer from a mental disease or defect at the time of the conduct relevant under the charges. A ground excluding criminal responsibility under Article 31(1)(a) of the Statute is not applicable.
>
> *(para. 2580)*

While excluding the Defence experts' reports for reasons of unreliability linked to flawed methodology might well have been justified, this did not necessarily mean that the Prosecution experts' methodology and findings were not beyond criticism. The trial transcripts indeed reveal some problematic aspects of the evidence presented by the Prosecution experts, none of whom met with the defendant. One of them conceded that they were 'not able to personally conduct a mental state examination of Mr Ongwen' because he 'did not wish to meet with' them (*Prosecutor v Ongwen*, 2018, 17), adding that they had no prior experience of working with child soldiers (14) and that they did not speak Acholi, the language of the defendant (20). Relatedly, the cultural dimension of mental health issues was generally overlooked, as illustrated by the discussions around *cen*, an Acholi spiritual concept described by experts as an 'aura or emanation' (*Prosecutor v Ongwen*, 2017, 19), and 'a possible manifestation of PTSD in the Acholi culture' (*Prosecutor v Ongwen*, 2018, 27). The expert witness called by the Victims' Representative pointed to the 'difficult[y] for westerners to understand [cen] because it just doesn't fit with our belief system, but it is a form of non-well-being. It is a form of pain and agony that is really very deep' (*Prosecutor v Ongwen*, 2018b, 26; for an analysis of control and spirituality – including possession by spirits such as *cen* – within the Lord's Resistance Army and its potential impact on mental capacity, see Nistor, Merrylees and Holá, 2020; on cen, see Bens, 2022, 106–8; on culture and trauma, see Vredeveldt, Given-Wilson and Memon, 2023). Ultimately, the Trial Chamber reached the ambivalent conclusion that 'there was general agreement among all experts that the cultural context must be taken into account in assessments of mental health, but that at the same time the standard criteria to determine mental disorders were universally accepted' (*Prosecutor v Ongwen*, 2021, para. 2461).

The Prosecution's expert conclusions might well be sound and accurately capture the defendant's mental capacity at the time he committed the crimes. Yet, the points raised above are by no means minor flaws and they do shed significant doubt on the accuracy of some of the experts' testimonies and on the validity of some of their conclusions. Even if Dominic Ongwen did not want to meet with the experts, and even if little could be done about this, it seems that – at the very least – these experts should all have had expertise in medically examining (former) child soldiers and should all have spoken the language of the defendant.

If the ICC is to achieve its global mandate, it is crucial that the different actors involved in the investigation and prosecution of atrocities be familiar with the defendants', the witnesses' and the victims' languages, beliefs and cultures.

The defence of intoxication

Another defence that relates to the mental capacity of the defendant is that of voluntary intoxication. Under article 31(1)(b) of the ICC Statute:

> a person shall not be criminally responsible if, at the time of that person's conduct:
>
> (b) The person is in a state of intoxication that destroys that person's capacity to appreciate the unlawfulness or nature of his or her conduct, or capacity to control his or her conduct to conform to the requirements of law, unless the person has become voluntarily intoxicated under such circumstances that the person knew, or disregarded the risk, that, as a result of the intoxication, he or she was likely to engage in conduct constituting a crime within the jurisdiction of the Court.

As with mental disease or defect, the decisive criterion for the validity of this defence is whether the person's capacity or appreciation and control was destroyed at the time of the commission of the alleged acts (Eser, 2016, 1142). Eser notes that

> [t]his rather lengthy provision can be broken down into two positive elements by requiring a certain state of intoxication (1) by which the person's capacity of appreciation and control is destroyed (2), and a negative element by excluding exculpation if the person was voluntarily intoxicated (3) unless that person was not aware of the risk that he could engage in criminal conduct as a ramification of intoxication.
>
> *(Eser, 2016, 1141)*

In any event, and as with mental disease or defect, '[i]mpairment, even of a substantial nature, is insufficient to exclude a person's liability' (Cryer et al., 2019, 385). This admittedly narrow scope is probably the reflection of the controversies attached to this defence and the debates its inclusion generated during the drafting of the Rome Statute: as Cryer et al. report, 'some delegations were opposed to its inclusion at all, considering intoxication as an aggravating factor rather than a possible defence' (ibid.). Still, under the Statute as adopted, if successfully raised, intoxication provides a full defence and the person will be entirely shielded from criminal responsibility and thus acquitted. Yet, this might remain purely theoretical as, in practice, the

> relevance of the defence is limited. Intoxication may be relevant to isolated acts, for instance where soldiers commit crimes under the influence of drugs or alcohol, but in the context of leadership responsibility this provision is somewhat bizarre. It is hard to establish in relation to the orchestration, planning and implementation of collective mass atrocity crime.
>
> *(Stahn, 2019, 150)*

Schabas also opines that:

> While many individual war crimes may be committed by soldiers and thugs under the influence of drugs and alcohol, it is highly unlikely that the Prosecutor of the International Criminal Court would choose to devote the institution's precious resources to an expensive trial of a drunkard. The nature of the crimes within the Court's jurisdiction, involving planning and preparation, and the policy of States and organizations, is virtually inconsistent with a plea of voluntary intoxication.
>
> *(Schabas, 2010, 486; see also Schabas, 2020, 243)*

The specific case of child soldiers, discussed above in the context of the defence of mental disease or defect, could here also provide an apt illustration of how this defence could be raised before the Court since '[c]hild soldiers are often given drugs or alcohol as a control mechanism, to loosen their inhibitions and increase their ferocity' (Drumbl, 2012, 80; also in Cryer et al., 2019, 384). As Stahn reports, '[i]n the Sierra Leonean civil war, warring factions used alcohol and drugs to control child soldiers or enhance their brutality in combat' (Stahn, 2019, 149).

With the trial of Dominic Ongwen, himself a former child soldier, the mental health of the defendant has admittedly become a live issue before the International Criminal Court, demonstrating that the judicial approach to defence claims related to the mental capacity of the defendant mirrors the text of the law by strictly requiring evidence that this capacity was destroyed at the time of the commission of the alleged crimes. While this understanding is not necessarily questionable, further attention might need to be devoted to evidentiary matters, to ensure that the medical expertise of the defendant is adequately conducted according to a methodology that is not only scientifically sound but also cognisant of the defendant's culture, language and personal circumstances.

Conclusion

Mental health is not an absent concept in international criminal law. It explicitly appears in the definitions of certain international crimes, which feature mental harm as one of their legal elements, as well as in specific rules designed to protect victims – particularly, although not exclusively, victims of sexual violence – and to facilitate the testimonies of traumatised witnesses. The mental health of the defendant is also taken into consideration, both at the time of the trial since he or she must be fit to stand trial, and at the time of the commission of the crimes since the absence of mental capacity would constitute an exculpatory ground.

These theoretical recognitions of mental health issues notwithstanding, this chapter has shown that the case law reveals a more cautious judicial attitude: so far, the judges at the International Criminal Court have been rather strict in their consideration of mental health, both in their admissions of testimonies of traumatised witnesses and in their assessments of the mental capacity of the accused, as reflected in the judgment issued against Dominic Ongwen. If the legacy of this judgment is one of uncertainty as the psychological expertise of the defendant admittedly contained some gaps, if not major flaws, it has at least contributed to achieve one key step: the issue of mental health in international criminal law and justice has – finally – gathered momentum.

References

Legal instruments

Cambodian National Assembly, (2004). Law on the Establishment of the Extraordinary Chambers in the Courts of Cambodia (NS/RKM/1004/006).

International Criminal Court, (2002). Rules of Procedure and Evidence. *Official Records of the Assembly of States Parties to the Rome Statute of the International Criminal Court, First Session, New York, 3–10 September 2002* (ICC. ASP/1/3 and Corr.1), part II.A.

International Criminal Court, (2002). Elements of Crimes. *Official Records of the Assembly of States Parties to the Rome Statute of the International Criminal Court, First Session, New York, 3–10 September 2002* (ICC. ASP/1/3 and Corr.1), part II.B.

International Criminal Court, (2018). Regulations of the Court. *Official Documents of the International Criminal Court* (ICC-BD/01-05-16).

United Nations, (1948). Convention for the Prevention and Punishment of the Crime of Genocide [Genocide Convention]. Approved and Proposed for Signature, Ratification or Accession by the General Assembly of the United Nations, Resolution 260 A (III) of 9 December 1948 (Entry into Force: 12 January 1951).

United Nations, (1989). Convention on the Rights of the Child Adopted and Opened for Signature, Ratification or Accession by the General Assembly of the United Nations. Resolution 44/25 of 20 November 1989 (Entry into Force: 2 September 1990).

United Nations, (1993). Statute of the International Tribunal for the Former Yugoslavia. Approved by the Security Council of the United Nations in Resolution 827, 25 May 1993.

United Nations, (1994). Statute of the International Tribunal for Rwanda. Decided by the Security Council of the United Nations, Resolution 955, 8 November 1994.

United Nations, (2002). Statute of the Special Court for Sierra Leone. Established Pursuant To Security Council Resolution, 1315, 14 August 2000.

United Nations Diplomatic Conference of Plenipotentiaries on the Establishment of an International Criminal Court, (1998). Rome Statute of the International Criminal Court, U.N. Doc. A/Conf.183/9, 17 July 1998 (Entry into Force, 1 July 2022).

Case Law

International Criminal Court

Prosecutor v Jean-Pierre Bemba Gombo, Case No. ICC-01/05-01/08, Trial Chamber III, Transcripts, ICC-01/05-01/08-T-100-ENG, 13 April 2011.

Prosecutor v Jean-Pierre Bemba Gombo, ICC-01/05-01/08, Trial Chamber III, Judgment, 21 March 2016.

Prosecutor v Jean-Pierre Bemba Gombo, ICC-01/05-01/08 A, Appeals Chamber, Judgment, 8 June 2018.

Prosecutor v Germain Katanga, ICC-01/04-01/07, Trial Chamber II, Judgment, 7 March 2014.

Prosecutor v Thomas Lubanga Dyilo, ICC-01/04-01/06, Trial Chamber I, Judgment, 14 March 2012.

Prosecutor v Thomas Lubanga Dyilo, ICC-01/04-01/06 A 5, Appeals Chamber, Judgment, 1 December 2014.

Prosecutor v Mathieu Ngudjolo Chui, ICC-01/04-02/12, Trial Chamber II, Judgment, 18 December 2012.

Prosecutor v Bosco Ntaganda, ICC-01/04-02/06, Trial Chamber VI, Judgment, 8 July 2019.

Prosecutor v Bosco Ntaganda, ICC-01/04-02/06 A3, Appeals Chamber, Judgment, 30 March 2021.

Prosecutor v Dominic Ongwen, Case No. ICC-02/04-01/15, Trial Chamber IX, Transcripts, ICC-02/04-01/15-T-28-ENG, 16 January 2017

Prosecutor v Dominic Ongwen, Case No. ICC-02/04-01/15, Trial Chamber IX, Transcripts, ICC-02/04-01/15-T-163-Red-ENG, 20 March 2018.
Prosecutor v Dominic Ongwen, Case No. ICC-02/04-01/15, Trial Chamber IX, Transcripts, ICC-02/04-01/15-T-176-ENG, 15 May 2018 (2018b)
Prosecutor v Dominic Ongwen, ICC-02/04-01/15, Trial Chamber IX, Judgment, 4 February 2021.
Prosecutor v Dominic Ongwen, ICC-02/04-01/15 A2, Appeals Chamber, Judgment, 15 December 2022.

International Criminal Tribunal for the former Yugoslavia

Prosecutor v Radislav Krstić, Case No. IT-98-33-T, Trial Chamber, Judgment, 2 August 2001.
Prosecutor v Milomir Stakić, Case No., IT-97-24-T, Trial Chamber II, Judgment, 31 July 2003.

International Criminal Tribunal for Rwanda

Prosecutor v Jean-Paul Akayesu, Case No. ICTR-96-4-T, Trial Chamber I, Judgment, 2 September 1998.
Prosecutor v Juvénal Kajelijeli, Case No. ICTR-98-44A-T, Trial Chamber II, Judgment, 1 December 2003.
Prosecutor v Clément Kayishema and Obed Ruzindana, Case No ICTR-95-1-T, Trial Chamber II, Judgment, 21 May 1999.
Prosecutor v Alfred Musema, Case No. ICTR-96-13-T, Trial Chamber I, Judgment, 27 January 2000.
Prosecutor v André Ntagerura, Emmanuel Bagambiki, Samuel Imanishimwe, Case No. ICTR-99-46-T, Trial Chamber III, Judgment, 25 February 2004.
Prosecutor v Georges Anderson Nderubumwe Rutaganda, Case No. ICTR-96-3-T, Trial Chamber I, Judgment, 6 December 1999.
Prosecutor v Laurent Semanza, Case No. ICTR-97-20-T, Trial Chamber III, Judgment, 15 May 2003.
Prosecutor v Athanase Seromba, Case No. ICTR-2001-66-T, Trial Chamber, Judgment, 13 December 2006.

Policy Papers

Office of the Prosecutor, (2014). *Best Practices Manual for the Investigation and Prosecution of Sexual Violence Crimes in Situations of Armed Conflict – Lessons from the International Criminal Tribunal for Rwanda*. https://unictr.irmct.org/sites/unictr.org/files/publications/ICTR-Prosecution-of-Sexual-Violence.pdf.
The Office of the Prosecutor, International Criminal Court, (June 2014). *Policy Paper on Sexual and Gender-Based Crimes*. https://www.icc-cpi.int/iccdocs/otp/OTP-Policy-Paper-on-Sexual-and-Gender-Based-Crimes--June-2014.pdf.

Literature

Bens, J., (2022). *The Sentimental Court – The Affective Life of International Criminal Justice*. Cambridge: Cambridge University Press.
Brammertz, S. and Jarvis, M., (2016). *Prosecuting Conflict-Related Sexual Violence at the ICTY*. Oxford: Oxford University Press.
Cryer, R., Robinson, D. and Vasiliev, S., (2019). *An Introduction to International Criminal Law and Procedure*. 4th ed. Cambridge: Cambridge University Press.
Drumbl, M., (2012). *Reimagining Child Soldiers in International Law and Policy*. Oxford: Oxford University Press.
Eser, A., (2016). Article 31. In: O. Triffterer and K. Ambos, eds. *Rome Statute of the International Criminal Court – A Commentary*. 3rd ed. München, Oxford and Baden-Baden: C.H. Beck, Hart, Nomos, pp. 1125–1160.

Janssen, S., 2004. Mental Condition Defences in Supranational Criminal Law, *International Criminal Law Review* 4(1), 83–98.

Krug, P., 2000. The Emerging Mental Incapacity Defence in International Criminal Law: Some Initial Questions of Implementation, *American Journal of International Law* 94(2), 317–335.

Marschner, L., (2016). Implications of Trauma on Testimonial Evidence in International Criminal Trials. In: P. Alston and S. Knuckey, eds. *The Transformation of Human Rights Fact-Finding*. Oxford: Oxford University Press, pp. 213–230.

Meiches, B., 2022. Genocide and the Brain: Neuroscience, Mental Harm, and International Law, *Journal of Genocide Research* 24(1), 23–44.

Nistor, A.-L., Merrylees, A and Holá, B., (2020). Spellbound at the International Criminal Court: The Intersection of Spirituality & International Criminal Law. In: J. Fraser and B. McGonigle Leyh, eds. *Intersections of Law and Culture at the International Criminal Court*. Cheltenham: Edward Elgar Publishing Ltd., pp. 147–68.

Radosavljevic, D., 2013. Scope and Limits of Psychiatric Evidence in International Criminal Law, *International Criminal Law Review* 13(5), 1013–1035.

Rohan, C.M., (2010). Rules Governing the Presentation of Testimonial Evidence. In: K.A.A. Khan, C. Buisman and C. Gosnell, eds. *Principles of Evidence in International Criminal Justice*. Oxford: Oxford University Press, pp. 499–550.

Schabas, W.A., (2010). *The International Criminal Court: A Commentary on the Rome Statute*. Oxford: Oxford University Press.

Schabas, W.A., (2020). *An Introduction to the International Criminal Court*. 6th ed. Cambridge: Cambridge University Press.

Schot, S., (2022). *Testimonial Evidence of Traumatised Witnesses in Trials of International Crimes – Striking a Balance in the Interest of Fair Proceedings and Accurate Fact-Finding*. Ph.D. thesis. University of Groningen.

Smith, E., (2021). Trauma in the Witness Stand: Effective Evaluation of Trauma-Impacted Testimony at the International Criminal Court. In: A. Heinze and V.E. Dittrich, eds. *The Past, Present and Future of the International Criminal Court*. Brussels: Torkel Opsahl Academic EPublisher, pp. 439–59.

Stahn, C., (2019). *A Critical Introduction to International Criminal Law*. Cambridge: Cambridge University Press.

Vredeveldt, A., Given-Wilson, Z., and Memon, A., 2023. Culture, trauma, and memory in investigative interviews. *Psychology, Crime & Law*. https://doi.org/10.1080/1068316X.2023.2209262.

Xavier, I., 2016. The Incongruity of the Rome Statute Insanity Defence and International Crime, *Journal of International Criminal Justice* 14(4), 793–814.

PART 5
Issues, controversies, challenges

17
DECISION-MAKING CAPACITY IN MENTAL HEALTH LAW

Alex Ruck Keene and Katherine Reidy

Introduction

In most jurisdictions in which it is recognised as a discrete entity, 'mental health law' is a misnomer. It is not, in fact, law designed, in and of itself, to secure the mental health of individuals. Rather, it is law designed to regulate the circumstances under which individuals may be admitted, assessed and treated for mental disorder, either in their own interests, or the interests of others. Viewed through this prism, the critical questions for mental health law have traditionally been as to the circumstances under which it is permissible to admit and/or treat a person with a mental disorder against their will. In any jurisdiction where the law provides for this, the questions of whether the person is (1) capacitously declining to take the step sought by the professionals; (2) incapacitously seeking to express resistance to those steps; or (3) is incapable of making a decision at all will always be second-order questions. It is therefore unsurprising that in many jurisdictions mental health law has traditionally not had a primary focus upon the concept of decision-making capacity. At the same time the law relating to decision-making capacity in those jurisdictions, developing on a parallel track, has sought to respond historically to different concerns – for instance about securing the interests (whether welfare or financial) of those with life-long cognitive impairments, who have not been the traditional focus of mental health lawyers (for a historical overview, see Lush (2015)).

This chapter does not purport to serve either as a comprehensive or universal history of the place of decision-making capacity in mental health law. Rather, we use this chapter to explore two jurisdictions – England and Wales, and Ireland – which place different formal weights upon the place of decision-making capacity in mental health law. The two jurisdictions have many similarities in terms of their legal traditions and frameworks (relevantly, for present purposes, for instance, both have incorporated the European Convention on Human Rights into their domestic law, and both have ratified, but not incorporated, the United Nations Convention on the Rights of Persons with Disabilities). They also have some differences, most notably that Ireland has a written Constitution; that Ireland remains a member of the European Union whilst the United Kingdom (of which England and Wales forms the largest part) has left does not make any immediate difference for these purposes.

Taking these two jurisdictions, we examine how, notwithstanding what the black letter law may say, 'soft law' and professional practice may give a very different shape to the actual place of decision-making capacity within the formal structures established under the two mental health regimes. Reflecting on these two case studies, we offer thoughts about the potential implications of a greater formal reliance upon decision-making capacity within mental health law, thoughts which, whilst grounded in the two jurisdictions, are of wider relevance.

Three final introductory matters. First, we are aware that the preferred term in the context of the United Nations Convention on the Rights of Persons with Disabilities is 'psychosocial disability'. However, we use 'mental disorder' in this chapter because this is the term used in the relevant legislation in the jurisdictions we discuss. Second, we also proceed in this chapter on the basis that the concepts of mental disorder and mental capacity are fundamentally legitimate, even if their application can be open to misuse. Third, we focus on those aged 18 and above, because questions of capacity or competence interact with the ability of parents – in some cases – to provide consent on behalf of a minor in ways which are too complex for treatment within the compass of this chapter (for the position in England & Wales, see Parker, 2020).

England and Wales

The statutory frameworks

The United Kingdom is comprised of England and Wales, Scotland and Northern Ireland. The governing mental health legislation in England and Wales is the Mental Health Act 1983 (MHA 1983). There is separate legislation in Scotland and Northern Ireland relating to both mental health and mental capacity. The MHA 1983 is based in significant part on the Mental Health Act 1959; it was subject to amendments in 2007 discussed further below. Although it has a space for in-patient assessment and treatment of mental disorder on an informal basis, its primary function is to provide a statutory framework for the compulsory care and treatment of people for mental disorder when they are unable or unwilling to consent to that care and treatment, and when it is necessary for that care and treatment to be given to protect themselves or others from harm. The key point for the exercise of these powers is the inability or unwillingness of the patient who suffers from a mental disorder to consent to the relevant care and treatment. Inability to consent will also include people who do not have capacity, but the question whether an individual patient has or does not have decision-making capacity is not, in statutory terms, the key determinant of whether the powers conferred by MHA 1983 should be used. Indeed, the term 'capacity' appears in only a very few places in the MHA 1983, primarily in relation to electroconvulsive therapy (ECT) and treatment in the community under the provisions of Part 4A: in both places, it remains possible – in different ways – for treatment to be administered where there is a sufficiently compelling need even in the face of the person's capacitous refusal. The MHA 1983 contains – in Part 4 – a treatment framework for detained patients, which includes safeguards such as a statutory requirement for a second medical opinion.

The suitability of the MHA framework, and in particular its compatibility with the procedural requirements of the European Convention on Human Rights in relation to non-consensual treatment, has been called into serious question since it was most recently updated with effect from 2009 (by operation of amendments introduced in the Mental Health Act 2007). At the time of writing the Government has expressed its intention to tighten the safeguards significantly in line with recommendations of an independent Review of the MHA

1983 which reported in 2018 (Department of Health and Social Care, 2021). A key feature of the reforms is to increase the weight placed upon decision-making capacity in the context of decisions about treatment. They would do so in a number of ways, some likely to be included in primary legislation, and some in the Code of Practice, but in effect the reforms aim to: (1) support the expression in advance of choices about treatment; and (2) make it more complicated for a clinician not to follow either such an advance choice, or a capacitous choice expressed at the time that treatment is being proposed. Ultimately, however, even if those reforms are implemented, a refusal of treatment, whether expressed contemporaneously by a person with capacity or expressed in advance in the new innovation of a statutory 'Advance Choice Document' would not be determinative in the face of a sufficiently compelling clinical rationale. Separately, the reforms would not, in statutory terms, require any weight to be placed upon decision-making capacity when it comes to admission, so, whilst raising the bar for admission, the criteria remain focused upon the harm that the person (or others) would suffer if not admitted.

Sitting alongside the MHA 1983 is the Mental Capacity Act 2005 (MCA 2005). This was enacted in 2005, following a lengthy gestation period (Ruck Keene et al., 2019). It is based wholly upon a functional and decision-specific test of mental capacity. Where a person lacks capacity to make a relevant decision, the MCA 2005 provides a framework by which decisions can be made and actions taken. There is a gradation of formality depending upon the seriousness of the intervention: the majority of acts of care or treatment carried out under the auspices of the MCA 2005 are carried out on the basis of the 'general authority' granted by s.5, which requires a reasonable belief on the part of the person concerned that the other lacks capacity to consent to the relevant act and that the action is in their best interests. There is, however, no equivalent to the formal treatment regime contained within Part 4 MHA 1983. Since 2009, the MCA 2005 provides an administrative framework to authorise deprivation of liberty for purposes of providing care and treatment to someone incapable of consenting to the arrangements in question; at the time of writing, it applies in hospitals and care homes to those aged 18 or over. By virtue of changes proposed to the framework by the Mental Capacity (Amendment) Act 2019, it should in future apply (in principle) in any setting to those aged 16 and above.

On its face, there might appear to be a large overlap between those to whom the MHA 1983 and the MCA 2005 might apply. A systematic review conducted in 2007 (Okai et al., 2007) suggested that a high proportion of patients admitted informally to psychiatric hospitals might lack capacity to consent to their admission, and that the frequency with which psychiatric in-patients lacked capacity to make decisions as to their treatment did not differ greatly from that in general hospital in-patients (around one-third). There is no reason to think that the position is substantially different in 2023 (see also Curley et al., 2021).

The overlap is addressed in statutory terms in three ways:

(1) Some who lack capacity will not come within the definition of those for whom compulsory powers under MHA 1983 can be exercised. By operation of the statutory exclusion contained in s.1(2A) from the scope of the definition of 'mental disorder', central to the criteria for detention and treatment, people with intellectual disabilities, for example, who may thereby not be able to give their consent to treatment, will not generally be subject to the compulsory powers of MHA 1983, unless their conduct is identified as being 'abnormally aggressive or seriously irresponsible'.

(2) The MCA 2005 contains statutory provisions addressing which regime is to be used in the case of a person lacking the capacity to consent to admission for assessment or treatment for mental disorder in circumstances of confinement, as well as provisions to address the interaction between the two regimes when a person is subject to the MHA 1983 but currently detained in hospital. These are contained at present in Sch.1A to the MCA 2005; as of the coming into force of the Mental Capacity (Amendment) Act 2019, they will be contained in Sch.AA1. When it comes to admission, the focus of these provisions is upon whether the person is objecting to either their admission or any of the proposed treatment for mental disorder. The way in which these provisions are interpreted in practice is addressed below, as they are revealing of some core concerns in relation to the operation of capacity-based legislation.

(3) By s.28, the MCA 2005 specifically excludes anyone giving a patient medical treatment for mental disorder, or consenting to a patient being given medical treatment for mental disorder, if the patient is, at the relevant time, already detained and subject to the compulsory treatment provisions of the MHA 1983. Conversely, the MHA 1983 provides no treatment authority in relation to medical treatment which is not treatment for mental disorder. If a patient detained under the MHA 1983 requires treatment for an unrelated physical disorder, then treatment can only be provided upon the basis of (1) the patient's capacitous consent; or (2) the 'general authority' within the MCA 2005 addressed above.

The frameworks in practice

From the review above it can be seen that: (1) there are, in principle, statutory bright lines delineating the zones of operation of the MHA 1983 and the MCA 2005; and (2) within the zone of operation of the MHA 1983, capacity is never determinative. However, it would be seriously misleading to leave matters at that. For a start, the English Code of Practice to the MHA 1983 makes extensive reference to mental capacity, for instance, providing as follows, in relation to treatment in the – current – initial three-month period during which it is possible for a detained patient to be provided with medical treatment for mental disorder on the basis of the opinion of one clinician alone:

> During this time, the patient's consent should still be sought before any medication is administered, wherever practicable. The patient's consent, refusal to consent, or a lack of capacity to give consent should be recorded in the case notes. If a person has capacity to consent, but such consent is not forthcoming or is withdrawn during this period, the clinician in charge of the treatment must consider carefully whether to proceed in the absence of consent, to give alternative treatment or stop treatment.
> *(Department of Health, 2015, para. 24.41)*

A separate Code of Practice has been published for Wales, which is broadly similar but reflects differences between the secondary legislation relating to the MHA 1983 as between England and Wales. In both England and Wales, the Code of Practice is a statutory code, to which professionals such as clinicians have to have regard, and from whose provisions the House of Lords made clear (in *R (Munjaz) v Ashworth Hospital Authority* [2005] UKHL 58) they can only depart with cogent reasons. Doubts as to whether the attempts within the Code to guide clinicians towards placing greater weight upon capacity were enough grounded, in part, the recommendations of the 2018 independent review to place matters upon a statutory footing, but the Code is nonetheless (at a minimum) of what good practice was envisaged by the Government to be as at 2015. Similarly in the realm of good practice, the Care Quality Commission, which monitors mental health services in England, actively reviews whether services have the mechanisms in place to sort and check for advance decision documentation, notwithstanding the fact that (unlike the position in relation to advance decisions in respect of physical treatments) a decision in relation to medical treatment for mental disorder can never be binding (Care Quality Commission, 2020).

The courts have also weighed in in the years since the MHA 1983 was last reformed. Of particular relevance and interest for present purposes is the way in which courts have been asked to weigh in – in circumstances where there is no statutory requirement that any questions relating to admission and/or treatment for mental disorder are brought before a court of any kind. In practice, this means that applications to court will arise in one of two ways: (1) a challenge by a person (or on their behalf) to a decision taken by a professional discharging a function under the MHA 1983; or (2) an application by the professional or, more likely, the relevant hospital body, essentially seeking confirmation as to whether the steps that they are proposing are lawful.

In this context, it is striking that since the MCA 2005 came into effect on 1 October 2007, there have been very few challenges brought to treatment decisions taken by professionals, although, as the independent Review of the MHA 1983 noted, this may well be because the route of challenge, by way of judicial review, is inaccessible (Department of Health and Social Care, 2018, 76). At the same time, however, there have been a significant number of cases where the professionals have sought confirmation of the lawfulness of their actions. For present purposes, most interesting are (1) those where the treating body has sought confirmation that *not* carrying out treatment in the face of the person's capacitous refusal is lawful; and (2) those where the treating team could have used the mechanisms of the MHA 1983 but instead sought determination of the issue from the Court of Protection, asking the court to consider whether the person had capacity to consent to the relevant treatment and, if they did not, whether it was in their best interests for the treatment to be carried out. An example of the first type of decision is the case of *Nottinghamshire Healthcare NHS Trust v RC* [2014] EWCOP 1317, in which the Trust responsible for the man in question, RC, detained under the provisions of the MHA 1983, sought confirmation that (1) he had capacity to make an advance decision to refuse life-saving treatment in the form of blood transfusions; (2) that he currently had capacity to refuse such treatment; and (3) it was lawful not to impose blood transfusions upon him in circumstances where he was significantly self-harming resulting in profuse bleeding, notwithstanding the fact that the consequence might well be his death. Mostyn J agreed with all three propositions, holding (at para. 42) that:

> In my judgment it would be an abuse of power in such circumstances even to think about imposing a blood transfusion on RC having regard to my findings that he presently has capacity to refuse blood products and, were such capacity to disappear for any reason, the advance decision would be operative. To impose a blood transfusion would be a denial of a most basic freedom.

The majority of the second types of decision – i.e. where the matter is placed before the Court of Protection – relate to women with anorexia, in circumstances where it would be entirely lawful to admit the person under the MHA 1983 and (if necessary) feed them compulsorily under the provisions of that Act.[1] The strong impression that the judgments give, however, is that the treating teams consider that the concepts of capacity and best interests provide a more calibrated framework for determining what the right course of action is. In most, but not all, applications, the Court of Protection concludes that the woman in question lacks capacity to make decisions as to their nutrition and hydration (which gives rise to interesting questions about precisely how the concept of capacity operates in this context: Craigie and Davies, 2019). However, it does not then follow that either admission or treatment is then held to be in their best interests. In *A Mental Health Trust v ER & Anor* [2021] EWCOP 32, for instance, the NHS bodies treating ER sought declarations that she lacked capacity to make decisions concerning her anorexia, but also that she 'should not be forced to accept treatment for her anorexia which she does not wish for, and that she should not be forced to go into a psychiatric hospital or a specialist eating disorder unit against her wishes'. Lieven J agreed with this proposition (at para. 34), noting, in particular, that this accorded with ER's wishes and feelings – central to the understanding of best interests as now conceptualised under the MCA 2005 (Ruck Keene and Friedman, 2020). Conversely, in *Re E (Medical treatment: Anorexia)* [2012] EWCOP 1639, the treating Trust sought authority to force-feed the woman in question notwithstanding her clearly expressed opposition – including by way of an advance decision to refuse such treatment. Of note, perhaps, is the fact that E was, at the time the case came before the Court of Protection, a patient detained under the MHA 1983, but there is no suggestion on the face of the judgment that her treating team considered that they could simply rely upon the provisions of Part 4 of the MHA 1983 to compel feeding: rather, their argument, accepted ultimately by the court, was that such treatment was in her best interests.

It bears repeating that cases such as those analysed in the previous paragraphs are ones where the treating team, themselves, have *chosen* not to use the tools provided them by the MHA 1983 to treat – either in the face of the person's capacitous refusal or where they consider that the person lacks the relevant capacity but they consider that the right question to ask is not whether treatment is appropriate (the MHA test) but whether it is in the person's best interests. These cases are likely to be the tip of the iceberg, representing situations of sufficient tension between what is felt ethically to be the right course of action and the knowledge that criticism is likely to follow an active decision not to do something that the place for appropriate resolution is the court, not least so that the ultimate decision can rest on the broad (and for these purposes unsackable) shoulders of a judge. We do not, in truth, know how often at 'ground level' decisions are negotiated as between professionals and the individual, and how heavily within this decision-making capacity truly features, as opposed to (say) the consistency and strength of the expression of the patient's views or the extent to which following those views troubles the clinicians. And, in reality, professionals may well also be as much concerned with very pragmatic matters (does the person have someone at home who could provide support if they were discharged?) as with fine-grained discussions about capacity. Perhaps the best that can be said is that the Chair of the independent Review of the MHA 1983, Sir Simon Wessely, was clearly satisfied that in suggesting reforms to increase the weight placed upon decision-making capacity he would be building on what was

---

1 Force-feeding can constitute medical treatment for a manifestation of anorexia, a mental disorder: see, for instance, *South West Hertfordshire HA v KB* [1994] 2 FCR 1051.

already perceived to be good practice, rather than seeking a revolution in practice (see, for instance, Department of Health and Social Care, 2018, 21).

In England & Wales, therefore, we have a position in which it could plausibly be argued that the passage of parallel legislation – the MCA 2005 – has simultaneously placed a greater focus upon the concept of decision-making capacity and provided an alternative set of tools for clinicians to use. The presence of this alternative set of tools is undoubtedly a mixed blessing in some situations. This is the case above all in relation to deciding which framework to use to admit a person to hospital for purposes of assessment and treatment for mental disorder. A 2021 study (Gilburt, 2021) vividly describes the (often stark) disagreements between professionals involved, often based upon different understandings of what it means to be 'objecting' to admission (the touchstone to decide whether the MHA 1983 or the MCA 2005 should be used) – how, for instance, should the attempts by a person with dementia to leave a locked ward to pick up their children from school be interpreted if the evidence is that (a) their children are now adult; and (b) the person in question seeks to leave any place where they are, including their own home, to do so? However, the very fact that these debates are happening, and that feelings run so high, only serves to reinforce the thesis developed in this section, namely that, whatever the formal place of capacity within English mental health law, the reality is that, alongside and 'below' it, it has taken on a major significance.

Many would be likely to regard what might be characterised as fusion by the backdoor as a positive step, not least because it reduces the number of situations in which the coercive powers granted professionals under the MHA 1983 are being deployed against those capacitously refusing the intervention proposed. However, such an assumption may be one which requires unpicking, and, in this context, the reasons why the independent Review of the MHA 1983 did not propose taking a final leap towards pure capacity-based mental health legislation are perhaps significant. They will be unpicked in the last section of this chapter after the position in England & Wales is contrasted with that in Ireland.

Ireland

The statutory frameworks

The Mental Health Act 2001 (MHA 2001), which currently governs mental health law in Ireland, was commenced in full in 2006. This replaced previous provisions, including the Mental Treatment Act 1945, and was introduced to reform Irish mental health law, bringing it more in line with international human rights developments. In a similar vein to the MHA 1983 in England and Wales, Ireland's MHA 2001 primarily provides a statutory framework for the involuntary admission of persons suffering from mental disorders to approved centres. The Act introduced a number of significant changes in this regard, including the establishment of a Mental Health Commission to oversee the provision of mental health services, especially in relation to involuntary admission, and the introduction of mental health tribunals to review those involuntary orders.

Although the MHA 2001 brought many welcome changes to Irish mental health law, the legislation, as it currently stands, has been criticised for falling short of adequately protecting human rights as domestic and international law in this regard continue to evolve. Before discussing the Act further, the domestic legal framework within which it exists ought to be considered. Briefly, in 1937, Bunreacht na hÉireann, the Irish Constitution, was enacted, replacing the Constitution of the Irish Free State. Articles 40–44 guarantee fundamental rights of citizens; article 40.3.1 provides, 'The State guarantees in its laws to respect, and, as far as practicable, by its laws to defend and vindicate the personal rights of the citizen'.

Among those rights are the right to liberty (article 40.4.1), the right to bodily integrity (*Ryan v Attorney General* [1965] IR 294) and the right to autonomy (*Re a Ward of Court (No. 2)* [1996] 2 IR 79).

Although some of these rights are not explicitly mentioned in the Constitution, they have been established as unenumerated rights by the courts over the years. Importantly, constitutional rights prevail over legislation in Irish law and legislation may be invalidated if it is found to be unconstitutional. As will be discussed further below, concerns have been expressed about the constitutionality of various provisions of the Act as well as its compatibility with international instruments, including the United Nations Convention on the Rights of Persons with Disabilities (UNCRPD) 2006 and the European Convention of Human Rights (ECHR).

As mentioned, the MHA 2001 mainly applies to patients who have been involuntarily admitted under the Act. A patient must suffer from a 'mental disorder', as described by section 3, to be admitted under the Act. 'Mental disorder' is defined by that section as:

mental illness, severe dementia or significant intellectual disability where

(a) because of the illness, disability or dementia, there is a serious likelihood of the person concerned causing immediate and serious harm to himself or herself or to other persons, or

(b) (i) because of the severity of the illness, disability or dementia, the judgment of the person concerned is so impaired that failure to admit the person to an approved centre would be likely to lead to a serious deterioration in his or her condition or would prevent administration of appropriate treatment that could be given only by such admission, and (ii) the reception, detention and treatment of the person concerned in an approved centre would be likely to benefit or alleviate the condition of that person to a material extent.

Regrettably, 'impaired judgment', although a prerequisite for involuntary admission under section 3(b), is not defined in the Act (a recurrent theme), thus leaving the question of how it is to be assessed ambiguous; in practice, it seems to be the responsible consultant psychiatrist (RCP) who ultimately decides whether a patient's judgment is impaired (Guy, 2011). Further concerns have been raised in relation to section 3(a), commonly referred to as the 'harm' or 'risk' criterion. Under the current legislation, there is no reciprocal requirement for treatment, such as is the case with section 3(b)(i), creating a situation in which a person could potentially be detained under this criterion without the need for treatment. Indeed, psychiatric facilities are not designed to substitute prison facilities or to prevent crime or violence (Reidy and Kelly, 2021). In this regard, the Expert Group on the Review of the Mental Health Act 2001, in its 2015 report (as to which, see further below), has recommended that involuntary admission must benefit the patient materially and that those who refuse all treatment options, and are deemed to have capacity, should be discharged as there would no longer be a valid basis for detaining such persons.

Interestingly, although 'capacity' does not feature in relation to admission in the current legislation, 'consent' is referred to in relation to treatment. According to section 57(1) MHA 2001:

the consent of a patient shall be required for treatment except where, in the opinion of the consultant psychiatrist responsible for the care and treatment of the patient, the treatment is necessary to safeguard the life of the patient, to restore his or her health, to alleviate his or her suffering, and by reason of his or her mental disorder, the patient concerned is incapable of giving such consent.

While such a provision may initially appear to uphold patient rights, upon closer reading, several concerns become apparent. First, the term 'incapable' is not defined in the section, opening the way to differing interpretations as to the meaning of the term. Second, it is the treating consultant who decides whether the patient is capable of consenting to treatment. This difficulty is compounded by the lack of statutory entitlement to a second opinion in such instances where the RCP deems a patient 'incapable' of giving consent despite express requirement for an independent assessment by another RCP in sections 59 and 60, dealing with ECT and continued treatment respectively. Concern has been expressed in this regard about the independence of the process of capacity assessment and the potential for human rights violations (Donnelly, 2007).

In addition to the 2001 Act, there are Codes of Practice and Rules which are issued by the Mental Health Commission pursuant to s.33(3) of the Act which requires periodic preparation and review of such codes by the Commission. These Codes offer guidance to those working in mental health services to ensure consistent implementation of the 2001 Act. Regarding the issue of capacity in relation to admission, the *Code of Practice on Admission, Transfer and Discharge to and from an Approved Centre* (COP – S33(3)/01/2009) unfortunately does not offer any counsel on assessing capacity, nor is there mention of capacity or consent in relation to admission criteria. Instead, the Code simply refers to the 'best interests' of the patient (p. 27), echoing the terminology used in section 4 of the Act.

Conversely, the *Rules Governing the Use of Electro-Convulsive Therapy* (R-S59(2)-01-2016 Version 3) consider capacity to consent and outline criteria to be met in its assessment. These include the understanding by the patient of the nature of and reasons for the proposal of ECT, risks and benefits associated with ECT, possible consequences of not receiving it, retention of the information long enough to make a decision, freedom of choice and the ability to consent (p. 15). Where a patient is unable to consent, the decision to administer ECT must be approved by the RCP with the agreement of a second consultant psychiatrist as required by the 2001 Act (p. 16).

Although yet to be fully commenced at the time of. The Assisted Decision-Making (Capacity) Act 2015 (ADMCA 2015) was signed into Irish law in December 2015 to reform existing capacity legislation and to uphold the values of the UNCRPD which sets out as its purpose to 'promote, protect and ensure the full and equal enjoyment of all human rights and fundamental freedoms by all persons with disabilities, and to promote respect for their inherent dignity' (Article 1).

The 2015 Act repeals the Lunacy Regulation (Ireland) Act 1871, including the heavily criticised system of Wards of Court, and places much (but not all) of the law relating to capacity on a statutory footing.[2] With regard to capacity, the Act introduces a statutory definition,

---

2 It will not, it appears, codify the common law doctrine of necessity, relied upon at present in Ireland to carry out very many acts of care and treatment in relation to those who cannot consent: see further Ruck Keene (2021).

including a presumption of capacity. It sets out a functional approach to assessment and removes the current requirement described by the High Court in *Fitzpatrick v FK* [2008] IEHC 104 for a patient to 'believe' information provided to them, instead replacing this with a need for a patient to be able to 'communicate' their decision. Moreover, the 'will and preferences' of the patient are to be part of the guiding principles rather than 'best interests', which currently guide interpretation of the 2001 Act as per section 4(i) of that Act, and which are the subject of much debate. Other changes which the Act proposes include decision-making supports (assisted decision-making, co-decision-making and a decision-making representative), expansion of enduring powers of attorney and a statutory basis for advanced healthcare directives. The ADMCA 2015 has been received largely positively thus far. However, commencement has not solved all of the problems, for instance in relation to the challenge of lawful deprivation of liberty of those requiring care and treatment but lacking capacity to consent to their confinement.

In terms of reform, it is also important to highlight that the Irish Government approved in June 2021 the draft heads of bill to amend the MHA 2001, which are based largely on recommendations of the Expert Group, taking into account various legislative changes, including the incoming ADMCA 2015. However, at the time of writing, the draft heads of bill are under debate by the Oireachtas Committee and are due to be reviewed again. In light of this, the section below will refer mainly to the Expert Group's recommendations and the 2015 Act where relevant.

The frameworks in practice

At present in Ireland, there is a presumption of capacity at common law which may be rebutted. The courts have traditionally adopted a functional approach to assessing decision-making capacity, that is an issue- and time-specific approach, recognising that a person's capacity may fluctuate over time, and that not having capacity to make certain decisions does not necessarily preclude a person from having capacity to make others. Such an approach to assessing decision-making capacity was set out by the High Court in *Fitzpatrick & Anor v K. & Anor* [2008] IEHC 104. In that case, the defendant, who was a Jehovah's Witness, refused blood transfusions which were deemed necessary to save her life following significant post-partum haemorrhage. In her judgment, Laffoy J noted the presumption of capacity at common law and stated that the approach to assessing capacity was a functional one. She went on to adopt the approach taken in the English case of *Re C* [1994] 1 WLR 290, which set out the test as the understanding and retention of treatment information by the patient, belief of that information and weighing the information to arrive at a decision.

In setting out the framework for involuntary admission and treatment of patients with a mental disorder, the 2001 Act does not explicitly reject the use of a functional approach to assessing capacity. However, in more practical terms, concern has been expressed about a *de facto* status approach once a patient becomes involuntary (Guy, 2011). A status approach may be considered an 'all or nothing' approach, essentially equating involuntary status with incapacity. This approach can be seen in the Ward of Court system. Arguably, the application of such an approach to assessing decision-making capacity in those with mental illness has the potential to violate human and constitutional rights, including rights to autonomy and bodily integrity. While it may often be the case that an involuntary patient lacks capacity to make decisions relating to admission or treatment, it should not automatically be assumed without proper assessment. Indeed, a recent cross-sectional study, considering capacity of voluntary and involuntary patients in Ireland, found that the majority (92.3%) of involuntary patients lacked mental capacity for treatment decisions while 7.7% retained capacity notwithstanding their status (Curley et al., 2019). The authors acknowledge several limitations, including the possibility that those patients who demonstrated capacity at the time of assessment may not have had capacity when admitted initially, and only subsequently regained it during admission. Nevertheless, this highlights the need for more rigorous assessment of capacity in those involuntarily admitted under the 2001 Act. The introduction of a legislative basis for a functional approach to capacity assessment, such as provided for by the ADMCA 2015, will likely be welcome in this regard.

Although the case law in Ireland regarding consent to treatment is limited at present, many of the cases which have come before the courts have involved decisions around the constitutionality of various provisions of Part 4 of the 2001 Act. Such was the case in *M.X. v Health Service Executive* [2012] IEHC 491 where the constitutionality and compatibility with the ECHR of section 60 MHA 2001 was challenged. In *M.X.*, the plaintiff was an involuntary patient with a diagnosis of treatment-resistant schizophrenia who was being treated involuntarily with clozapine, an antipsychotic medication requiring regular blood-monitoring, which the patient was also subject to. It was the expert medical opinion that the patient did not have capacity to give consent at the time of treatment. It was acknowledged by the High Court in its judgment that the treatment in question was invasive, interfering with bodily integrity and dignity. The court, therefore, emphasised the need for the vindication of 'personal capacity rights' (para. 52) and, referring to European Court of Human Rights jurisprudence, highlighted the need for 'heightened scrutiny' (para. 72) in such cases. Mac Menamin J went on to hold that a constitutional reading of section 60 required the patient's rights be vindicated 'as far as practicable' (para. 73) and found that this was possible under the section through the need for a second opinion from an independent consultant at three-monthly intervals, and further, that the hearing before him was, in essence, part of the vindication of those rights (para. 81). He therefore held that section 60 could not be regarded as unconstitutional. However, the court recommended changes to Form 17, the relevant form, which provides for the administration of medication for more than three months to an involuntary patient, to allow for the recording of the patient's choice in order to fully give effect to the vindication of patients' rights. In relation to the ECHR, the Court held that the UNCRPD could be referred to as a 'guiding principle', rather than a rule, in the interpretation of the ECHR. The court found that the European case law did not go any further than Irish constitutional rights (para. 94).

As mentioned, the 2001 Act is concerned mainly with involuntary patients, thus affording very little, if any, statutory protection to voluntary patients. Of those sections that do pertain to voluntary patients, the majority refer to ways in which they may be detained. In particular, section 23 provides for a detention period of 24 hours where a voluntary patient indicates that he or she wishes to leave an approved centre, and a registered medical practitioner or registered nurse is of the opinion that the person is suffering from a mental disorder. Prior to detention, assessment by the RCP and a second opinion of another consultant psychiatrist is required by section 24. In this regard, the Steering Group on the Review of the Mental Health Act 2001 has criticised the Act for being, arguably, less protective of voluntary patients than the earlier, 1945 Act (Steering Group, 2012). This focus on involuntary patients, seemingly at the expense of those who are voluntary, is quickly apparent from section 2(i) which defines a voluntary patient as one 'receiving care and treatment in an approved centre who is *not* the subject of an admission order or a renewal order' (emphasis added).

In the case of *E.H. v Clinical Director of St. Vincent's Hospital* [2009] IESC 46, where the applicant sought a declaration that section 2 of the Act was incompatible with Article 5 ECHR, the Supreme Court held that the Act does not necessitate that a person 'freely and voluntarily gives consent to an admission order' and, on the basis that any interpretation of the Act should be 'informed by the... paternalistic intent of the legislation' (p. 161), held that section 2 did not contravene the patient's rights. Such a lack of requirement for consent or capacity assessment has variously been criticised. The Irish Human and Equality Rights Commission, among others, has highlighted that the current definition is at odds with international human rights standards, and has urged reform (Irish Human Rights and Equality Commission, 2012). In this vein, the Expert Group recommended that a voluntary patient be defined as:

> a person who has the capacity (with support if required) to make a decision regarding admission to an approved centre and who, where the person retains capacity, formally gives his/her informed consent to such admission, and subsequent continuation of voluntary inpatient status and treatment on an ongoing basis as required.
> *(p.28)*

Such a definition would appear more consistent with the ADMCA 2015 and the values it represents.

Although welcome, a definition of a voluntary patient such as that proposed by the Expert Group would likely inadequately address the issue of those who are compliant, who do not object to admission or treatment, or who do not meet criteria for involuntary admission, but who do not have capacity to consent. In such instances, a new 'intermediate' category has been recommended by the Expert Group. It is proposed that intermediate patients would not be involuntarily detained, but would nevertheless be afforded the same protections and mechanisms for review as involuntary patients. In this regard, it is worth noting *A.C. v Patricia Hickey General Solicitor and Ors & AC v Fitzpatrick & Ors* [2019] IESC 73, post-dating the report of the Expert Group. While the case related to an elderly patient with dementia admitted to a general hospital, rather than a person with a mental disorder admitted to a psychiatric unit, the Supreme Court nonetheless considered the issue of decision-making capacity and the detention of those lacking capacity. In so doing, it emphasised that a lack of capacity does not afford a patient any less protection of their constitutional rights than others, including the right to liberty (para. 394). Moreover, it noted that a lack of capacity:

> will not on its own amount to justification, since if the patient cannot give a valid consent then some other lawful authority is necessary if persons are to make decisions for her.
> *(para. 393)*

On the whole, recent decades have seen significant and generally positive changes in the field of mental health law in Ireland. However, as is evident, difficulties remain, especially regarding decision-making capacity in relation to both admission and treatment under the existing legislation. Reform of Irish mental health law is required. A comprehensive revision of the Act in its entirety has been variously recommended. Such an approach would be preferable to the often piecemeal amendments to which Irish legislation has historically been subject, and appears largely to be the approach adopted in the recent draft heads of bill as mentioned above.

Capacity and mental health law – a double-edged sword?

As we have seen in the balance of this chapter, decision-making capacity has assumed ever greater importance within mental health law in England & Wales and Ireland, in developments which are broadly in line with trends in other jurisdictions. Mental capacity is a concept that troubles the Committee on the Rights of Persons with Disabilities (Committee on the Rights of Persons with Disabilities, 2014; see also Szmukler and Kelly, 2016). However, neither the Committee nor anyone else has to date advanced a concept which commands greater legitimacy when answering the question 'should I take this person's words or actions as having determinative legal effect?' (Ruck Keene et al., 2023). The trend of legislative reforms in this area – many provoked by the important challenge of the CRPD – has therefore been firmly towards making mental capacity a touchstone of decisions relating to admission and treatment.

Some have proposed that admission and treatment for mental disorder should be based upon either consent or the functional inability of the person to consent to the step(s) and a justification that such is in their best interests. This could take place within the framework of separate mental health legislation, but the most common proposal has been to 'fuse' mental health and mental capacity law. As an example of this, Northern Ireland has passed – but not yet fully implemented – such legislation in the form of the Mental Capacity Act (Northern Ireland) 2016 (see further in this regard, Harper, Davidson and McLelland, 2016; Davidson, this vol.). The proponents of such legislation emphasise that it eliminates the inherent discrimination against those with mental illness who may be subject to conventional mental legislation within which (as we have seen) capacity carries very little weight. Under fusion legislation, the touchstone will always be decision-making capacity – if the person has it, then admission, care and treatment will either be consensual or cannot take place; if the person lacks it, then admission, care and treatment will be on the same basis regardless of whether it is to address the person's mental health or physical health needs.

Why, then, did the recent independent Review of the MHA 1983 in England & Wales not recommend that capacity be determinative? It identified the human rights arguments in favour of fusing mental health and mental capacity law, endorsing the observation of the then-President of the Supreme Court, Lady Hale, that such an approach comes:

> closest to reconciling our conflicting international human rights obligations. It is predicated on respect for human dignity and autonomy and individual values and preferences. It does not discriminate between the treatment and care of physical and mental disorders. It covers all kinds of decision-making.
>
> *(Hale, 2018)*

However, before recommending that entirely new legislation should be drafted, the Review proposed five 'confidence tests': (1) the views of (as the review called them) service users; (2) the impact in practice of the 'fusion' legislation introduced in Northern Ireland; (3) whether the assessment of capacity is reliable enough to provide the sole basis for care and treatment;

(4) that associated processes are adapted to support change; and (5) whether fusion law can take sufficient account of public interest.

We suggest these confidence tests are equally applicable outside the context of England & Wales. Of particular importance are the measures to support and secure a just approach to uncertainty in crisis situations,[3] where the application of the concept of decision-making capacity comes under particular strain (see also Szmukler and Weich, 2017).

We also suggest that to the confidence tests posed by the review should be added a sixth: what mechanisms are there in place to secure those with mental disorders the support they require to remain, and flourish, in the circumstances that they wish to be in? In other words, what mechanisms are in place to give true effect to Article 19 CRPD?[4] If those mechanisms do not exist, and those requiring support are not able to exercise a meaningful right to obtain it if it is not forthcoming, then debates about whether to place a greater weight upon capacity in the context of mental health law will reduce to little more than a debate about what to label the lock on the door of the institution where the person will end up in crisis.

References

Care Quality Commission (2020), *Monitoring the Mental Health Act in 2019–2020*. Available at: Monitoring the Mental Health Act in 2018/19 (cqc.org.uk) (Accessed: 11 September 2021).

Committee on the Rights of Persons with Disabilities (2014), *General Comment, No 1, Article 12: Equal Recognition Before the Law*.

Craigie, J. and Davies, A. (2019) 'Problems of control: Alcohol dependence, anorexia nervosa, and the flexible interpretation of mental incapacity tests', *Medical Law Review*, 27(2), pp. 215–241.

Curley, A., Murphy, R., Plunkett, R. and Kelly, B.D. (2019) 'Concordance of mental capacity assessments based on legal and clinical criteria: A cross-sectional study of psychiatry inpatients', *Psychiatry Research*, 276, pp. 160–166. https://doi.org/10.1016/j.psychres.2019.05.015.

Curley, A., Watson, C. and Kelly, B.D. (2021) 'Capacity to consent to treatment in psychiatry inpatients – A systematic review', *International Journal of Psychiatry in Clinical Practice*. https://doi.org/10.1080/13651501.2021.2017461.

Department of Health (2015) *Mental Health Act Code of Practice*. London: HMSO.

Department of Health and Social Care (2018), *Modernising the Mental Health Act: Increasing Choice, Reducing Compulsion. Final Report of the Independent Review of the Mental Health Act 1983*. Available at: Modernising the Mental Health Act: Final Report of the Independent Review of the Mental Health Act 1983 (publishing.service.gov.uk) (Accessed: 2 December 2021).

Department of Health and Social Care (2021) *Reforming the Mental Health Act Government Response to Consultation* (CP 501). London: HMSO.

Donnelly, M. (2007) 'Assessing legal capacity: Process and the operation of the functional test', *Irish Judicial Studies Journal*, 2, pp. 141–168. Available at: https://ssrn.com/abstract=1961205 (Accessed: 21 February 2022).

Expert Group on the Review of the Mental Health Act, 2001 (2015) *Report of the Expert Group on the Review of the Mental Health Act, 2001*. Department of Health Dublin. Available at: https://www.gov.ie/en/publication/637ccf-report-of-the-expert-group-review-of-the-mental-health-act-2001/ (Accessed: 29 October 2021).

Gilburt, H. (2021) 'Understanding clinical decision-making at the interface of the Mental Health Act (1983) and the Mental Capacity Act (2005): Report by the king's fund', Available at: https://www.york.ac.uk/media/healthsciences/images/research/prepare/reportsandtheircoverimages/Understanding%20the%20MHA%20&%20MCA%20interface.pdf (Accessed: 2 December 2021).

---

3 As to the concept of 'just uncertainty', see Pollitt et al. (2022).
4 Which recognises the equal right of all persons with disabilities to live independently and be included in the community, with the freedom to choose and control their lives.

Guy, A. (2011) 'Legal capacity in a mental health context in Ireland a critical review and a case for reform', MA Dissertation. TU Dublin. Available at: https://arrow.tudublin.ie/aaschssldis/65/ (Accessed: 20 October 2021).

Hale, B. 'Is it time for yet another Mental Health Act?' Speech to the Royal College of Psychiatrists Annual Conference, Birmingham on 24 June 2018. Available at: Is it time for yet another Mental Health Act? (supremecourt.uk) (Accessed: 2 December 2021)

Harper, C., Davidson, G. and McLelland, R. (2016) 'No longer "anomalous, confusing and unjust": The Mental Capacity Act (Northern Ireland) 2016', *International Journal of Mental Health and Capacity Law*, 22, pp. 57–70.

Irish Human Rights and Equality Commission (2012) *IHRC Says "Significant judgment" Delivered in Mental Health Act Case in Which It Appeared as Amicus Curiae*. Available at: https://www.ihrec.ie/ihrc-says-significant-judgment-delivered-in-mental-health-act-case-in-which-it-appeared-as-amicus-curiae/ (Accessed: 24 November 2021).

Lush, D. (2015) 'The civil law and the common law', in: Frimston, A. et al. (eds.) *The International Protection of Adults*. Oxford: Oxford University Press, pp. 37–52.

Okai, D., Owen, G., McGuire, H., Singh, S., Churchill, R. and Hotopf, M. (2007) 'Mental capacity in psychiatric patients: Systematic review', *The British Journal of Psychiatry*, 191(4), pp.291–297.

Parker, C. (2020) *Adolescent Mental Health Care and the Law*. London: Legal Action Group.

Pollitt, P., Benson, C., Ruck Keene, A. and Pow, R. (2022) 'A "just" approach to uncertainty in mental health and capacity practice and policy: Findings from a policy lab', Available at: Uncertainty-Policy-Lab-Final.pdf (mhj.org.uk) (Accessed: 8 March 2022).

Reidy, K. and Kelly, B.D. (2021) 'Involuntary status and mental capacity for treatment decisions under Sections 4, 3, and 57 of Ireland's Mental Health Act, 2001: Analysis and recommendations for reform', *Irish Journal of Psychological Medicine*, 22, pp. 1–6. https://doi.org/10.1017/ipm.2020.136.

Ruck Keene, A., (2021) 'Lessons from Abroad', in: Donnelly, M. and Gleeson, G., (eds.) *The Assisted Decision-Making (Capacity) Act 2015: Personal and Professional Reflections*, Cork: University College Cork.

Ruck Keene, A. and Friedman, M. (2020) 'Best interests, wishes and feelings and the court of protection 2015–2020', *Journal of Elder Law and Capacity*, Winter, pp. 31–53.

Ruck Keene, A., Kane, N.B., Kim, S.Y. and Owen, G.S. (2019) 'Taking capacity seriously? Ten years of mental capacity disputes before England's Court of Protection', *International Journal of Law and Psychiatry*, 62, pp. 56–76.

Ruck Keene, A., Kane, N.B., Kim, S.Y. and Owen, G.S. (2023) 'Mental capacity – Why look for a paradigm shift', *Medical Law Review*, p. fwac052. https://doi.org/10.1093/medlaw/fwac052

Steering Group on the Review of the Mental Health Act 2001 (2012), *Interim Report of the Steering Group on the Review of the Mental Health Act 2001*. Available at: http://hdl.handle.net/10147/234554 (Accessed: 24 November 2021).

Szmukler, G. and Kelly, B.D. (2016) 'We should replace conventional mental health law with capacity-based law', *British Journal of Psychiatry*, 209(6), pp. 449–453. https://doi.org/10.1192/bjp.bp.116.191080.

Szmukler, G. and Weich, S. (2017) 'Has the Mental Health Act had its day?', *The British Medical Journal*, 359. https://doi.org/10.1136/bmj.j5248.

18
RISK OF HARM AND INVOLUNTARY PSYCHIATRIC TREATMENT

Matthew Large, Sascha Callaghan and Christopher James Ryan

Introduction

The criteria that must be satisfied before a person can be involuntarily detained and treated for mental illness under statutes that allow this differ markedly from jurisdiction to jurisdiction and may vary depending on whether the compulsory treatment is to be provided as an inpatient or outpatient. However, there are at least some similarities across most pieces of legislation.

First, involuntary detention and treatment is restricted to people with some abnormality of the mind or brain.[1] Second, in many jurisdictions, the mental abnormality must affect decision-making capacity with respect to a decision to refuse psychiatric treatment.[2] Third, it is frequently the case that the involuntary detention and treatment must be the least restrictive avenue for providing needed treatment.[3] This third criterion may require that the treatment will actually be available to the person should they be made an involuntary patient[4] and that the treatment is likely to be effective. A fourth criterion sometimes present is that there must be a judgement that the involuntary treatment is in the person's best interests.[5]

This chapter is concerned with yet another criterion that is common in modern mental health legislation. In broad terms, this criterion might be referred to as a "harm criterion", though as we shall demonstrate, beyond the fact that this criterion refers to the prevention of harm to persons, its content and interpretation vary enormously and, we argue, these differences matter.

---

1 See for example: *Mental Health Act 1983* (UK) s 3(2)(a); *Mental Health Act 2007* (NSW) ss 3, 15.
2 See for example: *Mental Health Act 2013* (Tas) s 25(c); *Mental Health (Care and Treatment) (Scotland) Act 2003* (Scot) s 44(4)(b); Ala Code § 22-52-10.4(a)(iv).
3 See for example: *Mental Health Act 2007* (NSW) s 12(1)(b); Fla Stat § 394.467(1)(b).
4 See for example: *Mental Health Act 1983* (UK) s 3(2)(d).
5 See for example: DC Code Ann. § 21-545(b)(2).

Involuntary psychiatric treatment

How harm criteria vary

In the mental health legislation of most jurisdictions, to qualify for involuntary detention and treatment, a mentally ill person must present a risk of harm either to themselves or to other people. While the possibilities of self-harm and harm to others arguably involve rather different ethical and evidentiary considerations, the two forms of harm are almost always lumped together and treated as substantively equivalent, such as in the *Mental Health Act 1983* (UK) which refers to admission that is "necessary for the health or safety of the patient *or* for the protection of other persons" [emphasis added].[6] This format is typical.

Harm criteria vary across a number of dimensions. The most prominent dimension and the one we will concern ourselves with is the degree of potential harm required for involuntary treatment.

At one end of the spectrum is a very simple requirement that the admission and treatment is necessary for the "health or safety" of the patient or, with regard to harm to others, that the admission and treatment is necessary "for the protection of other persons".[7] These very low thresholds are seen in both the English and Welsh, and Scottish laws.[8] As written, at least, both pieces of UK legislation, even when read in the context of the relevant Code of Practice (UK Department of Health, 2015; Scottish Executive, 2005), provide no real qualifier as to the degree of harm that is envisaged with any diminution of the patient's health or safety (or welfare), though the Scottish legislation does provide that such risk to the health, safety or welfare must be "significant". One does not have to imagine any particularly severe harm occurring before some diminution of the patient's "health or safety" is called into play.[9] Similarly, it does not seem that you'd need to envisage a particularly severe harm to others before that person might need protection or it might be seen as "significant".[10]

A little further along the spectrum are statutes such as those in the Australian state of New South Wales (NSW) – where all three authors reside – which require that involuntary treatment must be necessary for the protection of the person or others from "*serious* harm",[11] raising the bar slightly above the English, Welsh and Scottish legislation. The interpretation of this requirement by Australian courts, however, and subsequent interpretative guidelines, demonstrates that doctors have considerable flexibility when applying these criteria.

A 2011 ruling in the New South Wales Supreme Court suggested that "serious harm" was broad enough to include "the harm associated with the illness itself" (including, presum-

---

6 *Mental Health Act 1983* (UK) s 3(2)(c).
7 *Mental Health Act 1983* (UK) s 3(2)(c).
8 *Mental Health (Care and Treatment) (Scotland) Act 2003* (Scot) s 64(5)(c).
9 The *Mental Health Act 1983: Code of Practice* expands on this stating that "the
   factors to be considered in deciding whether patients should be detained for their own health and safety include any evidence suggesting that patients are at risk of: suicide; self-harm; self-neglect or being unable to look after their own health or safety; jeopardising their own health or safety accidentally, recklessly or unintentionally; or that their mental disorder is otherwise putting their health or safety at risk". Also to be considered is "any evidence suggesting that the patient's mental health will deteriorate if they do not receive treatment, including the views of the patient or carers, relatives or close friends (especially those living with the patient) about the likely course of the disorder" (UK Department of Health, 2015).
10 The *Mental Health Act 1983: Code of Practice* expands on this also stating it is necessary to consider "the nature of the risk to other people arising from the patient's mental disorder, the likelihood that harm will result and the severity of any potential harm, taking into account" among other things "psychological as well as physical harm" (ibid.).
11 *Mental Health Act 2007* (NSW) s 14(1).

ably, the psychological harm that a person may suffer as a result of hallucinations, delusions or a severe disturbance of mood, which fall within the Act's definition of mental illness). However, the Court also indicated that this was not unbounded, noting that "it would be necessary to consider the extent to which the illness was a harm for the person and to assess its seriousness" – meaning that symptoms of mental illness were not to be taken to be "seriously harmful" *per se*, and that evidence of some other kind of harm would be required.[12] While these statements were not legally binding, the ruling indicated that Courts might be willing to take an expansive approach to the types of harm that might justify involuntary treatment in that state. In guidelines issued subsequently, following a coronial inquest, it was noted that serious harm is intended to be a broad concept that may include: "physical harm"; "emotional/psychological harm"; "financial harm"; "self-harm and suicide"; "violence and aggression including sexual assault or abuse"; "stalking or predatory intent"; "harm to reputation[13] or relationships"; "neglect of self"; and "neglect of others (including children)" (Verrall, 2021). In addition, the legislation further specifies that an assessment of potential harm may include consideration of "any likely deterioration in the person's condition and the likely effects of any such deterioration".[14]

Given its extremely broad terms, in practice the harm criterion in the NSW *Mental Health Act* applies few breaks on well-intentioned doctors who feel that a person with a mental illness might benefit from admission, provided there is no less restrictive option reasonably available.[15]

Other jurisdictions restrict involuntary treatment to situations where treatment is deemed necessary to avert a risk of physical or bodily harm. In Ontario, for a patient to be admitted involuntarily, a doctor must be of the opinion

> that the patient is suffering from mental disorder of a nature or quality that likely will result in ... serious bodily harm to the patient, ... serious bodily harm to another person, or ... serious physical impairment of the patient.[16]

References to harm as potential future bodily injury are particularly common in the United States. In the District of Columbia, for example, a court or jury must find that the person "is likely to injure himself or others if not committed".[17]

The legislation of many US states additionally lays down criteria upon which the likelihood of that future physical harm must be gauged. In Colorado, commitment requires a court to find by clear and convincing evidence that the person "is a danger to others or to himself or herself or is gravely disabled".[18] In this statute, danger to self requires a "substantial risk" evidenced by recent threats or attempts at suicide or serious self-harm, and "danger

---

12 *Re J (No. 2)* [2011] NSWSC 1224, [101] (White J).
13 The inclusion of serious harm to reputation among the Chief Psychiatrist's examples is interesting, particularly since *obiter* in *Re J (No. 2)* had cast doubt upon the possibility that reputational harm was among the harms envisaged by Parliament. See: *Re J (No. 2)* [2011] NSWSC 1224, [93] (White J).
14 *Mental Health Act 2007* (NSW) s 14(2). Similar provisions in British Columbia *Mental Health Act*, RSBC 1996, c 288, s 22(3)(c)(ii).
15 *Mental Health Act 2007* (NSW) s 12(1)(b).
16 *Mental Health Act*, RSO 1996, c M-7, s 20(5)(a).
17 DC Code Ann § 21-545(b)(2).
18 Colo Rev Stat § 27-65-111(1).

to others" requires evidence of recent homicidal or other violent behaviour or including an attempt or threat to do serious physical harm.[19]

Similarly, in Florida, a court must find by clear and convincing evidence that there "is substantial likelihood that in the near future he or she will inflict serious bodily harm on self or others, as evidenced by recent behavior causing, attempting, or threatening such harm" or "is likely to suffer from neglect or refuse to care for himself or herself, and such neglect or refusal poses a real and present threat of substantial harm to his or her well-being".[20] In Georgia, the person must present "a substantial risk of imminent harm to that person or others, as manifested by either recent overt acts or recent expressed threats of violence which present a probability of physical injury to that person or other persons", or be "so unable to care for that person's own physical health and safety as to create an imminently life-endangering crisis".[21]

The examples demonstrate a range of harm criteria for involuntary treatment, falling anywhere from a possible impact on a person's or another's health and welfare to a grave and sometimes imminent threat to a person's or another's physical safety. And in addition to the actual letter of the law, there is the way in which health practitioners at the coalface interpret the requirements.

Indeed, much of the way that involuntary treatment occurs might depend less on the phrasing of the legislation than it does on the way that the health practitioners responsible for the day-to-day coercive treatment decisions frame those provisions in their mind (Anfang and Appelbaum, 2006). All three authors regularly provide teaching around the use and operation of the various pieces of mental health legislation in operation in Australia. In our experience, it is unusual for a psychiatrist or other healthcare practitioner who regularly uses the coercive provisions to be able to provide an accurate summary of the legislative provisions that they regularly engage. With respect to the harm criteria in the authors' home state of NSW, practitioners tend to refer to "risk of harm" when the word "risk" does not appear in the law. While the notion of "risk" is focussed on what may happen in the future, the legislation permits involuntary treatment where it is necessary to protect a person from harms they are experiencing *at the time* they present. It is not clear the extent to which practitioners appreciate any distinction between current and future harm. Conversely, practitioners will often overlook requirements for harms to be "serious" or "physical" where relevant, relying instead on habits of practice in which particular types of presentation and intuited "risks" tend to result in detention and involuntary treatment, without parsing the letter of the law.

In what follows we make clear that it is not possible to use one or any combination of clinical or demographic features in a patient's presentation to usefully judge future likelihood of serious self-harm, suicide or serious harm directed at others. This reality is a huge problem for laws that demand such judgements to be made. However, it is also a problem in areas without strict legal requirements to assess risk of future harm, but where tribunals, policy makers and, most importantly, clinicians understand this kind of assessment to be necessary in any case.

---

19 Colo Rev Stat § 27-65-102(4.5).
20 Fla Stat § 394.467(1)(a)(2).
21 Ga Code Ann § 37-3-1(9.1).

Understanding risk assessment for future harmful acts

When viewed as a predictive or statistical test of future harm, a risk assessment results in a two-by-two contingency table depending on the occurrence or non-occurrence of the act of harm. The cells of the contingency table consist of (i) true positives (people who are detained who would cause or come to harm), (ii) false positives (people who are detained who would not cause or come to harm), (iii) false negatives (people who are not detained who would cause or come to harm), and (iv) true negatives (people not detained who would not cause or come to harm) (Table 18.1).

This combination of two risk categories (higher- and lower-risk) and two outcomes (harmful behaviour and no harmful behaviour) can be used to generate the well-known risk assessment metrics of sensitivity (the proportion of people who cause or come to harm who are categorised in the higher-risk group), specificity (the proportion of people who do not cause or come to harm who are categorised in the lower-risk category), the odds ratio (OR) (approximating the increased likelihood that a person in the higher-risk category will cause or come to harm compared to a person in the lower-risk category) and the positive predictive value (PPV) (the proportion of people in the higher-risk category who go on to cause or come to harm) (Singh, 2013). There are a variety of other metrics that can be used to assess the strength of risk assessment, most notably the area under the (receiver operator) curve (AUC) which is a summary statistic of the trade-off between sensitivity and specificity which (like an odds ratio) is a single number quantifying the ability of the risk assessment to discriminate between higher- and lower-risk people with respect to harmful outcomes or the effect-size (Szmukler et al., 2012). In this chapter we have focussed on sensitivity, specificity, odds ratio, and the positive predictive value. We also report PPV in its inverse form (1/PPV) which is the number needed to detain (NND) one person who would go on to cause or come to harm (Large et al., 2011). NND is an important statistic because it indicates the number of people who might be needlessly detained and treated involuntarily to potentially prevent one harmful act. It should be noted that NND is not the same, and is inevitably lower, possibly much lower, than the number needed to treat, as is used to describe the benefits of medical treatment, because detention, particularly civil detention is likely to be so short-lived as not to prevent all harmful outcomes, and because treatments for violence and self-harm do not work very well (Fox et al., 2020). In this context NND and number needed to treat are further differentiated by the possibility that hospitalisation is actually counter-therapeutic and might paradoxically increase the likelihood of suicidal acts (Large et al., 2017b) or violence (Iozzino et al., 2015).

A detailed history of the efforts of mental health professionals to predict future harmful acts to the self or others in mental health care is beyond the scope of this chapter. One good starting point is the well-established finding by Paul Meehl that predictions made on the

Table 18.1 Contingency table generated by risk assessment and outcome

		Risk Assessment	
		Lower-risk	Higher-risk
Harmful outcome	Occurs	False negatives	True positives
	Does not occur	True negatives	False positives

basis of tangible observations (actuarial methods) generally exceed predictions made by clinicians (Meehl, 2013). Meehl's finding contributed to enthusiasm for modelling predictions of future harmful behaviour of people with mental illness. Arguably the two most well-known examples of this modelling are Alex D. Pokorny's prospective study of people discharged from psychiatric units (Pokorny, 1983) and the MacArthur Violence Risk Assessment Study (Steadman et al., 1998). Pokorny examined outcome in terms of suicide and suicide attempts and the MacArthur Violence Risk Assessment Study examined a range of harms to others. Both studies are very well known, have been heavily cited, including in replication studies, and continue to be discussed in commentaries in the peer-reviewed literature (Nielssen et al., 2017; Torrey et al., 2008). Since the Pokorny and Steadman studies, literally hundreds of studies of the prediction of various forms of self-harm/suicide and violence have been published in the peer-reviewed literature. In the last decade this huge body of primary research has been synthesised in multiple meta-analyses such that we can now be quite certain about the predictive strength of clinically meaningful variables and methods for assessing risk of violence, self-harm, and suicide.

Risk assessment for suicide and self-harm

Pokorny was not the first author to seriously consider the prospects for successful suicide-risk assessment. However, 40 years on, his study remains one of the largest and most thorough studies of the topic. In the mid-1970s Pokorny assembled and developed a comprehensive suite of suicide scales and suicide risk items that he then used to assess 4800 consecutive first-admitted patients to a Houston Veterans Administration psychiatric hospital. He then followed up the cohort for an average of five years, during which time a number had adverse outcomes, including suicide. Pokorny used various clinical and actuarial methods, including discriminant analysis and logistic regression to explore ways of categorising future suicides (Pokorny, 1983; Pokorny, 1993). The most widely discussed model, described in the 1983 Pokorny paper (p. 245), correctly identified 35 true positive suicides among 1241 higher-risk people while 28 false negative suicides were classified among the 3463 lower-risk people. From this data 35/63 suicides were classified as higher-risk (sensitivity = 56%), and 3435 of 4641 non-suicides were classified as lower-risk (specificity = 74%). Higher-risk patients had an increased odds ratio of suicide of 3.6 over lower-risk patients and the PPV of the optimal model was 2.8% indicating a NND of 36. This suggests that if the optimal model had been applied at the point of admission, 35 higher-risk patients would be false positive classifications for every true positive suicide in the following five years. Meanwhile 44% of the suicides would have been categorised as lower-risk. Pokorny rightly considered that "each trial missed many cases [of suicide] and identified far too many false positive cases to be workable" (Pokorny, 1983). He concluded that it is "inescapable that we do not possess any item or any combination of items that permit us to identify to a useful degree the particular persons who will commit suicide" (Pokorny, 1983).

In clinical practice suicide risk assessment often relies heavily on the presence or absence of suicidal thoughts or behaviours (such as suicide attempts) rather than statistical models. Contemporary theories of suicide hold that the causal steps towards suicide include suicidal ideas progressing to suicidal behaviours and then suicide (Van Orden et al., 2010). However, in recent years, several meta-analyses have found that suicidal thoughts and behaviours are only weakly associated with future suicide. A 2016 meta-analysis of longitudinal studies found both suicide thoughts and suicide behaviours were associated with suicide with an odds ratio for suicide of about two. The authors concluded that suicide ideas and behaviours "only provide a marginal improvement in diagnostic accuracy (for suicide) above chance" (Ribeiro et al., 2016). More recently the association between suicide ideas and suicide was examined in a meta-analysis that included a much larger sample of 71 longitudinal or controlled studies (McHugh et al., 2019). This study found that suicide ideas had sensitivity for suicide of 41%, a specificity for suicide of 86%, an odds ratio of 3.4, and a PPV of 1.7% over an average nine years' follow-up. This suggests that 59 people with suicide ideas would need to be hospitalised for every one person who would go on to suicide in the next decade. A third meta-analysis synthesised data from a sample of 51 studies that examined the associations between both suicidal ideas and suicidal behaviour, and later suicide (Large et al., 2021). This study contradicted conventional wisdom that suicide behaviour is more strongly associated with suicide than suicide ideas and confirmed the unexpected finding of Ribeiro and associates, that suicide behaviours (such as suicide attempts) are not statistically closer to suicide than suicidal ideas (Ribeiro et al., 2016).

The failure of these conventional indicators of suicide – suicide ideas and suicide attempts – to predict suicide is now known to be part of a picture of generally weak associations between other putative risk factors and suicide. A landmark study that synthesised 50 years of research into suicide risk factors reported on 365 longitudinal studies (Franklin et al., 2017) and examined numerous individual risk factors and domains including demographics, internalising factors (such as anxiety and depression), prior suicidal thoughts and behaviours, externalising behaviours (such as violence and drug use), and social factors, across a wide variety of populations and settings. The authors reached what they described as the unexpected finding that "no broad category or subcategory [of suicide risk factors] accurately predicted far above chance levels" (Franklin et al., 2017).

In response to the failure of individual risk factors to meaningfully predict suicide, various authors have re-examined the potential for suicide modelling based on the combination of various risk factors, either by experimental models or with the use of so-called suicide risk scales. In turn these studies have also been subject to meta-analyses to determine the underlying strength of such methods. In the first of these meta-analyses, Large et al. synthesised the predictive strength of 53 longitudinal studies of suicide risk categorisation made by combining two or more clinical risk factors carried by populations of psychiatric patients (Large et al., 2016). This study found that higher-risk categorisation had a sensitivity of 56%, a specificity of 79%, an odds ratio of 4.84, and a PPV of 5.5% over five years. This indicated an NND of 18 people, meaning that 17 higher-risk people who would not suicide would have to be detained to hospitalise one person who would suicide in the following five years. Other more recent studies have focussed on the use of suicide risk scales with similar results. These studies have variously concluded that "the scales lack sufficient evidence to support their use" (Chan et al., 2016), "are not clinically useful" (Carter et al., 2017), and "do not fulfil requirements for diagnostic accuracy" (Runeson et al., 2017).

The topic has also been approached with more statistically advanced and broader meta-analytic approaches – each yielding a similar result. One meta-analysis of 102 exploratory suicide prediction models (models that have the potential to inflate the predictive strength because of capitalisation on chance findings) had the counter-intuitive finding that suicide risk models that incorporate more risk factors are no better at predicting suicide than less complex models incorporating fewer risk factors (Corke et al., 2021). This suggests that more clinical information rather than less information is not more helpful in a predictive sense. A finding that a larger number of objective observations of risk factors at the outset are unhelpful in furthering prediction has theoretical and practical implications and suggests that much of the uncertainty about suicide is largely stochastic or aleatory, that is, subject to random factors (Large et al., 2017a). This finding can be seen as particularly significant because it not only holds for suicide but holds for the prediction of non-lethal self-harm such as suicide attempts (Taylor et al., 2020). The authors of this study concluded "risk scales should have little role in the management of people who have self-harmed" (Taylor et al., 2020). The failure of even quite complex suicide risk modelling to meaningfully predict suicide attempts and deaths was most recently and compellingly illustrated by Blesher and associates who synthesised data from high-quality prospective studies of suicide prediction modelling and concluded from these suicide prediction models that their "accuracy of predicting a future suicide event is near zero" (Belsher et al., 2019).

Finally, and returning to Meehl's contention about the superiority of actuarial over clinical prediction methods, among the 102 exploratory suicide prediction models included in the Corke and associates meta-analysis (Corke et al., 2021) were 10 studies that examined the predictive strength of unaided clinical judgement. These studies had the lowest odds ratio of any suicide prediction method. This suggests that clinicians cannot by some intuitive or heuristic process know which of their patients is more likely to die by suicide.

Risk assessment for violence

The MacArthur Violence Risk Assessment Study was not the first to examine the predictive properties of violence risk assessment, but it remains one of the most highly cited and discussed studies in the field. The authors examined 1136 people discharged from three psychiatric hospitals between 1992 and 1995. Each subject was comprehensively assessed for a wide variety of potential risk factors. Episodes of future violence were assessed using multiple informants at ten-week intervals for the next year. The study resulted in the publication of numerous papers, the first of which suggested that discharged patients without symptoms of substance abuse were no more violent than similar people in the neighbourhoods to which the patients were discharged (Steadman et al., 1998). Despite this conclusion, several later papers related to the MacArthur study examined methods for predicting violence (Monahan et al., 2000; Steadman et al., 2000). The most highly cited of these prediction studies found that 92 of 204 higher-risk patients and 84 of 735 low- or medium-risk patients (as classified using an iterative decision tree) were violent in the following year (Monahan et al., 2000). From this data it can be calculated that 92 of 176 violent people were classified as higher-risk (sensitivity 52%), that 651 of 763 non-violent people were classified as lower-risk (specificity 85%), and that higher-risk patients had an increased odds ratio of violence of 6.5 over lower-risk patients. The PPV of the study was 45% suggesting an NND of two and that one higher-risk non-violent patient would have to be detained for every hospitalised higher-risk violent patient.

Despite the similarity in the predictive metrics between the sensitivity (59% vs 53%), specificity (75% vs 85%) and odds ratios (3.6 vs 6.5) of the Pokorny and the MacArthur studies, the authors of the MacArthur study concluded that "a clinically useful actuarial method exists to assist in violence risk assessments" (Monahan et al., 2000). Tangentially, despite suicide and violence risk assessment having near identical predictive strength, differences of opinion about the utility of risk assessment still seem to be influenced by whether the harm in question is to the self or to others. Inexplicably, there is ongoing enthusiasm for violence risk assessment tools (Singh et al., 2014) alongside firm advice not to use scales that are conceptually and statistically similar to predict self-harm and suicide (Chan et al., 2016; Carter et al., 2017).

In the years after the MacArthur study, other researchers examined a wide variety of methods for predicting violence. A 2012 meta-analysis synthesised the available primary literature and measured the potential for clinical methods to predict violence and other harmful antisocial behaviours (Fazel et al., 2012). The researchers located 30 studies examining violent outcomes, 20 studies of future sex offending, and 23 studies of more broadly defined criminal offending. The results of this data synthesis demonstrated that as a group, risk assessment studies have a similar ability to discriminate between high- and lower-risk people to that demonstrated in the MacArthur study. This was true for violent offending (sensitivity = 92%, specificity = 36%, odds ratio = 6.07), sexual offending (sensitivity = 88%, specificity = 34%, odds ratio = 3.88), and criminal offending (sensitivity = 41%, specificity = 80%, odds ratio = 2.84). The authors also examined the PPV and NND of each domain, finding NND of 2, 5, and 2 people in order to detain one future violent, sex, or criminal offender respectively (Fazel et al., 2012). As noted above, in the context of civil commitment, NND is likely to be much lower than the number needed to treat (to prevent one harmful act) because in most instances detention under mental health legislation would be brief, and treatment to prevent violence is notoriously imperfect. As a result of the quantitative and qualitative considerations, Fazel and associates concluded that risk assessment tools were best at identifying lower-risk people but their "use as sole determinants of detention, sentencing, and release is not supported by the current evidence" (Fazel et al., 2012). In a follow-up study the same authors cast further doubt on the practical utility of violence risk assessment (Singh et al., 2013). This follow-up study examined the effects of authorship bias on odds ratios reported in violence risk studies. The authors found that violence risk assessment only worked about half as well in real world settings where the assessors had not developed a risk assessment instrument themselves (odds ratio of 3 synthesised from 92 studies) when compared to the original research reports (odds ratio of 6 synthesised from 12 studies). Irrespective of the acceptance of evidence drawn from original or replication violence risk assessment studies, clinicians should be aware of the marked limitations of violence risk assessment, particularly in the context of involuntary detention, as illustrated below.

Base rates and the prediction of harmful acts

After 50 years of primary research by multiple research groups in various international settings and after syntheses by modern meta-analytic methods, the limited potential for prediction of specific harmful acts including serious self-harm, suicide, and various forms of violence is now well established. The predictive metrics of suicide risk assessment and violence risk assessment appear to be quite similar with odds ratios in the range of 4 to 6. To put this in context, this represents a predictive strength that is marginally greater than the approximately fourfold increase in suicide associated with being male and rather less than the tenfold increase that male sex confers on risk for homicide (Large, 2018).

While odds ratios (and other measures such as the AUC) quantify the ability of risk assessments to discriminate between higher- and lower-risk groups, the weakness of a risk assessment as a practical and ethical method of identifying individuals in need of commitment under mental health law is better illustrated by a consideration of the NND, indicating the number of people who are liable to be fruitlessly detained on the basis of a risk assessment in

Involuntary psychiatric treatment

order to detain one person who will act harmfully (in the sense of undertaking an act such as serious self-harm, suicide, or violence).

For this purpose, we have imagined a risk assessment instrument with a realistically superior combination of a sensitivity of 75% and specificity of 75%. Unlike sensitivity and specificity and other measures of discrimination between higher and lower groups, the PPV (and thus the NND) is strongly affected by the base rate of the particular harmful behaviour. For this illustration we have considered estimated base rates of various harms found in the peer-reviewed literature (Large et al., 2011; Walsh et al., 2015; Chung et al., 2017; Nielssen et al., 2011). We have assumed a base rate of 20% (similar to self-harm behaviour in first-episode psychoses), 10% (similar to annual rates of assault by people with schizophrenia), 1% (similar to the rate of serious violent offending in schizophrenia and suicide rates in the first year post psychiatric discharge), 0.1% (similar to the rate of suicide in psychiatric hospitals), 0.01% (similar to the annual rate of homicide in treated psychosis and the annual rate of suicide in the community), and 0.001% (approximating the annual proportion of people with psychosis who will kill a stranger).

Using these base rates, the sensitivity and specificity of our realistic and superior risk assessment instrument, and Bayes' theorem it can be calculated that two people with first-episode psychosis would need to be detained to admit one person who would make an act of non-fatal but serious self-harm, four people with schizophrenia would have to be detained to admit one person who would commit an assault in the next year, 34 people would need to be detained to admit one person with schizophrenia who would commit serious crime in the next year or one person who would go on to suicide in the year post discharge, 334 inpatients would have to be subject to more rigorous observations or restrictive treatment to contain one person who would go on to suicide as an inpatient. Over three thousand people would need to be detained to admit one patient with schizophrenia who would kill another person in the next year and over 30,000 would need to be detained if the victim was to be a stranger (Figure 18.1).

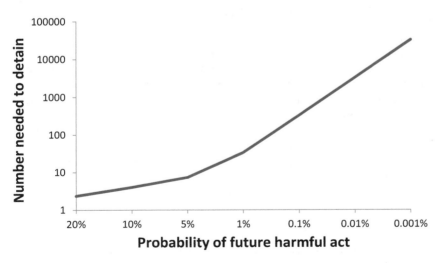

Figure 18.1 Number of people (false positives) needed to detain one person (true positive) with a future harmful act determined by an excellent risk assessment tool with a sensitivity and specificity of 75%

This illustrates that risk assessment is at its weakest when feared, rare, and extremely harmful events are at stake. We now know what was unclear in the mid- 1970s, that when tested against harmful outcomes, many harmful acts are committed by lower-risk people, and the vast majority of those categorised as at higher risk will never be harmful or experience harm.

Potential effects risk-based commitment on true positives, false positives, false negatives, and true negatives

As above, any person subjected to an assessment of their risk of harm for the purpose of civil commitment will fall into one of four groups: true positives, false positives, false negatives, and true negatives. In this section the effects on individuals in these four groups are discussed.

True positives

People detained because of an assessment that they are at higher risk of a future harm that they would go on to perform can be considered true positives. In the context of civil commitment, a risk assessment guides them into hospital where they will be contained and supervised and where they will be treated with medication and/or other therapies over the period of their admission. In this best-case scenario this containment and treatment would prevent a future harmful act even after discharge. However, detention in a hospital is no guarantee that treatment will prevent harmful acts. Nowadays hospital admissions tend to be brief opening the possibility for harmful acts after discharge, and rates of violence (Iozzino et al., 2015) and suicide (Walsh et al., 2015) in hospital are disturbingly high. Rates of violence in hospitals of almost 20% per admission also mean that scenarios in which a person is admitted because of higher risk of self-harm and is then injured by others in hospital, might not be rare.

False positives

People who are detained because of an assessment that they are at higher risk of a future harmful act that they would not go on to perform can be considered false positives. This group suffer all the same harms associated with inpatient treatment and have the same treatment and containment as true positives, but do not benefit from any reduction in harmful acts. In one sense these patients carry the burden of treatments and interventions so that a smaller number, for some outcomes a very much smaller number, of true positives can receive treatment. Such a higher-risk categorisation and subsequent hospital detention can have numerous more subtle harms including experiencing loss of social supports, and the stigma and self-stigma of being a patient in a mental hospital. False positives vastly outnumber true positives for all but the most common and least harmful outcomes, and have the worst cost- benefit exchange of any of the four groups.

False negatives

People who are not detained because of an assessment that they are lower risk but who do go on to perform a harmful act can be thought of as false negatives. These patients are deprived of treatment resources and suffer the consequences of committing a harmful act. Some of these patients will remain untreated and unwell even as a result of refusing treatment because of mental incapacity to consent and others might simply not receive needed treatment because treatment resources were being expended on inpatient care for false positive patients. To the extent that treatments actually work, false negative patients are disadvantaged.

True negatives

People who are not detained because of an assessment that they are at lower risk and who would not go on to perform a harmful act can be considered true negatives. In many studies true negatives are the numerically largest of the four groups. True negatives do not carry an unnecessary burden of treatment to prevent harms but they derive no benefit at all from the risk assessment. Some in this group will be deprived of treatments that would assist them more generally because of the diversion of resources to higher-risk patients. Like all of the other patients, they also lose out because of the limited healthcare resources used in the process of risk assessment – most notably in the cost of therapeutic time performing a risk assessment.

Revising the harm criterion in the light of this research

In 2023, with the benefit of all this evidence, it seems very unreasonable to detain a person based on an assessment of a person's probabilistic risk of future harm to the self or others. Risk assessment produces too many false positives and the limited sensitivity of risk assessment means that about half of all harmful acts are by people considered to be lower-risk. What should be done about this?

One possible alternative might be to require that the harms from which the patient or community need protection must be present at the time of assessment – that is associated with continuing or deteriorating mental illness. If terms like 'dangerousness' or 'risk of harm' are to be retained, they might be restricted to currently clinically observable characteristics of the patient, rather than a statistical probability of future harm. This would limit detention to those who are presently harmful to themselves or others, based solely on the presence of current harmful behaviour, such as acute behavioural disturbance or ongoing self-harm, without recourse to statistical risk factors which are now known to be unreliable. This change would likely limit involuntary psychiatric treatment to a smaller group of patients, who would only be detained for the period in which they were exhibiting harmful behaviour. The effects of such a limitation might be profound, not the least because very few patients could be considered contemporaneously harmful to themselves or others for long enough periods to have meaningful psychiatric treatment.

This kind of approach might exacerbate concerns that current risk provisions unfairly restrict access to necessary treatment of people who are unable to seek it for themselves, when such treatment is clearly necessary for their health and wellbeing. Although there would be fewer false positives, more people who would never cause or experience harm would not receive treatment and there would be an inevitable increase in the number of false negatives.

Another option might be to permit limited involuntary treatment where a person with treatable symptoms of mental illness is unable to provide consent for treatment where the treatment is necessary to protect the person's health and wellbeing. Such treatment would need to be available, and proportional to the harm (for example, it must be thought likely to reduce the harm or likelihood of deterioration, or to restore capacity for the patient to provide consent).

In line with the requirements of the United Nations Convention on the Rights of Persons with Disabilities, the views, preferences, and values of people living with mental illness must also be taken into account in making treatment decisions. This kind of needs-based framework is already in place in several jurisdictions, including from where we write in Australia, in Western Australia and Queensland. While a discussion of the merits of substitute decision-making and assisted decision-making is beyond the scope of the chapter, clinicians need to be cautious when interpreting risk of harm criteria and reforms to mental health laws should reflect what is now known about the weakness of risk assessment in mental health.

References

Anfang S.A. and Appelbaum P.S. (2006) Civil commitment–The American experience. *Isr J Psychiatry Relat Sci* 43(3): 209–218.

Belsher B.E., Smolenski D.J., Pruitt L.D., et al. (2019) Prediction models for suicide attempts and deaths: A systematic review and simulation. *JAMA Psychiatry* 76(6): 642–651.

Carter G., Milner A., McGill K., et al. (2017) Predicting suicidal behaviours using clinical instruments: Systematic review and meta-analysis of positive predictive values for risk scales. *Br J Psychiatry* 210(6): 387–395.

Chan M.K., Bhatti H., Meader N., et al. (2016) Predicting suicide following self-harm: Systematic review of risk factors and risk scales. *Br J Psychiatry* 209(4): 277–283.

Chung D.T., Ryan C.J., Hadzi-Pavlovic D., et al. (2017) Suicide rates after discharge from psychiatric facilities: A systematic review and meta-analysis. *JAMA Psychiatry* 74(7): 694–702.

Corke M., Mullin K., Angel-Scott H., Xia S. and Large M. (2021) Meta-analysis of the strength of exploratory suicide prediction models; from clinicians to computers. *BJPsych Open* 7(1): e26.

Fazel S., Singh J.P., Doll H. and Grann M. (2012) Use of risk assessment instruments to predict violence and antisocial behaviour in 73 samples involving 24 827 people: Systematic review and meta-analysis. *BMJ* 345: e4692.

Fox K.R., Huang X., Guzman E.M., et al. (2020) Interventions for suicide and self-injury: A meta-analysis of randomized controlled trials across nearly 50 years of research. *Psychol Bull* 146(12): 1117–1145.

Franklin J.C., Ribeiro J.D., Fox K.R., et al. (2017) Risk factors for suicidal thoughts and behaviors: A meta-analysis of 50 years of research. *Psychol Bull* 143(2): 187–232.

Iozzino L., Ferrari C., Large M., Nielssen O. and de Girolamo G. (2015) Prevalence and risk factors of violence by psychiatric acute inpatients: A systematic review and meta-analysis. *PLOS ONE* 10(6): e0128536.

Large M., Corderoy A. and McHugh C. (2021) Is suicidal behaviour a stronger predictor of later suicide than suicidal ideation? A systematic review and meta-analysis. *Aust N Z J Psychiatry*. 55(3): 254–267.

Large M., Galletly C., Myles N., Ryan C.J. and Myles H. (2017a) Known unknowns and unknown unknowns in suicide risk assessment: Evidence from meta-analyses of aleatory and epistemic uncertainty. *BJPsych Bull* 41(3): 160–163.

Large M., Kaneson M., Myles N., et al. (2016) Meta-analysis of longitudinal cohort studies of suicide risk assessment among psychiatric patients: Heterogeneity in results and lack of improvement over time. *PLOS ONE* 11(6): e0156322.

Large M.M. (2018) The role of prediction in suicide prevention. *Dial Clin Neurosci* 20(3): 197–205.

Large M.M., Chung D.T., Davidson M., Weiser M. and Ryan C.J. (2017b) In-patient suicide: Selection of people at risk, failure of protection and the possibility of causation. *BJPsych Open* 3(3): 102–105.

Large M.M., Ryan C.J., Singh S.P., Paton M.B. and Nielssen O.B. (2011) The predictive value of risk categorization in schizophrenia. *Harv Rev Psychiatry* 19(1): 25–33.

McHugh C.M., Corderoy A., Ryan C.J., et al. (2019) Association between suicidal ideation and suicide: Meta-analyses of odds ratios, sensitivity, specificity and positive predictive value. *BJPsych Open* 5: e18.

Meehl P.E. (2013) *Clinical versus Statistical Prediction. A Theoretical Analysis and Review of the Evidence.* Echo Point Books & Media.

Monahan J., Steadman H.J., Appelbaum P.S., et al. (2000) Developing a clinically useful actuarial tool for assessing violence risk. *Br J Psychiatry* 176: 312–319.

Nielssen O., Bourget D., Laajasalo T., et al. (2011) Homicide of strangers by people with a psychotic illness. *Schizophr Bull* 37(3): 572–579.

Nielssen O., Wallace D. and Large M. (2017) Pokorny's complaint: The insoluble problem of the overwhelming number of false positives generated by suicide risk assessment. *BJPsych Bull* 41(1): 18–20.

Pokorny A.D. (1983) Prediction of suicide in psychiatric patients: Report of a prospective study. *Arch Gen Psychiatry* 40(3): 249–257.

Pokorny A.D. (1993) Suicide prediction revisited. *Suicide Life Threat Behav* 23(1): 1–10.

Ribeiro J.D., Franklin J.C., Fox K.R., et al. (2016) Self-injurious thoughts and behaviors as risk factors for future suicide ideation, attempts, and death: A meta-analysis of longitudinal studies. *Psychol Med* 46(2): 225–236.

Runeson B., Odeberg J., Pettersson A., et al. (2017) Instruments for the assessment of suicide risk: A systematic review evaluating the certainty of the evidence. *PLOS ONE* 12(7): e0180292.

Scottish Executive. (2005) *Mental Health (Care and Treatment) (Scotland) Act 2003: Code of Practice.* Scottish Government.

Singh J.P. (2013) Predictive validity performance indicators in violence risk assessment: A methodological primer. *Behav Sci Law* 31(1): 8–22.

Singh J.P., Desmarais S.L., Hurducas C., et al. (2014) International perspectives on the practical application of violence risk assessment: A global survey of 44 countries. *Int J Forensic Ment Health* 13(3): 193–206.

Singh J.P., Grann M. and Fazel S. (2013) Authorship bias in violence risk assessment? A systematic review and meta-analysis. *PLOS ONE* 8(9): e72484.

Steadman H.J., Mulvey E.P., Monahan J., et al. (1998) Violence by people discharged from acute psychiatric inpatient facilities and by others in the same neighborhoods. *Arch Gen Psychiatry* 55(5): 393–401.

Steadman H.J., Silver E., Monahan J., et al. (2000) A classification tree approach to the development of actuarial violence risk assessment tools. *Law Hum Behav* 24(1): 83–100.

Szmukler G., Everitt B. and Leese M. (2012) Risk assessment and receiver operating characteristic curves. *Psychol Med* 42(5): 895–898.

Taylor A.K., Steeg S., Quinlivan L., et al. (2020) Accuracy of individual and combined risk-scale items in the prediction of repetition of self-harm: Multicentre prospective cohort study. *BJPsych Open* 7(1): e2.

Torrey E.F., Stanley J., Monahan J., Steadman H.J. and MacArthur Study Group. (2008) The MacArthur violence risk assessment study revisited: Two views ten years after its initial publication. *Psychiatr Serv* 59(2): 147–152.

UK Department of Health. (2015) *Mental Health Act 1983: Code of Practice.* The Stationary Office.

Van Orden K.A., Witte T.K., Cukrowicz K.C., et al. (2010) The interpersonal theory of suicide. *Psychol Rev* 117(2): 575–600.

Verrall P. (2021) *NSW Mental Health Act (2007) No. 8 Guidebook.* Health Education and Training Institute.

Walsh G., Sara G., Ryan C.J. and Large M. (2015) Meta-analysis of suicide rates among psychiatric inpatients. *Acta Psychiatr Scand* 131(3): 174–184.

19
COMPULSORY COMMUNITY TREATMENT

Is it the least restrictive alternative?

John Dawson

Introduction

This chapter addresses the law governing compulsory community mental health care, focusing on the legal framework typically provided in the common law jurisdictions of the UK, Canada, Australia and New Zealand.

One of the most significant questions facing mental health law over the last half century has been how the law should respond to the deinstitutionalisation of mental health services – to the massive down-sizing of psychiatric hospitals and the associated build-up of community mental health services. Should it respond by establishing a new framework for compulsory community care?

The older law governing the administration of psychiatric hospitals laid the foundations for compulsory community care, by allowing patients detained in hospital to be granted 'leave' or 'conditional discharge' from hospital. Subsequently, that framework has been superseded, or supplemented, in most jurisdictions, by a more elaborate Community Treatment Order (CTO) (or Outpatient Commitment) scheme. The general features of such schemes, and the dilemmas they typically present, are the subject of this chapter.

Central among these dilemmas is the imponderable impact CTOs have on people's rights. A CTO's primary effect is usually to require a person to 'comply' with psychiatric treatment (especially medication) after their release from detention in hospital. Plainly this affects their rights: to liberty, to refuse treatment and to respect for private life, at the very least. The dilemma, then, is not whether rights are limited, but whether this can be justified.

To justify such measures, under human rights law, it would usually be necessary to establish that only 'proportionate' limits are imposed on rights – to satisfy the principle of proportionality (Huscroft, 2014). Then, to make the case that the limits are proportionate, it would usually be necessary to show that the scheme, in limiting rights, has taken the least restrictive, or least drastic, approach to the achievement of its aims – limiting rights only to the extent necessary. Here the key argument would be that compulsory community care is the least restrictive approach, when the likely alternative is continuing detention of the person concerned in hospital, with compulsory treatment continuing there – an even more restrictive approach.

The dilemma, then, is whether this is a convincing justification. Is compulsory community care really the least restrictive alternative, when a person detained in hospital for compulsory treatment could be released entirely from compulsion upon release from hospital, while being *offered* the option of *voluntary* community care? Would that not be an even less restrictive approach?

The main question, then, is whether the offer of voluntary community care would be a *viable* alternative. Is it viable, for instance, with respect to a person who has undergone many previous compulsory hospital admissions, followed by 'failure to comply' voluntarily with the community treatment plan? Perhaps they have repeatedly 'dropped out of care' on release from hospital, and subsequently been readmitted, on a compulsory basis, following marked deterioration in their health, with all the potential consequences for their safety, and perhaps for the safety of others. Is the mere offer of community care really a viable alternative, in these circumstances?

This question is perhaps the central one concerning the rights-consistency of CTOs. It is relevant, firstly, to whether a CTO scheme should be enacted at all. Then, if such a scheme is enacted, it is relevant to the scheme's drafting: particularly the drafting of the criteria governing a person's placement on a CTO, and of the powers that can be exercised over them, to 'enforce' the conditions set for their community care. And this question – of use of the least restrictive *viable* alternative – is relevant to how the scheme is ultimately administered, by the clinicians, tribunals and courts who make the critical decisions in its process. How should the legal criteria be interpreted and applied? What view should be taken of the precise scope of the powers conferred? And how should those powers be exercised, in light of the scope of the discretion still conferred by the statutory scheme (Dawson, 2010b)?

The legal response to deinstitutionalisation

What, then, is the background to the enactment of these CTO schemes, and what is their typical legal structure?

As the process of deinstitutionalisation of large psychiatric hospitals gathered pace, despite opposition, during the 1970s, 80s and 90s, the question arose as to how the law would respond to this major change in the structure of mental health service delivery. Would the law maintain its own institutional focus, despite this change? Would the law continue to act mainly as a vehicle for regulating detention and treatment in designated psychiatric institutions? Or would it now become mainly a vehicle for authorising compulsory *treatment*, with no limit imposed on the range of places in which a person could be required to live while subject to its powers? If so, their treatment – while still involuntary – could occur either in hospital or in various community settings, including perhaps their own home.

Under the old law, even at the peak of the institutional era, *some* basic legal foundation had usually existed for compulsory community care. The provisions of the Mental Health Act (MHA) would usually authorise a detained patient to be granted 'leave' from hospital, or be placed on 'conditional discharge', on 'such terms as the Superintendent (or Home Secretary) thought fit' (or some formulation of that kind). The relevant provisions of the Act were typically brief, and vague, and conferred considerable discretion on hospital staff.

The Lunacy Act 1890 (UK), for instance, which became the model for mental health legislation in much of the British Empire, provided that two visitors, and a medical officer, of an asylum, acting in concert, could 'permit a patient in an asylum to be absent on trial so long as they think fit', and, if the patient did not return by the specified date, they could be 'retaken as in the case of an escape' (s 55). Similarly, the Mental Defectives Act 1911 (NZ) provided that the Superintendent of an institution could permit a 'patient to be absent ... on leave under proper control ... on such conditions as the said Superintendent thinks fit' (s 80).

In more modern times, the 'conditions' or 'terms' imposed would often include the person continuing to take psychiatric treatment (especially medication) as prescribed, and presenting periodically at a hospital or clinic for the assessment and monitoring of their condition. Then, to enforce those conditions, the law would provide a blunt power of 'recall' to hospital, or 'revocation' of leave. That power could be used if the person failed to comply with the conditions of their leave, or were again considered to need detention in hospital. In that situation, the law would usually permit them to be swiftly 'retaken', and re-detained in hospital, with involuntary treatment continuing there. Generally, a person subject to this scheme would be aware of the existence of the recall power, of course. So, even if it was rarely used in practice, the prospect that it might be used could cause them to 'comply' with the conditions imposed. Here, under the old legislation, was the basic legal framework for compulsory community care, even if little by way of a community service was provided, at the time, to match the promise of such care.

As the difficult process of deinstitutionalisation accelerated, 'leave' schemes of this kind were often used 'creatively' by hospital staff. The English case of *Hallstrom* (1986) provides an example. There, the 'leave' scheme under the MHA 1983 (UK) permitted a civilly committed patient to be granted leave from hospital for a maximum of six months. If not re-hospitalised during that six-month period, the patient then had to be fully released from control under the Act. To avoid this constraint, hospital staff would, in some instances, recall a patient granted leave, to the hospital, for a single night, immediately before expiry of the six-month period. Then the patient would be put back on leave from the hospital for a further six months (with that process even repeated several times). Similar 'creative' practices were followed in New Zealand (Dawson, 1991), and perhaps elsewhere. This practice was declared unlawful in England in *Hallstrom*: where the patient's recall had occurred solely for the purpose of extending their leave, not because they genuinely required treatment in hospital due to their current clinical condition (Dawson, 2010a).

Overall, these older 'leave' schemes had very limited legal structure. They were generally vague as to the conditions that could be imposed on leave, and, except for providing the blunt power of 'recall', were generally silent as to the powers conferred to 'enforce' those conditions – such as the requirement to continue taking medication outside hospital.

This history partly explains how, in some jurisdictions, the later enactment by parliament of a more structured CTO scheme might attract little controversy, at the time. In comparison with a prior, vague, discretionary, 'leave' scheme, a new CTO scheme, involving more legal structure, could be seen as an advance in human rights terms. The new law would clarify and sharpen the legal criteria, the process, the powers, the review entitlements and so on – potentially rendering it less draconian from a rights point of view.

The legal structure of a CTO regime

A more structured CTO regime would then specify, in more detail (Dawson, 2016b):

- the criteria for a person's placement under compulsory community mental health care
- the maximum duration of a CTO (before it needs to be renewed)

- the process through which the relevant decisions could be made, and the division of authority, in that process, between responsible clinicians and courts or tribunals
- the conditions that could be imposed on a person's community care
- the powers exercisable over them in the community, to 'enforce' those conditions
- the process to be followed in their recall to hospital, including the entitlement to have re-detention via this route reviewed by a court or tribunal
- the implications of such recall for continuation of the CTO
- the process through which the CTO could be renewed (or continued)
- the processes through which the person could be released from the CTO, even during its life, generally involving concurrent powers, conferred on both clinicians and courts or tribunals, to release the person from the order.

Even within this structure, the operation of such schemes presents difficulties. Which individuals are most likely to benefit from compulsory community care? How can we measure (or know) whether, and in what respect, they do benefit? What conditions can be acceptably imposed on a person's community tenure? Is it possible for those conditions to be enforced, in a manner that does not excessively intrude on their rights? Can the conferral of sufficient benefits on *other people* (such as family, or potential victims) justify limiting the patient's rights (Mullen, 2006a)?

Compulsory hospitalisation raises similar questions, but compulsion seems especially hard to justify when the clinicians have concluded that a person can be safely released from detention in hospital, if certain conditions are met. At this point, the clinicians seem to have decided that the individual is no longer so unwell, or so 'risky', that they require hospital-level care. Why, then, should they not be fully released, at this point, from control under the MHA? They can be offered continuing treatment, and ongoing contact with mental health professionals, and supported accommodation, and other elements of a community treatment plan. And the person can present themselves to hospital and request their own readmission. So, why is continuing compulsion necessary, under a CTO, if they no longer require hospital-level care?

The usual answer given is that use of the CTO is necessary because it permits certain conditions to be imposed on the person's community care, and it makes certain powers available to monitor and enforce 'compliance' with those conditions. Without that compliance, it may be said, the person's condition will deteriorate, with likely adverse consequences, so it is justified to keep them under the proportionate limits that are imposed by a humanely administered regime of compulsory community care.

The usual reasons advanced for the use of CTOs

A major review of the research on CTOs, conducted at the Institute of Psychiatry in London some years ago, found that (Churchill et al., 2007, at 109):

> There is remarkable consistency in the characteristics of patients on CTOs across jurisdictions embedded in very different cultural and geographic settings.... [P]atients are typically males, around 40 years of age, with a long history of mental illness, previous admissions, suffering from a schizophrenia-like or serious affective illness, and likely to be displaying psychotic symptoms, especially delusions at the time of the CTO. Criminal offences and violence are not dominant features among CTO patients....

[They] are more likely to be severely mentally ill with high hospital admission rate histories, poor medication compliance, and aftercare needs.

This reveals the typical profile of people on CTOs. Thus, the reasons given by clinicians for using CTOs – in review proceedings before courts and tribunals, for instance – typically address the position of people with this kind of profile, whose compulsion is seen to be justified on the basis of the reasoning discussed above.

Where a person presents this kind of background – a lengthy history of serious illness, multiple readmissions and a pattern of ceasing to take medication considered necessary after hospital discharge – a CTO will often be seen as vital to maintaining their 'continuity of care'. It will be seen as necessary to ensure they have regular contact with the staff of a community psychiatric service, especially community nurses; to provide the authority to insist they continue taking medication as prescribed; to permit early identification of their relapse into a more acute phase of illness; and to permit their timely readmission to hospital, if required. A common aim will be to 'stabilise' their condition, breaking a pattern of relapse and readmission, with a view to improving the long-term prognosis of their condition, and ameliorating its consequences for them and others.

In the process, use of the CTO might improve the person's capacity to meet their own goals, such as maintaining interpersonal relationships that they value. It might promote their capacity for self-care. It might reduce the risks of harm they pose, to their self or others, or prevent their victimisation. It might permit them to maintain settled accommodation. And it might, in some instances, permit them to avoid conflict with the criminal law, which, if it occurred, might lead to their imprisonment or placement in secure forensic care – even more restrictive outcomes. These reasons are all commonly advanced by clinicians for use of CTOs (Romans, 2004; Manning, 2011).

Through what mechanisms might a CTO advance such aims? Firstly, it might assist through the therapeutic relationships it helps maintain. It may promote continuity in a person's relationship with a community psychiatric nurse, for instance, who will visit them at their accommodation, and supervise (and even administer by injection) their medication. And it may help maintain their relationship with a psychiatrist, and other health professionals (including those concerned with their general health), by requiring them to attend appointments at a clinic or outpatient department. A central aim of these professionals will usually be to promote the benefits that compliance with medication can bring to a person with a serious mental illness who has experienced repeated relapse and rehospitalisation.

Secondly, it is sometimes suggested, CTOs achieve their apparent aims by communicating to the person certain important messages: about the seriousness with which other people view their condition, and the seriousness with which those people are determined to pursue their care. The CTO can be viewed as a powerful form of communication of this kind (Romans, 2004).

Thirdly, the CTO may bind into place a structure for care. The explicit conferral on a community mental health service provider of authority over the person's treatment may commit that provider more firmly to the delivery of that care. It may signal to them that this person specially deserves their professional attention and should not be permitted to 'drop out of care'. It may support family members' insistence that the person continues to take medication. And it may give housing providers the confidence to offer accommodation – in the knowledge that the person housed will be required to maintain contact with the mental health service, and comply with treatment, and can be recalled to hospital swiftly in a crisis. In all these respects, a CTO might support a 'structure for care' (Romans, 2004).

Generally, the responsible clinicians will try to insist, as a condition of the CTO, that the person: maintain contact with the members of a community team; present for appointments at a clinic or outpatient department; continue to take medication as prescribed; live in accommodation of a kind that provides the necessary level of support; and otherwise follow the elements of the community treatment plan. The legislation then provides certain powers (or 'levers') that clinicians can employ – implicitly or explicitly – to insist that the person adheres to these conditions.

Even so, clinicians face a dilemma as to the rigour and frequency with which they will invoke the 'enforcement' powers provided. They face the dilemma, especially, of needing to maintain their relationship with the person under the order. That relationship may be the vehicle through which their therapeutic aims are most likely to be achieved, and that relationship may be damaged by the 'active' (or 'aggressive') use of the powers the CTO confers. Use of its coercive powers may promote 'compliance' with the community treatment plan in the short term, but damage therapeutic relations in the longer term. So, active use of these powers is not necessarily the right approach. Clinicians have to try to balance these conflicting concerns (Mullen, 2006b).

Ultimately, it may be the implicit threat of the use of the recall power – rather than its actual use – that is critical to the operation of a CTO scheme. This implicit threat may work on the mind of the person under the order, even if it is never brought to the fore in their encounter with the clinician.

The legal criteria for a person's placement on a CTO

Those general aims or purposes are therefore reflected in the criteria set by law for a person to qualify for a CTO.

Generally, two distinct sets of legal criteria apply. The first may be described as the general criteria. These must be met by any person placed under the MHA, whether detained in hospital or placed on a CTO. The second is specific to the use of CTOs.

To satisfy the general criteria, it will usually be necessary for clinicians to establish, after conducting a proper assessment, that the person is 'mentally disordered' or 'mentally ill', in the sense defined by the legislation, and is considered to present certain 'dangers', 'risks' or 'needs' (such as need for treatment in hospital). In addition, in some jurisdictions, especially those in North America, a third general standard will need to be met. This concerns the capacity (or competence) of the person to consent to their psychiatric treatment (Dawson, 2006). If found to have such capacity, they may not qualify for placement on the MHA, or placement on a CTO; or their consent may be required before they can be placed on a CTO. If, on the other hand, they are considered to lack the capacity to consent, they will not be disqualified from placement under the MHA or a CTO. But, in some jurisdictions, including some provinces of Canada, the consent of a substitute decision-maker (SDM) to their placement on a CTO will be required instead. An SDM is appointed to make healthcare decisions on their behalf, when they lack this capacity, and the SDM's authority may extend to consenting on their behalf to their placement on a CTO (Gray, 2008). In that case, consultation will be required between the clinicians, the person, the SDM and the community service providers, to make the arrangements for the CTO (Dawson, 2016b).

These general civil commitment criteria, concerning mental disorder, risk and capacity to consent to treatment, that apply to a person's placement under the MHA as a whole, are then supplemented by specific criteria governing the use of CTOs. These generally concern the necessity for the person to remain under compulsory outpatient treatment following discharge from hospital, and the availability, for this individual, of a suitable programme of community care.

The first of these criteria might be described as the 'necessity' requirement. The existence of this requirement is important to the claim that CTOs constitute the least restrictive approach. For it to be satisfied, the clinicians will usually need to show that the person's continuing treatment, care or supervision in the community is 'necessary' (or 'required') to avoid the kind of serious deterioration in their mental health that will lead to their compulsory readmission to hospital if they 'drop out of community care'. In that situation, the CTO is said to be 'necessary' because it is predicted that, 'but for' the person's placement on the order, they would soon be compulsorily readmitted to hospital, or would face another – even more restrictive – outcome (such as imprisonment).

In addition, the 'necessity' criteria will usually require the voluntary approach to be unsuitable, or ineffective, or have been refused, or not reliably followed, or require that the person is unlikely, due to illness, to comply. The criteria in England and Wales say it must be 'necessary' to 'be able to exercise the power to recall the patient to hospital' (MHA 1983 (UK), s 17A(5)(d)). These criteria are all focused on the idea that the CTO provides a 'necessary' – and therefore proportionate and justified – response to the person's situation, in light of the history and consequences of their illness and their record of compliance with treatment.

Some Canadian provincial statutes are highly prescriptive in this regard. In effect, they require the person to have recently experienced a 'revolving door' pattern of care. Their criteria stipulate that the person must have been compulsorily admitted to hospital a certain number of times, over a certain period of years (such as admitted on two or more separate occasions in the last two years). The intention is to try to ensure that the CTO will only be used as an alternative to compulsory hospital admission (Gray, 2008; Dawson, 2016b).

Further specific criteria then require that a suitable outpatient service be available, and viable, for the person proposed for the CTO. To this end, it generally needs to be shown that appropriate community services exist; that the service providers will accept the person into their care; and that there is a good prospect that this person will survive safely outside hospital under that care. Not all the necessary services may be provided by a public sector mental health service. Some, such as supported accommodation services, will more usually be provided by the not-for-profit (or even private) sector. So their agreement to offer accommodation of the necessary kind may also need to be shown.

Some statutes require a community treatment plan to be prepared, to cover these arrangements, that is then attached to the CTO, to make the responsibilities of the respective parties reasonably clear (though the plan may still be drafted in broad terms, to keep it flexible). The law may require this plan to be 'signed off' by the community service providers (of which there may be many, drawn from various agencies). Their 'signing it off' in this way would probably not impose an enforceable legal duty upon them to provide the services listed in the plan, or render them liable in negligence for failure to do so (Dawson, 2006); otherwise, they might not sign the plan. But, particularly where the law requires that the CTO be made by a court or tribunal, it will usually be necessary to provide evidence that the relevant community services will be available, and will be suitable, before the order can be made.

The powers to 'enforce compliance' with the conditions of community care

The power of recall to hospital is then probably the most significant power provided with a view to ensuring that the person complies with the community treatment plan. Additional powers are also usually provided, and the scope of these powers is one of the most contentious aspects of CTO law.

The extent of the 'enforcement' powers that the law confers is especially relevant to the claim that CTOs adopt the least restrictive approach. This is because it can always be argued that some particular power is not essential to the operation of the scheme; or that the scheme's aims could be achieved in a less drastic manner; or that a particular power could be pitched in less draconian terms. It might be said, for instance, that a certain power should be available only in more restricted circumstances, or only where a certain process has been followed – because this would impact less on rights. The detailed terms of the enforcement powers are therefore vulnerable to challenge on human rights (or constitutional) grounds (Dawson, 2010b).

Along with the circumstances in which a person on a CTO power can be recalled to hospital, the most contentious aspects of these powers are those to:

- enter private property, to visit the person and monitor their condition
- 'take' the person to a clinic or outpatient appointment, to be seen by health professionals, without requiring them to be admitted to hospital
- detain or confine the person in a residence, or accommodation, of a specified kind (e.g., accommodation 'with 24-hour supervision')
- administer medication outside hospital
- use 'reasonable force', and call the police or peace officers to assist, in exercising any of those other powers.

Access to a person under a CTO who is living outside hospital can usually be obtained by the members of a community team with the person's consent, or the consent of other occupiers of the premises. But almost all CTO schemes provide an explicit power of entry, with police assistance if needed, for the purposes of activating the recall power. In addition, entry on to private property by the staff of a nominated community team ('with notice', 'at reasonable times', 'for the purposes of supervising treatment') is also authorised by some schemes (Dawson, 2016a). Alternatively, general legislation, or the common law principle of necessity, that permits immediate intervention when people are highly vulnerable, or a medical emergency exists, or there is an immediate threat to people or property, might permit entry. If not, it may be necessary to activate the recall power simply to obtain access to the individual: if, for instance, they are living alone and do not open the door. The legislation may then permit certain categories of mental health professional, with special training, to 'take' or 'transport' the person to a clinic and return them to their residence, with no need for hospital admission and no effect on the duration of the CTO.

Some CTO schemes turn the question of power on its head by expressing matters in terms of duties being imposed on the person on the CTO. So, the person might be placed under a duty to accept visits at their residence from health professionals, to attend appointments and to accept treatment listed in the plan. When the law uses those terms, difficult questions can arise as to whether a correlative power to enforce the person's compliance with the duties imposed is conferred, by implication, on the members of the community team. The law is generally sceptical of the notion of 'implied powers', especially when they would impinge on fundamental rights. In particular, it may be very hard to say precisely who is authorised to exercise such an implied power when the law is expressed in terms of duties imposed on the person under the order, not in terms of some body or official specifically possessing a correlative power.

Only a few schemes say specifically that a person can be directed to live in a certain kind of residence or, even less, that their detention in a community facility is authorised (Dawson and O'Reilly, 2015; Dawson, 2016a). It might be thought that a general power to impose 'conditions' on a person's CTO, or to include certain 'requirements' in their treatment plan, would authorise 'directed residence' of this kind. But, regarding any such implied power to detain at a community residence, the difficulty arises again as to who is entitled to exercise the power. No CTO scheme of which I am aware specifically confers a power of detention on the staff of a community residence (who, in addition, will often be employed by a different agency than the members of a community mental health team). Nor is any clear power usually conferred on police, or neighbours, or family members, to take the person forcibly back to a stipulated residence, should they try to leave.

Nor does any CTO scheme of which I am aware specifically authorise the administration of medication by 'force' outside a hospital setting (or an equivalent setting, such as a properly supervised clinic). No scheme authorises administration of medication via restraint of the person and injection, outside hospital, for instance. That practice would not be considered lawful, ethical or safe – except perhaps in an immediate emergency, where the person under the CTO faced an imminent threat of serious harm if not sedated (in which case, immediate intervention would probably have been authorised, in any case, under the common law of necessity) (Dawson, 1999). Thus, generally, administration of medication to an objecting – and especially a resisting – person, outside hospital, will not be authorised by the CTO regime. Nor is it likely that the person's restraint for such purposes would be considered a 'reasonable' use of force.

Such practices are especially likely to be considered unlawful because the power of recall to hospital is available, and can be used, to ensure medication is administered, if thought absolutely necessary. That power is especially likely to be used if the person is considered to have a 'dangerous relapse profile': that is, a history of suffering especially rapid, serious or dangerous deterioration in their mental health after ceasing medication (Mullen, 2006b).

The person can be returned to hospital, via this recall power, and then, in that environment, their position can be properly assessed. It is possible to carefully observe their condition, following administration of medication – via overnight admission, for example. They can then be released from hospital, continuing on the CTO. This would usually be a much safer approach for both patient and staff, if the difficult decision is taken that medication must be 'enforced'.

Nevertheless, 'enforcing treatment' in that way can be highly distressing for the person concerned. The police may be involved in returning them to hospital; the police may be poorly trained in such matters; and they may use considerable force, even handcuffs. Plus there is the trauma of being subjected to 'forced medication' at the hospital. All parties are usually keen to avoid this option and, even when assistance from police seems urgently required, they may be very reluctant to be involved.

In thinking about proportionality and the use of the least restrictive alternative, distressing practices of this kind – and the continuing threat of them – need to be firmly borne in mind. Practices of this kind can definitely occur in the operation of a CTO scheme.

The UK Supreme Court on enforcement powers and the least restrictive alternative

An example of a dispute concerning the scope of the enforcement powers is provided by a pair of cases – *MM* and *PJ* – that came before the UK Supreme Court (UKSC) in 2018. The main issue was whether a power to detain a person in a community facility was conferred by either the conditional discharge scheme (for forensic patients) or the CTO scheme (for civilly committed patients) under the MHA 1983 (UK).

These cases did not directly present the question whether compulsory community treatment breached human rights. Nor did these cases require the court to determine directly whether such a scheme constituted a less restrictive alternative to compulsory hospital care. But, in the way of British constitutionalism, the rights questions were strongly relevant to interpretation of the scope of the 'enforcement' powers conferred.

The two cases have rather similar facts. Both MM and PJ are described as middle-aged men with mild intellectual (or learning) disabilities, plus an 'autistic spectrum disorder' and a history of involvement with the criminal justice system. MM had a history of setting fires. PJ had been convicted of a serious assault and threatening to kill. Both had initially been directed into compulsory mental health care by the criminal courts, as restricted patients (a quasi-criminal, or forensic, form of legal status).

At the time of the litigation, only MM remained in that restricted patient status. PJ had been released from it, but had later been civilly committed under the MHA. So, the two men were now in different forms of involuntary patient status. But both were being considered for discharge from a secure ward of a psychiatric hospital, the plan being to place them in a special community facility which ran a programme for men in their position.

At this facility, they would be under continuous supervision and control by staff, and not allowed to leave, except under constant supervision. It was therefore agreed, in the course of the litigation, that they would – in law – be detained (or deprived of liberty). So, would their detention in this facility be lawful, under the powers conferred?

The conditions set for MM's release from hospital were imposed under this provision:

Mental Health Act 1983 (UK), section 73: Power to discharge restricted patients
(4) Where a patient is conditionally discharged under this section— ...
(b) the patient shall comply with such conditions (if any) as may be imposed at the time of discharge by the tribunal or at any subsequent time by the Secretary of State.

This is an old-style 'leave' provision, providing no specific guidance as to the kinds of condition that can be imposed. Did it authorise community detention on discharge from hospital?

Both the English Court of Appeal (2017) and the UKSC (2018) found this a relatively straightforward matter. It could be decided by applying (what is often called) the principle of legality (Meagher and Groves, 2017): the principle that any power that imposes limits on a person's fundamental rights must be very clearly specified by law. A broad legal provision like section 73, both courts held, was not sufficiently clear to authorise the limits involved here – on individual liberty, freedom of movement, freedom of association, and so on. Or, to put it in the language of the European Convention on Human Rights, the authority to impose such limits on liberty was not sufficiently 'specified by law' (article 5). In this manner, the principle of legality readily disposed of the case.

The courts found PJ's case more difficult, as to whether community detention was authorised under the civil CTO regime. Here the ruling provision was:

Mental Health Act 1983 (UK), section 17B(2)
Conditions [of a Community Treatment Order]
(2) ... the order may specify conditions ... if the responsible clinician ... thinks them necessary or appropriate for one or more of the following purposes:
    (a) ensuring that the patient receives medical treatment;
    (b) preventing risk of harm to the patient's health or safety;
    (c) protecting other persons.

So, what if the responsible clinician had formed a professionally sound view that PJ's detention at the community facility was 'necessary' for the purpose of protecting other people from his propensity for violence, and only subject to that condition could he be safely released from secure hospital care?

The Court of Appeal held such a condition could be imposed, when: it was for the listed purpose of 'protecting other persons'; it permitted the right balance to be struck between promoting the interests of the patient and protecting the public, without the need for PJ's detention in hospital; and the clinician was satisfied, in the circumstances, that no greater restriction would be imposed on his freedom of movement than was imposed by secure hospital care. In effect, his community detention would be lawful if no more restrictive of his rights.

Fewer restrictions might be imposed on a person's liberty when living in a community facility, and they might have more opportunity for supervised outings, than when living on a secure hospital ward – even though, in both cases, they might be continuously detained. There can be degrees of restriction on liberty, even while a person is detained.

Thus, the Court of Appeal held that, even though section 17B conferred no express power to impose conditions amounting to detention, the purpose of the CTO regime was to permit a compulsory patient's 'gradual reintegration' into the community, and that purpose would be 'frustrated' if a less restrictive form of detention in the community was not possible. In this situation, a power to impose community detention was available 'by necessary implication' to avoid 'frustration' of the statutory scheme.

The UKSC reversed that decision, holding there was no power to impose community detention under a CTO. In its view, community detention was not less restrictive. Nor was it consistent with the purposes of the CTO regime. The UKSC suggests that the Court of Appeal had become trapped in a false dichotomy, by comparing PJ's detention in a secure hospital only with his detention in a community facility. It had not taken into account the third option that was available – his compulsory treatment in the community subject to certain other strict conditions, but not detention.

The UKSC seems especially concerned about the precedential effect of approving a power of community detention, when the MHA applied to people in a much wider range of situations than those illustrated by PJ. Most people under the MHA will present various forms of serious mental illness, not learning disabilities or an autistic spectrum disorder. Once the precedent is set, however, and the power of detention is approved, it could be extended to a much wider group. The overall outcome, then, would not be less restrictive of people's rights.

The UKSC also takes a different view of the purposes of the CTO regime. Its purpose was not necessarily to promote 'the gradual reintegration of the patient into the community'. Its main purpose was to ensure continuity of care. Some people under the MHA, like MM and PJ, will spend long periods in hospital, but most involuntary patients will stay in hospital for much shorter periods: a matter of days or weeks. Otherwise, they live in the community. They do not therefore require 'reintegration', and that is not the primary purpose of compulsory community care. Its purpose, instead, is to stabilise the patient's mental health, prevent relapse in illness and promote recovery through continuing medication and other measures.

The UKSC also thought that other features of the MHA pointed to this conclusion. The Act provided no express power to detain a patient on a CTO, even though it did provide an express power to detain a compulsory patient in hospital. That was a telling indication. Plus, a CTO conferred no express power to convey, detain or retake a patient to a community facility. No 'enforcement' powers were conferred on the staff of community facilities, for example. And no power was conferred to impose treatment without consent on a competent patient outside hospital, except in an emergency. These all pointed to the absence of a power to detain in a community facility.

Thus, the UKSC held that no power of community detention was conferred – even when the law expressly said that conditions could be imposed on a person's CTO for certain purposes, and their detention in the community seemed to fit those purposes. The court thought that any power of community detention would need to be even more explicitly conferred than that.

In reaching this decision, the Court was not required to determine directly whether community detention imposed a disproportionate impact on human rights. But, in light of the court's view as to what constituted the least restrictive approach, and the way in which it read the relevant provisions, the implicit message seems to be that conferral of any such power would be disproportionate, and unjustified.

Do Community Treatment Orders 'work'?

What then of research as to whether CTOs 'work'? The usual reasoning required by human rights law, to justify placing limits on rights, requires it to be shown that the means used to limit the rights are rationally connected to the ends that the measures in question seek to achieve.

Human rights law does not always require such a means-ends connection to be established by the results of empirical research, or, in this case, to be established by the results of socio-legal studies showing that CTOs do achieve their aims. Convincing arguments as to their effect may suffice. Nevertheless, the efficacy of CTOs has been the subject of extensive empirical research (Churchill, 2007; Rugkåsa, 2014, 2016; Kisely, 2016, 2017, 2021).

Many different criteria for measuring the success of CTOs have been used in this research (Dawson, 2003). Different study designs have been employed. Different jurisdictions' CTO schemes have been studied, with their different legal arrangements, service systems and funding models. The studies have occurred at different times. The results found in one jurisdiction, at one point in time, certainly cannot be considered definitive of the results likely to be found in some other jurisdiction, or at another time.

Nevertheless, the major message from the research is that the more closely the research method used resembles the gold standard used in the discipline of evidence-based medicine to test the efficacy of medical interventions – that is, the standard of the randomised controlled trial (or RCT) – the less convincing is the evidence for the efficacy of CTOs. RCTs of CTO regimes are difficult to conduct, for legal, ethical and practical reasons (Dawson, 2002, 2011). But three have been conducted, in North Carolina (Swartz, 1999), New York (Steadman, 2001) and England (Burns, 2013). Although criticisms have been made of their methods, none reached a positive finding as to the benefits of the CTO scheme in the jurisdiction studied, on the primary, pre-selected outcome measure employed – which was, basically, the rate of readmission to hospital of patients under CTOs, compared with the rate for patients who were simply offered voluntary outpatient care on discharge from hospital. Generally, CTO patients were not found to experience significantly reduced rates of readmission to hospital.

Studies using methods considered less convincing in the discipline of evidence-based medicine as a means for testing treatment efficacy have, on the other hand, tended to produce more positive results. These studies tend to use a 'before and after' method, in which the position of, say, 150 people, is analysed before and after they go on a CTO – to see if differences emerge on various outcome measures. Or these studies use a matched pairs (or matched cohorts) design, in which the outcomes are compared for two groups of people who are (or are not) on a CTO, but otherwise share certain characteristics: age, gender, diagnosis, numbers of prior admissions and so on.

These research designs have well-known limitations. 'Before and after' studies of a single group of patients are vulnerable to the problem of 'regression to the mean'. That is, they are vulnerable to the likelihood that the people studied were put on a CTO at a time of crisis in their life, or a time of acute illness – when they were 'hitting bottom', in effect. So, their condition was thereafter likely to improve, in any case, as they 'regressed to their mean', or recovered from their crisis. Thus, simply establishing that they were admitted to hospital more frequently before they went on a CTO than afterwards is not sufficient to show that this change was caused by the CTO. They might have been readmitted less frequently anyway, as they recovered from the crisis that precipitated their placement on a CTO.

In addition, putting a person on a CTO is often the trigger for more intensive community services to be directed towards them. Thereafter, improvement in their condition may be observed. But, what if they had simply been *offered* more intensive services, without the CTO. Perhaps that would have led to improvement in their condition also. For such reasons, the results of these uncontrolled 'before and after' studies cannot be considered definitive.

Related research designs, that involve study of the position of matched pairs or groups of people 'before and after' one group go on a CTO, do use a control group. But these designs suffer from another limitation: that the two groups – having been matched on a certain range of parameters (gender, diagnosis, prior admissions, etc.) – may not have been matched on some other parameter that could in fact be the cause of any difference in outcome observed. Perhaps the key matter determining success or failure in use of CTOs is a person's degree of 'insight' into their need for treatment, for instance, or the extent of their substance use. Yet, on those parameters, the two groups might not have been matched – precluding any strong conclusion being reached as to the likely causes of any differences in outcome observed between the two groups.

Nevertheless, some studies of this kind have found positive results for CTOs on various outcomes – including rates of readmission to hospital, contacts with community services and treatment adherence (Rugkåsa, 2014, 2016; Kisely, 2016, 2017, 2021). But, overall, the results of such studies are uneven, and meta-analysis of the outcome research on CTOs as a whole has not produced evidence that rates of readmission to hospital are reduced (Kisely, 2017, 2021). At present, therefore, the empirical research does not support the idea that a 'rational connection' exists between means and ends, in the case of CTOs. Any such connection will therefore need to be established by arguments that convince despite the results of this research, not because of it.

Conclusions

When the research evidence is not strong that CTOs achieve their apparent aims, and there is no convincing case that they act – in the majority of situations – as an alternative to compulsory hospital care (especially in light of the pressure that exists in most places on hospital beds), it is doubtful whether use of CTOs can be justified in accordance with the demands of human rights law. Certainly, their expansive use cannot be justified, nor their use with people who have no history of repeatedly passing through the 'revolving door'.

Where such schemes do exist, the criteria for their use should be strictly interpreted and applied. The powers conferred should be narrowly construed. Their discretionary elements should be constrained. Wherever possible, police involvement should be avoided. They should be the subject of clear and detailed official guidelines. And they should be used only when a community mental health service is available that is sufficiently comprehensive, and intensive, to satisfy the promise of good community care.

References

Burns, T., Rugkåsa, J., Molodynski, A., et al. (2013) 'Community treatment orders for patients with psychosis: A randomised controlled trial', *Lancet*, 381(9878), 1627–1633.
Churchill, R., Owen, G., Singh, S., et al. (2007) *International Experiences of Using Community Treatment Orders*. London: Institute of Psychiatry, available at http://psychrights.org/research/digest/OutPtCmmtmnt/UKRptonCTO.pdf.
Dawson, J. (1991) 'Community treatment orders', *Otago Law Review*, 7, 410–425.
Dawson, J. (1999) 'The law of emergency psychiatric detention', *New Zealand Law Review*, 275–303.
Dawson, J. (2002) 'Randomised controlled trials of mental health legislation', *Medical Law Review*, 10(3), 308–321.
Dawson, J., Romans, S., Gibbs, A., Ratter, N. (2003) 'Ambivalence about community treatment orders', *International Journal of Law and Psychiatry*, 26(3), 243–255.
Dawson, J. (2006) 'Fault-lines in Community Treatment Order legislation', *International Journal of Law and Psychiatry*, 29(6), 482–494.
Dawson, J. (2010a) 'Community treatment orders', in Gostin, L., et al. (eds.) *Principles of Mental Health Law and Policy*. Oxford: Oxford University Press, pp. 513–554.
Dawson, J. (2010b) 'Compulsory outpatient treatment and the calculus of human rights', in McSherry, B. and Weller, P. (eds.) *Rethinking Rights-Based Mental Health Laws*. Oxford: Hart, pp. 327–354.
Dawson, J., Burns, T., Rugkasa, J. (2011) 'Lawfulness of a randomised trial of the new community treatment order regime for England and Wales', *Medical Law Review*, 19(1), 1–26.
Dawson, J., O'Reilly, R. (2015) 'Residence conditions on community treatment orders', *Canadian Journal of Psychiatry*, 60(11), 523–527.
Dawson, J. (2016a) 'Community treatment order legislation in the Commonwealth', in Molodynski, A., Rugkåsa, J. and Burns, T. (eds.) *Coercion in Community Mental Health Care International Perspective*. Oxford: Oxford University Press, pp. 23–44.
Dawson, J. (2016b) 'Community treatment orders', in Chandler, J. and Flood, C. (eds.) *Law and Mind: Mental Health Law and Policy in Canada*. Toronto: LexisNexis, pp. 139–160.
Gray, J., Shone, M., Liddle, P. (2008) *Canadian Mental Health Law and Policy* (2nd ed.). Toronto: LexisNexis.

Huscroft, G., Miller, B., Webber, G. (eds.) (2014) *Proportionality and the Rule of Law: Rights, Justification, Reasoning*. Cambridge: Cambridge University Press.

Kisely, S. (2016) 'Canadian studies on the effectiveness of community treatment orders', *Canadian Journal of Psychiatry*, 61(1), 7–14, doi: 10.1177/0706743715620414.

Kisely, S., Campbell, L., O'Reilly, R. (2017) 'Compulsory community and involuntary outpatient treatment for people with severe mental disorders', *Cochrane Database of Systematic Reviews*, CD004408, doi: 10.1002/14651858.CD004408.

Kisely, S., Yu, D., Maehashi, S., Siskind, D. (2021) 'A systematic review and meta-analysis of predictors and outcomes of community treatment orders in Australia and New Zealand', *Australian and New Zealand Journal of Psychiatry*, 55(7), 650–665, doi: 10.1177/0004867420954286.

Manning, C., Molodynski, A., Rugkåsa, J., Dawson, J., Burns, T. (2011) 'A national CTO survey: How clinicians in England and Wales view and use CTOs', *The Psychiatrist*, 35(9), 328–333.

Meagher, D., Groves, M. (2017) *The Principle of Legality in Australia and New Zealand*. Sydney: The Federation Press.

Mullen, R., Gibbs, A., Dawson, J. (2006a) 'Family perspective on community treatment orders: A New Zealand study', *International Journal of Social Psychiatry*, 52(5), 469–478.

Mullen, R., Dawson, J., Gibbs, A. (2006b) 'Dilemmas for clinicians in use of community treatment orders', *International Journal of Law and Psychiatry*, 29(6), 535–550.

Romans, S., Dawson, J., Mullen, R., Gibbs, A. (2004) 'How mental health clinicians view community treatment orders: A national New Zealand survey', *Australian and New Zealand Journal of Psychiatry*, 38(10), 836–841.

Rugkåsa, J., Dawson, J., Burns, T. (2014) 'Community treatment orders: What is the state of the evidence?', *Social Psychiatry and Psychiatric Epidemiology*, 49(12), 1861–1187.

Rugkåsa, J. (2016) 'Effectiveness of community treatment orders: The international evidence', *Canadian Journal of Psychiatry*, 61(1), 15–24, doi: 10.1177/0706743715620415.

Steadman, H.J., Gounis, K., Dennis, D., et al. (2001) 'Assessing the New York City involuntary outpatient commitment pilot program', *Psychiatric Services*, 52(3), 330–336.

Swartz, M.S., Swanson, J.W., Wagner, H.R., et al. (1999) 'Can involuntary outpatient commitment reduce hospital recidivism? Findings from a randomized trial with severely mentally ill individuals', *American Journal of Psychiatry*, 156(12), 1968–1975.

Cases Cited

R v Hallstrom ex parte W [1986] QB 109.
Secretary of State for Justice v MM; Welsh Ministers v PJ [2017] EWCA Civ 194.
MM v Secretary of State for Justice [2018] UKSC 60.
Welsh Ministers v PJ [2018] UKSC 66.

20
SOCIO-ECONOMIC INCLUSION AND MENTAL HEALTH LAW

Terry Carney

Introduction

Socio-economic inclusion as an objective of public policy design is commonly taken as a given. Indeed it is difficult to construct an argument opposing such a virtuous goal. But socio-economic inclusion is not necessarily representative of 'inclusion' more generally and its achievement is difficult to define or realise, raising doubts about its conceptual utility (Wright and Stickley, 2013, Wang et al., 2017).

This chapter considers the ways socio-economic inclusion is framed as an international human right for people with mental health conditions or psychosocial disabilities and the extent to which this objective is able to be advanced by mental health law. It argues that law has an important but limited contribution to make in addressing the manifold levels and ways in which lack of socio-economic inclusion is implicated as cause and consequence of mental health conditions or psychosocial disability.

The analysis opens with a discussion of analytical concepts of socio-economic inclusion and its relationship to ideas about equality and social participation. The argument then turns to examine normative frames, including disability theories and international human rights obligations and the role of domestic law in securing socio-economic rights. The conclusion draws out some of the implications of the argument that law has a limited contribution to make to advancing socio-economic inclusion in mental health.

Analytical framing of inclusion
What is socio-economic inclusion?

Socio-economic inclusion at first blush appears to be a deceptively straightforward concept. However, its characteristics or parameters blur at the edges as we move out from core concepts of economic inequality and social status.

For access to government services or subsidies, inequalities of income and wealth commonly serve as a 'ticket to service' for poorer citizens and as a barrier for the better off (who are denied eligibility under any means test). Mental health care under Medicaid in the USA is an example of such rationing by way of means tests (Fry, 2021). Yet health and mental health in most countries is also (or mainly) delivered as a market commodity. It is delivered as a market commodity with or without measures to cushion and spread the cost burden through access to private health insurance, government subsidies or universal mandates. For market-based services such as these, inequity is compounded (reverse equity).

In market-based services, greater ability to pay opens access to higher quality or more expensive forms of private sector care. The main exceptions to reverse equity are the small number of people who are income poor and asset rich but have the misfortune of holding an illiquid asset, along with those in need of a service that the market is unable to provide at an affordable price. Newly developed pharmaceutical drugs and care for chronic conditions are two classic examples of social goods that may over-stretch the capacity of being funded by individuals alone (or even with the help of cost-spreading by private health insurance markets), leading to exclusion unless government steps in to subsidise that risk.

Inequalities of inclusion associated with social status are more subtle. A social status is often the root cause of economic inequality. But the status may also give rise to compounding bases of exclusion which are non-economic in character. Some status inequalities of exclusion are familiar targets of anti-discrimination (equal opportunity) laws, such as those that stem from race, gender, sexuality, age or minority status. Equal opportunity laws are, however, a fairly weak reed in countering income or employment inequality associated with such a supposedly protected status, with quotas arguably a more effective tool (Vornholt et al., 2018: 44–46). Other status inequalities are no less severe in their impact but are less recognised.

Stigma associated with caste or cultural attributes is one example. LGBTQ+ status is another, particularly if that status is also criminalised. The stigma associated with mental illness is real in all societies (even those western countries that have made progress towards its reduction). In some countries the very condition continues to consign individuals to the exclusion and 'othering' of outsiders (Silver, 2010: 190).

The lesson to be drawn so far, then, is that the subtle aspects of the lived life of inclusion or exclusion for someone with a mental illness are poorly captured in standard concepts and metrics (Davey and Gordon, 2017).

Socio-economic inclusion and health inequality

Socio-economic *inequality* in health outcomes has been well documented since at least the landmark 'Black Report' of the United Kingdom Department of Health and Social Security Working Group in 1980 (Gray, 1982).

Challenge enough lies in untangling the multiplicity of economic, locational, social and cultural factors responsible for disparate health outcomes standing in the way of equitable inclusion and realisation health (Mazeikaite et al., 2021). Mental health likewise is unevenly distributed for a multitude of reasons. These include lower socio-economic status (Tibber et al., 2021), but also many other factors. There are compounding effects as well. Elevated levels of mental illness are found to be associated with groups experiencing a higher incidence of those 'life shocks' known to adversely impact mental health (Hashmi et al., 2020).

Inequality unquestionably is deeply implicated in any understanding of mental health inclusion, but it is hardly the last word.

Social inclusion as 'social citizenship' participation

On a wider register, inclusion and its corollary might better be understood through a '*social inclusion*' lens.

Social inclusion was first propounded by T.H. Marshal more than 70 years ago in expounding the rights of social citizenship (cf. Hamer et al., 2019). Social citizenship is conceived as the capacity (or otherwise) to have the option of participating as fully as possible in civil society (see for example: Guiraudon, 2009). This way of understanding inclusion has the added advantage that it resonates with the 'equality principle' enshrined in Article 12 of the Convention on the Rights of Persons with Disabilities 2007 (CRPD), a key human rights touchstone in assessing mental health laws. A more capacious frame such as social citizenship may more adequately capture the multiple pathways and reciprocal connections between the social and the economic strands of socio-economic exclusion by concentrating on the level of adequacy of participatory outcomes, as earlier expounded by Parker for disability (Parker, 2007).

Analytical framing of inclusion is helpful for understanding the complexity of the concept and its genesis and consequences, but for the purposes of the law it is normative literature that arguably is most relevant. Disability scholarship and international human rights standards are the two main sources of that guidance, as now discussed.

Normative framing of inclusion

An expansive disability and human rights scholarship

International human rights treaties and disability scholarship have both tracked in an expansive direction in recent decades.

International disability and healthcare norms and standards began to be laid down in 1946 when health was identified as an essential human right under the constitution of the World Health Organization (WHO) (Hendriks, 2019: 211), steadily expanding in scope before culminating in 2007 with the CRPD. As Lucy Series (2020) and others have charted in their detailed histories, the CRPD includes a number of path-breaking provisions. These include those about rights to live independently and in the community (Art. 19) and to habilitation and rehabilitation (Art. 26) (further: Series, 2020: 78). It also includes provisions on the intersectionality of disability for women (Art. 7); offers a nuanced expression of the right to health (Art. 25); and covers disability and international development (Arts 32, 11) (Degener, 2017: 44, 47, 48 respectively).

Disability scholarship challenged the medical model of disability for conceiving disadvantage as an exclusively biological function of the person. It advanced a 'social model' locating disadvantage as a social construct, the remedy for which lies in measures of 'accommodation' from the environment external to the person and elimination of discrimination. This analysis has culminated most recently in a less settled human rights model of disability (Degener, 2016, 2017). The human rights model of disability which Degener identifies as infusing the CRPD, is among other things said to embrace 'civil and political as well as economic, social and cultural rights' (Degener, 2017: 35). This is a breadth of rights that resonates closely with T.H. Marshall's notion of civil citizenship, and thus tracks closest to philosophical arguments favouring a universalist grounding of disability inclusion (Bickenbach, 2020: 59).

The claimed attraction of the human rights model is that it offers normative direction about how to achieve greater inclusion: '[w]hereas the social model of disability can explain why two-thirds of the one billion disabled persons in this world live in relative poverty, the human rights model offers a roadmap for change' (Degener, 2017: 47). That is another important feature, if the lived experience of exclusion is to be remedied.

The CRPD and other human rights instruments

Article 12(1) of the International Covenant on Economic, Social and Cultural Rights requires governments to recognise 'the right of everyone to the enjoyment of the highest attainable standard of physical and mental health'. This is mirrored in the Article 25 CRPD obligation to 'promote the right to the highest attainable healthcare on an equal basis with others'. Expressed in terms of Eric Fromm's (1942) well-known aphorism, these socio-economic rights are differentiated from 'civil' rights – characterised as freedom 'from' (external restraints) – on the basis that socio-economic rights are designed to advance the freedom 'to' (realise human capacities); alternatively they can be described as advancing a *positive* rather than the negative freedom of civil rights which are designed 'to prevent a certain behaviour – to create an *absence* rather than a *presence*' (McLaughlin, 2007). Although the 'interdependence and indivisibility' of these two sets of rights is one of the fundamental principles of the human rights framework (Steiner and Alston, 1996), socio-economic rights do have distinctive implications.

By comparison with civil rights (such as freedom from torture), socio-economic rights like the right to health lack the concrete precision that enables easy establishment of compliance or breach. In contrast to civil rights, socio-economic rights are also subject to progressive realisation in recognition of the economic costs of compliance (Carney, 2018). As a consequence of this lack of precision, evaluation of rights compliance instead often turns to more concrete issues, such as whether involuntary mental health treatment complies with the CRPD, as later discussed.

Before doing so, it is important not to overlook the important *distributional equity* consequence of concentrating public expenditure and legal provisions on the treatment of acute episodes of mental illness. Skewing of focus in this fashion all too frequently comes at the expense of severe neglect of the mental wellbeing and mental health needs of the vastly larger population of people experiencing lower-level or more chronic mental ill-health (McSherry, 2008). Government funding which unduly concentrates on episodes of acute severe illness effectively denies citizens with less severe illness their right to 'enjoyment of the highest attainable standard of ... mental health'.

In appreciating the contribution of this class of rights, we cannot overlook the powerful political and economic reasons which count against incorporation of socio-economic rights into domestic human rights law (Weller, 2009). Sandra Fredman offers some interesting deliberative democracy-shaped ways in which law can be developed to assist to secure realisation of socio-economic rights (Fredman, 2010a, Fredman, 2010b). However, this leaves unresolved the problem posed by the *withdrawal* of government from direct service delivery, stemming from the pre-eminence of neoliberalism as the preferred form of governance, as illustrated in debates about realising the 'right' to health (O'Connell, 2010). This has been a particular concern in many countries around the world as governments under-invest in public mental health, leaving care increasingly to the market.

Inclusion through mental health repeal or fusion?

The equality clause (Article 12) of the CRPD 2007 is interpreted by its United Nations (UN) monitoring committee to require repeal of all laws authorising involuntary mental health treatment (Callaghan and Ryan, 2016, Minkowitz, 2010), though progress around the world has been slight so far (Stavert, 2018). A principled argument for fusion of mental health and capacity law (Dawson and Szmukler, 2006) also continues to attract interest as a basis for putting mental health care onto the same footing as general health (Szmukler, 2020).

A difficulty with both the repeal and the fusion options is that of overlooking wider and more powerful actors. There are a multitude of strong reasons for repeal of involuntary mental health laws, but redressing socio-economic inequality of access to mental health care arguably is not one of them, at least not unless coupled with addressing wider contextual forces. Due to neoliberal policies of shrinking the role of the state and its fiscal outlays, mental health laws which once inappropriately treated too many and for too long, have at worst been transformed into barriers to accessing any treatment (at lowest), or to anything other than short-term care of the acute episode followed by premature discharge (Carney et al., 2011, Carney, 2003).

Other health conditions also tend to be under-diagnosed and under-treated. General health care is commonly skewed towards clinical care at the expense of under-investment in preventive public health programmes, and tends to favour research and investment in diseases that catch public attention and sympathy ahead of less socially attractive or newsworthy conditions.

So while the idea of putting formal equality of access to mental health services on the same voluntary basis as for general health care (on the basis of fusion or abolition of involuntary care) would answer objections based on discrimination and infringement of civil rights, it would contribute only at the margins regarding equity and inclusion (beyond removing stigma and other barriers). The same is arguably true of Wilson's (2020) compromise 'third model', entailing entirely voluntary access to all mental health services in the absence of risk of harm to self or others. Substantive equality of access to mental wellbeing and mental health care, not mere 'formal equality of access', is what must be debated and assessed.

If repeal or fusion of mental health legislation is unpromising, the obvious question is whether other legal options hold greater prospects of advancing mental health inclusion, as now discussed.

The role of law in health and mental health inclusion and equality

If conceptualisation of 'inclusion', disability scholarship and international human rights treaty formulations of disability rights have been moving ahead at a cracking pace, the same cannot be said about the role of domestic law in translating these grand aspirations into the lived lives of people with mental health conditions or psychosocial disabilities.

Law as leveraging voice

The toolbox of law is quite diverse, but the run-of-the-mill tools available to assist individual citizens resolve general community concerns are the ones that commonly first come to mind in mental health as well. Redress for harm (and even discrimination), enforcing bargains, holding government administration to account, and regulation of behaviour, are some of the better-known types of laws for delivering justice to individual citizens.

But turning to law to resolve any form of socio-economic exclusion is likely to raise eyebrows. This is so not just when law is contemplated as a way of addressing the harder-to-grasp manifestation of a case of 'inequality', but even as a way of redressing mundane examples of socio-economic exclusion such as unavailability or denial of access to mental health services or other public resources. Leveraging resources and dealing with systemic exclusion is not what law is known for.

Yet socio-legal studies in mental health show that while people with mental health conditions or psychosocial disabilities are very concerned about infringements of civil rights under laws authorising involuntary detention and/or treatment, their strongest concerns are about impacts on access to employment, housing and services generally (Carney et al., 2011, Carney, 2012). This is no surprise. Employment, for example, has been shown to be a critical component of inclusive mental health policy (Hendriks, 2019). This extends beyond non-discrimination in hiring, to include equality of access both to labour market programmes (Bråthen et al., 2020, Harris et al., 2014) and equitable social security. In social security this, for example, involves ensuring that disability pension eligibility does not discriminate against fluctuating and episodic psychiatric conditions (Rafael et al., 2017, Waddington and Priestley, 2021).

In a comprehensive review of disability paradigms and implications for enhancing resources to address mental health and wellbeing, Gooding (2019a) reviewed international examples of the way positive human rights might leverage greater access to services and support for people with mental health conditions or psychosocial disabilities. Examples canvassed include the 'care demander' role attributed to Sweden's independent advocacy assistant in helping the making of decisions (the personal advocate PO Skåne) and hypothecated tax levies to fund mental health services in Ghana and the US state of California. There is also a slew of other measures for support of people with mental health conditions and psychosocial disabilities (Then et al., 2023) but these are mainly non-legislative in character and lacking in a well-developed or sound evidence base.

As is common with most civil society support for decision-making, the claims for the publicly funded PO Skåne do not rest on robust evidence-based research (but see Berggren, 2021). They do however have more than intuitive appeal. There is evidence that people with greater stores of social capital in the form of the size, skills and backgrounds of their immediate circle of family or friends, do tend to be disproportionately advantaged in their ability to access services (Koutsogeorgou et al., 2014, Carey et al., 2021) and thus in their recovery (Sweet et al., 2018). They are also less likely to be subject to restrictive substitute-decision-making guardianship orders (Cripps, 2015). But further research is needed to confirm the soundness of such policies.

Hypothecated levies, for their part, at best buttress or help to entrench the will of governments of the day to prioritise boosted (or at least more adequate) funding of mental health. At worst they can degenerate to become a 'paper archway' – swamped by overall government budget revenue and expenditure streams to such a degree that future administrations can readily subvert their supposedly guaranteed revenue by making cuts to allied programmes. While dedicated levies may have political and even public appeal, there is little indication that they do much in the longer term to progress socio-economic inclusion.

This equivocal assessment of resource leveraging and hypothecated levies does not mean, however, that law cannot make other contributions. One such contribution is through its often neglected educative role of serving to provide a 'mobilizing narrative' (Conaghan, 2007: 162). Another possibility is by legislating an obligation for public bodies to have 'due regard' in their decision-making to socio-economic disadvantage (Fredman, 2010b), or by requiring publication of constructive 'steps' being taken to progress the obligation in international law for progressive realisation of socio-economic rights of the kind already discussed for the CRPD (Fredman, 2010a). A final example is that of conferring the deliberative democracy remedy of a 'right to challenge' – i.e. enter into a public dialogue on – a perceived inequity or vulnerability (Keogh et al., 2010). However, the potential appeal of such innovative measures is also yet to be demonstrated by robust evidence of effectiveness.

Mental health law and distributional equity

In health, national laws impacting distributional equity typically involve funding of treatment or care (medical benefits/insurance, hospital and outpatient treatment) and regulation of health professions (standards of care).

Distributional equity of mental health outcomes are special for two reasons. First, they are often outside or the poor cousins of general health provision – mental health conditions or psychosocial disabilities are not covered by or are less well remunerated under medical benefits schemes (meaning the poor have less access); people experience less well-funded access to public mental health services (there is greater rationing of access to any care or optimal length of care); and they experience neglect or under-investment in promotion of mental health wellbeing compared to funding for public health promotion generally (sectoral inequity). Second, unlike general health wellbeing and care, in mental health the law also plays a 'gatekeeper' role, especially regarding government-run involuntary admission for acute residential treatment and – in many countries – also involuntary community treatment orders (or more generically 'mandatory outpatient treatment') (O'Reilly et al., 2019). The distributional impact of that legal gatekeeping is uneven.

Most people experiencing a mental health condition or psychosocial disability will never or only comparatively rarely encounter these services for more acute or severe episodes, leaving their ongoing care at the mercy of often poorly resourced mental health and related services. Other than the previously mentioned role of law and government in funding public or private schemes of medical reimbursement, it is market forces that determine the distributional outcomes (and cost burdens or exclusion from services borne by lower-income citizens).

In short, most mental health legislation serves to *stratify* the types of care available (compounding rather than alleviating socio-economic exclusion) and funding laws to redress market-driven distributional inequity are comparatively rare.

A case study of structuring mental health administration and access

Consistent with the disability mantra 'nothing about us, without us', so central to the development of the CRPD (Series, 2020: 80–81), mental health inclusion has come to be identified with two initiatives in particular.

First, it is the basis for handing greater policy-making and administration to people with lived experience of mental health conditions or psychosocial disabilities. Second, it is the rationale for disaggregation of administration to regions and localities that better map to geographic communities of interest (as for example in Scotland: Gallagher, 2018). The latter reflects the principle of subsidiarity – that locals are better placed to judge their needs and interests – but devolution also carries risks of unwarranted regional disparities. A case study from Australia exemplifies how this reform package might be constructed.

Australia's 2021 Royal Commission from the second most populous state of Victoria offers a recent template of how the value of inclusion and equity might be expressed in mental health and how it might be progressed. One of four sub-clusters of its 65 recommendations was thematically headed 'A system attuned to promoting inclusion and addressing inequities'. It opened its elaboration of this theme by writing that:

> The future mental health and wellbeing system will be responsive to people and populations in Victoria with the greatest need, providing services that are safe, tailored and localised. The system will adapt to new and changing inequities, supporting those who may be experiencing disadvantage.
>
> *(Victorian MH Royal Commission, 2021: Executive summary, 25, theme 3.2)*

The Report immediately acknowledged whole-of-society implications of this aspiration, noting that it 'requires looking beyond the system to examine the varied factors that shape mental health and wellbeing' (ibid.). To promote that whole-of-government response it proposed a 'Mental Health and Wellbeing Outcomes Framework [to] create accountability for mental health and wellbeing outcomes across services and government' (ibid.: 28). Among groups identified for attention the report mentioned the LGBTIQ+ and indigenous communities, and young people. Issues to be targeted included provision of information 'regardless of first or preferred language, hearing, literacy or neurocognitive ability' and concrete proposals to address stigma and discrimination (ibid. 28; rec. 41).

To tackle inequality 'where people live, work, learn and connect', the Report of the Royal Commission recommended localisation ('community collectives… to promote social connection and inclusion in Victorian communities': rec. 15) and devolution to regional boards to commission and tailor to local needs the mental health and wellbeing services for their area. A proposed Mental Health and Wellbeing Act (enacted in 2022, commencing September 2023) would impose legal obligations and benchmarking of progress towards reduction of use of coercion and expansion of voluntary services, with the benchmarks monitored and overseen by a new independent Mental Health and Wellbeing Commission comprising significant membership of people with lived experience (Victorian MH Royal Commission, 2021, Recs 42(2)(e)(f), 53(2)(a)(b), 44 respectively).

Such measures may or may not succeed in promoting inclusion and equity in mental health, but Victoria's worked example of reform certainly attests to the breadth and complexity of the task of operationalising inclusion in domestic law and policy. The global position is no easier.

Inclusion and socio-economic equality internationally

If socio-economic equality is problematic in western developed countries, it is nothing compared to the magnitude of the issue in the developing world. The UN's Sustainable Development Goals of 2015 now recognise mental health, joining earlier pronouncements by the WHO and others (Hendriks, 2019: 211–212).

Operationalising recognition of mental health in low- and middle-income countries continues to be a huge challenge, however. Western models of free-standing services (and associated laws) are seen as too costly and out of keeping with more holistic, community-based delivery models (Jenkins, 2019). A clinical model of professional psychiatric care is a particular problem not only because of its expense (Hendriks, 2019: 213) but also because the medical model is out of keeping with CRPD and other human rights endorsements of the social model of disability (Degener, 2017). Low-cost initiatives that build social capital, such as Zimbabwe's 'friendship benches', have been shown to be an effective initiative (Gooding, 2019a), along with various configurations of peer support programmes. Digital ehealth and other such initiatives have been touted as a cost-effective way of addressing access, but these take many forms and are poorly regulated (Gooding, 2019b). They also lack robust evidence of effectiveness or even cost-efficiency (Carter et al., 2021) and suffer severely from the 'digital divide' of unequal access to smartphones, affordable internet plans or any/reliable internet (Yu, 2020).

Social protection policies in low- and middle-income countries have been found to cater to a small fraction of people with disabilities, fewer than one in five on one estimate (Côte, 2021: 354). This is partly because only a low proportion of gross domestic product is able to be afforded. But it is also because design of disability payments mimics those of most developed economies in being predicated on being a fallback to full employment (Côte, 2021). This narrow linking of social security eligibility to incapacity for employment and a need for rehabilitation and employment assistance is outdated and out of tune with economic realities. It is at odds with the human rights model of disability which calls for *inclusive* policy settings. As Côte (2021: 355) explains:

> This implies policies across sectors that combine the removal of barriers (awareness raising, non-discrimination, accessibility) with the provision of required support (assistive devices, rehabilitation, support services, social protection).

'Inclusive design' of social protection is one policy plank for the pursuit of greater socio-economic inclusion for people in low- and medium-income countries who are experiencing mental health conditions or psychosocial disability, as Côte has sketched (ibid., 264–265).

There are also some serious and distinctive ethical challenges for global mental health outside the developed global north. The first of these is how to frame models of care that are less reliant on high-cost professional clinicians without debasing quality. A second is how to deal with barriers to access due to unscientific cultural beliefs such as attributing causal responsibility to witchcraft or deep stigmatisation of people with mental health conditions or psychosocial disabilities.

A third ethical challenge is how to formulate more communitarian, equity-focused and culturally appropriate ethical guidance in place of the dominant 'principlist' frame of western bioethics with its concentration on autonomy, justice, beneficence and non-maleficence (Palk and Stein, 2020: 273–277). The latter of course is also pertinent in western developed countries, as illustrated by debate about whether community treatment orders (assertive outpatient care orders) meet CRPD or ethical standards, with Newton-Howes (2019), for example, concluding that they do not comply and should be used far less extensively than presently.

Conclusion

Driven by expansive human rights treaties and disability scholarship, socio-economic inclusion and equality are prominent aspects of social and policy dialogue in mental health. Summed up as equal participation, these sentiments also drive international development debate about promotion of inclusion in mental health low- and middle-income countries (Hendriks, 2019). Three lessons might be drawn.

One lesson from this brief review is that inclusive mental health entails engaging with all major spheres of the lived life of people with mental health conditions or psychosocial disabilities, not just mental health or even social services, but also employment, housing and other key domains of life.

The second lesson is that policy should no longer be initiated and imposed by government, as has been the practice in the past. Principles of genuine co-design are called for, where people with mental health conditions or psychosocial disabilities drive the process of initiating and shaping public policy settings (Williams and Smith, 2021); and where the 'inclusive by design' principle is adhered to (Treviranus, 2018). Inclusion by design originated in artificial intelligence and automated decision-making contexts, but its core focus on ensuring that 'outlier' characteristics and values are not overlooked or marginalised and that fairness is honoured (Trewin et al., 2019), applies equally in mental health policy.

The third lesson is that the issue of socio-economic inclusion is implicated as both cause and consequence of the experience of mental health conditions or psychosocial disability. As Gooding observes:

> The expanded scope of the human rights model of disability means taking into account the social and economic determinants of impairment, distress and disablement. Racism, sexism, homophobia, poverty, and so on, are undoubtedly contributing factors for many people. Practices of 'informal safeguarding', community development and other efforts to foster social inclusion will not address the deeper structural causes of disadvantage.
> *(Gooding, 2019a: 16)*

Reforming mental health law; re-organising services to be fully compliant with principles of recovery-oriented practice, a trauma-informed approach, localised and user controlled; and pursuit of the equality principle through supported decision-making are among the important measures which can engage the law in contributing to reduction of socio-economic inequality as cause and consequence.

However, measures such as these are only a small part of the answer. Socio-economic inequality is a complex and change-resistant phenomenon, irrespective of the sector of the community or group experiencing it. Scholarship on socio-economic inclusion and equality continues to grapple with how meaningfully to articulate and progress distributive justice goals, given that law at best is a minor player. I conclude by suggesting that a 'joined-up' framework is needed – one which better integrates consideration of the often separate conceptual domains of regulatory (law), distributive (economic), discretionary spending (services), and 'soft policies' ('new regulation') – and would go some way to facilitating broader dialogue on the politics of socio-economic inclusion and equality.

Under such an approach the task of promoting advancement of particular aspects of the goal of socio-economic inclusion would be pursued pragmatically. The particular task would be allocated to whatever is the optimal *domain* (e.g. law, civil society, family) and apply the best available *form* of governance (e.g. hard law vs. soft law; civil society unaided vs. civil society 'shaped' by incentives/supports).

In short, an evidence-based approach tailored to particular sub-goals appears best adapted to achieve 'lived lives' outcomes for any given country or community.

References

Berggren, U. J. 2021. The Swedish personal ombudsman: Support in decision-making and accessing human rights. *In*: Sunkel, C., Mahomed, F., Stein, M. A. & Patel, V. (eds.) *Mental Health, Legal Capacity, and Human Rights*. Cambridge: Cambridge University Press, 230–243.

Bickenbach, J. 2020. Disability, health, and difference. *In*: Cureton, A. & Wasserman, D. (eds.) *The Oxford Handbook of Philosophy and Disability*. New York: Oxford University Press, 46–62.

Bråthen, M., Wel, K. A. & Løyland, B. 2020. Mental health and access to active labor market programs. *Nordic Journal of Working Life Studies*, 10(3), 23–41.

Callaghan, S. & Ryan, C. 2016. An evolving revolution: Evaluating Australia's compliance with the convention on the rights of Person's with disabilities in mental health law. *University of New South Wales Law Journal*, 39, 596–624.

Carey, G., Malbon, E. & Blackwell, J. 2021. Administering inequality? The national disability insurance scheme and administrative burdens on individuals. *Australian Journal of Public Administration*. 10.1111/1467-8500.12508.

Carney, T. 2003. Mental health in postmodern society: Time for new paradigms? *Psychiatry, Psychology and Law*, 10, 12–32.

Carney, T. 2012. Mental health tribunals-rights, protection & treatment; or 'space' for tribunals as governance? *International Journal of Law and Psychiatry*, 35(1), 1–10.

Carney, T. 2018. A right to health? *In*: White, B., Mcdonald, F. & Willmott, L. (eds.) *Health Law in Australia*. 3rd ed. Sydney: Thompson Reuters.

Carney, T., Tait, D., Perry, J., Vernon, A. & Beaupert, F. 2011. *Australian Mental Health Tribunals: 'Space' for Fairness, Freedom, Protection & Treatment?* Sydney: Themis Press.

Carter, H., Araya, R., Anjur, K., Deng, D. & Naslund, J. A. 2021. The emergence of digital mental health in low-income and middle-income countries: A review of recent advances and implications for the treatment and prevention of mental disorders. *Journal of Psychiatric Research*, 133, 223–246.

Conaghan, J. 2007. Following the path to equality through law: Reflections on Baker et al., equality: From theory to action. *Res Publica*, 13(2), 159–170.

Côte, A. 2021. Disability inclusion and social protection. *In*: Schüring, E. & Loewe, M. (eds.) *Handbook on Social Protection Systems*. Cheltenham and Camberley: Edward Elgar, 354–367.

Cripps, D. A. 2015. The social gradient of adult guardianship in South Australia. *Psychiatry, Psychology and Law*, 22(3), 436–443.

Davey, S. & Gordon, S. 2017. Definitions of social inclusion and social exclusion: The invisibility of mental illness and the social conditions of participation. *International Journal of Culture and Mental Health*, 10(3), 229–237.

Dawson, J. & Szmukler, G. 2006. Fusion of mental health and incapacity legislation. *British Journal of Psychiatry*, 188, 504–509.

Degener, T. 2016. Disability in a human rights context. *Laws*, 5(3), 35.

Degener, T. 2017. A human rights model of disability. *In*: Blanck, P. & Flynn, E. (eds.) *Routledge Handbook of Disability Law and Human Rights*. London: Routledge, 31–49.

Fredman, S. 2010a. New horizons: Incorporating socio-economic rights in a British Bill of Rights. *Public Law*, 2010, 297–320.

Fredman, S. 2010b. Positive duties and socio-economic disadvantage: Bringing disadvantage onto the equality agenda. *European Human Rights Law Review*, 2010, 290–304.

Fromm, E. 1942. *The Fear of Freedom*. London: Routledge & Kegan Paul.

Fry, C. E. 2021. Medicaid waivers and access to behavioral health services: What is known and what can be expected. *Psychiatric Services*, appi. ps. 202000865.

Gallagher, M. 2018. From associations to action: Mental health and the patient politics of subsidiarity in Scotland. *Palgrave Communications*, 4, 1–11.

Gooding, P. 2019a. Can laws "commit" governments to provide mental health services? A role for human rights in securing resources. *In*: Okpaku, S. (ed.) *Innovations in Global Mental Health*. Cham: Springer, 11.

Gooding, P. 2019b. Mapping the Rise of Digital Mental Health Technologies: Emerging issues for law and society. *International Journal of Law and Psychiatry*, 67, 101498.

Gray, A. M. 1982. Inequalities in health. The black report: A summary and comment. *International Journal of Health Services: Planning, Administration, Evaluation*, 12(3), 349–380.

Guiraudon, V. 2009. Equality in the Making: Implementing European non-discrimination law. *Citizenship Studies*, 13(5), 527–549.

Hamer, H. P., Rowe, M. & Seymour, C. A. 2019. 'The right thing to do': Fostering social inclusion for mental health service users through acts of citizenship. *International Journal of Mental Health Nursing*, 28(1), 297–305.

Harris, S. P., Owen, R., Fisher, K. R. & Gould, R. 2014. Human rights and neoliberalism in Australian welfare to work policy: Experiences and perceptions of people with disabilities and disability stakeholders. *Disability Studies Quarterly*, 34.

Hashmi, R., Alam, K. & Gow, J. 2020. Socioeconomic inequalities in mental health in Australia: Explaining life shock exposure. *Health Policy*, 124(1), 97–105.

Hendriks, A. 2019. Mental health, disability rights, and equal access to employment. In: Davidson, L. (ed.) *The Routledge Handbook of International Development, Mental Health and Wellbeing*. Routledge, 153–170.

Jenkins, R. 2019. Global mental health and sustainable development 2018. *BJPsych International*, 16(2), 34–37.

Keogh, M., Fox, N. & Flynn, E. 2010. How far towards equality' A vulnerabilities approach to the rights of disabled people. *UCD Working Papers in Law, Criminology & Socio-Legal Studies Research Paper No. 29/2010*.

Koutsogeorgou, E., Leonardi, M., Bickenbach, J. E., Cerniauskaite, M., Quintas, R. & Raggi, A. 2014. Social capital, disability, and usefulness of the international classification of functioning, disability and health for the development and monitoring of policy interventions. *Disability and Society*, 29(7), 1104–1116.

Mazeikaite, G., O'donoghue, C. & Sologon, D. M. 2021. What drives cross-country health inequality in the EU? Unpacking the role of socio-economic factors. *Social Indicators Research*, 155(1), 117–155.

Mclaughlin, E. 2007. From negative to positive equality duties: The development and constitutionalisation of equality provisions in the UK. *Social Policy and Society*, 6(1), 111–121.

Mcsherry, B. 2008. Mental health and human rights: The role of the law in developing a right to enjoy the highest attainable standard of mental health in Australia. *Journal of Law and Medicine*, 15(5), 773–781.

Minkowitz, T. 2010. Abolishing mental health laws to comply with the convention on the rights of persons with disabilities. In: Mcsherry, B. & Weller, P. (eds.) *Rethinking Rights-Based Mental Health Laws*. Oxford: Hart, 151–177.

Newton-Howes, G. 2019. Do community treatment orders in psychiatry stand up to principalism: Considerations reflected through the prism of the convention on the rights of persons with disabilities. *The Journal of Law, Medicine and Ethics*, 47(1), 126–133.

O'Connell, P. 2010. The human right to health in an age of market hegemony. In: Harrington, J. & Stuttaford, M. (eds.) *Global Health and Human Rights: Legal and Philosophical Perspectives*. Oxford: Routledge, 190–209.

O'reilly, R. L., Hastings, T., Chaimowitz, G. A., Neilson, G. E., Brooks, S. A. & Freeland, A. 2019. Community treatment orders and other forms of mandatory outpatient treatment. *The Canadian Journal of Psychiatry*, 64(5), 356–374.

Palk, A. C. & Stein, D. J. 2020. Ethical issues in global mental health. In: D. J. Stein, I. Singh (eds.) *Global Mental Health and Neuroethics*. Amsterdam: Elsevier, 265–285.

Parker, S. 2007. Searching for the absent citizen: Enabling and disenabling discourses of disability. *Australian Journal of Human Rights*, 12, 1–25.

Rafael, L., Marie, S. & Victoria, S. 2017. To what extent is the assistance and support provided by social services capable of enhancing active citizenship for persons with psychosocial disabilities? A comparative perspective. In: Halvorsen, R., Hvinden, B., Bickenbach, J., Ferri, D. & Guillén Rodriguez, A. M. (eds.) *The Changing Disability Policy System*. London: Routledge, 108–126.

Series, L. 2020. Disability and human rights. In: Watson, N. & Vehmas, S. (eds.) *Routledge Handbook of Disability Studies*. 2nd ed. London: Routledge, 72–88.

Silver, H. 2010. Understanding social inclusion and its meaning for Australia. *Australian Journal of Social Issues*, 45(2), 183–211.

Stavert, J. 2018. Paradigm shift or paradigm paralysis? National mental health and capacity law and implementing the CRPD in Scotland. *Laws*, 7(3), 26.

Steiner, J. & Alston, P. 1996. *International Human Rights in Context: Law, Politics, Morals, Clarendon Press*. Oxford: Clarendon Press.

Sweet, D., Byng, R., Webber, M., Enki, D. G., Porter, I., Larsen, J., Huxley, P. & Pinfold, V. 2018. Personal well-being networks, social capital and severe mental illness: Exploratory study. *The British Journal of Psychiatry*, 212(5), 308–317.

Szmukler, G. 2020. Involuntary detention and treatment: Are we edging toward a "paradigm shift"? *Schizophrenia Bulletin*, 46(2), 231–235.

Then, S.-N., Duffy, J., Bigby, C., Carney, T., Wiesel, I., Sinclair, C. & Douglas, J. 2023. *Supported Decision-Making: The Current State of Knowledge*. Royal Commission into Violence, Abuse, Neglect and Exploitation of People with Disability. Sydney.

Tibber, M. S., Walji, F., Kirkbride, J. B. & Huddy, V. 2021. The association between income inequality and adult mental health at the subnational level—A systematic review. *Social Psychiatry and Psychiatric Epidemiology*, 1–24.

Treviranus, J. 2018. *The Three Dimensions of Inclusive Design: A Design Framework for a Digitally Transformed and Complexly Connected Society*. PhD, University College Dublin.

Trewin, S., Basson, S., Muller, M., Branham, S., Treviranus, J., Gruen, D., Hebert, D., Lyckowski, N. & Manser, E. 2019. Considerations for AI fairness for people with disabilities. *AI Matters*, 5(3), 40–63.

Victorian MH Royal Commission 2021. Royal commission into Victoria's mental health system: Final Report. Melbourne.

Vornholt, K., Villotti, P., Muschalla, B., Bauer, J., Colella, A., Zijlstra, F., Van Ruitenbeek, G., Uitdewilligen, S. & Corbiere, M. 2018. Disability and employment–Overview and highlights. *European Journal of Work and Organizational Psychology*, 27(1), 40–55.

Waddington, L. & Priestley, M. 2021. A human rights approach to disability assessment. *Journal of International and Comparative Social Policy*, 37(1), 1–15.

Wang, J., Lloyd-Evans, B., Giacco, D., Forsyth, R., Nebo, C., Mann, F. & Johnson, S. 2017. Social isolation in mental health: A conceptual and methodological review. *Social Psychiatry and Psychiatric Epidemiology*, 52(12), 1451–1461.

Weller, P. 2009. Human rights and social justice. *Public Space: The Journal of Law and Social Justice*, 4, 74–91.

Williams, T. & Smith, G. 2021. Mental health and the NDIS: Making it work for people with psychosocial disability. *In*: Cowden, M. & Mccullagh, C. (eds.) *The National Disability Insurance Scheme*. Singapore: Palgrave Macmillan, 161–191.

Wilson, K. E. 2020. The abolition or reform of mental health law: How should the law recognise and respond to the vulnerability of persons with mental impairment? *Medical Law Review*, 28(1), 30–64.

Wright, N. & Stickley, T. 2013. Concepts of social inclusion, exclusion and mental health: A review of the international literature. *Journal of Psychiatric and Mental Health Nursing*, 20(1), 71–81.

Yu, P. 2020. The algorithmic divide and equality in the age of artificial intelligence. *Florida Law Review*, 72, 331–389.

21
THE RIGHT TO MENTAL HEALTH CARE IN MENTAL HEALTH LEGISLATION

Brendan D. Kelly

Introduction

On 7 May 1959, British scientist and novelist C. P. Snow delivered the Rede Lecture in Cambridge, which was subsequently published as *The Two Cultures and the Scientific Revolution* (Snow, 1959). Snow argued that the humanities and science had split into 'two cultures', with proponents of the humanities bemoaning scientists' lack of familiarity with the humanities, but failing to recognise their own disengagement from science, and vice versa. The division between the 'two cultures' was, Snow argued, deeply detrimental to all who sought to solve the problems that humanity faced.

In this chapter, I argue that 'two cultures' have emerged with respect to rights to mental health and mental health care. On one side, organisations such as the United Nations (UN) and World Health Organization (WHO) issue declarations that fail to engage sufficiently with the social, medical, and scientific evidence base for mental health care or with the realities of service provision. On the other side, many mental health service-users and service-providers, seized by the urgency of providing health and social care to those in need, increasingly regard UN and WHO statements as too detached from reality to inform change, as evidenced by muted responses to the UN Convention on the Rights of Persons with Disabilities (CRPD) (United Nations, 2006), despite the vast academic literature it continues to generate.

There are, in essence, 'two cultures' with respect to rights to mental health and mental health care. Nobody benefits from this situation and important opportunities are missed, most notably with respect to the CRPD.

In the middle, people with mental illness and their families often chart the most sensible course, finding positions to value on both sides, even though the balance between ideology and evidence in views adopted by international bodies is increasingly tilted in favour of ideology. I argue that each of the 'two cultures' needs to seek greater understanding of the other's position in order to make rights to mental health and mental health care into useful realities, rather than futile battlegrounds of rhetoric.

The chapter starts with a brief background to human rights in this field, explores the draft views of the WHO and Office of the UN High Commissioner for Human Rights (OHCHR) on reforming mental health legislation, discusses the idea of a 'right' to involuntary mental health care, and concludes with a call for greater understanding between the 'two cultures', more inter-disciplinary research, and enhanced collaboration in planning and delivering services in order to better protect rights in mental health care.

Background to the right to mental health

Key ideas underpinning human rights have lengthy histories in many political and religious traditions, with particular growth in interest during the eighteenth century (Freeman, 2002). In theory, increased articulation of civil and political rights throughout the eighteenth and nineteenth centuries should have, automatically and without discrimination, included the rights of people with mental illness. The historical experiences of the mentally ill, however, and especially their increased rates of institutionalisation, highlight the need for pro-active protection of human rights and dignity, especially among those who lack opportunity to assert these rights adequately for themselves. The need to provide dedicated safeguards for such rights was not to be formally recognised until well into the twentieth century (Kelly, 2016).

Against this background, and at a more general level, the Universal Declaration of Human Rights (UDHR) was adopted by the UN General Assembly at the Palais de Chaillot in Paris on 10 December 1948 (United Nations, 1948). The UDHR was presented as a non-binding statement of rights which recognises that 'recognition of the inherent dignity and of the equal and inalienable rights of all members of the human family is the foundation of freedom, justice and peace in the world' (preamble).

The UDHR states that 'all human beings are born free and equal in dignity and rights. They are endowed with reason and conscience and should act towards one another in a spirit of brotherhood' (article 1). These rights are universal:

> Everyone is entitled to all the rights and freedoms set forth in this Declaration, without distinction of any kind, such as race, colour, sex, language, religion, political or other opinion, national or social origin, property, birth or other status.
>
> *(article 2)*

The UDHR makes reference to 'health and well-being':

> Everyone has the right to a standard of living adequate for the health and well-being of himself and of his family, including food, clothing, housing and medical care and necessary social services, and the right to security in the event of unemployment, sickness, disability, widowhood, old age or other lack of livelihood in circumstances beyond his control.
>
> *(article 25(1))*

The inclusion of economic and social rights in the UDHR was controversial and in 1966 two separate covenants were adapted by the UN General Assembly: the *International Covenant on Civil and Political Rights* (United Nations, 1966a) and the *International Covenant on Economic, Social and Cultural Rights* (United Nations, 1966b). The difference between the two covenants was that civil and political rights were to be implemented immediately, while social and cultural rights were to be implemented progressively. The *International Covenant on Economic, Social and Cultural Rights* recognises 'the right of everyone to the enjoyment of the highest attainable standard of physical and mental health' (article 12).

Detailed histories of the idea of a 'right to health' are provided elsewhere (Tobin, 2012; Wolff, 2012). For the purpose of the present chapter, key statements include the Constitution of the WHO, which says that 'health is a state of complete physical, mental and social well-being and not merely the absence of disease or infirmity':

> The enjoyment of the highest attainable standard of health is one of the fundamental rights of every human being without distinction of race, religion, political belief, economic or social condition.
> *(World Health Organization, 2020; p. 1)*

This statement places considerable responsibilities on governments to protect and promote good health (Gruskin et al., 2013), not least because the right includes both freedoms and entitlements, as outlined by the UN Committee on Economic, Social and Cultural Rights (CESCR) in 2000:

> The right to health is not to be understood as a right to be *healthy*. The right to health contains both freedoms and entitlements. The freedoms include the right to control one's health and body, including sexual and reproductive freedom, and the right to be free from interference, such as the right to be free from torture, non-consensual medical treatment and experimentation. By contrast, the entitlements include the right to a system of health protection which provides equality of opportunity for people to enjoy the highest attainable level of health.
> *(United Nations Committee on Economic, Social and Cultural Rights, 2000; paragraph 8)*

The CESCR adds that 'the right to health must be understood as a right to the enjoyment of a variety of facilities, goods, services and conditions necessary for the realization of the highest attainable standard of health' (paragraph 9). Overall, the CESCR document makes the 'right to health' more practical, attainable, and actionable (Backman and Bueno de Mesquita, 2012). This is especially helpful when non-binding statements of rights can occasionally appear utopian or aspirational, rather than pragmatic or effectual.

In 2006, the CRPD articulated a right to health specifically in the context of 'persons with disabilities':

> States Parties recognize that persons with disabilities have the right to the enjoyment of the highest attainable standard of health without discrimination on the basis of disability. States Parties shall take all appropriate measures to ensure access for persons with disabilities to health services that are gender-sensitive, including health-related rehabilitation.
> *(United Nations, 2006; article 25)*

Various other declarations about the right to health apply in specific regions around the world, including the Charter of Fundamental Rights of the European Union, which states:

> Everyone has the right of access to preventive health care and the right to benefit from medical treatment under the conditions established by national laws and practices. A

high level of human health protection shall be ensured in the definition and implementation of all Union policies and activities.

(European Union, 2000; Article 35)

The strengths and limitations of such declarations are explored in detail elsewhere (McHale and Fox, 2007; Tobin, 2012; Wolff, 2012), along with increased application of the right to health in the area of mental health, especially over the past two decades (Department of Mental Health and Substance Dependence, 2004; Kelly, 2013). This growing literature supports not only the importance of this right in the field of mental health, but also the ethical argument for a right to mental health care, based on benefit to individuals and society (Green, 2000) and clear deficits in current service provision (Flaskerud, 2009). Fulfilling this right in practice is likely to be complex and to require an evolving combination of public activism, policy change, and law reform (Kelly et al., 2020).[1]

Draft guidance on mental health legislation

Against this background, it is regrettable that a recent publication from the WHO and OHCHR presents significant cause for concern about the persistence of 'two cultures' in this area, demonstrated by a lack of engagement with systematic, clinical evidence, and a lack of critical, reflective thought. While forms of evidence other than scientific and medical findings are clearly essential for developing policy, no form of evidence should be de-emphasised when considering a topic as fundamental as the right to mental health care.

These issues are especially evident in the draft document about mental health, human rights, and legislation published for consultation by the WHO and OHCHR in June 2022, titled *Guidance on Mental Health, Human Rights, and Legislation*. The OHCHR sought input from 'Member States, and relevant regional and international intergovernmental organizations; national human rights institutions, equality bodies, United Nations funds, programmes, and specialized agencies, organizations of persons with disabilities and other civil society organizations, experts, academia and any other interested party' (World Health Organization/Office of the United Nations High Commissioner for Human Rights, 2022).[2]

It is important to emphasise that this was a draft document that was yet to be completed by the WHO and OHCHR and was, therefore, unlikely to represent the final position of either organisation. Even so, pre-consultation drafts often provide useful insights, and this particular draft presented many points of interest, including much that was valuable on topics such as 'rethinking legislation', 'person-centered, recovery-oriented and rights-based mental health', and 'developing, implementing and evaluating legislation on mental health'. Throughout the document, however, the 'two cultures' issue was in clear evidence, starting with the opening paragraph:

> Many people with mental health conditions and psychosocial disabilities, in particular, face wide-ranging human rights violations and discrimination, including in mental

---

1 See, for example: https://sd27.senate.ca.gov/news/20220429-stern-bill-establish-right-mental-health-care-and-housing-heals-severely-mentally-ill (Accessed 28 February 2023).
2 https://www.ohchr.org/en/calls-for-input/calls-input/draft-guidance-mental-health-human-rights-legislation-who-ohchr (Accessed 28 February 2023).

health care settings. Often, discriminatory practices are underpinned by legal frameworks, which fail to uphold human rights and to acknowledge the pernicious effects of institutionalisation, the over-emphasis on biomedical approaches and treatment options, and the use of involuntary psychiatric interventions.

(World Health Organization/Office of the United Nations High Commissioner for Human Rights, 2022; p. 8)

It is a matter of regret that the WHO and OHCHR did not present evidence to support this negative view and did not counter-balance it by articulating any of the benefits of current mental health legislation or psychiatric interventions. There is overwhelming evidence that psychiatric medications are just as effective as their counterparts in general medicine, and sometimes more so (Leucht et al., 2012). People with schizophrenia who take antipsychotic medication have half the risk of dying during 14 years of follow-up, compared to those who do not receive antipsychotics (Taipale et al., 2020). This includes significantly lower risks of death from cardiovascular disease as well as suicide. These findings remain significant and substantial even after controlling for age, gender, substance abuse, medical comorbidities, other medication use, and various other factors.

To put these results another way, cumulative mortality rates during 14 years of follow-up are 46% for people with schizophrenia who are not on antipsychotics, 26% for those on any antipsychotic, and 16% for those on clozapine (which is used for treatment-resistant schizophrenia). Treatments with similar benefits in cancer medicine or cardiology would be hailed as breakthroughs. That is not to say that antipsychotic medications help everyone equally (they do not), are without side-effects (they are not), or suffice on their own (they do not – they must form part of multi-disciplinary care). But accumulated scientific evidence shows clear, substantial benefits with antipsychotics in terms of both quality and quantity of life, so it is puzzling that this is not reflected in the WHO/OHCHR draft.

The scant weight attached to evidence in the draft was noted by others, including the National Secular Society:

> While cultural sensitivity and holistic, person-centred and rights-based approaches are welcome inclusions into mental health care, we caution that use of the phrase 'reductionist Western biomedical model' may lead to policies which reject objective, scientific and evidence-based healthcare in lieu of 'alternative medicine' models that are not supported by evidence and may be based on religious views. Sometimes, 'alternative medicine' models are pushed by people with a specific religious or personal agenda who do not prioritise the healthcare needs of the patient …The guidance should stress that, while cultural sensitivity is important, best practice mental health care should be objective and evidence-based.[3]

Hopefully, this will be addressed in more advanced versions, following consultation. The report, as originally drafted, returned repeatedly to what it termed the 'biomedical model':

---

3 https://www.ohchr.org/sites/default/files/documents/issues/health/draftguidance/submissions/2022-08-08/National_secular_society_response.docx (Accessed 28 February 2023).

The biomedical model, in which the predominant focus of care is on diagnosis, medication and symptom reduction, continues to be the most prevalent approach across existing mental health systems. As a result, social determinants that impact people's mental health are overlooked, resulting in persons with mental health conditions and psychosocial disabilities continuing to face higher rates of unemployment, poverty, homelessness, and incarceration.

(World Health Organization/Office of the United Nations High Commissioner for Human Rights, 2022; p. 16)

Rather than overlooking the social determinants of mental health, the papers referenced by the WHO and OHCHR highlighted these precise issues, as do many other publications throughout the psychiatric literature (see, for example, Kelly, 2005; Burns, 2013a; Burns, 2013b; Torrey, 2014; Kelly, 2022). These are social needs that psychiatrists and other mental health professionals have repeatedly highlighted over many decades, but which social care providers and policy-makers have repeatedly failed to meet. This is not the fault of what the WHO and OHCHR conveniently term the 'biomedical model'; these are social and political issues which mental health professionals highlight repeatedly, but lack the tools to solve.

Capacity, consent, and care

Other areas of the WHO/OHCHR draft guidance presented similar reasons for concern. The WHO and OHCHR wrote that:

It is important that the law clearly prohibits substitute decision-making in the provision of mental health care and support. This includes repealing the provisions that allow guardians and family members to make decisions for people receiving mental health care or support, as well as eliminating all instances in which the law allows the treating doctor to decide for the person in their 'best interests'. The law should also expressly prohibit health professionals from making decisions without the person's informed consent.

(World Health Organization/Office of the United Nations High Commissioner for Human Rights, 2022; p. 47)

There is general agreement that models of supported decision-making need to be developed, improved, and expanded, but there is minimal guidance about how to proceed when supported decision-making proves insufficient. On occasion, it is simply not possible, despite extensive efforts, to establish a person's 'will and preference' for periods of time. Regrettably, the draft WHO/OHCHR document chose to avoid dealing with such difficult cases in sufficient detail. Hopefully, this will be addressed in later drafts, but the avoidance of challenging topics was a repeated pattern in the pre-consultation draft and is common across other documents from the WHO and UN (e.g., United Nations Committee on the Rights of Persons with Disabilities, 2014).

The draft guidance went on to state that 'another common exception to informed consent, particularly used in mental health care, is the lack of "capacity" or "competency" to provide consent. As noted, this exception is contrary to the CRPD' (p. 54). Notwithstanding the particular interpretation of the CRPD presented by the UN Committee on the Rights of Persons with Disabilities (United Nations Committee on the Rights of Persons with Disabilities, 2014), there is a widespread view among mental health service users and providers that the concept of 'capacity' is a valid one and is not 'contrary to the CRPD' (Dawson, 2015; Freeman et al., 2015; Gergel et al., 2021).

In England and Wales, the foreword to the *Independent Review of the Mental Health Act, 1983* noted that 'some will point out that we have not gone as far as to recommend fully implementing the [CRPD], or to be precise, how that is interpreted by the Committee charged with its implementation':

> And they are right. We haven't. For example, the Committee's recommendations would include not just dropping the [Mental Health Act, 1983], it [would] also require us to end all forms of substituted decision making, which would have to include for example dropping the Mental Capacity Act as well. I agree that the Mental Capacity Act (MCA), or more specifically the Deprivation of Liberty Safeguards (DOLS), needs urgent reform, which is happening as we speak. But the idea that those who lack capacity to take decisions for themselves should have no protections, save supported decision making, against exploitation, excessive detention and so on, seems to me to be something that most people and Parliament will find difficult. I do not think that we are compelled to follow this interpretation, and we will not.
>
> *(Independent Review of the Mental Health Act 1983, 2018; p. 12)*

The WHO and OHCHR, in their draft guidance, expressed the view that 'the CRPD Committee and other human rights mechanisms have asserted that all coercive practices in mental health services are prohibited under the CRPD' (p. 61). Following this, they recommended that 'legislation should clearly prohibit all involuntary measures', but noted that 'no country has yet eliminated all forms of coercion in mental health systems'.

As a result, the draft WHO/OHCHR document explicitly recommended that every country pursue a course of action that no country had found possible to date; i.e., completely eliminating coercion in psychiatric services. Rather than citing systematic evidence to support their suggestion, the draft WHO/OHCHR recommendation appeared to be based, in large part, on one particular interpretation of the CRPD – an interpretation that is poorly supported by the CRPD itself, is widely contested (see above), and conflicts fundamentally with the position of other UN bodies (see below).

The ultimate goal is undisputed: non-coercive care is always ideal, it should be pursued more rigorously, and all incidents of coercion should be regulated closely, recorded in detail, and reviewed with a view to future prevention. But while many countries have implemented coercion-reduction programmes,[4] none have managed to eliminate it completely, as the WHO and OHCHR acknowledged.

Later in the draft document, the WHO and OHCHR articulated a very particular, unsourced account of highly coercive treatment of 'a person who is suicidal':

---

4 E.g., http://hdl.handle.net/10147/627078 (Accessed 28 February 2023).

When a person is threatening immediate harm to themselves (e.g., threatening to cut themselves or jumping out of a building), traditionally, legislation will consider them at risk to themselves and therefore authorize the use of coercion. First responders, often police officers and firefighters, will intervene to contain the situation. This may include the use of physical or chemical restraints. The person will then be taken to an inpatient service where, in many cases, they will be involuntarily admitted and kept for many days, even weeks. On many occasions, due to risk considerations, the person will be placed in a seclusion room at the beginning of their stay.

(World Health Organization/Office of the United Nations High Commissioner for Human Rights, 2022; p. 63)

Again, the WHO and OHCHR did not provide evidence to support this account or indicate if they regarded this trajectory as typical or atypical.

While it is likely that the situation varies across countries, it is worth noting that in Ireland, for example, 82% of people who present to emergency departments with self-harm or suicidal ideation are not admitted to inpatient care, but are directed to community supports instead (Health Service Executive, Mental Health Division, 2017). Among all people admitted to inpatient psychiatric care in Ireland, 84% of admissions are voluntary rather than involuntary (Daly and Craig, 2021), and, among those admitted, fewer than 9% experience seclusion (O'Callaghan et al., 2021). While further progress can be made on these parameters, and there are undoubtedly differences between countries, this picture of psychiatry is markedly different to the one articulated by the WHO and OHCHR in their draft guidance – and markedly more protective of rights, including the right to appropriate mental health care.

Listening to mental health service-users and the evidence more generally

Perhaps the most concerning issue in the WHO/OHCHR draft *Guidance on Mental Health, Human Rights, and Legislation* related to 'challenging and complex crisis situations'. The WHO/OHCHR noted 'there is an aphorism in law that says, "hard cases make bad law", which aims to convey the idea that highly unusual or difficult-to-solve cases are ill-suited to be used as the basis of general rules':

However, in the field of mental health, it is common to present complex and challenging situations, often referred to … as 'hard cases', as evidence that a total paradigm shift from substituted decision-making to supported decision-making is not possible, particularly in the context of mental health provision.

(pp. 62–63)

The occurrence of 'hard cases' does not, of course, suggest that a 'paradigm shift from substituted decision-making to supported decision-making is not possible', and it is a matter of regret that the WHO and OHCHR did not present evidence to support this statement.

But while a 'paradigm shift' is perfectly possible, 'hard cases' will still occur (even when best practice is followed) and will require solutions that are rooted in legislation, given the gravity of the issues involved. Saying that 'hard cases make bad law' does not prevent such cases occurring, does not assist with resolving them, and is not a reason to avoid dealing with them in guidance. The WHO/OHCHR continued:

> These examples, regularly used in legal and clinical discussions, include cases where an individual is suicidal, the individual is behaving aggressively or violently, or when the individual is experiencing psychosis, or has intense support needs. The traditional medical framing of these cases as 'hard cases' fails to acknowledge that these complex and challenging situations are often the result of the failures of existing mental health systems, many of which are unable to adequately respond to trauma, distress and crisis.
>
> (p. 63)

Again, stating that 'hard cases' are 'often the result of the failures of existing mental health systems' is true, and emphasises the need for better preventive health and social care. But saying this does not assist with resolving 'hard cases' when they occur, as they do, even in highly resourced, well-functioning systems. And nor is it a reason to avoid dealing adequately with 'hard cases' in guidance such as this. Regrettably, while the draft WHO/OHCHR document provided much information about good practice, it failed to provide sufficient guidance for occasions when 'hard cases' were not resolved by the good practice measures it outlined. This was a serious omission which will hopefully be addressed in future revisions.

The draft guidance stated that 'if de-escalation fails and a situation of violence arises, crisis intervention teams could provide protection against interpersonal violence and support law enforcement to ensure the person is safely taken into custody where the person could be offered appropriate accommodations and support' (p. 62). This suggested that, if good practice proved insufficient, it was better that 'law enforcement' take people with mental illness and disturbed behaviour into 'custody', rather than mental health professionals ensuring they go to health care settings where support and treatment are more likely to be available.

In essence, the draft guidance had clear difficulty dealing with the issue of violence. As a result, it avoided the issue when possible (on the basis that 'hard cases make bad law'); outsourced the response to other sectors that are less skilled than mental health staff and would likely decline involvement anyway (such as 'law enforcement'); and, on occasion, seemed to contradict itself. For example, the draft guidance suggested that 'law enforcement' might need to 'ensure the person is safely taken into custody where the person could be offered appropriate accommodations and support' (p. 62), but also stated that 'police intervention' should be 'free from discrimination and any use of force or coercion' (p. 97). The draft guidance did not explain how 'law enforcement' can keep a person in 'custody' without 'any use of force or coercion'.

The root problem here is the 'two cultures'. Clinicians deal with all kinds of issues (including 'hard cases') on a daily basis, are fully aware of the realities of care provision in imperfect systems, and, as a result, often find the WHO/OHCHR approach so far removed from reality as to be irrelevant. On the other side, the relentless and disproportionate criticism of psychiatry in these documents alienates mental health workers and enormously diminishes the impact of UN and WHO guidance, owing, not least, to their creation of a 'biomedical' strawman to support many of their more tenuous positions. This is a pity, because much needs to change in mental health services, generally (but not always) along the lines suggested by the UN and WHO.

The other causes of the 'two cultures' problem are a failure by the WHO and OHCHR to engage sufficiently with systematic evidence (including medical research, scientific studies, and reports about the realities of care provision); uncritical acceptance and selective quotation of statements by other UN bodies (creating an 'echo chamber' which amplifies questionable interpretations and positions); systematic neglect of the role of families, friends, and communities in situations of mental distress; and a failure to reflect the true diversity of views among mental health service-users about such key concepts as capacity and treatment without consent (Freeman et al., 2015).

The latter point appeared to reflect a prioritisation of pre-existing ideology over evidence, and a more general tendency of UN bodies to reflect certain views of mental health service-users rather than others, as demonstrated by Gergel and colleagues in their study of service-users' views about self-binding directives:

> The endorsement by the majority of service user respondents of involuntary treatment on the basis of impaired decision-making abilities counters a widespread view, upheld by the UN Committee on the Rights of Persons with Disabilities, that psychiatric use of capacity assessment and involuntary treatment necessarily violate fundamental human rights. Researchers, clinicians, and policy makers should consider that some service users with severe mental health conditions wish to request their own future involuntary treatment, using self-binding directives as a way to self-manage their illness and increase autonomy. When assessing the ethical viability of self-binding directives, mental capacity, and involuntary treatment, human rights advocates need to take a broad range of service user views into account.
>
> *(Gergel et al., 2021; p. 600)*

Service-users' endorsement of 'capacity' is especially interesting in light of the view of the UN Committee on the Rights of Persons with Disabilities that 'mental capacity is not, as is commonly presented, an objective, scientific and naturally occurring phenomenon. Mental capacity is contingent on social and political contexts, as are the disciplines, professions and practices which play a dominant role in assessing mental capacity' (United Nations Committee on the Rights of Persons with Disabilities, 2014; p. 4). Precisely the same comments could be made about the word 'disability' which has been used to deny 'legal capacity' for even longer than 'capacity' has, but which the Committee appears to accept.

The draft WHO/OHCHR guidance echoed the Committee's views about 'capacity' and recommended 'an assessment of support needs' instead:

> For example, during a crisis, assessing the person's support needs can help to determine if the person wants to go to an inpatient mental health service, a community crisis house, or simply be supported to stay at home.
>
> *(p. 67)*

This appeared to be asking someone about their preferences, which is vital but is not 'an assessment of support needs', and so it did not provide significant assistance if the concept of 'capacity' is to be jettisoned. The UN Committee on the Rights of Persons with Disabilities seems clear that it does not feel a responsibility to provide an alternative to 'capacity' in order to assess 'support needs':

> The provision of support to exercise legal capacity should not hinge on mental capacity assessments; new, non-discriminatory indicators of support needs are required in the provision of support to exercise legal capacity.
>
> *(p. 7)*

The Committee does not specify who should develop such 'non-discriminatory indicators of support needs' or what they might be. This omission raises an ethical concern about issuing vetoes but assuming no responsibility to suggest alternatives.

This issue was also apparent in the draft WHO/OHCHR document which sought to veto 'all involuntary measures' (p. 61). The WHO and OHCHR made this draft recommendation despite the facts that (a) 'no country has yet eliminated all forms of coercion in mental health systems' (p. 61) (and therefore it might not be possible); (b) 'sometimes there will be no optimal solution' (p. 65) (which are precisely the times when guidance is needed); and (c) its guidance on dealing with 'hard cases' in the absence of involuntary care was a mixture of repeating good practice measures which are often used already (pp. 63–64), avoiding difficult questions that arise when such measures do not work (on the basis that 'hard cases make bad law'; p. 62), outsourcing the response to a less experienced sector ('law enforcement'; p. 62), and making a deeply puzzling recommendation about a person being taken into 'custody' by 'law enforcement' (p. 62) without 'any use of force or coercion' (p. 97).

Issuing these kinds of vetoes without suggesting meaningful alternatives that address complex situations is deeply unhelpful. These are difficult circumstances, but that is precisely why guidance is needed. Broader, deeper engagement with mental health service-users, families, community leaders, and service-providers would help generate more useful guidance, protect rights, promote mental health, and support people through crises. Hopefully, more developed versions of the WHO/OHCHR guidance will address these matters. Avoiding difficult questions does not help anyone and can undermine the right to health in a population with especially complex needs.

The right to involuntary care

The issue of admission and treatment without consent is, perhaps, the most difficult question in this field and – again – highlights the 'two cultures' problem.

In 1990, H. Richard Lamb wrote about 'involuntary treatment for the homeless mentally ill' in the *Notre Dame Journal of Law, Ethics and Public Policy*. Lamb concluded by painting a picture that is familiar to many people with mental illness, their families, their friends, and mental health workers all around the world:

> Suppose I were acutely or chronically psychotic to the point of incompetency to make a decision about treatment and were living on the streets, vulnerable to every predator, eating out of garbage cans, and in and out of jail. I would fervently hope that the agent of society who saw my plight would not simply tell me that I have a right to live my life that way but instead would do something to rescue me – 'against my will' if necessary. Society owes us that much.
>
> Thus, the mentally ill have another crucial right. When, because of severe mental illness, they present a serious threat to their own welfare or that of others and at the same time are not able to ask for or even to accept treatment, they have a right to involuntary treatment. Not to grant them that right is inhumane.
>
> *(Lamb, 1990; p. 280)*

That passage was written in 1990, before the UN *Principles for the Protection of Persons with Mental Illness and the Improvement of Mental Health Care* (United Nations, 1991), before the CRPD (United Nations, 2006), and before the draft WHO/OHCHR recommendation that 'legislation should clearly prohibit all involuntary measures' (p. 61).

Notwithstanding this most recent draft recommendation, the need for treatment without consent at certain times was and still is broadly and consistently recognised today, as it was in Lamb's time. Not only has 'no country … yet eliminated all forms of coercion in mental health systems', as the WHO and OHCHR pointed out in their draft guidance, but in 2014, eight years after the CRPD, the UN Human Rights Committee outlined conditions under which it considers deprivation of liberty to be acceptable:

> The existence of a disability shall not in itself justify a deprivation of liberty but rather any deprivation of liberty must be necessary and proportionate, for the purpose of protecting the individual in question from serious harm or preventing injury to others. It must be applied only as a measure of last resort and for the shortest appropriate period of time, and must be accompanied by adequate procedural and substantive safeguards established by law. The procedures should ensure respect for the views of the individual and ensure that any representative genuinely represents and defends the wishes and interests of the individual.
>
> *(UN Human Rights Committee, 2014; paragraph 19)*

The WHO and OHCHR could usefully include this wording in the final version of their guidance about mental health legislation, limiting deprivation of liberty to certain, defined circumstances, with rigorous oversight. Simply hoping that a renewed emphasis on good practice and support will prevent all 'hard cases' and completely remove the need for treatment without consent and substitute decision-making is not evidence based, realistic, or protective of rights.

There has been no stage in human history when some people with mental illness were not severely ill to the point of refusing care, excluded from society, homeless, and profoundly neglected (Kelly, 2022). Hopefully, ours will be the first generation in history to develop services to a degree that prevents all such cases, but, in the meantime, we need to consider those who suffer *today*, many of whom see the need for treatment without consent themselves, from time to time (Freeman et al., 2015; Gergel et al., 2021). Their voices matter.

In 2016, two years after the UN Committee on the Rights of Persons with Disabilities issued its 'General Comment No. 1', the UN Subcommittee on Prevention of Torture and Other Cruel, Inhuman or Degrading Treatment or Punishment endorsed the need for treatment without consent under limited, specific circumstances, and agreed with Lamb (Lamb, 1990; Lamb, 2000) that denying such treatment could amount to a denial of rights:

14. Exceptionally, it may be necessary to medically treat a person deprived of liberty without her or his consent if the person concerned is not able to: (a) Understand the information given concerning the characteristics of the threat to her or his life or personal integrity, or its consequences; (b) Understand the information about the medical treatment proposed, including its purpose, its means, its direct effects and its possible side effects; (c) Communicate effectively with others.
15. In such a situation, the withholding of medical treatment would constitute inappropriate practice and could amount to a form of cruel, inhuman or degrading treatment or punishment. It may also constitute a form of discrimination. The measure must be

a last resort to avoid irreparable damage to the life, integrity or health of the person concerned, and must be mandated by a competent authority within a strict framework that sets out the criteria and duration for the treatment and review and supervision mechanisms.

(UN Subcommittee on Prevention of Torture and Other Cruel, Inhuman or Degrading Treatment or Punishment, 2016)

Again, this is wording that the WHO and OHCHR could usefully incorporate into their final guidance on mental health legislation, acknowledging that 'hard cases' occur and providing guidance for those situations, while also including material about best practice, promoting a paradigm shift to supported decision-making, and articulating a goal of zero-coercion in mental health care – although these goals should not be met at the expense of the minority of people who need treatment without consent or substitute decision-making for periods of time. *Everyone* matters.

More broadly, the WHO and OHCHR could usefully recognise that while an emphasis on individual rights such as the right to health care is urgently needed, individual legal 'rights' are not the only or even the best way to articulate and meet certain human needs (Osiatyński, 2009). There is growing recognition that legal intervention, although necessary, will have limited impact on addressing stigma or achieving global access to care and support (Petrila, 2010; Glover-Thomas and Chima, 2015). An exclusive focus on individual rights also fails to recognise the complexity of how socialisation influences personal autonomy (Kong, 2017). In addition, access to litigation is not equally distributed to all (Donnelly, 2010).

Notwithstanding these caveats, individual rights still matter hugely and have been shamefully neglected in health systems (Bartlett, 2010). The CRPD offers a valuable opportunity to address this issue and promote the right to mental health care, but the interpretation of the CRPD by the UN Committee on the Rights of Persons with Disabilities may well end up hurting the very people the CRPD purports to help (Appelbaum, 2019). Regrettably, that interpretation was echoed throughout the WHO/OHCHR draft guidance on mental health legislation and, as a result, potentially undermined the right to health for many people with serious mental illness.

Conclusions

In 2018, India commenced a new piece of mental health legislation, the Mental Healthcare Act, 2017. India's legislation states that it was designed to comply with the CRPD, but includes admission without consent (section 89) and substitute decision-making (section 89(7)), both of which are inconsistent with the UN Committee on the Rights of Persons with Disabilities' interpretation of the CRPD (United Nations Committee on the Rights of Persons with Disabilities, 2014).

The Indian legislation, however, also includes 'a right to access mental healthcare and treatment' (section 18(1)) and various other progressive measures that are highly consistent with the CRPD itself (Kelly et al., 2020). In addition, the 2017 Act recognises that articulating an individual legal right is not enough: the Act also commits the Indian government to providing sufficient mental health services (section 18) and human resources to make the system work (section 31), notwithstanding the considerable problems that Indian mental health services face (Gautham et al., 2020).

Despite the inevitable challenges of this undertaking, the Indian legislation takes a pragmatic approach to the CRPD and provides an explicit right to mental health care. The inclusion of measures relating to accommodation and community rehabilitation within this right (section 18(4)) acknowledges the social factors that shape mental illness, care, and outcomes, as the WHO and OHCHR also pointed out in their draft guidance:

> Mental health cannot be considered in isolation of an individual's multiple and intersecting layers of identity and oppression. A person's age, sex, sexual orientation, gender identity, disability, caste, racial or ethnic origin, socio-economic status, migrant or refugee status, and other markers of identity and experience cumulate to influence mental health and access to quality mental health care and support.
>
> *(p. 15)*

Later, when discussing 'hard cases', the WHO and OHCHR add that:

> the traditional medical framing of [certain] cases as 'hard cases' fails to acknowledge that these complex and challenging situations are often the result of the failures of existing mental health systems, many of which are unable to adequately respond to trauma, distress and crisis.
>
> *(p. 63)*

Psychiatry, of course, has recognised the roles of systems of care and socio-economic factors in shaping mental distress long before the UN and WHO existed (Blazer, 2005).

Today, psychiatrists and many others continue to highlight the structural inequalities, socio-economic circumstances, and system failings that shape the landscape of risk for mental illness and psychological distress, how they are diagnosed and treated, whether people are supported appropriately, and what the outcomes are (see, for example, Kelly, 2005; Burns, 2013a; Burns, 2013b; Torrey, 2014; Kelly, 2022). It is a matter of satisfaction that the WHO and OHCHR have also come to recognise these factors as significant. Achieving social justice (Callard et al., 2012) and protecting human dignity are key roles for mental health services and legislation (Kelly, 2016), along with preventing and treating mental illness. These should be priorities for mental health legislation and should be duly reflected in guidance.

With this in mind, and notwithstanding useful descriptions of good practice in the draft WHO/OHCHR guidance, it was a matter of regret that the draft guidance did not adequately address the most difficult situations that occur even in well-resourced systems. These include occasions when supported decision-making is not enough or when treatment without consent is unavoidable. As the WHO and OHCHR pointed out in their draft document, a paradigm shift needs to occur towards supported decision-making, and all countries need to implement coercion-reduction programmes with the goal of zero coercion, but as long as the WHO/OHCHR recommendations avoid dealing adequately with difficult situations, they will remain just one side of the 'two cultures' problem, alienated from service-providers and many mental health service-users.

Hopefully, the final WHO/OHCHR guidance will improve on the original draft and recognise that 'hard cases' will still occur and require guidance. There will be occasions when, notwithstanding best efforts and good practice, a person's will and preference will not be ascertainable for periods of time. There will be occasions when, despite best efforts and good practice, treatment without consent is needed for periods of time, at least until (and if) mental health services are transformed along the lines outlined by the WHO and OHCHR. Even then, it is not known if these difficult situations will be entirely eliminated, will become less common, or will simply be dealt with by 'law enforcement' (p. 62), with inevitably greater emphasis on 'custody' rather than care.

As a result, it was a matter of great concern that the draft guidance from the WHO and OHCHR recommended prohibiting substitute decision-making (p. 47) and treatment without consent (p. 61), and then noted that 'sometimes there will be no optimal solution' (p. 65). These are the precise occasions when guidance is needed most – difficult situations in which optimal solutions are elusive.

It was also gravely concerning that the draft guidance said that 'if de-escalation fails and a situation of violence arises, crisis intervention teams could provide protection against interpersonal violence and support law enforcement to ensure the person is safely taken into custody where the person could be offered appropriate accommodations and support' (p. 62). The idea of 'custody' appears inconsistent with the later statement that 'police intervention' must be free from 'any use of force or coercion' (p. 97). This issue will hopefully be resolved in the final document, but even its appearance in a draft for consultation presents real cause for concern.

Ultimately, it is vital that any paradigm shift takes account of *all* service-users' needs – those of the majority, whose needs will be met through good practices outlined by the WHO and OHCHR, and those of the minority, who will require substitute decision-making or treatment without consent for periods of time. Hoping that a paradigm shift which has yet to occur will eliminate all such cases is not an evidence-based way to proceed. As the WHO and OHCHR pointed out in the draft guidance, no country has managed to entirely eliminate coercion from mental health care (p. 61). It is reasonable to hope that such a thing is possible, but hope is not a strategy.

As a result of these issues, the draft WHO/OHCHR guidance did not protect the right to mental health care for many people, and, as originally written, would have worsened the 'two cultures' problem by failing to reflect 'the endorsement by the majority of service user respondents of involuntary treatment on the basis of impaired decision-making abilities' (Gergel et al., 2021; p. 600). The CRPD is clear that 'persons with disabilities' must receive 'the same range, quality and standard of free or affordable health care and programmes as provided to other persons' (United Nations, 2006; article 25(a)). The draft guidance, as originally written, would have undermined this right for people with severe mental illness.

Just as no one would deny social, medical, or surgical care to persons with impaired decision-making ability, legislation must ensure that all approved mental health treatments, ranging from psychotherapy to medication, are available to all who need them. For people whose ability to decide is impaired for periods of time (e.g., owing to severe mental illness), additional safeguards are needed in legislation, but the complexity of these situations should not be used as an excuse to avoid dealing with them or to simply state that 'sometimes there will be no optimal solution' (p. 65). Guidance is an opportunity to create solutions, not admit defeat. A failure to address these issues in the final guidance would be a profound failure to protect the equal right to care.

In summary, a paradigm shift towards supported decision-making should occur, as suggested by the WHO and OHCHR in their draft guidance, but should be studied closely (to ensure it works) and should not occur at the expense of the minority of people whose needs are not met, and whose rights are not protected, by this approach. One size does not fit all. Everyone matters, including people whose wills and preferences cannot be clarified for periods of time (even with extensive support) and people who require treatment without consent for periods of time (despite best practice at earlier stages in their care). These situations will hopefully be rare, short-lived, and managed in such a way as to respect rights – but these situations will continue to occur. Simply hoping that they will not happen is unrealistic and unhelpful for people who face these problems. Legislative guidance is needed to support their wellbeing and rights.

The WHO/OHCHR guidance should retain the goal of zero-coercion in mental health care, but should also retain admission and treatment without consent under very limited circumstances, using wording outlined by the UN Human Rights Committee (2014) and UN Subcommittee on Prevention of Torture and Other Cruel, Inhuman or Degrading Treatment or Punishment (2016) (above). This issue is too important to avoid in guidance or to omit from law.

The matter of issuing a veto on involuntary care (p. 61) without providing an adequate alternative was also addressed by the Bureau of Mental Health Policy of the Ministry of Health and Welfare of the Republic of Korea, in their response to the WHO/OHCHR draft:

> As mentioned in the draft guidance, a zero-coercion policy requires developing a non-coercive approach and its implementation manual, which can address difficult circumstances case by case. This zero-coercion policy needs to be supported by a relevant system and workforce to make it actually work in mental health institutions. It would therefore be very helpful if the WHO-OHCHR guidance provides some guidelines on how the government can commit by law to this zero-coercion policy. Similarly, more effective guidelines are also needed on the requirements of crisis support services to better implement these services without any coercive actions in emergent situations.[5]

On the other side of the 'two cultures' problem, clinicians need to engage more with the development and operation of guidance from the WHO, OHCHR, and UN more generally. Such guidance will remain detached from the realities of care provision unless service-providers participate in its development and operation. In this spirit, I submitted many of the points made in this chapter to the WHO and OHCHR during the consultation period about their draft guidance, in the hope of informing their final document.[6]

Addressing the 'two cultures' problem in the longer term will require a multi-pronged approach, including more inter-disciplinary research and enhanced collaboration in planning and delivering care. In 2022, the WHO published a document titled *World Mental Health Report: Transforming Mental Health for All* (World Health Organization, 2022) focusing on the need to transform services along these lines. Updating mental health legislation is a key part of this process and a vital way to advance the right to mental health care. The 2022 draft WHO/OHCHR guidance on mental health, human rights, and legislation made a good start, but also had significant problems that required resolution in order to advance the right to mental health care for all, equally and without discrimination. This issue is simply too important to get wrong.

---

5 https://www.ohchr.org/sites/default/files/documents/issues/health/draftguidance/submissions/2022-08-16/Min_health_welfare_rep_korea_response.docx (Accessed 28 February 2023).
6 https://www.ohchr.org/sites/default/files/documents/issues/health/draftguidance/submissions/2022-08-30/B_kelly_trinity_college_ireland_response.docx (Accessed 28 February 2023).

References

Appelbaum, P.S. (2019) 'Saving the UN convention on the rights of persons with disabilities – from itself', *World Psychiatry*, 18(1), pp. 1–2. https://doi.org/10.1002/wps.20583

Backman, G. and Bueno de Mesquita, J. (2012) 'The right to health', in Dudley, M., Silove, D. and Gale, F. (eds.) *Mental health and human rights: Vision, praxis, and courage*. Oxford: Oxford University Press, pp. 578–584.

Bartlett, P. (2010) 'Thinking about the rest of the world: Mental health and rights outside the "first world"', in McSherry, B. and Weller, P. (eds.) *Rethinking rights-based mental health laws*. Oxford and Portland, OR: Hart Publishing, pp. 397–418.

Blazer, D.G. (2005) *The age of melancholy: 'Major depression' and its social origins*. New York and Hove: Routledge (Taylor & Francis Group).

Burns, T. (2013a) *Our necessary shadow: the nature and meaning of psychiatry*. London: Allen Lane.

Burns, J.K. (2013b) 'Mental health and inequity: A human rights approach to inequality, discrimination and mental disability', in Grodin, M.A., Tarantola, D., Annas, G.J. and Gruskin, S. (eds.) *Health and human rights in a changing world*. New York and London: Routledge (Taylor & Francis Group), pp. 449–462.

Callard, F., Sartorius, N., Arboleda-Flórez, J., Bartlett, P., Helmchen, H., Stuart, H., Taborda, J. and Thornicroft, G. (2012) *Mental illness, discrimination and the law: Fighting for social justice*. Chichester: Wiley-Blackwell.

Daly, A. and Craig, S. (2021) *Annual report on the activities of Irish psychiatric units and hospitals 2020*. Dublin: Health Research Board.

Dawson, J. (2015) 'A realistic approach to assessing mental health laws' compliance with the UNCRPD', *International Journal of Law and Psychiatry*, 40, pp. 70–79. https://doi.org/10.1016/j.ijlp.2015.04.003

Department of Mental Health and Substance Dependence. (2004) *The role of international human rights in national mental health legislation*. Geneva: World Health Organization.

Donnelly, M. (2010) *Healthcare decision-making and the law: Autonomy, capacity and the limits of liberalism*. Cambridge: Cambridge University Press.

European Union. (2000) 'Charter of fundamental rights of the European Union', *Official Journal of the European Communities*, C 364/1.

Flaskerud, J.H. (2009) 'The "human right" to mental health care', *Issues in Mental Health Nursing*, 30(12), pp. 796–797. https://doi.org/10.3109/01612840903019740

Freeman, M. (2002) *Human rights*. Cambridge and Malden MA: Polity Press in Association with Blackwell Publishing Ltd.

Freeman, M.C., Kolappa, K., de Almeida, J.M.C., Kleinman, A., Makhashvili, N., Phakathi, S., Saraceno, B. and Thornicroft, G. (2015) 'Reversing hard won victories in the name of human rights: A critique of the general comment on article 12 of the UN convention on the rights of persons with disabilities', *Lancet Psychiatry*, 2(9), pp. 844–850. https://doi.org/10.1016/S2215-0366(15)00218-7

Gautham, M.S., Gururaj, G., Varghese, M., Benegal, V., Rao, G.N., Kokane, A., Chavan, B.S., Dalal, P.K., Ram, D., Pathak, K., Lenin Singh, R.K., Singh, L.K., Sharma, P., Saha, P.K., Ramasubramanian, C., Mehta, R.Y., Shibukumar, T.M. on behalf of the NMHS Collaborators Group. (2020) 'The national mental health survey of India (2016): prevalence, socio-demographic correlates and treatment gap of mental morbidity', *International Journal of Social Psychiatry*, 66(4), pp. 361–372. https://doi.org/10.1177/0020764020907941

Gergel, T., Das, P., Owen, G., Stephenson, L., Rifkin, L., Hindley, G., Dawson, J. and Ruck Keene, A. (2021) 'Reasons for endorsing or rejecting self-binding directives in bipolar disorder: A qualitative study of survey responses from UK service users', *Lancet Psychiatry*, 8(7), pp. 599–609. https://doi.org/10.1016/S2215-0366(21)00115-2 (licence: https://creativecommons.org/licenses/by/4.0/)

Glover-Thomas, N. and Chima, S.C. (2015) 'A legal "right" to mental health care? Impediments to a global vision of mental health care access', *Nigerian Journal of Clinical Practice*, 18, pp. S8–S14. https://doi.org/10.4103/1119-3077.170822

Green, S.A. (2000) 'An ethical argument for a right to mental health care', *General Hospital Psychiatry*, 22(1), pp. 17–26. https://doi.org/10.1016/s0163-8343(99)00047-x

Gruskin, S., Mills, E.J. and Tarantola, D. (2013) 'History, principles and practice of health and human rights', in Grodin, M.A., Tarantola, D., Annas, G.J. and Gruskin, S. (eds.) *Health and human rights in a changing world*. New York and London: Routledge (Taylor & Francis Group), pp. 32–42.

Health Service Executive, Mental Health Division. (2017) *National clinical programme for the assessment and management of patients presenting to the emergency department following self-harm: Review of the operation of the programme 2017*. Dublin: Health Service Executive, Mental Health Division.

Independent Review of the Mental Health Act 1983. (2018) *Modernising the Mental Health Act: Increasing choice, reducing compulsion: Final report of the Independent Review of the Mental Health Act 1983*. London: GOV.UK.

Kelly, B.D. (2005) 'Structural violence and schizophrenia', *Social Science and Medicine*, 61(3), pp. 721–730. https://doi.org/10.1016/j.socscimed.2004.12.020

Kelly, B.D. (2013) 'Is there a human right to mental health?', *Psychiatry Professional*, 2(1), pp. 10–14.

Kelly, B.D. (2016) *Dignity, mental health and human rights: Coercion and the law*. Abingdon, Oxon: Routledge.

Kelly, B.D. (2022) *In search of madness: A psychiatrist's travels through the history of mental illness*. Dublin: Gill Books.

Kelly, B.D., Duffy, R.M. and Gulati, G. (2020) 'Is there a human legal right to mental health?', *Studies in Arts and Humanities*, 6(1), pp. 5–13.

Kong, C. (2017) *Mental capacity in relationship: Decision-making, dialogue, and autonomy*. Cambridge: Cambridge University Press.

Lamb, H.R. (1990) 'Involuntary treatment for the homeless mentally ill', *Notre Dame Journal of Law, Ethics and Public Policy*, 4(2), pp. 269–280.

Lamb, H.R. (2000) 'Deinstitutionalization and public policy', in Menninger, R.W. and Nemiah, J.C. (eds.) *American psychiatry after world war II: 1944–1994*. Washington, DC and London: American Psychiatric Press, Inc., pp. 259–276.

Leucht, S., Hierl, S., Kissling, W., Dold, M. and Davis, J.M. (2012) 'Putting the efficacy of psychiatric and general medicine medication into perspective: review of meta-analyses', *British Journal of Psychiatry*, 200(2), pp. 97–106. https://doi.org/10.1192/bjp.bp.111.096594

McHale, J. and Fox, M. (2007). *Health care law: Text and materials*. 2nd edn. London: Sweet & Maxwell Limited.

O'Callaghan, A.K., Plunkett, R. and Kelly, B.D. (2021) 'The association between perceived coercion on admission and formal coercive practices in an inpatient psychiatric setting', *International Journal of Law and Psychiatry*, 75, p. 101680. https://doi.org/10.1016/j.ijlp.2021.101680

Osiatyński, W. (2009) *Human rights and their limits*. Cambridge: Cambridge University Press.

Petrila, J. (2010) 'Rights-based legalism and the limits of mental health law: The United States of America's experience', in McSherry, B. and Weller, P. (eds.) *Rethinking rights-based mental health laws*. Oxford and Portland, OR: Hart Publishing, pp. 357–378.

Snow, C.P. (1959) *The two cultures and the scientific revolution*. New York: Cambridge University Press.

Taipale, H., Tanskanen, A., Mehtälä, J., Vattulainen, P., Correll, C.U. and Tiihonen, J. (2020) '20-year follow-up study of physical morbidity and mortality in relationship to antipsychotic treatment in a nationwide cohort of 62,250 patients with schizophrenia (FIN20)', *World Psychiatry*, 19(1), pp. 61–68. https://doi.org/10.1002/wps.20699

Tobin, J. (2012) *The right to health in international law*. Oxford: Oxford University Press.

Torrey, E.F. (2014) *American psychosis: How the federal government destroyed the mental illness treatment system*. Oxford: Oxford University Press.

United Nations. (1948) *Universal declaration of human rights*. Paris: United Nations.

United Nations. (1966a) *International covenant on civil and political rights*. New York: United Nations.

United Nations. (1966b) *International covenant on economic, social and cultural rights*. New York: United Nations.

United Nations. (1991) *Principles for the protection of persons with mental illness and the improvement of mental health care*. Geneva: Office of the United Nations High Commissioner for Human Rights.

United Nations. (2006) *Convention on the rights of persons with disabilities*. New York: United Nations.

United Nations Committee on Economic, Social and Cultural Rights (CESCR). (2000) *CESCR general comment no. 14: The right to the highest attainable standard of health (art. 12)*. Geneva and New York: Office of the United Nations High Commissioner for Human Rights.

United Nations Committee on the Rights of Persons with Disabilities. (2014) *General comment no. 1. Article 12: Equal recognition before the law*. New York: United Nations.

United Nations Human Rights Committee. (2014) *General comment no. 35 (article 9)*. New York: United Nations.

United Nations Subcommittee on Prevention of Torture and Other Cruel, Inhuman or Degrading Treatment or Punishment. (2016) *Approach of the subcommittee on prevention of torture and other cruel, inhuman or degrading treatment or punishment regarding the rights of persons institutionalized and treated medically without informed consent*. New York: United Nations.

Wolff, J. (2012) *The human right to health*. New York and London: W.W. Norton and Company.

World Health Organization (2020) *Basic documents: Forty-ninth edition (including amendments adopted up to 31 May 2019)*. Geneva: World Health Organization.

World Health Organization. (2022) *World mental health report: Transforming mental health for all*. Geneva: World Health Organization.

World Health Organization/Office of the United Nations High Commissioner for Human Rights. (2022) *Guidance on mental health, human rights, and legislation (draft)*. Geneva: World Health Organization/Office of the United Nations High Commissioner for Human Rights.

22
MENTAL HEALTH, DISCRIMINATION AND EMPLOYMENT LAW

Mark Bell

Introduction

Research from across a range of jurisdictions has found that persons who experience mental health problems encounter significant barriers to participation in the labour market. Those who disclose mental health problems face the risk of discrimination in the recruitment process. Where mental health problems arise during employment, then discriminatory attitudes and behaviour can be encountered from others, such as managers and co-workers. Discrimination can also take the form of a failure to provide reasonable accommodation in the organisation of work, where adjustments would allow the person to continue in employment. The anticipation of discrimination means that some people living with mental health problems reach the conclusion that it will not be possible to find and retain employment. The extent of the barriers faced by people with mental health problems is reflected in international data showing that, amongst workers with disabilities, the groups with the lowest rates of employment are "individuals with mental health difficulties or intellectual impairments" (WHO, 2011, p. 237).

This chapter will explore the role of employment law in combating discrimination related to mental health, mainly through a focus on laws that prohibit disability discrimination. Given that this chapter is not devoted to a specific jurisdiction, it will provide examples from a range of sources. The 2006 United Nations (UN) Convention on the Rights of Persons with Disabilities (CRPD) is an indispensable point of reference given its normative status in disability rights. Within Europe, Directive 2000/78 (hereafter the 'Employment Equality Directive') has been particularly influential in shaping the content of national laws on disability discrimination in the European Union (EU) and beyond.

The first section commences with a short review of data on the labour market position and experience of people with mental health problems. The second section considers how such discrimination has been addressed by disability discrimination laws. It focuses on the extent to which mental health problems fall within the definition of 'disability' adopted by such laws. The next section examines the prohibition of discrimination, including the duty on employers to provide reasonable accommodation for persons with disabilities. The final section considers how employment law can, through a range of instruments, promote inclusive workplaces.

Throughout the chapter, the term 'mental health problems' will be used to refer to the variety of psychological conditions that can affect workers' health. This includes conditions such as depression, anxiety, schizophrenia and personality disorders. A range of other terms are found in the literature and, when citing research findings, then the terminology used in the original source will be adopted. This chapter will use the term 'psychosocial' disabilities when referring to the disabilities that can arise from such conditions.

Setting the scene: Mental health and the labour market

A consistent body of international data reveals that persons with mental health problems are in a disadvantageous position in the labour market compared to others. Over the past decade, the Organisation for Economic Co-operation and Development (OECD) has been publishing data on the comparative position in industrialised economies. Recently, it reported that "on average, the employment rate for persons with a mental health condition was 20% less than for those without. ... For those with more severe mental health issues ... the gap is even larger, averaging almost 38%" (OECD, 2021a, p. 24). Even so, 44.8% of those with severe mental distress and 60.1% of those with moderate mental distress were in employment (OECD, 2021a, p. 25), confirming the importance of addressing how such people are treated in working life. Those with mental health conditions had lower levels of income than other workers: on average, the level of pay was 83% of that received by workers without mental health conditions (OECD, 2021a, p. 28). Lower levels of pay may be connected to the higher prevalence of part-time working for people with mental health conditions: 19.5% compared to 13.6% for those without mental health conditions (OECD, 2021a, p. 30). Across the OECD, women were over-represented in those reporting mental health conditions. The data did not, however, indicate that, amongst those with mental health conditions, women had lower employment outcomes than men (OECD, 2021a, pp. 32–33). For those in employment, a prominent issue is absence due to ill-health. The OECD (2021a, p. 36) found that 47.6% of those with mental health conditions had been absent from work during the past year, compared to 30.4% of those without such conditions. Moreover, amongst workers experiencing sickness absence, the duration of such absences was longer on average for those with mental health conditions (OECD, 2021a, p. 36).

The picture painted in the comparative data assembled by the OECD echoes that found in other studies. Levels of participation in employment are lower than those of the general population and, in some states, data indicates that those with mental health problems have lower employment rates than those with other types of disability (e.g. the UK: Longhi, 2017, pp. 16–17; Ireland: CSO, 2016). In the EU, data on those with chronic depression showed an employment rate of 50%, compared to 77% for those not experiencing this condition (OECD/EU, 2018, p. 31). Data in the UK found that median pay for men with a mental impairment was lower than that for men with a physical impairment, but that there was no such gap in respect of women (Longhi, 2017, pp. 19–20). For both men and women, there were higher rates of being paid less than the 'living wage' amongst those with a mental impairment compared to those with a physical impairment (Longhi, 2017, pp. 23–24). Significant levels of sickness absence are frequently reported for those with mental health problems (Henderson and Madan, 2014, p. 158; Venema et al., 2009, p. 66).

Most of the existing data was gathered prior to the Covid pandemic. The OECD has reported evidence that the prevalence of symptoms of anxiety and depression has increased sharply and that this is a common trend across diverse countries (OECD, 2021b, p. 4). Evidently, there were heightened pressures for those working in frontline jobs, especially for many of those working in healthcare and other occupations that entail providing care. For many other workers, the pandemic was associated with a rapid increase in working from home. Research that pre-dates the pandemic already found that remote work is associated with a higher rate of work intensity and a greater likelihood to perform work during free time, compared to those who work at the employer's premises (Eurofound, 2020a, p. 24). Working from home during the pandemic was, though, different in context to the situation of those who were already doing that in earlier periods of time. EU research indicates that parents, and especially mothers, were caught between the demands of work and family life in the pandemic: 29% of women with children under the age of 11 reported that it was hard to concentrate on their job because of family, compared to 11% of men in the same situation; while 38% of such women worried about work when they were not working, compared to 29% of men (Eurofound, 2020b, 22).

In seeking to explain why persons with mental health problems fare less well in the labour market than others, much of the academic literature draws attention to the role played by stigma (Mellifont, 2021, p. 62). Thornicroft (2006, p. 181) criticised this insofar as it led to an emphasis on social attitudes and self-perception rather than an analysis of discrimination. He argued that there was a close relationship between stigma and discrimination. To this end, he distinguished between 'enacted' and 'felt' stigma (2006, p. 156). Enacted stigma entailed "episodes or events of discrimination against people who are considered unacceptable", whereas felt stigma included "the experience of shame of having a condition, and the fear of encountering enacted stigma" (2006, p. 156). Authors also use the terms 'experienced' and 'anticipated' discrimination (Ebuenyi et al., 2019; Yoshimura et al., 2018). An abundance of research indicates that people with mental health problems frequently experience and anticipate discrimination in employment, and that this is a global phenomenon. A study of people with a diagnosis of schizophrenia across 27 countries found that 29% linked their diagnosis to difficulties in finding or keeping a job; 69% anticipated discrimination in finding or keeping employment (Thornicroft et al., 2009, pp. 410–412). In the UK, a large study of mental health service-users found that 16.2% reported experiencing discrimination when seeking work and 15.3% reported discrimination in keeping work (Yoshimura et al., 2018, p. 1102); 53.7% anticipated discrimination in employment and 45% refrained from applying for work as a result (Yoshimura et al., 2018, p. 1102). This tallied with earlier research that found that 46% of mental health service-users reported not looking for work due to anticipated discrimination (Thornicroft et al., 2014, p. 180). The higher rates of anticipated discrimination (compared to experienced discrimination) are also reflected in a major study of persons with disabilities in Australia. It found that, relative to other types of disability, those with psychosocial or physical disabilities were the most likely to report experiencing discrimination and taking steps to avoid it occurring (Temple et al., 2018, p. 5). Ebuenyi et al. (2019) point out that many of the existing studies are in high-income countries, but their research in Kenya also revealed elevated rates of discrimination amongst persons with mental illness: 56.3% experienced discrimination in finding or keeping a job, while 59.2% refrained from applying for work due to anticipated discrimination (Ebuenyi et al., 2019, p. 3).

The relationship between experienced and anticipated discrimination is complex (Thornicroft, 2006, p. 152). In some cases, it is the experience of discrimination in the past that informs the person's anticipation of discrimination in the future. Yet there is also evidence of significant rates of anticipated discrimination amongst those who have no prior experience of workplace discrimination (Yoshimura *et al.*, 2018, p. 1106). One of the causes of anticipated discrimination is the persistence of prejudices and stereotypes about mental health in wider society. Public opinion surveys in a range of EU Member States have revealed that there are many people who have a negative outlook on working with someone who has mental health problems (Bell and Waddington, 2016, pp. 73–76). Unsurprisingly, one consequence of stigma is that individuals sometimes conceal mental health problems to avoid the risk of discrimination (Mellifont, 2021, p. 64; Yoshimura *et al.*, 2018, p. 1100). This is also reflected in evidence of 'presenteeism', which concerns situations where workers continue in employment even though they are experiencing ill-health, often due to concerns about the consequences of disclosing a need for sick leave for mental health reasons (De Lorenzo, 2013, p. 224).

Notwithstanding the considerable evidence of difficulties affecting people with mental health problems in the labour market, there is a consensus in the academic literature that, overall, the benefits of being in employment outweigh disadvantages. Having a job supports the person's "participation, integration and economic well-being." (Axiotidou and Papakonstantinou, 2021, p. 176; Scheid, 2005, p. 672). At the same time, this is contingent upon the nature of the working environment. Poor quality work and/or a lack of supportive management can cause or exacerbate mental health problems (OECD, 2012, p. 203).

Mental health and disability discrimination law

Older legislation on disability and employment tended to adopt a 'charity' or 'welfare' approach characterised by setting quotas or reserving certain positions for people with disabilities (Heyer, 2015, p. 32). Such laws assumed that people with disabilities were limited in their capacity to work or to obtain jobs in the open (i.e. competitive) labour market due to impairment. A turning point in the model of disability discrimination laws occurred with the adoption of the Americans with Disabilities Act (ADA) of 1990. Its premise was that most people with disabilities were able to participate in employment, but that they were obstructed from doing so by discrimination. This arose from "stigma and stereotypes" (Heyer, 2015, p. 32), but it also took the form of a failure to provide reasonable accommodation.

The rights-based model found in the ADA proved influential and other jurisdictions began to introduce similar instruments. In Europe, a notable example was the UK's Disability Discrimination Act (DDA) 1995. An anti-discrimination approach to disability rights was endorsed by the EU with the adoption of the Employment Equality Directive of 2000. This had the effect of requiring all Member States to enact domestic legislation prohibiting discrimination on grounds of disability in employment and vocational training, including a duty to provide reasonable accommodation. Internationally, the CRPD subsequently incorporated the prohibition of discrimination, but it did so within a broader "human rights model" that accompanied the right to non-discrimination with civil, political, economic, social and cultural rights (Degener, 2016, p. 36).

The previous section illustrated that people with mental health problems frequently report experiencing discrimination when searching for a job or within the employment relationship. Disability discrimination laws hold considerable potential to tackle such problems. Nevertheless, experience in a range of jurisdictions has shown that people with mental health problems have, at times, struggled to enforce the protection that these laws confer. The first issue to arise is the meaning of disability in such laws. Mental health problems vary in their severity and their duration. In particular, stress is a phenomenon experienced by many workers and it is a common cause of sickness absence. Yet not all instances of stress might be regarded as constituting a psychosocial disability. Establishing that the worker has a psychosocial disability (for the purposes of the law) can also be hindered by the effects of stigma. As mentioned above, some people with mental health problems seek to avoid discrimination by concealing their mental health status (Yoshimura et al., 2018, p. 1104). In situations where a worker has concealed mental health problems, then it may be harder for her to establish that she has a disability and that the employer was aware of this. Lockwood et al. (2014, p. 176) found that tribunals and courts tended to view a failure to disclose a medical condition in good time as a "lack of cooperation" on the part of the employee. As discussed in the next section, this is particularly important for triggering the duty to provide reasonable accommodation.

Disability discrimination legislation varies considerably in its approach to the meaning of disability. If there is an express definition, then it is relatively common that this accepts the possibility that disability may arise from a mental health problem (albeit using a variety of terms to indicate this) (Bell and Waddington, 2016, p. 51). Depending upon the jurisdiction, individuals may experience difficulty in establishing that their condition satisfies the criteria for disability found in the law. Early experience in the USA and the UK was that many claims of disability discrimination failed on this point; this problem affected all types of disability, including psychosocial disabilities (James, 2004, p. 521; Emens, 2006, p. 450). The ADA was subsequently amended in an effort to reduce the obstacles to satisfying the definition of disability (Kaminer, 2016, p. 224) and there were also modifications made to the UK's DDA and Equality Act (Fraser Butlin, 2011). The problems that litigants in some jurisdictions had faced with the definition of disability informed the adoption of a different approach in the CRPD (Broderick and Ferri, 2019, p. 66). Article 1 states:

> Persons with disabilities include those who have long-term physical, mental, intellectual or sensory impairments which in interaction with various barriers may hinder their full and effective participation in society on an equal basis with others.

This is a non-exhaustive definition of persons with disabilities. It identifies disability as arising from the interaction between impairment and barriers; disability is not reduced to an examination of an individual's condition. Take, for example, a person who returns to work following a period of sickness absence for depression, but who then finds that she is subject to negative treatment by her colleagues. Disability is caused by the combination of impairment (depression) and barriers (stigmatising behaviour). Such an approach tends to diminish the focus on individual impairment, albeit that this is not completely removed from the equation. In its General Comment on Equality and Discrimination, the UN Committee on the Rights of Persons with Disabilities (CmRPD) emphasised the need for anti-discrimination legislation to be inclusive:

> Such laws can only be effective if they are based on a definition of disability that includes those who have long-term physical, including psychosocial, intellectual or sensory impairments, and should include past, present, future and presumed disabilities, as well as persons associated with persons with disabilities. Persons victimized by

disability-based discrimination seeking legal redress should not be burdened by proving that they are "disabled enough" in order to benefit from the protection of the law.
(CmRPD, 2018, para. 73)

This quotation also indicates that the CmRPD interprets the reference in the CRPD to 'mental' impairments as including psychosocial disabilities. Although the emphasis in the CRPD is on breadth and inclusiveness, it is notable that it refers to "long-term" impairments. Kelly (2015, p. 95) points out that temporary mental illnesses are thus at risk of falling outside the CRPD. That said, the CmRPD has confirmed that temporary conditions may be disabilities:

the Committee considers that the difference between illness and disability is a difference of degree and not a difference of kind. A health impairment which initially is conceived of as illness can develop into an impairment in the context of disability as a consequence of its duration or its chronicity.
('SC v Brazil' (2014) para. 6.3)

The CRPD definition of disability has proven influential in shaping the approach of the EU Court of Justice (CJEU). In 'HK Danmark' (2013, paras 38–39), it held that:

the concept of 'disability' must be understood as referring to a limitation which results in particular from physical, mental or psychological impairments which in interaction with various barriers may hinder the full and effective participation of the person concerned in professional life on an equal basis with other workers.

In addition, it follows from the second paragraph of Article 1 of the UN Convention that the physical, mental or psychological impairments must be 'long-term'.

Although this case concerned complainants with a physical disability, the Court referred explicitly to 'psychological impairment' in its definition of disability. In 'Milkova' (2017), the complainant had bipolar disorder. The Court accepted that "the mental illness from which Ms Milkova suffers does constitute a 'disability' within the meaning of Directive 2000/78" (para. 37).

Finally, it is relevant to mention Article 14 of the European Convention on Human Rights (ECHR). This provides that:

The enjoyment of the rights and freedoms set forth in this Convention shall be secured without discrimination on any ground such as sex, race, colour, language, religion, political or other opinion, national or social origin, association with a national minority, property, birth or other status.

The list of protected characteristics is non-exhaustive and the European Court of Human Rights (ECtHR) has interpreted Article 14 as including disability and health status ('Kiyutin v Russia' (2011) para. 63). In 'Cînta v Romania' ((2020) para. 70), the Court confirmed that "mental health" is covered by the reference in Article 14 to "other status". Article 14 is not a 'free-standing' right to non-discrimination in any sphere of life, but the Court has accepted that discrimination in employment matters falls within the scope of the Convention ('IB v Greece' (2013) para. 70). Consequently, an individual who was not protected under domestic law from workplace discrimination because of her mental health could potentially have recourse to Article 14 as an alternative source of legal protection (Broderick and Ferri, 2019, pp. 440–446).

The prohibition of discrimination

The previous section has established that disability discrimination legislation will frequently offer protection from employment discrimination to persons with psychosocial disabilities. This section focuses on the meaning of the prohibition of discrimination with a particular emphasis on the duty to provide reasonable accommodation. Article 2 CRPD states:

> "Discrimination on the basis of disability" means any distinction, exclusion or restriction on the basis of disability which has the purpose or effect of impairing or nullifying the recognition, enjoyment or exercise, on an equal basis with others, of all human rights and fundamental freedoms in the political, economic, social, cultural, civil or any other field. It includes all forms of discrimination, including denial of reasonable accommodation.

Article 27 CRPD on work and employment specifies that discrimination should be prohibited in "all matters concerning all forms of employment", which includes "protection from harassment". In its General Comment on Equality and Discrimination, the CmRPD (2018, para. 18) stated that there are four main forms of discrimination that should be prohibited in law: direct discrimination; indirect discrimination; harassment; and denial of reasonable accommodation. In addition, the CmRPD requires states to recognise that these forms of prohibited discrimination can occur on a combination of disability and one or more other grounds, e.g. discrimination against women with disabilities may be based on the combination of disability and sex (2018, para. 19). Therefore, states should ensure that there are measures to address multiple and intersectional forms of discrimination. This is important given that, in some states, there may be stereotypes or institutional practices that discriminate against persons with mental health problems from minority ethnic communities.

Although the four forms of discrimination identified by the CmRPD are commonly found in many national laws on employment discrimination, their definition and interpretation in case-law varies according to the jurisdiction. The discussion below will mainly focus on the approach found in the EU Employment Equality Directive as an illustration of how these concepts can be defined.

Direct discrimination

Article 2(2)(a) of the Directive provides that direct discrimination occurs where one person is treated less favourably than another is, has been or would be treated in a comparable situation, on grounds of disability. An example of such discrimination would be a situation where a job offer is withdrawn after the employer learns that the applicant has had time off in the past for depression (e.g. 'J v DLA Piper UK LLP' (2010)). In Ireland, there was a finding of direct discrimination in a case where the claimant had been off work for around six months due to an anxiety-related illness ('Mr. O v A Named Company' (2003)). His request to resume work on a phased basis by increasing his duties over several weeks was refused, but there was evidence that a colleague with a different medical condition had been granted such flexibility in the past. This illustrated that less favourable treatment can entail a comparison between the treatment of people with different disabilities, as well as a comparison with those who do not have a disability.

Indirect discrimination

Indirect discrimination (also referred to as disparate impact in the USA) broadly concerns situations where measures are facially neutral, but they have unequal effects in practice on persons with particular characteristics. For example, the law might provide that workers can be dismissed if they accumulate more than 120 days of paid sick leave in a 12-month period ('HK Danmark' (2013)). This rule is the same for all workers, but it has a greater impact on any group of workers who are more likely to experience higher levels of sickness absence, such as workers with psychosocial disabilities. Article 2(2)(b) of the Employment Equality Directive provides the following definition:

> indirect discrimination shall be taken to occur where an apparently neutral provision, criterion or practice would put persons having a ... particular disability ... at a particular disadvantage compared with other persons unless:
>
> (i) that provision, criterion or practice is objectively justified by a legitimate aim and the means of achieving that aim are appropriate and necessary, or
> (ii) as regards persons with a particular disability, the employer ... is obliged, under national legislation, to take appropriate measures in line with the principles contained in Article 5 [reasonable accommodation] in order to eliminate disadvantages entailed by such provision, criterion or practice.

To continue the example above, laws and/or workplace policies on sickness absence are measures that may be indirectly discriminatory on grounds of disability, depending on the circumstances. This has been at the centre of several cases of indirect disability discrimination before the CJEU. In 'DW v Nobel Plastiques Ibérica SA' (2019), the complainant had multiple periods of sick leave for a physical impairment, as well as seven months off work due to an anxiety disorder. She was one of 10 workers who were selected for dismissal for "economic, technical, production and organisational reasons". The selection was based on four criteria, one of which was rate of absenteeism. Amongst the issues in the case was whether the use of this criterion was indirectly discriminatory on grounds of disability. The Court held that it did put disabled workers at a particular disadvantage because

> a disabled worker is, in principle, more exposed to the risk of having a high rate of absenteeism as compared to a worker without a disability, since he is exposed to the additional risk of being absent owing to an illness connected with his disability.
>
> *(para. 59)*

Indirect discrimination will not arise, however, if the provision, criterion or practice can be objectively justified. In earlier case-law, the Court had accepted that "combating absenteeism at work" is a legitimate aim, but that measures taken in pursuit of this aim need to take into account their particular impact upon workers with disabilities ('Ruiz Conejero' (2018) para. 44). In DW's case, the Court drew attention to sub-paragraph (ii) in the Directive's definition of indirect discrimination, which makes a link to the employer's duty to provide reasonable accommodation. The Court held that if DW's employer had already taken appropriate measures to provide her with reasonable accommodation, then the criteria used when selecting workers for dismissal did not constitute indirect discrimination (para. 73). Such cases indicate that the Court is not opposed to the principle that sickness absence will, eventually, result in detriment or dismissal for workers. It has, though, sought to ensure that such measures are implemented with due regard to the particular situation of workers with disabilities.

Harassment

The third form of discrimination recognised in the Employment Equality Directive is harassment. This occurs "when unwanted conduct related to any of the grounds … takes place with the purpose or effect of violating the dignity of a person and of creating an intimidating, hostile, degrading, humiliating or offensive environment" (Article 2(3)). The prohibition on harassment would obviously include situations where derogatory language is used about a person because of psychosocial disability, or related conduct such as being mocked or silenced in the workplace. Empirical research has provided evidence of such conduct in some workplaces (Mac Gabhann *et al.*, 2010, p. 51; Thornicroft, 2006, p. 57). In the USA, von Schrader's analysis of charges lodged under the ADA involving psychiatric disabilities found that 22.1% concerned harassment (2017, p. 3).

Reasonable accommodation

The fourth form of discrimination recognised in the CRPD is denial of reasonable accommodation. While the Employment Equality Directive includes a duty to provide reasonable accommodation, it does not expressly state that a breach of this duty is to be regarded as an act of discrimination. Nevertheless, in 'DW v Nobel Plastiques Ibérica' (2019), the CJEU stated that "it must be borne in mind that", according to the CRPD, discrimination on grounds of disability includes denial of reasonable accommodation (para. 72). In a similar vein, the ECtHR has held that the prohibition of discrimination in Article 14 ECHR must be interpreted in the light of the CRPD and, specifically, the CRPD position that denial of reasonable accommodation is a form of discrimination ('GL v Italy' (2020) para. 62). Article 2 CRPD states:

> "Reasonable accommodation" means necessary and appropriate modification and adjustments not imposing a disproportionate or undue burden, where needed in a particular case, to ensure to persons with disabilities the enjoyment or exercise on an equal basis with others of all human rights and fundamental freedoms.

Article 5 of the Employment Equality Directive is broadly similar, but focused on the context of employment:

> employers shall take appropriate measures, where needed in a particular case, to enable a person with a disability to have access to, participate in, or advance in employment, or to undergo training, unless such measures would impose a disproportionate burden on the employer.

Reasonable accommodation holds considerable potential to dismantle or mitigate the barriers that hinder people with psychosocial disabilities from participating in employment.

Ultimately, it entails the search for practical and effective measures, which require flexibility with regard to things like location, hours and duties. A review of empirical research on "workplace accommodations for people with mental illness" found that the most common adjustments provided were:

- assistance from an employment support worker (either during recruitment or employment);
- flexible working time (including reduced hours);
- modified training and supervision;
- modified job duties;
- physical accommodations to the workplace (e.g. quieter work space).

(McDowell and Fossey, 2015, p. 199)

Where workers are experiencing difficulties related to the working environment, then working from home is a potential adjustment. One effect of the pandemic is that it has normalised working from home in many job roles, which makes it likely that this type of accommodation will be more widely available in the future.

Although the practical contribution that reasonable accommodation can make is evident, the interpretation of the legal duty has, at times, proven contentious. In the UK, Lockwood *et al.* (2014, p. 178) found that the application of the duty of reasonable accommodation was a frequent ground for appeal in discrimination cases that concerned mental health. The first issue that arises is whether the employer knew, or ought to have known, of the worker's need for accommodation. The CmRPD describes accommodation as an "individualized reactive duty" that is "often but not necessarily requested by the person" (2018, para. 24). In the context of psychosocial disability, stigma means that many persons choose not to disclose mental health problems (McDowell and Fossey, 2015, p. 200). This becomes a problem in litigation on reasonable accommodation because there are examples from a range of jurisdictions of disputes over whether the employer was sufficiently aware of the worker's psychosocial disability and/or her need for accommodation (Bell and Waddington, 2016, p. 81). As indicated above by the CmRPD, a request from an individual is not the only way to trigger the duty to provide accommodation. Employers should be alert to information that indicates a potential need for accommodation. Where a worker is on extended sick leave, then it would be reasonable for the employer to explore with the worker accommodations that might enable their return to work.

There are two main components to the duty to provide reasonable accommodation: (i) identifying an adjustment or modification; (ii) determining whether this creates a disproportionate burden for the employer (Broderick and Ferri, 2019, pp. 106–114). The first stage involves the search for any measures that can remove or mitigate the barriers being encountered by the worker. The CmRPD has clarified that this part of the process should not be modified by the term 'reasonable': what matters is whether the adjustment would be relevant, appropriate and effective (2018, para. 25). There is a risk that employers' ideas about what constitutes an accommodation are bounded by the types of adjustment associated with physical disability, such as modifying premises or providing assistive technologies (Lockwood, 2014, p. 179). In respect of psychosocial disabilities, supports of a different nature might be necessary. For example, in 'Croft Vets Ltd v Butcher' (2013), the English Employment Appeals Tribunal accepted that an adjustment could include an employer providing funding for therapy sessions, in respect of an employee off work with depression and anxiety. Given that the employer would provide funding for other types of adjustment, then funding for therapy should not be excluded from the outset. In the context of the USA, Kaminer (2016, p. 242) observed that often people with psychiatric disabilities were seeking to be able to transfer away from a particular co-worker or manager where this relationship was giving rise to stress. Yet courts there had generally been unsympathetic to the idea that an accommodation includes being able to alter with whom you work.

This stage of the accommodation process entails an exploration of what steps can be effective. The procedure that the employer adopts for conducting this inquiry is significant. It is common for employers to engage the assistance of experts, such as occupational health advisors or medical practitioners. While these have an important role to play, the CmRPD holds that there is an obligation "to enter into dialogue with an individual with a disability" (2018, para. 24). One of the hallmarks of the CRPD is its recognition of the need for participation by people with disabilities and a rejection of paternalistic models where their voice is marginalised. The preamble states that "persons with disabilities should have the opportunity to be actively involved in decision-making processes about policies and programmes, including those directly concerning them". In this vein, people with disabilities should be able to convey their own views on what steps would mitigate the barriers that they are encountering at work. A review of the situation in the EU Member States found that national legislation was often silent on what procedures should be followed by an employer when considering a request for accommodation and it was typically unclear whether a failure to consult the employee would constitute a breach of the accommodation duty (Ferri and Lawson, 2016, p. 78).

If, during the first stage, an adjustment or modification has been identified that may mitigate the barrier affecting the person with a psychosocial disability, then the second stage is the consideration of whether this gives rise to a disproportionate burden for the employer. It is valuable to bear in mind that many accommodations are free or entail only a modest financial cost (McDowell and Fossey, 2015, p. 200). In the USA, the Job Accommodation Network (JAN) has been collecting data on this since 2004. Consistent with previous results, its 2020 survey found that 56% of employers reported that the accommodations needed by their employees did not entail any financial cost; 39% said that there was a one-off cost and that the median cost incurred was USD$500 (JAN, 2020). Furthermore, in many jurisdictions, there are public subsidies or tax benefits that can offset some of the employer's costs (Ferri and Lawson, 2016, p. 89). Nevertheless, it is clear that the law permits the need for accommodation to be balanced by consideration of the impact upon the employer. Beyond financial considerations, the CmRPD refers to the need to consider "third-party benefits, negative impacts on other persons and reasonable health and safety requirements" (2018, para. 26). Moreover, the burden of proof to justify denial of accommodation should lie with the employer (2018, para. 26).

Promoting inclusion: The labour market and workplaces

Kanter (2015, p. 882) points out that, in comparison to earlier instruments (such as the ADA), the CRPD moved beyond a narrow focus on anti-discrimination. Although the prohibition of discrimination is a central element of the Convention, it does not assume that this will be sufficient to bring about equality for people with disabilities. Instead, there are duties on the state to take the measures necessary "to ensure and promote the full realization of all human rights and fundamental freedoms for all persons with disabilities" (Article 4(1)).

In respect of work and employment, states must "promote employment opportunities and career advancement for persons with disabilities in the labour market, as well as assistance in finding, obtaining, maintaining and returning to employment" (Article 27(1)(e)). States must "employ persons with disabilities in the public sector" and "promote the employment of persons with disabilities in the private sector through appropriate policies and measures, which may include affirmative action programmes, incentives and other measures" (Article 27(1)(g)-(h)). The nature of these duties is that they require action to ensure that the labour market is inclusive of persons with disabilities. This means that the state cannot adopt a passive stance and simply provide welfare benefits. In 'Gröninger v Germany' (2014), the CmRPD found that the state had failed to comply with its obligations in Article 27 where it appeared that the main forms of labour market support available were unemployment benefits and counselling.

This section explores further the steps that can be taken to promote the inclusion of persons with mental health problems within the labour market, as well as measures at the level of specific companies/organisations that foster an inclusive and safe working environment.

Promoting inclusion in the labour market

Given the duties on states described above, it is helpful that Article 5(4) CRPD provides that "specific measures which are necessary to accelerate or achieve de facto equality of persons with disabilities shall not be considered discrimination under the terms of the present Convention". The CmRPD (2018, para. 28) has interpreted this as providing scope for "outreach and support programmes, allocation and/or reallocation of resources, targeted recruitment, hiring and promotion, quota systems, advancement and empowerment measures". One approach to "specific measures" is *supported employment* (ILO, 2015, p. 74). This is based upon providing tailored support to facilitate individuals to find and retain employment. Its exact form varies significantly between countries, but it is often described as a sequential process with the following main elements: (i) assessment of the individual's competencies and preferences; (ii) finding employers with potential jobs; (iii) analysis of the job functions; (iv) matching individuals to available jobs; (v) job coaching (Hoekstra *et al.*, 2004, p. 41). The job coaching stage entails "intensive, individualized coaching" in order to assist the person to learn how to perform the job, both at the outset and often with ongoing support (Hoekstra *et al.*, 2004, p. 42). Comparative research within Europe indicates that supported employment is used in some countries to assist those with severe mental health problems and/or those who have spent time as in-patients in psychiatric medical facilities (European Commission, 2012). Hoekstra *et al.* (2004) found that people with psychiatric disabilities tended to need more support at the initial stage of assessing competencies because of low self-esteem and a lack of confidence. Such schemes go beyond reasonable accommodation insofar as they may entail negotiation between the employer and the agency facilitating supported employment to design a role with duties that match the competencies of the individual. Moreover, the job is arranged for the individual rather than being acquired through an open competition.

Supported employment can be distinguished from *sheltered employment*. The former aims to ensure inclusion in the open labour market, whereas the latter is fundamentally based on a model of segregation, where persons with disabilities are not working alongside those without disabilities. Sheltered employment continues to be common in many states and, depending on the national context, it may be a form of employment for persons with severe psychosocial disabilities (ILO, 2015, p. 73). Yet it is at odds with the commitment in Article 27(1) CRPD to the right of persons with disabilities to work in "a labour market and work environment that is open, inclusive and accessible to persons with disabilities" (May-Simera, 2018). The question of whether sheltered employment should be permitted was highly contentious during the drafting of the CRPD and, ultimately, it is not specifically mentioned in its text (Broderick and Ferri, 2019, pp. 235–237). The CmRPD (2018, para. 67(a)) has expressed its view that the Convention requires states to "facilitate the transition away from segregated work environments for persons with disabilities and support their engagement in the open labour market".

Fostering an inclusive and safe working environment

The working environment can be designed to promote mental well-being and to support those workers who encounter mental health problems. Unfortunately, it is also true that the organisation of work can be a cause of mental ill-health. In the EU, a 2014 public opinion survey found that "exposure to stress" was identified by respondents as the leading health and safety risk in their workplace (European Commission, 2014, p. 70). When asked about any health problems that were either caused by or made worse by their work, 27% of respondents cited stress, depression or anxiety (European Commission, 2014, p. 72). Scheid observed that organisational culture plays an important role: if "competition, pressure, and control are widely prevalent", then the workplace may not be conducive for those with mental health problems (2005, p. 674). With an eye to such concerns, the International Labour Office (ILO) (2017, p. 6) has identified a role for "primary" mental health interventions that focus on preventing occupational exposure to psychosocial risks through the design of the working environment. This includes issues such as ensuring that workers are protected from bullying and harassment, that workloads are not excessive and that workers are enabled to take sufficient rest. The question of rest is receiving more attention since the pandemic because of the rise in remote working. Being able to work from another location can offer valuable flexibility for workers and, as mentioned earlier, working from home is sometimes provided as an adjustment to assist workers with mental health problems. Yet it also needs to be taken into account that research has linked mobile or home working to higher rates of stress, headaches and sleep disorders (Eurofound, 2020a, p. 35). A key issue here is the risk of an organisational culture of permanent connectivity, i.e. always being available via digital devices. Some states have sought to address such risks through the creation of an enforceable 'right to disconnect' and there are also examples of companies developing workplace policies designed to ensure that workers can switch off (Eurofound, 2021).

The legal backdrop for employers' initiatives to support mental well-being is occupational safety and health (OSH) law. The ILO has stated that "the fostering and promotion of a preventative safety and health culture is a fundamental basis for improving OSH performance in the long term" (ILO, 2010, p. 5). It is clear that OSH law includes the duty to prevent psychosocial risks to the worker. The ILO's Occupational Safety and Health Convention 1981 (no. 155) has been ratified by 74 countries. Article 3(e) provides that "health, in relation to work, indicates not merely the absence of disease or infirmity; it also includes the physical and mental elements affecting health which are directly related to safety and hygiene at work". States are obliged to formulate and implement a national policy on OSH; ILO Recommendation No. 164 specifies that this should address the "prevention of harmful physical or mental stress due to conditions of work" (Para. 3(e)).

In the EU, Council Directive 89/391/EEC established a duty on employers "to ensure the safety and health of workers in every aspect related to the work" (Article 5(1)). This duty includes an obligation to develop "a coherent overall prevention policy which covers technology, organization of work, working conditions, social relationships and the influence of factors related to the working environment" (Article 6(2)(g)). The Directive applies to all types of risks to workers' health, including those of a psychosocial nature. The CJEU has recently drawn attention to the duty on employers to evaluate and prevent "psychosocial risks, such as stress or burnout" ('Radiotelevizija Slovenija' (2021) para 62).

Such duties have been reinforced by a recent decision of the ECtHR. In 'Špadijer v Montenegro' (2021), the applicant was a prison officer who experienced instances of harassment inside and outside of her workplace after she alerted the prison authorities to inappropriate conduct by several colleagues. There was evidence that her treatment caused her to develop significant mental health problems, including post-traumatic stress disorder and an adjustment disorder. Although the domestic courts accepted that the instances had occurred, and were linked to the impact on her mental health, they did not find any breach of national legislation (para. 95). The ECtHR held that:

> Under Article 8 States have a duty to protect the physical and moral integrity of an individual from other persons. To that end they are to maintain and apply in practice an adequate legal framework affording protection against acts of violence by private individuals …, including in the context of harassment at work.
>
> *(para. 87)*

On the facts, it held that the manner in which her case was handled constituted a breach by the state of its positive duty to protect "physical and psychological integrity" (para. 87). While this case relates to the obligations of states, it implies that there must be an effective legal framework that protects persons from bullying and harassment in the workplace. This reinforces the existing duties on employers found in OSH law.

Conclusions

This chapter started by reviewing the existing data on people with mental health problems in the labour market. Internationally, a stark picture exists of significant disadvantage. There is ample evidence that experienced and anticipated discrimination are major factors in explaining this position. The main legal response over the past 30 years has been to enact legislation that prohibits discrimination on grounds of disability. Such laws include psychosocial disabilities and offer valuable protection to many, if not all, persons who experience mental health problems. These laws have had a normative effect on organisational practices, such as human resources policies (Scheid, 2005, p. 687). Aside from the ultimate option of going to court to enforce rights, the existence of such laws strengthens the bargaining position of workers. When organisations consider requests for an adjustment to working arrangements, this is not merely a matter of managerial discretion, but it is underpinned by a legal obligation. Notwithstanding the benefits conferred by the law, there remain reasons to doubt whether the prohibition of discrimination will, by itself, be sufficient to render workplaces inclusive for persons with mental health problems.

There are well-known limitations to the impact of anti-discrimination law where this rests upon enforcement by individuals. By design, such laws are reactive in nature; for the most part, they offer a remedy where discrimination has already occurred. Bagenstos (2009, p. 127) has pointed out that, in the USA, litigation under the ADA "overwhelmingly focuses on the discharge of employees with disabilities rather than the failure to hire them". Analysis of claims brought under the ADA by persons with psychiatric disabilities confirmed this pattern: 58.5% concerned termination of employment (von Schrader, 2017, p. 3). Moreover, there are significant barriers for the individual complainant to overcome. People need to be aware of their legal rights and the avenues for enforcement. If bringing litigation, it is often valuable to possess the financial resources necessary to benefit from professional legal representation. It is not sufficient for an individual to believe that she was treated less favourably for discriminatory reasons; there must be proof to sustain this and the relevant information may lie in the hands of the employer. Pursuing discrimination litigation can be lengthy and arduous, so it often entails emotional costs for complainants.

Such factors are reasons why most individuals who encounter discrimination do not bring complaints; very few proceed as far as initiating litigation. Research in Ireland found that, where persons with a disability had experienced discrimination, 66.5% took no action, 29.5% took verbal or written action (such as raising it with a manager), while 4.8% made an official complaint or initiated legal action (CSO, 2019). Comparative data paints a mixed picture with regard to disability discrimination litigation and persons with psychosocial disabilities. In the USA, a significant and sustained proportion of complaints under the ADA relate to such conditions (Scheid, 2005, p. 671). Von Schrader (2017, pp. 1–2) reported that, between 2005 and 2014, 14.2% of ADA charges included at least one psychiatric disability, which was approximately 50,400 charges; 43% of these concerned depression and 31% anxiety disorders. In contrast, comparative research on EU Member States found few examples of discrimination litigation relating to psychosocial disability (Bell and Waddington, 2016, p. 63). The UK and Ireland were outliers insofar as disability discrimination litigation in these states did often concern persons with psychosocial disabilities. It is, though, difficult to pinpoint the reason for such differences in the pattern of litigation.

One response to the above picture is to focus on reforms that make it easier for individuals to use the law. This is a common trajectory in all branches of anti-discrimination law. An institutional response to the difficulties faced by litigants can be found in the practice of many jurisdictions to create specialised bodies for the promotion of equal treatment (Crowley, 2018). These organisations are often intended to provide support and advice for persons who believe that they have experienced discrimination. Depending on their mandate, such bodies may be able to provide legal support for complainants and/or bring complaints in their own name. In some jurisdictions, specialised bodies have also acquired investigatory powers and/or adjudicatory functions. This may provide a forum that is easier (and cheaper) for complainants to access than the court system.

Certainly, there is much that can be done to seek to maximise the impact of the individual right to non-discrimination. The law is, though, inherently constrained by the need to identify specific instances of discrimination, which often (but not always) implies identifiable victims of such discrimination. The first section of this chapter cited research that found high levels of anticipated discrimination amongst persons with mental health problems. This led such persons to avoid certain situations because of their expectation that they would encounter discrimination, including refraining from seeking employment. This is a good illustration of the limits to the change that can be accomplished through an individual right to non-discrimination. We might hope that, over time, anti-discrimination law reduces the likelihood of experiencing discrimination at work and that this will then encourage more persons with mental health problems to seek employment. It is evident, however, that this is an incremental process and, to date, it has not been a sufficient way of increasing the rate of employment participation for such persons.

For this reason, it is necessary for the law to take other, complementary steps to promote inclusion for people with mental health problems. Indeed, the CRPD requires states to go beyond non-discrimination. This may be through targeted initiatives, such as supported employment schemes, or wider measures to promote change in organisational practice. As regards the latter, OSH law already places duties on employers to prevent psychosocial risks to workers. Yet there are often weak links between the enforcement of anti-discrimination law and OSH law. In most countries, there are dedicated agencies with a mandate to promote workplace safety, but some existing research suggests that these bodies may not recognise discrimination as relevant to their mandate (Smith *et al.*, 2019). In the context of mental health, there is a clear connection between preventing psychosocial risks and ensuring that the working environment supports and accommodates workers with mental health problems. Arguably, there is a need to enhance coordination between these two branches of employment law to forge an integrated approach to promoting inclusive workplaces.

References

Axiotidou, M. and Papakonstantinou, D. (2021) 'The Meaning of Work for People with Severe Mental Illness: A Systematic Review', *Mental Health Review Journal*, 26(2), pp. 170–179.
Bagenstos, S. (2009) *Law and the Contradictions of the Disability Rights Movement*. New Haven: Yale University Press.
Bell, M. and Waddington, L. (2016) *The Employment Equality Directive and Supporting People with Psychosocial Disabilities in the Workplace*. Luxembourg: Publications Office of the European Union.
Broderick, A. and Ferri, D. (2019) *International and European Disability Law and Policy – Text, Cases and Materials*. Cambridge: Cambridge University Press.
Central Statistics Office (CSO) (2016) *Census of Population 2016 – Profile 9 Health, Disability and Carers*. Available at: https://www.cso.ie/en/releasesandpublications/ep/p-cp9hdc/p8hdc/p9chs/ (Accessed: 16 November 2021).
CSO (2019) *Equality and Discrimination*. Available at: https://www.cso.ie/en/releasesandpublications/er/ed/equalityanddiscrimination2019/ (Accessed: 23 November 2021).
'Cînta v Romania' (2020) Application no. 3891/19, (ECtHR).
Council Directive 89/391/EEC of 12 June 1989 on the Introduction of Measures to Encourage Improvements in the Safety and Health of Workers at Work (1989) OJ L183/1.
Council Directive 2000/78/EC of 27 November 2000 Establishing a General Framework for Equal Treatment in Employment and Occupation (2000) OJ L303/16.
CmRPD (2018) *General Comment No. 6 (2018) on Equality and Non-Discrimination*. CRPD/C/GC/6.
'Croft Vets and Others v Butcher' [2013] Eq LR 1170, (EAT).
Crowley, N. (2018) *Equality Bodies Making a Difference*. Luxembourg: Publications Office of the European Union.
De Lorenzo, M. (2013) 'Employee Mental Illness: Managing the Hidden Epidemic', *Employee Responsibilities and Rights Journal*, 25(4), pp. 219–238.
Degener, T. (2016) 'A Human Rights Model of Disability', in: Blanck, P. and Flynn, E. (ed.), *Routledge Handbook of Disability Law and Human Rights*. Abingdon: Routledge, pp. 31–49.
'DW v Nobel Plastiques Ibérica SA' (2019), Case C-397/18, ECLI:EU:C:2019:703.
Ebuenyi, I. *et al.* (2019) 'Experienced and Anticipated Discrimination and Social Functioning in Persons with Mental Disabilities in Kenya: Implications for Employment', *Frontiers in Psychiatry*, 10, Article 181, pp. 1–9.
Emens, E. (2006) 'The Sympathetic Discriminator: Mental Illness, Hedonic Costs, and the ADA', *Georgetown Law Journal*, 94, pp. 399–487.

European Commission (2012) *Supported Employment for People with Disabilities in the EU and EFTA-EEA: Good Practices and Recommendations in Support of a Flexicurity Approach*. Luxembourg: Publications Office of the European Union.

European Commission (2014) *Flash Eurobarometer 398 (Working Conditions)*. Luxembourg: Publications Office of the European Union.

Eurofound (2020a) *Telework and ICT-Based Mobile Work: Flexible Working in the Digital Age*. Luxembourg: Publications Office of the European Union.

Eurofound (2020b) *Living, Working and Covid-19*. Luxembourg: Publications Office of the European Union.

Eurofound (2021) *Right to Disconnect: Exploring Company Practices*. Luxembourg: Publications Office of the European Union.

Ferri, D. and Lawson, A. (2016) *Reasonable Accommodation for Disabled People in Employment. A Legal Analysis of the Situation in EU Member States, Iceland, Liechtenstein, and Norway*. Luxembourg: Publications Office of the European Union.

Fraser Butlin, S. (2011) 'The UN Convention on the Rights of Persons with Disabilities: Does the Equality Act 2010 Measure up to UK International Commitments?', *Industrial Law Journal*, 40, pp. 428–438.

'GL v Italy' (2020) Application no. 59751/15, (ECtHR).

'Gröninger v Germany' (2014) Complaint No. 2/2010, CRPD/C/D/2/2010.

Heyer, K. (2015) *Rights Enabled – The Disability Revolution, from the US, to Germany and Japan, to the United Nations*. Ann Arbor: University of Michigan Press.

Henderson, M. and Madan, I. (2014) 'Mental Health and Work', in: Davies, S. (ed.), *Annual Report of the Chief Medical Officer 2013, Public Mental Health Priorities: Investing in the Evidence*. London: Department of Health, pp. 157–169.

'HK Danmark' (2013) Joined Cases C-335/11 and C-337/11, ECLI:EU:C:2013:222.

Hoekstra, E. *et al.* (2004) 'Supported Employment in the Netherlands for People with an Intellectual Disability, a Psychiatric Disability and a Chronic Disease: A Comparative Study', *Journal of Vocational Rehabilitation*, 21, pp. 39–48.

'IB v Greece' (2013), Application no. 552/10, (ECtHR).

International Labour Office (ILO) (2010) *Plan of Action (2010–2016) to Achieve Widespread Ratification and Effective Implementation of the Occupational Safety and Health Instruments (Convention No. 155, its 2002 Protocol and Convention No. 187)*. Geneva: ILO.

ILO (2015) *Decent Work for Persons with Disabilities: Promoting Rights in the Global Development Agenda*. Geneva: ILO.

ILO (2017) *Mental Health in the Workplace: Key Issues and Good Company Practices*. Geneva: ILO.

'J v DLA Piper UK LLP', [2010] IRLR 936, (EAT).

James, G. (2004) 'An Unquiet Mind in the Workplace: Mental Illness and the Disability Discrimination Act 1995', *Legal Studies*, 24(4), pp. 516–539.

Job Accommodation Network (2020) *Benefits and Costs of Accommodation*. Available at: https://askjan.org/topics/costs.cfm (Accessed: 22 November 2021).

Kaminer, D. (2016) 'Mentally Ill Employees in the Workplace: Does the ADA Amendments Act Provide Adequate Protection?', *Health Matrix: Journal of Law-Medicine*, 26, pp. 205–253.

Kanter, A. (2015) 'The Americans with Disabilities Act at 25 Years: Lessons to Learn from the Convention on the Rights of People with Disabilities', *Drake Law Review*, 63, pp. 819–883.

Kelly, B. (2015) *Dignity, Mental Health and Human Rights: Coercion and the Law*. Abingdon: Ashgate.

'Kiyutin v Russia' (2011), Application no. 2700/10, (ECtHR).

Lockwood, G., Henderson, C., and Thornicroft, G. (2014) 'Mental Health Disability Discrimination: Law, Policy and Practice', *International Journal of Discrimination and the Law*, 24(3), pp. 168–182.

Longhi, S. (2017) *The Disability Pay Gap*. Manchester: Equality and Human Rights Commission.

Mac Gabhann, L. *et al.* (2010) *Hear My Voice: The Experience of Discrimination of People with Mental Health Problems in Ireland*. Dublin: Dublin City University.

May-Simera, C. (2018) 'Reconsidering Sheltered Workshops in Light of the United Nations Convention on the Rights of Persons with Disabilities (2006)', *Laws*, 7(1: 6).

McDowell, C. and Fossey, E. (2015) 'Workplace Accommodations for People with Mental Illness: A Scoping Review', *Journal of Occupational Rehabilitation*, 25(1), pp. 197–206.

Mellifont, D. (2021) 'Facilitators and Inhibitors of Mental Discrimination in the Workplace: A Traditional Review', *Studies in Social Justice*, 15(1), pp. 59–80.

'Milkova' (2017) Case C-406/15, ECLI:EU:C:2017:198.

'Mr. O v A Named Company' (2003) DEC-E2003-052, (Equality Tribunal).

Organisation for Economic Coordination and Development (OECD) (2012) *Sick on the Job? Myths and Realities about Mental Health and Work*. Paris: OECD Publishing.

OECD (2021a) *Fitter Minds, Fitter Jobs: From Awareness to Change in Integrated Mental Health, Skills and Work Policies*. Paris: OECD Publishing.

OECD (2021b) *Tackling the Mental Health Impact of the COVID-19 Crisis: An Integrated, Whole-of-Society Response*. Available at: https://www.oecd.org/coronavirus/policy-responses/tackling-the-mental-health-impact-of-the-covid-19-crisis-an-integrated-whole-of-society-response-0ccafa0b/ (Accessed: 2 December 2021).

OECD/EU (2018) *Health at a Glance: Europe 2018: State of Health in the EU Cycle*. Paris: OECD Publishing.

'Radiotelevizija Slovenija' (2021) Case C-344/19, ECLI:EU:C:2021:182.

'Ruiz Conejero' (2018) Case C-270/16, ECLI: EU:C:2018:17.

'SC v Brazil' (2014) Communication No. 10/2013, CRPD/C/12/D/10/2013.

Scheid, T. (2005) 'Stigma as a Barrier to Employment: Mental Disability and the Americans with Disabilities Act', *International Journal of Law and Psychiatry*, 28(6), pp. 670–690.

Smith, B., Schleiger, M., and Elphick, L. (2019) 'Preventing Sexual Harassment in Work: Exploring the Promise of Workplace Safety Laws', *Australian Journal of Labour Law*, 32, pp. 219–249.

'Špadijer v Montenegro' (2021) Application No. 31549/18, (ECtHR).

Temple, J., Kelaher, M., and Williams, R. (2018) 'Discrimination and Avoidance in Australia: Evidence from a National Cross Sectional Survey', *BMC Public Health*, 18, pp. 1–13.

Thornicroft, G. (2006) *Shunned: Discrimination Against People with Mental Illness*. Oxford: Oxford University Press.

Thornicroft, G. et al. (2009) 'Global Pattern of Experienced and Anticipated Discrimination Against People with Schizophrenia: A Cross-Sectional Survey', *The Lancet*, 373(9661), pp. 408–415.

Thornicroft, G., Evans-Lacko, S., and Henderson, C. (2014) 'Stigma and Discrimination', in: Davies, S. (ed.), *Annual Report of the Chief Medical Officer 2013, Public Mental Health Priorities: Investing in the Evidence*. London: Department of Health, pp. 179–195.

Venema, A., van den Heuvel, S., and Geuskens, G. (2009) *Health and Safety at Work. Results of the Labour Force Survey 2007 Ad hoc Module on Accidents at Work and Work-Related Health Problems*. Hoofddorp: TNO.

von Schrader, S. (2017) *The Patterns and Context of ADA Discrimination Charges Filed by Persons with Psychiatric Disabilities*. Available at: https://www.northeastada.org/docs/NEADA-research-brief-psychiatric-disability.pdf (Accessed: 23 November 2021).

World Health Organisation (WHO) and the World Bank (2011) *World Report on Disability*. Geneva: WHO.

Yoshimura, Y., Bakolis, I., and Henderson, C. (2018) 'Psychiatric Diagnosis and Other Predictors of Experienced and Anticipated Workplace Discrimination and Concealment of Mental Illness among Mental Health Service Users in England', *Social Psychiatry and Psychiatric Epidemiology*, 53(10), pp. 1099–1109.

23
FAMILY IN MENTAL HEALTH LAW
Responding to relationality

Mary Donnelly

Introduction

In her final letter to her husband Leonard in 1941, Virginia Woolf writes:

> Dearest, I feel certain I am going mad again. I feel we can't go through another of those terrible times. And I shan't recover this time.

Leonard Woolf was Virginia's carer during her periods of mental illness (with what might now be described as bi-polar disorder). But their relationship was so much more than this. Leonard was also Virginia's publisher, manager, husband and companion (Lee, 1997). Her letter continues 'I don't think two people could have been happier till this terrible disease came.' This poignant letter provides just one entry point to a consideration of family in situations of mental illness. Spouses and partners, parents and children, siblings and grandparents, friends and lovers may all respond in different ways where someone in their circle has a mental illness. Given this infinite variety, it is no surprise that mental health legislation has struggled to identify the most appropriate way to address the role of family in situations of involuntary admission.

There is a complex dialectic at the heart of discussions of family in mental illness. On the one hand, family are often best placed to provide support for the person with mental illness and to influence his or her recovery. Yet, family may sometimes also (often without intending to do so) undermine resilience and impede recovery. It is essential that we attend to this dialectic and that we recognise that while the needs of individuals and of families will often overlap, they do not always do so. This has implications for how we evaluate legal frameworks and how we think about mental health law reform.

The chapter begins by exploring the complexities of relationality in mental illness, recognising the different roles which family assumes and is assigned across different cultural and temporal contexts. It then examines the treatment of family in 'traditional' mental health legislation, using the example of the Mental Health Act 1983 (UK) where the 'Nearest Relative' framework can be traced back to the early days of de-institutionalisation. This is followed by an analysis of some recent law reform efforts which stay within the traditional

DOI: 10.4324/9781003226413-29

model but seek to expand individual choice of support options. Having identified traditional (albeit developing) responses to the role of family and some of the limitations of these, the chapter then turns to broader reform possibilities. Here, it draws primarily on the Report of the Royal Commission into Victoria's Mental Health System (VRC Report, 2021). This offers a more expansive vision of the role of mental health law, which also involves new ways of engaging with family.

Before beginning the substantive discussion, a brief note is required on the meaning of 'family' in this chapter. Sometimes, when speaking about specific legal provisions, family is understood as the particular legal formulation at issue, which is usually based on the traditional ties of blood or marriage (sometimes described as 'family of origin'). However, in general, 'family' is used as a shorthand to encompass 'family of choice' (i.e. people in a close relationship which is not based on blood ties or marriage) as well as family of origin (Smart, 2007).

Relationality and mental illness

There is no single narrative of the role of family in mental illness (Donnelly and Murray, 2013). As well as the infinite range of human relationships, there are broader differences between competing accounts of the role of family across times and cultures (Gilbar and Miola, 2014; Gopalkrishnan, 2018). The discussion below is primarily focused on the role of family in the West (although recognising that there are different responses to mental illness among different ethnic communities in the West (Szmukler and Bloch, 1997; Lefley, 1998, 2000)). It begins by considering the evolution of views of family in mental illness. This is followed by discussion of how the role of family maps onto conceptual understandings of relationality and then by an exploration of contemporary experiences of families in situations of mental illness.

Evolving views of family in mental illness

One common temporal division in mental health law scholarship distinguishes between the pre-carceral, carceral and post-carceral eras (Unsworth, 1991: 255). Family features in a different way in each. Property concerns dominate in the pre-carceral era with the primary focus being the transfer (whether to the State or to family) of the benefits and responsibilities of property ownership in situations of mental illness (Unsworth, 1991: 258–259). Although some responsibilities to provide care were imposed on those in authority, for example through the *parens patriae* jurisdiction (Seymour, 1994), most of the time, care of people with mental illness was left to their families. Where families did not provide this, almshouses and other religious institutions provided some respite, but for many, the result was almost inevitably destitution and homelessness: what Brendan Kelly describes as the 'wandering lunatic' (2016: 18). Asylums, workhouses and other sites of incarceration were, in the first instance, an attempt to address this problem (Kelly, 2016). The steady growth in asylums which took place during the carceral era derived in no small way from families' enthusiasm to hand over the care of family members with mental illness. As David Rothman describes (in a United States context), 'once the family's tolerance was exhausted, they gave their burden over to the asylum, grateful for the relief it provided' (1990: xlvi). And for at least some of those admitted, this was the end of the matter, even in cases where the asylum attempted discharge into family care (Kelly, 2016: 4).

While these family responses to mental illness may seem incomprehensible to modern eyes, it is important to remember the broader social context in which they took place. Mental illness was a source of profound stigma and shame, both for the person who was mentally ill and for their family (Scull, 1993, 2015) and this created a compulsion to hide this shame by whatever means possible. This was reinforced by the shift to a capitalist, production-focused society which placed new pressures on relationships with economically non-productive family members (Series, 2022: 34). Nonetheless, it is no surprise that the 'legalism' of early mental health legislation was premised at least in part on the need to protect mentally ill people from their families (Unsworth, 1991). This view of family as inherently dangerous was exacerbated by other factors, including the attribution of mental illness to genetics or upbringing and the linkages drawn, especially in psychotherapy, between family failings and individual mental illness, for example, Frieda Fromm-Reichmann's cold and domineering 'schizophrenogenic mother' (1948) and Phyllis Chesler's patriarchal family structures (1972).

There were many reasons for the move away from incarcerating people with mental illness. Writing in respect of the UK, Lucy Series points to the role of scandals, sociological critiques (including Erving Goffman's coruscating analysis of 'total institutions' (1961)), the development of independent living and disability rights pressure groups (some of which were led by family members), the anti-psychiatry movement and the growth in theories of normalisation and person-centred care (2022: 55–65). The development of new pharmacological treatments also held out the promise that mental illness could be cured or at least managed outside of an institutional setting (Gronfien, 1985). In this new policy environment, family came increasingly to be seen less as 'the enemy' and more as necessary allies in the provision of appropriate care. This changing approach is exemplified in the Report of the Royal Commission on the Law Relating to Mental Illness and Mental Deficiency (1958) (the Percy Report), which provided the policy underpinnings for the shift to care in the community and was given legislative effect in the Mental Health Act 1959 (UK).

The Percy Commission consulted extensively, including with people with lived experience of mental illness and their families (Rapaport and Manthorpe, 2009: 254). The final Report presents families as having a vital role to play in delivering the new model of community care (Hewitt, 2009; Rapaport and Manthorpe, 2009: 260). This emerging understanding led to a new focus on 'burden' research, which sought to investigate the impact of one family member's mental illness on broader family health and wellbeing (Grad and Sainsbury, 1963; Hoenig and Hamilton, 1966; Platt, 1985; Faden, 1989; Sartorius et al., 2005). While criticisms can be levelled against some of the earlier research, which was often insufficiently cognisant of broader social factors, one very clear finding across all studies was that a family member's mental illness did not just affect the person themselves, but also had a negative impact on their broader family, especially if the family was involved in the person's care.

Recognising relationality

The recognition of family in the shift to community care reflects a broader philosophical turn towards recognising relationality and connectedness. Contemporary thinking reflects a move away from an individualist perspective and a greater recognition of the inherently social context in which people live their lives and the defining influence of relationships with others (Harding, 2017). The foundations for this shift lie primarily in feminist philosophy, which fundamentally challenged individualist conceptions of the self, emphasising instead the inevitability of dependency, connectedness and relationality (Baier, 1985; Fineman, 2005; Kittay,

1999; see also MacIntyre, 1999). Various ways of responding to the realities of relationality have been proposed. One is the elevation of an ethic of care (Noddings, 1984; Kittay, 1999; Herring, 2013); a second is the identification of relational autonomy (Mackenzie and Stoljar, 2000); and a third is the recognition of the normative force of vulnerability as a universal aspect of the human condition (Goodin, 1985; Fineman, 2008; Mackenzie et al., 2013).

Each of these approaches has something to offer in conceptualising the role of family in mental illness (Donnelly and Murray, 2013). The contribution of care (and of carers) has long been neglected in philosophical discourse, notwithstanding the fact that, as Eva Kittay has argued, the ability to give and receive care is as fundamental to human dignity as the ability to reason which has so preoccupied philosophers (Kittay, 2011: 52). As discussed below, care can be an essential part of recovery from mental illness and, without care, the only alternative for some people with serious mental illness is homelessness and destitution. However, an ethic of care alone cannot provide an adequate conceptual framework to address the role of family in mental illness (Donnelly and Murray, 2013: 398). This is because the relationship between a person with a mental illness and their family does not always fit neatly within the contours of 'care' (Henderson, 2001). Moreover, a focus on care alone risks obscuring the 'cared-for' person, including failing to respect their autonomy and dignity. This is especially problematic in mental illness, which has long been characterised by the denial of these rights (whether through societal or legal strictures or indeed because of the impact of the illness itself (Gergel, this vol.)).

A focus on relational autonomy provides something of a counterweight to these concerns. Although this concept is variously defined (Christman, 2004), at its core, it attempts to address the realities of relationality while remaining grounded in respect for individual autonomy (Mackenzie and Stoljar, 2000). Autonomy has been a foundational norm in disability rights advocacy 'where it provides a necessary counterweight to centuries of paternalist presumptions' (Donnelly, 2022: 23). Yet, traditional liberal conceptions of autonomy cannot address the range of factors (structural, societal, cultural and educational as well as capacity-related) which prevent a person from being able to make autonomous decisions. Relational autonomy provides a helpful way of thinking about family in situations of mental illness because it recognises that autonomy is not a given but rather, 'is made possible by constructive relationships' (Nedelsky, 2011: 118). Thus, it provides a conceptual basis for support-based legal frameworks which seek to assist a person with mental illness to make autonomous decisions, including during times of crisis. At the same time, a key feature of relational autonomy is that it does not presume that all relationships are positive or 'constructive'. Thus, the 'relational project' is 'intrinsically evaluative and aimed at transformation' (Nedelsky, 2011: 32). In respect of mental illness, this requires that a person with mental illness must also be supported to extricate themselves from relationships which diminish autonomy.

Vulnerability theory adds another helpful layer when thinking about mental illness. This theory begins from the premise that vulnerability is universal and inevitable (Fineman, 2008; Mackenzie et al., 2013). This in turn draws attention to the actions which a state can take to respond to vulnerability, including an obligation to build resilience (Fineman, 2008). The contribution of vulnerability theory in responding to mental illness is that it addresses both the vulnerable individual and those, including family, who are placed in a position of 'derivative dependency' because of their efforts to care for and support their family member (Fineman, 2008: 117). In practical terms, this focus requires asking 'what can be done to create or enhance frameworks in which both individuals *and* families can contribute to mental health and recovery' (Donnelly and Murray, 2013: 401).

Some of these conceptual understandings are reflected in the United Nations Convention on the Rights of Persons with Disabilities (CRPD). Article 12(3), which requires States Parties to 'take appropriate measures to provide persons with disabilities with the support they may require in exercising their legal capacity', reflects a relational understanding of autonomy (Bach and Kerzner, 2010). There is also a reference in the Preamble to family as 'the natural and fundamental group unit of society' and an affirmation that 'persons with disabilities and their family members should receive the necessary protection and assistance to enable families to contribute towards the full and equal enjoyment of the rights of persons with disabilities' (2006, para. 24). This might be seen as reflecting elements of vulnerability theory. However, beyond this, the role of family is largely ignored by the CRPD. As Rosemary Kayess and Phillip French point out, this downplaying of the role of family was a deliberate choice; following a keen argument among members of the Ad Hoc Committee, it was concluded that there should not be any overt recognition of family because, in most societies, family needs tend to be privileged above those of the person with disability and family members are sometimes principally responsible for, or collude in, the breach of rights of persons with disabilities (2008, 25–26).

Leaving aside the question of whether this was an appropriate call for the Ad Hoc Committee to make, its effect is that the CRPD is of limited use in trying to conceptualise, or advance, the role of relationality in situations of mental illness. Bearing this in mind, we now turn to the contemporary experiences of family in situations of mental illness.

Family in contemporary context

Although there is no single or simple narrative of family in contemporary context, some themes emerge. In the West, we are now well over half a century into the post-carceral era and the long-term institutional admission which grounded traditional mental health law is largely consigned to history (except in forensic settings). The vast majority of people receive care in the community or through short-term hospital admission. In Ireland, for example, the average length of stay for discharges from inpatient mental health services in 2021 was 55.6 days, while the median length of stay was 14 days (Daly and Craig, 2022: 8). This is not intended to diminish the importance of protection against wrongful involuntary admission; respect for the rights to liberty, autonomy and equality require that these protections be robust and meaningful. However, it is also the case that, for many people living with mental illness, the primary difficulty is no longer incarceration, but an absence of services and support, both in terms of direct access to health services and in respect of all the other elements, such as housing, income, employment and the social structures that make life liveable and recovery possible (Carney, this vol.). Thus, for many, the reality is that 'community care' is either family care or homelessness, isolation and neglect.

For those who do have access to family support (in its broadest sense), it is now widely recognised that these relationships can play an important role in recovery and preventing relapse (Onken et al., 2002; Tew et al., 2012; Ward, 2017). This has led to an increase in family therapy/recovery interventions and there is a body of evidence which suggests that these can be highly effective (Ward, 2017). Family and carer involvement is also encouraged in professional guidance and Codes of Practice (e.g. Code of Practice to the Mental Health Act 1983 (2015)). There is, however, also evidence that family relationships can adversely impact recovery (Ward, 2017) and that the person with a mental illness may sometimes have quite a different view of the role their family members play in their recovery (Waller, 2019).

The position can become even more complex in situations of chronic mental illness or during an acute phase of an intermittent illness. Here, family members may be required to act as carers. This shifts the relationship to a different register, which may continue for a short or a longer time, depending on the circumstances (Henderson, 2001). This in turn may give rise to tensions. As Henderson describes, the parties to the relationship 'may not always agree, or indeed ever [agree], about the nature of care or the need for it' (2001: 155). These tensions are heightened in situations of involuntary admission/use of coercion. In such situations, families report ambivalence and discomfort, but also feelings of relief (Jankovic, 2011; Norvoll, 2018; Stuart et al., 2020). For the person who has been admitted, there may be feelings of betrayal and/or abandonment, especially where their family members have been instrumental in initiating the admission (McGuinness, 2018; Akther, 2019; Sugiura, 2020).

There is also a strong body of evidence across a wide range of jurisdictions which suggests that the structures of mental healthcare pose significant challenges for families. Stuart et al.'s systematic review of carers' experience of involuntary admission identifies several key concerns (2020). A prominent theme was the absence of support from mental health services. Carers identified how, in the period prior to admission, they were 'overwhelmed by too much responsibility, isolated from sources of support, and expected to manage situations they were ill-equipped to deal with, including self-harm and threats of suicide, until assistance became available' (Stuart et al., 2020: 4). This problem was especially challenging for carers who were new to the mental health system or for younger and less experienced carers (Stuart et al., 2020: 5). Carers also described their frustrations in their relationships with health professionals and their distress at the quality of care provided (Stuart et al., 2020: 6).

A notable concern which emerges from most studies is carers' lack of access to information and exclusion from care decisions, something which becomes especially acute around plans for discharge (Jankovic, 2011; Stuart, 2020). Sometimes, this lack of information reflects a systems-level failure to engage properly with families or confusion about the scope of health professionals' legal duties (Hansson et al., 2022). However, these concerns also reflect an ongoing ethical tension regarding the role of confidentiality where the person with mental illness does not wish information to be shared with family members (Hansson et al., 2022). This is not easy to resolve. On the one hand, confidentiality is a long-established foundational principle of the clinician/patient relationship and basic equality principles indicate that confidentiality should be no less important just because a person has a mental illness. Moreover, confidentiality can be an essential element in building and sustaining trust within a therapeutic relationship. On the other hand, family members who act as carers are directly and personally affected by their family member's mental illness (Szmukler and Bloch, 1997: 404; Stuart, 2020: 6). It can be argued that this requires some degree of reformulation of the scope of the ethical duty of confidentiality (Hansson et al., 2022). Szmukler and Bloch argue that an ethical duty to share information with carers may be appropriate in some circumstances, based on 'the seriousness of the risk to the family's well-being, available alternatives, the patient's capacity to recognise actual and potential harms, and pre-existing family values' (Szmukler and Bloch, 1997: 404–405). Other relevant factors might include the pre-existing relationship between the person and their carer/s and any harm that would be caused to the person by sharing the information. As we will see below, finding ways to resolve this ethical tension is an ongoing challenge for mental health law.

All of the problems identified above are exacerbated for young carers (i.e. carers under 18), who are sometimes overlooked in mental health research, policy and law (although almost one-third of young carers provide support in situations of mental illness (Dharampal and Ani, 2020: 113)). Studies suggest that tasks undertaken by young carers include housework, healthcare and emotional support (Dharampal and Ani, 2020: 113). Young carers report being confused by the legal system, being ignored by mental health professionals and being left without supports or even basic information about medical changes following their parent's discharge from hospital (Dharampal and Ani, 2020: 117–118). It is also clear that the health and wellbeing of young carers is often substantially diminished by their caring role (Martinsen et al., 2019; Dharampal and Ani, 2020; Lacey et al., 2022).

Bearing in mind this complex picture, we turn now to the ways in which family is treated in traditional mental health legislation.

Family in mental health legislation

'Traditional' mental health legislation typically emerged during the carceral era and is principally concerned with regulating non-consensual admission to psychiatric facilities and non-consensual treatment for a 'mental disorder' which, depending on the jurisdiction, may be in hospital or in the community. This basic framework is replicated in many jurisdictions across the world (WHO, 2020). Within this, there is a good deal of variation in treatment of the role of family (Mullen et al., 2006; Donnelly and Murray, 2013). The discussion here focuses on the nearest relative provisions in the Mental Health Act 1983 (UK) (MHA). These remain largely unchanged from those recommended by the Percy Report in the very early days of the move to community care.

The 'Nearest Relative' framework

The 'Nearest Relative' framework is based on the identification of a single point of contact – the patient's[1] 'nearest relative' (NR) – who is invested with authority by law. The NR (who must be over 18 years and living in the UK) is determined in accordance with a set statutory hierarchy with spouse/civil partner/cohabitant (for more than 6 months) at the apex (MHA, s. 26(4)).[2] An application to displace the NR may be made to the county court by another relative or by an Approved Mental Health Professional (AMHP) and, subsequent to an amendment introduced by the Mental Health Act 2007 (MHA 2007 (EW)), by the patient him or herself (MHA, s. 29(2)).

The NR plays an important gatekeeper role (Laing et al., 2018). S/he may initiate an application for admission for assessment or treatment (MHA, s. 11(1)) or request an AMHP to carry out an MHA assessment (MHA, s. 13(4)).[3] The latter will typically happen where the NR considers that community mental health services are not being sufficiently responsive

---

1 While recognising the difficulties with the term 'patient', I adopt it in discussion of the MHA 1983 to reflect the wording of the Act.
2 This is followed by the patient's child, parent, sibling, grandparent, grandchild, uncle or aunt, nephew or niece (MHA, s. 26 as am by the Mental Health Act 2007, s. 26) with priority given to the eldest person in each class. However, where the patient ordinarily resides with, or is cared for by one or more relatives, this relative/s is given priority over other relatives (MHA, s. 26(4)). A person who is not a relative but with whom the patient has been ordinarily residing for more than 5 years at the time of admission is treated as a relative, although they come last in the hierarchy and cannot be treated as the nearest relative of someone who is married or has a civil partner (MHA, s. 26(7)).
3 In such circumstances, an assessment must be carried out and if the AMHP determines that an application for admission should not be made, they must inform the NR of the reasons for this in writing (MHA, s. 13(4)).

to their relative's situation (Laing et al., 2018: 39). The NR may also object to an application for admission by the AMHP (MHA, s. 11(4)(a)).[4] Where this occurs, the only way an admission can proceed is through an application to the county court to have the NR removed. The NR also has a gatekeeper role around discharge. S/he may make an order to have the patient discharged from detention, guardianship or a community treatment order (CTO) (MHA, s. 23(2)). However, this power is restricted where the responsible clinician certifies that the patient, if discharged, would be likely to act in a manner dangerous to him or herself or to others (MHA, s. 25(1)).[5] Where this happens, the NR is prohibited from making another discharge order for a 6-month period (MHA, s. 25(1)).

The NR is statutorily entitled to designated information, including the information about legal rights which must be provided to the patient (MHA, s. 132(4)).[6] S/he is also entitled to information about the patient's discharge (MHA, s. 133(1)).[7] This information may help a NR to support the person by identifying and explaining relevant information (although there is no express statutory linkage between the requirement to provide information and a requirement to provide support) (Keywood, 2010: 327). In respect of both statutory requirements, the patient may object to the information being shared and this objection prevents any sharing.

For its time, the NR framework was a considered and innovative response to relationality. However, as recognised by the Independent Review of the Mental Health Act 1983 (the Wessely Review), it is now 'outdated, variable and insufficient' (2018: 85). The most immediate problem is the imposition of a statutorily designated NR without meaningful patient involvement in the appointment. This was somewhat improved by an amendment allowing the patient to apply to court to have their nearest relative removed (MHA, s. 29(4)(za) as ins by MHA 2007, s. 23).[8] However, as Kirsty Keywood identifies, court application is a 'rather weak advocacy tool', placing the onus on the already disadvantaged patient to instigate and follow through (Keywood, 2010: 328). The lack of choice has been identified as problematic by NRs who indicate that the responsibilities imposed by the role may sometimes be unwelcome and/or assumed only because of a sense of duty (Yeates, 2007; Dixon, 2022). There is a dearth of studies of patients' experiences of the NR framework. However, it is highly likely that, for many patients, the NR is not the optimal person to provide support.

Looking beyond the lack of patient choice in appointment, various studies over an extended time-period identify systemic failures in the NR framework. NRs experience dissatisfaction and confusion around their role which in turn substantially impedes their capacity to support their family member (Yeates, 2007; Shaw et al., 2018; Dixon et al., 2022). Dixon

---

4 So as to facilitate the exercise of this right, the AMHP must consult with the person appearing to be the NR where an AMHP proposes to make an application for admission unless it appears to the AMHP that the consultation is not reasonably practicable or would involve unreasonable delay (MHA, s. 11(4)(b)).
5 In order to facilitate this, the NR must give 72 hours' notice in writing of his or her intention to order a discharge: MHA, s. 25(1).
6 Under MHA, s. 132, the manager of the hospital must take such steps as are practicable to ensure that the patient understands: the provision of the MHA under which the person is detained and the effect of this provision and the tribunal rights that apply; and various of the other statutory protections which apply.
7 If practicable, this must be given at least 7 days prior to discharge: MHA, s. 133(1).
8 This followed judicial recognition that the statutory framework as it stood was incompatible with the European Convention on Human Rights: *R(M) v Secretary of State for Health* (2003); *JT v United Kingdom* (2000).

et al. identify both subjective and objective burdens experienced by NRs. Subjective burdens include experiences of 'distress, relief, of feeling conflicted and frustrated with mental health services and staff' (2022: 13–14). Objective burdens included NRs' 'accounts that their concerns were ignored or minimised, that services failed to share information, and did not offer adequate support' (2022: 14).

Reforming the traditional model

The past decade has seen widespread mental health law reform. In part, this has been because of the impetus provided by the CRPD, although the movement for reform has also emerged from evident deficiencies in the operation of the traditional model (Donnelly, 2023). Perhaps the most obviously relevant reform for the discussion in this chapter is increased provision for individual choice of representative/supporter. The recommendations of the Wessely Review in England and Wales provide a useful example of this shift. The Review recommends replacing the NR by a 'Nominated Person' (NP) who is appointed (and may be removed) by the patient 'either prior to detention, at the point of assessment for detention or whilst detained' (2018: 85). The Review also recognises that not everyone will be able to identify a NP and so it also makes provision for a fallback 'Interim Nominated Person' (INP), who is to be appointed by the AMHP in accordance with guidelines (to be developed) aimed at ensuring that the INP is the most suitable person for the role (2018: 86). Once the patient regains capacity, s/he may replace the INP (and, in the interim, any objecting family member may go to court to seek replacement) (2018: 86). The Review is also clear that a person with capacity should be able to use the nomination process to opt out of having either a NP or an INP (2018: 86).

Alongside better choice, the Wessely Review proposes enhanced status for the NP/INP. This includes expanding the scope of consultation with the NP to include an obligation to consult on transfers between hospitals and on care plans (the latter with the patient's consent) and a right to appeal clinical treatment decisions where the patient is unable to do so and where the NP/INP believes that the patient would not agree to the treatment or that the treatment is not in the patient's best interests (2018: 87). The latter recommendation reflects the Review's recognition that 'closest family and friends will often be an invaluable source of information about the patient's wishes and preferences, as well as what treatment does and does not work best for them' (2018: 97). The Review also proposes that a NP/INP who has been found to have inappropriately objected to admission should not be removed, but that the county court should be permitted to temporarily overrule the NP on this point alone while allowing them to continue to support the patient in all other ways (2018: 88). These recommendations are given effect in the Draft Mental Health Bill 2022 (England and Wales) which is being progressed at the time of writing.

We are also seeing some jurisdictions buttress better choice through legislative provision for advance directives. These can operate alongside a nominated person model and can help reduce resort to coercion (Morrissey, 2022). In Ireland, for example, the Assisted Decision-Making (Capacity) Act 2015 (ADMCA) provides for advance healthcare directives (AHDs) which allow the directive-maker to make a legally enforceable treatment refusal (ADMCA, s. 84(2)) and to request treatment and to have this request taken into consideration if the treatment in question is relevant to the person's condition (ADMCA, s. 84(3)) (Donnelly, 2017). A notable feature of the ADMCA is that the directive-maker may appoint a designated healthcare representative (DHR) who is statutorily empowered to ensure that the person's AHD is complied with (ADMCA, s. 88(1)(a)). The directive-maker may also confer on the DHR the power to advise and interpret the directive-maker's will and preferences regarding treatment by reference to the AHD and/or to consent to or refuse treatment, up to and including life-sustaining treatment, based on the directive-maker's known will and preferences by reference to the AHD (ADMCA, s. 88(1)(b)). In some circumstances, the AHD remains operative in respect of mental health treatment even where a person has been involuntarily admitted under the Mental Health Act 2001 (ADMCA, s. 85(7) as am by Assisted Decision-Making (Capacity) (Amendment) Act 2022, s. 74).[9]

Mental health law reforms of the kind described above reflect the principles of relational autonomy. As well as enhancing personal choice, these reforms also increase the family's ability to advocate for their family member. By allowing the person to nominate and plan ahead, these reforms may also provide a way around some of the ethical dilemmas around confidentiality and information sharing which were identified above. The potential of these reforms is summarised by Margaret Sweeney, who has a diagnosis of paranoid schizophrenia and who plans to appoint her husband as her DHR:

> Having a vulnerability to psychosis makes me, at certain stages of my life, move from a position of capability, possibility and ability to a position of disability, dependency and mental confusion. This is why [the ADMCA] means so much to me. So that during those vulnerable periods of my life, my wishes are protected.
> *(Norton and Sweeney, 2022: 190)*

Yet, it is also clear that these reforms will not address all of the challenges experienced by people with mental illness or the families who support them. A much broader and well-resourced system change is required if lack of early and ongoing support is to be tackled in a meaningful way (Laing, 2021: 176). A similar point may be made about AHDs. While potentially very beneficial for some people, a good deal of work needs to be done to facilitate uptake within an integrated and properly resourced care plan. It must also be recognised that AHDs are by no means a universal solution, especially for people experiencing serious mental illness for the first time, whose experience of involuntary admission may have a profound impact on their recovery, or for people whose lives are more chaotic. Ultimately, as Judy Laing recognises, without a '[f]irm financial commitment to bolster the legal changes' we are unlikely to see the level of improvement which is needed to underpin law reform initiatives of the kind identified above (2021, 176). This then takes us to the last part of this chapter and the question of whether it is possible to use mental health law to create a better space for people with mental illness and their families.

Finding a better space?

An emerging theme in the scholarship of mental illness/distress is that new paradigms are needed which are better attuned to the realities of contemporary life (Rose, 2019; Rose and Rose, 2023). A similar argument may be made about mental health law, where variations on

---

9 There are two grounds for involuntary admission under the Mental Health Act 2001: s. 3(1)(a) provides for admission on the basis that the person is at risk of harm to him or herself or to others while s. 3(1)(b) provides for admission on the basis that the person's capacity is impaired and that the admission is likely to be of therapeutic benefit. Where a person is admitted under s. 3(1)(b), his or her AHD continues to have legal force in respect of treatment for the person's mental illness; however, this is not the case for those admitted under s. 3(1)(a).

Family in mental health law

the traditional model have dominated for almost 150 years and are looking increasingly out-of-touch with modern needs. Laing rightly identifies that '[p]ositive rights and resources must be at the heart of successful mental health law reform if it is going to lead to any lasting and meaningful improvements for people with mental illness and their families' (2021: 176). This requires a paradigm shift. A recent attempt to articulate such a shift can be found in the Report of the Royal Commission into Victoria's Mental Health System (VRC Report, 2021) and the subsequent legislative measures introduced in Victoria. The VRC Report is rich and multi-faceted with many lessons for mental health law reform (McSherry, this vol.; Donnelly, 2023). The discussion here focuses on the VRC Report's response to the role of families. However, to put this in context, a brief outline of the broader elements of the reform is needed.

The Royal Commission was appointed in 2019 with the aim (in the words of the then Victorian Premier) of fixing a 'broken system' (VRC Interim Report, 2019: 11). A distinguishing feature of the Royal Commission's work is that it was authorised to undertake a whole system review, with law reform being just one part of a much broader engagement. The Royal Commission published an Interim Report in 2019 and a final Report, which runs to five volumes, in February 2021. This sets out 65 recommendations intended to deliver 'transformational reform' (Executive Summary, 2021: 18 *et seq*). Drawing on the work of Braithwaite et al. (2013), the Royal Commission adopted a systems approach to its analysis. In this, the Royal Commission recognised both the interdependency and the complexity of the mental health system. This means that system change cannot be achieved by simply directing the system to produce an outcome (e.g. through legislative reform). Instead, change can only be achieved by 'shifting the underlying conditions that hold the most influence over how the system, and those people within the system, operate' (VRC Report Vol. 1: 58). Reflecting this approach, the Royal Commission focused on the identification of 'systems levers' (i.e. parts of a system 'where a seemingly small or discreet shift in one part of the system produces big changes across the system' (VRC Report Vol. 1: 77)).

One key systems lever identified by the Royal Commission was the introduction of a Mental Health and Wellbeing Act to shift the legislative focus away from compulsion towards the delivery of treatment and the enhancement of wellbeing (VRC Report Vol. 4: 35–36). Thus, the primary objective of the proposed Act was the delivery of the highest attainable standard of mental health (VRC Report Vol. 4: 36–37). Another systems lever was the establishment of the Victorian Collaborative Centre for Mental Health and Wellbeing, based on models from cancer and cardiac care (McSherry, this vol.). The Centre was to provide 'adult clinical and non-clinical services, emphasise the participation and inclusion of people with lived experience, and conduct interdisciplinary research' (VRC Interim Report: 392) with 'a mandate to influence mental health treatment, care and support across Victoria, with a view to changing some of the "deeper" characteristics of the system' (VRC Report Vol. 1: 77).

Families, carers and supporters played a central role in the Royal Commission's approach, which started from the premise that 'most people live within relationships of care and support' and that this should be 'the starting point for the design of the future mental health and wellbeing system' (VRC Report Vol 3: 72). In developing this analysis, the Royal Commission was careful to distinguish between the lived experience of families and carers and the lived experience of consumers[10] of mental health services (VRC Report Vol. 3: 74).

---

10 This reflects the terminology used in the Report.

It noted that '[w]hile at times these groups may have shared interests, they speak from their own perspective and experiences, and at times they may have conflicting views' (VRC Report Vol. 3: 74). This was an important methodological choice by the Royal Commission and is reflected in the Commission's recommendations (Donnelly, 2023).

Many of the concerns raised by the families who gave evidence to the Royal Commission were similar to those identified in the studies discussed above, including lack of information and support around admission and an absence of options in crisis situations. However, given the system-wide scope of the review, the Royal Commission also elicited feedback about a broader range of issues, including lack of housing options for their family member; lack of opportunities for respite; and lack of information about broader support options (VRC Report Vol. 3: 80). The VRC Report also includes powerful personal testimony from families, including young carers, on the impact of their caring role on their lives and on their own health and wellbeing.[11]

The Royal Commission found that caring for someone living with a mental illness is different to other caring roles for a variety of reasons, including:

> [T]he need to provide higher degrees of emotional support; managing crises; maintaining vigilance to prevent self-harm or suicide attempts; having strained relationships; dealing with the unpredictable and episodic nature of caregiving; and stigma and isolation.
>
> *(VRC Report Vol. 3: 81)*

On this basis, the Royal Commission concluded that families, carers and supporters need support in their own right and that the particular needs of young carers must be recognised (VRC Report Vol. 3: 81). Although the Royal Commission did not explicitly use a vulnerability analysis of the kind described in this chapter, this aspect of its work can be regarded as an attempt to address the 'derivative dependency' of family members.

In proposing solutions, the Royal Commission recommended that families should be much more closely involved in the operation of the mental health system. It identified the following three key strategies to achieve this:

- ensuring that working with families, carers and supporters is an essential part of the commissioning of mental health and wellbeing services
- improving information sharing with families, carers and supporters, including developing standards for services and practitioners
- introducing system-wide training for the mental health and wellbeing workforce to facilitate working with families, carers and supporters (VRC Report Vol. 3: 96).

While these strategies stretch well beyond what law can achieve, they also influence key aspects of the legal framework. Thus, the Royal Commission recommended that recognition and promotion of the value of families, carers and supporters should be one of the guiding principles underpinning the Mental Health and Wellbeing Act (VRC Report Vol. 4: 37). While underpinning principles are an increasingly common feature of mental health law, an

---

11 A notable feature of the Royal Commission's approach is its wide-ranging consultation and the inclusion of detailed personal testimonies (Donnelly, 2023).

explicit reference to families in such principles is unusual. The Royal Commission approach may also be distinguished from more traditional approaches because the legislative principles are scaffolded by an explicit requirement that the Victorian Department of Health and Victorian mental health and wellbeing services must make decisions in line with the Act's objectives (VRC Report Vol. 4: 37) and by the establishment of new enforcement bodies.

The explicit statutory recognition of the needs of families, carers and supporters is based on ethical principles which favour a more deeply relational approach. This choice needs to be viewed alongside other elements of the VRC Report, especially the recommendations that the consumer of mental health services must be central in all aspects of mental health policy and service delivery and that active steps must be taken towards the removal of all forms of coercive and restrictive practices in mental health (VRC Report Vol. 4: 300–301). Thus, the Royal Commission has tried to respond to the needs of families while also retaining an essential focus on the individual.

It remains to be seen whether the ambitious recommendations of the Royal Commission will achieve their goals. However, there has already been some progress. The Collaborative Centre is now established, with both carers and people with mental illness represented on the Board.[12] A Mental Health and Wellbeing levy came into effect on 1 January 2022 providing a steady income stream (in addition to State funds) for delivering on the Royal Commission's recommendations.[13] Finally, the Mental Health and Wellbeing Act 2022 has received Royal Assent, although it has not yet come into force at the time of writing.

Conclusion

For most people, mental health and mental illness are experienced relationally, with all the positive and negative aspects that this brings. Strong family relationships can help maintain mental health, assist in recovery from mental illness and provide necessary support during difficult times. Yet, relationality can also have a dark side. Some family relationships can be difficult or distant or may come under unbearable strain in situations of mental illness. Adding to this, all relationships (good and bad) are lived against a backdrop of a mental health system which is frequently under-resourced, unwieldy and restricted in the range of available options.

Mental health law has the challenging task of finding the best way to respond to relationality. A review of the Nearest Relative framework suggests that traditional mental health law has not been very good at this task. The increased choice being introduced through recent law reform projects should certainly improve the situation. Allowing each person to nominate their chosen supporter/s and to use advance healthcare directives to direct their choices during an acute phase should offer substantial improvements for both people with mental illness and their family members. However, as argued here, these improvements will not be sufficient to address the deep and structural problems that families encounter in trying to support their family member. A paradigm shift is needed to a

---

12 Under the Victorian Collaborative Centre for Mental Health and Wellbeing Act 2021, s. 11(6), two members of the Board (out of a maximum of 10) must be persons who identify as caring for or supporting, or as having cared for or supported, a person with mental illness or psychological distress and two must be persons who identify as experiencing, or having experienced, mental or psychological distress.
13 The levy is paid as payroll tax surcharge by employers with national payrolls of more than $10 million per annum.

mental health system that better serves the diverse needs of people with mental illness and their families. In imagining what this might look like, this chapter has drawn on the work of the Royal Commission into the Victorian Mental Health System (2019, 2021). Here we see an approach which looks at law as just one part of a broader system. We also see a normative shift towards delivering the highest attainable standard of mental health and away from the coercive practices which have characterised the traditional model. In this model, families, carers and supporters are recognised as separate rights-holders, although the Royal Commission also showed a good deal of ingenuity in trying to find ways to ensure that family interests do not become dominant over those of the person living with mental illness.

It is too soon to evaluate how the choices made by the Royal Commission around the role of families, carers and supporters will work in practice. It is certainly too much to expect that the new frameworks can resolve all of the tensions that arise in this space. Nonetheless, the inclusion of family (alongside consumers of mental health services) in researching, planning and structuring the mental health system offers the potential for innovation and the development of fresh perspectives which can better meet the needs of people with mental illness and the families who care for them.

References

Akther, S.F. et al. (2019) Patients' Experience of Assessment and Detention under Mental Health Legislation: Systematic Review and Qualitative Meta-Synthesis. *BJPsych Open*, 5(3), 10.1192/bjo.2019.19.

Assisted Decision-Making (Capacity) Act 2015 (Ireland).

Assisted Decision-Making (Capacity) (Amendment) Act 2022 (Ireland).

Bach, M. and Kerzner, L. (2010) *A New Paradigm for Protecting Legal Autonomy and the Right to Legal Capacity: Advancing Substantive Equality for Persons with Disabilities through Law, Policy and Practice*. Toronto: Law Commission of Ontario. Available at: https://www.lco-cdo.org/wp-content/uploads/2010/11/disabilities-commissioned-paper-bach-kerzner.pdf.

Baier, A. (1985) *Postures of the Mind: Essays on Mind and Morals*. Minneapolis: University of Minnesota Press.

Braithwaite, J. et al. (2013) Health Care as a Complex Adaptive System. In: Hollnagel, E., Braithwaite, J., and Wears, R., eds. *Resilient Health Care, Ashgate Studies in Resilience Engineering*. Surrey: Taylor and Francis: 59–73.

Carney, T. (2023) Socio-Economic Inclusion and Mental Health Law. In: Kelly, B. and Donnelly, M., eds. *Routledge Handbook of Mental Health Law*. Abingdon: Routledge: 371–383.

Chesler, P. (1972) *Women and Madness*. New York: Doubleday.

Christman, J. (2004) Relational Autonomy, Liberal Individualism, and the Social Construction of Selves'. *Philosophical Studies*, 117(1/2), 143–164.

Department of Health (2015) *Code of Practice to the Mental Health Act 1983*. London: TSO.

Daly, A. and Craig, S. (2022) *Annual Report on the Activities of Irish Psychiatric Units and Hospitals 2021*. Dublin: Health Research Board.

Dharampal, R. and Ani, C. (2020) The Emotional and Mental Health Needs of Young Carers: What Psychiatry Can Do. *BJPsych Bulletin*, 44(3), 112–120.

Dixon, J., Stone, K. and Laing, J. (2022) Beyond the Call of Duty: A Qualitative Study into the Experiences of Family Members Acting as Nearest Relative in Mental Health Act Assessments. *British Journal of Social Work*, 1–19, 10.1093/bjsw/bcab258.

Donnelly, M. (2023) Making the Future Happen: Law Reform Lessons from the Victorian Royal Commission. In: Maker, Y. and Wilson, K., eds. *The Future of Mental Health, Disability and Criminal Law*. Abingdon: Routledge.

Donnelly, M. (2022) Support Relationships in Law: Framing, Fictions and the Responsive State. In: Donnelly, M., Harding, R., and Taşcıoğlu, R., eds. *Supporting Legal Capacity in Socio-legal Context*. Oxford: Hart Publishing: 21–38.

Donnelly, M. (2017) Developing a Legal Framework for Advance Healthcare Planning: Comparing England and Wales and Ireland. *European Journal of Health Law*, 24(1), 67–84.

Donnelly, M. and Murray, C. (2013) The Role of Family in Mental Health Law: A Framework for Transformation. *Child and Family Law Quarterly*, 25(4), 380–405.

Draft Mental Health Bill 2022, CP 699. England and Wales.

Faden, G., Bebbington, P. and Kuipers, L. (1989) The Burden of Care: The Impact of Functional Psychiatric Illness on the Patient's Family. *British Journal of Psychiatry*, 150(3), 285–292.

Fineman, M. (2005) *The Autonomy Myth: A Theory of Dependency*. New York: The New Press.

Fineman, M. (2008) The Vulnerable Subject: Anchoring Equality in the Human Condition. *Yale Journal of Law and Feminism*, 20, 1–23.

Fromm-Reichman, F. (1948) Notes on Development of Treatment of Schizophrenics by Psychoanalytic Psychotherapy. *Psychiatry*, 11(3), 263–273.

Gergel, T. (2023) The Future of Mental Health Law: The Need for Deeper Examination and Broader Scope. In: Kelly, B. and Donnelly, M., eds. *Routledge Handbook of Mental Health Law*. Abingdon: Routledge: 704–726

Gilbar, R. and Miola, J. (2014) One Size Fits All? On Patient Autonomy, Medical Decision-Making, and the Impact of Culture. *Medical Law Review*, 23(3), 375–399.

Goffman, E. (1961) *Asylums*. New York: Anchor Books.

Goodin, R. (1985) *Protecting the Vulnerable: A Re-analysis of Our Social Responsibilities*. Chicago: University of Chicago Press.

Gopalkrishnan, N. (2018) Cultural Diversity and Mental Health: Considerations for Policy and Practice. *Frontiers in Public Health*, 6, 10.3389/fpubh.2018.00179.

Grad, J. and Sainsbury, P. (1963) Mental Illness and the Family. *Lancet*, 1(7280), 544–547.

Gronfien, W. (1985) Psychotropic Drugs and the Origins of Deinstitutionalization. *Social Problems*, 32(5), 437–454.

Hansson, K. et al. (2022) The Duty of Confidentiality during Family Involvement: Ethical Challenges and Possible Solutions in the Treatment of Persons with Psychotic Disorders. *BMC Psychiatry*, 22(1), 812, 10.1186/s12888-022-04461-6.

Harding, R. (2017) *Duties to Care: Dementia, Relationality and the Law*. Cambridge: Cambridge University Press.

Henderson, J. (2001) 'He's Not My Carer – He's My Husband': Personal and Policy Constructions of Care in Mental Health. *Journal of Social Work Practice*, 15(1), 149–159.

Herring, J. (2013) *Caring and the Law*. Oxford: Bloomsbury Publishing.

Hewitt, D. (2009) *The Nearest Relative Handbook*. 2nd edn. London: Jessica Kingsley Publishers Ltd.

Hoenig, J. and Hamilton, M. (1966) The Schizophrenic Patient in the Community and His Effect on the Household. *International Journal of Social Psychiatry*, 12(3), 165–176.

Jankovic, J. et al. (2011) Family Caregivers' Experiences of Involuntary Psychiatric Hospital Admissions of Their Relatives – A Qualitative Study. *PLOS ONE*, 6(10), e25425.

JT v United Kingdom [2000]. ECHR 133.

Kayess, R. and French, P. (2008) Out of Darkness into Light? Introducing the Convention on the Rights of Persons with Disabilities. *Human Rights Law Review*, 8(1), 1–34.

Kelly, B. (2016) *Hearing Voices: The History of Psychiatry in Ireland*. Dublin: Irish Academic Press.

Keywood, K. (2010) Nearest Relatives and Independent Mental Health Advocates: Advocating for Mental Health? In: Gostin, L. et al., eds. *Principles of Mental Health Law*. Oxford: OUP: 325–345

Kittay, E. (1999) *Love's Labour: Essays on Women, Equality, and Dependency*. Abingdon: Routledge.

Kittay, E. (2011) The Ethics of Care, Dependence and Disability. *Ratio Juris*, 24(1), 49–58.

Laing, J. et al. (2018) The Nearest Relative in the Mental Health Act 2007: Still an Illusory and Inconsistent Safeguard? *Journal of Social Welfare and Family Law*, 40(1), 37–56.

Laing, J. (2021) Reforming the Mental Health Act 1983: Will More Rights Lead to Fewer Wrongs? *Medical Law Review*, 30(1), 158–176.

Lacey, R., Xue, B. and McMunn, A. (2022) The Mental and Physical Health of Young Carers: A Systematic Review. *Lancet Public Health*, 7(9), e787–e796.

Lee, H. (1997) *Virginia Woolf*. London: Vintage Books.

Lefley, H. (1998) Families, Culture and Mental Illness: Constructing New Realities. *Psychiatry*, 61(4), 335–355.

Lefley, H. (2000) Cultural Perspectives on Families, Mental Illness, and the Law. *International Journal of Law and Psychiatry*, 23(3–4), 229–243.

MacIntyre, A. (1999) *Dependent Rational Animals: Why Human Beings Need the Virtues*. Chicago: Carus Publishing.

Mackenzie, C. and Stoljar, N., eds. (2000) *Relational Autonomy: Feminist Perspectives on Autonomy, Agency and the Relational Self*. New York: Oxford University Press.

Mackenzie, C., Rogers, W. and Dodds, S., eds. (2013) *Vulnerability: New Essays in Ethics and Feminist Philosophy*. New York: Oxford University Press.

Martinsen, E. et al. (2019) The Silent World of Young Next-of-Kin in Mental Healthcare. *Nursing Ethics*, 26(1), 213–223.

McGuinness, D. et al. (2018) Individuals' Experiences of Involuntary Admissions and Preserving Control: Qualitative Study. *BJPsych Open*, 4(6), 501–509.

McSherry, B. (2023) Interdisciplinary Collaboration in the Mental Health Sector: The Role of the Law. In: Kelly, B. and Donnelly, M., eds. *Routledge Handbook of Mental Health Law*. Abingdon: Routledge: 617–628.

Mental Health Act 1983 (United Kingdom).

Mental Health and Wellbeing Act 2022 (Victoria).

Morrissey, F. (2022) Advance Healthcare Directives: Respecting the Voice of the Person in Mental Healthcare. In: Donnelly, M. and Gleeson, C., eds. *The Assisted Decision-Making (Capacity) Act 2015: Personal and Professional Reflections*. Dublin: Donovan Print. Available at: https://decisionsupportservice.ie/assisted-decision-making-capacity-act-2015-personal-and-professional-reflections.

Mullen, R., Gibbs, A. and Dawson, J. (2006) Family Perspective on Community Treatment Orders: A New Zealand Study. *International Journal of Social Psychiatry*, 52(5), 469–478.

Nedelsky, J. (2011) *Law's Relations: A Relational Theory of Self, Autonomy and Law*. New York: Oxford University Press.

Noddings, N. (1984) *Caring: A Feminine Approach to Ethics and Moral Education*. Berkeley: University of California Press.

Norton, M.J. and Sweeney, M. (2022) Advance Healthcare Directives: Protecting the Rights and Values of the Person with Schizophrenia. In: Donnelly, M. and Gleeson, C., eds. *The Assisted Decision-Making (Capacity) Act 2015: Personal and Professional Reflections*. Dublin: Donovan Print. Available at: https://decisionsupportservice.ie/assisted-decision-making-capacity-act-2015-personal-and-professional-reflections.

Norvoll, R., Hem, M.H. and Lindemann, H. (2018) Family Members Existential and Moral Dilemmas with Coercion in Mental Healthcare. *Qualitative Health Research*, 28(6), 900–915.

Onken, S. et al. (2002) *Mental Health Recovery: What Helps and What Hinders?* Alexandria: National Association of State Mental Health Program Directors National Technical Assistance Center.

Platt, S. (1985) Measuring the Burden of Psychiatric Illness on Family: An Evaluation of Some Rating Scales. *Psychological Medicine*, 15(2), 383–393.

R(M) v Secretary of State for Health [2003] EWHC 1094 (Administration).

Rapaport, J. and Manthorpe, J. (2009) Fifty Years One: The Legacy of the Percy Report. *Journal of Social Work*, 9(3), 251–267.

Report of the Royal Commission on the Law Relating to Mental Illness and Mental Deficiency (1958) CMD 169. London: HMSO.

Rose, N. (2019) *Our Psychiatric Future*. Cambridge: Polity Press.

Rose, N. and Rose, D. (2023) Is 'Another' Psychiatry Possible? *Psychological Medicine*, 53(1), 46–54.

Rothman, D. (1990) *The Discovery of the Asylum: Social Order and Disorder in the New Republic*. New York: Little Brown.

Royal Commission into Victoria's Mental Health System Final Report, PP 202, Session 2018–2021 (February 2021). Available at: https://finalreport.rcvmhs.vic.gov.au/

Royal Commission into Victoria's Mental Health System Interim Report, PP 87, Session 2018–2019 (November 2019). Available at: http://rcvmhs.archive.royalcommission.vic.gov.au/interim-report.html

Sartorius, N. et al. (2005) *Families and Mental Disorder: From Burden to Empowerment.* New York: John Wiley & Sons.

Scull, A. (1993) *The Most Solitary of Afflictions: Madness and Society in Britain 1700–1900.* New Haven: Yale University Press.

Scull, A. (2015) *Madness in Civilisation: A Cultural History of Madness from the Bible to Freud.* New Jersey: Princeton University Press.

Seymour, J. (1994) Parens Patriae and Wardship Powers: Their Nature and Origins. *Oxford Journal of Legal Studies.* 14(1), 159–188.

Series, L. (2022) *Deprivation of Liberty in the Shadows of the Institution.* Bristol: Bristol University Press.

Shaw, L. et al. (2018) Experiences of the 'Nearest Relative' Provisions in the Compulsory Detention of People under the Mental Health Act: A Rapid Systematic Review. *Health Services and Delivery Research.* 6(39), 10.3310/hsdr06390.

Smart, C. (2007) *Personal Life: New Directions in Sociological Thinking.* Cambridge: Polity Press.

Stuart, R. et al. (2020) Carers' Experiences of Involuntary Admission under Mental Health Legislation: Systematic Review and Qualitative Meta-synthesis. *BJPsych Open.* 6(2), e19.

Sugiura, K. (2020) Experiences of Involuntary Psychiatric Admission Decision-Making: A Systematic Review and Meta-synthesis of the Perspectives of Service Users, Informal Carers, and Professionals. *International Journal of Law and Psychiatry*, 73, 101654.

Szmukler, G. and Bloch, S. (1997) Family Involvement in the Care of People with Psychoses: An Ethical Argument. *British Journal of Psychiatry*, 171, 401–405.

Tew, J. et al. (2012) Social Factors and Recovery from Mental Health Difficulties: A Review of the Evidence. *British Journal of Social Work*, 42(3), 443–460.

United Nations Convention on the Rights of Persons with Disabilities (2006) A/RES/61/106/Annex 1.

Unsworth, C. (1991) Mental Disorder and the Tutelary Relationship: From Pre- to Post-carceral Legal Order. *Journal of Law and in Society*, 18(2), 254–278.

Victorian Collaborative Centre for Mental Health and Wellbeing Act 2021.

Waller, S. et al. (2019). Family Focused Recovery: Perspectives from Individuals with a Mental Illness. *International Journal of Mental Health Nursing*, 28(1), 247–255.

Ward, B. et al. (2017) Family-Focussed Practice within a Recovery Framework: Practitioners' Qualitative Perspectives. *BMC Health Services Research*, 17(1), 234, 10.1186/s12913-017-2146-y.

Wessely, S. (Chair) (2018) *Modernising the Mental Health Act: Increasing Choice, Reducing Compulsion: Final Report of the Independent Review of the Mental Health Act 1983.* London: Crown.

World Health Organisation. (2020). *Mental Health.* Atlas. Available at: https://www.who.int/publications/i/item/9789240036703.

Yeates, V. (2007) Ambivalence, Contradiction and Symbiosis: Carers' and Mental Health Users' Rights. *Law and Policy*, 29(4), 407–532.

24
CONSENTING FOR PREVENTION
The ethics of ambivalent choice in psychiatric genomics

Camillia Kong

In 2011 my niece Ava was born, a healthy and happy baby. At about 12 months my sister and her husband began noticing unusual aspects of Ava's development: she was crawling fine, but then, at some point she seemed to stop. She could climb the stairs, but suddenly she would sit at the bottom, waiting to be carried up. Her eyes didn't seem to follow that of others and all the usual markers of childhood development – walking, first words – seemed to be delayed. Her breathing started to sound laboured. After many tests and referrals, Ava was diagnosed with Rett Syndrome, a rare genetic neurodevelopmental disorder that occurs almost exclusively in girls, altering brain development which affects speech, eye and body movement, and causes muscle deterioration. Having Rett Syndrome means that Ava will need care for the rest of her life.

The effect of Ava's diagnosis on my sister was profound. She described the period after diagnosis as a period of mourning: of the hopes that she had for Ava, her family, herself, of seeing Ava passing through milestones in life, maturing and flourishing as a woman. From the outside the fact that a parent would grieve the life they had hoped for their child remains intuitively understandable. Emily Rapp dreamed of her son Ronan, born with Tay-Sachs, as being clever, inventive, growing to be physically fearless, adventurous, and loved by all who went out with him – 'I was not above my own prodigy dreams', she writes (Rapp, 2013, p. 16). My sister's love for Ava has led her to pursue every available support and possible therapy to alleviate physical discomfort, every manner of including, accepting, accommodating Ava in their daily routines and family life. But this did not stop my sister from mourning the 'hypothetical child' without Rett Syndrome and continuing to move between poles of acceptance and regret, unconditional love and a desire to ameliorate her condition.

The onset of serious cognitive disabilities raises what Garland-Thomson calls 'a terrible paradox', where children like Ronan and Ava are welcome children with an unwelcome disability (Garland-Thomson, 2012, p. 349). From the perspective of those living with disabilities, who refuse to see themselves as objects of regret and presumed suffering, acknowledging this paradox can appear deeply disrespectful. It can be seen as fundamentally rejecting who they are as persons – as bodies and minds that function differently, enriching our common world. However, the fact of this paradox also speaks to certain features of human life in our pursuit of flourishing, and as such, is intuitively plausible.

It is through this lens that I want to explore the deeper moral unease around the issue of consenting to psychiatric genomics research, with its current preoccupation with the early intervention and prevention of cognitive disabilities. One powerful response to the paradox of 'wanted child but unwanted disability' is to work towards the control and elimination of certain conditions. The aspiration to improve knowledge of the biology behind, as well as advance therapies for, mental and neurodevelopmental disorders, has led to an increasingly genetic turn, both in scientific research and clinical agendas. For the scientific community, psychiatric genomics is thought to be a promising avenue for the early treatment or even prevention of these disorders (Insel and Scolnick, 2006). By enhancing our knowledge of the genetic architecture underlying mental and neurodevelopmental disorders, the hope is that genetic variations may be identified which can be appropriate targets for early intervention strategies, such as through drug treatment or programmes that foster protective variants or preventative mechanisms for at-risk groups. In addition, advancements in precision medicine may result in improved diagnostic testing through the identification of family history risk factors, biomarkers, and the use and application of polygenic risk scores which may enable individuals to make informed reproductive choices (Bloss, Jeste, and Schork, 2011; Sabatello, 2018; criticisms of this agenda by Hoge and Appelbaum, 2012; Kong, Dunn, and Parker, 2017).

In theory, participation in psychiatric genomics research is relatively low-risk and undemanding through the simple provision of a biological sample (usually saliva or blood) to identify and quantify the genetic variations associated with specific phenotypes (or traits) related to certain conditions through genome-wide association studies (GWAS). The putatively low stakes of this research are deceptive, however. The provision of biological samples is itself laden with complicated ethical issues: for instance, the metaphysics of these bodily components in certain cultural contexts highlight an interpretive gulf in conceptual schemas and substantive meaning even around the basic datum sought in psychiatric genomics research, leading to profound implications for informed consent procedures (Kamaara, Kong, and Campbell, 2020; Kong, 2019a).

In its preventative and curative clinical focus individuals who are asked to participate in psychiatric genomics research are effectively consenting to research that seeks to prevent conditions they live with. This initially appears unproblematic: people regularly consent to participate in research that seeks to eliminate long-standing, chronic conditions. The prima facie case for this preventative agenda in psychiatric genomics has also been made from multiple angles: from the public health perspective that such interventions would reduce the disease burden on society (Merikangas and Risch, 2003; Insel, 2009), to bioethical arguments that potential parents have an ethical duty of 'procreative beneficence' to ensure their children have the best opportunities in future and improve general well-being (Savulescu, 2001). The logical conclusion of these bioethical claims is that prospective moral harm might be avoided if certain lives – lives like Ava's and Ronan's – do not come into being, particularly if genetic variations relevant to undesirable conditions can be identified as early as pre-implantation or prenatal genetic testing.

Yet how this early intervention and prevention lens can be reconciled with an orientation of radical acceptance of and respect for individuals with cognitive disabilities remains unclear. Conditions of neurodevelopmental disorders, learning disabilities, or autism, can often be seen as constitutive of personal identity, significantly heightening the ethical stakes of such individuals' participation in psychiatric genomics research as a result. Put baldly, individuals are 'consenting for prevention': consenting to participate in research that may implicitly express the undesirability of constitutive parts of their identity and ways of functioning in the world. This chapter therefore seeks to answer the question: on what ethical grounds can persons with cognitive disabilities consent (or if they cannot consent, their family members consenting on their behalf) to participate in psychiatric genomics research?

Debates on the ethics of consent are limited in providing an answer to this important question, where the focal point tends to revolve around ethically justifiable procedures, epistemic conditions, and criteria on which consent is based. The law is similarly unhelpful. A human rights prism, represented in the United Nations Convention on the Rights of Persons with Disabilities (CRPD), and its empowering ethos towards persons with disabilities, implies the importance of a participatory ethos towards research. This would suggest a reorientation around the 'capacity to consent' procedures, premised more on inclusivity and education rather than screening and safeguarding, to help foster individuals' understanding and ability to enable them to participate in research. Such an orientation would make it putatively easier for individuals to consent to involvement in psychiatric genomics studies.

Ultimately, how persons with lived experience and family members negotiate divergent and conflicting orientations towards disability is key to shedding some light on the ethical dilemma of 'consenting for prevention'. In this chapter, I concentrate on genomics research around cognitive disabilities associated with neurodevelopmental and learning disabilities and autism, where it is questionable to distinguish between the *person-with-x* and the counterfactual *person-without-x*, where the latter is purportedly 'more authentic', as opposed to serious mental disorder with a later manifestation, such as schizophrenia.[1] My argument starts with a deflationary point that consenting for prevention must reflect individual choice. As others have highlighted, however, careful attention must be directed towards the social conditions of choice (Shakespeare, 2005), and fully informed choice in this context means challenging the presumptive rightness of the preventative or curative imperatives that are predominantly espoused in genomic interventions and research. But I want to further suggest that the ethical framing of choice in this context must be attuned to inherently conflictual and sometimes ambivalent evaluative stances towards disability, where subjective and relational perspectives can encompass a full spectrum of regretting, accepting, and embracing features of impairment, and do not provide easy or clear-cut answers to the ethical issue of consenting for prevention. I will argue that consenting for prevention, either by individuals or their family members, can often reflect a negotiation between the poles of acceptance and amelioration of cognitive disability, and this negotiation is ethically warranted for two reasons: first, at a subjective level it is important not to overdetermine what constitutes valid agency on the part of individuals living with disability; second, at a relational or parental level, it is to recognise how tensions expressed in consenting for prevention may reveal an

---

1 One could make the same argument in cases of serious mental disorder as well. But in the context of schizophrenia, it has been noted how family members look to the person prior to their first psychotic episode and how the deterioration of the person's ability to cope seems alien to who the person was previously. The reason for this focus is because one might arguably look to the person and their identity prior to conditions with a later manifestation, such as schizophrenia, whereas the person who is born with a learning disability, autism, or other neurodevelopmental conditions is ostensibly *that* person (where there is no counterfactual, prior individual without the condition). This is not to say that the identity of persons with schizophrenia is not closely tied to aspects of the mental illness (i.e., persons can be deeply attached to the voices or hallucinations that they experience), such that these too can be constitutive parts of their identity.

evaluative framing grounded in the (valid) pursuit of human goodness and flourishing and its vulnerability to tragic reversals.

I start by exploring in the first section of this chapter the limits of a human rights orientation in providing a coherent answer to my central question, revealing the limits of the law and the answers it can provide in this fraught ethical dilemma. Whilst the CRPD seemingly emphasises the importance of subjective choice and the participation of individuals with disabilities, I explore more specifically the importance of choice in its ambiguity: not as a determinate expression of one's subjective viewpoint, wishes, values, etc., but as providing space for ambivalent, incommensurable evaluations that reflect uncertainty and ways of coping with the challenges that can come with living with certain conditions. The subsequent two sections explore this ambivalent space in the context of parents consenting for prevention and how these choices may express the paradox of 'wanted child but unwanted disability'. I suggest that Aristotle's account of human flourishing and tragedy helps illuminate the deeper evaluative roots that embody this contradictory stance.

Limits of a human rights approach and subjective ambivalence towards disability

In recent years the empowering ethos of human rights law has been important for promoting the respectful treatment that is owed to persons with disabilities. The CRPD functions as a key normative vector for much legal scholarship as well as legal reform of mental capacity and mental health regimes, with a particular focus on mechanisms that enhance the participation, inclusion, and dignity of persons who have typically been subject to paternalistic and coercive treatment. Whilst these developments are crucial, the human rights approach to disability can lend itself to divergent, incoherent strands. Closer examination of these tensions reveals the limits of human rights law in resolving the central ethical dilemma around consenting for prevention in psychiatric genomics research.

The CRPD has arguably provided three important shifts: first is a normative emphasis on individuals' empowerment, autonomy, and participation in decisions about their lives, treatment, and so on, in opposition to the paternalistic orientation that has traditionally guided the treatment of those with cognitive disabilities. Regardless of the type or gravity of a decision, persons are owed the 'dignity of risk': the freedom to make choices that might be risky, imprudent, or potentially fail. Second, the social model of disability presumed in the CRPD moves away from the medicalisation of individuals and their conditions: much less than needing to be 'fixed', individuals require and deserve structural and societal accommodations and supports. According to the social model, impairments of the mind and body are value-neutral traits whilst disability is constructed through societal barriers. Third, the notion of universal legal capacity grounds the rights articulated in the CRPD, which brings to the fore sceptical questions about the link between legal capacity and tests of mental capacity or competence which can assess whether persons are able to make decisions about their lives.

This claim about universal legal capacity has both strong and weak interpretations: strong versions are typified in the CRPD Committee's General Comment on Article 12, which deems mental capacity law regimes as fundamentally discriminatory such that legal status and rights cannot be contingently linked to any decision-making threshold or tests (CRPD Committee, 2014). Weak interpretations, by contrast, suggest that certain mechanisms of mental capacity regimes – such as substituted decision-making frameworks – are necessary by virtue of hard cases where the subjective will and preferences of individuals might be difficult to ascertain or lead to clear subjective danger, harm, or abuse (Freeman et al., 2015; Dawson, 2015; Kong, 2015, 2022b).

Some contradictions within a human rights prism to disability become apparent when applied to the context of consenting to be part of psychiatric genomics research. On one hand, we can see that the emphasis on equal participation and the right to make one's own decisions would suggest that persons ought to have the right to be involved in research should they choose to do so. Article 31 of the CRPD, for example, states that research and data should be used 'to identify and address the barriers faced by persons with disabilities in exercising their rights' and 'ensure their accessibility to persons with disabilities and others'. Emphasis on the 'dignity of risk' cautions against the excessive safeguarding orientation that has tended to be the prevailing treatment of persons with disabilities. Part of this empowering ethos extends to revising informed consent procedures – where the participatory and inclusive emphasis in the CRPD challenges more conventional, exclusionary use of decision-making thresholds to ensure informed consent has been legitimately obtained (Kong, Efrem, and Campbell, 2019). These normative imperatives suggest the importance of individuals' participation in psychiatric genomics research and deploying consent tools through a prism of 'education' rather than 'screening'. Whereas conventional informed consent tools for psychiatric genomics research operationalise a binary, threshold concept of capacity to consent – effectively 'testing' individuals to see what they understand about the research – a more inclusive educative prism would facilitate iterative learning, dialogue, creative communicative tools, and relational support, such that consent becomes more of a process and spectrum (Campbell et al., 2017). Given that the consent tools around psychiatric genomics research can involve participants' grasp of complex concepts – such as genetics, DNA, sample storage, and cell line immortalisation[2] – a CRPD lens would, in theory, make participation more accessible and inclusive to individuals of varying cognitive abilities.

On the other hand, the human rights imperative towards more inclusive consent procedures sits incoherently with the negative evaluations of disability that are expressed in the preventative and curative clinical agenda of psychiatric genomics. The CRPD is explicitly committed to the social model of disability that posits the social construction of disabling barriers and focuses on accommodating mind and body difference to secure the equal treatment of persons with cognitive impairments. A core element of the social model is scepticism (in varying degrees) of the medicalisation of disability; yet the ontology of disability presupposed in psychiatric genomics locates disorder firmly within the biogenetic architecture of the individual. As a result, a human rights approach appears to provide an incoherent answer to the problem of consenting for prevention: individuals should be free to consent and indeed, positively enabled to be included in a research and clinical agenda that is, at the same time, fundamentally at odds with core descriptive and normative commitments around disability. To suggest otherwise on ideological grounds would be to revert to an unjustifiable paternalistic orientation towards persons with disabilities who *would* wish to be part of such research. Or it would be to make problematic judgements that those who do consent to participate in psychiatric genomics research, knowing full well its preventative agenda, are effectively choosing heteronomously, inauthentically, or against their better interests (Kong, 2019b).

---

2 This can be aggravated by poor literacy, unfamiliarity with the research process, and completely different conceptual explanatory schemas around certain conditions (see Campbell et al, 2017).

This conundrum shows us two things: first, a limited focus on informed consent in psychiatric genomics only gets us so far, skirting over the ambiguous, conflicting evaluations of disability and the fundamental ethical questions these evoke. Second, the normative limitations of the human rights framework are evident in its incoherent answer to the dilemma of consenting for prevention, where depending on how stridently one might wish to interpret the CRPD and its commitments to the social model, it seems difficult to countenance the ethical permissibility of participating in psychiatric genomics research.

My view is that involvement in psychiatric genomics research should ultimately be based on individual choice. Whilst discussions in bioethics have long attended to the ways in which informed consent preserves the significance of individual autonomy, my emphasis here is how choice must be situated within enriched evaluations of disability that challenge oversimplistic binaries of celebration or amelioration, acceptance or treatment. On one hand, the clinical imperatives fuelling psychiatric genomics research frequently focus on the negative experience of families or on epistemically dubious claims about the purported suffering of individuals living with certain conditions. As written elsewhere, challenging these narratives of suffering are a crucial first step towards resisting reductive narratives around what it means to live with a neurodevelopmental or learning disability or autism (Kong, 2022a; Sabatello, 2019). Psychiatric genomics is not isolated in its predominant evaluations which indicate the undesirability of disability. Writing about prenatal screening, Tom Shakespeare similarly shows how these procedures equate reproductive choice with aborting a disabled foetus, with information overwhelmingly weighted towards the putative challenges and burdens of raising a child with disability as opposed to the first-hand testimony of persons with lived experience or those of their families (Shakespeare, 2005). It is precisely these perspectives that are vital if we are to understand the moral complexities around the question of whether persons with disabilities (or their families) ought to participate in psychiatric genomics research.

Equally, we cannot overdetermine the content of these perspectives and presume that they follow a straightforward narrative that celebrates disability. Experiences of autism and learning or neurodevelopmental disability diverge and vary. Whilst for some, embodiment and mind difference is a constitutive, non-contingent part of one's identity, others speak of a more complicated relationship with their disability which does not reflect a simplistic subjective valuing of disability. First-hand accounts can often illustrate complex negotiations between accepting and rejecting their mind difference, between the intrinsic and socially constructed nature of their disability, between embodiment and environmental, social, and relational contexts. Attending to this spectrum of experience is vital if choice is to reflect the significance of evaluative framings in an enriched way and runs contrary to any notion that subjective agency is only valid if it accords with an emancipatory logic, where socially oppressive norms around disability are actively resisted.

For example, Naoki Higashida writes about his experiences as an autistic individual and the challenges of living in a neurotypical society (2017, 2013). Naoki's narrative attests to the constitutive nature of his autism to his identity – the notion that a 'cure' could fix him by ridding him of his autism is akin to 'an operation to effect a root and branch change to who and what you are and remove all meaning from everything you thought was beautiful and precious' (Naoki, 2017, p. 261). His rich account simultaneously affirms the irreplaceable value of how different minds perceive and interact with the world whilst describing his own periodic ambivalence and distress of being autistic in a neurotypical world. As Naoki indicates, the medicalisation of autism has cultivated negative, stigmatising societal attitudes that are then internalised, affecting his own self-acceptance and self-esteem. He recounts his own profound desire as a child to no longer have his autism, writing:

> A long time ago I used to dream that I was a neurotypical child. In these dreams I was forever laughing, chatting away and swapping jokes with my friends and family. My Dream Me forgot all about My Real Me here in the waking world. Then I would wake up and return to myself, but I'd be clueless about where I was or what on earth I was doing in this place. When I finally realised I'd been dreaming, I'd well up and tears would spill down my face.
> (Naoki, 2017, p. 179)

And though Naoki's account is one where he ultimately accepts and comes to value his autism, he is alive to the challenges which, at various times, have not precluded his own desire to rid himself of what he sees as a constitutive part of his identity. As he states, '[E]ven though I envy My Dream Me, these days it's a bit of a relief to get back to who I really am' (Naoki, 2017, p. 180).

Naoki's occasional ambivalence, where he yearns to be 'normal' as opposed to autistic, reflects a complex dynamic where constitutive identity involves mediating between socially constructed as well as innate challenges. The phenomenology of being a person with core perceptual divergences in a neurotypical world indicates challenges that can go beyond social prejudice, where a person's very perceptual architecture may depart in fundamental ways, meaning they cannot share features of a common life which help most of us navigate the world relatively unobstructed, such as a sense of time, spatial awareness, and social meaning (Ratcliffe, 2012). This does mean that it is incumbent on others to cultivate an ethical orientation comprised of attitudinal and interpretive skills that help make sense of such divergent ways of experiencing the world, to help forge that commonality (Kong, 2023). But the reality remains that, even in the most idealised and socially equitable circumstances, limits to one's understanding create residual challenges for the individual whose mind difference means moving and perceiving the world in radically different ways (see Shakespeare, 2013). For some, this may lead to a more nuanced relationship with their disability that oscillates between a yearning to be and rejection of being 'normal', even as that disability is nonetheless understood as a core part of who they are. Or it may even involve a subjective commitment to pursuing the things that appear to be 'normal' as an assertion that they too belong and are not the exception in a neurotypical society (Kong, 2019b; Schriempf, 2001).

Making space for these complex dialectical negotiations between internal discomfort with oneself and responding to social prejudice are also important in the context of psychiatric genomics research. The temptation is to assume that those individuals wishing to ameliorate features of their cognitive disability or autism – even to the point of wishing they could be 'normal' as opposed to a person with a particular mind difference – have internalised oppressive social narratives such that the authenticity of these choices may be in question. This angle, however, understands individual's agency and choice-making in a deterministic fashion, reducing free choice to that which challenges and rejects socially oppressive norms around disability. The more complex – and I would suggest realistic – picture is where personal identity and its emanating agency can also reflect the acceptance and inhabitation of social norms that one purportedly ought to reject (Lester and Tritter, 2005). Persons with lived experience may therefore wish to consent to participate in research that prevents core aspects of their identity, based on evaluations of disability which reflect their own subjective ambivalence. This possibility means that there must be space for consenting for prevention at the individual level, despite the questionable ontology and evaluation of disability in the psychiatric genomics agenda. To suggest otherwise is to normatively prescribe overly reductive tramlines of legitimate agency in a manner that belies the multi-faceted and sometimes contradictory navigation of disability as a constitutive part of self.

Ambivalence in families

Despite the valid unease around preventative genetic technologies from the perspective of those with lived experience, I have highlighted that choice can be situated within subjective ambivalence, even in cases where the purported impairment can be seen as a core part of their identity. The ethical nuances of consenting for prevention emerge more fully when we consider the experiences of parents, and for the remainder of the chapter I want to concentrate on the ethical justification behind this more relational perspective (see also Widdershoven et al., 2017). I have little doubt, for example, that my sister would have consented on Ava's behalf to participate in research into the genetics of Rett Syndrome – the imperative to prevent or cure her condition would have been a central reason *for* rather than against it. Equally, my sister is tireless in advocating for Ava and her inclusion in society, in challenging the discrimination that Ava experiences in her daily life. How are we to make sense of these seemingly contradictory impulses – can the desire to find a treatment for Ava sit side by side with acceptance of her? How does making sense of this contradiction provide further insight into the evaluative framing about disability within which informed choice about psychiatric genomics research must be situated?

Andrew Solomon sheds some light into this dynamic in his book, *Far from the Tree*. He explains how the hopes and aspirations attached to having children are often bound up with the idea of transmitting some of our traits to the next generation – what he calls 'vertical identities'. This manifests itself, not just in our genes, but also constituents of our socio-cultural identity, our ethnicity, religious faith, and so on. The challenge, however, is when a child has an obvious *horizontal* identity: an acquired trait that seems foreign to the parents that may reflect genetic mutations, prenatal influences, or extreme variation in values and preferences. Whereas vertical identities tend to be affirmed and respected, both within families and in society, horizontal identities are often treated as defects, often due to the discomfort that these identities may present to parents (rather than to the child).

The challenge of disability as a horizontal identity is captured in the different evaluations that characterise prospective and retrospective viewpoints of parents. Jeff McMahan suggests that the prospective parent who views genetic screening for disability as permissible expresses the evaluative principle that it would be a better outcome to have a 'normal' as opposed to a 'disabled' child, on the presumption that the chances of higher well-being correlate with having a child without disability, all other things being equal. This amounts to an impersonal (if ultimately contentious) evaluation premised on the purported well-being of the prospective child, but perhaps even more so to hypothetical projections of the well-being of the prospective parents as they assess the putative burdens and responsibilities of having a child with potentially demanding disability (McMahan, 2005).

By contrast, retrospective perspectives of parents often reflect an altogether different evaluation of disability that is premised on the reality of how and what it means to parent a child with disability. In contrast to prospective views, retrospective evaluations tend to express the judgement that their child with disability enhances the lives of those around them in positive ways. Solomon's book provides rich examples of such retrospective evaluations where parents would not 'trade' their child for an abstract non-disabled child. For instance, Bill Zirinsky and Ruth Schekter had two children with severe and undiagnosed degenerative disabilities, Sam and Juliana. Both died at about nine years old. After the death of Juliana, Bill recounted that he 'would have chosen the easier path' (Solomon, 2012, p. 378). However,

> [N]ow, knowing what I know, I would want Sam again, and I would want Juliana again. How could I trade the love I experienced with these two human beings? I was closer to Sam than any human being in my life. I spent more time lying on a bed with him, looking in his eyes, than anyone I've ever been with. I've spent a huge amount of time with Juliana, just hanging out with her, just loving her. So that's like asking any parent whether they would trade the love that they know for some abstract 'better' child. I would do it again.
>
> *(Solomon, 2012, p. 378)*

The experiences of parents like Bill and Ruth illustrate how, when faced with an abstract 'normal' child or *their* real child with disability, they would often choose the latter – even if it means undergoing the same tragic losses. These retrospective evaluations express a more holistic view that 'those disabled people *who actually exist* are not burdensome but enrich the lives of their parents and others' (McMahan, 2005, p. 166).

Prospective and retrospective judgements are on a par according to McMahan – both are equally defensible and rational but premised on incommensurable evaluations about life with a disabled child – though he does validate the concern about the negative valuation of disability in prospective views, which he ultimately suggests might be mitigated through public recognition or the social promotion of more positive evaluations that ground retrospective perspectives (McMahan, 2005). Such recommendations tend to be weak, however. Within the psychiatric genomics agenda, for example, little, if any, research is designed with an equal emphasis on the experiences of persons living with disability, let alone to accommodate the positive evaluations that may characterise the retrospective perspective of parents. Without some substantive attempts to integrate such experiences, it seems highly unlikely that the mere social acknowledgement of the values expressed in retrospective evaluations is sufficient to mitigate the overwhelmingly negative evaluation of disability presupposed in the psychiatric genomics agenda.

Many have also posed counterarguments to McMahan's analysis (Kittay, 2005, 2019; Barnes, 2014), and some have highlighted that the absence of nuanced information about the real experiences and life of what it means to parent a disabled child suggests that evaluations of the prospective parent fail to be informed in the fullest sense (Shakespeare, 2005). Whilst this is ultimately true, what interests me more, however, are divergences within retrospective evaluations – amongst parents who do have a disabled child. This matters because a common justification for the curative and preventative orientation of psychiatric genomics is to relieve the putative burden and suffering of families (Hens, Peeters, and Dierickx, 2016). Strong empirical evidence indicates more positive evaluations about life parenting a child with disability, such that parents do not regret the existence of their child and adapt to any potential challenges; however, it is also important to note that retrospective evaluations are far from uniform. For some, raising a child with severe cognitive disability is too much responsibility, as shown in the account of Julia Hollander, whose daughter, Imogen, was born with severe cerebral palsy. After months of struggling and eventually reaching close to breaking point, Hollander handed her child over to a foster carer. She described the 'confusing business [of] mourning for someone who is alive' (Solomon, 2012, p. 395). She also recounts her ambivalence about parenting Imogen:

> Every time she's around, I experiment with being the mother of the disabled child. People walking along the pavement get out of the way and smile at you, that smile that goes, 'You poor thing, I'm glad I'm not you!' I can imagine polishing my halo at the end of every day. At the very same time, I can imagine being the most furious person in the world.
>
> *(Solomon, 2012, p. 399)*

Hollander's frank account has been the subject of virulent criticism, which reflects as much about the socio-cultural norms around motherhood (and her putative violation of them) as it does the discomfort with the narrative of pity, frustration, and deficit she uses to describe her child with disability. One need not go so far as to endorse Hollander's choices or her evaluation of what life with Imogen looks like to nonetheless acknowledge the sometimes ambivalent and contradictory spaces that can characterise familial experiences of grappling with the horizontal identities of one's disabled children. Solomon's chapter on autism sums up well the pitfalls that come from overly reductive narratives about disability either way:

> Two diametrically opposite fictions contribute to a single set of problems. The first comes from the autism parents' literature of miracles. In its most extreme form, it describes beautiful boys and girls emerging from their affliction as if it were a passing winter frost, and, after wild parental heroics, dancing off into springtime fields of violets, fully verbal, glowing with the fresh ecstasy of unselfconscious charm. Such narratives of false hope eviscerate families who are struggling with the diagnosis. The other plotline is that the child does not get better, but the parents grow enough to celebrate him rather than seek to improve him and are fully content with that shift. This whitewashes difficulties that many families face and can obfuscate autism's authentic deficits. While the lives of many people who have autism remain somewhat inscrutable, the lives of many people whose children have autism are mostly avowedly hard – some, excruciatingly so. Social prejudice aggravates the difficulty, but it is naïve to propose that it's all about social prejudice; having a child who does not express love in a comprehensible way is devastating, and having a child who is awake all night, who requires constant supervision, and who screams and tantrums but cannot communicate the reasons for or the nature of his upset – these experiences are confusing, overwhelming, exhausting, unrewarding. The problem can be mitigated by some combination of treatment and acceptance, specific to each case. It is important not to get carried away by either the impulse only to treat or the impulse only to accept.
>
> *(Solomon, 2012, p. 288)*

Amongst the parents interviewed in Solomon's book is an immense adaptability in their quest to establish bonds of mutuality with one's disabled or autistic child. But part of understanding the richness of such adaptability comes through acknowledging the messy realities that transcend the reductive impulse to either champion disability or concentrate solely on its challenges and their amelioration – for some parents, the quest for mutuality is an ongoing struggle. A more rounded evaluation of the curative and preventative psychiatric genomics agenda must simultaneously be responsive to the three-dimensional realities and uphold an aspirational normative vision that accords respect and worth to the lives of persons with disability. Acknowledging the coexistence of valuing and loving your child whilst seeking amelioration of constitutive facets of that particular child may be key to advancing this more nuanced evaluation.

Avoiding the reductive impulse to either champion disability or concentrate solely on its challenges and their amelioration helps us in two ways: first, we better understand the phenomenology of the paradox of 'wanted child but unwanted disability' and the negotiation of agency in this ambiguous terrain. Second, we can help articulate more clearly the ethical grounding of such ambivalent motivation and choices – these revolve around moral claims of the contingency of human flourishing and our response in the face of tragic reversals. Understanding the liminal experiences of parents and families requires making conceptual and ethical space for their sense of reversals in human goodness, particularly as they grapple with the paradox of 'wanted child but unwanted disability'. Here I think philosophical discussions of luck and tragedy are particularly helpful in carving out and making sense of this space – especially as much of the preventative and curative agenda of psychiatric genomics is related to fundamental questions about the extent to which we can control and mitigate the arbitrariness of luck at the genetic level.

Consenting for prevention through the lens of Aristotelian tragedy

In her memoir, Rapp writes of her anguish when her son, Ronan, is diagnosed with Tay-Sachs disease. Despite a negative prenatal screen, the test had failed to detect rare genetic mutations that resulted from her Moroccan heritage, making her and her husband both unsuspecting carriers of the disease. Rapp describes her desire to 'untangle [Ronan's] DNA, restitch it, rebraid it, fix it, make it right, take it back somehow, change the odds' (Rapp, 2013, p. 88). The rare genetic odds make her ponder the nature of luck: of how luck is contrary to goodness, like when 'good' people experience irrevocable reversals and heartbreak. Fear of the endless possibilities created by luck animates the motivation to control it, remove it through self-improvement, deny it of its power to disrupt our lives. She concludes, 'We quite simply, do not have any control, not really, and this is the hardest lesson to learn' (Rapp, 2013, p. 88). On one hand, her deepest wish is to eradicate the source of Ronan's disease and decaying body; on the other is the acknowledgement that such aspirations to exert control and eradicate luck as much as possible, to insulate herself from its influence, are all illusory and indeed, flatten human value to that of control and self-transformation.

That the experience of parents loving children with serious disabilities leads to profound questions around the interplay between luck and human goodness is not unusual. Narratives like Rapp's capture an ancient philosophical debate around the extent to which our pursuit of human good(s) can be self-sufficient and insulated from contingency and vulnerability. How much luck is enough to imperil human goodness? Are human goods fragile by their very nature, or are our ultimate goods ones which embody self-sufficiency and control? As Nussbaum argues, our fraught relationship with luck, where openness to fortune intermingles with resilience, attests to two incommensurable kinds of values – of 'what is ours and what belongs to the world ... of making and being made' which pull us in sometimes opposite directions. Pindar describes the flourishing life as a plant, but 'the tenderness of a plant is not the dazzling hardness of a gem' (Nussbaum, 2001, p. 2). The paradox of 'wanted child but unwanted disability', of parental impulses of acceptance and amelioration of disability, can embody this dialectic between 'making' and 'being made' in the pursuit of human flourishing, which may well lead some to consent for prevention, knowing full well that the curative and preventative focus of psychiatric genomics seeks to eliminate the child they have grown to love. From one end of the spectrum, Plato claims that flourishing is bound up with an ultimate good that is within one's rational control, free of contingency and attachment, thus making it effectively invulnerable to luck. By contrast, the Aristotelian conception of luck and tragedy stems from a moral theory that acknowledges the fragility of the goods that comprise a flourishing life, observed through an approach that ultimately seeks to 'save the appearances', or the kernel of truth within the empirical phenomena and commonsense intuitions. The virtue of bringing Aristotle to bear in my discussion is in its ability to help shed light on the ethical truth that may be embedded in the paradoxical imperatives characterising parental experiences, capturing this complex phenomenology as well as the ethical grounding for such ambivalent motivation and agency.

In his exploration of the nature of *eudaimonia* or human flourishing, Aristotle in *Nicomachean Ethics I* emphasises that engaging in a certain kind of virtuous *activity* is necessary to become *eudaimon*. But this requires external goods, such as friends, a certain level of resources, the thriving of our children, political citizenship. Though not exclusively coextensive with the good, these external goods and attachments help enrich our lives and help enable the noble acts that are conducive to goodness, likewise enhancing our enjoyment of virtuous activity (as seen in Aristotle's discussion of virtue friendship and political citizenship). Our lack of self-sufficiency distinguishes human activities and pursuits from that of the gods. In making space for external goods and attachments in the flourishing life, Aristotle is suggesting that aspects of the good life are vulnerable. Luck and fortune can sometimes have a profound effect in our pursuit of *eudaimonia*: 'many changes occur in life' and 'all manner of chances' which may mean 'the most prosperous may fall into great misfortunes', where Aristotle cites Priam as an example of one who has 'experienced such chances and has ended wretchedly' (Aristotle, 1984a, 1109a6–9). Virtuous character *can* be disrupted by reversals in fortune – these reversals can be so extreme that one is no longer considered *eudaimon*. The nobility of the person of virtuous character might still shine through in their response to such misfortune nonetheless. But equally, Aristotle does not shy away from the possibility that reversals in fortune may present serious impediments to virtuous activity, making *eudaimonia* more elusive in certain circumstances.

This space for vulnerability, contingency, and tragic reversals in his moral theory likewise informs his perspective on the ethical function of tragedy in poetry and drama. Aristotle suggests that tragic drama arouses feelings of pity and fear which can be illuminating. In the *Rhetoric* Aristotle describes pity as 'the feeling of pain at an apparent evil, destructive or painful, which befalls one who does not deserve it' and its self-directed fear is that of which 'we might expect [these apparent evils] to befall ourselves or some friend of ours' (Aristotle, 1984b, 1385b13–15). These evils overlap with the loss of external goods outlined in *NE*, such as bodily injury, poor health, friendlessness, deformity, mutilation, the decline and death of one's children and city, 'evil coming from a source from which good ought to have come' (1386a11–12). Witnessing the tragic hero's reversals in luck evokes responses of pity and fear because we observe the unexpected happenings which compromise the hero's ability to achieve a flourishing life. The force of contingency forces her to act in limited circumstances or curtails the actions that are constitutive of the good life, sometimes causing her to choose wrongly in the face of such circumstances.

The feelings of fear and pity elicited by the dramatic arc of tragic heroes have an important philosophic and ethical function. It is philosophic in the sense that it depicts and enhances our understanding of human possibilities (Nussbaum, 1992). To trigger this learning and reflection demands seeing similarities between ourselves and the tragic protagonist. We identify with her; we can see ourselves in her shoes. We see ourselves as parents or potential parents of children whose thriving is thwarted, or citizens witnessing the decay of a beloved city, or virtuous individuals forced to act out of necessity, resulting in devastating consequences – generally agents of good character who are likewise vulnerable to undeserved bad happenings. She stands for the possibilities for us humans – not just of how changes in one's circumstances occur, but how one potentially acts and responds to such circumstances.

Our responses to perceived tragedy also have an ethical function. The experience of fear and pity provides a subjective hook for spectators of tragic drama, broadening insight into the nature of the good, making it all the more real: on one hand, we are faced with the force of contingency in the unfolding of a human life, the vulnerability of the human good to reversals in fortune through unexpected circumstances. On the other hand, observing the fact of fragile goods in isolation could lead to resignation, quietist acquiescence to the force of fortune and what is given by the world. But this is not Aristotle's point – in Rorty's words:

> [T]ragic drama shows that what is central to excellence in action – what is intrinsic to the very nature of action – carries the possibility of a certain kind of arrogance and presumption. ... The lesson of tragedy is not that we should know more, think more carefully; or that we should become more modest and less impetuously stubborn than the protagonists of tragic dramas. Because it is no accident that excellence sometimes undoes itself, one of the dark lessons of tragedy is that there are no lessons to be learnt, in order to avoid tragedy.
>
> *(Rorty, 1992, pp. 17, 18)*

In other words, it is in our nature to pursue human goods, to seek excellence in our lives, to try and achieve flourishing. But paradoxically, efforts to safeguard and insulate our goods through strategies which try to control and limit tragedy in our lives can ultimately result in moral hubris – namely the presumption that tragic reversals and misfortune are avoidable entirely by our own efforts. When unconstrained by humility, the drive for control can blind us from certain truths about the nature of human goods and how they fit into our lives. But contact with the uncontrollable through first-hand experience and second-hand observation cultivates that all-important humility and attunement towards the suffering of others. For Aristotle, responses of pity and fear, combined with the impulse to share in the sorrow of other, effectively deepens our understanding of the power of chance in the thriving of virtuous character, of the unchosen barriers which block the achievement of human goodness and flourishing, and importantly, of the mutual assistance we require to meet, if not overcome, such barriers (Nussbaum, 1992). Such 'overcoming' is not necessarily equivalent to exerting greater control of unchangeable circumstances, but, rather, engaging in actions that allow the nobility of character to 'shine through'.

How tragedy illuminates something about the nature of human goods likewise helps capture several important points about what is being expressed in the choice to consent for prevention in psychiatric genomics research. First, we can see with greater clarity the phenomenology at play within the paradox of 'wanted child but unwanted disability' and how it is an exemplar of our vulnerable pursuit of human flourishing. Tragedy in Aristotle's sense tracks well the phenomenology of the parental quest for mutuality with a child with serious disability – the sense of loss, of misfortune and bad luck when they find out that their child will not thrive the 'conventional way', especially if it is apparent that their child will miss out on some goods that are seen as integral to the flourishing life. Regret, confusion, and a sense of acting within the conditions of necessity comingle with love, care, and acceptance. The tenuous nature of control involved in pursuing excellence contains inherent tensions, as illustrated acutely in Rapp's case. For instance, even with all her and her husband's efforts to control, know, plan, display foresight – all is undone by a tragic reversal of circumstances when her son is diagnosed with Tay-Sachs. And this sense of incommensurability – of unconditional love and acceptance battling with sorrow and regret, of 'heightened presence and constant mourning' – teaches Rapp how to 'move around in the world, even if it made me feel vulnerable and raw, bright and strange' (Rapp, 2013, pp. 177, 149). She describes the human temptation towards moral arrogance when good fortune accompanies the pursuit of human excellence, writing:

> Saying 'I'm so lucky' might feel to some like a priestly incantation, the casting of a protective spell that makes people believe that they're standing on solid ground, far from catastrophe, while the unlucky folks within shouting distance squirm around in the quicksand with their cancer and diseases and dying babies. … It is mistaken for thankfulness, but it's not; it's smug and congratulatory, as if bad luck were a mischievous old gossipy lady with bad breath and kleptomania whom *you*, super smarty-pants you, were wise enough to kick out of your house before she slipped the family jewels into her big ugly purse while everyone else was stupid enough to let her in and serve her expensive chocolates and cups of champagne.
>
> *(Rapp, 2013, pp. 92–93)*

From the initial sense of bad luck, of feeling the raw edge of unfulfilled expectation, comes the realisation that this is the nature of hoping for, investing in, and pursuing human goods that may or may not come to fruition. Openness to the world is a necessary orientation to experience these goods; such openness equally makes the achievement of human flourishing fragile. Rapp's experience of the beauty and wonder of Ronan's brief life comes in equal measure to her attunement to his debilitating illness and the terrible realisation that she would bear witness to his death.

Even so, nobility of character can still shine through in these circumstances. And this leads to my second point: Aristotelian tragedy can help articulate more clearly the ethical grounding and moral significance of agency in such ambivalent spaces. Through this lens we can point to a deeper reason why prospective and retrospective perspectives are not ethically on a par, contra McMahan. Whilst the choice that emerges from a prospective evaluation expresses an (understandable) impulse to exert as much control as possible and insulate oneself from (what is perceived as) misfortune, retrospective evaluations are often attuned to the ways in which human goodness involves making choices and acting in ways that navigate between 'what is made' and 'being made'. Nobility of character emerges with the insight about the fragile nature of goods and the *adaptation* of this account to make space for *all* bodies and minds, not least one's own child. Such differences may make certain notions of flourishing out of reach, but for many families, there is a recognition that their disabled child has made a profound contribution to their understanding of human possibilities (Kittay, 2019). This should not be understood as attributing an instrumental function to persons with impairments, as implying the existence of such persons is worthwhile only for the broader learning of others. But Naoki, for example, gives his own reasons for why he believes people with autism exist in the world:

> Those who are determined to live with us and not give up on us are deeply compassionate people, and this kind of compassion must be a key to humanity's long-term survival. Even when the means of self-expression and/or intelligence are lacking, we still respond to love. Knowing we are cherished is a source of hope. ... Every single time someone treats me with kindness, my determination to live well from tomorrow is rejuvenated. This is how I feel empowered to give something back to my family and society, even if my contribution is modest.
>
> *(Naoki, 2017, pp. 262, 264)*

The compassion and love that characterises Naoki's family, the intuitive efforts of parents to convey inclusion and acceptance whilst, at the same time, fighting for therapies to foster unique potential or delay and prevent the atrophy of mind or body, may be examples of nobility in the face of tragic circumstances, as defined in the Aristotelian sense. Indeed, such responses embody his ethical doctrine around the constancy of virtue, that 'the expression of nobility in the midst of great suffering can carry its own form of *eudaimonia*, despite the loss of goods that normally constitute happiness' (Rorty, 1992, p. 18). The experiences of parents who struggle to but still forge bonds of mutuality with children possessing horizontal identities may reveal a path towards an *extraordinary* rather than ordinary sense of *eudaimonia*: the agency that expresses acceptance and inclusion with periodic regret and sadness, may show us yet another class of noble action that can constitute its own form of flourishing. This quest reflects the pursuit of something inherently valuable – the health and flourishing of our children – and about the need for compassion, understanding, and mutual support in light of one's tenuous hold on valuable human goods. Ethical agency is precisely about negotiating the uncertain poles of control and luck and finding some space for greater self-sufficiency and acceptance. As Solomon writes, 'Having exceptional children exaggerates parental tendencies; those who would be bad parents become awful parents, but those who would be good parents often become extraordinary' (Solomon, 2012, p. 6).

Conclusion

The expressive content of psychiatric genomics research can be devaluing to individuals living with disability and for this reason, I would recommend caution against individuals as well as parents consenting to involve their children in research that fundamentally seeks to cure or prevent constitutive parts of their identity. As I have written elsewhere, I take it as putatively right that an orientation of respect towards the subjective experience of cognitive disability and mental disorder must be better integrated in psychiatric genomics research, meaning the ways in which research is formulated and structured requires serious revision (Kong, 2022a). From my analysis above, the worry about the curative and preventative agenda of psychiatric genomics ultimately remains unresolved.

However, what I have tried to do in this chapter is look beyond the problematic evaluation of disability within psychiatric genomics and instead articulate the ethical grounding implicit in consenting for prevention. Since the CRPD has formed such an influential normative vector in advocacy, law reform, and academic discussion, a human rights law prism may seem the logical approach in answering this ethical dilemma. But alongside the incoherent answer that results, an ideological commitment to the social model of disability in human rights law could potentially dismiss the choices of those individuals who have a more equivocal experience of their disability – those who see their disability as constitutive of themselves but also yearn to be 'normal' in a neurotypical society. The complex motives as to why one may consent to psychiatric genomics research ultimately resides in the subjective ambivalence towards one's disability, as well as the equivocation of parents who see their child's disability as a tragic loss, but eventually find a way out of the paradox of 'wanted child but unwanted disability'.

This does not mean that we ignore the harm that can be and is endemic to the negative evaluations of disability intrinsic to the curative and preventative agenda of psychiatric genomics. But I have tried to understand the grey area where the desire to temper or remove perceptions of barriers in the flourishing of others can sit alongside love and acceptance in the choice to participate. As Aristotle shows, the navigation of these seemingly contrary poles reveals the prima facie value of certain human goods – of which includes social belonging and the flourishing of our children – the vulnerability of those goods to luck, and the possibility of moral virtue in light of this contingency. The question of consenting for prevention is but a microcosm of more foundational questions about luck and human goodness and hence why the ethical dilemma around genetic interventions remains so fraught. Ultimately, encountering and living through the vulnerability of these goods reveals opportunities for *eudaimonia* in the extraordinary sense. Cognitive disability as experienced by persons themselves and their parents forces us to explore such avenues of *eudaimonia*, recognising that these may not be found in simplistic binaries of championing or ameliorating disability, but in the ambivalent spaces between.

References

Aristotle (1984a) *Nicomachean ethics*. Trans. W.D. Ross, revised J.O. Urmson. In *The Complete Works of Aristotle; The Revised Oxford Translation*, ed. Barnes, J. Princeton: Princeton University Press.

Aristotle (1984b) *Rhetoric*. Trans. W. Rhys Roberts. In *The Complete Works of Aristotle*, ed. Barnes, J. Princeton: Princeton University Press.

Barnes, E. (2014) 'Valuing disability, causing disability', *Ethics*, 125(1), pp. 88–113.

Bloss, C.S., Jeste, D.V. and Schork, N.J. (2011) 'Genomics for disease treatment and prevention', *Psychiatric Clinics*, 34(1), pp. 147–166.

Campbell, M.M., et al. (2017) 'Using iterative learning to improve understanding during the informed consent process in a South African psychiatric genomics study', *PLOS ONE*, 12(11), p. e0188466.

Committee on the Rights of Persons with Disabilities (2014) General comment no. 1, article 12: Equal recognition before the law. 11th session, March 31–April 11, 2014. https://documents-dds-ny.un.org/doc/UNDOC/GEN/G14/031/20/PDF/G1403120.pdf?OpenElement (accessed 21 July 2022).

Dawson, J. (2015) 'A realistic approach to assessing mental health laws' compliance with the UNCRPD', *International Journal of Law and Psychiatry*, 40, pp. 70–79.

Freeman, M.C., et al. (2015) 'Reversing hard won victories in the name of human rights: A critique of the general comment on article 12 of the UN convention on the rights of persons with disabilities', *The Lancet Psychiatry*, 2(9), pp. 844–850.

Garland Thomson, R. (2012) 'The case for conserving disability', *Journal of Bioethical Inquiry*, 9(3), pp. 339–355.

Hens, K., Peeters, H. and Dierickx, K. (2016) 'Genetic testing and Counselling in the case of an autism diagnosis: A caregivers perspective', *European Journal of Medical Genetics*, 59(9), pp. 452–458.

Hoge, S.K. and Appelbaum, P.S. (2012) 'Ethics and neuropsychiatric genetics: A review of major issues', *International Journal of Neuropsychopharmacology*, 15(10), pp. 1547–1557.

Insel, T.R. and Scolnick, E.M. (2006) 'Cure therapeutics and strategic prevention: Raising the bar for mental health research', *Molecular Psychiatry*, 11(1), pp. 11–17.
Insel, T.R. (2009) 'Translating scientific opportunity into public health impact: A strategic plan for research on mental illness', *Archives of General Psychiatry*, 66(2), pp. 128–133.
Kamaara, E., Kong, C. and Campbell, M. (2020) 'Prioritising African perspectives in psychiatric genomics research: Issues of translation and informed consent', *Developing World Bioethics*, 20(3), pp. 139–149.
Kittay, E.F. (2005) 'At the margins of moral personhood', *Ethics*, 116(1), pp. 100–131.
Kittay, E.F. (2019) *Learning from my daughter: The value and care of disabled minds*. New York: Oxford University Press.
Kong, C. (2015) 'The Convention on the Rights of Persons with Disabilities and Article 12: Prospective feminist lessons against the "will and preferences" paradigm', *Laws*, 4(4), pp. 709–728.
Kong, C. (2019a) 'Cultural translation, human meaning, and genes: Why interpretation matters in psychiatric genomics', in Frimpong-Mansoh, Y. A. and Atuire, C. A. (eds.) *Bioethics in Africa: Theories and praxis*. Wilmington: Vernon Press, pp. 95–112.
Kong, C. (2019b) 'Constructing female sexual and reproductive agency in mental capacity law', *International Journal of Law and Psychiatry*, 66, p. 101488.
Kong, C. (2022a) 'Balancing prevention and respect: The ethical stakes of a psychiatric genomics lens for mental disorder and intellectual disability', in Tsermpini, E. E., et al. (eds.) *Psychiatric genomics*. London: Elsevier.
Kong, C. (2022b) 'The significance of strong evaluation and narrativity in supporting capacity', in Donnelly, M., et al. (eds.) *Supporting legal capacity in socio-legal context*. Oxford: Hart, pp. 57–74.
Kong, C. (2023) 'The phenomenology and ethics of P-centricity in mental capacity law', *Law and Philosophy* 42(2), pp. 145–175.
Kong, C., Dunn, M. and Parker, M. (2017) 'Psychiatric genomics and mental health treatment: Setting the ethical agenda', *American Journal of Bioethics*, 17(4), pp. 3–12.
Kong, C., Efrem, M. and Campbell, M. (2019) 'Education versus screening: The use of capacity to consent tools in psychiatric genomics', *Journal of Medical Ethics*, 46(2), pp. 137–143.
Lester, H. and Tritter, J.Q. (2005) 'Listen to my madness': Understanding the experiences of people with serious mental illness', *Sociology of Health and Illness*, 27(5), pp. 649–669.
McMahan, J. (2005) 'Preventing the existence of people with disabilities', in Wasserman, D., et al. (eds.) *Quality of life and human difference: Genetic testing, health care, and disability*. Cambridge: Cambridge University Press, pp. 142–171.
Merikangas, K.R. and Risch, N. (2003) 'Genomic priorities and public health', *Science*, 302(5645), pp. 599–601.
Naoki, H. (2017) *Fall down seven times, get up eight*. Trans. Mitchell, D. and Yoshida, K.A. London: Spectre.
Naoki, H. (2013) *The reason I Jump*. Trans. Mitchell, D. London: Spectre.
Nussbaum, M.C. (2001) *The fragility of goodness: Luck and ethics in Greek tragedy and philosophy*. Cambridge: Cambridge University Press.
Nussbaum, M.C. (1992) 'Tragedy and self-sufficiency: Plato and Aristotle on fear and pity', in Rorty, A. O. (ed.) *Essays on Aristotle's poetics*. Princeton: Princeton University Press, pp. 261–290.
Rapp, E. (2013) *The still point of the turning world*. London: Two Roads.
Ratcliffe, M. (2012) 'Phenomenology as a form of empathy', *Inquiry*, 55(5), pp. 473–495.
Rorty, A.O. (1992) 'The psychology of Aristotelian tragedy', in Rorty, A. O. (ed.) *Essays on Aristotle's poetics*. Princeton: Princeton University Press, pp. 1–22.
Sabatello, M. (2018) 'Precision medicine, health disparities, and ethics: The case for disability inclusion', *Genetics in Medicine*, 20(4), pp. 397–399.
Sabatello, M. (2019) 'Cultivating inclusivity in precision medicine research: Disability, diversity, and cultural competence', *Journal of Community Genetics*, 10(3), pp. 363–373.
Savulescu, J. (2001) 'Procreative beneficence: Why we should select the best children', *Bioethics*, 15(5–6), pp. 413–426.
Schriempf, A. (2001) '(Re)fusing the amputated body: An interactionist bridge for feminism and disability', *Hypatia*, 16(4), pp. 53–79.
Shakespeare, T. (2013) *Disability rights and wrongs revisited*. London: Routledge.

Shakespeare, T. (2005) 'The social context of individual choice', in Wasserman, D., et al. (eds.) *Quality of life and human difference: Genetic testing, health care, and disability*. Cambridge: Cambridge University Press, pp. 217–236.

Solomon, A. (2012). *Far from the tree: Parents, children and the search for identity*. New York: Simon and Schuster.

Widdershoven, G., Voskes, Y. and Meynen, G. (2017) 'Psychiatric genomics and the role of the family: Beyond the doctor–patient relationship', *American Journal of Bioethics*, 17(4), pp. 20–22.

PART 6

Developments in specific regions and jurisdictions

25
CHANGE OR IMPROVEMENT?[1]
Mental health law reform in Africa

Heléne Combrinck

Introduction

Although the adoption of the Convention on the Rights of Persons with Disabilities (CRPD) in 2006 offered significant promise for advancing the rights of persons with disabilities in general, it can be said that persons with psychosocial disabilities[2] had particular reason for optimism. The recognition of universal legal capacity in Article 12 of the CRPD, accompanied by state obligations to provide access to support for exercising legal capacity, appeared to open new prospects for persons with psychosocial disabilities to reclaim their autonomy and assert the rights guaranteed in the Convention. The potential for persons with psychosocial disabilities inherent in the CRPD is not limited to Article 12: together with legal capacity, the right to liberty and security of the person (Article 14), the prohibition of torture and cruel, inhuman or degrading treatment (Article 15), the right to freedom from exploitation, violence and abuse (Article 16) and the protection of physical and mental integrity (Article 17) can be said to embody the 'paradigm shift' brought about by the Convention in respect of psychosocial disability.

One of the consequences of ratifying the CRPD is that States Parties are obliged to review and reform existing laws and policies. Several 'new' mental health laws have accordingly seen the light, and as 16 years have passed since the birth of the Convention, an examination of recently enacted mental health legislation is due. This chapter therefore aims to evaluate the Mental Health Acts of three African jurisdictions, viz. Uganda, Zambia and Kenya, for their compliance with the standards set in the CRPD and regional African human rights instruments. The selection of the three jurisdictions is based on the relatively recent revision of

---

1 This question is derived from a passage in *Wretched of the Earth* (1961) by Frantz Fanon. Fanon was a psychiatrist and political philosopher whose work included an analysis of the psychopathology of colonialism. He lived and worked in Algeria and Tunisia during the last years of his life. The full extract reads: 'They realise at last that change does not mean reform, that change does not mean improvement'.
2 It is acknowledged that 'psychosocial disability' is not synonymous with 'mental illness'. However, the two terms are used interchangeably in this chapter due to the strong focus on mental illness in the legislation analysed here.

DOI: 10.4324/9781003226413-32

their mental health legislation. Moreover, the legal systems of these anglophone countries are founded in English common law, which facilitates comparison.

The interpretation of the CRPD provisions holding particular meaning for persons with psychosocial disabilities has proved to be contentious. From the outset, the Committee on the Rights of Persons with Disabilities (CRPD Committee) made it clear that practices such as involuntary admission and treatment and substitute decision-making are not compatible with Article 12 and related provisions. This is not only clear from the Committee's interpretive guidelines to Article 12 (Committee on the Rights of Persons with Disabilities, 2014) but also from its concluding observations to State Party reports. This perspective has drawn criticism from various authors for being unrealistic and impractical where, for example, a person with a psychosocial disability in crisis or distress is likely to harm themselves or others (Freeman et al., 2015; Kelly, 2022). On the other hand, a second group of commentators have expressed their concurrence with the CRPD Committee's 'principled' position (Wilson, 2020). The apparent dichotomy between the two schools of thought complicates the measurement of mental health legislation against the CRPD, which will be taken into account in this analysis of Mental Health Acts.

Following the introduction, the chapter first sets out the broader background to mental health legislation in Africa. It subsequently considers the normative framework contained in key human rights instruments from the African region. An overview of the constitutional dispensations of the three countries follows, accompanied by a synopsis of the disability-specific legislation adopted (or awaiting adoption) in each jurisdiction. The next section then contains the thematic analysis of the three Mental Health Acts and the chapter concludes with a final section which draws together the findings of this evaluation.

Background: mental health legislation in African contexts

Given the enormous diversities across the continent, it is unwise to reduce psychosocial disability and mental health legislation 'in Africa' to one monolithic essence. However, a number of trends may be discerned. The first notable aspect, shared by the majority of African countries, is 'the multiple and strange entanglements between psychiatry and colonialism' (Mills, 2017; see also Ibrahim, 2017). The connection between the development of mental health laws and colonial administration resulted in, for example, early legislative measures addressing mental illness in anglophone African jurisdictions greatly resembling those employed in England. The emphasis in these laws was on 'control and containment' rather than on the provision of individual mental health care (Quinn, 2022). In fact, this outdated legislation still prevails in certain African countries, such as the Lunatic Detention Act presently in effect in The Gambia.

The second trend, encountered in many middle- to lower-income countries in the Global South, is a relatively low budget allocation in the mental health sector. For example, in 2022 a Kenyan taskforce reporting on the state of mental health in the country recommended that the mental health budget should be increased from the current 0.01% of the total health budget to 2% (Mutiso, undated). The failure by African governments to give greater prominence to mental health services naturally results in inadequate service provision, as seen in a chronic lack of medical professionals such as psychiatrists and psychologists and the severe underdevelopment of community-based programmes (Bartlett, 2010).

Given these stark realities, traditional and religious healers often present the only care and treatment alternatives available to persons with psychosocial disabilities. The benefit of consulting these healers, usually locally based, is that they may bring insight into distinctive cultural considerations. On the other hand, since this sector is almost completely unregulated, the threat of egregious human rights violations is ubiquitous, as seen in the so-called 'prayer camps' in countries such as Ghana and Nigeria.[3]

The disproportionate stigma and discrimination experienced by persons with psychosocial disabilities also prevail in many African contexts, often closely intertwined with long-held sociocultural perceptions about witchcraft, possession by demons and bad omens. This may be exacerbated by limited popular knowledge about psychosocial disability and mental illness. It is clear from this brief overview that mental health law reform in African countries is often a particularly complex and contested environment (see also Kamundia and Grobbelaar-Du Plessis, 2021).

Regional African human rights standards

African Charter on Human and Peoples' Rights

The principal human rights instrument in this region is the African Charter on Human and Peoples' Rights (African Charter). This document, which was adopted by the Organisation of African Unity in 1981, came into operation in 1986. The Charter has been ratified by virtually all Member States of the African Union, with Morocco the only exception out of 55.

Chapter 1 of the Charter guarantees civil and political rights as well as a more limited range of socio-economic rights. According to Article 2 of the Charter, every individual is entitled to enjoy the rights and freedoms guaranteed in the Charter 'without distinction of any kind such as race, ethnic group, colour, sex, language, religion, political or any other opinion, national and social origin, fortune, birth *or other status*' (emphasis added). Disability is markedly absent from this list of grounds, which is perhaps unsurprising given the genesis of the African Charter early in the 1980s and the fact that disability rights were at this time only beginning to emerge as a human rights concern at international level (Quinn and Degener, 2002). The question whether disability may be seen as an 'other status', viz. a prohibited ground analogous to the specifically listed ones, was raised in the communication of *Purohit and Moore v The Gambia*, which is discussed below.

The Charter further recognises that every individual is equal before the law and entitled to equal protection of the law (Article 3). The inherent right to dignity, guaranteed in Article 5, includes a prohibition of torture and cruel, inhuman or degrading punishment and treatment. The right to liberty and security of the person (Article 6) is of particular importance in the context of mental health legislation, since it pertains to the issue of involuntary admission. This article provides that no one may be deprived of their freedom 'except for reasons and conditions previously laid down by law'.[4]

---

3 Prayer camps can be described as private religious institutions, mostly Christian, operated by self-proclaimed prophets asserting that they have the ability to heal physical and psychosocial disabilities. Widespread human rights violations such as forced starvation, poor hygiene and restraining practices – for example, shackling of persons with psychosocial disabilities – have consistently been found in Ghanaian prayer camps (Edwards, 2014; Kamundia, 2022).
4 This provision is similar to those found in other regional human rights instruments: see e.g. Article 7 of the Inter-American Convention and Article 5 of the European Convention.

Article 16(1) guarantees the right to enjoy the best attainable state of physical and mental health while Article 18 sets out certain state obligations in respect of three marginalised groups, viz. women, children and persons with disabilities. Article 18(3) requires states to ensure the elimination of discrimination against women and the protection of the rights of women and of children. Finally, Article 18(4) states that 'the aged and the disabled' will also have the right to special protective measures.

The approach to disability rights in Article 18(4) has been criticised on a number of grounds. First, in blending together 'the aged and the disabled', it creates the impression that older persons and persons with disabilities are inevitably closely connected (Mute and Kalekye, 2016–2017). Article 18, which is predominantly focused on the family, further combines the rights of older persons and persons with disabilities with those of women and children. In addition, the entitlement set out here (viz. the right to 'special protective measures') overemphasises the presumed need for protection without reference to substantive rights (Kamga, 2013).

As can be expected, the provisions of the African Charter are relatively broad and 'generic' and the interpretation of the Charter by its monitoring body, viz. the African Commission on Human and Peoples' Rights (African Commission), therefore takes on specific importance. Unlike its European and Inter-American counterparts, the African Commission has unfortunately not yet developed a significant body of jurisprudence on disability rights generally or on psychosocial disability in particular. The one notable exception is the communication brought in Purohit and Moore v The Gambia, which is discussed in the next section.

Interpretation of the African Charter: *Purohit and Moore v The Gambia*

The complainants in this matter were two mental health advocates who approached the Commission with a complaint on behalf of persons detained under Gambian legislation. They specifically took issue with the 'Lunatics Detention Act' (LDA),[5] which *inter alia* allowed for persons described as 'lunatics'[6] to be detained for indefinite periods in psychiatric institutions without any safeguards such as ongoing reviews of treatment regimens or the right to contest the legal basis for detention (*Purohit and Moore v The Gambia*). The complainants accordingly alleged violations by the Gambian government of several rights in the African Charter, including the right to human dignity and protection against cruel, inhuman and degrading treatment (Article 5), the right to liberty and security of the person (Article 6) and the right to health (Article 16).

The Commission's view was that the conduct of the Gambian government constituted violations of the Charter provisions as averred by the complainants, with the exception of Article 6. The Commission reiterated that infringements of the right to personal liberty had to be authorised by law and be consistent with state duties under the Charter. All domestic legislation aimed at limiting this right should be aligned with international human rights standards. Although conceding that the detention of persons with mental illness under the Gambian LDA did not meet these criteria, the Commission concluded that Article 6 did not apply where 'persons in need of medical assistance or help are institutionalised'. For this reason, its finding was that no violation of this provision had taken place.

---

5 The LDA was enacted in 1917 and last revised in 1964.
6 Section 2 of the LDA defines a 'lunatic' as including 'an idiot or person of unsound mind'.

Change or improvement?

Although the Commission's views (adopted in 2003) predated the CRPD, certain aspects may be highlighted. First, the African Commission made a number of strong statements regarding state (and individual) duties to respect, protect and fulfil the rights of persons with psychosocial disabilities. It clarified that disability-based discrimination fell within the purview of Article 2[7] and emphasised that the references to 'lunatics' and 'idiots' in the LDA deprived persons with mental illness of their dignity. On the negative side, the Commission's reading of Article 6 is somewhat disappointing.

Protocol to the African Charter on Human and Peoples' Rights on the Rights of Persons with Disabilities in Africa

The general sparseness of Articles 18(3) and 18(4) of the African Charter has led to the introduction of two additional Protocols. In 2003, the Protocol to the African Charter on Human and Peoples' Rights on the Rights of Women in Africa (also known as the Maputo Protocol) was adopted; it came into effect in 2005. In 2018, the Protocol to the African Charter on Human and Peoples' Rights on the Rights of Persons with Disabilities in Africa (African Disability Protocol) was adopted by the African Union. This Protocol has not yet attracted the 15 ratifications required for it to come into operation: to date, only five countries have ratified the document.

The origins and evolution of the African Disability Protocol have been documented extensively (Kamga, 2013; Mute and Kalekye, 2016–2017) and a detailed history is beyond the scope of this chapter. In brief, the arguments for an Africa-specific disability rights instrument included the significant normative shortcomings in existing African human rights documents, exemplified by the fact that these documents were to a considerable extent influenced by the charity and medical models of disability. Despite some opposition, the African Union adopted the Disability Protocol in January 2018. Whereas many of its provisions are strongly reminiscent of the CRPD, the document does contain some refinements apposite to African circumstances (Appiagyei-Atua, 2017). The following section therefore considers the scope of application of the CRPD and the African Disability Protocol respectively, as well as legal capacity, the right to personal liberty and harmful practices.

Comparison between the CRPD and the African Disability Protocol

The first point of comparison may be found in certain of the definitions underpinning the two instruments. Comparing the description of 'persons with disabilities' in the CRPD with that in the African Protocol, one notes that in terms of the Protocol an impairment does not have to be a 'long-term' one as indicated in Article 1 of the CRPD. (The inclusion of this aspect in the CRPD may arguably have a limiting effect on the protection offered under the Convention.)

Furthermore, the definition of 'reasonable accommodation' in the Protocol leaves out the contested qualifier – featuring in the CRPD – that the required modifications or adjustments should not present 'a disproportionate or undue burden'. In addition, the Protocol deci-

---

7 Although the African Commission agreed that Article 2 had been violated, it did not provide clarity on the question of disability as an analogous ground. The adoption of the African Disability Protocol may imply that this issue has now been settled.

sively spells out that the term 'legal capacity' refers to 'the ability to hold rights and duties and to exercise those rights and duties'. This is noteworthy in light of the forceful debates about the meaning of legal capacity during the drafting process of the CRPD (Dhanda, 2007). From these examples, it appears that the drafters of the Protocol made an attempt to clarify issues which have proven to be somewhat ambiguous in the CRPD.

When it comes to legal capacity, Article 7(1) of the Protocol to a large extent mirrors the wording of Article 12(1) of the CRPD. Article 7(2) then lists a number of measures to be taken by States Parties, the first of which is to ensure that persons with disabilities enjoy legal capacity on an equal basis with others in all aspects of the law. This corresponds with Article 12 (2) of the CRPD. Further state duties listed here include ensuring that 'non-state actors and other individuals' do not violate the right to exercise legal capacity by persons with disabilities (Article 7(2)(b)). This is in keeping with the principle, well established in international human rights law, that the protection of rights requires states to respond to rights violations by non-state actors.

Article 7(2)(e) requires States Parties to review laws and policies which have the purpose or effect of limiting the enjoyment of legal capacity by persons with disabilities. This provision complements the undertaking by States Parties in terms of Article 4(c) of the Protocol to address disability-based discrimination found in existing laws, policies and practices. (The latter is similar to Article 4(1)(b) of the CRPD.) Furthermore, in terms of Article 7(2)(f) of the Protocol, persons with disabilities have an equal right to hold identity documents and other documents enabling them to exercise their right to legal capacity; this is an innovation, important in African contexts, which does not expressly appear in the CRPD.

Article 9(5) of the Protocol follows the example of the CRPD in providing that 'the existence of a disability or perceived disability shall in no case justify deprivation of liberty'. The phrase 'perceived disability' in the Protocol is a welcome addition here. It will also be recalled that the African Commission, in its views in the *Purohit* communication, made the statement that the institutionalisation of 'persons in need of medical assistance or help' does not constitute a violation of Article 6 of the African Charter. This provision in the Protocol therefore steps in to fill the space left in 2003 by the African Commission. Enonchong (2017) is of the opinion that the result may be that 'automatic detention' of persons with psychosocial disabilities will no longer be possible in African jurisdictions.

Article 11 of the Protocol, which addresses harmful practices, does not have a direct equivalent in the CRPD, although it touches on certain aspects covered in Article 8 of the latter. 'Harmful practices' are described in the Protocol as including behaviour, attitudes and practices based *inter alia* on tradition, culture or religion, which 'negatively affect the human rights and fundamental freedoms of persons with disabilities or promote discrimination'. Examples of such practices specifically enumerated in Article 11(1) include 'witchcraft, abandonment, concealment, ritual killings or the association of disability with omens'.

In sum, the symmetries between Article 7 of the Protocol and Article 12 of the CRPD imply that the former may not shed any additional light on the existing differences of opinion about involuntary admission and treatment and substitute decision-making. However, the Protocol may nevertheless contribute to the development of disability rights standards at the African regional level. Realising the potential of the Protocol will to a large degree depend on the monitoring of its implementation by the African Commission. The following section therefore takes a look at the arrangements for overseeing implementation of the Protocol.

Implementation and interpretation of the African Disability Protocol

According to Article 34(3) of the Protocol, the African Commission is tasked with the interpretation of the Protocol. The Commission also has the power to refer disputes arising from the implementation and interpretation of the Protocol to the African Court on Human and Peoples' Rights.[8] In other words, the African Disability Protocol is reliant on the same imperfect oversight mechanisms as the African Charter itself. This could prove to be one of the major weaknesses of the Protocol: the potential power of the African regional human rights institutions – most notably the African Commission – has been severely eroded by a dearth of resources as well as an absence of political will on the part of States Parties to comply with their treaty obligations. (For example, although the African Commission recommended in the *Purohit* matter that The Gambia should urgently review and reform its mental health laws, at the time of writing this has not yet taken place.)

The ultimate test of this instrument will therefore lie in whether state hesitation to give effect to its provisions and the structural shortcomings of African regional human rights institutions can be overcome.

Constitutional and legislative frameworks: Uganda, Zambia and Kenya

Introduction

A comparative assessment of legislation, as undertaken in this chapter, cannot take place in an acontextual vacuum: it is essential to also explore the broader legislative scheme in order to understand where these Mental Health Acts 'fit in'. For this reason, this section provides a brief overview of the Constitutions of the three selected countries as well as the disability-specific legislation enacted in each jurisdiction.[9]

Constitutional provisions

The Constitutions of Uganda, Zambia and Kenya all date from the post-independence period. The Ugandan Constitution was enacted in 1995 (with subsequent amendments) and the Zambian one, also since amended, in 1991. The Kenyan Constitution, dated 2010, is an extensive revision of its 1963 predecessor. Although the three countries followed different paths of development after the end of colonial rule (for example, both Uganda and Kenya experienced periods of armed conflict whereas Zambia did not), their Constitutions bear marked similarities. These include: the principle of constitutional supremacy; a 'catalogue' of human rights; the prohibition of discrimination based on certain listed grounds, which in each case includes disability; the right to approach courts in instances where rights are threatened or have been infringed; and the inclusion of a specific article dedicated to persons with disabilities in the Ugandan and Kenyan Constitutions.

---

8 It should be noted that direct access of individuals and non-organisations to the African Court on Human and Peoples' Rights is at present severely curtailed. The Protocol establishing the Court requires States Parties to submit a declaration accepting the Court's jurisdiction in this regard. Due to the relatively low number of States Parties that have to date submitted a declaration, the African Court is not discussed in detail here.

9 This discussion is limited, given that the consideration of policy documents and plans go beyond the scope of the chapter.

In terms of variations between the documents in the context of human rights protection, the first may be found in the relationship between international law and domestic law. In Uganda and Zambia, treaties ratified by these countries must be enacted in national legislation in order to form part of domestic law – the so-called dualist approach. The Kenyan constitution, on the other hand, takes a monist approach in that ratified international law treaties are directly incorporated in its domestic law (Orago, 2013). This holds clear implications for the domestic implementation of both the CRPD and the African Disability Protocol.

Looking at the individual rights included in the three constitutions, another difference which stands out relates to the right to personal liberty. All three Constitutions guarantee this right; however, certain exceptional circumstances where a deprivation of liberty is permitted are set out. Both the Ugandan and the Zambian Constitutions include, among these exceptions, situations where 'a person is of unsound mind' and the detention is aimed at their treatment or care or protection of the community.

Despite these differences, it can generally be said that the constitutional dispensations of the three countries not only form a solid foundation for the development of rights-based legislation but in fact compel lawmakers to ensure that this approach is followed. This is apparent from the enshrinement of rights in the Constitutions as read with the provisions declaring constitutional supremacy.

Disability-specific legislation

As indicated earlier, the three jurisdictions have in recent years enacted disability-specific legislation. The Zambian Persons with Disabilities Act[10] (PDA) dates from 2012, whereas the similarly named Ugandan Act[11] came into effect on 14 February 2020. In Kenya, the Persons with Disabilities Bill[12] is at present under parliamentary consideration. The two current Acts and the Bill represent a review or revision of existing disability-specific legislation. The following section considers the ambit of protection of the rights of persons with disabilities in each Act, the monitoring bodies for implementation and the right to legal recourse where the rights of persons with disabilities have been infringed.

Protection of the rights of persons with disabilities

The three enactments all pay specific attention to guarantees of the rights of persons with disabilities. As a foundational principle, Section 3(2) of the Ugandan Persons with Disabilities Act (PDA) requires the government and all persons in Uganda to respect, uphold and promote the rights of persons with disabilities as enshrined in the Constitution and the CRPD. The Act incorporates the right of persons with disabilities to enjoy family life as well as a prohibition of inhuman and degrading treatment of persons with disabilities (including harmful traditional or cultural practices). It further prohibits disability-based discrimination in various sectors, including education, health services, employment and access to justice.

The compendium of rights in the Zambian PDA extends well beyond the prohibition of disability-based discrimination as emphasised in the Ugandan PDA. Significantly, Section

---

10 Act No. 6 of 2012.
11 Act 3 of 2020.
12 Bill No. 61 of 2021.

8(1) of the Zambian Act states – without any qualifiers – that persons with disabilities are entitled to enjoy legal capacity on an equal basis with others in all aspects of life. The right of persons with disabilities to choose their place of residence or to live with their family is also secured under the Act; however, this right is subject to an exception, viz. where a person with disability is 'required to be in a specialised institution due to the nature of the disability'.

Part II of the Kenyan Bill, which is dedicated to the rights of persons with disabilities, is considerably more extensive than the Ugandan and Zambian Acts. Section 5 of the Kenyan Bill echoes Article 12 of the CRPD in that it affirms the right of persons with disabilities to enjoy legal capacity.

Monitoring and oversight

The Ugandan PDA proclaims that the National Council for Persons with Disabilities, established under legislation dating from 2003, continues in existence. The functions of the Council include the monitoring of the implementation as well as liaison, for purposes of planning, with government on the needs and problems of persons with disabilities. The Zambian PDA likewise makes provision for the continued existence of the Zambia Agency for Persons with Disabilities while the Kenyan Bill creates the National Council for Persons with Disabilities. The oversight functions of the latter two bodies to a substantial extent resemble those of the Ugandan Council.

Recourse for violations of rights

The Ugandan PDA empowers the National Council for Persons with Disabilities, as one of its functions, to conduct inquiries and investigations relating to violations of the rights of persons with disabilities or failures to comply with the Act. It may also issue orders for corrective measures to address such violations or non-compliance. The contravention of certain provisions (for example, the prohibition of inhuman and degrading treatment of persons with disabilities) constitutes a criminal offence. While the PDA itself does not expressly refer to the right to approach the courts, regard should be had to the Ugandan Constitution which states that persons alleging the violation (or threatened violation) of their constitutional rights may approach a competent court for relief.

For its part, the Zambian PDA entrusts the Zambia Agency for Persons with Disabilities with the mandate to conduct inquiries into matters relating to 'the welfare, habilitation and rehabilitation' of persons with disabilities. Further, the Agency may request the Attorney-General[13] to take 'appropriate legal action' in instances of discriminatory practices which constitute serious infringements of the rights of persons with disabilities and raise issues of public interest. Turning to the Constitution, persons aggrieved by infringements of their constitutional rights may bring an application for redress to the High Court, which has the power to make orders or give directives aimed at the enforcement of the right(s) concerned. This provision is mirrored by the Kenyan Bill, which similarly sets out the jurisdiction of the High Court to hear claims relating to violations of the rights of persons with disabilities.

---

13 Article 177 of the Zambian Constitution describes the Attorney-General as the chief legal adviser to the government.

Conclusion

Looking at the two Acts and the Kenyan Bill, one notes a broadly comparable approach. These enactments explain how certain rights are applicable to persons with disabilities and also make provision for institutional frameworks for implementation of the legislation.

Analysis of mental health legislation in Uganda, Zambia and Kenya

Introduction

Because the background to the legislative drafting process could contribute to insight into the legislation itself, a brief overview is provided here. It may be said that the process of drafting new mental health laws is often characterised by vigorous debates and hesitance or even opposition from different interest groups. This certainly holds true for the Ugandan and Zambian Acts. For instance, while the Ugandan Mental Health Bill was serving before parliament in 2018, a coalition of civil society organisations, led by Mental Health Uganda (MHU), presented a position statement describing their concerns (Allen, 2018).

The position statement recounted that MHU and other organisations of persons with disabilities had since 2009 provided the government with recommendations on the development of a new legislative framework (MHU et al., 2018). The coalition was of the view that despite this guidance the Bill serving in parliament at the time did not reflect the concerns raised by civil society. Disputed issues included involuntary admission and treatment, so-called 'special treatment options' such as seclusion and restraint, and the lack of a framework for the development of community-based mental health care services. The Bill was eventually adopted without substantial changes to these provisions.

The enactment of the Zambian Mental Health Act (MHA) was also preceded by a lengthy period of government interaction with the disability sector. However, the draft Mental Health Bill published in 2019 did not correspond with points of agreement reached during previous consultations (Raw, 2019). At this time several stakeholders recommended an extensive overhaul of the Bill, with specific emphasis placed on the provision dealing with legal capacity (Combrinck and Chilemba, 2021). Despite optimism that the misgivings of civil society would be addressed in a redrafted Bill, the final version as enacted still featured the controversial provisions.

It appears that the Kenyan experience was a different one: not only did the Bill progress through parliament in the comparatively short period of four years, but the document has found approval with civil society organisations (Physicians for Human Rights, 2022) as well as the Kenya National Commission on Human Rights (Kemboi, 2022).

In the following section, the three Mental Health Acts are analysed with reference to legal capacity and related themes. The selection of these themes in part drew on the 'Checklist for rights-based mental health legislation' included in the draft guidelines on mental health, human rights and legislation published in June 2022 by the World Health Organization and Office of the High Commissioner for Human Rights.

Recognition of legal capacity

Notably, the three Acts all contain an affirmation of universal legal capacity. However, this recognition is in each case to a greater or lesser extent subject to limitations. For example, the Ugandan MHA endorses universal legal capacity and confirms the right of persons with mental illness to manage their own affairs. Persons with mental illness may, however, be prevented from managing their personal lives by a court finding that they are unable to do so.

Similarly, the Zambian MHA proclaims that all 'mental patients'[14] enjoy legal capacity, 'subject to the other requirements of this Act'. This affirmation is immediately undercut by the next subsection (Section 4(2)), which states that where the nature of the patient's mental illness leads to the absence of mental capacity, he or she does not have legal capacity and is 'legally disqualified' from any acts where legal capacity is required.

The Kenyan MHA acknowledges the right of persons with mental illness to recognition before the law and to enjoy legal rights on an equal basis with others. One notes that this provision does not contain an 'internal' qualifier within the section itself, unlike its Ugandan and Zambian counterparts. Legal capacity is nevertheless constrained by other arrangements under the Act such as the fact that a supporter may provide the necessary consent where the person with mental illness is incapable of making an informed decision regarding appropriate treatment.

Eliminating coercion: informed consent and involuntary admission and treatment

It appears that the three legislatures, in drafting the Acts, made cautious efforts to navigate the troublesome terrain between consent and coercion. The point of departure is in each instance that admission and/or treatment may only occur with the informed consent of the person with mental illness. However, the three Acts also allow certain exceptions where involuntary admission and treatment may occur. For example, the Ugandan MHA states that where a person with mental illness is being considered for emergency admission and treatment the medical practitioner concerned must 'where possible' obtain consent. Failing this, the practitioner must provide emergency treatment which is in the best interest of the patient to preserve life or to avert the deterioration of their health.

The Ugandan Act creates three categories of patients, viz. involuntary patients, voluntary patients and so-called assisted patients. Involuntary patients are persons with mental illness who are *prima facie* in need of treatment and care from a mental health unit but who are 'for the time being incapable of expressing themselves as willing or unwilling to receive treatment'.

The category of 'assisted patients' encompasses persons with mental illness who voluntarily present themselves at a mental health unit but are incapable of making informed decisions due to their mental health status. According to Section 30, the person with mental illness should be accompanied to the mental health facility by a relative or concerned person[15] who must give written consent to the treatment.

The Zambian MHA sets out the circumstances where admission and treatment may legitimately be provided. The first instance is where the 'mental patient' or their supporter has given their consent. Second, the Board of the National Mental Health Council may authorise admission and treatment. The third situation is where a failure to provide mental health

---

14 The term 'mental patient' is defined in Section 2 as 'a person diagnosed by a mental health practitioner as having a mental illness, mental disorder, mental impairment or mental disability'. The term is used here solely to correspond with the Act.
15 Section 2 of the Ugandan MHA defines 'a concerned person' as a person who is not a relative of the person with mental illness but who has a reasonable and justifiable concern for his or her wellbeing.

services may result in death or irreversible harm to a 'mental patient'; the infliction of serious harm on the patient or another person; or serious property loss or damage. Although the latter two situations therefore allow for admission and treatment without the consent of the 'mental patient', mental health practitioners are enjoined to minimise admission or treatment without informed consent. A further mitigation is found in the general guideline in the Act that all 'mental patients' must be treated in the least restrictive environment and with the least intrusive treatment.

Section 14 of the Kenyan MHA explains that involuntary admission of a person with mental illness may take place where a qualified mental health practitioner determines that there is a serious likelihood of immediate or impending harm to that person due to their mental illness. Involuntary admission may also be considered where a failure to admit the person will likely result in a major worsening of their condition or frustrate the administration of treatment which can only be provided on an in-patient basis.

Supported or substitute decision-making

The legislative approach to decision-making by persons with psychosocial disabilities is the second minefield often associated with Article 12 of the CRPD. If one accepts – as do the three Acts at issue here – that involuntary admission and treatment may on occasion be justified, the next question is immediately how decision-making should occur in these instances. This section therefore examines the legislative scheme around decision-making by looking at who may act as 'support persons',[16] and what their role would be.

The Ugandan MHA states that a person with mental illness may appoint a personal representative to act on their behalf in the event of a loss of 'capacity to execute a particular task'. Where a voluntary patient subsequently lacks the capacity to consent to treatment, the necessary consent may be obtained from their representative. (This form of appointment of a personal representative could be seen as a form of 'advance planning'.)

A personal representative may also be assigned by a court where the person with mental illness has not made such an appointment. In the event of an order to the effect that a person with mental illness is incapable of managing his or her affairs, the court should appoint a 'suitable relative' as a representative. The functions of the representative in this context are to manage the estate of the person with mental illness or to act as their guardian.[17] The arrangements in the Ugandan Act therefore unambiguously take the form of substitute decision-making (Dinymoi and Lubaale, 2021).

Looking at the Zambian MHA, it may at first glance appear that its drafters intended to introduce a form of supported decision-making: in terms of Section 4(3) a court may appoint a 'supporter' where a 'mental patient' lacks legal capacity. In addition, Section 16 specifies that the rights of 'mental patients' include the right to supported decision-making in respect of treatment. However, closer scrutiny of the role of the supporter reveals that substitute decision-making still prevails: Section 23(1) states that where a 'mental patient' is

---

16 The term 'support person' is used here as a generic term indicating a range of options, from support in the sense of supplementing the decision-making capacity of persons with psychosocial disabilities to substitute decision-making in the form of a court-appointed guardian.
17 The Kenyan MHA also makes provision for court orders for the management of the estate of a person with mental illness.

'unable to consent to the treatment', their supporter may give the required consent on their behalf. (The heading to Section 23 is in fact 'proxy consent to treatment'.) This is further confirmed by the definition of 'supporter' in the Act, viz. 'a person who *represents* a mental health service user or mental patient's rights or interests' (emphasis added). That said, the Zambian Act recognises the right of a 'mental patient' to give an advance directive – with legally binding effect – setting out their choices regarding treatment. This advance directive must be given at a point in time when the 'mental patient' is 'competent to make an informed decision'.

The Kenyan MHA envisages two categories of support persons, viz. a 'duly appointed supporter' or a representative. Their respective roles and functions may be explained as follows. A 'supporter' is a person who is appointed by the person with mental illness to make decisions on their behalf according to their will and preference. A 'representative' fulfils this function where the person with mental illness did not appoint a supporter and therefore acts as an alternative in the absence of a supporter.

The Act includes certain circumstances where the supporter – or representative, as the case may be – may step into the shoes of the person with mental illness. These include situations where the person with mental illness is 'incapable of making an informed decision' on the appropriate form of treatment; where the person with mental illness is incapable of exercising their right to take part in the formulation of their treatment plans; and where the person with mental illness is unable at that particular time to consent to the extension of the period of involuntary admission.

The Kenyan MHA imposes a duty of care on a supporter; moreover, they must ensure that all decisions are compatible with the will and preference of the person with mental illness. In determining this 'will and preference', the supporter must consider whether the decision concerned aligns with the long-term values and wishes of the person receiving support. They must also consider the rights guaranteed in the Kenyan Constitution and international human rights law and make ongoing attempts to establish the will and preference of the person with mental illness. However, it should be noted that the same duties are not imposed on a representative who may fulfil certain of these functions in the absence of a supporter.

It therefore appears that the appointment of a supporter in effect constitutes an advance directive by the person with mental illness. Where a supporter has not been appointed, the 'support', which is in effect substitute decision-making, is provided by a representative as outlined.

Monitoring and oversight

The three Acts all establish bodies tasked with monitoring the implementation of the legislation. These institutions are respectively the Uganda Mental Health Advisory Board (UMHAB), the National Mental Health Council (ZNMHC) in Zambia and the Kenya Board of Mental Health (KBMH).

The monitoring bodies all have a broad mandate to oversee the operation of the respective Acts and to promote and protect the rights of persons with mental illness. Their functions include setting standards for mental health care services and playing a role in certain prescribed procedures such as determining whether patients require continued treatment without their consent (in the case of the UMHAB), authorisation of admission, treatment and care by mental health facilities under the Zambian Act[18] and receiving reports of abuse of a person with mental illness (the Kenyan Board).

Interestingly, the three bodies are mandated with tasks going beyond the strict parameters of monitoring implementation of the Acts. For example, the ZNMHC must assist in the development of community-based mental health services and must promote deinstitutionalisation. The responsibilities of the KBMH include advising the national government and county structures on the levels of access to mental health care services in Kenya and preparing reports on the prevalence of mental illness.

Safeguards

The three Acts contain safeguards aimed at protecting the rights of persons with mental illness (and that arguably enhance the accountability of mental health practitioners and facilities). These safeguards include, amongst others, guiding principles for service provision, limits on the duration of certain forms of treatment and complaints mechanisms to challenge decisions relating to admission and treatment. The first two safeguards will briefly be discussed here.

An example of the guiding principles may be found in the Zambian MHA, which states that the decision on whether a person is a 'mental patient' may not be based on any considerations not directly relevant to their mental health status. For instance, reliance may not be placed on political or socio-economic status or membership of cultural or religious groupings.

The three Acts contain several instances where limits are imposed on the duration of treatment. Under the Ugandan MHA a person with mental health illness who has been admitted for emergency medical treatment must be assessed within 12 hours of admission and this emergency treatment may not exceed three days. Likewise, the provision of emergency treatment under the Kenyan MHA may not be continued beyond the period required to 'stabilise' and treat the person with mental illness, or in any event no longer than 72 hours.

Evaluation

The three Mental Health Acts considered here undoubtedly constitute progress and hold much that is positive. First, the three Acts aim to shape the normative frameworks aimed at guiding the implementation of the legislation, as seen in the statements of principles on determination of the mental health status of persons with mental illness.

These normative frameworks contain a strong emphasis on the protection of the rights of persons with psychosocial disabilities and the prohibition of discrimination. This is apparent from the substantive chapters in the Acts setting out these rights. The prominence given to rights may also be seen in, for example, the affirmation in the Kenyan Act that persons with mental illness have the right to make use of all civil and political and socio-economic rights secured under the Kenyan Constitution and any other legislation. The three Acts can therefore (arguably) be described as 'rights-based legislation'.

---

18 In addition to creating the ZNMHC, the Act also establishes a Board to play a general oversight role in respect of the Council and to fulfil functions relating to the implementation of the Act.

Further, the three Mental Health Acts provide clarity on concepts and procedures which may previously have been overlooked or not dealt with decisively. The recognition in all of the Acts of some form of advance planning or directives is to be welcomed. The introduction in the Kenyan MHA of parameters for establishing 'will and preference' may also prove to be helpful in practice. The fact that the legislation makes provision for complaints mechanisms and/or recourse to courts to oppose decisions relating to treatment and care is a further strong point.

The drafters of the Acts have made demonstrable efforts to address broader systemic issues: for example, the Kenyan MHA allocates priority to community health care and treatment as opposed to institutionalisation. The Zambian Act requires that mental health service provision should be integrated within general health services and where possible provided on an equal basis with 'physical' health services.

On the other hand, certain concerns do arise. The first observation is that the Mental Health Acts appear to largely stand in isolation, without a meaningful connection to the disability-specific legislation discussed above or general health legislation. Moreover, the relationship (if any) between the oversight bodies created under the respective Persons with Disabilities Acts and those established in terms of the mental health legislation is unclear. One exception is found in the Zambian Act: it lists liaison with the Zambian Agency for Persons with Disabilities among the functions assigned to the National Mental Health Council. That said, there are admittedly some intersections between the Mental Health Acts and other legislation. For example, the Zambian Persons with Disabilities Act states that when it comes to 'mental disabilities', the Act is subject to the Mental Health Act of 2019.

The larger concerns lie in the manner in which the more controversial facets of legal capacity such as involuntary treatment and substitute decision-making are dealt with in the three Acts. This is not unexpected, given the divergent approaches to these issues mentioned earlier.

Regarding supported and substitute decision-making, there appears to be scant evidence of 'support' in the sense of supplementing rather than replacing the decision-making capacities of persons with psychosocial disabilities. Instead, the different options presented in the three Acts may be said to amount to either advance directives or substituted decisions on behalf of a person with mental illness.

When it comes to legal capacity, lawmakers in the three jurisdictions have made efforts to carve out exceptions to universal legal capacity. In the process, conceptual dissonances are created in the description of situations where a person with psychosocial disability (who, according to the legislation itself, has full legal capacity) is nevertheless unable to give informed consent to admission or treatment. An example can be found in Section 45 of the Ugandan MHA, which refers to 'an involuntary patient *who is capable of giving consent*' (emphasis added). Considering that an 'involuntary patient' is conceptualised elsewhere in the Act as a person with mental illness who is incapable of expressing themselves as willing or unwilling to receive treatment, the disjuncture becomes apparent.

The treatment of legal capacity in the Zambian MHA has proved particularly troubling. As noted, the Act confirms universal legal capacity – but it is effectively made dependent on mental capacity. This conflation of mental and legal capacity and the creation of a category of 'legally disqualified' persons have received condemnation from legal commentators (Kalunga, undated). Moreover, the conditional recognition of legal capacity in the Zambian MHA appears to contradict the unqualified guarantee of legal capacity in its Persons with Disabilities Act. It is therefore unsurprising that the issue is currently the focus of a constitutional challenge to the new legislation brought by mental health activists.

Finally, it is alarming to note that all the Acts allow for 'special treatment' such as seclusion and restraint, albeit as an option of last resort. The continued reliance on these practices runs counter to the call for their elimination by the UN Special Rapporteur on torture and other cruel, inhuman and degrading treatment or punishment.

Conclusion

This chapter set out to analyse the mental health laws in three African jurisdictions for compliance with the CRPD and regional human rights instruments. The final verdict is a mixed one. While there is a significant shift towards rights-based legislation which conforms to CRPD standards, it may be said that these reforms have not gone far enough.

This is where the compromise between the 'purist' and the 'pragmatic' approaches to Article 12 of the CRPD as proposed by Davidson (2021) becomes appealing. She suggests that efforts to reduce involuntary interventions by means of community-based alternatives offering individual support are at present not generally viable in middle- and lower-income countries. Her proposal is therefore that interim or 'holding' legislation be introduced with the aim of decreasing involuntary interventions while simultaneously making progress towards eventual full alignment with the CRPD. This incremental approach should be accompanied by the development of evidence-based alternative support mechanisms. While the three Mental Health Acts were probably not intended as interim measures, it could be said that they fit into this category as described by Davidson.

Taking a step back, the chapter has also shown that the disability rights framework in the African region remains imperfect. Even when the African Disability Protocol comes into effect, the question remains whether the African Commission will have the capacity to oversee its implementation.

It is discouraging to note that the Kenyan MHA is currently the only Act among the three already in force. The commencement of both the Zambian MHA and its Ugandan counterpart is being impeded by delays in finalising the Regulations which are required for the operation of the Acts. The commencement of the Ugandan MHA has also been held back by the low recruitment of psychiatric professionals and the fact that the Uganda Mental Health Advisory Board is not yet in place (Chemonges, 2022). These obstacles again raise the spectre of a lack of political will, which poses the risk that the legislation will become 'a printed exercise in futility' (Fombad, 2016).

While it is generally true that law reform simply for the sake of change should be avoided, this statement is particularly applicable to mental health law reform. (The reasons for this include the potential impact of such legislation on an already marginalised group.) It can be said that Uganda, Zambia and Kenya have made some progress on the road to meaningful reform; however, the mental health laws and their implementation in these three countries – and indeed, all of Africa – will have to receive ongoing scrutiny to avoid the 'paradigm shift' promised by the CRPD becoming a 'paradigm crawl'.

References

Allen, S. (2018) 'Mental health law proposal in Uganda will breach human rights, says civil society coalition', Available at: https://validity.ngo/2018/09/09/mental-health-law-proposal-in-uganda-will-breach-human-rights-says-civil-society-coalition/ (Accessed: 10 December 2022).

Appiagyei-Atua, K. (2017) 'A comparative analysis of the United Nations convention on the rights of persons with disabilities and the African draft protocol on the rights of persons with disabilities', *Law, Democracy and Development*, 21, pp. 153–175.

Bartlett, P. (2010) 'Thinking about the rest of the world: Mental health and rights outside the "first world"', in McSherry, B. and Weller, P. (eds) *Rethinking rights-based mental health laws*. Oxford: Hart Publishing, pp. 397–418.

Chemonges, T. (2022) *MPs demand more attention for mental health in the country*. Available at: https://parliamentwatch.ug/news-amp-updates/mps-demand-more-attention-for-mental-health-in-the-country/ (Accessed: 17 November 2022).

Combrinck, H. and Chilemba, E. (2021) '"The revolution will not be televised": Recent developments in mental health law reform in Zambia and Ghana', in Stein, M.A. et al. (eds.) *Mental health, legal capacity and human rights*. Cambridge: Cambridge University Press, pp. 184–198.

Committee on the Rights of Persons with Disabilities. (2014) 'General comment no. 1 - article 12: Equal recognition before the law', Available at: https://www.ohchr.org/en/documents/general-comments-and-recommendations/general-comment-no-1-article-12-equal-recognition-1 (Accessed: 12 October 2022).

Davidson, L. (2021) 'From pipe dream to reality: A practical legal approach towards the global abolition of psychiatric coercion', in Stein, M.A. et al. (eds.) *Mental health, legal capacity and human rights*. Cambridge: Cambridge University Press, pp. 70–94.

Dhanda, A. (2007) 'Legal capacity in the disability rights convention: Stranglehold of the past or lodestar for the future', *Syracuse Journal of International Law and Commerce*, 34, pp. 429–462.

Dinymoi, A.M.I. and Lubaale, E.C. (2021) 'The right to decision-making for persons with mental disabilities in Uganda', *Speculum Iuris*, 35(2), pp. 226–244.

Edwards, J. (2014) 'Ghana's mental health patients confined to prayer camps', *The Lancet*, 383(9911), pp. 15–16. https://doi.org/10.1016/S0140-6736(13)62717-8.

Enonchong, L. (2017) 'Mental disability and the right to personal liberty in Africa', *The International Journal of Human Rights*, 21(9), pp. 1351–1377. https://doi.org/10.1080/13642987.2017.1322067.

Fombad, C.M. (2016) 'Introduction', in Fombad, C.M. (ed.) *The implementation of modern African constitutions: Challenges and prospects*. Pretoria: Pretoria University Press, pp. 1–9.

Freeman, M.C. et al. (2015) 'Reversing hard won victories in the name of human rights: A critique of the general comment on article 12 of the UN convention on the rights of persons with disabilities', *The Lancet Psychiatry*, 2(9), pp. 844–850. https://doi.org/10.1016/S2215-0366(15)00218-7.

Ibrahim, M. (2017) 'Mental health in Africa: Human rights approaches to decolonization', in Morrow, M. and Malcoe, L.H. (eds.) *Critical inquiries for social justice in mental health*. Toronto: Toronto University Press, pp. 113–137.

Kalunga, F.K. (undated) *A 'legally-disqualified person': The mischief created by Zambia's parliament in the 2019 Mental Health Act*. Available at: https://www.commonwealthlawyers.com/africa/a-legally-disqualified-person-the-mischief-created-by-zambias-parliament-in-the-2019-mental-health-act-by-felicity-kayumba-kalunga/ (Accessed: 10 December 2022).

Kamga, S.A.D. (2013) 'A call for a protocol to the African charter on human and peoples' rights on the rights of persons with disabilities in Africa', *African Journal of International and Comparative Law*, 21(2), pp. 219–249. https://doi.org/10.3366/ajicl.2013.0060.

Kamundia, E. and Grobbelaar-Du Plessis, I. (2021) 'Supported decision-making and legal capacity in Kenya', in Stein, M.A. et al. (eds.) *Mental health, legal capacity and human rights*. Cambridge: Cambridge University Press, pp. 199–212.

Kamundia, E. (2022) *Shackled in Ghana for mental health conditions*. Available at: https://www.hrw.org/news/2022/12/08/shackled-ghana-mental-health-conditions (Accessed: 17 January 2023).

Kelly, B.D. (2022) *Response: Draft guidance on mental health, human rights and legislation*. Available at: https://www.ohchr.org/en/calls-for-input/calls-input/draft-guidance-mental-health-human-rights-legislation-who-ohchr (Accessed: 7 January 2023).

Kemboi, C. (2022) *An analysis of the Mental Health (Amendment) Act, 2022*. Nairobi: Kenya National Commission on Human Rights.

Mills, C. (2017) 'Global psychiatrization and psychic colonization: The coloniality of global mental health', in Morrow, M. and Malcoe, L.H. (eds.) *Critical inquiries for social justice in mental health*. Toronto: Toronto University Press, pp. 87–109.

Mental Health Uganda et al. (2018) Position statement: The Mental Health Bill, 2014, and the Report of the Sectoral Committee on Health. Available at: https://validity.ngo/wp-content/uploads/2018/09/Position-Statement-Mental-Health-Bill-2014-1.pdf (Accessed: 10 December 2022).

Mute, L. and Kalekye, E. (2016–2017) 'An appraisal of the draft protocol to the African charter on human and people's rights on the rights of persons with disabilities in Africa', *East African Law Journal*, 68, pp. 68–90.

Mutiso, M. (undated) *A new post-election dawn: What does the future hold for mental health in Kenya?* Available at: https://unitedgmh.org/knowledge-hub/a-new-post-election-dawn-what-does-the-future-hold-for-mental-health-in-kenya/ (Accessed: 12 December 2022).

Orago, N.W. (2013) 'The 2010 Kenyan constitution and the hierarchical place of international law in the Kenyan domestic legal system: A comparative perspective', *African Human Rights Law Journal*, 13, pp. 415–440.

Physicians for Human Rights. (2022) *Eleven human rights organizations laud landmark new mental health amendment act in Kenya*. Available at: https://phr.org/news/11-human-rights-organizations-laud-landmark-new-mental-health-amendment-act-in-kenya/ (Accessed: 27 November 2022).

'Purohit and Moore v The Gambia', African Commission on Human Rights, Communication No 241/2001, Sixteenth Activity Report 2002–2003.

Quinn, G. (2022) *Observations on the draft guidance on mental health, human rights and legislation: WHO & UN OHCHR*. Available at: https://www.ohchr.org/en/calls-for-input/calls-input/draft-guidance-mental-health-human-rights-legislation-who-ohchr (Accessed: 7 January 2023).

Quinn, G. and Degener, T. (2002). *The current use and future potential of United Nations human rights instruments in the context of disability*. New York: United Nations.

Raw, A. (2019) You only have rights if you are a person: How Zambia is legislating away the rights of persons with psychosocial disabilities. Available at: https://africanlii.org/article/20190620/you-only-have-rights-if-you-are-person-how-zambia-legislating-away-rights-persons (Accessed: 24 October 2022).

United Nations (2006) *Convention on the rights of persons with disabilities*. New York. United Nations.

Wilson, K.E. (2020) 'The abolition or reform of mental health law: How should the law recognise and respond to the vulnerability of persons with mental impairment?', *Medical Law Review*, 28(1), pp. 30–64. https://doi.org/10.1093/medlaw/fwz008.

26
MENTAL HEALTH LAW AND PRACTICE IN GHANA
An examination of the implementation of Act 846

Lily Kpobi, Charlotte Kwakye-Nuako, and Leveana Gyimah

Introduction

Availability of and access to mental health services in many low- and middle-income countries in Africa and elsewhere still fall below what is considered optimal (Rathod et al., 2017). Various reasons have been posited to account for this, including limitations in numbers of trained health professionals, health facilities, and other resources for mental health (Freeman, 2016). At the root of these constraints is often a generally low political will and interest in mental health, and consequently, inadequate mental health legislation (Breuer et al., 2016). Several low- and middle-income countries continue to use outdated laws which often reinforce stigma and discrimination towards mental health services and service users. The absence of appropriate legislation has meant that funding and policy development to support mental health services have also been lacking (Omar et al., 2010). Unlike in high-income countries, the portion of the health budget devoted to mental health in many low- and middle-income countries is generally comparatively low, sometimes even less than 1% of the total health budget (WHO, 2021, 2022).

According to the World Health Organization (WHO), the presence of appropriate mental health laws and policies has been found to play a significant role in promoting good clinical practice, strengthening community-based rehabilitation and integration, and preventing human rights abuses (WHO, 2019, 2022). When the laws encourage the apposite inclusion of alternative health care systems, there are better opportunities for reducing the treatment gap in contexts where formal resources may be constrained. These suggest that having strong mental health legislation is important for ensuring availability, access, and equity in mental health care in countries.

While having good legislation is desirable, enacting mental health laws in many African countries has historically not been simple (Freeman, 2016). From the difficulties of the colonial era to the upheaval of military rule on the continent, mental health systems have often been neglected. In addition to these, cultural and religious beliefs and practices have also influenced perceptions about mental health, and consequently, the extent to which laws and policies have been developed in that area (Gopalkrishnan, 2018).

In this chapter, we examine the development of mental health legislation in Ghana and discuss how the current law is being implemented. We first present a brief history of mental health legislation in Ghana from pre-colonial times through colonial regulations and into the postcolonial and military eras. We then discuss Ghana's current Mental Health Act, 2012 (Act 846) and how it has positively impacted on existing statutory provisions on mental health. The third section of this chapter then explains the process of implementation of the law at the health systems level of the country, including the successes and challenges of implementation. We conclude the chapter by making recommendations for fully implementing the provisions of the Act and consequently improving mental health in Ghana and other similar contexts.

An overview of mental health care in Ghana: from pre-colonial to modern health care

While not backed by formal legislation, historically the treatment of illness (including mental illness) in Ghana formed part of the work of traditional healers and herbalists. In many cases, the healers were considered spiritual leaders within the communities in which they worked and were thus believed to have skills – many of them supernatural – for treating both physical and spiritual maladies (Kpobi et al., 2014). While the treatment for milder behavioural problems would typically involve social or communal processes, severe mental illness was mostly treated through exorcism at traditional shrines, sometimes together with herbal medications. According to Twumasi (1975), the consultations at the shrine were both biopsychosocial and spiritual in nature. All treatment regimens typically required the involvement of a family member, and this helped to facilitate reintegration into the community (Asare, 2010). Persons were made to confess their known sins to re-establish lost relationships (psychosocial) and were made to use herbs in various forms (physical healing). An important part of the ritual was the consultation of the gods for diagnosis and intervention, thus completing the spiritual part of their healing.

Following the formalisation of colonial rule in Ghana, traditional health practices were banned, and European health beliefs and practices were promoted by the colonial British government. Through the passing of the Lunatic Asylum Ordinance by then-Governor Sir Edward Griffiths in 1888, the colonial government began to arrest persons with mental illness and vagrants, who were subsequently detained in a converted courthouse in the former Victoriaborg area of Accra (Osei, 2006). This converted courthouse became known as the Lunatic Asylum. As was similarly practised in Britain in those days, the approved interventions for mental health care at that time generally involved detaining persons with mental health problems in government-run facilities which were designed to 'protect' the society from the patients. There were no specific medical interventions (Kpobi et al., 2014).

Due to overcrowding in the converted lunatic asylum, the colonial government soon built a bigger asylum in 1906 which could house over 200 persons. The new Accra Lunatic Asylum was situated in what was then the outskirts of the town. With the evolution of psychiatry over the years, this facility expanded and became the first psychiatric hospital in Ghana – the present-day Accra Psychiatric Hospital.

The Lunatic Asylum Ordinance of 1888 persisted until 1972 when the Mental Health Decree of 1972 (NRCD 30) was passed by the then-military government which had overthrown Ghana's second republican government. The NRCD 30 provided for the establishment of more psychiatric facilities (including Pantang Psychiatric Hospital) and the constitution of visiting committees to monitor care practices and outcomes. At that time, the focus had shifted to institutional care, and dialogue about voluntary treatment had commenced (Osei, Asare, and Roberts, 2021).

NRCD 30 also provided for what was seen as some basic human rights for what were still considered 'inmates'. For instance, Sections 2(b) and 2(c) of the Decree required that every patient be kept clean, well-nourished, and clothed. It also made provision for the care of the vulnerable such as female patients and children under 16 years (Section 26). Moreover, NRCD 30 allowed guardians to obtain a court order before a magistrate to commit a person into temporary treatment.

While NRCD 30 was an improvement on the Lunatic Asylum Ordinance, it soon became outdated and therefore inadequate to meet the mental health needs of Ghana's populace. Moreover, during that time the Pentecostal movement had started to spread across the African continent (Anderson, 2005; Asamoah-Gyadu, 2020), and Ghana experienced its share of a proliferation of Pentecostal and charismatic churches with their attendant faith healing centres (called 'prayer camps'), some of whose practices raised serious concerns about human rights violations. The focus of these religious establishments was on demon possession and so the preferred mode of treatment was exorcism with little or no medical intervention and attention to human rights. Although some benefits were recognised from the 'community-based' nature of the prayer camps, practices such as the use of mechanical restraints, corporal punishment to exorcise spirits, forced fasting, and the deprivation of other needs, which were found to be happening at some prayer camps, presented real challenges to their integration into health services (Arias *et al.*, 2016).

In addition to the concerns about traditional and faith healing practices, there was also increasing discontent with the social and political systems of the time resulting from economic hardships, changes in social structures, and the difficulties of military rule. As a result, formal systems and structures were unpopular and viewed with suspicion or discontent. This changing social and religious landscape meant that a renewed interest in alternative health care interventions started to grow in popularity.

Following independence from colonial rule, the postcolonial governments in 1965 and again in 1975 constructed two additional psychiatric facilities in Ankaful and Pantang respectively. These three facilities – Accra Psychiatric Hospital, Pantang and Ankaful hospitals – remain the only specialist psychiatric institutions in the country. They are all located on the southern coast of Ghana but serve people from other parts of the country and the West African region. To provide access to some services to people living in other parts of the country, from 1981 until the early 2000s, small psychiatric units were opened in some regional hospitals further north of the coast such as at the Komfo Anokye Teaching Hospital in Kumasi in the Ashanti Region, and the Tamale Hospital (now Tamale Teaching Hospital) in the Northern Region (Asare, 2010).

Due to the limited number of specialist psychiatric facilities and professionals in Ghana, from 1986 psychiatric care in underserved parts of the country was largely provided by a limited number of community health workers who were placed within district hospitals and community health centres (Ewusi-Mensah, 2001). These community health workers engaged in case-finding, follow-up care, and family support, and sometimes intervened in human rights issues. Although community psychiatric nursing has been in existence for several years, it was poorly developed and largely unsupported until the last decade. In subsequent sections below, we discuss the integration of psychiatric care into primary health care through such community-based practices. As we highlight below, these developments are largely the result of the promulgation of the new mental health law in 2012. To put these in context, we first discuss the journey to the passage of this new mental health legislation.

After Ghana entered into the fourth democratic republic in 1992 and promulgated a new constitution that emphasised the rights of all persons including the mentally ill, there began several attempts to amend NRCD 30 to improve mental health services in the country. More serious targeted efforts to replace the 1972 mental health legislation, however, started in 2003 through the work of both public and private sector groups, mental health professionals at various levels, and individual advocates. In March 2012, the parliament of Ghana successfully passed the new Mental Health Act 846. The new Act adopts a rights-based, decentralised approach to mental health care, and provides for the development of more community-based mental health services. In the following section, we examine the new Mental Health Act, 2012 (Act 846), the activities leading to its passage, changes it has made to existing laws, and how it is being implemented ten years after it was promulgated.

Developing new legislation for mental health

Despite the need to promulgate a new law, the journey to passing Ghana's current Mental Health Act was an arduous one. Writing about the process, Akwasi Osei, the immediate-past Chief Executive Officer of the Mental Health Authority, describes some of the factors which derailed the smooth passage of the Bill into law (Osei, 2008; Osei et al., 2021). According to him, by 2003 several plans had been made to revise the existing mental health law and this coincided with plans of the World Health Organization (WHO) to encourage countries to enact or revise their mental health legislation (WHO, 2005). Thus, in 2004 a Technical Drafting Committee was formed by the then-Minister of Health with the assistance of a WHO technical committee that began working on drafting the proposed new Bill. The Bill, however, was not laid before Parliament until 2011. There were several reasons for this. First, the Ministry of Health was reportedly concerned that the psychiatrists desired to create a parallel mental health system instead of working to properly integrate mental health into the existing Ghana Health Service (Osei, 2008). Second, other health-related Bills were still under development at the time, and the Minister chose to delay the introduction of the Mental Health Bill to Parliament until the other health Bills were ready, in order to present them together (Osei, 2008).

While these delays were ongoing, a consultant was contracted to review the Mental Health Bill and other health-related Bills to ensure their coherence before presentation to Parliament. All of this took quite a lot of time and significantly delayed the process (Osei, 2008, 2011). After several years of delay, the new Bill was passed by Ghana's legislative branch of government – Parliament – in March 2012, and the new Act was assented to by the President of the Republic on 31 May 2012. Ghana's new Mental Health Act (Act 846) thus came into effect.

Ghana's Mental Health Act, 2012 (Act 846)

According to the Memorandum that was attached to the Bill laid before Parliament, Act 846 was to replace the old (1972) Mental Health Act, accord it with best practices, and align it with international best standards of mental health care. It was also to facilitate an expansion of mental health services to include private and religious facilities so as to enable proper monitoring of their activities and prevent potential abuse at such facilities. Third, the law was to promote the deinstitutionalisation of mental health care and provide for expansion of community-based services. In this section, we provide a detailed discussion of the Act to highlight the differences it promoted in mental health care, as well as the ways in which it has affected the procedure for mentally ill offenders (MIOs).

The first part of Act 846 addresses issues of governance and the appointment of a Board. In terms of governance, a Mental Health Authority (MHA) is established under the law as a legal person with the power to own property and oversee the general governance of mental health-related issues in the country. The Mental Health Authority has the objectives of proposing, implementing, and promoting mental health policies. It is also mandated to diffuse mental health care to the regional and district levels, and provide safe and rights-centred care for persons who are mentally ill, as well as to ensure the recruitment, retention, and adequate remuneration of workers. Furthermore, the Authority is to promote culturally acceptable humane mental health care, which includes exploring appropriate collaborations with alternative health providers such as traditional or faith-based healers. To fulfil this mandate, there have been efforts to build partnerships with healers as a step towards providing integrated mental health care.

The MHA has an 11-member Governing Board of the Authority with a tenure of 4 years. It includes a chairperson and the Chief Executive Officer (CEO) of the Authority. The membership of the Board is drawn from the Ministry of the Interior, Ministry of Health, the Ghana Health Service, tertiary medical training institutions, and civil society organisations (CSOs). The Board is appointed with the mandate of ensuring "the proper and effective performance of the functions of the Authority" (s. 4(3) of Mental Health Act, 2012 (Act 846)). Since the passing of the Act, there have been two governing boards of the Authority. At the time of writing this chapter, a new board had just been inaugurated 18 months into the second term of the current political administration.

Act 846 also establishes mental health services at the national, regional, and district levels. This aligns with the main objective of the law to promote the dispersion of mental health care to the regional and district facilities, in order to facilitate integrating mental health into primary health care. The law also emphasises community-based services. As a result, since about 2015, approximately 1000 community mental health workers have been trained and posted across the country to serve at community health centres (Osei *et al.*, 2021). This is a marked improvement from the less than 100 community psychiatric nurses that worked in a few communities previously (Ae-Ngibise *et al.*, 2010; Ofori-Atta *et al.*, 2010). Additionally, the law establishes visiting committees in line with the agenda to deinstitutionalise mental health care. These visiting committees are supposed to oversee and visit facilities and residences where people with mental health problems reside or are kept. Although there are reportedly plans to inaugurate them, at the time of writing this chapter, none had ever been constituted.

Sections 24–33 of Act 846 focus on the establishment, composition, and functions of a quasi-judicial Mental Health Review Tribunal. This Tribunal is a relic from the old Mental Health Act (NRCD 30) but has been expanded to require the inclusion of at least one service user as a member. It is to be headed by a lawyer of at least 10 years' experience. However, as an administrative tribunal, it does not have the powers of a high court.

Sections 39–53 deal with both voluntary treatment (39–41) and involuntary treatment (42–53). Section 42, for instance, allows for a recommendation to the court for temporary treatment and the processes to be used by the courts in such an application as well as an appeal process. Similarly, Section 48 provides for involuntary service users to be treated under a certificate of urgency. This purportedly is to allow for public protection and safety, especially where the person with a mental disorder is thought to pose a risk to themselves and/or others. However, a recent study identified that most health care workers (apart from psychiatrists) were found to have little knowledge of the existence or use of this certificate of urgency (Anokye et al., 2018).

Act 846 on protecting the human rights of the mentally ill

Following Chapter 5 of Ghana's 1992 constitution, provisions for the protection of human rights are highlighted in Act 846. In the constitution, Article 12(2) provides that

> every person in Ghana, whatever his race, place of origin, political opinion, colour, religion, creed or gender shall be entitled to the fundamental human rights and freedoms of the individual contained in this chapter but subject to the respect of the rights and freedoms of others and for the public interest.

This makes provision for people living with mental health problems to enjoy the rights enshrined in the constitution just as any other persons in the country. Conversely, this blanket right is whittled down in Article 14 which restricts the right to liberty for persons with mental disorders who are considered a risk to themselves and the public.

In Sections 54–63 of Act 846, however, there are some provisions for the rights of persons with mental disorders to be protected. These include issues about standards of treatment, the use of seclusion and restraint, confidentiality, privacy, autonomy, access to information about themselves, as well as the right to employment. This part of the Act constitutes one of the dominant reasons why the law was promulgated—it aptly adopts a human rights approach to mental health care and emphasises the protection of the rights of people with mental health problems. In this way, Act 846 promotes the realisation of several articles of the United Nations Convention on the Rights of People with Disabilities (UN CRPD) including Article 5, Article 12, and Article 15.

An important aspect of human rights is nomenclature. Act 846 uses more appropriate language to describe mental health and consequently persons living with mental health problems. This is contrary to what pertains, for instance, in Ghana's Criminal and Other Offences Act, 1960 (Act 29). Promulgated in the 1960s, Act 29 uses damaging labels such as "idiot" and "imbecile" to describe people in need of mental health care. To illustrate, Section 102 of Act 29 criminalises sexual contact with persons who are mentally ill, stating it as follows:

> Whoever has carnal knowledge or has unnatural carnal knowledge of any idiot, imbecile or a mental patient in or under the care of a mental hospital whether with or without his or her consent, in circumstances which prove that the accused knew at the time or the commission of the offence that the person had a mental incapacity commits an offence and shall be liable on summary conviction to imprisonment for a term of not less than five or more than twenty-five years.

The penalty for this offence (5–25 years) makes it a second-degree felony; however, the presence of such derogatory language means that lawmakers inadvertently infringe on the rights of the people who are the objects of the law's protection. Act 846 uses more appropriate modern terminology such as "intellectual disability" or "developmental disabilities" among others. This is one area where professionals have been advocating for the incorporation of appropriate terminology in Act 29.

Act 846 also protects vulnerable groups and these are specified as females, children, the aged, and persons with developmental disabilities. It also addresses issues of capacity, competence, and guardianship. In Act 846, capacity is used to refer to the perceived possession of appropriate cognitive abilities suitable to make reasonable decisions about self and dependents. With regards to competence, Act 846 views a person who is unable to manage their own finances, business, occupation, marriage, and testamentary capacity as a person who is incompetent (Section 68(1)(4)). The law thus provides that their capacity to engage in and handle such activities be assessed by a qualified clinical team. Where the person is deemed incompetent, the law provides for the appointment of a guardian via two pathways: a social welfare officer or family member may apply to the court for the appointment of a guardian, or anyone else can apply when they observe that guardians responsible for managing the affairs of the individual with mental illness are doing so in a detrimental manner (Section 68(3)). Additionally, the law provides for psychosocial rehabilitation for offenders with mental disorders. All these are essential to protecting the human rights of persons living with mental health problems.

Funding for mental health care

The law also addresses the sore issue of funding for mental health in Ghana (see Sections 80–92). It provides for the creation of a Mental Health Fund, and dictates the sources of money for the fund, its management, as well as general financial management for the MHA. Despite these provisions, and even with numerous advocacy efforts over the years, the Mental Health Fund, though established, does not yet have an appropriate levy to feed it. Funding for the implementation of the law was one of the key areas identified when Act 846 was first promulgated (Doku, Wusu-Takyi and Awakame, 2012; Walker and Osei, 2017), and this challenge persists ten years after the law was promulgated. The passage of the legislative instrument that would give effect to several provisions of the law apparently left out provisions on mental health funding. While this omission was purportedly due to some conflicting procedures before Parliament, it is a further marker of the low interest in mental health generally.

Transitional provisions and offences

Sections 93–100 address acts carried out under the old law that were saved in this new law as well as transitional provisions. In this section are also provisions for offences. For instance, a person who is found to have neglected a person with mental health problems or to be discriminating against them faces up to 2 years of a custodial sentence, and/or a fine of GHC6000 (approximately £400 currently). As we write this chapter, there has been no known litigation on this section of the law. Section 96 further makes provision for the Minister of Health to make the requisite regulations to be passed to give effect to portions of the Act. Despite numerous delays and errors, Parliament has since passed the Mental Health Regulations, 2019 (L.I. 2385). This Legislative Instrument (LI) gives effect and explains different activities that the Mental Health Authority is expected to carry out as part of its mandate.

The impact of Act 846 on the criminal law in respect of mentally ill offenders

Act 846, in several ways, repeals some of the existing laws relating to how persons with mental illness are treated in the criminal justice system. As already mentioned, it has changed the nomenclature on persons with mental illness in the substantive criminal law, but more importantly, it has changed the procedure of how they are to be dealt with in judicial matters. Although these procedures are not clearly stated, using the rules of interpretation one can deduce these changes. One of the canons of interpretation is that the provisions of a new law that are contrary to existing law are meant to repeal the old law. Again, the presumption is that laws that are specific to particular issues are preferred to laws that apply generally. Thus, in the Ghanaian case of *Bonney & 4,174 others vs. Ghana Ports and Harbours Authority* (Civil Appeal No. J4/39/2012), the Supreme Court speaking through Owusu JSC, quoted *Halsbury's Laws of England* 4th edition volume 44 to define the rule *generalia specialbus non derogant* (general laws do not prevail over specifics) in this way:

> Whenever there is a general enactment in a statute which if taken in its most comprehensive sense, would override a particular enactment in the same statute, the particular enactment must be operative, and the general enactment must be taken to affect only the ports [sic] of the statute to which it may properly apply.

Applying this principle, Act 846 is a later law, and so there is a legal presumption that Parliament knew the body of laws that existed, and has therefore repealed the old laws with the promulgation of Act 846 which addresses issues of mental disorder and MIOs. Although criminal acts are defined and punished in various laws, a large portion of Ghana's laws on crime are captured in the Criminal and Other Offences Act, 1960 (Act 29) and the procedure for criminal trials is encapsulated in the Criminal and Other Offences (Procedure) Act, 1960 (Act 30). For instance, in Section 27 of Act 29, the law presumes all people as sane until they prove otherwise. It provides as follows:

> When a person is accused of a crime, the special verdict provided by the Criminal Procedure Code in the case of insanity shall only be applicable—
>
> (a) if he was prevented, because of idiocy, imbecility, [sic] or any mental derangement or disease affecting the mind, from knowing the nature or consequences of the act in respect of which he is accused; or
> (b) if he did the act in respect of which he is accused under the influence of an insane delusion of such a nature as to render him, in the opinion of the jury or of the Court, an unfit subject for the punishment of any kind in respect of such act.

The law recognises the dual requirement of capacity to appreciate the act as criminal at the time of commission and competence to stand trial. It identifies developmental disorders and other mental illnesses as possible candidates for the special verdict of 'guilty but insane'. However, it also recognises that for such a person to qualify for the verdict, the person would have to prove that as a result of the disorder they were prevented from knowing the nature and consequence of the criminal act they committed. The Ghanaian standard for insanity deviates from the M'Naghten test of not knowing the 'nature and quality' of an act, and rather substitutes it for the 'nature or consequences' of the criminal act. Thus, a person may obtain a special verdict if they do not know the nature of the offence committed or cannot appreciate the consequences of the act committed by virtue of their mental illness.

Although Act 846 endorses the procedure set out in the Criminal and Other Offences Procedure Act, 1960 (Act 30), it also improves upon it. The procedure in Section 133 of

Act 30 is to have the judge refer the suspect who may be having mental health issues to a psychiatric facility for evaluation and safekeeping until they are ready to stand trial. This only applied to courts and not to the police. However, Section 76(1) of Act 846 states that a person who is suspected of mental illness while in police custody is to be sent for psychiatric evaluation rather than to remain in custody. Subsection 3 of the same section provides that "an offender suspected to have a mental disorder at the time of the commission of the offence shall be sent to a psychiatric hospital for assessment and if found to have mental disorder shall be committed to treatment". Act 846 thus gives the mandate to both the police and the courts to divert persons found to be mentally ill. With regard to the diversion by the courts, it is, however, unclear who is to send the individual for treatment. A combined reading of Section 27 of Act 29 and Section 133 of Act 30 suggests that once the police have arraigned the person before the magistrate or judge, the accused person may request for evaluation as to their sanity at the time the crime was committed.

A second effect of Act 846 on the law on MIOs is that it gives the mental health practitioner the power to discharge persons committed to a mental health facility after reassessment. In Section 76(7) of Act 846 it reads:

An offender assessed and found to have had a mental disorder at the time of the offence and found by the court not to be responsible for a criminal act due to mental disorder, who on reassessment by the mental health facility is found no longer to have a mental disorder, or is no longer in need of in-patient treatment shall be discharged if the offence is a minor offence otherwise a report shall be made to the court for a further directive.

This power of mental health facilities to discharge mentally ill offenders with minor disorders is restricted to the courts. It is thus contrary to Section 137 (3)-(7) of Act 30 which gives the power to the minister responsible for health on behalf of the President, to commit an MIO to a mental health facility, and to allow for their discharge under certain conditions irrespective of the offence committed.

Per the rules of interpretation explained above, a law that is more recent and specific takes precedence over an older law or a law with general application. In that sense, the law on the criminal procedure is general to all criminal procedures whereas Act 846 is specific for issues of mental health. Arguably, the procedure for dealing with MIOs should follow the procedure set out in Act 846, particularly in aspects of the procedure that differ from what is prescribed in Act 30. The Mental Health Authority may seek a statutory interpretation at the High Court to clarify this. In our view, the provision in the Mental Health Act should prevail since it gives effect to the general human rights-based approach, and also reduces the time that it would take for the MIOs with minor offences to be released from forensic psychiatric wards.

In addition to the procedures for MIOs, Act 846 provides a better solution to the treatment of persons who attempt suicide, and changes the substantive criminal provision. Currently, suicide attempt is criminalised under Section 57(2) of Ghana's Criminal and Other Offences Act, 1960 (Act 29). It is punishable as a misdemeanour, meaning that the suspect faces a custodial jail term of between 3 and 36 months. Section 76(10) of Act 846 makes provision for persons who attempt suicide to be diverted from the courts to psychiatric facilities for evaluation and intervention. Once again, the position of Act 846 provides a more humane and rights-centred approach to such individuals than the 1960 law. What remains is for the courts to apply the rules of interpretation.

Generally, from the above, it is clear that Act 846 is a comprehensive and well-thought-through law which places greater emphasis on determining appropriate means of intervention to ensure the promotion of human rights and justice, and less on punishment as encouraged in other (older) laws. While these written rules and procedures are noteworthy, the appropriate implementation of the Act is what would make the difference in transforming mental health in Ghana. In the following section, we highlight some of the achievements and challenges that have been experienced in implementing Act 846 in Ghana.

Implementing Act 846: achievements and challenges

In this section, we discuss some practical examples of how the new Act has been implemented, looking at both legal and health systems implementation. We have discussed criminal procedures in the section above; however, Act 846 has also been applied in civil cases. With respect to the legal application of the Act in civil proceedings, there are examples of issues of mental health arising in probate actions where, for instance, court actions are taken by family members to contest the will of a deceased relative. In such instances, the cases typically revolve around the mental capacity of the testator to make a will at the time they did. In most cases, the argument is made that the testator showed signs of dementia or some other mental health problems typically thought to be related to ageing or loss of memory. A case in point is *Gee nee Whang and another vs Vanderpuye Manison* (Civil Appeal No. J4/b/2015 S.C.), where the respondent (a son of the deceased) contested the will of the deceased as having been made when the deceased lacked testamentary capacity. The court found that at the time of making the will, the testator did not have testamentary capacity and that all activities were done before he was diagnosed by a psychiatrist with dementia. They also found that the signature of the testator had been forged. The will could not be proved in solemn form and was thus inadmissible to probate. This is one of many cases that have contested testamentary capacity on grounds of mental illness.

In clinical practice, the Act protects against the exploitation of individuals in the management of their estate. For persons living with dementia who may require assistance due to declining cognitive skills, an assessment of the individual by a team of health professionals is required through an application to the law court to ascertain the status of the said individual before granting the request. This is contrary to the previous practice of power granted to relevant third parties simply by the issuance of a letter by the health professional to the institution in charge of the individual's estate. Again, under Act 846, issues of guardianship of persons with severe mental illness who are considered unable to manage their personal affairs are considered, with the status of the guardianship reviewed annually or earlier upon the recommendation of the medical team rather than being in place in perpetuity.

Although Act 846 makes provisions for involuntary admissions in situations of risk to self and property, this contradicts the UN CRPD which advocates for 'no exceptions' to involuntary care (Funk and Bold, 2020). As Hoare and Duffy (2021) have argued, however, advocating for absolutely no involuntary treatment has often been found impractical in clinical settings. This notwithstanding, such legal provisions are expected to guide clinical practice to better protect service users from potential for abuse and neglect.

As we discussed above, Act 846 takes a human rights-based approach to mental health care and policies. To build the capacity for mental health professionals in recognising and acting on human rights issues, and to promote respect for the basic rights of people seeking treatment for mental health problems, the Mental Health Authority together with the WHO have recently implemented the Quality Rights (QR) initiative to provide training to mental health workers. The QR initiative is a WHO programme which was developed in response to the frequent instances of human rights abuses against people with mental health problems globally (Funk and Drew, 2017). This initiative attempts to minimise and eradicate such abuses through capacity building on human rights approaches to delivering mental health care. The QR initiative seeks to transform mental health services by creating awareness of practices that promote human rights and recovery-oriented care among multi-sectoral groups including health, education, social services, and community members. Its successful launch and implementation in Ghana were greatly facilitated by the provisions of Act 846, particularly the role of the Mental Health Authority in promoting the respect for human rights of all persons receiving mental health interventions.

Ghana was the first country to roll out the QR initiative on a national scale in 2019 (WHO, 2019). The rollout began with a national launch attended by mental health professionals, policymakers, members of health institutions, and other national and international stakeholders, as well as representatives of agencies such as the WHO. During the launch, an electronic self-paced training platform (the Quality Rights e-training platform) was introduced for use in training key stakeholders including health professionals, teachers, persons with lived experience of mental illness, and their caregivers. This was the initial stage of the rollout which sought to create awareness and provide guidance on how to include person-centred human rights care in the mental health interventions, particularly at the community level. This was significant due to past incidents of alleged abuse of people living with mental health issues in communities.

Beyond the e-training approach, in-person group sessions were also conducted to engage a selection of professionals from health, education, and social welfare, and persons with lived experience of mental illness in in-depth discussions on the principles and practice of human rights care in line with the UN CRPD. Additionally, psychiatric facilities have recently undergone assessment on the quality-of-service provision and respect for human rights (Moro *et al.*, 2022). The aim of these assessments was to understand the gaps in service provision in order to improve the health system and interventions provided. The process of strengthening the mental health system through these facility assessments and implementation of measures to address the gaps is still ongoing.

As we have discussed above, there has been a focus on building capacity for human rights-based care among mental health professionals in the country. To build upon that aspect, the provisions of Act 846 have also seen greater emphasis on the deinstitutionalisation of mental health services in Ghana, with a remarkable expansion of community mental health care across previously unserved parts of the country. There has been an increase in the number of mental health professionals employed to work in public health facilities, including more psychologists, psychiatrists, and physician assistants in psychiatry (called Clinical Psychiatric Officers) at regional and district levels. There has also been an increase in community mental health nurses dispatched to serve within communities and settlements in rural parts of the country.

While more community mental health workers have been trained and posted to work in primary health care facilities, there has been limited support by way of resources and logistics to facilitate their work. The general absence of dedicated ring-fenced funding to support community mental health interventions has meant a continued reliance on higher-level tertiary or specialist care which is not easily accessible for many people and communities. With the limited support from the health system, there has been a continued increase in the number of trained mental health workers emigrating from the country to work in Europe and North America (Nartey, 2022). This 'brain-drain' phenomenon has had adverse effects on the availability of adequate numbers of health workers to support the struggling mental health system (Oladeji and Gureje, 2016).

As discussed above, Section 3 of Act 846 further encourages the establishment of working relationships between community health workers and traditional or faith healers located in different parts of the country. Given the pluralistic nature of health-seeking in Ghana, there is a high level of engagement with traditional and herbal medicines. These services often run parallel to the formal health system. Since 2018, community mental health workers have been tasked to find ways to work with the informal health sector as a way of increasing reach to service users, but also as a way of monitoring for potential human rights abuses (MHA, 2018). A recent ethnographic documentary project highlighted that in this instance also, the inadequate logistic support often results in ethical dilemmas for the health workers, particularly around the use of mechanical restraints, as there are often no in-patient facilities available in rural communities to provide alternatives (Colucci, 2021). This contrasts with the training of initiatives such as Quality Rights, and highlights the need to include systems-level change together with transforming human resources. Although the Authority has provided guidelines for community mental health workers to establish collaborations with traditional and faith healers, these guidelines do not appear to promote actual mutual collaboration. Instead, the guidelines seek to facilitate the transformation of traditional cultural ideas of illness and wellness regarding mental health to align with biomedical perspectives. Equal working partnerships between healers and health workers have therefore been difficult to establish.

Generally, the implementation of Act 846 has had some achievements but is also faced with serious challenges. Many of these challenges are related to the absence of adequate funding support to sustain the rapid transformation of services and interventions. They are also driven by the inadvertent (and perhaps unanticipated) power dynamics between existing cultural ideas of leadership and westernised perspectives which retain hegemony in the postcolonial formal sector. These barriers were not addressed in the new Act, and may be contributors to the limited uptake of programmes such as collaborative partnerships with traditional and faith healers.

Recommendations for improving the implementation of Act 846

The current law – Act 846 – is a good one and seeks to uphold the human rights of people with mental health problems. As discussed above, there are some portions of the law that provide a better option for criminal procedure than what pertains to Act 30. There is therefore a need to seek interpretation of these portions of the law to ensure that the rights of people with mental disorders are adequately upheld in court.

Mental health is a life-course experience requiring multi-sectoral engagement to address the needs of the populace. As emphasised in the WHO Atlas (2020) global report as well as the World Mental Health Report (WHO, 2022), the implementation of mental health policies, plans, and laws require collaboration between multiple sectors. This goes beyond the health sector to include service users and family or carer advocacy groups, social affairs/social welfare, justice, education, housing, employment, and government and non-government agencies. There is also the need to include the media, academia, and local and international organisations that deliver or advocate for mental health services. This can span between the private sector, professional associations, faith-based organisations/institutions, and traditional/indigenous healers. To achieve this fusion of health needs with resources requires strong leadership and a robust governance structure. Through such structures, countries can address mental health needs from the lowest to the highest level of care across the life course. The establishment of the governance structures of the MHA such as the Mental Health Review Tribunal and the visiting committees across the regions and districts are therefore critical to support the full implementation of the law.

As part of its efforts at multisectoral collaboration, it would be beneficial for the Mental Health Authority to work with organisations such as the Narcotics Control Commission which has a dedicated fund for research and treatment of persons with substance use disorders. Such partnerships would help promote mental health and also fill the gaps in implementation created by the MHA's lack of resources.

Conclusions

In this chapter, we have narrated Ghana's journey through mental health legislation, looking at the processes and challenges which have resulted in the promulgation and partial implementation of the current Mental Health Act. Much of the discussion has centred on the operationalisation of Act 846 and its legislative instrument (LI). Unfortunately, the full implementation of these legal instruments has not been realised a decade since the passing of the Act. Although there has been some remarkable progress in terms of the establishment of the administrative structures for overseeing mental health services in the country, as well as some strides in human resource capacity, what is still lacking is the provision of appropriate ring-fenced funding and governance structures to support mental health work. These structures are important for improving patient care and protecting human rights. The passage of the LI without the complementary Mental Health Levy as proposed in the Act appears to have been a great setback as successive governments over the years have not committed the required resources to meet the mental health budget.

These challenges notwithstanding, there have been significant transformations in the mental health system within the last decade which, if sustained and improved, bodes well for mental health work generally. To keep this momentum going, there is a need for multisectoral collaboration between state and non-state agencies to identify and strengthen structures capable of supporting the full implementation of the Act to ensure its sustainability. A comprehensive review of the current Act and its instruments is certainly warranted in order to synthesise lessons learned over the decade of its existence, and to facilitate appropriate planning for the future.

The strides and challenges that Ghana has experienced in developing appropriate legislation for mental health contain lessons which may be useful for other developing countries in the region and elsewhere. First, the emphasis on community-based care in Act 846 has been beneficial in integrating mental health services at the primary level and decentralising psychiatric care from specialist institutions to community centres. This is important given the difficulties of access that are experienced in many developing countries where specialist facilities are limited and costly. By providing some interventions at the primary level, more people could benefit from early interventions.

Related to this point, Act 846 facilitated the training and posting of larger numbers of community mental health officers to work in the community-based facilities across Ghana. In addition to the biomedical interventions that these health workers can offer, the added mandate of establishing working relationships with non-biomedical practitioners is also important as there is greater opportunity for collaborative care, as well as the potential elimination of human rights violations. Further, it provides room for the inclusion of psychosocial interventions at the community level – something that has been largely absent in the implementation strategies which have emphasised the expansion of psychiatric (thus medicalised) care. Given the dominance of medical pluralism in many low- and middle-income countries, and the popularity of alternative approaches to mental health care, such partnerships with traditional and faith healers are valuable and necessary.

Reacting to the debate about involuntary treatment, McGovern (2022) cautions on the risk of the legalisation of such treatment becoming the norm rather than the exception in difficult clinical situations as they run the risk of fostering a tendency for abuse. Instead, McGovern advocates that there must always be an active exploration of alternatives that put the patient at the centre of care in difficult clinical situations. Similarly, Moro *et al.* (2022) have advocated for the use of measures such as advance directives and substituted decision-making during periods of acute mental illness as a plausible alternative to involuntary treatment. Although still largely unresolved, these debates have resulted in health professionals in Ghana (and in other countries globally) exploring potential paradigm shifts to make mental health service users an integral part of decisions that concern them – including particularly in decisions about their treatment. The debates about the utility of such provision have resulted in revisions in clinical guidelines in some countries (Hoare and Duffy, 2021; Moro *et al.*, 2022; McGovern, 2022). Although, in recent years, similar conversations about revising clinical guidelines to reflect the evolving perspectives about involuntary treatment have begun in Ghana, no specific revisions have yet been made.

Ghana's experiences in the last decade reflect the benefits of developing and implementing appropriate legislation for mental health services within a developing country context. But although these strides are noteworthy, Ghana's experiences highlight the fact that, to ensure the success of these activities, the importance of providing dedicated ring-fenced funding specifically for mental health cannot be overemphasised. Despite the heavy burden that mental health problems constitute both locally and globally, due to the low priority and low political interest in mental health issues in many countries, there is a danger of mental health needs being overlooked unless they are specifically targeted. Providing dedicated funding structures to support mental health services is therefore crucial for transformation of services, but also importantly, for the sustainability of the gains.

Improving mental health outcomes in any developing (or indeed any developed) country must therefore include concrete processes for the proper implementation and sustainability of legislative structures to support improvement of services, experiences, and outcomes. This can be achieved through the actual provision of resources, funding support, and the development of integrated services to improve access to care. Without these, there is the danger of losing out on the benefits that improved legislation can bring to service users.

References

Ae-Ngibise, K. *et al.* (2010) '"Whether you like it or not people with mental problems are going to go to them": A qualitative exploration into the widespread use of traditional and faith healers in the provision of mental health care in Ghana'. *International Review of Psychiatry*, 22(6), pp. 558–567. https://doi/10.3109/09540261.2010.536149.

Anderson, A. (2005) 'The origins of Pentecostalism and its global spread in the early twentieth century'. *Transformation*, 22(3), pp. 175–185.

Anokye, R. *et al.* (2018) 'Knowledge of mental health legislation in Ghana: A case of the use of certificate of urgency in mental health care'. *International Journal of Mental Health Systems*, 12(1), pp. 1–7. https://doi.org/10.1186/s13033-018-0215-1.

Arias, D. et al. (2016). 'Prayer camps and biomedical care in Ghana: Is collaboration in mental health care possible?'. *PLoS One*, 11(9), e0162305. https://doi.org/10.1371/journal.pone.0162305

Asamoah-Gyadu, J. K. (2020) *Pentecostalism in Africa: Experiences from Ghana's charismatic ministries*. Oxford: Regnum Books International.

Asare, J. B. (2010) 'Mental health profile of Ghana'. *International Psychiatry: Bulletin of the Board of International Affairs of the Royal College of Psychiatrists*, 7(3), pp. 67–68.

Breuer, E. *et al.* (2016) 'Planning and evaluating mental health services in low- and middle-income countries using a theory of change'. *The British Journal of Psychiatry*, 208(Suppl 56), pp. s55–s62. https://doi.org/10.1192/bjp.bp.114.153841.

Colucci, E. (Director) (2021) *Nkabom: A little medicine, a little prayer* [Film]. Middlesex University.

Doku, V. C. K., Wusu-Takyi, A. and Awakame, J. (2012) 'Implementing the Mental Health Act in Ghana: Any challenges ahead?' *Ghana Medical Journal*, 46(4), pp. 241–250.

Ewusi-Mensah, I. (2001) 'Post-colonial psychiatric care in Ghana'. *Psychiatric Bulletin*, 25(6), pp. 228–229.

Funk, M., and Drew, N. (2017). 'WHO QualityRights: Transforming mental health services'. *The Lancet Psychiatry*, 4(11), 826–827.

Funk, M. and Bold, N.D. (2020). 'WHO's QualityRights initiative: Transforming services and promoting rights in mental health'. *Health and Human Rights*, 22(1), 69–76.

Freeman, M. (2016) 'Global mental health in low and middle income, especially African countries'. *Epidemiology & Psychiatric Sciences*, 25(6), pp. 503–505. https://doi.org/10.1017/S2045796016000482.

Ghana. (2012). *Mental Health Act 846 of 2012*.

Gopalkrishnan, N. (2018) 'Cultural diversity and mental health: Considerations for policy and practice'. *Frontiers in Public Health*, 6, p. 179. https://doi.org/10.3389/fpubh.2018.00179.

Hoare, F., and Duffy, R. M. (2021). 'The World Health Organization's QualityRights materials for training, guidance and transformation: Preventing coercion but marginalising psychiatry'. *The British Journal of Psychiatry*, 218(5), 240–242.

Kpobi, L., Osei, A. and Sefa-Dedeh, A. (2014) 'Overview of mental healthcare in Ghana'. In Ofori-Atta, A. and Ohene, S. (eds.), *Changing trends in mental health care & research in Ghana: A reader of the department of psychiatry, university of Ghana medical school*. Accra: Sub-Saharan Press, pp. 4–12.

McGovern, P. (2022) 'The World Health Organisation's quality rights initiative: Rights and recovery-oriented services should be at the centre not the margins of psychiatry'. *The British Journal of Psychiatry*, 1–3. https://doi.org/10.1192/bjp.2022.25.

Mental Health Authority [MHA] (2018) 'Guidelines for traditional and faith based healers in mental health'. https://mhaghana.com/wp-content/uploads/2019/05/guidelines-for-traditional-and-faith-based-healers.pdf (Accessed October 2021)

Moro, M. F. *et al.* (2022) 'A nationwide evaluation study of the quality of care and respect of human rights in mental health facilities in Ghana: Results from the World Health Organisation quality rights initiative'. *BMC Public Health*, 22(1), pp. 1–14. https://doi.org/10.1186/s12889-022-13102-2.

Nartey, L. (2022) 'Gov't is concerned about brain drain in health sector – Nsiah Asare', *3News*, 13 May. Available at: https://3news.com/govt-is-concerned-about-brain-drain-in-health-sector-nsia-asare/ (Accessed: 13 May 2022).

Ofori-Atta, A. et al. (2010) 'A situation analysis of mental health services and legislation in Ghana: Challenges for transformation'. *African Journal of Psychiatry*, 13(2), pp. 99–108. https://doi/10.4314/ajpsy.v13i2.54353.

Oladeji, B. D. and Gureje, O. (2016) 'Brain drain: A challenge to global mental health'. *BJPsych International*, 13(3), pp. 61–63.

Omar, M. A. et al. (2010) 'Mental health policy process: A comparative study of Ghana, South Africa, Uganda and Zambia'. *International Journal of Mental Health Systems*, 4(1), pp. 1–10. https://doi.org/10.1186/1752-4458-4-24.

Osei, A. (2006) 'Accra psychiatric hospital is 100'. *The Daily Graphic*, 1 June, p. 9.

Osei, A. (2011) 'Pass mental health bill now – Chief psychiatrist'. *Joy Online*, 23 January. Available at: https://www.myjoyonline.com/pass-mental-health-bill-now-chief-psychiatrist (Accessed: 2 May 2022).

Osei, A. O. (2008) 'Pass the mental health bill now'. *The Daily Graphic*, 1 August.

Osei, A. O., Asare, J. B. and Roberts, M. A. (2021) *History of mental health care in Ghana*. Accra: Sedco Publishing.

Rathod, S. et al. (2017) 'Mental health service provision in low- and middle-income countries'. *Health Services Insights*, 10, p. 1178632917694350. https://doi.org/10.1177/1178632917694350.

Twumasi, P. A. (1975) *Medical systems in Ghana*. Accra: Ghana Publishing.

Walker, G. H. and Osei, A. (2017) 'Mental health law in Ghana'. *BJ Psych International*, 14(2), pp. 2011–2012.

WHO (2005) *WHO resource book on mental health and human rights and legislation*. Geneva: WHO.

WHO (2019) *The WHO special initiative for mental health (2019–2023): Universal health coverage for mental health*. Available at: https://www.who.int/publications/i/item/special-initiative-for-mental-health-(2019-2023) (Accessed: 13 May 2022).

WHO (2021) 'Mental health ATLAS 2020'. Available at: https://www.who.int/publications/i/item/9789240036703 (Accessed: 13 May 2022).

WHO (2022) *World mental health report: Transforming mental health for all*. Geneva: WHO. Available at: https://www.who.int/publications/i/item/9789240049338 (Accessed 31 July 2022).

27
REGULATING MENTAL HEALTH CARE IN SOUTH AFRICA

Assessing the right to legal capacity and the right to the highest attainable standard of health in South African law and policy

Elizabeth Kamundia and Ilze Grobbelaar-du Plessis

Introduction

This chapter will examine the regulation of mental health care in South Africa. Firstly, delving into the normative framework of the right to the highest attainable standard of health and legal capacity, the focus of the assessment will be on the impact of South Africa's mental health law and policy on the exercise of legal capacity by persons with psychosocial disabilities regarding making mental health treatment decisions. This will entail an examination of the Constitution of the Republic of South Africa, 1996 ('the Constitution'), legislation regulating health care in South Africa, in particular the Mental Health Care Act 2002 and the National Mental Health Policy Framework and Strategic Plan 2013–2020. The in-depth evaluation of the South African Mental Health Care Act 2002 about practices that may be considered to comprise supported decision-making will assess the extent to which the human rights focus of South Africa's Mental Health Care Act 2002 enhances the protection of the legal capacity of persons with psychosocial disabilities in mental health care decision-making in South Africa.

The chapter will finally argue that the generic recognition of human rights of persons with psychosocial disabilities is not sufficient to ensure that persons with psychosocial disabilities enjoy the right to access health care based on free and informed consent and to exercise legal capacity in health care decision-making.

Regulating health care in South Africa

To situate mental health care in the broader South African health care context, the following section will start with an examination of the various categories of laws governing health in South Africa. In this regard, South African public health and welfare laws can be sub-divided into five categories.

Applicable international law, the Constitution and the subsequent National Health Act 2003 establish the right of everyone to access health care services, which can be categorised as the first type of law on health care in South Africa. The second type of law on health care in South Africa can be categorised as legislation aimed at regulating health system input, including medical education and research, professional training and the licensing and accreditation of health care organisations (Organisation for Economic Co-operation and Development, 2012). Laws under this category include the Health Professions Act 1974 and the Traditional Health Practitioners Act 2007. The third category of law on health care sets up a legal framework for health insurance under the Medical Schemes Act 1998. The fourth category of law on health care focuses on securing and maintaining health, as well as providing protection against harmful substances. An example under this category is the Hazardous Substances Act 1973. The fifth and final category of law concerns access to health care by specific groups such as women, children and other vulnerable groups including persons with psychosocial disabilities (South African Human Rights Commission, 2006–2009). An example under this category is the Children's Act 2005. Finally, the Mental Health Care Act 2002 is a case apart as it provides not only for 'the care, treatment and rehabilitation of persons who are mentally ill', but also contains expansive provisions for the care and administration of the property of such persons (Kamundia, 2019).

Chapter VIII of the Mental Health Care Act 2002 addresses the administration of property of a 'mentally ill person' or a 'person with severe or profound intellectual disability'. Persons with disabilities have the right to own or inherit property and to control their own financial affairs in South Africa. For this purpose Chapter VIII of the Mental Health Care Act 2002 provides for the appointment of a *curator bonis* or an administrator for the care and administration of property of 'mentally ill' persons, 'mentally ill' minors or persons with severe or profound intellectual disabilities as well as the process of application of such administrators through the High Court (UN Doc CRPD/C/ZAF/1, 2014). However, South African law does not provide for enduring powers of attorney, which means that families of persons deemed as 'incapacitated' are at present forced to incur considerable legal fees to establish curatorships to manage the financial affairs of these individuals (UN Doc CRPD/C/ZAF/1, 2014, paras 123–124). In this regard the South African Law Reform Commission (SALRC) proposed the need for alternative and additional measures of supported decision-making for adults with decision-making impairments, and proposed a Bill on Supported Decision-making (Law Reform Commission, 2015). The issue of the administration of the property of persons with psychosocial disabilities, however, falls outside the scope of this chapter.

While the various laws discussed above have implications on access to health care by persons with psychosocial disabilities in South Africa, this chapter will focus on the laws and policies on health care that also address rights that are related to legal capacity. These include the right to non-discrimination and the freedom and security of the person. The chapter, therefore, will focus on applicable international law and the Constitution, the Mental Health Care Act 2002 and the South African National Mental Health Policy Framework and Strategic Plan 2013–2020.

The normative framework on the right to the highest attainable standard of health and legal capacity: international law and the Constitution

This section will examine the right to the highest attainable standard of health and the right to legal capacity in line with applicable international law within the South African constitutional context. The section will demonstrate the generic recognition of the human rights of persons with psychosocial disabilities in South Africa, and will set the basis for the discussion of the normative framework of the chapter, which will argue that a generic recognition of the human rights of persons with psychosocial disabilities is not sufficient to ensure equal enjoyment of the right to access to health care on the basis of free and informed consent and to exercise legal capacity in health care decision-making.

The application of international law in South Africa on health and legal capacity

International law has a direct and indirect effect on legal capacity and health law and policy-making in South Africa (*The Constitution*, S 39(1)(b) & S 231(1) and (2); South African Human Rights Commission (SAHRC), Public Inquiry, 2009; Grobbelaar-du Plessis, 2013). For the purposes of this chapter, it is important to note that South Africa is a state party to the International Covenant on Economic, Social and Cultural Rights (UN Doc 6 ILM 368, 1967) and the Convention on the Rights of Persons with Disabilities (UN Doc A/RES/61/106, 2006). South Africa has also ratified regional instruments that comprise provisions on health including the African Charter on Human and Peoples' Rights (OAU Doc 21 I.L.M. 58, 1982) and the African Charter on the Rights and Welfare of the Child (OAU Doc CAB/LEG/24.9/49, 1990). South Africa is yet to ratify the Protocol to the African Charter on Human and Peoples' Rights on the Rights of Persons with Disabilities in Africa.

Since South Africa follows a dualistic approach to international law (The Constitution, S 231(2); '*Glenister v President of the Republic of South Africa*', 2009) in relation to international instruments, it is important to note that legislation to domesticate the Convention on the Rights of Persons with Disabilities (CRPD) in South Africa has not yet been enacted (Grobbelaar-du Plessis, 2013). However, an important development in this regard was the request received by the SALRC in 2018 from the Department of Justice and Constitutional Development to investigate the domestication of the CRPD. In response to the request received, the SALRC developed an issue paper (the first stage of a three-stage process interspersed with public consultation) asking for public comments in 2021 on the issues that need law reform (Law Reform Commission, 2021). The second stage is to develop a discussion paper on the responses received on the issue paper, and the responses to the discussion paper will then result in the drafting of a final view in the form of a report on domesticating the CRPD and a draft Disability Bill (UN Doc CRPD/C/ZAF/1, 2014, para. 125).

Whilst awaiting the domestication of the CRPD through the legislative process, it is important to note the redeeming effect of Section 233 of the Constitution of the Republic of South Africa (1996) on the South African dualistic approach to international law. The provision provides for the interpretation of legislation by all South African courts that must prefer any reasonable interpretation of the legislation that is consistent with international law over any alternative interpretation that is inconsistent with international law (Dugard, 2013). This means that the interpretation of any domestic legislation must be consistent with international law, and for the purposes of this chapter, the CRPD.

Constitutional framework on health care and on the right to legal capacity in South Africa

The Constitution refers to 'health' in different provisions and in a variety of contexts, some of which relate to the exercise of legal capacity in mental health care decision-making.

Section 27(1)(a) provides that everyone has the right to have access to health care services, including reproductive health care. Although the Constitution provides for universal access to health care services, it does not provide for the right to attain the highest standard of physical and mental health (Human Rights Commission, 2009). In other words, the Constitution does not provide for entitlement to all the goods and services that are required to attain 'the highest standard' of physical and mental health. Also relevant is Section 184(3), which determines that the South African Human Rights Commission (SAHRC) must require relevant organs of the State to provide the SAHRC with information relative to measures that they have taken towards the realisation of the rights in the Bill of Rights (Chapter 2 of the Constitution) concerning a variety of issues, including health care on an annual basis.

On the right to equality before the law, Section 9(1) of the Constitution provides that '[e]veryone is equal before the law and has the right to equal protection and benefit of the law' which relates to the exercise of legal capacity in mental health care decision-making. The Constitution also has a robust equality and non-discrimination clause, that provides for both vertical and horizontal application to non-discrimination (Grobbelaar-du Plessis, 2013). Section 9(3) provides for a vertically applicable right by prohibiting the State from unfairly discriminating directly or indirectly against anyone on a list of prohibited grounds that includes disability. Section 9(4) provides for a horizontal application to non-discrimination by prohibiting any person from unfairly discriminating directly or indirectly against anyone on the same list of prohibited grounds which includes disability. The Constitution therefore prohibits indirect and direct discrimination on the ground of disability under both Sections 9(3) and 9(4) (Grobbelaar-du Plessis, 2013). It is further important to note that the manner in which the CRPD is to be incorporated into South African law is through the concept of equality (Law Reform Commission, 2021, p. xiv).

The other section in the Bill of Rights of the South African Constitution that relates to the exercise of legal capacity in health care is Section 12(1), which provides that everyone has the right to the freedom and security of the person. This right includes a number of freedoms, including freedom from arbitrary arrest or detention, from violence and from torture and/or cruel punishment (The Constitution, S 12(1)(a)-(e); Currie and Woolman, 1996; Currie and De Waal, 2013).

As seen from the judgments of the Constitutional Court, there are three possible interpretations of Section 12(1) (*Ferreira v Levin*, 1996; *S v Coetzee*, 1997; *De Lange v Smuts*, 1998). The first is to the effect that '[f]reedom of the person means the liberty of the subject to pursue his or her chosen ends without interference' (*Ferreira v Levin* Ackermann J, 1996; Currie and Woolman, 1996). This means that every individual has the freedom to make his/her own decisions without taking direction from others. The second possible interpretation of Section 12(1) of the Constitution is to the effect that, while the right to freedom and security of the person primarily protects a person's physical integrity, freedom of the person may also be read as a 'residual' right that protects 'freedoms of a fundamental nature that do not find protection anywhere in the Bill of Rights' (*Ferreira v Levin* Chaskalson P, 1996; Currie and Woolman, 1996). The third interpretive possibility of Section 12(1) is to the effect that the right protects physical freedom and integrity only and should not be read as a residual right (*Ferreira v Levin* Mokgoro, J, 1996; Currie and Woolman, 1996). However, the majority of the Constitutional Court supported the second possible interpretation in the case of *Ferreira v Levin* (1996).

Section 12(2)(b) provides that everyone has the right to bodily and psychological integrity, which includes the right to security in, and control over, their bodies. 'Security in' has been argued to denote 'the protection of bodily integrity against intrusions by the state and others' while 'control over' implies 'protection of what could be called bodily autonomy or self-determination against interference' (*Ferreira v Levin* (1996)). Both elements are crucial to mental health treatment decision-making since 'the right to control over one's body includes control over one's mind' (*Ferreira v Levin* (1996) 39–46). Having security over one's body implies that one will be left unmolested by others, including not being subjected to treatments to which one has not consented. While not every action that involves touching another person's body in the provision of health care is sufficient to warrant constitutional attention, it is clear that psychiatric interventions (for example electroshock treatments) often involve a level of intrusion that is high enough to warrant constitutional attention (*Ferreira v Levin* (1996) 39–44). Having control over one's body implies that one is allowed to make choices that one wishes to make regarding your own body. Often, forced medical interventions are commenced when it is felt (either for moralistic or paternalistic reasons) that an individual is making poor decisions (for example giving away one's property as a result of being taken advantage of by others (*Re Matter of Captain PGM*, 2015) or living in unhygienic conditions) (*WK v AW*, 2014; Kamundia, 2016/2017).

This chapter holds the view that the recognition of the constitutional right to bodily and psychological integrity means relinquishing paternalistic interventions in the lives of individuals, which interpretation is consistent with the principles of the CRPD (UN Doc CRPD/C/GC/1, 2014). The Committee on the Rights of Persons with Disabilities (CRPD Committee) also opines that forced treatment by psychiatric and other health and medical professionals is a violation of the right to equal recognition before the law and an infringement of article 17 of the CRPD on the right to personal integrity (UN Doc CRPD/C/GC/1, 2014, para. 42).

It is important to note that health treatment for persons with disabilities in South Africa is provided on the basis of their free and informed consent. In this regard the National Health Act 2003 stresses the importance of obtaining the patient's consent to a health service and requires health care providers to take all reasonable steps to ensure that the patient makes an informed decision. However, the Act provides for informed consent by a person with legal capacity to do so, and invokes the Mental Health Care Act 2002 when a person does not have legal capacity (UN Doc CRPD/C/ZAF/1, 2014, para. 267). South Africa's initial report to the CRPD Committee under article 35 of the CRPD proposes to review the Mental Health Care Act 2002 in order to bring the National Health Act 2003 in line with article 12(3) of the CRPD and the obligation to provide persons with disabilities with the support they require to exercise their decision-making (UN Doc CRPD/C/ZAF/1, 2014, para. 267). The SALRC in their December 2021 issue paper on domestication of the CPRD, makes reference to the Mental Health Care Act 2002, but does not provide guidance on its alignment with article 12 of the CRPD (Law Reform Commission, 2021). This is expected to be addressed in the discussion paper on the strength of the responses received during public consultation.

The normative framework on the right to the highest attainable standard of health and the right to legal capacity: legislative and policy framework

The Mental Health Care Act 2002 was promulgated in 2004 in the same year that the SALRC commenced with an extensive participatory investigation on assisted decision-making for adults with impaired decision-making capacity. At the time of the preparation of the

SALRC Discussion Paper, the mental health law had not been promulgated. The SALRC concluded their investigation in 2015 with a report and a proposed Bill on supported decision-making (Law Reform Commission, 2015). Unfortunately, the SALRC excluded health care treatment decision-making by 'mentally ill' persons from their investigation, which they reported to be regulated by mental health legislation (Law Reform Commission, 2004, para. 1.0; Law Reform Commission, 2015, para. 2.37). However, in the 2021/2 extensive participatory investigation of the SALRC, additional areas such as mental health legislation will be considered in the review of civil and criminal legislation during the domestication process of the CRPD (Law Reform Commission, 2021, para. 4.38).

In the meantime, in order to establish whether current mental health legislation is consistent with articles 12 (equal recognition before the law) and 25 (right to the highest attainable standard of health care) of the CRPD, the focus of the next section will be on the extent to which the Mental Health Care Act 2002 protects the legal capacity of persons with psychosocial disabilities in making mental health treatment decisions. However, it is important to note that the Act predates the CRPD and therefore does not reflect the full gamut of rights contained in the CRPD.

Mental Health Care Act 17 of 2002

South Africa's Mental Health Care Act 2002 is divided into ten chapters and aims at regulating and providing mental health care, establishing Review Boards in respect of health establishments and providing for the care and administration of the property of persons with 'mental illness' and persons with severe or profound intellectual disability (Grobbelaar-du Plessis, 2013). Chapter III of the Act is especially pertinent as it is dedicated to the rights and duties relating to mental health care users. Recognised rights include: human dignity and privacy; protection against unfair discrimination; protection from exploitation and abuse; and the right to representation. The Act also recognises the right to give consent to care, treatment and rehabilitation; however, this is a limited right as the Act also allows for treatment without consent under Sections 26 and 32. Under Section 4(c) of the Act, state organs responsible for health services must implement their policies and measures in a way that 'promotes the rights and interests of mental health care users'. However, for the purposes of this chapter one firstly has to determine who falls within the scope of the Act. Secondly, an examination will follow on how treatment and health care decisions are made under the Act. The assessment is made on how well the Act measures up to the obligations imposed in articles 12 and 25 of the CRPD.

Persons subject to the Mental Health Care Act

Section 3 of the Mental Health Care Act 2002 states that the object of the Act is to regulate access to, and provide for, mental health care, treatment and rehabilitation services to various categories of users. These include voluntary, assisted and involuntary mental health care users, state patients, mentally ill prisoners and persons with intellectual disabilities. When the Act refers to persons with psychosocial disabilities, it refers to 'mental health care user' and 'person with mental illness'. From the terminology used, and from various provisions that deny persons with psychosocial disabilities the right to exercise legal capacity in treatment decision-making (Mental Health Care Act 2002 S 26(b)(i) & (ii), 27(1)(a), 31(4), 32, and 33(1)(a)), it can be argued that the Act is anchored in the medical model of understanding mental health issues. However, Chapter III of the Act is dedicated to human rights, and it explicitly recognises 'persons with mental illness' as holders of rights (Kamundia, 2019).

Making treatment decisions under the South Africa Mental Health Care Act

The Mental Health Care Act 2002 has three distinct mental health care categories, namely voluntary, assisted and involuntary admission. As will be explained below, all three categories sanction substitute decisions on behalf of the individual.

The Act is predicated on the idea that, at times, individuals have the 'capacity' to make mental health care and treatment decisions while, at other times, individuals lack the 'capacity' to make decisions (Mental Health Care Act 2002 S 28(2)(a), 31 & 38). At different stages, different actors, including the Review Board and the head of the health establishment, are given the powers to assess the capacity of an individual to make his/her own treatment decisions. In instances where individuals are seen to 'lack capacity', the Act permits substitute decision-making, contrary to article 12 of the CRPD. The SALRC report on assisted decision-making echoes this position, and states that 'one of the major disabling consequences of mental incapacity is the inability or limited ability to make legally effective decisions. Diminished decision-making capacity may in turn reduce a person's ability to control his or her life' (Law Reform Commission, 2004, para. 2.1).

The CRPD Committee in its General Comment No. 1 on article 12 of the CRPD on equal recognition before the law asserts that 'perceived or actual deficits in mental capacity must not be used as justification for denying legal capacity' (UN Doc CRPD/C/GC/1, 2014, para. 13). This means that an individual may not, under any circumstances, be denied the right to exercise legal capacity, including the right to mental health care decision-making. Since all three categories of mental health care decision-making in the Act provide for substitute decisions on behalf of the individual, it may follow that the Act is contrary to the obligations imposed by the CRPD.

'Mental capacity' is seen under the Act, as well as under General Comment No. 1, as varying from one person to another, which 'may be different for a given person depending on many factors, including environmental and social factors' (UN Doc CRPD/C/GC/1, 2014, para. 13). On its part, Section 8(2) of the Act states that 'every mental health care user must be provided with care, treatment and rehabilitation services that improve the mental capacity of the user to develop to full potential and to facilitate his or her integration into community life'. Section 8(2) of the Act does not identify the specific care, treatment and rehabilitation services that would improve the mental capacity of the user to develop to full potential. This chapter argues that if the proposed services (geared towards improving the mental capacity of the user to develop to full potential and his/her integration into community life) were carried out in accordance with the will and preferences of the person with a psychosocial disability, then such services could form part of supported decision-making (Kamundia, 2019).

The word 'consent' is mentioned numerous times in the Act; however, ironically the Act does not provide for a requirement that the person with a psychosocial disability must give consent to treatment (Mental Health Care Act 2002 S 1 (xi), 9, 26, 29(3), 30(5)(a) (ii), 34(3)(a), 35(3)(b) and 38(2)). At the same time, and under certain conditions, the Act allows for care, treatment and rehabilitation to be given without the consent of the mental health care user (Mental Health Care Act 2002 S 26(b), 32), contrary to article 25(d) of the CRPD. In such circumstances, substitute decision-makers under the Act include a spouse, the next of kin, a partner, an associate, a parent or a guardian of the user, the head of a health establishment, the Review Board and the High Court. Substitute decision-makers under the Act are not required to take the will and preferences of the person with a psychosocial disability into account. Following from this, it is important to highlight voluntary, assisted and involuntary mental health care in Chapter V of the Act:

(i) Voluntary admission

Section 25 of the Act regulates voluntary care, where a person who submits himself/herself voluntarily to a health establishment for mental health treatment is entitled to receive appropriate services or to be referred to an appropriate health establishment. The Act, however, does not provide for a situation where a person is admitted on a voluntary basis and later changes his/her mind and wants to leave the health establishment. From interpreting the provisions on assisted mental health care and treatment and on involuntary care and treatment, the voluntary mental health care user will presumably not be able to simply leave the health establishment at will, but would likely be assessed and, if it was deemed necessary, converted into a mental health user who requires assisted or involuntary care and treatment (Mental Health Care Act 2002 S 26(b)(i) & (ii) & 32).

(ii) Treatment for mental health users who are 'incapable of making informed decisions' or assisted mental health care, treatment and rehabilitation

The Act has a category of mental health care users who are termed 'assisted'. These are users who are believed to be suffering from a 'mental illness' or severe or profound mental disability, who require treatment for their health or safety or for the health and safety of other people and who are 'incapable of making an informed decision on the need for the care, treatment and rehabilitation services' (Mental Health Care Act 2002 S 26(b)(i) & (ii)). In these circumstances, an application must be made to the head of the health establishment by the spouse, next of kin, partner, associate, parent or guardian of a mental health care user, who must have seen the user within seven days of making the application (Mental Health Care Act 2002 S 27(1)(a) & (b)). Once the application is made, two mental health care practitioners must concur that conditions for inpatient care exist. The head of the health establishment must also be 'satisfied that the restrictions and intrusions on the rights of the mental health care user to movement, privacy and dignity are proportionate to the care, treatment and rehabilitation services required' (Mental Health Care Act 2002 S 27(8)(a) & (b)). It must be noted that the Act has an explicit provision on 'recovery of capacity of assisted mental health care users to make informed decisions' (Mental Health Care Act 2002 S 31).

Assisted mental health care treatment is therefore arguably treatment without the consent of the person. Instead of finding a way to discover/ascertain the will and preference of the individual regarding treatment, the law merely substitutes the individual's decision-making with that of other persons. It is commendable that the Act safeguards individuals against treatment without consent by providing that the restrictions and intrusions should be proportionate to the care that is required (Mental Health Care Act 2002 S 8(3) & 27(8)(b)). Nevertheless, Section 26(b)(i) & (ii) of the Act on assisted mental health care treatment falls short of the obligations imposed by article 25 of the CRPD. In this regard the interpretive guidelines under General Comment No. 1 provide that psychiatric professionals are obligated to obtain free and informed consent of persons with disabilities prior to any treatment (UN Doc CRPD/C/GC/1, 2014, para. 41).

It is clear that the Act permits substituted decision-making which is inconsistent with the CRPD. It should be noted that assisted care and involuntary care are separate categories under the Act. Under assisted care, the mental health care user, while 'incapable of making informed decisions due to mental health status', agrees to the health intervention. However, under involuntary care, the mental health care user is not willing to receive the health interventions.

(iii) *Involuntary care, treatment and rehabilitation*

Contrary to article 25 of the CRPD on the right to health care by persons with disabilities on the basis of their free and informed consent, treatment and rehabilitation may be provided without the consent of the mental health care user on an involuntary basis. In this regard, Section 32 of the Act states that:

> A mental health care user must be provided with care, treatment and rehabilitation services without his or her consent at a health establishment on an outpatient or inpatient basis if–
>
> (a) an application in writing is made to the head of the health establishment concerned to obtain the necessary care, treatment and rehabilitation services and the application is granted;
> (b) at the time of making the application, there is reasonable belief that the mental health care user has a mental illness of such a nature that–
>   (i) the user is likely to inflict serious harm to himself or herself or others; or
>   (ii) care, treatment and rehabilitation of the user is necessary for the protection of the financial interests or reputation of the user; *and*
>   (iii) at the time of the application the mental health care user is incapable of making an informed decision on the need for the care, treatment and rehabilitation services and is unwilling to receive the care, treatment and rehabilitation required.

It is important to note that Section 32 of the Act uses 'and' (in italics in the foregoing paragraph), which raises the threshold for involuntary treatment significantly, where all the conditions have to exist before one can be subjected to involuntary treatment. Often, however, the determination of one's likelihood to inflict serious harm is rooted in the mental illness itself (Paré, 2011, p. 109), contrary to article 12 of the CRPD. It is worth noting that South Africa did not make a reservation or declaration upon ratifying the CRPD (United Nations Treaty Collection, 2022).

The foregoing provisions seem to be geared towards protection of the mental health user. The legitimate concern for the protection of the user, however, does not justify violating the user's right to equal recognition before the law. In this regard the first general interpretative comment makes it clear that 'there are no permissible circumstances under international human rights law in which a person may be deprived of the right to recognition as a person before the law, or in which this right may be limited' (UN Doc CRPD/C/GC/1, 2014, para. 5).

According to Section 34 of the Act, within 72 hours after the involuntary care and treatment has started, the mental health user must be assessed to consider whether or not involuntary care should continue. The findings of the assessment must be available within 24 hours after the expiry of the 72-hour assessment period. Furthermore, inpatient involuntary care can only take place in a psychiatric hospital. It is worth noting that the specified time frames in the Act are safeguards reducing the length of time during which a person with a psychosocial disability is deprived of his/her liberty in the course of treatment. The section also provides that following the assessment, the head of the establishment may reach a conclusion that the mental health care user does not warrant involuntary care and assessment, in which case the user will be discharged.

In South Africa involuntary care may also be provided on an outpatient basis. In such instances, the head of the establishment must inform the Review Board in writing. If the mental health user fails to comply with the terms and conditions of such discharge, the discharge will be cancelled and the user will be required to return to the health establishment on an involuntary inpatient basis (Mental Health Care Act 2002 S 34 (3)(b)(ii)). If the head of the health establishment reaches the conclusion that involuntary care should be provided on an inpatient basis, within seven days of the expiry of the 72-hour assessment period, the head of the health establishment must submit a written request to the Review Board to approve further involuntary care. The Review Board must consider the application for involuntary care and treatment within 30 days. If the Review Board decides to grant the request, the Board must submit to the Registrar of a High Court a written notice for consideration by the High Court. If the Review Board receives an appeal before reaching a decision on further involuntary care and treatment, it must set aside the review proceedings and consider the appeal (Mental Health Care Act 2002 S 34(3)(c); 34(7) & 34(8)).

Under Section 35 of the Act, a mental health care user or the spouse, next of kin, partner, associate, parent or guardian of the mental health care user may appeal to the Review Board against the decision of the head of the health establishment about involuntary care and treatment. If the Review Board does not uphold the appeal, it must submit the relevant documents to the Registrar of the High Court for the purposes of a review by the court. The High Court must consider the relevant documents and any other representation made by the mental health care user, or the spouse, next of kin, partner, associate, parent or guardian of the mental health care user or any other relevant person. The High Court must thereafter order further hospitalisation of the mental health care user or the immediate discharge of the mental health care user (Mental Health Care Act 2002 S 35(2); 35(3); 35(4); 36 & 36(c)).

The fact that the mental health care user (or the user's spouse, next of kin, partner, associate, parent or guardian of the mental health care user) may appeal against the decision of the head of the health establishment to provide assisted care and treatment is an important safeguard of the Act (Mental Health Care Act 2002 S 29). The Review Board must provide an opportunity for all parties to be heard on the merits of the appeal. These parties include the mental health care user (or other applicant on his/her behalf), the relevant medical practitioners and the head of the establishment. This provides an opportunity for the mental health care user to be heard, which arguably promotes the agency of the mental health care user. Should the Review Board uphold an appeal, all mental health care treatment must be stopped according to accepted clinical practices, and the user must be discharged from the health establishment. However, the only kind of support anticipated to be provided to the mental health care user in the appeal process, is legal representation (Mental Health Care Act

2002 S 15). In practice, a mental health care user might require other kinds of support in the appeal process, including communication and peer support (Kamundia, 2019).

The Act provides for oversight mechanisms on involuntary treatment with varying appeal mechanisms from the head of the establishment to the Review Boards and, finally, to the High Court. Arguably, appeal mechanisms enhance accountability as well as checks and balances. It also makes the exercise of legal capacity by persons with psychosocial disabilities in mental health treatment decision-making and the provision of treatment on the basis of free and informed consent more likely. At the same time, it is regrettable that, under South Africa's Mental Health Care Act 2002, the High Court can make orders only for either further hospitalisation or the discharge of the person with a psychosocial disability. The Act does not provide for any support that the user may require subsequent to the Court's decision. Furthermore, the Review Board does not have a mental health care user or a person with any lived experience of psychosocial disability in its membership (Mental Health Care Act 2002 S 20). This arguably runs contrary to article 4(3) of the CRPD, which requires that, in decision-making processes concerning issues relating to persons with disabilities, States Parties should closely consult with and actively involve persons with disabilities.

The foregoing extensive provisions on involuntary treatment run contrary to article 12 of the CRPD. In its State report to the CRPD Committee under article 35 of the CRPD, South Africa identified several pieces of legislation in which provisions relating to consent were not consistent with accepted human rights standards. It is worth noting with concern that the Mental Health Care Act 2002 is not one of the laws explicitly identified by the South African government in the report as having a 'problematic' notion of 'informed consent' (UN Doc CRPD/C/ZAF/1, 2014, para. 125).

South Africa National Mental Health Policy Framework and Strategic Plan 2013–2020

The development of South Africa's Mental Health Policy followed important reforms in policy and legislation in the wake of the demise of apartheid and the election of the first democratic government in 1994. South Africa's Mental Health Policy is preceded by important reforms in the health sector including the White Paper for the Transformation of the Health System, 1997, the Mental Health Policy Guidelines, 1997 and the Mental Health Care Act 2002. The policy aims to respond to ongoing challenges that exist despite the reforms in the health sector. These challenges include the facts that mental health care is under-funded and under-resourced, that there is inequity in the distribution of mental health services, a lack of public awareness on mental health, the existence of widespread stigma against persons with psychosocial disabilities and lack of accurate data regarding mental health provision.

South Africa's Mental Health Policy was developed through a consultative process that involved more than 400 stakeholders, including 'research groups, academia, professional associations and statutory health institutions, the World Health Organization, non-governmental organizations, mental health care user groups, clinicians, [and] national and provincial departments that play a role in mental health' (South Africa National Mental Health Policy Framework and Strategic Plan 2013–2020, Acknowledgements by the Director General). It is commendable that mental health care user groups were involved in the development of the policy although it is not clear to what extent their views influenced the final text of the policy. The policy applies to persons with mental illness, persons who have substance use disorders in circumstances where there is co-morbidity with 'mental disorder' and persons with intellectual disabilities where co-morbidity exists between intellectual disability and 'mental disorders' (South Africa National Mental Health Policy Framework and Strategic Plan 2013–2020, S 1).

The objectives of the policy include the scaling up of decentralised integrated primary mental health services, including community-based care, primary health care, clinic care and district hospital level care, to empower mental health care users and others to participate in promoting well-being and recovery within their community and to promote and protect the human rights of people living with mental illness. The policy is explicit regarding the implementation thereof to be framed within the ambit of the CRPD (South Africa National Mental Health Policy Framework and Strategic Plan 2013–2020, S 7.5).

However, the policy lapsed in 2020 and it was reported during October 2021 that the National Department of Health will have a revised and updated policy framework by the following financial year. This oversight, amidst the Covid-19 pandemic, was disconcerting and widely criticised (Daily Maverick Citizen, 2021). The SAHRC, in their 2017 investigation into the status of mental health care in South Africa and report in 2018, also criticised the implementation of the policy framework (Human Rights Commission, 2017). However, the proposed updated framework promises to be aligned with the World Health Organization's Comprehensive Mental Health Action Plan of 2013–2030.

For the purposes of this chapter, it is important to assess whether the policy employs a human rights-based approach to mental health care. The first part of the assessment below will demonstrate the various ways through which the policy takes a human rights-based approach to mental health care and the second part of the assessment will highlight the shortcomings of the policy.

Demonstrating how the South African Mental Health Policy takes a human rights-based approach to mental health care

Firstly, the policy explicitly mentions human rights in its mission statement, objectives, values and principles when referring to partnerships between providers, users, carers and communities, which have to uphold the human rights of people with mental illness.

The policy explicitly advocates for the promotion and protection of the human rights of people with mental illness as a key value and principle. Section 6 of the policy further identifies specific rights that should be upheld in the provision of mental health care. These are: equality, non-discrimination, dignity, privacy, autonomy, information and participation. This could be seen as a positive step towards protecting the rights of persons with psychosocial disabilities generally, and more specifically their right to exercise legal capacity in making mental health treatment decisions. Furthermore, the policy also identifies rights that should be pursued on a basis of progressive realisation. These include the 'rights to education, access to land, adequate housing, health care services, sufficient food, water and social security, including social assistance for the poor, and environmental rights for adult mental health care users' (South Africa National Mental Health Policy Framework and Strategic Plan 2013–220, S 6).

For younger users under the age of 18, the policy identifies that their non-conditional rights (including basic nutrition, shelter, basic health care services and social services) should be promoted and protected. In this regard it is important to note the interrelatedness of human rights, where the promotion and protection of these rights will relate to the right to legal capacity of persons with psychosocial disabilities. Indeed, General Comment No. 1 specifically highlights a direct link between the right to legal capacity and some of the rights identified as being central under the policy. Such rights include equality, non-discrimination and privacy (UN Doc CRPD/C/ZAF/1, 2014, paras 32–34, 47). It is also commendable that the policy places particular importance on the right to housing, and on providing a range of options of state-funded housing. The policy states that:

> Deinstitutionalisation has progressed at a rapid rate in South Africa, without the necessary development of community-based services. This has led to a high number of homeless mentally ill, people living with mental illness in prisons and revolving door patterns of care.
>
> *(South Africa National Mental Health Policy Framework and Strategic Plan 2013 – 2020, S 2.5)*

This means that persons with psychosocial disabilities have been moved from institutions before the government has set up mechanisms and infrastructure to house and support them within the community. As a result, these individuals end up homeless, or experience mental health relapses and are re-admitted to the institutions. The right to housing is especially important for persons with psychosocial disabilities who are unemployed or who have no families, and who are, therefore, at risk of being homeless in the absence of State interventions. Developing housing options for persons with psychosocial disabilities is, therefore, an important aspect regarding enabling them to exercise legal capacity on an equal basis with others (Kamundia, 2019).

Secondly, the policy also has a stand-alone section on human rights emphasising the promotion and protection of human rights of 'people living with mental illness' through the active implementation of the Mental Health Care Act 2002. It further highlights the need to ensure that provisions of the CRPD 'are actively implemented for persons with mental disability in South Africa' (South Africa National Mental Health Policy Framework and Strategic Plan 2013–2020, S 7.6). The reference to the CRPD underscores the intention of utilising a human rights-based approach to mental health care in South Africa.

Thirdly, in the mission statement of the policy, the role of mental health care users is recognised in ensuring that their rights are upheld. In this regard, the policy provides that 'mental health care users should be involved in the planning, delivery and evaluation of mental health services' and that 'self-help and advocacy groups should be encouraged' (South Africa National Mental Health Policy Framework and Strategic Plan 2013–2020, S 6). The policy therefore regards mental health care users as capable subjects who can contribute to the delivery of mental health care services. The policy furthermore takes note of the voices of users or persons with psychosocial disabilities within the policy and notes with regard to community mental health services the need for capacity development for users to provide appropriate self-help and peer-led services (South Africa National Mental Health Policy Framework and Strategic Plan 2013–2020, S 7.1). Although the principle of participation is commendable, supported decision-making goes beyond this principle where the persons with psychosocial disabilities should be involved in all processes that concern them. Participation, however, assists with the facilitation of the exercise of the right to legal capacity in treatment decision-making.

Finally, the Ekurhuleni Declaration on Mental Health, 2012 which takes a human rights-based approach to mental health, forms part of the mental health policy as an appendix to the policy.

Shortcomings of the South African Mental Health Policy from a human rights-based approach

The first shortcoming of the South African Mental Health Policy is that although violations of the rights of persons with psychosocial disabilities are recognised, the policy does not identify the right to legal capacity as one of the rights commonly violated in relation to this group. The policy does not address coercive practices, involuntary care and aspects of consent to treatment. While the policy is progressive on the provisions of mental health care services within the community, it makes no mention of supported decision-making. In this regard the policy fails to sufficiently protect and recognise the right of persons with disabilities to make their own treatment decisions, with or without support.

The policy also requires that units in hospitals are built to 'ensure adequate infrastructure and security to protect the human rights of mental health care users, and to protect the rights and safety of clinical staff working in these units' (South Africa National Mental Health Policy Framework and Strategic Plan 2013–2020, p. 36). While infrastructure is an important aspect to address, it is also important to note that interventions that are directly aimed at enhancing the autonomy of the individual with regard to treatment decisions and other areas of an individual's life are also important to address in the policy (Minkowitz, 2007). In this regard and in the contexts of limited resources, this is a second shortcoming of the policy. It is important to focus on improving the delivery of a diverse range of community-based services (including peer support). The approach selected (to rather focus on physical infrastructure to address human rights) does not address interventions that recognise the agency of the mental health care user and does not in the long term enhance the person's role in his/her own recovery process (Lester *et al.*, 2006).

Thirdly, evaluating from the terminology used, the policy may be criticised for taking an 'illness' rather than a 'disability' approach to mental health care. In this regard, CRPD jurisprudence suggests that both illnesses and conditions can constitute a disability (Fanning, 2018). This was evident in *S.C. v. Brazil* (2013), where the CRPD Committee found that an illness could qualify as a disability under the CRPD (UN Doc CRPD/C/12/D/10/2013, para. 2.2). This means that people with illnesses are not automatically excluded from protection under the CRPD and that 'a health impairment which is initially conceived of as illness can develop into an impairment in the context of disability because of its duration or its chronic development' (UN Doc CRPD/C/12/D/10/2013, para. 6.3). In the specific context of persons with mental health conditions, the CRPD Committee has, however, not clarified when such conditions amount to disability.

Although the policy takes an 'illness' rather than a 'disability' approach to mental health care, it does, however, make the important link between mental health and disability. For example, the policy mandates the Department of Health to engage with non-health sectors, including the Department of Disability, within the Ministry of Children, Women and the Disabled, 'with a view to strengthening the place of mental health within the broader disability agenda, and improving the rights of disabled citizens' (South Africa National Mental Health Policy Framework and Strategic Plan 2013 – 2020, S 7.5). Furthermore, the policy requires that advocacy towards changing 'discriminatory attitudes toward mental disability' should be framed within human rights frameworks including the provisions of the CRPD and the human rights-based framework of South African law.

Conclusion

This chapter examined the regulation of mental health care in South Africa with a focus on applicable international law, the Constitution, the Mental Health Care Act 2002 and the National Mental Health Policy Framework and Strategic Plan 2013–2020. The focus was on the extent to which the existing legal framework on mental health care enhances the protection of legal capacity in mental health care decision-making. Furthermore, the chapter considered whether supported decision-making is reflected in the South African legal system.

From the discussion it is clear that South Africa focuses on human rights in its mental health laws and policies. However, it was also clear from the discussion that the South African mental health legal system deviates in significant ways from a human rights-based approach to mental health care. Significantly, the Mental Health Care Act 2002 allows for care, treatment and rehabilitation to be given without the consent of the mental health care user. This goes against the interpretive General Comment No. 1, which deems legal capacity to be a universal attribute inherent in all persons by virtue of their humanity (UN Doc CRPD/C/GC/1, 2014, para. 8). It is important to note that the SALRC in their 2021 issue paper on domestication of the CPRD, made several references to the CRPD Committee's interpretative General Comments to be used as guidelines during the investigation processes, public consultation and comments for the purposes of law reform and the drafting of the Disability Bill (Law Reform Commission, 2021).

Furthermore, it is clear that the Mental Health Care Act 2002 does not explicitly make reference to supported decision-making. However, this is not surprising, since the Mental Health Care Act 2002 was promulgated in 2002, prior to the coming into force of the CRPD. In this regard, the Act did not provide for the necessary emphasis on support in communication, peer support or other kinds of support to the user.

On a positive note, the chapter has demonstrated that the Mental Health Care Act 2002 requires that every mental health care user be provided with care, treatment and rehabilitation services that improve the mental capacity of the user to develop to full potential and to facilitate his/her integration into community life (Mental Health Care Act 2002 S 8(2)). In this regard, approaches towards enabling a user to develop to his/her full potential could form part of supported decision-making to the extent that such approaches are carried out in accordance with the will and preferences of the person with a psychosocial disability.

Finally, it is worth emphasising that a lack of public awareness on mental health and the existence of widespread stigma against persons with psychosocial disabilities significantly hinders their enjoyment of human rights. It is essential, therefore, to emphasise the importance of awareness raising on the rights of persons with psychosocial disabilities among the public and among medical practitioners, including their right to exercise legal capacity and the right to health care on the basis of free and informed consent. In this regard, it is therefore important for stakeholders to take note of the invitations of the SALRC to take part in their participatory processes for public comment during the development of a discussion paper for the purposes of draft legislation on disability, as well as the review of civil and criminal legislation in the domestication process of the CRPD (Law Reform Commission, 2021).

References

Treaties and Conventions

African Charter on Human and Peoples' Rights OAU Doc 21 ILM 58 (1982).
African Charter on the Rights and Welfare of the Child OAU Doc CAB/LEG/24.9/49 (1990).
Committee on the Rights of Persons with Disabilities (2015) *Initial State Party Report of South Africa* (24 November 2015). [Online] CRPD/C/ZAF/1. Available at: https://tbinternet.ohchr.org/_layouts/15/treatybodyexternal/Download.aspx?symbolno=CRPD%2fC%2fZAF%2f1&Lang=en (Accessed: 3 April 2022).
Convention on the Rights of Persons with Disabilities UN Doc A/RES/61/106 (2006)
Department of Health (2013–2020) *National Mental Health Policy Framework and Strategic Plan*. Pretoria: Department of Health.
International Covenant on Economic, Social and Cultural Rights UN Doc 6 ILM 368 (1967).
Protocol to the African Charter on Human and Peoples' Rights on the Rights of Persons with Disabilities in Africa.

Government Publication – Act of Parliament

Children's Act 2005, c. 38. Available at: https://www.gov.za/sites/default/files/gcis_document/201409/a38-053.pdf (Accessed: 3 April 2022).
The Constitution of the Republic of South Africa 1996, c. 108. Amended 2005, c. 5. Available at: https://www.justice.gov.za/legislation/constitution/saconstitution-web-eng.pdf (Accessed: 3 April 2022).
Hazardous Substances Act 1973, c. 15. Available at: https://www.gov.za/sites/default/files/gcis_document/201504/act-15-1973.pdf (Accessed: 3 April 2022).
Health Professions Act 1974, c. 56. Available at: https://www.hpcsa.co.za/Uploads/Legal/legislation/health_professions_ct_56_1974.pdf (Accessed: 3 April 2022).
Medical Schemes Act 1998, c. 131. Available at: https://www.gov.za/sites/default/files/gcis_document/201409/a131-98.pdf (Accessed: 3 April 2022).
Mental Health Care Act 2002, c. 17. Available at: https://www.gov.za/sites/default/files/gcis_document/201409/a17-02.pdf (Accessed: 3 April 2022).
National Health Act 2003, c. 61. Available at: https://www.gov.za/sites/default/files/gcis_document/201707/40955gon627.pdf (Accessed: 3 April 2022).
Traditional Health Practitioners Act 2007, c. 22 Available at: https://www.gov.za/sites/default/files/gcis_document/201409/a22-07.pdf (Accessed: 3 April 2022).

Case Law

De Lange v Smuts, N.O. [1998] (3) SA 785 (CC).
Ferreira v Levin, N.O. and Others [1996] (1) SA 984 (CC).
Glenister v President of the Republic of South Africa [2009] (1) SA 287, 2009 (2) BCLR 136 (CC).
Re Matter of Captain PGM [2015] eKLR (HC, 13 March 2015).
S v Coetzee [1997] (3) SA 527 (CC).
S.C. v Brazil [2013] CRPD/C/12/D/10/2013
WK v AW [2014] eKLR (HC, 15 December 2014) [Online]. Available at: http://kenyalaw.org/caselaw/cases/view/107004 (Accessed: 3 April 2022).

Government Publication – Other Official Publications

Department of Health (1997) *White Paper for the Transformation of the Health System in South Africa*. Pretoria: Department of Health.
Department of Health (2013–2020) *National Mental Health Policy Framework and Strategic Plan*. Pretoria: Department of Health.

United Nations Publications

Committee on the Rights of Persons with Disabilities (2014a) *Communication No. 10/2013* (28 October 2014). [Online] CRPD/C/12/D/10/2013. Available at: https://tbinternet.ohchr.org/_layouts/15/treatybodyexternal/Download.aspx?symbolno=CRPD%2FC%2F12%2FD%2F10%2F2013&Lang=en (Accessed: 3 April 2022).

Committee on the Rights of Persons with Disabilities (2014b) *General Comment No. 1 Article 12 Equal Recognition Before the Law* (11 April 2014). [Online] CRPD/C/GC/1. Available at: https://www.ohchr.org/en/treaty-bodies/crpd/general-comments (Accessed: 3 April 2022).

Committee on the Rights of Persons with Disabilities (2015) *Initial State Party Report of South Africa* (24 November 2015). [Online] CRPD/C/ZAF/1. Available at: https://tbinternet.ohchr.org/_layouts/15/treatybodyexternal/Download.aspx?symbolno=CRPD%2fC%2fZAF%2f1&Lang=en (Accessed: 3 April 2022).

Journal Articles

Grobbelaar-du Plessis, I. (2013) 'South Africa', *African Disability Rights*. Yearbook, pp. 307–341.

Kamundia, E. (2016/2017) 'The Right to Own and Manage Property and Finances by Persons with Psychosocial Disabilities in Kenya', *East African Law Journal*, pp. 1–2. Available at: http://rodra.co.za/images/countries/kenya/research/East%20African%20Law%20Journal%20-%20Special%20issue%20on%20disability%20rights%202017-2017.pdf (Accessed: 3 April 2022).

Lester, H., Tait, L., England, E. and Tritter, J. (2006) 'Patient Involvement in Primary Care Mental Health: A Focus Group Study', *The British Journal of General Practice* 56(527), pp. 415–422.

Minkowitz, T. (2007) 'The United Nations Convention of the Rights of Persons with Disabilities and the Right to be Free from Non-Consensual Psychiatric Interventions', *Syracuse Journal of International Law & Commerce* 34(2), pp. 405–428.

Paré, M. (2011) 'Of Minors and the Mentally Ill: Re-positioning Perspectives on Consent to Health Care', *Windsor Yearbook of Access to Justice* 29(1), pp. 107–109.

Books

Currie, I. and De Waal, I. (2013) *The Bill of Rights Handbook*, 6th edn. South Africa: Juta Academic.

Currie, I. and Woolman, S. (1996) 'Freedom and Security of the Person', in Chaskalson, M. *et al* (eds.), *Constitutional Law of South Africa*, pp. 39–34 Juta: Cape Town.

Dugard, J. (2013) *International Law: A South African Perspective*, 4th edn. South Africa: Juta Academic.

Fanning, J. (2018) *New Medicalism and the Mental Health Act*. Oxford: Hart Publishing.

Reports

South African Human Rights Commission (2006–2009) *7th Report on Economic and Social Rights*. Braamfontein: South African Human Rights Commission.

South African Human Rights Commission (2009) *Public Inquiry: Access to Health Care Services*. Braamfontein: South African Human Rights Commission.

South African Human Rights Commission (2017) *Report of the National Investigative Hearing into the Status of Mental Health Care in South Africa*. Braamfontein: South African Human Rights Commission.

South African Law Reform Commission (2004) *Assisted Decision-Making: Adults with Impaired Decision-Making Capacity Discussion Paper 105*. Pretoria: Law Reform Commission.

South African Law Reform Commission (2015) *Assisted Decision-Making Report Project 122*. Pretoria: Law Reform Commission.

South African Law Reform Commission (2021) *Domestication of the United Nations Convention on the Rights of Persons with Disabilities Issue Paper: No. 39 Project 148*. Pretoria: Law Reform Commission.

Organization for Economic Cooperation and Development (2012) *OECD Reviews of Health Care Quality: Korea 2012 Raising Standards*. Available at: https://www.oecd.org/publications/oecd-reviews-of-health-care-quality-korea-9789264173446-en.htm (Accessed: 3 April 2022).

Thesis (PhD) – Print

Kamundia, E. (2019) *Supported Decision-Making as a Human Rights Principle in Mental Health Care: An International and Comparative Analysis.* PhD Thesis. University of Pretoria.

Newspaper

Jeranji, T. (2021) 'South Africa's Policy Framework and Strategic Plan Has Lapsed, So What Happens Next?', *Daily Maverick Citizen*, 11 October.

Web Page

United Nations Treaty Collection (2022) *Depositary Status as at 18-03-2022 Chapter IV Human Rights.* Available at: https://treaties.un.org/pages/ViewDetails.aspx?src=IND&mtdsg_no=IV-15&chapter=4&clang=_en#EndDec (Accessed: 18 March 2022).

28
UNTAPPED POTENTIAL OF CHINA'S MENTAL HEALTH LAW REFORM

Bo Chen

Introduction

This chapter presents mental health law reform in China's mainland as a case study to engage the international debate around mental health laws and the United Nations Convention on the Rights of Persons with Disabilities (CRPD). Among many controversies, one of the most debated questions is whether involuntary detention and treatment authorised by mental health laws can comply with international human rights law (Wilson, 2021). The position of abolishing compulsory mental health laws of the United Nations Committee on the Rights of Persons with Disabilities (CRPD Committee) is explicitly made on various occasions, including the first General Comment of the CRPD (CRPD Committee, 2014). In the Concluding Observations to China in 2012, the CRPD Committee

> advises the State party to adopt measures to ensure that all health care and services provided to persons with disabilities, including all mental health care and services, is based on the free and informed consent of the individual concerned, and that laws permitting involuntary treatment and confinement, including upon the authorization of third party decision-makers such as family members or guardians, are repealed.

That said, there has been an international trend where States Parties to the CRPD have enacted legislation in which involuntary mental health interventions are still permissible, for example India; meanwhile, other States Parties, such as Ireland, Australia, and Canada, entered declarations or reservations in relation to provisions in the CRPD requiring abolishing involuntary interventions upon their ratification of the Convention. Against this background, a number of approaches have been suggested to resolve the different perspectives, including the exploration of alternative measures to coercion in psychiatry (Gooding et al., 2020), the fusion model of mental health and capacity law (Dawson and Szmukler, 2006), and the disability-neutral approach in state intervention to save lives (Flynn and Arstein-Kerslake, 2017). One of the proposals is to develop good quality, voluntary mental health services before involuntary detention and treatment can be abolished. Arguably the hope is, if the voluntary services are sufficiently resourced and well-functioning, there would be no need to initiate the involuntary system even if it is still in place (McSherry and Weller, 2010).

As will be discussed in the chapter, China's Mental Health Law (MHL), which entered into force in 2013, not only introduced the 'voluntary principle' and narrowed the scope of involuntary detention and treatment but also calls for increased attention and resources to the voluntary services. However, the chapter also suggests that this law reform has not fully achieved its potential.

Before moving to a doctrinal examination of the law reform, the following section will briefly provide fundamental background, including demographic information on persons with mental health issues and the mainstream mental health services available in China. The chapter will then present the ongoing and generally accepted practice of 'medical protective admission' as an example to suggest that law reform has not been well translated into practice. The chapter ends with a few concluding reflections.

Background

Home to 'over 170 million adults suffering from at least one type of mental disorder' and 16 million people who have severe mental illness (Qian, 2012), China is an Eastern Asian country, with a population of around 1.4 billion and a territory of 9.6 million square kilometres. The MHL is applicable in its thirty-one provinces, centrally administered municipalities, and autonomous regions of minorities, excluding the special regions which have their own mental health services systems and legal systems such as Hong Kong and Macao. Despite its international image as an economic giant, the gross domestic product per capita of China is 16,400 US dollars (USD) estimated in 2020, ranked 102nd globally (CIA, 2022). There are also enormous gaps between economic and social development in coastal (eastern) and inland (western) regions (Wei, 2013).

Albeit there is some visibility of traditional Chinese medicine in the formal health care system, the mental health system is primarily western or modern in style (Yip, 2005). China 'embraced' the western system in 1897 when an American missionary built the first psychiatric hospital in Guangzhou, an important port city and one of the first cities where foreigners were allowed to do business in China. However, that period of history was not the best time for modern psychiatry to grow in China: the Qing dynasty was overthrown by the revolution by which the Republic of China was founded in 1911; regional warlords competed (1916–1928); Japan invaded China (1937–1945), as a part of World War II; and then there was the civil war between the Communist Party and the Nationalist Party (1927–1949). By 1 October 1949, when the regime of the People's Republic of China was founded, there were around one hundred psychiatrists and one thousand beds in psychiatric hospitals, providing services to over four hundred million people in the country (Liu et al., 2011).

The development of mental health services did not accelerate immediately after the decades of war and the foundation of the regime of the People's Republic of China. In the first decade after 1949, the new government built more psychiatric hospitals, and the idea of community mental health service was promoted in the first National Mental Health Meeting in 1958. The Great Leap Forward (1958–1960) and the Cultural Revolution (1966–1976), however, stopped most social development projects in the country. According to a review article on mental health services and resources in China, the total number of psychiatric hospitals in 1965 dropped to only 55% of the number in 1961 (Li et al., 2012). When the Cultural Revolution ended, the opening and reform towards a market economy (1978 onwards) became the new national policy priority and altered communist China fundamentally. It provided a relatively stable political and social environment for mental health services to develop. On the other hand, the sharp, and arguably unprepared, transformation into a market economy cut most full public funding to health care service providers and pushed hospitals to make profits in order to be self-sustaining (Li et al., 2012).

After decades of development, inpatient treatments in institutionalised facilities, seen as the 'alien forms grafted onto Chinese society rather than an indigenous product' in the past (Pearson, 1996), have become the most important form of mental health services one can get in China (Ma, 2014). However, psychiatry in China differs from its western counterparts, in that the psycho-social consideration of mental illness has been mostly absent. This is partly because social science subjects in higher education were banned in the mid-1950s. Considered to be 'too Western' (Pearson, 1996), psychology, sociology, anthropology, and social work were no longer taught or researched in universities It was not until the Chinese leadership set aside the ideological revolution and shifted to focus on economic development in the 1980s that this scenario started to change.

To better cope with the stress that accompanied economic growth and modernity, the government supported the teaching and practice of psychology (Yang, 2017). Pilot projects on community service were undertaken and promoted in all versions of the National Mental Health Work Plan. Social workers are integrated into the mental health team in some regions (Chen and Huang, 2014). However, these are very recent developments. The biomedical model is still dominant in the mental health system without competing and effective alternative approaches to understanding and coping with mental distress.

Against this background, solving the problem that a large number of patients had no or limited access to treatment has been regarded as the policy priority. Research shows that 'undersupply of the mental health service is the most pivotal issue for policy-makers' in China (Qian, 2012). All versions of the National Mental Health Work Plan and other relevant policy documents reflect this concern. For example, the baseline for the treatment rate of schizophrenia set in the Guidelines 2008–2015 was 15% to 30%, and the aim was 60% in 2010 and 80% in the National Mental Health Work Plan 2015–2020. The policy goal of promoting treatment is crucial in understanding service providers' attitudes about service users' right to decision-making and autonomy. Under this policy goal, refusing treatment is more likely to be seen as a barrier to accessing treatment and, therefore, coercion is seen as necessary to facilitate treatment. This policy priority is argued to be supported by psychiatric research. As more recent data is unavailable, a study published in 2009 reveals that from 2001 to 2004 91.8% of people with a diagnosis of mental disorders and 27.6% of people with a diagnosis of psychotic disorders never sought help in China (Liu et al., 2011). Another study, based on the data from the World Health Organization (WHO) World Mental Health Surveys, reveals that the treatment rate of common mental disorders (including anxiety disorder, emotional disorder, substance use disorder, but excluding schizophrenia) was only 11.3% (Zhang, 2006).

Taking its enormous population into account, the National Mental Health Work Plan 2015–2020 (2015) revealed that China's mental health workforce (1.49 psychiatrists and 17.1 psychiatric beds for every 100,000 population) is considerably lower than the European average level: 9.7 psychiatrists and 62.7 psychiatric beds for every 100,000 population (WHO, 2021, pp. 61, 78). Inadequate investment is argued to be a direct reason for the under-supply of mental health services. Data in 2017 shows that the government investment for psychiatric hospitals is around 1.07 USD per capita; in contrast the number in high-income countries is about 35.06 USD at the same period of time (Que et al., 2019). As public health funding is mainly the responsibility of local governments whose financial resources vary from region to region, the problem of inadequate investment is worse in underdeveloped areas. An authoritative policy paper acknowledges that in some western regions 'the existing national mental health policies become just well-written documents' (Liu et al., 2011, p. 214).

Paradoxically, when greater awareness of mental health has been raised and government funding has increased, this has led to a movement of building new institutions or expanding the existing institutions. Data from 2004 reveals that there were 557 psychiatric hospitals (among which 359 had 100 beds or more and 44 had 500 beds or more), and 1.0 beds in psychiatric hospitals for every 10,000 population (Liu et al., 2011). Another piece of research in 2016 reports that the number of psychiatric hospitals increased to 728 (with 323 beds per hospital on average) and psychiatric beds per 10,000 population rose to 1.7 (Patel et al., 2016). A policy paper reveals that 9.1 billion RMB (approximately 1.3 billion euros) was spent to construct or expand 550 psychiatric institutions from 2010 to 2012 (Xie, 2017). The problem, however, is that community services have failed to receive equal attention and funding to that invested in large-scale psychiatric hospitals. For decades, psychiatrists and policymakers have acknowledged the importance of community services, but the reality remains that for most Chinese people 'the only form of service patients and their family can receive is the institutionalised treatment and care' (Ma, 2014). Community service was encouraged by the government as early as 1958 by the Five-Year Plan for Mental Health (1958–1962) and emphasised in all the following policies. Yet, nearly sixty years later the National Mental Health Work Plan 2015–2020 admits that the community rehabilitation system for mental disorders has not been built.

The fact that public investment goes to psychiatric hospitals rather than community service does not necessarily mean that hospitalised care has become accessible. Although insurance coverage is improving, treatment in psychiatric hospitals is still expensive for most Chinese people (Li et al., 2012). As a commentator puts it, '[a] Western outsider might simply assume from what he or she knew of socialism that China would provide health care free to all her citizens. This has never been the case' (Pearson 1996). For example, it has been revealed by a study that in 2004 only 26% of the total population had health insurance in China, and one treatment session in a psychiatric hospital usually costs half of the personal income of a year (Li et al., 2012). It has to be noted here that being covered by public health insurance does not mean that treatment would be free, as there is a mechanism to determine whether and how much of the cost should be covered by the State. In both urban and rural regions, the lack of community services leaves no choice for family members who bear most, if not all, responsibilities of care.

The traditional Confucian values of family self-reliance and lifelong interdependence have further reinforced this family-oriented care model. More importantly, from the lens of traditional political thought, the social recognition and even the meaningfulness of Chinese people are based on the fulfilment of the role within the family, and the notion of self or self-identity lies on family rather than the individual (Fei, 1992). Therefore, since mental illness is perceived as damaging a person's social functioning and the notion of self, other parties in society, particularly psychiatrists, take family members as the legitimate agent in expressing needs and describing conditions on behalf of the person concerned (Ma, 2015). From this traditional perspective, family members should 'control' and 'direct' the lives of people with mental health issues (Ma, 2015). This may be in tension with the liberal understanding of self and the emphasis on the patient-state relationship of the mental health laws in the West (Donnelley and Murray, 2013). Nevertheless, the collective notion of self may also have a theoretical potential of being closer to the concept of relational autonomy (Series, 2015), which is arguably promoted by the CRPD.

The history of communist governance adds another layer of complexity to the situation. Before China's economic reform of the market to open up to globalisation, people's lives had been tied closely with the State, either through their employers, mostly government or state-owned factories, or through collective communes in villages. Putting political abuse of psychiatry aside, under the totalitarian system, a person could only be treated in hospital and covered by health insurance with approval from employers or other forms of government/ Party officials (Ding, 2010). Although public control has largely retreated from people's private lives in the market economy, the power of governments, especially in underdeveloped areas, is still arbitrary. It appears that the professionalism of psychiatry is not strong enough to refuse an order from the government to detain someone. Many cases were revealed by the media of 'petitioners' (Minzner, 2006) being sent to psychiatric hospitals by the local government to silence or punish them (Ding, 2014).

In summary, after China's reform into a market economy, the government prioritised the problem of untreated patients as a major threat to social stability and economic growth, thereby promoting policies that control people with mental health issues, through their families at home or in institutions. In recent years, with the growing financial ability of the Chinese government and the enactment of the MHL, investment in mental health services has increased. However, as there is no voice advocating against the expansion of psychiatry, most public investments go into the construction of segregated psychiatric hospitals. The above overview of the mental health services in China, including some social elements underneath, are crucial in understanding the changes brought by the MHL in 2013.

Detention and treatment decision-making under the Mental Health Law 2013

This section explores the current framework for mental health detention and treatment under the MHL. It argues that the MHL has taken some steps forward, at least in theory, in promoting autonomy and reducing the over-reliance on involuntary inpatient treatment in the Chinese mental health system. The MHL adopts the voluntary principle for mental health treatment. Compared to its predecessors, the MHL has also narrowed the substantive criteria for involuntary interventions. These changes are arguably in line with the proposal that States and mental health laws internationally should shift focus to improve voluntary services which would hopefully maximise the autonomy of persons with mental health issues.

It is worth noting first that mental health legislation in common law jurisdictions usually only regulates detention and involuntary treatment. By contrast, the MHL covers broader issues. Its eighty-five articles are divided into seven chapters, covering a wide range of issues, including psychological well-being promotion and mental disorder prevention, diagnosis and treatment of mental disorders, rehabilitation of mental disorders, and measures necessary to implement the law, such as financial contributions.

Although this chapter focuses on the provisions for detention and treatment, some other provisions are also broadly relevant. For example, family members' significant decision-making status and responsibility, as will be discussed later, may be seen as reflections of the general principle in Article 21 of the MHL, which requires that family members 'should care for one another, create a good and amiable home environment and raise awareness of mental disorder prevention', and when a family member is suspected to have a mental disorder, other family members 'shall help them to immediately see a doctor, look after their life and take care of them'.

The MHL also includes some other provisions that are unlikely to appear in mental health legislation in other jurisdictions. For example, Article 11 provides that the State encourages and supports the training of specialised personnel in mental health, the protection of the legal rights and interests of mental health workers, and the strengthening of the professional mental health workforce. However, Zhao and Dawson (2014) rightly point out that many provisions like this 'must be reviewed as largely aspirational' (p. 670). As the MHL allocates responsibilities for developing and managing mental health services across so many agencies, there is the risk that no-one will take responsibility, since clauses like Article 11 lack clarity as to the standard or the legal consequence for failing to fulfil the obligation.

During the 28-year period it took to create the MHL, seven municipal mental health regulations were developed and implemented in seven cities, which are Shanghai (whose mental health regulation entered into force in 2002), Ningbo (2006), Hangzhou (2007), Beijing (2007), Wuxi (2007), Wuhan (2010), and Shenzhen (2012). These cities are among the most economically and socially developed across China or at least in their regions. These mental health regulations were developed and implemented while the MHL was being drafted. As such they are particularly important in understanding the MHL and the changes it made.

In short, these regulations authorised two types of involuntary admissions: emergency admissions and medical protective admissions. Emergency admissions are essentially procedures that, when some sorts of risks are observed, authorise detention for diagnostic assessment, after which the decision for the continued detention for treatment is still most likely decided by family members. Medical protective admissions, on the other hand, are also mostly decided by family members, without any requirement of evident harm or dangerousness to themselves or others but based on clinical determinations of insight or capacity. Therefore, except for those detentions that have been addressed by criminal procedures since 2014, family members, following medical recommendations, were the primary decision-makers for the civil commitment under the municipal mental health regulations.

Unlike the preceding regulations, the MHL no longer places a general limitation on a service user's autonomy and decision-making rights, such as the loss of insight or 'the capacity for civil conduct' (a term in Chinese law roughly referring to mental capacity for civil affairs such as entering a contract). The only exception to the voluntary principle is the detention for involuntary treatment, when a diagnostic threshold and a dangerousness standard has been met.

Article 30 of the MHL states that inpatient treatment of mental disorders shall be voluntary in principle. However, if the result of the diagnostic assessment indicates that a person has a severe mental disorder, the medical facility may impose inpatient treatment when the person is: (1) self-harming, or at risk of self-harm; or (2) behaving in a way that harms others, or poses a risk to the safety of others.

Voluntary treatment

As a principle, a voluntary service user can choose or refuse inpatient treatment themselves. Accordingly, Article 44 says that they can also request discharge at any time, and medical facilities are required to comply. However, the MHL does not make it clear whether a voluntary service user has the right to refuse treatment during hospitalisation. In theory, his or her right to request discharge 'at any time' serves as a last resort if the service user does not want certain treatments to proceed. Nevertheless, Article 45 provides that when persons with mental disorders are unable to complete hospital discharge procedures themselves, these procedures shall be completed by their guardians. How this is determined in practice and whether this provision applies to voluntary service users is unclear.

What is clear, however, is that the MHL does not grant a mental health facility the power to detain a voluntary service user if the facility disagrees with the service user's request for discharge. The MHL provides in Article 44 that when the medical facility considers hospital discharge requested by voluntary service users and guardians to be inappropriate, the facility shall explain their reasons for opposing discharge to the patient and the guardians; and if the patient or the guardians insist on discharge, the registered physician shall write a detailed record of the discussion about discharge in the medical chart and provide recommendations about the medical management of the patient after discharge.

Similar to its predecessors, the MHL adopts 'patients or guardians' as the persons with the right to receive information. As a general rule, Articles 37–39 say that the facility is required to inform the patients or their guardians about the patients' rights and treatment plan, including its methods, goals, and potential adverse effects. From a legal perspective, mental health facilities will fulfil their obligations under these provisions by merely informing the guardians only.

In addition, the right of guardians may still prevail in certain situations. For example, Article 47 of the MHL requires that a mental health facility must allow service users and their guardians to access and copy their medical record. However, unlike the rule of accessing medical records in general health care, the right of a service user could be legally restricted, if accessing or copying medical records would be potentially detrimental to their treatment. The MHL does not clarify this standard, but it is very likely to be determined by the psychiatrist. By contrast, the guardian's right to access the medical records must be ensured, regardless of any situation.

Detention and involuntary treatment under the Mental Health Law

This subsection addresses the provisions for detention and involuntary treatment, specifically considering detention for diagnostic assessment, detention for treatment, and discharge.

Detention for diagnostic assessment

In addition to voluntary admission for diagnostic assessment in a mental health facility, Article 28 also provides that close family members 'may' take a person for a mental health assessment. This implies that no one in Chinese society can refuse diagnostic assessment in circumstances where their mental health is called into question. Reading Article 28 and Article 83 together, the MHL relies on family members, not necessarily equipped with any expertise in mental health, to determine the presence of a suspected mental disorder, defined as the disturbances or abnormalities of perception, emotion, thinking, or other mental processes. The wording of 'may' implies a certain degree of coercion, for example by threat or deception, is permitted in the process of taking a person with a suspected mental disorder to a facility. The implementation of this provision merits further discussion. However, it is reasonable to suggest that the decision to restrict a service user's liberty is at the discretion of a family member, without any meaningful threshold.

Article 28 says that when a person with a suspected mental disorder is at risk of harming themselves or others, a broader range of entities, including employers and the police, should or are obliged to immediately intervene and take the person to a mental health facility for diagnostic assessment. However, there is no clear time restriction for the assessment. Article 29 merely provides that, when receiving persons with suspected mental disorders deemed to pose a risk, medical facilities shall hold them and designate a registered psychiatrist for diagnostic assessment immediately who must issue a formal diagnostic result promptly.

A 72-hour limit to the diagnostic assessment was included in the Standing Committee of the National People's Congress (SCNPC) Draft Article 24, which was ultimately removed from the MHL. Nevertheless, both the new ('promptly') rule in MHL Article 28 and the old rule ('72-hour') apply to persons taken to be posing harm or risk to oneself or others. By contrast, for persons without such dangerousness who are taken for assessment by family members, the MHL does not provide any time limit for their diagnostic assessment. This arguably reflects a presumption that no conflict of interest between a service user and the family member would arise.

Even for those detained on the ground of dangerousness to themselves or others, the MHL does not provide any mechanism to substantiate the claimed dangerousness. This means a family member without any expertise in mental health can decide on deprivation of liberty for an unknown period of time, based on a suspected mental disorder where they claim or perceive dangerousness.

Detention for treatment

As discussed, detention for treatment, or 'involuntary inpatient treatment' in the language of the MHL, has to meet the diagnostic threshold of a severe mental disorder, of which the definition implies consideration of mental capacity, and the dangerousness standard. Unlike mental health legislation in some jurisdictions, the MHL does not require separate procedures or standards for detention and involuntary treatment. The concept of 'inpatient treatment' suggests that a service user has no control in respect of future treatment as long as he or she is detained. The only exception to this is provided by Article 43, which requires that the delivery of surgeries that result in loss of function of body organs and of experimental clinical treatments must obtain separate written consent from service users. If the service user is regarded as 'unable' to give consent, the consent of guardians can be substituted instead, with internal ethical approval from the facility. Again, this provision implies the consideration of mental capacity, but the MHL does not provide any further clarification on how to determine a service user's ability in this context. There is no literature on how this provision of substituted consent works in practice, and this requires further research. However, it seems reasonable to assume that the capacity determination will be more likely to apply to service users who refuse proposed interventions than those who comply.

In relation to the decision-maker for detention for treatment, the MHL differentiates service users who are dangerous to themselves from those who are dangerous to others. By reading Articles 30, 32, 35, and 36 together, if a service user having a severe mental disorder is considered to pose harm or dangerousness to others, the decision of detention for involuntary treatment will ultimately be made by the facility that receives the service user and carries out the diagnosis. Article 36 provides that if the guardians do not complete the

China's mental health law reform

hospital admission procedures, the employer, rural villagers' committee, or urban neighbourhood committee completes the hospital admission procedures instead and the medical facility records this situation in the patient's medical chart. In this scenario, the service user or the guardian could only apply for a reassessment and medical certification if they disagree with the decision for detention for treatment as provided in Articles 32 and 35.

By contrast, according to Articles 30–32, if the service user is dangerous to themselves but poses no dangerousness to others, detention for treatment is up to the guardian. A significant deficit in respect of the service users' rights under the MHL is that, where a service user disagrees with the diagnosis or the guardian's decision for detention, the MHL does not provide any internal complaint mechanism. In an earlier draft released by the Standing Committee of the National People's Congress before the final enactment of the MHL, if a service user disagrees with the guardian's decision for detention based on a diagnosis of severe mental disorder, he or she was entitled to apply for a reassessment by the same facility and, further, a medical certification by external experts about the initial diagnosis and the detention for treatment. However, this provision was removed from the final text of the MHL. According to the official explanation for this deletion, the legislators thought most service users would not be willing to accept inpatient treatment and allowing them to challenge the decision of their guardians would 'raise new problems in practice' (Xin, 2013, p. 93). They believed the external mechanism, the right to litigate in courts provided in Article 82, would serve as an adequate safeguard.

Discharge

The discharge provisions in the MHL adopt different approaches to decision-making depending on the basis for admission. For service users detained on the basis of imposing harm or dangerousness to themselves, Article 44 says that the guardian can request discharge at any time, and the mental health facility must comply. The facility can only advise why discharge is unwise from a professional perspective. If the advice is not accepted by the guardian, the facility can merely note this in the medical record and discharge the service user.

For those service users detained on the basis of posing a risk to others, Article 45 says that a mental health facility may decide when discharge is appropriate but the discharging procedures have to be completed by the service user or, in the cases where service users are 'unable' to complete hospital discharge procedures, the guardians. Problematically, the MHL is silent on the determination of such ability. If a service user under detention for treatment is automatically deemed unable to make any treatment decision or discharge, their liberty is left to their guardian to decide. This is the case even when the mental health facility believes he or she should be discharged (Chen, 2018). This provision may cause considerable problems in practice.

Cross-cutting issues

Through the discussions above, some cross-cutting issues emerge. Chief amongst these is that under the MHL, both diagnostic assessment and inpatient treatment can be voluntarily and involuntarily provided, creating potential complications. In theory, a person can consent to a diagnostic assessment on a voluntary basis but then be detained for treatment, if the diagnostic threshold of a severe mental disorder and the dangerousness standard are met. Therefore, voluntary diagnostic assessment could be viewed as risky from the service user's perspective. It is also possible that a person could be taken by the family member for diagnostic assessment against their will, but, if no dangerousness is found, they should be able to refuse the inpatient treatment and leave. These hypothetical cases are entirely possible by law.

Another cross-cutting issue is that, like its predecessors, the MHL grants guardians or family members significant decision-making power in respect of detention. Granting the power of deprivation of liberty to another individual is clearly at odds with international human rights law. At the very least, considering the significant power imbalance between service users and their guardians, the MHL should provide safeguards that recognise the potential for conflict and prevent abusive use of the MHL by family members. However, the MHL provides in Article 83 that guardians of persons with mental disorders under the MHL are persons who may assume the role of the guardian as specified in Chinese civil law, by which the list includes one's spouse, parents, and adult children. In Chinese law, a guardian has a wide range of responsibility for the person, including provision of care (or bearing the cost of living of the person) and even tort liability should the person cause injury to a third party or their property (Chen, 2022, p. 84). In theory, an appointment of a guardian requires a consideration of mental capacity in decision-making of the person under guardianship and a formal procedure as provided in China's Civil Procedure Law, so that not every mental health service user has a formal guardian. But it is a general practice that mental health facilities and even courts automatically see their close family members are guardians, possibly due to the wording of Article 83 (Chen, 2022, pp. 84–89). Without any formal safeguard or further guidance on how to appoint a guardian, the MHL leaves excessive discretion and significant potential for abuse by both psychiatrists and family members or guardians. Moreover, Article 83 may even bypass the safeguards provided under the adult guardianship system.

Section summary

As discussed above, under the MHL, the only exception to the voluntary principle is that inpatient treatment must meet both a diagnostic threshold of a severe mental disorder and a dangerousness standard to oneself or others. This is a significant change in the law, compared to the dominant practice of medical protective admissions, which does not require any evidence of dangerousness and is supported by the predecessors to the MHL. The MHL does not adopt any general threshold for a service user in exercising his or her right to information and decision-making, moving away from the old paradigm of 'medical protective admissions' that allows family members to decide on detention for treatment upon medical recommendations without any requirement of dangerousness to oneself or others.

Nevertheless, the doctrinal examination of the MHL in this article has identified a number of unanswered questions. The MHL does not provide any guidance on many critical determinations, including dangerousness and the ability to complete the procedures for inpatient treatment or discharge. For example, if the dangerousness threshold is interpreted loosely in practice, anyone with a label of a severe mental disorder could be at risk of detention for treatment. The scope for a loose interpretation could render the voluntary principle meaningless in practice. Another significant issue is the appointment of guardians, who wield enormous decision-making power over service users. The wording of the MHL seems to imply that every person with a severe mental disorder must have a guardian, which places the rights of service users in significant jeopardy.

Translation from 'law in the book' to 'law in action'

Despite the progress in law, it is equally important to assess the extent to which the progressive law reform has been translated into practice. However, such an assessment appears to be very difficult. For example, there is hardly any national or regional data that could suggest whether voluntary treatment has been put into more use or whether there has emerged reduced reliance on detention and involuntary treatment.

As a matter of fact, what counts as voluntary or involuntary appears to be mostly unclear in practice. Based on the data collected from 814 inpatients from 32 psychiatric hospitals in 29 provinces in 2017, Jiang et al. (2018) suggest that more than half of the involuntarily hospitalised patients meet the MHL-defined criteria, raising concerns of liberty violations to the service suers; whilst Ma and Shao (2019) argue the data should be interpreted differently as Jiang's finding excludes patients detained for being a risk to self. However, Ma and Shao (2019) also acknowledge that the clinical perception of 'risk' in China is vague: in their survey, '54.5% of respondents thought that somebody with a history of attacking others can be considered dangerous to others, and 33.1% of respondents thought that stopping taking medicine was a danger to the patients themselves'. While a more comprehensive analysis of the incomplete translation from law in the book to law in action is provided elsewhere (Chen, 2022), the analysis below will revisit this vague but popular perception in risk determinations. The emphasis of this chapter will be placed on 'medical protective admission', the mainstream method of involuntary admission before the MHL but no longer permissible under the MHL (at least by a strict reading) that is still widely accepted in both medical practice and courts (Chen, 2022). It is possible that this is because the risk evaluation criterion has not been taken seriously.

The MHL provides very vague guidance on how to evaluate the harm or dangerousness to oneself or others. It does not require any standard of evidence or include any term such as 'immediate', 'material', or 'significant' in respect of the risk. Empirical studies suggest it is not uncommon that diagnosis of certain mental disorders or symptoms, like schizophrenia or delusion, is believed to automatically entail harm or danger, thereby justifying the detention and involuntary treatment (Chen, 2022). The legal basis for this common practice is the fact that the MHL does not provide any specific guide or tool for risk assessment either. An authoritative textbook (Editorial Team, 2013) on the MHL for medical and psychiatric professionals prescribes broad medical discretion in risk assessment. For example, in answering the question 'Should involuntary detention for treatment be imposed on patients with schizophrenia who have no behaviour of harm but refuse treatment?', the *Training Textbook* explains:

> Obviously, 'harm to oneself' has a broader scope than suicide. 'Harm to self' must include all behaviours that may harm the patients, intentionally or unintentionally. These behaviours include, for example, *stiffness, excitement*, food or water refusal, and long periods of sleepless. So, patients with a diagnosis of schizophrenia may have no behaviour or risk of suicide or harming others. However, if a patient who refuses treatment has these above conditions [referring to stiffness, excitement, food or water refusal, and long periods of sleepless] that may potentially harm the patient, the criteria for detention for involuntary treatment based on imposing harm or dangerousness to him/herself is fulfilled [emphasis added].
>
> *(Editorial Team, 2013, p. 109)*

Admittedly, the *Training Textbook* also reminds psychiatrists to uphold the 'principle of accurate diagnosis' and to avoid an approach that is 'too loose' (Editorial Team, 2013, p. 109). The effectiveness of this reminder in practice, however, is questionable, especially when other psychiatrists undertaking reassessments and medical certifications are most likely to be trained with the same standards and interpretations and are not sufficiently independent from the mental health facility where the person is detained.

More importantly, Chinese courts have not provided a clear message in respect of a finding that imposing involuntary admission on patients without any evidence of harm or dangerousness is unlawful. For example, in one case a woman was taken to a mental health facility by her husband and treated against her will (*Sun v the Hospital 2015*). After discharge, she sued the hospital for violating her right to liberty, stressing that her condition did not fulfil the dangerousness standard. The hospital argued that the treatment was voluntary because the plaintiff was 'accompanied' by her husband who completed the procedure of hospitalisation. The court rejected the plaintiff's claim on the basis that there was not sufficient evidence to suggest the hospital's fault in the delivery of treatment, without any elaboration on whether the dangerousness standard was met. A particularly problematic point here is that the court assigned the duty of proof to the service user, which is by nature extremely difficult for her to prove she was not posing any risk. This case, and many other cases decided on the basis of similar reasoning, is not legally binding for future cases but rather reflects a judicial interpretation of the MHL which suggests that the practice that family members decide detention for treatment without any presence of harm or dangerousness, so-called 'medical protective admission', is still widely accepted by the courts. In another case, 'unrest and illegal petitioning' to the government is found by the Supreme Court in China to pose dangerousness to the petitioner herself and others (*Huang v the local government 2018*).

It is important to note that there are also several cases in which the courts found involuntary detention for treatment to be unlawful in cases with similar facts to the case above (*Jing v the Hospital 2016*; *Du v the Hospital and others 2015*; *Wang v the Hospital 2017*; *Zhang v the Hospital 2016*). In *Yu v the Hospital 2017*, a man's wife took her husband to a mental health facility, where the man was diagnosed as having an anxiety disorder. The facility wrote in his medical record 'no dangerous or impulsive behaviour is observed. [The plaintiff] has thoughts of suicide but has not acted on those thoughts'. In the medical record, his wife suggested that the plaintiff had emotional issues; he did not pose a risk to his family members but to himself. However, the medical record did not assess the level of 'risk' he posed or elaborate on his specific behaviours. Despite the medical record that had at least suggested the risk of suicide, the court found 'it cannot be established that the plaintiff has suicidal behaviour, is harming others, or damaging things'. On this basis, the court found a violation of the plaintiff's right to liberty.

Therefore, the chapter argues that existing courts' rulings on this matter have not provided a clear response regarding the general acceptance of medical protective admissions, in which the decisions are made by family members and no evident dangerousness is required. This arguably creates ambiguity in understanding the new norms provided in the MHL and may demotivate mental health facilities to make efforts to achieve MHL-compliance.

More interestingly, the decision-making power of family members even extends to the decisions that should be made by psychiatrists. According to the MHL, when the diagnostic threshold of a severe mental disorder is met, if a person poses danger to him or herself, the guardian decides on detention for treatment; by contrast, if the harm or dangerousness is to others, the psychiatrist should assume the role of decision-maker. However, there is empirical evidence suggesting psychiatrists are prone not to exercise their decision-making authority in detention for treatment (Chen, 2022). Again, the existing courts' rulings fail to give a clear response to the practice.

In *Ding v Hospital and Ding 2017*, a woman was taken to a mental hospital and treated for more than a month for engaging in a physical conflict with her ex-father-in-law, who called the police. The woman sued the hospital and her ex-father-in-law after being discharged by her own mother. The court found that the hospital was accountable because the hospital had detained the woman without seeking the consent of her guardian. It is worth noting that in this case the court regarded the mother of the plaintiff as the guardian but there was no indication in the judgment that there was a procedure through which the mother was formally appointed as the guardian. The court ruled:

> Even if under circumstances where the patient with a mental disorder is posing harm or dangerousness to others and involuntary detention for treatment should be imposed, it still needs the consent of the patient or the guardian. If the guardian obstructs hospitalisation, the procedure for inpatient treatment shall be completed by the police. If the guardian refuses hospitalisation, the plaintiff's work unit, village committee or neighbourhood committee shall complete the procedure.

The court's reasoning is problematic. When the harm or danger is towards others the MHL only grants the guardian the right to apply for a reassessment and medical certification, not a right to veto the detention. Since the dangerousness to others was confirmed by the police, the psychiatrist and the mental health facility have the authority to impose detention for treatment.

Why had the court believed that the hospital should seek consent from the guardian? It seems possible that the court read the second paragraph of Article 35 of the MHL without having a consistent understanding of other relevant provisions. Article 35 provides that if the reassessment or the certification affirms the proposal of inpatient treatment, 'the guardians shall agree to the imposition of inpatient treatment for the patient'. This provision reaffirms that the guardian should be informed about the detention for treatment and the guardian's right to apply for reassessment and certification as provided in Article 37. However, if the guardian still refuses to complete the procedure after reassessment and certification, Article 36 provides that his or her work-unit or relevant village/neighbourhood committee should complete the procedure, as quoted in the judgment. Therefore, it has become clear in law that when the identified dangerousness is to others and the psychiatric opinions favour detention for treatment, it will happen after all. The only method for a guardian to object is to apply for reassessment and medical certification.

Putting the legal details aside, it has become apparent that, when the dangerousness is to others, the courts, as well as the MHL itself, still place emphasis on the guardian's role. The court's approach in the above case indicates that family members are still the dominant decision-makers for detention for treatment even when the MHL authorises psychiatrists to decide. This pattern of 'psychiatrists propose, and family members decide' has been conceptualised as 'shared power and silenced service users' and received a deeper analysis elsewhere (Chen, 2022). The point here is that the medical practice after the MHL and related courts' ruling has not fully followed the progressive law reform brought by the MHL.

Concluding reflections

The chapter has argued that, compared to its predecessors, the MHL significantly expands the scope of voluntary decision-making. The MHL adopts the voluntary principle in inpatient treatment by removing the limitation of exercising decision-making rights on the basis of insight or capacity for civil conduct. Under the MHL, the only exception to the voluntary principle is based on the diagnostic threshold and the dangerousness standard. The necessity of treatment, which is commonly found in mental health laws in other jurisdictions, has no place under the MHL. It must be noted that, since substituted decision-making is still clearly provided, the MHL and applicable adult guardianship law is not CRPD-compliant. Nevertheless, it is a step closer to CRPD requirements, at least in theory. However, the chapter also argues that the practice has not been much altered, arguably because the power relationships among service users, family members, and psychiatrists remain unchanged.

One reflection of the unchanged power relationship is that psychiatrists still retain huge discretionary power over service users. Psychiatrists in China have the power of imposing coercion with extremely loose criteria and no oversight. They are also exercising more hidden and invisible power in deciding what is true or valuable to consider in admission and treatment and what language other stakeholders have to use. Unlike the decision-making structure in mental health treatment in many other jurisdictions, family members in China earn their status as decision-makers by bearing almost all responsibilities. They are primary caregivers and hospital fee payers for service users. According to Chinese law, they are also liable for civil compensation if the service user causes damage to a third party. Without accessible alternative forms of social support from the government or from society, family members are the sole source for the provision of the basic needs and support in all aspects of service users' lives. This enlarges the power imbalance between service users and family members, which is already obvious in Chinese law and culture.

It seems reasonable to argue that introducing periodic review and establishing a multidisciplinary review mechanism for mental health detentions and involuntary treatment may also be helpful in balancing the discretion of psychiatrists and family members. Indeed, the research on the design and feasibility of this proposal requires further investigation. More importantly, however, the chapter holds the position that effectively tackling the power imbalance and its social embodiment is beyond the capacity of a piece of mental health legislation and, therefore, requires a fundamental 'paradigm shift' enlightened by the CRPD, a detailed discussion of which is beyond the scope of the chapter. In brief, the development of community-based services and non-coercive support, the awareness-raising of a human rights approach of mental health and disability, and enhancement of participation of service users to all stages of decision-making should be prioritised (Chen, 2022).

References

Central Intelligence Agency, 2022. *China*. Available at: https://www.cia.gov/the-world-factbook/countries/china/ (Accessed: 14 February 2022).

Chen, B. and Huang, S., 2014. Promoting the autonomy of persons with mental disabilities through social worker's intervention: A qualitative study guided by the convention on the rights of persons with disabilities. *In*: W. Zhang, ed. *Disability Rights Studies in China* (Volume 1). Beijing: Social Science Academic Press, 120–140.

Chen, B., 2018. Xu vs. The hospital and his guardian – Involuntary inpatient treatment. *International Journal of Mental Health and Capacity Law*, 2016(22), 134–143.

Chen, B., 2022. *Mental Health Law in China: A Socio-Legal Analysis*. London: Routledge.

CRPD Committee, 2014. General comment no. 1, equal recognition before the law, UN Doc. CRPD/C/GC/1, 11 April 2014.

Davidson, H., 2017. When is a voluntary patient not a voluntary patient? An examination of the degree to which the Irish courts have sought to engage with the jurisprudence of the European Court of Human Rights, in relation to the treatment and detention of voluntary or 'informal' patients. *International Journal of Mental Health and Capacity Law*, 2016(22), 38–50.

Dawson, J. and Szmukler, G., 2006. Fusion of mental health and incapacity legislation. *The British Journal of Psychiatry*, 188(6), 504–509.

Delin Wang v Anding Hosptial of Tianjin Municipality - Medical damage liability dispute first instance case, Basic People' Court of Hexi District, Tianjin Municipality, Civil First Instance No 4915, 21 July 2017. (*Wang v the Hospital*, 2017) [Note: The title of this case is translated by the author of the chapter. original title in Chinese is 天津市河西区人民法院（2017）津0103民初4915号民事判决书.].

Ding v mental Hosptial of Xuzhou Municipality and Ding - Medical damage liability dispute first instance case, Basic People's Court of Gulou District, Xuzhou Municipality, Jiangsu Province, Civil First Instance No 3401, 29 June 2017. (*Ding v the Hospital and Ding*, 2017) [江苏省徐州市鼓楼区人民法院（2015）鼓民初字第3401号民事判决书].

Ding, C., 2010. Family members' informed consent to medical treatment for competent patients in China. *China: An International Journal*, 8(1), 139–150.

Ding, C., 2014. Involuntary detention and treatment of the mentally ill: China's 2012 mental health law. *International Journal of Law and Psychiatry*, 37(6), 581–588.

Donnelley, M. and Murray, C., 2013. The role of family in mental health Law: A framework for transformation. *Child and Family Law Quarterly*, 25, 380–405.

Editorial Team, 2013. *Training Textbook for Healthcare Professionals on the Mental Health Law of the People's Republic of China*. Beijing: China Legal Publishing House.

Fei, X., 1992. *From the Soil: The Foundations of Chinese Society*. Berkeley: University of California Press.

Flynn, E. and Arstein-Kerslake, A., 2017. State intervention in the lives of people with disabilities: The case for a disability-neutral framework. *International Journal of Law in Context*, 13(1), 39–57.

Gooding, P., McSherry, B., and Roper, C., 2020. Preventing and reducing 'coercion' in mental health services: An international scoping review of English-language studies. *Acta Psychiatrica Scandinavica*, 142(1), 27–39.

Jiang, F., Zhou, H., Rakofsky, J.J., Hu, L., Liu, T., Liu, H., Liu, Y., and Tang, Y., 2018. The implementation of China's mental health law-defined risk criteria for involuntary admission: A national cross-sectional study of involuntarily hospitalized patients. *Frontiers in Psychiatry*, 9, 560.

Li, K., Sun, X., Zhang, Y., Shi, G., and Kolstad, A., 2012. Mental health services in China: A review of delivery and policy issues in 1949–2009. *Chinese Mental Health Journal*, 26(5), 321–326.

Lianqiong Zhang v Stomatological Hospital of Jinmen Municipality - Right to health dispute first instance case, Basic People's Court of Dongbao District, Jinmen Municipality, Hubei Province, Civil First Instance No 238, 11 March 2016. (*Zhang v the Hospital*, 2016) [湖北省荆门市东宝区人民法院（2016）鄂0802民初238号民事判决书].

Lianshui Du v Chinese Medical Psychiatric Hospital and others - Personal liberty dispute, Basic People's Court of Lixia District, Jinan Municipality, Shandong Province, Civil First Instance No 1219, 08 September 2015. (*Du v the Hospital and Others*, 2015) [山东省济南市历下区人民法院（2015）历民初字第1219号民事判决书].

Liu, J., 2015. Dependent and non-community living: Rethinking the institutionalization trend of Chinese policies regarding persons with mental disabilities. In: W. Zhang, ed. *Disability Rights Studies in China* (Volume 2). Beijing: Social Science Academic Press, 205–215.

Liu, J., Ma, H., He, Y.-L., Xie, B., Xu, Y.-F., Tang, H.-Y., Li, M., Hao, W., Wang, X.-D., Zhang, M.-Y., Ng, C.H., Goding, M., Fraser, J., Herrman, H., Chiu, H.F.K., Chan, S.S., Chiu, E., and Yu, X., 2011. Mental health system in China: History, recent service reform and future challenges. *World Psychiatry*, 10(3), 210–216.

Ma, H. and Shao, Y., 2019. Commentary: The implementation of China's mental health law-defined risk criteria for involuntary admission: A national cross-sectional study of involuntarily hospitalized patients. *Frontiers in Psychiatry*, 10, 121.

Ma, Z., 2014. In the name of love and medicine? Understanding the experience of female psychiatric inmates from the perspective of rights. *In*: W. Zhang, ed. *Disability Rights Studies in China* (Volume 1). Beijing: Social Science Academic Press, 224–246.

Ma, Z., 2015. An Iron cage of civilization? Missionary psychiatry, the Chinese family and a colonial dialect of enlightenment. *In*: H. Chiang, ed. *Psychiatry and Chinese History*. Routledge, 71–90.

McSherry, B. and Weller, P., eds., 2010. *Rethinking Rights-Based Mental Health Laws*. Oxford: Hart Publishing.

Meifang Huang v Xiangxiang Municipal Government, Hunan Province - Mental health treatment and compensation, Retrial, Supreme People's Court of China, Administrative No 4637, 30 November 2018. (*Huang v the Local Government*, 2018) [最高人民法院（2018）最高法行申4637号行政裁定书].

Mengyan Jing v Mental Hospital of Luohe Municipality - Tort liability dispute, Intermediate People's Court of Luohe Municipality, Henan Province, Civil Appeal No 1357, 26 July 2016. (*Jing v the Hospital*, 2016) [河南省漯河市中级人民法院（2016）豫11民终1357号民事判决书].

Mental Health Atlas 2020. Geneva: World Health Organization; 2021.

Minkowitz, T., 2012. CRPD advocacy by the world network of users and survivors of psychiatry: The emergence of an user/survivor perspective in human rights. *Survivor Perspective in Human Rights* (August 14, 2012).

Minzner, C.F., 2006. Xinfang: An alternative to formal Chinese legal institutions. *Stanford Journal of International Law*, 42, 103–179.

Patel, V., Xiao, S., Chen, H., Hanna, F., Jotheeswaran, A.T., Luo, D., Parikh, R., Sharma, E., Usmani, S., Yu, Y., Druss, B.G., and Saxena, S., 2016. The magnitude of and health system responses to the mental health treatment gap in adults in India and China. *The Lancet*, 388(10063), 3074–3084.

Pearson, V., 1996. The Chinese equation in mental health policy and practice: Order plus control equal stability. *International Journal of Law and Psychiatry*, 19(3), 437–458.

Qian, J., 2012. Mental health care in China: Providing services for under-treated patients. *The Journal of Mental Health Policy and Economics*, 15(4), 179–186.

Que, J., Lu, L., and Shi, L., 2019. Development and challenges of mental health in China. *General Psychiatry*, 32(1), e100053.

Series, L., 2015. Relationships, autonomy and legal capacity: Mental capacity and support paradigms. *International Journal of Law and Psychiatry*, 40, 80–91.

Shuhua Sun v Fourth People's Hospital of Linyi Municipality - Medical damage liability dispute first instance case, Basic People's Court of Lanshan District, Linyi Municipality, Shandong Province: Civil First Instance Case No 2487, 16 November 2015. (*Sun v the Hospital*, 2015) [山东省临沂市兰山区人民法院（2015）临兰民初字第2487号民事判决书].

Wei, Y.D., 2013. *Regional Development in China: States, Globalization, and Inequality*. Oxfordshire: Routledge.

Wilson, K., 2021. *Mental Health Law: Abolish or Reform?* Oxford: Oxford University Press.

Xie, B., 2017. Strategic mental health planning and its practice in China: Retrospect and prospect. *Shanghai Archives of Psychiatry*, 29(2), 115–119.

Xin, C., 2013. *The Interpretations of the Mental Health Law of the People's Republic of China*. 1st ed. Beijing: Law Press China.

Yang, J., 2017. *Mental Health in China: Change, Tradition, and Therapeutic Governance*. New Jersey: John Wiley & Sons.

Yip, K.-S., 2005. An historical review of the mental health services in the People's Republic of China. *International Journal of Social Psychiatry*, 51(2), 106–118.

Yu v Mental Hospital of Zhumadian Municipality - Right to personal liberty dispute first instance case, Basic People's Court of Yicheng District, Zhumadian Muncipality, Henan Province, Civil First Instance No 4122, 26 June 2017. (*Yu v the Hospital*, 2017) [河南省驻马店市驿城区人民法院（2016）豫1702民初4122号民事判决书].

Zhang, M., 2006. Challenge to mental health services in China: Thinking from world mental health surveys. *Journal of Shanghai Jiaotong University (Medical Science)*, 26(4), 329–330.

Zhao, X. and Dawson, J., 2014. The new Chinese mental health Law. *Psychiatry, Psychology and Law*, 21(5), 669–686.

29
COLONIZATION, HISTORY AND THE EVOLUTION OF MENTAL HEALTH LEGISLATION IN INDIA, PAKISTAN, SRI LANKA AND BANGLADESH

Sangeeta Dey and Graham Mellsop

Introduction

Mental health legislation (MHL) in the Asian subcontinent has undergone significant changes over the last five years. In 2017, the World Health Organization (WHO) highlighted the role of legislation in "advancing the right to health" and the need for MHL to be up to date, focused on human rights and to include the right to treatment (Duffy *et al.*, 2019). This prompt led to the development or reforming of legislation in this region to align with WHO guidelines and the United Nations Convention on the Rights of Persons with Disabilities (UNCRPD). Such a change was overdue for this region because of concerns regarding custodial philosophy and human rights violations while caring for people with mental illness (Avasthi and Singh, 2015). The evolution of the legislations of India, Pakistan, Sri Lanka and Bangladesh discussed in this chapter share similarities due to their parallel histories of colonization. Those four countries are the biggest of the so-called subcontinent, with Nepal, Maldives and Bhutan being significantly smaller.

India, Pakistan, Sri Lanka and Bangladesh inherited their MHL from their British rulers. The challenges of daily practice in this region are also quite unique, and contrast with those faced by their Western counterparts. These four countries share a common socio-cultural background (Kala and Kala, 2008; Avasthi and Singh, 2015). Cultural and societal factors shape "what is normal and what is abnormal" in this region, which also influences the understanding and treatment of mental illnesses. It is common for mentally ill people to present to religious preachers first and not to the health professionals until quite late in their illness. Additionally, there have been problems of poor mental health literacy, limited clinical governance and sub-optimal quality assurance to ensure proper implementation of the legislative changes.

Mental health remains a low priority for health budgets in this region. Therefore, practical implementation of any newly developed MHL is still very much a dream and may not be achievable within the planned timeframes. The lack of infrastructure, funding, resources and regulated practice in much of this region has limited the proper implementation of evolving legislation.

History of MHL in South Asian countries

After the British rulers left in 1947, three countries (India, Pakistan and Bangladesh) in this region inherited the Lunacy Act from their rulers. As the name indicates, this legislation contained terms such as "lunatics" and "asylums". It is believed the origin of these terms can be traced back to the English Acts in 1845 (the Lunacy Act and Asylum Act 8 & 9 Vict., c. 100). The first specific legislation concerning mental illness was the Lunatic Removal Act 1851. The first Lunacy Act, known as Act 36 (XXXVI), was enacted in December 1858 by the British Parliament. This legislation went through various versions before the Lunacy Act 1912 was in place. The Lunacy Act 1912 was the first law that governed mental health in British India (Somasundaram, 1987; Firdosi and Ahmad, 2016) and was more focused on the protection of society, with human rights not at the forefront for people with mental illnesses.

In 1947, after the division of British India into Pakistan and India, both countries adopted the Lunacy Act 1912. In 1971 when Bangladesh became an independent country (previously known as East Pakistan), it also adopted this Act. In Sri Lanka, the Act was named the Ceylon Lunacy Ordinance in 1873 (De Alwis, 2017). Sri Lanka was controlled by the Dutch, Portuguese and British in the 16th century, and in 1815 it was united under British rule (colonial Sri Lanka) until 1948. After that, it was independent but remained part of the British Empire until 1972, when it finally became a republic. Sri Lanka subsequently went through a long civil war that lasted until 2009.

Since then, these countries have travelled a long way—politically, socially and economically. This journey has inevitably influenced the subsequent evolution of their legislation. The Lunacy Act, like any archaic legislation, was not informed by modern-day human rights law or psychiatric practice and has been described as "archaic and obsolete" (WHO, 2005). Therefore, at different paces, Bangladesh, India and Pakistan have replaced the Lunacy Act. Sri Lanka has not yet officially replaced this Act, but there is a draft that has been waiting for approval by parliament for over ten years (Draft Mental Health Act June 2007). In the meantime, Sri Lanka was influenced by a civil war and a natural disaster which also affected the evolution of their legislation.

From the late 1970s, worldwide MHL became increasingly influenced by international human rights law. With the adoption of the Principles for the Protection of Persons with Mental Illness (known as the MI Principles) in 1991, the journey began to ensure the least restrictive care (Gooding, 2017). In 2005, the WHO Review Board published guidance on developing human rights-centred MHL. However, this was before the UNCRPD came into force. Therefore, there were some concerns that this guidance may not fully align with the UNCRPD. In 2006, the UNCRPD was adopted and is now ratified by 182 countries. The South Asian countries discussed here were included in the signatories (the total number of signatories are 163) and led the evolution of MHLs in this region.

In 1987, India became the first country in this region to replace the outdated Lunacy Act. Pakistan replaced the Act in 2001 with an ordinance. Bangladesh inherited the Lunacy Act from Pakistan and replaced it in 2018. Sri Lanka has an updated mental health policy, but even though a draft legislation has been waiting for approval for over ten years, Sri Lanka has not yet replaced their legislation.

India

India, the second-most populous nation worldwide, has made a series of changes to its MHL. India's first MHL was introduced in 1858 when three Acts were adopted: the Lunacy (Supreme Courts) Act, the Lunacy (District Courts) Act and the Indian Lunatic Asylum Act (Duffy et al., 2019). To these, the Military Lunatic Act was added in 1877. Finally, these pieces of legislation were consolidated in 1912 under the Indian Lunacy Act, which drew heavily on the English Lunatic Act of 1845.

In 1950, three years after independence, the Indian Psychiatric Society first submitted a revision of the 1912 Lunacy Act. As a result, a mental health act was drafted, but this legislation took over 35 years to be adopted, finally becoming the Mental Health Act 1987. This was a modern version with up-to-date terminology and created central and State mental health authorities, prohibited non-consensual research and simplified discharge procedures. However, there were concerns about the content of this legislation from the outset. These concerns were driven by the fact that the delivery of mental health services had changed significantly over that time. After protracted debate, the Mental Health Act was finally enacted in 1987 but only came into operation in 1993. However, quality control did not occur, and there were ongoing concerns about the human rights of mentally ill patients that were insufficiently protected under this legislation (Trivedi et al., 2007).

In 2007, India ratified the UNCRPD, and this provided further impetus for updating their legislation. The demands of the UNCRPD required that existing legislation be replaced rather than revised, owing to the extent of the required changes. The passage of the Rights of Persons with Disabilities Act 2016 also had significant implications for people with psychosocial disabilities, owing to the inclusion of mental illness. The Mental Health Care Bill 2016 was passed on August 8, 2016, and has been adopted most recently as the Mental Healthcare Act (MHCA) 2017, which came into force on July 7, 2018 (MHCA, 2017).

The MHCA emphasized individual autonomy and replaced "involuntary admission" with "supported admission" (MHCA, 2017), and therefore does not legislate involuntary admission directly. The legislation supports the appointment of a "representative" nominated by the patient for "supported decision-making". Until now, this is the only legislation that has developed an Act for "supported admission" with the UNCRPD as the driving force for this change. At any time, the patient may revoke the appointment of the person appointed to support them in their decision-making.

The definition of mental illness is clear in this legislation, along with the criteria for supported admission. Supported admission is only allowed if the mental disorder is sufficiently severe to impose a risk to themselves or others or if they are unable to care for themselves. The supported admission requires agreement between two accredited mental health professionals that the individual meets the criteria. Both assessors must examine the person independently on the day of admission or in the preceding seven days. The admission must be to a registered mental health establishment.

For monitoring, the Mental Health Review Board (MHRB) must be informed within seven days (three days in the case of a minor or a woman) of a supported admission, and the person, their representative or an appropriate organization may appeal this decision. There is no provision for an automatic review before 30 days. However, if continued hospitalization is required after 30 days, the MHRB undertakes a review of whether this is justified within 21 days of the admission and decides whether such an admission is necessary. This review continues at a maximum frequency of 180 days. The State Mental Health Authority (SMHA) and the Central Mental Health Authority (CMHA) confer with the MHRB when requires. The MHRB is responsible for supported admissions, advanced directives, nominated representatives and any complaints. The MHRB consists of a representative of the district, a psychiatrist, a second mental health practitioner and two individuals who suffer from mental illness or who are caregivers or representatives of organizations advocating for those with mental illness. The CMHA maintains a register of all mental health establishments, develops quality and service standards for the establishments and trains all persons regarding the provisions and implementation of the Act.

The Act ensures informed consent of the patient with the support of their nominated representative. Mental health professionals are required to review the capacity of the person to give consent every seven days. Advanced directives are allowed to cover future situations where the patient may cease to have the capacity and may also apply in community settings. However, there is no clear guidance about ongoing care in the community and the use of legislation. This supported admission is a shift from substituted decision-making. Involuntary treatment in the community setting is only referred to in the context of emergencies.

A significant concern about the new legislation is that families are not always entitled to information as the nominated person may or may not be a family member. The idea of "collective responsibility" in this region implies family involvement, and there are concerns that the "family may not be able to have any right to information" if the nominated person is not a family member. In India, over 90% of patients with chronic mental illness live with their families (Pavitra *et al.*, 2019). The "right to refuse treatment" would unlikely be accepted either by the patient's family or mental health professionals because the concept of personal independence is reported as different culturally, and "family preferences often supersede the personal". This may affect the management of any unwilling patient that requires treatment and caregivers would be unable to admit them.

The severity criteria for admission do not include the likelihood of deterioration as a criterion, or the need for therapeutic purpose, and the criteria for admission are only risk-based. "Supported admission" also implies that all persons have the capacity, but the level of support from nominated representatives varies based on the level of capacity that is supposed to be reviewed every 7 to 14 days. This could be difficult to ensure without regular monitoring. Therefore, the reality on the ground can be quite different from what is expected on paper.

Several areas are lacking in clarity. For example, treatment of mentally ill offenders and any treatment against choice in the community is vague, as this is covered only in the context of emergencies. The issues of personality disorder and/or substance abuse are not clear apart from mentioning "mental conditions associated with the abuse of alcohol and drugs". Both public and private sectors can admit people, but it is unclear how the State will address the moral and ethical responsibility of bearing the cost like in many modern societies (Kumar, 2018).

There is no provision for "involuntary treatment" according to the Act. Supported admission is based on decision-making capacity with varying levels of support from the nominated representative, and is therefore not "involuntary treatment". Treatment without consent can only be given when one lacks the full capacity to make such a decision. The nominated representative, as a proxy decision-maker, can provide consent. However, if the nominated representative refuses, health professionals cannot proceed with treatment. This can lead to further problems and the abuse of mentally ill patients. The duration, review and appeal processes are similar to supported admission when there is a proxy decision-maker. There is also scope for emergency hospitalization for 72 hours, except in areas where due to local infrastructure, this can be extended up to 120 hours and must be authorized by a registered medical practitioner until the person has been assessed by a mental health professional.

There are also concerns about the underrepresentation of the psychiatrist in the MHRB, SMHA and CMHA and increased stigmatization by regulating and licensing general hospital units. The private sector is also concerned about the level of their responsibilities and the families' responsibilities in the absence of clear guidelines about the State's responsibility for ensuring care. Every sector agrees on the mammoth responsibility of implementing the Act and performing quality control. The increase in administrative work and the use of resources may also lead to reduced patient contact (Duffy et al., 2018).

In summary, the Indian Mental Health Act covers many of the requirements of modern legislation despite some flaws. The Act is one of the most developed and ambitious, with a shift from custodial care, the inclusion of patient rights, the autonomy of patients, regular monitoring of the process and development of State authority and decriminalization of suicide (Duffy et al., 2019). Patient autonomy stands out in this region, where collective responsibility is part of the culture. It is a bold step and is a rights-based MHL.

Pakistan

Pakistan is the sixth most populous country. Like the other three countries discussed in this chapter, religion plays a major role in Pakistani society, and Pakistan also has collectivist societal structures. Mentally ill people first presenting to a religious healer is a common phenomenon. Mental health literacy remains poor, and an illness could be considered a curse, requiring a spell from a religious healer. Help from the mainstream health system for mental illness usually occurs late after trying religious healers and alternative healers.

The Lunacy Act 1912 was adopted as legislation after the partition of the region into Pakistan and India (Indo-Pak subcontinent) in 1947. The main purpose of the Act was to save society and keep the mentally ill ("lunatics" or "idiots of unsound mind" according to the Act) in asylums (Inayat, 2017). However, since the Lunacy Act of 1912, many changes have occurred regarding training mental health professionals and developing private and public health sectors. Since 1970, there have been ongoing discussions about reforming this legislation (Tareen and Tareen, 2016). A new mental health act was proposed in 1992, and the current legislation, Mental Health Ordinance (MHO), finally replaced the Lunacy Act in 2001. Since the 18th amendment, it has been known as the Mental Health Act.

The new amendment was first enacted in Sindh, one of the four provinces of Pakistan, in 2013. Other provinces are slowly developing their own legislation based on the MHO. Pakistan now has the Punjab Mental Health Act 2014, the Khyber Pakhtunkhwa MHA 2017 and the Balochistan MHA 2019. The Islamabad MHA is currently being drafted. Pakistan also ratified the UNCRPD in 2008.

The 2001 law removed archaic terms such as "lunatic" and defined mental disorder as "mental illness, including mental impairment, severe personality disorder, severe mental impairment and any other disorder or disability of mind" (MHO, 2001, Sec. 2(1) (m) of (7)). Comprehensive definitions were provided for each. The term "asylum" was replaced by "health/psychiatric facility". A definition of "informed consent" has also been provided, and the ordinance deals with both voluntary and involuntary treatment.

The criteria for admission are "mental illness that requires hospitalisation, risk of harm to themselves or others, community and or voluntary treatment is not possible" (MHO, 2001, Sec. 10, Sub. 2 & 3). There are four types of detention for a patient's involuntary admission, namely: (1) admission for assessment, (2) admission for treatment, (3) urgent admission and (4) emergency holding.

Another term used is "Emergency Powers", which allows a clinician to provide treatment without initiating any of the legislative processes.

Where in case of an emergency, a medical practitioner is unable to obtain informed consent in writing, he may administer treatment that, in his professional opinion, is necessary for:

- Saving the patient's life; or
- Preventing serious deterioration of his condition; or
- Alleviating serious suffering by the patient; or
- Preventing the patient from behaving violently or being a danger to himself or others.

The duration for each type of detention is as follows:

(a) The period of detention for the purposes of assessment shall be up to 28 days from the date of application;
(b) The period of detention for the purposes of treatment is up to six months from the date of application made and is renewable;
(c) The period of detention for the purposes of urgent admission is up to 72 hours; and
(d) The period of detention for the purposes of emergency holding already in hospital is up to 24 hours.

The current legislation also includes sections on competency, capacity and guardianship and addresses the protection of human rights (Tareen and Tareen, 2016). A psychiatrist is involved in the initial assessment unless not available, in which case a medical practitioner with experience in psychiatry should be involved. Reports from two medical practitioners are necessary. Current Pakistani legislation is also quite clear about the reason for detention, for example, for only assessment, treatment or urgent admission or emergency holding for a brief period of 24 to 72 hours.

This MHL also allows a patient's relatives/family members to appeal against the order of detention within 14 days. Urgent admission (forced by the police or a magistrate) under MHL requires a review by a psychiatrist within 72 hours, and this legislation also provides the opportunity for an independent legal review. However, if a family challenges this, legal costs will be borne by the patient's family.

Despite these advances, there are ongoing concerns about the gap between the legislative framework and current practice in Pakistan (Tareen and Tareen, 2016). The Federal Mental Health Authority, founded in 2001 (whose aim was to develop national standards for the care of patients), was dissolved in 2010, and health was made a provincial subject rather than a federal one. Therefore, the implementation of the Act remains an area of concern.

The MHO is not in alignment with UNCRPD guidelines. There is no mention of advance care directives, supported decision-making, no provision for automatic review or independent reviews or requirement for institutional licensing (Dey et al., 2019). Procedural fairness is an ongoing concern, and a loophole for human rights violations. There is no recognized authority that a psychiatrist can approach in an emergency (Tareen and Tareen, 2016). This loophole also affects families who wish to access appropriate care when looking after patients with mental illness. Family members are still the mainstay of support in this region.

Due to a lack of proper implementation of MHL and in the absence of infrastructure, those with mental disorders are vulnerable to human rights abuses. A recent study among stakeholders also reported limited awareness of MHL among patients and family members (Khalily *et al.*, 2021). However, mental health professionals and voluntary organizations in Pakistan are creating awareness about these issues (Gilani *et al.*, 2005; Tareen and Tareen, 2016). Supported decision-making is an alternative, supported by appropriate legislation to address human rights concerns (Kokanović *et al.*, 2018). The introduction of advanced directives could also be an alternative protection. Another major concern in Pakistan was that those held in custody under blasphemy laws did not have any rights in this legislation. This was now included as "A person who attempts suicide, including an accused of blasphemy, shall be assessed by an approved psychiatrist and if found to be suffering from a mental disorder shall be treated appropriately under the provisions of this Act" (MHO, 2001, Chap. VII, cl. 49). The mentally ill person detained in prison without a proper pathway remains an issue, as the MHO is not safeguarding all mentally ill defendants.

Provincially, Sindh and Punjab made some progress theoretically, but legally still have a long way to go before the provincial implementation of their Acts. As the MHO 2001 has lapsed, there is a need for appropriate mental health legislative frameworks in each province. In Pakistan, only 0.4% of the health budget is spent on mental health, and no provincial acts are in place for Baluchistan, Azad Jammu or Kashmir (Khan and Khan, 2020).

Sri Lanka

Sri Lanka is an island nation and the least populous of the four (Kathriarachchi, Seneviratne and Amarakoon, 2019). Over the last two decades, Sri Lanka has reformed their mental health system and developed a mental health policy in 2005. Similar to the rest of the region, cultural and religious beliefs influence the presentation and treatment of mental illness. People go to traditional healers to expel demons possessing the mentally ill person. Sri Lanka also went through two decades of internal armed conflict causing significant hardship and natural disasters. Despite progress made in many areas of mental health care, Sri Lanka is still using the Lunacy Ordinance enacted in 1873 when Sri Lanka was a British colony.

The origin of legislation in Sri Lanka is also influenced by British colonization. In 1839, an ordinance was enacted to provide the legal framework for civil commitment (a legal process through which a State can deprive individuals of their liberty based on mental illness). The ordinance had gone through several phases before Regulation 3 of 1839 was enacted for the provision of care of insane persons—the Mental Diseases Ordinance for involuntary admission (De Alwis, 2017). The first asylum under this ordinance was built in 1847. The 1839 Ordinance gave power to district judges to commit mentally ill people involuntarily to a "lunatic asylum", but required evidence from a medical practitioner. In 1840, the requirement to obtain a medical expert opinion was removed (De Alwis, 2017). According to the ordinance, anyone of "unsound mind", as defined in the ordinance, needed to be incarcerated in an asylum or prison. This included mentally ill prisoners and those who were unfit to stand trial. The other option was to discharge under the care and custody of family or friends.

The current legislation is the Mental Diseases Ordinance (MDO) [3, 27 of 1956], first enacted in 1873. It is the origin of Sri Lankan legislation, last amended in 1956. Act no. 27 of the MDO 1956 substituted the word "Lunacy" with "Mental Diseases Act". Provisions in this act were for "emergency, voluntary and temporary admission" to a specific mental hospital (MDO, 1956). A comprehensive review by Edward Mapother, Medical Superintendent of the Maudsley Hospital in London (Mills and Jain, 2009), of asylums and mental health care in Sri Lanka is believed to be the driver for the Mental Diseases (Amendment) Act which mainly regulates the custody, hospitalization and detention of people with mental illness.

This law is still operating with minor modifications. Even though Sri Lanka has a mental health policy for comprehensive mental health care for citizens, it has not enacted any new legislation in alignment with modern mental health laws despite a draft being in place for over ten years. The ordinance maintains a centralized admission process ensuring "confinement of individual who is suspected of being of unsound mind and needs to be confined in an emergency due to risk to self or others". An individual could be admitted involuntarily if two medical practitioners make such recommendations without having to go before a district court.

There are two categories for detention. First is the presence of an unsound mind, which is defined as:

Every person shall be deemed to be of unsound mind who is so far deranged in mind as to render it necessary that he, either for his own sake or that of the public, should be placed under control.

The assessment of an unsound mind is undertaken by a civil court inquiry and is open to judicial appeal. A certificate by a medical practitioner should accompany an application by a person to the district court. The court continues the inquiry and hears the evidence. It may then either discharge or remand the person in custody or to a mental asylum for further observation. If any healthy family member or friend is prepared to take responsibility for the person of unsound mind, the court can order that the person be released to the relative.

There is also the concept of a temporary patient. A temporary patient is defined as "a person who is suffering from mental illness and is likely to benefit by temporary treatment in a mental hospital but is for the time being incapable of expressing himself as willing or unwilling to receive such treatment". This group may be received under this section as a temporary patient for the purpose of treatment (MDO, 1956, Chap. 559, XV11, p. 250, 251). A court is not involved in this process. A spouse, relative or any other person can submit an application to the hospital's superintendent accompanied by recommendations from two medical practitioners (with no greater interval than five days between examining the person and submitting the application). The order expires 14 days after the date when the last medical practitioner examined the person. The person may be committed for up to one year. If the temporary patient becomes capable of expressing themselves, then they shall not be detained for more than 28 days unless the circumstances change.

The ordinance does not specify that the assessor must be a psychiatrist. In practice, a psychiatrist (or medical practitioner working under a psychiatrist) is usually involved in the decision-making. District Court admissions for patients of unsound mind are, in current practice, mostly reserved for persons with mental illness who are homeless, found wandering and not safe.

The ordinance is silent regarding human rights and is therefore not in keeping with the times (Kathriarachchi *et al.*, 2019). However, the Mental Health Policy of Sri Lanka 2005 has a rights-based approach and calls for new legislation to incorporate human rights for detained persons.

The Draft Mental Health Act June 2007 has been waiting in parliament for over ten years. The draft states it is:

an act to protect the rights of persons with mental illness, provide for the care, treatment, continuing care, and rehabilitation of persons with mental illness; establish the Mental Health Advisory Council and Grievance Committee; establish district review committees; repeal the mental disease ordinance.

(Draft Mental Health Act, 2007, p. 4)

This draft includes voluntary, involuntary and emergency mental health service users, offenders and prisoners who require mental health services (Draft Mental Health Act, June 2007).

The Draft Mental Health Act June 2007 incorporates human rights safeguards, eliminates obsolete terminology and focuses on rehabilitation and the capacity to consent. This is in alignment with modern psychiatric law. The Draft Mental Health Act specifically highlights the importance of assessing capacity at regular intervals. An application for involuntary admission requires a statement by either a medical practitioner, the nearest relative or guardian of the person or a mental health worker or police officer. Each application then needs to be supported by a written statement by the admitting medical officer stating that the person is suffering from mental illness, and the involuntary admission for observation is necessary to save the person's life, prevent serious deterioration of their condition, alleviate serious suffering by the patient or to prevent the patient being a danger to themselves or others as a result of their mental illness. A second medical officer or a consultant psychiatrist must review the application before approving initial admission for 48 hours. The patient, their nearest relative or guardian can appeal to the hospital director within 15 days. The hospital director has the authority to approve or discharge the patient. This decision can also be appealed to the District Review Committee responsible within 15 days from the time of the director's authorization, and the next step is an appeal to the Grievance Review Committee within 15 days of the District Review Committee's decision. On admission, patients can have their own representative. Police have the power to take a person they feel is dangerous due to mental illness to hospital for assessment but cannot hold them in police custody for over three hours. All facilities require a valid licence to admit involuntary patients.

The period of detention could extend up to 30 days. Further detention for a period not exceeding three months is from a written recommendation by a consultant psychiatrist and another medical practitioner based on the same criteria. The further detention and treatment for a further period of up to six months shall be only on the recommendation of an independent consultant psychiatrist and another medical practitioner. The Mental Health Advisory Council is also consulted. The Draft Mental Health Act June 2007 also includes community care if responsible medical practitioners agree on treatment. For monitoring, this Act requires the establishment of a Mental Health Advisory Council and a Grievance Committee to uphold the rights and duties. The establishment of district review committees in each district for addressing and investigating complaints and dealing with applications is also required.

Mental health literacy has improved in Sri Lanka. However, due to bureaucratic processes and a lack of consensus among stakeholders several attempts to develop a new mental health act have been aborted in Sri Lanka despite a draft being in place.

Bangladesh

Bangladesh is a densely populated country; by population size, it ranks eighth in the world (Hasan *et al.*, 2021). Bangladesh was part of Pakistan after the separation of the Indo-Pakistan subcontinent and became an independent country in 1971. Cultural beliefs, religions and societal stigmas play a major role in the presentation and treatment of mental illness, as with other countries in this region. Traditional or religious healers are also, more often than not, treating the mentally ill person prior to help being sought from mainstream health systems. Family still play a major role in providing care for mentally ill people.

A recent study highlighted concerns about the effects of social stigma, inequalities and socio-cultural beliefs on the presentation and treatment of mental illness, and the tendency to avoid accessing care for mental illness despite increasing efforts from health professionals and non-governmental organizations to improve mental health literacy (Hasan *et al.*, 2021). This also includes awareness among health professionals at the primary care level. There is a gap between urban and rural areas, as in the rest of the region, with specialist support being much more available in urban areas (Hasan *et al.*, 2021).

Bangladesh also inherited the Lunacy Act 1912 at the time of independence. Despite being outdated legislation, it remained in place until recently. Bangladesh replaced it with the Bangladesh Mental Health Act 2018. This was a major step in developing a modern mental health law in alignment with the UNCRPD. The new act defines the criteria for involuntary admission and removed archaic terms used in previous legislation. The criteria are based on illness severity and refer to risk to self or others, including poor self-care and treatment noncompliance. Mental illnesses associated with substance abuse or intellectual disability are included as criteria for detention. The goals are assessment, admission and treatment of the mentally ill person, determination of mental capacity, guardianship of the person and property of such patient and supervision of mental health hospitals (Shawon, 2019; Karim and Shaikh, 2021). Mental disorder is defined as:

> conditions including mental disability, drug addiction and any other clinically recognized mental conditions, that being connected with a person's body and/or mind, hinder their normal living, whereas mental illness is defined as a form of mental illness other than mental disability or drug addiction.
>
> *(Karim and Shaikh, 2021, p. 86)*

The legislation includes voluntary, non-protesting and unwilling patients. A non-protesting patient is mainly based on their capacity to make decisions. A relative, parent or friend can initiate an application for involuntary admission. This is followed by an assessment by a medical officer within 24 hours. A medical officer can authorize emergency admission for up to 72 hours. After that, an assessment by a psychiatrist is required for ongoing involuntary admission. This status is reviewed every 28 days. The maximum duration of admission can be up to 180 days or more. After this, a mental health review and monitoring committee can extend the duration of stay if necessary. A non-willing patient requires assessment by a psychiatrist with or without an application by family or a police officer.

There is an intention to establish mental health review and monitoring committees in every district to monitor admission and treatment regularly. These committees will include government representatives and mental health clinicians. The patient's relatives and parents may appeal to this committee if they are not satisfied with the treatment. Both private and government hospitals must have a licence for admitting and treating involuntary patients. The government will fund legal representation for the patient. A medical practitioner would be punished if found to have provided a false certificate for mental illness. There is no community extension of this legislation.

The current law is very new to clinicians in Bangladesh, but has created hope among clinicians, especially concerning the law's reference to patient rights. English translation of the current law is not yet available. Some concerns have been raised regarding the fact that while patients' rights have been mentioned, insufficient attention has been paid to addressing treatment under unfavourable social circumstances. Issues of confidentiality, rights of mental health patients and community-based treatment are not addressed adequately. As with the other countries in the region, due to minimal allocation for mental health in the health budget, implementation of legislation and monitoring of the registered hospitals to avoid system abuse may not be a reality yet, but it is at least a proper step in that direction. Abuse by family members is not an uncommon phenomenon that requires more emphasis on the rights of mentally ill people, and the role of advanced directives also needs to be considered, which is absent in this legislation.

Conclusion

The WHO regards MHL as a key component of good health services. In view of the concern about human rights violations and abuse of mentally ill people, after adopting the UNCRPD in 2006, many countries are now reforming their MHL. The WHO has also published guidance to facilitate the process, but this was prior to the adoption of the UNCRPD. However, in 2017, the WHO reinforced the role of law in "advancing the right to health" (WHO, 2017). The goal of modern MHL is to ensure proper care for people with mental illness and at the same time ensure their rights are respected as they are for other citizens.

The four South Asian countries with British colonial histories discussed in this chapter are taking important steps to align their legislation with the UNCRPD and modern mental health law. All these countries inherited their legislation from their British colonial rulers. This encouraged custodial care and institutionalization. Given the sociopolitical differences and some cultural differences, each country is following their own journey. However, resource issues, problems with health infrastructure, bureaucracy, poor mental health literacy and gradual urbanization are common issues that all these countries are encountering, in addition to the ongoing stigma and myths that exist about mental illness. Therefore, despite enacting legislation, practical implementation with equitable resource allocation to provinces or states and regular monitoring to ensure that the rights of people with mental illness are protected will take significant resources and effort from all stakeholders in these countries. Ratification implies accountability and monitoring processes. All these countries ratified the UNCRPD, indicating their commitment to ensuring the rights of people with mental illness.

It is encouraging that all these countries have made changes and, apart from Sri Lanka, have already enacted their new legislation despite concerns about flaws and limitations. The main concerns from all these countries, highlighted in recent publications from the countries themselves, include those about the implementation of these modern mental health laws in such populous countries with poor resource allocation, different funding systems and gaps between urban and rural areas and private and public sectors. Supported decision-making rather than involuntary admission is thought to be more in alignment with the UNCRPD. In that respect, the Indian Mental Health Act has been the most progressive legislation. "Supported admission", by definition, allows a mentally disordered person to exercise their capacity with different levels of support, rather than taking their core human rights away from them.

Regional collaborative approaches in developing legislation in alignment with the UNCRPD may help address common concerns. A continuous monitoring system, coordinated approach, education of vulnerable groups, development of specialized tertiary facilities and access to mental health care at the provincial or State or district level are crucial for implementing the newly developed legislation.

Societies in this region are also mostly collectivistic. This has provided an excellent resource for the care of the mentally ill (Chadda and Deb, 2013). The concept of collectivism ensures significant family involvement in decision-making. Therefore, concerns have been raised by clinicians about some aspects of these modern mental health laws. However, this is also slowly changing as more and more people are living in urban areas as nuclear families. Abuse by family members is also not an uncommon phenomenon. However, given the predominant collectivistic culture in this region, the family still play a significant role, and this is a crucial area that needs attention.

Stigma and shame are associated with mental illness. This is a reality, despite advances in treatment and society. Societal awareness and empowering people with mental illness by creating awareness of their rights as citizens, rather than feeling marginalized, would lead to more shared decision-making and reduce concerns about human rights violations. The roles of advanced directives, capacity assessment and confidentiality also require further attention in the new legislation. An advanced directive, even though useful, requires acknowledgement that one may become ill again in the future and that itself creates a fear of being alienated. Therefore, education and awareness are crucial. The role of advanced directives needs to be clarified more in this legislation to facilitate the ability of the person to make decisions.

Appropriate governance, including the necessary policy and legislative frameworks to promote and protect the mental health of a population, can overcome barriers to the effective integration of mental health care.

References

Avasthi, A. and Singh, S. (2015) 'Human rights and psychiatry in South Asia', in Trivedi, J. and Tripathi, A. (eds.) *Mental health in South Asia: Ethics, resources, programs and legislation*. Dordrecht: Springer, pp. 3–18. https://doi.org/10.1007/978-94-017-9017-8

Chadda, R. K. and Deb, K. S. (2013) 'Indian family systems, collectivistic society and psychotherapy', *Indian Journal of Psychiatry*, 55(Suppl. 2), pp. S299–S309. https://doi.org/10.4103/0019-5545.105555

De Alwis, L. A. P. (2017) 'Development of civil commitment statutes (laws of involuntary detention and treatment) in Sri Lanka: A historical review', *Medico-Legal Journal of Sri Lanka*, 5(1), pp. 22–31. http://doi.org/10.4038/mljsl.v5i1.7351

Dey, S. et al. (2019) 'Comparing legislation for involuntary admission and treatment of mental illness in four South Asian countries', *International Journal of Mental Health Systems*, 13(1), pp. 1–9. https://doi.org/10.1186/s13033-019-0322-7

Draft Mental Health Act June, 2007. Available at: http://www.health.gov.lk/moh_final/english/public/elfinder/files/publications/list_publi/act/Act_Mental_health_act_Final_draft_English.pdf

Duffy, R. et al. (2019) 'Stigma, inclusion and India's Mental Healthcare Act 2017', *Journal of Public Mental Health*, 18(3), pp. 199–205. https://doi.org/10.1108/JPMH-02-2019-0021

Duffy, R. M. et al. (2018) 'New legislation, new frontiers: Indian psychiatrists' perspective of the Mental Healthcare Act 2017 prior to implementation', *Indian Journal of Psychiatry*, 60(3), pp. 351–354. https://doi.org/10.4103/psychiatry.IndianJPsychiatry_45_18

Firdosi, M. M. and Ahmad, Z. Z. (2016) 'Mental health law in India: Origins and proposed reforms', *BJPsych International*, 13(3), pp. 65–67. https://doi.org/10.1192/s2056474000001264

Gilani, A. I. et al. (2005) 'Psychiatry health laws in Pakistan: From lunacy to mental health', *PLOS Medicine*, 2(11). https://doi.org/10.1371/journal.pmed.0020317

Gooding, P. A. (2017) *New era for mental health law and policy, supported decision-making and the UN convention on the rights of persons with disabilities*. Cambridge: Cambridge University Press.

Hasan, M. et al. (2021) 'The current state of mental healthcare in Bangladesh: Part 1 – An updated country profile', *BJPsych International*, 18(4), pp. 78–82. https://doi.org/10.1192/bji.2021.41

Inayat, S. (2017) 'Mental health issues and relevant legislation in a developing country', *Pakistan Journal of Public Health*, 7(2), pp. 122–126.

Kala, A. K. and Kala, K. (2008) 'Mental health legislation in developing countries with special reference to South Asia: Problems and solutions', *Global Social Policy*, 8(3), pp. 308–311. https://doi.org/10.1177/1468018108008030204

Karim, E. M. and Shaikh, S. (2021) 'Newly enacted mental health law in Bangladesh', *BJPsych International*, 18(4), pp. 85–87. https://doi.org/10.1192/bji.2021.1

Kathriarachchi, S. T., Seneviratne, V. L. and Amarakoon, L. (2019) 'Development of mental health care in Sri Lanka: Lessons learned', *Taiwanese Journal of Psychiatry*, 33(2), pp. 55–65. https://doi.org/10.4103/TPSY.TPSY_15_19

Khalily, M. T. et al. (2021) '"Stakeholders" perspective on mental health laws in Pakistan: A mixed method study', *International Journal of Law and Psychiatry*, 74. https://doi.org/10.1016/j.ijlp.2020.101647

Khan, R. Q. and Khan, A. M. (2020) 'Crime and punishment: Pakistan's legal failure to account for mental illness', *BJPsych International*, 18(4), pp. 94–96. https://doi.org/10.1192/bji.2020.30

Kokanović, R. et al. (2018) 'Supported decision-making from the perspectives of mental health service users, family members supporting them and mental health practitioners', *Australian and New Zealand Journal of Psychiatry*, 52(9), pp. 826–833. https://doi.org/10.1177/0004867418784177

Kumar, M. T. (2018) 'Mental Healthcare Act 2017: Liberal in principles, let down in provisions', *Indian Journal of Psychological Medicine*, 40(2), pp. 101–107. https://doi.org/10.4103/IJPSYM.IJPSYM_23_18

Mental Diseases Ordinance, No 27 of (1956). Available at: http://www.commonlii.org/lk/legis/consol_act/md559196.pdf

Mental Healthcare Act 2017. Available at: https://prsindia.org/files/bills_acts/acts_parliament/2017/the-mental-healthcare-act,-2017.pdf

Mills, J. and Jain, S. (2009) '"A disgrace to a civilised community": Colonial psychiatry and the visit of Edward Mapother to South Asia, 1937–8', *Clio Medica (Amsterdam, Netherlands)*, 86, pp. 223–242.

Pavitra, K. S. et al. (2019) 'Family matters! – The caregivers' perspective of Mental Healthcare Act 2017', *Indian Journal of Psychiatry*, 61(Suppl. 4), pp. S832–S837. https://doi.org/10.4103/psychiatry.IndianJPsychiatry_141_19

Shawon, S. R. (2019) 'New mental health act in Bangladesh', *The Lancet Psychiatry*, 6(3), p. 199. https://doi.org/10.1016/S2215-0366(19)30028-8

Sindh Mental Health Act 2013. Available at: http://www.pas.gov.pk/uploads/acts/Sindh%20Act%20No.L%20of%202013.pdf

Somasundaram, O. (1987) 'The background of Indian Lunacy Act, 1912', *Indian Journal of Psychiatry*, 29(1), pp. 3–14.

Tareen, A. and Tareen, K. (2016) 'Mental health law in Pakistan', *BJPsych International*, 13(3), pp. 67–69. https://doi.org/10.1192/s2056474000001276

The Mental Health Ordinance 2001. Available at: http://punjablaws.gov.pk/laws/430a.html

The Punjab Mental Health (Amendment) Act 2014. Available at: http://papmis.pitb.gov.pk/uploads/bills/billpassed_2014_13.pdf

Trivedi, J., Narang, P. and Dhyani, M. (2007) 'Mental health legislation in South Asia with special reference to India: Shortcomings and solutions', Mental Health Review Journal, 12(3), pp. 22–29.

World Health Organization. (2005) *WHO resource book on mental health, human rights and legislation*. Geneva: World Health Organization.

World Health Organization. (2017) *Advancing the right to health: The vital role of law*. Geneva: World Health Organization.

30
INDIA'S MENTAL HEALTHCARE ACT, 2017
A promise for transformation and radical change

Arjun Kapoor and Manisha Shastri

Introduction

This chapter provides an overview of India's Mental Healthcare Act, 2017 (MHCA) and its transformative potential for reimagining India's mental health system. The MHCA as a legal framework brings about paradigmatic shifts in India's mental health landscape by (i) recognising the right to mental healthcare and treatment and (ii) protecting, promoting and fulfilling the rights of persons with mental illness. It shifts the existing discourse on mental healthcare to one which centres the autonomy and legal capacity of persons with mental illness. The MHCA was enacted in accordance with India's obligations under international laws, predominantly, the United Nations (UN) Convention on the Rights of Persons with Disabilities (CRPD) and the International Covenant on Economic, Social and Cultural Rights (CESCR). As a rights-based legislation, the MHCA is strategically positioned between India's progressive National Mental Health Policy, 2014 (NMH) and State-driven policy and programmatic interventions to bridge gaps in ensuring rights-based mental healthcare for all. It also presents an opportunity to reconceptualise and restructure India's flagship programmatic interventions such as the National Mental Health Programme (NMHP) and District Mental Health Programme (DMHP) to actualise the right to access mental healthcare and treatment. Finally, the MHCA's transformative potential is also reflected in its anti-discrimination provisions which have been relied upon by India's higher judiciary for evolving rights-based jurisprudence and recognising the fundamental rights of marginalised and vulnerable groups, through judicial pronouncements.

Historical context of the Mental Healthcare Act, 2017

The MHCA is a legislation which regulates mental healthcare and treatment while protecting and promoting the rights of persons with illness. It was enacted in 2017 in accordance with India's obligations under the CRPD (Duffy and Kelly, 2020). The significance of the MHCA and the shift it has brought in the discourse on mental health in India, and internationally, can be best understood by tracing the evolution of the legal and policy landscape for mental health in India.

The history of India's mental health legislation spans over 150 years beginning with the enactment of the four 'lunacy laws' by the British colonial government in the mid-19th century. In 1912, these laws were replaced by the Indian Lunacy Act, 1912 (ILA) which was in force till 1993 and legitimised the segregation of persons with mental illness into asylums and prisons. The ILA denied such persons equal recognition before the law and institutionalised the role of judicial officials in regulating treatment while treating such persons as 'dangerous' or 'criminals' (Addlakha, 2010; Duffy and Kelly, 2020). On the other hand, the history of mental health policies and programmes in India is just about four decades old, dating back to the early 1980s. Following the Declaration of Alma Ata (1978) which identified primary healthcare services as the key to ensuring health for all ('Declaration of Alma-Ata', 1978), there was a push for the integration of mental healthcare services into primary healthcare services and the adoption of community-based models for public health. Several administrative committees such as the Bhore Committee (1946), Mudaliar Committee (1959) and the Srivastava Committee (1975) were constituted before and after independence by the Government of India to determine the future steps for improving and strengthening the public health system in independent India. These committees made important observations regarding the quality and quantity of public health services and treatment available for persons with mental illness in the country. International developments along with recommendations submitted by these special committees led to the conception of the National Mental Health Programme as India's flagship programmatic intervention on mental health (Shastri, 2021).

The NMHP was launched in 1982 by the Ministry of Health and Family Welfare, with the objective of integrating primary mental healthcare into general health services. At the time of its launch, it was the first of its kind State-led initiative among low- and middle-income countries (LMICs) (Duggal, 1991). Since its inception the objectives of the NMHP have been revised several times. At present the NHMP is implemented based on objectives last revised in 2012 which include (i) establishing centres of excellence in mental health; (ii) setting up and strengthening postgraduate studies departments in mental health specialties; (iii) implementation of the District Mental Health Programme for detection, management and treatment of mental illness; (iv) building partnerships with non-governmental organisations and the public sector; and (v) conducting awareness campaigns and research (Government of India, 2017). Subsequently, in 1995 the Government launched the DMHP as a component under the NMHP. The DMHP is the first and only State-funded programme in India with the objective of decentralising mental health services at the sub-district level (Sarin and Jain, 2015). At present, the DMHP is being implemented in 704 of India's 773 districts (Ministry of Health and Family Welfare, 2022). Like the NMHP, the DMHP's objectives have also undergone several revisions over the years. Last revised in 2015, the DMHP's objectives now include: (i) provision of mental health services, including for prevention, promotion and long-term and continuing care at the sub-district and community level; (ii) improvement of institutional capacity, infrastructure, equipment and human resources; (iii) community awareness and participation in delivery of service; and (iv) integration of mental health services into general care services (Shastri and Varma, 2021). Over the past four decades, neither the NMHP nor the DMHP have achieved their stated goals and objectives for equitable access to mental healthcare for all citizens (Gupta and Sagar, 2018).

According to the National Mental Health Survey (NMHS), approximately 150 million people in India suffer from some form of mental illness, with a prevalence rate of 10.6% among adults, of which 70–92% persons are unable to access any form of mental healthcare and treatment (NIMHANS, 2016). Despite these disparities, India's annual budget for mental health is less than 1% of the total budget for healthcare (Keshav Desiraju India Mental Health Observatory, 2022). Further, as per estimates, India has 0.49 psychiatrists and 0.07 psychologists per 100,000 population, much below the prescribed international standards. The lack of infrastructure for service provision is also a challenge; per 100,000 population there are only 1.43 beds in mental health hospitals and 0.56 beds in general hospitals (World Health Organisation, 2017). This treatment gap as highlighted by the NMHS can be attributed to the failure of the NMHP and DMHP to provide access to quality mental health services in the country, as well as poor budgetary allocations and expenditure for mental health programmes. Further, both the NMHP and DMHP as policy and programmatic interventions have been designed and implemented based on a biomedical approach which in India's context *predominantly* relies on psychiatric medication or institutionalisation to address the mental health needs of the population while eschewing community-based models of care to address the social determinants of mental health and social recovery using rights-based approaches (Gupta and Sagar, 2018; Varma, 2021). Further, these programmes have been saddled with several implementation gaps due to limited infrastructure, deficiency of human resources and lack of political will to recognise mental health as a governance issue which restricts access to quality mental health services in low-resource rural settings across the country (Varma, 2021).

On the other hand, India's mental health landscape has also been tainted by a legacy of human rights violations specifically in psychiatric institutions. The Mental Health Act, 1987 (MHA) which repealed the ILA, was enacted with the objective of replacing the colonial-era ILA with a more progressive legal framework. However, the MHA's provisions continued to focus on the segregation and institutionalisation of persons with mental illness who were viewed as dangerous or lacking the capacity to make decisions pertaining to their treatment and care (Davar, 2015b). The MHA reinforced the colonial-era practice of empowering judicial magistrates to issue reception orders authorising the detention of persons with mental illness in institutions for treatment without consent, thus perpetuating stigmatising stereotypes of treating such persons as criminals. The MHA contained no provisions for informed consent, as it did not recognise or acknowledge the autonomy and agency of persons with mental illness. Its provisions included no substantive protections for the rights of persons with mental illness nor did it include provisions for judicial review of involuntary admissions and rights violations. The MHA also exempted government-run facilities from licensing requirements leading to rampant human rights violations such as inhumane conditions, solitary confinement, chaining, forceful treatments such as electroconvulsive therapy (Human Rights Watch, 2014; Singh, 2021) and physical abuse (Davar, 2015a).

The adoption of the United Nations Convention on the Rights of Persons with Disabilities in 2006 was a historic moment which had profound implications for India's law and policy framework on mental health and disabilities (United Nations, 2007). The CRPD, widely regarded as the gold standard for protecting and fulfilling the rights of persons with disabilities, provides a robust legal framework for States to transition from a medical and charity-based model of disability to the social and rights-based model which (i) centres the autonomy and legal capacity of persons with disabilities and (ii) shifts the locus of responsibility on to the State, governments and institutions to remove barriers to ensure equal participation of persons with disabilities. In 2007, India ratified the CRPD which obligated the State to amend existing domestic laws and policies in compliance with the Convention. Given the absence of a rights-based legal framework in the MHA, the Government of India decided to draft a new bill after a ten-year consultative and legislative process. Eventually, the MHCA was enacted repealing the MHA in compliance with India's obligations under the CRPD.

In 2014, the Government of India framed the country's first National Mental Health Policy with the active participation of service users, caregivers and civil society organisations. The NMH is a landmark achievement as it adopts an intersectoral approach which addresses the structural determinants of mental health such as unemployment, homelessness, marginalisation and exclusion. The NMH also lists key strategic areas such as strengthening of governance and service-delivery mechanisms, inter-departmental coordination and making available community-based rehabilitation services. The NMH through its provisions creates scope for the provision of mental healthcare and services in a range of settings, particularly communities, in order to make them more accessible and easily available, and to reduce stigma. The NMH's objective is not limited to the prevention of mental illness; it recognises the necessity of a 'holistic approach to alleviate distress' as stated in the preamble. While the NMH is progressive and envisions an integrated and holistic model of care, it remains to be translated into an actionable framework by State Governments. Even though the NMH addresses the needs of vulnerable populations, there have been few efforts from policymakers to prioritise and address the structural determinants of mental health through policy and programmatic interventions.

Actualising the transformative vision of the MHCA and NMH especially for ensuring the right to access mental healthcare and community living requires a fundamental reconceptualisation of India's policy and programmatic initiatives such as the NMHP and the DMHP. In this respect, the MHCA provides a legal framework for restructuring and strengthening the implementation of the NMHP, DMHP and other programmatic interventions. Drawing on international legal instruments such as the CRPD and ICESCR, the MHCA as a rights-based legal framework is strategically positioned between the NMH and the State-driven programmatic framework as it adopts a rights-based approach to protect the autonomy and legal capacity of persons with mental illness, recognises the right to access mental healthcare and emphasises a shift towards deinstitutionalisation and community-based living. It is in this context that we will now discuss some of the MHCA's transformative aspects and the radical shifts which have the potential to transform India's mental health system.

Mental Healthcare Act, 2017 – A paradigmatic shift for mental healthcare

The MHCA's enactment has transformative implications for mental healthcare in India should it be implemented in its true letter and spirit. The legislation's preamble states that it is a law 'to provide for mental healthcare and services for persons with mental illness and to protect, promote and fulfil the rights of such persons during delivery of mental healthcare and services'. Thus, the MHCA emphatically adopts a rights-based approach to regulate the mental healthcare treatment and services for all persons while protecting the rights of persons with mental illness by recognising their autonomy and status as equal persons before the law. A progressive and aspirational legislation, the MHCA through its legal framework brings about a radical shift in India's mental health landscape which can be broadly categorised into three significant themes.

Right to access mental healthcare and treatment

One of the MHCA's most fundamental and critical shifts is the recognition of the right to access mental healthcare and treatment for all persons without discrimination on any basis.

The MHCA places duties and obligations on the Union and State Governments to provide a range of mental health services and facilities as a bare minimum. In doing so, the MHCA adopts a public health approach as opposed to the erstwhile MHA and ILA which did not address the issue of equitable access to mental healthcare. The MHCA's recognition of the right to access mental healthcare is historic, as the right to health has never been statutorily recognised by any legislation in India before, even though the Supreme Court of India in various judgments has recognised the right to health as a fundamental right under the right to life in India's Constitution (Supreme Court of India, 2020). According to Section 18 of the MHCA, the right to access mental healthcare and treatment means that mental health services should be of 'affordable cost, of good quality, available in sufficient quantity, accessible geographically, without discrimination and acceptable to persons with mental illness and their family members'. Thus, the MHCA aligns itself with Article 12 of the CESCR and General Comment 14 on the CESCR which recognises 'the right of everyone to the enjoyment of the highest attainable standard of physical and mental health', and Article 25 of the CRPD which recognises the right to health for all persons with disabilities (United Nations, 1976, 2007; UN Office of Human Rights Commissioner, 2000).

The MHCA obligates the State to provide a range of mental health services such as in-patient and out-patient treatment facilities, halfway homes, supported and sheltered accommodations, community-based rehabilitation services, emergency services and services for children and elderly persons. It also mandates the integration of mental health with general health services at all levels of the public health system including general hospitals. Where there are no public services accessible in their districts, persons with mental illness have the right to claim reimbursements for costs of treatment at any other mental health establishment. The MHCA also guarantees free essential medicines to all persons with mental illness and free treatment to those who are below the poverty line, in situations of homelessness or destitute. These legal entitlements are particularly significant in India's context wherein most treatment and care services for mental health are disproportionately concentrated in urban areas and largely provided by the private sector (NIMHANS, 2016). As a result, persons with mental illness residing in semi-urban and rural parts of the country have limited to no access to mental healthcare services and treatment and have to travel long distances incurring a range of out-of-pocket expenditures (Rejani, Sumesh and Shaji, 2015; Tripathy et al., 2016), which may deplete limited financial resources of those belonging to marginalised and vulnerable communities (Sahithya and Reddy, 2018). These provisions are also in accordance with Article 25 of the CRPD, which mandates that health services be provided close to people's communities, particularly in rural areas.

The MHCA's provisions also clearly define the government's role in transforming the mental health system to ensure the realisation of the right to access mental healthcare and treatment. For instance, the MHCA obligates the Union and State Governments to implement programmes for prevention of mental illness, suicide prevention, anti-stigma and creating awareness through mass media including radio, TV, print and online media. The MHCA also recognises the larger systemic and infrastructural deficiencies in the country's mental health system by requiring the State to make efforts to meet internationally accepted guidelines for the number of mental health professionals and improve their skills through training and educational programmes. Lastly, one of the significant deficiencies in India's policy and programmatic framework is intersectoral coordination between different government departments. To this effect, the MHCA also mandates 'intra and inter-sectoral collaborations between various ministries and department, to ensure mental health is addressed in a holistic manner, beyond just the realm of medical services'. These provisions are essential for transforming India's mental health system which requires a range of policy and programmatic interventions to reduce inequities in accessing quality mental health services. The MHCA thus provides a statutory and rights-based legal framework to ensure that access to mental healthcare is a justiciable right which the State is duty-bound to provide its citizens and is accountable for any violations or denial of this right.

Decisional autonomy and rights of persons with mental illness

The second critical shift the MHCA brings about is the recognition of the decisional autonomy of persons with mental illness to make their own mental healthcare decisions. The MHCA dispels the stereotype that persons with mental illness lack decision-making capacity by locating them at the centre of all mental healthcare and treatment decisions. The MHCA creates a presumption that all persons with mental illness have the capacity to make decisions regarding their mental healthcare and treatment. Section 4 of the MHCA defines capacity as the ability to (i) understand the information relevant to take a decision regarding one's admission and treatment, (ii) reasonably foresee consequences of making or not making a decision and (iii) communicate one's decision by means of speech, expression, gesture or any other means. Thus, if mental health professionals believe that a person lacks capacity, then the former must provide proof of the same through a capacity assessment. The MHCA makes it clear that a person cannot be presumed to be lacking capacity if the decision made by them is perceived as wrong by others, nor does having a mental illness imply lack of capacity. Thus, the law protects such individuals from subjective determinations of incapacity by mental health professionals which are often based on their own conservative values and beliefs (Jacob, 2016). Consequently, any form of treatment can be provided to a person only after obtaining their informed consent by providing necessary information about alternatives, risks, benefits and side-effects of the treatment, to help them make an informed decision.

The law also makes it unequivocally clear that mental illness is not the same as unsound mind and that a person with mental illness can be of sound mind. This is significant since several laws in India still carry provisions that deny persons with mental illness various rights such as the right to vote, marry, open a bank account or enter into legal relationships on grounds of 'unsound mind' (Davar, 2015b). Thus, the MHCA dispels the historical and hegemonic discourse that persons with mental illness are irrational and lack decisional capacity, in favour of recognising their legal capacity. It acknowledges that capacity is dynamic, and that it may vary depending on the context, and in some situations, individuals may require a range of adequate supports for exercising their decisional capacity. In other words, the MHCA, in accordance with Article 12 of the CRPD on legal capacity, recognises that persons with impaired decision-making abilities can still exercise decisional capacity through supported decision-making, and further obligates duty-bearers and caregivers to provide such supports (Pathare and Kapoor, 2021). To protect the autonomy of persons who may lack capacity at any given time, the MHCA provides for two supported decision-making tools known as advance directives (ADs) and nominated representatives (NRs). An AD is a written document by any person which states how they wish to be treated and cared for or not, in situations where they are unable to make decisions pertaining to their mental healthcare and treatment. Mental health professionals are legally obligated to comply with an AD which is valid and registered with a Mental Health Review Board (MHRB) which is a district-level quasi-judicial authority for ensuring the MHCA's implementation. However, if a mental health professional or caregiver of a person with mental illness wishes to challenge the AD, they may approach the MHRB to modify, cancel or alter it. On the other hand, a NR is any individual appointed by a person with mental illness to provide support during their mental healthcare, admission and treatment, and also make decisions on their behalf, keeping in mind the person's will and preferences if their capacity is impaired at any point. While a person can appoint their own nominated representative, in case they are unable to do so, the MHCA provides a default list of individuals who can be appointed as a nominated representative.

The MHCA also recognises a range of rights related to mental healthcare such as the right to equality and non-discrimination, the right to information, the right to access medical records, the right to legal aid, the right to be protected from cruel, inhuman and degrading treatment, the right to communication and the right to confidentiality. Another significant shift is the MHCA's recognition of the right to medical insurance on the same basis as provided for physical illnesses. Previously persons with mental illness were not eligible for health insurance coverage; however, the MHCA adopts the principle of parity which mandates that coverage for mental illnesses be provided on par with physical illnesses.

Admissions under the MHCA are of two types: (i) independent wherein a person with mental illness can voluntarily apply to be admitted and (ii) supported admission wherein a nominated representative applies on behalf of the person with or without their consent. The MHCA provides for a range of safeguards for supported admissions when a person is admitted without obtaining their informed consent. In such cases, the person must lack capacity to make decisions or require high support due to a severe mental illness and fulfil any one of these conditions: (i) be at risk of harming their self, (ii) be at risk of harming another person or (iii) is unable to take care of their self. During such admissions, if a person lacks capacity, then the nominated representative may give temporary informed consent on the person's behalf until they regain capacity. All instances of supported admissions are mandated to be judicially reviewed by the MHRB to ensure that there is sufficient reason to admit the person and that their rights are not being violated. Thus, while the MHCA still retains substitute decision-making in exceptional situations, such instances are subject to judicial review before the MHRBs.

Lastly, another aspect of the MHCA which illustrates the shift towards a more rights-based, person-centred approach is its provisions for the representation and participation of persons with mental illness in quasi-judicial and statutory bodies to be established under the MHCA. These provisions are in line with Article 4 of the CRPD, which mandates that persons with disabilities be included in the development and implementation of policies and participate on an equal basis with others in decisions relating to themselves. The MHCA mandates the creation of regulatory and adjudicatory bodies – namely the Central Mental Health Authority (CMHA), State Mental Health Authorities (SMHAs) and the MHRBs – to monitor its implementation and redress any rights violations. These bodies also ensure accountability and transparency in the functioning of mental health establishments, compliance with minimum standards for services and qualifications of mental health professionals. The MHCA provides for representation of persons with mental illness, caregivers and civil society organisations on all these statutory bodies which is a first in the history of mental health legislation in India.

The MHCA's provisions on decisional autonomy are crucial as they recognise the autonomy and legal capacity of persons with mental illness in making their own treatment decisions – a right which was hitherto not recognised by mental health legislations in India. Significantly the MHCA's provisions also imply that decisional autonomy is critical for realising one's right to access mental healthcare and treatment, as without the same, a person cannot enjoy mental healthcare which is 'acceptable' and in accordance with their will and preferences. At the same time, realising the right to access mental healthcare and treatment is imperative to exercise one's decisional autonomy, as in the absence of accessible mental health and recovery services, infrastructure and trained workforce, individuals will be denied a range of supports required to make decisions to exercise their legal rights on an equal basis with others.

Right to community living and deinstitutionalisation

The third paradigm shift brought by the MHCA is the recognition of the right to community living and deinstitutionalisation. In other words, Section 19 of the MHCA recognises that all persons with mental illness have a 'right to live in, be part of and not be segregated from society'. The MHCA makes its intent on deinstitutionalisation clear by moving towards a model of community-based care wherein long-term institutional care should be used only in 'exceptional circumstances for as short a duration and only as a last resort when appropriate community-based treatment has been tried and failed'. Thus, the State has a duty to make available community-based facilities such as halfway homes, group homes, supported or sheltered accommodations for persons who no longer require long stay in psychiatric institutions, but continue residing there due to not having or being abandoned by their families. The MHCA refers to these facilities as 'less restrictive options' which meet the person's treatment needs and impose the least restriction on the person's rights, and requires that these be tried before resorting to institutionalisation. These provisions reflect the global shifts taking place in the discourse on mental health and the growing movement away from deinstitutionalisation towards the promotion and adoption of community-oriented paradigms of services and care for persons with mental illness (Padmakar *et al.*, 2020). The provisions draw upon Article 19 of the CRPD which recognises the 'equal right of all persons with disabilities to live in the community, with choices equal to others' and mandates that persons with disabilities have access to residential, community and in-home services (United Nations, 2007).

The right to community living is a crucial right as it requires the fulfilment of both the right to access mental healthcare and treatment and the decisional autonomy of persons with mental illness through supported decision-making. Community-based services are critical for several reasons. First, they facilitate early intervention and treatment in a more accessible and cost-effect manner, while being respectful of an individual's right to community life (Saxena and Sharan, 2008). Second, in a country like India where insufficient infrastructure and human resources for delivery of mental healthcare treatment and services are a grave concern, community-based mental health services reduce the burden on the formal mental healthcare system. There is also a growing body of evidence to show the effectiveness of mental health interventions at the community level (Joag *et al.*, 2020), delivered by non-specialists in low-resource settings such as LMICs (Kohrt *et al.*, 2018). Thus, the absence of community-based services and facilities can impede the decisional autonomy of persons (and violate their right to health and other legal rights) while the right to decisional autonomy and legal capacity can only be fully achieved if persons with mental illness are fully integrated with society, have access to a range of supports and can rehabilitate or recover with the help of community-based services (Pathare and Kapoor, 2021).

There are now various community-based interventions in India's context which leverage community resources and reduce dependence on the formal health system. For example, Atmiyata – a community-based intervention – aims to improve access to mental healthcare and social care in rural settings by training community volunteers to provide primary support and evidence-based counselling to persons experiencing distress or common mental health disorders. Atmiyata has also been recognised by the World Health Organization as one of the best practices for delivering community mental health services in the world (Shields-Zeeman et al., 2017; Damji, Shastri and Pathare, 2021; World Health Organisation, 2021). The Banyan's 'Home Again' programme focuses on rehabilitating homeless women with mental illness, by providing them support in the form of transit care centres, and facilitating access to healthcare services, housing and employment. The programme also provides support to women with mental illness by reuniting and rehabilitating them with their family and community, where possible (The New Indian Express, 2021). While these are initiatives and best practices led by civil society organisations, there continues to be a vacuum in terms of adequate State-led programmes and initiatives which focus on the social determinants of mental healthcare and social recovery as is evident by the NMHP and DMHP which are still biomedically driven in their conceptualisation and implementation.

MHCA's transformative potential for evolving rights-based jurisprudence

Since its enforcement, the MHCA has been instrumental in interpreting and evolving rights-based jurisprudence under India's Constitution. India's higher judiciary (Supreme Court and High Courts) has in various judgments relied on the MHCA's anti-discrimination provisions to recognise and protect the fundamental rights of marginalised and vulnerable groups. The judiciary in its interpretation of the MHCA's provisions has often adopted a socio-legal lens for laying down progressive jurisprudence which highlights MHCA's transformative potential beyond just mental healthcare and treatment.

In 2018, the Supreme Court of India delivered a landmark judgment, decriminalising homosexuality and reading down Section 377 of the India Penal Code, in the case of *Navtej Singh Johar v. the Union of India*. In its judgment, the Court invoked the right to non-discrimination and equality as granted under Section 21 of the MHCA as per which 'there shall be no discrimination on any basis including gender, sex, sexual orientation, religion, culture, caste, social or political beliefs, class or disability'. The Court relied on this provision to hold that an existing legislation prohibited discrimination based on sexual orientation. Further, the Court in its judgment cited Section 3 of the MHCA, as per which mental illness must be diagnosed based on internationally accepted standards, like the International Classification of Diseases (ICD-11), to counter arguments of homosexuality being a mental illness (Supreme Court of India, 2018b). The Court's judgment in this case also has a substantial implication for the practice of mental healthcare professionals. In its judgment the Court encouraged mental health professionals to reconsider their view on homosexuality, taking into consideration the 'repercussions of prejudice, stigma and discrimination'. The Court's observations in the case should be interpreted as a stand against the practice of conversion treatments which are commonly used in India, with the aim of 'curing' homosexuality or gender non-conformism (Patra, 2016). Since this judgment, Courts in the country have also ruled against the practice of conversion treatments. In June 2021, the High Court of Madras banned conversion treatments in the State of Tamil Nadu, declaring 'attempts to medically cure or change the sexual orientation of LGBTQIA+ people to heterosexual or the gender identity of transgender people to cisgender' as illegal (High Court of Madras, 2021; The Jurist, 2021). Following the Court order, the National Medical Commission has banned 'conversion therapy' as professional misconduct under the Indian Medical Council (Professional Conduct Etiquettes and Ethics) Regulations, 2002 (The Hindu, 2022).

In another landmark judgment titled *Common Cause v. Union of India* (2018), a constitutional bench of the Supreme Court upheld passive euthanasia for persons who are terminally ill and on life support with no possibility of recovery. The Court relied on the MHCA's provisions on advance directives while framing guidelines on enforcing advance directives for terminally ill persons who in the future may not have capacity to give informed consent for passive euthanasia when they are on life support (Supreme Court of India, 2018a). The Court also recognised that an advance directive 'as part of a regime of constitutional jurisprudence is an essential attribute of the right to life and personal liberty under Article 21'. Furthermore, the Court in its judgment also highlighted Section 115 of the MHCA, which decriminalises attempted suicide by creating a presumption that any person attempting suicide is under severe stress and thus cannot be prosecuted under Section 309 of the Indian Penal Code. The Court observed that this provision regards persons who have attempted suicide as 'victims of circumstances' (rather than offenders) who are 'in need of care, treatment and rehabilitation rather than penal sanctions'.

Another example of the judiciary's reliance on the MHCA's provisions is in the case of *Accused X v. the State of Maharashtra* (2019). The Supreme Court while delivering the judgment related to an accused, relied on the MHCA's provision on right to confidentiality and instructed the court registry to not disclose the name of the accused since they had a mental illness. In its judgment, the Court also cited Section 103 of the MHCA as per which the State is obligated to provide mental healthcare for those belonging to specific vulnerable groups, including prisoners, and directed the State to set up a mental health establishment in at least one prison (Supreme Court of India, 2019).

The Court's reliance on the anti-discrimination provisions under the MHCA is significant, as it paves the way for challenging other forms of discrimination faced by persons with mental illness. For instance, under the Hindu Marriage Act, 1955, and Special Marriage Act, 1954, mental illness is listed as a ground for divorce and disqualification of marriage – a provision which disproportionately impacts women through indirect discrimination (Pathare *et al.*, 2015). The Court's jurisprudence based on the MHCA's anti-discrimination provisions can thus evolve to challenge such provisions in other legislations which directly or indirectly discriminate against persons with mental illness including by denying them legal capacity and access to other rights on an equal basis with others (Kapoor and Pathare, 2018).

Conclusion

While the MHCA symbolises a monumental achievement in displacing the existing discourse on mental healthcare through a progressive and rights-based legal framework, this is only one side of the story. As all rights-based legislations in India, the MHCA's transformative potential is also threatened by implementation gaps, infrastructural deficits, lack of political will and resistance from duty-bearers who are accountable under the law.

For instance, some mental health professionals have criticised the legislation as being 'westernised', individualistic and patient-centric which is likely to break the family, 'the very backbone and fabric of our society or deny family members their rights by giving primacy to the individual's wishes' (Avasthi, 2010; Math *et al.*, 2019). Many mental health professionals continue to perpetuate the stereotype that persons with mental illness (specifically severe mental illness) do not have the capacity or insight to make their own treatment decisions. For example, the provisions on advance directives have been criticised on the grounds that persons with mental illness may make inappropriate choices, might not be aware of their best interests or may refuse treatment (Sarin, 2012). Similarly, the nominated representative is seen as a threat to the role of the family and as further negating the family's rights. While such criticism claims that the MHCA enables 'too much' autonomy and sets impractical goals, other criticisms point to the 'denial' of legal capacity or autonomy of persons with mental illness through provisions which retain substitute decision-making and involuntary treatment (supported admissions) and provide for judicial review of advance directives (Davar, 2015b; UN Committee, 2019). On the other hand, it has been argued that the MHCA recognises the practical constraints that emerge in low-resource and socio-culturally complex settings such as India and seeks to achieve a pragmatic balance between competing rights such as protecting decisional autonomy, ensuring access to healthcare and preventing harm to persons with mental illness or others (Pathare and Kapoor, 2021). Thus, the MHCA eschews an absolutist position in favour of the progressive realisation of the CRPD's guiding principles while embedding itself in India's socio-economic context.

The MHCA continues to face mammoth implementation challenges given the lack of political will to recognise mental health as a right, and a development and governance issue (Pathare and Kapoor, 2020). Even though the legislation came into force in 2018, many State Governments are yet to draft State rules, minimum quality standards for mental health establishments or set up statutory bodies such as the SMHAs and MHRBs which are integral for monitoring the MHCA's implementation (Keshav Desiraju India Mental Health Observatory, 2022). In some States where these statutory bodies have been established, they remain non-functional. The lack of action by these statutory authorities has created barriers for persons with mental illness and caregivers seeking to exercise their rights or support from authorities. For instance, in the absence of functional MHRBs, persons with mental illness are unable to register their advance directives, nor are they able to register complaints or grievances regarding the quality of mental healthcare services or any rights violations.

The inaction of nodal authorities and the lack of implementation has compelled stakeholders to approach the Courts for recourse, over a variety of issues ranging from the establishment of SMHAs and MHRBs, to insurance coverage for persons with mental illness, rehabilitation of persons who have recovered from mental illness and the notification of minimum standards to be followed by mental health establishments (Shastri, Kapoor and Pathare, 2021). The Delhi High Court recently passed a landmark judgment on the right to medical insurance for mental illness, instructing an insurance company to pay the petitioner her rightful insurance claims for treatment of her severe mental illness. The Court also directed the insurance regulatory authority to ensure that insurance companies comply with the legal obligations of providing medical insurance for mental illness on the same basis as is provided for physical illness (Kapoor and Mahashur, 2021).

Further, since 2018, the Supreme Court has been adjudicating a public interest litigation regarding the rehabilitation of persons with mental illness, who have recovered but continue languishing in mental health establishments either because they are homeless or have been abandoned by their families. Due to insufficient halfway homes and community rehabilitation facilities for such persons, in several instances they have been relocated to homes for elderly persons or beggars by States, or States have redesignated such facilities as halfway homes. The Court observed that the re-designation of old-age homes or beggar homes as halfway homes for persons recovered from mental illness would 'not amount to a valid discharge of its duties and obligations by the State Government of complying' with the provisions of the MHCA. In its order, the Court instructed all State Governments to set up rehabilitation homes for persons who have recovered from mental illness on priority; also directing the Union Government to monitor the progress being made by States and to appraise the Court of the same, periodically (Supreme Court of India, 2021).

While the Courts will continue to remain as the last resort for redressal of rights violations, these challenges suggest the need for collective action and a multi-pronged approach by civil society to advocate for the MHCA's implementation with duty-bearers and policymakers. Historically, most rights-based legislations in India such as the Right to Information Act, 2005; National Rural Employment Guarantee Act, 2005; Forest Rights Act, 2006; Right of Children to Free and Compulsory Education Act, 2009; and National Food Security Act, 2013 have been outcomes of decades-long social movements. Sustained advocacy by civil society organisations, groups and individuals with the State led to the enactment of these legislations. More importantly, these organisations continue to monitor and strengthen implementation of these laws across the country. In contrast, the MHCA was enacted in the absence of a cohesive and widespread movement which cut across different segments of civil society. This is largely because historically apart from the mental health and disability sectors, mental health had not been considered as a rights-based or development issue by other civil society actors or the bureaucracy, thus obviating the emergence of a widespread movement for the right to mental health. However, if the MHCA's vision is to be realised in tandem with a reconceptualisation of India's policy and programmatic framework for mental health, then it will first require a sustained movement bringing together different sectors, marginalised groups and civil society representatives to advocate for mental health as a governance issue which is inextricably linked to social justice and human rights. Civil society in India needs to recognise mental health as an intersectoral and multi-factorial issue and build alliances with other movements advocating for social justice and socio-economic rights. It is also crucial that advocacy efforts are informed by lived experiences and focus on overcoming resistance to integrating rights-based approaches for providing mental healthcare. Such efforts have to adopt strategies which focus on transforming attitudes and imparting necessary skills to mental health professionals, law enforcement officials and policymakers to implement the law in its letter and spirit.

Countries across the world can draw lessons from India's experiences of navigating the contested terrain of enacting and enforcing rights-based mental health legislation. The MHCA represents a unique and significant achievement of enacting a progressive mental health legislation in response to the CRPD's mandate despite contrasting interests of different stakeholder groups. However, at the same time, the MHCA is also grounded in practical realities of balancing competing principles such as individual autonomy on the one hand and overcoming challenges of providing rights-based mental healthcare in low-resource settings or addressing India's complex socio-cultural realities on the other. The MHCA seeks to strike a balance between these concerns, albeit within the framework of India's constitutional jurisprudence to prevent rights violations through legal safeguards and at the same time facilitating progressive realisation of human rights. LMICs embedded in similar shared realities can draw from these lessons if they seek to strike a similar balance in their respective contexts while prioritising the rights of persons with mental illness in accordance with the CRPD's guiding principles. In India's context, we believe these dynamic tensions are likely to lead to the development of rights-based jurisprudence on mental health and human rights as is already evident from the judiciary's proactive stance. If implementation of rights-based mental health legislation is considered as a political process, then in democratic countries like India, it is vital that the judiciary and civil society continue to play a role in maintaining checks and balances on the Executive to actualise the right to mental healthcare on the ground. While the MHCA is a promise for transformation and radical change, it is a promise which can only be fulfilled if there is a concerted effort and will on the part of all those who have a stake in its vision for India's mental health system and the future of its people.

References

Addlakha, R. (2010) *'Indigenisation' Not 'Indianisation' of Psychiatry: An Anthropological Perspective*. Available at: https://journals.sagepub.com/doi/abs/10.1177/0038022920100103 (Accessed: 25 May 2022).

Avasthi, A. (2010) 'Preserve and Strengthen Family to Promote Mental Health', *Indian Journal of Psychiatry*, 52(2), pp. 113–126. Available at: https://doi.org/10.4103/0019-5545.64582.

Damji, M., Shastri, M. and Pathare, S. (2021) 'Mobilizing for the Rights of Persons with Psychosocial Disabilities in India Lessons from the Centre for Mental Health Law & Policy's Work During the COVID-19 Pandemic', *HPOD*, 6 October. Available at: https://hpod.law.harvard.edu/news/entry/mobilizing-for-the-rights-of-persons-with-psychosocial-disabilities-in-india (Accessed: 23 May 2022).

Davar, B. (2015a) 'Law as a Social Determinant of Clinical Interactions in Mental Hospitals', *Cusp the Journal* [Preprint]. Available at: http://www.cuspthejournal.com/47.html (Accessed: 23 May 2022).

Davar, B. (2015b) 'Legal Frameworks for and against People with Psychosocial Disabilities', *Economic and Political Weekly*, 47(52), pp. 7–8.

'Declaration of Alma-Ata' (1978) Available at: https://www.who.int/teams/social-determinants-of-health/declaration-of-alma-ata (Accessed: 23 May 2022).

Duffy, R.M. and Kelly, B.D. (2020) *India's Mental Healthcare Act, 2017: Building Laws, Protecting Rights*. Singapore: Springer. Available at: https://doi.org/10.1007/978-981-15-5009-6.

Duggal, R. (1991) 'Bhore Committee (1946) and Its Relevance Today', *Indian Journal of Pediatrics*, 58(4), pp. 395–406. Available at: https://doi.org/10.1007/BF02750917.

Government of India, D.G. of H.S. (2017) *National Mental Health Programme*. Available at: https://dghs.gov.in/content/1350_3_NationalMentalHealthProgramme.aspx (Accessed: 14 December 2021).

Gupta, S. and Sagar, R. (2018) 'National Mental Health Programme–Optimism and Caution: A Narrative Review', *Indian Journal of Psychological Medicine*, 40(6), pp. 509–516. Available at: https://doi.org/10.4103/IJPSYM.IJPSYM_191_18.

High Court of Madras (2021) *Sushma and Agarval vs State of Tamil Nadu & Ors*.

Human Rights Watch (2014) *India: Women With Disabilities Locked Away and Abused*. Available at: https://www.hrw.org/news/2014/12/03/india-women-disabilities-locked-away-and-abused (Accessed: 23 May 2022).

Jacob, K.S. (2016) 'Social Context and Mental Health, Distress and Illness: Critical yet Disregarded by Psychiatric Diagnosis and Classification', Available at: https://www.indjsp.org/article.asp?issn=0971-9962;year=2016;volume=32;issue=3;spage=243;epage=248;aulast=Jacob (Accessed: 24 May 2022).

Joag, K. *et al.* (2020) 'Atmiyata, a Community-Led Intervention to Address Common Mental Disorders: Study Protocol for a Stepped Wedge Cluster Randomized Controlled Trial in Rural Gujarat, India', *Trials*, 21(1), p. 212. Available at: https://doi.org/10.1186/s13063-020-4133-6.

Kapoor, A. and Mahashur, S. (2021) *Right to Health Insurance: Ensuring Parity for Mental Illness in India*. Available at: https://www.jurist.org/commentary/2021/06/kapoor-mahashur-health-insurance-india/ (Accessed: 24 May 2022).

Kapoor, A. and Pathare, S. (2018) 'Section 377 and The Mental Healthcare Act, 2017: Breaking Barriers', *Indian Journal of Medical Ethics* [Preprint]. Available at: https://ijme.in/articles/

section-377-and-the-mental-healthcare-act-2017-breaking-barriers/?galley=html (Accessed: 23 May 2022).

Keshav Desiraju India Mental Health Observatory (2022) *MHCA 2017 Implementation Tracker.xlsx* Keshav Desiraju India Mental Health Observatory. Available at: https://indianlawsociety.sharepoint.com/:x:/s/IndianLawSociety/EZtaOMBK7qZFrnqK8U188QUBEDkgAdb83B5t6cwaYTFuYw?rtime=ivn5Fhmt2kg (Accessed: 13 October 2022).

Keshav Desiraju India Mental Health Observatory (2022) 'Union Budget for Mental Health 2022–23', Keshav Desiraju India Mental Health Observatory. Available at: https://cmhlp.org/wp-content/uploads/2022/02/IMHO-Union-Budget-for-Mental-Health-2022-23.pdf (Accessed: 23 May 2022).

Kohrt, B.A. *et al.* (2018) 'The Role of Communities in Mental Health Care in Low- and Middle-Income Countries: A Meta-review of Components and Competencies', *International Journal of Environmental Research and Public Health*, 15(6), p. 1279. Available at: https://doi.org/10.3390/ijerph15061279.

Math, S.B. *et al.* (2019) 'Mental Healthcare Act 2017 - Aspiration to Action', *Indian Journal of Psychiatry*, 61(Suppl 4), pp. S660–S666. Available at: https://doi.org/10.4103/psychiatry.IndianJPsychiatry_91_19.

Ministry of Health and Family Welfare (2022) *Allocation of Funds for Mental Health*. Government of India. Available at: https://pib.gov.in/pib.gov.in/Pressreleaseshare.aspx?PRID=1795422 (Accessed: 23 May 2022).

NIMHANS (2016) *National Mental Health Survey 2016*. Bengaluru: National Institute of Mental Health and Neuro Sciences. Available at: http://www.indianmhs.nimhans.ac.in/Docs/Summary.pdf (Accessed: 23 May 2022).

Padmakar, A. *et al.* (2020) 'Supported Housing as a Recovery Option for Long-Stay Patients with Severe Mental Illness in a Psychiatric Hospital in South India: Learning from an Innovative De-hospitalization Process', *PLOS ONE*, 15(4), p. e0230074. Available at: https://doi.org/10.1371/journal.pone.0230074.

Pathare, S. and Kapoor, A. (2020) 'Implementation Update on Mental Healthcare Act, 2017', in R.M. Duffy and B.D. Kelly (eds.) *India's Mental Healthcare Act, 2017: Building Laws, Protecting Rights*. Singapore: Springer, pp. 251–265. Available at: https://doi.org/10.1007/978-981-15-5009-6_11.

Pathare, S. and Kapoor, A. (2021) 'Decisional Autonomy and India's Mental Healthcare Act, 2017: A Comment on Emerging Jurisprudence', in C. Sunkel et al. (eds.) *Mental Health, Legal Capacity, and Human Rights*. Cambridge: Cambridge University Press, pp. 155–170. Available at: https://doi.org/10.1017/9781108979016.013.

Pathare, S., Nardodkar, R., Shields, L., Bunders, J.F. and Sagade, J. (2015) 'Gender, Mental Illness and the Hindu Marriage Act, 1955', *Indian Journal of Medical Ethics*, 12(1), pp. 7–13. Available at: https://doi.org/10.20529/IJME.2015.003.

Patra, S. (2016) 'Conversion Therapy for Homosexuality: Serious Violation of Ethics', *Indian Journal of Medical Ethics*, 1(3), pp. 194–195. Available at: https://doi.org/10.20529/IJME.2016.056.

Rejani, P.P., Sumesh, T.P. and Shaji, K.S. (2015) 'Cost of Care: A Study of Patients Hospitalized for Treatment of Psychotic Illness', *Indian Journal of Psychological Medicine*, 37(1), pp. 71–74. Available at: https://doi.org/10.4103/0253-7176.150823.

Sahithya, B.R. and Reddy, R.P. (2018) 'Burden of Mental Illness: A Review in an Indian Context', *International Journal of Culture and Mental Health*, 11(4), pp. 553–563. Available at: https://doi.org/10.1080/17542863.2018.1442869.

Sarin, A. (2012) 'On Psychiatric Wills and the Ulysses Clause: The Advance Directive in Psychiatry', *Indian Journal of Psychiatry*, 54(3), pp. 206–207. Available at: https://doi.org/10.4103/0019-5545.102332.

Sarin, A. and Jain, S. (2015) 'The 300 Ramayanas and the District Mental Health Programme', *Economic and Political Weekly*, 48(25), pp. 7–8.

Saxena, S. and Sharan, P. (2008) 'Community Mental Health - An Overview', *ScienceDirect* [Preprint]. Available at: https://www.sciencedirect.com/topics/medicine-and-dentistry/community-mental-health (Accessed: 23 May 2022).

Shastri, M. (2021) 'Deconstructing the DMHP: Part I', Keshav Desiraju India Mental Health Observatory. Available at: https://cmhlp.org/wp-content/uploads/2021/11/Issue-Brief-DMHP-I.pdf (Accessed: 23 May 2022).

Shastri, M., Kapoor, A. and Pathare, S. (2021) 'The Central Role India's Courts Have Played to Protect People With Mental Illness'. *The Wire Science*, 21 October. Available at: https://science.thewire.in/health/mental-health-care-act-2017-india-courts-progressive-jurisprudence/ (Accessed: 7 January 2022).

Shastri, M. and Varma, A. (2021) 'Deconstructing the DMHP: Part II', Keshav Desiraju India Mental Health Observatory. Available at: https://cmhlp.org/wp-content/uploads/2021/11/Issue-Brief-DMHP-II.pdf (Accessed: 23 May 2022).

Shields-Zeeman, L., Pathare, S., Walters, B.H., Kapadia-Kundu, N. and Joag, K. (2017) 'Promoting Wellbeing and Improving Access to Mental Health Care through Community Champions in Rural India: The Atmiyata Intervention Approach', *International Journal of Mental Health Systems*, 11(1), p. 6. Available at: https://doi.org/10.1186/s13033-016-0113-3.

Singh, S. (2021) 'Twenty Years after Gruesome Erwadi Tragedy, People with Disabilities Continue to Be Treated with Indignity', *The Indian Express*, 10 August. Available at: https://indianexpress.com/article/opinion/columns/twenty-years-after-gruesome-erwadi-tragedy-people-with-disabilities-continue-to-be-treated-with-indignity-7446249/ (Accessed: 23 May 2022).

Supreme Court of India (2018a) *Common Cause (A Regd. Society) vs Union of India on 9 March, 2018*. Available at: https://indiankanoon.org/doc/184449972/ (Accessed: 23 May 2022).

Supreme Court of India (2018b) *Navtej Singh Johar vs Union Of India Ministry Of Law And Ors*. Available at: https://indiankanoon.org/doc/168671544/ (Accessed: 23 May 2022).

Supreme Court of India (2019) *Accused X vs The State of Maharashtra on 12 April, 2019*. Available at: https://indiankanoon.org/doc/155869274/ (Accessed: 23 May 2022).

Supreme Court of India (2020) *Suo Moto Writ Petition (Civil) No(s). 7/2020*. Available at: https://images.assettype.com/barandbench/2020-06/cc6ffef3-b7bb-4b78-97f4-f3cdfead8133/Suo_Motu_Order.pdf (Accessed: 23 May 2022).

Supreme Court of India (2021) *Gaurav Kumar Bansal vs Mr. Dinesh Kumar on 25 February, 2019*. Available at: https://indiankanoon.org/doc/46614748/ (Accessed: 24 May 2022).

The Hindu (2022) '"Conversion Therapy" Is Misconduct, Declares National Medical Commission', *The Hindu*. Available at: https://www.thehindu.com/news/national/nmc-declares-conversion-therapy-to-be-professional-misconduct/article65842557.ece (Accessed: 13 October 2022).

The Jurist (2021) 'India's High Court Bans Conversion Therapy: A Much Needed Law', June. Available at: https://www.jurist.org/commentary/2021/06/bhavyata-kapoor-india-high-court-bans-conversion-therapy/ (Accessed: 23 May 2022).

The New Indian Express (2021) 'World Health Organisation Highlights Chennai NGO's "Home Again" Project', *The New Indian Express*, June. Available at: https://www.newindianexpress.com/cities/chennai/2021/jun/14/world-health-organisation-highlights-chennai-ngos-home-again-project-2315810.html (Accessed: 24 May 2022).

Tripathy, J.P. et al. (2016) 'Cost of Hospitalisation for Non-communicable Diseases in India: Are We Pro-Poor?', *Tropical Medicine and International Health*, 21(8), pp. 1019–1028. Available at: https://doi.org/10.1111/tmi.12732.

UN Committee on the Rights of Persons with Disabilities (2019) 'Concluding Observations on the Initial Report of India', UN. Available at: https://digitallibrary.un.org/record/3848327 (Accessed: 24 May 2022).

UN Office of Human Rights Commissioner (2000) *General Comment No. 14: The Right to the Highest Attainable Standard of Health, (Article 12) (2000)*. OHCHR. Available at: https://www.ohchr.org/en/resources/educators/human-rights-education-training/e-general-comment-no-14-right-highest-attainable-standard-health-article-12-2000 (Accessed: 23 May 2022).

United Nations (1976) 'International Covenant on Economic, Social and Cultural Rights', Available at: https://www.ohchr.org/Documents/ProfessionalInterest/cescr.pdf (Accessed: 26 January 2022).

United Nations (2007) 'Convention on the Rights of Persons with Disabilities', Available at: https://www.un.org/development/desa/disabilities/convention-on-the-rights-of-persons-with-disabilities/convention-on-the-rights-of-persons-with-disabilities-2.html (Accessed: 23 May 2022).

Varma, A. (2021) 'Deconstructing the DMHP: Part IV', Keshav Desiraju India Mental Health Observatory. Available at: https://cmhlp.org/wp-content/uploads/2021/11/Issue-Brief-DMHP-IV.pdf (Accessed: 23 May 2022).

World Health Organisation (2017) *Mental Health Atlas 2017.* Available at: https://cdn.who.int/media/docs/default-source/mental-health/mental-health-atlas-2017-country-profiles/ind.pdf?sfvrsn=2afad897_1&download=true (Accessed: 23 May 2022).

World Health Organisation (2021) *Community-Based Mental Health Services Using a Rights-Based Approach.* Available at: https://www.who.int/news-room/feature-stories/detail/community-based-mental-health-services-using-a-rights-based-approach (Accessed: 23 May 2022).

31
AN ALTERNATIVE TO MENTAL HEALTH LAW
The Mental Capacity Act (Northern Ireland) 2016

Gavin Davidson

Introduction

In this chapter, the focus is on the legislative framework developed in Northern Ireland to promote the autonomy, and protect the rights, of people whose ability to make decisions is impaired. The main law, the Mental Capacity Act (Northern Ireland) 2016 (MCA(NI)), is the equivalent of many capacity-based laws in other jurisdictions and its contents were perhaps most directly informed by the Mental Capacity Act 2005 for England and Wales. The unusual aspect of the legislative framework in Northern Ireland is that the MCA(NI) is intended to replace the current mental health law, the Mental Health (Northern Ireland) Order 1986, rather than work in parallel with it, for everyone aged 16 and over.

In December 2019, the MCA(NI) was partially implemented to provide safeguards for those deprived of their liberty in circumstances not covered by the mental health law. The Department of Health in Northern Ireland is committed to the full implementation of the MCA(NI) as specified in the current Mental Health Action Plan (Department of Health, 2020) and the new Mental Health Strategy 2021–2031 (Department of Health, 2021) but no specific date has yet been set. The development and partial implementation process have taken a long time, and there may be a number of factors involved including the scope of the changes needed and the associated training and implementation costs. The wider pressures on health and social care related to the Covid pandemic have certainly further contributed to the delay. When (and if) full implementation is achieved, there will be a comprehensive legislative framework for everyone aged 16 and over whose ability to make decisions is impaired. In order to provide the background to the law in Northern Ireland the chapter first provides some initial discussion of: the problems that are being addressed; alternative approaches to developing the necessary legislative framework; the language used; the political nature of these discussions; and the limitations of the law. The historical context of Northern Ireland and the process of developing the MCA(NI) will then be considered. Some of the key specific sections of the MCA(NI) are then presented before engaging with some of the ongoing debates about the law and its implementation, particularly in relation to: the extended scope of the law; the exclusion of those aged under 16; the application to the criminal justice system; the need for ongoing training and resources; the potential impact of the MCA(NI);

and the data and research that could be useful to inform future developments in Northern Ireland and possibly internationally as the first example of the implementation of the 'fusion approach'.

Background issues

There are a number of issues which form the background to considering the MCA(NI) including the ongoing debates about the language used, the meaning of various key terms and the most effective ways to promote and protect people's rights. There are a range of perspectives on these issues and they are sometimes discussed in a relatively adversarial way which may reflect how important they are and how strongly people feel about them. It may be, however, that there really is a relatively high degree of consensus that some form of legal framework is needed and that the central aim should be on promoting and protecting people's rights.

A possible starting point for considering the legal framework in Northern Ireland is to identify the problem or problems that are being addressed; in other words, why do we need a mental health and/or mental capacity-based law? This is a question which is certainly not unique to Northern Ireland, but it is interesting to note that many mental health law review processes focus on revising the existing approach rather than a wider range of possibilities. One way of framing why a legal framework is needed is to suggest that there are times when people's ability to make decisions is impaired to the extent that they are unable to make a necessary decision and so a process is needed to protect their rights and enable the necessary decision/s to be made. One of the more obvious, and perhaps relatively uncontroversial, examples is when a person is unconscious. There will probably be times when decisions about the unconscious person's health and welfare need to be made. The problem then arises about how those decisions should be made, in a fair and open way, that protects the person's rights. It can also be argued that, in addition to when people are unconscious, there is a range of other ways in which people's ability to make decisions is impaired to the extent that they are unable to make the relevant decision. The causes of impairment may be wide and varied, including physical health problems, mental health problems, alcohol and drug use, intellectual disabilities and dementia. There may be ongoing and helpful debates and exploration of the appropriate threshold for when a person is unable to make a decision and the most reliable and valid approaches to determining whether a person is unable to make the decision, but it seems reasonably clear that this problem arises and some form of legal framework is needed.

There are a range of possible approaches to developing the necessary legislative framework for decisions to be made when a person is unable to make them. One, and perhaps the most common approach, is to review the current legal framework, identify relevant developments in case law, explore similar laws and updates in other jurisdictions and then consider how the current laws could be further developed. A difficulty with this approach is that it may neglect more fundamental questions about whether the current laws are the best available approach. In many jurisdictions, historically there were different approaches taken for decision-making in the context of mental health problems, based on mental disorder and risk, and for most other aspects of decision-making, based on decision-making ability. One of the themes in this chapter is that having a separate mental health law for only some forms of impairment, with different criteria for decision-making, is discriminatory and so just revising and updating the current mental health law may be an improvement but will not address this basic inequity and arguably injustice. One possible solution is usually referred to as the 'fusion approach' which suggests having one law for all, with decision-making ability as the gateway criterion. This was beautifully articulated by Dawson and Szmukler (2006), and has been discussed and developed over many years (Campbell and Heginbotham, 1991; Szmukler and Holloway, 1998; Zigmond, 1998; Holloway and Szmukler, 2003).

A further issue relates to the language used in relation to mental health law, mental capacity law and the United Nations Convention on the Rights of Persons with Disabilities (UNCRPD), which is undoubtedly evolving but at times seems to have obscured and complicated the associated debates. The first is the use of mental capacity to refer to people's ability to make decisions. It may be that 'decision-making ability' may be a more accessible phrase. It might also help with some of the complexities with the use of legal capacity, especially in relation to Article 12 of the UNCRPD to refer to universal human rights. The use of legal capacity to positively assert everyone's right to make decisions, irrespective of their ability to do so, reflects a hugely important and progressive position but the use of 'capacity' in both 'mental capacity' and 'legal capacity' seems unhelpful. Another issue in the language used in these debates is the variable definitions and use of substitute and supported decision-making. A crucial distinction would seem to be between when a person, sometimes with considerable support, is making the decision themselves, and when, despite all possible support, the person is unable to make the relevant decision and so it is made by someone else. At times it has been suggested that the term 'supported decision-making' could be stretched to include when someone else is making the decision but this would seem to be misleading and may also prevent the clear identification of when additional safeguards need to be in place.

Another area of complexity relates to how, if a decision has to be made by someone else, it should be made. The two main possibilities seem to be that it should be based on the 'best interests' of the person or based on an estimate or interpretation of their 'will and preferences'. Again, there would seem to be a high degree of overlap between these two positions. A reasonable criticism of 'best interests' is that it has been misused in an overly paternalistic way to reflect more of the decision-maker's view of what they think would be best for the person rather than focusing on the person's subjective best interests. However, that is clearly not the intention in the use of 'best interests' in the MCA(NI). For example, Section 7 of the MCA(NI) specifies that in determining best interests, 'special regard' should be given to the person's past and present wishes and feelings; their beliefs and values; and other factors the person would likely have considered. It is therefore intended to be best interests from the person's own perspective, not what would be best clinically or in the view of others.

Even if an estimate of the person's will and preferences is used that does not prevent people interpreting that in an inappropriate and overly protective way. A possible criticism of using the interpretation of will and preferences as the basis for decision-making is that it may suggest that the person's expressed will and preferences should be absolute. There may be circumstances, for example when their ability to make the relevant decisions is so impaired by depression or alcohol, when respecting a person's clearly expressed will and preferences would lead to more fundamental infringements of their rights. As Kelly (2015) has argued, asserting the central importance of subjective best interests would seem a very positive basis on which to facilitate decision-making that would protect people's rights. It is reasonable to acknowledge that certainly often in the past, and possibly still to some extent, decision-making processes have not focused sufficiently on this subjective conceptualisation of best interests. It is less clear, however, whether abandoning the phrase, rather than clarifying its meaning and specifying how it should be determined, would better protect people's rights.

The next background issue relates to clarifying some of the complementary purposes of mental health and/or mental capacity law and policy. One purpose is to provide safeguards when a person is unable to make the relevant, necessary decisions. Another related purpose is to ensure that people's needs are appropriately assessed and responded to through the provision of support. It is an important point that the need for safeguards, when a person is unable to make the decision, can be reduced by funding and providing more effective support. It is great to see the evidence base for specific approaches to reducing the need for compulsory intervention, especially the use of force, developing (Gooding et al., 2020) and a greater social policy focus on the social determinants of mental health problems would also help. It seems reasonable to argue, however, that we should both do everything possible to support people to make their own decisions and also have safeguards in place for when a person is unable to make the relevant decision/s.

The final background issue to be mentioned, before focusing on the Northern Ireland context, is to highlight that there are a number of underlying political and philosophical issues which are central to these debates but which sometimes do not get fully acknowledged. Perhaps the most relevant is the Szaszian position that mental health problems are not the equivalent of physical health problems and that any associated impairment should not be used as the basis to enable decision-making when a person is unable to make the decision or to mitigate responsibility when a person commits a crime (Szasz, 1960). That position, which does not support any form of legal framework which is based on impairment related to mental health problems, is different from the position that safeguards are needed, that they should not be discriminatory and much more can be done to prevent the need for their use. In the ongoing debates, especially in relation to the UNCRPD, it sometimes appears that this important distinction is not clearly made.

The Northern Ireland context

Northern Ireland is located on the western edge of Europe and is roughly one-fifth of the whole island of Ireland. It was created in 1921 by the Government of Ireland Act 1920 which divided Ireland into the six counties of Northern Ireland in the north east of the island, which remained politically part of the United Kingdom, and the 26 counties of the independent Republic of Ireland. It's a relatively small country, about the same size as East Timor, and with a population of approximately 1.9 million people, similar to Latvia. Since its creation, a dominant, at times defining aspect of Northern Ireland has been the question of whether it should remain part of the UK or reunify with the rest of Ireland. This issue was the focus of many years of political violence, usually referred to as 'the Troubles', from 1969 to the Good Friday Agreement in 1998, during which time over 3,500 people were killed and 50,000 injured. Since 1998 there has been much greater focus on the impact of the Troubles on the mental health of people in Northern Ireland and, although the levels of violence are now much lower, the role of paramilitary activity on both sides of the conflict remains a concern.

There are a number of aspects of the Northern Ireland context which may have contributed to its openness to a capacity-based fusion law to replace mental health law. It is difficult to determine the relative importance of any of these factors but it does seem reasonable to hypothesise that a combination of factors, including timing, may have been relevant to the decision to go with this relatively unusual and radical approach. The first is the history of political conflict. As a result there is perhaps a heightened awareness of the potential for discrimination, including by the state, and the need to have independent legal processes to protect the rights of all citizens. One example is the work of the Northern Ireland Human Rights Commission which was established as a result of the Good Friday Agreement and which in 2003 commissioned a research report (Davidson et al., 2003) on the human rights issues relevant to mental health law, policy and practice in Northern Ireland. The report identified a number of concerns with the legal framework at that time which consisted mainly of the Mental Health (Northern Ireland) Order 1986, a traditional mental health law with mental disorder and risk (not decision-making ability) as the gateway criteria, and the common law. The concerns identified included:

> Involuntary intervention in whatever form causes considerable controversy in the field of mental health, and raises a plethora of human rights concerns. For example, pursuant to the prevailing mental health legislation in Northern Ireland, persons involuntarily detained may be treated against their will, even if mentally capable.
>
> *(p. 12)*

> It is debatable how many compulsory admissions could be prevented if community services were better developed but there appears to be great potential in Northern Ireland to establish more appropriate community alternatives so that people's liberty is not unnecessarily restricted.
>
> *(p. 25)*

> There are patients who are being treated in hospital or who are resident in care homes who are not there as a result of compulsion…There are human rights concerns in relation to those who lack sufficient mental capacity to understand why they are in hospital or care or that they may leave the institution. In some cases if the person tried to leave the assessment and detention process under the Order would be initiated. In other situations, the Trust [the five Health and Social Care Trusts are the statutory providers of services in NI] may seek to rely on the common law doctrine of necessity as regards the need to detain the person in their best interests.
>
> *(p. 25)*

> The lack of accessible independent review of a decision to detain a person under common law or to treat those who are passive and mentally incapable as voluntary patients may contravene Article 5(4) [of the European Convention on Human Rights (ECHR)]. Similarly the lack of certainty in the common law power may contravene the Convention's requirements. Moreover, the fact that a decision can be made by one professional with no obligation to present objective evidence to any authority does not appear to provide for sufficient protection against arbitrary detention…The lack of a review procedure leaves incapacitated adults vulnerable to decisions being made about their best interests which may be heavily influenced by the interests of the professionals who operate under budget pressure, or those of family or carers who may have conflicting interests. The right to respect for private life of the individual protected by Article 8 of the ECHR would suggest that time should be taken to identify his or her wishes to the extent that this is possible.
>
> *(p. 28)*

An alternative to mental health law

People who have the capacity to make decisions about their everyday life should be encouraged to make these decisions. This is consistent with the right to respect for private life, the right to freedom of expression and association and the right to marry and found a family. Those who do not have capacity also have these rights but may require assistance in exercising them and in order to prevent abuse, there is an obligation on public authorities to provide appropriate protection. In Northern Ireland at present there is a vacuum in law as regards decision-making for people with incapacity. There is no protection of their autonomy, a lack of clarity for those seeking to make decisions and a lack of access to justice when disputes arise.

(p. 69)

Unaccountable decisions about capacity can be made by doctors [and others] in Northern Ireland which impact very seriously on the autonomy of people with mental health difficulties. There is a lack of procedure which allows people or their representatives to consider the test applied and the reasons for the decision. There is no appeal process. Once a person is considered incapable, there is no legislation which states how the interests or views of the person are to be taken into account when making a decision. Where the person does not actively disagree with the decision, such as with whom he or she can have contact, or where he or she should live, then it is very unlikely that there will be any check on those making the decisions.

(p. 71)

Another aspect of the Northern Ireland context which may be relevant is that, as a consequence of concerns about discrimination in local government, the Health and Personal Social Services (NI) Order 1972 transferred responsibility for social care from locally elected councils to an integrated health and social care service. This was, at least partly, due to the concerns about sectarianism in the distribution of resources by local government but the potential benefits of integration were also recognised. This early example of integrated health and social care may therefore have contributed to a more holistic consideration of the rights and needs of people experiencing mental health problems. The integrated health and social care system, combined with the scale of the country, also meant that it was relatively straightforward to get together most of the people involved and interested in considerations about mental health and mental capacity law, and that facilitated positive relationships on which to enable discussion and build consensus.

A further aspect of the context which may have contributed to the fusion approach was simply timing. As will be outlined in the next section, the process of considering and developing the MCA(NI) really began in 2002 and was long, inclusive and careful. This enabled information about how the complex approaches developed in the neighbouring jurisdictions of Scotland (with parallel and arguably overlapping capacity, mental health and adult safeguarding laws) and England and Wales (with mental health law and capacity law with the addition of complex deprivation of liberty safeguards) were working.

A final note on the context was that this law was considered and passed by the Northern Ireland Assembly which is the devolved legislature for Northern Ireland. From 1972 to 1998 Northern Ireland had been subject to direct rule from the UK's Central Government in Westminster. The Assembly was established by the Northern Ireland Act 1998 and was again suspended from 2002 to 2007. It was then in place to consider and pass the MCA(NI) in 2016 before again being suspended from 2017 to 2020. It is debatable whether this process would have been different if it had not been through the Assembly but it does seem reasonable to assert that this legislative approach is different from, and possibly challenging for, the legal frameworks in the rest of the UK.

The process of developing the MCA(NI)

The formal process of reviewing the legal framework in Northern Ireland was part of a wider review of the law, policy and services for people with mental health problems and/or intellectual disabilities. The review began in October 2002 and was chaired by Professor David Bamford, a Professor of Social Work from Ulster University, with Professor Roy McClelland, a Consultant Psychiatrist and Professor of Mental Health from Queen's University Belfast, as the Deputy Chair. From the start, it was a very inclusive and in-depth process, which highlighted the importance of equity, rights, the perspectives of service users and carers, societal issues and international developments. The Bamford Review established a number of guiding principles which included: involvement and open access; integrity; inclusivity; quality; teamwork; coherence and integration; and the importance of research and information. It asserted that services should respect individual autonomy and demonstrate justice and fairness.

In order to conduct such a wide-ranging and inclusive review, ten Working Committees were established, including the Legal Issues Working Committee. The focus on equity, justice and human rights was reinforced throughout the Review's work including in the reports of the Learning Disability Working Committee, which was chaired by Siobhan Bogues, and the Human Rights and Equality Sub-Group, chaired by Lady Christine Eames. Sadly, during the Review, two of the key people involved died, Winston McCartney who was one of the service user representatives, in June 2005, and Professor David Bamford, in January 2006. Professor Roy McClelland then succeeded Professor Bamford as Chair of the Review and then of the Bamford Monitoring Group which provided independent oversight of the implementation process. The Bamford Review's final report was the Legal Issues Committee's report, 'A Comprehensive Legislative Framework', which was published in August 2007.

The Legal Issues Committee's report begins

> The comprehensive nature of the Bamford Review allows the same core values to run throughout its deliberations. This ensures an integrated and coordinated approach to its work. The vision underpinning the Review is a valuing of those with mental health needs or a learning disability, including their rights to full citizenship, equality of opportunity and self-determination.
>
> *(Bamford Review, 2007, p, 3)*

It identified a number of drivers for change which included: the perspectives of service users and carers; changes in wider society and in services; human rights; changes in mental health law in other jurisdictions; and the introduction of capacity-based laws in other jurisdictions. The report states that

> A rights-based approach is proposed as the guiding principle for reform of legislation, which should respect the decisions of all who are assumed to have capacity to make their own decisions. Grounds for interfering with a person's autonomy should be based primarily on impaired decision-making capacity.
>
> *(Bamford, 2007, p. 26)*

The report concludes

> The Review considers that having one law for decisions about physical illness and another for mental illness is anomalous, confusing and unjust…Northern Ireland should take steps to avoid the discrimination, confusion and gaps created by separately devising two separate statutory approaches, but should rather look to creating a comprehensive legislative framework which would be truly principles-based and non-discriminatory.
>
> *(Bamford Review, 2007, p. 36)*

In response to the Bamford Review's recommendation, between January and March 2009 the Department of Health conducted a public consultation on the possibility of developing two separate laws, one focused on mental health and the other on mental capacity, but with an overarching set of principles for both. The responses to the consultation were strongly supportive of staying with the Bamford Review's recommendation for a single, capacity-based comprehensive law for everyone and, in September 2009, the Department of Health announced that it would adopt that approach. The importance and value of service user, carer and cross-sectorial involvement is often discussed and reinforced but it is less common to be able to demonstrate its impact. This was perhaps an excellent example of how an inclusive, review process can develop progressive proposals and also how a genuine, public consultation process does have the potential to achieve change. It is also, though, an indication of how long these types of process can take as it was seven years from the start of the Bamford Review to the decision to develop a capacity-based law to replace the current Mental Health (Northern Ireland) Order 1986 and that was just the beginning of developing the new law itself.

The process of developing the new law was also an inclusive, careful and lengthy process. It was overseen by a Project Board and Project Team (referred to as the Bill Team) with a Reference Group which was made up of representatives of service users, carers, professionals and service providers. Following considerable discussion and debate, and an Equality Impact Public Consultation, which was conducted between July and October 2010, the first set of instructions for the new Bill were provided to the Office of Legislative Consul in June 2011. An interesting aspect of the process was that, although the Northern Ireland Assembly was restored in March 2007, responsibility for justice matters was not devolved to the Assembly until April 2010. As the proposed new law had major implications for justice matters, the newly established Department of Justice conducted its own public consultation between July and October 2012. There was then a joint Department of Health and Department of Justice public consultation on the proposals for new mental capacity legislation for Northern Ireland between May and September 2014. In May 2015, an Ad-Hoc Joint (Health and Justice) Committee of the Assembly was established to consider the Mental Capacity Bill, which was then introduced to the Assembly in June 2015. The Bill was passed by the Assembly on 15 March 2016 and the Mental Capacity Act (Northern Ireland) 2016 received Royal Assent, the final stage in the law-making process, on 9 May 2016. In the Assembly, on 15 March 2016, the Minister of Health, Social Services and Public Safety at that time, Simon Hamilton, stated:

> I have great pleasure today in moving the Final Stage of the Bill. Born out of the Bamford review, it is fair to say that the Bill had a rather long journey to the Chamber. Turning the vision that Professor Bamford and his colleagues had into detailed policy

proposals and then a workable legal framework, with no template to work from, was never going to be easy or quick. Careful analysis of often complex concepts was crucial to a successful outcome, and balanced judgements had to be made, all under the watchful eye of those involved in the Bamford review and the many stakeholders whose contribution has shaped the Bill from day one…it is important to remind ourselves of what we are trying to achieve. First and foremost, the Bill is about reducing the stigma that is still felt by many people suffering from mental disorder. It will introduce a new rights-based legal framework that applies equally to every adult where there is a need to intervene in their lives on health grounds. In other words, there will be no more separate rules for those with mental disorder. Instead, there will be rules that recognise everyone's fundamental right to make decisions for themselves if they have the capacity to do so.

(Northern Ireland Assembly, Official Report, Tuesday 15 March 2016)

In the same session, the then Minister of Justice, David Ford, also noted:

I will digress, if I may, slightly. When, as a very young and enthusiastic trainee social worker, I found my supervisor on my first student placement to be a principal social worker called David Bamford, I little believed that, 40-something years later, one of the things that I would do on my last day as Minister in the Chamber would be to sit through the Final Stage of a Bill that puts into practice the work that he suggested.

The Assembly was again suspended from January 2017 until January 2020 and, although that may have further slowed implementation, the first phase did proceed. That happened in two stages, on 1 October 2019 the provisions relating to conducting research with participants whose ability to consent may be impaired commenced; and then on 2 December 2019, the provisions relating to deprivation of liberty, offences and money and valuables in residential and nursing homes commenced. Until full implementation, however, the Mental Health (Northern Ireland) Order 1986 remains in place and is to be used when it applies. The intention to fully commence the Act, and so replace the Mental Health (Northern Ireland) Order 1986 for those aged 16 and over, was included as a specific action in the most recent Mental Health Action Plan (Department of Health, 2020) and referred to in the Mental Health Strategy 2021–2031 (Department of Health, 2021) but no date has yet been set for that to happen.

Key sections of the MCA(NI)

There are a number of sections of the MCA(NI) which may be relevant to highlight. In many ways it is a relatively conventional capacity-based law, largely based on the Mental Capacity Act 2005 for England and Wales, and perhaps the most important aspect of it is that, when fully implemented, it will replace, rather than be in parallel with a mental health law for those aged 16 and over. The Act is structured into 15 Parts with 308 Sections and 11 Schedules.

Sections 1 and 2 specify the principles that underpin the Act and must be taken into account for any proposed intervention. Section 1 includes four principles in relation to capacity and Section 2 sets out the best interests principle. They are perhaps more clearly presented in paragraph 3.2 of the Deprivation of Liberty Safeguards Code of Practice (Department of Health, 2019) which states:

The statutory principles are:

a. Principle 1 – A person is not to be treated as lacking capacity unless it is established that the person lacks capacity in relation to the matter in question.
b. Principle 2 – The question if a person is able to make a decision for himself or herself can only be determined by considering the requirements of the Act and no assumptions can be made merely on the basis of any condition that the person has or any other characteristics of the person.
c. Principle 3 – A person is not to be treated as unable to make a decision for himself or herself unless all practicable help and support to enable the person to make the decision has been given without success.
d. Principle 4 – A person is not to be treated as unable to make a decision merely because the person makes an unwise decision.
e. Principle 5 – Any act done, or decision made, must be made in the person's best interests.

(Department of Health, 2019, p. 18)

Section 3(1) of the Act specifies that a person 'lacks capacity' to make a decision at the relevant time if 'the person is unable to make a decision for himself or herself about the matter because of an impairment of, or a disturbance in the functioning of, the mind or brain'. In the Code of Practice this is referred to as the impairment or disturbance test. The functional test is then set out in Section 4(1) which states that

a person is 'unable to make a decision' for himself or herself about a matter if the person:

(a) is not able to understand the information relevant to the decision;
(b) is not able to retain that information for the time required to make the decision;
(c) is not able to appreciate the relevance of that information and to use and weigh that information as part of the process of making the decision; or
(d) is not able to communicate his or her decision (whether by talking, using sign language or any other means).

The Code of Practice further clarifies that there are therefore three elements to a person lacking capacity: the impairment or disturbance test; the functional test; and that there is a causal link between them, in other words that it is because of the impairment or disturbance that the person lacks the relevant capacity. It is interesting to note that the four main components of the functional test (understand, retain, use and weigh and communicate) are fairly standard for capacity tests but the addition of 'appreciate the relevance of that information' is more unusual. This maybe doesn't add much to 'use and weigh' but perhaps reinforces how this test should be considered for those whose ability to make the relevant decision may be impaired due to mental health problems.

Arguably, one of the most positive and progressive aspects of the Act is the third principle, the support principle, which requires all practicable help and support to be given to enable the person to make their own decision. Section 5 specifies a number of steps which are required under the support principle which include: the provision of information in an appropriate way which includes some consideration of the 'reasonably foreseeable consequences' of the options of not making a decision; consideration of the timing and environment for making a decision; and involving those who are likely to help the person make the decision and/or communicate the decision. To achieve the positive potential of the support principle it will be important that a broad definition of 'all practicable help and support' is adopted and that this crucial aspect of the Act is appropriately resourced.

Section 7 addresses the implementation of Principle 5, the determination of what would be in the best interests of the person. This includes consideration of all the relevant circumstances, involving the person as fully as possible and consulting any relevant people. It also specifies that special regard must be given to: the person's past and present wishes and feelings; any beliefs and values that might have influenced their decision if they had the relevant capacity; and any other factors that the person would be likely to consider if able to do so. The Code of Practice further reinforces this interpretation of best interests and states:

> It is more than a clinical or medical best interests test; it is a holistic consideration of all relevant factors that would be reasonable to consider under the circumstances. The best interests is not what the professional would do or agree to if he or she was in the same shoes or what the relatives think they would do. A best interests determination starts with consideration of what decision [the person] would have made if [the person] had capacity to make the decision.
>
> *(p. 40)*

It does though still allow the important safeguard that the person's expressed wishes, when they lack the ability to make the relevant decision, are not absolute.

Other key sections of the Act set out a number of other safeguards, in addition to the Act's principles, which are required depending on the level of intervention being considered. These include: the formal assessment of capacity (Section 13); consultation with the nominated person (Section 15); and, in relation to deprivation of liberty, the prevention of serious harm condition and authorisation by a panel (Schedule 1) or authorisation of short-term detention in hospital (Schedule 2); and the role of the Review Tribunal (Sections 225–230).

Once the MCA(NI) is fully implemented it will therefore provide safeguards for when a person, even with all practicable support, is unable to make the relevant decision/s across all settings. The MCA(NI)'s principles apply across all decisions, so even for the most routine of everyday decisions, it is necessary to consider the Act's five principles including supporting the person to make the relevant decision and, if the person is still unable to make the relevant decision, ensuring that the decision is in the person's best interests. For serious interventions (such as those involving major surgery, serious and prolonged pain and/or distress), and treatment with serious consequences, in addition to adherence to the MCA(NI)'s five principles, a formal assessment of capacity is required and consultation with the person's nominated person. If a nominated person hasn't been identified then there is a process in the MCA(NI) by which someone can be identified. For some specific interventions, a second opinion and the involvement of an independent mental capacity advocate are also required. For treatment with serious consequences where the nominated person reasonably objects, and for interventions which involve deprivation of liberty, an attendance requirement or a community residence requirement, then further safeguards are required. These include: the involvement of an independent mental capacity advocate; that a report is completed which proposes the intervention; that additional criteria are met (for deprivation of liberty and a community residence requirement the proposed intervention must be necessary to prevent serious harm; and for an attendance requirement it must be necessary to ensure the person attends to receive the specified intervention); and then the proposed intervention must be considered and authorised by a Health and Social Care Trust Panel. Under Schedule 2 of the MCA(NI), short-term (up to 28 days) detention in hospital which amounts to deprivation of liberty, can be authorised by an appropriate health care professional who, where possible, should be an Approved Social Worker (who has completed specialist training for this role). This authorisation process involves the professional submitting: a report; a statement of incapacity (not completed by the authoriser); a best interests determination statement; evidence of consultation with the nominated person (if the nominated person objects then another Approved Social Worker must be consulted); a medical report; and a statement of whether the person has the capacity to decide to the Review Tribunal (if not, the Attorney General considers this). Proposed intervention which amounts to deprivation of liberty in a hospital setting beyond 28 days would then have to be considered and, if necessary, authorised through the Trust panel process.

Conditions for the use of restraint are also specified in Section 12 of the MCA(NI). These are that: 'failure to do the relevant act would create a risk of harm' to the person; and that the relevant act is proportionate to 'the likelihood of harm' and the 'seriousness of the harm'. Restraint tends to be distinguished from deprivation of liberty by being immediate, brief and unplanned. The Code of Practice (Department of Health, 2019) also highlights that the use of seclusion, which goes beyond the remit of restraint, may involve deprivation of liberty and so would require the associated safeguards and authorisation.

The Act does specify that in some emergency circumstances, if waiting until all the safeguards are in place would create an unacceptable risk of harm to the person, then intervention should proceed but the safeguards should still be put in place as soon as possible. It's also important to note that, for the civil parts of the MCA(NI), the provisions mainly provide protection from liability, as long as the appropriate safeguards are in place, rather than powers to intervene.

Part 10 of the Act focuses on its application in the criminal justice system and it is important to note that, although the intention is that the capacity-based approach continues to apply for treatment decision-making processes, for the court powers in relation to detention and public protection, a version of traditional mental health law's mental disorder as a criterion and court powers will continue to be used.

Ongoing debates about the MCA(NI) and its implementation

There are a number of ongoing debates about the MCA(NI) including complexities and uncertainties about its implementation. The first is the uncertainty about when it will be fully implemented. Although the commitment to full implementation is referred to in the current Mental Health Action Plan (Department of Health, 2020) and the Mental Health Strategy 2021–2031 (Department of Health, 2021), no date has been set and there will be funding needed to implement the Act effectively. The funding will be required for a range of aspects of implementation including: the additional training needed across sectors; the effective operationalisation of the support principle; and the provision of independent advocacy.

This is in the context of more general concerns about funding for health and social care, and wider economic uncertainty. In 2019, the Northern Ireland Affairs Committee of the House of Commons highlighted that:

> Despite many of the positive changes made in the wake of the Bamford Review funding for mental health as a proportion of the health budget in Northern Ireland has remained comparatively low, despite the higher prevalence of need. In 2015–16, spending on mental health totalled £255 million, which represents 5.5 per cent of the overall health budget. In 2016–17, 5.2 per cent of the health budget was spent on the Mental Health Programme of Care by HSC Trusts (not including spend on mental health services delivered by GPs or the Public Health Agency, which the Department does not collect data on). By comparison, 13 per cent of total expenditure by clinical commissioning groups and specialised commissioning services (not including direct commissioning such as that by general practitioners) was spent on mental health by NHS England in 2015–16, with 13.3 per cent spent in 2016–17 and 2017–18. NHS Wales allocated 11.4 per cent of expenditure to mental health in 2017–18 and NHS Scotland allocated 7.6 per cent in 2019–20.
>
> *(Paragraph 116)*

Although it is hoped that the funding plan accompanying the new Mental Health Strategy will address this issue, the wider political and economic uncertainties may further slow this process.

A more general debate about the capacity-based approach is the possibility that it will expand the scope of compulsory intervention. In Northern Ireland, one of the aims of the MCA(NI) is to put statutory safeguards in place for all people who are unable to make the relevant decisions across settings and who are already subject to compulsory intervention but not through a procedure prescribed by law. So, for those people, the aim is not to increase compulsory intervention but to ensure there are appropriate safeguards in place. The MCA(NI) does though also extend the possibility of compulsory intervention into areas of impaired decision-making which were specifically excluded under Article 3(2) of the Mental Health (Northern Ireland) Order 1986 which stated that 'No person shall be treated under this Order as suffering from mental disorder, or from any form of mental disorder, by reason only of personality disorder, promiscuity or other immoral conduct, sexual deviancy or dependence on alcohol or drugs'. The MCA(NI) does not have these exclusions and so it does introduce the possibility of compulsory intervention with those whose ability to make decisions is sufficiently impaired by substance use and/or impairment or disturbance associated with a diagnosis of personality disorder. For more serious interventions, including deprivation of liberty under the MCA(NI), the prevention of serious harm condition has to be met, and that condition is wider than the risk criterion under the Mental Health (Northern Ireland) Order 1986 which is restricted, in Article 4(2)(b) to 'a substantial likelihood of serious physical harm to himself or to other persons' whereas the MCA(NI), in Article 25(5)(a) expands this to 'a risk of serious harm to P or of serious physical harm to other persons'. The MCA(NI) does therefore extend the potential scope of compulsory intervention but it is important to note that there are additional safeguards in place including that the intervention would have to be in the person's best interests and so there would need to be consideration of the evidence of the effectiveness and/or negative impact of such intervention. A related concern is that MCA(NI) could also be misused to inappropriately exclude people from support by concluding that if people have the relevant decision-making ability and decline support then no further attempts should be made to offer support. In practice this is a complex area of law, policy and ethics but there are perhaps circumstances when, even if a person has the relevant decision-making ability and refuses support, it may still be appropriate and important to explore ways to keep the offer of support open.

Concerns about the inappropriate expansion of compulsory intervention and/or about the inappropriate withdrawal of the offer of support can both be addressed by ensuring there is sufficient preparation, and ongoing training, for full implementation. The training process for partial implementation has been an ongoing and evolving process as some of the detail of the relevant procedures and practice issues were only fully explored once people started using the new law. The relevant literature on training (Jenkins et al., 2020) highlights the importance of ensuring approaches are interactive and applied, and there are ongoing interdisciplinary projects in Northern Ireland developing more creative and engaging approaches to prepare people for the new legal framework.

The exclusion of those aged under 16 has also been the subject of considerable debate. It means that, at present, following full implementation, the Mental Health (Northern Ireland) Order 1986 will remain in place only for those aged under 16 with the associated discrimination based on mental disorder. There does seem to be a reasonable consensus that the legal framework for those aged under 16 does need to be clarified and reformed, and a range of possible approaches including: new guidance; revising or developing new legislation for children; or extending the MCA(NI) to apply to all. There are undoubtedly complex issues and different perspectives to be explored but the MCA(NI) does further reinforce the need for the legal framework for decision-making by those aged under 16 to be considered and clarified.

As mentioned, the application of the capacity-based approach in the criminal justice system does include treatment decision-making, but decisions about detention and public protection by the courts retain a focus on mental disorder and risk. In the criminal justice system, decisions about detention are clearly not usually made by the person who is accused or convicted of a crime, but there are perhaps opportunities to consider whether there are other aspects of the relevant processes which could be further clarified and aligned with the MCA(NI) specifically in relation to unfitness to be tried and insanity. There is also the concern that, in some circumstances, by respecting a person's ability to make decisions about treatment, if that treatment could have reduced risk, it could lead to the person's detention being prolonged (Campbell and Rix, 2018).

A final aspect of the MCA(NI) and its implementation to highlight is the opportunity and need to collect data about how the Act is being implemented, the experiences of all involved and the associated outcomes. It would be particularly helpful if that included data which enabled international comparison. Although it is necessary and important to reform legal frameworks which are discriminatory, that may not be enough to effectively address the stigma and discrimination that people with mental health problems continue to experience and so, while the MCA(NI) may help with this process, it is only one component of the changes that are needed.

Conclusion

The MCA(NI) represents a positive and progressive attempt to create a legal framework that applies to everyone, aged 16 and over, and therefore avoids the discrimination involved in having separate laws and different criteria for compulsory intervention for people experiencing mental health problems. The development of the MCA(NI) was a long and inclusive process, and it was appropriate to prioritise the commencement of the provisions of the MCA(NI) relating to deprivation of liberty. Its full and progressive potential will not be achieved, however, until the MCA(NI) is fully implemented, replacing the Mental Health (Northern Ireland) Order 1986. The Department of Health is currently working on a plan for the next stages of implementation but there will be costs associated with training, support and advocacy, and so, in the context of wider economic uncertainty, this may continue to be an incremental process. This provides the opportunity for further research to inform implementation and to evaluate how effective the MCA(NI) will be in addressing stigma and in protecting people's rights. There remain a number of ongoing debates including about the framework needed for those aged under 16 and the application of the MCA(NI) across all settings including the criminal justice system. It would be unreasonable to expect that the MCA(NI) will be sufficient to address all the ongoing concerns about health and social care, but it is an important step towards a more equitable legal framework which may also provide valuable learning for other jurisdictions.

References

Bamford Review of Mental Health and Learning Disability (Northern Ireland) (2007). *A Comprehensive Legislative Framework*. Belfast: Bamford Review. Available online at www.health-ni.gov.uk/publications/bamford-published-reports.

Campbell, P., & Rix, K. (2018). Fusion legislation and forensic psychiatry: The criminal justice provisions of the Mental Capacity Act (Northern Ireland) 2016. *BJPsych Advances, 24*(3), 195–203.

Campbell, T., & Heginbotham, C. (1991) *Mental Illness: Prejudice, Discrimination, and the Law*. Aldershot: Dartmouth Publishing Group.

Davidson, G., McCallion, M., & Potter, M. (2003) *Connecting Mental Health and Human Rights*. Belfast: Northern Ireland Human Rights Commission.

Dawson, J., & Szmukler, G. (2006). Fusion of mental health and incapacity legislation. *British Journal of Psychiatry, 188*(6), 504–509.

Department of Health (2019) *Deprivation of Liberty Safeguards: Code of Practice*. Belfast: Department of Health.

Department of Health (2020) *Mental Health Action Plan*. Belfast: Department of Health.

Department of Health (2021) *Mental Health Strategy 2021–31*. Belfast: Department of Health.

Gooding, P., McSherry, B., & Roper, C. (2020). Preventing and reducing 'coercion'in mental health services: An international scoping review of English-language studies. *Acta Psychiatrica Scandinavica, 142*(1), 27–39.

Holloway, F., & Szmukler, G. (2003). Involuntary psychiatric treatment: Capacity should be central to decision making. *Journal of Mental Health, 12*(5), 443–447.

Jenkins, C., Webster, N., Smythe, A., & Cowdell, F. (2020). What is the nature of Mental Capacity Act training and how do health and social care practitioners change their practice post-training? A narrative review. *Journal of Clinical Nursing, 29*(13–14), 2093–2106.

Kelly, B. D. (2015). Best interests, mental capacity legislation and the UN convention on the rights of persons with disabilities. *BJPsych Advances, 21*(3), 188–195.

Northern Ireland Affairs Committee (2019). *Health Funding in Northern Ireland – Mental Health*. Accessed online on 16.04.21 at https://publications.parliament.uk/pa/cm201919/cmselect/cmniaf/300/30008.htm.

Northern Ireland Assembly (2016) Official Report – 15 March 2016. Belfast: Northern Ireland Assembly. Available online at http://aims.niassembly.gov.uk/officialreport/reports.aspx.

Szasz, T. S. (1960). The myth of mental illness. *American Psychologist, 15*(2), 113.

Szmukler, G. (2019). "Capacity", "best interests", "will and preferences" and the UN convention on the rights of persons with disabilities. *World Psychiatry, 18*(1), 34–41.

Szmukler, G., & Holloway, F. (1998). Mental health legislation is now a harmful anachronism. *Psychiatric Bulletin, 22*(11), 662–665.

Zigmond, A. S. (1998). Medical incapacity act. *Psychiatric Bulletin, 22*(11), 657–658.

32
ARGENTINA, CHILE, COLOMBIA, AND PERU
The relationship of mental health law and legal capacity

Pablo Marshall[1]

Introduction

Latin America has witnessed a series of reforms to legal capacity in the last decade, mainly inspired by the Convention on the Rights of Persons with Disabilities (2006) (hereinafter CRPD). They have been directed towards eliminating guardianship regimes that impede the autonomous exercise of the rights of persons with disabilities and towards the implementation of support models for decision-making. These reforms have directly or indirectly altered the long-established general rules that govern legal capacity in the Latin American Civil Codes (Marshall et al., 2023), putting systems of support for legal capacity in line with what is demanded by Article 12 CRPD (Series and Nilsson, 2018). It is too early to assess the impact of these reforms, but they represent a legal revolution. They have been cited as examples of eliminating the different forms of substitute decision-making as an essential step in the emancipation of people with disabilities (Vasquez, 2021; Martinez-Pujalte, 2019; Flynn, 2021).

Despite their general ambitions, and perhaps because of their general legal nature, these reforms have not explicitly incorporated support on decisions related to healthcare, and they have not modified the rules that regulate informed consent contained in general health laws. Additionally, the reforms have not expressly modified the regulation of involuntary hospitalisations and other emergency psychiatric treatments regulated in recently enacted mental health laws. This has created a tense coexistence between the general capacity system and the capacity system of health and mental health legislation (Marshall, 2023). While such cohabitation is not unfamiliar to other jurisdictions, as the literature on British mental health law illustrates (Hale, 2010), such tension has the potential to be resolved by further reform-

---

[1] Thanks to Violeta Purán for her research assistance. This work was supported by the National Agency of Research and Development (ANID) (Fondecyt Research Grant 1190434, 2019–2022). I would like to thank Celeste Fernández, Renato Constantino, and Constanza López for their comments and the Editors' suggestions that helped me to improve this chapter.

ing the regulation of legal capacity in mental health legislation (Vasquez, 2021). However, it also reflects the limited scope of the support system and the difficulties in implementing it in Latin American practice (Marshall, 2023).

The chapter examines the relationship between legal capacity rules and mental health legislation in four jurisdictions that have passed relatively recent mental health legislation. The four selected jurisdictions have ratified the CRPD and the Inter-American Convention for the Elimination of All Forms of Discrimination against Persons with Disabilities (1999). Three have recently made significant reforms to legal capacity (Argentina, Colombia, and Peru), and one has not reformed its general legal capacity regime but has recently enacted an unprecedented mental health law (Chile). For an overview of the relevant legal reforms, see Table 32.1.

The chapter begins with a general overview of mental health laws and the legal capacity reforms. It then seeks to examine how recent legal capacity reforms in Argentina, Colombia, and Peru have impacted mental health law, paying particular attention to the recognition of support for decision-making in the context of mental health. It also shows whether the decision-making support systems which the CRPD promotes can be directly implemented in mental health law without going through the reform of legal capacity – which the Chilean case suggests is a possibility, as will be discussed. It ends with a detailed comparative description of the regulation of involuntary hospitalisation, exploring the different degrees of commitment to the abolition or reform of coercive practices displayed by mental health law in the region.

Table 32.1 Relevant legal reforms in selected Latin American jurisdictions

Jurisdiction	Previous legal capacity law	Legal capacity reform	Previous regulation of involuntary hospitalisation	Current mental health law
Argentina	Civil Code (1871)	New Civil and Commercial Code (2014)	Law 22,914 (General Health Law) (1982)	Law 26,657 (Mental Health Law) (2010)
Chile	Civil Code (1857)	—	Law 20,584 (On the Rights and Duties of People in Relation to Actions Related to their Healthcare) (2012)	Law 21,331 (Mental Health Law) (2021)
Colombia	Law 1,306 (On the Protection of Persons with Mental Disabilities) (2009)	Law 1,996 (2019)	Law 1,306 (On the Protection of Persons with Mental Disability) (2009)	Law 1,616 (Mental Health Law) (2013)
Peru	Civil Code (1984)	Decree-Law 1384 (2018)	Law 29,889 (Mental Health Law) (2012)	Law 30,947 (Mental Health Law) (2019)

Source: Table created by the author.

The difficulty of addressing the reality of various jurisdictions in a single analysis should be noted. However, this is possible due to the similarity of the legal systems in question, all belonging to the tradition of European-continental law, and to the similar stage of development of the regulation of mental health law. The advantages of comparing jurisdictions, however, come at the cost of limiting the depth of the analysis by limiting itself to a description of the legislative and administrative regulation without reference to case-law or socio-legal studies. A common characteristic of the jurisdictions under study is that they have a weak system of judicial review of decisions, which, added to the absence of a system of binding judicial precedents in the continental legal tradition, means that the absence of a case-law analysis does not substantially impact in such a relevant way the value of the presentation that follows.

Mental health legislation

Understood as a set of rules that regulate mental health services and treatments, accommodating the needs and interests of people with mental disorders, their carers, and the public (Hale, 2010), mental health law was born in the region during the first half of the 20th century, mainly through the regulation of psychiatric hospitals: for example, through the Executive Decree 68, *General Code for the Organization and Care Provision of Mental Health Services, Hospitalization and Confinement of the Insane* (1927) in Chile or the Law 4953, on *Regional Hospitals and Asylums* (1906) in Argentina. Its development has followed the rise and fall of psychiatric hospitals and asylums, the process of dismantling them, and the establishment of community models of mental health after the beginning of the 21st century (Caldas de Almeida and Horvitz-Lennon, 2010). However, as an academic discipline that studies these rules in practice, mental health law is still absent in the region. Legal problems relating to health in general and mental health, in particular, have traditionally been addressed by other legal disciplines. Administrative law has been involved in the organisation and exercise of police powers in the health field. Private law has addressed contractual and non-contractual relationships between patients, health services, and health personnel from the perspective of civil responsibilities. Problems related to capacity determination, informed consent, emergency psychiatric treatment, involuntary hospitalisation, and legal control have only been studied marginally (e.g. Bustamante and Cavieres, 2018; Buitrago, 2019; Constantino and Bregaglio, 2020). They have been treated more substantively by bioethics and forensic psychiatry, disciplines housed in schools of medicine. The poor legal development of mental health law and dearth of literature in this area may be due to the novelty and weakness of the existing judicial control mechanisms in the region, which imply limited access to the courts and little need for professional legal representation.

A new interest in mental health has occurred due to the growing importance of the rights of people with disabilities. In the context of discussions about their rights, and in particular their right to autonomously exercise their legal capacity and to live in the community, mental health standards have aroused new interest. This new interest has been reinforced during the last ten years by the reforms to legal capacity and the enactment of new mental health laws that assume a human rights approach and a community rather than institutional emphasis. However, academic analysis of these developments is still in an embryonic state, whether doctrinal or socio-legal (e.g. Constantino, 2021).

As a new wave of mental health legislation, certain common elements recur in the laws that will be analysed. They are special laws focused on mental health and have been separated from general health laws. However, they are complemented by provisions in other regulations in civil, criminal, and social security fields, as recommended by the World Health Organization (World Health Organization, 2003). All laws mention informed consent as a mechanism to guarantee patients' autonomy; the principle of the less restrictive and invasive therapeutic alternative; a list of rights recognised for patients in the context of their mental health treatment; a guarantee of the confidentiality of mental health information and medical records; and rights to maintain a family relationship. At the same time, some of them have notable and distinctive elements, and they differ in some significant respects.

Argentina's Law 26,657 [National Mental Health Law] (2010) (hereinafter AMHL) was the first mental health law in the region to take a human rights approach, repealing the Law 22,914 [Public Health. Hospitalisation Discharges Mental Health Establishment] (1982). It considers mental health a multifactorial phenomenon and explicitly recognises the importance of a community approach based on social inclusion, rehabilitation, and recovery for those with 'mental disorders' (Moldavsky et al., 2011). Some relevant characteristics of the AMHL are the following. Firstly, there is a commitment to deinstitutionalisation, through the prohibition of new psychiatric hospitals and the mandate to adapt existing ones to the new principles and the creation of community-based services (Art. 27). There is a current debate on the definition of psychiatric hospital, because some argue that the existence of hospitals focused on mental health do not infringe the deinstitutionalisation mandate. A general diagnosis of the transition to deinstitutionalisation is that minimal progress has been made towards implementing a comprehensive vision for mental health (Hurley and Agrest, 2021). Secondly, there is a commitment to interdisciplinarity in mental health treatment, recognising equality among mental health professions (Arts 8 and 13); and finally, an acknowledgement of cultural diversity and the protection of personal and collective identity (Art. 9.e), which is particularly relevant in recognition of the rights of indigenous people. The AMHL created an administrative supervisory body whose main task is to prevent rights violations. The AMHL influenced the 2014 legal capacity reform, which can be seen in the increased respect for persons' autonomy, expressed in the regulation of informed consent and advance directives in the text of the new Civil Code (Lafferriere and Muñiz, 2016).

Colombia's Law 1,616 [Mental Health Law] (2013) (hereinafter COMHL) also follows a human rights-based and integrated approach. It emphasises the importance of mental health promotion and prevention, especially for children and adolescents, and social participation mechanisms in the design of public policies in this area, especially for associations of people with 'mental disorders', their families, and caregivers. It also considers interdisciplinary teams and emphasises mental health workers' training, education, and protection. However, COMHL lacks clinical standards and does not address the most sensitive issues related to capacity and coercion in mental health treatment, which continue to be regulated by Law 1,306 [On the Protection of Persons with Mental Disabilities] (2009). A significant issue in this respect is that Law 1,306 was recently repealed by Law 1996 [Regime for the Exercise of the Legal Capacity of Persons with Disabilities] (2019), which implements decision-making support mechanisms in Colombia, but without establishing a regulation that replaces Law 1,306. We can identify the first and most evident intersections between legal capacity reforms and mental health law. Given this express repeal, psychiatric emergencies are deregulated, and the legal basis for interventions now seems to be in the outdated general regulations for medical emergencies contained in Law 23 [Medical Ethics] (1981).

Peru's Law 30,947 [Mental Health Law] (2019) (hereinafter PMHL) was enacted only one year after the 2018 legal capacity reform. This proximity has brought a certain degree of harmony between their provisions, especially between the laws and the CRPD. The PMHL replaces relevant rules of Law 26,842 [General Health Law] (1997), modified by Law 29,889 [Mental Health Law] (2012), which already embraced a rights-based approach and a community health model. The new law also incorporates these two elements, emphasising a multifactorial definition of mental health and promoting prevention through the early detection of risk factors and groups. Unlike Colombian legislation, it does incorporate specific regulations on clinical standards on hospitalisation and informed consent. It does not contain detailed rules regarding involuntary treatment and hospitalisations (except for the hospitalisation by order of a court), which is attributed to the influence of civil society organisation in the debate around the law. They advocate for removal of some provisions that were considered openly contradictory with the progress achieved by legal capacity reform (Vasquez, 2021, pp. 131–133). However, involuntary hospitalisation was regulated in the Executive Regulation of the Law (Supreme Decree 007-2020-SA) (hereinafter RPMHL). Other particularities of the PMHL worth mentioning include (1) its commitment to deinstitutionalisation, projected for a period of three years (2020–2023) (Arts 30–33); (2) the inclusion of substance abuse problems within the scope of the law (Art. 18; also Art. 4 AMHL); and (3) the express prohibition of certain practices such as electroconvulsive therapies, pharmacological treatment, and isolation without the patient's consent (Art. 17.6 RPMHL). Regarding isolation, however, the PMHL recognises therapeutic reasons to deprive the person of visits and to restrict freedom of movement and communication (Art. 9.13 and 9.15).

In Chile, the new Law 21,331 [Recognition and Protection of the Rights of People in Mental Healthcare] (2021) (hereinafter CLMHL) has consolidated the legal regulations on mental health, which were previously scattered in several legal and administrative documents, most importantly Law 20, 584 [On the Rights and Duties of People in Relation to Actions Related to their Healthcare] (2012), including provisions on mental health, and Decree 570 [On the Hospitalisation of Mentally Ill Persons] (2001) (Bahamondes et al., 2014). Despite incorporating a catalogue of rights and the bases for greater respect for autonomy in psychiatric interventions, the law has been criticised on grounds including an insufficient emphasis on community approaches to mental health, lack of participation of civil society organisations in the debate around the law, the inadequate budget for its implementation, and the adoption of a biomedical health model. For a list of acroyms used through the chapter, see Table 32.2.

Table 32.2 List of acronyms (for Chapter 32)

Country	Law or Regulation	Acronym
Argentina	Law 26,657 [National Mental Health Law] (2010)	AMHL
Colombia	Law 1,616 [Mental Health Law] (2013)	COMHL
Chile	Law 21,331 [On the Recognition and Protection of the Rights of People in Mental Healthcare] (2021)	CLMHL
Peru	Law 30,947 [Mental Health Law] (2019)	PMHL
	Regulation of the Law (Supreme Decree 007-2020-SA)	RPMHL

Legal capacity reforms

Article 12 of the CRPD stipulates, under the title of 'Equal recognition as a person before the law', the equal recognition of legal personality; the right to exercise legal capacity on equal terms with others in all aspects of life; and the obligation to provide support for the exercise of legal capacity and safeguards. The practical implications of these rules are difficult to determine because there was a lively debate at the time of their adoption (Dhanda, 2007), which has now reopened after the CRPD Committee interpreted Article 12 in its General Comment No. 1 (2014). The issues remain disputed, especially concerning the implications for mental health law (Craigie et al., 2019; Flynn, 2019; Szmukler, 2019).

In this context, a series of legal reforms have been implemented in different countries to comply with the rights and obligations of Article 12 CRPD. In common law jurisdictions, these reforms have preserved instances of incapacitation governed by the functional approach (e.g. the Republic of Ireland in 2015, Northern Ireland in 2016, and Victoria in Australia in 2020) and the Committee has criticised the compatibility of these rules with the CRPD. On the other hand, Latin American reforms to legal capacity have been identified as the reforms that have brought the mandate of Article 12 to its most radical realisation, in line with the Committee's interpretation. In Colombia and Peru, these reforms have eliminated the institution of guardianship of people with disabilities and replaced it with a system of decision-making support that aims to be more respectful of the will and preferences of people with disabilities (Martinez-Pujalte, 2019; Constantino, 2020; Isaza, 2021).

Noting that substitute decision-making has recently been abolished concerning guardianship law in Colombia and Peru, Kay Wilson questions whether such reforms 'really [do] result in significant benefits and freedom for persons with disabilities in those jurisdictions'. She warns that 'mental health contains some unique challenges such as the effects of episodic illness, delusions, self-harm, suicide, and how to deal with persons in acute crises'. She suggests this may explain why other jurisdictions are reluctant to abolish mental health law (Wilson, 2021, p. 11). Taking this question seriously, we seek to assess the extent to which these reforms have eliminated instances of psychiatric coercion and eradicated substitute decision-making in mental health law.

The three reforms analysed are the new ArgentineCivil Code, the Legislative Decree 1,384 [legal capacity of persons with disabilities] (2018) that reformed the Peruvian Civil Code, and the Colombian Law 1,996 [Regime for the Exercise of the Legal Capacity of Persons with Disabilities] (2019). They differ in several respects. From a formal point of view, while the Argentine and Colombian reforms were carried out through legislative changes, the Peruvian reform was enacted by delegated legislation. More importantly, while the Argentine reform was carried out in the context of a general reform of the Civil Code, the Peruvian and Colombian reforms were carried out to give a more favourable legal status to the exercise of their legal capacity by persons with disabilities. Although in principle any person could need support for decision-making, these reforms have taken a restrictive approach. In Peru, certification of disability is required, and in Colombia, disability was included in the very title of the law. Finally, the Argentine and Peruvian reforms modified the general rules of the Civil Code about legal capacity and guardianship, while the Colombian reform created a particular and detailed piece of legislation that establishes a decision-making support system (Marshall et al., 2023).

Substantively, all the reforms have in common the recognition that people with disabilities enjoy legal capacity. This recognition is expressed in a general provision presuming capacity and a system of support and safeguards for its exercise. While the Peruvian and Colombian reforms abolished the institution of guardianship for people with disabilities, replacing it entirely with support measures, the Argentine reform preserved guardianship for exceptional cases in which the person is unable to interact with their environment and express their will in any way. However, the Argentine Civil Code stipulates that even in this exceptional case, the substitute decision must promote autonomy and favour decisions that respond to the will and preferences of the protected person (Marshall et al., 2023). For such cases, the Peruvian reform provided a rule of exceptional support, in which a court appoints a support person with powers of representation when the appointment of support is necessary for the exercise and protection of their rights. The judge must determine the scope and responsibilities of the support, and the will and preferences of the person must always be considered (Bregaglio and Constantino, 2020b, pp. 51–55). Other than in such exceptional cases, support measures can be judicially or conventionally determined according to the rules included in the Peruvian Civil Code that replace guardianship. One of the main criticisms to the Peruvian reform is that it maintains the restriction of legal capacity for drug addiction and alcoholism, which has raised alerts about its possible use to cover cases of persons with disabilities.

Similarly, under Article 48 of the new Colombian law, a judge can authorise certain acts on behalf of people who are unable to express their will and preferences by any possible means, mode, and format of communication, when the support person demonstrates that the legal act in question reflects the best interpretation of the will and preferences of the relevant person. As in Peru, the Colombian Law 1,996 (2019) allows the creation of relations of support for the exercise of legal capacity through agreements, declarations, and advanced directives. As can be seen, the Colombian legislation takes the idea of support for legal capacity to such an extreme that it allows, in theory, the elimination of substituted decision-making. The case of Argentine legislation is less clear and questionable (Marshall et al., 2023).

In the case of Peru, we can track an obvious influence of the legal capacity reform on mental health reform. Colombia is likely to follow Peru's example. On the other hand, Argentina's legal capacity reform has been unable to impact mental health legislation. Notwithstanding having debated several bills on the matter (Marshall, 2020), Chile has not reformed the rules of legal capacity for people with disabilities that date back to 1857. If Chile follows the path travelled by Argentina, where the AMHL preceded its legal capacity reform, the CLMHL could also set the stage for future Chilean reform of legal capacity.

Decision-making support in health and mental health law

In order to fulfil the promise of implementing Article 12 CRPD, the reforms should have carried out a systematic modification of legal capacity in all sectors of the legal system that regulate the different spheres of life of persons with disabilities. In the context of healthcare, this should have involved both the implementation of support decision-making measures for informed consent and the review of involuntary emergency psychiatric practices. This section describes the inclusion of decision-making support in informed consent. The transformation of involuntary hospitalisation is addressed in the next section.

Unlike other reforms in the region, the new Argentine Civil Code expressly established general rules on informed consent for medical treatments, advance health directives, and involuntary hospitalisation in a manner consistent with provisions about support for legal capacity. Although the Civil Code does not make any innovations regarding the AMHL, it clarifies some situations. Regarding informed consent, it regulates the case of a person who cannot express his will at the time of medical care and has not expressed it in advance. In this case, consent may be granted by the legal representative, the support person, or another family member accompanying the patient if there is an emergency with a specific and imminent risk of serious harm to their life or health (Art. 59). The Code states that competent persons can make advance directives and confer a mandate regarding their health in anticipation of their disability. They can also designate the person who must express consent for medical treatment (Art. 60). Although support mechanisms are expressly considered for health treatments, the reform to legal capacity did not include an express reform to the AMHL that would make said support measures operational. The administrative regulation of the AMHL neither mentions nor regulates decision-making support. The lack of implementation of decision-making supports in the context of mental health has been one of the criticisms of the legal capacity reform in Argentina. This shows that the operation of support as an attempt to respect people whose autonomy has been neglected requires efforts beyond mere legislative change.

The Peruvian reform to legal capacity did not define the extension of the support system to the sphere of health and mental health. The reform did not modify Law 26,842 [General Health Law] (1997), which establishes the general rules on informed consent. Despite being enacted only a year after the legal capacity reform, the PMHL did not provide any support mechanism and did not refer to the support for the exercise of legal capacity or the legal capacity reform. Although the same principles inspire the two legal instruments, they are not explicitly connected. Their unity of purpose is implicit, for example, in the reference to the standards of the CRPD (Art. 3.5 PMHL) and the commitment in the PMHL to 'adopt the necessary measures, including making reasonable adjustments, to eliminate the barriers that prevent the full exercise of mental health by people with disabilities, under equal conditions' (Art. 3.12). Another relevant aspect is that the PMHL makes legal representation applicable only to children and adolescents and not adults with disabilities (Art. 5.8). However, as mentioned above, there is no mention of support measures in the text of the PMHL. It was only the RPMHL, whose drafting was strongly influenced by civil society, which finally recognised the importance of support for decision-making in the context of mental health. The RPMHL makes substantive efforts to avoid substituted decision-making and provides instances of support for informed consent, advance planning, accessibility, and accommodation, including the participation of trusted persons (Vasquez, 2021). It is too early to judge the success of this ambitious reform, which committed to eliminating all coercion in mental health, especially in psychiatric emergencies. Such ambition anticipates long and arduous work that, to be successful, requires a genuine commitment between the various actors involved. Whether this unique commitment to respecting consent at any cost is successful remains to be seen.

Colombian Law 1,996 also does not explicitly mention the extension of support for decision-making to the sphere of health and mental health. The only aspects that expressly address health treatments are the regulation of advance directives (Art. 21) and certain particular cases of judicially appointed support (Art. 56). This could lead to the application of support to the field of health in general. Although it is perhaps too early to judge the Colombian case, since its regulations are still in the process of being implemented, the centrality of the sphere of mental health in the struggle for the autonomy of people with disabilities, expressed in various Constitutional Court rulings on this subject (Acevedo, 2021), raises the question of why the application of support was not expressly regulated. Although Law 1,996 explicitly repealed numerous legal provisions of Law 1,306, which previously limited autonomy and allowed involuntary treatment and interventions, it did not regulate the matter. Nor did it modify more general health legislation, such as Law 23 [Medical Ethics] (1981), Law 1,733 [Palliative

Care] (2014), and Law 1,751 [the Fundamental Right to Health] (2015). Therefore, the reform leaves the general regulation of health treatments compatible with substituted decision-making and does not expressly contemplate support for decision-making and safeguards.

What is worrying about the current situation in Colombia and Argentina, and to a lesser extent in Peru, is the uncertainty generated by the lack of specific regulation of support in health and mental health law. It is unclear to which cases support would be applied or how it would operate (Bregaglio and Constantino, 2020a). There may be interpretations that link the general regulation of support and safeguards with the regulation of health and mental health. In this task, judges may use techniques to harmonise legislation and interpretation under human rights. However, the results are uncertain because there are minimal instances of judicial review, and it is much more time-consuming than an express legislative or executive reform. Other challenges are created by the deficit in the training of judicial and medical personnel on the reform's content, operational aspects, and human rights approach to mental health more generally. This last aspect can also play an essential role in the lack of intervention of judges in implementing mental health legislation. Especially concerning the most controversial cases, those of persons who need communication support, the lack of an express regulation of those supports in mental health may be critical. The lack of unification mechanisms of the case law typical of Latin American legal systems will leave the evolution in this matter at the mercy of the discretion of a predominantly conservative judicial culture.

Several hypotheses can be put forward to explain the lack of regulation of support for health treatment. A simple explanation would be that the centrality of transforming the general regime of guardianship into one of support for decision-making made legislators lose sight of the regulation of support in different areas where a specific regulation of harmonisation was required. Besides health law, this may also be the case in criminal and public law, for example. There may also have been a belief that reform of health law required a systematic treatment that general reforms to legal capacity could not provide. However, these are only hypothetical reasonable explanations for the omission.

In an unusual direction for the region, the CLMHL established an obligation to provide support for consent in mental health treatment without having previously carried out a general reform on legal capacity. Article 4 of the law, which deals with informed consent, establishes that support will be articulated for decision-making to safeguard patients' will and preferences. Likewise, it establishes that healthcare teams will protect the person's will and preferences as a priority, using advance directives, intervention plans for psycho-emotional crises, and other protection tools. Additionally, the CLMHL states that one or more support persons may be designated for decision-making, who will assist the patient in weighing the therapeutic alternatives available to recover their mental health. Although administrative regulation of this law is still pending, the mobilisation of civil society after its enactment anticipates a commitment to the human rights approach. The creation during 2022 of a multidisciplinary board for a new rights-centred mental health strategy, where users have a place of preference, anticipates a lasting commitment, although without guaranteed success, to the paradigm of support and respect for the will and preferences.

Involuntary hospitalisation

Following the movement of people with psychiatric disabilities, CRPD's Committee has condemned the persistence of instances of involuntary hospitalisation (or commitment or internment) and other coercive interventions in the psychiatric field, indicating that such practices are contrary to the CRPD (2014, pp. 40–42; 2018, p. 30). Other United Nations (UN) human rights bodies have maintained that such practices can be respectful of human rights standards as long as they comply with the principles of necessity and proportionality and due safeguards are adopted (Human Rights Committee, 2014). This difference between UN human rights bodies is part of an ongoing debate involving opposing and irreconcilable positions regarding mental health interventions in the arena of international law but also in academia (Martin and Gurbai, 2019; Wilson, 2021, pp. 6–16). Notwithstanding this, no traces indicate the disappearance of coercive psychiatric measures such as involuntary hospitalisation from domestic legislation, not even those that claim the broadest compliance with international law standards in the field of disability.

The first thing to note about the mental health legislation of the jurisdictions analysed is that the Peruvian and Colombian laws do not regulate involuntary hospitalisation. In the case of PMHL, this is due to a deliberate omission, as the law only regulates voluntary hospitalisation and a case of hospitalisation by court order. As for support for decision-making, this omission was later corrected by the RPMHL. In the case of the COMHL, this is because involuntary hospitalisation was previously regulated in Law 1,306 (2009). However, the relevant provisions were repealed by the reform to legal capacity of 2019, leaving the general regulation on emergency hospitalisation of Law 23 (1981) as the only current regulation. In this scenario, there is still uncertainty about the applicable legal regime. For this reason, Colombian law will not be included in the following analysis.

In general terms, all three jurisdictions (Argentina, Chile, and Peru) highlight the importance of psychiatric hospitalisation and internment as an exceptional tool that should be subsidiary to other outpatient and community rehabilitation therapies which focus on people's social and family ties. It is also mentioned that hospitalisation can only have a therapeutic purpose; it must be necessary due to the absence of a less restrictive alternative (Art. 20 AMHL; Art. 13. CLMHL; Art. 27.1 PMHL) and that it cannot serve to resolve social or housing problems of people with mental health problems (Arts 15, 18 AMHL; Art. 12 CLMHL). This latter characteristic is linked to the community approach of the legislation in all three jurisdictions analysed and the commitment to deinstitutionalisation (Art. 28 AMHL; Art. 30 PMHL; Art. 26 CLMHL).

When referring to involuntary hospitalisation, the laws do so as a qualified case of hospitalisation with special requirements, in which informed consent will not be required due to the urgency of the case. Involuntary hospitalisation is regulated explicitly in the AMHL (Arts 20–25) and the CLMHL (Arts 13–17). It has been excluded from the PMHL, leaving behind a general regulation on emergencies contained in Article 40 of Law 26,842 [General Health Law] (1997), which has been used as a legal basis for the regulation of psychiatric emergencies by the RPMHL (Arts 26–28). Some differences that can be identified are: (a) the requirements for involuntary hospitalisation's orders; (b) the duration allowed by law for diagnosis, stabilisation, and treatment; (c) the judicial safeguards available; (d) the measures that may or may not be taken during involuntary hospitalisation; (e) consideration of the will and preferences of the person; and, lastly, (f) the origin of internments ordered by criminal courts as precautionary or security measures.

Requirements

Concerning the requirements for involuntary hospitalisation, Chilean and Argentine laws require a specific and imminent risk to the life or bodily integrity of the patient or third parties.

The Peruvian RPMHL makes a critical innovation in this respect by restricting the application of involuntary hospitalisation only to cases of risk to the patient and therefore excluding risks to third parties (Art. 27.2). This may be seen as a positive innovation to restrict involuntary hospitalisation, but it is too early to know whether the impact of this aspect of the law may prevent the abuse of hospitalisation at the cost of using the tools of criminal law as a substitute.

The second requirement is that a team of professional specialists must determine the risk. In the AMHL, two professionals from different disciplines must participate, one of whom must be a psychologist or psychiatrist (Art. 20.a AMHL). The CLMHL demands the involvement of two medical doctors from different specialisms who have the specific skills required, preferably a psychiatrist (Art. 13.1 CLMHL). Finally, the RPMHL simply states that hospitalisation orders must be issued by a medical doctor (Art. 27.7 RPMHL).

A third requirement is an innovation that prohibits discrimination against people with disabilities regarding determining the conditions for their hospitalisation (Art. 13 CLMHL; Art. 27.13 RPMHL).

Duration

Regarding the duration of the involuntary hospitalisation, neither Argentina nor Chile have established a time limit; instead, they have established safeguards to guarantee the exceptional nature and strict necessity of these measures. In contrast, the PMHL indicates that emergency psychiatric hospitalisations or internments may only last 12 hours, which may be extended up to a maximum of 72 hours, after which the medical team is obliged to attempt community care procedures. Only if these alternatives fail or are impossible, and the symptoms persist, will a more extended hospitalisation be considered for evaluation, diagnosis, and stabilisation that cannot be carried out on an outpatient basis.

Safeguards

Both Argentina and Chile have adopted a system of judicial and administrative safeguards to guarantee the rights of persons subject to involuntary hospitalisation. They have the objective of reviewing the intervention orders to ensure they comply with the requirements established by law.

Table 32.3 shows the safeguards system for involuntary hospitalisation in Chile and Argentina. While Argentina has a specialised review agency that can prosecute some cases, the review of hospitalisation conditions has been left to the family courts in Chile. The deadlines for reporting involuntary hospitalisation to the supervisory body are relatively short: 72 hours in Chile and 10 hours in Argentina, with the obligation to notify those voluntary hospitalisations that last more than 60 days. Both jurisdictions have a legal aid system and require that the hospitalisation be reviewed for relevance every 30 days. Finally, Argentina considers that if a hospitalisation has not been reassigned as voluntary within 90 days, a new therapeutic team should assume the management of the case.

In Peru, the RPMHL has chosen not to include a system of administrative or judicial safeguards; it only establishes that requests to repeal hospitalisation orders can be addressed to the professionals responsible for the hospitalisation and resolved using shared decision mechanisms (Art. 27.12). There are many reasons to be suspicious of this kind of regulation that waives the guarantee of the rights of mental health patients in an environment that has

Table 32.3 Safeguards for involuntary hospitalisation in Argentina and Chile

Country	Supervision body	Deadline for notification to supervision body	Legal aid	Periodic review	Other
Argentina	Administrative Revision Body (Art. 38); Court (Art. 21)	After 10 hours (Art. 21) [60 days in voluntary cases (Art. 23)]	Voluntary or estate appointed	No later than every 30 days (Art. 24)	After 90 days, a new therapeutic team designated by the judge (Art. 24)
Chile	Family Court (Art. 14)	After 72 hours (Art. 13)	Voluntary or judicially appointed	Every 30 days (Art. 14)	—

Source: Table created by the author.

historically been built on relationships of imbalance of power, not to mention abuse and neglect. The transition to a regime in which mental health decisions are made in consensual ways, respectful of the person's will and preferences, requires a more profound and probably more prolonged process that provides more guarantees of success before withdrawing the mechanisms of supervision and judicial protection from the mental health system.

Involuntary measures during hospitalisation

It has been generally claimed that during involuntary hospitalisation, therapeutic measures aimed at the patient's treatment will not generally require informed consent. However, the laws reviewed have taken precautions regarding measures that may or may not be taken using different techniques. The RPMHL establishes the strictest standard, with a ban on the application of psychoactive drugs or electroconvulsive therapy without informed consent. It also bans any restrictive measure, including the use of isolation rooms or impediments to free movement in health services premises (Art. 28). It should be noted that restraints are not mentioned.

The AMHL only prohibits isolation rooms and does not mention other restrictive therapeutic measures. Finally, the least strict standard can be found in the CLMHL, which only establishes the prohibition of irreversible procedures or treatments, such as sterilisation or psychosurgery, during involuntary hospitalisation. In addition, it is the only law that provides an express legal basis for restrictive measures for aggressive behaviour management through physical, mechanical, or pharmacological restraints (Art. 21).

Respect for will and preferences

Regarding respecting the will and preferences of the involuntarily hospitalised patient, the RPMHL states that it must be ensured that patients participate in decisions about their treatment. The AMHL states the same but qualifies that commitment with the clause 'within their possibilities', making clear the difference between patients' participation and the duty to respect will and preferences. Likewise, the CLMHL points out that healthcare teams will protect the person's will and preferences and use protection tools accordingly.

In this regard, Peru incorporates an important innovation. The RPMHL reasons on the basis that people may be able to consent to or refuse treatment during a psychiatric emergency and therefore establishes the need for extreme efforts to obtain the expression of the person's preferences, including the provision of support for decision-making. Only where the person is unable to express their consent, after real, considerable, and relevant efforts have been made to obtain it, can hospitalisation be authorised by the exceptional support with powers of representation designated by the person for this specific purpose. In case there is no designated support, the health service authority will request to a judge the exceptional designation of a support person with the power to authorise the hospitalisation. Again, this procedure shows Peruvian legislation's commitment to the will and preferences paradigm, adopting measures more likely to deliver decisions closer to the patients' will. It also contributes to safeguarding against informal decisions by the medical staff that may compromise the right of the patients.

Hospitalisation by order of a criminal court

Although not recognised by the AMHL, Article 34 of the Argentine Penal Code (1922) states that in case of 'alienation', the court may order confinement in an 'asylum', from which the patient will not be released except by judicial order once the danger of the person harming themselves or others has disappeared. This article generates an evident tension regarding the prohibition of asylums established in the AMHL and challenges the conception of mental health as a phenomenon requiring treatment that the AMHL embraces (Hegglin, 2017). Article 457 of the Chilean Criminal Procedure Code (2000), and Articles 72 to 74 of the Peruvian Criminal Code (1991) contemplate a similar standard. There is an interplay of criminal law, mental health law, and medical law regulation that has not been thoroughly studied and adapted to the standards set in the new mental health legislation. This is expressed in the fact that criminal judges continue to determine dangerousness based on what they can intuitively perceive in criminal hearings and the psychiatric records they can request. There has not been a concern about installing a risk assessment process, if this is possible, in the context of criminal justice.

However, the Peruvian mental health reform has attempted to balance risk and dangerousness with the therapeutic aims of psychiatric hospitalisation. Article 29 PMHL provides different rules on hospitalisation by court order. It is recognised that a criminal court judge can order preventive hospitalisation in a health facility to stabilise, evaluate, and diagnose the person involved. If the psychiatric evaluation identifies a mental health problem requiring hospitalisation, the judge may order hospitalisation as a security measure for a time-limited medical diagnosis. The said hospitalisation must be preceded by a hearing with the defence attorney no later than 48 hours after the evaluation. The medical service must keep the judge informed by sending information about the condition of the hospitalised person every three weeks. As can be seen, judicial hospitalisation is regulated more in line with the principles and limitations established in the PMHL. At the time of discharge, the hospital authorities must notify the judge to take the measures they deem pertinent. There is no clarity if these rules are going to replace in practice the security measures regulated in the Criminal Code (Constantino and Bregaglio, 2020).

Conclusion

This chapter has shown the extent to which the latest reforms to legal capacity carried out in Latin America are aligned with mental health law in the selected countries. The mental health laws analysed contain similar regulations regarding patients' rights and a variable emphasis on community treatments. It was possible to identify in the four jurisdictions a tendency to incorporate the standards of the CRPD in the regulation of mental health, including support for decision-making, advance directives, and in general, the protection of the patient's will and preferences at the time of treatment.

Concerning involuntary hospitalisation, contrary to what the CRPD's Committee has stated and demanded, instances of hospitalisation and emergency psychiatric treatment are maintained – without significant changes in Argentina and Chile, but with interesting advances towards eliminating coercion in Peru. The Colombian case is still developing, to the extent that the reform to legal capacity repealed the specific regulation of hospital admissions of people with disabilities.

The commitment these jurisdictions have shown concerning the adaptation of domestic legislation to the standards of the CRPD is a sign that there are regulatory alternatives to traditional approaches. This is especially so in terms of support and respect for the will and preferences of patients. These advances are unique in the world and, if successful, could provide lessons on moving towards eliminating or restricting coercive practices in psychiatry.

It must be recognised, however, that it is too early to assess these developments, especially as there is no academic work or publicly available information to draw more detailed conclusions. This could be pointed out as one of the problems of these jurisdictions. Decisions can be seen as respectful of human rights. However, the evidence of such respect is limited to regulatory change and subsequent documentation by human rights non-governmental organisations focused on regulatory compliance or the documentation of flagrant and gross violations. This affects compliance with human rights standards in the developing world, where there are few public resources to make informed decisions and produce evaluation studies of implemented policies. The problem of the lack of public information is reinforced by the absence of judicial decisions concerning matters related to mental health.

A manifest weakness can be identified in the jurisdictions studied, lacking a specialised safeguards system. None of them has specialised courts in mental health or capacity law, and the administrative agencies in charge of supervision do not have a specialised nature except for Argentina. Particularly in Peru, the regulation deliberately dispenses with judicial interventions designed to safeguard the rights of the patients. In Chile, on the other hand, the control of involuntary hospitalisation conditions is done by poorly equipped and trained family judges.

The continuation of the advances in mental health law in the region depends, first, on the evaluation and the lessons that can be drawn and, second, on the construction of a dialogue between the most important actors of the mental health system. As in the rest of the world, psychiatrists and patient organisations have not engaged in fruitful dialogue and lack a common diagnosis of the challenges posed by mental health law.

References

Acevedo, N. (2021) 'La autonomía relacional, la reforma a la capacidad legal y la toma de decisiones en salud en Colombia', in Bezerra de Menezes, J., Constantino, R. and Bariffi, F. J. (eds.) *A convenção sobre os direitos da pessoa com deficiência em aplicação na América latina e seus impactos no direito civil*, Sao Paulo: Foco, pp. 315–334.

Bahamondes, A. *et al.* (2014) 'Mental Health Legislation in Chile', *International Psychiatry* 11(4), 90–92. https://doi.org/10/gpbnkj.

Bregaglio, R. and Constantino, R. (2020a) 'El consentimiento médico informado de las personas con discapacidad intelectual y psicosocial en el Perú', *Revista Brasileira de Direito Civil* 26, 157–182.

Bregaglio, R. and Constantino, R. (2020b) 'Un modelo para armar: la regulación de la capacidad jurídica de las personas con discapacidad en el Perú a partir del Decreto Legislativo 1384', *Revista Latinoamericana en Discapacidad, Sociedad y Derechos Humanos* 4(1), 32–59.

Buitrago, J. E. T. G. (2019) 'El Consentimiento Informado En Psiquiatría: Fundamentación Operativa y Aspectos Legales En Colombia', *Drugs and Addictive Behavior (Histórico)* 4(2), 342–355. https://doi.org/10.21501/24631779.3372.

Bustamante, J. A. and Cavieres, A. (2018) 'Internación Psiquiátrica Involuntaria. Antecedentes, Reflexiones y Desafíos', *Revista Médica de Chile* 146(4), 511–517. https://doi.org/10.4067/s0034-98872018000400511.

Caldas de Almeida, J. M. and Horvitz-Lennon, M. (2010) 'Mental Health Care Reforms in Latin America: An Overview of Mental Health Care Reforms in Latin America and the Caribbean', *Psychiatric Services* 61(3), 218–221. https://doi.org/10.1176/ps.2010.61.3.218.

Committee on the Rights of Persons with Disabilities (2014) 'General Comment No 1'.

Constantino, R. (2020) 'The Flag of Imagination: Peru's New Reform on Legal Capacity for Persons with Intellectual and Psychosocial Disabilities and the Need for New Understandings in Private Law', *The Age of Human Rights Journal* 14(June), 155–180. https://doi.org/10.17561/tahrj.v14.5482.

Constantino, R. (2021) '¿Hogar, dulce hogar?: La privación de libertad de personas con discapacidad en casas particulares a partir de la sentencia Guillén Domínguez del Tribunal Constitucional peruano', *La Constitución frente a la sociedad contemporánea. Treinta años de la Maestría en Derecho Constitucional de la Pontificia Universidad Católica del Perú.* Available at: https://repositorio.pucp.edu.pe/index/handle/123456789/176300.

Constantino, R. and Bregaglio, R. (2020) 'La Complejidad Del Internamiento Involuntario En El Reglamento de La Ley de Salud Mental', *Enfoque, Derecho.Com.* Available at: https://www.enfoquederecho.com/2020/03/10/la-complejidad-del-internamiento-involuntario-en-el-reglamento-de-la-ley-de-salud-mental (Accessed 10 March 2020).

Craigie, J. et al. (2019) 'Legal Capacity, Mental Capacity and Supported Decision-Making: Report from a Panel Event', *International Journal of Law and Psychiatry* 62(January), 160–168. https://doi.org/10.1016/j.ijlp.2018.09.006.

Dhanda, A. (2007) 'Legal Capacity in the Disability Rights Convention: Stranglehold of the Past or Lodestar for the Future?', *Syracuse Journal of International Law and Commerce* 34, 429.

Flynn, E. (2019) 'The Rejection of Capacity Assessments in Favor of Respect for Will and Preferences: The Radical Promise of the UN Convention on the Rights of Persons with Disabilities', *World Psychiatry* 18(1), 50–51. https://doi.org/10.1002/wps.20605.

Flynn, E. (2021) 'Law, Language and Personhood: Disrupting Definitions of Legal Capacity', *Griffith Law Review* 30(3), 374–394. https://doi.org/10.1080/10383441.2022.2035947.

Hale, B. (2010) *Mental Health Law*, London: Sweet & Maxwell.

Hegglin, M. F. (2017) 'Las Medidas de Seguridad En El Sistema Penal Argentino: Su Contradicción Con Principios Fundamentales Del Derecho Penal y de La Convención Sobre Los Derechos de Las Personas Con Discapacidad', In Documenta-Análisis y Acción Para La Justicia Social (Ed.), *Inimputabilidad y Medidas de Seguridad a Debate: Reflexiones Desde América Latina En Torno a Los Derechos de Las Personas Con Discapacidad*, 15–52.

Human Rights Committee (2014) 'General Comment No. 35 (Article 9: Liberty and Security of Person)'.

Hurley, D. J. and Agrest, M. (2021) 'Argentina: A Mental Health System Caught in Transition', *International Journal of Mental Health* 50(2), 168–191. https://doi.org/10.1080/00207411.2020.1777375.

Isaza, F. (2021) 'La Ley 1996 de 2019: Una aproximación general a la reforma derivada del artículo 12 de la CDPD en Colombia', in Bezerra de Menezes, J., Constantino, R. and Bariffi, F. J. (eds.) *A convenção sobre os direitos da pessoa com deficiência em aplicação na América latina e seus impactos no direito civil*, Sao Paulo: Foco, pp. 295–313.

Lafferriere, J. N. and Muñiz, C. (2016) 'Los Procesos Civiles Relativos a La Capacidad: De La Ley de Salud Mental al Nuevo Código Civil y Comercial', *Revista Pensar En Derecho* 9, 141–196.

Marshall, P. (2020) 'State of the Reform of Legal Capacity in Chile', *International Journal of Mental Health and Capacity Law* 27, 58–94. https://doi.org/10.19164/ijmhcl.27.1198.

Marshall, P. (2023) 'Informed Consent and Decision Support: Legal Reforms in Latin America', in Espejo, N. and Bach, M. (eds.) *Legal Capacity, Disability and Human Rights*, London: Intersentia.

Marshall, P. et al. (2023) 'Are We Closing the Gap? Reforms to Legal Capacity in Latin America in the Light of the Convention on the Rights of Persons with Disabilities', *Vanderbilt Journal of Transnational Law* 55(5),119–179.

Martin, W. and Gurbai, S. (2019) 'Surveying the Geneva Impasse: Coercive Care and Human Rights', *International Journal of Law and Psychiatry* 64(May), 117–128. https://doi.org/10.1016/j.ijlp.2019.03.001.

Martinez-Pujalte, A. (2019) 'Legal Capacity and Supported Decision-Making: Lessons from Some Recent Legal Reforms', *Laws* 8(1), 4. https://doi.org/10.3390/laws8010004.

Moldavsky, D. et al. (2011) 'Mental Health in Argentina', *International Psychiatry* 8(3), 64–66. https://doi.org/10/gpbnkf.

Series, L. and Nilsson, A. (2018) 'Article 12 CRPD: Equal Recognition before the Law', in Bantekas, I., Stein, M. A. and Anastasiou, D. (eds.) *The UN Convention on the Rights of Persons with Disabilities: A Commentary*, Oxford, Oxford University Press, pp. 339–383.

Szmukler, G. (2019) '"Capacity" "Best Interests", "Will and Preferences" and the UN Convention on the Rights of Persons with Disabilities', *World Psychiatry* 18(1), 34–41. https://doi.org/10.1002/wps.20584.

Vasquez, A. (2021) 'The Potential of the Legal Capacity Law Reform in Peru to Transform Mental Health Provision', in Stein, M. et al. (eds.) *Mental Health, Legal Capacity, and Human Rights*, Cambridge: Cambridge University Press. https://doi.org/10.1017/9781108979016.

Wilson, K. (2021) *Mental Health Law: Abolish or Reform?* Oxford: Oxford University Press.

World Health Organization (2003) 'Mental Health, Legislation & Human Rights', Geneva. Available at: https://www.who.int/mental_health/policy/services/7_legislation%20HR_WEB_07.pdf.

33
MENTAL HEALTH POLICIES IN SPANISH AND PORTUGUESE-SPEAKING SOUTH AMERICAN COUNTRIES

Carla Aparecida Arena Ventura

Introduction

Since the early 1980s, new treatments, service delivery models, legislation, policies and technologies have dramatically reshaped the mental health service delivery system worldwide (Druss and Goldman, 2018). Despite advances, it is still necessary to invest in more resources and, at the same time, offer efficient and economic treatments, mainly in the public network (Osma et al., 2019), with special attention to social inequities and to the vulnerability experienced by people with mental disorders.

In this sense, legislation represents the legal framework upon which policies are created, and this chapter is based on the assumption that the discourse of rights will only be effective when transformed into practical health policy tools that can affect the practice of health professionals and the lives of persons with mental disorders. Therefore, it is essential to invest in the implementation of appropriate legislation and government policies, as well as in strengthening community awareness (Yu, 2018), in line with the movements of reform and reaffirmation of the rights of people with mental disorders and drug users.

In this way, the psychiatric reform movement is also the struggle for the right to exercise citizenship, for a more egalitarian society, for the horizontalization of power in arenas of conflict of interests and for the occupation of public spaces so that the voice of those who experience mental suffering becomes audible and validated (Sampaio and Bispo Júnior, 2021).

The Declaration of Caracas was a milestone in the psychiatric reform process in the region of the Americas, recommending the integration of mental health services into primary health care, transferring hospital care for people with mental disorders to community care and reaffirming the human rights of this population group. This movement unfolded in multiple ones with different results in the region, especially in Latin America. The Declaration arose from the recognition that traditional psychiatric hospitals failed to meet the complex needs of people with mental disorders and to deal with frequent violations of their human rights. This initiative to restructure psychiatric services was launched shortly after the Declaration of Caracas by the Pan American Organization and the World Health Organization. As a result, psychiatric reforms were successful in most Latin American and Caribbean countries. These countries organized community services and reduced the number and improved services in other psychiatric hospitals. The integration of mental health into primary care with a focus on health promotion and prevention has been an important component of these processes in many countries in the region (Caldas de Almeida and Horvitz-Lennon, 2010).

Psychiatric reforms are complex social processes, based on reflections about the foundations of psychiatry and related areas, such as the concepts of alienation, mental disorder, cure, treatment, medicalization, recovery and rehabilitation, among others. Therefore, these processes resignified concepts, mental health services and care strategies. From the hospitalization model, based on isolation and centered on discipline, control and surveillance, emerges a framework recognizing different identities and relationships with the territories and the existing institutions (Amarante and Torre, 2017). With respect to the juridical and political dimension, there were several possibilities of engagement, aiming at assuring the citizenship and social inclusion of persons with mental disorders. Finally, the sociocultural dimension reveals the strong process of social participation in the daily construction of policies in view of transforming the relationship of society with diversity and, in this case, with mental illnesses (Amarante and Torre, 2017).

These movements are even more relevant when one observes that the prevalence of mental disorders in the Americas is relatively high: the 12-month prevalence range varied from 7.2% in Guatemala to 29.6% in Brazil among the population of these countries (Kohn et al., 2018). The rate of severe mental disorders, however, ranged from 2.0% in Guatemala to 10.0% in Brazil. Furthermore, mental disorders and substance use disorders are responsible for 22.0% of years lived with disability in the Americas. The weighted average treatment gap in the Americas for any mental disorder was 71.2%; for severe disorders, 57.6%; and for severe to moderate disorders, 65.7%. In Latin America, the treatment gap for substance use disorders was 83.7%, compared to 69.1% in North America. With respect to children and adolescents, mental disorders are highly prevalent. According to one of the selected studies, the percentages are 16.2% in Puerto Rico, 38.3% in Chile, 39.4% in Mexico and 42.6% in the United States (Kohn et al., 2018).

The psychiatric reform movements resonated beyond the field of mental health, articulating with the ideals of the processes of democratization and social participation in the countries of the region, in the search for the transformation of the health and social protection system. In this context, it is essential to emphasize the interrelations between legislation and policies for the development of inclusive strategies for health service users, such as: supporting and encouraging the creation of user associations, creating income-generating cooperatives, developing active strategies to combat stigma and encouraging the orientation of existing services to recovery, which can be particularly difficult in developing countries due to the great socio-economic inequality that exists (Onocko-Campos, 2019).

At the political level, it is important to track the impact of new federal and state laws and ensure they are successfully implemented and upheld. On the clinical side, it is important to continue to support the widespread dissemination of effective treatments in the public and private sectors. Also, for people with mental disorders, it is relevant to ensure that they are receiving the care that meets their needs and helps them improve their physical and mental health and well-being (Druss and Goldman, 2018).

Considering the high burden of mental disorders in the Americas, especially in South American countries, and the need for legislation and policies to guarantee the rights of these people and improve their living conditions, this chapter aims to analyze the legislation and policies on mental health in South American countries that speak Spanish and Portuguese.

Method

A documentary analysis was performed. In this way, studies based on documents as primary material extract all the analysis from them, organizing and interpreting them according to the objectives of the proposed investigation (Pimentel, 2001). For this, documents related to mental health legislation and policies were collected through the WHO MiNDbank (More Inclusiveness Needed in Disability and Development) platform www.mindbank.info/collection/country. WHO MiNDbank is an online platform, created by the World Health Organization, that provides quick and easy access to international resources and national/regional policies, strategies, laws and service standards for mental health, substance abuse, disability, health general, non-communicable diseases (NCDs), human rights, development, children and youth and the elderly. Since its inception in 2014, MiNDbank has become an essential tool to support the work of policymakers, advocacy groups, academics and researchers (World Health Organization, n.d.). It is the single global point to access all comprehensive information related to mental health, substance abuse, disability, general health, human rights and development. In this research, we are using the WHO MiNDbank to refer to the countries: Argentina, Bolivia, Brazil, Chile, Colombia, Ecuador, Paraguay, Peru, Uruguay and Venezuela (World Health Organization, n.d.).

The WHO MiNDbank divides the legislation and policies into several themes, presented in a total of 451 policy documents. However, this study was based on the item "Mental Health Legislation, Regulations and Implementation Guides", in which there is no legislation referring to Venezuela and only one document about Bolivia, which did not respond to the objective of this study. Thus, 57 documents from this database were analyzed, from eight Latin-speaking countries, in the Latin-speaking region of the Americas. A search for these documents was carried out on the WHO MiNDbank from November 15 to November 30, 2021.

However, although the WHO MiNDbank platform does not contain documents related to the recognition of the rights of people with mental disorders for Bolivia, Ecuador, Paraguay and Venezuela, free searches were carried out on other platforms such as SciELO, Google Scholar and BVS, in order to locate such documents because of their fundamental importance to this study.

Results

Of the 57 documents included in the study, seven are from Argentina, 38 from Brazil, three from Chile, one from Colombia, one from Ecuador, one from Paraguay, two from Peru and four from Uruguay, as listed in Table 33.1.

The documents were analyzed and interpreted through thematic content analysis, which consists of discovering the frequency and presence of nuclei of meaning that reveal themes and significant categories related to the object under study. The thematic analysis unfolded in three stages: (a) pre-analysis, where the codes and sections of the narratives were organized and determined; (b) examination of the material, where the sentences and codes were reduced to thematic units, through the reading of the documents in relation to the objectives of the study; and (c) treatment and interpretation of the results (Minayo, 2014).

Table 33.1 Documents selected by country on the theme "Mental health legislation, regulations and implementation guides" (World Health Organization MiNDbank [More Inclusiveness Needed in Disability and Development] platform)

Code	Country	Document title	Publication date	Description
AR01	Argentina	Atención en las urgencias de salud mental. 2019/Service provision on mental health emergencies. 2019	January 1, 2019	This publication is part of the series "Recommendations for the Integrated Community-based Mental Health Network", and aims to bring suggestions and recommendations as work tools that guide the care of people who report or present mental illness (including problematic consumption of substances and/or dependencies), without any type of prejudice or discrimination in all health institutions and in the area or community scope of service of this institution. It is framed in the Convention on the Rights of Persons with Disabilities and in the National Mental Health Law No. 26.657, its normative decree No. 603/2013, understanding that mental health care should not be carried out in monovalent institutions, but in the area closest to the community of the person in need. These Recommendations include suggestions for clinical practice, as well as basic tools for health care teams in attending and responding to emergencies in mental health.
AR02	Argentina	Pautas para la organización y funcionamiento de dispositivos de salud mental. 2019	January 1, 2019	The purpose of these guidelines is to develop recommendations for the organization and operation of public, private and social security mental health facilities. The Community Care Model involves the work and creation of a community-based Integrated Mental Health Network. The guidelines must comply with Article 27 of the National Mental Health Law No. 26.657, which prohibits the creation of "new neuropsychiatric or monovalent, public or private institutions of hospitalization throughout the national territory", such as colonies, homes, therapeutic communities and psychiatric clinics. In the case of existing ones, they must adapt to the objectives and principles of the aforementioned law and to their gradual and definitive replacement by a network of community-based services.
AR03	Argentina	Salud Publica Ley 26.657: Derecho a la protección de la salud mental	November 25, 2010	National Mental Health Law: This law aims to guarantee the right to protection of the mental health of all people, and the full enjoyment of human rights of people with mental illness who are in the country, contained in international human rights instruments, the constitutional statute and observing the regulations more beneficial for the protection of these rights that can be established in the provinces and in the Autonomous City of Buenos Aires.

AR04	Argentina	Ley 7365: Ley de protección al paciente con enfermedad mental	October 18, 2002	People who suffer from mental illness enjoy the same rights in the Province as the other inhabitants of the Nation. That is, to be treated at all times with the solicitude, respect and dignity proper to one's condition of a person.
AR05	Argentina	Ley 25.421: Creación del programa de Asistencia Primaria de Salud Mental (APSM)	April 4, 2001	The Primary Care in Mental Health Program (APSM) is created, which will have the function of promoting and coordinating the actions resulting from the application of this law. The Ministry of Health is the body that inspects it, when required personally or through third parties, or when they are taxed by collective actions that include it. Based on the regulation of this law, institutions and organizations providing public and private health must have the necessary resources to provide primary mental health care to the population under their responsibility, ensuring the follow-up and continuity of actions and programs.
AR06	Argentina	Ley N° 2.440: Salud mental tratamiento y rehabilitación de las personas con sufrimiento mental	October 10, 1991	Rio Negro Province Mental Health Law
AR07	Argentina	Ley 4004: Personas con deficiencias mentales, alcohólicos crónicos y toxicómanos – Normas que regulan su internación y egreso de establecimientos asistenciales.	December 31, 1983	People with mental disabilities, chronic alcoholics and chemical dependents – norms that regulate admission and discharge from health facilities.
BR01	Brazil	Ordinance SNAS No. 189, from November 19, 1991	November 19, 1991	Changes the financing of mental health actions and services.

(*Continued*)

Table 33.1 (Continued)

Code	Country	Document title	Publication date	Description
BR02	Brazil	Ordinance SAS/MS N° 224, from January 29, 1992	January 30, 1992	Establishes norms and guidelines to regulate the functioning of all mental health services.
BR03	Brazil	Ordinance SAS No. 407, from June 30, 1992	December 30, 1992; republished for having been inaccurate, from the original, in the Official Diary of January 7, 1993; republished in Official Diary No. 43 of March 5, 1993, for having been incorrect	Creates a transitory procedure code for psychiatric hospitals that have not yet fully complied with Ordinance SNAS/MS No. 224/92.
BR04	Brazil	Ordinance SAS No. 408, from December 30, 1992	December 30, 1992; republished for having been incorrectly published in the Official Journal of the Union on January 7, 1993	It lists all psychiatric care procedure codes and regulates the registration of services.
BR05	Brazil	Ordinance SAS No. 145, from August 25, 1994	August 25, 1994; republished for having been incorrectly published in the Official Diary of August 29, 1994	It constitutes the Psychiatric Care Assessment Groups.

BR06	Brazil	Ordinance SAS No. 147, from August 25, 1994	August 25, 1994	Establishes the requirement of the psychiatric institution to expose the therapeutic project.
BR07	Brazil	Ordinance GM No. 1.077, from August 24, 1999	August 24, 1999	Provides for pharmaceutical assistance in psychiatric care.
BR08	Brazil	Ordinance GM No. 106, from February 11, 2000	February 11, 2000	Establishes the Therapeutic Residential Services.
BR09	Brazil	Ordinance GM No. 799, from July 19, 2000	July 19, 2000	Determines the evaluation of mental health care provided by the Unified Health System.
BR10	Brazil	Ordinance GM No. 175, from February 7, 2001	February 7, 2001	Defines the minimum team of outpatient services specialized in mental health that must act in the assistance and supervision of the activities of Therapeutic Residential Services.
BR11	Brazil	Act 10.216, from April 6, 2001	April 9, 2001	Provides for the protection and the rights of people with mental disorders and redirects the mental health care model.
BR12	Brazil	Ordinance GM No. 251, from January 31, 2002	January 31, 2002	Establishes guidelines and standards for hospital care in psychiatry, reclassifies psychiatric hospitals, defines and structures the gateway to psychiatric hospitalizations in the Unified Health System network.
BR13	Brazil	Ordinance GM No. 336, from February 19, 2002	February 19, 2002	Defines the rules and guidelines for the organization of services that provide mental health care.
BR14	Brazil	Ordinance SAS No. 189, from March 20, 2002	March 20, 2002; republished due to having inaccuracies in the original in Official Diary No. 56, of March 22, 2002, section 1, p. 108	Inserts new outpatient procedures in the SIA-SUS table, expanding the funding of those services.

(*Continued*)

Table 33.1 (Continued)

Code	Country	Document title	Publication date	Description
BR15	Brazil	Ordinance GM No. 626, from April 1, 2002	April 1, 2002	This ordinance legislates on the resources destined to the cost of Psychosocial Attention Services.
BR16	Brazil	Ordinance SAS No. 1.001, from December 20, 2002	December 20, 2002	Defines the classification of the Unified Health System psychiatric hospitals, with their corresponding remuneration.
BR17	Brazil	Ordinance GM No. 2.391, from December 23, 2002	December 26, 2002	Regulates the control of involuntary and voluntary psychiatric hospitalizations.
BR18	Brazil	Law No. 10.708, from July 31, 2003	July 31, 2003	Institutes psychosocial rehabilitation aid for patients with mental disorders who have been hospitalized.
BR19	Brazil	Ordinance GM No. 2.077, from October 31, 2003	October 31, 2003	This ordinance regulates Law No. 10.708, of July 31, 2003, which establishes the psychosocial rehabilitation aid provided for in the "De Volta Para Casa" Program.
BR20	Brazil	Ordinance GM No. 52, from January 20, 2004	January 20, 2004	Establishes the Annual Program for the Restructuring of Hospital Psychiatric Care in the Unified Health System – 2004.
BR21	Brazil	Ordinance GM No. 53, from January 20, 2004	January 20, 2004	Creates new procedures within the scope of the Annual Plan for the Restructuring of Hospital Psychiatric Care in the Unified Health System – 2004.
BR22	Brazil	Ordinance GM No. 358, from March 9, 2004	March 9, 2004	Establishes resources for the psychiatric care reform.
BR23	Brazil	Resolution No. 5, from May 4, 2003	May 14, 2004	Provides for the Guidelines for compliance with Security Measures, adapting them to the provision contained in Law No. 10.216 of April 6, 2001.

BR24	Brazil	Ordinance GM No. 1.935, from September 16, 2004	September 16, 2004	It allocates early financial incentives to Psychosocial Attention Centers in the implementation phase.
BR25	Brazil	Ordinance GM No. 2.068, from September 24, 2004	September 24, 2004	It allocates financial incentive for Therapeutic Residential Services.
BR26	Brazil	Ordinance GM No. 245, from February 17, 2005	February 17, 2005	It provides financial incentives for the implementation of Psychosocial Attention Centers.
BR27	Brazil	Ordinance GM No. 246, from February 17, 2005	February 17, 2005	It provides financial incentive for the implementation of Therapeutic Residential Services.
BR28	Brazil	Interministerial Ordinance No. 353, from March 7, 2005	March 7, 2005	Establishes the Working Group on Mental Health and Solidarity Economy.
BR29	Brazil	Ordinance No. 395, from July 7, 2005	July 7, 2005	Changes the remuneration of psychiatric hospitals that did not adhere to the Hospital Psychiatric Care Restructuring Program in SUS-2004.
BR30	Brazil	Ordinance No. 1.174, from July 7, 2005	July 7, 2005	Allocates emergency financial incentives to the Psychosocial Attention Centers Qualification Program.
BR31	Brazil	Ordinance GM No. 678, from March 30, 2006	March 30, 2006	Establishes the National Strategy for Assessment, Monitoring, Supervision and Technical Support for Psychosocial Attention Centers and other services of the public mental health network of the Unified Health System.
BR32	Brazil	Ordinance No. 2.759, from October 25, 2007	October 25, 2007	Establishes general guidelines for the Comprehensive Care Policy for the Mental Health of Indigenous Populations and creates the Management Committee.
BR33	Brazil	Ordinance No. 1.899, from September 11, 2008	September 11, 2008	Establishes the Working Group on Mental Health in General Hospitals.
BR34	Brazil	Ordinance No. 2.629, from October 28, 2009	October 28, 2009	Readjusts the values of procedures for mental health care in general hospitals and encourages short-term hospitalizations.

(Continued)

Table 33.1 (Continued)

Code	Country	Document title	Publication date	Description
BR35	Brazil	Joint Ordinance No. 6, from September 17, 2010	September 17, 2010	Establishes the Education through Work Program for Health/Mental Health.
BR36	Brazil	Resolution No. 448, from October 6, 2011	October 6, 2011	Resolves that governmental efforts and social forces be joined to increase the allocation of financial resources to the Psychosocial Attention Network.
BR37	Brazil	Ordinance No. 3.090, from December 23, 2011	December 23, 2011	Provides for the transfer of funding incentive resources and monthly funding for the implantation and/or implementation and operation of Therapeutic Residential Services.
BR38	Brazil	Ordinance No. 857, from August 22, 2012	August 22, 2012	Includes Type I Therapeutic Residency and Type II Therapeutic Residency in the SCNES Network Incentives Table of Psychosocial Attention Centers.
CL01	Chile	Proyecto de Ley "Del reconocimiento y protección de los derechos de las personas en la atención de salud mental" (2021)	May 11, 2021	Title I: General Provisions Article 1. This law aims to recognize and protect the fundamental rights of people with mental illness or mental or intellectual disability, especially their right to personal freedom, physical and mental integrity, health care and social and labor inclusion. The full enjoyment of these people's human rights is guaranteed within the framework of the Political Constitution of the Republic and the international human rights treaties and instruments ratified by Chile and in force. These instruments constitute fundamental rights and, therefore, it is the State's duty to respect, promote and guarantee them.
CL02	Chile	Ley 18.600 – Ley de deficientes mentales	Publication date: February 19, 1987. Last version published: April 1, 2018	Article 1. Prevention, rehabilitation and equal opportunities constitute rights of people with intellectual disabilities and duties toward the family and society in general. It is incumbent upon the State to coordinate and control the development of a mixed system of public and private participation, suitable for supporting families in fulfilling the obligations indicated in the previous paragraph. The State must also guarantee the prevention and early diagnosis of mental disability, in addition to creating, financing and maintaining subsidy systems, direct or indirect, for people with intellectual disabilities coming from families with fewer resources or for them, with the objective of making effective the rights and duties enshrined in the first paragraph.

CL03	Chile	Reglamento para la Internación de las personas con enfermedades mentales	July 14, 2000	Supreme Decree No. 570 of the Division of Sanitary Regulation and Rectory of the Ministry of Health was published on July 14, 2000 in the Official Diary of Chile. This decree approves the regulation of hospitalization of people with mental illness and the establishments that make it available.
CO01	Colombia	Ley 1616 DE 2013: por medio de la cual se expide la ley de salud mental y se dictan otras disposiciones	December 31, 2012 Official Diary No. 48.680 of January 21, 2013	The objective of this law is to guarantee the full exercise of the Right to Mental Health for the Colombian population, prioritizing childhood and adolescence through health promotion and the prevention of mental disorders.
EC01	Ecuador	Manual de atención primaria em salud mental	No date	The chapters include: – Mental health plan for pandemic influenza – Epidemiology of mental disorders – What is mental health? – Depression – Anxiety disorders – Organic brain disorders – Dissociative disorders – Hyperkinetic disorders – Drug addiction management.
PY01	Paraguay	Ley No. 836/80 de Código Sanitario – Capítulo VII: de la salud mental	December 31, 1980	Law number 836/80 of the Paraguayan Health Code offers 326 articles on health in Paraguay. More specifically, chapter No. 8, which contains six articles, focuses on mental health in Paraguay. The Paraguayan Health Code was created in December 1980.
PE01	Peru	Decreto Supremo No. 033-2015-SA: Acceso universal y equitativo a las intervenciones de promoción y protección para preservar salud mental	October 6, 2015	The adopted regulation aims to ensure that people with mental health problems have access to universal and equitable interventions for the promotion and protection of mental health. They must also have access to prevention, treatment, recovery and psychosocial rehabilitation, with an integrated vision and community approach to human rights, gender and multiculturalism at different levels of attention. This device incorporates legal services and nationwide service network. The new method of care will be made possible by the network of health services on an outpatient basis; that is, without hospitalization of people with mental health problems. For this, the mission of the medical team is the resocialization of the patient in the family and in the community.

(*Continued*)

Table 33.1 (Continued)

Code	Country	Document title	Publication date	Description
PE02	Peru	Ley No. 29889: Ley que modifica el arículo 11 de la ley 26842, Ley General de la salud, y garantiza los derechos de las personas con problemas de salud mental	June 24, 2012	Law No. 2.9889 was published on June 24, 2012 in the Official Diarr El Peruano. The objective of this law is to modify article 11 of Law 26.842, General Health Law, and to guarantee the rights of people with mental health problems.
UY01	Uruguay	Reglamentacion de la Ley 19.529 (Ley de Salud Mental), Decree No. 226/018	July 27, 2018	Its objective is to guarantee the right to protection of the mental health of inhabitants residing in the country, within the scope of the Unified National Health System.
UY02	Uruguay	Ley de Salud Mental (2017), Ley No. 19529	September 19, 2017	The objective of this law is to guarantee the right for protection of mental health of the inhabitants residing in the country, in a perspective of respect for the human rights of all people and, in particular, of users of mental health services within the scope of the Unified National Health System. Its provisions are of public order and social interest.
UY03	Uruguay	Ley No. 11.139 Patronato Del Psicópata	January 11, 1949	Act establishing a Board for Psychopaths in order to ensure that they receive the necessary support at all stages of their illness.
UY04	Uruguay	Ley No. 9.581 Psicopatas	August 24, 1936	The provisions of this Act shall apply to all patients with mental conditions, irrespective of the place where they are treated.

Thus, the documents were analyzed through thematic analysis and the nuclei that the documents had in common related to this study were identified and organized into six thematic categories: recognition of rights; community-oriented service; norms and regulations for psychiatric hospitalization; attention to the financing of mental health; benefit programs for well-being and the promotion of rights; other regulations on the care of people with mental disorders. The distribution of documents by categories is shown in Table 33.2, noting that some documents meet more than one category.

Recognition of rights

Of the documents referring to the recognition of any rights of people with mental disorders, whether rights adopted in the Convention on the Rights of Persons with Disabilities (CRPD) or not, three were found in Argentina, one in Brazil, one in Chile, one in Colombia, two in Peru and two in Uruguay, totaling ten documents.

In Argentina, the regulation for the recognition of these rights has as a precursor in the Ley 7365 – Ley de protección al paciente con enfermedad mental (Law No. 7.365 – Law for the Protection of Patients with Mental Illness), from October 18, 2002, which sought to equalize the same right to all people of the nation, so that they were treated with respect and dignity proper to their condition as a person (Argentina, 2002). In this sense, the national mental health law: Salud Pública Ley 26.657 – Derecho a la Protección de la Salud Mental (Public Health Law No. 26.657 – Right to Protection of Mental Health), from November 25, 2010, not only reaffirms Law No. 7.365 from 2002, but aims to guarantee the right to the protection of mental health for all people, as well as the full exercise of the human rights of people with mental disorders in the country, recognized in international human rights instruments and constitutional statute, and observing the most beneficial regulations for the protection of those rights (Argentina, 2010).

Subsequently, the series "Recommendations for the Integrated Community-based Mental Health Network" was published, with the objective of presenting suggestions and recommendations as working tools for the care of people with mental disorders, including the problematic consumption of substances and/or addictions. Among these recommendations is the "Atención em las Urgencias de Salud Mental" (Care in Mental Health Emergencies), from January 1, 2019, which presents suggestions for clinical practice and basic tools for health teams in attending and responding to emergencies in mental health (Argentina. Dirección Nacional de Salud Mental y Adicciones, 2019).

Law 10.216, from April 6, 2001, also known as the Psychiatric Reform Law in Brazil, provides for the protection and rights of people with mental disorders and redirects the mental health care model in the country. These rights and protection are ensured without any form of discrimination as to race, color, sex, sexual orientation, religion, political option, nationality, age, family, economic resources and the degree of severity or time of evolution of the disorder, or any other (Brasil, 2001a). It is considered a milestone for mental health in the country, as it redirects the care model, regulates special care for people with mental disorders hospitalized for long years and provides for the possibility of punishment for arbitrary or unnecessary involuntary hospitalization. Furthermore, all subsequent legislation on mental health followed the guidelines aligned with this Law 10.216/2001, mainly due to its status as a federal law.

In Chile, the Proyecto de Ley "Del reconocimiento y protección de los derechos de las personas en la atención de salud mental", (Bill "On the recognition and protection of the rights of people in mental health care"), aims to recognize and protect the fundamental

Table 33.2 Documents by categories (World Health Organization MiNDbank [More Inclusiveness Needed in Disability and Development] platform)

Country	Total documents per country	Recognition of rights	Community-oriented service	Rules and regulations for psychiatric hospitalization	Attention to mental health funding	Benefit programs for well-being and the promotion of rights	Other regulations on the care of people with mental disorders
Argentina	7	3 (AR01; AR03; AR04)	3 (AR01; AR02; AR05)	1 (AR07)			1 (AR06)
Brazil	38	1 (BR11)	9 (BR08; BR12; BR13; BR24; BR25; BR26; BR27; BR30; BR38)	4 (BR01; BR04; BR17; BR34)	7 (BR01; BR07; BR14; BR15; BR29; BR36; BR37)	5 (BR07; BR09; BR18; BR19; BR35)	14 (BR02; BR03; BR05; BR06; BR10; BR16; BR20; BR21; BR22; BR23; BR28; BR31; BR32; BR33)
Chile	3	1 (CL01)		1 (CL03)	1 (CL02)		
Colombia	1	1 (CO01)					
Ecuador	1						1 (EC01)
Paraguay	1			1 (PY01)		1 (PY01)	
Peru	2	2 (PE01; PE02)	1 (PE01)				
Uruguay	4	2 (UY01; UY02)					2 (UY03; UY04)
Total by category	57	10	13	7	8	6	18

rights of people with mental disorders or mental or intellectual disabilities, especially their right to personal freedom, physical and mental integrity, health care and social and labor inclusion. The exercise of these rights is guaranteed by the Political Constitution of the Republic and by treaties and international human rights instruments and laws ratified by Chile and in force. This project was approved and culminated in Law No. 21.331 from May 11, 2021, with the same title and provisions as the project (Chile, 2021), being identified as the most recent law, among the countries studied, that recognizes the rights of people with mental disorders.

The affirmation of the rights of people with mental disorders in Colombia dates back to the last decade, Law 1616 of 2013, with the objective of guaranteeing the full exercise of the right to mental health for the Colombian population, prioritizing childhood and adolescence through the promotion of health and prevention of mental disorders, and comprehensive and integrated care in mental health within the scope of the general social security system in health (Colombia, 2013). In Peru, Law No. 26.842 – Ley General de Salud (Law No. 26.842 – General Health Law), was amended by Law No. 29.889 from June 24, 2012 – Ley General de La Salud (Law No. 29.889 – General Health Law), in order to guarantee the rights of people with mental health problems, such as universal and equal access to interventions to promote and protect health, prevention, treatment, recovery and psychosocial rehabilitation, with an integral vision and community approach, human rights, gender and interculturality, at different levels of attention (Peru, 2012).

In this sense, the Supreme Decree No. 033-2015-SA – Acceso universal y equitativo a las intervenciones de promoción y protección para preservar salud mental (Supreme Decree No. 033-2015-SA – Universal and equitable access to promotion and protection interventions for preserve mental health), from October 6, 2015, regulates Law No. 29.889, aiming at guaranteeing the aforementioned rights, as well as incorporating legal services and a network of services throughout the country, a new method of attending the health services network on an outpatient basis (without hospitalization), being the resocialization of the patient in the family and in the community, the mission of the medical team (Peru, 2015).

Uruguay also has a recent mental health law, Ley N° 19529 – Ley de Salud Mental (Law No. 19.529 – Mental Health Law), from September 19, 2017, and regulated by Decree No. 226 from July 27, 2018. Its objective is to guarantee the right to the protection of mental health of the inhabitants residing in the country, in a perspective of respect for the human rights of all people and, in particular, of users of mental health services within the scope of the integrated national health system. In this perspective, its provisions are of public order and social interest (Uruguai, 2018, 2017).

Recognizing a right is the first step toward its exercise; therefore, the search for the existence of the right of people with mental disorders in countries that did not have documents in the WHO database was necessary. Although no laws constituting this right were found, other documents were found, which may be considered principles or vestiges for the emergence of this right.

On the subject in Bolivia, no mental health policy or specific laws were found; however, the Código de Salud de la República de Bolivia, July 18, 1978, which addresses mental health in general and succinctly in its Chapter IV "De La salud mental y deportiva", represents a first step for the recognition of rights (Bolivia, 1978; Organização Pan-Americana de Saúde (OPAS), 2012).

In Ecuador, having as a legal framework the Acuerdo Ministerial No. 01745 del 21 de octubre de 1999, the mental health policy is considered as a "state of subjective wellbeing" in favor of the development of all psychiatric potential, productive work and contribution to collective well-being (Henao et al., 2016; Ministerio de Salud del Ecuador et al., 2008).

The Sanitary Code of Paraguay, in its Chapter VII "De la Salud Mental", only states that the Ministries will develop mental hygiene programs, without mentioning any recognition of the rights of people with mental disorders (Paraguay, 1980). However, with the National Mental Health Policy 2011–2020 approved in 2010, access to specialized mental health care and deinstitutionalization was expanded. (Paraguay. Ministerio de Salud Pública y Bienestar Social. Dirección de Salud Mental, 2011).

In Venezuela, despite the existence of mental health services and attention to drug addiction (Bonvecchio et al., 2011), no specific national normative device for mental health was found.

Therefore, Bolivia and Venezuela not only do not have a law that recognizes the rights of people with mental disorders, or a mandatory national normative document for mental health, having only administrative mechanisms such as programs and plans. On the other hand, Ecuador and Paraguay, although they also do not have specific laws for the recognition of rights, do have mental health policies.

Therefore, we found documents approved before the CRPD, which are in consonance with the psychiatric reform values, as is the case of Argentina and Brazil, with legislation from 2002 and 2001, respectively. On the other hand, in Colombia, Peru, Uruguay and Chile, the documents found were approved after the CRPD. In addition, we did not find specific documents on the theme in countries such as Bolivia, Venezuela and Ecuador. In spite of these difficulties, we may affirm that, in general, countries in the region are striving to adjust their legislation and policies to assure the rights of persons with mental disorders.

Community-oriented service

Of the documents analyzed with a focus on community-based care, three were found in Argentina, nine in Brazil and one in Peru.

Law No. 25.421, of April 4, 2001, creates in Argentina the Programa de Asistencia Primaria de Salud Mental (APSM) (Primary Attention Program in Mental Health), with the function of promoting and coordinating the actions resulting from the application of this law by the Ministry of Health. All people have the right to receive primary mental health care, and institutions and organizations providing public and private health services must have, based on the regulation of this law, the necessary resources to provide primary mental health care to the population for which they are responsible, ensuring the monitoring and continuity of actions and programs (Argentina, 2001).

This way, both the Pautas para La Organización y Funcionamiento de Dispositivos de Salud Mental (Guidelines for the Organization and Functioning of Mental Health Devices) from 2019, with the aim of providing guidelines for the development of recommendations for the organization and operation of public and private health facilities as well as social security (Argentina. Ministerio de Salud Y Desarrollo Social. Secretaría de Gobierno de Salud., 2019), and the Atención en las Urgencias de Salud Mental (Care in Mental Health Emergencies) (2019) which presents suggestions and recommendations as work tools that guide the care of people who report or present mental illness, are instruments with the purpose to guarantee the rights of all people to effective and timely mental health care (Argentina. Dirección Nacional de Salud Mental y Adicciones, 2019).

In Brazil, several documents have shown relevance in terms of their importance for the development of community-based care: Ordinance GM No. 106, of February 11, 2000, which created the Therapeutic Residential Services (TRS) in Mental Health, within the scope of the Unified Health System (SUS), focuses on providing care to people with mental disorders. These services offer dwellings or houses inserted, preferably, in the community, intended to provide care for people with mental disorders, discharged from long-term psychiatric hospitalizations, who do not have social support and family ties, aiming at the social inclusion of these people (Brasil. Ministério da Saúde, 2000). The guidelines and norms for hospital care in psychiatry, introduced by Ordinance GM No. 251, of January 31, 2002, establish guidelines to consolidate the implementation of the community care model, with an extra-hospital basis, articulated in a diversified network of territorial services, aiming to promote social integration and ensure patients' rights, and organize services based on the principles of universality, hierarchy, regionalization and comprehensiveness of actions (Brasil. Ministério da Saúde, 2002a).

Still in Brazil, Ordinance GM No. 336, from February 19, 2002, establishes modalities of services for Psychosocial Care Centers (CAPS), according to size/complexity and population scope, but they fulfill the same function in public care in mental health (Brasil. Ministério da Saúde. Secretaria-Executiva. Secretaria de Atenção à Saúde, 2004; Brasil. Ministério da Saúde, 2002b). In addition, Ordinance GM No. 1.935, from September 16, 2004, provides an anticipated financial incentive for the Federal District, states and municipalities that are carrying out the process of implementing new Psychosocial Attention Centers (Brasil. Ministério da Saúde, 2004a).

Brazil was the country with most documents found in the platform MiNDbank, mainly resolutions related to financial support to the municipalities, states and the Federal District. Among them, we have: Ordinance GM No. 2.068/2004, providing financial support to the implementation of Therapeutic Residence Services (Brasil. Ministério da Saúde, 2004b) and Ordinance GM No. 245/2005 for the implementation of new Psychosocial Care Centers (Brasil. Ministério da Saúde, 2005a). Related to investments in the Psychosocial Care Centers, there is Ordinance No. 1.174/2005, for the development of a Program to Strengthen the Management of the Centers, including: regular clinical supervision (weekly), home care and community spaces, follow-up integrated with the primary health care network and participation of family and community (Brasil. Ministério da Saúde, 2005b).

The financial support to the Therapeutic Residence Services was established in Ordinance GM No. 246/2005 (Brasil. Ministério da Saúde, 2005c). However, only in 2012 did the Ordinance No. 857 define specific mechanisms for the follow-up and evaluation of these services (Brasil. Ministério da Saúde, 2012).

Although this Brazilian list of instruments on mental health is not exhaustive, they are extremely important instruments for the promotion of public mental health policies based on its guidelines, seeking improvements in the care of those who are not always able to speak for themselves.

Finally, in Peru, the Supreme Decree No. 033-2015-ASNo., from October 6, 2015, which approves the Regulation of Law No. 29.889 amending the General Health Law No. 26.842, aims to ensure that people with mental health problems have access to universal and equitable interventions for the promotion and protection of mental health, prevention, treatment, recovery and psychosocial rehabilitation, with an integrated vision and a community approach, of human rights, gender and interculturality at different levels of care. In addition, it incorporates legal services and a nationwide service network. The new method of care will be on an outpatient basis, that is, without hospitalization of people with mental health problems, with the mission of the medical team being the resocialization of the patient in the family and community (Peru, 2015).

Brazil, Argentina and Peru are the countries with most initiatives regarding the establishment of community-oriented services, following the principles of the Caracas Declaration. Brazil and Argentina offer different services linked to the community aiming to provide mental health care. Peru is also an interesting example, offering services within the primary health care network. In addition, the lack of documents and legislations from other countries about this theme is a great concern, as community-oriented services are the basis for the social inclusion and recovery of persons with mental illness.

Norms and regulations for psychiatric hospitalization

Within this category, seven citations were obtained in legislation between ordinances and laws. Of these, one was from Argentina, four were from Brazil, one was from Chile and one was from Paraguay.

The Argentine law that mentioned psychiatric hospitalization was Ley 4004, from December 31, 1983, and it refers to people with "mental disabilities", chronic alcoholics and chemical dependents, establishing norms that regulate the admission and discharge of institutions of health, emphasizing that hospitalizations of people with mental disorders will only be admitted in the following cases: (a) by court order; (b) at the request of the interested party or his legal representative; (c) by provision of the police authority in the cases and with the precautions established in the second paragraph of Article 482 of the Civil Code; (d) in case of urgency, at the request of the persons indicated in subsections 1 to 4 of Article 144 of the Civil Code (Argentina, 1983).

In Chile, the law that presents some arguments about psychiatric hospitalization is the Reglamento para la Internación de las Personas con Enfermedades Mentales from July 14, 2000, known as the supreme decree No. 570. This decree approves the regulation of hospitalization of people with mental disorders and of mental institutions and establishments that can carry out this type of hospitalization. In its Article 2, it is emphasized that the treatment to be given to people with mental disorders must be multidimensional and its components must be adapted to the different moments of the evolution of the underlying disorder and to the needs of those who experience it. Also, the treatment will be directed in order to neutralize causal factors and obtain relief or remission of symptoms or clinical signs of the underlying mental illness, to recover adaptation to the subject's usual life situation and, in some cases, to allow adequate awareness and emotional acceptance of the disturbance experienced, the eventual sequel and its significance for personal identity (Chile, 2000).

Another country that mentioned psychiatric hospitalization in its legislation was Paraguay, with Ley No. 836/80 de Código Sanitario from December 31, 1980. Article 45 establishes that the hospitalization of a person in establishments intended for the treatment of mental illness can only be accomplished after two doctors, one of them a psychiatrist, certify that the person has some mental disorder, and Article 46 recommends to avoid any type of orientation, treatment and application of psychological systems that may create or favor individual or group reactions that are harmful to mental health or that jeopardize people's emotional stability or jeopardize social coexistence (Paraguay, 1980).

Brazil, on the other hand, has several passages in its legislation on psychiatric hospitalization, many of them about funding and supervision, such as the Ordinance of the National

Social Assistance Secretariat (SNAS) No. 180, from November 19, 1991, which alters the funding of mental health actions and services (Brasil, 1991) and Ordinance SAS No. 408, from December 30, 1992, which lists all psychiatric care procedure codes and regulates the registration of services (Brasil, 1992a).

However, the ordinance that actually regulates psychiatric hospitalization is Ordinance GM No. 2.391, from December 23, 2002, which regulates the control of involuntary and voluntary psychiatric hospitalizations, determining that health establishments, whether members of SUS or not, should observe this Ordinance and Law No. 10.216/2001, proceeding with the notification of hospitalization to the Public Prosecutor's Office and to the managing bodies of SUS, for systematic follow-up. This notification is necessary because psychiatric hospitalization should only occur after all attempts to use other therapeutic possibilities and after exhausting all extra-hospital resources available in the care network. Hospitalization should be for the shortest possible time (Brasil, 2002a, 2001a).

Additionally, there is also Ordinance No. 2.629, from October 28, 2009, which readjusts the values of the procedures contained in the Table of Procedures, Medicines, Orthoses/Prostheses and Special Materials of the Unified Health System and establishes a 10% incentive in the value of Professional and Hospital Service for the procedure Treatment in Psychiatry – in a general hospital (per day) for hospitalizations that do not exceed 20 days, and that informs as the reason for leaving "acute patient discharge" (Brasil, 2009).

With the exception of Brazil, other legal documents are from several years ago and do not follow the recent guidelines for psychiatric hospitalizations as the last possible therapeutic resource. These norms are fundamental to reaffirm the human rights of persons with mental disorders, especially considering the probability of violations which occur during psychiatric hospitalizations.

Attention to the financing of mental health

Regarding the financing category, seven pieces of legislation presented this subject, with six excerpts from Brazil and one from Chile.

Right at the beginning of the psychiatric reform, Brazil already presented an ordinance with the objective of improving mental health care, the Ordinance of the National Department of Social Assistance (SNAS) No. 189, from November 19, 1991, which alters the financing of actions and services in the area of mental health (psychiatric hospitals) due to the need to improve the quality of care for people with mental disorders, diversifying therapeutic methods and techniques, aiming at comprehensive care for these people, as well as making procedures compatible with mental health actions with the proposed care model. It also concerns the Outpatient Information System of the Unified Health System (SIA/SUS), including new procedures, assistance in Psychosocial Care Nuclei/Centers, assistance in Therapeutic Workshops, home visits by a higher education professional, psycho diagnosis and enabling the construction of psychosocial care services in the country (Brasil, 1991). Ordinance GM No.No. 1.077, from August 24, 1999, provides for pharmaceutical assistance in psychiatric care, aiming to ensure the acquisition of essential mental health medicines for users of public mental health outpatient services (Brasil, 1999).

Some subsequent ordinances introduce new outpatient procedures, such as Ordinance SAS No. 189, from March 20, 2002, which included in the SIH-SUS Procedures Table the group of procedures for welcoming patients from the Psychosocial Attention Center and established rules for charging of the procedures (Brasil, 2002b). Some address financing, such as Ordinance GM No. 626, from April 1, 2002, which determines that all the resources of the Ministry of Health destined to finance the procedures contained in Ordinance SAS/MS No. 189/2002 (funding of Psychosocial Attention Services) are included in the Strategic Actions and Compensation Fund – FAEC (Brasil, 2002c, 2002b).

However, Ordinance No. 395, from July 7, 2005, determines that psychiatric hospitals that did not adhere to the Hospital Psychiatric Care Restructuring Program in SUS – 2004, by signing a Term of Commitment and Adjustment to reduce beds in the 1st stage of the Program (adjustment/rectification to modules of 40 beds), return to being remunerated according to the values defined in Ordinance No. 77/SAS, from February 1, 2002 (Brasil, 2005a). Resolution No. 448, from October 6, 2011, focuses on psychosocial attention and resolves to bring together government efforts and social forces to increase the allocation of financial resources to the Psychosocial Attention Network, to enhance the Public Policy for Reception and Attention to Problems of Mental Health (Brasil, 2011a).

Another country that cited funding in its legislation was Chile, with the Ley 18.600 – Ley de deficientes mentales, published on February 19, 1987, with its last update on April 1, 2018. The legislation mentions that the State must guarantee the prevention and early diagnosis of mental disability, in addition to creating, financing and maintaining subsidy systems, direct or indirect, for people with mental disorders coming from families with fewer resources or for them, with the objective of realizing the rights and duties enshrined in the first paragraph (Chile, 2018).

Based on the above, it is reinforced that despite a renewed focus on mental health in the last decade by WHO and development partners, financial assistance for mental health remains inadequate, with little attention, especially in country legislation. It is therefore essential to learn more about the current contributions of development to global mental health, in order to monitor future increases in resource allocation and distribution (Liese et al., 2019), considering the differences among and within countries.

Benefit programs for well-being and the promotion of rights

This category presented seven passages mentioned in the legislation of South American countries; six of these passages were included in the Brazilian legislation and one passage was in the Paraguayan legislation.

In Brazil, the first ordinance to address this issue was GM No. 1.077, from August 24, 1999, which provides for pharmaceutical assistance in psychiatric care (Brasil, 1999). The second ordinance, GM No. 799, from July 19, 2000, determines the evaluation of the care provided in mental health by the SUS (Brasil, 2000), establishing mechanisms for continued supervision of hospital and outpatient services, as well as proposing technical and alternative norms in continuity with the processes of reversal of the mental health care model in force in the country.

In relation to aid, Law No. 10.708, from July 31, 2003, institutes psychosocial rehabilitation aid for assistance, monitoring and social integration, outside the hospital unit, of patients with mental disorders who have been admitted to hospitals or psychiatric units. This aid is an integral part of a rehabilitation program called "De Volta Para Casa", under the coordination of the Ministry of Health and consists of the monthly payment of pecuniary aid, intended for patients discharged from hospitalizations (Brasil, 2003a).

Regulating this law, Ordinance GM No. 2.077, from October 31, 2003, institutes the psychosocial rehabilitation aid provided for in the "De Volta Para Casa" Program and guarantees the benefits of social reintegration to people with mental disorders submitted to long-term hospitalization, or residents of therapeutic residential service. For the purposes of Law No. 10,708, egress and possible beneficiaries are considered to be all persons with a mental disorder who are proven to have been hospitalized in a psychiatric hospital for an uninterrupted period equal to or greater than two years, which must be included in the Register of Potential Beneficiaries of the "De Volta Para Casa" Program (Brasil, 2003b, 2003a).

Another ordinance that creates a program is Joint Ordinance No. 6, from September 17, 2010, which institutes the Education Program through Work for Mental Health, aimed at promoting the creation of tutorial learning groups in the area of mental health care, alcohol and other drugs, based on education through work (Brasil, 2010). Finally, in Brazil, Ordinance No. 3.090, from December 23, 2011 (Brasil, 2011b), amends Ordinance No. 106/GM/MS, from February 11, 2000, which creates Therapeutic Residential Services (TRS), so that TRSs welcome people with long-term hospitalization, discharged from psychiatric hospitals and custodial hospitals. Long-term hospitalization is considered to be the hospitalization of two or more uninterrupted years (Brasil. Ministério da Saúde, 2000).

In this way, the function of the TRS goes beyond a response to chronification and social segregation, presenting itself as one of the care devices that addresses one of the most difficult modalities of the psychiatric reform, with regard to the contemporary difficulties of inhabiting, since these are homes for residents previously segregated in psychiatric hospitals (Roza Junior and Loffredo, 2018).

In Paraguay, Ley No. 836/80 de Código Sanitario – Capítulo VII: de la salud mental, from December 31, 1980, emphasizes in one of its chapters that the Ministry will develop mental hygiene programs to prevent, promote and recover mental, individual, family and collective well-being of people, and will establish the rules to be observed, exercising control of their faithful compliance (Paraguay, 1980).

In sum, in addition to the legislation, it is important to assure the development of policies and the allocation of budget to programs with the goal to ensure the well-being and social inclusion of persons with mental disorders.

Other regulations on the care of people with mental disorders

Other legislation that directly or indirectly regulates the care of people with mental disorders appear in 18 documents, of which 1 is an Argentine document, 14 Brazilian documents, 1 from Ecuador and 2 from Uruguay.

Briefly, in Argentina, the Ley No. 2.440, Salud Mental Tramiento y Rehabilitacion De Las Personas Com Sufrimiento Mental from October 10, 1991, emphasizes that the Province promotes a health system that, taking into account the integrity and integrality of the human being, guarantees the treatment and rehabilitation of people, of any age, with psychological suffering (Argentina, 1991).

In Brazil, Ordinance SAS/MS No. 224, from January 29, 1992, establishes norms and guidelines to regulate the functioning of all mental health services and incorporates new procedures to the Unified Health System (SUS) table (Brasil, 1992b), and in the same year, the ordinance of the Department of Health Care (SAS) No. 407, of June 30, 1992, creates a code of transitional procedure for psychiatric hospitals that have not yet fully complied with the SNAS Ordinance No. 224/92 (Brasil, 1993).

Aiming at the evaluation of services and the integral care of assisted users, the SAS Ordinance No. 145, from August 25, 1994, constitutes the Psychiatric Care Evaluation Groups (GAP) and creates a subsystem of supervision, control and evaluation of assistance in mental health

(Brasil, 1994a); Ordinance SAS No. 147, from August 25, 1994, establishes the requirement that the psychiatric institution expose the Therapeutic Project, defined as the set of objectives and actions, established and carried out by the multi-professional team, aimed at the recovery of the patient, from the moment of admission to discharge (Brasil, 1994b); Ordinance GM No. 175, from February 7, 2001, defines the minimum team of outpatient services specialized in mental health that must act in the assistance and supervision of activities (Brasil, 2001b); and SAS Ordinance No. 1.001, from December 20, 2002, defines the classification of psychiatric hospitals in the SUS, with their corresponding remuneration (Brasil, 2002d).

Aiming at the precepts of the psychiatric reform, Ordinance GM No. 52, from January 20, 2004, establishes the "Annual Program for the Restructuring of Hospital Psychiatric Care in SUS – 2004", so that the process of changing the care model is conducted in a way to ensure a safe transition, with a reduction in hospital beds, planned and accompanied by the concomitant construction of attention alternatives in the community model, deepening the strategy already established in previous measures of the SUS mental health policy (Brasil, 2004a).

Some ordinances aimed at improving care are: Ordinance GM No. 53, from January 20, 2004, which establishes new procedures in the SIH-SUS (Brasil, 2004b); Ordinance GM No. 358, from March 9, 2004, which establishes resources for psychiatric care reform (Brasil, 2004c); Resolution No. 5, from May 4, 2003, which provides for the guidelines for compliance with security measures, aiming to adapt security measures to the principles of SUS and to the guidelines provided for in Law No. 10.216/2001 (Brasil, 2004d, 2001a); Interministerial Ordinance No. 353, from March 7, 2005, which establishes the Mental Health and Solidarity Economy Working Group (Brasil, 2005b); Ordinance GM No. 678, from March 30, 2006, which establishes the National Strategy for Assessment, Monitoring, Supervision and Technical Support for CAPS and other community devices of the public mental health network (Brasil, 2006); and Ordinance No. 1.899, from September 11, 2008, which establishes the Working Group on Mental Health in General Hospitals (Brasil, 2008).

In Ecuador, the "Manual de Atención Primaria em Salud Mental" aims to develop actions to promote mental health during the flu pandemic, which reduce the vulnerability of specific groups, and can create an environment of trust that favors safety, in the health authorities, in leaders and in civil society itself, in order to sustain its ability to resolve the pandemic influenza (Equador, n.d.).

Uruguay has two laws. The Ley No. 11.139 Patronato del Psicópata from January 11, 1949, aims to create the "Council of the Psychopath", whose purposes, among others, will be to protect people with mental disorders in all phases of their care – hospital and external – and during their convalescence; to look after their well-being through reintegration into society, seeking housing and food, if they do not have them, and adequate work (Urugai, 1949); and offer the necessary help to solve their economic, professional and affective problems; and Ley No. 9.581 Psicopatas, from August 24, 1936, which, among its articles, defines that every person with a mental disorder will receive medical care and may be cared for in their private residence or in another private residence, in a private psychiatric establishment or in an official psychiatric establishment, whose technical organization will adjust to the regulations that are dictated (Uruguai, 1936).

Discussion and conclusions

People with mental disorders have the right to the enjoyment and protection of their fundamental human rights, which are encompassed in the three instruments that make up the

International Bill of Rights (the Universal Declaration of Human Rights, the International Covenant on Civil and Political Rights and the International Pact on Economic, Social and Cultural Rights) and also in the United Nations Convention on the Rights of Persons with Disabilities. These include: protection against discrimination; the right to health, including the right to access rehabilitation services; the right to dignity; the right to community integration; the right to reasonable accommodation; the right to liberty and personal security; the need for affirmative action to protect the rights of persons with disabilities, which includes persons with mental disorders; and protection from torture, cruelty and inhuman or degrading treatment (Jones, 2005; Sharan and Krishnan, 2017).

In this sense, mental health legislation aims to protect the basic human and civil rights of people with mental disorders, in addition to providing for treatments, human resources, professional training and service structure. With this, governments must assume responsibility for the activities necessary to improve mental health services and care, which leads to the elaboration of policies and programs, in addition to the legislation itself, on mental health. In general, the mental health policy promoted by the government or Ministry of Health aims to improve the mental health of its people and may include issues such as defending mental health goals, promoting mental well-being, prevention of mental disorders, treatments and rehabilitation, among others (Saxena et al., 2007; Sharan and Krishnan, 2017).

Given the above, facing the old and new challenges that will come requires effective policy responses. In this new century, the South American region needs to adopt an ambitious reform agenda focused on expanding access to ongoing mental health services, including promotion, prevention and rehabilitation, with special emphasis on the most vulnerable populations. Another important target of reform efforts is improving the quality of mental health care. Demographic trends suggest that the region needs to start planning for the complex mental health needs associated with an aging population (Caldas de Almeida and Horvitz-Lennon, 2010).

In relation to the Latin American countries examined in this chapter, the number of psychiatric beds in custodial hospitals is decreasing; there was a modest increase in psychiatric units in general hospitals; and mental health care is slowly becoming an integral component of primary health care. However, the overall picture is mixed: in most countries few community services are available, particularly for the young and the elderly, and the capacity to monitor and evaluate services and programs remains insufficient (Razzouk et al., 2012).

It is also worth mentioning that no mental health system can function with insufficient beds for acute hospitalizations. Another problem is represented by the shortage of human resources, mainly psychiatrists and specialized nurses, which leads to an overload of work for mental health professionals, representing in some countries a powerful factor for professionals to leave work (Razzouk et al., 2012).

Despite the difficulties faced in Brazil to establish its psychiatric reform after many complaints of violations, the country is going through the "psychiatry of deinstitutionalization", which aims to achieve a transformation in the field of knowledge, professional, educational and institutional practices of mental health. These transformations are in line with the paradigmatic transition and have a glimpse at the construction of an "emerging paradigm", as they distance themselves from the classic paradigm, inaugurating, both in practice and in discourse, creative and innovative contexts about the psychiatric suffering of the subjects. Psychosocial care can be seen as "prudent knowledge", capable of creating spaces for the inclusion of people with mental disorders in society (Machado and Colvero, 2003).

In this way, we see that the consolidation of health care models takes place in complementary areas: professional practices (new clinical technologies, training process, etc.), institutional (creation of new services, management practices, etc.) and systemic (legal framework, governance, financing and evaluation and control methods). The relationship between them is plastic. Organizational changes at the systemic level influence the daily routine of the services, at the same time that the reality of the units imposes changes in the hegemonic model, either from the consensus of the actors involved or the ascendancy of interest groups in the political decision-making process (Trapé and Campos, 2017).

To improve this network, Brazil has some programs and benefits, such as Social Security disability benefit programs, which constitute an essential safety net for individuals unable to work and earn a living due to their disability. Ideally, such programs seek to meet those who need it most, without discouraging those who can work from leaving the labor market or from looking for work. Striking a balance between meeting needs, stimulating work and containing public spending is a source of underlying tension that typifies these safety net programs (Bilder and Mechanic, 2003).

In relation to psychiatric hospitalizations, we see that Brazil has a well-defined legislation on the subject, and this is a milestone in the face of the Brazilian psychiatric reform, since, with regard to psychiatric hospitalizations, the law defines its modalities, as well as its justifications: (1) voluntary hospitalization: one that takes place with the consent of the user; (2) involuntary hospitalization: one that takes place without the user's consent and at the request of a third party; and (3) compulsory hospitalization: the one determined by the Justice. Therefore, any patient who is in a psychiatric ward falls into one of these categories: apart from those legally determined (compulsory) cases in which the patient's will does not interfere, hospitalization is only voluntary if the patient declares in writing to accept it; all other cases are involuntary (Barros and Serafim, 2009).

Decree 1384, from September 2018, more recently regulates the legal capacity of persons with disabilities in Peru, establishing that all persons over 18 years of age have full capacity to exercise their legal capacity, in all aspects of life (Menezes et al., 2021).

In sum, this chapter brings important data on the recognition of the rights of persons with mental disorders in South American countries, focusing on the legislation and policies regarding community-oriented services, psychiatric hospitalizations, the financing of the system and the existence of different programs for the promotion of rights and the care for people with mental disorders. The analysis of these data shows important movements to assure the rights of persons with mental disorders as well as several challenges that are still experienced by the analyzed countries, which require innovative approaches for the implementation of collaborative practices and effective legislation based on human rights principles in the region.

Finally, it is important to emphasize that this chapter was based on an analysis of documents found at the platform WHO MiNDbank, which is a very powerful resource, compiling legislation on mental health from all over the world. However, we cannot assure that this resource is exhaustive, including the most updated legislation from the studied Latin American countries. In this sense, it is relevant to promote further research to comprehend the relationship between the legislation and the actual exercise of rights of persons with mental disorders in the region.

References

Amarante, P., Torre, E. H. G., 2017. Loucura e diversidade cultural: inovação e ruptura nas experiências de arte e cultura da Reforma Psiquiátrica e do campo da Saúde Mental no Brasil. *Interface - Comunicação Saúde Educação* 21(63), 763–774. https://doi.org/10.1590/1807-57622016.0881.

Argentina, 2019a. Dirección Nacional de Salud Mental y Adicciones. Atención en las Urgencias de Salud Mental. 2019.

Argentina, 2019b. Ministerio de Salud Y Desarrollo Social. Secretaría de Gobierno de Salud. Pautas para la Organización y Funcionamiento de Dispositivos de Salud Mental. Aprobadas por: ANEXO I de RESOL-2019-715-APN-SGS#MSYDS.

Argentina, 2010. Ley 26.657. Ley Nacional de Salud Mental. Argentina.

Argentina, 2002. Ley 7365: Ley de protección al paciente con enfermedad mental. Argentina.

Argentina, 2001. Ley 25.421: Creacion del Programa de Asistencia Primaria de Salud Mental (APSM). Argentina.

Argentina, 1991. Ley N° 2.440, Salud Mental Tratamiento y Rehabilitacion De Las Personas Con Sufrimiento Mental.

Argentina, 1983. Ley 4004: Personas con deficiencias mentales, alcohólicos crónicos y toxicómanos -- Normas que regulan su internación y egreso de establecimientos asistenciales. Argentina.

Barros, D. M. de, Serafim, A. de P., 2009. Parâmetros legais para a internação involuntária no Brasil. *Archives of Clinical Psychiatry (São Paulo)* 36(4), 175–177. https://doi.org/10.1590/S0101-60832009000400008.

Bilder, S., Mechanic, D., 2003. Navigating the disability process: Persons with mental disorders applying for and receiving disability benefits. *Milbank Quarterly* 81(1), 75–106. https://doi.org/10.1111/1468-0009.00039.

Bolivia, 1978. Bolivia: Código de salud de la República de Bolivia, 18 de julio de 1978.

Bonvecchio, A., Becerril-Montekio, V., Carriedo-Lutzenkirchen, Á., Landaeta-Jiménez, M., 2011. Sistema de salud de Venezuela. *Salud Publica de México* 53, s275–s286. https://doi.org/10.1590/S0036-36342011000800022.

Brasil. Ministério da Saúde. *Secretaria-Executiva. Secretaria de Atenção à Saúde*, 2004. Legislação em saúde mental: 1990–2004, 5 ed., amp. ed. Brasília.

Brasil. Ministério da Saúde, 2012. Portaria n° 857, de 22 de agosto de 2012. Brasil.

Brasil. Ministério da Saúde, 2005a. Portaria/GM n° 245, de 17 de fevereiro de 2005. Destina incentivo financeiro para implantação de Centros de Atenção Psicossocial e dá outras providências. Brasil.

Brasil. Ministério da Saúde, 2005b. Portaria/GM n° 1174, de 7 de julho de 2005. Destina incentivo financeiro emergencial para o Programa de Qualificação dos Centros de Atenção Psicossocial - CAPS e dá outras providências. Brasil.

Brasil. Ministério da Saúde, 2005c. Portaria/GM n° 246, de 17 de fevereiro de 2005. Destina incentivo financeiro para implantação de Serviços Residenciais Terapêuticos e dá outras providências. Brasil.

Brasil. Ministério da Saúde, 2004a. Portaria/GM n° 1935, de 16 de setembro de 2004. Destina incentivo financeiro antecipado para Centros de Atenção Psicossocial em fase de implantação, e dá outras providências. Brasil.

Brasil. Ministério da Saúde, 2004b. Portaria/GM n° 2.068, de 24 de setembro de 2004. Destina incentivo financeiro para os Serviços Residenciais Terapêuticos e dá outras providências. Brasil.

Brasil. Ministério da Saúde, 2002a. Portaria/GM n° 251, de 31 de janeiro de 2002. Brasil.

Brasil. Ministério da Saúde, 2002b. Portaria/GM n° 336, de 19 de fevereiro de 2002. Brasil.

Brasil. Ministério da Saúde, 2000. Portaria/GM n° 106, de 11 de fevereiro de 2000. Institui os Serviços Residenciais Terapêuticos. Brasil.

Brasil, 2011a. Resolução n° 448, de 6 de outubro de 2011 (Resolution 448/2011). Brasil.

Brasil, 2011b. Portaria n° 3.090, de 23 de dezembro de 2011 (Ordinance 3.090/2011). Brasil.

Brasil, 2010. Portaria Conjunta n° 6, de 17 de setembro de 2010 (Joint Ordenance 6/2010). Brasil.

Brasil, 2009. Portaria n° 2.629, de 28 de outubro de 2009 (Ordinance 2.629/2009). Brasil.

Brasil, 2008. Portaria n° 1.899, de 11 de setembro de 2008 (Ordinance 1.899/2008).

Brasil, 2006. Portaria GM n° 678, de 30 de março de 2006 (Ordinance GM 678/2006).

Brasil, 2005a. Portaria n° 395, de 7 de julho de 2005 (Ordinance 395/2005). Brasil.

Brasil, 2005b. Portaria Interministerial nº 353, de 7 de março de 2005 (Interministerial Ordinance 353/2005).
Brasil, 2004a. Portaria GM nº 52, de 20 de janeiro de 2004 (Ordinance GM 52/2004).
Brasil, 2004b. Portaria GM nº 53, de 20 de janeiro de 2004 (Ordinance GM 53/2004).
Brasil, 2004c. Portaria GM nº 358, de 9 de março de 2004 (Ordinance GM 358/2004).
Brasil, 2004d. Resolução nº 5, de 4 de maio de 2003 (Resolution 5/2004).
Brasil, 2003a. Lei nº 10.708, de 31 de julho de 2003 (Law 10.708/2003). Brasil.
Brasil, 2003b. Portaria GM nº 2.077, de 31 de outubro de 2003 (Ordinance GM 2.077/2003). Brasil.
Brasil, 2002a. Portaria GM nº 2.391, de 23 de dezembro de 2002 (Ordinance GM 2.391/2002). Brasil.
Brasil, 2002b. Portaria SAS nº 189, de 20 de março de 2002 (Ordinance SAS 189/2002). Brasil.
Brasil, 2002c. Portaria GM nº 626, de 1º de abril de 2002 (Ordinance GM 626/2002). Brasil.
Brasil, 2002d. Portaria SAS nº 1.001, de 20 de dezembro de 2002 (Ordinance SAS 1.001/2002).
Brasil, 2001a. Lei nº 10.216 - Dispõe sobre a proteção e os direitos das pessoas portadoras de transtornos mentais e redireciona o modelo assistencial em saúde mental. Brasil.
Brasil, 2001b. Portaria GM nº 175, de 7 de fevereiro de 2001 (Ordinance GM 175/2001).
Brasil, 2000. Portaria GM nº 799, de 19 de julho de 2000 (Ordinance GM 799/2000). Brasil.
Brasil, 1999. Portaria GM nº 1.077, de 24 de agosto de 1999 (Ordinance GM 1.077/2000). Brasil.
Brasil, 1994a. Portaria SAS nº 145, de 25 de agosto de 1994 (Ordinance SAS 145/2002).
Brasil, 1994b. Portaria SAS nº 147, de 25 de agosto de 1994 (Ordinance SAS 147/1994).
Brasil, 1993. Portaria SAS nº 407, de 30 de junho de 1992 (Ordinance SAS 407/1992).
Brasil, 1992a. Portaria SAS nº 408, de 30 de dezembro de 1992 (Ordinance SAS 408/1992). Brasil.
Brasil, 1992b. Portaria SAS/MS n° 224, de 29 de janeiro de 1992 (Ordinance SAS 224/1992).
Brasil, 1991. Portaria SNAS nº 189, de 19 de novembro de 1991 (Ordinance SNAS 189/1991). Brasil.
Caldas de Almeida, J. M., Horvitz-Lennon, M., 2010. Mental health care reforms in Latin America: An overview of mental health care reforms in Latin America and the Caribbean. *Psychiatric Services* 61(3), 218–221. https://doi.org/10.1176/ps.2010.61.3.218.
Chile, 2021. Ley N. 21331, 11 MAY-2021, Del reconocimiento y protección de los derechos de las personas en la atención de salud mental. [WWW Document]. Minist. Salud. URL https://www.bcn.cl/leychile/navegar/imprimir?idNorma=1159383&idVersion=2021-05-11 (accessed 3.30.22).
Chile, 2018. Ley 18.600 - Ley de deficientes mentales. Chile.
Chile, 2000. Reglamento para la Internacion de las Personas con Enfermedades Mentales. Chile.
Colombia, 2013. Ley 1616 de 2013, por medio de la cual se expide la ley de Salud Mental y se dictan otras disposiciones. Colombia.
Druss, B. G., Goldman, H. H., 2018. Integrating health and mental health services: A past and future history. *American Journal of Psychiatry* 175(12), 1199–1204. https://doi.org/10.1176/appi.ajp.2018.18020169.
Equador, n.d. Manual de Atencion Primaria en Salud Mental [WWW Document]. https://aplicaciones.msp.gob.ec/salud/archivosdigitales/documentosDirecciones/dnn/archivos/ManualatencionPrimariaEnSaludMental.pdf (accessed 4.7.22).
Henao, S., Quintero, S., Echeverri, J., Hernández, J., Rivera, E., López, S., 2016. Políticas públicas vigentes de salud mental en Suramérica: un estado del arte. *Revista Facultad Nacional de Salud Pública* 34(2), 184–192. https://doi.org/10.17533/UDEA.RFNSP.V34N2A07.
Jones, M., 2005. Can international law improve mental health? Some thoughts on the proposed convention on the rights of people with disabilities. *International Journal of Law and Psychiatry* 28(2), 183–205. https://doi.org/10.1016/J.IJLP.2005.03.003.
Kohn, R., Ali, A. A., Puac-Polanco, V., Figueroa, C., López-Soto, V., Morgan, K., Saldivia, S., Vicente, B., 2018. Mental health in the Americas: An overview of the treatment gap. *Revista Panamericana de Salud Pública* 42. https://doi.org/10.26633/RPSP.2018.165.
Liese, B. H., Gribble, R. S. F., Wickremsinhe, M. N., 2019. International funding for mental health: A review of the last decade. *International Health* 11(5), 361–369. https://doi.org/10.1093/inthealth/ihz040.
Machado, A. L., Colvero, L. de A., 2003. Unidades de internação psiquiátrica em hospital geral: Espaços de cuidados e a atuação da equipe de enfermagem. *Revista Latino-Americano de Enfermagem* 11(5), 672–677. https://doi.org/10.1590/S0104-11692003000500016.

Menezes, J. B. de, Pimentel, A. B. L., Lins, A. P. de C. e, 2021. A capacidade jurídica da pessoa com deficiência após a Convenção sobre os Direitos das Pessoas com Deficiência: análise das soluções propostas no Brasil, em Portugal e no Peru. *Revista Direito e Práxis* 12(1), 296–322. https://doi.org/10.1590/2179-8966/2020/43240.

Minayo, M. C. de S., 2014. *O desafio do conhecimento: Pesquisa qualitativa em saúde*, 14ª. ed. São Paulo, SP: Hucitec.

Ministerio de Salud del Ecuador, Organización Panamericana de la Salud (OPS/OMS), Departamento de Salud Mental y Abuso de Sustancias (MSD) de la OMS, 2008. IESM-OMS Informe sobre el Sistema de Salud Mental en el Ecuador. Quito.

Onocko-Campos, R.T., 2019. Saúde mental no Brasil: Avanços, retrocessos e desafios. *Cadernos de Saude Publica* 35(11). https://doi.org/10.1590/0102-311x00156119.

Organização Pan-Americana de Saúde (OPAS), 2012. *Saúde nas Américas: Panorama regional e perfis de países*. Washington, DC.

Osma, J., Suso-Ribera, C., Peris-Baquero, Ó., Gil-Lacruz, M., Pérez-Ayerra, L., Ferreres-Galan, V., Torres-Alfosea, M.Á., López-Escriche, M., Domínguez, O., 2019. What format of treatment do patients with emotional disorders prefer and why? Implications for public mental health settings and policies. *PLOS ONE* 14(6), e0218117. https://doi.org/10.1371/journal.pone.0218117.

Paraguay, 2011. Ministerio de Salud Pública y Bienestar Social. Dirección de Salud Mental. Política Nacional de Salud Mental 2011–2020.

Paraguay, 1980. Ley N° 836/80 de Código Sanitario. Congreso Nacional.

Peru, 2015. Decreto Supremo N° 033-2015-SA: Acceso universal y equitativo a las intervenciones de promoción y protección para preservar salud mental. Peru.

Peru, 2012. Ley N° 29889 - Ley que modifica el artículo 11 de la ley 26842, Ley General de la Salud, y garantiza los derechos de las personas con problemas de salud mental. Peru.

Pimentel, A., 2001. O método da análise documental: Seu uso numa pesquisa historiográfica. *Cadernos de Pesquisas* 114, 179–195.

Razzouk, D., Gregório, G., Antunes, R., Mari, J. D. J., 2012. Lessons learned in developing community mental health care in Latin American and Caribbean countries. *World Psychiatry* 11(3), 191–195. https://doi.org/10.1002/j.2051-5545.2012.tb00130.

Roza Junior, J. A., Loffredo, A. M., 2018. Residências Terapêuticas e a cidade: Enfrentamentos de normas sociais vigentes. *Saúde em Debate* 42(116), 287–295. https://doi.org/10.1590/0103-1104201811623.

Sampaio, M. L., Bispo Júnior, J. P., 2021. Entre o enclausuramento e a desinstitucionalização: A trajetória da saúde mental no Brasil. *Trabalho, Educação e Saúde* 19. https://doi.org/10.1590/1981-7746-sol00313.

Saxena, S., Thornicroft, G., Knapp, M., Whiteford, H., 2007. Resources for mental health: Scarcity, inequity, and inefficiency. *Lancet* 370(9590), 878–889. https://doi.org/10.1016/S0140-6736(07)61239-2.

Sharan, P., Krishnan, V., 2017. Principles: Mental health resources and services. *International Encyclopedia of Public Health*, 15–21. https://doi.org/10.1016/B978-0-12-803678-5.00287-3.

Trapé, T.L., Campos, R.O., 2017. The mental health care model in Brazil: Analyses of the funding, governance processes, and mechanisms of assessment. *Revista de Saude Publica* 51. https://doi.org/10.1590/s1518-8787.2017051006059.

Urugai, 1949. Ley N° 11.139 Patronato del Psicópata.

Uruguai, 2018. Reglamentacion de la Ley 19.529 (LEY DE SALUD MENTAL). Decreto N° 226/018. Uruguai.

Uruguai, 2017. Ley N° 19529, Ley de Salud Mental (2017). Uruguai.

Uruguai, 1936. Ley N° 9.581 Psicopatas.

World Health Organization, n.d. WHO MiNDbank: More inclusiveness needed in disability and development [WWW Document]. World Heal. Organ. http://www.mindbank.info (accessed 6.27.22).

Yu, S., 2018. Uncovering the hidden impacts of inequality on mental health: A global study. *Translational Psychiatry* 8(1), 98. https://doi.org/10.1038/s41398-018-0148-0.

PART 7
Future directions

34
INTERDISCIPLINARY COLLABORATION IN THE MENTAL HEALTH SECTOR

The role of the law

Bernadette McSherry[1]

Introduction

Thirty-five years ago, Clive Unsworth (1987, p. 5) pointed out that "law actually constitutes the mental health system, in the sense that it authoritatively constructs, empowers, and regulates relationships between the agents who perform mental health functions". Recent law reform endeavours relating to compulsory mental health treatment have emphasised the importance of human rights in regulating relationships between mental health practitioners and their clients (McSherry and Weller, 2010). However, 'mental health law' may sometimes be viewed as synonymous with regulating compulsory detention and treatment and the lived experience of such treatment may be far from what human rights principles require.

This chapter explores a different view of the role of the law in shaping relationships in the mental health sector. It argues that while interdisciplinary collaboration in both research and clinical practice is not a new concept, the law can serve a useful role in supporting and developing its use. It provides examples of two legal schemes in the state of Victoria, Australia, the purpose of which is to support collaboration across multiple disciplines and services for the benefit of mental health consumers.

Defining interdisciplinary collaboration in the mental health sector

Michael Farrell and colleagues (2001, p. 281) have defined an interdisciplinary healthcare team as "a group of colleagues from two or more disciplines who co-ordinate their expertise in providing care to patients". This emphasis on coordination of expertise distinguishes such a team from a large multidisciplinary "team of professionals working together for the benefit

---

1 This chapter is written in the author's personal capacity and does not represent any deliberations pertaining to or the views of the other Commissioners or staff at the Royal Commission into Victoria's Mental Health System. The author would like to thank Andrew Simon-Butler for his editorial assistance.

of the patient/service user but retaining their professional autonomy" (McLean, 2007, p. 323).

In her book on the topic, Di Bailey (2012, p. 5) refers to the "'betweenness' and interaction that delineates collaboration in contemporary mental health care from the fragmented joint working seen in the past". Interdisciplinary collaboration is thus seen as ensuring members of the group, including mental health consumers and their families, come up with new ways of addressing care and treatment needs.

Similarly, interdisciplinary collaboration in research looks beyond disciplinary boundaries to integrate knowledge and methods from different disciplines. Felicity Callard and Des Fitzgerald (2015, p. 4) have referred to 'interdisciplinarity' as "a term that everyone invokes and none understands". Indeed, there are many variations as to what interdisciplinary research means in the literature on the topic. Thomas Cech and Gerald Rubin (2004, p. 1167) have defined such research as a "collaboration of [researchers] with largely nonoverlapping training and core expertise to solve a problem that lies outside the grasp of the individual [researcher]". In comparison, multidisciplinary research involves people from different disciplines working together while drawing on their own disciplinary knowledge (Cech and Rubin, 2004, p. 1166).

There are other terms that appear in the literature which may complicate what sort of collaboration is envisaged. 'Cross-disciplinary' research can refer to researchers exploring an area in one discipline from the perspective of another, while the term 'transdisciplinary' is sometimes used instead of 'interdisciplinary' to describe when researchers from different disciplines collaborate to create new conceptual, methodological and translational approaches that integrate and move beyond discipline-specific approaches to address a common problem. Other terms used in the literature include 'transversality' (Guattari, 2015) and 'post-disciplinarity' (Nystrom, 2007). Marilyn Stember (1991) argues that many researchers believe that they work in an interdisciplinary fashion, while in fact it is more common to work in a multidisciplinary way.

Whatever definitions are used, collaboration in general raises many issues relating to traditional disciplinary perspectives and deeply ingrained differences in how to approach issues to be resolved. In terms of research, there may be differences as to how it is viewed and conducted as well as in theoretical constructs and research methods employed. Lauren Rickards (2014, pp. 38–39) refers to interdisciplinary research as being interpreted in different ways. It can be viewed as encompassing both 'new knowledge' such as through integrating expertise to create new fields of knowledge and 'new perspectives' such as through providing new viewpoints into traditional avenues of learning and offering multiple rather than single solutions to problems.

Some of the barriers to interdisciplinary collaboration are explored below. First, however, it is worth outlining the importance of such collaboration in achieving positive mental health outcomes.

Advantages of interdisciplinary collaboration

Mental health challenges do not lend themselves to being addressed well by any single discipline or social sector. Research suggests that there are links between a range of social determinants and mental health, including positive social determinants such as education, housing and employment, and negative social determinants such as social inequality, discrimination, violence, childhood trauma and abuse, minority ethnicity and female gender (Patel et al., 2010; Wildeman, 2013).

Interdisciplinary collaboration can thus assist in supporting conceptual and practical ways of improving mental health. It is linked with a 'biopsychosocial' model of health care, in that it may be viewed as going beyond a 'biomedical' model in focusing on "a comprehensive integrative, flexible approach" (Thompson Klein, 1990, p. 140). By adapting responses to individual and community-based needs there can be an increased focus on several determinants of mental health rather than simply relying on pharmacological treatments. Interdisciplinary collaboration can also increase shared and supported decision-making, hence avoiding rigid hierarchical divisions between disciplines. When mental health consumers are engaged as active participants in mental health services, reported benefits include improvements in therapeutic relationships and the fostering of supportive organisational cultures, as well as their roles being associated with significant reductions in hospital stays among individuals they support (Trachtenberg, Parsonage, Shepherd and Boardman, 2013).

In terms of research, there is growing support for interdisciplinary collaboration as a means to solving complex global problems. Robert Frodeman (2010, p. xxxii), in advocating for 'interdisciplinarity', goes so far as to berate disciplinary knowledge as abdicating the aim of achieving "the perennial goal of living the good life". He writes (2010, pp. xxxii–xxxiii):

> By focusing on standards of excellence internal to a discipline academics have been able to avoid larger responsibilities of how knowledge contributes to the creation of a good and just society.

This position exulting interdisciplinarity may be seen as a counterbalance to what Catherine Lyall (2019, p. 117) refers to as "the prevailing ethos within research-intensive universities [of] discipline excellence first, then interdisciplinary collaboration". She argues that both should be equally encouraged rather than the latter being seen as secondary.

Andrea McCloughen and colleagues (2011, p. 47) refer to collaboration in the mental health sector as signifying a shift "away from traditional paternalistic and authoritative ways of illness treatment towards more mutually respectful systems of person-centred care that consider the knowledge and expertise held by both partners within a relationship". Collaboration between mental health consumers, practitioners and academics challenges traditional notions of expertise as residing within what have been referred to as the 'psy professions' (Rose, 2019, p. 151). Christopher van Veen and colleagues (2019, p. 70) have pointed out that traditionally there has been "an epistemological hierarchy of knowledge producers" in the mental health sector with university-trained researchers sitting at the apex. Interdisciplinary collaboration with mental health consumers as equal participants challenges dominant constructions of knowledge while providing opportunities to explore new ways of improving their lives.

Nikolas Rose (2019) has traced the rise of the mental health 'experts by experience' movement in the United Kingdom and United States from the 1970s onwards and how disability rights activist James Charlton's (1998) slogan 'nothing about us without us' became a platform for activists in the mental health sector. The central tenet of full and active participation of consumers in decision-making about their own mental health has provided the impetus for employing consumer-workers and consumer academics (Daya, Hamilton and Roper, 2020). At the same time, many mental health practitioners, including psychiatrists such as Bracken and colleagues (2012), have been advocating for collaboration with the mental health consumer movement. As Bracken and colleagues (2012, p. 432) have stated, there is a need "to reframe experiences of mental illness, distress and alienation by turning them into human, rather than technical, challenges". Interdisciplinary collaboration that is led by or otherwise fully engages mental health consumers as equal partners can assist with addressing those human challenges.

Despite increasing advocacy and support for interdisciplinary collaboration in both research and practice, there are, of course, several challenges to its feasibility that are outlined in the next section.

Challenges to interdisciplinary collaboration

As mentioned above, there may be deeply ingrained disciplinary differences that must be overcome for collaboration to work. There may also be organisational challenges such as where the culture of a particular service does not support interdisciplinary collaboration or time pressures are such that it becomes easier to simply 'stick' with traditional disciplinary approaches (Rickards, 2014; Lyall, 2019). In addition, advisory and/or peer networks are usually discipline-based. Jennifer Terpstra and colleagues (2010, p. 509) have pointed out that moving to an interdisciplinary research and practice model is difficult "when the infrastructure, culture, practice, and policies are deeply rooted in the traditional single-disciplinary approach".

Perhaps the most difficult challenges, however, are interpersonal ones. Julie Thompson Klein (1990, p. 141) states that "[g]ood interdisciplinary care depends on good teamwork". As with any team-based endeavours, there may be challenging group dynamics because of:

- too many inexperienced or uninterested team members;
- a lack of trust among certain team members;
- unequal power distributions; or
- an inappropriate mix of disciplines.

(Rickards, 2014)

In the mental health sector, the involvement of consumer workers in planning, delivery and evaluation of services has increased (Daya, Hamilton and Roper, 2020), but their full and active participation in interdisciplinary collaboration is still in its infancy. This is perhaps because consumer workers are not perceived to be 'professionals' in the same way that psychiatrists, psychologists and mental health nurses are considered so. As Vrinda Edan and colleagues point out (2021, p. 3276), "[c]onsumer-work is an atypical occupation: unlike the worker who may be employed for their IT skills but also has a mental illness, consumer-workers are employed because they have a diagnosis". They may thus be viewed as only being able to proffer personal perspectives, rather than representing a 'discipline' which is generally considered a branch of knowledge studied in higher education.

This view of consumer workers not being 'professionals' is however being challenged. 'Mad Studies' is offered in some universities in the United Kingdom and Canada and forms part of an emergent academic discipline led by mental health consumers (Faulkner, 2017). There is also a focus on consumer work being seen as a discipline in its own right (Bennetts, Cross and Bloomer, 2011; Byrne, Happell and Reid-Searl, 2017).

Indigo Daya and colleagues (2020) have set out a model of diverse consumer views relating to treatment and care which can help underpin interdisciplinary collaboration. Their message is that "engaging with only a single consumer or survivor as 'representative' is tokenistic and futile" (Daya, Hamilton and Roper, 2020, p. 309).

Awareness of these challenges is the first step to overcoming them. Clarification and role negotiation would seem essential for interdisciplinary collaboration to work. From a practical perspective, Thompson Klein (1990, p. 144) states that "[m]aking a comprehensive list of all needs and then ranking them has helped some [interdisciplinary] teams to see areas of commonality and disagreement more clearly".

For those working in the mental health sector, an excellent practical resource for making any form of team-based collaboration work may be found in Part 2 of Graham Meadows and colleagues' edited collection on *Mental Health and Collaborative Community Practice* (2021). The rest of this chapter considers what role the law can play in facilitating interdisciplinary collaboration in the mental health sector.

The role of the law

As explored elsewhere in this volume, much of the scholarly debates about mental health laws have focused on the appropriate scope and content of civil legislation relating to compulsory detention and treatment and the protection of human rights. Guardianship law, criminal law and employment law also raise important issues concerning breaches of human rights, or protection against such breaches.

A focus of mental health scholarship has been on the so-called 'negative' human rights that encompass freedom from interference. In recent decades, there has been attention to the association between mental health and 'positive' human rights, the protection, promotion and fulfilment of which requires positive action by States, including the allocation of resources (McSherry, 2008; Hunt, 2009; Carney, this volume). In particular, the human right to the enjoyment of the highest attainable standard of mental health has been recognised and discussed as an element of the broader right to health established in foundational human rights instruments such as the International Covenant on Economic, Social and Cultural Rights (McSherry, 2008; Chapman, Williams, Hannah and Pūras, 2016; RCVMHS, 2021, vol. 4, pp. 35–43).

There is an additional way in which the law may be used to shape relationships in the mental health sector which merits attention. Any interdisciplinary endeavour must be carefully coordinated in order to address potential problems. The law can serve a coordinating role here. This section outlines how almost twenty years ago, the Victorian state government in Australia established through legislation a 'Multiple and Complex Needs Panel' to help foster interdisciplinary collaboration in the mental health sector with some positive results. The chapter then turns to more recent Victorian legislation which endeavours to foster interdisciplinary collaboration in both mental health research and practice.

By way of background, the Australian mental health system is a complex web of public and private providers, hospitals, health facilities and supporting mechanisms. The public system is governed by both Commonwealth and state and territory governments, with the Commonwealth responsible for commissioning primary care services and providing subsidies for access to general practitioners, psychiatrists and psychologists via the Medicare Benefits Schedule. Indicative of the role of Australia's eight state and territory governments, Victoria has a population of approximately 6.7 million people with the Victorian government responsible for the state's specialist mental health system. This involves the provision of clinical and non-clinical support services in hospital, residential and community-based services.

The multiple and complex needs panel

One legislative scheme, established under the state's *Human Services (Complex Needs) Act 2003* (Vic) (now repealed and replaced by the *Human Services (Complex Needs) Act 2009* (Vic)), exemplifies how coordination of multiple services by a panel can help facilitate interdisciplinary collaboration. Section 1 of that Act provided that:

The purposes of this Act are–

(a) to facilitate the delivery of welfare services, health services, mental health services, disability services, drug and alcohol treatment services and housing and support services to certain persons with multiple and complex needs by providing for the assessment of such persons and the development and implementation of appropriate care plans;
(b) to establish the Multiple and Complex Needs Panel.

The independent statutory Panel consisted of a Chair, the Secretary of the then Victorian Department of Human Services (or their nominee) and twelve people appointed by the Minister who had:

significant knowledge of, or significant experience in providing, welfare services, health services, mental health services, disability services, drug and alcohol treatment services, offender services or housing and support services.

(section 6(5))

When this legislation was first introduced into Parliament, emphasis was placed on the fact that the individuals who would be subject to the scheme were "sometimes dangerous" and that they presented "significant levels of risk to the community, to staff and to themselves through challenging behaviours that include aggressive and assaultive behaviour, as well as self-harming, and risk taking" (Parliament of Victoria, 2003). The introduction of this legislation can thus be viewed as having dual purposes – the control of problem behaviour as well as the coordination of care and treatment services.

The Panel's responsibilities included determining if a particular individual was eligible for the scheme, authorising comprehensive assessments, determining, reviewing, varying and extending care plans and appointing a Care Plan Coordinator. Assessments and the development of draft care plans were undertaken by a Multidisciplinary Assessment and Care Planning Service (Hamilton and Elford, 2009, p. 10). While the term 'multidisciplinary' is used here and 'multi-disciplinary' appears in the legislation (section 20), it can be said that the overall work of the Multiple and Complex Needs Panel supported 'interdisciplinary' collaboration in that it emphasised 'shared work' (Hamilton and Elford, 2009, p. 33) in developing care plans and ensured consumers and, where appropriate, their families and carers were active participants throughout the process.

In 2007, the scheme was evaluated positively (KPMG, 2008), with 50 per cent of the individuals involved showing behavioural improvements, although whether these improvements were concerned with lowered levels of aggression and assault was not specified. Hospital-related data indicated a 76 per cent reduction in presentations to hospital emergency departments, a 34 per cent reduction in number of hospital admissions and a 57 per cent reduction in the time spent in hospital (Hamilton, 2010, p. 319).

In a report on the five years of the Panel, it was pointed out that care plan coordination was a key element to the overall success of the initiative (Hamilton and Elford, 2009). The central role of Care Plan Coordinators also suggests that the success of such initiatives may depend upon strong leadership (Rosenbaum, 2002; Steadman, 1992).

The legislation had a sunset clause which was extended once and then the *Human Services (Complex Needs) Act 2009* was enacted to continue the scheme but with significant changes. Instead of having an independent statutory panel coordinating care and treatment, the scheme was brought under the auspices of the Victorian Department of Human Services, Department of Health and the Department of Justice. This was on the basis that such an arrangement would enable a 'speedy response' and because one of the original intended purposes for having a panel was that it should have the power to detain people as needed for the purposes of assessment, but this never eventuated (Parliament of Victoria, 2009, p. 787).

While the Victorian opposition parties supported the changes to the scheme, when discussing the proposed 2009 legislation, Helen Shardey, the Member for Caulfield, pointed out that "[s]ome people are concerned that [the new arrangement] is bureaucratising things somewhat, but the devil will be in the detail and the implementation of this" (Parliament of Victoria, 2009, p. 1014). Unfortunately, given that any reviews of this initiative are not publicly available, it is unclear how successful this 'inhouse' model of coordination has been.

The Department of Families, Fairness and Housing's (DFFH) *Service Provision Framework: Complex Needs* (2021) provides an overview of the current Multiple and Complex Needs Initiative (MACNI). Reading through this Framework does support the Member for Caulfield's reference to 'bureaucratising things somewhat'.

There are seventeen areas across four divisions of the department, with each area having a Complex Needs Coordinator. In relation to MACNI, the *Service Provision Framework* sets out "[a]ccountabilities and responsibilities" for six "Division/Business Areas" including, within the Department, the "Complex Needs Team, Disability and Complex Needs Branch, Operations Support Group, Community Services Operations Division" (DFFH, 2021, pp. 25–28). In addition, there are eight regional Complex Needs Panels that consider all potential referrals for eligibility and which approve, monitor and review all care plans. Regional panels comprise senior programme managers, regionally funded sector representatives and a Regional Coordinator. A Central Eligibility and Review Group confirms the individual's eligibility for the initiative and if the individual is eligible, a Care Plan Coordinator is appointed.

Despite attempts to clarify the documentation required and tasks of the eight regional panels, the *Service Provision Framework* describes a labyrinthine process for coordinating services for what the Royal Commission into Victoria's Mental Health System (2021, vol. 1, p. 208) observed was "only available to a limited number of people at any one time". As Margaret Hamilton (2010, p. 320) pointed out about service delivery, "the issue of complexity resides more in the service system than inherently in the people it services". The same could be said about the current MACNI governance arrangements.

Having an independent statutory body coordinating and supporting interdisciplinary collaboration and service delivery helped ensure that different services communicated effectively and led to positive outcomes for those involved. Replacing an overarching Multiple and Complex Needs Panel as previously existed with numerous departmental groups and panels may not be the best way of achieving the "speedy response" that the Victorian Government envisaged in justifying its disbanding.

The Victorian Collaborative Centre for Mental Health and Wellbeing

The opportunity for large-scale interdisciplinary collaboration across research and practice in the mental health sector is now coming to fruition in Victoria as a result of the recommendations of the Royal Commission into Victoria's Mental Health System. On 22 February 2019, the Governor of Victoria formally established this Royal Commission and appointed Penny Armytage as Chair and Dr Alex Cockram, Professor Allan Fels AO and the author of this chapter as Commissioners.

The terms of reference required that it report on "how Victoria's mental health system can most effectively prevent mental illness, and deliver treatment, care and support so that all those in the Victorian community can experience their best mental health, now and into the future" (RCVMHS, 2019a). The Commission delivered an Interim Report that November which made nine recommendations (RCVMHS, 2019b). This was followed by its Final Report fifteen months later, which made sixty-five recommendations (RCVMHS, 2021). The Final Report was tabled on 2 March 2021 at a joint sitting of the Victorian Parliament at which the Premier of Victoria agreed to implement all the Royal Commission's recommendations.

One of the recommendations in the Commission's Interim Report was for the establishment of a new entity, the Victorian Collaborative Centre for Mental Health and Wellbeing. Accordingly, the Parliament passed in November 2021 the *Victorian Collaborative Centre for Mental Health and Wellbeing Act 2021* (Vic). The Centre came into operation on 1 October 2022 and a Board has been established to determine its direction and priorities.

In the Interim Report (RCVMHS, 2019b, p. 392) the Royal Commission stated that the Centre "will provide adult clinical and non-clinical services, emphasise the participation and inclusion of people with lived experience, and conduct interdisciplinary research". It also set out (RCVMHS, 2019b, p. 404) that it "presents an opportunity to bring together people with lived experience (including consumers, their carers and families), researchers and clinicians to work together to improve service delivery and research".

The Royal Commission envisaged that theCentre would be based in a new purpose-built facility in Victoria's capital city Melbourne (RCVMHS, 2019b, p. 411). Its intention was for "a new and dynamic entity" which would support interdisciplinary collaboration in both mental health research and practice and disseminate knowledge widely across mental health networks including in the state's rural and regional areas (RCVMHS, 2019b, p. 412). Whether the Royal Commission's vision for the Centre will be achieved in practice remains to be seen.

Hollingsworth and Hollingsworth (2000, p. 227) have pointed out in relation to research that:

> [t]he greater the research group's diversity and depth within an integrated structure, the greater the likelihood that [researchers] will not stray into unproductive areas. Frequent and intense interaction among people of like minds (with low levels of diversity) tends not to lead to major breakthroughs.

The Royal Commission stressed that mental health consumers must play a central part in both research and service delivery:

> People with lived experience should lead and be employed in a range of the Collaborative Centre's functions, in positions where they motivate and help determine outcomes.

They must be on the Collaborative Centre's board, they must form part of its operational management, and they must be involved in its design and establishment.
(*RCVMHS, 2019b, pp. 410–411*)

To that end, section 11 of the *Victorian Collaborative Centre for Mental Health and Wellbeing Act 2021* specifies that "at least 2 members of the Board are persons who identify as experiencing, or as having experienced, mental illness or psychological distress" and "at least 2 members of the Board are persons who identify as caring for or supporting, or as having cared for or supported, a person with mental illness or psychological distress". Section 23 empowers the Board to appoint two directors of the Centre, one of whom must "identify as experiencing, or as having experienced, mental illness or psychological distress".

There are of course existing mental health centres such as the Centre for Addiction and Mental Health in Ontario, Canada, the New York State Psychiatric Institute in the United States and the Institute of Psychiatry, Psychology and Neuroscience at King's College London, which all could be said to foster interdisciplinary collaboration in the mental health sector. There are, however, varying degrees of participation of people with lived experience in clinical care and research conducted in such collaborative centres. By legislatively specifying the central role of mental health consumers in the Victorian Collaborative Centre for Mental Health and Wellbeing, the potential exists for not only effective service delivery but also ground-breaking interdisciplinary research. Mental health consumers' active engagement in service delivery and research is important because, in Nikolas Rose's (2019, p. 187) words, "the alternative knowledge that service users have developed of the social and interpersonal foundations of mental distress … might genuinely meet the needs of those experiencing profound crises in their lives".

It remains to be seen how Victoria's new Collaborative Centre works in practice and whether the challenges outlined above, including the risk of "bureaucratising things somewhat", can be overcome. Much will depend on the leadership and commitment to the full and effective participation of people with lived experience across all functions and levels of the Collaborative Centre.

Conclusion

Interdisciplinary collaboration can be difficult to pin down and there is an ever-growing literature on the role of 'interdisciplinarity' in research and practice. In the mental health sector, it is perhaps most appropriately viewed as a means of ensuring mental health consumers along with members of a research team or mental health and other service providers, develop new ways of addressing care and treatment needs.

Despite challenges to achieving interdisciplinary collaboration, there are several benefits to integrating and applying knowledge from different disciplinary perspectives. The law can play a role in supporting and fostering this.

In Victoria, legislatively enacting the Multiple and Complex Needs Panel brought people from several disciplinary backgrounds together to coordinate service delivery for a small group of people. While that Panel no longer exists, the experience indicated that independent statutory bodies can facilitate effective interdisciplinary collaboration with beneficial results. Now, there is an opportunity for the Victorian Collaborative Centre for Mental Health and Wellbeing to follow this collaborative model with a broad remit of service delivery and research that has mental health consumers as central participants.

The term 'mental health law' may sometimes be viewed narrowly as synonymous with the regulation of compulsory treatment. This chapter has outlined a broader conception of the law as helping facilitate interdisciplinary collaboration in both research and practice in the mental health sector. While such collaboration is not new, interdisciplinary collaboration which has the lived experience and knowledge of mental health consumers at its heart is still developing and has the potential for transformative and beneficial systemic change.

References

Bailey, D. (2012) *Interdisciplinary working in mental health*. London: Palgrave Macmillan.

Bennetts, W., Cross, W. and Bloomer, M. (2011) 'Understanding consumer participation in mental health: Issues of power and change', *International Journal of Mental Health Nursing*, 20(3), pp. 155–164.

Bracken, P., Thomas, P., Timini, S., Asen, E., Behr, G., Beuster, C., Bhunoo, S., Browne, I., Chhina, N., Double, D., Downer, S., Evans, C., Fernando, S., Garland, M. R., Hopkins, W., Huws, R., Johnson, B., Martindale, B., Middleton, H., Moldavsky, D., Moncrieff, J., Mullins, S., Nelki, J., Pizzo, M., Rodger, J., Smyth, M., Summerfield, D., Wallace, J. and Yeomans, D. (2012) 'Psychiatry beyond the current paradigm', *The British Journal of Psychiatry*, 201(6), pp. 430–434.

Byrne, L., Happell, B. and Reid-Searl, K. (2017) 'Risky business: Lived experience mental health practice, nurses as potential allies', *International Journal of Mental Health Nursing*, 26(3), pp. 285–292.

Callard, F. and Fitzgerald, D. (2015) *Rethinking interdisciplinarity across the social sciences and neurosciences*. Basingstoke: Palgrave.

Cech, T. R. and Rubin, G. M. (2004) 'Nurturing interdisciplinary research', *Nature Structural and Molecular Biology*, 11(12), pp. 1166–1169.

Chapman, A., Williams, C., Hannah, J. and Pūras, D. (2016) 'Reimaging the mental health paradigm for our collective well-being', *Health and Human Rights*, 22(1), pp. 1–6.

Charlton, J. I. (1998) *Nothing about us without us: Disability oppression and empowerment*. Berkeley: University of California Press.

Daya, I., Hamilton, B. and Roper, C. (2020) 'Authentic engagement: A conceptual model for welcoming diverse and challenging consumer and survivor views in mental health research, policy and practice', *International Journal of Mental Health Nursing*, 29(2), pp. 299–311.

Department of Families, Fairness and Housing (DFFH) (2021) *Service provision framework: Complex needs – Including the multiple and complex need initiative (MACNI) and support for high-risk tendencies (SfHRT)*. Melbourne: Victorian Government.

Edan, V., Sellick, K., Ainsworth, S., Alvarez-Varquez, S., Johnson, B., Smale, K., Randall, R. and Roper, C. (2021) 'Employed but not included: The case of consumer-workers in mental health care services', *The International Journal of Human Resource Management*, 32(15), pp. 3272–3301.

Farrell, M. P., Schmitt, M. H. and Heinemann, G. D. (2001) 'Informal roles and the stages of interdisciplinary team development', *Journal of Interprofessional Care*, 15(3), pp. 281–295.

Faulkner, A. (2017) 'Survivor research and mad studies: The role and value of experiential knowledge in mental health research', *Disability and Society*, 32(4), pp. 500–520.

Frodeman, R. (2010) 'Introduction', in Frodeman, R., Thompson Klein, J. and Mitcham, C. (eds.), *The Oxford handbook of interdisciplinarity*. Oxford: Oxford University Press, pp. xxix–xxxix.

Guattari, F. (2015) 'Transdisciplinarity must become transversality', *Theory, Culture and Society*, 32(5–6), pp. 131–137.

Hamilton, M. (2010) 'People with complex needs and the criminal justice system', *Current Issues in Criminal Justice*, 22(2), pp.307–324.

Hamilton, M. and Elford, K. (2009) *The report on the five years of the multiple and complex needs panel 2004–2009*. Melbourne: Multiple and Complex Needs Panel.

Hollingsworth, R. and Hollingsworth, E. J. (2000) 'Major discoveries and biomedical research organisations: Perspectives on interdisciplinarity, nurturing leadership, and integrated structure and cultures', in Weingart, P. E. and Steher, N. (eds.), *Practising interdisciplinarity*. Toronto: University of Toronto Press, pp. 215–244.

Hunt, P. (2009) 'Missed opportunities: Human rights and the commission on social determinants of health', *Global Health Promotion*, 16(1 Suppl), pp. 36–41.
KPMG (2008) *Evaluation of multiple and complex needs initiative: Final report*. Melbourne: Department of Human Services.
Lyall, C. (2019) *Being an interdisciplinary academic: How institutions shape university careers*. Cham: Palgrave Macmillan.
McCloughen, A., Gillies, D. and O'Brien, L. (2011) 'Collaboration between mental health consumers and nurses: Shared understandings, dissimilar experiences', *International Journal of Mental Health Nursing*, 20(1), pp.47–55.
McLean, T. (2007) 'Interdisciplinary practice', in Lishman, J. (ed.), *Handbook for practice learning in social work and social care: Knowledge and theory*, 2nd ed. London: Jessica Kingsley Publishers, pp. 322–343.
McSherry, B. (2008) 'Mental health and human rights: The role of the law in developing a right to enjoy the highest attainable standard of mental health in Australia', *Journal of Law and Medicine*, 15(5), pp. 773–781.
McSherry, B. and Weller, P. (2010) 'Rethinking rights-based mental health laws', in McSherry, B. and Weller, P. (eds.), *Rethinking rights-based mental health laws*. Oxford: Hart Publishing, pp. 3–10.
Meadows, G., Farhall, J., Fossey, E., Happell, B., McDermott, F. and Rosenberg, S. (eds.) (2021) *Mental health and collaborative community practice*, 4th ed. Oxford: Oxford University Press.
Nystrom, P. (2007) 'Disciplinarity, inter-disciplinary and post-disciplinarity: Changing disciplinary patterns in the history discipline', https://dialnet.unirioja.es/descarga/articulo/2532824.pdf (Accessed 13 January 2022).
Parliament of Victoria (2003) *Hansard: Legislative assembly. Human services (complex needs) bill*, Second Reading, B. Pike, Minister for Health, 27 August, p. 81.
Parliament of Victoria (2009) *Hansard: Legislative assembly. Human services (complex needs) bill*, Second Reading, D. Andrews, Minister for Health, 12 March, p. 787.
Patel, V., Lund, C., Hatherill, S., Plagerson, S., Corrigall, J., Funk, M. and Flisher, A. J. (2010) 'Mental disorders: Equity and social determinants', in Blas, E. and Sivasankara Kurup, A. (eds.), *Equity, social determinants and public health programmes*. Geneva: World Health Organization, pp. 115–134.
Rickards, L. (2014) 'Interdisciplinary collaboration in context: academics and agendas', Melbourne Interdisciplinary Collaboration Exploration Final Report. University of Melbourne. https://research.unimelb.edu.au/__data/assets/pdf_file/0033/147795/MICE-Final-Report-2014.pdf (Accessed 13 January 2022).
Rose, N. (2019) *Our psychiatric future*. Cambridge: Polity Press.
Rosenbaum, D. P. (2002) 'Evaluating multi-agency anti-crime partnerships: Theory, design, and measurement issues', *Crime Prevention Studies*, 14, pp. 171–225.
Royal Commission into Victoria's Mental Health Service (RCVMHS) (2019a) *Terms of Reference*. http://rcvmhs.archive.royalcommission.vic.gov.au/Terms_of_Reference_signed.pdf (Accessed 13 January 2022).
Royal Commission into Victoria's Mental Health Service (RCVMHS) (2019b) *Interim report*. http://rcvmhs.archive.royalcommission.vic.gov.au/interim-report.html (Accessed 13 January 2022).
Royal Commission into Victoria's Mental Health Service (RCVMHS) (2021). *Final report*. https://finalreport.rcvmhs.vic.gov.au/download-report/ (Accessed 13 January 2022)
Steadman, H. J. (1992) 'Boundary spanners: A key component for the effective interactions of the justice and mental health systems', *Law and Human Behavior*, 16(1), pp. 75–87.
Stember, M. (1991) 'Advancing the social sciences through the interdisciplinary enterprise', *The Social Science Journal*, 28(1), pp. 1–14.
Terpstra, J. L., Best, A., Abrams, D. B. and Moor, G. (2010) 'Health sciences and health services', in Frodeman, R., Thompson Klein, J. and Mitcham, C. (eds.), *The Oxford handbook of interdisciplinarity*. Oxford: Oxford University Press, pp. 508–521.
Thompson Klein, J. (1990) *Interdisciplinarity: History, theory, and practice*. Detroit: Wayne State University Press.
Trachtenberg, M., Parsonage, M., Shepherd, G. and Boardman, J. (2013) *Peer support in mental health care: Is it good value for money*. London: Centre for Mental Health.
Unsworth, C. (1987) *The politics of mental health legislation*. Oxford: Clarendon Press.

van Veen, C., Teghtsoonian, K. and Morrow, M. (2019) 'Enacting violence and care: Neo-liberalism, knowledge claims, and resistance', in Daley, A., Costa, L. and Beresford, P. (eds.), *Madness, violence, and power*. Toronto: University of Toronto Press.

Wildeman, S. (2013) 'Protecting rights and building capacities: Challenges to global mental health policy in light of the convention on the rights of persons with disabilities', *Journal of Law, Medicine and Ethics*, 41(1), pp. 48–73.

35
THE MENTAL HEALTH AND JUSTICE PROJECT[1]
Reflections on strong interdisciplinarity

Gareth Owen

Introduction

This chapter will explore opportunities and challenges in interdisciplinary collaborations using the Mental Health and Justice project (MHJ) as a case study.

MHJ was a five-year interdisciplinary research initiative funded by the Wellcome Trust in the UK. The project addressed a cluster of public policy challenges arising at the complex interface where mental health and mental healthcare interact with principles of human rights. Its principal aim was to develop clinical, legal and public policy strategies for jointly satisfying two fundamental imperatives: the imperative to protect people in contexts where they can be vulnerable, and the imperative to respect their agency and autonomy.

The chapter will outline some background to the project and give some reflections on what is meant by 'strong interdisciplinarity' (which I will argue MHJ was an instance of), ways the project navigated scholarship versus activism and the course of the project.

These are personal reflections limited by the fact that, at the time of writing, the MHJ project remains in a final phase and the fact that I am still digesting what was a complex, intense, fascinating project.[2] My main reflections are that strongly interdisciplinary projects offer multi-faceted opportunities for outputs, influences and impacts and that tension points are inherent and require a process of dynamic *balance*. I suggest that models of strong interdisciplinarity need to evolve and that MHJ achieved its original strategic aims without being entirely bound to them. Furthermore, I suggest that there was a positive phenomenon of interdisciplinary collaboration as *education* that I try to capture.

---

1 Thanks to everyone who was involved in the MHJ research project and to the MHJ committee that continues to think about and care about its legacy and dissemination. Funding provided by Wellcome grant number 203376/Z/16/Z.
2 My roles in the project were as project lead and co-lead for two of the workstreams (workstreams 3 and 6).

DOI: 10.4324/9781003226413-43

This chapter has been made available under a CC-BY license.

Background

Some background on the project may help to put into context how it started on its five-year timeline.

I am a psychiatrist with an interdisciplinary background involving philosophy. I had done my PhD and postdoctoral fellowships in the Department of Psychological Medicine, King's College London (KCL) in a loosely grouped collection of academics interested in mental capacity and mental health law. This work had been funded mainly by the Wellcome Trust and involved researchers at the Institute of Psychiatry and the Law School at KCL. It developed over time to involve academics in philosophy (both in the research itself and in an interdisciplinary postgraduate masters education initiative) and also service user involvement. These collaborations were quite small. I had found them very fruitful and stimulating but they were not going anywhere very clearly within the existing university structures, and thus it was apparent that to create opportunity and growth an expanded collaboration with external grant investment was needed.

A formative experience for me had been working at the Parliamentary Office of Science and Technology (POST) in 2011 as a Wellcome Trust–POST fellow. I worked on the Mental Capacity Act (2005) at a time of post legislative scrutiny. The work involved speaking to a wide range of policy makers involved with the Act including its implementation. One of the curious things about this ground-breaking piece of legislation is that it is entirely the responsibility of the Department of Justice whilst interpretation and implementation falls to the Department of Health (now Department of Health and Social Care) due to the fact that assessments very largely get done by professionals working in health and social care. The fact that the Act had been conceived in a department of 'Justice' yet had to be interpreted in a department of 'Health' intrigued me and resonated with the interdisciplinary issues I was grappling with as a researcher on mental capacity. The two government departments were not collaborating very much in relation to the Mental Capacity Act and some of the problems in its post legislative course seemed traceable to this fact. Again, this resonated with administrative issues I was facing in the University with researching mental capacity across departments of psychiatry, law and philosophy. How to collaborate across 'Justice' and 'Health' on mental capacity and related areas? It was this question in the context of silos of communication across government departments that prompted my initial use of the term 'Mental Health and Justice'.

I initiated discussions with the Wellcome Trust about a large collaborative research project. At this time the Wellcome was putting a lot of emphasis on collaborations in research. They were becoming more interested in social science and had longstanding interests in the neurosciences but this was not well connected to real-world issues in mental health. We decided to run a large workshop at the Wellcome with a diverse group of participants and deliberately drew in researchers in social sciences, cognitive neurosciences and also policy makers and service user researchers. It was a 'big tent' event and it greatly helped in expanding the pool of potential collaborators and moving to identify themes and research topics. However, it also created a somewhat bewilderingly large canvass and body of unsculpted material. So work was left to clarify which areas were ready to take forward and which were falling away so as to forge and refine a collaborative research programme.

In addition to this there had been a big international event in human rights law – ratification of the United Nations (UN) Convention on the Rights of Persons with Disabilities (CRPD) – and this was challenging the Mental Capacity Act in radical ways. It was clear that a contemporary research initiative on 'Mental Health and Justice' was going to have to tackle the challenges posed by the CRPD; yet the CRPD challenge was not posing a specific researchable question.

What emerged from the original 'big tent' workshop was a research project oriented around the problem of empowerment versus protection in mental health. This was framed broadly to accommodate the research workgroups that were forming, to keep to the 'big tent' spirit of the initial workshop and also to acknowledge that the CRPD was now part of the landscape. Six research workstreams emerged with leads or co-leads with the requisite energy for, and interest in, interdisciplinarity:

1. Supporting Legal Capacity – this addressed the idea of supported decision-making as a way of resolving tensions between respecting and protecting a person with mental disabilities. It combined theoretical research into problems such as the relation of supported decision-making to undue influence with specific real-world studies such as supporting contraceptive decision-making in people with learning disability.
2. Community Participation – this addressed the right to independent living in the community emphasised by article 19 of the CRPD. It combined exploration of the concept itself with real-world participatory action research into its realisation in different socio-cultural contexts, particularly in challenging human rights settings in the West Bank of the occupied Palestine territory and in Ghana.
3. Advance Directives – this addressed the idea of 'self-binding' or 'Ulysses' advance directives for care and treatment in the context of bipolar and fluctuating capacity. It developed a real-life implementation study of an advance directive template that included a provision for self-binding.
4. Insight – this addressed the idea of unawareness of illness. It combined theoretical exploration of the concept with real-world study of how insight is used in legal discourse and in clinical settings. It sought to develop guidelines for increasing service user involvement in articulating areas of shared/divergent understanding and identifying strategies for support.
5. Metacognition – this addressed the relation between the psychological process of 'thinking about thinking' and clinical concepts of insight and the legal concept of ability to 'use or weigh' information. It developed new lab-based measurements to acquire quantifiable data as well as exploring if and how psychological and neuroscience measurements are used in the courts and in professional practice. The workstream also addressed social influences on metacognition, insight and decision-making capacity.
6. Contested Assessment – this addressed the functional model of decision-making capacity, addressing the challenge arising from radical interpretations of the CRPD and giving it more satisfactory interpretation based on court-based processes and reflections of experienced practitioners on their hard cases. It developed research-informed practical guidance on capacity assessment for clinical and social care professionals.

The workstreams (diverse as can be seen) were arranged as mini-collaborations within a larger collaborative structure. The workstreams had largely traditional academic aims of running studies and producing academic outputs but, unusually, each workstream was comprised of academics belonging to different established 'strong' disciplines (e.g. psychiatry, law, social science, philosophy, cognitive neuroscience) who had not worked together in this way before. The project also developed three key partnerships with organisations serving the aims of policy engagement (the King's Policy Institute), service user research involvement (McPin Foundation) and public engagement (Bethlem Gallery). These partnerships were planned from the start though with a degree of looseness built in as we knew that policy engagement, service user involvement in research and the public engagement approach we wanted to take (participatory arts) all had fluidities.

For a collaboration such as this, working on complex, heartfelt and controversial topics in mental health and justice, there were going to be opportunities as well as challenges.

What is 'strong interdisciplinarity'?

The MHJ project aimed for 'strong interdisciplinarity'. What do I mean by this term?

The standard definition of interdisciplinarity is that it involves bringing together two or more disciplines into a single activity where it is expected more will be gained than by one discipline alone. But disciplines have subdisciplines and some disciplines differ more than others (e.g. the difference between physics and chemistry compared to the difference between academic psychiatry and law). By 'strong interdisciplinarity' I mean bringing together disciplines with large differences as systems of knowledge which typically exist in separated administrative or departmental units within a university. Furthermore, the bringing together of disciplines should be characterised by co-working on problems over sustained periods of time. The MHJ project was strongly interdisciplinary in all these senses. It involved academics in established departments of psychiatry, law, social science, cognitive neuroscience and philosophy co-working on problems over five years where giving definition to the work was part of the work itself.

Ideally, interdisciplinarity needs some kind of self-understanding or theory of its own activity. If a clear, unambiguous theory of interdisciplinarity is needed for 'strong interdisciplinarity' then I think the MHJ project was not necessarily strong. However, given the lack of unity in the literature on interdisciplinary theory, and no compelling unified theory of interdisciplinarity, force fitting a non-compelling model to our processes was never going to be a strength. That said, it may be helpful here to consider two influential theories, or models, of interdisciplinarity in the literature and consider how the MHJ project measured relative to them.

The first model sees interdisciplinarity in problem-solving or epistemological terms. Karl Popper took this view when he wrote in a chapter entitled 'The Nature of Philosophical Problems and Their Roots in Science': "*We are not students of some subject matter, but students of problems. And problems may cut right across the borders of any subject matter or discipline*" (Popper, 1963, p. 88). Take the problem of who decides in health and social care situations where serious mental disorder or disability is in existence. That is a problem. But it is not a problem owned exclusively by the disciplines of academic psychiatry, law, social science, cognitive neuroscience or philosophy. The student of the problem however, following Popper, would be well advised to know how the problem looks from each of these disciplinary perspectives. Related to this problem-solving theory of interdisciplinarity is an intriguing notion of the 'superconcept'. This term has been coined by Alan Wilson (Wilson, 2010). The basic idea is that a concept developed in one discipline, for example, the concept of entropy developed in electrical engineering, can find similar expression in other disciplines (e.g. thermodynamics in physics) or application in other disciplines (e.g. biological systems or urban planning). Concepts like entropy or evolution are 'superconcepts'. Wilson says a superconcept is an idea which "cross[es] disciplines and which contribute[s] both to our depth of understanding and helps us to navigate the breadth [of knowledge]" (Gombrich, 2019; Wilson, 2010, section 4). Here the idea is not to deconstruct extant disciplines but rather to identify strong disciplines and then to identify a set of concepts that find application across them. Those superconcepts range from macro ones like entropy and evolution to those with a more circumscribed, or micro, domain.[3] Core thinking skills related to this model of interdisciplinarity include 'critical thinking' and 'mental models' – generic problem-solving and decision-making skills such as probabilistic thinking, analogical thinking, bias and fallacy detection that can find application in pretty much all subject areas (Gombrich, 2021). On this model of interdisciplinarity, the goal is to educate in scientific problem solving so a new generation of students are best equipped to solve the most pressing problems which, as Popper indicated, may well cut across the borders of subject matters.

The second model sees interdisciplinarity in socio-political and social justice terms (Parker et al., 2010). It starts with a social justice problem in which a social group is recognised as having a power disadvantage and a relative exclusion from the social construction of knowledge.[4] Examples include gender (Woodward and Woodward, 2015), disability, non-white race/ethnicity and combinations (intersections) of these. The social justice problem is then critiqued from different disciplinarity perspectives such that issues of power imbalance and epistemic disadvantage are surfaced and then righted through action. On radical versions of the model this critique may involve deconstructing, or abolishing, established disciplines showing them to be discriminatory or unjust systems of knowledge. The disciplines drawn upon for this model of interdisciplinarity tend to belong to the humanities and the social sciences and core skills include participatory understanding, empathy, ability to discern disparity/discrimination and activism – skills that can be applied across different areas of social justice.

Reflecting on the MHJ project I think there was a continuum between these two models in the project with no workstream adapting what might be considered a pure single model approach, and the project overall is probably best characterised as a hybrid. Notwithstanding, differences in approach existed in MHJ with the workstream on independent living being most aligned to the model of interdisciplinarity as social justice and the workstream on metacognition most aligned to the model of interdisciplinarity as problem solving. Other workstreams were variably in-between.

Superconcepts, as Wilson defines them, are interesting to reflect on using the MHJ case study. There were contenders for superconcepts in the project (e.g. mental capacity, advance decision-making, supported decision-making, metacognition, insight, independent living). Taking mental capacity as an example: originating in law, the concept outlived the critique from CRPD mental capacity abolitionists, showed a fair degree of transferability across professional and service user groups and kept arising in different forms across disciplines and workstreams. It also showed application. Personally speaking, I found research across MHJ moved my thinking on from my earlier interdisciplinary considerations of the concept of

---

3 For example, Wilson calls 'Christensen units' a superconcept. These are units of new technology that successful businesses have to adapt to as well as risk being destroyed by (Wilson, 2010, 5.2.1). Here the scope of application is much more circumscribed compared to entropy or evolution.
4 The socio-political approach to interdisciplinarity raises the question of values. It is important to note that this second model of interdisciplinarity is largely constrained to socio-political values relating to care and oppression. Haidt (2012) in his empirical work on values across cultures has identified the value cluster of care but also other value clusters he calls liberty, fairness, loyalty, authority and sanctity.

mental capacity (Owen et al., 2008) indicating that a superconcept is not static and can respond to new evidence and argument.

Socio-political considerations in interdisciplinarity also afford reflection based on MHJ experience. I think everyone in the MHJ project found that socio-political considerations were important and not fully separable from the interdisciplinary work. Working in mental health where upsetting realities of illness, stigma and discrimination are so present sensitised all of us. That said, some of us were more comfortable than others with socio-political and social justice considerations being tightly framed in terms of one value cluster (see footnote 4). One of the interesting and helpful symposiums we held in MHJ involved exploring the variety of meanings of justice and imperatives to action and some of the learning on MHJ involved realisation that felt imperatives to action can be collectively inconsistent. This raises the problem of reflective equilibrium in strong interdisciplinarity.

In summary, MHJ as a case study helps to see that interdisciplinarity is not just one thing. The project ranged across different models of interdisciplinarity and was not fully accounted for by any of them. For interdisciplinary projects I would recommend being aware of the kind of interdisciplinarity one is doing, or what different kinds are incorporated, or where on a continuum of kinds. The right emphasis will be hugely contextual. The in-between forms of interdisciplinarity (i.e. between the problem-solving kind and the socio-political kind) are harder to do because there are more emotional and conceptual tension points to navigate and less of a pre-defined blueprint to follow. But in the area of mental health the impactful interdisciplinary projects are very likely to require both knowledge-orientated problem solving and socio-political awareness and action. These blended, or hybrid, projects may need more planning and more continuous reflective practice built in. It would be helpful to see the socio-political literature on interdisciplinarity develop to become more diverse on values, in Haidt's moral psychology sense (Haidt, 2012), to guide collaborative processes and reflective equilibrium and help manage the risks of tendentiousness or polarisations. It would also be helpful to see the problem-solving literature on interdisciplinarity develop to accommodate the roles of values.

Scholarship and activism

In this section I want to reflect on how the MHJ project navigated between scholarship and action (or activism). This relates to the preceding discussion about interdisciplinarity but is a less abstract way of framing the discussion.

MHJ engaged a wide range of action organisations and persons outside the academy.[5] Rather than trying to capture all of these, I will focus on one engagement which was particularly significant for the MHJ project. This was the engagement with policy makers and with the mental health law reform process in England and Wales in particular.

---

5 These included organisations with specific mandates or campaigns to bring about social and political change (for example the UN Special Rapporteur on the right to health; the WHO Policy, Law and Human Rights Unit, the Mental Disability Advocacy Centre (Validity); non-governmental organisations (e.g. the Palestinian Counselling Centre); service user organisations with specific condition-specific charitable objectives (e.g. Bipolar UK, Supported Loving); state-funded clinical services (e.g. the South London and Maudsley NHS Foundation Trust); policy makers (e.g. the Independent Review of the Mental Health Act, the Scottish Mental Health Law Review, civil servants at the UK Ministry of Justice and Department of Health and Social Care, UK parliamentarians); courts (e.g. the Court of Protection)).

The Mental Health and Justice project

We also addressed action within the research methodology itself. Again, this was varied and I cannot cover it all, so I will give brief reflections on two examples which struck me personally. The first was a research method that might be best termed 'bracketing action' or 'bracketing belief'; the second might be termed 'enabling action' or 'enabling belief'. I will explain more what I mean below but let me first consider the engagement with the policy makers.

Engagement with policy makers

In its planning and inception, MHJ established a partnership with the King's Policy Institute for a series of 'policy labs' on topics related to protection and empowerment in mental health. Policy labs were a technique for policy deliberation that the Policy Institute had been developing (Hinrichs-Krapels et al., 2020). At the time I think it is safe to say we had no expectation of the UK government seeking substantial reform of mental health law. Within a few months of the project starting the then Prime Minister Theresa May announced, very unexpectedly, a major reform process. An independent review group was announced with Sir Simon Wessely as chair and MHJ had an opportunity for 'impact' using the policy lab mechanism that we had in place.

Two early policy labs were held with a diverse range of policy experts with briefing materials prepared on the main tension points in mental health law and the main policy options facing the independent review team (which was just being assembled) (Owen et al., 2018). The main approach we took was to present the deliberators with value choices that needed to be made in deciding the future course of law reform. Two key value choices were (1) individual autonomy and (2) legal formality and we represented these as orthogonal axes because we took the values to be largely independent of each other. This created a 2x2 grid with four prototype or 'ideal type' policy options (A–D). These were presented and summarised with examples. Figure 35.1 shows the scheme we used.

We understood compliance with the CRPD as the CRPD committee were stating it at the time (Committee on the Rights of Persons with Disabilities, 2014). This entailed abolition, or phasing out, of any formal legal system for mental health treatment without consent and maximum value placed on individual autonomy. This was option A. We also thought it important to be transparent about the option of what is sometimes called 'medicalism' or, in other words, permitting health professionals to make case-by-case judgements on mental health treatment (including treatment without consent) informally based on clinical context and relationship rather than formal legal rules and criteria. 'Medicalism' also placed value on public health and clinical expertise rather than individual autonomy. This was option C. Options B and D were both options for a mental health law with formal legal rules and criteria for treatment without consent. Option D was essentially the current provision in England and Wales with the Mental Health Act (1983) and option B was a mental capacity-based mental health law (sometimes called 'fusion'), a version of which Northern Ireland had recently enacted.

Following deliberations in the policy labs over workshops in November 2017 and February 2018, a consensus recommendation emerged that the direction of policy in mental health law should be legal formality with a shift towards an approach placing more value upon individual autonomy. In effect, this was a recommendation for a shift from D towards B.

We also used the policy labs for some deliberation on the positive right to health, but it became clear that moving mental health law in that direction was not a politically achiev-

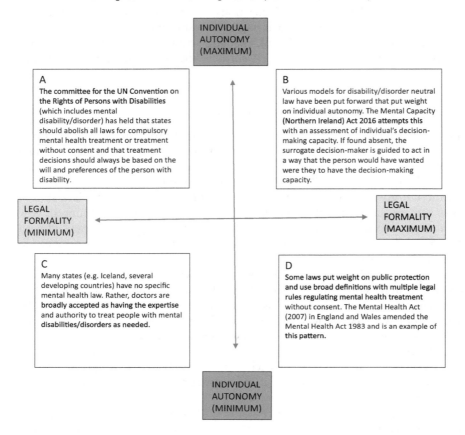

Figure 35.1 Scheme for Mental Health and Justice project policy lab on reform of the Mental Health Act

able option. I think this was mainly due to two things: one was the politics of social and economic rights and their association with 'big state' and 'big public spending' – something which was not government policy in the UK at the time. The other was that the human rights discourse (from both the European Court of Human Rights and the UN CRPD committee) was very largely about autonomy rights with either no formulations about social rights or only very generalised ones. Practitioners, even those working within socialised healthcare systems like the English and Welsh National Health Services, had no clear idea of what the language of a right to health meant in practice. We therefore found it very difficult to get political or practitioner buy-in on discussion of social rights or, for that matter, very much specificity on what a mental health act with a right to health framing would even look like legislatively in the UK. On reflection that was a problem: we were in effect talking about moving from D to B (see Figure 35.1) in a public spending and resource vacuum. Subsequent work was done to focus on advance choice and the case for resources for their enablement (service user support, professional training, IT infrastructure) but even five years after a government commitment to advance decision-making in mental health (Owen et al., 2019), resource commitment for even modest implementation remains tenuous.

Our approach to engagement with mental health law reform was essentially one of outlining and deliberating policy options rather than campaigning – acknowledging that it is not ultimately for researchers to decide. It has been disappointing to see that even modest investments to enable meaningful change to what law means in practice to people with severe mental health problems remain very difficult to secure. It is not surprising therefore to see the British Medical Association recently take a more campaigning approach to social rights (Sheather and Norcliffe, 2022).

Future policy engagement research will need to provide more detailed options on social rights and more sophisticated deliberative work on what policy makers and the public prioritise when they understand mental health law reform *without* public spending commitments. I consider this learning an important learning point of the MHJ project's engagement with mental health act law reform.

Let me now turn to the issue of how action was managed within the research methodology itself.

Action in the research itself

As already mentioned, the MHJ project had to address a new landscape with the CRPD. We needed a normative steer on a human rights approach to mental health law with an answer to the fundamental question: what action was the UN Human Rights system recommending in relation to treatment without consent? Two researchers who believed different things about what was right action on the matter agreed to approach the task using a method that in effect 'bracketed' or 'suspended' their beliefs and rigorously surveyed what the different Human Rights committees within the UN system were recommending. This method gave a result that was important for the MHJ project early on even if it was difficult in terms of suggesting a coherent way forward with a human rights approach. The research showed that Human Rights committees were collectively recommending inconsistent action and had no internal decision-making mechanism to resolve the inconsistency (Martin and Gurbai, 2019). Using this research method to understand that a genuine 'impasse' existed helped us as a project to step back from aiming to achieve a clear and distinct international human rights framing for MHJ (we were going to have to embrace messiness and ambiguity in the normative 'steer'). The research result also helped us give more focus to specific areas where consensus for action was more likely to be found.

Work on advance directives was showing up as one area where consensus for action was emerging. Researching this area had a rather different problem to the belief one above. The problem was that a large, English, multi-centre randomised control trial (RCT) of a type of advance directive had reported a mainly null result on reduction of use of the Mental Health Act (1983) (Thornicroft et al., 2013). On the evidence-based perspective there was therefore not a strong case for action. However, on service user, clinical ethics, human rights and policy perspectives we were finding that there was a strong consensus for action (Owen et al., 2019). Our work was also indicating that the complexity of the advance directive intervention and the plurality of values that stakeholders were attributing to it[6] raised questions about the RCT methodology being top of the evidence-generating hierarchy on this subject. To resolve this methodological problem the workstream 3 spent some time early on learning about participatory action research from the workstream 2 with a view to *developing*[7] an advance directive intervention within the complex mental health services of the South London and Maudsley NHS Trust. This was an interesting turn for clinical research which was more familiar with putting the RCT first (or preparing for the definitive RCT study). In effect, there was a prior commitment, within the research itself, to action based on an essentially ethics-based analysis rather than a conventionally causal or RCT-based one. The resulting method we developed (a combination of literature reviews, wide stakeholder consultation, doing through showing, detailed iterative process development, qualitative inquiry, network development with key partners and implementation science) was a sort of hermeneutic clinical research trial – very different indeed from the method of RCT first, action second.[8] But, as above, it has not (yet at least) had an impact on resource allocation – no doubt in large part due to the fact that RCT evidence with economic analysis remains the convention for how resource allocations in healthcare are made by governments.

In summary, the MHJ project navigated scholarship and activism in a variety of ways and with a variety of results. I have selected a few of these navigations to give a sense of the learning and to show that the balancing of action-impartial research and action-partial, or action-laden, research did not just exist as a matter of balancing between the academy and the 'outside world' but also within the research methodology itself. This balancing allowed us to innovate with policy engagement using policy labs, with methods to approach contested human rights questions and with complex interventions in clinical settings.

Course of the project

The project was an extraordinarily intense and fascinating one which followed a path laid down in its original project proposal of 2016. The varied outputs of the project are brought together on an MHJ project website https://mhj.org.uk[9] and reflections on how we met our original strategic aims are also given there. Outputs and outcomes will not be the focus here, rather I will reflect on the course of the project.

MHJ had to react to external events unforeseen in 2016. Unforeseen events fundamentally shaped the work including reform of mental health legislation in the several jurisdictions of the UK but also the Black Lives Matter (BLM) movement and the Covid-19 pandemic with its social distancing impacts and its marked increase in population anxiety levels during

---

6 For example, reduction of use of the Mental Health Act was just one of the things valued by stakeholders, others being: enhanced self-management, building shared understanding of the illness, building therapeutic alliance and communication, avoiding personally defined harms, reducing trauma of compulsory treatment, earlier presentation, shorter admissions and peace of mind.
7 The methodology we focused on – 'Outcome Mapping' (*Outcome Mapping Learning Community*, available at www.outcomemapping.ca/download/OM-faq-en.pdf) – literally derives from development. It comes out of working on development projects in developing countries where the question of whether to act is not being studied or tested (that being assumed). Rather it is a method that addresses the way to achieve action and outcomes.
8 Details of this 'trial' are available in the PhD thesis of Lucy Stephenson and associated publications.
9 The website will be archived by KCL from 2024.

the first lockdown (Hamilton and Coates, 2020) and changing anxieties thereafter. As such we were stretched across multiple dimensions and challenged.

One example of the importance of the fluid, 'third space' nature of the public engagement partnership with the Bethlem Gallery was the response to the BLM movement. In June 2020 a large MHJ social art installation on the perimeter of the Bethlem Royal Hospital inspired by the Mental Capacity Act and called 'Some Questions About Us' was graffitied (a version of the original work 'Some Questions About Us' now forms part of the Government Art Collection). The letters 'RIP Seni' were painted in red by an unknown person. This was a reference to the death of a young black man called Seni Lewis under police restraint in the Bethlem Hospital in 2010. The transformation of 'Some Questions About Us' to 'RIP Seni' in the early phase of the BLM movement set in motion a new set of reflections and processes for the project. 'RIP Seni' was preserved and donated to Bethlem Museum of the Mind's permanent collection and an MHJ film was coproduced with the Lewis family exploring the moving but challenging emotions evoked by the graffiti.[10]

In 2022 the very terms 'mental health' and 'justice' do not have quite the same meanings that they had in 2016. Both terms have become more culturally and politically salient. These are big issues to reflect on: too big probably and too early to expect full reflection on now. So, I will reflect tentatively and imperfectly on just a few: management of the collaboration, collaborative processes and collaborative working as education.

Management of the collaboration

The project was overseen by an academic management group which gave it a useful central, coordinating management hub (we had over 40 meetings). Management of the project (including management of budgets) was devolved to workstreams otherwise.

The academic management group had active involvement from the leads of all the workstreams as well as from the service user advisory group. Formal aspects of line management for each of the people working in the project (there were over 50) followed the policies of each of the universities, the partnering organisations and the contracts agreed between them. King's College London was the host university from a grants management point of view with a project administrator and myself overseeing the grant and the running of the academic management group. The project required considerable administrative work to set up, sustain and bring to a close and one reflection is that collaborative projects are best served by administrative support that 'gets' interdisciplinarity and is willing to 'stick with it' over time. I would say that continuity in the management of interdisciplinary collaborations is important.

The balance of central versus devolved management was especially important to MHJ because of its diverse workstreams and partnerships. Sometimes there needed to be a central or 'tight' style of management but usually I found it better for it to be 'loose'. In part this was because 'MHJ' was actually not a formal 'entity' from a governance point of view (e.g. it didn't have any single line management structure), in part because the workstreams

---

10 The film had its world premiere at Sheffield DocFest, was acquired by Guardian films and is available to be viewed for free on the Guardian website www.theguardian.com/news/ng-interactive/2021/aug/12/rip-seni-racism-graffiti-and-the-uks-mental-health-crisis-video.

To date, it has been screened at ten film festivals around the world including the London Short Film Festival.

themselves had strong identities and committed leadership and in part because high levels of engagement across the project allowed, to a large degree, a natural self-regulation to happen. There were times when the workstreams were all consuming centres of activity and progress and the central group less important and times when the academic management group was very important (e.g. in preparing the annual colloquia, policy labs, addressing interfaces and resolving problems). *Balance* was the theme of management: both understanding the balanced central and devolved management structure itself (its nuts and bolts) and knowing when the balance between central and devolved needed to shift. These balances were not always perfect but that there needed to be attention to balance I think was clear. Perfect, or ideal, balance is probably not the appropriate standard for governance of strongly interdisciplinary collaborations. In other words, expect some wobble and if no wobbles then consider whether you are actually achieving strong interdisciplinarity. But there are standards to aspire to on balance. I think these are around reasonableness, adaptive learning, trusted systems of communication and also the so-called 'via negativa'.[11]

The 'big tent' experience was part of the origin of MHJ's development as a research programme and was important to maintain but with this came a tension between, so to say, tightening the tent stays to keep a big tent pitched (especially during the stormy cross winds of the pandemic) and overtightening the stays (risking it being no longer a big tent). There was also the intellectual tension between fostering the richness of intellectual work within the big tent (i.e. maintaining the richness and diversity across the MHJ workstreams) and the overall conceptual coherence of the project (or to keep the tent metaphor: 'what' the MHJ tent was). The group found metaphors helpful in balancing these tensions – for example the metaphors of a 'garden' or 'octopus' emerged – as well as a reconciliation with ambiguity and uncertainty in any final formulation of the empowerment versus protection question. But, mostly, resolving these tensions was down to the resolution of the group itself and I think that, in large part, went back to the early 'big tent' identity which was formed, at the start, when sculpting the project. A final, no cost extension, for a dissemination year, was granted by the Wellcome Trust, which, at the time of writing the project is still in. That was helpful for planning further articulations and representations of what that 'big tent' MHJ object was/is,[12] what the field can become, and for the process of letting MHJ as a grant go.

Collaborative processes

As mentioned already, it is to be expected that collaborations like MHJ will bring challenges to those working in them as well as opportunities. I will briefly reflect on some of the key challenges or 'bumps' we faced.[13]

---

11 Nassim Taleb in his book, *Antifragile: Things That Gain from Disorder* (2013) defines the via negativa as a heuristic for what to avoid, what not to do, subtraction, not addition. In effect, the art of letting things go. Theodor Adorno in his abstract notion of 'negative dialectics', emphasised anti-system or anti-ideology as a way to act outside the sway, or lure, of unities. Theologians refer to via negativa as the approach to the divine which characterises it only in terms of what it is not.
12 A film on the whole MHJ project made by Sally Marlow and David Martin captures this nicely and is freely available on the MHJ website.
13 A longer and 'gritty' account of the collaborative processes as well as some key practical recommendations on organising strong interdisciplinary collaborations is given by Laura Heath, an independent organisation consultant who worked alongside the MHJ project for five years and interviewed many of the participants

After the joy and excitement of the MHJ award, the Wellcome Trust asked us to make a financial cut. That was an early bump to overcome because it meant us having to re-open a shaped collaborative structure or whole, remove research from it and put it back as a whole again. The fact that there were six workstreams made this easier to do in the respect that each workstream could be fairly asked to propose cuts to its research package in a way which it felt most comfortable with. But the task of putting it back together as a whole was more difficult and some lasting impact of having a reconstructed whole needing to fit into a new budget likely occurred.

Another bump related to organisational policy issues on equality, diversity and inclusion (EDI). MHJ lived through a period of rapid change in the EDI policy landscape in higher education in the UK and there were some uncertainties in relation to understanding need, protocol and expectation – both within the collaboration and within and across the organisations. EDI policies address complex matters of identity and power which carry strong emotions. The rapidity of the policy changes caused a bump. MHJ, like all collaborations, was entangled with a wider process of change which continues to be worked through and it may have been somewhat amplified in the project because of its emphasis on justice.

As already discussed, the very words 'mental health' and 'justice' have become more culturally and politically salient now than they were in 2016 when the project formed. That also raised a rather unexpected issue around the 'MHJ' brand which created a bump in relation to what was being assumed either by individuals or organisations. One thing that emerged for me was that we were dealing with an ambiguity in relation to what MHJ was a reference to: a grant (which has a specific reference) or an emerging field (which is a very open reference). These two things are very different. If the term 'MHJ' is to continue beyond the grant (which I hope it does) this will need to be disambiguated.

In summary, there were some bumps but adaptation occurred, and the group got through them. I think it was an indication that strongly interdisciplinary projects will have to be accepted with 'warts and all' but with an expectation of a will to adapt. With MHJ, I think that will to adapt, in large part, went back to the early 'big tent' mental health and justice identity as well as to a good will commitment, and sense of responsibility, to make things better (as well as not make them worse).

Collaborative working as education

A final reflection on MHJ I would like to capture relates to the education of all of those who worked on it. I don't mean this in any kind of didactic sense. I mean *the experience* of doing strong interdisciplinarity and the education afforded thereof.

Firstly, a curious feature of the project was a generational (or seniority/juniority) difference in that educational experience. For senior researchers who were leading the workstreams and running the whole project, the rarity of *large-scale* strongly interdisciplinary projects meant that none of us had been brought up in this way of working. Most of us had their research habits and skills shaped (from doctoral research days onwards) by more solo, uni-disciplinarity or weakly interdisciplinary ways of working. In addition, we had only relatively sketchy blueprints or guidelines (discussed above) on how to lead and run strong interdisci-

---

over time. Laura was commissioned by the MHJ project to write a report on MHJ collaborative processes. These reports are freely available on the MHJ website. My account here draws on her work.

plinary projects. It was not even necessarily a case of 'see one, do one, teach one' because to see one there actually has to be one and it was not clear that there was a proto-MHJ project to 'see'. Also, there was not a, so to say, 'practical guide to strong interdisciplinarity for the new user' so we were in largely unchartered waters. That all said, nothing is completely new under the sun and we (i.e. the senior researchers) were able to draw on a blend of experience and learn on the way. It was possible to do a 'good enough' job of steering a course within the workstreams and across them.[14]

With the junior researchers, it was wonderful to see a phenomenon develop of semi-autonomous assembly, peer support and interdisciplinary collaboration. The junior researchers had the lion's share of research time and the peer support and work in progress group they formed was an important and enduring part of the project and its course. I think they literally *grew up* in strong interdisciplinarity in the workstreams and across them in a way that was new and unusual. The junior researchers (seven doctoral candidates) have done their doctoral research as, say, a psychologist or a psychiatrist at ease with the idea that a lawyer or a philosopher or social scientist is in the team. And all of them have been able to assume that research is also about meaningful contact with service users and that it engages with the issue of action (as discussed above) and balances values. That is quite a new educational experience, I think. Talking to a MHJ junior researcher recently who was thinking on how their doctorate compared to university peers (not working in an interdisciplinary collaboration) brought that home to me.

For all the researchers (senior and junior), the MHJ project has provided a substantial and helpful base of experience in *doing* strong interdisciplinarity which can be carried forward. The junior researchers will be very interesting ones to watch in the future on interdisciplinary achievement – both inside and outside of the academy – because they have 'grown up' in it and had their intellectual habits and expectations formed accordingly.[15]

Finally, it was noteworthy how art featured in the educational experience of doing strong interdisciplinarity. At the inception of the project our hunch was that the participatory arts would be important because they were fitted to the subject area of MHJ where the very ambiguity of the human condition and the inherent tensions between freedom and dependency, protection and empowerment are exposed. We thought that art could mobilise a different type of learning on the grey areas that would crop up in the workstreams and so we linked a Bethlem Gallery artist with each of the workstreams. That hunch about a different kind of learning was borne out and one good example was the interplay of a Bethlem artist with the workstream on advance directives that brought a new kind of appreciation of self-binding advance directives: both as sculpted objects and as a form of 'wrapping' rather than only 'binding'.[16] But something in addition also happened in MHJ with how art featured in the educational experience which was not part of our original 'hunch'. This was to do with the way art can flow with events, and take them up into its own activity in a way that science cannot achieve. The BLM movement was a major cultural event and its interplay with MHJ

---

14 On strong interdisciplinarity, the Wellcome 'Hearing the voices' project was a helpful point of external reference.
15 The remark (I think attributable to Churchill) that 'we form institutions and institutions form us' captures what I am struggling to articulate here.
16 The artwork was published by *The Lancet Psychiatry* together with a survey study of attitudes to the idea of self-binding co-produced with the service user organisation Bipolar UK.

within the participatory arts stream (see footnote 10) was a moving and enduring part of the MHJ educational experience. There was no clear anticipation of BLM at the start of MHJ and no research workstream was designed around it but the partnership with the Bethlem Gallery was able to respond to it as it unfolded in real time and create innovating forms of learning and influence.

Conclusion

It is too early to conclude what the MHJ project will transmit and not for me to judge it. The academic management group has reported on the original strategic aims of the project and it was a positive experience for us to reflect on how these have been met.[17]

What I hope, and relevant to how it started, is that the project has been an example of the kinds of influences, impacts and innovations that strongly interdisciplinary projects promise to provide. If so, then the project can be added to the background of experience for the research community (put in the extended interdisciplinary academic library, so to speak, for looking up by those wanting to work in an interdisciplinary way). We need to be able to say, and with good reason, about strong interdisciplinarity: 'this is what it can do', 'these are some things to do and not to do when running projects', 'do a project after being well taught in one' and 'do another one'!

On the problem of empowerment versus protection in mental health it is something of a cliché to refer to the number of lives affected by mental disorders or disabilities and quote figures like 1 in 4, etc. but the experience of doing MHJ has made me think that it is better to think that *everyone* is affected, directly or indirectly, by the problem of empowerment versus protection in mental health. The pandemic has shown how this is true but there are other examples.[18]

The MHJ project has been able to make just a small contribution to this vast problem of protection versus empowerment. It has been a wide-ranging 'big tent' type of contribution. I hope it helps further ships set sail. We all know that we need to keep struggling to achieve sustainability and growth in mental health and justice.

References

Committee on the rights of persons with disabilities. 2014. General Comment No. 1.
Gombrich, C. 2019. An outline of Alan Wilson's philosophy of knowledge, with special attention given to the importance of interdisciplinarity and its role in undergraduate education. *Interdisciplinary Science Reviews*, 44(3–4), 342–360.
Gombrich, C. 2021. Should future learning be problem-based? Royal Society of Edinburgh. Available from: https://rse.org.uk/resources/resource/blog/should-future-learning-be-problem-based/2022 (Accessed June 14th 2022).
Haidt, J. 2012. *The Righteous Mind*. Why Good People Are Divided by Politics and Religion. Pantheon.
Hamilton, M. & Coates, S. 2020. *Coronavirus and Anxiety, Great Britain: 3 April 2020 to 10 May 2020*. Office for National Statistics.
Hinrichs-Krapels, *et al.* 2020. Using policy labs as a process to bring evidence closer to public policy-making: A guide to one approach. *Palgrave Communications*, 6(1), 101.

---

17 The academic management group formally ended in January 2021.
18 Dementia, for example, is now the leading cause of death in the UK. I have yet to meet someone unaffected by the empowerment/protection problems arising from dementia.

Martin, W. & Gurbai, S. 2019. Surveying the Geneva impasse: Coercive care and human rights. *International Journal of Law and Psychiatry*, 64, 117–128.
Outcome mapping learning community. Available from: https://www.outcomemapping.ca/download/OM-faq-en.pdf (Accessed June 2022).
Owen, G., Freyenhagen, F., Richardson, G. & Hotopf, M. 2008. Mental capacity and decisional autonomy: An interdisciplinary challenge. *Inquiry*, 52(1), 79–107.
Owen, G., et al. 2018. The future of the Mental Health Act. King's College London. Available from: https://www.kcl.ac.uk/policy-institute/assets/future-of-the-mental-health-act.pdf (Accessed June 13th 2022).
Owen, G. S., et al. 2019. Advance decision-making in mental health - Suggestions for legal reform in England and Wales. *International Journal of Law and Psychiatry*, 64, 162–177.
Parker, J., Samantrai, R. & Romero, M. 2010. *Interdisciplinarity and Social Justice: Revisioning Academic Accountability*. SUNY Press.
Popper, K. 1963. *Conjectures and Refutations*. Routledge.
Sheather, J., Norcliffe Brown, D. 2022. *Health and Human Rights in the New World (Dis)Order: A Report from the British Medical Association*. BMA: British Medical Association. Avaible from: https://www.bma.org.uk/media/5491/20220104-bmas-human-rights-report-v4-compressed.pdf (Accessed June 13th 2022).
Talib, N. 2013. *Anti-Fragile: Things That Gain From Disorder*. Penguin.
Thornicroft, G., et al. 2013. Clinical outcomes of joint crisis plans to reduce compulsory treatment for people with psychosis: A randomised controlled trial. *Lancet*, 381(9878), 1634–1641.
Wilson, A. 2010. *Knowledge Power: Interdisciplinary Education for a Complex World*. Routledge.
Woodward, K., & Woodward, S. 2015. Gender studies and interdisciplinarity. *Palgrave Communications* 1, 15018. https://doi.org/10.1057/palcomms.2015.18

36
'DIGITISING THE MENTAL HEALTH ACT'

Are we facing the app-ification and platformisation of coercion in mental health services?

Piers Gooding

Introduction

In 2019, an industry publication called the *Medical Futurist* (2019) imagined a near future:

> [P]atients might go to the hospital with a broken arm and leave the facility with a cast and a note with a compulsory psychiatry session due to flagged suicide risk. That's what some scientists aim for with their A.I. system developed to catch depressive behavior early on and help reduce the emergence of severe mental illnesses.

This is one imagined future for mental health services. Others have rejected a forecast of expanded risk predictions and coercive intervention (see e.g. McQuillan, 2018), instead promoting co-operative support relationships augmented by selective use of data-driven technology (see e.g. Bossewitch, 2016; Cosgrove et al., 2020).

These contested futures are beginning to appear in the mainstream – often in the pages not of mental health journals but of financial news. Consider Elon Musk's claim that his 'AI-brain-chips company could "solve" autism and schizophrenia' (Hamilton, 2019) or the *MIT Technology Review* description of a mobile app 'that can tell you're depressed before you know it yourself' (Metz, 2018). The latter app, called *Mindstrong*, was developed with funding from Jeff Bezos' capital firm (Murtha, 2018), and its inaugural director and co-founder, Thomas Insel, joined the company after leaving a role at Google, where he had pursued a 'Big Data' approach to mental health (Reardon, 2017). Insel had previously been the director of the US National Institute of Mental Health (NIMH). Between 2009 and 2015, NIMH (2017) disbursed US$445 million to projects concerned with 'technology-enhanced mental health interventions'.

Despite the attention-grabbing claims of the *Medical Futurist*, and indeed of Musk, many such proposals are the stuff of speculative fiction. Often, there is scant evidence for the technical feasibility of their claims, except in the most exploratory of terms. Even claims about the *Mindstrong* app are promissory, and like many algorithmic and data-driven proposals in men-

DOI: 10.4324/9781003226413-44

This chapter has been made available under a CC-BY-NC-ND license.

tal healthcare, they lack a robust evidence base; its website supports the product with reference to a single study with a total sample of 27 people (Corbyn, 2021; Dagum, 2018). This point is important because even critical responses to new technologies, such as an analysis of their legal and ethical downsides, risks amplifying the sensational claims behind them. This inadvertent hype can exaggerate the technical feasibility of a proposal and risks promoting a 'distorted picture of science's potential' (Horgan, 2021). An even greater risk, according to historian of computational technology David Brock (2019), is that 'wishful worries' about speculative futures can distract us from the 'actual agonies' of technology-use today.

Indeed, for the purposes of this chapter, there are several forms of digital data-driven technologies that are being used today, which are starting to reshape processes of mental health-related law in some countries. These technologies may not be as sensational as 'AI brain-chips' or forms of algorithmic pre-vision, but these more mundane technical systems – in particular, video-conference software, online platforms for managing healthcare labour, and electronic health records – have significant legal ramifications for people facing involuntary psychiatric intervention. This chapter will turn to these sociotechnical systems[1] as a way to reflect on the digital futures of mental health-related law.

Specifically, the chapter will focus on the explicit policy aim to 'digitise mental health legislation' in England and Wales, with reference to the *Mental Health Act 1983* (England and Wales) (MHA). I will look at three developments: (1) the rise of digital platforms to coordinate MHA assessments of those facing involuntary intervention, (2) the use of videocall technology to make remote medical assessments to authorise intervention under the Act, and (3) remote video hearings of mental health tribunals. Some of these developments are not unique to England and Wales, and brief comparative points will be made with other jurisdictions. Yet, the chapter will focus on English and Welsh law and policy given 'digitising mental health legislation' (HM Government, 2018, p. 213) is an explicit policy aim, unlike elsewhere.

Beyond a descriptive account of the evolving law, policy, and practice, the final section will reflect on these experiments and look to the levers in policy and law that can help govern them responsibly. I will consider human rights concerns raised by 'digitising' mental health legislation, and draw in a political economy perspective to reflect on the role of the private sector in emerging configurations of digitised health and social services. I will argue that although courts appear responsive to the impact of videocall platforms on the direct application of the MHA – specifically for remote medical assessments and tribunal hearings – there appear to be less obvious means to monitor and respond to the use of digital platforms in administering MHA-related crisis work, and in the broader 'platformisation' of health and social services (Faulkner-Gurstein and Wyatt, 2021). Even as there remain open questions about the role of videocall technologies in hearings and assessments (for example, concerning access to justice for those subject to MHA orders or the experimental use of remote

---

1 'Sociotechnical systems' refers to a 'system involving the interaction of hard systems and human beings, in ways that either cannot be separated or are thought to be inappropriate to separate'('Socio-Technical System', n.d.). It offers a concept for analysing the dynamic interaction of people and technology, rather than narrowly focusing on merely the technology itself. The concept has origins as an extension Sociotechnical Theory, which emerged from organisational development in organising complex work, and which offers language for describing, analysing, and designing organisations, and has become a widely used concept for studies in human computer interaction (Baxter and Sommerville, 2011). For the purposes of this paper it is used to refer to the digital systems under discussion, and the people and social structures that interact with them.

medical assessments for people under community treatment orders (CTOs) in Scotland), more pressing questions arise regarding the checks and balances in place for the use of private digital platforms for facilitating the setup by mental health practitioners of compulsory treatment and hospital detention.

Background: 'Digitising the Mental Health Act' in England and Wales

Today, electronic records and official forms are more easily transferable across communication systems than ever before. The growing interconnectedness and complexity of these systems has driven efforts by governments – and, increasingly, private market actors – to digitise processes of involuntary psychiatric intervention. The COVID-19 pandemic has accelerated these developments. Social distancing prerogatives have helped strengthen information communication infrastructure and remote technologies in many health and social care systems. The pandemic has also arguably created a 'seller's market' for private technology vendors seeking to disrupt traditional forms of service delivery (see e.g. Teräs et al., 2020).

In 2018, the British government recommended 'digitising … the Mental Health Act' (HM Government, 2018, p. 213) following its major review of the MHA for the Department and National Health Service (NHS) England and Improvement. The recommendation aimed to provide 'patients with a modern and consistent way to access information about the Act, their rights, safeguards and treatment processes' (HM Government, 2018, p. 213). Digitising administrative requirements, it was suggested, could help reduce delays (including during the assessment process), maximise the time professionals could spend with their patients, and 'improve patient access to care records, care plans, treatment preferences and advance choice documents, and the details and wishes of nominated persons' (HM Government, 2018, p. 213). Clinical decision tools could be integrated, including those that prompt clinicians to carry out 'observations or assessments before tribunal deadlines', and patients could 'benefit from digital access to information, self-care tools and easily navigable forms of clinical and non-clinical support' (HM Government, 2018, p. 213). These aims sat within the broader recommendation 'to test, evaluate and roll-out a fully digitised, consistent approach to the MHA' (HM Government, 2018, p. 213).

Digital platforms for professionals conducting MHA assessment setup and claim form processes

Within this context, private sector actors and government agencies have created various online platforms designed to assist the mental health professionals who are seeking to apply the MHA and impose involuntary psychiatric intervention over a person (see s12 Solutions, 2022; Thalamos, 2022a; Stevens et al. 2022). For example, one for-profit company, *s12 Solutions* (2022), established an online platform that allows social workers, nurses, psychologists, and others who are interacting with a person in crisis to locate and communicate with authorised medical practitioners (s12 Solutions, 2022). Such practitioners may assess the person and authorise involuntary intervention, as well as completing and submitting payment claim forms for their work. At the time of writing, the company reports that its product is used by approximately 75% of England's Mental Health Trusts (S12 Solutions, 2022).

s12 Solutions is so named because Section 12 of the MHA establishes provisions regarding medical recommendations for involuntary intervention. Subsection 2 requires one of the medical practitioners making a recommendation for the involuntary admission of patients to hospital to be authorised by the Secretary of State as having 'special experience in the diagnosis or treatment of mental disorder' (*Mental Health Act 1983* (England and Wales) [12(2)]). The role of a digitised triaging platform like *s12 Solutions*, according to Stevens and colleagues (2020, p. 16), is to enable 'authorised mental health practitioners' or AMHPs[2] to 'contact section 12 doctors, to arrange MHA assessments'. Further, within the platform:

> approval of involved doctors is checked against the national database on a weekly basis ... Section 12 doctors can enter their availability on a personal calendar and 'build a profile containing their location, specialities and languages spoken, and monitor their activity via a dashboard'. Doctors can also use the platform to record the assessments they have attended, to provide supporting evidence for Continuing Professional Development. In addition, the app provides data capture and reporting about the MHA assessment process.
>
> *(Stevens et al. 2020, p. 16)*

The platform was endorsed by a Chief Executive of one NHS Trust (s12 Solutions, 2020), who, according to *s12 Solutions*, described the company as '[t]he Uber of finding doctors for the health service' (S12 Solutions, 'What is S12 Solutions?' Twitter (21 Jan 2020) https://twitter.com/S12Solutions/status/1219262300667961349 [accessed 19/05/2021]).

Loosening regulation of the electronic communication of statutory forms under the MHA

Two years after the 2018 recommendation to digitise the MHA, and following the outbreak of COVID-19, mental health treatment regulations were amended in December 2020 to allow electronic communication of statutory forms under the MHA (*The Mental Health (Hospital, Guardianship and Treatment) (England) (Amendment) Regulations 2020*). Another for-profit company, which provides a platform for streamlining professionals' administrative activities under the MHA, *Thalamos* (2022b), noted the legislative amendment on its website, stating that 'we have even helped change the law'. The amendment advanced the 2018 Review of the MHA in its aim to speed up applications for compulsory intervention orders, while also aiding with pandemic-related imperatives to socially distance. The changes were made, according to the Department of Health and Social Care (England and Wales) (2020, s 7.5):

> because developments in information technology allow for integrated and secure information systems in the NHS, which serve patients by keeping relevant clinical information about them so that services can respond to the needs of patients quickly and appropriately. Such systems have the potential in this case to help professionals follow the requirements of the Act in ways that do not use their time unnecessarily, for example by waiting to receive signed paper forms.

---

2 Approved Mental Health Professionals were introduced by the *Mental Health Act 2007*, which amended the *Mental Health Act 1983*. Their role is primarily to coordinate the assessment of individuals who are being considered for detention under the *Mental Health Act 1983*. They are typically social workers but may be nurses, occupational therapists, and psychologists, with varying accreditation requirements.

Research concerning the online triaging and form-processing platforms sheds some light on the changes created by these amendments, and appears largely positive.

A 2022 study on the availability of 'Section 12 approved doctors' in England and Wales, for example, specifically asked a range of approved doctors, AMHPs, NHS managers, 'Chair of Approvals Panels', and other key informants (n=52), about using the *s12 Solutions* app (Stevens et al., 2022). The interviewees reported three main advantages of the app:

1. it provides information about the availability of section 12 doctors and their sub-specialisms;
2. facilitates the payment of fees to section 12 doctors;
3. and supports the 'smooth running' of MHA assessments, which reduces AMHPs' workloads (Stevens et al., 2022, p. 60).

These noted benefits are consistent with an earlier evaluation by the Wessex Academic Health Science Network (2020). This Network is an NHS-managed public-private entity self-described as a partnership of 'NHS and academic organisations, local authorities, the third sector and industry' (The AHSN Network, 2022). I will return to the Academic Health Science Network later in the chapter.

A small number of interviewees in Stevens and colleagues' (2022b, 3) study expressed concerns about the *s12 Solutions* app. These concerns include that:

- dependence on the internet could limit its application in some areas;
- the app could potentially mean that AMHPs would be less likely to seek the involvement of a section 12 doctor who knows the patient, because of easy access to large numbers of section 12 doctors;
- reluctance by some AMHPs or section 12 doctors to use the technology;
- some AMHPs may wish to use their lists of known and trusted section 12 doctors; and
- a small number of technical problems had been experienced.

(Stevens et al., 2022b, iii)

Several interviewees also expressed a preference for the app to be developed and owned by the Department of Health and Social Care and raised concerns about how much it costs and whether public services should pay for it (Stevens et al., 2022b, 3). Perhaps for this reason, one Clinical Commissioning Group (an NHS organisation set up to organise the delivery of NHS services in England) created its own app, though little information about the app is publicly available (Stevens et al., 2022b, iii).

Elsewhere, some mental health services users have raised concerns about the unknown impact of the digitised triage process on those who use services or are subjected to involuntary interventions (Mental Elf, 2020). The potential for AMHPs to seek a section 12 doctor out of convenience rather than a doctor with whom the person is familiar would be a significant issue in this regard. However, this concern would seemingly extend beyond the *s12 Solutions* app to the NHS-run national MHA Approvals Register Database, which provides a list of 9000+ section 12 doctors. Nevertheless, no research appears to have explored this concern in much depth nor sought the views of service users or those whose MHA detention was facilitated by digital platforms.

One major legal concern to arise following platform-use for mental health crisis work is the use of videocalls by section 12 authorised doctors to conduct remote personal assessments of those facing MHA interventions.

Videocall assessments for authorising detention: England

Administering involuntary psychiatric interventions via online platforms affords the possibility of remote expert assessments of an individual to determine if an intervention should occur. Remote MHA assessments were encouraged by the NHS in the early stages of the pandemic but in 2021 they were ruled by the High Court of England to have been unlawful (*Devon Partnership NHS Trust v Secretary of State for Health and Social Care* (January 2021); Dyer, 2021).

Under the MHA, applications for detention can only be made by an AMHP who has 'personally seen' the patient in a recent 14-day period (Section 11). Supporting medical recommendations must come from practitioners who have 'personally examined' the patient (Section 12). These provisions, at first glance, appear ambiguous as to whether assessments via videocall could meet the threshold of being 'personally seen' or 'examined'. In May 2020, prior to the High Court decision, NHS England (2020) and Department of Health and Social Care for England released guidance stating that 'the provisions of the Mental Health Act *do allow* for video assessments to occur' (emphasis added), but that '[e]ven during the COVID-19 pandemic it is always preferable to carry out a Mental Health Act assessment in person'. A caveat was added that 'providers should be aware that only courts can provide a definitive interpretation of the law' (NHS England, 2020).

Subsequently, the Devon Partnership NHS Trust sought clarification from the High Court, which found 'that the phrases "personally seen" in s. 11(5) and "personally examined" in s. 12(1) require the physical attendance of the person in question on the patient' (*Devon Partnership NHS Trust v Secretary of State for Health and Social Care* (January 2021) [s.62]). The court made clear that any change to the law in England and Wales on this matter would be for Parliament.

Subsequently, the Department of Health and Social Care (2021) released a white paper titled 'Reforming the Mental Health Act', which addressed the prospect of remote MHA assessments, among other issues. In a section on use of remote technology, the paper stated:

> At the time of the White Paper's publication, the position of the Government and NHS [England and Improvement] was that the Act may be interpreted to allow for this. However, the High Court found otherwise.
>
> In parallel … the Government held discussions with stakeholders to consider whether the Act should be amended to allow … for the use of remote assessments. We have decided not to do so. The broad consensus was that the presence of professionals in the room with people is required. It is in the interest of patients, and preserves established good practice.
>
> *(Department of Health and Social Care, 2021 [28])*

During the period in which videocall assessments *were* being used, a survey of AMHPs by the British Association of Social Workers (BASW, 2020) looked at the impact of the COVID-19 pandemic on AMHP services. Several benefits of remote assessments were listed, including reducing the risk of COVID-19 infection for all concerned, undertaking out-of-area assessments over large distances, and being able to assess people in care homes that did not allow visitors (BASW, 2020, 29). Concerns were raised among the 100 AMHPs who were surveyed, 'that some professionals will want to use [digital technology during MHA assessments] "for convenience rather than necessity"' and that '[i]t hampers effective communication, including the observation and assessment on non-verbal cues and behaviour' (BASW, 2020, 29). Reportedly, '[o]nly a small number of respondents felt that these assessments worked well' (BASW, 2020, 29).

Elsewhere in the UK, the potential for remote assessments during this time have been considered more favourably. In Scotland, the *Mental Health (Care and Treatment) (Scotland) Act 2003* does *not* require assessments to be conducted in person, yet the Code of Practice for the Act does appear to envision that detention assessments would be conducted face-to-face in all circumstances (Scottish Executive, 2003 [parts 5, 6, 7 & 20]; noted in Schölin et al., 2021). The Mental Welfare Commission for Scotland has subsequently recommended that remote assessments *should* be permitted in limited circumstances; particularly for the renewal of a community treatment order, which 'might be preferably undertaken remotely with the consent of the patient' (Schölin et al., 2021, 604).

The recommendation is justified by 'the possibility of patients who have existing relationships with psychiatrists to have assessments undertaken remotely', again stressing that 'the method of assessment should not be forced on the patient, but respect the patient's preferences' (Schölin et al., 2021, 604). It is outside the scope of this chapter to consider the implications for law and practice in Scotland of this recommendation. Suffice to say that ethical and legal challenges remain, including with obtaining the informed consent of the person concerned (see Schölin et al., 2021), as well as with regard to the unique compulsory powers afforded by CTOs in community settings (Fennell, 2010), and what it might mean to extend forms of medical power via digital modes into peoples' homes and residences (see relatedly, Series, 2022; Crowther and McGregor, 2022).

Videoconferencing in tribunals that authorise involuntary psychiatric intervention

A third major area of digitisation was the increased use of videoconferencing software in the formal proceedings of mental health tribunals, a trend in no way unique to England and Wales. Since the COVID-19 pandemic began, remote hearings have ramped up in several countries, such as Scotland (Stavert and McKay, 2020), Australia (Wilson, 2020), and the US (Vitiello and Williams, 2021). In England and Wales, contingency planning was implemented for tribunals across the Courts and Tribunals Judiciary early in the pandemic (Rider, 2020). Practice directions required that hearings should be held remotely where it was reasonably practicable and in accordance with their overriding objective. This temporary directive did not appear to be extended beyond September 2021 (Wilson, 2022, 'Coronavirus' [s 1.5]).

An immediate question to be asked is whether the transition to remote tribunals impacted outcomes, such as discharge rates. According to the Care Quality Commission (2022, 66–67), it did not: the First-Tier Tribunal (Mental Health) continued to hear cases throughout the pandemic using remote hearings and the change 'to remote hearings appear[ed] to have had no effect on outcome, with similar proportions of discharges to hearings in 2020/21 compared to the previous year'.

Case law reveals some legal issues with the transition to remote hearings, particularly concerning access to justice. One case, *Re D [2020] MHLO 51 (FTT)* (a non-binding First-Tier Tribunal decision) involved the tribunal's decision being set aside because 'it was not clear whether or not the patient had a reasonable opportunity to hear all the evidence that was given at the hearing: it was not possible to be sure that the patient had a fair hearing' [4].

The patient's microphone had been muted for much of the time after giving her evidence at the outset because she 'would not stop talking' (*Re D [2020] MHLO 51 (FTT)* [4]). The judge suggested steps for ensuring a 'reasonable opportunity to hear all the evidence that was given', including going back to the person at the end of each witness statement to ensure that she had heard and understood the evidence given (*Re D [2020] MHLO 51 (FTT)* [4]).

In *GL v Elysium Healthcare [2020] UKUT 308 (AAC)*, a patient, GL, had his adjournment request refused and the tribunal proceeded with a telephone hearing in his absence. The Upper Tribunal determined that the tribunal's decision was unlawful because:

1. The tribunal had assumed that GL's flatmate (who was in a different room to the patient, behind a closed door, as they were both self-isolating due to COVID-19) would not overhear the proceedings [11].
2. The tribunal had disregarded or afforded too little weight to the patient's anxiety about being overheard or others learning his history. In the past, GL had been seriously assaulted by another patient who learned of his past offending. The tribunal should have considered whether his anxiety would have impacted his ability to participate [12].
3. The tribunal had wrongly approached GL's request as if he was concerned about the mode of hearing (via telephone) rather than the specific circumstances giving rise to the risk of being overheard [14].

The cases demonstrate that although discharge rates overall may not have been impacted by the move to remote hearings, there remained significant risks to procedural fairness with the move to remote hearings.

There is limited research on patient and clinician experiences of remote hearings. One (non-peer reviewed) survey conducted by the Mental Health Tribunal and the Royal College of Psychiatrists (2021a) recorded the views of 223 clinicians and 30 patients. Of the clinician respondents, 33% thought remote hearings were better for them – 'a more efficient use of clinical time' (Royal College of Psychiatrists, 2021a, 1). (What the remaining 57% of clinicians reported is unstated.) A total of 58% of clinicians reported that hearings were disrupted in some way due to technological issues and 29% reported that hearings had no disruption (Royal College of Psychiatrists, 2021a, 1). Clinicians gave examples of when they thought remote hearings would be useful, including: 'if the patient had indicated they would not attend, or could not attend (due to behaviour, being in seclusion or segration [sic]) and also [in instances in which] the patient was in a more familiar environment on the ward than in the tribunal room' (Royal College of Psychiatrists, 2021a, 2).

The 30 patients who provided feedback reported similar satisfaction with remote hearings as with face-to-face hearings (Royal College of Psychiatrists, 2021a); 40% of patient respondents reported no problems with technological issues (though it is not reported if the remaining patients reported disruption due to technological issues, or to what extent). Not all patients were aware of the process of a remote hearing. To improve patient experiences, the report authors recommended (Royal College of Psychiatrists, 2021a, 3):

1. The [Tribunal] panel to continue to ask order of evidence and reasonable adjustments from the [responsible clinician], patient and patient's representative;
2. Patients to be offered breaks during the hearing;
3. Information leaflets about remote hearings written by the Tribunal to be given to patients.

These recommendations were to be integrated into Tribunal Members' training during 2021–2022, and the tenor of the document suggests an overall plan to continue remote hearings (for example, the report recommends that NHS Trusts invest in technology infrastructure for patients) (Royal College of Psychiatrists, 2021a, 2–3).

Videoconferencing in authorising involuntary psychiatric interventions: United States

By way of international comparison, in the US, the majority of civil commitment hearings were conducted remotely by the end of 2020 (Sorrentino et al., 2020). 'Remotely' entailed not simply videocalls with the relevant person, which have been used in varying ways since the 1990s (see e.g. American Psychiatric Association, 1998), but the entire courtroom meeting remotely, including judge and courtroom personnel (attorney, witnesses, and so on). When the pandemic began, the Judicial Conference of the US gave temporary approval to the use of video and telephone conferencing during COVID-19 civil commitment hearings, and indeed all civil proceedings (*Coronavirus Aid, Relief, and Economic Security Act. S. 3548, 116th Cong., 2d Sess. (2020) (enacted)*). The approval built upon a 2016 Position Statement by the American Psychiatric Association (APA, 2016), which argued that videoconferencing was an 'acceptable and cost-effective alternative that protects the privacy of the patient without compromising their due process rights'.

However, Evan Vitiello and Joseph Williams (2021, p. 610) highlight that 'courts have not been aligned with each other regarding the legality of a commitment tele-hearing arrangement'. They cite decisions in the US Fourth Circuit (*United States v. Baker*, 45 F.3d 837 (4th Cir. 1995)) and the Virginia Supreme Court (*Shellman v. Commonwealth of Virginia* (Va. 2012)) which offered support for a virtual commitment hearing format but contrast them with other courts that have restricted videoconferencing usage for commitment proceedings. For example, the Florida Supreme Court held that respondents have a veto on videoconferenced commitment hearings (*Doe v. State, 217 So. 3d 1020* (Fla. 2017)), and Oregon's Court of Appeals required trial courts to make a clear justification for holding a commitment hearing via videocall where the respondent objects to the format (*re G.N., 215 P.3d 902* (Or. Ct. App. 2009)). There has been no US Supreme Court ruling on the lawfulness of the remote mode of civil commitment hearings, nor on the procedural safeguards that might be required, reflecting a similar state of flux as in the UK and elsewhere.

Discussion: Reflections on technological experimentation and mental health law

Government agencies are increasingly adopting digital technological approaches to mediate the relationship between citizens and mental health services, including involuntary or coercive interventions. Even when the service user or person subject to intervention does not engage *directly* with such digital systems, such as app-based triaging and MHA practitioner payments like the *s12 Solutions* and *Thalamos*, the new systems directly shape people's experience of mental health law and practice. This may be for better, in improving service responsiveness, or it may be for worse, such as by increasing the potential for a person in crisis to be assessed by a clinician unknown to them.

Simultaneously, governments are attempting to regulate and govern the rapidly expanding technology sector in recognition of the ethico-legal issues these technologies raise.

According to some, these government efforts are hampered by narratives pushed by the technology industry that 'policymakers are people that don't understand the technology itself' (Jordan and Klein, 2020), and similar derisive claims are sometimes leveled at academics.

However, efforts to govern technological developments are occurring in the mental health context in a range of ways. In England and Wales, the High Court's recognition of the qualitative difference between in-person and videocall medical assessment concerning detention under the MHA is a prime example, as is the subsequent consultation by the Department of Health and Social Care that demurred from recommending legislative change to allow remote assessments. The decision by the Mental Welfare Commission for Scotland to allow remote assessment for consenting adults on CTOs is noteworthy, and questions are likely to be raised regarding the affordances of digital technologies in extending processes of coercive intervention in the community. Another example of active governance is the temporary contingency measures to allow for remote Mental Health Tribunal hearings under Section 3 of the *Tribunals, Courts and Enforcement Act 2007* (England and Wales), which was time-limited, being initially authorised for six months, with options to renew or revoke at any time should it become inappropriate or unnecessary (Byrom and Beardon, 2021 [2.5]). Courts appear to be taking a precautionary approach, identifying that a fair trial clearly requires that a person can fully engage in the remote hearing process. This sentiment was articulated by the judge in *Re D [2020]* (*MHLO 51 (FTT)*), who highlighted 'the difficulty for all concerned of managing hearings on video, and the extra care that needs to be taken by all participants to ensure that justice is being done consistently'.

Regarding the use of apps or digital platforms for professionals conducting MHA assessment setup and claim form processes, it is perhaps slightly harder to identify levers for responsible governance and oversight – at least from a legal perspective. This is not to suggest that the courts or tribunals in the UK have 'got it right' in exercising oversight of remote medical assessments or hearings; rather, it is to say that the levers in law for governing such processes are readily apparent. This seems to be less the case regarding the 'app-ification' or 'platformisation' of mental health crisis work.

The apps or platforms discussed earlier in the chapter are not subject to direct oversight by the mental health tribunals and tend not to be characterised as enabling a direct application of the MHA in the way assessments and hearings do. Instead, the use of apps and platforms to set up MHA assessment are viewed in policy terms as facilitating the administration of practitioner activity or as 'workforce development', as one report suggests (Stevens et al., 2022). Yet, as discussed above, safety issues and concerns about the rights of those subject to interventions via the app remain, and these real or potential harms may be missed by such an administrative framing. Nor does it appear that the application of the platform model in public policy is necessarily well understood (Faulkner-Gurstein and Wyatt, 2021), posing barriers to transparency and scrutiny. Procurement and commissioning processes may constitute a 'soft law' lever for governments to balance their role as regulators and procurers of emerging technologies and innovations in mental health crisis work. Procurement processes have also been a site for civil society representatives such as professional associations or service user advocacy groups to direct their attention, as the next section will note. However, serious issues have emerged on these fronts, with evidence that the NHS's current procurement and commissioning arrangements, particularly involving data-driven approaches to mental health law, are far from ideal.

Safety and accountability amid digitisation and privatisation

The reported description of *s12 Solutions* by an NHS Trust Executive as the 'Uber of finding doctors for the health service' is striking. Uber is synonymous with disruptive 'platform' businesses that, at least in one major iteration of the digital platform, connect 'producers' and 'consumers'/platform users (Faulkner-Gurstein and Wyatt, 2021). The comment is perhaps indicative of the alignment between the use of digital technology in government agencies and trends to privatise health and social services, including a growing reliance on the private sector to solve problems, especially through technological means (Petersen, 2018, pp. 66–77).

s12 Solutions was founded by an AMHP herself who was reportedly frustrated with the inefficient MHA communication process between relevant professionals (Stevens et al., 2022). More recently, the company was acquired by a larger, for-profit electronic health records company (Matlow, 2021) in an acquisition deal reportedly worth USD$8.23M ('S12 Solutions Company Profile,' n.d.). The business was originally supported with funding from the NHS Innovation Accelerator, as well as other sub-programmes of NHS England, including its Innovation and Technology Payment Evidence Generation Fund, NHS England's Clinical Entrepreneur programme, and DigitalHealth.London's Accelerator (s12 Solutions, 2022), helping to secure the programmes reported uptake in 75% of NHS Trusts.

The involvement of the private sector in the NHS is a hotly contested topic, and beyond the scope of this paper. However, I will briefly consider the concern of some commentators that traditional accountability measures may be ill-equipped to ensure private digital technology providers align with the public good, particularly where the divide between public and private entities becomes blurred (United Nations General Assembly, 2018). These possibilities, at a minimum, seem important to articulate, especially where for-profit entities are taking a role in digitising processes that involve restrictions on a person's liberty, legal capacity, autonomy, and other fundamental rights, as occurs with involuntary psychiatric intervention.

Philip Alston, the former UN 'Special Rapporteur on extreme poverty and human rights', has raised concerns about digitisation in the provision of social and healthcare services more generally; he argues that growing privatisation, often accompanied by processes of digitisation, has rendered existing mechanisms of accountability increasingly marginal (United Nations General Assembly, 2018). The rise of private sector actors in social protection services, according to Alston, has been accompanied by a 'deeply problematic lack of information about the precise role and responsibility of private actors in proposing, developing and operating digital technologies in welfare states around the world' (United Nations General Assembly, 2019). The current UN Special Rapporteur for the Rights of Persons with Disabilities, Gerard Quinn, has argued that government funding for digital initiatives in the disability context – including mental health services – should be dependent upon submissions regarding stringent evidence of safety and efficacy, and in accordance with human rights (Human Rights Council, 2021). Quinn's and Alston's comments are general in nature, and I am not suggesting in any way that the companies discussed earlier in this paper have acted improperly.

Where serious concerns *can* be raised is with the NHS-managed public-private partnerships that have helped to resource such digital platform companies, and the ecosystem of public-private entities from which they emerge. For example, in 2021, the Royal College of Psychiatrists (UK) called for an 'urgent and transparent investigation' into the 'NHS Innovation Accelerator' and Academic Health Science Network, both of which have provided financial and institutional support to *s12 Solutions, Thalamos,* and other for-profit operators concerning digitised MHA arrangements (see NHS England, n.d.). Public concerns about these quasi-government entities related specifically to a programme called 'Serenity Integrated Mentoring'.

Serenity Integrated Mentoring: A case study in the perils of innovation-speak

'Serenity Integrated Mentoring' (or SIM) was a programme run in England by police and public mental health services directed at individuals who are frequently detained under section 136 of the MHA (Jackson and Brewster, 2018). Such individuals were defined by the private company behind SIM as 'high intensity users' (Jackson and Brewster, 2018). The SIM programme involved police and mental health crisis services collaborating to develop 'case management plans that allowed a seamless move from offers of therapeutic engagement (by the mental health team) to use of coercive measures (by the police) with those who persisted with frequent crisis presentations' (House, 2022, p. 1). The individuals were chosen based on local health authority MHA data for the previous year to 'define which borough/geographical area had the highest proportion of high intensity users of [Section] 136' (Jackson and Brewster, 2018, 6). SIM did not use app-based technology, though a key component of the programme was electronic health records being shared between government agencies that were used to flag individuals in emergency service encounters.

In May 2021, major concerns were reported about the programme following advocacy by a service user-led group, the StopSIM Coalition (n.d.). According to one media report:

> When tagged under the system, patients can be denied care, prevented from seeing doctors or psychiatrists, and sent home. An NHS doctor told [media] that he had to turn away a woman who had attempted suicide on multiple occasions because she had been assigned to the SIM scheme. He considered resigning as a result.
> *(Strudwick, 2021)*

The Royal College of Psychiatrists (2021) released a highly critical statement about the programme, reporting that:

> [where a person] remained unwell and continued to self-harm, attempt suicide or report suicidality, in some cases they were prosecuted and imprisoned or community protection notices were applied which required them to stop self-harming or calling for help, with imprisonment as a potential sanction if they breached the notice.

The StopSIM coalition raised three major concerns: the harm of police contact and criminalisation of those in crisis, application of the 'mentoring' without the free and informed consent of the person, and sharing of confidential information with police (House, 2022).

Concerning data protection, StopSIM charged that the programme 'allows "sensitive data" (information like medical records, ethnicity, religion, sexuality, gender reassignment and financial information) to be shared between services without the subject's consent … (for example, as a consequence of calling [emergency services] when feeling suicidal)' (StopSIM Coalition, n.d.). This claim was denied by the company (Moreton, 2021), and steps towards General Data Protection Regulation (GDPR) compliance were outlined in early NHS programme material (Jackson and Brewster, 2018, 5). However, Allan House (2022, p. 2) has reported troubling evidence of what he described as the company's 'authoritarian' approach to sharing confidential clinical data. 'Crisis plans' were developed by sharing clinical information with police at any time, because patients in the scheme were portrayed as 'constantly an emergency case' – conceivably circumventing GDPR restrictions on non-urgent data sharing – and staff were instructed to 'please don't tell the patient they have any right to choose who reads it. Know your GDPR' (cited in House, 2022, p. 2).

These are very serious allegations, and an NHS-led investigation is underway at the time of writing to clarify precisely what happened, as noted below. Regardless, by 2021, the SIM programme had been reportedly rolled out to 23 NHS mental health trusts and 18 police forces in England (Moreton, 2021). The programme had expanded with the institutional and financial support of the NHS Innovation Accelerator programme and the NHS-managed Academic Health Science Networks. The company director behind SIM was made an 'NHS Innovation Accelerator Fellow', which entitles recipients to financial and institutional support 'to further scale [Fellows'] promising innovations' (Ducey, 2018); and the NHS had commissioned the Academic Health Science Networks to 'support the spread and adoption of SIM' between April 2018 and March 2020 ('AHSN Network statement on SIM (Serenity Integrated Mentoring)', 2021).

This rollout occurred despite a lack of robust assessment of impact on patient safety or outcomes (Royal College of Psychiatrists, 2021). Instead, research by the Academic Health Science Network – again, a public-private entity – focused principally on SIM's impact on cost minimisation, with a small number of descriptive case studies (see e.g. Health Innovation Network South London, 2020). The Academic Health Science Networks are self-described in one such report as 'the only bodies that connect NHS and academic organisations, local authorities, the third sector and industry' and as 'catalysts that create the right conditions to facilitate change across whole health and social care economies, with a clear focus on improving outcomes for patients' (Health Innovation Network South London, 2020).

The SIM programme was also the recipient of several awards within a broader eco-system of for-profit entities concerned with privatisation and healthcare technology. This included a 'Patient Safety Award' by the *Health Service Journal* (2017) (not to be confused with the academic *Health Services Journal*), a UK online media company that is a subsidiary of a private consulting firm that advertises its role in 'NHS Service Improvement' through '[c]onsultancy services, and bespoke insights and analytics, designed to improve patient experiences and market access' (Wilmington Healthcare, 2022).

After concerted advocacy by the StopSIM coalition and others, the company behind the SIM programme appears to have closed permanently; its website was removed and its social media presence wiped.[3] An overarching concern of the StopSIM coalition was that outsourcing service provision to a private company meant the programme fell between gaps of traditional accountability mechanisms (StopSIM Coalition, n.d.):

> Usually when a new treatment is introduced into the NHS there is a careful process of checking that it is safe and effective before it is rolled out to patients. This includes trialling it with a small number of people and assessing how well it meets their needs as well as catching any unintended consequences or side effects. SIM bypassed this process by being sold as an 'innovation' or 'quality improvement' measure and so research into the safety and effects of SIM has not been done.

---

3 An archived version of the Network website is available here: https://web.archive.org/web/20201126102513/https://highintensitynetwork.org/ (accessed 25/08/21).

At the time of writing, the National Clinical Director for Mental Health has directed NHS Mental Health Trusts to review their use of SIM (AHSN Network, 2022). It is unclear whether this review will extend to the role of the NHS Innovation Accelerator and Academic Health Science Network, as recommended by the Royal College of Psychiatrists and the StopSIM coalition.

Governing sociotechnical systems in the public interest: Finding the right(s) framework?

In providing an account of SIM, I am not suggesting that this programme is at all comparable in nature or in terms of the harms it has caused, to the digital platforms discussed earlier that assist professionals to conduct MHA assessments. Instead, I am suggesting that the current NHS procurement and commissioning of private sector practices concerning mental health crisis work – particularly through the NHS Innovation Accelerator and Academic Health Science Network, which again have provided institutional resources to promote the widespread uptake of the apps/platforms noted earlier – appear manifestly inadequate. These concerns align with critiques of accountability deficits common to privatisation and digitisation of public services, noted above.

This situation is clearly unsatisfactory in terms of the rights of those engaging with public mental health services, but nor would it seem desirable to those wishing to innovate mental health crisis work in good faith. This latter group are likely to want robust evidentiary and safety requirements that have the confidence of service user groups and professional associations alike, among others – a confidence that does not appear to be enjoyed by public-private partnerships like Academic Health Science Networks or the NHS Accelerator, at least at present.

Currently, some parts of the programme evaluations conducted by the Academic Health Science Networks tend to read like promotional material rather than rigorous and independent research. As one example, an evaluation of the *s12 Solutions* app by the Wessex Academic Health Science Network (2020 s.11.3), contains a section on the UK's General Data Protection Regulation, which is established by the *Data Protection Act 2018* (UK). This is likely to be a core domestic legal concern regarding the digitisation of health services. The evaluators first list the data protection issues of the traditional AMHP system, which arise because paper- or email-based forms pass by numerous individuals and in multiple settings (Wessex Academic Health Science Network, 2020, 68). In contrast, the *s12 Solutions* app presents a standardised claim form that is sent directly to the claim form processor. This is straightforward enough, yet the authors go on to state that '[t]herefore, patient and staff privacy are maintained and the risk of a *GDPR breach is eliminated*' (Wessex Academic Health Science Network, 2020, 68 (emphasis added)). This conclusion is overstated and unrealistic. GDPR compliance only every aims to *minimise* – not eliminate – the risk of personal data breaches.[4] 'Data controllers' under the *Data Protection Act 2018*, s102(b), for example, are required to 'implement appropriate technical and organi-

---

4 Notably, the authors refer to a '*GDPR breach*', which is arguably narrower than a 'data breach'. A personal data breach might not lead to a *breach of the GDPR* if the principles of the *Data Protection Act 2018* are followed (for example, there is no 'GDPR breach' in the strict sense where the controller informs the data subject of the *data breach* without undue delay (*Data Protection Act 2018* s68(1)). However, it doesn't appear that this is the

sational measures … to ensure that … risks to the rights and freedoms of data subjects are minimised'. This may be a minor issue of expression in an otherwise large report. Yet, in the context of the safety and accountability failures of the SIM programme, and broader concerns about for-profit data intermediaries in British healthcare (Faulkner-Gurstein and Wyatt, 2021) and internationally (United Nations General Assembly, 2018), the error is troubling.

Several issues warrant further exploration amid these broader changes. One is the impact of electronic health records, which are subject to a growing body of evidence showing how they create new practices and workflows, often unexpectedly (Kariotis et al., 2022; Ventres et al., 2006). For example, structured data entry forms can disrupt the inclusion of narrative information (Kariotis et al., 2022), and the potential for AMHPs using apps to opt for MHA assessors based on convenience rather than familiarity with the person, is another example of a potentially adverse outcome (albeit a speculative one). Scholarship on electronic health records is relatively sparse in the mental health context (Kariotis et al., 2022) but could inform legal and policy arrangements for digitised mental health crisis support. Certainly, Academic Health Science Network evaluations have highlighted *improvements* in workflow created by the electronic record keeping of triage apps (Health Innovation Network South London, 2020), and promising evidence has emerged from subsequent scholarly evaluations (Stevens et al., 2022), but little attention has been paid to potentially adverse impacts on workflow, which have only started to be explored (BASW, 2020; Stevens et al., 2022).

Efforts to strengthen transparency and scrutiny over for-profit data intermediaries have also included analysing 'platformisation' more generally, particularly in the context of public policy. Rachel Faulkner-Gurstein and David Wyatt (2021) make a compelling case that the NHS itself is being managed as a sort of platform, in which the organisational form and operational logic of digital platforms is applied to public services. Although it is beyond scope to outline their argument, they offer techniques for analysing the heterogenous range of platforms in the public policy context – their function, beneficiaries, and data usages – which could inform the development of governance levers in law and policy. Faulkner-Gurstein and Wyatt (2021, p. 16) capture the 'dualistic conception of the public benefit' underlying the digital transformation of English and Welsh health services, which is 'conceived both in medical and economic terms':

> The platform … model has facilitated the development of new treatments and medicines, potentially leading to better patient outcomes. But platformization also extends the notion of public benefit into murky areas where developing a research infrastructure uses the strategies of private firms. … [P]latformization makes these intertwined logics difficult to evaluate. The delegation of authority to private firms means that some public funds and resource are supporting private profit-making. And yet as part of the platform, these private initiatives attempt to define themselves as part of the public good.

Risks emerging from this entwinement include public resources being appropriated by private-sector technology and other firms, and the delegation of accountability to private firms

---

meaning adopted by the evaluation authors as the report's conclusion includes the more tempered statement that the programme 'significantly reduces the opportunity for GDPR breaches' (p. 78).

in opaque ways. Benefits will also emerge, but they remain largely promissory and speculative. The balance sheet is yet to be written.

Finally, the inclusion of people with lived experiences (or lack thereof) in the development, implementation, and oversight of digital data-driven mental health services requires further examination (Carr, 2020); and little appears to be known about service user views on many of the developments discussed in this chapter, with notable exceptions (see Tomison 2021). This conforms with broader patterns in research into data-driven and algorithmic technology in mental healthcare, which shows troublingly low levels of involvement – let alone partnership with, or leadership – of service user perspectives (Gooding and Kariotis, 2021).

Conclusion

The world is facing the app-ification of mental healthcare and the Uber-isation of the mental health profession (Zeavin, 2021). The extent and form of this potential change remains uncertain, as does its impact on processes of involuntary psychiatric intervention. Yet, 'digital mental health services' have clear coercive potential (Butorac and Carter, 2021) and experimentation is underway (see Gooding, 2019). Sarah Carr (2020, p. 125) describes the significance of these changes when she writes that:

> Possibly more than any other group of patients, people with mental health problems can experience particular forms of power and authority in service systems and treatment … The implications of these specific power dynamics as well as potential biases in mental health systems must be considered for the ethical development and implementation of any data-driven technology in mental health.

Global economic downturns and fiscal constraint will increase pressures on health systems to minimise costs, to which technological solutions will be invariably proposed. A common appeal lies in expected efficiency gains and improved services for those who want or are deemed to need them. It is hard to object to cutting down wait times in service provision for those in extreme crisis, or allowing a person to seek advocacy or access remote tribunal hearings where it suits them, including through high-quality internet facilities in acute public mental health settings (see e.g. Care Quality Commission, 2022). At the same time, many of these aims are tied to economic and political interests concerned with cost minimisation, privatisation, and the generation of capital through data accumulation and the uptake of apps, driven by expectations of the economic value attributed to platforms and data (Crawford, 2021; Faulkner-Gurstein and Wyatt, 2021).

For those concerned with mental health-related law, it will be difficult to avoid entering this thicket as the 21st century rolls on. And one needn't contemplate utopian or dystopian visions of the future to do so – there is much to get on with today.

References

American Psychiatric Association (1998). Telepsychiatry via videoconferencing resource document [Internet]. https://citeseerx.ist.psu.edu/viewdoc/download?doi=10.1.1.173.2939&rep=rep1&type=pdf (accessed 5/5/22)

American Psychiatric Association (2016). Position statement on location of civil commitment hearings [Internet]. https://www.psychiatry.org/File%20Library/About-APA/Organization-Documents-Policies/Policies/Position-2016-Location-of-Civil-Commitment-Hearings.pdf (accessed 5/5/2022)

Legislation

Data Protection Act 2018. GOV.UK. https://www.legislation.gov.uk/ukpga/2018/12/pdfs/ukpga_20180012_en.pdf

Mental Health Act 1983 (England and Wales). Queen's printer of Acts of Parliament. https://www.legislation.gov.uk/ukpga/1983/20/contents

Mental Health (Care and Treatment) (Scotland) Act 2003 asp 13. Acts of the Scottish Parliament. https://www.legislation.gov.uk/asp/2003/13/contents

The Mental Health (Hospital, Guardianship and Treatment) (England) (Amendment) Regulations 2020 (2020). Queen's printer of Acts of Parliament. https://www.legislation.gov.uk/uksi/2020/1072/made

Case Law

United Kingdom

GL v Elysium Healthcare [2020] UKUT, 308 (AAC)

Re, D. [2020] MHLO 51 (FTT)

United States

Doe v. State, 217 So. 3d 1020 (Fla. 2017)

re G.N., 215 P.3d 902 (Or. Ct. App. 2009)

Shellman v. Commonwealth of Virginia (Va. 2012)

United States v. Baker, 45 F.3d 837 (4th Cir. 1995)

Literature

AHSN Network (2022). *Freedom of Information (FOI) Requests*. AHSN Network. https://www.ahsn-network.com/freedom-of-information-foi-requests

AHSN Network Statement on SIM (Serenity Integrated Mentoring). (June 2021). AHSN Network. https://www.ahsnnetwork.com/ahsn-network-statement-on-sim-serenity-integrated-mentoring

BASW (2020). *The Impact of the Covid-19 Pandemic on Approved Mental Health Professional (AMHP) Services in England.* https://www.basw.co.uk/system/files/resources/amhp_covid-19_report_2020.pdf

Baxter, G., & Sommerville, I. (2011). Socio-technical systems: From design methods to systems engineering. *Interacting with Computers, 23*(1), 4–17. https://doi.org/10.1016/j.intcom.2010.07.003

Bossewitch, J.S. (2016). *Dangerous Gifts: Towards a New Wave of Mad Resistance.* Columbia University. https://doi.org/10.7916/D8RJ4JFB

Brock, D. (2019). *Los Angeles Review of Books.* https://lareviewofbooks.org

Butorac, I., & Carter, A. (2021). The coercive potential of digital mental health. *The American Journal of Bioethics, 21*(7), 28–30. https://doi.org/10.1080/15265161.2021.1926582

Byrom, N., & Beardon, S. (2021). *Understanding the Impact of COVID-19 on Tribunals: The Experience of Tribunal Judges.* Tribunals Judiciary. https://www.judiciary.uk/wp-content/uploads/2021/06/2021_06_02_REPORT_Understanding-the-impact-of-COVID-19-on-tribunals-the-experiences-of-judges-1.pdf

Care Quality Commission (2022). *Monitoring the Mental Health Act in 2020/21.* Controller of Her Majesty's Stationery Office.

Carr, S. (2020). 'AI gone mental': Engagement and ethics in data-driven technology for mental health. *Journal of Mental Health, 29*(2), 125–30. https://doi.org/10.1080/09638237.2020.1714011

Corbyn, Z. (2021). The dawn of tappigraphy: Does your smartphone know how you feel before you do? *The Observer.* https://www.theguardian.com/technology/2021/nov/07/the-dawn-of-tappigraphy-does-your-smartphone-know-how-you-feel-before-you-do

Cosgrove, L., Karter, J., Mcginley, M., & Morrill, Z. (2020). Digital phenotyping and digital psychotropic drugs: Mental health surveillance tools that threaten human rights. *Health and Human Rights Journal, 22*(2), 33–39.

Crawford, K. (2021). *The Atlas of AI: Power, Politics, and the Planetary Costs of Artificial Intelligence.* Yale University Press.

Crowther, N., & McGregor, L. (2022). *A Digital Cage Is Still a Cage: How Can New and Emerging Digital Technologies Advance, Rather Than Put at Risk, the Human Rights of Older People Who Draw on Social Care?* University of Essex.

Dagum, P. (2018). Digital biomarkers of cognitive function. *NPJ Digital Medicine, 1*, 1–3. https://doi.org/10.1038/s41746-018-0018-4

Department of Health and Social Care (2021). Reforming the Mental Health Act: Government response. GOV.UK. https://www.gov.uk/government/consultations/reforming-the-mental-health-act/outcome/reforming-the-mental-health-act-government-response

Department of Health and Social Care (2020). *Explanatory Memorandum to the Mental Health (Hospital, Guardianship and Treatment) (England) (Amendment) Regulations 2020 (No. 1072).* HM Government.

Ducey, H. (2018). Understanding how and why the NHS adopts innovation: Serenity integrated mentoring in Surrey. NHS innovation accelerator. https://nhsaccelerator.com/insight/understanding-nhs-adopts-innovation-serenity-integrated-mentoring-surrey/

Dyer, C. (2021). Mental Health Act: Doctors should not use video assessments to detain patients during pandemic, say judges. *BMJ, 372*, n228. https://doi.org/10.1136/bmj.n228

Faulkner-Gurstein, R.F., & Wyatt, D. (2021). Platform NHS: Reconfiguring a public service in the age of digital capitalism. *Science, Technology and Human Values.* Online First. https://doi.org/10.1177/01622439211055697

Fennell, P.W.H. (2010). Institutionalising the community: The codification of clinical authority and the limitations of rights based approaches. In McSherry, B., & Weller, P. (Eds.), *Rethinking Rights-Based Mental Health Laws,* (13–50). Hart Publishing

Gooding, P. (2019). Mapping the rise of digital mental health technologies: Emerging issues for law and society. *International Journal of Law and Psychiatry, 67*, 101498. https://doi.org/10.1016/j.ijlp.2019.101498

Gooding, P., & Kariotis, T. (2021). Ethics and law in research on algorithmic and data-driven technology in mental health care: Scoping review. *JMIR Mental Health, 8*(6), e24668. https://doi.org/10.2196/24668

Hamilton, I.A. (2019). Elon Musk said his AI-brain-chips company could "solve" autism and schizophrenia. Business insider Australia. https://www.businessinsider.com.au/elon-musk-said-neuralink-could-solve-autism-and-schizophrenia-2019-11

Health Innovation Network South London (2020). *SIM London: Support for a Better Life (April 2018–2020).* Academic Health Science Network.

Health Service Journal (2017). HSJ patient safety awards 2017: Managing long term conditions. HSJ.co.uk. https://www.hsj.co.uk/patient-safety/hsj-patient-safety-awards-2017-managing-long-term-conditions/7018933.article

HM Government (2018). *Modernising the Mental Health Act: Increasing Choice, Reducing Compulsion: Final Report of the Independent Review of the Mental Health Act 1983.* Crown.

Horgan, J. (2021). *Premature Freak-Outs about Techno-Enhancement.* Scientific American.

House, A. (2022). Serenity integrated mentoring and the high intensity network: A scheme that raises serious questions for practice and governance in UK psychiatry. *BJPsych Bulletin,* 1–4. https://doi.org/10.1192/bjb.2022.6

Human Rights Council (2021). Report of the special rapporteur on the rights of persons with disabilities (UN Doc A/HRC/49/52).

Jackson, A., & Brewster, J. (2018). The implementation of SIM London: Sharing best practice for spread and adoption. Health Innovation Network: South London.

Jordan, A., & Klein, N. (2020). Branding, privacy, and identity: Growing up in surveillance capitalism. *Journal of Children and Media, 14*(2), 259–266. https://doi.org/10.1080/17482798.2020.1735148

Kariotis, T.C., Prictor, M., Chang, S., & Gray, K. (2022). Impact of electronic health records on information practices in mental health contexts: Scoping review. *Journal of Medical Internet Research, 24*(5), e30405. https://doi.org/10.2196/30405

Matlow, D. (2021). Vitalhub signs S12 contract with Northamptonshire. Stockwatch.com. https://www.stockwatch.com/News/Item/Z-C!VHI-3184892/C/VHI.

McQuillan, D. (2018). Mental health and artificial intelligence: Losing your voice. openDemocracy.

Mental elf (2020). Digitising the Mental Health Act: A Public Debate #DigitalMHA

Metz, R. (2018). The smartphone app that can tell you're depressed before you know it yourself. *MIT's Technology Review*. https://www.technologyreview.com/2018/10/15/66443/the-smartphone-app-that-can-tell-youre-depressed-before-you-know-it-yourself/

Moreton, S. (2021). ACP-UK rapid response: Concerns about the high intensity network (HIN) and serenity integrated mentoring (SIM). ACP UK. https://acpuk.org.uk/rapid-response-concerns-about-the-high-intensity-network-hin-and-serenity-integrated-mentoring-sim-2/

Murtha, J. (2018). Jeff Bezos's VC arm contributes to mindstrong's $15M round. Chief healthcare executive. https://www.chiefhealthcareexecutive.com/view/jeff-bezoss-vc-arm-contributes-to-mindstrongs-15m-round

NIMH - National Institute of Mental Health. (2019). NIMH » Technology and the future of mental health treatment.

NHS England (2020). *Legal guidance for mental health, learning disability and Autism, and specialised commissioning services supporting people of all ages during the coronavirus pandemic: Version 2* (publications approval reference: 001559). National Health Service.

NHS England (n.d.). Innovations. NHS innovation accelerator. https://nhsaccelerator.com/innovations/

Petersen, A. (2018). *Digital Health and Technological Promise: A Sociological Inquiry*. Routledge.

Reardon, S. (2017). Former US mental-health chief leaves Google for start-up. *Nature*. https://doi.org/10.1038/nature.2017.21976

Rider, E. (2020). Pilot practice direction: contingency arrangements in the first-tier tribunal and the upper tribunal. Courts and Tribunals Judiciary. England and Wales.

Royal College of Psychiatrists (2021a). Patient and clinician feedback about remote mental health tribunal hearings. https://www.rcpsych.ac.uk/improving-care/campaigning-for-better-mental-health-policy/reforming-the-mental-health-act/remote-mht-research

Royal College of Psychiatrists (2021b). RCPsych calls for urgent and transparent investigation into NHS innovation accelerator and AHSN following HIN suspension. https://www.rcpsych.ac.uk/news-and-features/latest-news/detail/2021/06/14/rcpsych-calls-for-urgent-and-transparent-investigation-into-nhs-innovation-accelerator-and-ahsn-following-hin-suspension

S12 Solutions (2020). S12 and David Bradley: Chief Exec of the South London and Maudsley NHS Trust.

S12 Solutions (2022). S12 Solutions. https://s12solutions.com/ (accessed 3/4/2022)

S12 Solutions (n.d.). Company profile: Acquisition & investors | PitchBook. Pitchbook.com. https://pitchbook.com/profiles/company/437312-35

Series, L. (2022). *Deprivation of Liberty in the Shadows of the Institution, Law, Society, Policy*. Bristol University Press.

Schölin L, Connolly M, Morgan G, et al. (2021). Limits of remote working: The ethical challenges in conducting Mental Health Act assessments during.

Scottish Executive. Mental health (Care and Treatment) (Scotland) Act 2003 Code of Practice Volume 2 – Civil compulsory powers.

Socio-Technical System (n.d.). Oxford reference. https://doi.org/10.1093/oi/authority.20110803100515814

Sorrentino, R.M., DiCola, L.A., & Friedman, S.H. (2020). COVID-19, civil commitment, and ethics. *Journal of the American Academy of Psychiatry and the Law*, 48(4), 436. https://doi.org/10.29158/JAAPL.200080-20

Stavert, J., & McKay, C. (2020). Scottish mental health and capacity law: The normal, pandemic and 'new normal'. *International Journal of Law and Psychiatry*, 71, 101593. https://doi.org/10.1016/j.ijlp.2020.101593

Stevens, M., Martineau, S., Manthorpe, J., Steils, N., & Bramley, S. (2020). *The Availability of Section 12 Doctors for Mental Health Act Assessments: A Scoping Review of the Literature*. King's College London. https://doi.org/10.18742/PUB01-037

Stevens, M., Martineau, S., Steils, N., & Manthorpe, J. (2022). *The Availability of Section 12 Doctors for Mental Health Act Assessments: Interview Perceptions and Analysis of the National MHA Approvals Register Database*. King's College London. https://doi.org/10.18742/PUB01-072

StopSIM Coalition (n.d.). STOPSIM. https://stopsim.co.uk/

Strudwick, P. (2021). Campaigners call for inquiry after mental health patients turned away by NHS under controversial scheme I.
Thalamos (2022a). Thalamos. https://www.thalamos.co.uk/ (accessed 3/4/2022)
Thalamos (2022b). Thalamos, 'Our Approach'. https://www.thalamos.co.uk/about/our-approach/ (accessed 3/4/2022)
Teräs, M., Suoranta, J., Teräs, H., & Curcher, M. (2020). Post-Covid-19 education and education technology 'solutionism': A seller's market. *Postdigital Science and Education*, *2*(3), 863–78. https://doi.org/10.1007/s42438-020-00164-x
The Medical Futurist (2019). Artificial intelligence in mental health care. *The Medical Futurist*. https://medicalfuturist.com/artificial-intelligence-in-mental-health-care
Tomison, A. (2021). Recognising the importance of responsible innovation: How Thalamos is developing clinical safety and lived experience by design. *Thalamos*. https://www.thalamos.co.uk/2021/08/12/recognising-the-importance-of-responsible-innovation-how-thalamos-is-developing-clinical-safety-and-lived-experience-by-design/
United Nations General Assembly (2019). Report of the special rapporteur on extreme poverty and human rights 11 October (No. A/74/493).
United Nations General Assembly (2018). Report of the special rapporteur on extreme poverty and human rights 26 September (No. A/73/396).
Ventres, W., Kooienga, S., Vuckovic, N., Marlin, R., Nygren, P., & Stewart, V. (2006). Physicians, patients, and the electronic health record: An ethnographic analysis. *Annals of Family Medicine*, *4*(2), 124–31. https://doi.org/10.1370/afm.425
Vitiello, E.M., & Williams, J.B. (2021). Videoconferencing of involuntary commitment hearings in the COVID Era. *Journal of the American Academy of Psychiatry and the Law Online*, *49*(4), 610–17. https://doi:10.29158/JAAPL.210032-21
Wessex Academic Health Science Network (2020). *Independent Evaluation of the S12 Solutions Platform in Hampshire and Southampton*. National Health Service.
Wilmington Healthcare (2022). What we do | Wilmington healthcare. https://wilmingtonhealthcare.com/what-we-do/
Wilson, J. (2022). Mental health law online: Annual review 2021.
Wilson, K. (2020). The COVID-19 pandemic and the human rights of persons with mental and cognitive impairments subject to coercive powers in Australia. *International Journal of Law and Psychiatry*, *73*, 101605. https://doi.org/10.1016/j.ijlp.2020.101605
Zeavin, H. (2021). *The Distance Cure: A History of Teletherapy*. MIT Press.

37
MENTAL HEALTH LAW
A global future?[1]

Jean V. McHale

Introduction

Does mental health law have a "global future"? Health, as has been graphically demonstrated by the Covid-19 pandemic, is not something which should be seen simply as the concern of individual jurisdictions. Instead, it should be regarded both as a global challenge and a global responsibility. Global heath challenges have led to calls for the development of global health law not simply as an academic discipline but also in the form of a legal instrument establishing a Global Health Convention (Gostin: 2014: Luca-Burchi and Toebes 2018). But to what extent will the future of mental health law be truly "global" and if so, what will be the implications of such a global future?

To attempt to address these questions this chapter begins by considering what the nature of mental health law is itself in terms of legal frameworks and as an academic discipline. It suggests that while there is a myriad of applicable international human rights frameworks and related governance applicable to mental health it is suggested that these international frameworks, while important in framing protections and debate, fall short of "global mental health law". Finally, it explores whether the future for mental health at global level is indeed that of a truly "global mental health law" emerging as a distinct academic area and perhaps with its own distinct legal force at global level.

Does mental health law have a future?

Before considering what is a "global future for mental health law" we need to begin by exploring just what exactly is meant by "mental health law" at present. What is mental health law concerned with? Is it a separate discipline/area of law or is it a part of a broader area of law concerning health? In terms of a distinct body of law concerning the care and treatment

---

1 The author would like to thank the editors of this collection, Mary Donnelly and Brendan Kelly, and also James Sullivan-McHale and the members and audience at the Health and Medicine Panel at the Law and Society Conference in Lisbon 2022 for their very helpful comments on an earlier draft of this chapter. Any views expressed and errors which may remain are entirely the responsibility of the author.

DOI: 10.4324/9781003226413-45

of persons with mental illness this is commonly recognised across jurisdictions. Very often this is subject to distinct legislative frameworks, e.g., in relation to detention and where treatment for mental illness can be compelled. But today, as we shall see below, the precise boundaries of law concerning care and treatment of those with mental illness are frequently seen as much broader than this.

Mental health law as an academic discipline has had its own discrete identity over a very long period in some jurisdictions in the Global North.[2] One reason perhaps for such distinct early engagement with mental health law may be at least partly due to the nature of the evolution of the discipline in certain jurisdictions. Frequently health law itself can be seen as emerging organically from existing core legal principles such as criminal law, public law and tort law (Laurie, Harmon, and Dove 2019).[3] In contrast, in some jurisdictions disciplinary distinct mental health legislation provides an automatic framework which may in turn facilitate its evolution as an academic discipline. Mental health law also can be seen as distinctive due to its direct engagement with the criminal justice system through use of compulsory orders for hospital detention[4] following criminal law proceedings and sentencing (Peay 2011 (although it could be argued that public health law is also analogous, in that some aspects of public health law incorporate compulsion for the individual and broader public protection.[5]

What then comprises mental health law in the academy today? There have been notable texts published delineating its nature and differences in approach across jurisdictions. Some mental health law textbooks have different intended audiences, whether academic lawyers and legal practitioners (Bartlett and Sandland 2014; Gostin et al. 2010: Hale 2020) or clinicians (Guthell and Appelbaum 2019), in turn impacting on the way in which the subject is framed within a particular volume. In the case of Perlin, Cucolo and Lynch's book in the US, the term "mental disability law" is used to describe what others might have regarded as coming within the realm of mental health law, something which interestingly pre-dates the introduction of the United Nations (UN) Convention on the Rights of Persons with Disabilities, discussed below (UN 2008) (Perlin, Cucolo, Lynch 2017).

Traditionally mental health scholarship engages with statutory structures relating to compulsory treatment and detention (Dawson and Gledhill 2013) but also with informal admission, with oversight of statutory powers and notable leading cases (Weaver and Meyer 2019). This area also interfaces with matters of capacity and consent to treatment in general (Series 2024), broader related matters such as privacy and medical research (Gostin et al. 2010), with socialal care and socio-legal analysis (Chen 2022). While there has historically been a movement from medicalism to an approach of "legalism" driven by a fundamental rights-based approach reflected across some jurisdictions (Jones 1980; Brown 2016), such a "movement" has taken time and in some respects is still under development (Duffy and Kelly 2020; Ugochukwu et al. 2020).

---

2 The existence of mental health law in the form of discrete principles has, e.g., been traced to the Twelve Tables of Roman Law circa 451 BC: see Allan 2000. Academic treaties while much more recent have still been in place for a considerable period, e.g., in the UK F.B. Matthew's book *Mental Health Services: A Handbook on Lunacy and Mental Treatment and Mental Deficiency* (which later became *Mental Health Services: Law and Practice* (Matthews 1948).
3 See, for example, the discussion of principles of consent to medical treatment, e.g., Laurie, Harmon, and Dove 2019 at chapter 4.
4 E.g., in England and Wales, the Mental Health Act 1983, Part III.
5 See, for example, discussion in Gostin and Wiley (2016).

Mental health law

One question is whether, in the long term, mental health law will itself survive as a distinct academic discipline, and indeed whether it should do. A number of existing medical/health care law/health law textbooks include chapters on mental health law.[6] Is it the case that mental health law will ultimately be subsumed within health or health care law? Some regard the very existence of mental health law as a separate area as problematic, a relic of an era when physical and mental health were regarded as distinctly different entities. The very existence of mental health law as a separate concept, it has been suggested, is stigmatising those with mental illness (Allan 2002: 44). Writing in the 1990s Rosenman and Campbell called for the abolition of mental health laws and for treatment of those with mental illness to be dealt with under health law principles (Rosenman 1994; Campbell 1994). Similar debates are ongoing today in the context of international law principles in relation to the UN Convention on the Rights of Persons with Disabilities, as we shall see below. There is also the prospect that even if mental health law remains as a separate area, the disciplinary boundaries will be further blurred or extinguished, for example by a growing movement towards "fusion" of mental health and mental capacity law principles (Dawson and Szmukler 2006; Dawson and Szmukler 2011).[7]

Alternatively in the longer term, will mental health law itself be seen as simply a subset of human rights law? Mental health law has been notably impacted by international human rights law, as we shall see in the following section. The interface between health law and human rights law is well documented. In the UK legal scholars Kennedy and Grubb famously saw medical law[8] itself as being a subset of human rights law (Kennedy and Grubb 2000). However, some twenty years later whilst human rights have certainly been at least to some extent influential in framing responses in some jurisdictions, to date medical, health and health care law remain distinct disciplines (McHale 2019). Thus, it remains questionable as to whether in the short term, at least, mental health law while clearly impacted by human rights law would be seen as fundamentally a subset of human rights law. A final possibility is that mental health law will become incorporated within disability law, an area itself with long-standing broader academic engagement (Bagenstos 2004–5; Lawson 2020; Blanck 2017; Broderick and Ferri 2019). The focus on recognising the position of those with disabilities at international level through the United Nations Convention on the Rights of Persons with Disabilities can also be seen as a catalyst for developments in relation to this in the academy, which we explore in the next section.

Mental health law may have a future in the form of legal principles relating to the care and treatment of mental illness. But that future may be as part of another albeit related category such as health, human rights or disability law.

If we look to characterise mental health law in global terms, then what would this mean? Are there principles which would meet with agreement as to precisely what mental health law is and should be? Can we say that there is in existence already, or that there is a movement towards, a body of scholarship which has become global health law itself? Is it the case that it is the development of and operation of international human rights norms in the area

---

6 For example, in the UK Laurie, Harmon and Dove (2019), chapter 14.
7 See also here the development of "fusion" law in the form of the Mental Capacity Act 2016 in Northern Ireland; see Harper, Davison and McLelland (2016).
8 What some regard as the precursor of healthcare and health law; see Hervey and McHale (2015), chapter 2.

of mental health which already provides a global framing – a form of "global mental health law"? This premise is explored in the next section.

Mental health law: a matter of international human rights law

It can be argued that in fact we already have "global mental health law" in that mental health law can be seen as a sub-category of international human rights law which is itself in turn a sub-category of international law (Craven 2000; Sheeran 2013). Human rights have provided an important framing for mental health law and policy from the last half of the 20th century until today (Gostin and Gable 2010). Health and mental health are directly addressed in international human rights statements (Toebes 1999) such as the right to a standard of living adequate for health and well-being contained in the Universal Declaration of Human Rights.[9] The International Covenant on Economic and Social Rights similarly contains the requirement for recognition of the highest attainable standard of physical and mental health.[10] The right to health has been developed in General Comment 14 produced by the UN Committee on Economic, Social and Cultural Rights.[11] There is not, however, overall agreement as to precisely what these mean and the consequent method of interpretation (Tobin 2012; Hunt 2016; Lougarre 2014). However, rights to health care stated in international declarations are phrased in terms of rights to *access* health care and also address non-discriminatory access. This is very different than saying that an individual has a right to a particular treatment as such. The UN Rapporteur on the Right to Health, Paul Hunt, notably stated that mental health is "among the most grossly neglected elements of the right to health" (Hunt 2005). More developed and detailed approaches are provided in the UN Principles for the Protection of Persons with Mental Illness and the Improvement of Mental Health Care in 1991 (UN 1991–2). These provisions include the entitlement to receive the best quality of care available (Rosenthal and Rubenstein 1993). However, a further obstacle, as Stavert comments, is the fact that rights declarations concerned with socio-economic rights raise issues of positive enforcement and resource allocation (Stavert 2017: 338).

There are also other developments in relation to mental health governance at international level and regional groupings level. The importance of mental health at a global level has been emphasised in policy terms in the 21st century. So, for example, the *World Health Organization (WHO) Resource Book on Mental Health, Human Rights and Legislation* provided guidance for states in developing and implementing legislation to human rights standards along with a checklist on mental health legislation which states can be assessed against (WHO 2005). This was followed by the WHO Mental Health Action Plan in 2013 (WHO 2013) and the Report "World Mental Health Report: Transforming Mental Health for All" (WHO 2022).

---

9 Article 25, Universal Declaration of Human Rights, adopted 10 December 1948 under General Assembly Resolution 217 A (III), UN Doc. A/810, 71.
10 Article 12(1), International Covenant on Economic, Social and Cultural Rights, New York, 19 December 1966, in force 3 January 1976, see further on the right to health, Tobin (2012).
11 Committee on Economic, Social and Cultural Rights, Twenty-second session Geneva, 25 April–12 May 2000, https://docstore.ohchr.org/SelfServices/FilesHandler.ashx?enc=4slQ6QSmlBEDzFEovLCuW1A VC1NkPsgUedPlF1vfPMJ2c7ey6PAz2qaojTzDJmC0y%2B9t%2BsAtGDNzdEqA6SuP2r0w%2F6sVBG TpvTSCbiOr4XVFTqhQY65auTFbQRPWNDxL

Mental health law

There have also been movements to address mental health through the United Nations Sustainable Development Goals[12](Patel 2018). The recent work of the European Union (EU) Commission in this area is also rooted in the Sustainable Development Goals and WHO Non-Communicable Disease Targets. In 2018 a Steering Group on Health Promotion, Disease Prevention and Management of Non-Communicable Diseases was created.[13] This is an expert group comprised of representatives from the health ministries of EU member states with the task of supporting member states to meet the health targets of the Sustainable Development Goals and mental health has been prioritised for the application of good practice. It has been followed by ranking of best practices with financial support being given to the three highest rated schemes (European Commission: 2019). (The EU also has potential to develop its own body of mental health law although to date this has not emerged as a separate area (McHale 2011).)

Aside from the general scope of United Nations human rights bodies and related instruments and engagement with UN principles at regional level, there is also notable engagement with human rights through specific statements applicable to regional groups of states such as in relation to the European Convention of Human Rights. This Convention contains a number of rights which have formed the basis of claims brought against member states in relation to mental health concerning, for example, the right not to be subject to torture, inhuman and de-grading treatment (European Convention of Human Rights Article 3; *Aerts v. Belgium* (1998) 29 EHRR 50; *Kucheruk v. Ukraine* Application 2570/04, 2017) and the deprivation of liberty (European Convention of Human Rights, Article 5; *Winterwerp v. Netherlands* 6301/73 [1979] ECHR 4; *MH v. UK* 11577/06 [2013] ECHR 1008). At Council of Europe level, violation of human rights in Bulgaria of those in psychiatric hospitals and social care institutions has also been highlighted by the European Committee for the Prevention of Torture.[14]

Various provisions in the Council of Europe Convention on Human Rights and Biomedicine (Council of Europe 1997) relate to more detailed provisions relevant to health law and specifically mental health law (Zilgavis 2001; Raposo 2016).[15] These include reference to safeguarding dignity (Article 1, Biomedicine Convention), rights to consent to treatment (Articles 5–9, Biomedicine Convention), private life and the right to information (Article 12, Biomedicine Convention), the prohibition of discrimination (Articles 11–13, Biomedicine Convention) and rights in the context of research (Articles 15–18, Biomedicine Convention). Article 7 concerns the "Protection of persons who have a mental disorder". This states that

---

12 "Transforming Our World: the 2030 Agenda for Sustainable Development" https://sdgs.un.org/2030agenda

13 Commission Decision of 17.7.2018 setting up a Commission expert group "Steering Group on Health Promotion, Disease Prevention and Management of Non-Communicable Diseases" and repealing the Decision setting up a Commission expert group on rare diseases and the Decision establishing a Commission expert group on Cancer Control, Brussels, 17.7.2018 .C (2018) 4492 final.

14 *Report to the Bulgarian Government on the visit to Bulgaria carried out by the European Committee for the Prevention of Torture and Inhuman or Degrading Treatment or Punishment (CPT) from 10 to 21 August 2020*, Strasbourg, 2 December 2020.

15 Council of Europe Convention for the Protection of Human Rights and Dignity of the Human Being with Regard to Biology and Medicine: Convention on Human Rights and Biomedicine (Biomedicine Convention), Oviedo, 4 April 1997, in force 1 December 1999, ETS No. 164, http://conventions.coe.int/.

Subject to protective conditions prescribed by law, including supervisory, control and appeal procedures, a person who has a mental disorder of a serious nature may be subjected, without his or her consent, to an intervention aimed at treating his or her mental disorder only where, without such treatment, serious harm is likely to result to his or her health.

While many of the Council of Europe member states have to date still not ratified or become signatories to the Convention,[16] nonetheless this document has been of influence in some member states and has been referred to in cases before the European Court of Human Rights. There was also considerable controversy regarding the Draft Additional Protocol concerning the protection of human rights and dignity of persons with mental disorder with regard to involuntary placement and involuntary treatment produced in 2018, as to whether this was compliant with the United Nations Convention on the Rights of Persons with Disabilities (Council of Europe 2018 and see Nilsson and Doyle-Guilloud's chapters in this volume).

Health rights are also contained in international statements concerning certain population groups. Attempts to safeguard rights in relation to mental health with regard to specific groups such as children, older persons and those with disabilities particularly illustrate some of the challenges in attempting to establish mental health law as a subset of international human rights law. For example, there are notable challenges as to reaching clear consensus at a level of detail as to the position of involvement of "international mental health law" regarding children (see Parker, this volume). In the context of some jurisdictions, capacity of children is seen as a developing notion and approaches to the age of maturity may differ. Also, there may be differences across jurisdictions regarding the nature and indeed strength of parental powers to make decisions regarding those children.[17]

The position of children is specifically recognised through the UN Convention on the Rights of the Child (UN 1999) (Akhtar, Nyamutata and Faulkner 2020). Various provisions in Article 23 of this Convention make specific reference to children who may have mental disability or who require treatment for their mental health. Article 24(1) of this Convention also makes specific reference to the right to the highest standard of health and that states should ensure children are not deprived of access to health care services. Article 25 sets out the right of the child who is subject to placement for their care, protection, and treatment to periodic review of their placement. While this Convention also provides a backdrop for individual jurisdictions to frame their approaches[18] in relation to the care and treatment of children with mental illness, as with any international human rights principles their practical

---

16 The following states have not signed this Convention: Austria, Belgium, Germany, Ireland, Malta, and the United Kingdom.
17 See, e.g., Bridgeman (2020); European Fundamental Rights Agency (2017): Consenting to medical treatment without parental consent | European Union Agency for Fundamental Rights (europa.eu)
18 The Scottish Parliament introduced the United Nations Convention on the Rights of the Child (Incorporation) (Scotland) Bill to incorporate the UN Convention on the Rights of the Child into domestic law. Though this was challenged, see further *Reference by the Attorney General and the Advocate General for Scotland – United Nations Convention on the Rights of the Child (Incorporation) (Scotland) Bill. Reference by the Attorney General and the Advocate General for Scotland – European Charter of Local Self-Government (Incorporation) (Scotland) Bill* [2021] UKSC 42.

efficacy is dependent upon measures taken at member state level to ensure domestic law is in line with them.[19]

One Convention which has had a notable impact on the engagement with human rights in the area of mental health and could be seen as a game changer is that of the UN Convention on the Rights of Persons with Disabilities.[20] Stavert has commented that:

> Globally it is, however, the UN Convention on the Rights of Persons with Disabilities (CRPD) that arguably nowadays takes the lead in terms of the rights of persons with mental health issues. Heralded as a revolutionary treaty its approach is very different to that of previous human rights treaties, which have tended to recognise the rights of persons with mental health issues primarily in terms of justifying those circumstances when the denial of their rights is permitted.
>
> *(Stavert 2017: 332)*

The UN Convention on the Rights of Persons with disabilities (CRPD) was adopted on 13 December 2006 (Bartlett 2009; Lewis and Pathare 2020) and along with its Optional Protocol came into effect on 3 May 2008.[21] As Kayess and French have commented, persons with disability are not seen as a protected category in the main international human rights declarations and it was only the UN Convention on the Rights of the Child which refers in Article 23 to "mentally and physically disabled children" (Kayess and French 2008). The UNCRPD is notable for the involvement of those with disabilities in the drafting of the Convention (Morrissey 2012). The Convention does not include a definition of what constitutes a disability. However, the Preamble to the Convention states in paragraph (e) that

> *Recognising* that disability is an evolving concept and that disability results from the interaction between persons with impairments and attitudinal and environmental barriers that hinder their full and effective participation in society on an equal basis with others.
>
> *(UN 2006)*

---

19 So, for example, commenting on use of the Convention in the English courts in relation to the mental health of children, Justice MacDonald has argued that "it is in my experience rarely, if ever, cited in support of arguments seeking ensure that the therapeutic and other services necessary for children who are found to have suffered significant harm are provided by local authorities", per Mac Donald J, "Do Children Have a Right to Mental Health?" The annual lecture of The Wales Observatory on Human Rights of Children and Young People delivered by the Honourable Mr Justice MacDonald at the College of Law and Criminology, Swansea University on 20 July 2017 https://www.swansea.ac.uk/media/2017-Observatory-Annual-Lecture-MR-JUSTICE-MACDONALD.pdf.
20 See further, e.g., discussion in Gooding (2018); Kelly (2015), at chapter 4; and Szmukle, Daw and Callard (2014).
21 The Convention has had a notable impact in the development of policy in this area, e.g., European Commission, European Disability Strategy (2010–2020) https://eur-lex.europa.eu/LexUriServ/LexUriServ.do?uri=COM%3A2010%3A0636%3AFIN%3Aen%3APDF; and "Union for Equality; Strategy for the Rights of Persons with disabilities" 2021-2030; https://ec.europa.eu/social/main.jsp?catId=738&langId=en&pubId=8376&furtherPubs=yes

In addition, Article 1 of the Convention "Purpose" states that

> The purpose of the present Convention is to promote, protect and ensure the full and equal enjoyment of all human rights and fundamental freedoms by all persons with disabilities, and to promote respect for their inherent dignity.
>
> Persons with disabilities include those who have long-term physical, mental, intellectual, or sensory impairments which in interaction with various barriers may hinder their full and effective participation in society on an equal basis with others.

The Convention is a combination of traditional civil and political rights, such as the right to life (Article 10), equality and non-discrimination (Article 5), liberty and security of the person (Article 14) and integrity of the person (Article 17). At the same time, it includes socio-economic rights such as rights to health (Article 25) and habitation and rehabilitation (Article 26). Reference is made to distinct groups such as women and children with disabilities (Articles 6 and 7). The Convention addresses matters such as accessibility intended to remove barriers which can be seen as inhibiting the ability of disabled people to enjoy rights.

The very existence of this Convention can be seen as problematic or as liberating in relation to current norms and legal provisions in the area of mental health law. Article 12(2) in relation to equal recognition before the law provides that:

> States Parties shall recognize that persons with disabilities enjoy legal capacity on an equal basis with others in all aspects of life.

This has led to discussion as to whether recognition of legal capacity may mean that individuals are able to refuse treatment for mental illness.[22] The CRPD Committee in its "General Comment on Article 12: Equal Recognition before the Law" stated that if a person has an impairment which includes mental or psychosocial impairments, this is not to be a basis for the denial of legal capacity or of imposing substitute decision making; it went on to say that:

> Respecting the right to legal capacity of persons with disabilities on an equal basis includes respecting the rights of persons with disabilities to liberty and security of the person. The denial of the legal capacity of persons with disabilities and their detention in institutions against their will, either without their consent or with the consent of a substitute decision maker is an ongoing problem. This practice constitutes arbitrary deprivation of liberty and violates Article 12 and 14 of the Convention.[23]

The Convention also requires provision of support in relation to legal capacity (Article 12(3)). The implications of such a statement are of course major in relation to whether a core element of mental health law, namely the compulsory detention and treatment of persons with mental illness, would be thus in contravention of the Convention (Nilsson

---

22 See, e.g., *Stanev v. Bulgaria* (2012) ECHR 36760/96 and *Shtukaturov v. Russia* ECHR Application No 4409/05 27 March 2008, discussion in Morrissey at p. 427.
23 Ibid. at para. 40. https://www.ohchr.org/en/documents/general-comments-and-recommendations/general-comment-no-1-article-12-equal-recognition-1 and see further Szmulker (2017).

2021). There is a further challenge with a separate Convention in this form. Identifying as having a disability of itself does equate with difference, and while this may be welcomed as empowering by some, equally others may not wish to be personally identified in such a manner.

One other area which in the future may have an increasing impact on the development of international law norms in relation to mental health is in relation to the fundamental human rights of older persons. There have been calls over several years to develop a specific United Nations Convention on the Rights of Older Persons. In 1991 the United Nations Principles for Older Persons (United Nations 1991) were issued followed by a Proclamation on Ageing in 1992, and the Political Declaration and Madrid International Plan of Action on Ageing in 2002 (United Nations 2002). The Council of Europe issued in 2014 a Recommendation on the Promotion of the Rights of Older People (Council of Europe 2014).[24] A UN Independent Expert on the enjoyment of all human rights by older persons took office in June 2014.[25]

Any proposed Convention here is not uncontroversial. It can be argued that such a Convention is itself potentially entrenching stereotypes of older persons and it is uncertain as to the extent to which this would be generally welcomed. Some persons may not welcome classification as being "old". There is also by no means uniformity of support for such a statement of rights across jurisdictions (Dabbs Scubbia 2014; Poffe 2015). Nonetheless, for example, the Inter-American Convention on the Human Rights of Older Persons provides one model of such a Convention.[26] There is a mixture of traditional civil and political rights but accompanied with and developed in new forms such as rights to privacy and intimacy (Article 16) and liberty (Article 13), and Article 19 provides a right to physical and mental health without discrimination. Notably included are commitments in relation to a right "to give free and informed consent on health matters" (Article 11) and rights of persons to long-term care (Article 12).

Thus, there are high-level principles of human rights at international level and in the form of regional groupings such as the Council of Europe which are applicable to mental health. These can be seen as loosely forming "international mental health law". At the same time, as with any such statements at international human rights level these do not easily translate into specific provisions automatically capable of being utilised at individual state level. Application of international human rights provisions involves broader principles of proportionality and of the margin of appreciation (Legg 2012) which courts recognise and can entrench differences in law and policy at state level.

It is also the case that enforcing such human rights principles is dependent on a range of issues, firstly, whether an individual state has been willing to sign a particular international instrument. Moreover, inevitably the focus here is due to the jurisdictional aspects, as Gostin notes the focus is on the position of sovereign states and consequently does not necessarily translate to non-state actors (Gostin 2014). Secondly, as Stavert has argued,

---

24 Council of Europe Recommendation CM/Rec (2014)2 and explanatory memorandum on the Promotion of Human Rights for Older Persons, https://rm.coe.int/1680695bce
25 Following adoption of Resolution 24/20 of the Human Rights Council establishing the mandate of the Independent Expert on the enjoyment of all human rights by older persons.
26 https://www.oas.org/en/sla/dil/inter_american_treaties_A-70_human_rights_older_persons.asp

there is a strong correlation between respect given to the rule of law by a particular member state and the protection that state gives to human rights (Stavert 2017 at p. 336). This has consequent impact on the extent to which states respect and protect those with mental illness and in turn can differ across jurisdictions. Thirdly, even if such a commitment has been made by a member state the right may be limited or qualified in some way. Fourthly, as Stavert comments, the interpretation of rights may at times be challenging in the light of a range of diverse socio-cultural values (Stavert 2017: 342). Furthermore, while rights may exist in principle their enforceability is dependent upon individual awareness of those rights combined with the necessary resources to support such claims (Stavert 2017: 329–349).

Ultimately, existing international human rights conventions and related provisions do not provide a uniform global mental health law as such which can be easily directly transposed. Were there to be better liaison between international human rights bodies, and detailed collaboration and the prospect generally for more rapid change in law at member state level, then perhaps this could be viewed differently. Moreover, these conventions themselves are developed through existing international frameworks which in turn are international political constructs which may not, as we shall come on to see in the next section, necessarily be reflective of a "global" approach to law. But given the existing limitations of the current position, would it be possible to seek to develop a "global mental health law"? We turn to this question in the next section of this chapter.

A "global" mental health law future?

Is "global mental health law" the future? First, as discussed above there is the question of what mental health law itself is and whether it will remain as a distinct and different discipline. Will it be subsumed into health law or "fused" with mental capacity law? As we have seen this remains uncertain, but it is suggested that any reports of the demise of mental health law as a distinct academic area are likely to be greatly exaggerated and that the discipline has some time at least ahead of it. The very existence of distinct health professionals working in this area may drive a demand for specific legal analysis, training and related textbooks such that it remains as a separate area at least from a professional perspective, regardless of whether the general approach taken in the academy in the future is to subsume it under health or disability law.

Secondly, it could be argued that global mental health law is already in existence in that there is engagement with fundamental provisions of international human rights law which impact on mental health law at domestic level. International human rights law provides a framework for mental health law. While the UNCRPD provides a possible future, as we have seen above there are challenges in taking this as the focus. Moreover, it is suggested that this falls far short of what we would see as being "global mental health law" itself as a distinct disciplinary area.

Is it then the case that "global mental health law" could emerge either as a distinct academic area alone or also as an area with its own distinct legal force at global level? It is clearly the case that there is a space for mental health law to operate through a global prism rather than simply through existing international legal instruments. As we have seen above, already there is recognition by the international community and the WHO of the global dimension of mental health. But what actually is "global law" as compared with international law? As Twining has commented:

Sometimes "global law" is confusingly equated with public international law: but not all international law is truly global; on some theories, international law is only one form of "global law".

(Twining 2011: 22–23)[27]

Twining himself is, however, notably cautious as to the broad concept of global law (Twining 2019: 14). This is an area where we need to tread carefully in terms of conceptualisation. It is clear that this is extending beyond the "Westphalian duo" which is the national and the international realm (Twining 2011: 39). Walker suggests that global law cannot be seen simply as law which goes beyond the state (Walker 2015: 18). Moreover, there is already a broad concept from Jessup, that of transnational law, which as Walker notes was developed "so as to convey the sheer range, interconnectedness, and mutability of law that 'transcends national frontiers'" (Jessup 1956: 136). However, global law can be said to extend beyond this. In conceptualising global law, Walker states, it:

> is not this notion of transnational law in the round but the much less commodious category of law which operates at the external "global edge" of the transnational domain.
>
> *(Walker 2015: 18)*

He goes on to say that:

> Rather what qualified law as global law and what all forms of global law have in common, is a practical endorsement of or commitment to the universal or otherwise global – in general – warrant of some laws or other dimensions of law.
>
> *(Walker 2015: 18)*

What is notable about this approach is that global law is not derived from one specific source. It thus may be derived from, for example, specific institutions but equally:

> It may be found in the cross-site acknowledgement and development of a shared body of doctrine or general legal worldview. What is more these are by no means sealed categories and often we will find that they interact combine and build upon one another.
>
> *(Walker 2015: 21)*

There are different conceptions to global law as Walker notes, either encouraging convergence or that of the accommodation of general divergence (Walker 2015, chapter 3). It has been argued that global law can be seen as containing distinct principles. Domingo has identified as principles of global law those of justice, reasonableness, solidarity, subsidiarity and horizontality and goes on to say that:

> These global principles are opposed respectively to the principles of totality, individuality, centralism, and verticality, which have been the foundation of modern international law. From each of these principles, and especially from the proto-principle of justice,

---

27 See also Capaldo (2015).

are derived many others – the principles of property, security, legality, proportionality – that can also affect global law.

(Domingo 2010)

Walker comments that:

The new global law then describes a trend which, in viewing law as a less grounded and less embedded form, a more malleable and more precarious category, captures and expresses nothing less than a new shift in the legal analyst's relationship to law itself.

(Walker 2015: 205)

What does this then mean for mental health law in the future at global level? First, it is possible that there is a distinct evolution of global mental health law as an entity drawing upon the existing backdrop of international legal principles and those principles operating amongst groups of states such as the Council of Europe. This may though draw more organically and broadly in terms of what Walker suggests of a "general legal world view" (Walker 2015). Some existing international law normative approaches may be seen in terms of a hierarchal approach[28] which sits somewhat uncomfortably in recognising widely differing approaches to health and care, to families and to decision-making processes in mental health across jurisdictions.

Is there then a case for "global mental health law"? Global mental health is a matter of international engagement and academic discussion (Okpaku and Biswas 2014). In addition, there is already a "Movement for Global Mental Health".[29] Established following a *Lancet* series on Global Mental Health in 2007 (Prince et al. 2007) its website states that:

The Movement for Global Mental Health is a network of individuals and organisations that aim to improve services for people living with mental health problems and psychosocial disabilities worldwide, especially in low- and middle-income countries where effective services are often scarce. Two principles are fundamental to the Movement: scientific evidence and human rights. [30]

The *Lancet* articles suggested utilisation of standards and interventions with the aim of reducing gaps in the treatment of mental health experienced in some less economically advantaged countries.[31] However, such an approach met criticism from some in psychiatry on the basis that this did not engage sufficiently with cultural and social dimensions of mental health.[32]

We have seen above that the WHO has and is engaging with mental health policy. But this is within standard international law frameworks. There does not seem to be yet a movement towards "global mental health law" as such. However, today I suggest that rather than undue reliance on the hierarchical approach of the national/international law division we should explore how mental health law could be effectively conceptualised within a specific

---

28 The problems of such an approach are highlighted by Walker.
29 https://www.globalmentalhealth.org/pages/about
30 https://www.thelancet.com/series/global-mental-health
31 There was subsequent engagement with this later in relation to the sustainable development goals.
32 See discussion in Gajaria et al. (2019).

global framework. One possibility is for global mental health law to be constructed as part of a broader ongoing movement by some legal scholars at international level to establish as an academic discipline and as a legal framework "global health law" (Gostin 2014; Luca-Burchi and Toebes 2018). As Gostin and Sridhar note, "Global health law has been defined as the legal norms, processes, and institutions that are designed primarily to attain the highest possible standard of physical and mental health for the world's population" (Gostin and Sridhar 2014).

Gostin argues that governments should be held "accountable to assure the conditions in which people can be healthy" (Gostin 2014: 414). He goes on to assert that:

> Put simply three conditions of life would give everyone a fairer opportunity for good health: (1) public services on a populational level; (2) healthcare services to all individuals; and (3) the socio-economic determinants that undergird healthy and productive lives.
>
> *(Gostin 2014: 415)*

This emphasis on socio-economic determinants of health is of course something which is integral to public health discourse[33] and major socio-economic deprivation can undermine effective health responses – as illustrated recently in relation to the disproportionate impacts of Covid-19 globally. Gostin also sees "global health as justice"; this is something which necessarily extends beyond the responsibilities of national governments in relation to health and that "values of good governance" are something which also apply to the private sector (Gostin 2014: 431). There is a broader issue, which goes beyond this chapter concerning the role of private sector providers in providing mental health care, and issues of governance and effective scrutiny. Gostin also notes that a major challenge at global level is "to ensure that programmes and activities are financed in ways that are predictable and scalable to health needs" (Gostin 2014: 431).

In terms of its components Gostin suggests that global health law should include the right to health but go further than existing statements with more detail as to relevant goods and services individuals are entitled to through human rights law. Emphasis is placed here upon the health needs of those in marginalised groups and also the need for "upstream priority setting" and for health policies to engage with health prevention and social determinants of health. He states that this must also include:

> Mutual responsibility—creating clear domestic and international responsibilities on states parties to ensure the health of their inhabitants, and a duty for wealthier states to build capacities in partnership with lower-income states.
>
> *(Gostin 2014)*

This also should be accompanied by "innovative financing" supporting health resources by, e.g., taxing unhealthy foods, placing health through all policies, and facilitating global governance through a wide range of different international sectors and finally "good governance", for example focusing on targets and monitoring (Gostin 2014: 439).

---

33 See, e.g., DHSS (1980) and Marmot (2010).

The concept of global health law today can be seen as drawing upon an existing mixture of hard and soft law human rights legal instruments but not simply as this (Luca-Burchi 2018). Gostin along with certain other commentators see global health law as going beyond the scope of an academic area of study and instead something which should be taken forward as its own distinct legal instrument. The establishment of a World Health Organization Framework Convention on Global Health has been proposed along with a New Global Fund for Health (Gostin 2012). The first such binding WHO Framework Convention is that in relation to Tobacco Control.[34] The advantage of utilising the WHO Framework Convention approach is that of relative speed and reduced complexity of implementation in comparison with that of a United Nations Convention.

While some have welcomed the development of "global health law" others have been more critical. Murphy has identified as concerns a "neglect" of the practical operation of international human rights law in both legal and non-legal settings and how it relates to other fields including ethics and politics (Murphy 2018). Seeking to implement a Global Health Law Convention as a WHO legal instrument as in the form of the Framework Convention on Tobacco Control may in itself be seen as problematic. The operation and effectiveness of the WHO over time has been subject to considerable criticism; Mason Meier for example has suggested that there has been "institutional neglect of human rights for the public's health" (Mason Meier 2010).

Writing in 2013 Haynes et al. expressed concerns as to the likelihood of the WHO taking forward such a Convention given political dynamics and "WHO's current lack of vigour and the chokehold that some donors exercise over the organization's agenda" (Haynes et al. 2013). In the years since Haynes et al.'s article was published, reliance on the very effectiveness of global responses to health has been shaken by the developments from early 2020 onwards in the Covid-19 pandemic (Farrar with Ahujav 2021). Given this, trust in health leadership at global health level may need some time to rebuild. Despite this it is interesting that the WHO is currently pressing ahead with work on a Pandemic Preparedness Treaty.[35]

Hoffman and Rottingen in their systematic review of the literature in this area identified a range of further problems with the proposed Global Health Convention (Hoffman and Røttingen 2013): firstly, the prospect that there would simply be duplication of existing measures taken by a range of actors. Secondly, is it feasible? Cost is seen as a problem in terms of both its negotiation and implementation. Individual states may not welcome it and moreover it has been suggested that various powerful organisations could see it as a threat and oppose it. They have questioned whether a Convention would have sufficient impact, given how difficult it can be to ensure that international obligations are met. Furthermore, global health could as a consequence be impacted by "the whole set of principles, rules, norms, and procedures that are part of legal regimes" (Hoffman and Røttingen 2013). So, for example, they note that in terms of access to justice this can be challenging particularly for less economically advantaged states and that

---

34 World Health Organisation *Framework Convention on Tobacco Control* (2003) https://fctc.who.int/publications/i/item/9241591013
35 "World Health Assembly agrees to launch process to develop historic global accord on pandemic prevention, preparedness, and response" https://www.who.int/news/item/03-03-2023-countries-begin-negotiations-on-global-agreement-to-protect-world-from-future-pandemic-emergencies

> Emphasis in legal systems is on ensuring good process rather than good results, because so often there is little clarity on what constitutes the correct outcome.
> *(Hoffman and Røttingen 2013)*

Thirdly, an alternative, perhaps coupled with the strengthening of the WHO, would be to situate a Framework Convention for Global Health elsewhere, e.g., within the UN Security Council or the Human Rights Council or Economic and Social Council. While there has been traction to move forward to a global health law legal instrument by some, Luca-Burchi has suggested the need for a note of pragmatism in relation to approaches to global health law. He is against an approach to global health law which is totally directed at binding legal treaties and highlights the importance of soft law instruments including in relation to standard setting in this area (Luca-Burchi 2018: 520–527).

If global health law as a concept continues to gain further academic and legal traction and moreover if it is accepted that mental health should not be seen as separate from physical health, then there might not be a case for a separate global mental health law future at all. Instead, global health law can be seen as accommodating all aspects of health. Alternatively, if it is the case that in the future mental health still remains as a distinct area from that of general health law or other related legal principles, then a Global Health Convention could still facilitate such issues being addressed. A future global mental health law could, for example, itself evolve from a specific protocol attached to a Global Health Convention. Or it may be that rather than a movement to a defined new legal instrument operating at global level, taking Luca-Burchi's approach (Luca-Burchi 2018), global health law might evolve further soft law approaches which could be seen as having a part to play in building on the work of international actors such as the WHO and the European Union in their responses to mental health in the context of broader policy such as sustainable development goals, which we noted above. Gable has also commented in relation to the existing role of and ongoing potential of global mental health governance both through formal (e.g., international bodies) and informal actors (Gable 2014). Informal governance, as Gable notes, has advantages; by expanding the role of international actors beyond existing legal instruments this may facilitate the harmonisation of norms and also bring to the table a wide range of organisations such as civil society organisations and non-governmental organisations. However, there are of course, as he notes, disadvantages; namely, without legal enforcement governments cannot be held to account, a range of actors may have diverging priorities which may undermine mental health improvements and new political regimes may too easily be able to retrench from steps taken (Gable 2014).

Any such developments, whether at Convention or through the medium of soft law, would need to recognise the role and also related pressures of global actors and stakeholders, not least the pharmaceutical industries. But this will be challenging. The diverse approaches to health and illness, to autonomous decisions and to the involvement of family across jurisdictions are unlikely to lend themselves easily to a "global" approach to health in general and to mental health in particular.

Conclusions

The future of mental health law and whether and to what extent it should be seen as separate from areas such as "health law" remains a moot point. Mental health law as a separate discipline may indeed disappear in the future. But legal structures and norms which impact on the mental health of individuals and of communities will almost certainly exist in one form of another. While human rights litigation and related international documents are vital to address concerns and to facilitate redress for wrongs these too have their limitations. When we move from those issues of mental health care which fall within traditional civil and political rights and issues, e.g., concerning lawful detention, to broader more fluid questions around service provision and choice then human rights themselves can be problematic to utilise. Exploring the nature and potential for global mental health law as a discipline may assist in setting out the expected parameters and the recognition of the challenge of conflicting rights and collective responsibilities.

Whether there should be not only a distinct discipline but also a specific legal instrument is a different matter. As with the growth of other human rights Conventions in recent years there may be the danger of reaching "Convention saturation point", where there is undue proliferation of Conventions, many containing virtually identical or subtly different provisions.[36] Rather than resulting in clear paradigms and statements for states to follow, this may simply lead to confusion. Moreover, it could also dilute the effectiveness of specific statements. In relation to mental health, as with health in general, there is also the question of reaching consensus as to what should be included and precisely how specific such a Convention would be. Too specific – would this lead to agreement particularly given the diverse approaches currently at domestic level? Too general – this could ultimately mean that its utility was limited other than at what is a highly rhetorical level. Any new Convention would also need to address the interface between therapeutic-related measures and those concerning the criminal justice system. At the same time implementation of this is likely to be challenging given different approaches across jurisdictions, not least in relation to the nature of what constitutes autonomous decision making. There is furthermore the question of the extent to which all these normative approaches themselves can be seen as driven through a lens which itself is problematic and dated. We need to stop and reflect on the appropriateness of the models of medical and legal engagement in this area. There is already discussion of the need to decolonise approaches in relation to mental health (Mills 2014). In relation to what are appropriate legal structures in this area further exploration is needed of the paradigms utilised in relation to broader decolonising of law discourse, for example in relation to international law, and how they can help to inform our scholarship and policy in the area of global mental health law going forward (Pahuja 2011). This is itself an important academic project to take forward in the future.

Disciplines can develop through gradual evolution, but academics, those with lived experience, practitioners and policy makers can and should set out what they would like to see as the parameters. In so doing we need to understand how far we have come with international law and also its limitations in relation to health and mental health law. By recasting the debate around the nature and scope of mental health law in a "global" context and recognising that in so doing we need to go beyond the scope of international human rights we are presented with potential, but also notable challenges. There is also the risk that this is a debate which is ultimately undertaken by "usual suspects" albeit simply casting it from a different perspective. We need to situate the discourse recognising that health and mental health can be and needs to be viewed through the prism of different traditions, social and cultural, legal and political taking a genuinely broader "global" perspective. We need to work organically. This

---

36 See, for example, the discussion regarding the feasibility of a UN Convention on the rights of older persons.

will be a difficult and challenging task. But we need to be prepared to face those challenges and look forward to seeing what a global mental health law future will look like. In a world which is increasingly integrated at so many levels, political, social and economic, this is a dialogue we need to enter.

References

Akhtar, R, Nyamutata, C and Faulkner, E (2020) *International Child Law*. London: Routledge.
Allan, A (2002) "The past, present and future of mental health law: A therapeutic jurisprudence analysis". *Law Context: A Socio-Legal Journal* 20, pp. 24–52.
Bagenstos, SR (2004–5) "The future of disability law". *Yale Law Journal* 114(1), pp. 1–84.
Bartlett, P (2009) "The United Nations convention on the rights of persons with disabilities and the future of mental health law". *Psychiatry* 8(12), pp. 496–498.
Bartlett, P and Sandland, R (2014) *Mental Health Law: Policy and Practice*, 4th ed. Oxford: Oxford University Press.
Blanck, P (ed.) (2017) *Routledge Handbook of Disability Law and Human Rights*. Abingdon: Routledge.
Broderick, A and Ferri, D (2019) *International and European Disability Law and Policy*. Cambridge: Cambridge University Press.
Bridgeman, J (2020) *Medical Treatment of Children, and the Law: Beyond Parental Responsibilities*. London: Routledge.
Brown, J (2016) "The changing purpose of mental health law: From medicalism to legalism to new legalism". *International Journal of Law and Psychiatry* 47, pp. 1–9.
Campbell, TD (1994) "Mental health law: Institutionalised discrimination". *Australian and New Zealand Journal of Psychiatry* 28(4), pp. 554–559.
Capaldo, GZ "What is global law?" https://blog.oup.com/2015/08/what-is-global-law-jurisprudence/.
Chen, B (2022) *Mental Health Law in China: A Socio-Legal Analysis Routledge Research in Health Law*. London: Routledge.
Craven, M (2000) "Legal differentiation and the concept of human rights treaty in international law". *European Journal of International Law* 11(3), pp. 489–551.
Council of Europe (1997) *Convention on Human Rights and Biomedicine*.
Council of Europe (2004) *Recommendation CM/Rec (2004) of the Committee of Ministers to Member States Concerning the Protection of Human Rights and Dignity of Persons with Mental Disorder*.
Council of Europe (2014) *Recommendation on the Promotion of the Human Rights of Older Persons*. CM Rec 2014/2 and explanatory recommendation.
Council of Europe (2018) *Draft Additional Protocol Concerning the Protection of Human Rights and Dignity of Persons with Mental Disorder with Regard to Involuntary Placement and Involuntary Treatment*.
Dabbs Sciubba, J (2014) "Explaining campaign timing and support for a UN convention on the rights of the older person". *International Journal of Human Rights* 18(4), pp. 462–478.
Dawson, J and Gledhill, K (2013) *New Zealand's Mental Health Act in Practice*. Wellington: Victoria University Press.
Dawson, J and Szmukler, G (2006) "Fusion of mental health and incapacity legislation". *British Journal of Psychiatry* 188(6), pp. 504–509.
Department of Health and Social Security (1988) *Report of the Working Group on Inequalities in health*. London: DHSS (the Black Report).
Domingo, R (2010) *The New Global Law*. Cambridge: Cambridge University Press.
Duffy, RM and Kelly, BM (2020) *India's Mental Health Act 2017: Building Laws, Protecting Rights*. Singapore: Springer.
European Commission (2019) *Mental Health: Good Practice and Implementable Research Results*. Brussels: European Union.
Farrar, J with Ahuja, A (2021) *Spike: The Virus vs the People: The Inside Story*. London: Profile Books.
Fair Society Healthy Lives. (2010). *The Marmot Review: Strategic Review of Health Inequalities in England Post 2010*. https://www.instituteofhealthequity.org/resources-reports/fair-society-healthy-lives-the-marmot-review/fair-society-healthy-lives-full-report-pdf.pdf.

Gable, L (2014) "Global health governance, international law, and mental health". In Okpaku, SP (ed.) *Essentials of Global Mental Health*. Cambridge: Cambridge University Press.

Gajaria, A, Izenberg, JM, Nguyen, V, Rimal, P, Acharya, B and Hansen, H (2019) "Moving the global mental health debate forward: How a structural competency framework can apply to global mental health training". *Academic Psychiatry* 43(6), pp. 617–620.

Gooding, P (2018) *A New Era for Mental Health Law and Policy: Supported Decision-Making and the UN Convention on the Rights of Persons with Disabilities*. Cambridge: Cambridge University Press.

Gostin, LO and Gable, L (2010) "Human rights of persons with mental disabilities". In Gostin, LO, McHale, JV, Fennell, P, Mackay, RD and Bartlett, P (eds.) *Principles of Mental Health Law and Policy*. Oxford: Oxford University Press. pp 103–167.

Gostin, LO (2001) "Public health, ethics and human rights: A tribute to the late Jonathan Mann". *Journal of Law, Medicine and Ethics*, 29(2), pp. 121–130.

Gostin, LO (2012) "A framework convention on global health: Health for all, justice for all". *JAMA* 307(19), pp. 2087–2092.

Gostin, LO (2014) *Global Health Law*. Cambridge: Harvard University Press.

Gostin, LO, McHale, JV, Fennell, P, Mackay, RD and Bartlett, P (eds.) (2010) *Principles of Mental Health Law and Policy*. Oxford: Oxford University Press.

Gostin, LO and Sridhar, D (2014) "Health and the law". *New England Journal of Medicine* 370, pp. 1732–1740.

Gostin, LO and Wiley, LF (2016) *Public Health Law: Power, Duty, and Restraint*, 3rd ed. Oakland California: University of California Press.

Guthell, TG and Appelbaum, PS (2019) *Clinical Handbook of Psychiatry and the Law*, 5th ed. Lippincott: Williams and Wilkin.

Haynes, L, Legge, D, London, L, McCoy, D, Sanders, D and Schuftan, C (2013) "Will the struggle for health equity and social justice be best served by a framework convention on global health?" *Health and Human Rights* 15(1). https://www.hhrjournal.org/2013/10/will-the-struggle-for-health-equity-and-social-justice-be-best-served-by-a-framework-convention-on-global-health/.

Hoffman, SJ and Røttingen, JA (2013) "Dark sides of the proposed framework convention on global health's many virtues: A systematic review and critical analysis". *Health and Human Rights* 15(1). https://cdn2.sph.harvard.edu/wp-content/uploads/sites/13/2013/06/Hoffman.pdf.

Hale, B (2020) *Mental Health Law*, 6th ed. London: Sweeet and Maxwell.

Hervey, TK and McHale, JV (2015) *European Health Law: Themes and Implications*. Cambridge: CUP.

Hunt, P (2005) *Report of the Special Rapporteur on the Right of Everyone to the Enjoyment of the Highest Attainable Standard of Physical and Mental Health*. UN Commission on Human Rights. Doc. E/CN.4/2005/51.

Jessup, P (1956) *Transnational Law* New Haven: Yale University Press.

Jones, K (1980) "The limitations of the legal approach to mental health". *International Journal of Law and Psychiatry* 3(1), pp. 1–15.

Luca-Burchi, G (2018) "Global health law: Present and future". In Luca-Burchi, G and Toebes, B (eds.) *Research Handbook on Global Health Law*. London: Edward Elgar.

Kayess, R and French, P (2008) "Out of darkness into light? Introducing the convention on the rights of persons with disabilities". *Human Rights Law Review* 8(1), pp. 1–34.

Kelly, BD (2015) *Dignity, Mental Health, and Human Rights: Coercion and the Law*. Farnham: Ashgate.

Kennedy, I and Grubb, A (2000) *Medical Law Text and Materials*, 3rd ed. London: Butterworths.

Laurie, GT, Harmon, S and Dove, E (2019) *Mason and McCall Smith's Law and Medical Ethics* Oxford: Oxford University Press, Chapter 14.

Legg, A (2012) *The Margin of Appreciation in International Human Rights Law: Deference and Proportionality*. Oxford: Oxford University Press.

Harper, C, Davison, G and McLelland, R (2016) "No longer 'anomalous, confusing, and unjust'": the Mental Capacity Act (Northern Ireland) 2016". *International Journal of Mental Health and Capacity Law* 22, pp. 1–70.

Hunt, P (2016) "Interpreting the international right to health in a human rights-based approach to health". *Health and Human Rights Journal*. https://www.hhrjournal.org/2016/12/interpreting-the-international-right-to-health-in-a-human-rights-based-approach-to-health/.

International covenant on economic, social and cultural rights, New York, 19 December 1966, in force 3 January 1976.

Lawson, A (2020) "Disability law as an academic discipline: Towards cohesion and mainstreaming?" *Journal of Law and in Society* 47(4), pp. 558–587.

Lewis, O. and Pathare, S (2020) "Chronic illness, disability and mental health". In Gostin, LO and Meier, BM (eds.) *Foundations of Global Health and Human Rights*. Oxford: Oxford University Press. pp. 285–307.

Lougarre, C (2014) "John Tobin, the right to health in international law" *Modern Law Review* 77(2), pp. 336–342.

Matthew, FB (1948) *Mental Health Services a Handbook on Lunacy and Mental Treatment and Mental Deficiency*. London: Shaw and Sons.

Mason Meier, B (2010) "The World Health Organization, the evolution of human rights, and the failure to achieve Health for All". In Harrington, J and Stuttaford, M (eds.) *Global Health and Human Rights: Legal and Philosophical Perspectives*. Abingdon: Routledge. pp. 168–189.

MacDonald, J (2017) "Do children have a right to mental health? The annual lecture of the wales observatory on human rights of children and young people delivered by the Honourable Mr Justice MacDonald at the College of Law and Criminology, Swansea University on 20 July 2017". https://www.swansea.ac.uk/media/2017-Observatory-Annual-Lecture-MR-JUSTICE-MACDONALD.pdf.

McHale, JV (2011) "Mental health and the EU: The next new regulatory frontier?" *Medical Law Review* 19(4), pp. 606–635.

McHale, JV (2019) "Health law in the UK as a subset of human rights law: Idealistic aspiration or coherent reality?" *Journal of Medical Law and Ethics*,7, pp. 179–200.

Mills, C (2014) *Decolonizing Global Mental Health: The Psychiatrization of the Majority World*. London: Routledge.

Morrissey, F (2012) "The United Nations convention on the rights of persons with disabilities: A new approach to decision-making in mental health law". *European Journal of Health Law* 19, pp. 423–440.

Murphy, T (2018) "Hardwired human rights: A health and human rights perspective on global health law". In Luca-Burchi, G and Toebes, B (eds.) *Research Handbook on Global Health Law*. London: Edward Elgar. pp 82–103.

Nilsson, A (2021) *Compulsory Mental Health Interventions and the CRPD*. London: Bloomsbury.

Okpaku, SO and Biswas, S " (2014) History of global mental health". In Okpaku, SP (ed.) *Essentials of Global Mental Health*. Cambridge: Cambridge University Press. pp. 1–11.

Pahuja, S (2011) *Decolonising International Law: Development, Economic Growth, and the Politics of Universality*. Cambridge: Cambridge University Press.

Patel, V, Saxena, S, Lund, C et al. (2018) "The Lancet commission on global mental health and sustainable development". *Lancet* 392(10157), pp. 1553–1598.

Peay, J (2011) *Mental Health and Crime*. Abingdon: Routledge.

Perlin, M, Cucolo, HE and Lynch, AJ (2017) *Mental Disability Law: Cases and Materials*, 3rd ed. Durham North Carolina: Carolina Academic Press.

Poffé, L (2015) "Towards a new United Nations human rights convention for older persons?" *Human Rights Law Review* 15, p. 591.

Prince, M, Pate, LV, Saxena, S, Maj, M, Maselko, J, Phillips, MR and Rahman, A (2007) "No health without mental health". *Lancet* 370(9590), pp. 859–877.

Rapose, VL (2016) "The convention of human rights and biomedicine revisited: Critical assessment". *International Journal of Human Rights*, 20, pp. 1277–1294.

Rosenman, S (1994) "Mental health law: An idea whose time has passed". *Australian and New Zealand Journal of Psychiatry* 28(4), pp. 560–565.

Rosenthal, E and Rubenstein, L (1993) "International human rights advocacy under the 'principles for the protection of persons with mental illness'". *International Journal of Law & Psychiatry* 16(3–4), pp. 257–300.

Series L. "Of Powers and Safeguards". In Krajewska, A and McHale, JV (eds.) *Rethinking Health Law: from Medical to Health and Social Care Law*, forthcoming, Edward Elgar 2024.

Sheeran, S (2013) "The relationship of international human rights law and general international law: A hermeneutic constraint or pushing the boundaries?" In Sheeran, S and Rodley, N (eds.) *Routledge Handbook on International Human Rights Law*. London: Routledge.

Szmulker, G (2017) "The UN convention on the rights of persons with disabilities: 'Rights, will and preferences' in relation to mental disabilities". *International Journal of Law and Psychiatry* 54, pp. 90–97.

Szmulker, G, Daw, R and Callard, F (2014) "Mental health law and the UN convention on the rights of persons with disabilities". *International Journal of Law and Psychiatry* 37(3), pp. 245–252.

Szmukler, G and Dawson, J (2011) "Reducing discrimination in mental health law: The fusion of mental incapacity and mental health legislation". In Kallert, TW, Mezzich, JE and Monahan, J (eds.) *Coercive Treatment in Psychiatry: Clinical, Legal and Ethical Aspects*. Wiley-Blackwell.

Stavert, J (2017) "Mental health law in a global context". In White, RG, Jaain, S and Orr, DMR (eds.) *The Palgrave Handbook of Sociocultural Perspectives on Global Mental Health*. London: Palgrave Macmillan. pp 329–349.

Tobin, J (2012) *The Right to Health in International Law*. Oxford: Oxford University Press.

Toebes, B (1999) *The Right to Health as a Human Right in International Law*. Cambridge: Intersentia.

Twining, W (2009) *General Jurisprudence: Understanding Law from a Global Perspective*. Cambridge: Cambridge University Press.

Twining, W (2011) "Globalisation and legal scholarship: Montesquieu lecture". Tilberg Law Lecture Series Nijmegen: Wolf Legal Publishers.

Ugochukwu, O, Mbaezue, N, Akinmayowa, S, Lawal, C, Azubogu, T, Lateef Sheikh, T and Vallières, F (2020) "The time is now: Reforming Nigeria's outdated mental health laws". *The Lancet Global Health* 8(8), pp. E989–E990.

United Nations (1989) Convention on the rights of the child adopted 20 November 1989, by general assembly resolution 44/25.

United Nations (1991–1992) *The Protection of Persons with Mental Illness and the Improvement of Mental Health Care: Resolution / Adopted by the General Assembly*. UN General Assembly (46th Sess.: 1991–1992).

United Nations (2002) *Political Declaration and Madrid International Action Plan on Ageing Second World Assembly on Ageing, Madrid Spain, 8–12th April 2002*. New York: United Nations.

United Nations (2007) *Convention on the Rights of Persons with Disabilities Preamble*, paragraph (a).

Weaver, R and Meyer, G (2019) *Law and Mental Health, A Case-Based Approach*, 2nd ed. New York: The Guilford Press.

Walker, N (2015) *Intimations of Global Law*. Cambridge: Cambridge University Press.

WHO (2005). *Resource on Mental Health, Human Rights and Legislation*. Geneva: World Health Organization.

World Health Organisation (2021) *Mental Health Action Plan 2013–2030*. Geneva: World Health Organization.

World Health Organisation (2022) *World Mental Health Report: Transforming Mental Health for All*. Geneva: World Health Organization.

Zalgiris, P (2001) "The European convention on biomedicine: Its past, present and future". In Garwood-Gowers, A, Tingle, J and Lewis, T (eds.) *Healthcare Law: The Impact of the Human Rights Act 1998*. London: Cavendish. 31–49.

38
THE FUTURE OF MENTAL HEALTH LAW
Abolition or reform?

Kay Wilson

Mental health law[1] permits the state to authorize the involuntarily detention and treatment of persons with severe mental impairments[2] (e.g. Mental Health Act 1983 which applies in England and Wales). Not surprisingly, mental health law, which interferes with such personal matters as medical decision-making, has always been controversial and the subject of reviews and reforms about the scope of such invasive powers and when and how they should be used. However, never – until the entry into force of the Convention on the Rights of Persons with Disabilities (CRPD) in 2008[3] – has the very existence of mental health law been challenged, or been as fiercely criticized on the grounds of being an unjustified loss of liberty, bodily integrity and discrimination. While the text of the CRPD is deliberately silent on whether mental health law should be abolished, as States Parties and negotiators from Disabled Persons Organizations were unable to agree during the CRPD negotiations (Ward, 2021), it has resulted in a vacuum in which the future of mental health law now hangs in the balance, and in which the existence of mental health law has been both attacked and defended.

On the one hand, the CRPD Committee, the treaty body responsible for monitoring the implementation of the CRPD, and certain disability and human rights advocates and schol-

---

1 While the term 'mental health law' applies to all laws that relate to mental health, this chapter is particularly concerned about legal provisions which permit the involuntary detention and psychiatric treatment of persons with mental impairment, whether contained in a stand-alone Mental Health Act or dispersed within other legislation.
2 The terminology which refers to persons with mental impairments has always been problematic and contentious. By persons with mental impairment I mean persons with psychiatric conditions including schizophrenia, bipolar disorder, depression, anxiety disorders, eating disorders, obsessive-compulsive disorder and post-traumatic stress disorder which may be treatable by psychiatric intervention, rather than persons with cognitive impairments such as intellectual disability, autism and dementia. While I have no difficulty with the idea that society can disable persons, 'persons with disabilities' seems too general. I have instead chosen 'mental impairment' as opposed to 'mental illness' or 'psycho-social' disability in this paper because it is the term used in the *Convention on the Rights of Persons with Disabilities*, open for signature 30 March 2007, UNTS 2515 (entered into force 3 May 2008), Art. 1 CRPD.
3 Convention on the Rights of Persons with Disabilities, open for signature 30 March 2007, UNTS 2515 (entered into force 3 May 2008).

ars (whom I call abolitionists) have claimed that to be CRPD compliant, States Parties must immediately abolish mental health law and offer supported decision-making (which persons with mental impairments are entitled to reject). Minkowitz (2021) has even gone so far as to call for reparations for psychiatric violence caused by involuntary detention and treatment. On the other hand, while few would argue that the CRPD does not require *any* changes to mental health law, there is growing support for the idea that the CRPD does not go so far as requiring the abolition of mental health law, although it may require significant legal and systemic reform, and that the complete abolition of mental health law would be both unnecessary and undesirable (e.g. Wilson, 2021; Alexandrov and Schuck, 2021; Ward, 2021; Yamin, 2021; Bo, 2020). Certainly, States Parties have resisted the abolition of mental health law and many have issued interpretive declarations that they do not interpret the CRPD that way. Even States Parties, such as Peru, who have come closer to implementing the abolitionist vision of the CRPD than any other states so far, have not completely abolished mental health law, still permitting involuntary detention and psychiatric treatment in emergency situations (Encalada, 2021). Still other scholars accept that the *immediate abolition* of mental health law is unrealistic, but argue that States Parties should instead aim for a slower progressive realization to implement it and take steps to gradually phase out mental health law, without letting the perfect get in the way of the good (e.g. Davidson, 2020; Maylea et al., 2021).

The resulting debate raises a number of perplexing questions. What does the CRPD actually require States Parties to do? Does the CRPD contain a broader vision of disability rights than the abolition of mental health law? What *should* the future of mental health law be? Does mental health law have *any* merit? What are the options for reform? Is meaningful reform even possible? How can the best outcome for persons with mental impairments be achieved? The purpose of this chapter then is to consider each of these issues and what they mean for the future of mental health law both as a matter of principle (what the law should be) and pragmatism (what states are actually likely to do). In doing so, I will draw on the arguments in my recent book *Mental Health Law: Abolish and Reform?* (OUP, 2021) – that mental health law should not be abolished, but be significantly reformed to decrease coercion and increase social support to persons with mental impairments. I also frame my discussion within what I call the 'interpretive compass' of dignity (including autonomy), equality and participation, which underpins the CRPD and international human rights law generally.

What does the CRPD actually require States Parties to do? Does the CRPD contain a broader vision of disability rights than the abolition of mental health law?

As already noted, the CRPD negotiations over the abolition of mental health law were fraught and even threatened to derail the negotiation of the whole convention. Consequently, the text of the CRPD neither expressly permits nor prohibits involuntary detention and psychiatric treatment. Nonetheless, abolitionists have still claimed victory and that the CRPD, particularly the rights to non-discrimination (Article 4) and the rights to equality (Article 5), legal capacity (Article 12), liberty (Article 14), bodily integrity (Article 17), independent living (Article 19), health (Article 25) and the ban on torture and cruel and unusual punishment (Article 15), collectively require the immediate abolition of mental health law.

However, on closer examination, the requirements of the CRPD are not so clear-cut and I argue that the abolitionist interpretation represents a selective and extreme interpretation of the CRPD, rather than a more balanced and holistic approach (Wilson, 2021).

Similarly, Gerald Neuman criticizes the abolitionist approach as an 'absolutist' interpretation which is out-of-step with wider human rights law (Neuman, 2021). Unfortunately, the unresolved issues about the abolition of mental health law during the negotiations means that the CRPD contains a number of ambiguities, making it a classic 'incompletely theorized agreement' rather than a coherent exposition of disability rights (Kayess and French, 2008). Much has been made over whether Article 12(4) requires the abolition of all substitute decision-making, or permits it with strict controls for short periods of time in emergency situations; whether Article 14 prohibits the detention of all persons with disabilities regardless of whether they are at risk of harming themselves or others; whether Article 17 prohibits all non-consensual interference with bodily integrity, or is limited to unbeneficial or overly intrusive treatment; and whether Article 15 means that non-consensual treatment is always torture or cruel, inhuman and degrading treatment, regardless of whether it is medically necessary and intended to relieve suffering. I do not intend to reiterate or explore these technical arguments, which no one has yet been able to definitively resolve here, other than to point out that the interpretation of the CRPD is ambiguous and that the abolitionist interpretation is one of many. Rather, I argue that disputes about the interpretation of the CRPD reflect two competing priorities and visions, based on how mental impairment and disability are conceptualized and what vision of disability rights the CRPD seeks to create.

For the abolitionists, the CRPD is based on the British Social Model of Disability which views disability as being entirely created by social, attitudinal and environmental barriers (Traustadottir, 2009). The British Social Model of Disability, originally created by wheelchair users, takes the position that the discrimination created by society is always worse than the impairment (which is more or less neutral). In fact, some abolitionists conceptualize mental impairment itself as an alternative state of consciousness, rather than a mental impairment which has symptoms that affect cognition, emotion and impulse control (e.g. Roper and Gooding, 2019; Oaks, 2012). Therefore, if mental impairment is illusory, the biggest harm for persons with mental impairments is mental health law and the loss of liberty and decision-making power it permits. Further, abolitionists argue that the commitment to individual autonomy and choice extends not just to whether or not to consent to hospital admission and psychiatric treatment, but also to whether to accept or reject decision-making support and what and how much support to accept regardless of an individual's ability. Where, after considerable efforts, a person is unable to make or communicate an intelligible decision, a facilitator can make a decision based on what they consider the person's will and preferences would have been, after consultation with those closest to them (General Comment No. 1, para. 26; Arstein-Kerslake and Flynn, 2016). From this perspective, the most important principle in the CRPD is individual liberty which should be respected in all cases, regardless of the effect of the person's impairment on their functioning, or the consequences of their decisions to the individual or society.

As we have seen in the COVID-19 pandemic, there are a minority of persons in most western societies who take the view that the principle of individual liberty is always the most important value and that the state should *never* circumscribe individual decision-making, even if that involves serious consequences such as death, disability or long-term health issues. That is, the individual is always sovereign. However, in the health sphere most states can and do legislate on a range of matters where the boundaries between the social interest and individual choice are controversial – from public health orders and vaccine mandates, to euthanasia, physician-assisted dying and abortion (Wilson and Rudge, 2023). The debate about the future of mental health law can be seen in that wider social and politically charged context.

Of course, 'for every problem there is a solution which is neat, plausible and wrong', wrote journalist Henry Louis Mencken in 1920, and I argue so it is with the call for the abolition of mental health law. An alternative, holistic and, I argue, a more nuanced understanding of the CRPD is that the rights to legal capacity (Article 12), liberty (Article 14) and bodily integrity (Article 17) are only part of the vision of disability rights in the CRPD. From this perspective the CRPD is also about recognizing and protecting the right to life of persons with mental impairments (Article 10; Wilson, 2018), the right to the highest attainable standard of mental and physical health, including the prevention of further impairments (Article 25), habilitation and rehabilitation (Article 26) and to be able to generally have a good life including education, employment, relationships, leisure and the ability to participate in the community. That is, in international human rights law all rights are seen as 'universal, indivisible, interdependent and interrelated' (Vienna Declaration, 1993). It recognizes that while social, environmental and attitudinal barriers play a big part in excluding persons with mental impairments (and should be rectified), the impairments themselves can also cause pain, inertia and distress, and in some cases interfere with a person's judgment, identity and ability to see a future for themselves, or have a sense of their own worth. In other words, rather than simply promoting 'negative liberty' or *freedom from* state interference in all circumstances, the CRPD as a whole creates a richer vision of 'positive liberty' or the *freedom to* live a good life (Alexandrov and Schuck, 2021) and that pure non-interference may not deliver that, especially in the so-called 'hard' cases where distilling a person's will and preferences may be quite murky. While it could be argued that it should always be for the individual to choose what a 'good life' is for them, human rights law is not the same as liberalism and does in its broad constellation of rights and principles create a broad blueprint of what most people conceptualize as being a 'good' life, which should not be discarded lightly. Persons with mental impairments ought to be entitled to the same quality of life that persons without disabilities take for granted and not be deprived of it because their impairment may impede their recognition of the desire for and enjoyment of those rights. An additional issue for persons with mental impairment is that sometimes a person's immediate wishes may contradict or undermine *their own* pre-existing overarching life goals and understanding of the 'good life'. This has led to some scholars distinguishing between a person's 'will' which is more enduring and should be given more respect, and their more fleeting 'preferences' when the two are in conflict (e.g. Smukler, 2017, 2019).

Further, most individual human rights are not absolute and must be limited and reconciled against other human rights and the rights of others and society. Therefore, while the CRPD is quite rightly about setting out and amplifying the rights of persons with disabilities (which have been long forgotten and overlooked), the implementation of those rights can have implications for others. The human rights of friends, family, supporters and the community at large, which are protected by other human rights treaties such as the International Covenant on Civil and Political Rights 1976, cannot be completely excluded from the development of mental health law and policy.

One way of 'balancing' conflicting rights, especially in constitutional and human rights courts, has been to do a 'proportionality' analysis between the different competing rights and rights-holders; that is, a kind of *quantitative* analysis or reconciliation to recognize each right to its maximum or optimum width and therefore seek to maximize all rights. Anna Nilsson recently used proportionality analysis, using the work of Robert Alexy (Nilsson, 2021) to argue (as I do) that mental health law should be reformed, rather than abolished. Another approach, which I use, is to do a *qualitative* analysis, based on the work of Ronald

Dworkin (2013) that interpretation must include consideration of moral and social traditions and Jeremy Waldron (2011) that most rights contain internal limitations, by exploring the meaning of certain core concepts in the CRPD in order to better interpret and understand the scope and contours of each right, before trying to weigh different rights and the rights of competing rights-holders against each other. Given the many 'gaps' in the CRPD, understanding the deeper meaning of its core concepts seems to be a good starting point before seeking to 'balance' different rights. While Nilsson (2021) essentially treats the CRPD as a non-discrimination treaty and focuses only on equality and discrimination analysis, my approach is broader and encompasses the three core concepts which underpin the CRPD, being the principles of dignity (including autonomy), equality and participation which I call the 'interpretive compass'. I have chosen these principles as they are embedded in the foundations of human rights law and the principles on which the whole of the CRPD is intended to be interpreted in Article 3 of the CRPD (many of which are repetitive, but I argue can be summarized as dignity (including autonomy), equality and participation). Further, in General Comment No. 1 (2014), the CRPD Committee, the treaty body responsible for monitoring the implementation of the CRPD, has called for the abolition of mental health law by explicitly basing its interpretation of equality before the law (Article 12) on the general principles in Article 3 of the CRPD (General Comment No. 1, para. 4). However, as Craigie (2019) has recently observed:

> it is unclear how the step from these principles to the conclusions in General Comment No.1 was made. Indeed, it seems plausible that the application of these principles might sometimes yield conflicting guidance that would need resolution. The requirements to respect the inherent dignity and value the independence of persons, for example, do not always point in the same direction. Much depends on the situation that is being considered, and how these principles are understood.
>
> *(pp. 160–161)*

While I am only able to give a broad overview of the interpretive compass here, a fuller and detailed description and justification is contained in my book.

Dignity (including autonomy)

Dignity is a key principle which permeates the CRPD, including its object and purpose. It is also often regarded as the foundation of all human rights law. In fact, the CRPD was originally called the International Convention on the Protection and Promotion of the Rights and *Dignity* of Persons with Disabilities, but dignity was removed and put into the purpose (Article 1) and principles (Article 3) to make the title shorter. Dignity is also particularly significant in the mental health and disability context because persons with disabilities are particularly exposed to dignity violations and have even been regarded as less than human.

However, the CRPD provides little normative content on which to understand the concept of dignity, making it necessary to go beyond a purely textual analysis. Further, the concept of dignity is ambiguous, contested and is 'multi-vocal' in that it probably has more than one meaning. After consulting a wide range of literature from disciplines from philosophy, law, medicine, psychology and disability studies as well as documents recording the negotiations of the CRPD, I identified a number of key features of the concept of dignity on which there is broad agreement. These are that inherent dignity requires the recognition of inalienable intrinsic human worth of all persons simply for being human; dignity requires equality as all persons have inherent dignity; dignity requires that persons seek to behave with dignity; all persons must be treated with dignity; the state should be organized to support dignity; and that inherent dignity involves respect for autonomy (although, I argue, is not synonymous with it) (Wilson, 2021, ch. 4). Of these, the complex relationship between dignity and autonomy is probably the most relevant with respect to the abolition or reform of mental health law. That is because the CRPD recognizes *both* dignity and the independence of persons. So what happens when a person tries to exercise their autonomy in a way which may conflict with their dignity, such as by rejecting much-needed medical treatment while their mental state continues to deteriorate?

In this regard, I argue that the concept of inherent dignity is wider than the concept of autonomy and in some circumstances is capable of acting as a limit on autonomy. I begin my analysis by providing a deeper analysis of the meaning of the rather problematic concept of autonomy. While the CRPD refers to making one's own choices and decisions, there is no express right to autonomy in the CRPD, or in international human rights law. The difficulty is that autonomy is more a matter of fact rather than a right which has a strong internal dimension which a person must develop: it can be recognized or not by the law, but not given by the law if it does not exist (Megret, 2008; Nedelsky, 2011). Even persons without disabilities may not always be autonomous. Also, autonomy by its nature could only ever be a very qualified right; it cannot be the right to do whatever a person wants without limits (Maclean, 2009). Giving primacy to autonomy also assumes that humans are by their nature decision-makers who always know what they want (Stone, 2020), which is surely inaccurate and unrealistic. By contrast, the abolitionist approach regards the right to autonomy as being the removal of all external constraints on decision-making, including mental health law, even though support may not be sufficient to essentially 'make a person autonomous' as a matter of fact, or discern their will and preferences without guessing. That is not to say that supported decision-making should not be used, but that it is not a panacea and that it has its limits. As Terry Carney points out, creating the conditions for autonomy is not necessarily the same as having autonomy (Carney, 2017).

If inherent dignity is, as I argue, wider than autonomy in human rights law and has an objective meaning, it is also capable of limiting autonomy in some circumstances, especially where there is good reason to think that a person's autonomy has been compromised or diminished in some way, such as by a severe mental impairment. To the extent that dignity is a collective norm which defines what it means to be human and limits individual autonomy, it has an illiberal dimension. While some find that discomforting (Duwell, 2014), human rights, in setting basic universal standards of acceptable conduct and treatment, does by its nature place some limits on individual choice at the edges. Situations where inherent dignity may justify involuntary detention and treatment, or less coercive intervention, would include where a person's acts are self-destructive, degrading or which offend widely accepted norms of dignified behavior fit for a human. Brendan Kelly, for instance, uses the example of persons with mental impairments living in extreme filth and squalor which places their physical health at risk, especially where they lack 'insight' into their condition (Kelly, 2014).

Of course, the treatment of persons with mental impairment by the mental health system, and medical patients in healthcare settings generally, with a lack of dignity, is a separate issue and is well documented and ought to be immediately addressed by significant systemic reform. Examples include miscommunication and being talked down to by staff; not being offered any or adequate treatment, being punished and humiliated by staff (particularly by use of seclusion and restraint); not being 'heard'; lack of privacy and overcrowded and impoverished environments; or being expected to have more independence and autonomy than a person is capable of and being ashamed to ask for help. Staff who are polite, courteous, patient, friendly, helpful, respectful, encouraging and treat individuals as a person are important for supporting dignity in mental healthcare.

Equality

Equality and non-discrimination are often described as being 'at the heart of the CRPD' (Goldschmidt, 2017), with the word 'equality' the 'leitmotif of the CRPD', being repeated at least 31 times throughout the convention (Megret and Msipa, 2014). The CRPD is not a comprehensive human rights treaty in relation to all disability rights, but was limited to being an 'implementation treaty' explaining how existing human rights were intended to apply to persons with disabilities without officially creating any new rights. However, the CRPD provides little information about the meaning of 'equality' and 'non-discrimination', and those terms, like 'dignity' and 'autonomy', are highly contested in law, politics and philosophy. While the CRPD Committee's General Comment No. 6 on equality and non-discrimination provides some guidance, it still leaves many questions open about how the concepts of equality and non-discrimination apply to the abolition of mental health law.

There is, however, widespread agreement that the concepts of equality and non-discrimination in the CRPD and in the disability context are ambiguous and undertheorized (Byrne, 2018; Rioux and Riddle, 2011; Dawson, 2015). While the CRPD text and most of the literature treats the concepts of 'equality' and 'non-discrimination' as being synonymous and interchangeable, the two are not exactly the same, with discrimination being the narrower of the two. Non-discrimination ensures that particular resources, opportunities, goods and services are not distributed in a discriminatory way based on particular personal traits, like race, sex and disability, rather than addressing inequitable outcomes or structural inequality. That is, non-discrimination does not necessarily guarantee equality. For example, in the CRPD discrimination is defined in Article 2 as:

> any distinction, exclusion or restriction on the basis of disability which has the purpose or effect of impairing or nullifying the recognition, enjoyment or exercise, on an equal basis with others, of all human rights and fundamental freedoms in the political, economic, social, cultural, civil or any other field. It includes all forms of discrimination, including denial of reasonable accommodation.

The prohibition on discrimination is similar to that in other comparable treaties, except it does not include any references to direct and indirect discrimination. This was deliberate in that the negotiators wanted to avoid expressly incorporating the Human Rights Committee's exception with respect to indirect discrimination which allows differential treatment which is objective, reasonable and proportionate and made with a legitimate aim (Negotiation Archives, Fourth Session). That said, the definition of discrimination does not specifically exclude it either. This has left remaining questions as to what extent the Human Rights Committee's exception for indirect discrimination applies and whether the CRPD is capable of excluding it, given that the CRPD Committee avoided the issue again in General Comment No. 6 and has sent mixed messages in its jurisprudence (Gurbai, 2020). Jessica

Lynn Corsi has argued that it may apply at least in relation to special measures (Corsi, 2018). Whether the Human Rights Committee's exception to indirect discrimination applies to the CRPD is relevant to the debate about whether the CRPD requires States Parties to abolish mental health law because such an interpretation could arguably allow involuntary detention and treatment where it applies to everyone, even though persons with disabilities are likely to be disproportionately more likely to be caught by that legislation. This is the view taken by those abolitionists who see the CRPD as prohibiting non-discrimination rather than all forms of coercion (e.g. Stavert, 2018; Martin, 2014).

Making the denial of reasonable accommodation a form of discrimination is new to the CRPD and is an important development for the protection of the rights of persons with disabilities by promoting an individualized application of the equality paradigm. The CRPD also goes beyond previous treaties by embracing the concepts of multidimensional and intersectional approaches which recognize that disability interacts with other aspects of a person's identity, such as race, gender and age (Broderick, 2015).

It is also important to note that the definition of discrimination in Article 2 of the CRPD is very broad and includes 'all forms of discrimination'. Theresia Degener also observes that 'the CRPD encompasses all concepts of equality and thus imposes formal, substantive and transformative duties on State Parties' (Degener, 2016). While it is understandable that the drafters of the CRPD and the CRPD Committee would want to create the widest possible interpretation of the concepts of equality and discrimination, the result is that the CRPD contains an eclectic and all-encompassing model of 'equality' and 'non-discrimination' which is unclear, complex and prone to inherent tensions, especially when trying to apply it to the proposed abolition of mental health law.

According to Amartya Sen the most important question when considering the term 'equality' is 'equality of what'? This is because most claims for equality are not general claims, but are for equality in particular respects, while permitting inequality in others (Sen, 1995). It is useful to keep this question in mind when considering equality in the debate about the future of mental health law. Further, most accounts of equality begin with the Aristotelian approach that like is treated alike and differences are to be treated differently in proportion to their unlikeness (Gosepath, 2011). The first limb of treating 'like the same as like' is probably the most straightforward and can be understood as 'formal equality'. That is, that the law should treat everyone the same regardless of social context (Gosepath, 2011). However, treating like the same as like as a matter of formal equality where there are differences (that is, ignoring the second limb) can exacerbate inequality. Accordingly, most contemporary models of equality seek more than formal equality and seek some kind of 'substantive equality' of outcomes. Rather, they look beyond equality of treatment or opportunity and acknowledge that people situated differently (due to corporeal and socio-historical differences) may need better targeted interventions to give them substantive equality. More recently, the notion of 'transformative equality' has emerged which is the most amorphous approach to equality. Transformative equality aims to look beyond formal and substantive equality and redress socio-historical causes of inequality through social structures and power relations (Minkowitz, 2017; Degener, 2016).

Accordingly, it is not surprising that a number of multi-dimensional models which seek to cover many aspects of equality and non-discrimination have been developed (Fredman, 2016; Baker, 2004) with the CRPD Committee favoring a model of 'inclusive equality' which is very similar to that proposed by Fredman and also includes a focus on dignity and inclusion. Inclusive equality:

embraces a substantive model of equality and extends and elaborates on the content of equality in: (a) a fair redistributive dimension to address socio-economic disadvantages; (b) a recognition dimension to combat stigma stereotyping, prejudice and violence and to recognize the dignity of human beings and their intersectionality; (c) a participative dimension to reaffirm the social nature of people as members of social groups and the full recognition of humanity through inclusion in society; and (d) an accommodating dimension to make space for difference as a matter of human dignity.
(General Comment No. 6, para. 11)

However, applying these different models of equality and non-discrimination to the abolition of mental health law can be problematic. For instance, if the 'equality of what?' is legal capacity, treating persons with and without mental impairment 'the same' (even if adequate support is offered) may perpetuate inequality with respect to other CRPD rights such as the right to life including the prevention of suicide and accident (Wilson, 2018); access to healthcare and rehabilitation; being able to participate effectively in education; obtaining and continuing employment; living independently and participating in and being included in the community. That is, formal equality which doesn't adequately recognize the differences and difficulties encountered by persons with mental impairments may actually create or increase substantive inequality and the poverty and powerlessness of persons with disabilities in society. While support for decision-making and legal capacity can assist, the use of support with respect to making decisions around hospital admission and psychiatric treatment requires further research and has many drawbacks from finding the right supporters to ensuring support is done properly. As already noted, persons with mental impairments can refuse support, whether they need it or not.

Further, what does being treated on 'an equal basis with others' mean? Which *others*? Who is the appropriate comparator? It is unclear who is similarly situated with persons with mental impairments. It may be that mental impairment with its fluctuating and diverse mental states which can deteriorate over time and association with suicide and self-harm makes it a unique experience which does not permit comparison. Alternatively, maybe persons with mental impairments could be properly compared with all persons who lack mental capacity for whatever reason (as in a Mental Capacity Model discussed below). Further, the difference between persons with and without mental impairments may not be clear-cut or binary. While it is certainly true that persons without mental impairments also make risky and impulsive decisions, those decisions aren't necessarily of the same quality. For instance, if persons without mental impairment started to behave unpredictably, erratically, out-of-character, irrationally, overly passively or in accordance with delusions, then it is likely that people around them would question their mental health and encourage them to at least seek a psychiatric assessment or professional help. Finally, equality with the non-disabled norm may not be very good (for instance, in the United States there is no access to universal healthcare), or may mean that specific needs associated with a person's impairments are not met (Shakespeare, 2018).

There is also debate about whether involuntary detention and psychiatric treatment is a detriment or benefit. If it is conceived of as a benefit in terms of giving persons with mental impairments access to healthcare as a social service (which the symptoms of their mental impairment may prevent them seeking), is life-saving, redresses a pre-existing (social or corporeal) disadvantage and improves their quality of life, then mental health law may not be discriminatory. While there are some abolitionists who consider that all forms of psychiatric treatment are almost always damaging, it should be noted that many people do consider them helpful and do seek them voluntarily, even if significant social intervention is also required. For instance, the Australian Institute of Health and Welfare estimates around 4 million prescriptions were issued in Australia in 2016–2017 (AIHW, 2018). Further, numerous studies show that between 40% and 80% of people are grateful for their involuntary admission and treatment in retrospect, or at least accept it was needed, especially where the admission procedures were fair and the treatment was successful (Priebe, 2009; Owen, 2009; Katsakou, 2012).

Participation

Participation is a core principle of the CRPD and is reflected in the disability rights slogan 'nothing about us without us'. It applies to participation in individual decisions and at a policy-making level. In general, the principle of participation is fairly uncontroversial and I have no difficulty with the idea that persons with disabilities should be genuinely consulted and have their views taken seriously in the decision-making process. I would even agree with the CRPD Committee that the views of persons with disabilities should be given due weight and should not be departed from without good reason (General Comment No. 7). However, participation does not mean that States Parties must do everything persons with disabilities and their representatives say, or that the views of persons with disabilities should always outweigh other wider policy interests or the human rights of other rights-holders.

The other point about participation is that it is difficult to determine how representative an individual's views, or those of a disability organization, actually are in the decision-making process and whether proper representativeness is even possible. Even during the CRPD negotiations it appears that some groups may not have been represented, especially those with dementia (Nilsson and Series, 2018) and very high support needs (MacQuarrie and Laurin-Bowie, 2013). While certain groups of persons with mental impairments are in favor of the abolition of mental health law, many other people probably do not even know about the disability rights movement, let alone consider themselves a part of it (Shakespeare, 2013). In addition, other mental health advocates have questioned whether the abolition of mental health law is what they really want. For instance, Anne Plumb has argued that even though many people object to the way they have been treated, does that mean that no intervention is preferable when no intervention can leave people in a very bad place (Plumb, 2015)?

Similarly, as observed by Graham Morgan, who has been diagnosed with schizophrenia:

> for me, compulsory treatment in the community probably keeps me alive and yet I am aware there is limited evidence that this form of intervention is effective. However, I think there is ample evidence that detention in hospital when desperate, when you cannot bear another day, when the television is beaming horrific messages and instructions into your brain is needed…if left to exercise my legal capacity, I would have died and no peer support, no compassionate friend or loving professional, no aspect of Open Dialogue or eCPR would have made any difference.
>
> *(Craigie, 2019, p. 163)*

Other research suggests that while some persons with mental impairment are very concerned about their autonomy, others are less so. For example, recent research by Fauzia Knight and colleagues (2018) indicates that persons with mental impairments have four types of narrative positions describing the type of support for decision-making they preferred. These were: the 'Inward Expert' who wanted their clinicians to recognize their personal expertise in understanding their condition; the 'Outward Entrustor' who was more interested in developing a caring and trusting relationship with their clinician than in exercising control; the 'Self-Aware Observer' who sought help to manage their unwell identity and who sought collaborative relationships with clinicians; and 'Social Integrators' who were concerned with acquiring support through medical advice, peer and social support and community participation. These positions were fluid so that some Inward Experts became Outward Entrustors when they were more acutely unwell.

Therefore it is important to acknowledge that there are a wide range of views and experiences in the mental health field and that probably no single view is entirely 'representative' of all others.

What *should* the future of mental health law be? Does mental health law have any merit?

So the question then is what should the future of mental health law be? There is no doubt that mental health law as it is currently drafted and implemented can create trauma from unwanted detention and treatment and poor practices for some people which impedes their recovery. On the other hand, abolishing mental health law – especially for emergency situations – may have other serious and unintended consequences with respect to suicide, self-harm and people committing offenses and going to prison. It is also likely that for some it would lead to neglect and abandonment as it is certainly easier and cheaper to withdraw mental health services from a difficult person with serious problems on the basis that they refuse to consent. While in western societies we are often more concerned about being too coercive and intervening wrongly, that does not mean that sins of omission are not just as serious or are necessarily any better.

Nor would simply abolishing mental health law necessarily give persons with mental impairments the access to the alternatives and choices they want. It is interesting to note that many of the objections from persons with mental impairments are not necessarily complaints about unwanted treatment or lack of autonomy, so much as bad treatment in poor facilities (resulting in a loss of dignity as discussed above). For example, Andrew Turtle from Australia complains of a lack of consultation with his parents and treating psychiatrist and psychologist and the reliance of the public mental health system on drug treatments and sedatives rather than having access to a full range of non-medical therapeutic options, like mindfulness walks, gym access and laughter therapy (Sunkel et al., 2021). Other complaints are about not feeling safe in mental health wards, including sexual assault from other patients and staff (Roper and Gooding, 2019). Sylvio Gravel from Canada complains about the reliance on police as first responders to persons with mental health problems, a lack of community-based mental health resources, a lack of peer supporters and the need for continuity of care and coordination of services (Sunkel et al., 2021). Charlene Sunkel from South Africa has complained about the 'prison-like' environment and attitudes in the mental health system that did not make her feel safe, cared for or respected, even though she acknowledges that she needed treatment (Sunkel et al., 2021). What this suggests is that there is much work to be done to make mental health services more effective, dignified and acceptable to persons with mental health problems. The ability to say 'no' is a response to woeful treatment and abuse, as much as a claim for the right to be left alone.

It is also important to note that while alternatives to coercion exist, none of those alternatives have involved the complete abolition of mental health law. For instance, the constitutional bans on coercion in 2011–2012 in Germany still permitted involuntary detention and treatment in emergencies, and while rates of involuntary treatment dropped there were reported increases in restraints (Gooding, 2018). In Trieste in Italy which has a system based on complete deinstitutionalization and community care, rates of involuntary detention and treatment are lower than the rest of Europe, but involuntary detention and treatment is still permitted for serious cases (Mezzina, 2018). While studies of peer respite services have indicated that they can reduce hospital admissions by up to 70%, those who had longer respite (and presumably more serious and complicated issues) still ended up in hospital (Gooding, 2018). As noted above, no country has yet completely abolished mental health law in emergencies, even if they have abolished substituted decision-making in guardianship law. While the offering of non-coercive alternatives to psychiatry to address 'unmet need' may have the side-effect of reducing overall coercion, hospital-based psychiatric support is still likely to be needed in situations of psychiatric crisis, even if it is supplemented with general community support aimed at preventing emergencies and helping persons with mental impairments live more fulfilling lives (Gooding, 2018).

Mental health law, in structuring the mental health system, has the capacity to do many things (positive and negative) and is also very dependent on the resources and culture of the mental health services it offers. As Clive Unsworth (1987) observes, mental health law can authorize involuntary detention and treatment, while at the same time limiting and protecting people with mental impairment from unchecked medical power, providing external oversight, inspection and monitoring, harnessing and directing healthcare resources, and allocating responsibility between medical professionals, the family and the state.

Rather than abolish mental health law completely, which no state has done or is likely to do, what is perhaps more useful is to reform mental health law so that voluntary treatment is the 'norm', coercion is the exception and support is integrated into the provision of a wide range of services and the development of a supportive community. That is, there is consensus that the way forward is the maximization of autonomy with safeguards (Bo, 2020).

What are the options for reform? Is meaningful reform even possible?

While the abolition of mental health law is one approach, there are a whole range of options for reform. Two alternatives which I have explored are what I call the Mental Capacity with Support Model and the Support Except Where There Is Harm Model (explained below). Of these, I prefer the Mental Capacity with Support Model and give that greater consideration. Both involve the offering of support, but permit involuntary detention and psychiatric treatment in certain limited circumstances as a last resort. I argue that the options for reform are better and more compatible with the object and purpose of the CRPD to ensure the enjoyment of *all* of a person's human rights and dignity (Article 1) and the interpretive compass than abolition.

While there are many different Mental Capacity with Support Models (Murray, 2017), all involve reforming mental health law so that involuntary detention and treatment is only permitted by those who are assessed as lacking mental capacity. That is, a person's actual ability to make a decision at a particular time is determinative, rather than a blanket assumption of their mental incapacity and risk of causing harm to self or others as currently occurs under mental health law. The result is that those persons who have mental capacity would be able to exercise autonomy and make their own mental health decisions, the same as any other patient. Involuntary detention and treatment can be further narrowed to those decisions where a person lacks mental capacity *and* is making a decision which is likely to risk harm to self or others, rather than extending to any decision by a person who lacks mental capacity however benign. Further, by incorporating the offering of support, the Mental Capacity with Support Model contains a mechanism to enlarge the group of persons who are assessed to lack mental capacity and make their own decisions. Given that most people who are assessed as lacking mental capacity still have at least partial mental capacity, there is a lot of scope to use support to increase the group of persons who are able to make their own decisions (Curley, 2019) and thereby reduce the 'binary divide' between those with and without mental capacity (Richardson, 2013).

Integrating support into the Mental Capacity with Support Model takes into account the environmental and contextual factors in decision-making such as professionals who do not bother to consult, present information in a cursory or inappropriate way and give insufficient time for persons to respond or seek advice from those they trust. Yet, unlike the abolitionist approach which relies on divining the will and preferences of the person even where it can become somewhat artificial, the Mental Capacity with Support Model still includes a 'success criterion' for the effectiveness of the support: it is successful when a person can demonstrate functional capacity (Scholten and Gather, 2017). Further, just because a person is assessed to lack mental capacity does not mean that they have *no say* at all in their hospital admission and treatment. Their wishes and feelings (arguably broader than 'will' and 'preferences') are still required to be given weight in determining their best interests. In fact, some are going so far as to advocate that the wishes and feelings of persons with mental impairments who lack mental capacity should be respected, unless there is good reason to depart from them (Jackson, 2018). However, the advantage of 'best interests' is that it is an objective test, is more transparent about why a decision is made and avoids the hidden exercise of power. By contrast a 'will' and 'preferences' approach assumes that the person with mental impairment is the author of the decision, when they may not be, or their will and preferences are unclear or contradictory.

While the CRPD Committee has rejected the Mental Capacity with Support Model as not being CRPD compliant, the text of the CRPD itself does not expressly criticize functional tests of mental capacity or require the abolition of substitute decision-making or the best interests approach (Murray, 2017). However, it is arguable that the Mental Capacity with Support Model is actually CRPD compliant, because Article 12(4) permits substituted decision-making for the shortest possible time and subject to safeguards. As John Dawson argues, mental capacity can be a way of mediating between conflicting negative rights to non-interference by the state and positive rights to life, health, social benefits and inclusion (Dawson, 2015). Advance directives, in which persons express their will and preferences when they are well, are also more conceptually compatible with the Mental Capacity with Support Model than abolition, because advance directives rely on competence (Wilson, Purushothaman & Kolur, 2022). That is, a person's decisions when they are competent overrides their preferences when they are incompetent (Scholten and Gather, 2017), whereas an abolitionist approach assumes that a person is never incompetent.

With respect to the interpretive compass the Mental Capacity with Support Model is consistent with the principles of dignity (including autonomy), equality and non-discrimination and participation. First, as already noted, capacity assessments recognize the autonomy of those who have mental capacity and may also include those with borderline mental capacity if they receive adequate support. However, dignity has many dimensions and is wider than autonomy, especially where there is reason to believe that autonomy may be diminished in some way, such as by failing a capacity assessment. As Fallon-Kund and Bickenbach (2016) observe, sometimes capacity assessments may be necessary to limit autonomy so as to preserve human dignity. This is especially the case where there is extreme self-neglect and harm unfit for a human. While abolitionists argue that *any difference* in treatment between persons with and without mental impairment is insidious discrimination, as discussed above the meaning of equality and discrimination is more nuanced and complicated than this. Rather, I argue that by focusing on a person's actual mental capacity, rather than presuming incapacity by law (as most mental health laws do), the Mental Capacity with Support Model is concerned with an individual's actual abilities rather than social prejudices about persons with mental impairments. It recognizes that persons with and without mental impairments are not similarly situated and therefore, in accordance with theories of substantive equality, differential treatment is permissible to the extent of the difference. The Mental Capacity with Support Model removes the discrimination between persons with mental and physical disorders and involves an appropriate comparator – those who lack mental capacity for any reason from undue influence and deception to misinformation, physical illness, tiredness, shock, pain or drugs (Donnelly, 2008). That is, it makes mental capacity assessment simply the way society responds to persons who may have permanently or temporarily diminished autonomy for any reason. Given that all persons may have compromised capacity at some stage in their lives (as part of the human experience), it can apply equally to everyone in the right circumstances.

However, the CRPD Committee has made two specific criticisms of capacity tests (General Comment No. 1 paras 14 and 15). The first is that it is discriminatorily applied to persons with disabilities (discussed above). The second is that it is not possible to assess the inner workings of the human mind, pointing out that it isn't value neutral and relies on the social and political context of the assessors. Nevertheless, this seems exaggerated. While it is not possible to know *exactly* the inner workings of the human mind, it is usually possible to make *some* assessment from what persons are able to communicate about their decision and how they made it. In fact, the abolitionist approach does exactly that when it seeks to determine what a person's will and preferences are and even more so when a supporter or facilitator seeks to '*interpret*' a person's will and preferences. The strength of the support paradigm, whether it is used on its own or as part of the Mental Capacity with Support Model, is that it requires far more time to be spent exploring the inner workings of the mind of the person and getting 'evidence' from those around them to get a more holistic understanding of them. But it also gives the supporter, facilitator and assessor a measure of epistemic privilege in 'judging' those inner workings.

Capacity assessments are perhaps the most tricky where a person's wishes and feelings may involve a risky decision or rejecting a doctor's advice. However, courts have become more inclined to find mental capacity where a person makes decisions which go against prevailing social norms and have tried to not set the bar of mental capacity too high (*PBU & NJE* [2018] VSC 546). The Mental Capacity with Support Model can also be improved, *inter alia*, by ensuring that the person who is assessing mental capacity is not the same person as the treating clinician, is well qualified in assessment (such as being a psychologist) and is trained to avoid their attitudes and values tainting an assessment.

The Mental Capacity with Support Model would also significantly increase the participation of persons with mental impairment in personal healthcare decision-making, especially through the use of support to help a person make, understand and explain their decision.

The other alternative is the Support Except Where There Is Harm Model which prioritizes support and choice in the first instance, but permits limited involuntary detention and treatment where there is a risk of harm. Like the other models, the Support Except Where There Is Harm Model has a number of variations, which range from modifications to existing mental health law (Wellesley Report, 2018) to something that looks a lot like the abolition of mental health law with some ability for intervention in emergency situations (ALRC, 2014; Bach and Kerzner, 2010). It seems to be an approach which is favored by law reform commissions and has received less attention in the scholarly literature. The Support Except Where There Is Harm Model is consistent with autonomy in that it prioritizes the giving of support and the implementation of a person's clear decisions in the first instance, unless there is likely to be harm. As argued above, the prevention of harm can be used to restore a person's dignity. While those who take an abolitionist approach would see the differential treatment of those with mental impairments who are at risk of harm as being discriminatory, once again it could also be argued that differential treatment is not unequal if the persons concerned are not similarly situated. Similarly, the Support Except Where There Is Harm Model is aimed to maximize individual participation in decision-making through the use of support.

Of course, abolitionists are skeptical about whether meaningful reform of mental health law is even possible and hence argue that the system is so broken that abolition is the only option. It is certainly true that changing attitudes and practices is difficult. As Maylea (2021) has pointed out, the reform of the Victorian Mental Health Act 2014 failed to make significant differences to the experiences of users of mental health services. However, I argue that this is overly pessimistic. New legislation, on its own, is ever rarely enough and requires investment in systemic reform including staff training, provision of peer support and advocacy, extra resources so that staff have time to explain rights and give support, and a system with greater choices of treatment options and community services (Maylea, 2021). In addition to reforming mental health law, the CRPD and the call for the abolition of mental health law has created a new willingness by governments to reform the mental health system to include greater non-psychiatric options and a larger lived experience workforce (such as the Royal Commission into Victoria's Mental Health System, 2021). Further, the power of continued advocacy and education by persons with mental impairments in sharing their lived experience cannot be under-estimated.

Conclusion

This chapter has provided an overview of the debate about the future of mental health law since the negotiation of the CRPD and whether it should be abolished or reformed. In circumstances where the CRPD contains many unresolved disagreements between the parties, conceptual gaps and remains incompletely theorized, what it requires of States Parties is inconclusive. The debate revolves around two competing visions of the CRPD: the first in which disability is socially constructed and autonomy, liberty and legal capacity are prioritized; the second where disability has both a social and corporeal dimension and the maximization of *all* disability rights is emphasized with the aim of giving persons with mental impairments more meaningful and fulfilling lives. The second, broader and more nuanced and holistic vision of disability rights can be understood in terms of the 'interpretive compass' of the CRPD which aims to explore the meaning and contours of the core CRPD and human rights concepts of dignity (including autonomy), equality and non-discrimination and participation. Exploring each of these concepts demonstrates the complexity of interpreting the CRPD and that abolition, while having a certain simplistic appeal, may not be the best option for realizing all of the rights of persons with mental impairments. Instead, the chapter argues for a middle course and that the merits of the Mental Capacity with Support Model are also consistent with the CRPD and the values of the interpretive compass. A model which is based on legal and systemic reform for the reduction of coercion and increase in social support is superior to abolition.

References

Alexandrov, Nikita and Natalie Schuck, 'Coercive Interventions Under the New Dutch Mental Health Law: Towards a CRPD-Compliant Law?' (2021) 76 *International Journal of law and Psychiatry* 101685

Arstein-Kerslake, Anna and Eilonoir Flynn, 'The General Comment on Article 12 of the Convention on the Rights of Persons with Disabilities: A Roadmap for Equality Before the Law' (2016) 20(4) *The International Journal of Human Rights* 471

Australian Institute of Health and Welfare, *Mental Health Services in Australia 2018*, https://www.aihw.gov.au/reports/mental-health-services/mental-health-services-in-australia/report-contents/summary-of-mental-health-services-in-australia

Australian Law Reform Commission, *Equality, Capacity and Disability in Commonwealth Laws* (Australian Government, 2014)

Bach, Michael and Lana Kerzner, *A New Paradigm for Protecting Autonomy in the Right to Legal Capacity* (Law Commission of Ontario, 2010)

Baker, John et al, *Equality: From Theory to Action* (Palgrave MacMillian, 2004)

Bo, Chen, 'Controversy and Consensus: Does the UN Convention on the Rights of Persons with Disabilities Prohibit Mental Health Detention and Involuntary Treatment?' (2020) 1(1) *Foundation for Law and International Affairs Review* 39

Broderick, Andrea, *The Long and Winding Road to Equality and Inclusion for Persons with Disabilities: The United Nations Convention on the Rights of Persons with Disabilities* (Intersentia, 2015)

Byrne, Bronagh, 'Dis-Equality: Exploring the Juxtaposition of Disability and Equality' (2018) 6(1) *Social Inclusion* 9

Carney, Terry, 'Supported Decision-Making in Australia: Meeting the Challenge of Moving from Capacity to Capacity-Building?' (2017) 35(2) *Law in Context. A Socio-Legal Journal* 44

Committee on the Rights of Persons with Disabilities 'General Comment No 1 (2014) Article 12: Equal Recognition Before the Law' (10 April 2014) UN Doc CRPD/C/GC/1

Convention on the Rights of Persons with Disabilities, Open for Signature 30 March 2007, UNTS 2515 (Entered into Force 3 May . 2008)

Corsi, Jessica Lynn, 'Art 5 Equality and Non-Discrimination' in Ilias Batekas (ed), *The UN Convention on the Rights of Persons with Disabilities: A Commentary* (Oxford University Press 2018).

Craigie, Jillian et al, 'Legal Capacity, Mental Capacity and Supported Decision-Making: Report from a Panel Event' (2019) 62 *International Journal of Law and Psychiatry* 160

CRPD Committee, *General Comment No 6: Equality and Non-Discrimination* (Article 5), 9 March 2018

CRPD Committee, *General Comment on Article 4.3 and 33.3 of the Convention on the Participation with Persons with Disabilities in the Implementation and Monitoring of the Convention*, 16 March 2018

CRPD Negotiation Archives, https://www.un.org/development/desa/disabilities/resources/ad-hoc-committee-on-a-comprehensive-and-integral-international-convention-on-the-protection-and-promotion-of-the-rights-and-dignity-of-persons-with-disabilities.html

Curley, Aoife et al, 'Categorical Mental Capacity for Treatment Decisions among Psychiatry Inpatients in Ireland' (2019) 64 *International Journal of Law and Psychiatry* 53

Davidson, Laura, 'A Key, Not a Straightjacket: The Case for Interim Mental Health Legislation Pending Complete Prohibition of Psychiatric Coercion in Accordance with the Convention on the Rights of Persons with Disabilities' (2020) 22(1) *Health and Human Rights Journal* 163

Dawson, John, 'A Realistic Approach to Assessing Mental Health Laws Compliance with the UNCRPD' (2015) 40 *International Journal of Law and Psychiatry* 70

Degener, Theresia, 'Disability in a Human Rights Context' (2016) 5(3) *Laws* 35

Donnelly, Mary, 'From Autonomy to Dignity:Treatment for Mental Disorders and the Focus for Patient Rights' (2008) 26(2) *Law in Context* 37

Duwell, Marcus, 'Human Dignity: Concepts, Discussions, Philosophical Perspectives' in Marcus Duwell and others (eds), *The Cambridge Handbook of Human Dignity* (Cambridge University Press 2014).

Dworkin, Ronald, *Taking Rights Seriously* (Bloomsbury Publishing, 2013) 20

Encalanda, Alberto, 'The Potential of the Legal Capacity Law Reform in Peru to Transform Mental Health Provision' in Michael Stein et al (eds), *Mental Health, Legal Capacity and Human Rights* (Cambridge University Press, 2021) 124

Fallon-Kund, Marie and Jerome Bickenbach, 'Strengthening the Voice of Persons with Mental Health Problems and Legal Capacity Proceedings' (2016) 5(3) *Laws* 29

Fredman, Sandra, 'Emerging from the Shadows: Substantive Equality and Article 14 of the European Convention on Human Rights' (2016) 16 *Human Rights Law Review* 273

Goldschmidt, Jenny, 'New Perspectives on Equality: Towards Transformative Justice through the Disability Convention?' (2017) 35(1) *Nordic Journal of Human Rights* 1

Gooding, Piers et al, *Alternatives to Coercion in Mental Health Settings: A Literature Review* (Melbourne Social Equity Institute, University of Melbourne, 2018)

Gosepath, Stefan, 'Equality' in Edward N Zalta (ed), *The Stanford Encyclopedia of Philosophy* (Spring 2011 ed, 2011)

Gurbai, Sandor, 'Beyond the Pragmatic Definition? The Right to Non-discrimination of Persons with Disabilities in the Context of Coercive Interventions' (2020) *Health and Human Rights Journal*, https://cdn1.sph.harvard.edu/wp content/uploads/sites/2469/2020/06/Gurbai.pdf

Independent Review of the MHA 1983, 'Modernising the Mental Health Act: Increasing Choice, Reducing Compulsion' (UK Government, Final Report, December 2018) (hereafter 'Wellesley Report')

International Covenant on Civil and Political Rights, Opened for Signature 16 December 1966, UNTS 999 (entered into force 23 March 1976)

Jackson, Emily, 'From 'Doctor Knows Best' to Dignity: Placing Adults Whole Lack Capacity at the Centre of Decisions About Their Medical Treatment' (2018) 81(2) *The Modern Law Review* 247

Katsakou, Christina et al, 'Psychiatric Patient's Views on Why Their Involuntary Hospitalisation Was Right or Wrong: A Qualitative Study' (2012) 47 *Social Psychiatry and Psychiatric Epidemiology* 1169

Kayess, Rosemary and Phillip French, 'Out of Darkness into Light? Introducing the Convention on the Rights of Persons with Disabilities' (2008) 8(1) *Human Rights Law Review* 1

Kelly, Brendan, 'Dignity, Human Rights and the Limits of Mental Health Legislation' (2014) 31 *Irish Journal of Psychological Medicine* 75

Knight, Fauzia et al, 'Supported Decision-Making: The Expectations Held by People with Experience of Mental Illness' (2018) 28(6) *Qualitative Health Research* 1002

Maclean, Alasdair, *Autonomy, Informed Consent and Medical Law: A Relational Challenge* (Cambridge University Press, 2009)

MacQuarrie, Anna and Connie Laurin-Bowrie, 'Our Lives, Our Voices: People with Intellectual Disabilities and Their Families' in Maya Sabatello and Marriane Schulze (eds), *Human Rights and Disability Advocacy* (University of Pennsylvannia Press, 2013) 25

Martin, Wayne et al, *Achieving CRPD Compliance: Is the Mental Capacity Act of England and Wales Compatible with the UN Convention on the Rights of Persons with Disabilities? If Not, What Next?* (University of Essex, Essex Autonomy Project, 2014)

Maylea, Chris et al, 'Consumers' Experiences of Rights-Based Mental Health Laws: Lessons from Victoria, Australia' (2021) 78 *International Journal of Law and Psychiatry* 101737

Megret, Frederic and Dianah Msipa, 'Global Reasonable Accommodation: How the Convention on the Rights of Persons with Disabilities Changes the Way We Think About Equality' (2014) 30 *South African Journal of Human Rights* 253

Megret, Frederic, 'The Disabilities Convention: Human Rights of Persons with Disabilities or Disability Rights?' (2008) 30(2) *Human Rights Quarterly* 494

Mental Health Act 1983 (UK)

Mezzina, R, 'Forty Years of the Law 180: The Aspirations of a Great Reform, Its Successes and Continuing Need' (2018) 27(4) *Epidemiology and Psychiatric Sciences* 336

Minkowitz, Tina, 'Reparation for Psychiatric Violence: A Call to Justice' in Michael Stein et al (eds), *Mental Health, Legal Capacity and Human Rights* (Cambridge University Press, 2021) 44

Minkowitz, Tina, 'CRPD and Transformative Equality' (2017) 13(1) *International Journal of Law in Context* 77

Murray, Brian Joseph, 'Mental Capacity: Different Models and Their Controversies' (2017) 23 *British Journal of Psychiatry* 366

Nedelsky, Jennifer, *Laws Relations: A Relational Theory of Self, Autonomy, and Law* (Oxford University Press, 2011)

Neuman, Gerald, 'Divergent Human Rights Approaches to Capacity and Consent', in Michael Stein et al (eds), *Mental Health, Legal Capacity and Human Rights* (Cambridge University Press, 2021) 56

Nilsson, Anna and Lucy Series, 'Art, 12 CRPD Equal Recognition before the Law' in Lias Bantekas et al (eds), *The UN Convention on the Rights of Persons with Disabilities: A Commentary* (Oxford University Press, 2018)

Nilsson, Anna, *Compulsory Mental Health Interventions and the CRPD: Minding Equality* (Hart, 2021)

Oaks, David, 'Whose Voices Should Be Heard? The Role of Mental Health Consumers, Psychiatric Survivors, and Families' in Michael Dudley et al (eds), *Mental Health and Human Rights* (Oxford University Press, 2012) 566

Owen, Gareth et al, 'Retrospective Views of Psychiatric in-Patients Regaining Mental Capacity' (2009) 195(5) *British Journal of Psychiatry* 403, 405

PBU & NJE [2018] VSC 564

Plumb, Anne, 'UN Convention on the Rights of Persons with Disabilities: Out of the Frying Pan into the Fire?' in Helen Spandler et al (eds), *Madness, Distress and the Politics of Disablement* (Policy Press, 2015)

Priebe, Stefan et al, 'Patients' Views and Readmissions 1 Year After Involuntary Hospitalisation'(2009) 194 *British Journal of Psychiatry* 49–54

Richardson, Genevra, 'Mental Capacity in the Shadow of Suicide: What Can the Law Do?' (2013) 9(1) *International Journal of Law in Context* 87

Rioux, Marcia and Christopher Riddle, 'Values in Disability Policy and Law: Equality' in Marcia H. Rioux et al (eds), *Critical Perspectives on Human Rights and Disability Law* (Martinus Nijhoff Publishers, 2011) 37

Roper, Cath and Piers Gooding, 'This Is Not a Story: From Ethical Loneliness to Respect for Diverse Ways of Knowing Thinking and Being' in Elionoir Flynn et al (eds), *Global Perspectives on Legal Capacity Reform: Our Voices, Our Stories* (Cambridge University Press, 2019) 154

Royal Commission into Victoria's Mental Health System, Final Report, 2021.

Scholten, Matthe and Jakov Gather, 'Adverse Consequences of Article 13 of the UN Convention on the Rights of Persons with Disabilities for Persons with Mental Disabilities and an Alternative Way Forward' (2017) 1 *Journal of Medical Ethics* 1.

Sen, Amartya, *Inequality Reexamined* (Oxford University Press, 1995)

Shakespeare, Tom et al, 'Rehabilitation as a Disability Equality Issue: A Conceptual Shift for Disability Studies?' (2018) 6(1) *Social Inclusion* 61

Shakespeare, Tom, *Disability Rights and Wrongs Revisited* (Routledge, 2013)

Stavert, Jill, 'Paradigm Shift of Paradigm Paralysis? National Mental Health and Capacity Law and Implementing the CRPD in Scotland' (2018) 7(3) *Laws* 26

Stone, Meredith et al, 'Estranged Relations: Coercion and Care in Narratives of Supported Decision-Making in Mental Healthcare' (2020) 46(1) *Medical Humanities* 62, 69

Sunkel, Charlene et al, 'Lived Experience Perspectives from Australia, Canada, Kenya, Cameroon and South Africa – Conceptualising the Realities' in Michael Stein et al (eds), *Mental Health, Legal Capacity and Human Rights* (Cambridge University Press, 2021) 316

Szmukler, George, '"Capacity", "Best Interests", "Will and Preferences" and the UN Convention on the Rights of Persons with Disabilities' (2019) 18(1) *World Psychiatry* 34

Szmukler, George, 'The UN Convention on the Rights of Persons with Disabilities: "Rights, Will and Preferences"' in *Relation to Mental Health Disabilities*' (2017) 54 *International Journal of Law and Psychiatry* 90

Traustadottir, Rannveig, 'Disability Studies, the Social Model and Legal Developments' in Oddny Mjoll Arnadottir and Gerard Quinn (eds), *The UN Convention on the Rights of Persons with Disabilities: European and Scandinavian Perspectives* (Martinus Nijhoff Publishers, 2009)

Unsworth, Clive, *The Politics of Mental Health Legislation* (Claredon Press, 1987)

Vienna Declaration and Programme of Action Adopted by the World Conference on Human Rights in Vienna 1993

Waldron, Jeremy, 'Dignity, Rights, and Responsibilities' (2011) 43(1) *Ariz. St. L. J.* 1112

Ward, Adrian, 'Towards Resolving Damaging Uncertainties: Progress in the United Kingdom and Elsewhere' in Michael Stein et al (eds), *Mental Health, Legal Capacity and Human Rights* (Cambridge University Press, 2021) 171

Wilson, Kay, *Mental Health Law: Abolish or Reform?* (OUP, 2021)

Wilson, Kay, 'The Call for the Abolition of Mental Health Law: The Challenges of Suicide, Accidental Death and the Equal Enjoyment of the Right to Life' (2018) 18 *Human Rights Law Review* 651

Wilson, Kay, Purushothaman, S, and Kolur, U, 'Psychiatric Advance Directives and Consent to Electroconvulsive Therapy (ECT) in Australia: A Legislative Review and Suggestions for the Future' (2022) 85 *International Journal of Law and Psychiatry* 101836

Wilson, Kay, and Rudge, Christopher, 'COVID-19 Vaccine Mandates: A Coercive But Justified Public Health Necessity' (2023) 46(2) *University of New South Wales Law Journal* 381

Yamin, Alicia, 'The Alchemy of Agency: Reflections on Supported Decision-Making, the Right to Health and Health Systems as Democratic Institutions' in Michael Stein et al (eds), *Mental Health, Legal Capacity and Human Rights* (Cambridge University Press, 2021) 17

39
THE FUTURE OF MENTAL HEALTH LAW[1]

The need for deeper examination and broader scope

Tania L. Gergel

Introduction

This chapter aims to outline the most prominent developments in mental health law and examine some challenges arising from these developments, while also considering areas of law rarely included within discussions of mental health law, despite their great significance for individuals with mental illness. Although a comprehensive account is not possible, I will outline major global trends, using illustrative examples, and examine how we might progress towards addressing the many remaining concerns.

The last 20 years have seen some major shifts in mental health law, both internationally and within individual countries. Central to this has been the United Nations (UN) Convention on the Rights of Persons with Disabilities (CRPD), passed in 2006 and ratified by 185 States, as of May 2022 (Convention on the Rights of Persons with Disabilities [Online],). The CRPD prioritises maximising the autonomy of those with disabilities, by instituting changes within law, healthcare, and society, which could facilitate social inclusion and a paradigm shift from substitute to supported decision-making (Doyle Guilloud, this vol.). In doing so, it presents both significant challenges and opportunities in relation to mental health law.

I will begin by briefly summarising recent changes in laws and ideas discussed in great depth within this Handbook, reviewing some related difficulties and starting to think about how these might be addressed. In particular, we must acknowledge major environmental factors which may obstruct implementation of legal change and the potential unintended consequences and omissions which legal changes may themselves involve. Most important, perhaps, are the continuing lack of resources, stigma, and discrimination in mental health, outlined very powerfully within the recently launched *Lancet* 'Commission on ending stigma and discrimination in mental health' (Lancet, 2022b). The *Lancet*'s most recent 'Global

---

1 TG is funded by the Wellcome Trust, UK (grant number 203376/Z/16/Z), as part of the Mental Health and Justice project. I am grateful to Trudo Lemmens, Scott Kim, and Niall Boyce for providing information in relation to euthanasia and criminalisation of suicide, and to Brendan Kelly and Mary Donnelly for their guidance and support in the preparation of this chapter.

Burden of Disease' report identifies 'mental disorder' as the health condition with the seventh highest global Disability Adjusted Life Years (DALYs), including the second highest global years of healthy life lost due to disability (YLDs) (Lancet, 2020). Nevertheless, 'worldwide, government spending on mental health is, on average, a paltry 2% of the total health budget' (Lancet, 2022a). To progress towards realising the legal and human rights aspirations of the CRPD these environmental factors must be identified and addressed.

Alongside CRPD-related issues such as decision-making capacity and supported decision-making which dominate current mental health law debates, we must also recognise legal and human rights issues beyond the usual scope of such debates, but with huge relevance for those with mental health conditions. Notably, there are recent developments in medically assisted dying or euthanasia, both generally and relating more specifically to mental health conditions. This issue, with its deeply important legal and ethical challenges, should be incorporated within mainstream ethico-legal mental health debates. Another issue rarely discussed is that attempting suicide remains illegal in multiple countries. Given that severe mental illness is a significant contributory factor in so many suicide attempts, to protect the rights of those with mental health conditions, this issue should not be neglected.

Central to all these issues is the principle of autonomy, one of the four cornerstones of medical ethics. This makes it all the more important to recognise that maximising autonomy is not a straightforward process. Efforts to modify mental health law to improve human rights and justice for those with mental health conditions can only progress effectively through considering the complexities of understanding autonomy in relation to mental illness. We must ensure that an excessively narrow focus on a particular view or element of autonomy does not result in potential harms and injustices being overlooked.

The CRPD as a catalyst for change

The CRPD advocates equality for those with disabilities through 'equal enjoyment of all human rights and fundamental freedoms by all persons with disabilities, and to promote respect for their inherent dignity' (Article 1). Equality, according to the CRPD, includes socio-economic factors, such as the right to 'full and effective participation and inclusion in society' and 'equality of opportunity' (Article 3). The CRPD notion of discrimination is broad, encompassing anything which obstructs full inclusion and participation in the 'political, economic, social, cultural, civil or any other field' (Article 2). Given that the human rights advocated within the CRPD itself are concise but broad in scope, a further Committee on the Rights of Persons with Disabilities, currently comprising 18 independent experts, was created to monitor implementation of the CRPD, to issue recommendations to member states, and to publish General Comments offering a broader interpretation of the CRPD provisions. It was the first of these comments (GC1), on 'Article 12: Equal recognition before the law', which has stimulated the most intensive discussion in relation to mental health law (2014).

Article 12 calls for States Parties to 'ensure that all measures that relate to the exercise of legal capacity provide for appropriate and effective safeguards to prevent abuse in accordance with international human rights law' and lays down some broad guidelines concerning such measures. GC1 interprets Article 12 as requiring governments to move from a 'substitute decision-making paradigm' to a paradigm 'based on supported decision-making' (para. 3). It advocates the abolition of 'substitute decision-making regimes such as guardianship, conservatorship and mental health laws that permit forced treatment' (para. 7) and presents these laws as restricting the right to exercise 'legal capacity' on an equal basis with others. GC1 prioritises 'legal capacity' and 'takes the position that, while mental capacity may change and fluctuate due to factors such as a person's age, impairment or emotional state, the legal capacity of every individual is unassailable' (Doyle Guilloud, this vol.). It presents mental capacity, defined as 'the decision-making skills of a person', as a flawed 'highly controversial' concept, 'contingent on social and political contexts', and argues that using impaired decision-making (mental) capacity to justify denying any type of legal capacity is inherently discriminatory and contravenes the fundamental right to 'equal recognition before the law' (Gergel et al., 2021). Both the CRPD and the Committee's interpretation reflect the drive to move away from models of coercive treatment and substitute decision-making which developed during the 20th century and have been central to debates surrounding mental healthcare and the law.

The CRPD is underpinned by a primarily social, rather than medical, model of disability (Doyle Guilloud, this vol.), while the abolitionist position espoused within GC1 is based on an entirely social model of disability 'which views disability as being entirely created by social, attitudinal, and environmental barriers' (Wilson, this vol.). The CRPD Preamble states the need to recognise 'that disability is an evolving concept and that disability results from the interaction between persons with impairments and attitudinal and environmental barriers that hinders their full and effective participation in society on an equal basis with others'. Thus, even the CRPD and UN Committee's concept of illness and disability departs from mainstream contemporary psychiatry, which generally adheres to the 'biopsychosocial' model influential within modern medicine (Huda, 2021, Borrell-Carrió et al., 2004).

Coercion – how do things stand and how might we move forwards?

Involuntary treatment and detention have always played a major role in how society manages the care of those with severe mental health conditions (Kelly, this vol.). The ethical case for GC1's calls for complete abolition of involuntary treatment can seem compelling. Undoubtedly, despite any regulatory safeguards, experiencing involuntary treatment and detention is usually disturbing and traumatic for service users and even for clinicians responsible for its implementation (Diana Paksarian et al., 2014, Butterworth et al., 2022, Borgeat and Zullino, 2004). Moreover, human rights abuses associated with coercive treatment of mental health service users remain, both under the auspices of mental health law and outside of legal frameworks. Although the CRPD is now ratified by almost all member states of the United Nations, shocking abuses still occur, due to reasons such as lack of resources, stigma, and mistaken beliefs about mental illness. For example, a 2020 'Human Rights Watch' report found 'evidence of shackling across 60 countries across Asia, Africa, Europe, the Middle East, and the Americas' (*Living in Chains* 2020). Even in developed countries with legal safeguards, abuse occurs, as demonstrated by a recent exposé on abusive treatment of individuals detained under the Mental Health Act 1983 at the Edenfield Centre in Manchester, England (Lee, 2022a).

While a cluster of factors, including some progress in human rights law and understanding of mental illness and treatments, and some decrease in stigma, have led to certain improvements and safeguards and slightly decreased need for involuntary treatment, it is evident that we still have far to go.

It is interesting that near global ratification of the CRPD has brought no absolute abolition of legal provision for involuntary treatment for mental illness. As Doyle Guilloud explains, 'at the domestic level, the response has varied from complete rejection, to outright refusal, to major (if not complete) shifts in law and policy' (Doyle Guilloud, this vol.). India, despite its 'best effort to give effect to the Convention in national mental health legislation', still has statutory provision for substitute decision-making (Kelly, this vol.). In China, where reformed mental health law has narrowed the scope of involuntary treatment and increased provision of voluntary services, remaining legal loopholes and societal factors significantly hamper its implementation (Chen, this vol.). At regional level, an additional protocol proposed by the Council of Europe Committee on Bioethics, still under consideration, which 'provides for the involuntary detention and treatment of persons with a "mental disorder" based on need for treatment or dangerousness to others' and 'also endorses the concept of legal incapacity' has created controversy and internal division (Doyle Guilloud, this vol.). As Wilson explains 'even States Parties, such as Peru, who have come closer to implementing the abolitionist vision of the CRPD than any other states so far, have not completely abolished mental health law, still permitting involuntary detention and psychiatric treatment in emergency situations' (Wilson, this vol.).

This situation does not look set to change in the near future and most mental health law remains closer to UN 1991 Principles which constituted major legal advances pre-CRPD by allowing for involuntary treatment, but imposing protective conditions (Kelly, this vol.). So, what changes should we target for coercion within mental healthcare? Would it be realistic or ethical to move towards a zero-coercion model of mental health law, in line with GC1? Clearly, implementation of involuntary treatment and detention needs to change. However, as we consider significant reduction or even abolition, we also need to consider the validity of the abolitionist argument and the potentially negative consequences of such changes.

GC1's call for all legally sanctioned substitute decision-making to be abolished prioritises the UN Committee's model of autonomy above all else. Yet there are many reasons to question the assumption that all statutory provision for involuntary treatment necessarily constitutes a fundamental violation of human rights, especially when a lack of insight into illness and a failure to recognise the need for treatment are often features of severe mental illness (David and Ariyo, 2021). As Lewis puts it: 'This narrow type of autonomy is said to be more important than every other value: health, wellbeing, happiness, living a pain-free life and the right to non-discrimination. In some cases it may be, but in every scenario?' (Craigie et al., 2019). Significant concerns are raised that 'an interpretation precluding any involuntary interventions' may well deprive those with severe mental illness of treatment and stands to threaten or even violate 'an individual's right to health, justice, liberty, and even life', through depriving them of treatment and the 'personal, financial, reputational and occupational damage that may occur' (Duffy, this vol., Freeman et al., 2015). Indeed, although the UN Committee present their abolitionist stance as part of realising the 'right to health', espoused in CRPD Article 14, Norwegian law actually uses Article 14 itself to justify retention of some legal provision for 'compulsory care or treatment' (Doyle Guilloud, this vol.). Moreover, increasing evidence during the last 15 to 20 years suggests that service users may well retrospectively accept that treatment was beneficial and acknowledge the necessity of involuntary treatment during severe episodes of illness (Larsen and Terkelsen, 2014, Krieger et al., 2018, Borgeat and Zullino, 2004, Craigie et al., 2019, Pathare et al., 2015).

In practical terms, reducing restrictive practices and inpatient care in mental healthcare can, in itself, have adverse consequences for health and may even cause increased reliance on involuntary treatment. Widespread reduction in provision of inpatient care is rarely offset by a corresponding increase in provision for community treatment and care, while resources allocated to mental healthcare remain vastly inadequate throughout the world (Lancet, 2022a, Kelly, this vol.). Absence of care leads to increased incidence of severe episodes and, ironically, may well increase usage of coercive interventions, given that care remains unavailable until people experience a health crisis. As Carney explains, shrinking budgets for mental healthcare mean mental health law often becomes the only route for individuals to access treatment and, even then, only for short acute periods (Carney, this vol.). Another risk is that raising thresholds for accessing treatment or abolishing involuntary treatment will result in increased involvement of the criminal justice system for those with mental health conditions (Duffy, this vol.). It is already true that 'figures from those detained in prisons in many jurisdictions suggest that the majority of offenders have mental health difficulties' (Peay, this vol.). It would be both deeply ironic and damaging if attempts to use international law to maximise the autonomy of those with mental health conditions inadvertently resulted in their increased criminalisation.

It therefore appears that many reasons remain for retaining some statutory provision for substitute decision-making within mental healthcare. Moving forwards, therefore, what can be changed to ensure that implementation of coercion maximises the rights of service users? Increasing research shows that, even when service users retrospectively accept the benefit or necessity of involuntary treatment, many still view this treatment as having been administered in ways which were, for example, unnecessarily disrespectful or abusive and made them feel unsafe (Valenti et al., 2014, Larsen and Terkelsen, 2014). There is an increasing drive towards changing how coercive treatment is practised (Krieger et al., 2018), reducing coercion where possible, giving patients more control and maximising dignity, an idea enshrined in the CRPD Article 1's statement of purpose – 'to promote respect for their inherent dignity'. Part of this drive is ensuring that blanket condemnation of coercive practices does not lead to an inability to differentiate between unethical practices and those which have the potential to be used in a way which does not violate human rights (Duffy, this vol.). Another important factor is to consider patients' 'emotional safety' (Veale et al.). It is suggested that 'even in the ethically challenging context of involuntary treatment, there are possibilities to increase patient freedoms, enhance their sense of safety and convey respect' (Valenti et al., 2014, Butterworth et al., 2022, Plunkett and Kelly, 2021, Kelly, this vol.).

It is also highly likely that, no matter how liberal the law and its aspirations, such goals can only be achieved through huge culture shifts bringing decreased stigma and changing attitudes towards mental illness. One shift could well be moving from the current and stigma-reinforcing legal focus on dangerousness and risk management towards provision of treatment (Kelly, this vol.). Moreover, we cannot reduce coercive treatment without increased provision of community services and the type of support which maximises possibilities for moving towards a supported decision-making paradigm (Wilson, this vol.).

Other options for using the law to enhance autonomy
'Fusion'

As Kelly argues, the case is strong for viewing the continuing focus on dangerousness and risk management within most mental health law as unjust (Kelly, this vol.). The principal idea proposed for addressing such injustice is moving from the dangerousness criterion towards a system based on impaired mental/decision-making capacity (DMC). Widely known as 'fusion' and gaining increasing prominence, some claim that this system would allow equality between mental and physical health by making substitute decision-making within any medical context contingent on a clinical judgement of impaired DMC in relation to specific treatment decisions (Szmukler, 2017). 'Fusion' might also reflect the increasing significance of DMC within psychiatry, even where laws are not capacity-based (Ruck Keene and Reidy, this vol.).

'Fusion' may represent a way to make mental health law more equitable (Davidson, this vol.). However, many questions about its practicability and potential still need to be addressed. Given that psychiatric assessment of DMC is central to 'fusion', the issue of accuracy of assessment is critical. While some evidence supports the reliability of psychiatric capacity assessment (Cairns et al., 2005b, Okai et al., 2007), other evidence suggests that major uncertainties surrounding accuracy remain (Charland, 2016, Verhofstadt et al., 2019a, Ferracuti and Parmigiani, this vol.). These include great variability in assessment methods (Calcedo-Barba et al., 2020, Okai et al., 2007) and the proportion of patients judged to retain DMC in different studies (Curley et al., 2022). For example, while a 2005 British study reported that 43.8% of their inpatient participants lacked DMC in relation to treatment (DMC-T) (Cairns et al., 2005a), a 2020 meta-review based primarily on inpatient participants suggests that up to 75% of psychiatric patients, even when hospitalised for severe mental illness, may retain DMC and that '[d]ecisional capacity impairments in psychotic patients are temporal, identifiable, and responsive to interventions directed towards simplifying information, encouraging training and shared decision making' (Calcedo-Barba et al., 2020). Moreover, 'fusion' cannot offer a complete solution for proponents of the abolitionist position, insofar as GC1 would still render substitute decision-making based on impaired DMC as a denial of 'legal capacity' and therefore as a violation of human rights.

Other questions concern the feasibility of implementing 'fusion' and its potential for making a significant difference. Although Northern Ireland has introduced fusion via the Mental Capacity Act 2016, remaining difficulties and questions mean that it is not yet implemented (Davidson, this vol.). Would a move towards DMC-based mental health law make a substantive difference to issues such as involuntary treatment? Given the variability and evaluative elements of DMC and its assessment, would the majority of patients who would have been treated involuntarily under risk-based laws simply now be assessed as lacking DMC-T? Is there a danger that 'fusion' could lead to longer periods of detention in those who retain DMC-T, but refuse treatment, both within the criminal justice system (Davidson, this vol.), and within healthcare? For example, following a landmark case in Canada (Starson v Swayze, 2003 SCC 32), where the Supreme Court upheld Starson's right to refuse treatment on grounds that he had DMC-T, Starson was lawfully detained involuntarily for many years in Ontario psychiatric hospitals without treatment.

The recent Independent Review of the Mental Health Act in England and Wales proposed five 'confidence tests' to evaluate feasibility of 'fusion'. These were examining service user views, the impact of 'fusion' legislation in Northern Ireland, the reliability of DMC assessment, the possibility of adapting associated processes, and public interest (Ruck Keene and Reidy, this vol.). However, even if DMC-based laws might come closer to exemplifying UN principles (Kelly, this vol.), as with the CRPD, how much change can they initiate if socioeconomic frameworks are not modified to support those with mental illness? As Ruck-Keene and Reidy argue, if no mechanisms exist supporting the CRPD's right to independent living and social inclusion (Article 19), then 'fusion' debates 'will reduce to little more than a debate about what to label the lock on the door of the institution where the person will end up in crisis' (Ruck Keene and Reidy, this vol.).

Tania L. Gergel

Advance decision-making (ADM) in mental health

Advance decision-making (ADM) in mental health, also known as psychiatric advance directives or advance statements, is based on Dworkin's principle of 'precedent autonomy', allowing that 'an individual's preferences when autonomous trump their preferences when lacking autonomy and that this can extend self-determination to incapacity' (Gergel and Owen, 2015). ADM can help to ensure that, despite ongoing legal provision for involuntary treatment, people have the right to contribute in advance to decisions about management of care and treatment when severely unwell, and it could be an important way of increasing autonomy within mental healthcare. ADM even appears to accord with the UN Committee to some extent, given that GC1 states that 'all persons with disabilities have the right to engage in advance planning', although the fact that ADM is implemented when an individual is assessed as lacking in DMC during a health crisis also appears to render ADM in violation of GC1's prohibition of denying 'legal capacity' (Gergel et al., 2021, Stephenson et al., 2020).

There has been growing support for mental health ADM. While some states in the USA and the Netherlands have already had legal provision for mental health ADM for some time, countries such as India, Australia (in some states and territories), Chile, and Peru have recently introduced this (Gergel et al., 2021, Marshall and Gómez Yuri, 2022). The UK government has also now committed to introducing statutory provision for ADM in England and Wales, following the recent Independent Review of the Mental Health Act (Stephenson et al., 2020). Research has confirmed that key stakeholders are interested in ADM as a way to improve management of mental illness, and has produced some evidence for effectiveness in reducing coercion, including reduction in involuntary admission rates in ethnic minority populations, and improving the therapeutic alliance (Stephenson et al., 2020, Frances, 2021, Ariyo et al., 2021). In the words of Allen Frances:

> Advance directives are perhaps the only intervention in psychiatry that is without a downside. Relapses are much shorter and less harmful when treated promptly. Accepting that future relapses can occur provides patients with the strongest possible incentive to reduce their probability by participating fully in preventive disease management. And ideological and legal controversies about the role of coercion in psychiatry usually dissolve in the cooperation forged by jointly facing clinical reality.
>
> *(Frances, 2021)*

Moreover, not all mental health ADM aims to reduce the use of hospitalisation or enforced treatment. 'Self-binding directives' (SBDs) or 'Ulysses contracts' are a form of ADM which 'instruct clinicians to overrule treatment refusal during future severe episodes by using involuntary treatment'. SBDs are particularly interesting, not simply in terms of potential for maximising autonomy and reducing illness-related harms, but also insofar as they depend upon acceptance and support for statutory provision of involuntary treatment. Opposition to SBDs based on GC1's abolitionist stance may well contravene the wishes of the individuals themselves (Duffy, this vol.). SBDs have been promoted and discussed since the 1970s and some very limited provision for SBDs has been introduced in parts of Europe, North America, and Australasia. There is now also research demonstrating patient support for SBDs, which should go some way to addressing the remaining ethico-legal concerns (Gergel et al., 2021, Hindley et al., 2019). Interestingly, qualitative analysis of reasons given by individuals with bipolar disorder for endorsing SBDs actually indicated service user support for the notion of impaired DMC, as well as involuntary treatment. Although the survey question did not mention DMC, endorsement responses were dominated by the view that their severe episodes of illness involved a 'determinate shift (from valid thinking when well) that substantially compromised decision-making abilities'.

In conclusion, there is strong support for ADM in mental health and a small, but increasing, amount of research exploring its outcomes (Stephenson et al., 2022). Nevertheless, it has also been recognised that take-up can remain low, even when law supports ADM, suggesting that introduction of statutory provision alone is not sufficient for facilitating ADM. It is also critical that education and frameworks are provided to ensure the availability and practicability of mental health ADM (James et al., 2022, Gieselmann et al., 2018, Stephenson et al., 2020).

Co-production and mental health law

Another way to try to ensure that mental health law reflects the priorities of service users themselves is increasing use of co-production with mental health law. Underpinned by the principle of 'nothing about us without us', 'co-production' is the active involvement of people with lived experience of illness. Co-production is expanding in many areas of mental health (Gergel and Kabir, 2017), including the development and administration of law. Innovative involvement of the disability community was central to developing the CRPD itself (Doyle Guilloud, this vol.) and follow-on initiatives such as the World Health Organization (WHO) QualityRights Initiative (Duffy, this vol.). McSherry and Carney both discuss the need for co-production and recent Australian initiatives ensuring that involvement of those with lived experience becomes a legislative requirement (McSherry, this vol.; Carney, this vol.). Co-production has been an important element of law reform in countries including India, England and Wales, and Northern Ireland (Gov.uk, 2018; Davidson, this vol.; Dey and Mellsop, this vol.).

Going forwards, development of mental health law must incorporate expertise through experience. Yet we must also be aware of some of the challenges facing service user involvement in the law and elsewhere. One problem is that the value of service user expertise may be questioned by other stakeholders, with worries that it only reflects 'personal perspectives', rather than broad areas of knowledge (Gergel and Kabir, 2017). Another issue is ensuring that co-production is truly representative, not tokenistic (Gergel and Kabir, 2017), and includes input from a broad range of service users and user organisations. Moreover, to produce practicable recommendations, it must be truly collaborative and include input from clinicians alongside service users. For example, even those who are deeply supportive of service user involvement in drafting the CRPD and General Comments, express major concerns that the extreme abolitionist position expressed in GC1 and the resultant controversies stemmed from exclusion of clinical input and failure to include a broad range of service user views (Freeman et al., 2015).

Reforming mental health law – environmental factors, unintended consequences, and omissions

As discussed above, mental health legislation does not exist within a vacuum. With mental health law dominated by a drive towards using law to realise the aspirations of the CRPD, feasibility and applicability of laws depend upon and are affected by multiple environmental factors, while legal changes and even debates can have unintended consequences or omit significant factors. To make progress, it is essential that these issues are explored and addressed.

As can be seen, for example, in the Asian subcontinent, factors such as insufficient resources, culture, social structure, and stigma can obstruct both legal change and implementation of new laws. India's new Mental Healthcare Act 2017 represents a 'bold step' away from outdated laws stemming back to colonial rule and is a 'rights-based mental health law'. Nevertheless, its implementation has been hindered through insufficient funding, while certain elements of the new law are incompatible with existing social structures. The case is similar regarding 'ongoing concerns about the gap between the legislative framework and current practice in Pakistan'. Meanwhile, poor understanding and unscientific cultural beliefs regarding mental illness mean that people still approach religious leaders, rather than seeking medical intervention (Carney, this vol.; Dey and Mellsop, this vol.).

Others raise concerns that the dominance of controversies surrounding involuntary treatment and mental capacity within legal debates leads to the neglect of other critical issues, particularly how to realise the CRPD's positive rights to socio-economic inclusion (Kelly, this vol.). Carney suggests that, even though socio-economic exclusion is both a cause and consequence of mental illness, inclusion is largely overlooked in relation to law due to the difficulties of measuring it, together with a shortage of resources (Carney, this vol.). An excessive focus on coercion and capacity within legal debate may even be contributing to the comparative neglect of issues of inclusion (Craigie et al., 2019). Fulfilling the CRPD's principles of non-discrimination and inclusion will depend upon increasing prioritisation of socio-economic rights and dominant service user concerns, such as resources and how the law 'impacts on access to employment, housing and services generally' (Bell, this vol.; Carney, this vol.). Kelly suggests that we may also need to look beyond mental health legislation and that 'some rights might be better protected, and some needs better met, through mental health policy, social policy, and broader societal awareness and reform' (Kelly, this vol.).

Another issue often neglected in relation to mental health law is legal equality. While Article 7 of the 1948 Universal Declaration of Human Rights states 'All are equal before the law and are entitled without any discrimination to equal protection of the law' (Nations, 1948), these rights are rarely realised within the application and even structure of mental health law. From an international perspective, although the rights advocated in the CRPD should be universally applicable, factors such as insufficient resources and prevalent cultural beliefs make implementation harder or even unattainable in many low- and middle-income countries (Carney, this vol.; Duffy, this vol.). Within individual nations, inequalities within the application and structure of law affect a number of particular populations.

Legal debate needs urgently to address the fact that coercive practices are disproportionately associated with social deprivation, male gender, and ethnic minorities, as well as particular symptoms and diagnoses (Keown et al., 2016, Ferracuti and Parmigiani, this vol.). Structural racism, exclusion and prejudice towards ethnic minorities, and a lack of cultural competency amongst mental health professionals are other factors which hinder mental health equity (Michael Mensah et al., 2021, Gone and Kirmayer, 2020, Venkataramu et al., 2021) and are highly relevant to mental health law, both in terms of protecting rights and decreasing disproportionate use of involuntary treatment. Disproportionately high involuntary detention, treatment, and police involvement amongst ethnic minorities is widely recognised (Keown et al., 2016). For example, a principal aim of the recent Independent Review of the Mental Health Act in England and Wales was addressing 'the disproportionate number of people from black and minority ethnic groups detained under the Act, police involvement, admission to secure hospitals, and poorer outcomes' (Gov.uk, 2018). It remains to be seen whether the proposed changes will have a significant impact on this situation. The law also needs to do more to address the fact that the needs of older adults are not yet adequately reflected in mental health law (Weller, this vol.) and to address issues of prejudice based on gender and sexuality in relation to mental health (Argüello, 2020).

Mental health law should offer protection to those who experience mental illness. Excluding certain conditions, such as personality and substance abuse disorder, from the remit of mental health law in many countries (Dey and Mellsop, this vol.) can result in poorer health and social outcomes and increased criminalisation. Conditions are either explicitly excluded from detention under mental health laws, or through defining mental illness within the law in terms 'tailored to psychosis, thought disorder or mood disorders' (O'Loughlin, this vol.). Some possible progress is being made in this direction, for example, in Northern Ireland, through broad changes to mental health laws (Davidson, this vol.), or in New Zealand through the recent Substance Addiction (Compulsory Assessment and Treatment) Act 2017. This innovative law offers compulsory treatment for 'severe substance addiction' when necessary and when provision of treatment is available, on the grounds of impaired DMC-T (Health, 2017). However, far more must be done to ensure that particular conditions do not fall beneath the radar of mental health law.

Moving beyond 'mental health law' – suicide, euthanasia, mental illness, and the law

Despite the continuing criminalisation and stigmatisation of suicide and increasing movements towards legalising physician-assisted suicide for those with psychiatric conditions, these issues are very rarely included within mainstream discussions of 'mental health law'. Given the strong association between mental illness and suicide, the case seems strong for directing more attention towards these issues going forwards. Moreover, another reason for drawing these issues into broader discussions of mental health law is that the risk factors identified above in relation to mental health law in terms of environmental factors, unintended consequences, and omissions, could all potentially contribute towards causation of both suicide attempts and the type of chronic and apparently hopeless situations which might lead an individual towards requesting euthanasia. Although I cannot explore all aspects of practice or debate, I will aim to give a broad indication and consider some of the most pressing concerns.

A recent review reports that 'suicides account for 1.4% of premature deaths worldwide'. Suicide is a global phenomenon and 'the majority of suicides worldwide are related to psychiatric diseases'. It is estimated that 'half of all completed suicides are related to depressive and other mood disorders' (Bachmann, 2018). The link between severe mental illness and suicide has been well documented (Bertolote and Fleischmann, 2002, UGMH, 2021). For bipolar disorder, for example, the mental disorder with probably the highest suicide risk, it is estimated that 'about one-third to one-half of bipolar patients attempt suicide at least once in their lifetime and approximately 15–20% die due to suicide' (Dome et al., 2019, Miller and Black, 2020). Suicidal ideation and actions are viewed as key diagnostic criteria associated with multiple categories of mental disorder in both the WHO's International Classification of Diseases and the American Psychiatric Association's DSM-V, and high suicide rates are also linked to psychotic, eating, personality, substance abuse, and other mental disorders (Bachmann, 2018, Bertolote and Fleischmann, 2002). It is also highly likely that both suicide rates and the links to mental illness are under-reported, given the stigma and even, in some countries, illegality of suicide, combined with the fact that suicide often occurs in early episodes of illness and may well occur before diagnosis. For bipolar disorder, for example, the average delay between onset of illness and diagnosis is estimated to be close to a decade (Fritz et al., 2017, Scott and Leboyer, 2011, Lublóy et al., 2020). Suicide risks are intensified by the global phenomenon of lack of resources for healthcare, lack of inclusion, stigma, discrimination, and abuse associated with mental illness.

Clearly this relation between suicide and mental disorder should be carefully considered in any matters relating to law and suicide. Yet it is frequently overlooked or downplayed in debates surrounding both euthanasia and the criminalisation of attempting suicide. Surely a key question in relation to both issues must be, given that suicidality is a core feature of mental illness, could it ever be just for the law either effectively to aid illness by facilitating suicide or to punish and stigmatise individuals for their illness, through criminalisation of suicide?

Criminalisation of suicide

Historically, suicide has been stigmatised from both cultural and religious viewpoints and viewed, for example, as a criminal act of selfishness and cowardice. While most countries have now reformed laws criminalising attempted suicide, such laws do still exist (Mishara and Weisstub, 2016), and calls for reform are complicated by cultural and religious sensitivities. A 2021 report by the International Association for Suicide Prevention together with United for Global Mental Health was part of working towards the 'United Nations Sustainable Development Goal: Good Health and Wellbeing's target to reduce suicides globally'. It details the current state of affairs, outlines key concerns, and calls for decriminalisation. Efforts towards decriminalisation are being made – 'in recent years legislation criminalising suicide has been successfully repealed or superseded by new legislation in the Cayman Islands, Cyprus, Singapore and India' (UGMH, 2021, Lancet, 2014). Nevertheless, as of 2021, attempting suicide is a criminal offence in at least 20 countries worldwide, with a further 20 countries prosecuting suicide attempts under Sharia law (UGMH, 2021).

Laws criminalising suicide are usually part of a penal or criminal code which often dates back to laws imposed by colonial powers, when 'suicide or attempted suicide was considered a crime against the state, as well as against religion'. They were written 'when mental health was grossly misunderstood and human rights abuses regarding mental health were commonplace' and one obstacle facing reform is that this situation still remains in many of these countries (UGMH, 2021). In Pakistan, for example, both factors still influence law and practice, with suicide and attempted suicide still 'deemed criminal offences under section 309 of the Pakistan Penal Code', and a 2018 amendment to mental health law decriminalising attempting suicide yet to be practically implemented. Such is the stigma and fear surrounding disclosure of suicide that Pakistan has only included suicide among annual mortality data since 2017 (Khan and Khan, 2020).

Failure to collect accurate data concerning suicide and suicide attempts is one major harm which results from such laws, with suicide prevention initiatives hampered by underrepresentation or even concealing of suicide prevalence rates. This remains the case, even in many countries where suicide is no longer illegal. Despite suicide being a worldwide epidemic, 'only 87 countries have quality data concerning suicide' (Mishara and Weisstub, 2016, UGMH, 2021, Wu et al., 2022). Criminalising suicide also contributes to perpetuating stigma and stops people from seeking help (Khan and Khan, 2020), with research suggesting that laws penalising suicide were associated with higher national suicide rates (Wu et al., 2022, UGMH, 2021). At the World Health Assembly in 2019, all health ministers agreed that decriminalising suicide was an effective way to reduce deaths by suicide when they approved the World Health Organization Mental Health Action Plan for 2021–2030. Moreover, legal procedures and even imprisonment of those who attempt suicide have severe adverse effects on their mental health.

It is also important to note that, even in countries where suicide is no longer deemed a criminal offence, ongoing stigma and prejudice can result in criminalisation of suicidality. In the US, for example, there have been cases of a pregnant woman attempting suicide being prosecuted for murder, or where military personnel attempting suicide face criminal charges and even imprisonment (Mishara and Weisstub, 2016). In the UK, there has been considerable recent controversy over the now withdrawn SIM (Serenity Integrated Mentoring) scheme which involved the police in 'mentoring' of those who had experienced police involvement during a mental health emergency and, effectively, resulted in criminal sanctions as a response to suicidality (Thomson et al., 2022, House, 2022). Even outside of SIM, however, criminalisation of those who are suicidal has been longstanding and still continues, using mechanisms such as 'antisocial behaviour orders, community protection notices and criminal behaviour orders'. Although suicide was decriminalised fully in the UK 55 years ago, there are examples of people being charged with 'breach of the peace for causing alarm to a police officer by disclosing suicidal thoughts, criminal damage for dislodging fencing while jumping from a bridge, or wasting police time for calls made by healthcare staff to police' (Thomson et al., 2022). As Thomson and others argue, these practices are both unethical and damaging, and need urgently to be addressed.

The criminalisation of suicide does not typically fall within the remit of mental health law debates and is also an area which must be approached with cultural awareness, especially given that many calls for reform come from ex-colonial nations, historically responsible for the initial criminalisation. Nevertheless, given the associations between mental illness and suicide, ongoing stigma and lack of resources for healthcare and societal inclusion, and the harms engendered by criminalisation of suicide, we must devote more attention towards campaigning for the remaining laws which criminalise suicide to be overturned (Mishara and Weisstub, 2016). We must also direct attention towards preventing criminalisation of suicidality through other legal avenues, in countries where attempting suicide is officially no longer a criminal offence. Looking beyond the law, an important part of this is to prioritise increasing our understanding of suicide, allowing us to address continuing stigmatisation and misconceptions. We must work towards a future where those who are suicidal can request and receive help without fear of reprisal, legal or otherwise.

What price 'autonomy'? Euthanasia and mental illness

Physician-assisted suicide and mental illness – how things stand

While five US states and Switzerland have already legalised euthanasia for terminal medical conditions, the BeNeLux countries Belgium, Luxembourg, and the Netherlands have, since 2002, legalised physician-assisted suicide (PAS) for both terminal and non-terminal medical conditions (Verhofstadt et al., 2019b, Verhofstadt et al., 2017). Canada joined these countries in March 2021, with Bill C-7 amendments to their 2015 MAiD (medical assistance in dying) Laws, removing the 'foreseeable death requirement' (Whitelaw et al., 2022, Webster, 2022).

As Lemmens reports about the law in Belgium and the Netherlands:

Generally, patients can request euthanasia if all of the following criteria are fulfilled: (1) they have a medical condition; (2) which causes unbearable (physical or psychological) suffering; (3) the situation is medically hopeless (Belgium) or there is no prospect of improvement (Netherlands); and (4) the suffering cannot be alleviated (Belgium) or there is no reasonable alternative solution (Netherlands).

(Lemmens, 2018)

The inclusion of conditions which cause unbearable *psychological* suffering allows those with chronic mental health conditions the possibility of requesting physician-assisted suicide (Kelly, 2017, Lemmens, 2018). In March 2023, Canada's 2021 revisions to the MAiD laws will expand to include patients with mental illness. Although final reviews are still ongoing, Canada's MAiD laws are more 'permissive', with fewer safeguards, than their BeNeLux counterparts (Webster, 2022).

Instances of euthanasia-assisted suicide (EAS) in Belgium and the Netherlands have increased dramatically, with such deaths now accounting for a far greater percentage of overall deaths in Belgium and the Netherlands than in US states which have legalised PAS only for terminal conditions (Lemmens, 2018). EAS accounted for 4.5% of all deaths (7666) in the Netherlands in 2021 (Euthanasie, 2021), with rates going as high as 14.43% in some districts (Groenewoud et al., 2021), while Belgium had its highest ever number in 2021, with 2699 euthanasia-related deaths (l'euthanasie, 2022).

A major increase in requests for PAS amongst psychiatric patients has generated growing opposition to the inclusion of mental illness as a basis for PAS (Verhofstadt et al., 2019b, Lemmens, 2018). In the Netherlands psychiatric cases have steadily increased from 1% of all EAS in 2016 to 1.5% in 2021 and EAS for dementia accounts for 2.8% (Euthanasie, 2021).

In Belgium, some recent controversies have seen a slight decline (Lemmens, 2018), with psychiatric cases accounting for 0.9% of 2699 total EAS deaths in 2021 compared to 2.3% of 1928 deaths in 2014 (l'euthanasie, 2022). One high-profile controversy was the case of Tina Nys, a 38-year-old woman, who suffered a relapse after a very long period of stability and was then diagnosed with autism, but not treated, two months before being 'euthanized in the presence of her traumatized family members' (Lemmens, 2018). This case, in which 'the patient was euthanized without it having been substantiated that her psychiatric illness had no prospect of improvement and that her suffering could not be alleviated' became the first criminal trial in Belgium of PAS clinicians, although they were not convicted (De Hert et al., 2022). Alongside this came controversies raised by a 2015 study published by the Belgian psychiatrist, Thienpont, who admits to a very flexible approach towards granting euthanasia requests and was revealed to be responsible for approving almost 50% of Belgian cases of PAS for mental illness in the period leading up to publication (Lemmens, 2018).

In Canada euthanasia rates are now increasing even faster than in Belgium and the Netherlands and have far less stringent safeguards in general and especially in relation to the upcoming inclusion of mental illness as a sole or primary criterion in MAiD laws (Webster, 2022, Guly, 2022). Numbers have already increased from 2838 in MAiD's first year (2017) to '10,064 – accounting for more than 3 percent of all deaths in Canada that year' in 2021 (Subramanya, 2022). Concerns have been raised over a number of controversial cases such as Alan Nichols, who died via MAiD in July 2019, after being detained involuntarily under the Mental Health Act in June 2019 (Nichols, 2020), or recent reports of MAiD being suggested unprompted by Veteran Affairs Canada to a Canadian armed forces veteran seeking help for post-traumatic stress disorder and a traumatic brain injury (Lee, 2022b). The impending addition of mental illness to MAiD criteria, following a Senate amendment which pressured parliament to overturn its original exclusion of mental illness, remains deeply controversial (Guly, 2022). Even those who advocate for the inclusion of mental illness have expressed deep concerns about the lack of adequate safeguards and insufficient impartiality within Canada's expert panel on MAiD and Mental Illness, who were commissioned to review and issue recommendations concerning the upcoming legislation (Kirby, 2022, Guly, 2022).

Expansion of PAS/MAiD to include non-terminal conditions and disabilities, both physical and psychiatric, has been justified on the basis of prioritising equality and autonomy, insofar as restriction to those suffering from terminal conditions is presented as discriminating against those who suffer from chronic health conditions/disabilities. In Canada, for example, the 2021 expansion of MAiD laws was due to a ruling following a constitutional challenge, which stipulated that 'the restriction to a reasonably foreseeable death is an unjustifiable impingement on the right to life, liberty, and security of the person and the right to equality' (Whitelaw et al., 2022). However, given the numerous legal and ethical concerns about this expansion, we must consider whether, ironically, it actually risks abusing the autonomy and equality it supposedly protects. Might it be the case, as Charland suggested, that 'nascent science, inadequate regulations, economic pressures and incentives, and an overly zealous commitment to autonomy and individualism at all costs, make us worry whether autonomy may actually be turning on its own and is poised to devour its most vulnerable subjects' (Charland, 2016)?

Problems and challenges facing euthanasia for mental illness

The legalisation of euthanasia based on a sole or primary reason of mental illness or 'psychological suffering' faces significant legal, ethical, and practical challenges, while strong evidence suggests that we currently lack sufficient knowledge and resources relating to mental illness to allow a safe and ethical clinical and social environment for this practice. Here is a brief summary of key concerns relating to euthanasia for mental illness or 'psychological suffering' and an account of how many concerns seem to be substantiated by increasing evidence of abuse and controversy within the countries which have legalised this practice (Charland, 2016).

One factor underpinning all concerns relating to PAS for mental illness is a comparative lack of knowledge. Compared to many physical disorders, mental disorder is poorly understood and unpredictable (Kelly, 2017, Naudts et al., 2006, Nicolini et al., 2022). We lack, or are severely limited in, our ability to understand and measure what would constitute irremediable suffering, to establish that all options and hope of future improvement have been exhausted, and, accordingly, to make informed decisions about the validity of this practice. An additional factor relevant to all concerns is the global lack of resources devoted both to care and support for those with mental illness and to research into mental illness which could expand our understanding. Given that this shows no immediate signs of being significantly alleviated, how could we ever be justified in saying that we have considered all clinical and socio-economic interventions which could potentially improve outcomes? Insufficient knowledge and resources must constitute critical factors to consider in relation to all euthanasia-based concerns.

One of the greatest concerns about PAS for mental illness is the fact that suicidality is itself an intrinsic feature of many types of severe mental illness, as explained above in relation to the criminalisation of suicide. Suicide prevention, through treating illness and protecting individuals from harming themselves, is central to mental healthcare. So, could we ever truly overcome concerns that PAS is responding to a symptom of illness instead of aiming to find alternative interventions to help recovery or improvement (Kelly, 2017; Verhofstadt, Van Assche, et al., 2019)?

Medical evidence suggests that psychiatric illness is usually treatable, episodic, and transient, meaning that there can never be certainty regarding the absence of possible improvement or recovery (Verhofstadt et al., 2019b, Nicolini et al., 2022). As Kelly argues, 'with mental illness there is no point at which we can say that a person's illness is untreatable or that their suffering cannot be alleviated, either now or at some future point' (Kelly, 2017). A recent review of PAS cases involving 'treatment resistant depression' concludes that '[o]ur findings suggest that the objective standard for irremediability in psychiatric EAS cannot be met, raising implications for policy and practice around the world' (Nicolini et al., 2022), while others discuss the potential complexities of establishing irremediability in relation to personality disorders, a common diagnosis in PAS requests (Nicolini et al., 2020). The Canadian Mental Health Association has now made an about-turn in relation to MAiD, by accepting the proposed inclusion of mental illness, albeit with numerous safeguards which do not actually look feasible. However, a main reason for their initial strong opposition to its inclusion was the episodic nature of mental illness and uncertainties regarding prognosis, stating 'Mental illness is very often episodic. Death, on the other hand, is not reversible. In Dutch and Belgian studies, a high proportion of people who were seeking MAID for psychiatric reasons, but did not get it, later changed their minds' (Webster, 2022).

Another major concern is that, according to the generally accepted biopsychosocial model of mental illness, socio-environmental factors can be a major contributory factor in its onset, deterioration, and continuation. Given the lack of resources currently allocated to mental healthcare and the major socioeconomic challenges facing so many people with mental illness, many factors which contribute to 'psychological suffering' may well be alleviated through better provision of resources (Kelly, 2017, Verhofstadt et al., 2019b). It is deeply disturbing to recognise that, for both mental illness and other health conditions and disabilities, death might become an alternative to providing improved resources or treatments. The reality of these concerns is borne out by existing evidence. The controversial Belgian psychiatrist Thienpont admitted 'accepting social determinants of health as sources of unbearable suffering' when approving PAS requests (Lemmens, 2018), while a recent qualitative study examining the concept of 'unbearable suffering' through the testimonials of 26 psychiatric patients requesting PAS in Belgium, found that socio-economic factors, including financial issues like the unaffordability of paying for continued treatment, were major contributory factors (Verhofstadt et al., 2017). This study also reported 'the experience of solitude or loneliness because of a lack of social support from "society in general"' as reasons for requesting PAS, while a review of 66 Dutch PAS cases concluded that 'most of the patients had personality disorders and were identified as socially isolated and lonely' (Kim et al., 2016). As Verhofstadt states:

> Some correlates of suffering (such as low income) indicate the need for a broad medical, societal and political debate on how to reduce the burden of financial and socio-

economic difficulties and inequalities in order to reduce patients' desire for euthanasia. Euthanasia should never be seen (or used) as a means of resolving societal failures.

(Verhofstadt et al., 2017)

A connected concern is the issue of normalisation, whereby, as PAS becomes increasingly accepted and repeated, death is more readily considered or offered as a solution (Lemmens, 2018, Whitelaw et al., 2022, Naudts et al., 2006). The increasing numbers of PAS cases for mental illness in Belgium and the Netherlands suggest that this is a very real phenomenon rather than some theoretical 'slippery slope' concern. In Canada, the situation regarding MAiD for mental illness seems potentially even worse, since there will be no requirement for the physician to pursue other treatment options with patients and it is even the case that 'physicians and nurse practitioners would have a "professional obligation" to initiate conversations about MAiD if they believe a patient might be eligible' (Benson, 2022, Kirkey, 2022).

Alongside normalisation comes the very legitimate concern that increased provision for PAS for disabilities including mental illness will result in devaluing the life of those with disabilities, with euthanasia increasingly becoming a substitute for failing to provide adequate resources, support, and treatment (Lemmens, 2018) – in the words of a recent UN report,

when life-ending interventions are normalized for people who are not terminally ill or suffering at the end of their lives, such legislative provisions tend to rest on – or draw strength from – ableist assumptions about the inherent "quality of life" or "worth" of the life of a person with a disability.

(Mulligan, 2022)

This is a particular concern for people with severe mental illness, who are already often amongst the most disadvantaged and disenfranchised members of society (Whitelaw et al., 2022). Research found that being a burden to family, friends, or society was given amongst reasons for requesting PAS by psychiatric patients in Belgium (Verhofstadt et al., 2017), where such guilt is not necessarily viewed as a legally invalid reason for this request (Verhofstadt, Van Assche, et al., 2019). As Naudts says, 'Patients who primarily have a mental disorder are at substantial risk of judging themselves to be a burden on their carers' (Naudts et al., 2006) and it seems that legally sanctioned provision of PAS is already reinforcing this view.

Further concerns are the risk of undue influence, either from family or clinicians, pushing people towards seeking PAS and the increased risk and complexity relating to particular patient populations (Kirkey, 2022). Clinical opinion regarding PAS varies greatly and there is a risk that clinical endorsement of PAS in itself suggests a lack of hope of recovery or alleviation of suffering to patients (Kelly, 2017). Moreover, the controversies surrounding Thienpoint show that 'change in practice can be driven by a small number of medical practitioners, and in a direction that arguably moves away from the original intent of the regulatory regime' (Lemmens, 2018).

There are particular issues surrounding dementia, PAS, and rising numbers. In the Netherlands, for example, numbers have risen from 12 cases in 2009 to 215 cases in 2021 (2.8% of all euthanasia cases) (Lemmens, 2018, Euthanasie, 2021). There are concerns about an 'expansion of the access criteria' for dementia cases and worries about imposing euthanasia on an elderly population, many of whom might not be able to fully comprehend what is happening and whose 'unbearable suffering' is difficult to establish, given the lack of awareness associated with severe dementia. It is also feared that expansion of PAS in dementia cases may lead to devaluing 'quality of life in the context of dementia' and have an 'impact on societal perception of cognitive disabilities more broadly' (Lemmens, 2018). There have already been many controversial and shocking cases, especially in relation to administering treatment according to advance directives requesting euthanasia (Lemmens, 2018, Groenewoud et al., 2022, Miller et al., 2019).

Particular concerns have been raised about PAS amongst the prison population, especially given the prevalence of mental disorders, an extremely insufficient provision of treatment and care, and the proliferation of 'external factors' which can contribute to suffering. In the words of Franke et al., 'strong safeguards are necessary to prevent a slippery slope toward AD (assisted death) becoming the preferred method for ending suffering from untreated or incurable mental disorders in detention because other options (e.g., sufficient mental health care) are lacking' (Franke, Urwyler, & Prüter-Schwarte, 2022).

Finally, there are major procedural concerns that adequate safeguards regarding assessment of eligibility for PAS are either currently lacking or actually not possible. The most significant questions concern the difficulties of measuring 'psychological suffering' and assessing decision-making capacity (DMC) in relation to PAS. It is argued that there is insufficient understanding of the type and level of suffering which would prompt psychiatric patients to consider PAS, as well as no clear consensus regarding multiple clinical issues (Verhofstadt et al., 2019a, Nicolini et al., 2022, Nicolini et al., 2020). As van Veen and others write in relation to MAiD and mental illness:

Challenges regarding the definition, diagnosis and treatment of irremediable psychiatric suffering complicate the process of establishing it in the context of MAiD. Development of consensus clinical criteria for irremediable psychiatric suffering in this context and further research to understand 'treatment fatigue' among patients with psychiatric disorders may help address these challenges.

(van Veen et al., 2022)

Assessing whether someone has capacity to consent to PAS in relation to mental illness is particularly complex. Yet DMC, despite its centrality, is rarely discussed in relation, for example, to MAiD, where discussions 'tend to be very general and ideological and conveniently overlook practical details' (Charland, 2016). Assessment of DMC in mental illness in general is still a relatively new area with many uncertainties and remains 'a matter of considerable controversy among many researchers and clinicians' (Charland, 2016). There are significant difficulties in establishing whether DMC is 'affected by a psychiatric disorder' (Verhofstadt et al., 2019b, Naudts et al., 2006) and major concerns about how clinicians' personal values might influence capacity assessments, so that a '"sliding standard of competence" poses the risk of further paternalistic, non-voluntary euthanasia' (Naudts et al., 2006, Charland, 2016, Lemmens, 2018).

Such concerns are substantiated by evidence from Belgium and the Netherlands suggesting that safeguards are insufficiently observed (Verhofstadt et al., 2019b, Lemmens, 2018, Kim and Lemmens, 2016). As Kim and Lemmens report: 'there is a gap between the idealized basis upon which MAID is advocated for patients with psychiatric conditions and the reality of its practice' (Kim and Lemmens, 2016). Analysis of Netherlands PAS cases shows that DMC assessment was often superficial, was subject to disagreement both in relation to DMC and irremediability, and that low thresholds for DMC may 'reflect the normative position of the review committees' (Doernberg et al., 2016, Kim et al., 2016). Although many cases of PAS in the Netherlands and Belgium do involve a second consultation with a specialist clinician, this second consultation is not legally binding and PAS often proceeds despite clinical disagreement (Lemmens, 2018).

In conclusion, the numerous concerns, many based on worrying evidence from current practice in countries where PAS for mental illness is legal, suggest that there are strong arguments for prohibition or abolition of such legalisation and that current knowledge and resources are, indeed, insufficient to facilitate safe and ethical practice. Nevertheless, numbers of PAS cases for mental illness in Belgium and the Netherlands have increased and this practice will soon be legalised in Canada. Moreover, there is a strong possibility that these existing models might impel other countries towards considering this practice, especially as people become more sympathetic to euthanasia in general. It is imperative, therefore, that during the next decade, this issue receives increased attention and resources, and becomes a major element of debate within mental health law and ethics.

Conclusion

There is still much to be done to address the constitution, application, and debates surrounding mental health law, especially relating to the prevalence and practice of involuntary treatment. Moreover, progress towards realising the CRPD's aspirations for justice, autonomy, equality, and inclusion, will also depend upon prioritising the multiple interconnected environmental factors and considering legal issues beyond the traditional remit of mental health law, such as criminalisation of suicide and euthanasia. It is also critical that the dominance of a particular libertarian view of autonomy manifest, for example, in assumptions about rights to abolition of all involuntary health interventions or euthanasia, does not inadvertently produce harmful outcomes or even threaten the autonomy of people with mental illness.

Nevertheless, there may be some grounds for optimism about addressing stigma, increasing resources, and legal reform. While certainly true, as the *Lancet* Commission reports, that stigma and discrimination surrounding mental health is an ongoing global issue, the very existence of high profile initiatives such as the *Lancet* Commission demonstrates the increasing prioritisation of the rights and well-being of those with mental health conditions (Lancet, 2022b). While resources for mental health research remain vastly insufficient, it is heartening to note, for example, that the Wellcome Trust, one of the world's largest funders for medical research, has recently identified mental health as one of three core health challenges and priorities for health research alongside infectious diseases and climate and health (Wellcome Trust [Online]). Moreover, as we have seen, considerable progress is also being made in mental health law itself. Recent years have seen the introduction of new mental health laws, reforms to existing laws, increasing safeguards, and movements towards change, largely motivated by the passing of the CRPD in 2006. Initiatives such as growing recognition and provision for mental health advance decision-making and co-production within law have great potential for maximising the autonomy of people with mental illness and ensuring relevance to their concerns. There has been some progress towards decriminalisation of suicide, together with increased awareness and campaigns. Despite the enormity and urgency of the remaining challenges, these recent changes and initiatives suggest a growing global recognition of the importance of mental health law and the human rights of people with mental health conditions.

TG is funded by the Wellcome Trust, UK (grant number 203376/Z/16/Z), as part of the Mental Health and Justice project. I am grateful to Trudo Lemmens, Scott Kim, and

Niall Boyce for providing information in relation to euthanasia and criminalisation of suicide, and to Brendan Kelly and Mary Donnelly for their guidance and support in the preparation of this chapter.

References

2014. General comment on article 12 of the UNCRPD. Committee on the rights of persons with disabilities.
2020. *Living in Chains* [Online]. Available: https://www.hrw.org/report/2020/10/06/living-chains/shackling-people-psychosocial-disabilities-worldwide [Accessed 21/10/22].
Argüello, T. M. 2020. Decriminalizing LGBTQ+: Reproducing and resisting mental health inequities. *CNS Spectrums*, 25(5), 667–686.
Ariyo, K., Henderson, C., Gilbert, S. & Smith, S. 2021. Advance directives reduce friction over involuntary treatment. *The Lancet Psychiatry*, 8(9), 749.
Bachmann, S. 2018. Epidemiology of suicide and the psychiatric perspective. *International Journal of Environmental Research and Public Health*, 15(7), 1425.
Benson, S. 2022. 'These are real people': Medical ethicist urges Parliamentarians to dig deeper on inappropriate MAiD applications. *The Hill Times*, 22/8/22.
Bell, M. 2023. Mental Health, discrimination and employment law. In Kelly, B. D. and Donnelly, M. (eds.) *Routledge Handbook of Mental Health Law*. London: Routledge.
Bertolote, J. M. & Fleischmann, A. 2002. Suicide and psychiatric diagnosis: A worldwide perspective. *World Psychiatry*, 1(3), 181–185.
Borgeat, F. & Zullino, D. 2004. Attitudes concerning involuntary treatment of mania: Results of a survey within self-help organizations. *European Psychiatry*, 19(3), 155–158.
Borrell-Carrió, F., Suchman, A. L. & Epstein, R. M. 2004. The biopsychosocial model 25 years later: Principles, practice, and scientific inquiry. *Annals of Family Medicine*, 2(6), 576–582.
Butterworth, H., Wood, L. & Rowe, S. 2022. Patients' and staff members' experiences of restrictive practices in acute mental health in-patient settings: Systematic review and thematic synthesis. *BJPsych Open*, 8(6), e178.
Cairns, R., Maddock, C., Buchanan, A., David, A. S., Hayward, P., Richardson, G., Szmukler, G. & Hotopf, M. 2005a. Prevalence and predictors of mental incapacity in psychiatric in-patients. *The British Journal of Psychiatry*, 187, 379–385.
Cairns, R., Maddock, C., Buchanan, A., David, A. S., Hayward, P., Richardson, G., Szmukler, G. & Hotopf, M. 2005b. Reliability of mental capacity assessments in psychiatric in-patients. *The British Journal of Psychiatry*, 187, 372–378.
Calcedo-Barba, A., Fructuoso, A., Martinez-Raga, J., Paz, S., Sánchez De Carmona, M. & Vicens, E. 2020. A meta-review of literature reviews assessing the capacity of patients with severe mental disorders to make decisions about their healthcare. *BMC Psychiatry*, 20(1), 339.
Carney, T. 2023. Socio-economic inclusion and mental health law. In Kelly, B. D. and Donnelly, M. (eds.) *Routledge Handbook of Mental Health Law*. London: Routledge.
Charland, L., Lemmens, T. & Wada, K. 2016. Decision-making capacity to consent to medical assistance in dying for persons with mental disorders. *Journal of Ethics in Mental Health*, 9, 1–14.
Chen, B. 2023. Untapped potential of China's mental health law reform. In Kelly, B. D. and Donnelly, M. (eds.) *Routledge Handbook of Mental Health Law*. London: Routledge.
Convention on the rights of persons with disabilities [Online]. Available: https://www.un.org/development/desa/disabilities/convention-on-the-rights-of-persons-with-disabilities.html [Accessed 19/10/22].
Craigie, J., Bach, M., Gurbai, S., Kanter, A., Kim, S. Y. H., Lewis, O. & Morgan, G. 2019. Legal capacity, mental capacity and supported decision-making: Report from a panel event. *International Journal of Law and Psychiatry*, 62, 160–168.
Curley, A., Watson, C. & Kelly, B. D. 2022. Capacity to consent to treatment in psychiatry inpatients – A systematic review. *International Journal of Psychiatry in Clinical Practice*, 26(3), 303–315.
David, A. & Ariyo, K. 2021. Insight is a useful construct in clinical assessments if used wisely. *Journal of Medical Ethics*, 47, 185–6.

Davidson, G. 2023. An alternative to mental health law: The Mental Capacity Act (Northern Ireland) 2016. In Kelly, B. D. and Donnelly, M. (eds.) *Routledge Handbook of Mental Health Law*. London: Routledge.

De Hert, M., Loos, S., Sterckx, S., Thys, E. & Van Assche, K. 2022. Improving control over euthanasia of persons with psychiatric illness: Lessons from the first Belgian criminal court case concerning euthanasia. *Frontiers in Psychiatry*, 13, 933748.

Dey, S. & Mellsop, G. 2023. Colonisation, history and the evolution of mental health legislation in India, Pakistan, Sri Lanka and Bangladesh. In Kelly, B. D. and Donnelly, M. (eds.) *Routledge Handbook of Mental Health Law*. London: Routledge.

Doernberg, S. N., Peteet, J. R. & Kim, S. Y. 2016. Capacity evaluations of psychiatric patients requesting assisted death in the Netherlands. *Psychosomatics*, 57(6), 556–565.

Dome, P., Rihmer, Z. & Gonda, X. 2019. Suicide risk in bipolar disorder: A brief review. *Medicina (Kaunas, Lithuania)*, 55(8), 403. doi: 10.3390/medicina55080403.

Doyle Guilloud, S. 2023. The United Nations convention on the rights of persons with disabilities and mental health laws: Requirements and responses. In Kelly, B. D. and Donnelly, M. (eds.). *Routledge Handbook of Mental Health Law*. London: Routledge.

Duffy, R. M. 2023. Responses to the World Health Organization's quality rights initiative. In Kelly, B. D. and Donnelly, M. (eds.) *Routledge Handbook of Mental Health Law*. London: Routledge.

Euthanasie, R. T. 2021. Annual report 2021. Available: https://english.euthanasiecommissie.nl/the-committees/documents/publications/annual-reports/2002/annual-reports/annual-reports [Accessed 20/10/22]

Ferracuti, S. & Parmigiani, G. 2023. Mental capacity in forensic psychiatry in a comparative context. In Kelly, B. D. and Donnelly, M. (eds.) *Routledge Handbook of Mental Health Law*. London: Routledge.

Frances, A. 2021. Advance directives reduce friction over involuntary treatment. *The Lancet Psychiatry*, 8(9), 749–750.

Franke, I., Urwyler, T., Pruter-Schwarte, C. 2022. Assisted dying requests from people in detention: Psychiatric, ethical, and legal considerations–A literature review. *Frontiers in Psychiatry*, 13.

Freeman, M. C., Kolappa, K., De Almeida, J. M. C., Kleinman, A., Makhashvili, N., Phakathi, S., Saraceno, B. & Thornicroft, G. 2015. Reversing hard won victories in the name of human rights: A critique of the general comment on article 12 of the UN convention on the rights of persons with disabilities. *The Lancet Psychiatry*, 2(9), 844–850.

Fritz, K., Russell, A. M. T., Allwang, C., Kuiper, S., Lampe, L. & Malhi, G. S. 2017. Is a delay in the diagnosis of bipolar disorder inevitable? *Bipolar Disorders*, 19(5), 396–400.

Gergel, T., Das, P., Owen, G., Stephenson, L., Rifkin, L., Hindley, G., Dawson, J. & Ruck Keene, A. 2021. Reasons for endorsing or rejecting self-binding directives in bipolar disorder: A qualitative study of survey responses from UK service users. *The Lancet Psychiatry*, 8(7), 599–609.

Gergel, T. & Kabir, T. 2017. Reframing a model – The benefits and challenges of service user involvement in mental health research. In Bluhm, R. (ed.) *Knowing and Acting in Medicine*. London and New York: Rowman and Littlefield. 77–96.

Gergel, T. & Owen, G. S. 2015. Fluctuating capacity and advance decision-making in bipolar affective disorder - Self-binding directives and self-determination. *International Journal of Law and Psychiatry*, 40, 92–101.

Gieselmann, A., Simon, A., Vollmann, J. & Schone-Seifert, B. 2018. Psychiatrists' views on different types of advance statements in mental health care in Germany. *The International Journal of Social Psychiatry*.

Gone, J. P. & Kirmayer, L. J. 2020. Advancing indigenous mental health research: Ethical, conceptual and methodological challenges. *Transcultural Psychiatry*, 57(2), 235–249.

GOV.UK. 2018. Independent review of the Mental Health Act. Available at https://www.gov.uk/government/groups/independent-review-of-the-mental-health-act [Accessed 20/10/22]

Groenewoud, A. S., Atsma, F., Arvin, M., Westert, G. P. & Boer, T. A. 2021. Euthanasia in the Netherlands: A claims data cross-sectional study of geographical variation. *BMJ Supportive and Palliative Care*. doi: 10.1136/bmjspcare-2020-002573

Groenewoud, A. S., Leijten, E., Van Den Oever, S., Van Sommeren, J. & Boer, T. A. 2022. The ethics of euthanasia in dementia: A qualitative content analysis of case summaries (2012–2020). *Journal of the American Geriatrics Society*, 70(6), 1704–1716.

Guly, C. 2022. MAiD expert panel final report provides no 'safeguards' for people with mental illness. *The Lawyer's Daily*. Canada: LexisNexis.

Health, M. O. 2017. Substance Addiction (Compulsory Assessment and Treatment) Act, 2017.

Hindley, G., Stephenson, L., Ruck Keene, A., Rifkin, L., Gergel, T. & Owen, G. 2019. "Why have I not been told about this?": A survey of experiences of and attitudes to advance decision-making amongst people with bipolar. *Wellcome Open Research*. 4: 16.

House, A. 2022. Serenity integrated mentoring and the high intensity network: A scheme that raises serious questions for practice and governance in UK psychiatry. *BJPsych Bulletin*, 47(1), 1–4.

Huda, A. S. 2021. The medical model and its application in mental health. *International Review of Psychiatry*, 33(5), 463–470.

James, R., Maude, P. & Searby, A. 2022. Clinician knowledge and attitudes of mental health advance statements in Victoria, Australia. *International Journal of Mental Health Nursing*. 31, 116–1175.

Kelly, B. D. 2017. Invited commentary on... When unbearable suffering incites psychiatric patients to request euthanasia. *British Journal of Psychiatry*, 211(4), 248–249.

Kelly, B. D. 2023. History and development of mental health law. In Kelly, B. D. and Donnelly, M. (eds.) *Routledge Handbook of Mental Health Law*. London: Routledge.

Keown, P., Mcbride, O., Twigg, L., Crepaz-Keay, D., Cyhlarova, E., Parsons, H., Scott, J., Bhui, K. & Weich, S. 2016. Rates of voluntary and compulsory psychiatric in-patient treatment in England: An ecological study investigating associations with deprivation and demographics. *The British Journal of Psychiatry*, 209(2), 157–161.

Khan, R. Q. & Khan, A. M. 2020. Crime and punishment: Pakistan's legal failure to account for mental illness. *BJPsych International*, 18(4), 94–6.

Kim, S. Y., De Vries, R. G. & Peteet, J. R. 2016. Euthanasia and assisted suicide of patients with psychiatric disorders in the Netherlands 2011 to 2014. *JAMA Psychiatry*, 73(4), 362–368.

Kim, S. Y. H. & Lemmens, T. 2016. Should assisted dying for psychiatric disorders be legalized in Canada? *CMAJ*, 188, E337–E339.

Kirby, J. 2022. MAiD expert panel recommendations are inadequate, contends panel member who resigned. *The Hill Times*, 16/6/22.

Kirkey, S. 2022. Canadian doctors encouraged to bring up medically assisted death before their patients do. *National Post*.

Krieger, E., Moritz, S., Weil, R. & Nagel, M. 2018. Patients' attitudes towards and acceptance of coercion in psychiatry. *Psychiatry Research*, 260, 478–485.

L'euthanasie, C. F. D. C. E. D. É. D. 2022. EUTHANASIE – Chiffres de l'année 2021.

Larsen, I. B. & Terkelsen, T. B. 2014. Coercion in a locked psychiatric ward: Perspectives of patients and staff. *Nursing Ethics*, 21(4), 426–436.

Lee, J. A. P. 2022a. 'Toxic culture' of abuse at mental health hospital revealed by BBC secret filming.

Lee, M. 2022b. Canadian soldier with PTSD 'outraged' when VA suggested euthanasia. *The New York Post*, 22/8/22.

Lemmens, T. 2018. Charter scrutiny of Canada's medical assistance in dying law and the shifting landscape of Belgian and Dutch euthanasia practice. *Supreme Court Law Review* (2nd Series), 85, 459–544.

Lublóy, Á., Keresztúri, J. L., Németh, A. & Mihalicza, P. 2020. Exploring factors of diagnostic delay for patients with bipolar disorder: A population-based cohort study. *BMC Psychiatry*, 20(1), 75.

Marshall, P. & Gómez Yuri, H. 2022. Advance directives in mental health and the revocation problem. *Acta Bioethica*, 28(2), 205–214.

McSherry, B. 2023. Interdisciplinary collaboration in the mental health sector: The role of the law. In Kelly, B. D. and Donnelly, M. (eds.) *Routledge Handbook of Mental Health Law*. London: Routledge.

Mensah, M., Lucy, O.-N. & Shim, R. S. 2021. Racism and mental health equity: History repeating itself. *Psychiatric Services*, 72(9), 1091–1094.

Miller, D. G., Dresser, R. & Kim, S. Y. H. 2019. Advance euthanasia directives: A controversial case and its ethical implications. *Journal of Medical Ethics*, 45(2), 84–89.

Miller, J. N. & Black, D. W. 2020. Bipolar disorder and suicide: A review. *Current Psychiatry Reports*, 22(2), 6-020-1130-0.

Mishara, B. L. & Weisstub, D. N. 2016. The legal status of suicide: A global review. *International Journal of Law and Psychiatry*, 44, 54–74.

Mulligan, C. & Bond, M. 2022. Ethics of medically-assisted death questioned as some turn to it as an alternative to poverty. Available at https://toronto.citynews.ca/2022/10/14/ethics-medically-assisted-death-maid/ (Accessed 22/10/22)

Naudts, K., Ducatelle, C., Kovacs, J., Laurens, K., Van Den Eynde, F. & Van Heeringen, C. 2006. Euthanasia: The role of the psychiatrist. *British Journal of Psychiatry*, 188, 405–409.

Nichols, G. N. T. 2020. *The Tragic Euthanasia Death of Alan Nichols* [Online]. Canada. Available: https://actionlife.org/life-issues/euthanasia/item/944-the-tragic-euthanasia-death-of-alan-nichols [Accessed 14/11/22].

Nicolini, M. E., Jardas, E. J., Zarate, C. A., Gastmans, C. & Kim, S. Y. H. 2022. Irremediability in psychiatric euthanasia: Examining the objective standard. *Psychological Medicine*, 1–19.

Nicolini, M. E., Peteet, J. R., Donovan, G. K. & Kim, S. Y. H. 2020. Euthanasia and assisted suicide of persons with psychiatric disorders: The challenge of personality disorders. *Psychological Medicine*, 50(4), 575–582.

Okai, D., Owen, G., Mcguire, H., Singh, S., Churchill, R. & Hotopf, M. 2007. Mental capacity in psychiatric patients: Systematic review. *The British Journal of Psychiatry*, 191, 291–297.

O'Loughlin, A. 2023. Personality disorder in mental health law and criminal law. In Kelly, B. D. and Donnelly, M. (eds.) *Routledge Handbook of Mental Health Law*. London: Routledge.

Paksarian, D., Ramin, M., Kotov, R., Cullen, B., Nugent, K. L., Bromet, E. J. 2014. Perceived trauma during hospitalization and treatment participation among individuals with psychotic disorders. *Psychiatric Services*, 65(2), 266–269.

Pathare, S., Shields, L., Nardodkar, R., Narasimhan, L. & Bunders, J. 2015. What do service users want? A content analysis of what users may write in psychiatric advance directives in India. *Asian Journal of Psychiatry*, 14, 52–56.

Peay, J. 2023. Mental illness and criminal law: Irreconcilable bedfellows? In Kelly, B. D. and Donnelly, M. (eds.) *Routledge Handbook of Mental Health Law*. London: Routledge.

Plunkett, R. & Kelly, B. D. 2021. Dignity: The elephant in the room in psychiatric inpatient care? A systematic review and thematic synthesis. *International Journal of Law and Psychiatry*, 75, 101672.

Ruck Keene, A. & Reidy, K. 2023. Decision-making capacity in mental health law. In Kelly, B. D. and Donnelly, M. (eds.) *Routledge Handbook of Mental Health Law*. London: Routledge.

Scott, J. & Leboyer, M. 2011. Consequences of delayed diagnosis of bipolar disorders. *L'Encephale*, 37(Suppl 3), S173–S175.

Starson v Swayze (2003) SCC 32

Stephenson, L., Gergel, T., Ruck Keene, A., Rifkin, L. & Owen, G. 2022. Preparing for Mental Health Act reform: Pilot study of co-produced implementation strategies for advance choice documents [version 1; peer review: 2 approved]. *Wellcome Open Research*, 7.

Stephenson, L. A., Gergel, T., Ruck Keene, A., Rifkin, L. & Owen, G. 2020. The PACT advance decision-making template: Preparing for Mental Health Act reforms with co-production, focus groups and consultation. *International Journal of Law and Psychiatry*, 71, 101563.

Subramanya, R. 2022. Scheduled to die: The rise of Canada's assisted suicide program. *Common Sense*. Canada.

Szmukler, G. 2017. *Men in White Coats - Treatment under Coercion*. OUP.

Thomson, A. B., Eales, S., Mcallister, E. & Molodynski, A. 2022. Criminal sanctions for suicidality in the 21st Century UK. *The British Journal of Psychiatry*, 221, 653–654.

The Lancet. 2014. Suicide in India: From criminalisation to compassion. *The Lancet*, 384(9961), 2174.

The Lancet. 2020. *The Lancet Global Burden of Disease (GBD) 2019* [Online]. Available: https://www.thelancet.com/gbd#2019GBDIssue [Accessed 9/11/22].

The Lancet. 2022a. Can we end stigma and discrimination in mental health? *The Lancet*, 400(10361), 1381.

The Lancet. 2022b. *Launch of the Lancet Commission Report on Ending Stigma and Discrmination in Mental Health* [Online]. Available: https://unitedgmh.org/knowledge-hub/lancet-commission-launch-ending-stigma-and-discrimination-in-mental-health/ [Accessed 9/11/22].

UGMH. 2021. *Decriminalising suicide: Saving lives, reducing stigma*. United for Global Mental Health.

United Nations. 1948. Universal declaration of human rights.

Valenti, E., Giacco, D., Katasakou, C. & Priebe, S. 2014. Which values are important for patients during involuntary treatment? A qualitative study with psychiatric inpatients. *Journal of Medical Ethics*, 40(12), 832–836.

Van Veen, S. M. P., Ruissen, A. M., Beekman, A. T. F., Evans, N. & Widdershoven, G. A. M. 2022. Establishing irremediable psychiatric suffering in the context of medical assistance in dying in the Netherlands: A qualitative study. *Canadian Medical Association Journal*, 194(13), E485–E491.

Veale, D. et al. 2022. No safety withouth emotional safety. *The Lancet Psychiatry*, 10(1), 65–70.

Venkataramu, V. N., Vajawat, B., Raghuraman, B. S. & Chaturvedi, S. K. 2021. Cultural competency training for psychiatry residents and mental health professionals: A systematic review. *International Journal of Social Psychiatry*, 67(7), 833–839.

Verhofstadt, M., Chambaere, K., Leontjevas, R. & Peters, G.-J. Y. 2019a. Towards an assessment instrument for suffering in patients with psychiatric conditions: Assessing cognitive validity. *BJPsych Open*, 5(3), e35.

Verhofstadt, M., Thienpont, L. & Peters, G.-J. Y. 2017. When unbearable suffering incites psychiatric patients to request euthanasia: Qualitative study. *British Journal of Psychiatry*, 211(4), 238–245.

Verhofstadt, M., Van Assche, K., Sterckx, S., Audenaert, K. & Chambaere, K. 2019b. Psychiatric patients requesting euthanasia: Guidelines for sound clinical and ethical decision making.

Webster, P. 2022. Worries grow about medically assisted dying in Canada. *The Lancet*, 400(10355), 801–802.

Wellcome. *Wellcome's vision and strategy* [Online]. Available: https://wellcome.org/who-we-are/strategy [Accessed 12/11/22].

Weller, P. 2023. Mental health laws and older adults. In Kelly, B. D. and Donnelly, M. (eds.) *Routledge Handbook of Mental Health Law*. London: Routledge.

Whitelaw, S., Lemmens, T. & Van Spall, H. G. C. 2022. The expansion of medical assistance in dying in the COVID-19 pandemic era and beyond: Implications for vulnerable Canadians. *Canadian Journal of General Internal Medicine*, 17(2), 17–21.

Wilson, K. 2023. The future of mental health law: Abolition or reform? In Kelly, B. D. and Donnelly, M. (eds.) *Routledge Handbook of Mental Health Law*. London: Routledge.

Wu, K. C.-C., Cai, Z., Chang, Q., Chang, S.-S., Yip, P. S. F. & Chen, Y.-Y. 2022. Criminalisation of suicide and suicide rates: An ecological study of 171 countries in the world. *BMJ Open*, 12(2), e049425.

INDEX

Note: Page numbers in *italics* indicate figures, **bold** indicates tables, and references following "n" refer to notes.

Additional Protocol to the Oviedo Convention 111–14, 115
adjustment disorder 267–8, 416
adult safeguarding 194–5, 207, 561; Care Act 2014 198–200; in England and Wales 197–202, *197*; historical developments 197–8; inherent jurisdiction 201–2; law in practice 202–7; legislation in England *197*; Mental Capacity Act 2005 200–1
Adults with Incapacity (Scotland) Act 2000 (AWIA) 166, 168–9, 171–2
advance decision-making (ADM) 721; in Australia 710; for autonomy 710–11; in Chile 710; in England and Wales 331–2, 710; hospitalisation and 710; in India 710–11; in mental health 710–11; in the Netherlands 710; in Peru 710
advance directives 28, 130–1, 133, 429, 473, 578–9, 631, 637, 642, 697; in Argentina 474; in Ghana 490; in India 545, 549–50; medical powers of 186; psychiatric 710; requesting euthanasia 720
Africa 21, 477, 479, 706; African Charter on Human and Peoples' Rights (*see* African Charter on Human and Peoples' Rights); dignity in 461–3; human rights standards 461–2; mental health law reform in 459–74; right to liberty in 461–2; substitute decision-making in 460, 464, 470–1, 473; *see also* Kenya; Uganda; Zambia
African Charter on Human and Peoples' Rights 461–2, 495; interpretation of 462–5; Protocol to the African Charter on Human and Peoples' Rights on the Rights of Women in Africa 463–5; rights in 462; violation of 464
African Charter on the Rights and Welfare of the Child 462, 495
African Disability Protocol 474; CRPD *vs.* 463–4, 466; Implementation and interpretation of 465; origins and evolution 463
Algeria 459n1
Americans with Disabilities Act (ADA) of 1990 406
anti-social personality disorder (ASPD) 235, 255, 258, 715
Anttila, M. 138
Appelbaum, B. C. 289
Appelbaum, P. S. 126, 289
Argentina 584; 2012 Gender Recognition Law 224; advance directives in 474; care of people with mental disorders 607; community-oriented service in 602–4; decision-making support in health and mental health law 577–9; dignity in 599; documents 589, **590–1, 600**; equality in 574; involuntary hospitalisation in 580–3; judicial and administrative safeguards in 581–2, **582**; legal capacity reforms in 576–7; legal reforms in **572**; mental health legislation in 573–5, **575**; psychiatric hospitalization 604; recognition of rights in 599–602
Argentinian Gender Identity Law (2012) 219
Aristotelian tragedy 448–52
Arnardottir, O.M. 102

Index

Ashley, F. 220
Ashworth, A. 255, 256
Assisted Decision-Making (Capacity) Act 2015 (Ireland) 188
assorted personality disorder 255
asylums 17, 31, 34, 42, 196, 357, 422, 573, 583; in England 18, 21–2; in Germany 19; in Ghana 478–9; in India 529, 541; in Ireland 20–1; in Italy 23; in Pakistan 531; in Sri Lanka 533–4
attention-deficit hyperactivity disorder 89
Australia 49, 239, 288, 345, 356, 405, 621; 2021 Royal Commission 377; advance decision-making in 710; Institute of Health and Welfare 694; lack of consultation with parents 695; older adults in 183–4; OPCAT monitoring in 39–40; prescriptions for antipsychotic medication 181; responses to CRPD 117, 511; videoconferencing in 651
Austria 117; involuntary psychiatric hospitalization in 288, 289
autism spectrum disorders 257n1, 439–40, 443, 447, 452, 645, 685n2, 716; in children 159; in England and Wales 174, 203; in Ireland 174; medicalisation of 443–4; in Norway 259–60; and personality disorder 257; in Scotland 168, 170–1, 174–5; trans men with 226
autonomy 25–6, 28, 39, 41, 48, 58, 59–62, 126, 154, 207, 255, 294, 336, 425, 441, 635, 705, 721; advance decision-making for 710–11; bodily of 225; in China 513, 515, 516; co-production for 711; in CRPD 689–91, 694–8; decisional 545–7, 550; dominant models of legislation 58; in England and Wales 117; enhancing 708; environmental factors, unintended consequences, and omissions for 711–13; fusion for 708–9; in Ghana 482; in Greece 139; independent 187; in India 529–31, 540, 542–3, 545–7, 550–1; loss of 182–3; in Northern Ireland 556, 561–2, 574–5, 577–8; older adults 181–90; overriding 64; personal 90–3, 287, 396; precedent 710; professional 71, 272, 618; promotion of 70n45, 72; protection of 90–3, 96–7; rational 187; relational 187–8, 424, 430, 515; respecting 59, 73–4; restoring 75; risks abusing 717; in Scotland 167–75; social 187; in South Africa 497, 504, 506; supported 76; trans persons 213, 215, 220, 222–3, 225–6, 228

Bagenstos, S. 417
Bailey, D. 618
Bangladesh 527, 528; abuse in 536–7; mental health legislation in 535–7
Bartlett, P. 62, 64, 94, 103

Basaglia, F. 22–3
Basaglia Law 23
Beck, U. 4
Belgium: euthanasia-assisted suicide in 716; gender recognition in 224, 227; involuntary psychiatric hospitalization in 289; mental illness in 719–21; official languages 87; physician-assisted suicide in 715–16, 718–21
beneficence, principle of 64, 73, 379, 439
Benjamin, H. 214
best interests 25, 28, 57, 65–8, 71–4, 106, 257, 290, 300, 329, 331–2, 335–6, 339, 389, 429, 469; advantage of 697; best interpretation of 59n9; in case law under the Human Rights Act (1998) 65n28; of children 150–2, 153–5, 162; decision-making 206; in England and Wales 65; in India 550; in Northern Ireland 558, 564–8; objective and subjective 186; trans persons 221, 227
Bhore Committee (1946) (India) 541
Bickenbach, J. 698
biopsychosocial model of health care 619, 706, 718
Black Lives Matter (BLM) movement 638–9, 642–3
Blandford, G. F. 21–2
Bolam test 66–7, 71–2
Bold, N. D. 126–7, 133
Bolivia: document 589; gender recognition in 224; recognition of rights in 601, 602
borderline personality disorder (BPD) 235–6, 255
Bracken, P. 619–20
Bradley, E. 205
Braithwaite, J. 431
Braye, S. 202
Brazil 588, 609; care of people with mental disorders in 607–8; community-oriented service in 602–4; documents 489, **591–6**, **600**; financing of mental health in 605; gender recognition in 224; programs for well-being and promotion of rights in 606, 607; psychiatric hospitalization 604–5; recognition of rights in 599, 602
British Social Model of Disability 687
Brock, D. 646
Bulgaria: abuse and ill–treatment in mental health hospitals 193; responses to CRPD 113; violation of human rights in 669

Cahalan, S. 262
Cairns, R. 289
Callaghan, S. M. 59
Callard, F. 618
Cambridge, P. 195
Campbell, A. 112

Index

Canada 511, 620, 625, 709, 715; compulsory community treatment in 356, 361; euthanasia-assisted suicide in 716–17; medical assistance in dying in 715–17, 719; physician-assisted suicide in 715–17; reliance on police 695; reservations and declarations by 117; responses to CPRD 117; right to refuse unwanted medical treatment 185
Care Act 2014 (England) 196, *197*, 197n4, 198–200, 203, 206–7
Care Quality Commission (CQC) 38, 42, 331, 651; duty to monitor 45; functions of 35; as member of UK National Preventive Mechanism 35–6, 48–9; mental health monitoring and human rights 44–50; on OPCAT 50; protecting and promoting human rights standards 47–50; regulating standards of health and social care 43–4; SPT guidelines for NPMs 45–6
Carney, G. 182
Carr, S. 660
Carta, M. G. 140–2
Cascardi, M. 289
Cech, T. 618
Charlton, J. 619
children 21, 42, 66, 102, 109, 149–50, 162–3, 168, 221, 421, 670–2; African Charter on 462; with attention-deficit hyperactivity disorder 89; autism in 159; best interests and the evolving capacities of 150–2, 153–5, 162; in China 520; in Colombia 574; decision-making in mental health care 150–5; deprivation of liberty 156–62; in England and Wales 150, 154, 162–3; in Ghana 479, 483; hospitalisation 155; in India 544, 551; informed consent in psychiatric genomics 438–53; inpatient psychiatric care 155; institutional care 156–7; learning disability and 159; legal capacity *vs.* decisional capacity 154–5; mental capacity in 151, 154–5; non-consensual care, mental health and rights 152–4; in Northern Ireland 569; in Peru 578; right to liberty 156; safeguarding 194, 206; sexual violence on 265, 312–13; in South Africa 494, 495; in South American Countries 588–9, 601; trans children 214, 227; trauma 201, 313–15, 317, 319–20, 618
Chile 584, 588; abuse in 141; advance decision-making in 710; documents 589, **596–7, 600**; financing of mental health in 605, 606; involuntary hospitalisation in 580–3; judicial and administrative safeguards in 581, **582**; legal capacity reforms in 577; legal reforms in **572**; mental health legislation in 573, 575, **575**; psychiatric hospitalization in 604; QualityRights research in **136**, 140–1; recognition of rights in 599–602

Chilean Criminal Procedure Code (2000) 583
China 511–15, 707; abuse in 515, 520; autonomy in 513, 515, 516; care homes or welfare institutions in 195; children in 520; coercion in 513, 517, 524; CRPD Committee 511; demonic possession and disturbances to cosmic forces in 18; Japan invaded 512; mental health law reform in 511–24; right to liberty in 522; suicide in 521–2; *see also* Mental Health Law 2013 (China)
cisgender 222, 225–6, 549
coercion 26, 41, 64, 75, 87, 107–9, 113–19, 133–4, 201–2, 308, 378, 390–9, 426, 429, 433–4, 645, 653–4, 692, 696, 706–8; abolishing 287; avoiding 126, 130–1; benefits and risks associated with 65, 65n26; in China 513, 517, 524; coercive care 59–61, 88, 95–7; coercive psychiatry 96–7; in Colombia 574; eliminating 469–70; in Finland 138; personality disorder and 243, 249; in Peru 584; psychiatric 576; psychological 275; in Scotland 175; in South Africa 506; in Tunisia 140
cognitive-behaviour therapy (CBT) 19
Colombia 224, 584, 589, **597**; children in 574; coercion in 574; decision-making support in 578–9; documents **597, 600**; gender recognition in 224; involuntary hospitalisation in 580; legal capacity reforms in 576–7; legal reforms in **572**; mental health legislation 574–5, **575**; recognition of rights in 599, 601, 602; substitute decision-making in 576
colonization 527; British 533; *see also* Bangladesh; India; Pakistan; Sri Lanka
Colorado, harm in 344–5
Columbia, harm in 344
Committee on Bioethics 97, 111–14, 707
Committee on the Rights of the Child (CCRC) 150, 157, 162
Committee on the Rights of Persons with Disabilities (CRPD Committee) 39, 51, 101, 150–1; anti-discrimination laws 104; China and 511; in England and Wales 117–18; implications of CRPD's human rights 105–6; interpretation of CRPD 95, 97, 105–18, 153, 156; legal capacity 153–4; medical necessity doctrine, use of 41; South Africa's report to 497; view on abolishing institutionalisation 47
community-oriented service 599; in Argentina 602–4; in Brazil 602–4; in Peru 602–4
Community Treatment Order (CTO) 244, 356–7, 379, 428, 647, 651; advanced for use of 359–61; criteria for measuring success of 367–9; criteria for a person's placement on 361–2; enactment of 357–8; enforce compliance, powers to 363–4; legal structure of regime 358–9; UK Supreme Court and 365–7

729

compulsory community treatment 356–7, 365; deinstitutionalisation, legal response to 357–8; powers to 'enforce compliance' with conditions of community care 363–4; *see also* Community Treatment Order (CTO)
compulsory hospitalisation 85, 93–5, 97, 359
concertina effect 206
co-production: for autonomy 711; in England and Wales 711; in India 711; mental health law and 711; in Northern Ireland 711
coronavirus pandemic 174, 195, 405, 504, 638, 647–51, 653, 665, 677–8, 687; Disability Rights Monitor Report in 2020 on 42; global failures of response 181; health and social care related to 556; and persons with 172–3; Scottish measures 172
Cote, A. 379
Council of Europe Commissioner for Human Rights 114–15, 218
Council of Europe Committee on Bioethics 707
Craigie, J. 689
criminal law 200, 233–4, 238–9, 360, 583, 621, 666; forensic psychology and 272, 277–9, 281, 282; impact of Act 846 on 483–6; insanity for 257, 258, 259; international 306–7, 315, 321–2; mental illness and 255–7, 263–9; personality disorder and 246–8; and psychiatric expertise 262
Criminal and Other Offences Act (1960) 482, 484, 485
Cultural Revolution (1966–1976) 512
Curley, A. 290
Czech Republic 117, **137**, 142

Davidson, L. 474
Davies, W. 266
Dawson, J. 516, 558
Daya, I. 620
de Bhailis, C. 106
decision-making 73n57, 200–1, 205, 263–4, 268, 413, 503, 513, 522–4, 676; ability 557–8, 569; advance 637, 710–11, 721; arrangements 184; assisted 354, 497, 499; automated 380; balanced 74; best interests 206; in children's mental health care 150–5; clinical 72–3; collaborative 220; competent and incompetent 93; detention and treatment 515–20; forensic experts 293; health care 493, 495–7, 499, 698; holistic approach to 66; impairment 107, 393, 398, 494, 497, 545, 562, 706; incapacity 561; individual participation in 699; investment 296; legal capacity vs. decisional capacity 154–5; medical 67, 685; medical model of 67; with older adults 182–3; ownership over 73n57; parental 151–2, 159–63; persons with disabilities in 46; political 610; powers of State 156; psychiatric 263; qualified 25; in relation to involuntary treatment 65; rights of persons 101–2; shared 213, 220, 228, 538; to socio-economic disadvantage 376; substitute (*see* substitute decision-making); supported (*see* supported decision-making); third party 511; treatment 505, 569; unidimensional 56
decision-making capacity (DMC) 62, 68–70, 91, 106, 118, 285, 290, 327–40, 327–8, 342, 499, 631, 705, 720; -based mental health law 709; in England and Wales 328–33; in Ireland 333–40; older adults 185
Declaration of Alma Ata (1978) (India) 541
Degener, T. 104–5
Denmark: gender recognition in 224; involuntary psychiatric hospitalization in 289
Department of Health and Social Care (2021) 650
deprivation of liberty 26, 44, 59, 85, 91–2, 101, 108, 116, 163, 466, 518, 520, 669, 672; arbitrary, protection against 83–4; ban on 110, 156; of children 156–62; and children's institutional care 156–7; CRPD's position on mental health laws 105; dignity and 87; under ECHR 157–9; elimination of mechanisms of 108; in Germany 158; impact of 46; interpretation of 150; justifying 95, 107, 395, 464; lawfulness of 242; limiting 395; MCA 2005 and 329; national approach 159–61; in Northern Ireland 566–8, 570; OPCAT affirming 38–9; relevance of consent 161–2; right to liberty and 156; on treaty bodies and experts on 47; unlawful 41, 87; wrongful 57
Deprivation of Liberty safeguards (DoLS) 35–6, 44–6, 48, 390, 561, 565
Devitt, P. 75
Dhanda, A. 58, 106
digitise mental health legislation 645–7; digital platforms 647–8; electronic communication of statutory form 648–9; in England and Wales 645–60; governing sociotechnical systems in the public interest 658–60; safety and accountability 655–6; Serenity Integrated Mentoring 656–8; videocall assessments 649–50; videoconferencing 650–3
dignity 28, 31, 48, 58, 67, 90, 97, 170, 311, 337, 339, 424, 697–9; in Africa 461–3; in Argentina 599; concerns about 46; in CRPD 105, 111, 689–91, 705, 708; deprivations of liberty and 87; inherent 39, 335, 385, 461, 672, 689–90; interpretive compass of 686; lack of 690; learning disability and 170, 173; loss of 41, 65, 695; older adults 181–3, 185, 188–90; personality disorder and 243; privacy and 46; protection of 96, 97, 385, 397, 670; respect for 40, 44, 96, 97; of risk 441, 442;

safeguarding 669; in South Africa 498, 500, 504; trans persons 216, 225; violating 26, 411
diminished responsibility 256, 258; defence of 257n1; in England and Wales 261–2, 267–8; to personality disorder 247
Disability Adjusted Life Years (DALYs) 705
disabled person's organisations (DPOs) 102, 118
discrimination 403, 416–17, 686–9, 704–5, 721; analysis 95–7; anticipated 405–6, 416; anti-discrimination 26, 104, 372, 406–7, 413, 416–18, 540, 548–9; direct 409–10, 417; disability discrimination law 406–9; experienced 405–6, 416; gender 180; harassment 411; indirect 410–11; inherent 339; in Ireland 409, 417; in Kenya 405; need to engage in analysis 95–7; prohibition of 409–13; reasonable accommodation 411–12; social and labour 215; trans person 225–7; against women 462; workplace 406; *see also* non-discrimination
Donnelly, M. 68, 722
Draft Mental Health Act June 2007 (Sri Lanka) 534–5
Draft Mental Health Bill 2022 (England and Wales) 118, 429
Drew, N. 126
dual-role transvestism 214
Duffy, R. 486
Dworkin, R. 688–9

Ebuenyi, I. 405
Ecuador: care of people with mental disorders in 607, 608; documents 589, **597**, **600**; recognition of rights in 601–2
Edan, V. 620
Egypt **136**; abuse in 139; QualityRights research in 138–9
elderly *see* older adults
electro-convulsive therapy (ECT) 19, 39, 335
Ely Hospital inquiry 196
employment law 403–4, 418, 621; inclusive and safe working environment 415–16; mental health and labour market 404–6; promoting inclusion in labour market 414–15
Encalada, A.V. 118
England and Wales 18, 20, 34–6, 42–4, 49, 56n4, 64, 193–4, 256, 273, 275, 339, 362, 368, 561, 648–9; abuse, neglect, and mental health in 194–7; adult safeguarding in 197–202, *197*; advance decision-making in 710; African jurisdictions and 460; asylums in 18, 21–2; autism spectrum disorders in 203; autonomy in 117; best interests in 65; Care Act 2014 198–200; care of people with mental disorders in 65; children in 150, 154, 162–3; children's mental health care in 150, 154, 162–3; Code of Practice 330; co-production in 711; CRPD and 117–18; CRPD Committee in 117–18; decision-making capacity in 339; digitise mental health legislation in 645–60; diminished responsibility in 261–2, 267–8; Draft Mental Health Bill 2022 429; frameworks in practice 330–3; *Hallstrom* case 358; harm in 343; historical developments 197–8; human rights frameworks in 36–40; ill-treatment in 42–3, 46–7, 49–51; Independent Review of the Mental Health Act 390, 709, 712–13; inherent jurisdiction 201–2; insanity defences in 257–9; involuntary pharmacological treatment in 64; involuntary psychiatric hospitalization in 289; justification of involuntary treatment in 61–2; law in practice 202–7; learning disability in 42, 49, 174, 193–6, 200, 203, 205, 258; legal framework in 203, 207; mental disability and ill-treatment 40–2; mental health monitoring in 34–51; mental health trusts and police forces in 657; mental impairment in 65; M'Naghten Rules in 259; NHS services in 205, 655; older adults in 185–6; personality disorder in 239, 249; role of legislation in 21–2; Serenity Integrated Mentoring in 656–8; statutory frameworks 328–30; videocall assessments for authorising detention 650–1, 654; videoconferencing in 651; Wessely Review 429; *see also* Care Quality Commission (CQC)
English and Welsh Mental Health Act (Wessely Review) 174, 233, 243–6, 428, 429
equality 26, 48, 373, 413, 425–6, 641, 672, 697–9, 712; in Argentina 574; in CRPD 104, 107, 109, 166, 686, 689, 691–4; de facto 414; formal 58, 375, 692, 693; frameworks 47; gender 223; inclusive 105, 692–3; in India 546, 548; before the law 153; between mental and physical health 708; with non-disabled norm 693; in Northern Ireland 562–3; of opportunity 705; of outcome 58; persons with learning disabilities 167, 172, 174; risks abusing 717; role of law in 376; in Scotland 167, 172, 174; socio-economic 378–80; in South Africa 496, 504–5; substantive 375, 692, 698; transformative 692
ethics and law in mental healthcare: best interests 65–8; clinical ethics 56, 74–5, 637; clinical practice 71–6; coercive care 59–61; Convention on the Rights of Persons with Disabilities 58–9; ethical excellence 55; ethical losses 64–5; evolution of mental health law 56–8; insight 68–70; involuntary pharmacological treatment 63–4; involuntary treatment, justification of 61–2; in mental health law 721; risk to self or to others 70–1

731

European Committee for the Prevention of Torture, Inhuman and Degrading Treatment or Punishment (CPT) 37, 50, 86, 193
European Convention on Human Rights (ECHR) 3, 27, 37, 57, 115, 150, 167, 204, 242, 365, 408, 560; and CRPD 110–11; deprivation of liberty under 157–9; into domestic law 327; gender recognition in 222; learning disabilities and 167, 171; medical paternalism and 57; procedural requirements of 328; right to liberty by 83
European Court of Human Rights (ECtHR) 27, 40–1, 47, 57, 112–13, 150, 152, 160, 163, 222, 228, 240, 408, 411, 416; and CRPD 110–11; deprivation of liberty under 157–62; discrimination analysis 95–7; jurisprudence 156–7, 224–5; personal autonomy 90–3; protection against arbitrary deprivation of liberty 83–4; protection against inhuman and degrading treatment 87–90; stricter scrutiny 94; third-party intervention in 115; *Winterwerp* criteria 84–7
European Network of (Ex-)Users and Survivors of Psychiatry (ENUSP) 112, 126
European Society for Sexual Medicine 220
euthanasia 687, 705, 713–15; advance directives and 720; passive 549; problems and challenges facing 717–21
euthanasia-assisted suicide (EAS): in Belgium 716; in Canada 716–17; in the Netherlands 716, 719–21

Fallon-Kund, M. 698
family in mental health 421–2, 430–4; in contemporary context 425–7; and distributional equity 377; in Ireland 425; mental health law in 421–34; Nearest Relative framework 427–9; relationality, recognising 423–5; traditional model, reforming 429–30; views in mental illness 422–3
Fanneran, T. 205
Farrell, M. 617
Faulkner-Gurstein, R. 659
Favalli, S. 110–11
Fawzy, E. 138, 141, 142
Fennell, P. 34, 67–8
Finland 137; coercion in 138; involuntary psychiatric hospitalization in 289; QualityRights research in 138
Fitton, E. 69
Fitzgerald, D. 618
Florida 653; harm in 345
Flynn, E. 106
forensic psychiatry 87, 88, 245, 266, 272, 485, 573; assessments of criminal responsibility 291–4; assigned professional roles 275–7; conducting evaluation 273–4; conveying ethical obligations 279–82, 285; criminal law and 272, 277–9, 281, 282; forensic care 360; malingering 277–8; strive to keep errors 278–9
Foss, D. 205
Foster, C. 72–3
France: French language 86; gender recognition in 224; involuntary psychiatric hospitalization in 289
FREDA Principles 48
Fredman, S. 692
Freeman, M.C. 103, 116, 126
French, P. 104
Friedman, M. 180
Frodeman, R. 619
Fromm, E. 374
Funk, M. 126–7, 133

gender dysphoria 213–18, 220, 223–4, 226–8
gender identity 212, 216–19, 223, 397, 549; assessment of 220, 226; declaration of 222; disorder 213, 214–15, 223–8; disorder of childhood 214; non-binary 215; other disorders 214; through medical treatment 214; unspecified 214
gender recognition 213, 216, 219, 228; abusive requirements in 222–3; in Belgium 224, 227; in Bolivia 224; in Brazil 224; in Colombia 224; in Denmark 224; in European Convention on Human Rights 222; in France 224; in Greece 224; in Iceland 224; in Luxembourg 224; in Malta 224; to minors in Ireland 227; in Norway 224; pathologising procedures for 223–5; in Portugal 224, 227; progress vs. stagnation 224–5; in Switzerland 224; in the UK 224; in Uruguay 228
Gender Recognition Act 2004 (UK) 224
Gender Recognition Law 2012 (Argentina) 224
Georgia 117, 345
Germany 117; asylums in 19; constitutional bans on coercion in 696; deprivation of liberty in 158; German language 86–7; involuntary psychiatric hospitalization in 289
Ghana 376, 461, 489–90; abuse in 477, 480, 486–8, 490; advance directives in 490; asylums in 478–9; autonomy in 482; children in 479, 483; Criminal and Other Offences Act (1960) 482, 484, 485; mental health care in 478–80; mental health law in 477–90; new legislation for mental health 480; prayer camps 461n3, 477–8; right to liberty in 482; suicide in 485; *see also* Mental Health Act 2012 (Ghana)
Gjerberg, E. 75
Goldstein, A.M. 279
Gooding, P. 106–7, 376

Index

Gostin, L. 57
Great Leap Forward (1958–1960) 512
Greece **136**; autonomy in 139; gender recognition in 224; humours, idea of 18; involuntary psychiatric hospitalization in 289; QualityRights research in 139–40
Grey, M. 182
Grisso, T. 279, 289
Groning, L. 260–1
Guardianship and Administration Act 2019 (Victoria) 187
Guardianship law 621
Guidry-Grimes, L. 69–70
Guilloud, D. 706–7
Gurbai, S. 69

Hale, B. 339
Hale, L. 2
Hall, M. 185
Hallstrom case 358
Hamilton, M. 623
harm 342; base rates and prediction of 350–2; in Colorado 344–5; in Columbia 344; criteria 343–5, 353–4; in England and Wales 343; false negatives 352–3; false positives 352; in Florida 345; in New South Wales 343–4; in Ontario 344; to others 4, 343, 568; risk assessment for 346–7; in Scotland 343; true negatives 353; true positives 352; *see also* self-harming behaviour; suicide
Harrison, F. 183–4
Heilbrun, K. 279
Hem, M. H. 75
Henderson, C. 407
Herring, J. 185, 188
highest attainable standard of health 108–10, 130, 374, 386, 431, 434, 544, 621, 668, 688; international law and Constitution 494–7; legislative and policy framework 497–507; in Scotland 171, 173; in South Africa 493–507; in trans persons 217, 221
Hippocratic theory 18
Hirschfeld, M. 213
Hoare, F. 486
Hoekstra, E. 414
Hollingsworth, E. J. 624
Hollingsworth, R. 624
hospitalisation 247, 502–3; abuse of 581–2; advance decision-making and 710; children 155; clinical standards on 575; compulsory 85, 93–5, 97, 359; counter-therapeutic 346; criteria for 531–2; against individual's will 91; involuntary (*see* involuntary hospitalization); judicial 583; procedure of 522; psychiatric 583; refusal of 89, 91–2, 517, 523; rehospitalisation 360; risk of 63n23

Hostiuc, S. 290
Hughes, D. 270
Hughes, K. 195
Human Rights Act 1998 (HRA) 37, 65, 167, 198, 206
Human Services (Complex Needs) Act 2009 (Vic) 622
humours, idea of 18
Husum, T. L. 75

Iceland, gender recognition in 224
ill-treatment 42, 90, 196, 198; in England and Wales 42–3, 46–7, 49–51; mental disability and 40–2; preventing 36–8, 50; *see also* abuse and neglect
impaired decision-making (mental) capacity 154, 168, 393, 398, 497, 545, 562, 568, 706
Independent Review of Learning Disability and Autism in the Mental Health Act (Rome Review) 168, 170–1, 174, 175
Independent Review of the Mental Health Act (England and Wales) 390, 709, 712–13
India 31, 124, 511, 707, 714; abuse in 530, 533, 542; advance decision-making in 710–11; advance directives in 545, 549–50; asylums in 529, 541; autonomy in 529–31, 540, 542–3, 545–7, 550–1; best interests in 550; children in 544, 551; co-production in 711; CRPD and 29, 529, 542–3; equality in 546, 548; legal capacity in 540, 542–3, 545–50; mental health law in 29–30, 529–31; model of pragmatic realisation 29; non-discrimination in 546; personality disorder in 530; QualityRights research in 135–7, **136**, 396–7; substitute decision-making in 530, 532–23, 546, 550; suicide in 531, 549; supported decision-making in 529, 547; *see also* Mental Health Care Act 2017 (India)
Indian Lunatic Asylum Act 529
Indian Psychiatric Society 529
informed consent 24–6, 38–40, 47, 109–10, 119, 213, 218–19, 299, 338, 530–2, 573; acquisition 294; ambivalence in families 445–8; Aristotelian tragedy 448–52; clinical standards on 575; conventional tools 442; exception to 389–90; free and 106, 109–10, 138, 157, 219, 224, 227, 493, 495, 497, 500–1, 503, 507, 511, 656, 673; implications for procedures 439, 442; improving decisional capacity to research 290–1; inclusion of decision-making support in 577–9; and involuntary admission and treatment 469–70; involuntary hospitalisation and 580, 582; limits of a human rights approach 441–5; mental capacity principles 184; older adults 179, 181–4, 188–90; for

733

passive euthanasia 549; in psychiatric genomics 438–53; psychiatric treatment in absence of 105; removal of requirement for 118; rules regulating 571, 574; scope and limitations of 181–4; in Sweden 221; temporary 546; trans persons 219–22, 224, 227, 228; to treatment/research in vulnerable populations 285–7, 289
inherent jurisdiction 155, *197*, 201–3, 205, 207
inpatient psychiatric care 92, 150; children 155, 161; in Northern Ireland 391
insanity 19, 21–2, 256, 264, 291, 294–5, 317, 484, 569; in American perspective 274–5; for criminal law 257, 258, 259; in England and Wales 257–9; in Norway 259–61; not guilty by reason of insanity 247
insight 68–70, 71, 368, 387, 445, 461, 468, 524, 550, 631, 633; assessments 69; bespoke 657; broadening 450; lack of 68n39, 69, 91, 690, 707; loss of 516; psychological or psychiatric 269; reduced 289
insulin coma therapy 19, 22
Intellectual Disability (Compulsory Care and Rehabilitation) Act 2003 175
Inter-American Court of Human Rights (IACtHR) 224, 225–6
interdisciplinary collaboration 629, 639–40, 642; advantages of 618–20; challenges to 620–1; defined 617–18; Human Services (Complex Needs) Act 2009 (Vic) 622; in mental health sector 617–18; role of law 621–5; and supported decision-making 619; Victorian Collaborative Centre for Mental Health and Wellbeing 624–5
International Covenant on Civil and Political Rights (ICCPR) 102
International Covenant on Economic, Social and Cultural Rights (ICESCR) 102
International Criminal Court (ICC) 306–7, 314, 321
international criminal law 306–7, 315, 321–2
International Disability Caucus (IDC) 102, 126
International Labour Office (ILO) 415
International Military Tribunal for the Far East in Tokyo (1946) 306
International Military Tribunal in Nuremberg (1945) 306
involuntary hospitalisation 85, 92, 97, 571–3, **572**, 577, 579–80, 584, 610; arbitrary or unnecessary 599; in Argentina 580–3; in Chile 580–3; in Colombia 118, 580, 581, 583; criteria in European countries *289*; duration of 581; healthcare policy to limit 62; judicial and administrative safeguards 581–2, **582**; measures 582; by order of criminal court 583; in Peru 118; requirements for 580–1; violation of 95–6; will and preferences of 582–3

involuntary psychiatric hospitalization: in Austria 288, 289; in Belgium 289; in Denmark 289; in England and Wales 289; in Finland 289; in France 289; in Germany 289; in Greece 289; in Ireland 289; in Italy 288, 289; in Luxembourg 289; in the Netherlands 289; in Portugal 289; in Sweden 289
involuntary psychiatric treatment 59n11; limiting 353; older adults 179; *see also* involuntary psychiatric hospitalization
Ireland 17, 29, 327, 339, 511; advance healthcare directives in 429; asylums in 20–1; autism spectrum disorders in 174; criteria for involuntary admission 30; decision-making capacity in 333–40; decision-making support in 336–7; declaration in relation to Articles 12 and 14 126; direct discrimination in 409, 417; early laws 20; family in contemporary context in 425; frameworks in practice in 336–8; gender recognition to minors in 224, 227; human rights in mental health legislation 27–8; involuntary psychiatric hospitalization in 289; learning disability and autism in 174; legislative developments in 31; mental health law in 28, 29–30, 333–40; personality disorder in 239; responses to CRPD 117; role of legislation in 20–1; statutory frameworks in 333–6; supported decision-making, levels of 188
Italy: asylums in 23; involuntary detention and treatment in 696; involuntary psychiatric hospitalization in 288, 289; role of legislation in 22–3

Japan, invasion of China 512
Jenkin, P. 43
Jiang, F. 521
judicial and administrative safeguards: in Chile 581, **582**

Kanter, A.S. 413, 117
Kayess, R. 104
Kelly, B. D. 75, 290, 408, 558, 708, 722
Kennedy, K. M. 72
Kenya **137**, 459; constitutional provisions in 465–6; disability-specific legislation in 466–8; discrimination in 405; involuntary admission and treatment in 470; mental health legislation in 460, 468–74; monitoring bodies in 471–2; monitoring and oversight 467; recognition of legal capacity in 468–9; rights of persons with disabilities 467; safeguards in 472; supported or substitute decision-making in 471; violations of rights in 467–8
Kingston, P. 205
Klein, J. T. 620
Klein, T. 621

Knight, F. 694–5
Kohn, N. 198
Kong, C. 204
Kraepelin, E. 18–19, 30
Kuwait 117

labour market 376, 403–4, 416; due to impairment 406; inclusive and safe working environment 415–16; mental health and labour market 404–6; promoting inclusion in 414–15
Lancet Commission 704
Lansdown, G. 154
Lantta, T. 138
Latin American jurisdictions *see specific countries*
Lawson, A. 40
learning disability 166–7, 175n1, 265, 365–6, 439–40, 443, 562, 631; in children 159; coronavirus pandemic and persons with 172–3; CRPD and 167; dignity and 170, 173; in England and Wales 42, 49, 193–6, 200, 203, 205, 258; equality in 167, 172, 174; and European Convention on Human Rights 167, 171; human rights framework for 167; in Ireland 174; legal framework for 168–70; mental capacity and 170; non-discrimination and 166, 169, 171, 173–4; recommendations adopting CRPD 171; in Scotland 166–75; in the UK 174
least restrictive alternative principle 24, 28, 57, 112, 169, 357, 364–5
legal capacity 39–40, 91, 95, 97, 108, 117, **128**, 130–1, 137, 393, 425, 571–5, 655, 688, 699, 705–6; in Argentina 576–7; CCRPD's interpretation of 153–4; in Chile 577; in Colombia 576–7; to decide about care 110, 118; defined 464; in India 540, 542–3, 545–50; in Kenya 468–9; in Northern Ireland 558; older adults 187; in Peru 576–8; prohibition of denying 710; recognition of 105–6, 114, 468–9, 672; reforms 576–9, 580, 583–4; removal of 101; in Scotland 167–70, 174; in South Africa 493–9, 503–7; in South American countries 610; supporting 631, 693; in Uganda 468–9; universal 441, 459, 473; in Victoria 576; vs. decisional capacity 154–5; in Zambia 467, 468–9, 473
legalism 57, 57n5, 423, 666
Lewis, A. 239
Lewis, O. 111, 112, 707
LGBTQI+ 226
liberty 39, 41, 83, 85, 97, 101, 107–9, 113, 116, 170, 173, 334, 338, 459; in Africa 461–2; of children 156; in China 522; deprivation of liberty and 156; in Ghana 482; importance of 156; against interferences 158; safeguards 163;

in South American countries 609; *of see also* deprivation of liberty
Libya 117
Local Government Act 1972 198
Lockwood, G. 407
Lunacy (District Courts) Act (India) 529
Lunacy (Supreme Courts) Act (India) 529
Luxembourg: gender recognition in 224; involuntary psychiatric hospitalization in 289; physician-assisted suicide in 715
Lyall, C. 619

Ma, H. 521
MacArthur Violence Risk Assessment Study 347, 349
Mackay, R. 270
Maker, Y. 40, 41
Malta: gender recognition in 224
Mandarelli, G. 290
Manthorpe, J. 182–3
Martin, W. 69
Marzanski, M. 182
Maylea, C. 699
McCloughen, A. 619
McConville, Scott B. 69
McGorry, Patrick D. 69
McGovern, P. 490
McLean, S. 72
McSherry, B. 376
McSherry, M. 40, 41
medical assistance in dying (MaiD) 715–17, 719
medicalism 57, 635, 666
medically assisted dying 687, 705
medical model 103, 105, 130, 135, 228, 373, 378, 389, 498, 513, 619; African Disability Protocol 463; of decision-making 67; of disability 171; entrenchment 111; medicalism and 57; in Norway 259, 260; Western 388
medical necessity doctrine 40, 41, 58n6, 64n25, 67
Medical Treatment Planning and Decisions Act 2016 (Victoria) 187
Meiches, B. 309
Melle, I. 256, 263
Melzer, N. 126
Mencken, H. L. 688
Mendez, Juan E. 40
mental capacity 35, 66n30, 91–2, 106, 199–203, 317–20, 393, 441, 499, 558; assessing 44; capacity to stand trial 290–1; in children 151, 154–5; criminal responsibility 291–5, **293**, *295*; defined 706; financial capacity 295–9, **297–8**; informed consent to clinical research 287–90; in informed consent to treatment 285–7, *286*; learning disability and 170; older adults 179, 182, 184–7; other decisional tasks

Index

299–300; in Peru 118; in Scotland 170; in trans persons 213; variables influencing *287*
Mental Capacity Act 2005 (England and Wales) 35–6, 44, 46, 48–9, 58n8, 65–8, 66n29, 154–5, 185, 186, *197*, 199–207, 245–8, 329–33, 390, 556, 564, 630, 639
Mental Capacity Act 2008 (Singapore) 204
Mental Capacity Act (Northern Ireland) 2016 (MCA(NI)) 204, 339, 556–7, 570, 709; background issues 557–9; context 559–62; key sections of 564–7; number of ongoing debates and implementation 567–9; process of developing 562–4
Mental Capacity with Support Model 696–8, 700
Mental Health Act 1959 (UK) 21, 42, 328
Mental Health Act 1978 (Italy) 23
Mental Health Act 1983 (England and Wales) 35–6, 43–5, 48–9, 61–2, 65, 68, 117, 150, 155, 161, 174, *197*, 198, 203, 205, 207, 233, 249, 257, 328, 333, 339, 343–4, 358, 362, 365–7, 390, 421–8, 635, *636*, 637, 638, 645–60, 653–6, 658, 685, 706, 712; appropriate treatment to therapeutic benefit 243–6; digital platforms for professionals conducting 647–8; digitising 645–7; ethos of a therapeutic disposal under 261–2; frameworks in practice 330–3; nearest relative framework in 427–9; personality disorder and criminal law 243–8; regulation of the electronic communication of statutory forms 648–9; statutory frameworks of 328–30; treatability to appropriate treatment in 240–3; videocall assessments 650–1; videoconferencing in tribunals 651–3
Mental Health Act 1987 (India) 124, 529, 531, 537, 542–4
Mental Health Act 2001 (Ireland) 27–8, 30, 35, 174, 239, 333–4, 333–8, 337, 430n9
Mental Health Act 2007 (UK) 61–2, 65, 240, 328
Mental Health Act 2012 (Ghana) 478, 480–2; achievements and challenges 486–8; on criminal law in respect of mentally ill offenders 483–6; funding for mental health care 483; on protecting human rights of mentally ill 482–3; recommendations for improving implementation of 488–9; transitional provisions and offences 483
Mental Health Act 2014 (Punjab, Victoria) 188, 531, 699
Mental Health Act 2017 (Khyber Pakhtunkhwa) 531
Mental Health Act 2018 (Bangladesh) 536
Mental Health Act 2019 (Balochistan, Peru) 118, 531, 473
Mental Health Act Commission (MHAC) 43–4

Mental Health Act (Islamabad) 531
Mental Health Bill 1999 (Ireland) 27
Mental Health Care Act 17 of 2002 (South Africa) 498; persons subject to 498–9; treatment decisions under 499–503
Mental Health Care Act 2017 (India) 3, 28–9, 133, 531, 537, 550–2, 712; decisional autonomy and rights of persons with mental illness 545–7; historical context of 540–3; MHCA's transformative potential 548–9; paradigmatic shift for mental healthcare 543–8; right to access mental healthcare and treatment 543–5; right to community living and deinstitutionalisation 547–8; rights-based jurisprudence 548–9
Mental Health (Care and Treatment) Act 2003 (Scotland) 166–75
Mental Health Europe (MHE) 112
Mental Health and Justice project (MHJ) 629–32; action in research 637–8; collaborative processes 640–1; collaborative working as education 641–3; course of 638–43; engagement with policy makers 635–7; management of collaboration 639–40; policy lab on reform of mental health act *636*; scholarship and activism 634–8; for strong interdisciplinarity 632–4
Mental Health Law 2013 (China) 524; cross-cutting issues in 519–20; detention for diagnostic assessment 517–18; detention for treatment 518–19; detention and treatment decision-making under 515–16; discharge provisions in 519; law in book to action 521–3; voluntary treatment 516–17
mental health monitoring 34–6, 42–3; Care Quality Commission (*see* Care Quality Commission (CQC)); CRPD (*see* United Nations (UN) Convention on the Rights of Persons with Disabilities (CRPD)); ECHR (*see* European Convention on Human Rights (ECHR)); Human Rights Act 1998 37; human rights frameworks to prevent ill–treatment 36; mental disability and ill–treatment 40–2; OPCAT (*see* Optional Protocol to the Convention Against Torture (OPCAT))
Mental Health Policy (2005) (Sri Lanka) 534
Mental Health and Wellbeing Act 2022 (Victoria) 3–4, 34, 378, 431–3
Mental Welfare Commission for Scotland guidance 168
metacognition 631, 633; impaired 286
MHA.359 see Mental Health (Care and Treatment) Act 2003 (Scotland)
Minkowitz, T. 59, 686
Miola, J. 72–4

M'Naghten Rules (England and Wales) 2, 257, 259–60
Morgan, G. 694
Moro, M. F. 141, 490
Mudaliar Committee (1959) (India) 541

narcissistic personality disorder 235, 259, 263
Nathan, T. 266
National Assistance Act 1948 198
National Institute for Health and Care Excellence (NICE) 237
National Mental Health Policy (South Africa); framework and strategic Plan 2013–2020 503–4; from human rights-based approach 506–7; human rights-based approach to mental health care 504–6
National Mental Health Work Plan 2015–2020 513
Nazi Germany 19
Nearest Relative framework 421, 427–9, 433
Netherlands, the: advance decision-making in 710; euthanasia-assisted suicide in 716, 719–21; involuntary psychiatric hospitalization in 289; physician-assisted suicide in 715–16; responses to CRPD 116–17
Neuman, G. 687
New South Wales (NSW) 343; harm in 343–4
Newton-Howes, G. 379
New Zealand 35, 175, 239, 288, 356, 358, 713
NHS services in England and Wales 205, 655
Nilsson, W. 689
Nomidou, A. 139, 141
non-discrimination 26, 96, 379, 406, 408, 417–18, 672, 697, 699, 707; in CRPD 102, 107, 109, 686, 689, 691–4, 712; in India 546; persons with learning disabilities 166, 169, 171, 173–4; in Scotland 166, 169, 171, 173–4; in South Africa 494, 496, 504–5
nongovernmental organisations (NGOs) 102, 114, 125
Northern Ireland 238, 339, 713; abuse in 561; autonomy in 556, 561–2, 574–5, 577–8; best interests in 558, 564–8; children in 569; co-production in 711; CRPD and 558; deprivation of liberty in 566–8, 570; equality in 562–3; 'fusion' legislation in 339–40, 635, 709; inpatient psychiatric care in 391; legal capacity in 558; mental health law in 556–70; personality disorder in 568; supported decision-making in 558; see also Mental Capacity Act (Northern Ireland)
Norway 258n2; autism spectrum disorders in 259–60; diagnostic disagreements in 238; gender recognition in 224; insanity defence in 259–61; medical model in 259, 260; QualityRights research in 126; responses to CRPD 115–17

Offender Personality Disorder (OPD) Pathway 240, 248
Office of the Public Advocate (OPA) 189
Office of the UN High Commissioner for Human Rights (OHCHR) 384–400
older adults 20, 179–80, 207, 312–14, 544, 550, 589, 609, 713; abuse and neglect in 180, 182–3, 186, 193, 198, 201; in Australia 183–4; autonomy in 181–90; decision-making with 182–3; decision-making capacity in 185; decision-making support 188–90; with dementia 195, 198, 338; dignity in 181–3, 185, 188–90; in England and Wales 185–6; financial capacity in 295–6; informed consent 179, 181–4, 188–9; legal capacity and 187; mental capacity in 179, 182, 184–7; and mental health 180–1; substitute decision-making 186–7; supported decision-making with 182, 187–9
O'Mahoney, C. 40
Ontario 625, 709; harm in 344
Optional Protocol to the Convention Against Torture (OPCAT) 37–8, 37–40, 45, 47, 107; affirming deprivation of liberty 38–9; CQC on 50; UK ratified 36
Orr, D. 202
O'Sullivan, S. 267
Owen, G. S. 289

Pakistan 527, 712; asylums in 531; criminalisation of suicide in 714; mental health legislation in 528, 531–3; personality disorder in 531; suicide in 533; supported decision-making in 532–3
Paraguay: documents 589, **597**, **600**; programs for well-being and promotion of rights in 606, 607; psychiatric hospitalization in 604; recognition of rights in 602
parens patriae doctrine 56, 56n2, 422
Pathare, S. 135
Pedersen, R. 75
personality disorder 166, 201, 233–4, 248–9, 260, 289, 404, 718; anti-social 235, 255, 258; anxious and fearful 235; appropriate treatment to therapeutic benefit 243–6; assorted 255; autism spectrum disorders and 257; borderline 235, 255; categories of 235; coercion and 243, 249; and criminal law 246–8; dangerous people diagnosed with 238–40; defining 234–6; dignity and 243; diminished responsibility to 247; dramatic, emotional or erratic 235; in

England and Wales 239, 249; in India 530; in Ireland 239; mental health law in 233–49; models of 234, 236–8; narcissistic 259, 263; in Northern Ireland 568; odd or eccentric 235; other specified 235; in Pakistan 531; of psychopathic type 263; trans persons with 226; treatability to appropriate treatment 240–3; unspecified 235

Peru 572, 584, 686, 707; abuse in 575, 581; advance decision-making in 710; children in 578; coercion in 584; community-oriented service in 602–4; CRPD Committee in 118–19; decision-making support in 578, 579, 580, 581, 583; documents 589, **597–8, 600**; involuntary hospitalisation in 118; legal capacity in 118, 576–8; legal reforms in **572**; mental capacity in 118; mental health legislation in 575, **575**; persons with disabilities in 610; recognition of rights in 599, 601, 602; responses to CRPD 118–19; substitute decision-making in 576; supported decision-making in 118

physical restraint 22, 88, 134, 139; defined 60n12

physician-assisted suicide (PAS); in Belgium 715–16, 718–21; in Canada 715–17; in Luxembourg 715; in the Netherlands 715–16; in Switzerland 715

Pickard, H. 246

Pilgrim, D. 236

Plato 20–1, 30

Pokorny, A.D. 347

Poland: responses to CRPD 117

Portugal 117, 528; gender recognition in 224, 227; involuntary psychiatric hospitalization in 289; Portuguese-speaking South American countries 589–610; responses to CRPD 113

Powers of Attorney Act 2014 (Victoria) 187

Poythress, N. G. 289

Preston-Shoot, M. 202

proportionality principle 66, 85, 112, 170, 172–3, 356, 364, 580, 673, 676, 688

Protocol to the African Charter on Human and Peoples' Rights on the Rights of Persons with Disabilities in Africa 495

psychiatric genomics 438–9, 446; consenting for prevention in 441–52; informed choice about 445; social prejudice in 444

psychiatric hospitalization: in Argentina 604; in Brazil 604–5; in Chile 604; in Paraguay 604

QualityRights Initiative 124–7, 142, 711; and abuse **129**, 130–1, 133–4, 139, 141; assessment themes, standards and criteria **128–9**; assessment tool kit 127; in Chile **136**, 140–1; in Egypt 138–9; elements of 133–5; evaluation tools 131; in Finland 138; in Greece 139–40; guidance tools 131–2; in India 135–7, **136**, 396–7; limitations of the research to date 141; in Norway 126; objectives of 125; research carried out using material **136–7**; self-help tool 132–3; strengths of research to date 141–2; tools created by **125**; training material 127–31; in Tunisia 140

Queensland 354

Quigley, M. 67

Rains, S. 288

recognition of rights: in Argentina 599–602; in Bolivia 601, 602; in Brazil 599, 602; in Chile 599–602; in Colombia 599, 601, 602; in Ecuador 601–2; in Paraguay 602; in Peru 599, 601, 602; in Uruguay 599, 601, 602; in Venezuela 117

relationality 433; and mental illness 422–3; NR framework and 428; realities of 424; recognising 423–5

Rickards, L. 618

Rider, G. N. 220

right to mental health care 17, 29, 31, 384–5, 397–9, 499; capacity, consent, and care 389–94; draft guidance on 387–9; histories of 385–7; involuntary care 394–6

Ritterband, L. 289

Roper, C. 75, 376

Rose, N. 619, 625

Rosenhan, D. 262

Royal Commission into Victoria's Mental Health System 4, 422, 431, 434, 617n1, 623

Rubin, G. 618

Ruck Keene, A. 204

rule of law 25, 30, 37, 124, 255, 674

Ryan, C. 59

Safeguarding Adults Boards (SABs) 199

Safeguarding Adults Reviews (SARs) 199–200, 203, 205

St. Amand, C. M. 220

Salie, M. 104

Samsi, K. 182–3

Schwend, S. 215

Scotland: autism spectrum disorders in 168, 170–1, 174–5; autonomy in 167–75; coercion in 175; equality in 167, 172, 174; harm in 343; highest attainable standard of health in 171, 173; learning disability in (*see* learning disability); legal capacity in 167–70, 174; mental capacity in 170; mental health law in 168, 170, 173; non-discrimination in 166, 169, 171, 173–4; videoconferencing in 651

Scotland Act 1998 167

Seierstad, A. 259
self-harming behaviour 4, 93, 343n9, 344–6, 350–3, 426, 576, 622, 656, 693–5; dialectical behavioural therapy for 237; emergency departments with 391; possibilities of 343; preventing 85, 89, 432; risk of 516; risk assessment for 347–9
Serenity Integrated Mentoring (SIM) 656–8, 715
Series, L. 373
service user reference panel (SURP) 46
sexual violence 307–10, 314, 322; on children 265, 312–13; psychological impact of crimes of 311–13
Shao, Y. 521
Slovakia 117
social model of disability 58, 103–5, 373, 378, 441–2, 453, 687, 706
socio-economic equality 378–80
socio-economic inclusion 712; case study 377–8; CRPD and human rights instruments 374; defined 371–2; distributional equity 377; equality and 378–80; expansive disability and human rights scholarship 373; and health inequality 372; mental health law and 371–80; role of law 375–7; as 'social citizenship' participation 372–4; through mental health repeal or fusion 374–5
South Africa 695; abuse in 498; application of international law in 494–7; autonomy in 497, 504, 506; children in 494, 495; coercion in 506; dignity in 498, 500, 504; equality in 496, 504–5; highest attainable standard of health in 493–507; legal capacity in 493–9, 503–7; mental health law in 493–507; non-discrimination in 494, 496, 504–5; persons with disabilities in 497; regulating health care in 493–4; report to CRPD Committee 497; right to highest attainable standard 494–5, 497–507; right to legal capacity in 495–7; substitute decision-making in 499–501; supported decision-making in 493, 494, 498–9, 505–7
South America, Portuguese-speaking countries in 587–9, 608–10; abuse in 589; care of people with mental disorders 607–8; children in 588–9, 601; community-oriented service 602–4; documentary analysis 589; financing of mental health 605–6; legal capacity in 610; mental health law in 599, 601; programs for well-being and promotion of rights 606–7; psychiatric hospitalization 604–5; recognition of rights 599–602; right to liberty in 609; *see also specific countries*
Spain: involuntary psychiatric hospitalization in 289; Spanish-speaking South American countries 589–610

Special Rapporteur 26, 36, 40–1, 108–9, 112–15, 126, 129–30, 216, 223, 474, 655
Sri Lanka 527, 528, 537; asylums in 533–4; mental health legislation in 528, 533–5; mental health literacy in 535; Mental Health Policy of 534
Srivastava Committee (1975) (India) 541
Standards of Care (SOC) for trans health care 216–18, 220–2, 228
Stember, M. 618
Stevens, M. 648, 649
stricter scrutiny 85, 94
structured risk assessment instruments (SRAIs) 71
substitute decision-making 3, 29, 58n8, 106–7, 354, 389–92, 396, 398, 441, 687, 696–7, 704–9; in Africa 460, 464, 470–1, 473; in Canada 361; in Colombia 576; CRPD and 115; in India 530, 532–23, 546, 550; in Kenya 471; older adults 186–7; paradigm 705; in Peru 576; in South Africa 499–501; in Uganda 470; in Zambia 470–1
suicide 93, 318, 343n9, 344–5, 388, 576, 705, 713–15; in China 521–2; criminalisation of 714–15; decriminalization of 28; in Ghana 485; in India 531, 549; in Pakistan 533, 714; prevention 544, 693; in prison 89; risk assessment for 347–51; threat 204, 426; true positives 352; *see also* euthanasia-assisted suicide; physician-assisted suicide
supported decision-making 58n8, 59n10, 106, 470, 537, 572, 576, 631, 686, 704–5, 708; accepting or rejecting 687; as advance directives 545; and advance planning 131, 134; application of 106, 167; in Argentina 577–9; in Colombia 574, 578–9; equality principle through 380; in India 529, 547; in informed consent 577–9; from institutional care to 40; interdisciplinary collaboration and 619; in Ireland 188, 336–7; in Kenya 471; Mental Welfare Commission for Scotland guidance on 168; models of 29, 59, 389; need for 182; nominated representatives 545; in Northern Ireland 558; Office of the Public Advocate guidance on 189; with older adults 182, 187–9; older adults 189–90; in Pakistan 532–3; paradigm shift to 396–9; in Peru 118, 578, 579; provision of 118; in South Africa 493, 494, 498–9, 505–7; substituted decision-making to 391; in Uganda 470; Victoria's law 189; in Zambia 470–1
Support Except Where There Is Harm Model 699
Sweden 26; independent advocacy assistant 376; informed consent models in 221; involuntary psychiatric hospitalization in 289; psychiatry and uncertainty in 263; responses to CPRD 117

Switzerland 117; gender recognition in 224; physician-assisted suicide in 715
Szmukler, G. 70, 558

Terpstra, J. 620
Theilen, J. T. 215
Thornicroft, G. 405, 407
trans children 214, 227
trans depathologisation activism 215–16, 219, 222, 228
trans identities 213, 215–16, 228; depathologisation of 223, 225, 228; pathologisation of 222, 226
trans persons 212–13, 227–8; abusive requirements in gender recognition procedures 222–3; on autism spectrum disorders 226; autonomy in 213, 215, 220, 222–3, 225–6, 228; best interests in 221, 227; bodily autonomy of 225; children 214; defined 212n1; depathologisation activism 215–16, 219; dignity in 216, 225; discrimination 225–7; gender-non-conforming 226; heterosexual 227; highest attainable standard of health in 217, 221; inclusion in medical classifications 215–17; informed consent models in health care 219–22, 224, 227, 228; intersectional exclusion in 225–7; LGB+ 226; mental capacity in 213; mental health in health care 217–19; minors 226, 227; neurodivergent and mentally ill 226; non-binary 227; pathologisation 213–15, 223–7; with personality disorder 226; really trans 225; with stigmatised personality disorders 226; trans-related diagnoses 215–17; truly 213, 214, 225–6, 227–8
transsexuality/transsexualism 213–15, 223
transvestism, dual-role 214
treatability, concept of 233, 239–41, 246, 247
Tunisia **136**, 142, 459n1; coercion in 140; QualityRights Research in 140
Twumasi, P. A. 478

Uganda 459, 474; constitutional provisions in 465–6; disability-specific legislation in 466–8; evaluation of mental health legislation in 473; involuntary admission and treatment in 469; Mental Health Act 468–74; monitoring bodies in 471–2; monitoring and oversight 467; recognition of legal capacity in 468–9; rights of persons with disabilities 467; safeguards in 472; supported or substitute decision-making in 470; violations of rights in 467–8
UK National Preventive Mechanism (NPM) 50–1; advantage of 36; Care Quality Commission as member of 35–6, 48–9; functions of 36, 45; procedural requirements for 47; SPT and 38, 45–51
UK Disability Discrimination Act (DDA) 1995 406
Ulysses Clause 131, 134
United Kingdom: autism in 174; gender recognition in 224; learning disability in 174; *see also* England and Wales; Northern Ireland; Scotland
United Nations Convention Against Torture and other Cruel, Inhuman or Degrading Treatment (UN CAT) 37–40
United Nations (UN) Convention on the Rights of the Child (CRC) 149–54, 156–7, 159, 161–2
United Nations (UN) Convention on the Rights of Persons with Disabilities (CRPD) 3, 26, 37–41, 57, 83, 124, 150, 166, 186–7, 193, 268, 328, 334, 354, 373, 384, 403, 425, 440, 495, 527, 571, 599, 609, 630, 666–7, 670–1, 685, 704; adoption of 459; African Disability Protocol vs. 463–4, 466; and Australia 117, 511; autonomy in 689–91, 694–8; and Bulgaria 113; and Canada 117; as catalyst for change 705–13; coercive care, paradox of 59–61; coercive treatment of mental health service 706–8; Council of Europe Commissioner for Human Rights and 114–15; dignity in 105, 111, 689–91, 705, 708; disability, definition of 103–4; domestic responses 115–19; drafting of 102–3; and England and Wales 117–18; equality in 104, 107, 109, 166, 686, 689, 691–4; European Convention on Human Rights and 110–11; European Court of Human Rights and 110–11; fundamentals 103–5; and human rights instruments 374; human rights model of disability 104–5; impact of 28–9, 44; implications of CRPD's human rights 105–6; and India 29, 529, 542–3; interpretation of CRPD 95, 97, 105–18, 153, 156; and Ireland 117; learning disabilities and 167, 171; medical model entrenchment 111–14; negotiations over abolition of mental health law 686–9; and the Netherlands 116–17; non-discrimination in 102, 107, 109, 686, 689, 691–4, 705, 712; and Northern Ireland 558; and Norway 115–17; notion of discrimination 705; participation in 694–5; and Peru 118–19; Poland and 117; position on mental health laws 105; prohibition on disability-based detention and treatment 105–10; recommendations adopting CRPD 171; reservations and/or interpretative declarations 115–17; substitute decision-making and 115; and Venezuela 117; voice, inclusion and 58–61

Index

United States 291, 313, 422, 588, 625; forensic practice in 281; harm criteria in 344; mental health 'experts by experience' movement in 619; psychiatry and uncertainty in 262; videoconferencing in 651, 653; *see also specific states*
unspecified personality disorder 235
UN Sub-Committee on Prevention of Torture (SPT) 38, 47; guidelines for National Preventive Mechanisms 45–6; National Preventive Mechanism and 38, 45–51; visit to UK 48
Unsworth, C. 617, 695
Uruguay: care of people with mental disorders in 607, 608; documents 589, **598**, **600**; gender recognition in 228; recognition of rights in 599, 601, 602
Uzbekistan 117

Valimaki, M. 138
Van der Burg, W. 72
van Veen, C. 619
Venezuela: documentary analysis in 589; recognition of rights in 602; responses to CPRD 117
Victoria (Australia) 34, 187–8, 422, 431–4; law of supported decision-making 189; legal capacity reforms in 576; opposition parties 623; role of law in 621–2; value of inclusion and equity 377–8
Victorian Collaborative Centre for Mental Health and Wellbeing Act 2021 431, 433n12, 624–5
Victorian Department of Health and Victorian mental health and wellbeing services 433
videocall 646, 649, 653; assessments 650–1, 654; in England and Wales 650–1, 654
videoconferencing: in England and Wales 651; in tribunals 651–3; in United States 653
Vitiello, E. 653
von Schrader, S. 417
vulnerability theory 424–5

Waldron, J. 689
Wall, J. 188
Watson, C. 290
Weller, P. 40
Wessex Academic Health Science Network (2020) 649, 658
Western Australia 354
Wicks, E. 90
Williams, J. 653
Wilson, A. 633
Wilson, K. E. 59, 375, 707
Winterwerp criteria 84–7, 91, 93, 94, 96
World Health Organization (WHO) 19, 30; Division of Mental Health and Prevention of Substance Abuse 24; guidance on mental health legislation 384–400; Mental Health Action Plan 2013–2030 135; QualityRights Initiative (*see* QualityRights Initiative); *Ten Basic Principles* 24–5; United Nations *Principles* and 23–6; World Health Report 25
World Professional Association for Transgender Health (WPATH) 216–18, 220–2, 228
Wyatt, D. 659

years of healthy life lost due to disability (YLDs) 705
Yogyakarta Principles 216, 221, 223

Zambia 459, 474; abuse in 459, 472; constitutional provisions in 465–6; disability-specific legislation in 466–8; evaluation of mental health legislation in 473; involuntary admission and treatment in 469–70; legal capacity in 467, 468, 473; Mental Health Act 468–74; monitoring bodies in 471–2; monitoring and oversight 467; recognition of legal capacity in 468–9; rights of persons with disabilities 466–7; safeguards in 472; supported or substitute decision-making in 470–1; violations of rights in 467–8
zero-coercion model 396, 399, 707
Zhao, X. 516